13

50 47

ASIA
10-11

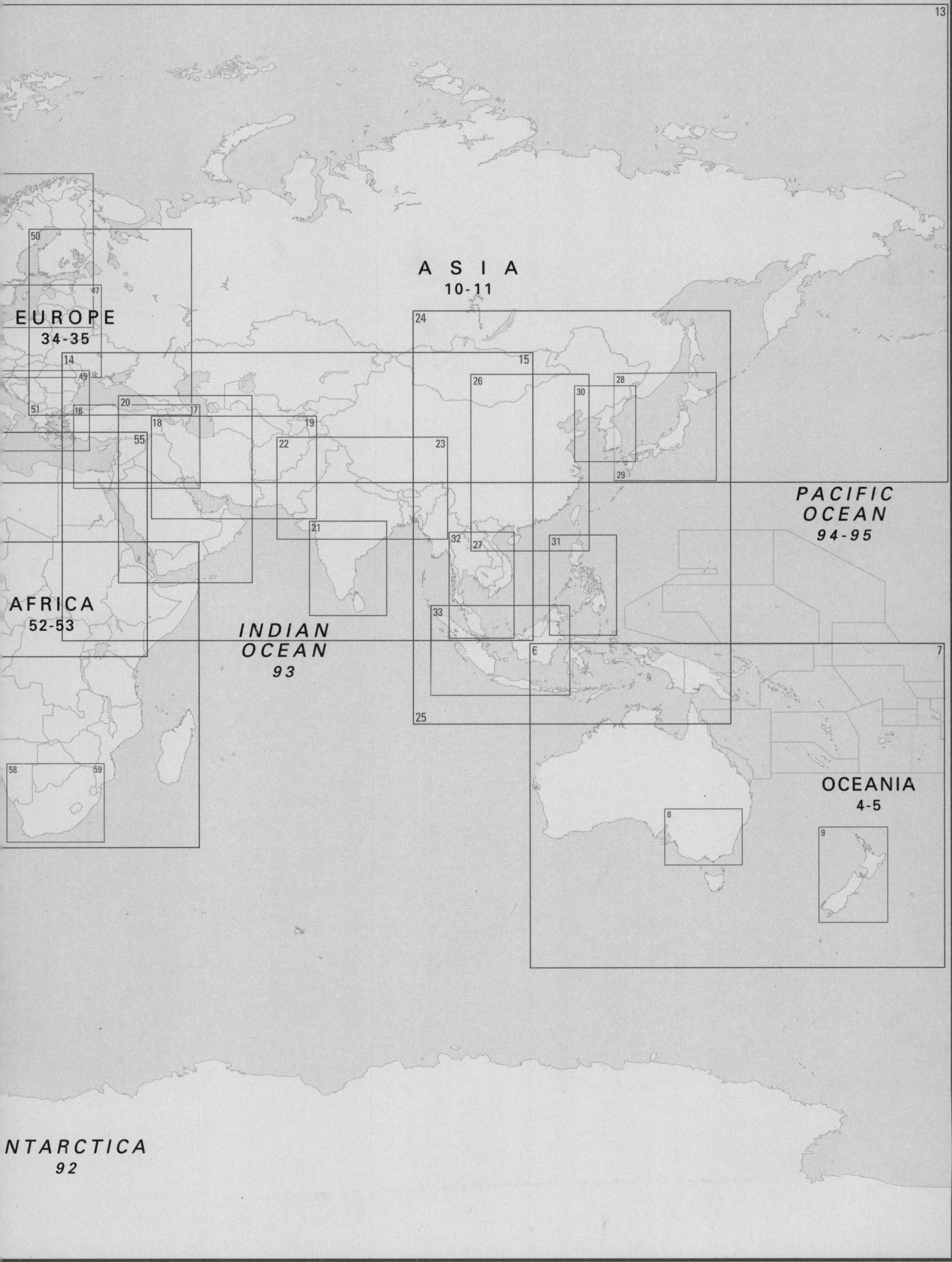

EUROPE
34-35

24 15

14 49 26 28 30

20 17 16 51 18 19 55 22 23 29

PACIFIC
OCEAN
94-95

21 32 27 31

AFRICA
52-53

33

INDIAN
OCEAN
93

6 7

25

58 59

OCEANIA
4-5

8 9

NTARCTICA
92

THE TIMES ATLAS OF THE WORLD

NEW GENERATION EDITION

TIMES BOOKS

WORLD INFORMATION

4–27 GUIDE TO STATES AND TERRITORIES

28–41 THE PHYSICAL EARTH

28–29 Southeast ASIA and AUSTRALASIA

30–31 ASIA

32–33 EUROPE

34–35 AFRICA

36–37 NORTH AMERICA and THE ARCTIC

38–39 CENTRAL and SOUTH AMERICA

40–41 SOUTH AMERICA and ANTARCTICA

42–43 GEOGRAPHICAL COMPARISONS

44–45 CLIMATE: VEGETATION

46–47 POPULATION

48 EARTHQUAKES AND VOLCANOES: ENERGY

49–64 CITY PLANS

50–51 Auckland, Melbourne, Sydney, Jakarta, Singapore, Manila, Bangkok, Hong Kong, Beijing, Shanghai, Seoul, Karachi

52–53 Tōkyō

54–55 Delhi, Bombay, Tehrān, Mecca, Jerusalem, İstanbul, Athens, Moscow, St Petersburg, Berlin, Brussels, Amsterdam

56–57 London

58–59 Paris

60–61 Rome, Milan, Madrid, Barcelona, Cairo, Cape Town, Montréal, Toronto, Chicago, Washington, Los Angeles, San Francisco

62–63 New York

64 México, Lima, Rio de Janeiro, São Paulo, Buenos Aires, Caracas

THE TIMES ATLAS OF THE WORLD
NEW GENERATION EDITION

TIMES BOOKS, London
77–85 Fulham Palace Road,
London W6 8JB

First published 1997
Reprinted 1998, 1999

Printed in Italy by Rotolito Lombarda

British Library Cataloguing in Publication Data. A catalogue record for this book is available from the British Library.

ISBN 0 7230 0962 7

MH 10390 Imp 004

The maps in this product are also available for purchase in digital format, from Bartholomew Mapping Services,
Tel: +44 (0) 141 306 3155
Fax: +44 (0) 141 306 3104
E-mail: batholomew@harpercollins.co.uk

COUNTRY-FINDER

A

Afghanistan **19**
Albania **49**
Algeria **54–55**
American Samoa **5**
Andorra **45**
Angola **56–57**
Anguilla **83**
Antigua and Barbuda **83**
Argentina **88**
Armenia **17**
Aruba **83**
Australia **6–7**
Austria **46**
Azerbaijan **17**
Azores **34**

B

The Bahamas **83**
Bahrain **18**
Bangladesh **23**
Barbados **83**
Belarus **47**
Belgium **42**
Belize **82**
Benin **54**
Bermuda **83**
Bhutan **23**
Bolivia **86–87**
Bosnia-Herzegovina **48–49**
Botswana **57**
Brazil **86–88**
British Indian Ocean Territory **10**
Brunei **33**
Bulgaria **49**
Burkina **54**
Burundi **56**

C

Cambodia **32**
Cameroon **54–55**
Canada **62–63**
Cape Verde **54**
Cayman Islands **83**
Central African Republic **56**
Chad **55**
Chile **88**
China **15, 24–25**
Christmas Island **25**
Cocos Islands **25**
Colombia **86**
Comoros **57**
Congo **56**
Congo (Zaire) **56–57**
Cook Islands **5**
Costa Rica **83**
Côte d'Ivoire **54**
Croatia **48–49**
Cuba **83**
Cyprus **16**
Czech Republic **46–47**

D

Denmark **37**
Djibouti **56**
Dominica **83**
Dominican Republic **83**

E

Ecuador **86**
Egypt **55**
El Salvador **82**
Equatorial Guinea **54**
Eritrea **56**
Estonia **37**
Ethiopia **56**

F

Falkland Islands **88**
Faroe Islands **36**
Fiji **7**
Finland **36–37**
F.Y.R.O.M. (Macedonia) **49**
France **44**
French Guiana **87**
French Polynesia **5**
French Southern and Antarctic Lands **3**

G

Gabon **56**
The Gambia **54**
Gaza **16**
Georgia **51**
Germany **46**
Ghana **54**
Gibraltar **45**
Greece **49**
Greenland **63**
Grenada **83**
Guadeloupe **83**
Guam **25**
Guatemala **82**
Guernsey **44**
Guinea **54**
Guinea-Bissau **54**
Guyana **86–87**

H

Haiti **83**
Honduras **82–83**
Hungary **46–49**

I

Iceland **36**
India **14–15**
Indonesia **25**
Iran **18–19**
Iraq **17**
Isle of Man **38**
Israel **16**
Italy **48**

J

Jamaica **83**
Japan **28–29**
Jersey **44**
Jordan **16–17**

K

Kazakstan **12**
Kenya **56**
Kiribati **7**
Kuwait **17**
Kyrgyzstan **14–15**

L

Laos **25**
Latvia **37**
Lebanon **16**
Lesotho **59**
Liberia **54**
Libya **54–55**
Liechtenstein **46**
Lithuania **37**
Luxembourg **42**

M

Macau **27**
Macedonia, see F.Y.R.O.M.
Madagascar **57**
Madeira **54**
Malawi **57**
Malaysia **33**
Maldives **15**
Mali **54**
Malta **48**
Marshall Islands **4**
Martinique **83**
Mauritania **54**
Mauritius **53**
Mayotte **57**
Mexico **82**
Micronesia, Federated States of **4**
Moldova **47**
Monaco **44**
Mongolia **24**
Montserrat **83**
Morocco **54**
Mozambique **57**
Myanmar **24–25**

N

Namibia **57**
Nauru **7**
Nepal **22–23**
Netherlands **42**
Netherlands Antilles **83**
New Caledonia **7**
New Zealand **9**
Nicaragua **82–83**
Niger **54–55**
Nigeria **54–55**
Niue **7**
Norfolk Island **7**
North Korea **30**
Northern Mariana Islands **24–25**
Norway **36–37**

O

Oman **20**

P

Pakistan **14–15**
Palau **25**
Panama **83**
Papua New Guinea **6**
Paraguay **88**
Peru **86**
Philippines **31**
Pitcairn Islands **5**
Poland **46–47**
Portugal **45**
Puerto Rico **83**

Q

Qatar **18**

R

Republic of Ireland **41**
Réunion **53**
Romania **47, 49**
Russian Federation **12–13**
Rwanda **56**

S

St Helena **53**
St Kitts-Nevis **83**
St Lucia **83**
St Pierre and Miquelon **67**
St Vincent and the Grenadines **83**
San Marino **48**
São Tomé and Príncipe **54**
Saudi Arabia **20**
Senegal **54**
Seychelles **53**
Sierra Leone **54**
Singapore **32**
Slovakia **46–47**
Slovenia **48**
Solomon Islands **7**
Somalia **56**
South Africa, Republic of **58–59**
South Korea **30**
Spain **45**
Sri Lanka **21**
Sudan **55**
Suriname **87**
Swaziland **59**
Sweden **36–37**
Switzerland **46**
Syria **16–17**

T

Taiwan **27**
Tajikistan **14–15**
Tanzania **56–57**
Thailand **32**
Togo **54**
Tokelau **7**
Tonga **7**
Trinidad and Tobago **83**
Tunisia **54–55**
Turkey **16–17**
Turkmenistan **14**
Turks and Caicos Islands **83**
Tuvalu **7**

U

Uganda **56**
Ukraine **51**
United Arab Emirates **20**
United Kingdom **34**
United States of America **70–71**
Uruguay **91**
Uzbekistan **14**

V

Vanuatu **7**
Vatican City **48**
Venezuela **89**
Vietnam **24–25**
Virgin Islands (UK) **83**
Virgin Islands (USA) **83**

W

Wallis and Futuna **7**
West Bank **16**
Western Sahara **54**
Western Samoa **7**

Y

Yemen **20**
Yugoslavia **49**

Z

Zambia **57**
Zimbabwe **57**

ATLAS OF THE WORLD

1 SYMBOLS

THE WORLD
2–3 *1:80M*

OCEANIA
4–5 *1:35M*

6–7 AUSTRALIA and Southwest PACIFIC *1:20M*
8 Southeast AUSTRALIA *1:5M*
9 NEW ZEALAND *1:5M*

ASIA
10–11 *1:35M*

12–13 RUSSIAN FEDERATION *1:21M*
14–15 THE MIDDLE EAST and South ASIA *1:20M*
16–17 East MEDITERRANEAN *1:5M*
18–19 THE GULF, IRAN and AFGHANISTAN *1:7M*
20 ARABIAN PENINSULA *1:12.5M*
21 South INDIA *1:7M*
22–23 PAKISTAN, North INDIA and BANGLADESH *1:7M*
24–25 East and Southeast ASIA *1:20M*
26–27 Central CHINA *1:7.5M*
Hong Kong *1:750 000*
28–29 JAPAN *1:5M*
30 Northeast CHINA, NORTH KOREA and SOUTH KOREA *1:5M*
31 PHILIPPINES *1:7M*
32 THAILAND, CAMBODIA and Peninsular MALAYSIA *1:7.5M*
Singapore *1:550 000*
33 West INDONESIA *1:10M*

EUROPE
34–35 *1:18M*

36–37 SCANDINAVIA and the BALTIC STATES *1:5M*
Iceland *1:5M*
Faroe Islands *1:5M*
38–39 ENGLAND and WALES *1:2M*
40 SCOTLAND *1:2M*
41 IRELAND *1:2M*
42–43 BELGIUM, NETHERLANDS and North GERMANY *1:2M*
44 FRANCE *1:5M*
45 SPAIN and PORTUGAL *1:5M*
46–47 North Central EUROPE *1:5M*
48–49 ITALY and the BALKANS *1:5M*
50–51 West RUSSIA, BELARUS and UKRAINE *1:7M*

AFRICA
52–53 *1:28M*

54–55 North AFRICA *1:16M*
Cape Verde *1:16M*
56–57 Central and South AFRICA *1:16M*
58–59 REPUBLIC OF SOUTH AFRICA *1:5M*

NORTH AMERICA
60–61 *1:25M*

62–63 CANADA *1:17M*
64–65 West CANADA *1:7M*
66–67 East CANADA *1:7M*
68–69 THE GREAT LAKES *1:3.5M*
70–71 UNITED STATES OF AMERICA *1:12M*
72–73 West UNITED STATES OF AMERICA *1:7M*
74–75 Southwest UNITED STATES OF AMERICA *1:3.5M*
Hawaiian Islands *1:6M*
Oahu *1:1.5M*
76–77 Central UNITED STATES OF AMERICA *1:7M*
78–79 East UNITED STATES OF AMERICA *1:7M*
80–81 Northeast UNITED STATES OF AMERICA *1:3.5M*
82–83 CENTRAL AMERICA and the CARIBBEAN *1:14M*
84 Central MEXICO *1:7M*

SOUTH AMERICA
85 *1:30M*

86–87 North SOUTH AMERICA *1:15M*
Galapagos Islands *1:15M*
88 South SOUTH AMERICA *1:15M*
South Georgia *1:15M*
89 VENEZUELA and COLOMBIA *1:7.5M*
90 Southeast BRAZIL *1:7.5M*
91 Central CHILE, Central ARGENTINA and URUGUAY *1:7.5M*

92 ANTARCTICA *1:28M*
93 INDIAN OCEAN *1:58M*
94–95 PACIFIC OCEAN *1:58M*
96 ATLANTIC OCEAN *1:58M*

97–144 INDEX

IN THIS GUIDE to States and Territories all independent states and major territories appear. The states and territories are arranged in alphabetical order using the same English-language conventional name form as is used on the maps. The name of the capital city is given in either its local form or in English-language form, whichever is more commonly used and understood. This reflects the names on the maps where alternative forms are also shown in brackets.

The statistics used for the area and population, and as the basis for languages and religions, are from the latest available sources. The information for the internal divisions in federal states may be for a less recent date than that for the entire country, but are the latest available.

The order of the different languages and religions reflects their relative importance within the country; generally all languages and religions with over one or two per cent speakers or adherents are mentioned.

For independent states membership of the following international organizations is shown by the abbreviations below. Territories are not shown as having separate membership of these international organizations.

ASEAN	Association of Southeast Asian Nations
CARICOM	Caribbean Community
CIS	Commonwealth of Independent States
COMM.	Commonwealth
EU	European Union
NAFTA	North American Free Trade Area
OAU	Organization of African Unity
OECD	Organization for Economic Cooperation and Development
OPEC	Organization of Petroleum Exporting Countries
SADC	Southern African Development Community
UN	United Nations

AFGHANISTAN

Status : REPUBLIC
Area : 652,225 sq km (251,825 sq mls)
Population : 20,141,000
Capital : KĀBUL
Language : DARI, PUSHTU, UZBEK, TURKMEN
Religion : SUNNI MUSLIM, SHI'A MUSLIM
Currency : AFGHANI
Organizations : UN

MAP PAGE: 19

A LANDLOCKED COUNTRY in central Asia, Afghanistan borders Pakistan, Iran, Turkmenistan, Uzbekistan, Tajikistan and China. Its central highlands are bounded by the Hindu Kush to the north and desert to the south and west. Most farming is on the plains round Kabul, the most populated area, and in the far northeast. The climate is dry, with extreme temperatures. Civil war has disrupted the rural-based economy. Exports include dried fruit, nuts, carpets, wool, hides and cotton.

ALBANIA

Status : REPUBLIC
Area : 28,748 sq km (11,100 sq mls)
Population : 3,645,000
Capital : TIRANA
Language : ALBANIAN (GHEG, TOSK DIALECTS), GREEK
Religion : SUNNI MUSLIM, GREEK ORTHODOX, R.CATHOLIC
Currency : LEK
Organizations : UN

MAP PAGE: 49

ALBANIA LIES IN the western Balkans of south Europe, on the Adriatic Sea. It is mountainous, with coastal plains which support half the population. The economy is based mainly on agriculture and mining, chiefly chromite. The fall of communism brought reform and foreign aid for the ailing economy.

ALGERIA

Status : REPUBLIC
Area : 2,381,741 sq km (919,595 sq mls)
Population : 28,548,000
Capital : ALGIERS
Language : ARABIC, FRENCH, BERBER
Religion : SUNNI MUSLIM, R.CATHOLIC
Currency : DINAR
Organizations : OAU, OPEC, UN

MAP PAGE: 54-55

ALGERIA IS ON the Mediterranean coast of North Africa. The second largest country in Africa, it extends southwards from the coast into the Sahara Desert. Over 85 per cent of the land area is a dry sandstone plateau, cut by valleys and rocky mountains, including the Hoggar Massif in the southeast. Though hot, arid and largely uninhabited, the region contains oil and gas reserves. To the north lie the Atlas Mountains, enclosing the grassland of the Chott Plateau. The mountains separate the arid south from the narrow coastal plain which has a Mediterranean climate and is well suited to agriculture. Most people live on the plain and on the fertile northern slopes of the Atlas. Hydrocarbons have been the mainstay of the economy. Though reserves are dwindling, oil, natural gas and related products still account for over 90 per cent of export earnings. Other industries produce building materials, food products, iron, steel and vehicles. Agriculture employs a quarter of the workforce, producing mainly food crops. Political unrest including Islamic militancy in the early 1990s weakened the economy.

AMERICAN SAMOA

Status : US TERRITORY
Area : 197 sq km (76 sq mls)
Population : 56,000
Capital : PAGO PAGO
Language : SAMOAN, ENGLISH
Religion : PROTESTANT, R.CATHOLIC
Currency : US DOLLAR

MAP PAGE: 5

LYING IN THE South Pacific Ocean, American Samoa consists of five islands and two coral atolls. The main island is Tutuila.

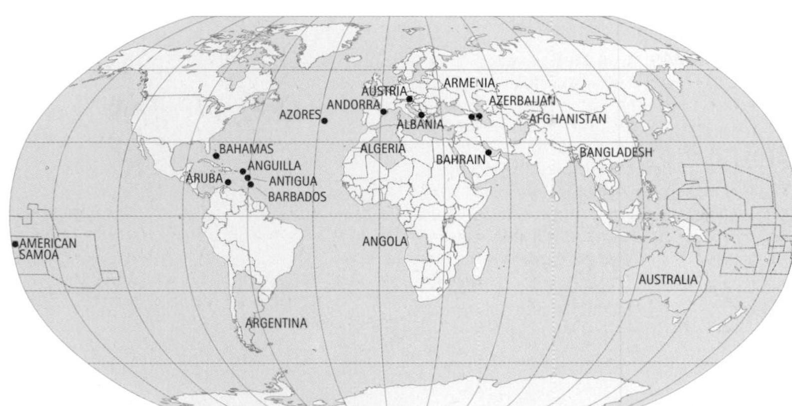

ANDORRA

Status : PRINCIPALITY
Area : 465 sq km (180 sq mls)
Population : 68,000
Capital : ANDORRA LA VELLA
Language : CATALAN, SPANISH, FRENCH
Religion : R.CATHOLIC
Currency : FRENCH FRANC, SPANISH PESETA
Organizations : UN

MAP PAGE: 45

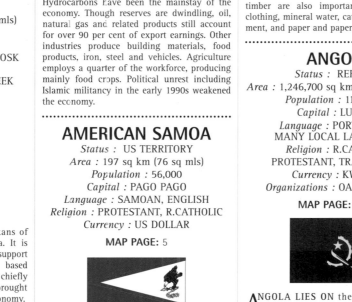

A LANDLOCKED STATE in southwest Europe, Andorra nestles in the Pyrenees between France and Spain. It consists of deep valleys and gorges, surrounded by mountains. Winter lasts six months, with heavy snowfalls; spring and summer are warm. One-third of the population lives in the capital. Tourism (about 12 million visitors a year), trade and banking are the main activities. Livestock, tobacco and timber are also important. Exports include clothing, mineral water, cattle, electrical equipment, and paper and paper products.

ANGOLA

Status : REPUBLIC
Area : 1,246,700 sq km (481,354 sq mls)
Population : 11,072,000
Capital : LUANDA
Language : PORTUGUESE, MANY LOCAL LANGUAGES
Religion : R.CATHOLIC, PROTESTANT, TRAD.BELIEFS
Currency : KWANZA
Organizations : OAU, SADC, UN

MAP PAGE: 56-57

ANGOLA LIES ON the Atlantic coast of southern central Africa. Its northern province, Cabinda, is separated from the rest of the country by part of Zaire. Much of Angola is high plateau, with a fertile coastal plain where most people live. The climate is equatorial in the north but desert in the south. Over half the workforce are farmers, growing cassava, maize, bananas, coffee, cotton and sisal. Angola is rich in minerals. Oil and diamonds account for 90 per cent of exports. Civil war has slowed economic development.

ANGUILLA

Status : UK TERRITORY
Area : 155 sq km (60 sq mls)
Population : 8,000
Capital : THE VALLEY
Language : ENGLISH
Religion : PROTESTANT, R.CATHOLIC
Currency : E. CARIB. DOLLAR

MAP PAGE: 83

ANGUILLA LIES AT the northern end of the Leeward Islands in the Caribbean Sea. Tourism and fishing are the basis of the economy.

ANTIGUA AND BARBUDA

Status : MONARCHY
Area : 442 sq km (171 sq mls)
Population : 66,000
Capital : ST JOHN'S
Language : ENGLISH, CREOLE
Religion : PROTESTANT, R.CATHOLIC
Currency : E. CARIB. DOLLAR
Organizations : CARICOM, COMM., UN

MAP PAGE: 83

THE STATE COMPRISES Antigua, Barbuda and Redonda, three of the Leeward Islands in the eastern Caribbean. Antigua, the largest and most populous, is mainly hilly scrubland, with many beaches and a warm, dry climate. The economy relies heavily on tourism.

ARGENTINA

Status : REPUBLIC
Area : 2,766,889 sq km (1,068,302 sq mls)
Population : 34,768,000
Capital : BUENOS AIRES
Language : SPANISH, ITALIAN, AMERINDIAN LANGUAGES
Religion : R.CATHOLIC, PROTESTANT, JEWISH
Currency : PESO
Organizations : UN

MAP PAGE: 88

ARGENTINA OCCUPIES ALMOST the whole of the southern part of South America, from Bolivia to Cape Horn and from the Andes to the Atlantic Ocean. The second largest South American state has four geographical regions: the subtropical forests and swampland of the Chaco in the north; the temperate fertile plains or Pampas in the centre, which support most of the farming and the bulk of the population; the wooded foothills and valleys of the Andes in the west; and the cold, semi-arid plateaux of Patagonia, south of the Colorado river. Farming was the making of Argentina and still plays an important part in terms of export earnings. Beef, mutton and wool are the main produce but grains, sugarcane, soybeans, oilseeds and cotton are also important. Industry now makes the biggest contribution to the economy. Oil and gas are being produced and some mineral resources, chiefly iron ore, are being exploited. Manufacturing has expanded to include not only food processing but also textiles, motor vehicles, steel products, iron and steel, industrial chemicals and machinery.

ARMENIA

Status : REPUBLIC
Area : 29,800 sq km (11,506 sq mls)
Population : 3,599,000
Capital : YEREVAN
Language : ARMENIAN, AZERI, RUSSIAN
Religion : ARMENIAN ORTHODOX, R.CATHOLIC, SHI'A MUSLIM
Currency : DRAM
Organizations : CIS, UN

MAP PAGE: 17

A LANDLOCKED STATE in southwest Asia, Armenia is in southwest Transcaucasia and borders Georgia, Azerbaijan, Iran and Turkey. It is mountainous, with a central plateau-basin, and dry, with warm summers and cold winters. One-third of the population lives in Yerevan. War over Nagorno-Karabakh, the majority-Armenian enclave in Azerbaijan, has crippled the economy. Manufacturing and mining were the main activities. Agriculture was also important, producing mostly grapes (for brandy), vegetables, wheat and tobacco.

ARUBA

Status : NETHERLANDS TERRITORY
Area : 193 sq km (75 sq mls)
Population : 70,000
Capital : ORANJESTAD
Language : DUTCH, PAPIAMENTO, ENGLISH
Religion : R.CATHOLIC, PROTESTANT
Currency : FLORIN

MAP PAGE: 83

THE MOST SOUTHWESTERLY of the islands in the Lesser Antilles, Aruba lies just off the coast of Venezuela. Tourism and offshore finance are the most important activities.

AUSTRALIA

Status : FEDERATION
Area : 7,682,300 sq km (2,966,153 sq mls)
Population : 18,054,000
Capital : CANBERRA
Language : ENGLISH, ITALIAN, GREEK, ABORIGINAL LANGUAGES
Religion : PROTESTANT, R.CATHOLIC, ORTHODOX, ABORIGINAL
Currency : DOLLAR
Organizations : COMM., OECD, UN

MAP PAGE: 6-7

AUSTRALIA, THE WORLD'S sixth largest country, occupies the smallest, flattest and driest continent. The western half of the continent is mostly arid plateaux, ridges and vast deserts. The central-eastern area comprises lowlands of river systems draining into Lake Eyre, while to the east is the Great Dividing Range, a belt of ridges and plateaux running from Queensland to Tasmania. Climatically more than two-thirds of the country is arid or semi-arid. The north is tropical monsoon: the south is subtropical in the west, temperate in the east. A majority of Australia's highly urbanized population lives in cities along on the east, southeast and southwest coasts. Australia is richly endowed with natural resources. It has vast mineral deposits and various sources of energy. Over 50 per cent of the land is suitable for livestock rearing, though only 6 per cent can be used for crop growing. Forests cover 18 per cent of the land and fishing grounds off the coasts are teeming with marine life. Agriculture was the main sector of the economy, but its contribution to national income has fallen in recent years, as other sectors have grown. Sheep-rearing is still the main activity and Australia is the world's leading wool producer. It is also a major beef exporter and wheat grower. Wool, wheat, meat (beef and mutton), sugar and dairy products account for a third of export earnings. Minerals have overtaken agricultural produce as an export earner. As well as being among the world's leading producers of iron ore, bauxite, nickel and uranium, Australia also exploits lead, gold, silver, zinc and copper ores, tungsten and gems. Its is a major producer of coal; petroleum and natural gas are also being exploited. Manufacturing and processing has shifted from being based on agricultural produce (chiefly food processing and textiles) to being based on mineral production. The main products are: iron and steel, construction materials, petrochemicals, motor vehicles, electrical goods. Along with manufacturing, trade and services are the key growth sectors of the economy. Tourism is a major foreign exchange earner, with 1.5 million visitors a year.

AUSTRALIAN CAPITAL TERRITORY

Status: FEDERAL TERRITORY
Area: 2,400 sq km (927 sq mls)
Population: 299,000
Capital: CANBERRA

NEW SOUTH WALES

Status: STATE
Area: 801,600 sq km (309,499 sq mls)
Population: 6,009,000
Capital: SYDNEY

NORTHERN TERRITORY

Status: TERRITORY
Area: 1,346,200 sq km (519,771 sq mls)
Population: 168,000
Capital: DARWIN

QUEENSLAND

Status: STATE
Area: 1,727,200 sq km (666,876 sq mls)
Population: 3,113,000
Capital: BRISBANE

SOUTH AUSTRALIA

Status: STATE
Area: 984,000 sq km (379,925 sq mls)
Population: 1,462,000
Capital: ADELAIDE

TASMANIA

Status: STATE
Area: 67,800 sq km (26,178 sq mls)
Population: 472,000
Capital: HOBART

VICTORIA

Status: STATE
Area: 227,600 sq km (87,877 sq mls)
Population: 4,462,000
Capital: MELBOURNE

WESTERN AUSTRALIA

Status: STATE
Area: 2,525,000 sq km (974,908 sq mls)
Population: 1,678,000
Capital: PERTH

AUSTRIA

Status : REPUBLIC
Area : 83,855 sq km (32,377 sq mls)
Population : 8,053,000
Capital : VIENNA
Language : GERMAN, SERBO-CROAT, TURKISH
Religion : R.CATHOLIC, PROTESTANT
Currency : SCHILLING
Organizations : EU, OECD, UN

MAP PAGE: 46

A LANDLOCKED STATE in central Europe, Austria borders the Czech Republic, Italy, Slovenia, Hungary, Germany, Switzerland and Liechtenstein. Two-thirds of the country, from the Swiss border to eastern Austria, lies within the Alps, with the low mountains of the Bohemian Massif to the north. The only lowlands are in the east. The Vienna Basin and Danube river valley in the northeast contain almost all the agricultural land and most of the population. Austria also has a large forested area, minerals, chiefly iron ore, and fast-flowing rivers for hydroelectric power. The climate varies according to altitude, but in general summers are warm and winters cold with heavy snowfalls. Industry is the mainstay of the economy. Manufactures include machinery, iron and steel, electrical goods, chemicals, food products, vehicles, and paper products. Agricultural output covers 90 per cent of food needs. Crops include cereals, fruit (chiefly grapes) and vegetables as well as silage, sugar beet and rapeseed. Dairy and timber products are exported. With 15 million visitors a year, tourism is a major industry.

AZERBAIJAN

Status : REPUBLIC
Area : 86,600 sq km (33,436 sq mls)
Population : 7,499,000
Capital : BAKU
Language : AZERI, ARMENIAN, RUSSIAN, LEZGIAN
Religion : SHI'A MUSLIM, SUNNI MUSLIM, RUSSIAN AND ARMENIAN
Currency : MANAT
Organizations : CIS, UN

MAP PAGE: 17

AZERBAIJAN IS IN east Transcaucasia, southwest Asia, on the Caspian Sea. Its region of Nakhichevan is separated from the rest of the country by part of Armenia. It has mountains in the northeast and west, valleys in the centre and a coastal plain. The climate is continental. It is rich in energy and mineral resources. Oil production onshore and offshore is the main industry and the basis of heavy industries. Agriculture is still important, with cotton and tobacco the main cash crops. War with Armenia has reduced output.

AZORES

Status : PORTUGUESE TERRITORY
Area : 2,247 sq km (868 sq mls)
Population : 237,800
Capital : PONTA DELGADA
Language : PORTUGUESE
Religion : R.CATHOLIC, PROTESTANT
Currency : PORT. ESCUDO

MAP PAGE: 34

A GROUP OF islands in the Atlantic Ocean around 1500 kilometres (1000 miles) west of Portugal.

THE BAHAMAS

Status : MONARCHY
Area : 13,939 sq km (5,382 sq mls)
Population : 278,000
Capital : NASSAU
Language : ENGLISH, CREOLE, FRENCH CREOLE
Religion : PROTESTANT, R.CATHOLIC
Currency : DOLLAR
Organizations : CARICOM, COMM., UN

MAP PAGE: 83

THE BAHAMAS IS an archipelago of about 700 islands and 2,400 cays in the northern Caribbean between the Florida coast of the USA and Haiti. Twenty-two islands are inhabited, and two thirds of the population live on the main island of New Providence. The climate is warm for much of the year, with heavy rainfall in the summer. Tourism is the islands' main industry. Banking, insurance and ship registration are also major foreign exchange earners. Exports include oil transhipments, chemicals, pharmaceuticals, crayfish and rum.

BAHRAIN

Status : MONARCHY
Area : 691 sq km (267 sq mls)
Population : 586,000
Capital : AL MANĀMAH
Language : ARABIC, ENGLISH
Religion : SHI'A MUSLIM, SUNNI MUSLIM, CHRISTIAN
Currency : DINAR
Organizations : UN

MAP PAGE: 18

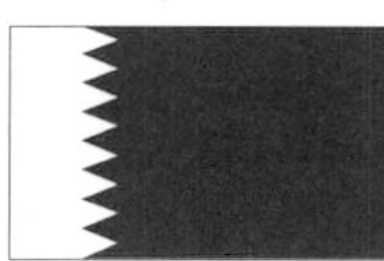

BAHRAIN'S 33 ARID islands lie in a bay in The Gulf, southwest Asia, off the coasts of Saudi Arabia and Qatar. Bahrain Island, the largest, has irrigated areas in the north where most people live. Oil is the main sector of the economy. Banking is also strong.

BANGLADESH

Status : REPUBLIC
Area : 143,998 sq km (55,598 sq mls)
Population : 120,433,000
Capital : DHAKA
Language : BENGALI, BIHARI, HINDI, ENGLISH, LOCAL LANGUAGES
Religion : SUNNI MUSLIM, HINDU, BUDDHIST, CHRISTIAN
Currency : TAKA
Organizations : COMM., UN

MAP PAGE: 23

THE SOUTH ASIAN state of Bangladesh is in the northeast of the Indian subcontinent, on the Bay of Bengal. It consists almost entirely of the low-lying alluvial plains and deltas of the Ganges and Brahmaputra rivers. The southwest is swampy, with mangrove forests in the delta area. The north, northeast and southeast have low forested hills. With a cultivable area of 70 per cent and few other natural resources, Bangladesh has a strong agricultural base, engaging two-thirds of the workforce. Food crops include rice, wheat, fruit and pulses; cash crops include jute, sugar cane, oilseeds, spices and tea. The main industries produce fertilizers, iron and steel, paper and glass as well as agricultural, marine and timber products. Exports include garments, raw and manufactured jute, fish and prawns, leather and tea. Bangladesh faces problems of overpopulation, low world commodity prices and the vagaries of climate. Floods and cyclones during the summer monsoon season often destroy crops. As a result, the country relies on foreign aid and remittances from its workers abroad.

BARBADOS

Status : MONARCHY
Area : 430 sq km (166 sq mls)
Population : 264,000
Capital : BRIDGETOWN
Language : ENGLISH, CREOLE (BAJAN)
Religion : PROTESTANT, R.CATHOLIC
Currency : DOLLAR
Organizations : UN, COMM., CARICOM

MAP PAGE: 83

THE MOST EASTERLY of the Caribbean islands, Barbados is small and densely populated, with a fairly flat terrain, white-sand beaches and a tropical climate. The economy is based on tourism, financial services light industries and sugar production.

BELARUS

Status: REPUBLIC
Area: 207,600 sq km (80,155 sq mls)
Population: 10,141,000
Capital: MINSK
Language: BELORUSSIAN, RUSSIAN, UKRAINIAN
Religion: BELORUSSIAN ORTHODOX, R.CATHOLIC
Currency: ROUBLE
Organizations: CIS, UN

MAP PAGE: 47

BELARUS IS A landlocked state in east Europe, bounded by Lithuania, Latvia, Russia, Ukraine and Poland. Belarus consists of low hills and forested plains, with many lakes, rivers and, in the south, extensive marshes. It has a continental climate. Agriculture contributes a third of national income, with beef cattle and grains as the major products. Manufacturing produces a range of items, from machinery and crude steel to computers and watches. Output has fallen since the ending of cheap Soviet energy supplies and raw materials.

BELGIUM

Status: MONARCHY
Area: 30,520 sq km (11,784 sq mls)
Population: 10,113,000
Capital: BRUSSELS
Language: DUTCH (FLEMISH), FRENCH, GERMAN (ALL OFFICIAL), ITALIAN
Religion: R.CATHOLIC, PROTESTANT
Currency: FRANC
Organizations: EU, OECD, UN

MAP PAGE: 42

BELGIUM LIES ON the North Sea coast of west Europe. Beyond low sand dunes and a narrow belt of reclaimed land are fertile plains which extend to the Sambre-Meuse river valley from where the land rises to the forested Ardennes plateau in the southeast. Belgium has mild winters and cool summers. It is densely populated and has a highly urbanized population. The economy is based on trade, industry and services. With few mineral resources, Belgium imports raw materials for processing and manufacture, and exports semi-finished and finished goods. Metal working, machine building, food processing and brewing, chemical production, iron and steel, and textiles are the major industries. External trade is equivalent to over 70 per cent of national income. Exports include cars, machinery, chemicals, foodstuffs and animals, iron and steel, diamonds, textiles and petroleum products. The agricultural sector is small, but provides for most food needs and a tenth of exports. A large services sector reflects Belgium's position as the home base for over 800 international institutions.

BELIZE

Status: MONARCHY
Area: 22,965 sq km (8,867 sq mls)
Population: 217,000
Capital: BELMOPAN
Language: ENGLISH, CREOLE, SPANISH, MAYAN
Religion: R.CATHOLIC, PROTESTANT, HINDU
Currency: DOLLAR
Organizations: CARICOM, COMM., UN

MAP PAGE: 82

BELIZE IS ON the Caribbean coast of central America and includes cays and a large barrier reef offshore. Belize's coastal areas are flat and swampy; the north and west are hilly, and the southwest contains the Maya mountain range. Jungle covers about half of the country. The climate is tropical, but tempered by sea breezes. A third of the population lives in the capital. The economy is based primarily on agriculture, forestry and fishing. Exports include sugar, clothing, citrus concentrates, bananas and lobsters.

BENIN

Status: REPUBLIC
Area: 112,620 sq km (43,483 sq mls)
Population: 5,561,000
Capital: PORTO-NOVO
Language: FRENCH, FON, YORUBA, ADJA, LOCAL LANGUAGES
Religion: TRAD.BELIEFS, R.CATHOLIC, SUNNI MUSLIM
Currency: CFA FRANC
Organizations: OAU, UN

MAP PAGE: 54

BENIN IS IN west Africa, on the Gulf of Guinea. The Atakora range lies in the northwest; the Niger plains in the northeast. To the south are plateaux, then a fertile plain and finally an area of lagoons and sandy coast. The climate is tropical in the north, but equatorial in the south. The economy is based mainly on agriculture and transit trade. Agricultural products, chiefly cotton, coffee, cocoa beans and oil palms, account for two thirds of export earnings. Oil, produced offshore, is also a major export.

BERMUDA

Status: UK TERRITORY
Area: 54 sq km (21 sq mls)
Population: 63,000
Capital: HAMILTON
Language: ENGLISH
Religion: PROTESTANT, R.CATHOLIC
Currency: DOLLAR

MAP PAGE: 83

IN THE ATLANTIC Ocean to the east of the USA, Bermuda is a group of small islands. The climate is warm and humid. The economy is based on tourism, insurance and shipping.

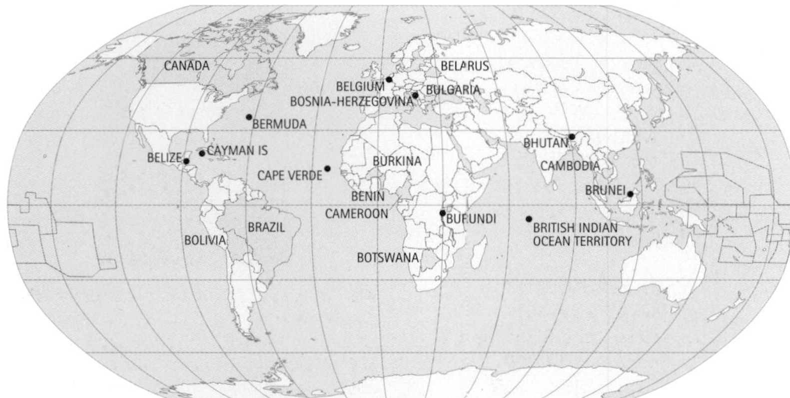

BHUTAN

Status: MONARCHY
Area: 46,620 sq km (18,000 sq mls)
Population: 1,638,000
Capital: THIMPHU
Language: DZONGKHA, NEPALI, ASSAMESE, ENGLISH
Religion: BUDDHIST, HINDU
Currency: NGULTRUM, INDIAN RUPEE
Organizations: UN

MAP PAGE: 23

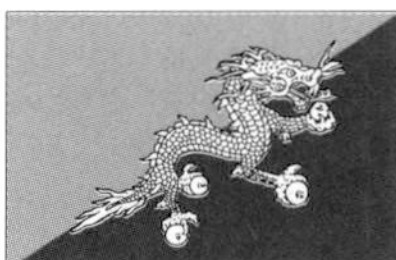

BHUTAN NESTLES IN the eastern Himalayas of south Asia, between China and India. It is mountainous in the north, with fertile valleys in the centre, where most people live, and forested lowlands in the south. The climate ranges between permanently cold in the far north and subtropical in the south. Most of the working population is involved in livestock raising and subsistence farming, though fruit and cardamon are exported. Electricity, minerals, timber and cement are the main exports. Bhutan relies heavily on aid.

BOLIVIA

Status: REPUBLIC
Area: 1,098,581 sq km (424,164 sq mls)
Population: 7,414,000
Capital: LA PAZ
Language: SPANISH, QUECHUA, AYMARA
Religion: R.CATHOLIC, PROTESTANT, BAHA'I
Currency: BOLIVIANO
Organizations: UN

MAP PAGE: 86-87

A LANDLOCKED STATE in central South America, Bolivia borders Brazil, Paraguay, Argentina, Chile and Peru. Most Bolivians live in the high plateau within the Andes ranges. The lowlands range between dense Amazon forest in the northeast and semi-arid grasslands in the southeast. Bolivia is rich in minerals, and sales (chiefly zinc, tin, silver and gold) generate half of export income. Natural gas and timber are also exported. Subsistence farming predominates, though sugar, soya beans and, unofficially, coca are exported.

BOSNIA-HERZEGOVINA

Status: REPUBLIC
Area: 51,130 sq km (19,741 sq mls)
Population: 4,484,000
Capital: SARAJEVO
Language: SERBO-CROAT
Religion: SUNNI MUSLIM, SERBIAN ORTHODOX, R.CATHOLIC, PROTESTANT
Currency: DINAR
Organizations: UN

MAP PAGE: 48-49

BOSNIA-HERZEGOVINA LIES IN the western Balkans of south Europe, on the Adriatic Sea. It is mountainous, with ridges crossing the country northwest-southeast. The main lowlands are around the Sava valley in the north. Summers are warm, but winters can be very cold. Civil war has ruined the economy, which was based on agriculture, sheep rearing and forestry. All production has ceased, the currency is worthless and only the black economy operates. Much of the population relies on UN relief.

BOTSWANA

Status: REPUBLIC
Area: 581,370 sq km (224,468 sq mls)
Population: 1,456,000
Capital: GABORONE
Language: ENGLISH (OFFICIAL), SETSWANA, SHONA, LOCAL LANGUAGES
Religion: TRAD.BELIEFS, PROTESTANT, R.CATHOLIC
Currency: PULA
Organizations : COMM., OAU, SADC, UN

MAP PAGE: 57

BOTSWANA, A LANDLOCKED state in south Africa, borders South Africa, Namibia, Zambia and Zimbabwe. Over half of the country lies within the upland Kalahari desert, with swamps to the north and salt-pans to the northeast. Most people live near the eastern border. The climate is subtropical, but drought-prone. The economy was founded upon cattle rearing, and beef is an important export, but now it is based on mining and industry. Diamonds account for 80 per cent of export earnings. Copper-nickel matte is also exported.

BRAZIL

Status: REPUBLIC
Area: 8,511,965 sq km (3,286,488 sq mls)
Population: 155,822,000
Capital: BRASÍLIA
Language: PORTUGUESE, GERMAN, JAPANESE, ITALIAN, AMERINDIAN LANGUAGES
Religion: R.CATHOLIC, SPIRITIST, PROTESTANT
Currency: REAL
Organizations: UN

MAP PAGE: 86-88

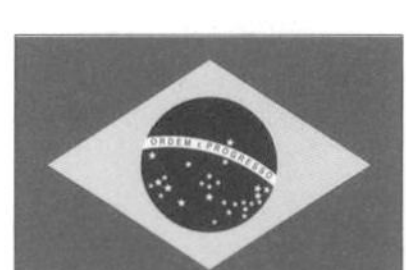

BRAZIL, IN EASTERN South America, covers almost half of the continent - making it the world's fifth largest country - and borders ten countries and the Atlantic Ocean. The northwest contains the vast Amazon Basin, backed by the Guiana Highlands. The centre west is largely a vast plateau of savannah and rock escarpments. The northeast is mostly semi-arid plateaux, while the east and south contain the rugged mountains and fertile valleys of the Brazilian Highlands and narrow, fertile coastal plains. The Amazon basin is hot, humid and wet; the rest of Brazil is cooler and drier, with seasonal variations. The northeast is drought-prone. Most Brazilians live in urban areas along the coast and on the central plateau, chiefly São Paulo, Rio de Janeiro and Salvador. Brazil is well endowed with minerals and energy resources. Over 50 per cent of the land is forested and 7 per cent is cultivated. Agriculture employs a quarter of the workforce. Brazil is the world's largest producer of coffee and a leading producer of sugar, cocoa, soya beans and beef. Timber production and fish catches are also important. Brazil is a major producer of iron, bauxite and manganese ores, zinc, copper, tin, gold and diamonds as well as oil and coal. Manufacturing contributes a quarter of national income. Industrial products include food, machinery, iron and steel, textiles, cars, pharmaceuticals, chemicals, refined oil, metal products and paper products. The main exports are machinery, metallic ores, cars, metal products, coffee beans, soya products, electrical and electronic goods, and orange juice. Despite its natural wealth and one of the largest economies in the world, Brazil has a large external debt and growing poverty gap.

BRITISH INDIAN OCEAN TERRITORY

Status: UK TERRITORY
Area: 60 sq km (23 sq mls)
Population: 3,100

MAP PAGE: 10

THE TERRITORY CONSISTS of the Chagos Archipelago in the middle of the Indian Ocean. The islands are uninhabited apart from the joint British-US military base on Diego Garcia.

BRUNEI

Status: MONARCHY
Area: 5,765 sq km (2,226 sq mls)
Population: 285,000
Capital: BANDAR SERI BEGAWAN
Language: MALAY, ENGLISH, CHINESE
Religion: SUNNI MUSLIM, BUDDHIST, CHRISTIAN
Currency: DOLLAR (RINGGIT)
Organizations: ASEAN, COMM., UN

MAP PAGE: 33

THE SOUTHEAST ASIAN state of Brunei lies on the northwest coast of the island of Borneo, on the South China Sea. Its two enclaves are surrounded inland by Malaysia. The western part is hilly with a narrow coastal plain which supports some crops and most of the population. The eastern part is mountainous and more forested. Tropical rainforest covers over two thirds of Brunei. The economy is dominated by the oil and gas industries.

BULGARIA

Status: REPUBLIC
Area: 110,994 sq km (42,855 sq mls)
Population: 8,402,000
Capital: SOFIA
Language: BULGARIAN, TURKISH, ROMANY, MACEDONIAN
Religion: BULGARIAN ORTHODOX, SUNNI MUSLIM
Currency: LEV
Organizations: UN

MAP PAGE: 49

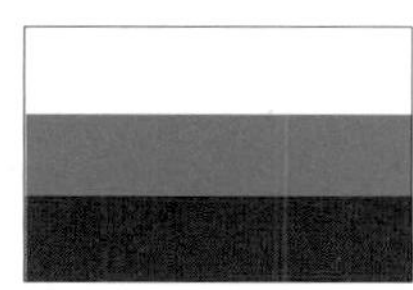

BULGARIA, IN SOUTH Europe, borders Romania, Yugoslavia, Macedonia, Greece, Turkey and the Black Sea. The Balkan Mountains separate the Danube plains in the north from the Rhodope massif and the lowlands in the south. The climate is subject to regional variation. The economy is based on agriculture and manufacturing, chiefly machinery, consumer goods, chemicals and metals. Disruption of Soviet-dominated trade has reduced output.

BURKINA

Status: REPUBLIC
Area: 274,200 sq km (105,869 sq mls)
Population: 10,200,000
Capital: OUAGADOUGOU
Language: FRENCH, MORE (MOSSI), FULANI, LOCAL LANGUAGES
Religion: TRAD.BELIEFS, SUNNI MUSLIM, R.CATHOLIC
Currency: CFA FRANC
Organizations: OAU, UN

MAP PAGE: 54

BURKINA, A LANDLOCKED country in west Africa, borders Mali, Niger, Benin, Togo, Ghana and Côte d'Ivoire. The north of Burkina lies in the Sahara and is arid. The south is mainly semi-arid savannah. Rainfall is erratic and droughts are common. Settlements centre on the country's rivers. Livestock rearing and farming are the main activities. Cotton, livestock, groundnuts and some minerals are exported. Burkina relies heavily on aid.

BURUNDI

Status: REPUBLIC
Area: 27,835 sq km (10,747 sq mls)
Population: 5,982,000
Capital: BUJUMBURA
Language: KIRUNDI (HUTU, TUTSI), FRENCH
Religion: R.CATHOLIC, TRAD.BELIEFS, PROTESTANT, SUNNI MUSLIM
Currency: FRANC
Organizations: OAU, UN

MAP PAGE: 56

THE DENSELY POPULATED east African state of Burundi borders Rwanda, Zaire, Tanzania and Lake Tanganyika. It is hilly with high plateaux and a tropical climate. Burundi depends upon subsistence farming, coffee exports and foreign aid.

CAMBODIA

Status: MONARCHY
Area: 181,000 sq km (69,884 sq mls)
Population: 9,836,000
Capital: PHNUM PENH
Language: KHMER, VIETNAMESE
Religion: BUDDHIST, R.CATHOLIC, SUNNI MUSLIM
Currency: RIEL
Organizations: UN

MAP PAGE: 32

CAMBODIA LIES IN southeast Asia, on the Gulf of Thailand. It consists of the Mekong river basin, with the Tonle Sap (Great Lake) at its centre. To the north, northeast and east are plateaux and to the southwest are mountains. The climate is tropical monsoon, with forests covering half the land. Most people live on the plains and are engaged in farming (chiefly rice growing), fishing and forestry. Devastated by civil war, Cambodia is dependent on aid.

CAMEROON

Status: REPUBLIC
Area: 475,442 sq km (183,569 sq mls)
Population: 13,277,000
Capital: YAOUNDÉ
Language: FRENCH, ENGLISH, FANG, BAMILEKE, MANY LOCAL LANGUAGES
Religion: TRAD.BELIEFS, R.CATHOLIC, SUNNI MUSLIM, PROTESTANT
Currency: CFA FRANC
Organizations: OAU, UN, COMM.

MAP PAGE: 54-55

CAMEROON IS IN west Africa, on the Gulf of Guinea. The coastal plains, southern and central plateaux are covered with tropical forest. The northern lowlands are semi-arid savannah, and the western highlands, around Mount Cameroon, support a range of crops. A majority of Cameroonians are farmers. Cocoa, coffee and cotton are the main cash crops, though crude oil, sawn wood and logs account for over half of export earnings.

CANADA

Status: FEDERATION
Area: 9,970,610 sq km (3,849,674 sq mls)
Population: 29,606,000
Capital: OTTAWA
Language: ENGLISH, FRENCH, AMERINDIAN LANGUAGES, INUKTITUT (ESKIMO)
Religion: R.CATHOLIC, PROTESTANT, GREEK ORTHODOX, JEWISH
Currency: DOLLAR
Organizations: COMM., NAFTA, OECD, UN

MAP PAGE: 62-63

THE WORLD'S SECOND largest country, Canada covers the northern two-fifths of North America and has coastlines on the Atlantic, Arctic and Pacific Oceans. On the west coast, the Cordilleran region contains coastal mountains, interior plateaux and the Rocky Mountains. To the east lie the fertile prairies. Further east, covering about half the total land area, is the Canadian, or Laurentian, Shield, fairly flat U-shaped lowlands around the Hudson Bay extending to Labrador. The Shield is bordered to the south by the fertile Great Lakes-St Lawrence lowlands. In the far north climatic conditions are polar. In general, however, Canada has a continental climate. Winters are long and cold with heavy snowfalls, while summers are hot with light to moderate rainfall. Most Canadians live in the south, chiefly in the southeast, in the urban areas of the Great Lakes-St Lawrence basin, principally Toronto and Montreal. Canada is well endowed with minerals, energy resources, forests and rich coastal waters. Only 5 per cent of land is classified as arable, but that is still a large area. Canada is among the world's leading exporter of wheat. Other major agricultural exports are apples, beef cattle, potatoes, oilseeds and feed grain. Canada is also a leading exporter of wood from its vast coniferous forests, and fish and seafood from its rich Atlantic and Pacific fishing grounds. It is a top producer of iron ore, uranium nickel, copper, zinc and other minerals, as well as crude oil and natural gas. Its abundant raw materials are the basis of for manufacturing industries. The principal ones are car manufacture, food processing, chemical production, lumber, woodpulp and paper making, oil refining, iron and steel, and metal refining. Canada is an important trading nation. External trade is equivalent to about 30 per cent of national income. Exports include cars, crude materials, minerals fuels (chiefly oil and gas), food (chiefly wheat), newsprint, lumber, wood pulp, industrial machinery and aluminium. Canada has an important banking and insurance sector.

ALBERTA

Status: PROVINCE
Area: 661,190 sq km (255,287 sq mls)
Population: 2,672,000
Capital: EDMONTON

BRITISH COLUMBIA

Status: PROVINCE
Area: 947,800 sq km (365,948 sq mls)
Population: 3,570,000
Capital: VICTORIA

MANITOBA

Status: PROVINCE
Area. 649,950 sq km (250,947 sq mls)
Population: 1,117,000
Capital: WINNIPEG

NEW BRUNSWICK

Status: PROVINCE
Area: 73,440 sq km (28,355 sq mls)
Population: 751,000
Capital: FREDERICTON

NEWFOUNDLAND

Status: PROVINCE
Area: 405,720 sq km (156,649 sq mls)
Population: 581,000
Capital: ST JOHN'S

NORTHWEST TERRITORIES

Status: TERRITORY
Area: 3,426,320 sq km (1,322,910 sq mls)
Population: 63,000
Capital: YELLOWKNIFE

NOVA SCOTIA

Status: PROVINCE
Area: 55,490 sq km (21,425 sq mls)
Population: 925,000
Capital: HALIFAX

ONTARIO

Status: PROVINCE
Area: 1,068,580 sq km (412,581 sq mls)
Population: 10,795,000
Capital: TORONTO

PRINCE EDWARD ISLAND

Status: PROVINCE
Area: 5,660 sq km (2,158 sq mls)
Population: 132,000
Capital: CHARLOTTETOWN

QUEBEC

Status: PROVINCE
Area: 1,540,680 sq km (594,860 sq mls)
Population: 7,226,000
Capital: QUÉBEC

SASKATCHEWAN

Status: PROVINCE
Area: 652,330 sq km (251,866 sq mls)
Population: 1,002,000
Capital: REGINA

YUKON TERRITORY

Status: TERRITORY
Area: 483,450 sq km (186,661 sq mls)
Population: 33,000
Capital: WHITEHORSE

CAPE VERDE

Status: REPUBLIC
Area: 4,033 sq km (1,557 sq mls)
Population: 392,000
Capital: PRAIA
Language: PORTUGUESE, PORTUGUESE CREOLE
Religion: R.CATHOLIC, PROTESTANT, TRAD.BELIEFS
Currency: ESCUDO
Organizations: OAU, UN

MAP PAGE: 54

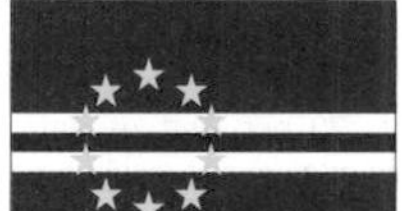

CAPE VERDE COMPRISES ten semi-arid volcanic islands and five islets off the coast of west Africa. The economy is based on fishing and subsistence farming, but relies on workers' remittances and foreign aid.

CAYMAN ISLANDS

Status: UK TERRITORY
Area: 259 sq km (100 sq mls)
Population: 31,000
Capital: GEORGE TOWN
Language: ENGLISH
Religion: PROTESTANT, R.CATHOLIC
Currency: DOLLAR

MAP PAGE: 83

IN THE CARIBBEAN, northwest of Jamaica, there are three main islands: Grand Cayman, Little Cayman and Cayman Brac. They form one of the world's major offshore financial centres, though tourism is also important.

CENTRAL AFRICAN REPUBLIC

Status: REPUBLIC
Area: 622,436 sq km (240,324 sq mls)
Population: 3,315,000
Capital: BANGUI
Language: FRENCH, SANGO, BANDA, BAYA, LOCAL LANGUAGES
Religion: PROTESTANT, R.CATHOLIC, TRAD. BELIEFS, SUNNI MUSLIM
Currency: CFA FRANC
Organizations: OAU, UN

MAP PAGE: 56

THE LANDLOCKED CENTRAL African Republic borders Chad, Sudan, Zaire, Congo and Cameroon. Most of the country is savannah plateaux, drained by the Ubangi and Chari river systems, with mountains to the north and west. The climate is hot with high rainfall. Most of the population live in the south and west, and a majority of the workforce is involved in subsistence farming. Some cotton, coffee, tobacco and timber are exported. However, diamonds and some gold account for more than half of export earnings.

CHAD

Status: REPUBLIC
Area: 1,284,000 sq km (495,755 sq mls)
Population: 6,361,000
Capital: NDJAMENA
Language: ARABIC, FRENCH, MANY LOCAL LANGUAGES
Religion: SUNNI MUSLIM, TRAD.BELIEFS, R.CATHOLIC
Currency: CFA FRANC
Organizations: OAU, UN

MAP PAGE: 55

CHAD IS A landlocked state of central Africa, bordered by Libya, Sudan, Central African Republic, Niger, Nigeria and Cameroon. It consists of plateaux, the Tibesti massif in the north and Lake Chad basin in the west. Climatic conditions range between desert in the north and tropical forest in the southwest. Most people live in the south and near Lake Chad. Farming and cattle herding are the main activities, cattle and raw cotton the chief exports. Impoverished by civil war and drought, Chad relies upon foreign aid.

CHILE

Status: REPUBLIC
Area: 756,945 sq km (292,258 sq mls)
Population: 14,210,000
Capital: SANTIAGO
Language: SPANISH, AMERINDIAN LANGUAGES
Religion: R.CATHOLIC, PROTESTANT
Currency: PESO
Organizations: UN

MAP PAGE: 88

CHILE HUGS THE Pacific coast of the southern half of South America. Between the High Andes in the east and the lower coastal ranges is a central valley, with a mild climate, where most Chileans live. To the north is arid desert, to the south is cold, wet forested grassland. Chile is a leading exporter of copper, and is rich in other minerals and nitrates. Agriculture, forestry and fishing are important activities. Timber products, chemicals products and other manufactures account for a third of exports.

CHINA

Status: REPUBLIC
Area: 9,560,900 sq km (3,691,484 sq mls)
Population: 1,221,462,000
Capital: BEIJING
Language: CHINESE (MANDARIN OFFICIAL), MANY REGIONAL LANGUAGES
Religion: CONFUCIAN, TAOIST, BUDDHIST, SUNNI MUSLIM, R.CATHOLIC
Currency: YUAN
Organizations: UN

MAP PAGE: 15, 24-25

CHINA, THE WORLD'S third largest country, occupies almost the whole of east Asia, borders fourteen states and has coastlines on the Yellow, East China and South China seas. It has an amazing variety of landscapes. The southwest contains the high Tibetan plateau, flanked by the Himalayas and Kunlun mountains. The northwest is mountainous with arid basins and extends from the Tien Shan and Altai ranges and vast Taklimakan desert in the west to the Mongolian plateau and Gobi desert in the centre-east. Eastern China is predominantly lowland and is divided broadly into the basins of the Huang He (Yellow River) in the north, Chang Jiang (Yangtze) in the centre and Xi Jiang (Pearl River) in the southeast. The main exceptions are the Manchurian uplands, loess plateau, Qin Ling range, southeast mountains and the Yunnan plateau in the far south. Climatic conditions and vegetation are as diverse as the topography. Northern China has an extreme continental climate, much of the country experiences temperate conditions, while the southwest enjoys a moist, warm subtropical climate. More than 70 per cent of China's huge population live in rural areas, chiefly in the northern part of the eastern lowlands and along the coast. Agriculture and livestock rearing involves two thirds of the working population. China is the world's largest producer of rice, wheat, soya beans and sugar and is self-sufficient in cereals, fish and livestock. Cotton, soya bean and oilseeds are the major cash crops. China is rich in coal, oil, natural gas and many minerals, chiefly iron ore, wolfram (tungsten ore), tin and phosphates. Industrial and agricultural production were given a boost by the economic reforms of the 1980s which introduced a degree of private enterprise. Industry also benefited from the setting up of joint ventures and the inflow of foreign investment. The major industries produce iron and steel, machinery, textiles, processed foods, chemicals and building materials. China's chief exports are textiles and clothing, petroleum and products, machinery and transport equipment, agricultural products, metal products, iron and steel.

ANHUI (ANHWEI)
Status: PROVINCE
Area: 139,000 sq km (53,668 sq miles)
Population: 58,340,000
Capital: HEFEI

BEIJING (PEKING)
Status: MUNICIPALITY
Area: 16,800 sq km (6,487 sq miles)
Population: 11,020,000
Capital: BEIJING

FUJIAN (FUKIEN)
Status: PROVINCE
Area: 121,400 sq km (46,873 sq miles)
Population: 31,160,000
Capital: FUZHOU

GANSU (KANSU)
Status: PROVINCE
Area: 453,700 sq km (175,175 sq miles)
Population: 23,140,000
Capital: LANZHOU

GUANGDONG (KWANGTUNG)
Status: PROVINCE
Area: 178,000 sq km (68,726 sq miles)
Population: 65,250,000
Capital: GUANGZHOU

GUANGXI ZHUANG (KWANGSI CHUANG)
Status: AUTONOMOUS REGION
Area: 236,000 sq km (91,120 sq miles)
Population: 43,800,000
Capital: NANNING

GUIZHOU (KWEICHOW)
Status: PROVINCE
Area: 176,000 sq km (67,954 sq miles)
Population: 33,610,000
Capital: GUIYANG

HAINAN
Status: PROVINCE
Area: 34,000 sq km (13,127 sq miles)
Population: 6,860,000
Capital: HAIKOU

HEBEI (HOPEI)
Status: PROVINCE
Area: 187,700 sq km (72,471 sq miles)
Population: 62,750,000
Capital: SHIJIAZHUANG

HEILONGJIANG (HEILUNGKIANG)
Status: PROVINCE
Area: 454,600 sq km (175,522 sq miles)
Population: 36,080,000
Capital: HARBIN

HENAN (HONAN)
Status: PROVINCE
Area: 167,000 sq km (64,479 sq miles)
Population: 88,620,000
Capital: ZHENGZHOU

HONG KONG
Status: SPECIAL ADMINISTRATIVE REGION
Area: 1,075 sq km (415 sq mls)
Population: 6,190,000
Capital: HONG KONG
Language: CHINESE (CANTONESE, MANDARIN), ENGLISH
Religion: BUDDHIST, TAOIST, PROTESTANT
Currency: DOLLAR

HUBEI (HUPEI)
Status: PROVINCE
Area: 185,900 sq km (71,776 sq miles)
Population: 55,800,000
Capital: WUHAN

HUNAN
Status: PROVINCE
Area: 210,000 sq km (81,081 sq miles)
Population: 62,670,000
Capital: CHANGSHA

JIANGSU (KIANGSU)
Status: PROVINCE
Area: 102,600 sq km (39,614 sq miles)
Population: 69,110,000
Capital: NANJING

JIANGXI (KIANGSI)
Status: PROVINCE
Area: 166,900 sq km (64,440 sq miles)
Population: 39,130,000
Capital: NANCHANG

JILIN (KIRIN)
Status: PROVINCE
Area: 187,000 sq km (72,201 sq miles)
Population: 25,320,000
Capital: CHANGCHUN

LIAONING
Status: PROVINCE
Area: 147,400 sq km (56,911 sq miles)
Population: 40,160,000
Capital: SHENYANG

NEI MONGOL (INNER MONGOLIA)
Status: AUTONOMOUS REGION
Area: 1,183,000 sq km (456,759 sq miles)
Population: 22,070,000
Capital: HOHHOT

NINGXIA HUI (NINGHSIA HUI)
Status: AUTONOMOUS REGION
Area: 66,400 sq km (25,637 sq miles)
Population: 4,870,000
Capital: YINCHUAN

QINGHAI (TSINGHAI)
Status: PROVINCE
Area: 721,000 sq km (278,380 sq miles)
Population: 4,610,000
Capital: XINING

SHAANXI (SHENSI)
Status: PROVINCE
Area: 205,600 sq km (79,383 sq miles)
Population: 34,050,000
Capital: XI'AN

SHANDONG (SHANTUNG)
Status: PROVINCE
Area: 153,300 sq km (59,189 sq miles)
Population: 86,100,000
Capital: JINAN

SHANGHAI
Status: MUNICIPALITY
Area: 6,300 sq km (2,432 sq miles)
Population: 13,450,000
Capital: SHANGHAI

SHANXI (SHANSI)
Status: PROVINCE
Area: 156,300 sq km (60,348 sq miles)
Population: 29,790,000
Capital: TAIYUAN

SICHUAN (SZECHWAN)
Status: PROVINCE
Area: 569,000 sq km (219,692 sq miles)
Population: 109,980,000
Capital: CHENGDU

TIANJIN (TIENTSIN)
Status: MUNICIPALITY
Area: 11,300 sq km (4,363 sq miles)
Population: 9,200,000
Capital: TIANJIN

XIZANG (TIBET)
Status: AUTONOMOUS REGION
Area: 1,228,400 sq km (474,288 sq miles)
Population: 2,280,000
Capital: LHASA

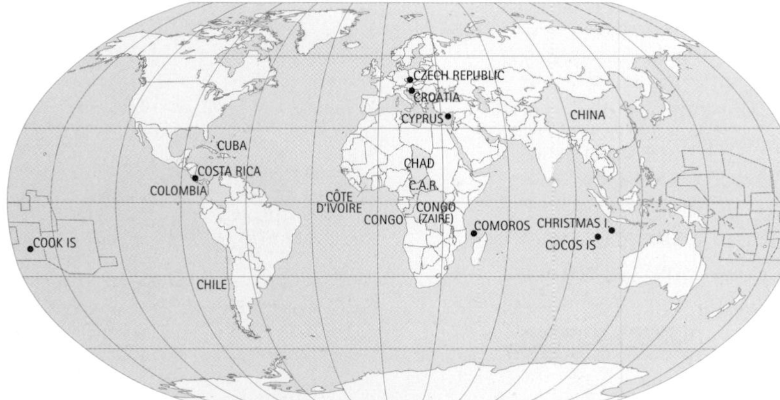

XINJIANG UYGUR (SINKIANG UIGHUR)

Status: AUTONOMOUS REGION
Area: 1,600,000 sq km (617,763 sq miles)
Population: 15,810,000
Capital: ÜRÜMQI

YUNNAN

Status: PROVINCE
Area: 394,000 sq km (152,124 sq miles)
Population: 38,320,000
Capital: KUNMING

ZHEJIANG (CHEKIANG)

Status: PROVINCE
Area: 101,800 sq km (39,305 sq miles)
Population: 42,360,000
Capital: HANGZHOU

CHRISTMAS ISLAND

Status: AUSTRALIAN TERRITORY
Area: 135 sq km (52 sq mls)
Population: 2,000
Capital: THE SETTLEMENT
Language: ENGLISH
Religion: BUDDHIST, SUNNI MUSLIM, PROTESTANT, R.CATHOLIC
Currency: AUSTR. DOLLAR

MAP PAGE: 25

COCOS ISLANDS

Status: AUSTRALIAN TERRITORY
Area: 14 sq km (5 sq mls)
Population: 1,000
Capital: HOME ISLAND
Language: ENGLISH
Religion: SUNNI MUSLIM, CHRISTIAN
Currency: AUSTR. DOLLAR

MAP PAGE: 25

THE COCOS ISLANDS are two separate coral atolls in the east of the Indian Ocean between Sri Lanka and Australia. Most of the population live on West Island and Home Island.

COLOMBIA

Status: REPUBLIC
Area: 1,141,748 sq km (440,831 sq mls)
Population: 35,099,000
Capital: BOGOTÁ
Language: SPANISH, AMERINDIAN LANGUAGES
Religion: R.CATHOLIC, PROTESTANT
Currency: PESO
Organizations: UN

MAP PAGE: 86

A STATE IN northwest South America, Colombia has coastlines on the Pacific Ocean and the Caribbean Sea. Behind coastal plains lie three ranges of the Andes, separated by high valleys and plateaux where most Colombians live. To the southeast are the prairies and then the jungle of the Amazon. Colombia has a tropical climate, though temperatures vary with altitude. Only 5 per cent of land can be cultivated, but a range of crops are grown. Coffee (Colombia is the world's second largest producer), sugar, bananas, cotton and flowers are exported. Petroleum and its products are the main export. Coal, nickel, gold, silver, platinum and emeralds (Colombia is the world's largest producer) are mined. Industry involves mainly processing minerals and agricultural produce. In spite of government efforts to stop the drugs trade, coca growing and cocaine smuggling are rife.

COMOROS

Status: REPUBLIC
Area: 1,862 sq km (719 sq mls)
Population: 653,000
Capital: MORONI
Language: COMORIAN, FRENCH, ARABIC
Religion: SUNNI MUSLIM, R.CATHOLIC
Currency: FRANC
Organizations: OAU, UN

MAP PAGE: 57

THE STATE COMPRISES three volcanic islands Grande Comore, Anjouan and Mohéli and some coral atolls in the Indian Ocean, off the east African coast. The tropical islands are mountainous, with poor soil. Subsistence farming predominates, but vanilla, cloves and ylang-ylang (an essential oil) are exported.

CONGO

Status: REPUBLIC
Area: 342,000 sq km (132,047 sq mls)
Population: 2,590,000
Capital: BRAZZAVILLE
Language: FRENCH (OFFICIAL), KONGO, MONOKUTUBA, LOCAL LANGUAGES
Religion: R.CATHOLIC, PROTESTANT, TRAD. BELIEFS, SUNNI MUSLIM
Currency: CFA FRANC
Organizations: OAU, UN

MAP PAGE: 56

CONGO, IN CENTRAL Africa, is for the most part forest or savannah-covered plateaux drained by the Ubangi-Congo river systems. Sand dunes and lagoons line the short Atlantic coast. The climate is hot and tropical. Most Congolese live in the southern third of the country. Oil is the main source of export revenue. Diamonds, lead, zinc and gold are also mined. Hardwoods are the second biggest export earner. Half of the workforce are farmers, growing food crops and cash crops including sugar, coffee, cocoa and oil palms.

CONGO (ZAIRE)

Status: REPUBLIC
Area: 2,345,410 sq km (905,568 sq mls)
Population: 43,901,000
Capital: KINSHASA
Language: FRENCH, LINGALA, SWAHILI, KONGO, MANY LOCAL LANGUAGES
Religion: R.CATHOLIC, PROTESTANT, SUNNI MUSLIM, TRAD. BELIEFS
Currency: ZAÏRE
Organizations: OAU, UN

MAP PAGE: 56-57

THE CENTRAL AFRICAN state of Congo consists of the basin of the Congo river flanked by plateaux, with high mountain ranges to the north and east and a short Atlantic coastline to the west. The climate is tropical with rainforest close to the Equator and savannah to the north and south. Congo has fertile land that grows a range of food crops and cash crops, chiefly coffee. It has vast mineral resources, copper and diamonds being the most important. However economic mismanagement and political turmoil have ruined the economy.

COOK ISLANDS

Status: NEW ZEALAND TERRITORY
Area: 293 sq km (113 sq mls)
Population: 19,000
Capital: AVARUA
Language: ENGLISH, MAORI
Religion: PROTESTANT, R.CATHOLIC
Currency: DOLLAR

MAP PAGE: 5

COSTA RICA

Status: REPUBLIC
Area: 51,100 sq km (19,730 sq mls)
Population: 3,333,000
Capital: SAN JOSÉ
Language: SPANISH
Religion: R.CATHOLIC, PROTESTANT
Currency: COLÓN
Organizations: UN

MAP PAGE: 83

COSTA RICA HAS coastlines on the Caribbean Sea and Pacific Ocean. From the tropical coastal plains the land rises to mountains and a temperate central plateau where most people live. Farming is the main activity and exports include bananas, coffee, sugar, flowers and beef. There is some mining and a strong manufacturing sector, producing a range of goods from clothing (the main export) and electrical components to food products and cement.

CÔTE D'IVOIRE

Status: REPUBLIC
Area: 322,463 sq km (124,504 sq mls)
Population: 14,230,000
Capital: YAMOUSSOUKRO
Language: FRENCH (OFFICIAL), AKAN, KRU, GUR, LOCAL LANGUAGES
Religion: TRAD.BELIEFS, SUNNI MUSLIM, R.CATHOLIC
Currency: CFA FRANC
Organizations: OAU, UN

MAP PAGE: 54

CÔTE D'IVOIRE (IVORY Coast) is in west Africa, on the Gulf of Guinea. In the north are plateaux and savannah, in the south are low undulating plains and rainforest, with sandbars and lagoons on the coast. Temperatures are warm, and rainfall is heavier in the south. Most of the workforce is engaged in farming. Côte d'Ivoire is a major producer of cocoa and coffee, and agricultural products (including cotton and timber) are the main export. Gold and diamonds are mined and some oil is produced offshore.

CROATIA

Status: REPUBLIC
Area: 56,538 sq km (21,829 sq mls)
Population: 4,495,000
Capital: ZAGREB
Language: SERBO-CROAT
Religion: R.CATHOLIC, ORTHODOX, SUNNI MUSLIM
Currency: KUNA
Organizations: UN

MAP PAGE: 48-49

THE SOUTH EUROPEAN state of Croatia has a long coastline on the Adriatic Sea and many offshore islands. Coastal areas have a Mediterranean climate, inland is colder and wetter. Croatia was strong agriculturally and industrially, but secessionist and ethnic conflict, the loss of markets and the loss of tourist revenue have caused economic difficulties.

CUBA

Status: REPUBLIC
Area: 110,860 sq km (42,803 sq mls)
Population: 11,041,000
Capital: HAVANA
Language: SPANISH
Religion: R.CATHOLIC, PROTESTANT
Currency: PESO
Organizations: UN

MAP PAGE: 83

CUBA COMPRISES THE island of Cuba, the largest island in the Caribbean, and many islets and cays. A fifth of Cubans live in and around Havana. Sugar, with molasses and rum, account for two thirds of export earnings. Severe recession followed the disruption of traditional trade with east Europe and the ending of Russian subsidies.

CYPRUS

Status: REPUBLIC
Area: 9,251 sq km (3,572 sq mls)
Population: 742,000
Capital: NICOSIA
Language: GREEK, TURKISH, ENGLISH
Religion: GREEK (CYPRIOT) ORTHODOX, SUNNI MUSLIM
Currency: POUND
Organizations: COMM., UN

MAP PAGE: 16

THE MEDITERRANEAN ISLAND of Cyprus has hot summers and mild winters. The economy of the Greek south is based mainly on specialist agriculture and tourism, though shipping and offshore banking are also major sources of income. The Turkish north depends upon agriculture, tourism and aid from Turkey.

CZECH REPUBLIC

Status: REPUBLIC
Area: 78,864 sq km (30,450 sq mls)
Population: 10,331,000
Capital: PRAGUE
Language: CZECH, MORAVIAN, SLOVAK
Religion: R.CATHOLIC, PROTESTANT
Currency: KORUNA
Organizations: UN, OECD

MAP PAGE: 46-47

THE LANDLOCKED CZECH Republic in central Europe consists of rolling countryside, wooded hills and fertile valleys. The climate is temperate, but summers are warm and winters fairly cold. The country has substantial reserves of coal and lignite, timber and some minerals, chiefly iron ore, graphite, garnets and silver. It is highly industrialized and major manufactures include industrial machinery, consumer goods, cars, iron and steel, chemicals and glass. Since separation from Slovakia in January 1993, trade between the two countries has declined, exacerbating the difficulties the economy was already experiencing from the introduction of a free-market economy. There is, however, a growing tourist industry.

DENMARK

Status: MONARCHY
Area: 43,075 sq km (16,631 sq mls)
Population: 5,228,000
Capital: COPENHAGEN
Language: DANISH
Religion: PROTESTANT, R.CATHOLIC
Currency: KRONE
Organizations: EU, OECD, UN

MAP PAGE: 37

THE KINGDOM OF Denmark in north Europe occupies the Jutland Peninsula and nearly 500 islands in and between the North and Baltic seas. The country is low-lying, with a mixture of fertile and sandy soils, and long, indented coastlines. The climate is cool and temperate, with rainfall throughout the year. A fifth of the population lives in Greater Copenhagen on the largest of the islands, Zealand. Denmark's main natural resource is its agricultural potential; two thirds of the total area is fertile farmland or pasture. Agriculture, forestry and fishing are all important sectors of the economy. The chief agricultural products are cheese and other dairy products, beef and bacon, much of which is exported. Some oil and natural gas is produced from fields in the North Sea. Manufacturing, largely based on imported raw materials, now accounts for over half of exports. The main industries are iron and metal working, food processing and brewing, chemicals and engineering. Exports include machinery, food, chemicals, furniture, fuels and energy, and transport equipment.

DJIBOUTI

Status: REPUBLIC
Area: 23,200 sq km (8,958 sq mls)
Population: 577,000
Capital: DJIBOUTI
Language: SOMALI, FRENCH, ARABIC, ISSA, AFAR
Religion: SUNNI MUSLIM, R.CATHOLIC
Currency: FRANC
Organizations: OAU, UN

MAP PAGE: 56

DJIBOUTI LIES IN northeast Africa, on the Gulf of Aden. It consists mostly of low-lying desert, with some areas below sea level and a mountainous area to the north. Temperatures are high and rainfall is low. Most people live in the coastal strip. There is some camel, sheep and goat herding, and cattle, hides and skins are the main exports. With few natural resources, the economy is based on services and trade. The deep-water port and the railway line to Addis Ababa account for about two thirds of national income.

DOMINICA

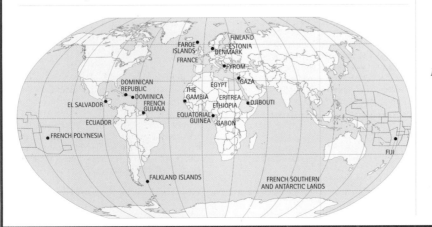

Status: REPUBLIC
Area: 750 sq km (290 sq mls)
Population: 71,000
Capital: ROSEAU
Language: ENGLISH, FRENCH CREOLE
Religion: R.CATHOLIC, PROTESTANT
Currency: E. CARIB. DOLLAR, POUND STERLING, FRENCH FRANC
Organizations: CARICOM, COMM., UN

MAP PAGE: 83

DOMINICA IS THE most northerly of the Windward Islands in the eastern Caribbean. It is mountainous and forested, with a coastline of steep cliffs, and features geysers and hot springs. The climate is tropical and rainfall abundant. A quarter of Dominicans live in the capital. The economy is based on agriculture, with bananas (the major export), coconuts and citrus fruits the most important crops. There is some forestry, fishing and mining. Manufactured exports include soap, coconut oil, rum and bottled water. Tourism is growing.

DOMINICAN REPUBLIC

Status: REPUBLIC
Area: 48,442 sq km (18,704 sq mls)
Population: 7,915,000
Capital: SANTO DOMINGO
Language: SPANISH, FRENCH CREOLE
Religion: R.CATHOLIC, PROTESTANT
Currency: PESO
Organizations: UN

MAP PAGE: 83

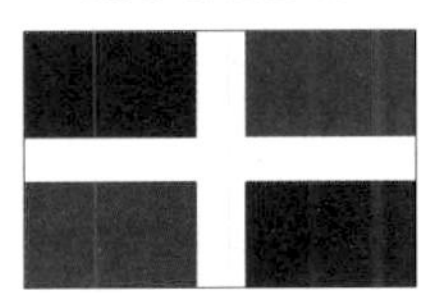

THE STATE OCCUPIES the eastern two thirds of the Caribbean island of Hispaniola. It has a series of mountain ranges, including the highest peaks in the region, fertile valleys and a large coastal plain in the east. The climate is hot tropical, with heavy rainfall. A third of the population lives in the capital. Sugar, coffee and cocoa are the main cash crops. Bauxite, nickel (the main export), gold and silver are mined, and there is some light industry. Tourism is the main foreign exchange earner.

ECUADOR

Status: REPUBLIC
Area: 272,045 sq km (105,037 sq mls)
Population: 11,460,000
Capital: QUITO
Language: SPANISH, QUECHUA, AMERINDIAN LANGUAGES
Religion: R.CATHOLIC, PROTESTANT
Currency: SUCRE
Organizations: UN

MAP PAGE: 86

ECUADOR IS IN northwest South America, on the Pacific coast. It consists of a broad coastal plain, the high ranges of the Andes and the forested upper Amazon basin to the east. The climate is tropical, moderated by altitude. Most people live on the coast or in the mountain valleys. Ecuador is one of the continent's leading oil producers. Mineral reserves include gold, silver, zinc and copper. Most of the workforce depends on agriculture. Ecuador is the world's leading producer of bananas. Shrimps, coffee and cocoa are also exported.

EGYPT

Status: REPUBLIC
Area: 1,000,250 sq km (386,199 sq mls)
Population: 59,226,000
Capital: CAIRO
Language: ARABIC, FRENCH
Religion: SUNNI MUSLIM, COPTIC CHRISTIAN
Currency: POUND
Organizations: OAU, UN

MAP PAGE: 55

EGYPT, ON THE eastern Mediterranean coast of North Africa, is low-lying, with areas below sea level in the west, and in the Qattara depression, and mountain ranges along the Red Sea coast and in the Sinai peninsula. It is a land of desert and semi-desert, except for the Nile valley, where 99 per cent of Egyptians live, about half of them in towns. The summers are hot, the winters mild and rainfall is negligible. Less than 4 per cent of land (chiefly around the Nile floodplain and delta) is cultivated, but farming employs half the workforce and contributes a sixth of exports. Cotton is the main cash crop. Rice, fruit and vegetables are exported, but Egypt imports over half its food needs. It has major reserves of oil and natural gas, phosphates, iron ore, manganese and nitrates. Oil and its products account for half of export earnings. Manufactures include cement, fertilizers, textiles, electrical goods, cars and processed foods. Workers' remittances, Suez canal tolls and tourist receipts are major sources of income, though attacks on tourists by Islamic militants has reduced the latter.

EL SALVADOR

Status: REPUBLIC
Area: 21,041 sq km (8,124 sq mls)
Population: 5,768,000
Capital: SAN SALVADOR
Language: SPANISH
Religion: R.CATHOLIC, PROTESTANT
Currency: COLÓN
Organizations: UN

MAP PAGE: 82

A DENSELY POPULATED state on the Pacific coast of central American, El Salvador has a coastal plain and volcanic mountain ranges that enclose a plateau where most people live. The coast is hot, with heavy summer rainfall, the highlands are cooler. Coffee (the chief export), sugar and cotton are main cash crops. Shrimps are also exported. Manufactures include processed foods, cosmetics, pharmaceuticals, textiles and clothing.

EQUATORIAL GUINEA

Status: REPUBLIC
Area: 28,051 sq km (10,831 sq mls)
Population: 400,000
Capital: MALABO
Language: SPANISH, FANG
Religion: R.CATHOLIC, TRAD.BELIEFS
Currency: CFA FRANC
Organizations: OAU, UN

MAP PAGE: 54

THE STATE CONSISTS of Rio Muni, an enclave on the Atlantic coast of central Africa, and the islands of Bioco, Annobón and Corisco group. Most people live on the coastal plain and upland plateau of the mainland; the capital is on the fertile volcanic island of Bioco. The climate is hot, humid and wet. Cocoa and timber are the main exports, but the economy depends heavily upon foreign aid.

ERITREA

Status: REPUBLIC
Area: 117,400 sq km (45,328 sq mls)
Population: 3,531,000
Capital: ASMARA
Language: TIGRINYA, ARABIC, TIGRE, ENGLISH
Religion: SUNNI MUSLIM, COPTIC CHRISTIAN
Currency: ETHIOPIAN BIRR
Organizations: OAU, UN

MAP PAGE: 56

ERITREA, ON THE Red Sea coast of northeast Africa, consists of high plateau in the north and a coastal plain that widens to the south. The coast is hot, inland is cooler. Rainfall is unreliable. The agricultural-based economy has suffered from 30 years of war and occasional poor rains. Coffee and cotton were the main cash crops, though food crops were important to reduce food aid.

ESTONIA

Status: REPUBLIC
Area: 45,200 sq km (17,452 sq mls)
Population: 1,530,000
Capital: TALLINN
Language: ESTONIAN, RUSSIAN
Religion: PROTESTANT, RUSSIAN ORTHODOX
Currency: KROON
Organizations: UN

MAP PAGE: 37

ESTONIA IS IN north Europe, on the Gulf of Finland and Baltic Sea. The land, one third of which is forested, is generally low-lying, with many lakes. The climate is temperate. About one third of Estonians live in Tallinn. Forests and oil-shale deposits are the main natural resources. Agriculture is limited to livestock and dairy farming. Industries include timber, furniture production, shipbuilding, leather, fur and food processing.

ETHIOPIA

Status: REPUBLIC
Area: 1,133,880 sq km (437,794 sq mls)
Population: 56,677,000
Capital: ADDIS ABABA
Language: AMHARIC, OROMO, LOCAL LANGUAGES
Religion: ETHIOPIAN ORTHODOX, SUNNI MUSLIM, TRAD.BELIEFS
Currency: BIRR
Organizations: OAU, UN

MAP PAGE: 56

ETHIOPIA, IN NORTHEAST Africa, borders Eritrea, Djibouti, Somalia, Kenya and Sudan. The western half is a mountainous region traversed by the Great Rift Valley. To the east is mostly arid plateaux. The highlands are warm with summer rainfall, though droughts occur; the east is hot and dry. Most people live in the centre-north. Secessionist wars have hampered economic development. Subsistence farming is the main activity, though droughts have led to famine. Coffee is the main export and there is some light industry.

FALKLAND ISLANDS

Status: UK TERRITORY
Area: 12,170 sq km (4,699 sq mls)
Population: 2,000
Capital: STANLEY
Language: ENGLISH
Religion: PROTESTANT, R.CATHOLIC
Currency: POUND

MAP PAGE: 88

LYING IN THE southwest Atlantic Ocean, northeast of Cape Horn, the Falklands consists of two main islands, West Falkland and East Falkland, where most of the population live, and many smaller islands. The economy is based on sheep farming and the sale of fishing licences, though oil has been discovered offshore.

FAROE ISLANDS

Status: DANISH TERRITORY
Area: 1,399 sq km (540 sq mls)
Population: 47,000
Capital: TÓRSHAVN
Language: DANISH, FAEROESE
Religion: PROTESTANT
Currency: DANISH KRONE

MAP PAGE: 36

A SELF GOVERNING territory, the Faeroes lie in the north Atlantic Ocean between the UK and Iceland. The islands benefit from the Gulf Stream which has a moderating effect on the climate. The economy is based on deep-sea fishing and sheep farming.

FIJI

Status: REPUBLIC
Area: 18,330 sq km (7,077 sq mls)
Population: 784,000
Capital: SUVA
Language: ENGLISH, FIJIAN, HINDI
Religion: PROTESTANT, HINDU, R.CATHOLIC, SUNNI MUSLIM
Currency: DOLLAR
Organizations: UN

MAP PAGE: 7

FIJI COMPRISES TWO main islands, of volcanic origin and mountainous, and over 300 smaller islands in the South Pacific Ocean. The climate is tropical and the economy is based on agriculture (chiefly sugar, the main export), fishing, forestry, gold mining and tourism.

FINLAND

Status: REPUBLIC
Area: 338,145 sq km (130,559 sq mls)
Population: 5,108,000
Capital: HELSINKI
Language: FINNISH, SWEDISH
Religion: PROTESTANT, FINNISH (GREEK) ORTHODOX
Currency: MARKKA
Organizations: EU, OECD, UN

MAP PAGE: 36-37

FINLAND IS IN north Europe, on the Gulf of Bothnia and the Gulf of Finland. It is low-lying apart from mountainous areas in the northwest. Forests cover 70 per cent of the land area, lakes and tundra over 20 per cent. Only 8 per cent is cultivated. Summers are short and warm, and winters are long and severe, particularly in the north. Most people live in the southern third of the country, along the coast or near the many lakes. Timber is the main resource and products of the forest-based industries account for a third of exports. Finland has a large fishing industry and its agricultural sector produces enough cereals and dairy products to cover domestic needs. It has some mineral deposits, chiefly zinc, copper, nickel, gold and silver. Finland is a highly industrialised country, though it must import most of the raw materials. Apart from the timber and related industries, it has important metal working, shipbuilding and engineering industries. Other industries produce chemicals, pharmaceuticals, plastics, rubber, textiles, electronic equipment, glass and ceramics.

F.Y.R.O.M. (MACEDONIA)

Status: REPUBLIC
Area: 25,713 sq km (9,928 sq mls)
Population: 2,163,000
Capital: SKOPJE
Language: MACEDONIAN, ALBANIAN, SERBO-CROAT, TURKISH, ROMANY
Religion: MACEDONIAN ORTHODOX, SUNNI MUSLIM, R.CATHOLIC
Currency: DENAR
Organizations: UN

MAP PAGE: 49

FYROM, FORMERLY THE Yugoslav republic of Macedonia, is a landlocked state of south Europe, bordered by Yugoslavia, Bulgaria, Greece and Albania. Lying within the south Balkans, it is a rugged country, traversed north-south by the Vardar valley. It has fine hot summers, but very cold winters. The economy is based on industry, mining and, to a lesser degree, agriculture. But conflict with Greece and UN sanctions against Yugoslavia have reduced trade, caused economic difficulties and discouraged investment.

FRANCE

Status: REPUBLIC
Area: 543,965 sq km (210,026 sq mls)
Population: 58,143,000
Capital: PARIS
Language: FRENCH, FRENCH DIALECTS, ARABIC, GERMAN (ALSATIAN), BRETON
Religion: R.CATHOLIC, PROTESTANT, SUNNI MUSLIM
Currency: FRANC
Organizations: EU, OECD, UN

MAP PAGE: 44

FRANCE LIES IN southwest Europe, with coastlines on the North Sea, Atlantic Ocean and Mediterranean Sea; it includes the Mediterranean island of Corsica. Northern and western regions consist mostly of flat or rolling countryside, and include the major lowlands of the Paris basin, the Loire valley and the Aquitaine basin, drained by the Seine, Loire and Garonne river systems respectively. The centre-south is dominated by the Massif Central. Eastwards, beyond the fourth major lowland area of the Rhône-Saône valley, are the Alps and the Jura mountains. In the southwest, the Pyrenees form a natural border with Spain. The climate of northern parts is temperate and wet, but in the centre and east it is continental, with warmer summers and milder winters. Along the south coast a Mediterranean climate prevails, with hot, dry summers and mild winters with some rainfall. Some 75 per cent of the population live in towns, but Greater Paris is the only major conurbation, with a sixth of the French population. Rich soil, a large cultivable area and contrasts in temperature and relief have given France a strong and varied agricultural base. It is a major producer of both fresh and processed food and the world's second largest exporter of agricultural products, after the USA. Major exports include cereals (chiefly wheat), dairy products, wines and sugar. France has relatively few mineral resources, though iron ore, potash salts, zinc and uranium are mined. It has coal reserves, some oil and natural gas, but it relies mainly for its energy needs on nuclear and hydroelectric power and imported fuels. France is the world's fourth largest industrial power after the USA, Japan and Germany. Heavy industries include iron, steel and aluminium production and oil refining. Other major industries are food processing, motor vehicles, aerospace, chemicals and pharmaceuticals, telecommunications, computers and armaments as well as luxury goods, fashion and perfumes. The main exports are machinery, agricultural products, cars and other transport equipment. France has a strong services sector and tourism is a major source of revenue and employment.

FRENCH GUIANA

Status: FRENCH TERRITORY
Area: 90,000 sq km (34,749 sq mls)
Population: 147,000
Capital: CAYENNE
Language: FRENCH, FRENCH CREOLE
Religion: R.CATHOLIC, PROTESTANT
Currency: FRENCH FRANC

MAP PAGE: 87

FRENCH GUIANA, ON the northeast coast of South America, is densely forested and is mountainous in the south. The climate is tropical with high rainfall. Most people live in the coastal strip and most workers are involved in subsistence farming, though sugar is exported. Livestock rearing and fishing are also important. Timber and mineral resources are largely unexploited and industry is limited. French Guiana depends upon French aid.

FRENCH POLYNESIA

Status: FRENCH TERRITORY
Area: 3,265 sq km (1,261 sq mls)
Population: 220,000
Capital: PAPEETE
Language: FRENCH, POLYNESIAN LANGUAGES
Religion: PROTESTANT, R.CATHOLIC, MORMON
Currency: PACIFIC FRANC

MAP PAGE: 5

EXTENDING OVER A vast area of the southeast Pacific Ocean, French Polynesia comprises more than 130 islands and coral atolls. The main island groups are the Marquesas, the Tuamotu Archipelago and the Society Islands. The capital, Papeete, is on Tahiti in the Society Islands. The climate is subtropical and the economy is based on tourism.

FRENCH SOUTHERN AND ANTARCTIC LANDS

Status: FRENCH TERRITORY
Area: 7,781 sq km (3,004 sq mls)

MAP PAGE: 3

THIS TERRITORY INCLUDES Crozet Island, Kerguelen, Amsterdam Island and St Paul Island. All are uninhabited apart from scientific research staff. In accordance with the Antarctic Treaty, French territorial claims in Antarctica have been suspended.

GABON

Status: REPUBLIC
Area: 267,667 sq km (103,347 sq mls)
Population: 1,320,000
Capital: LIBREVILLE
Language: FRENCH, FANG, LOCAL LANGUAGES
Religion: R.CATHOLIC, PROTESTANT, TRAD.BELIEFS
Currency: CFA FRANC
Organizations: OAU, UN

MAP PAGE: 56

GABON, ON THE Atlantic coast of central Africa consists of low plateaux, with a coastal plain lined by lagoons and mangrove swamps. The climate is tropical and rainforests cover 75 per cent of the land. Half of the population lives in towns, chiefly Libreville and Port Gentil. The economy is heavily dependent on mineral resources, mainly oil but also manganese and uranium. Timber, chiefly okoumé, is exported. Agriculture is mainly at subsistence level, but oil palms, bananas, sugarcane and rubber are grown.

THE GAMBIA

Status: REPUBLIC
Area: 11,295 sq km (4,361 sq mls)
Population: 1,118,000
Capital: BANJUL
Language: ENGLISH (OFFICIAL), MALINKE, FULANI, WOLOF
Religion: SUNNI MUSLIM, PROTESTANT
Currency: DALASI
Organizations: COMM., OAU, UN

MAP PAGE: 54

THE GAMBIA, ON the coast of west Africa, occupies a strip of land along the lower Gambia River. Sandy beaches are backed by mangrove swamps, beyond which is savannah. The climate is tropical, with rainfall in the summer. Over 70 per cent of Gambians are farmers, growing chiefly groundnuts (the main export) but also seed cotton, oil palms and food crops. Livestock rearing and fishing are important, while manufacturing is limited. Re-exports, mainly from Senegal, and tourism are major sources of income.

GAZA

Status: AUTONOMOUS REGION
Area: 363 sq km (140 sq mls)
Population: 756,000
Capital: GAZA
Language: ARABIC
Religion: SUNNI MUSLIM, SHI'A MUSLIM
Currency: ISRAELI SHEKEL

MAP PAGE: 16

GAZA IS A narrow strip of land on the southeast corner of the Mediterranean Sea, between Egypt and Israel. The territory has limited autonomy from Israel. The economy is based on agriculture and remittances from work in Israel.

GEORGIA

Status: REPUBLIC
Area: 69,700 sq km (26,911 sq mls)
Population: 5,457,000
Capital: T'BILISI
Language: GEORGIAN, RUSSIAN, ARMENIAN, AZERI, OSSETIAN, ABKHAZ
Religion: GEORGIAN ORTHODOX, RUSSIAN ORTHODOX, SHI'A MUSLIM
Currency: LARI
Organizations: CIS, UN

MAP PAGE: 51

GEORGIA IS IN northwest Transcaucasia, southwest Asia, on the Black Sea. Mountain ranges in the north and south flank the Kura and Rioni valleys. The climate is generally mild, but subtropical along the coast. Agriculture is important, with tea, grapes, citrus fruits and tobacco the major crops. Mineral resources include manganese, coal and oil, and the main industries are iron and steel, oil refining and machine building. However, economic activity has been seriously affected by separatist wars and political unrest.

GERMANY

Status: REPUBLIC
Area: 357,868 sq km (138,174 sq mls)
Population: 81,642,000
Capital: BERLIN
Language: GERMAN, TURKISH
Religion: PROTESTANT, R.CATHOLIC, SUNNI MUSLIM
Currency: MARK
Organizations: EU, OECD, UN

MAP PAGE: 46

THE WEST EUROPEAN state of Germany borders nine countries and has coastlines on the North and Baltic seas. It includes the southern part of the Jutland peninsula and Frisian islands. Behind the indented coastline and covering about one third of the country is the north German plain, a region of fertile farmland and sandy heaths drained by the country's major rivers. The central highlands are a belt of forested hills and plateaux which stretches from the Eifel region in the west to the Erzgebirge (Ore mountains) along the border with the Czech Republic. Farther south the land rises to the Swabian and Jura mountains, with the high rugged and forested Black Forest in the southwest and the Bavarian plateau and Alps to the southeast. The climate is temperate, with continental conditions in eastern areas where winters are colder. Rainfall is evenly spread throughout the year. Divided in 1945 after defeat in the second world war, Germany was reunified in 1990, barely a year after the collapse of communism in eastern Europe. It had been thought that west Germany, the world's third largest industrial economy and second largest exporter, would easily absorb east Germany, less than half the size and with a quarter of the population. But the initial cost of unification was high. The overhaul of east German industry led to 30 per cent unemployment there, while the high level of investment and the rising social security bill led to tax increases in the west. In addition unification coincided with recession in the west German economy and rising unemployment, which created social tensions. However, by 1994 there were signs that the economy was pulling out of the recession. Germany lacks minerals and other industrial raw materials, with the exception of lignite and potash. It has a small agricultural base, though a few products (chiefly wines and beers) enjoy an international reputation. It is predominantly an industrial economy, dominated by the mechanical and engineering, iron and steel, chemical, pharmaceutical, motor, textile and high-tech industries. It also has a large service sector, with tourism, banking and finance being important.

BADEN-WÜRTTEMBERG

Status: STATE
Area: 35,751 sq km (13,804 sq miles)
Population: 10,344,009
Capital: STUTTGART

BAYERN (BAVARIA)

Status: STATE
Area: 70,554 sq km (27,241 sq miles)
Population: 12,014,674
Capital: MÜNCHEN

BERLIN

Status: STATE
Area: 889 sq km (343 sq miles)
Population: 3,467,322
Capital: BERLIN

BRANDENBURG

Status: STATE
Area: 29,056 sq km (11,219 sq miles)
Population: 2,545,511
Capital: POTSDAM

BREMEN

Status: STATE
Area: 404 sq km (156 sq miles)
Population: 678,731
Capital: BREMEN

HAMBURG

Status: STATE
Area: 755 sq km (292 sq miles)
Population: 1,708,528
Capital: HAMBURG

HESSEN (HESSE)

Status: STATE
Area: 21,114 sq km (8,152 sq miles)
Population: 6,016,251
Capital: WIESBADEN

MECKLENBURG-VORPOMMERN (MECKLENBURG-WEST POMERANIA)

Status: STATE
Area: 23,559 sq km (9,096 sq miles)
Population: 1,829,587
Capital: SCHWERIN

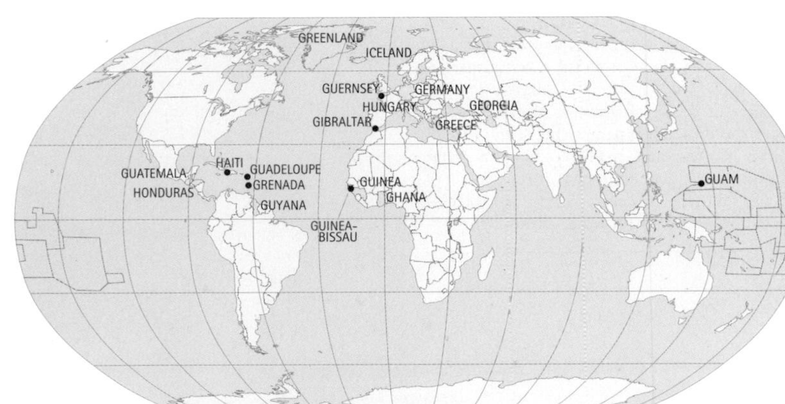

NIEDERSACHSEN (LOWER SAXONY)

Status: STATE
Area: 47,351 sq km (18,282 sq miles)
Population: 7,795,149
Capital: HANNOVER

NORDRHEIN-WESTFALEN (NORTH RHINE-WESTPHALIA)

Status: STATE
Area: 34,070 sq km (13,155 sq miles)
Population: 17,908,473
Capital: DÜSSELDORF

RHEINLAND-PFALZ (RHINELAND-PALATINATE)

Status: STATE
Area: 19,849 sq km (7,664 sq miles)
Population: 3,983,282
Capital: MAINZ

SAARLAND

Status: STATE
Area: 2,570 sq km (992 sq miles)
Population: 1,083,119
Capital: SAARBRÜCKEN

SACHSEN (SAXONY)

Status: STATE
Area: 18,341 sq km (7,081 sq miles)
Population: 4,557,210
Capital: DRESDEN

SACHSEN-ANHALT (SAXONY-ANHALT)

Status: STATE
Area: 20,607 sq km (7,956 sq miles)
Population: 2,731,463
Capital: MAGDEBURG

SCHLESWIG-HOLSTEIN

Status: STATE
Area: 15,731 sq km (6,074 sq miles)
Population: 2,730,595
Capital: KIEL

THÜRINGEN (THURINGIA)

Status: STATE
Area: 16,251 sq km (6,275 sq miles)
Population: 2,496,685
Capital: ERFURT

GHANA

Status: REPUBLIC
Area: 238,537 sq km (92,100 sq mls)
Population: 17,453,000
Capital: ACCRA
Language: ENGLISH (OFFICIAL), HAUSA, AKAN, LOCAL LANGUAGES
Religion: PROTESTANT, R.CATHOLIC, SUNNI MUSLIM, TRAD. BELIEFS
Currency: CEDI
Organizations: COMM., OAU, UN

MAP PAGE: 54

A WEST AFRICAN STATE on the Gulf of Guinea, Ghana is a land of plains and low plateaux covered with savannah and, in the west, rainforest. In the east is the Volta basin. The climate is tropical, with high rainfall in the south, where most people live. Ghana is a major producer of cocoa. Timber is also an important commodity. Bauxite, gold, diamonds and manganese ore are mined, and there are a number of industries around Tema.

GIBRALTAR

Status: UK TERRITORY
Area: 6.5 sq km (2.5 sq mls)
Population: 28,000
Capital: GIBRALTAR
Language: ENGLISH, SPANISH
Religion: R.CATHOLIC, PROTESTANT, SUNNI MUSLIM
Currency: POUND

MAP PAGE: 45

GIBRALTAR LIES ON the south coast of Spain at the western entrance to the Mediterranean Sea. The economy depends on tourism, offshore banking and entrepôt trade.

GREECE

Status: REPUBLIC
Area: 131,957 sq km (50,949 sq mls)
Population: 10,458 ,000
Capital: ATHENS
Language: GREEK, MACEDONIAN
Religion: GREEK ORTHODOX, SUNNI MUSLIM
Currency: DRACHMA
Organizations: EU, OECD, UN

MAP PAGE: 49

GREECE OCCUPIES THE southern part of the Balkan Peninsula of south Europe and many islands in the Ionian, Aegean and Mediterranean Seas. The islands make up over one fifth of its area. Mountains and hills cover much of the country. The most important lowlands are the plains of Thessaly in the centre-east and Salonica in the northeast. Summers are hot and dry. Winters are mild and wet, colder in the north with heavy snowfalls in the mountains. One third of Greeks live in the Athens area. Agriculture involves one quarter of the workforce and exports include citrus fruits, raisins, wine, olives and olive oil. A variety of ores and minerals are mined and a wide range of manufactures are produced including food and tobacco products, textiles, clothing, chemical products and metal products. Tourism is an important industry and there is a large services sector. Tourism, shipping and remittances from Greeks abroad are major foreign exchange earners. The war in former Yugoslavia and UN embargo on trade to Serbia have lost Greece an important market and regular trade route.

GREENLAND

Status: DANISH TERRITORY
Area: 2,175,600 sq km (840,004 sq mls)
Population: 58,000
Capital: NUUK
Language: GREENLANDIC, DANISH
Religion: PROTESTANT
Currency: DANISH KRONE

MAP PAGE: 63

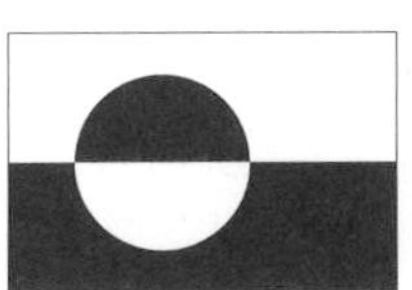

SITUATED TO THE northeast of North America between the Atlantic and Arctic Oceans, Greenland is the largest island in the world. It has a polar climate and over 80 per cent of the land area is permanent ice-cap. The economy is based on fishing and fish processing.

GRENADA

Status: MONARCHY
Area: 378 sq km (146 sq mls)
Population: 92,000
Capital: ST GEORGE'S
Language: ENGLISH, CREOLE
Religion: R.CATHOLIC, PROTESTANT
Currency: E. CARIB. DOLLAR
Organizations: CARICOM, COMM., UN

MAP PAGE: 83

THE CARIBBEAN STATE comprises Grenada, the most southerly of the Windward Islands, and the southern Grenadines. Grenada has wooded hills, beaches in the southwest, a warm climate and good rainfall. Agriculture is the main activity, with bananas, nutmeg and cocoa the main exports. Tourism and manufacturing are important. Grenada relies on grant aid.

GUADELOUPE

Status: FRENCH TERRITORY
Area: 1,780 sq km (687 sq mls)
Population: 428,000
Capital: BASSE TERRE
Language: FRENCH, FRENCH CREOLE
Religion: R.CATHOLIC, HINDU
Currency: FRENCH FRANC

MAP PAGE: 83

GUADELOUPE, IN THE Caribbean's Leeward group, consists of two main islands, Basse Terre and Grande Terre, connected by a bridge, and a few outer islands. The climate is tropical, but moderated by trade winds. Bananas, sugar and rum, tourism and French aid are the main sources of foreign exchange.

GUAM

Status: US TERRITORY
Area: 541 sq km (209 sq mls)
Population: 149,000
Capital: AGANA
Language: CHAMORRO, ENGLISH, TAGALOG
Religion: R.CATHOLIC
Currency: US DOLLAR

MAP PAGE: 25

LYING AT THE south end of the North Mariana Islands in the Western Pacific Ocean, Guam has a humid tropical climate. The island has a large US military base and the economy relies on that and tourism which is beginning to develop.

GUATEMALA

Status: REPUBLIC
Area: 108,890 sq km (42,043 sq mls)
Population: 10,621,000
Capital: GUATEMALA
Language: SPANISH, MAYAN LANGUAGES
Religion: R.CATHOLIC, PROTESTANT
Currency: QUETZAL
Organizations: UN

MAP PAGE: 82

THE MOST POPULOUS country in Central America after Mexico, Guatemala has a long Pacific and a short Caribbean coastline. Northern areas are lowland tropical forests. To the south lie mountain ranges with some active volcanoes, then the Pacific coastal plain. The climate is hot tropical in the lowlands, cooler in the highlands, where most people live. Farming is the main activity, coffee, sugar and bananas are the main exports. There is some mining and manufacturing (chiefly clothing and textiles). Tourism is important. Guerrilla activity is rife in certain areas.

GUERNSEY

Status: UK TERRITORY
Area: 78 sq km (30 sq mls)
Population: 64,000
Capital: ST PETER PORT
Language: ENGLISH, FRENCH
Religion: PROTESTANT, R.CATHOLIC
Currency: POUND

MAP PAGE: 44

ONE OF THE Channel Islands lying off the west coast of the Cherbourg peninsula in northern France.

GUINEA

Status: REPUBLIC
Area: 245,857 sq km (94,926 sq mls)
Population: 6,700,000
Capital: CONAKRY
Language: FRENCH, FULANI, MALINKE, LOCAL LANGUAGES
Religion: SUNNI MUSLIM, TRAD.BELIEFS, R.CATHOLIC
Currency: FRANC
Organizations: OAU, UN

MAP PAGE: 54

GUINEA IS IN west Africa, on the Atlantic Ocean. The coastal plains are lined with mangrove swamps. Inland are the Fouta Djallon mountains and plateaux. To the east are savannah plains drained by the upper Niger river system, while to the southeast are mountains. The climate is tropical, with high coastal rainfall. Agriculture is the main activity, with coffee, bananas and pineapples the chief cash crops. Bauxite, alumina, iron ore, gold and diamonds are the main exports, but Guinea relies upon foreign aid.

GUINEA-BISSAU

Status: REPUBLIC
Area: 36,125 sq km (13,948 sq mls)
Population: 1,073,000
Capital: BISSAU
Language: PORTUGUESE, PORTUGUESE CREOLE, LOCAL LANGUAGES
Religion: TRAD.BELIEFS, SUNNI MUSLIM, R.CATHOLIC
Currency: CFA FRANC
Organizations: OAU, UN

MAP PAGE: 54

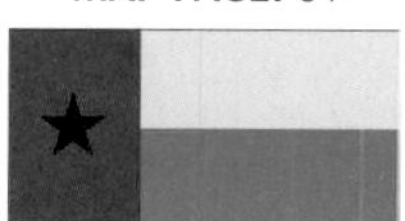

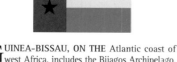

GUINEA-BISSAU, ON THE Atlantic coast of west Africa, includes the Bijagos Archipelago. The mainland coast is swampy and contains many estuaries. Inland are forested plains and to the east are savannah plateaux. The climate is tropical. The economy is based mainly on subsistence farming. There is some fishing, but little industry. Forestry and mineral resources are largely unexploited. The main exports are cashews, groundnuts, oil palms and their products. Donors largely suspended support in 1991 because of payment arrears.

GUYANA

Status: REPUBLIC
Area: 214,969 sq km (83,000 sq mls)
Population: 835,000
Capital: GEORGETOWN
Language: ENGLISH, CREOLE, HINDI, AMERINDIAN LANGUAGES
Religion: PROTESTANT, HINDU, R.CATHOLIC, SUNNI MUSLIM
Currency: DOLLAR
Organizations: CARICOM, COMM., UN

MAP PAGE: 86-87

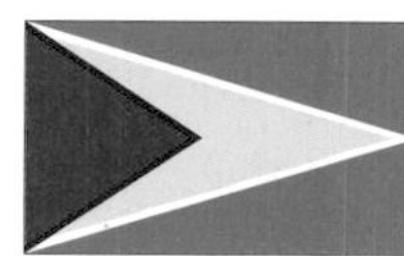

GUYANA, ON THE northeast coast of South America, consists of the densely forested highlands in the west, and the savannah uplands of the southwest. A lowland coastal belt supports crops and most of the population. The generally hot, humid and wet conditions are modified along the coast by sea breezes. The economy is based on agriculture, mining, forestry and fishing. Sugar, bauxite, gold and rice are the main exports. Other exports are shrimps and timber.

HAITI

Status: REPUBLIC
Area: 27,750 sq km (10,714 sq mls)
Population: 7,180,000
Capital: PORT-AU-PRINCE
Language: FRENCH, FRENCH CREOLE
Religion: R.CATHOLIC, PROTESTANT, VOODOO
Currency: GOURDE
Organizations: UN

MAP PAGE: 83

HAITI, OCCUPYING THE western third of the Caribbean island of Hispaniola, is a mountainous state, with small coastal plains and a central valley. The climate is tropical, hottest in coastal areas. Haiti has few natural resources, is overpopulated and relies on exports of local manufactures and coffee, and remittances from workers abroad. Political unrest and UN sanctions from 1991 to 1994 hit the economy badly.

HONDURAS

Status: REPUBLIC
Area: 112,088 sq km (43,277 sq mls)
Population: 5,953,000
Capital: TEGUCIGALPA
Language: SPANISH, AMERINDIAN LANGUAGES
Religion: R.CATHOLIC, PROTESTANT
Currency: LEMPIRA
Organizations: UN

MAP PAGE: 82-83

HONDURAS, IN CENTRAL America, is a mountainous and forested country with lowland areas along its long Caribbean and short Pacific coasts. Coastal areas are hot and humid with heavy summer rainfall, inland is cooler and drier. Most people live in the central valleys. Coffee and bananas are the main exports, along with shrimps, lead, zinc and timber. Industry involves mainly agricultural processing. Honduras depends on foreign aid.

HUNGARY

Status: REPUBLIC
Area: 93,030 sq km (35,919 sq mls)
Population: 10,225,000
Capital: BUDAPEST
Language: HUNGARIAN, ROMANY, GERMAN, SLOVAK
Religion: R.CATHOLIC, PROTESTANT
Currency: FORINT
Organizations: UN, OECD

MAP PAGE: 46-49

A LANDLOCKED COUNTRY in central Europe, Hungary borders Austria, Slovakia, Ukraine, Romania, Yugoslavia, Croatia and Slovenia. The Danube river flows north-south through central Hungary. To the east lies a great plain, flanked by highlands in the north. To the west low mountains and Lake Balaton separate a small plain and southern uplands. The climate is continental, with warm summers and cold winters. Rainfall is fairly evenly distributed thoughout the year. Half the population lives in urban areas, and one fifth lives in Budapest. Hungary has a predominantly industrial economy. The main industries produce metals, machinery, transport equipment (chiefly buses), textiles, chemicals and food products. Some minerals and energy reources are exploited, chiefly bauxite, coal and natural gas. Farming remains important, though output has fallen. Fruit, vegetables, cigarettes and wine are the main agricultural exports. Tourism is an important foreign exchange earner. Progress towards creating a market economy has been proved slow.

ICELAND

Status: REPUBLIC
Area: 102,820 sq km (39,699 sq mls)
Population: 269,000
Capital: REYKJAVIK
Language: ICELANDIC
Religion: PROTESTANT, R.CATHOLIC
Currency: KRÓNA
Organizations: OECD, UN

MAP PAGE: 36

THE NORTHWEST EUROPEAN island of Iceland lies in the Atlantic Ocean, near the Arctic Circle. It consists mainly of a plateau of basalt lava flows. Some of its 200 volcanoes are active, and there are geysers and hot springs, but one tenth of the country is covered by ice caps. Only coastal lowlands can be cultivated and settled, and over half the population lives in the Reykjavik area. The climate is fairly mild, moderated by the North Atlantic Drift and southwesterly winds. The mainstay of the economy is fishing and fish processing, which account for 80 per cent of exports. Agriculture involves mainly sheep and dairy farming. Iceland is self-sufficient in meat and dairy products, and exports wool and sheepskins. Diatomite is the only mineral resource but hydro-electric and geothermal energy resources are considerable. The main industries produce aluminium, ferro-silicon, electrical equipment, books, fertilizers, textiles and clothing. Tourism is growing in importance.

INDIA

Status: REPUBLIC
Area: 3,287,263 sq km (1,269,219 sq mls)
Population: 935,744,000
Capital: NEW DELHI
Language: HINDI, ENGLISH (OFFICIAL), MANY REGIONAL LANGUAGES
Religion: HINDU, SUNNI MUSLIM, SIKH, CHRISTIAN, BUDDHIST, JAIN
Currency: RUPEE
Organizations: COMM., UN

MAP PAGE: 14-15

MOST OF THE South Asian state of India occupies a peninsula that juts out into the Indian Ocean between the Arabian Sea and Bay of Bengal. The heart of the peninsula is the Deccan plateau, bordered on either side by ranges of hills, the Western Ghats and the lower Eastern Ghats, which fall away to narrow coastal plains. To the north is a broad plain, drained by the Indus, Ganges and Brahmaputra rivers and their tributaries. The plain is intensively farmed and is the most populous region. In the west is the Thar Desert. The Himalayas form India's northern border, together with parts of the Karakoram and Hindu Kush ranges in the northwest. The climate shows marked seasonal variation: the hot season from March to June; the monsoon season from June to October; and the cold season from November to February. Rainfall ranges between heavy in the northeast Assam region and negligible in the Thar Desert, while temperatures range from very cold in the Himayalas to tropical heat over much of the south. India is among the ten largest economies in the world. It has achieved a high degree of self-sufficiency and its involvement in world trade is relatively small, though growing. Agriculture, forestry and fishing account for one third of national output and two thirds of employment. Much of the farming is on a subsistence basis and involves mainly rice and wheat growing. India is a major world producer of tea, sugar, jute, cotton and tobacco. Livestock is raised mainly for dairy products and hides. India has substantial reserves of coal, oil and natural gas and many minerals including iron, manganese and copper ores, bauxite, diamonds and gold. The manufacturing sector is large and diverse. The main manufactures are chemicals and chemical products, textiles, iron and steel, food products, electrical goods and transport equipment. The main exports are diamonds, clothing, chemicals and chemical products, textiles, leather and leather goods, iron ore, fish products, electronic goods and tea. However, with a huge population - the second largest in the world - India receives foreign aid to support its balance of payments.

INDONESIA

Status: REPUBLIC
Area: 1,919,445 sq km (741,102 sq mls)
Population: 194,564,000
Capital: JAKARTA
Language: INDONESIAN (OFFICIAL), MANY LOCAL LANGUAGES
Religion: SUNNI MUSLIM, PROTESTANT, R.CATHOLIC, HINDU, BUDDHIST
Currency: RUPIAH
Organizations: ASEAN, OPEC, UN

MAP PAGE: 25

INDONESIA, THE LARGEST and most populous country in southeast Asia, consists of 13,677 islands extending along the Equator between the Pacific and Indian oceans. Sumatra, Java, Sulawesi, Kalimantan (two thirds of Borneo) and Irian Jaya (western New Guinea) make up 90 per cent of the land area. Most of Indonesia is mountainous and covered with rainforest or mangrove swamps, and there are over 300 volcanoes, some still active. Two thirds of the population live in the lowland areas of Java and Madura. In general the climate is tropical monsoon. Indonesia is rich in energy resources, minerals, forests and fertile soil. It is among the world's top producers of rice, palm oil, tea, coffee, rubber and tobacco. It is the world's leading exporter of natural gas and a major exporter of oil and timber. In recent years manufacturing output has risen. A range of goods are produced including textiles, clothing, cement, fertilizer and vehicles. Tourism has also increased. However, given its huge population, Indonesia remains a relatively poor country.

IRAN

Status: REPUBLIC
Area: 1,648,000 sq km (636,296 sq mls)
Population: 67,283,000
Capital: TEHRĀN
Language: FARSI (PERSIAN), AZERI, KURDISH, REGIONAL LANGUAGES
Religion: SHI'A MUSLIM, SUNNI MUSLIM, BAHA'I, CHRISTIAN, ZOROASTRIAN
Currency: RIAL
Organizations: OPEC, UN

MAP PAGE: 18-19

IRAN IS IN southwest Asia, on The Gulf, the Gulf of Oman and Caspian Sea. Eastern Iran is high plateaux country, with large salt pans and a vast sand desert. In the west the Zagros Mountains form a series of ridges, while to the north lie the Elburz Mountains. Most farming and settlement is on the narrow plain along the Caspian Sea and the foothills of the north and west. The climate is one of extremes, with hot summers and very cold winters. Most of the light rainfall is in the winter months. Agriculture involves one quarter of the workforce. Wheat is the main crop but fruit (chiefly dates) and pistachio nuts are grown for export. Fishing in the Caspian Sea is important and caviar is exported. Petroleum (the main export) and natural gas are Iran's leading natural resources. There are also reserves of coal, iron ore, copper ore and other minerals. Manufactures include carpets, clothing, food products, construction materials, chemicals, vehicles, leather goods and metal products. The 1979 revolution and 1980-88 war with Iraq slowed economic development.

IRAQ

Status: REPUBLIC
Area: 438,317 sq km (169,235 sq mls)
Population: 20,449,000
Capital: BAGHDĀD
Language: ARABIC, KURDISH, TURKMEN
Religion: SHI'A MUSLIM, SUNNI MUSLIM, R.CATHOLIC
Currency: DINAR
Organizations: OPEC, UN

MAP PAGE: 17

IRAQ, WHICH LIES on the northwest shores of The Gulf in southwest Asia, has at its heart the lowland valley of the Tigris and Euphrates rivers. In the southeast where the two rivers join are marshes and the Shatt al Arab waterway. Northern Iraq is hilly, rising to the Zagros Mountains, while western Iraq is desert. Summers are hot and dry, while winters are mild with light though unreliable rainfall. The Tigris-Euphrates valley contains most of the arable land and population, including one in five who live in Baghdad. One third of the workforce is involved in agriculture, with dates, cotton, wool, hides and skins exported in normal times. However, the 1980-88 war with Iran, defeat in the 1991 Gulf war and international sanctions have ruined the economy and caused considerable hardship. Petroleum and natural gas sales, which had accounted for 98 per cent of export earnings, were severely restricted. Much of the infrastructure was dam aged and industrial output - which had included petroleum products, cement, steel, textiles, bitumen and pharmaceuticals - was reduced.

ISLE OF MAN

Status: UK TERRITORY
Area: 572 sq km (221 sq mls)
Population: 72 ,000
Capital: DOUGLAS
Language: ENGLISH
Religion: PROTESTANT, R.CATHOLIC
Currency: POUND

MAP PAGE: 38

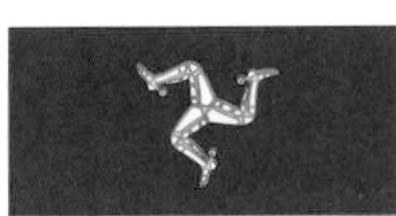

ISRAEL

Status: REPUBLIC
Area: 20,770 sq km (8,019 sq mls)
Population: 5,545,000
Capital: JERUSALEM
Language: HEBREW, ARABIC, YIDDISH, ENGLISH, RUSSIAN
Religion: JEWISH, SUNNI MUSLIM, CHRISTIAN, DRUZE
Currency: SHEKEL
Organizations: UN

MAP PAGE: 16

ISRAEL LIES ON the Mediterranean coast of southwest Asia. Beyond the coastal plain of Sharon are the hills and valleys of Judea and Samaria with the Galilee highlands to the north. In the east is the rift valley, which extends from Lake Tiberias to the Gulf of Aqaba and contains the Jordan river and Dead Sea. In the south is the Negev, a triangular semi-desert plateau. Most people live on the coastal plain or in northern and central areas. Much of Israel has warm summers and mild winters, during which most rain falls. Southern Israel is hot and dry. Agricultural production was boosted by the inclusion of the West Bank of the Jordan in 1967. Citrus fruit, vegetables and flowers are exported. Mineral resources are few but potash, bromine and some oil and gas are produced. Manufacturing makes the largest contribution to the economy. Israel produces finished diamonds, textiles, clothing and food products as well as chemical and metal products, military and transport equipment, electrical and electronic goods. Tourism and foreign aid are important to the economy.

ITALY

Status: REPUBLIC
Area: 301,245 sq km (116,311 sq mls)
Population: 57,187,000
Capital: ROME
Language: ITALIAN, ITALIAN DIALECTS
Religion: R.CATHOLIC
Currency: LIRA
Organizations: EU, OECD, UN

MAP PAGE: 48

MOST OF THE south European state of Italy occupies a peninsula that juts out into the Mediterranean Sea. It includes the main islands of Sicily and Sardinia and about 70 smaller islands in the surrounding seas. Italy is mountainous and dominated by two high ranges: the Alps, which form its northern border; and the Apennines, which run almost the full length of the peninsula. Many of Italy's mountains are of volcanic origin and its two active volcanoes are Vesuvius near Naples and Etna on Sicily. The main lowland area is the Po river valley in the northeast, which is the main agricultural and industrial area and is the most populous region. Italy has a Mediterranean climate with warm, dry summers and mild winters. Sicily and Sardinia are warmer and drier than the mainland. Northern Italy experiences colder, wetter winters, with heavy snow in the Alps. Italy's natural resources are limited. Only about 20 per cent of the land is suitable for cultivation. Some oil, natural gas and coal are produced, but most fuels and minerals used by industry must be imported. Italy has a fairly diversified economy. Agriculture flourishes, with cereals, wine, fruit (including olives) and vegetables the main crops. Italy is the world's largest wine producer. Cheese is also an important product. However, Italy is a net food importer. The north is the centre of Italian industry, especially around Turin, Milan and Genoa, while the south is largely agricultural with production based on smaller, less mechanized farms. Thus average income in the north is much higher than that in the south. Another feature of the Italian economy is the size of the state sector, which is much larger than that of other European Union countries. Italy's leading manufactures include industrial and office equipment, domestic appliances, cars, textiles, clothing, leather goods, chemicals and metal products and its famous brand names include Olivetti, Fiat and Benetton. Italy has a strong service sector. With over 25 million visitors a year, tourism is a major employer and accounts for 5 per cent of national income. Finance and banking are also important.

JAMAICA

Status: MONARCHY
Area: 10,991 sq km (4,244 sq mls)
Population: 2,530,000
Capital: KINGSTON
Language: ENGLISH, CREOLE
Religion: PROTESTANT, R.CATHOLIC, RASTAFARIAN
Currency: DOLLAR
Organizations: CARICOM, COMM., UN

MAP PAGE: 83

JAMAICA, THE THIRD largest Caribbean island, has beaches and densely populated coastal plains traversed by hills and plateaux rising to the forested Blue Mountains in the east. The climate is tropical, cooler and wetter on high ground. The economy is based on tourism, agriculture, mining and light manufacturing. Bauxite, alumina, sugar and bananas are the main exports. Jamaica depends on foreign aid.

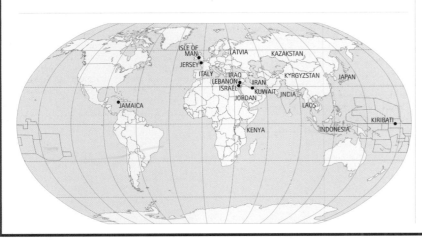

JAPAN

Status: MONARCHY
Area: 377,727 sq km (145,841 sq mls)
Population: 125,197,000
Capital: TŌKYŌ
Language: JAPANESE
Religion: SHINTOIST, BUDDHIST, CHRISTIAN
Currency: YEN
Organizations: OECD, UN

MAP PAGE: 28-29

JAPAN, WHICH LIES in the Pacific Ocean off the coast of east Asia, consists of four main islands - Hokkaido, Honshu, Shikoku and Kyushu - which extend northeast-southwest over 1,600 km (995 miles). It includes more than 3,000 smaller volcanic islands in the surrounding Sea of Japan, East China Sea and Pacific Ocean. The central island of Honshu occupies 60 per cent of the total land area and contains 80 per cent of the population, mostly in the east-central Kanto plain which includes Tokyo, Kawasaki and Yokohama. Behind the long and deeply indented coastline, nearly three quarters of Japan is mountainous and heavily forested. The most rugged range crosses Honshu and includes the country's highest point, Mount Fuji, which reaches a height of 3,776 m (12,388 ft). Japan has over 60 active volcanoes, and is subject to frequent major earthquakes, monsoons, typhoons and tidal waves. The climate is generally temperate maritime, with warm summers and mild winters, except in western Hokkaido and northwest Honshu, where the winters are very cold with heavy snow. Rain falls mainly in June and July, and typhoons sometimes occur in September. Japan has few natural resources. It has a limited land area of which only 14 per cent is suitable for cultivation, and production of its few industrial raw materials (chiefly coal, oil, natural gas and copper) is insufficient for its industry. Most raw materials must be imported, including about 90 per cent of energy requirements. Yet, in a fairly short space of time, Japan has become the world's second largest industrial economy. Its economic success is based on manufacturing, which employs one third of the workforce and accounts for one third of national output. Japan has a range of heavy and light industries centred mainly round the major ports of Yokohama, Osaka and Tokyo. It is the world's largest manufacturer of cars, motorcycles and merchant ships, and a major producer of steel, textiles, chemicals and cement. It is a leading producer of many consumer durables, such as washing machines, and electronic equipment, chiefly office equipment and computers. Recent years have seen the spread of Japanese business overseas, with many industrial plants sited in the European Union and the USA. Japan has a strong service sector, banking and finance are particularly important and Tokyo is one of the world's major stock exchanges. Owing to intensive agricultural production, Japan is 70 per cent self-sufficient in food. The main food crops are rice, barley, fruit, wheat and soya beans. Livestock raising (chiefly cattle, pigs and chickens) and fishing are also important. Japan has one of the largest fishing fleets in the world. In spite of its forestry resources, Japan has to import timber as well as food.

JERSEY

Status: UK TERRITORY
Area: 116 sq km (45 sq mls)
Population: 87,000
Capital: ST HELIER
Language: ENGLISH, FRENCH
Religion: PROTESTANT, R.CATHOLIC
Currency: POUND

MAP PAGE: 44

ONE OF THE Channel Islands lying off the west coast of the Cherbourg peninsula in northern France.

JORDAN

Status: MONARCHY
Area: 89,206 sq km (34,443 sq mls)
Population: 5,439,000
Capital: 'AMMĀN
Language: ARABIC
Religion: SUNNI MUSLIM, CHRISTIAN, SHI'A MUSLIM
Currency: DINAR
Organizations: UN

MAP PAGE: 16-17

JORDAN, IN SOUTHWEST Asia, has a short coastline on the Gulf of Aqaba. Much of Jordan is rocky desert plateaux. In the west, behind a belt of hills, the land falls below sea level to the Dead Sea and Jordan river. Much of Jordan is hot and dry, the west is cooler and wetter and most people live in the northwest. Phosphates, potash, fertilizers, pharmaceuticals, fruit and vegetables are the main exports. Jordan relies upon tourism, workers' remittances and foreign aid, all of which were affected by the 1991 Gulf crisis.

KAZAKSTAN

Status: REPUBLIC
Area: 2,717,300 sq km (1,049,155 sq mls)
Population: 16,590,000
Capital: ALMATY
Language: KAZAKH, RUSSIAN, GERMAN, UKRAINIAN, UZBEK, TATAR
Religion: SUNNI MUSLIM, RUSSIAN ORTHODOX, PROTESTANT
Currency: TANGA
Organizations: CIS, UN

MAP PAGE: 12

STRETCHING ACROSS CENTRAL Asia, Kazakstan covers a vast area of steppe land and semi-desert. The land is flat in the west rising to mountains in the southeast. The climate is continental and mainly dry. Agriculture and livestock rearing are the main activities, with cotton and tobacco the main cash crops. Kazakstan is very rich in minerals, such as oil, natural gas, coal, iron ore, chromium, gold, lead and zinc. Mining, metallurgy, machine building and food processing are major industries.

KENYA

Status: REPUBLIC
Area: 582,646 sq km (224,961 sq mls)
Population: 30,522,000
Capital: NAIROBI
Language: SWAHILI (OFFICIAL), ENGLISH, MANY LOCAL LANGUAGES
Religion: R.CATHOLIC, PROTESTANT, TRAD.BELIEFS
Currency: SHILLING
Organizations: COMM., OAU, UN

MAP PAGE: 56

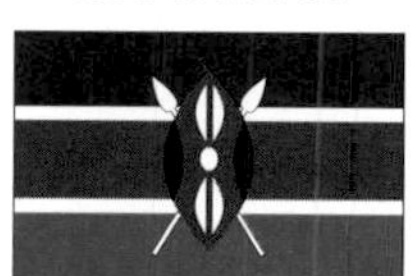

KENYA IS IN east Africa, on the Indian Ocean. Beyond the coastal plains the land rises to plateaux interrupted by volcanic mountains. The Rift Valley runs northwest of Nairobi to Lake Turkana. Most people live in central Kenya. Conditions are tropical on the coast, semi-desert in the north and savannah in the south. Agricultural products, chiefly tea and coffee, provide half export earnings. Light industry is important. Tourism is the main foreign exchange earner; oil refining and re-exports for landlocked neighbours are others.

KIRIBATI

Status: REPUBLIC
Area: 717 sq km (277 sq mls)
Population: 79,000
Capital: BAIRIKI
Language: I-KIRIBATI (GILBERTESE), ENGLISH
Religion: R.CATHOLIC, PROTESTANT, BAHA'I, MORMON
Currency: AUSTR. DOLLAR
Organizations: COMM.

MAP PAGE: 7

KIRIBATI COMPRISES 32 coral islands in the Gilbert, Phoenix and Line groups and the volcanic island of Banaba, which straddle the Equator in the Pacific Ocean. Most people live on the Gilbert islands, and the capital, Bairiki, is on Tarawa, one of the Gilbert Islands. The climate is hot, wetter in the north. Kiribati depends on subsistence farming and fishing. Copra and fish exports and licences for foreign fishing fleets are the main foreign exchange earners.

KUWAIT

Status: MONARCHY
Area: 17,818 sq km (6,880 sq mls)
Population: 1,691,000
Capital: KUWAIT
Language: ARABIC
Religion: SUNNI MUSLIM, SHI'A MUSLIM, OTHER MUSLIM, CHRISTIAN, HINDU
Currency: DINAR
Organizations: OPEC, UN

MAP PAGE: 17

KUWAIT LIES ON the northwest shores of The Gulf in southwest Asia. It is mainly low-lying desert, with irrigated areas along the Bay of Kuwait where most people live. Summers are hot and dry, winters are cool with some rainfall. The oil industry, which accounts for 80 per cent of exports, has largely recovered from the damage caused by Iraq in 1991. Income is also derived from extensive overseas investments.

KYRGYZSTAN

Status: REPUBLIC
Area: 198,500 sq km (76,641 sq mls)
Population: 4,668,000
Capital: BISHKEK
Language: KIRGHIZ, RUSSIAN, UZBEK
Religion: SUNNI MUSLIM, RUSSIAN ORTHODOX
Currency: SOM
Organizations: CIS, UN

MAP PAGE: 14-15

A LANDLOCKED CENTRAL Asian state, Kyrgyzstan is rugged and mountainous, lying in the western Tien Shan range. Most people live in the valleys of the north and west. Summers are hot and winters cold. Agriculture (chiefly livestock farming) is the main activity. Coal, gold, antimony and mercury are produced. Manufactures include machinery, metals and food products. Disruption of Russian-dominated trade has caused economic problems.

LAOS

Status: REPUBLIC
Area: 236,800 sq km (91,429 sq mls)
Population: 4,882,000
Capital: VIENTIANE
Language: LAO, LOCAL LANGUAGES
Religion: BUDDHIST, TRAD.BELIEFS, R.CATHOLIC, SUNNI MUSLIM
Currency: KIP
Organizations: UN

MAP PAGE: 25

A LANDLOCKED COUNTRY in southeast Asia, Laos borders Vietnam, Cambodia, Thailand, Myanmar and China. Forested mountains and plateaux predominate. The climate is tropical monsoon. Most people live in the Mekong valley and the low plateau in the south, and grow food crops, chiefly rice. Electricity, timber, coffee and tin are exported. Foreign aid and investment and the opium trade are important.

LATVIA

Status: REPUBLIC
Area: 63,700 sq km (24,595 sq mls)
Population: 2,515,000
Capital: RĪGA
Language: LATVIAN, RUSSIAN
Religion: PROTESTANT, R.CATHOLIC, RUSSIAN ORTHODOX
Currency: LAT
Organizations: UN

MAP PAGE: 37

LATVIA IS IN north Europe, on the Baltic Sea and Gulf of Riga. The land is flat near the coast but hilly with woods and lakes inland. Latvia has a modified continental climate. One third of the people live in Riga. Crop and livestock farming are important. Industry is varied but specialist products include telephones, diesel trains, buses and paper. Latvia has few natural resources. Economic priorities are creating a market economy and reducing economic dependence on Russia.

LEBANON

Status: REPUBLIC
Area: 10,452 sq km (4,036 sq mls)
Population: 3,009,000
Capital: BEIRUT
Language: ARABIC, FRENCH, ARMENIAN
Religion: SHI'A, SUNNI AND OTHER MUSLIM, PROTESTANT, R.CATHOLIC
Currency: POUND
Organizations: UN

MAP PAGE: 16

LEBANON LIES ON the Mediterranean coast of southwest Asia. Beyond the coastal strip, where most people live, are two parallel mountain ranges, separated by the Bekaa Valley. In general the climate is Mediterranean. Civil war crippled the traditional sectors of banking, commerce and tourism, but some fruit production and light industry survived. Reconstruction is under way.

LESOTHO

Status: MONARCHY
Area: 30,355 sq km (11,720 sq mls)
Population: 2,050,000
Capital: MASERU
Language: SESOTHO, ENGLISH, ZULU
Religion: R.CATHOLIC, PROTESTANT, TRAD.BELIEFS
Currency: LOTI
Organizations: COMM., OAU, SADC, UN

MAP PAGE: 59

LESOTHO IS A landlocked state surrounded by the Republic of South Africa. It is a mountainous country lying within the Drakensberg range. Most people live in the western lowlands and southern Orange and Caledon river valleys. In general Lesotho has hot moist summers and cool, dry winters, with lower temperatures in the mountains. Subsistence farming and herding are the main activities. Exports include livestock, vegetables, wool and mohair. The economy depends heavily on South Africa for transport links and employment.

LIBERIA

Status: REPUBLIC
Area: 111,369 sq km (43,000 sq mls)
Population: 2,760,000
Capital: MONROVIA
Language: ENGLISH, CREOLE, MANY LOCAL LANGUAGES
Religion: TRAD. BELIEFS, SUNNI MUSLIM, PROTESTANT, R.CATHOLIC
Currency: DOLLAR
Organizations: OAU, UN

MAP PAGE: 54

LIBERIA IS ON the Atlantic coast of west Africa. Beyond the coastal belt of sandy beaches and mangrove swamps the land rises to a forested plateau, with highlands along the Guinea border. A quarter of the population lives along the coast. The climate is hot with heavy rainfall. The 1989-93 civil war ruined the economy. Before the war exports included iron ore, diamonds and gold along with rubber, timber and coffee. Ship registration was a major foreign exchange earner. Liberia now relies on foreign aid.

LIBYA

Status: REPUBLIC
Area: 1,759,540 sq km (679,362 sq mls)
Population: 5,407,000
Capital: TRIPOLI
Language: ARABIC, BERBER
Religion: SUNNI MUSLIM, R.CATHOLIC
Currency: DINAR
Organizations: OAU, OPEC, UN

MAP PAGE: 54-55

LIBYA LIES ON the Mediterranean coast of north Africa. The desert plains and hills of the Sahara dominate the landscape and the climate is hot and dry. Most people live in cities near the coast, where the climate is cooler with moderate rainfall. Farming and herding, chiefly in the northwest, are important but the main industry is oil, which accounts for about 95 per cent of export earnings. There is some heavy industry. In 1993 the UN imposed economic sanctions because of alleged sponsorship of terrorism.

LIECHTENSTEIN

Status: MONARCHY
Area: 160 sq km (62 sq mls)
Population: 31,000
Capital: VADUZ
Language: GERMAN
Religion: R.CATHOLIC, PROTESTANT
Currency: SWISS FRANC
Organizations: UN

MAP PAGE: 46

A LANDLOCKED STATE between Switzerland and Austria in central Europe, Liechtenstein occupies the floodplains of the upper Rhine valley and part of the Austrian Alps. It has a temperate climate with cool winters. Dairy farming is important, but manufacturing is dominant. Major products include precision instruments, dentistry equipment, pharmaceuticals, ceramics and textiles. There is also some metal working. Finance, chiefly banking, is very important. Tourism and postal stamps provide additional revenue.

LITHUANIA

Status: REPUBLIC
Area: 65,200 sq km (25,174 sq mls)
Population: 3,715,000
Capital: VILNIUS
Language: LITHUANIAN, RUSSIAN, POLISH
Religion: R.CATHOLIC, PROTESTANT, RUSSIAN ORTHODOX
Currency: LITAS
Organizations: UN

MAP PAGE: 37

LITHUANIA IS IN north Europe, on the eastern shores of the Baltic Sea. It is mainly lowland with many lakes, small rivers and marshes. The climate is generally temperate. About 15 per cent of people live in Vilnius. Agriculture, fishing and forestry are important, but manufacturing dominates the economy. The main products are processed foods, light industrial goods, machinery and metalworking equipment. Progress towards a market economy is slow. The economy remains heavily dependent on Russia.

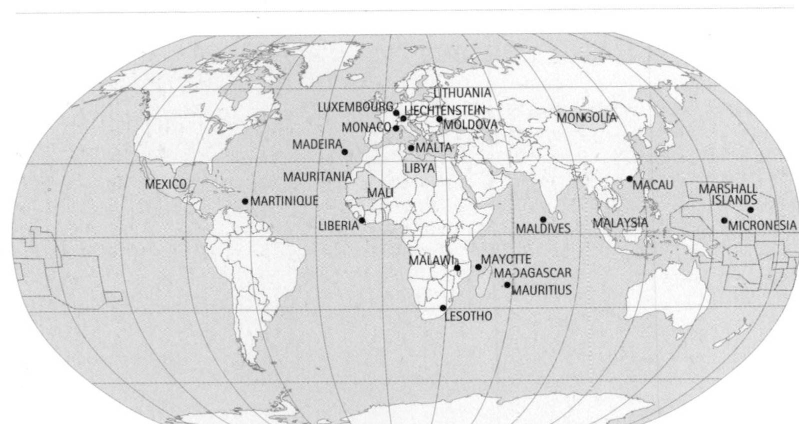

LUXEMBOURG

Status: MONARCHY
Area: 2,586 sq km (998 sq mls)
Population: 410,000
Capital: LUXEMBOURG
Language: LETZEBURGISH, GERMAN, FRENCH, PORTUGUESE
Religion: R.CATHOLIC, PROTESTANT
Currency: FRANC
Organizations: EU, OECD, UN

MAP PAGE: 42

LUXEMBOURG, A LANDLOCKED country in west Europe, borders Belgium, France and Germany. The hills and forests of the Ardennes dominate the north, with rolling pasture to the south, where the main towns, farms and industries are found. Summers are warm and winters mild, though colder in the north. The iron and steel industry is still important, but light industries (including textiles, chemicals and food products) are growing. Luxembourg is a major banking centre and the home base of key European Union institutions.

MACAU

Status: PORTUGUESE TERRITORY
Area: 17 sq km (7 sq mls)
Population: 418,000
Capital: MACAU
Language: CANTONESE, PORTUGUESE
Religion: BUDDHIST, R.CATHOLIC, PROTESTANT
Currency: PATACA

MAP PAGE: 27

AN ENCLAVE ON the south coast of China, Macau consists of an area of the mainland and the two islands of Taipa and Coloane. The territory is scheduled to revert to China in 1999.

MADAGASCAR

Status: REPUBLIC
Area: 587,041 sq km (226,658 sq mls)
Population: 14,763,000
Capital: ANTANANARIVO
Language: MALAGASY, FRENCH
Religion: TRAD.BELIEFS, R.CATHOLIC, PROTESTANT, SUNNI MUSLIM
Currency: FRANC
Organizations: OAU, UN

MAP PAGE: 57

MADAGASCAR AND ADJACENT islets lie off the east coast of south Africa. The world's fourth largest island is in the main a high plateau with a coastal strip to the east and scrubby plain to the west. The climate is tropical with heavy rainfall in the north and east. Most people live on the plateau. Exports include coffee, vanilla, cloves, sugar and shrimps. The main industries are agricultural processing, textile manufacturing, oil refining and mining (chiefly chromite). Tourism and foreign aid are important.

MADEIRA

Status: PORTUGUESE TERRITORY
Area: 794 sq km (307 sq mls)
Population: 253,000
Capital: FUNCHAL
Language: PORTUGUESE
Religion: R.CATHOLIC, PROTESTANT
Currency: PORT. ESCUDO

MAP PAGE: 54

AN ISLAND GROUP in the Atlantic Ocean to the southwest of Portugal. Tourism is important to the economy.

MALAWI

Status: REPUBLIC
Area: 118,484 sq km (45,747 sq mls)
Population: 9,788,000
Capital: LILONGWE
Language: CHICHEWA, ENGLISH, LOMWE
Religion: PROTESTANT, R.CATHOLIC, TRAD. BELIEFS, SUNNI MUSLIM
Currency: KWACHA
Organizations: COMM., OAU, SADC, UN

MAP PAGE: 57

LANDLOCKED MALAWI IN central Africa is a narrow hilly country at the southern end of the East African Rift Valley. One fifth of the country is covered by Lake Malawi, which lies above sea level. Most people live in the southern regions. The climate is mainly subtropical with varying rainfall. The economy is predominantly agricultural. Tobacco, tea and sugar are the main exports. Manufacturing involves mainly chemicals, textiles and agricultural products. Malawi relies heavily on foreign aid.

MALAYSIA

Status: FEDERATION
Area: 332,665 sq km (128,442 sq mls)
Population: 20,140,000
Capital: KUALA LUMPUR
Language: MALAY, ENGLISH, CHINESE, TAMIL, LOCAL LANGUAGES
Religion: SUNNI MUSLIM, BUDDHIST, HINDU, CHRISTIAN, TRAD. BELIEFS
Currency: DOLLAR (RINGGIT)
Organizations: ASEAN, COMM., UN

MAP PAGE: 33

THE FEDERATION OF Malaysia, in southeast Asia, comprises two regions, separated by the South China Sea. Peninsular Malaysia occupies the southern Malay peninsula, which has a chain of mountains dividing the eastern coastal strip from the wider plains to the west. To the east, the states of Sabah and Sarawak in the north of the island of Borneo are mainly rainforest-covered hills and mountains with mangrove swamps along the coast. Both regions have a tropical climate with heavy rainfall. About 80 per cent of the population lives in Peninsular Malaysia, mainly on the coasts. The country is rich in natural resources. It is the world's largest producer of tin, palm oil, pepper and tropical hardwoods, and a major producer of natural rubber, coconut and cocoa. It also has vast reserves of minerals and fuels. However high economic growth in recent years has come from manufacturing which now provides most exports and involves mainly processing industries, electronics assembly and engineering (chiefly car production). With over 7 million visitors a year, tourism is also a major industry.

PENINSULAR MALAYSIA

Status: DIVISION
Area: 131,585 sq km (50,805 sq mls)
Population: 14,942,697
Capital: KUALA LUMPUR

SABAH

Status: STATE
Area: 76,115 sq km (29,388 sq mls)
Population: 1,583,726
Capital: KOTA KINABALU

SARAWAK

Status: STATE
Area: 124,965 sq km (48,249 sq mls)
Population: 1,708,737
Capital: KUCHING

MALDIVES

Status: REPUBLIC
Area: 298 sq km (115 sq mls)
Population: 254,000
Capital: MALE
Language: DIVEHI (MALDIVIAN)
Religion: SUNNI MUSLIM
Currency: RUFIYAA
Organizations: COMM., UN

MAP PAGE: 15

THE MALDIVE ARCHIPELAGO comprises 1,190 coral atolls (202 of which are inhabited), in the Indian Ocean, southwest of India. The climate is hot, humid and monsoonal. The islands depend mainly on fishing and fish processing, light manufacturing (chiefly clothing) and tourism.

MALI

Status: REPUBLIC
Area: 1,240,140 sq km (478,821 sq mls)
Population: 10,795,000
Capital: BAMAKO
Language: FRENCH, BAMBARA, MANY LOCAL LANGUAGES
Religion: SUNNI MUSLIM, TRAD.BELIEFS, R.CATHOLIC
Currency: CFA FRANC
Organizations: OAU, UN

MAP PAGE: 54

A LANDLOCKED STATE in west Africa, Mali is low-lying, rising to mountains in the northeast. Northern regions lie within the Sahara desert. To the south, around the Niger river, are marshes and savannah grassland. Rainfall is unreliable. Most people live along the Niger and Senegal rivers. Exports include cotton and groundnuts. Some gold is produced. Mali relies heavily on foreign aid.

MALTA

Status: REPUBLIC
Area: 316 sq km (122 sq mls)
Population: 371,000
Capital: VALLETTA
Language: MALTESE, ENGLISH
Religion: R.CATHOLIC
Currency: LIRA
Organizations: COMM., UN

MAP PAGE: 48

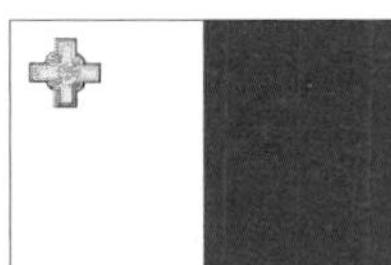

THE ISLANDS OF Malta and Gozo lie in the Mediterranean Sea, off the coast of south Italy. Malta, the main island, has low hills and an indented coastline. Two thirds of the population lives in the Valletta area. The islands have hot, dry summers and mild winters. The main industries are tourism, ship building and repair, and export manufacturing (chiefly clothing). Vegetables, flowers, wine and tobacco are also exported.

MARSHALL ISLANDS

Status: REPUBLIC
Area: 181 sq km (70 sq mls)
Population: 56,000
Capital: DALAP-ULIGA-DARRIT
Language: MARSHALLESE, ENGLISH
Religion: PROTESTANT, R.CATHOLIC
Currency: US DOLLAR
Organizations: UN

MAP PAGE: 4

THE MARSHALL ISLANDS consist of over 1,000 atolls, islands and islets, within two chains, in the North Pacific Ocean. The main atolls are Majuro (home to half the population), Kwajalein, Jaluit, Enewetak and Bikini. The climate is tropical with heavy autumn rainfall. The islands depend on farming, fishing, tourism, financial services, and US aid and rent for a missile base.

MARTINIQUE

Status: FRENCH TERRITORY
Area: 1,079 sq km (417 sq mls)
Population: 379,000
Capital: FORT-DE-FRANCE
Language: FRENCH, FRENCH CREOLE
Religion: R.CATHOLIC, PROTESTANT, HINDU, TRAD.BELIEFS
Currency: FRENCH FRANC

MAP PAGE: 83

MARTINIQUE, ONE OF the Caribbean's Windward Islands, has volcanic peaks in the north, a populous central plain, and hills and beaches in the south. The tropical island depends on fruit growing (chiefly bananas), oil refining, rum distilling, tourism and French aid.

MAURITANIA

Status: REPUBLIC
Area: 1,030,700 sq km (397,955 sq mls)
Population: 2,284,000
Capital: NOUAKCHOTT
Language: ARABIC, FRENCH, LOCAL LANGUAGES
Religion: SUNNI MUSLIM
Currency: OUGUIYA
Organizations: OAU, UN

MAP PAGE: 54

MAURITANIA IS ON the Atlantic coast of northwest Africa and lies almost entirely within the Sahara desert. Oases and a fertile strip along the Senegal river to the south are the only areas suitable for cultivation. The climate is generally hot and dry. A quarter of Mauritanians live in Nouakchott. Livestock rearing and subsistence farming are important. The economy is heavily dependent on iron ore mining and fishing, which together account for 90 per cent of export earnings, and foreign aid.

MAURITIUS

Status: REPUBLIC
Area: 2,040 sq km (788 sq mls)
Population: 1,122,000
Capital: PORT LOUIS
Language: ENGLISH, FRENCH CREOLE, HINDI, INDIAN LANGUAGES
Religion: HINDU, R.CATHOLIC, SUNNI MUSLIM, PROTESTANT
Currency: RUPEE
Organizations: COMM., OAU, UN, SADC

MAP PAGE: 53

THE STATE COMPRISES Mauritius, Rodrigues and some 20 small islands in the Indian Ocean, east of Madagascar. The main island of Mauritius is volcanic in origin and has a coral coast rising to a central plateau. Most people live on the west side of the island. The climate is warm and humid. Mauritius depends mainly on sugar production, light manufacturing (chiefly clothing) and tourism.

MAYOTTE

Status: FRENCH TERRITORY
Area: 373 sq km (144 sq mls)
Population: 110,000
Capital: DZAOUDZI
Language: MAHORIAN (SWAHILI), FRENCH
Religion: SUNNI MUSLIM, R.CATHOLIC
Currency: FRENCH FRANC

MAP PAGE: 57

LYING IN THE Indian Ocean off the east coast of Central Africa, Mayotte is part of the Comoros Archipelago, but remains a French Territory.

MEXICO

Status: REPUBLIC
Area: 1,972,545 sq km (761,604 sq mls)
Population: 90,487,000
Capital: MÉXICO
Language: SPANISH, MANY AMERINDIAN LANGUAGES
Religion: R.CATHOLIC, PROTESTANT
Currency: PESO
Organizations: NAFTA, OECD, UN

MAP PAGE: 82

THE LARGEST COUNTRY in central America, Mexico extends southwards from the USA to Guatemala and Belize, and from the Pacific Ocean to the Gulf of Mexico. The greater part of the country is high plateaux flanked by the western and eastern Sierra Madre mountain ranges. The principal lowland is the Yucatán peninsula in the southeast. The climate varies with latitude and altitude: hot and humid in the lowlands, warm in the plateaux and cool with cold winters in the mountains. The north is arid, while the far south has heavy rainfall. Mexico City is one of the world's largest conurbations and the centre of trade and industry. Agriculture involves a quarter of the workforce and exports include coffee, fruit and vegetables. Shrimps are also exported and timber production is important for allied industries. Mexico is rich in minerals, including copper, zinc, lead and sulphur, and is the world's leading producer of silver. It is one of the world's largest producers of oil, from vast oil and gas resources in the Gulf of Mexico. The oil and petrochemical industries are still the mainstay, but a variety of manufactures are now produced including iron and steel, motor vehicles, textiles and electronic goods. Tourism is growing in importance.

FEDERATED STATES OF MICRONESIA

Status: REPUBLIC
Area: 701 sq km (271 sq mls)
Population: 105,000
Capital: PALIKIR
Language: ENGLISH, TRUKESE, POHNPEIAN, LOCAL LANGUAGES
Religion: PROTESTANT, R.CATHOLIC
Currency: US DOLLAR
Organizations: UN

MAP PAGE: 4

MICRONESIA COMPRISES 607 atolls and islands in the Carolines group in the North Pacific Ocean. A third of the population lives on Pohnpei. The climate is tropical with heavy rainfall. Fishing and subsistence farming are the main activities. Copra and fish are the main exports. Income also derives from tourism and the licensing of foreign fishing fleets. The islands depend on US aid.

MOLDOVA

Status: REPUBLIC
Area: 33,700 sq km (13,012 sq mls)
Population: 4,432,000
Capital: CHIȘINĂU
Language: ROMANIAN, RUSSIAN, UKRAINIAN, GAGAUZ
Religion: MOLDOVAN ORTHODOX, RUSSIAN ORTHODOX
Currency: LEU
Organizations: CIS, UN

MAP PAGE: 47

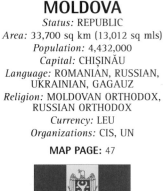

MOLDOVA IS IN east Europe, sandwiched between Romania and Ukraine. It consists of hilly steppe land, drained by the Prut and Dnestr rivers; the latter provides access to the Black Sea through Ukrainian territory. Moldova has long hot summers and mild winters. The economy is mainly agricultural, with tobacco, wine and fruit the chief products. Food processing and textiles are the main industries. Ethnic tension, which erupted into civil war in 1992, has slowed economic reform.

MONACO

Status: MONARCHY
Area: 2 sq km (0.8 sq ml)
Population: 32,000
Capital: MONACO
Language: FRENCH, MONEGASQUE, ITALIAN
Religion: R.CATHOLIC
Currency: FRENCH FRANC
Organizations: UN

MAP PAGE: 44

THE PRINCIPALITY, IN south Europe, occupies a rocky peninsula and a strip of land on France's Mediterranean coast. It depends on service industries (chiefly tourism, banking and finance) and light industry.

MONGOLIA

Status: REPUBLIC
Area: 1,565,000 sq km (604,250 sq mls)
Population: 2,410,000
Capital: ULAANBAATAR
Language: KHALKA (MONGOLIAN), KAZAKH, LOCAL LANGUAGES
Religion: BUDDHIST, SUNNI MUSLIM, TRAD.BELIEFS
Currency: TUGRIK
Organizations: UN

MAP PAGE: 24

MONGOLIA IS A landlocked country in east Asia between Russia and China. Much of it is high steppe land, with mountains and lakes in the west and north. In the south is the Gobi desert. Mongolia has long, cold winters and short, mild summers. A quarter of the population lives in the capital. Mongolia is rich in minerals and fuels. Copper accounts for half export earnings. Livestock breeding and agricultural processing are important. The demise of the Soviet Union caused economic problems and Mongolia depends on foreign aid.

MONTSERRAT

Status: UK TERRITORY
Area: 100 sq km (39 sq mls)
Population: 11,000
Capital: PLYMOUTH
Language: ENGLISH
Religion: PROTESTANT, R.CATHOLIC
Currency: E. CARIB. DOLLAR
Organizations: CARICOM

MAP PAGE: 83

MOROCCO

Status: MONARCHY
Area: 446,550 sq km (172,414 sq mls)
Population: 27,111,000
Capital: RABAT
Language: ARABIC, BERBER, FRENCH, SPANISH
Religion: SUNNI MUSLIM, R.CATHOLIC
Currency: DIRHAM
Organizations: UN

MAP PAGE: 54

LYING IN THE northwest corner of Africa, Morocco has both Atlantic and Mediterranean coasts. The Atlas ranges separate the arid south and disputed Western Sahara from the fertile regions of the west and north, which have a milder climate. Most Moroccans live on the Atlantic coastal plain. The economy is based mainly on agriculture, phosphate mining and tourism. Manufacturing (chiefly textiles and clothing) and fishing are important.

MOZAMBIQUE

Status: REPUBLIC
Area: 799,380 sq km (308,642 sq mls)
Population: 17,423,000
Capital: MAPUTO
Language: PORTUGUESE, MAKUA, TSONGA, MANY LOCAL LANGUAGES
Religion: TRAD.BELIEFS, R.CATHOLIC, SUNNI MUSLIM
Currency: METICAL
Organizations: OAU, SADC, UN, COMM.

MAP PAGE: 57

MOZAMBIQUE LIES ON the east coast of southern Africa. The land is mainly a savannah plateau drained by the Zambezi and other rivers, with highlands to the north. Most people live on the coast or in the river valleys. In general the climate is tropical with winter rainfall, but droughts occur. Reconstruction began in 1992 after 16 years of civil war. The economy is based on agriculture and trade. Exports include shrimps, cashews, cotton and sugar, but Mozambique relies heavily on aid.

MYANMAR

Status: REPUBLIC
Area: 676,577 sq km (261,228 sq mls)
Population: 46,527,000
Capital: YANGON
Language: BURMESE, SHAN, KAREN, LOCAL LANGUAGES
Religion: BUDDHIST, SUNNI MUSLIM, PROTESTANT, R.CATHOLIC
Currency: KYAT
Organizations: UN

MAP PAGE: 24-25

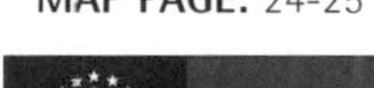

MYANMAR IS IN southeast Asia, on the Bay of Bengal and Andaman Sea. Most people live in the valley and delta of the Irrawaddy river, which is flanked on three sides by mountains and high plateaux. The climate is hot and monsoonal, and rainforest covers much of the land. Most people depend on agriculture. Exports include teak and rice. Myanmar is rich in oil and gemstones. Political unrest has affected economic development.

NAMIBIA

Status: REPUBLIC
Area: 824,292 sq km (318,261 sq mls)
Population: 1,540,000
Capital: WINDHOEK
Language: ENGLISH, AFRIKAANS, GERMAN, OVAMBO
Religion: PROTESTANT, R.CATHOLIC
Currency: DOLLAR
Organizations: COMM., OAU, SADC, UN

MAP PAGE: 57

NAMIBIA LIES ON the Atlantic coast of southern Africa. Mountain ranges separate the coastal Namib Desert from the interior plateau, bordered to the south and east by the Kalahari desert. Namibia is hot and dry, but some summer rain falls in the north which supports crops, herds and most of the population. The economy is based mainly on agriculture and diamond and uranium mining. Fishing is increasingly important.

NAURU

Status: REPUBLIC
Area: 21 sq km (8 sq mls)
Population: 11,000
Capital: YAREN
Language: NAURUAN, GILBERTESE, ENGLISH
Religion: PROTESTANT, R.CATHOLIC
Currency: AUSTR. DOLLAR
Organizations: COMM.

MAP PAGE: 7

NAURU IS A coral island in the South Pacific Ocean, with a fertile coastal strip, a barren central plateau and a tropical climate. The economy is based on phosphate mining, but reserves are near exhaustion.

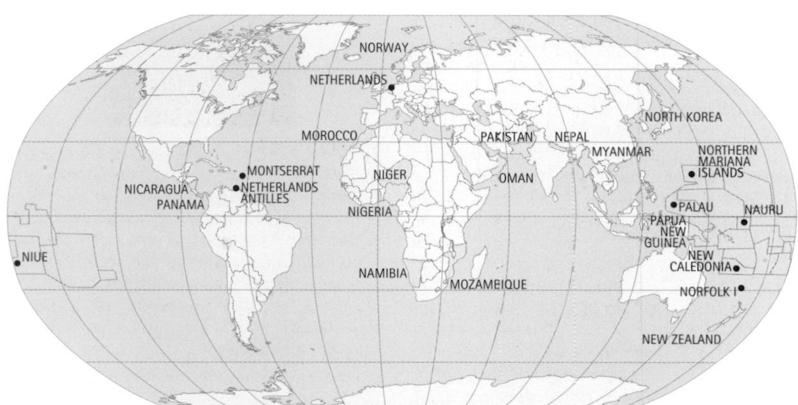

NEPAL

Status: MONARCHY
Area: 147,181 sq km (56,827 sq mls)
Population: 21,918,000
Capital: KATHMANDU
Language: NEPALI, MAITHILI, BHOJPURI, ENGLISH, MANY LOCAL LANGUAGES
Religion: HINDU, BUDDHIST, SUNNI MUSLIM
Currency: RUPEE
Organizations: UN

MAP PAGE: 22-23

THE SOUTH ASIAN country of Nepal lies in the southern Himalayas between India and China. High mountains (including Everest) dominate northern Nepal. Most people live in the temperate central valleys and subtropical southern plains. The economy is based largely on agriculture and forestry. Manufacturing (chiefly textiles) and tourism are important. Nepal relies upon foreign aid.

NETHERLANDS

Status: MONARCHY
Area: 41,526 sq km (16,033 sq mls)
Population: 15,451,000
Capital: AMSTERDAM/THE HAGUE
Language: DUTCH, FRISIAN, TURKISH
Religion: R.CATHOLIC, PROTESTANT, SUNNI MUSLIM
Currency: GUILDER
Organizations: EU, OECD, UN

MAP PAGE: 42

THE NETHERLANDS LIES on the North Sea coast of west Europe. Apart from hills in the far southeast, the land is flat and low-lying, much of it below sea level. The coastal region contains the delta of five rivers and polders (reclaimed land), protected by sand dunes, dikes and canals. The climate is temperate, with cool summers and mild winters. Rainfall is spread evenly throughout the year. The Netherlands is a densely populated country, with the majority of people living in the western Amsterdam-Rotterdam-The Hague area. Horticulture and dairy farming are important activities, with exports of eggs, butter and cheese. The Netherlands is Europe's leading producer and exporter of natural gas from reserves in the North Sea, but otherwise lacks raw materials. The economy is based mainly on international trade and manufacturing industry. Industrial sites are centred mainly around the port of Rotterdam. The chief industries produce food products, chemicals, machinery, electric and electronic goods and transport equipment. Financial services and tourism are important.

NETHERLANDS ANTILLES

Status: NETHERLANDS TERRITORY
Area: 800 sq km (309 sq mls)
Population: 205,000
Capital: WILLEMSTAD
Language: DUTCH, PAPIAMENTO
Religion: R.CATHOLIC, PROTESTANT
Currency: GUILDER

MAP PAGE: 83

THE TERRITORY COMPRISES two separate island groups: Curacao and Bonaire off the northern coast of South America, and Saba, Sint Eustatius and the southern part of Sint Maarten in the northern Lesser Antilles.

NEW CALEDONIA

Status: FRENCH TERRITORY
Area: 19,058 sq km (7,358 sq mls)
Population: 186,000
Capital: NOUMÉA
Language: FRENCH, LOCAL LANGUAGES
Religion: R.CATHOLIC, PROTESTANT, SUNNI MUSLIM
Currency: PACIFIC FRANC

MAP PAGE: 7

AN ISLAND GROUP, lying in the southwest Pacific, with a sub-tropical climate. The economy is based on nickel mining, tourism and agriculture.

NEW ZEALAND

Status: MONARCHY
Area: 270,534 sq km (104,454 sq mls)
Population: 3,542,000
Capital: WELLINGTON
Language: ENGLISH, MAORI
Religion: PROTESTANT, R.CATHOLIC
Currency: DOLLAR
Organizations: COMM., OECD, UN

MAP PAGE: 9

NEW ZEALAND, IN Australasia, comprises two main islands separated by the narrow Cook Strait, and a number of smaller islands. North Island, where three quarters of the population lives, has mountain ranges, broad fertile valleys and a volcanic central plateau with hot springs and two active volcanoes. South Island is also mountainous, the Southern Alps running its entire length. The only major lowland area is the Canterbury Plains in the east. The climate is generally temperate, though South Island has cooler winters with upland snow. Rainfall is distributed throughout the year. Farming is the mainstay of the economy. New Zealand is one of the world's leading producers of meat (beef, lamb and mutton), wool and dairy products. Specialist foods, such as kiwi fruit, and fish are also important. Coal, oil and natural gas are produced, but hydroelectric and geothermal power provide much of the country's energy needs. Other industries produce timber, wood pulp, iron, aluminium, machinery and chemicals. Tourism is the largest foreign exchange earner.

NICARAGUA

Status: REPUBLIC
Area: 130,000 sq km (50,193 sq mls)
Population: 4,539,000
Capital: MANAGUA
Language: SPANISH, AMERINDIAN LANGUAGES
Religion: R.CATHOLIC, PROTESTANT
Currency: CÓRDOBA
Organizations: UN

MAP PAGE: 82-83

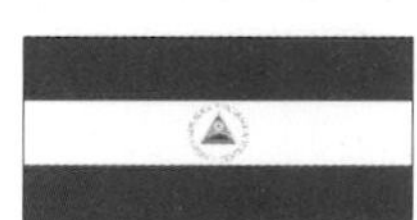

NICARAGUA LIES AT the heart of Central America, with both Pacific and Caribbean coasts. Mountain ranges separate the east, which is largely jungle, from the more developed western regions, which include Lake Nicaragua and some active volcanoes. The highest land is in the north. The climate is tropical. The economy is largely agricultural.

Traditional exports include cotton, coffee, bananas and gold. The aid-dependent economy has suffered from civil war (1978-89) and US sanctions.

NIGER

Status: REPUBLIC
Area: 1,267,000 sq km (489,191 sq mls)
Population: 9,151,000
Capital: NIAMEY
Language: FRENCH (OFFICIAL), HAUSA, FULANI, LOCAL LANGUAGES
Religion: SUNNI MUSLIM, TRAD.BELIEFS
Currency: CFA FRANC
Organizations: OAU, UN

MAP PAGE: 54-55

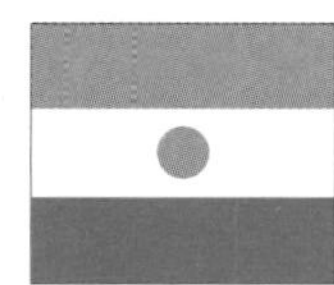

A LANDLOCKED STATE of west Africa, Niger lies mostly within the Sahara desert, but with savannah land in the south and Niger valley. The Air massif dominates central regions. Much of the country is hot and dry. The south has some summer rainfall, though droughts occur. The economy depends on subsistence farming and herding, uranium exports and foreign aid.

NIGERIA

Status: REPUBLIC
Area: 923,768 sq km (356,669 sq mls)
Population: 111,721,000
Capital: ABUJA
Language: ENGLISH, CREOLE, HAUSA, YORUBA, IBO, FULANI
Religion: SUNNI MUSLIM, PROTESTANT, R.CATHOLIC, TRAD. BELIEFS
Currency: NAIRA
Organizations: COMM., OAU, OPEC, UN

MAP PAGE: 54-55

NIGERIA IS IN west Africa, on the Gulf of Guinea, and is the most populous country in the African continent. The Niger delta dominates coastal areas, fringed with sandy beaches, mangrove swamps and lagoons. Inland is a belt of rainforest that gives way to woodland or savannah on high plateaux. The far north is the semi-desert edge of the Sahara. The climate is tropical with heavy summer rainfall in the south but low rainfall in the north. Most people live in the coastal lowlands or in western Nigeria. About half the workforce is involved in agriculture, mainly growing subsistence crops, and Nigeria is virtually self-sufficient in food. Cocoa and rubber are the only significant export crops. The economy is heavily dependent on vast oil resources in the Niger delta and shallow offshore waters, which account for about 90 per cent of export earnings. Nigeria also has natural gas reserves and some mineral deposits, but these are as yet largely undeveloped. Industry involves mainly oil refining, chemicals (chiefly fertilizer), agricultural processing, textiles, steel manufacture and vehicle assembly. Economic mismanagement in the oil boom of the 1970s and political instability have left Nigeria with a heavy debt, poverty and rising unemployment.

NIUE

Status: NEW ZEALAND TERRITORY
Area: 258 sq km (100 sq mls)
Population: 2,000
Capital: ALOFI
Language: ENGLISH, POLYNESIAN (NIUEAN)
Religion: PROTESTANT, R.CATHOLIC
Currency: NZ DOLLAR

MAP PAGE: 7

NORFOLK ISLAND

Status: AUSTRALIAN TERRITORY
Area: 35 sq km (14 sq mls)
Population: 2,000
Capital: KINGSTON
Language: ENGLISH
Religion: PROTESTANT, R.CATHOLIC
Currency: AUSTR. DOLLAR

MAP PAGE: 7

NORTH KOREA

Status: REPUBLIC
Area: 120,538 sq km (46,540 sq mls)
Population: 23,917,000
Capital: P'YŎNGYANG
Language: KOREAN
Religion: TRAD.BELIEFS, CHONDOIST, BUDDHIST, CONFUCIAN, TAOIST
Currency: WON
Organizations: UN

MAP PAGE: 30

OCCUPYING THE NORTHERN half of the Korean peninsula in east Asia, North Korea is a rugged and mountainous country. The principal lowlands and the main agricultural areas are the Pyongyang and Chaeryong plains in the southwest. More than half the population lives in urban areas, mainly on the coastal plains, which are wider along the Yellow Sea to the west than the Sea of Japan to the east. North Korea has a continental climate, with cold, dry winters and hot, wet summers. About half the workforce is involved in agriculture, mainly growing food crops on cooperative farms. A variety of minerals and ores, chiefly iron ore, are mined and are the basis of the country's heavy industry. Exports include minerals (chiefly lead, magnesite and zinc) and metal products (chiefly iron and steel). North Korea depends heavily on aid, but has suffered since support from Russia and China was ended in in 1991 and 1993 respectively. Agricultural, mining and maufacturing output have fallen. Living standards are much lower than in South Korea from which it was separated in 1945.

NORTHERN MARIANA ISLANDS

Status: US TERRITORY
Area: 477 sq km (184 sq mls)
Population: 47,000
Capital: SAIPAN
Language: ENGLISH, CHAMORRO, TAGALOG, LOCAL LANGUAGES
Religion: R.CATHOLIC, PROTESTANT
Currency: US DOLLAR

MAP PAGE: 24-25

A CHAIN OF islands in the Western Pacific Ocean, tourism is increasingly important to the economy.

NORWAY

Status: MONARCHY
Area: 323,878 sq km (125,050 sq mls)
Population: 4,360,000
Capital: OSLO
Language: NORWEGIAN
Religion: PROTESTANT, R.CATHOLIC
Currency: KRONE
Organizations: OECD, UN

MAP PAGE: 36-37

A COUNTRY OF NORTH Europe, Norway stretches along the north and west coasts of Scandinavia, from the Arctic Ocean to the North Sea. Its extensive coastline is indented

with fjords and fringed with many islands. Inland, the terrain is mountainous, with coniferous forests and lakes in the south. The only major lowland areas are along the southern North Sea and Skagerrak coasts, where most people live. The climate on the west coast is modified by the North Atlantic Drift. Inland, summers are warmer but winters are colder. Norway has vast petroleum and natural gas resources in the North Sea. It is west Europe's leading producer of oil and gas, which account for over 40 per cent of export earnings. Related industries include engineering (such as oil and gas platforms) and petrochemicals. More traditional industries process local raw materials: fish, timber and minerals. Agriculture is limited, but fishing and fish farming are important. Norway is the world's leading exporter of salmon. Merchant shipping and tourism are major sources of foreign exchange.

OMAN

Status: MONARCHY
Area: 309,500 sq km (119,499 sq mls)
Population: 2,163,000
Capital: MUSCAT
Language: ARABIC, BALUCHI, FARSI, SWAHILI, INDIAN LANGUAGES
Religion: IBADHI MUSLIM, SUNNI MUSLIM
Currency: RIAL
Organizations: UN

MAP PAGE: 20

THE SULTANATE OF southwest Asia occupies the southeast coast of Arabia and an enclave north of the United Arab Emirates. Oman is a desert land, with mountains in the north and south. The climate is hot and mainly dry. Most people live on the coastal strip on the Gulf of Oman. The majority depends on farming and fishing, but the oil and gas industries dominate the economy. Copper is mined.

PAKISTAN

Status: REPUBLIC
Area: 803,940 sq km (310,403 sq mls)
Population: 129,808,000
Capital: ISLAMABAD
Language: URDU (OFFICIAL), PUNJABI, SINDHI, PUSHTU, ENGLISH
Religion: SUNNI MUSLIM, SHI'A MUSLIM, CHRISTIAN, HINDU
Currency: RUPEE
Organizations: COMM., UN

MAP PAGE: 14-15

PAKISTAN IS IN the northwest part of the Indian subcontinent in south Asia, on the Arabian Sea. Eastern and southern Pakistan are dominated by the great basin drained by the Indus river system. It is the main agricultural area and contains most of the population. To the north the land rises to the mountains of the Karakoram and part of the Hindu Kush and Himalayas. The west is semi-desert plateaux and mountain ranges. The climate ranges between dry desert and polar ice cap. However, temperatures are generally warm and rainfall is monsoonal. Agriculture is the main sector of the economy, employing about half the workforce and accounting for over two thirds of export earnings. Cultivation is based on extensive irrigation schemes. Pakistan is one of the world's leading producers of cotton and an important exporter of rice. However, much of the country's food needs must be imported. Pakistan produces natural gas and has a variety of mineral deposits including coal and gold, but they are little developed. The main industries are textiles and clothing manufacture and food processing, with fabrics and ready-made clothing the leading exports. Pakistan also produces leather goods, fertilizers, chemicals, paper and precision instruments. The country depends heavily upon foreign aid and remittances from Pakistanis working abroad.

PALAU

Status: REPUBLIC
Area: 497 sq km (192 sq mls)
Population: 17,000
Capital: KOROR
Language: PALAUAN, ENGLISH
Religion: R.CATHOLIC, PROTESTANT, TRAD.BELIEFS
Currency: US DOLLAR
Organizations: UN

MAP PAGE: 25

PALAU COMPRISES OVER 300 islands in the western Carolines group of the North Pacific Ocean. Two thirds of the people live on Koror. The climate is tropical. Palau depends on farming, fishing, tourism and US aid.

PANAMA

Status: REPUBLIC
Area: 77,082 sq km (29,762 sq mls)
Population: 2,631,000
Capital: PANAMÁ
Language: SPANISH, ENGLISH CREOLE, AMERINDIAN LANGUAGES
Religion: R.CATHOLIC, PROTESTANT, SUNNI MUSLIM, BAHA'I
Currency: BALBOA
Organizations: UN

MAP PAGE: 83

PANAMA IS THE most southerly state in Central America and has Pacific and Caribbean coasts. It is hilly, with mountains in the west and jungle near the Colombian border. The climate is tropical. Most people live on the drier Pacific side. The economy is based mainly on services related to the canal, shipping, banking and tourism. Exports include bananas, shrimps, sugar and petroleum products.

PAPUA NEW GUINEA

Status: MONARCHY
Area: 462,840 sq km (178,704 sq mls)
Population: 4,074,000
Capital: PORT MORESBY
Language: ENGLISH, TOK FISIN (PIDGIN), LOCAL LANGUAGES
Religion: PROTESTANT, R.CATHOLIC, TRAD.BELIEFS
Currency: KINA
Organizations: COMM., UN

MAP PAGE: 6

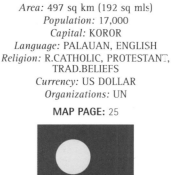

PAPUA NEW GUINEA, in Australasia, occupies the eastern half of New Guinea and includes many island groups. Papua New Guinea has a forested and mountainous interior, bordered by swampy plains, and a tropical monsoon climate. Most of the workforce are farmers. Timber, copra, coffee and cocoa are important, but exports are dominated by minerals, chiefly copper and gold. The country depends on foreign aid.

PARAGUAY

Status: REPUBLIC
Area: 406,752 sq km (157,048 sq mls)
Population: 4,828,000
Capital: ASUNCIÓN
Language: SPANISH, GUARANÍ
Religion: R.CATHOLIC, PROTESTANT
Currency: GUARANÍ
Organizations: UN

MAP PAGE: 88

PARAGUAY IS A landlocked country in central South America, bordering Bolivia, Brazil and Argentina. The river Paraguay separates a sparsely populated western zone of marsh and flat alluvial plains from a more developed, hilly and forested region to the east. The climate is subtropical. The mainstay of the economy is agriculture and agricultural processing. Exports include cotton, soya bean and edible oil products, timber and meat. The largest hydro-electric dam in the world is at Itaipú on the river Paraná.

PERU

Status: REPUBLIC
Area: 1,285,216 sq km (496,225 sq mls)
Population: 23,560,000
Capital: LIMA
Language: SPANISH, QUECHUA, AYMARA
Religion: R.CATHOLIC, PROTESTANT
Currency: SOL
Organizations: UN

MAP PAGE: 86

PERU LIES ON the Pacific coast of South America. Most people live on the coastal strip and the slopes of the high Andes. East of the Andes is high plateau country and the Amazon rainforest. The coast is temperate with low rainfall, while the east is hot, humid and wet. Agriculture involves one third of the workforce. Sugar, cotton, coffee and, illegally, coca are the main cash crops. Fishmeal and timber are also important, but copper, zinc, lead, gold, silver, petroleum and its products are the main exports.

PHILIPPINES

Status: REPUBLIC
Area: 300,000 sq km (115,831 sq mls)
Population: 70,267,000
Capital: MANILA
Language: ENGLISH, FILIPINO (TAGALOG), CEBUANO
Religion: R.CATHOLIC, AGLIPAYAN, SUNNI MUSLIM, PROTESTANT
Currency: PESO
Organizations: ASEAN, UN

MAP PAGE: 31

THE PHILIPPINES, IN southeast Asia, consists of 7,100 islands and atolls lying between the South China Sea and the Pacific Ocean. The islands of Luzon and Mindanao occupy two thirds of the land area. They and nine other fairly large islands are mountainous and forested. There are ten active volcanoes and earthquakes are common. Most people live in the intermontane plains on the larger islands or on the coastal strips. The climate is hot and humid with heavy monsoonal rainfall. Coconuts, sugar, pineapples and bananas are the main agricultural exports. Fish and timber are also important. The Philippines produces copper, gold, silver, chromium and nickel as well as oil, though geothermal power is also used. The main industries process raw materials and produce electrical and electronic equipment and components, footwear and clothing, textiles and furniture. Tourism is being encouraged. Foreign aid and remittances from workers abroad are important to the economy, which faces problems of high population growth rate and high unemployment.

PITCAIRN ISLANDS

Status: UK TERRITORY
Area: 45 sq km (17 sq mls)
Population: 71
Capital: ADAMSTOWN
Language: ENGLISH
Religion: PROTESTANT
Currency: DOLLAR

MAP PAGE: 5

AN ISLAND GROUP in the southeast Pacific Ocean consisting of Pitcairn Island and three uninhabited islands. It was originally settled by mutineers from HMS Bounty.

POLAND

Status: REPUBLIC
Area: 312,683 sq km (120,728 sq mls)
Population: 38,588,000
Capital: WARSAW
Language: POLISH, GERMAN
Religion: R.CATHOLIC, POLISH ORTHODOX
Currency: ZŁOTY
Organizations: UN, OECD

MAP PAGE: 46-47

POLAND LIES ON the Baltic coast of central Europe. The Oder and Vistula deltas dominate the coast, fringed with sand dunes. Inland much of Poland is low-lying (part of the North European plain), with woods and lakes. In the south the land rises to the Sudeten and western Carpathian mountains which form the borders with the Czech Republic and Slovakia respectively. The climate is continental, with warm summers and cold winters. Conditions are milder in the west and on the coast. A third of the workforce is involved in agriculture, forestry and fishing. Agricultural exports include livestock products and sugar. The economy is heavily industrialized, with mining and manufacturing accounting for 40 per cent of national income. Poland is one of the world's major producers of coal. It also produces copper, zinc, lead, nickel, sulphur and natural gas. The main industries are ship building, car manufacture, metal and chemical production. The transition to a market economy has resulted in 15 per cent unemployment and economic hardship.

PORTUGAL

Status: REPUBLIC
Area: 88,940 sq km (34,340 sq mls)
Population: 10,797,000
Capital: LISBON
Language: PORTUGUESE
Religion: R.CATHOLIC, PROTESTANT
Currency: ESCUDO
Organizations: EU, OECD, UN

MAP PAGE: 45

PORTUGAL LIES IN the western part of the Iberian peninsula in southwest Europe, has an Atlantic coastline and is flanked by Spain to the north and east. North of the river Tagus are mostly highlands with forests of pine and cork. South of the river is undulating lowland. The climate in the north is cool and moist, influenced by the Atlantic Ocean. The south is warmer, with dry, mild winters. Most Portuguese live near the coast, with one third of the total population in Lisbon and Oporto. Agriculture, fishing and forestry involve 12 per cent of the workfork. Wines, tomatoes, citrus fruit, cork (Portugal is the world's largest producer) and sardines are important exports. Mining and manufacturing are the main sectors of the economy. Portugal produces pyrite, kaolin, zinc, tungsten and other minerals. Export manufactures include textiles, clothing and footwear, electrical machinery and transport equipment, cork and wood products, and chemicals. Service industries, chiefly tourism and banking, are important to the economy as are remittances from workers abroad.

PUERTO RICO

Status: US TERRITORY
Area: 9,104 sq km (3,515 sq mls)
Population: 3,674,000
Capital: SAN JUAN
Language: SPANISH, ENGLISH
Religion: R.CATHOLIC, PROTESTANT
Currency: US DOLLAR

MAP PAGE: 83

THE CARIBBEAN ISLAND of Puerto Rico has a forested, hilly interior, coastal plains and a tropical climate. Half the population lives in the San Juan area. The economy is based on export manufacturing (chiefly chemicals and electronics), tourism and agriculture.

QATAR

Status: MONARCHY
Area: 11,437 sq km (4,416 sq mls)
Population: 551,000
Capital: DOHA
Language: ARABIC, INDIAN LANGUAGES
Religion: SUNNI MUSLIM, CHRISTIAN, HINDU
Currency: RIYAL
Organizations: OPEC, UN

MAP PAGE: 18

THE EMIRATE OCCUPIES a peninsula that extends northwards from east-central Arabia into The Gulf in southwest Asia. The peninsula is flat and barren with sand dunes and salt pans. The climate is hot and mainly dry. Most people live in the Doha area. The economy is heavily dependent on petroleum, natural gas and the oil-refining industry. Income also comes from overseas investment.

REPUBLIC OF IRELAND

Status: REPUBLIC
Area: 70,282 sq km (27,136 sq mls)
Population: 3,582,000
Capital: DUBLIN
Language: ENGLISH, IRISH
Religion: R.CATHOLIC, PROTESTANT
Currency: PUNT
Organizations: EU, OECD, UN

MAP PAGE: 41

A STATE IN northwest Europe, the Irish republic occupies some 80 per cent of the island of Ireland in the Atlantic Ocean. It is a lowland country of wide valleys, lakes and peat bogs, with isolated mountain ranges around the coast. The west coast is rugged and indented with many bays. The climate is mild due to the North Atlantic Drift and rainfall is plentiful, though highest in the west. Nearly 60 per cent of people live in urban areas, Dublin and Cork being the main cities. Agriculture, the traditional mainstay, involves mainly the production of livestock, meat and dairy products, which account for about 20 percent of exports. Manufactured goods form the bulk of exports. The main industries are electronics, pharmaceuticals and engineering as well as food processing, brewing and textiles. Natural resources include petroleum, natural gas, peat, lead and zinc. Services industries are expanding, with tourism a major foreign exchange earner. The economy could benefit from peace in Northern Ireland, which is part of the United Kingdom.

RÉUNION

Status: FRENCH TERRITORY
Area: 2,551 sq km (985 sq mls)
Population: 653,000
Capital: ST-DENIS
Language: FRENCH, FRENCH CREOLE
Religion: R.CATHOLIC
Currency: FRENCH FRANC

MAP PAGE: 53

THE INDIAN OCEAN island of Réunion is mountainous, with coastal lowlands and a warm climate. It depends heavily on sugar, tourism and French aid. Some uninhabited islets to the east are administered from Réunion.

ROMANIA

Status: REPUBLIC
Area: 237,500 sq km (91,699 sq mls)
Population: 22,680,000
Capital: BUCHAREST
Language: ROMANIAN, HUNGARIAN
Religion: ROMANIAN ORTHODOX, R.CATHOLIC, PROTESTANT
Currency: LEU
Organizations: UN

MAP PAGE: 47, 49

ROMANIA LIES ON the Black Sea coast of east Europe. Mountains separate the Transylvanian plateau from the populous plains of the east and south and the Danube delta. The climate is continental. Romania is rich in fuels and metallic ores. Mining and manufacturing (chiefly metallurgy and machine building) predominate but agriculture is

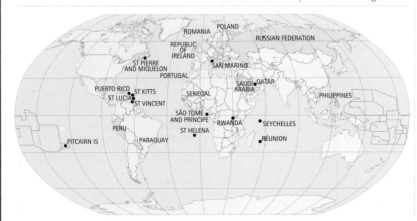

important. Pre-1989 mismanagement and economic reforms of the 1990s have caused hardship.

RUSSIAN FEDERATION

Status: REPUBLIC
Area: 17,075,400 sq km (6,592,849 sq mls)
Population: 148,141,000
Capital: MOSCOW
Language: RUSSIAN, TATAR, UKRAINIAN, LOCAL LANGUAGES
Religion: RUSSIAN ORTHODOX, SUNNI MUSLIM, OTHER CHRISTIAN, JEWISH
Currency: ROUBLE
Organizations: CIS, UN

MAP PAGE: 12-13

RUSSIA OCCUPIES MUCH of east Europe and all of north Asia, and is the world's largest state, nearly twice the size of the USA. It borders thirteen countries to the west and south and has long coastlines on the Arctic and Pacific oceans to the north and east. European Russia, which lies west of the Ural mountains, is part of the North European plain. To the south the land rises to uplands and the Caucasus Mountains on the border with Georgia and Azerbaijan. East of the Urals lies the flat Siberian plain. Much of central Siberia is plateaux. In the south is Lake Baikal, the world's deepest lake, and the Altai and Sayan ranges on the border with Azerbaijan and Mongolia. Eastern Siberia is rugged and mountainous with active volcanoes, notably in the Kamchatka peninsula. Russia's major rivers are the Volga in the west and the Ob, Yenisey, Lena and Amur in Siberia. The climate and vegetation range between Arctic tundra in the north and semi-arid steppe towards the Black and Caspian Sea coasts in the south. In general, the climate is continental with extreme temperatures. The majority of the population (the sixth largest in the world), industry and agriculture are concentrated in European Russia, but there has been increased migration to Siberia to exploit its vast natural resources. The economy is heavily dependent on exploitation of its raw materials and heavy industry. Russia has a wealth of mineral resources, though they are often difficult to exploit because of the climate. It is one of the world's leading producers of petroleum, natural gas and coal as well as iron and manganese ores, platinum, potash, asbestos and many precious and rare metals. Mining provides important exports and is the basis of heavy industry. Russia is a major producer of steel and machinery such as tractors, motor vehicles and generators, as well as chemicals and textiles. Other light industries are less important to the economy. Forests cover about 40 per cent of the land area and supply an important timber, paper and pulp industry. About 8 per cent of land is suitable for cultivation. However farming is generally inefficient and much of food needs, especially grains, must be imported. Fishing is important and Russia operates a large fleet throughout the world. Economic reforms begun in the late 1980s to liberalize the economy met with mixed success, largely because of political unrest. The transition to a free market economy, which was speeded up in the 1990s has been painful, with rising unemployment.

RWANDA

Status: REPUBLIC
Area: 26,338 sq km (10,169 sq mls)
Population: 7,952,000
Capital: KIGALI
Language: KINYARWANDA, FRENCH, ENGLISH
Religion: R.CATHOLIC, TRAD.BELIEFS, PROTESTANT, SUNNI MUSLIM
Currency: FRANC
Organizations: OAU, UN

MAP PAGE: 56

A DENSELY POPULATED and landlocked state in east Africa, Rwanda consists mainly of mountains and plateaux to the east of the Rift Valley. The climate is warm with a summer dry season. Rwanda depends upon subsistence farming, coffee and tea exports, light industry and foreign aid, but the 1990-93 civil war and ethnic conflict have devastated the country.

ST HELENA

Status: UK TERRITORY
Area: 411 sq km (159 sq mls)
Population: 7,000
Capital: JAMESTOWN
Language: ENGLISH
Religion: PROTESTANT, R.CATHOLIC
Currency: POUND STERLING

MAP PAGE: 53

ST HELENA AND its dependencies, Ascension and Tristan da Cunha are isolated island groups lying in the south Atlantic Ocean. Ascension is over 1000 kilometres (620 miles) northwest of St Helena and Tristan da Cunha over 2000 kilometres (1240 miles) to the south.

ST KITTS-NEVIS

Status: MONARCHY
Area: 261 sq km (101 sq mls)
Population: 42,000
Capital: BASSETERRE
Language: ENGLISH, CREOLE
Religion: PROTESTANT, R.CATHOLIC
Currency: E. CARIB. DOLLAR
Organizations: CARICOM, COMM., UN

MAP PAGE: 83

ST KITTS-NEVIS are in the Leeward group in the Caribbean Sea. Both volcanic islands are mountainous and forested with sandy beaches and a warm, wet climate. Some 75 per cent of the population lives on St Kitts. Agriculture is the main activity, with sugar, molasses and sea island cotton the main products. Tourism and manufacturing (chiefly garments and electronic components) are important.

ST LUCIA

Status: MONARCHY
Area: 616 sq km (238 sq mls)
Population: 145,000
Capital: CASTRIES
Language: ENGLISH, FRENCH CREOLE
Religion: R.CATHOLIC, PROTESTANT
Currency: E. CARIB. DOLLAR
Organizations: CARICOM, COMM., UN

MAP PAGE: 83

ST LUCIA, PART OF the Windward group in the Caribbean Sea, is a volcanic island with forested mountains, hot springs, sandy beaches and a wet tropical climate. Agriculture is the main activity, with bananas accounting for over half export earnings. Tourism, agricultural processing and manufacturing (chiefly garments, cardboard boxes and electronic components) are increasingly important.

ST PIERRE AND MIQUELON

Status: FRENCH TERRITORY
Area: 242 sq km (93 sq mls)
Population: 6,000
Capital: ST-PIERRE
Language: FRENCH
Religion: R.CATHOLIC
Currency: FRENCH FRANC

MAP PAGE: 67

A GROUP OF islands off the south coast of Newfoundland in eastern Canada.

ST VINCENT AND THE GRENADINES

Status: MONARCHY
Area: 389 sq km (150 sq mls)
Population: 111,000
Capital: KINGSTOWN
Language: ENGLISH, CREOLE
Religion: PROTESTANT, R.CATHOLIC
Currency: E. CARIB. DOLLAR
Organizations: CARICOM, COMM., UN

MAP PAGE: 83

ST VINCENT, WHOSE TERRITORY includes 32 islets and cays in the Grenadines, is in the Windward Islands group in the Caribbean Sea. St Vincent is forested and mountainous, with an active volcano, Mount Soufrière. The climate is tropical and wet. The economy is based mainly on agriculture and tourism. Bananas account for about half export earnings. Arrowroot is also important.

SAN MARINO

Status: REPUBLIC
Area: 61 sq km (24 sq mls)
Population: 25,000
Capital: SAN MARINO
Language: ITALIAN
Religion: R.CATHOLIC
Currency: ITALIAN LIRA
Organizations: UN

MAP PAGE: 48

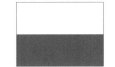

LANDLOCKED SAN MARINO lies on the slopes of Mt Titano in northeast Italy. It has a mild climate. A third of the people live in the capital. There is some agriculture and light industry, but most income comes from tourism and postage stamp sales.

SÃO TOMÉ AND PRÍNCIPE

Status: REPUBLIC
Area: 964 sq km (372 sq mls)
Population: 127,000
Capital: SÃO TOMÉ
Language: PORTUGUESE, PORTUGUESE CREOLE
Religion: R.CATHOLIC, PROTESTANT
Currency: DOBRA
Organizations: OAU, UN

MAP PAGE: 54

THE TWO MAIN islands and adjacent islets lie off the coast of west Africa in the Gulf of Guinea. São Tomé is the larger island and supports over 90 per cent of the population. Both São Tomé and Principe are mountainous and tree-covered, and have a hot and humid climate. The economy is heavily dependent on cocoa, which accounts for over 90 per cent of export earnings.

SAUDI ARABIA

Status: MONARCHY
Area: 2,200,000 sq km (849,425 sq mls)
Population: 17,880,000
Capital: RIYADH
Language: ARABIC
Religion: SUNNI MUSLIM, SHI'A MUSLIM
Currency: RIYAL
Organizations: OPEC, UN

MAP PAGE: 20

SAUDI ARABIA OCCUPIES most of the Arabian peninsula in southwest Asia. The terrain is desert or semi-desert plateaux, which rise to mountains running parallel to the Red Sea in the west and slope down to plains in the southeast and along The Gulf in the east. Most people live in urban areas, one third in the cities of Riyadh, Jiddah and Mecca. Summers are hot, winters are warm and rainfall is low. Saudi Arabia has the world's largest reserves of oil and gas, located in the northeast, both onshore and in The Gulf. Crude oil and refined products account for over 90 per cent of export earnings. Other industries and irrigated agrculture are being encouraged, but most food and raw materials are imported. Saudi Arabia has important banking and commercial interests. Each year 2 million pilgrims visit Islam's holiest cities, Mecca and Medina, in the west.

SENEGAL

Status: REPUBLIC
Area: 196,720 sq km (75,954 sq mls)
Population: 8,347,000
Capital: DAKAR
Language: FRENCH (OFFICIAL), WOLOF, FULANI, LOCAL LANGUAGES
Religion: SUNNI MUSLIM, R.CATHOLIC, TRAD.BELIEFS
Currency: CFA FRANC
Organizations: OAU, UN

MAP PAGE: 54

SENEGAL LIES ON the Atlantic coast of west Africa. The north is arid semi-desert, while the south is mainly fertile savannah bushland. The climate is tropical with summer rains, though droughts occur. One fifth of the population lives in Dakar. Groundnuts, phosphates and fish are the main resources. There is some oil refining and Dakar is a major port. Senegal relies heavily on aid.

SEYCHELLES

Status: REPUBLIC
Area: 455 sq km (176 sq mls)
Population: 75,000
Capital: VICTORIA
Language: SEYCHELLOIS (SESELWA, FRENCH CREOLE), ENGLISH
Religion: R.CATHOLIC, PROTESTANT
Currency: RUPEE
Organizations: COMM., OAU, UN

MAP PAGE: 53

THE SEYCHELLES COMPRISES an archipelago of 115 granitic and coral islands in the western Indian Ocean. The main island, Mahé, contains about 90 per cent of the population. The climate is hot and humid with heavy rainfall. The economy is based mainly on tourism, transit trade, and light manufacturing, with fishing and agriculture (chiefly copra, cinnamon and tea) also important.

SIERRA LEONE

Status: REPUBLIC
Area: 71,740 sq km (27,699 sq mls)
Population: 4,509,000
Capital: FREETOWN
Language: ENGLISH, CREOLE, MENDE, TEMNE, LOCAL LANGUAGES
Religion: TRAD. BELIEFS, SUNNI MUSLIM, PROTESTANT, R.CATHOLIC
Currency: LEONE
Organizations: COMM., OAU, UN

MAP PAGE: 54

SIERRA LEONE LIES on the Atlantic coast of west Africa. Its coast is heavily indented and lined with mangrove swamps. Inland is a forested area rising to savannah plateaux, with the mountains to the northeast. The climate is tropical and rainfall is heavy. Most of the workforce is involved in subsistence farming. Cocoa and coffee are the main cash crops, but rutile (titanium ore), bauxite and diamonds are the main exports. Civil war and economic decline have caused serious difficulties.

SINGAPORE

Status: REPUBLIC
Area: 639 sq km (247 sq mls)
Population: 2,987,000
Capital: SINGAPORE
Language: CHINESE, ENGLISH, MALAY, TAMIL
Religion: BUDDHIST, TAOIST, SUNNI MUSLIM, CHRISTIAN, HINDU
Currency: DOLLAR
Organizations: ASEAN, COMM., UN

MAP PAGE: 32

THE STATE COMPRISES the main island of Singapore and 57 other islands, lying off the southern tip of the Malay Peninsula in southeast Asia. A causeway links Singapore to the mainland across the Johor Strait. Singapore is generally low-lying and includes land reclaimed from swamps. It is hot and humid, with heavy rainfall throughout the year. There are fish farms and vegetable gardens in the north and east of the island, but most food needs must be imported. Singapore also lacks mineral and energy resources. Manufacturing industries and services are the main sectors of the economy. Their rapid development has fuelled the nation's impressive economic growth over the last three decades to become the richest of Asia's four 'little dragons'. The main industries include electronics, oil refining, chemicals, pharmaceuticals, ship building and repair, iron and steel, food processing and textiles. Singapore is a major financial centre. Its port is one of the world's largest and busiest and acts as an entrepot for neighbouring states. Tourism is also important.

SLOVAKIA

Status: REPUBLIC
Area: 49,035 sq km (18,933 sq mls)
Population: 5,364,000
Capital: BRATISLAVA
Language: SLOVAK, HUNGARIAN, CZECH
Religion: R.CATHOLIC, PROTESTANT, ORTHODOX
Currency: KORUNA
Organizations: UN

MAP PAGE: 46-47

A LANDLOCKED COUNTRY in central Europe, Slovakia borders the Czech Republic, Poland, Ukraine, Hungary and Austria. Slovakia is mountainous along the border with Poland in the north, but low-lying along the plains of the Danube in the southwest. The climate is continental. Slovakia is the smaller, less populous and less developed part of former Czechoslovakia. With few natural resources, uncompetitive heavy industry and loss of federal subsidies, the economy has suffered economic difficulties.

SLOVENIA

Status: REPUBLIC
Area: 20,251 sq km (7,819 sq mls)
Population: 1,984,000
Capital: LJUBLJANA
Language: SLOVENE, SERBO-CROAT
Religion: R.CATHOLIC, PROTESTANT
Currency: TÓLAR
Organizations: UN

MAP PAGE: 48

SLOVENIA LIES IN the northwest Balkans of south Europe and has a short coastline on the Adriatic Sea. It is mountainous and hilly, with lowlands on the coast and in the Sava and Drava river valleys. The climate is generally continental, but Mediterranean nearer the coast. Dairy farming, mercury mining, light manufacturing and tourism are the main activities. Conflict in the other former Yugoslav states, which has affected tourism and international trade, has caused serious economic problems.

SOLOMON ISLANDS

Status: MONARCHY
Area: 28,370 sq km (10,954 sq mls)
Population: 378,000
Capital: HONIARA
Language: ENGLISH, SOLOMON ISLANDS PIDGIN, MANY LOCAL LANGUAGES
Religion: PROTESTANT, R.CATHOLIC
Currency: DOLLAR
Organizations: COMM., UN

MAP PAGE: 7

THE STATE CONSISTS of the southern Solomon, Santa Cruz and Shortland islands in Australasia. The six main islands are volcanic, mountainous and forested, though Guadalcanal, the most populous, has a large area of flat land. The climate is generally hot and humid. Subsistence farming and fishing predominate. Exports include fish, timber, copra and palm oil. The islands depend on foreign aid.

SOMALIA

Status: REPUBLIC
Area: 637,657 sq km (246,201 sq mls)
Population: 9,250,000
Capital: MOGADISHU
Language: SOMALI, ARABIC (OFFICIAL)
Religion: SUNNI MUSLIM
Currency: SHILLING
Organizations: OAU, UN

MAP PAGE: 56

SOMALIA IS IN the Horn of northeast Africa, on the Gulf of Aden and Indian Ocean. It consists of a dry scrubby plateau, rising to highlands in the north. The climate is hot and dry, but coastal areas and the Jubba and Shebele river valleys support crops and the bulk of the population. Subsistence farming and herding are the main activities. Exports include livestock and bananas. Drought and war have ruined the economy.

SOUTH AFRICA

Status: REPUBLIC
Area: 1,219,080 sq km (470,689 sq mls)
Population: 41,244,000
Capital: PRETORIA/CAPE TOWN
Language: AFRIKAANS, ENGLISH, NINE LOCAL LANGUAGES (ALL OFFICIAL)
Religion: PROTESTANT, R.CATHOLIC, SUNNI MUSLIM, HINDU
Currency: RAND
Organizations: COMM., OAU, SADC, UN

MAP PAGE: 58-59

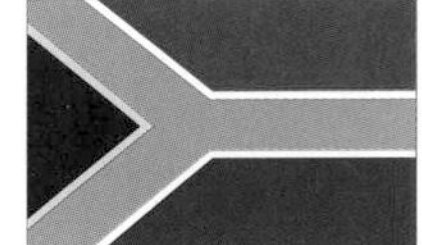

SOUTH AFRICA OCCUPIES most of the southern part of Africa. It borders five states, surrounds Lesotho and has a long coastline on the Atlantic and Indian oceans. Much of the land is a vast plateau, covered with grassland or bush and drained by the Orange and Limpopo river systems. A fertile coastal plain rises to mountain ridges in the south and east, including Table Mountain near Cape Town and the Drakensberg range in the east. Gauteng is the most populous province, with Johannesburg and Pretoria its main cities. South Africa has warm summers and mild winters. Most of the country has rainfall in summer, but the coast around Cape Town has winter rains. South Africa is the largest and most developed economy in Africa, though wealth is unevenly distributed. Agriculture provides one third of exports, including fruit, wine, wool and maize. South Africa is rich in minerals. It is the world's leading producer of gold, which accounts for one third of export earnings. Coal, diamonds, platinum, uranium, chromite and other minerals are also mined. The main industries process minerals and agricultural produce, and manufacture chemical products, motor vehicles, electrical equipment and textiles. Financial services are also important.

SOUTH KOREA

Status: REPUBLIC
Area: 99,274 sq km (38,330 sq mls)
Population: 44,851,000
Capital: SEOUL
Language: KOREAN
Religion: BUDDHIST, PROTESTANT, R.CATHOLIC, CONFUCIAN, TRADITIONAL
Currency: WON
Organizations: UN, OECD

MAP PAGE: 30

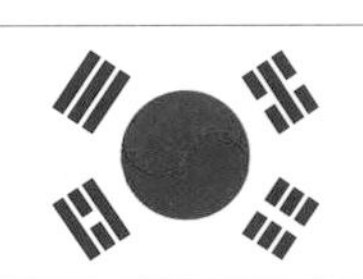

THE STATE CONSISTS of the southern half of the Korean Peninsula in east Asia and many islands lying off the western and southern coasts in the Yellow Sea. The terrain is mountainous, though less rugged than that of North Korea. Population density is high and most people live on the western coastal plains and in the Han basin in the northwest and Naktong basin in the southeast. South Korea has a continental climate, with hot, wet summers and dry, cold winters. Arable land is limited by the mountainous terrain, but because of intensive farming South Korea is nearly self-sufficient in food. Sericulture is important as is fishing, which contributes to exports. South Korea has few mineral resources, except for coal and tungsten. It is one of Asia's four 'little dragons' (Hong Kong, Singapore and Taiwan being the others), which have achieved high economic growth based mainly on export manufacturing. In South Korea industry is dominated by a few giant conglomerates, such as Hyundai and Samsung. The main manufactures are cars, electronic and electrical goods, ships, steel, chemicals, and toys as well as textiles, clothing, footwear and food products. Banking and other financial services are increasingly important.

SPAIN

Status: MONARCHY
Area: 504,782 sq km (194,897 sq mls)
Population: 39,210,000
Capital: MADRID
Language: SPANISH, CATALAN, GALICIAN, BASQUE
Religion: R.CATHOLIC
Currency: PESETA
Organizations: EU, OECD, UN

MAP PAGE: 45

SPAIN OCCUPIES THE greater part of the Iberian peninsula in southwest Europe, with coastlines on the Atlantic Ocean (Bay of Biscay and Gulf of Cadiz) and Mediterranean Sea. It includes the Balearic and Canary island groups in the Mediterranean and Atlantic, and two enclaves in north Africa. Much of the mainland is a high plateau, the Meseta, drained by the Duero, Tagus and Guadiana rivers. The plateau is interrupted by a low mountain range and bounded to the east and north also by mountains, including the Pyrenees which form the border with France and Andorra. The main lowland areas are the Ebro basin in the northeast, the eastern coastal plains and the Guadalquivir basin in the southwest. Three quarters of the population lives in urban areas, chiefly Madrid and Barcelona, which alone contain one quarter of the population. The plateau experiences hot summers and cold winters. Conditions are cooler and wetter to the north, though warmer and drier to the south. Agriculture involves about 10 per cent of the workforce and fruit, vegetables and wine are exported. Fishing is an important industry and Spain has a large fishing fleet. Mineral resources include iron, lead, copper and mercury. Some oil is produced, but Spain has to import most energy needs. The economy is based mainly on manufacturing and services. Manufacturing industries account for one third of national income and are based mainly around Madrid and Barcelona. The principal products are machinery and transport equip-

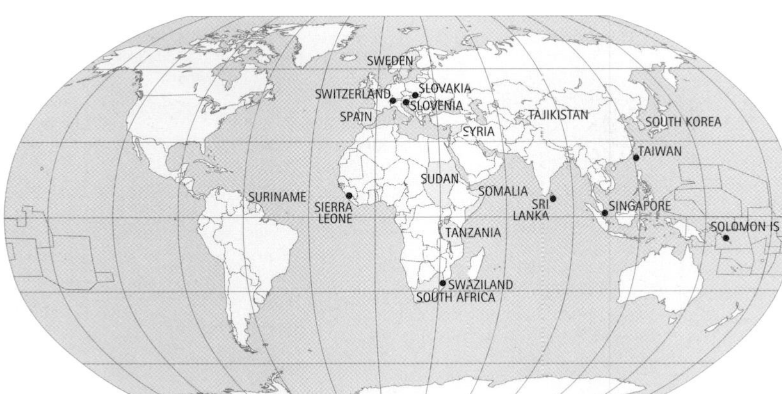

ment. Spain is a leading manufacturer of motor vehicles (SEAT). Other manufactures are agricultural products, chemicals, steel and other metals, paper products, wood and cork products, clothing and footwear, and textiles. With some 50 million visitors a year, tourism is a major industry, accounting for 10 per cent of national income and employing about the same percentage of the workforce. Banking and commerce are also important.

SRI LANKA

Status: REPUBLIC
Area: 65,610 sq km (25,332 sq mls)
Population: 18,354,000
Capital: COLOMBO
Language: SINHALESE, TAMIL, ENGLISH
Religion: BUDDHIST, HINDU, SUNNI MUSLIM, R.CATHOLIC
Currency: RUPEE
Organizations: COMM., UN

MAP PAGE: 21

SRI LANKA LIES in the Indian Ocean off the southeast coast of India in south Asia. It has rolling coastal plains with mountains in the centre-south. The climate is hot and monsoonal and most people live on the west coast. Manufactures (chiefly textiles and clothing), tea, rubber, copra and gems are exported. The economy relies on aid and workers' remittances. Tourism has been damaged by separatist activities.

SUDAN

Status: REPUBLIC
Area: 2,505,813 sq km (967,500 sq mls)
Population: 28,098,000
Capital: KHARTOUM
Language: ARABIC, DINKA, NUBIAN, BEJA, NUER, LOCAL LANGUAGES
Religion: SUNNI MUSLIM, TRAD. BELIEFS, R.CATHOLIC, PROTESTANT
Currency: DINAR
Organizations: OAU, UN

MAP PAGE: 55

AFRICA'S LARGEST COUNTRY, Sudan is in northeast Africa, on the Red Sea. It lies within the Upper Nile basin, much of which is arid plain but with swamps to the south. Mountains lie to the northeast and south. The climate is hot and arid with light summer rainfall, though droughts occur. Most people live along the Nile and are farmers and herders. Cotton, gum arabic, livestock and other agricultural products are exported. In southern Sudan civil war has ruined the economy.

SURINAME

Status: REPUBLIC
Area: 163,820 sq km (63,251 sq mls)
Population: 423,000
Capital: PARAMARIBO
Language: DUTCH, SURINAMESE (SRANAN TONGO), ENGLISH, HINDI, JAVANESE
Religion: HINDU, R.CATHOLIC, PROTESTANT, SUNNI MUSLIM
Currency: GUILDER
Organizations: CARICOM, UN

MAP PAGE: 87

SURINAME, ON THE Atlantic coast of northern South America, consists of a swampy coastal plain (where most people live), central plateaux and the Guiana Highlands. The climate is tropical and rainforest covers much of the land. Bauxite mining is the main industry. Alumina and aluminium are the chief exports, with shrimps, rice, bananas and timber. Suriname depends on Dutch aid.

SWAZILAND

Status: MONARCHY
Area: 17,364 sq km (6,704 sq mls)
Population: 908,000
Capital: MBABANE
Language: SWAZI (SISWATI), ENGLISH
Religion: PROTESTANT, R.CATHOLIC, TRAD.BELIEFS
Currency: EMALANGENI
Organizations: COMM., OAU, SADC, UN

MAP PAGE: 59

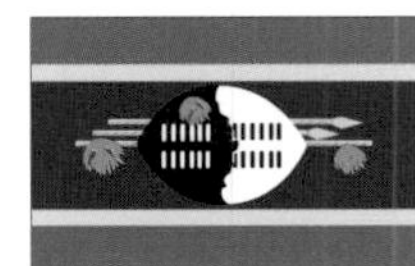

LANDLOCKED SWAZILAND IN southern Africa lies between Mozambique and South Africa. Savannah plateaux descend from mountains in the west towards hill country in the east. The climate is subtropical, temperate in the mountains. Subsistence farming predominates. Asbestos, coal and diamonds are mined. Exports include sugar, fruit and wood pulp. Tourism and workers' remittances are important.

SWEDEN

Status: MONARCHY
Area: 449,964 sq km (173,732 sq mls)
Population: 8,831,000
Capital: STOCKHOLM
Language: SWEDISH
Religion: PROTESTANT, R.CATHOLIC
Currency: KRONA
Organizations: EU, OECD, UN

MAP PAGE: 36-37

SWEDEN, THE LARGEST and most populous of the Scandinavian countries, occupies the eastern part of the peninsula in north Europe and borders the North and Baltic Seas and Gulf of Bothnia. Forested mountains cover the northern half of the country, part of which lies within the Arctic Circle. Southwards is a lowland lake region, where most of the population lives. Farther south is an upland region, and then a fertile plain at the tip of the peninsula. Sweden has warm summers and cold winters, though the latter are longer and more severe in the north and milder in the far south. Sweden's natural resources include coniferous forests, mineral deposits and water resources. There is little agriculture, though some dairy products, meat, cereals and vegetables are produced in the south. The forests supply timber for export and for the important pulp, paper and furniture industries. Sweden is one of the world's leading producers of iron ore. Copper, zinc, lead, uranium and other metallic ores are also mined. Mineral industries, chiefly iron and steel, are the basis for the production of a range of products, but chiefly machinery and transport equipment of which cars and trucks (Volvo and Saab) are the most important export. Sweden also manufactures chemicals, electrical goods (Electrolux) and telecommunications equipment (Ericsson). Like their Scandinavian neighbours, Swedes enjoy a high standard of living.

SWITZERLAND

Status: FEDERATION
Area: 41,293 sq km (15,943 sq mls)
Population: 7,040,000
Capital: BERN
Language: GERMAN, FRENCH, ITALIAN, ROMANSCH
Religion: R.CATHOLIC, PROTESTANT
Currency: FRANC
Organizations: OECD

MAP PAGE: 46

SWITZERLAND IS A landlocked country of southwest Europe that is surrounded by France, Germany, Austria, Liechtenstein and Italy. It is also Europe's most mountainous country. The southern half of the nation lies within the Alps, while the northwest is dominated by the Jura mountains. The rest of the land is a high plateau, which contains the bulk of the population and economic activity. The climate varies greatly, depending on altitude and relief, but in general summers are mild and winters are cold with heavy snowfalls. Switzerland has one of the highest standards of living in the world. Yet it has few mineral resources and, owing to its mountainous terrain, agriculture is based mainly on dairy and stock farming. Most food and industrial raw materials have to be imported. Manufacturing makes the largest contribution to the economy and though varied is specialist in certain products. Engineering is the most important industry, producing precision instruments such as scientific and optical instruments, watches and clocks, and heavy machinery such as turbines and generators. Other industries produce chemicals, pharmaceuticals, metal products, textiles, clothing and food products (cheese and chocolate). Banking and other financial services are very important and Zurich is one of the world's leading banking cities. Tourism and international organisations based in Switzerland are also major foreign currency earners.

SYRIA

Status: REPUBLIC
Area: 185,180 sq km (71,498 sq mls)
Population: 14,186,000
Capital: DAMASCUS
Language: ARABIC, KURDISH, ARMENIAN
Religion: SUNNI MUSLIM, OTHER MUSLIM, CHRISTIAN
Currency: POUND
Organizations: UN

MAP PAGE: 16-17

SYRIA IS IN southwest Asia, on the Mediterranean Sea. Behind the coastal plain lies a range of hills and then a plateau cut by the Euphrates river. Mountains flank the borders with Lebanon and Israel, east of which is desert. The climate is Mediterranean in coastal regions, hotter and drier inland. Most Syrians live on the coast or in the river valleys. Cotton, cereals and fruit are important, but the main exports are petroleum and its products, textiles and chemicals. Syria receives support from Gulf states.

TAIWAN

Status: REPUBLIC
Area: 36,179 sq km (13,969 sq mls)
Population: 21,211,000
Capital: T'AI-PEI
Language: CHINESE (MANDARIN OFFICIAL, FUKIEN, HAKKA), LOCAL LANGUAGES
Religion: BUDDHIST, TAOIST, CONFUCIAN, CHRISTIAN
Currency: DOLLAR

MAP PAGE: 27

THE EAST ASIAN state consists of the island of Taiwan, separated from mainland China by the Taiwan Strait, and several much smaller islands. Much of Taiwan itself is mountainous and forested. Densely populated coastal plains in the west contain the bulk of the population and most economic activity. Taiwan has a tropical monsoon climate, with warm, wet summers and mild winters. Agriculture is highly productive. Taiwan is virtually self-sufficient in food and exports some products. Coal, oil and natural gas are produced and a few minerals are mined but none of them are of great significance to the economy. Taiwan depends heavily on imports of raw materials and exports of manufactured goods. The latter is equivalent to 50 per cent of national income. The country's main manufactures are electrical and electronic goods, including television sets, watches, personal computers and calculators. Other products include clothing, footwear (chiefly track shoes), textiles and toys. In contrast to mainland China, Taiwan has enjoyed considerable prosperity.

TAJIKISTAN

Status: REPUBLIC
Area: 143,100 sq km (55,251 sq mls)
Population: 5,836,000
Capital: DUSHANBE
Language: TAJIK, UZBEK, RUSSIAN
Religion: SUNNI MUSLIM
Currency: ROUBLE
Organizations: CIS, UN

MAP PAGE: 14-15

LANDLOCKED TAJIKISTAN IN central Asia is a mountainous country, occupying the western Tien Shan and part of the Pamir ranges. In less mountainous western areas summers are warm though winters are cold. Most activity is in the Fergana basin. Agriculture is the main sector of the economy, chiefly cotton growing and cattle breeding. Mineral and fuel deposits include lead, zinc, uranium and oil. Textiles and clothing are the main manufactures. Civil war has damaged the economy, which depends heavily on Russian support.

TANZANIA

Status: REPUBLIC
Area: 945,087 sq km (364,900 sq mls)
Population: 30,337,000
Capital: DODOMA
Language: SWAHILI, ENGLISH, NYAMWEZI, MANY LOCAL LANGUAGES
Religion: R.CATHOLIC, SUNNI MUSLIM, TRAD. BELIEFS, PROTESTANT
Currency: SHILLING
Organizations: COMM., OAU, SADC, UN

MAP PAGE: 56-57

TANZANIA LIES ON the coast of east Africa and includes Zanzibar in the Indian Ocean. Most of the mainland is a savannah plateau lying east of the great Rift Valley. In the north are Mount Kilimanjaro and the Serangeti National Park. The climate is tropical and most people live on the narrow coastal plain or in the north. The economy is mainly agricultural. Coffee, cotton and sisal are the main exports, with cloves from Zanzibar. Agricultural processing and diamond mining are the main industries, though tourism is growing Tanzania depends heavily on aid.

THAILAND

Status: MONARCHY
Area: 513,115 sq km (198,115 sq mls)
Population: 59,401,000
Capital: BANGKOK
Language: THAI, LAO, CHINESE, MALAY, MON-KHMER LANGUAGES
Religion: BUDDHIST, SUNNI MUSLIM
Currency: BAHT
Organizations: ASEAN, UN

MAP PAGE: 32

A COUNTRY IN southeast Asia, Thailand borders Myanmar, Laos, Cambodia and Malaysia and has coastlines on the Gulf of Thailand and Andaman Sea. Central Thailand is dominated by the Chao Phraya river basin, which contains Bangkok, the only major urban centre, and most economic activity. To the east is a dry plateau drained by tributaries of the Mekong river, while to the north, west and south, extending halfway down the Malay peninsula, are forested hills and mountains. Many small islands line the coast. The climate is hot, humid and monsoonal. About half the workforce is involved in agriculture. Thailand is the world's leading exporter of rice and rubber, and a major exporter of maize and tapioca. Fish and fish processing are important. Thailand produces natural gas, some oil and lignite, metallic ores (chiefly tin and tungsten) and gemstones. Manufacturing is the largest contributor to national income, with electronics, textiles, clothing and footwear, and food processing the main industries. With over 5 million visitors a year, tourism is the major source of foreign exchange.

TOGO

Status: REPUBLIC
Area: 56,785 sq km (21,925 sq mls)
Population: 4,138,000
Capital: LOMÉ
Language: FRENCH, EWE, KABRE, MANY LOCAL LANGUAGES
Religion: TRAD. BELIEFS, R.CATHOLIC, SUNNI MUSLIM, PROTESTANT
Currency: CFA FRANC
Organizations: OAU, UN

MAP PAGE: 54

TOGO IS A long narrow country in west Africa with a short coastline on the Gulf of Guinea. The interior consists of plateaux rising to mountainous areas. The climate is tropical, drier inland. Agriculture is the mainstay of the economy. Cotton, coffee and cocoa are exported, but phosphates are the main exports. Oil refining and food processing are the main industries. Lomé is an entrepôt trade centre.

TOKELAU

Status: NEW ZEALAND TERRITORY
Area: 10 sq km (4 sq mls)
Population: 2,000
Language: ENGLISH, TOKELAUAN
Religion: PROTESTANT, R.CATHOLIC
Currency: NZ DOLLAR

MAP PAGE: 7

TONGA

Status: MONARCHY
Area: 748 sq km (289 sq mls)
Population: 98,000
Capital: NUKU'ALOFA
Language: TONGAN, ENGLISH
Religion: PROTESTANT, R.CATHOLIC, MORMON
Currency: PA'ANGA
Organizations: COMM.

MAP PAGE: 7

TONGA COMPRISES SOME 170 islands in the South Pacific Ocean, northeast of New Zealand. The three main groups are Tongatapu (where 60 per cent of Tongans live), Ha'apai and Vava'u. The climate is warm with good rainfall and the economy relies heavily on agriculture. Exports include coconut products, root crops, bananas and vanilla. Fishing, tourism and light industry are increasingly important.

TRINIDAD AND TOBAGO

Status: REPUBLIC
Area: 5,130 sq km (1,981 sq mls)
Population: 1,306,000
Capital: PORT OF SPAIN
Language: ENGLISH, CREOLE, HINDI
Religion: R.CATHOLIC, HINDU, PROTESTANT, SUNNI MUSLIM
Currency: DOLLAR
Organizations: CARICOM, COMM., UN

MAP PAGE: 83

TRINIDAD, THE MOST southerly Caribbean island, lies off the Venezuelan coast. It is hilly in the north, with a populous central plain. Tobago, to the northeast, is smaller, more mountainous and less developed. The climate is tropical. Oil and petrochemicals dominate the economy. Asphalt is also important. Sugar, fruit, cocoa and coffee are produced. Tourism is important on Tobago.

TUNISIA

Status: REPUBLIC
Area: 164,150 sq km (63,379 sq mls)
Population: 8,896,000
Capital: TUNIS
Language: ARABIC, FRENCH
Religion: SUNNI MUSLIM
Currency: DINAR
Organizations: OAU, UN

MAP PAGE: 54-55

TUNISIA IS ON the Mediterranean coast of north Africa. The north is mountainous with valleys and coastal plains, where most people live. Beyond a central area of salt pans are Saharan plains. The north has a Mediterranean climate, the south is hot and arid. Oil and phosphates are the main resources. Olive oil, citrus fruit and textiles are also exported. Tourism is important.

TURKEY

Status: REPUBLIC
Area: 779,452 sq km (300,948 sq mls)
Population: 61,644,000
Capital: ANKARA
Language: TURKISH, KURDISH
Religion: SUNNI MUSLIM, SHI'A MUSLIM
Currency: LIRA
Organizations: OECD, UN

MAP PAGE: 16-17

TURKEY OCCUPIES THE Asia Minor peninsula of southwest Asia and has coastlines on the Black, Mediterranean and Aegean seas. It includes eastern Thrace, which is in south Europe and separated from the rest of the country by the Bosporus, Sea of Marmara and Dardanelles. The Asian mainland consists of the semi-arid Anatolian plateau, flanked to the north, south and east by mountains. Over 40 per cent of Turks live in central Anatolia and the Marmara and Aegean coastal plains. The coast has a Mediterranean climate, but inland conditions are more extreme with hot, dry summers and cold, snowy winters. Agriculture involves about half the workforce and exports include cotton, tobacco, fruit, nuts and livestock. Turkey is one of the world's major producers of chrome. Coal and lignite, petroleum, iron ore and boron are also exploited. Apart from food products, the main manufactures are textiles (the chief export), iron and steel, vehicles and chemicals. With over 7 million visitors a year, tourism is a major industry. Remittances by workers aboard are also important.

TURKMENISTAN

Status: REPUBLIC
Area: 488,100 sq km (188,456 sq mls)
Population: 4,099,000
Capital: ASHGABAT
Language: TURKMEN, RUSSIAN
Religion: SUNNI MUSLIM
Currency: MANAT
Organizations: CIS, UN

MAP PAGE: 14

TURKMENISTAN, IN CENTRAL Asia, lies mainly within the desert plains of the Kara Kum. Most people live on the fringes: the foothills of the Kopet Dag in the south, Amudarya valley in the north and Caspian Sea plains in the west. The climate is dry with extreme temperatures. The economy is based mainly on irrigated agriculture, chiefly cotton growing. Turkmenistan is rich in oil, natural gas (the main export) and minerals.

TURKS AND CAICOS ISLANDS

Status: UK TERRITORY
Area: 430 sq km (166 sq mls)
Population: 14,000
Capital: GRAND TURK
Language: ENGLISH
Religion: PROTESTANT
Currency: US DOLLAR

MAP PAGE: 83

THE STATE CONSISTS of 40 or so low-lying islands and cays in the northern Caribbean. Only eight islands are inhabited, two fifths of people living on Grand Turk and Salt Cay. The climate is tropical. The islands depend on fishing, tourism and offshore banking.

TUVALU

Status: MONARCHY
Area: 25 sq km (10 sq mls)
Population: 10,000
Capital: FONGAFALE
Language: TUVALUAN, ENGLISH (OFFICIAL)
Religion: PROTESTANT
Currency: DOLLAR
Organizations: COMM.

MAP PAGE: 7

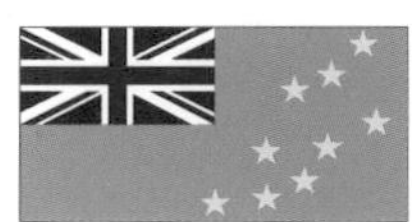

TUVALU COMPRISES NINE coral atolls in the South Pacific Ocean. One third of the population lives on Funafuti and most people depend on subsistence farming and fishing. The islands export copra, stamps and clothing, but rely heavily on UK aid.

UGANDA

Status: REPUBLIC
Area: 241,038 sq km (93,065 sq mls)
Population: 19,848,000
Capital: KAMPALA
Language: ENGLISH, SWAHILI (OFFICIAL), LUGANDA, MANY LOCAL LANGUAGES
Religion: R.CATHOLIC, PROTESTANT, SUNNI MUSLIM, TRAD. BELIEFS
Currency: SHILLING
Organizations: COMM., OAU, UN

MAP PAGE: 56

A LANDLOCKED COUNTRY in east Africa, Uganda consists of a savannah plateau with mountains and lakes. It includes part of Lake Victoria from which the Nile flows northwards to Sudan. The climate is warm and wet. Most people live in the southern half of the country. Agriculture dominates the economy. Coffee is the main export, with some cotton and tea. Uganda relies heavily on aid.

UKRAINE

Status: REPUBLIC
Area: 603,700 sq km (233,090 sq mls)
Population: 51,639,000
Capital: KIEV
Language: UKRAINIAN, RUSSIAN, REGIONAL LANGUAGES
Religion: UKRAINIAN ORTHODOX, R.CATHOLIC
Currency: HRYVNIA
Organizations: CIS, UN

MAP PAGE: 51

UKRAINE LIES ON the Black Sea coast of east Europe. Much of the land is steppe, generally flat and treeless, but with rich black soil and drained by the river Dnieper. Along the border with Belarus are forested, marshy plains. The only uplands are the Carpathian mountains in the west and smaller ranges on the Crimean peninsula. Summers are warm and winters are

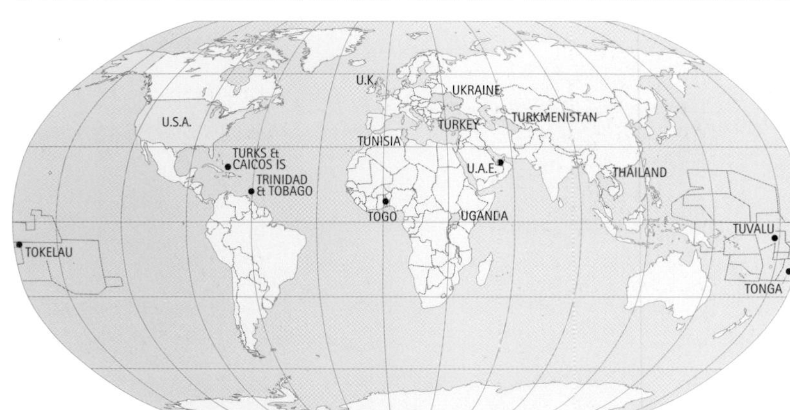

cold, with milder conditions in the Crimea. About a quarter of the population lives in the mainly industrial provinces of Donetsk, Kiev and Dnepropetrovsk. The Ukraine is rich in natural resources: fertile soil, substantial mineral deposits and forests. Agriculture, livestock raising and viticulture are important, but mining and manufacturing predominate, contributing over 40 per cent of national income. Coal mining, iron and steel production, engineering and chemicals are the main industries. Output has fallen and few state enterprises have been privatized since Ukraine became independent in 1991.

UNITED ARAB EMIRATES
(UAE)

Status: FEDERATION
Area: 77,700 sq km (30,000 sq mls)
Population: 2,314,000
Capital: ABU DHABI
Language: ARABIC (OFFICIAL), ENGLISH, HINDI, URDU, FARSI
Religion: SUNNI MUSLIM, SHI'A MUSLIM, CHRISTIAN
Currency: DIRHAM
Organizations: OPEC, UN

MAP PAGE: 20

THE UAE IS in east-central Arabia, southwest Asia. Six emirates lie on The Gulf while the seventh, Fujairah, fronts the Gulf of Oman. Most of the land is flat desert with sand dunes and salt pans. The only hilly area is in the northeast. Three emirates - Abu Dhabi, Dubai and Sharjah - contain 85 per cent of the population. Summers are hot and winters are mild with occasional rainfall in coastal areas. Fruit and vegetables are grown in oases and irrigated areas. The state's wealth is based on hydrocarbons, mainly within Abu Dhabi, but with smaller supplies in Dubai, Sharjah and Ras al Khaimah. Dubai is a thriving entrepot trade centre.

ABU DHABI
Status: EMIRATE
Area: 64,750 sq km (25,000 sq miles)
Population: 800,000

AJMAN
Status: EMIRATE
Area: 260 sq km (100 sq miles)
Population: 76,000

DUBAI
Status: EMIRATE
Area: 3,900 sq km (1,506 sq miles)
Population: 500,000

FUJAIRAH
Status: EMIRATE
Area: 1,170 sq km (452 sq miles)
Population: 63,000

RAS AL KHAIMAH
Status: EMIRATE
Area: 1,690 sq km (653 sq miles)
Population: 130,000

SHARJAH
Status: EMIRATE
Area: 2,600 sq km (1,004 sq miles)
Population: 314,000

UMM AL QAIWAIN
Status: EMIRATE
Area: 780 sq km (301 sq miles)
Population: 27,000

UNITED KINGDOM
(UK)

Status: MONARCHY
Area: 244,082 sq km (94,241 sq mls)
Population: 58,258,000
Capital: LONDON
Language: ENGLISH, SOUTH INDIAN LANGUAGES, CHINESE, WELSH, GAELIC
Religion: PROTESTANT, R.CATHOLIC, MUSLIM, SIKH, HINDU, JEWISH
Currency: POUND
Organizations: COMM., EU, OECD, UN

MAP PAGE: 34

A COUNTRY OF northwest Europe, the United Kingdom occupies the island of Great Britain, part of Ireland and many small adjacent islands in the Atlantic Ocean. Great Britain comprises the countries of England, Scotland and Wales. England covers over half the land area and supports over four-fifths of the population, chiefly in the southeast region. The landscape is flat or rolling with some uplands, notably the Cheviot Hills on the Scottish border, the Pennines in the centre-north and the Cumbrian mountains in the northwest. Scotland consists of southern uplands, central lowlands, highlands (which include the UK's highest peak) and islands. Wales is a land of mountains and river valleys. Northern Ireland contains uplands, plains and the UK's largest lake, Lough Neagh. The climate is mild, wet and variable. The UK has few mineral deposits, but has important energy resources. Over 40 per cent of land is suitable for grazing, over 25 per cent is cultivated, and 10 per cent is forested. Agriculture involves mainly sheep and cattle raising and dairy farming, with crop and fruit growing in the east and southeast. Productivity is high, but about one third of food needs must be imported. Both forestry and fishing are also important. The UK produces petroleum and natural gas from reserves in the North Sea and is self-sufficient in energy in net terms. It also has reserves of coal, though the coal industry has contracted in recent years. Manufacturing accounts for over 20 per cent of national income and relies heavily on imported raw materials. Major manufactures are food and drinks, motor vehicles and parts, aerospace equipment, machinery, electronic and electrical equipment, and chemicals and chemical products. However, the economy is dominated by service industries, including banking, insurance, finance, business services, retail and catering. London is one of the world's major banking, financial and insurance capitals. Tourism is a major industry, with over 18 million visitors a year. International trade is also important, equivalent to a third of national income and the UK has a large merchant fleet.

ENGLAND
Status: CONSTITUENT COUNTRY
Area: 130,423 sq km (50,357 sq miles)
Population: 48,532,700
Capital: LONDON

NORTHERN IRELAND
Status: CONSTITUENT REGION
Area: 14,121 sq km (5,452 sq miles)
Population: 1,631,800
Capital: BELFAST

SCOTLAND
Status: CONSTITUENT COUNTRY
Area: 78,772 sq km (30,414 sq miles)
Population: 5,120,200
Capital: EDINBURGH

WALES
Status: PRINCIPALITY
Area: 20,766 sq km (8,018 sq miles)
Population: 2,906,500
Capital: CARDIFF

UNITED STATES OF AMERICA
(USA)

Status: REPUBLIC
Area: 9,809,386 sq km (3,787,425 sq mls)
Population: 263,034,000
Capital: WASHINGTON D.C.
Language: ENGLISH, SPANISH, AMERINDIAN LANGUAGES
Religion: PROTESTANT, R.CATHOLIC, SUNNI MUSLIM, JEWISH, MORMON
Currency: DOLLAR
Organizations: NAFTA, OECD, UN

MAP PAGE: 70-71

THE USA COMPRISES 48 contiguous states in North America, bounded by Canada and Mexico, and the states of Alaska, to the northwest of Canada, and Hawaii, in the Pacific Ocean. The populous eastern states consist of the Atlantic coastal plain (which includes the Florida peninsula and the Gulf of Mexico coast) and the Appalachian mountains. The central states form a vast interior plain drained by the Mississippi-Missouri river system. To the west lie the Rocky Mountains, separated from the Pacific coastal ranges by the intermontane plateaux. The coastal ranges, which are prone to earthquakes, extend northwards into Alaska. Hawaii is a group of some 20 volcanic islands. Climatic conditions range between arctic in Alaska to desert in the intermontane plateaux. Most of the USA is temperate, though the interior has continental conditions. The USA has abundant natural resources. It has major reserves minerals and energy resources. About 20 per cent of the land can be used for crops, over 25 per cent is suitable for livestock rearing and over 30 per cent is forested. The USA has the largest economy in the world, which is based mainly on manufacturing and services. Though agriculture accounts for only about 2 per cent national income, productivity is high and the USA is a net exporter of food, chiefly grains and fruit. Major industrial crops include cotton, tobacco and sugarbeet. Livestock rearing, forestry and fishing are also important. Mining is well developed. The USA produces iron ore, bauxite, copper, lead, zinc, phosphate and many other minerals. It is a major producer of coal, petroleum and natural gas, though being the world's biggest energy user it must import significant quantities of petroleum and its products. Manufacturing is well diversified. The main products are: iron, steel and aluminium metals and products, machinery, transport equipment (chiefly motor vehicles and aircraft), electrical and electronic goods, food products, chemicals, textiles and clothing. Tourism is a major foreign currency earner. Other important service industries are banking and finance, and Wall Street in New York is a major stock exchange.

ALABAMA
Status: STATE
Area: 135,775 sq km (52,423 sq miles)
Population: 4,273,084
Capital: MONTGOMERY

ALASKA
Status: STATE
Area: 1,700,130 sq km (656,424 sq miles)
Population: 607,007
Capital: JUNEAU

ARIZONA
Status: STATE
Area: 295,274 sq km (114,006 sq miles)
Population: 4,428,068
Capital: PHOENIX

ARKANSAS
Status: STATE
Area: 137,741 sq km (53,182 sq miles)
Population: 2,509,793
Capital: LITTLE ROCK

CALIFORNIA
Status: STATE
Area: 423,999 sq km (163,707 sq miles)
Population: 31,878,234
Capital: SACRAMENTO

COLORADO
Status: STATE
Area: 269,618 sq km (104,100 sq miles)
Population: 3,822,676
Capital: DENVER

CONNECTICUT
Status: STATE
Area: 14,359 sq km (5,544 sq miles)
Population: 3,274,238
Capital: HARTFORD

DISTRICT OF COLUMBIA
Status: FEDERAL DISTRICT
Area: 176 sq km (68 sq miles)
Population: 543,213
Capital: WASHINGTON

DELAWARE
Status: STATE
Area: 6,446 sq km (2,489 sq miles)
Population: 724,842
Capital: DOVER

FLORIDA
Status: STATE
Area: 170,312 sq km (65,758 sq miles)
Population: 14,399,985
Capital: TALLAHASSEE

GEORGIA
Status: STATE
Area: 153,951 sq km (59,441 sq miles)
Population: 7,353,225
Capital: ATLANTA

HAWAII
Status: STATE
Area: 28,314 sq km (10,932 sq miles)
Population: 1,183,723
Capital: HONOLULU

IDAHO
Status: STATE
Area: 216,456 sq km (83,574 sq miles)
Population: 1,189,251
Capital: BOISE

ILLINOIS
Status: STATE
Area: 150,007 sq km (57,918 sq miles)
Population: 11,846,544
Capital: SPRINGFIELD

INDIANA
Status: STATE
Area: 94,327 sq km (36,420 sq miles)
Population: 5,840,528
Capital: INDIANAPOLIS

IOWA
Status: STATE
Area: 145,754 sq km (56,276 sq miles)
Population: 2,851,792
Capital: DES MOINES

KANSAS
Status: STATE
Area: 213,109 sq km (82,282 sq miles)
Population: 2,572,150
Capital: TOPEKA

KENTUCKY
Status: STATE
Area: 104,664 sq km (40,411 sq miles)
Population: 3,883,723
Capital: FRANKFORT

LOUISIANA
Status: STATE
Area: 134,273 sq km (51,843 sq miles)
Population: 4,350,579
Capital: BATON ROUGE

USA continued

MAINE
Status: STATE
Area: 91,652 sq km (35,387 sq miles)
Population: 1,243,316
Capital: AUGUSTA

MARYLAND
Status: STATE
Area: 32,134 sq km (12,407 sq miles)
Population: 5,071,604
Capital: ANNAPOLIS

MASSACHUSETTS
Status: STATE
Area: 27,337 sq km (10,555 sq miles)
Population: 6,092,352
Capital: BOSTON

MICHIGAN
Status: STATE
Area: 250,737 sq km (96,810 sq miles)
Population: 9,594,350
Capital: LANSING

MINNESOTA
Status: STATE
Area: 225,181 sq km (86,943 sq miles)
Population: 4,657,758
Capital: ST PAUL

MISSISSIPPI
Status: STATE
Area: 125,443 sq km (48,434 sq miles)
Population: 2,716,115
Capital: JACKSON

MISSOURI
Status: STATE
Area: 180,545 sq km (69,709 sq miles)
Population: 5,358,692
Capital: JEFFERSON CITY

MONTANA
Status: STATE
Area: 380,847 sq km (147,046 sq miles)
Population: 879,372
Capital: HELENA

NEBRASKA
Status: STATE
Area: 200,356 sq km (77,358 sq miles)
Population: 1,652,093
Capital: LINCOLN

NEVADA
Status: STATE
Area: 286,367 sq km (110,567 sq miles)
Population: 1,603,163
Capital: CARSON CITY

NEW HAMPSHIRE
Status: STATE
Area: 24,219 sq km (9,351 sq miles)
Population: 1,162,481
Capital: CONCORD

NEW JERSEY
Status: STATE
Area: 22,590 sq km (8,722 sq miles)
Population: 7,987,933
Capital: TRENTON

NEW MEXICO
Status: STATE
Area: 314,937 sq km (121,598 sq miles)
Population: 1,713,407
Capital: SANTA FE

NEW YORK
Status: STATE
Area: 141,090 sq km (54,475 sq miles)
Population: 18,184,774
Capital: ALBANY

NORTH CAROLINA
Status: STATE
Area: 139,396 sq km (53,821 sq miles)
Population: 7,322,870
Capital: RALEIGH

NORTH DAKOTA
Status: STATE
Area: 183,123 sq km (70,704 sq miles)
Population: 643,539
Capital: BISMARCK

OHIO
Status: STATE
Area: 116,104 sq km (44,828 sq miles)
Population: 11,172,782
Capital: COLUMBUS

OKLAHOMA
Status: STATE
Area: 181,048 sq km (69,903 sq miles)
Population: 3,300,902
Capital: OKLAHOMA CITY

OREGON
Status: STATE
Area: 254,819 sq km (98,386 sq miles)
Population: 3,203,735
Capital: SALEM

PENNSYLVANIA
Status: STATE
Area: 119,290 sq km (46,058 sq miles)
Population: 12,056,112
Capital: HARRISBURG

RHODE ISLAND
Status: STATE
Area: 4,002 sq km (1,545 sq miles)
Population: 990,225
Capital: PROVIDENCE

SOUTH CAROLINA
Status: STATE
Area: 82,898 sq km (32,007 sq miles)
Population: 3,698,746
Capital: COLUMBIA

SOUTH DAKOTA
Status: STATE
Area: 199,742 sq km (77,121 sq miles)
Population: 732,405
Capital: PIERRE

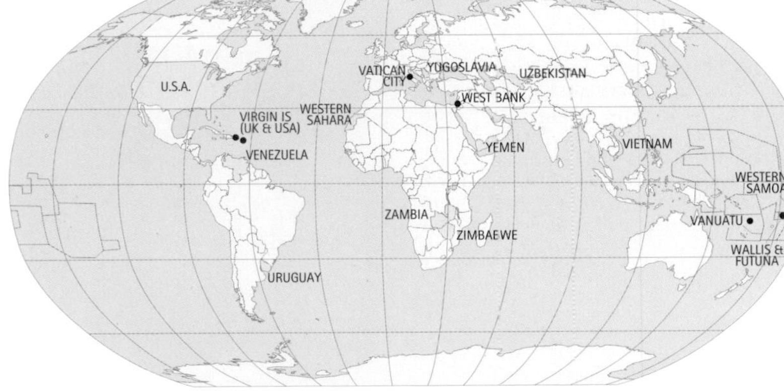

TENNESSEE
Status: STATE
Area: 109,158 sq km (42,146 sq miles)
Population: 5,319,654
Capital: NASHVILLE

TEXAS
Status: STATE
Area: 695,673 sq km (268,601 sq miles)
Population: 19,128,261
Capital: AUSTIN

UTAH
Status: STATE
Area: 219,900 sq km (84,904 sq miles)
Population: 2,000,494
Capital: SALT LAKE CITY

VERMONT
Status: STATE
Area: 24,903 sq km (9,615 sq miles)
Population: 588,654
Capital: MONTPELIER

VIRGINIA
Status: STATE
Area: 110,771 sq km (42,769 sq miles)
Population: 6,675,451
Capital: RICHMOND

WASHINGTON
Status: STATE
Area: 184,674 sq km (71,303 sq miles)
Population: 5,532,939
Capital: OLYMPIA

WEST VIRGINIA
Status: STATE
Area: 62,758 sq km (24,231 sq miles)
Population: 1,825,754
Capital: CHARLESTON

WISCONSIN
Status: STATE
Area: 169,652 sq km (65,503 sq miles)
Population: 5,159,795
Capital: MADISON

WYOMING
Status: STATE
Area: 253,347 sq km (97,818 sq miles)
Population: 481,400
Capital: CHEYENNE

URUGUAY
Status: REPUBLIC
Area: 176,215 sq km (68,037 sq mls)
Population: 3,186,000
Capital: MONTEVIDEO
Language: SPANISH
Religion: R.CATHOLIC, PROTESTANT, JEWISH
Currency: PESO
Organizations: UN

MAP PAGE: 91

URUGUAY, ON THE Atlantic coast of central South America, is a low-lying land of prairies. The coast and the River Plate estuary in the south are fringed with lagoons and sand dunes. Almost half the population lives in Montevideo. Uruguay has warm summers and mild winters. The economy was founded on cattle and sheep ranching, and meat, wool and hides are major exports. The main industries produce food products, textiles, petroleum products, chemicals and transport equipment. Offshore banking and tourism are important.

UZBEKISTAN
Status: REPUBLIC
Area: 447,400 sq km (172,742 sq mls)
Population: 22,843,000
Capital: TASHKENT
Language: UZBEK, RUSSIAN, TAJIK, KAZAKH
Religion: SUNNI MUSLIM, RUSSIAN ORTHODOX
Currency: SOM
Organizations: CIS, UN

MAP PAGE: 14

A REPUBLIC OF central Asia, Uzbekistan borders the Aral Sea and five countries. It consists mainly of the flat desert of the Kyzyl Kum, which rises eastwards towards the mountains of the western Pamirs. Most settlement is in the Fergana basin. The climate is dry and arid. The economy is based mainly on irrigated agriculture, chiefly cotton production. Industry specializes in fertilizers and machinery for cotton harvesting and textile manufacture. Uzbekistan is rich in minerals and has the largest gold mine in the world.

VANUATU
Status: REPUBLIC
Area: 12,190 sq km (4,707 sq mls)
Population: 169,000
Capital: PORT VILA
Language: ENGLISH, BISLAMA (ENGLISH CREOLE), FRENCH (ALL OFFICIAL)
Religion: PROTESTANT, R.CATHOLIC, TRAD.BELIEFS
Currency: VATU
Organizations: COMM., UN

MAP PAGE: 7

VANUATU OCCUPIES AN archipelago of some 80 islands in Oceania. Many of the islands are mountainous, of volcanic origin and densely forested. The climate is tropical with heavy rainfall. Half the population lives on the main islands of Efate, Santo and Tafea, and the majority of people live by farming. Copra, beef, seashells, cocoa and timber are the main exports. Tourism is growing and foreign aid is important.

VATICAN CITY
Status: ECCLESIASTICAL STATE
Area: 0.4 sq km (0.2 sq ml)
Population: 1,000
Language: ITALIAN
Religion: R.CATHOLIC
Currency: ITALIAN LIRA

MAP PAGE: 48

THE WORLD'S SMALLEST sovereign state, the Vatican City occupies a hill to the west of the river Tiber in the Italian capital, Rome. It is the headquarters of the Roman Catholic church and income comes from investments, voluntary contributions and tourism.

VENEZUELA
Status: REPUBLIC
Area: 912,050 sq km (352,144 sq mls)
Population: 21,644,000
Capital: CARACAS
Language: SPANISH, AMERINDIAN LANGUAGES
Religion: R.CATHOLIC, PROTESTANT
Currency: BOLÍVAR
Organizations: OPEC, UN

MAP PAGE: 89

VENEZUELA IS IN northern South America, on the Caribbean Sea. Its coast is much indented, with the oil-rich area of Lake Maracaibo at the western end and the swampy Orinoco delta in the east. Mountain ranges run parallel to the coast then turn southwestwards to form the northern extension of the Andes chain. Central Venezuela is lowland grasslands drained by the Orinoco river system, while to the south are the Guiana Highlands which contain the Angel Falls, the world's highest waterfall. About 85 per cent of the population lives in towns, mostly in the coastal mountain areas. The climate is tropical, with summer rainfall. Temperatures are lower in the mountains. Venezuela is an important oil producer, and sales account for about 75 per cent of export earnings. Bauxite, iron ore and gold are also mined and manufactures include aluminium, iron and steel, textiles, timber and wood products, and petrochemicals. Farming is important, particularly cattle ranching and dairy farming. Coffee, cotton, maize, rice and sugarcane are major crops.

VIETNAM

Status: REPUBLIC
Area: 329,565 sq km (127,246 sq mls)
Population: 74,545,000
Capital: HA NÔI
Language: VIETNAMESE, THAI, KHMER, CHINESE, MANY LOCAL LANGUAGES
Religion: BUDDHIST, TAOIST, R.CATHOLIC, CAO DAI, HOA HAO
Currency: DONG
Organizations: UN, ASEAN

MAP PAGE: 24-25

VIETNAM EXTENDS ALONG the east coast of the Indochina peninsula in southeast Asia, with the South China Sea to the east and south. The Red River (Song-koi) delta lowlands in the north are separated from the huge Mekong delta in the south by narrow coastal plains backed by the generally rough mountainous and forested terrain of the Annam highlands. Most people live in the river deltas. The climate is tropical, with summer monsoon rains. Over three quarters of the workforce is involved in agriculture, forestry and fishing. Rice growing is the main activity, and Vietnam is the world's third largest rice exporter, after the USA and Thailand. Coffee, tea and rubber are the main cash crops. The north is fairly rich in minerals including some oil, coal, iron ore, manganese, apatite and gold. The food processing and textile industries are important, but the steel, oil and gas and car industries are growing rapidly. The 1992 economic reform programme, inflow of foreign investment and the 1994 lifting of the US trade embargo are boosting an economy which suffered from decades of war and strife.

VIRGIN ISLANDS (UK)

Status: UK TERRITORY
Area: 153 sq km (59 sq mls)
Population: 19,000
Capital: ROAD TOWN
Language: ENGLISH
Religion: PROTESTANT, R.CATHOLIC
Currency: US DOLLAR

MAP PAGE: 83

THE CARIBBEAN TERRITORY comprises four main islands and some 36 islets at the eastern end of the Virgin Islands group. Apart from the flat coral atoll of Anegada, the islands are volcanic in origin and hilly. The climate is subtropical and tourism is the main industry.

VIRGIN ISLANDS (USA)

Status: US TERRITORY
Area: 352 sq km (136 sq mls)
Population: 105,000
Capital: CHARLOTTE AMALIE
Language: ENGLISH, SPANISH
Religion: PROTESTANT, R.CATHOLIC
Currency: US DOLLAR

MAP PAGE: 83

THE TERRITORY CONSISTS of three main islands and some 50 islets in the Caribbean's western Virgin Islands. The islands are mostly hilly and of volcanic origin and the climate is subtropical. The economy is based on tourism, with some manufacturing on St Croix.

WALLIS AND FUTUNA

Status: FRENCH TERRITORY
Area: 274 sq km (106 sq mls)
Population: 14,000
Capital: MATA-UTU
Language: FRENCH, POLYNESIAN (WALLISIAN, FUTUNIAN)
Religion: R.CATHOLIC
Currency: PACIFIC FRANC

MAP PAGE: 7

THE SOUTH PACIFIC territory comprises the volcanic islands of the Wallis archipelago and Hoorn Islands. The climate is tropical. The islands depend upon subsistence farming, the sale of licences to foreign fishing fleets, workers' remittances and French aid.

WEST BANK

Status: TERRITORY
Area: 5,860 sq km (2,263 sq mls)
Population: 1,219,000
Language: ARABIC, HEBREW
Religion: SUNNI MUSLIM, JEWISH, SHI'A MUSLIM, CHRISTIAN

MAP PAGE: 16

THE TERRITORY CONSISTS of the west bank of the river Jordan and parts of Judea and Samaria in southwest Asia. The land was annexed by Israel in 1967, but the Jericho area was granted self-government under an agreement between Israel and the PLO in 1993.

WESTERN SAHARA

Status: TERRITORY
Area: 266,000 sq km (102,703 sq mls)
Population: 283,000
Capital: LAÂYOUNE
Language: ARABIC
Religion: SUNNI MUSLIM
Currency: MOROCCAN DIRHAM

MAP PAGE: 54

SITUATED ON THE northwest coast of Africa, the territory of Western Sahara is controlled by Morocco.

WESTERN SAMOA

Status: MONARCHY
Area: 2,831 sq km (1,093 sq mls)
Population: 171,000
Capital: APIA
Language: SAMOAN, ENGLISH
Religion: PROTESTANT, R.CATHOLIC, MORMON
Currency: TALA
Organizations: COMM., UN

MAP PAGE: 7

WESTERN SAMOA CONSISTS of two main mountainous and forested islands and seven small islands in the South Pacific Ocean. Seventy per cent of people live on Upolu. The climate is tropical. The economy is based on agriculture, with some fishing and light manufacturing. Traditional exports are coconut products, timber, taro, cocoa and fruit, but cyclones in recent years devastated the coconut palms. Tourism is increasing, but the islands depend upon workers' remittances and foreign aid.

YEMEN

Status: REPUBLIC
Area: 527,968 sq km (203,850 sq mls)
Population: 14,501,000
Capital: ṢAN'Ā
Language: ARABIC
Religion: SUNNI MUSLIM, SHI'A MUSLIM
Currency: DINAR, RIAL
Organizations: UN

MAP PAGE: 20

YEMEN OCCUPIES THE southwestern Arabian Peninsula, on the Red Sea and Gulf of Aden. Beyond the Red Sea coastal plain the land rises to a mountain range then descends to desert plateaux. Much of Yemen is hot and arid, but rainfall in the west supports crops and most settlement. Farming and fishing are the main activities, with cotton the main cash crop. Oil production is increasingly important. Remittances from workers abroad are the main foreign exchange earner.

YUGOSLAVIA

Status: REPUBLIC
Area: 102,173 sq km (39,449 sq mls)
Population: 10,544,000
Capital: BELGRADE
Language: SERBO-CROAT, ALBANIAN, HUNGARIAN
Religion: SERBIAN ORTHODOX, MONTENEGRIN ORTHODOX, SUNNI MUSLIM
Currency: DINAR
Organizations: UN

MAP PAGE: 49

THE SOUTH EUROPEAN state comprises only two of the former Yugoslav republics: the large and populous but landlocked Serbia and the much smaller Montenegro on the Adriatic Sea. The landscape is for the most part rugged, mountainous and forested. Northern Serbia (including the formerly autonomous province of Vojvodina) is low-lying, drained by the Danube river system. The climate is Mediterranean on the coast, continental inland. War and economic sanctions have ruined Serbia's economy and damaged that of Montenegro.

ZAIRE

see CONGO *page 9*

MAP PAGE: 124-125

ZAMBIA

Status: REPUBLIC
Area: 752,614 sq km (290,586 sq mls)
Population: 9,373,000
Capital: LUSAKA
Language: ENGLISH, BEMBA, NYANJA, TONGA, MANY LOCAL LANGUAGES
Religion: PROTESTANT, R.CATHOLIC, TRAD. BELIEFS, SUNNI MUSLIM
Currency: KWACHA
Organizations: COMM., OAU, SADC, UN

MAP PAGE: 57

A LANDLOCKED STATE in central Africa, Zambia borders seven countries. It is dominated by high savannah plateaux and flanked by the Zambezi river in the south. Most people live in the central Copperbelt. The climate is tropical with a rainy season from November to May. Agriculture, which involves 70 per cent of the workforce, is mainly at subsistence level. Copper is still the mainstay of the economy, though reserves are declining. Lead, zinc, cobalt and tobacco are also exported. Manufacturing and tourism are important.

ZIMBABWE

Status: REPUBLIC
Area: 390,759 sq km (150,873 sq mls)
Population: 11,526,000
Capital: HARARE
Language: ENGLISH (OFFICIAL), SHONA, NDEBELE
Religion: PROTESTANT, R.CATHOLIC, TRAD.BELIEFS
Currency: DOLLAR
Organizations: COMM., OAU, SADC, UN

MAP PAGE: 57

ZIMBABWE, A LANDLOCKED state in south-central Africa, consists of high plateaux flanked by the Zambezi river valley and Lake Kariba in the north and the Limpopo in the south. Climatic conditions are temperate because of altitude. Most people live in central Zimbabwe. Tobacco, cotton, sugar, tea, coffee and beef are produced for export as are a variety of minerals including gold, nickel, asbestos and copper. Manufacturing provides a wide range of goods. Tourism is a major foreign exchange earner.

GEOGRAPHICAL STATISTICS

MOUNTAINS

m		ft
4,509	MT WILHELM	14,793
4,073	MT VICTORIA	13,364
4,000	MT HAGEN	13,124
3,754	MT COOK	12,316
2,230	MT KOSCIUSKO	7,316

INLAND WATERS

sq km		sq miles
0–8,900	LAKE EYRE	0–3,435
0–5,780	LAKE TORRENS	0–2,230
0–4,770	LAKE GAIRDNER	0–1,840
0–2,410	LAKE FROME	0–930

ISLANDS

sq km		sq miles
808,510	NEW GUINEA	312,085
757,050	BORNEO	292,220
189,040	CELEBES (Sulawesi)	72,970
150,460	SOUTH ISLAND	58,080
134,045	JAVA	51,740
114,690	NORTH ISLAND	44,270
68,330	TASMANIA	26,375
36,500	NEW BRITAIN	14,090
33,915	TIMOR	13,090

RIVERS

km		miles
3,750	MURRAY-DARLING	2,330
1,480	LACHLAN	920
840	FLINDERS	520
820	GASCOYNE	510
650	VICTORIA	400

DRAINAGE BASINS

sq km		sq miles
910,000	MURRAY-DARLING	351,000
108,000	FLINDERS	42,000
85,000	LACHLAN	33,000
80,000	GASCOYNE	31,000
78,000	VICTORIA	30,000

MAXIMUM WATER DEPTHS

m		ft
9,175	CORAL SEA	30,102
7,440	BANDA SEA	24,409
6,220	CELEBES SEA	20,410
5,514	SOUTH CHINA SEA	18,091
4,570	TASMAN SEA	14,993
3,310	TIMOR SEA	10,860

SEE MAPS pages 4–9, 33

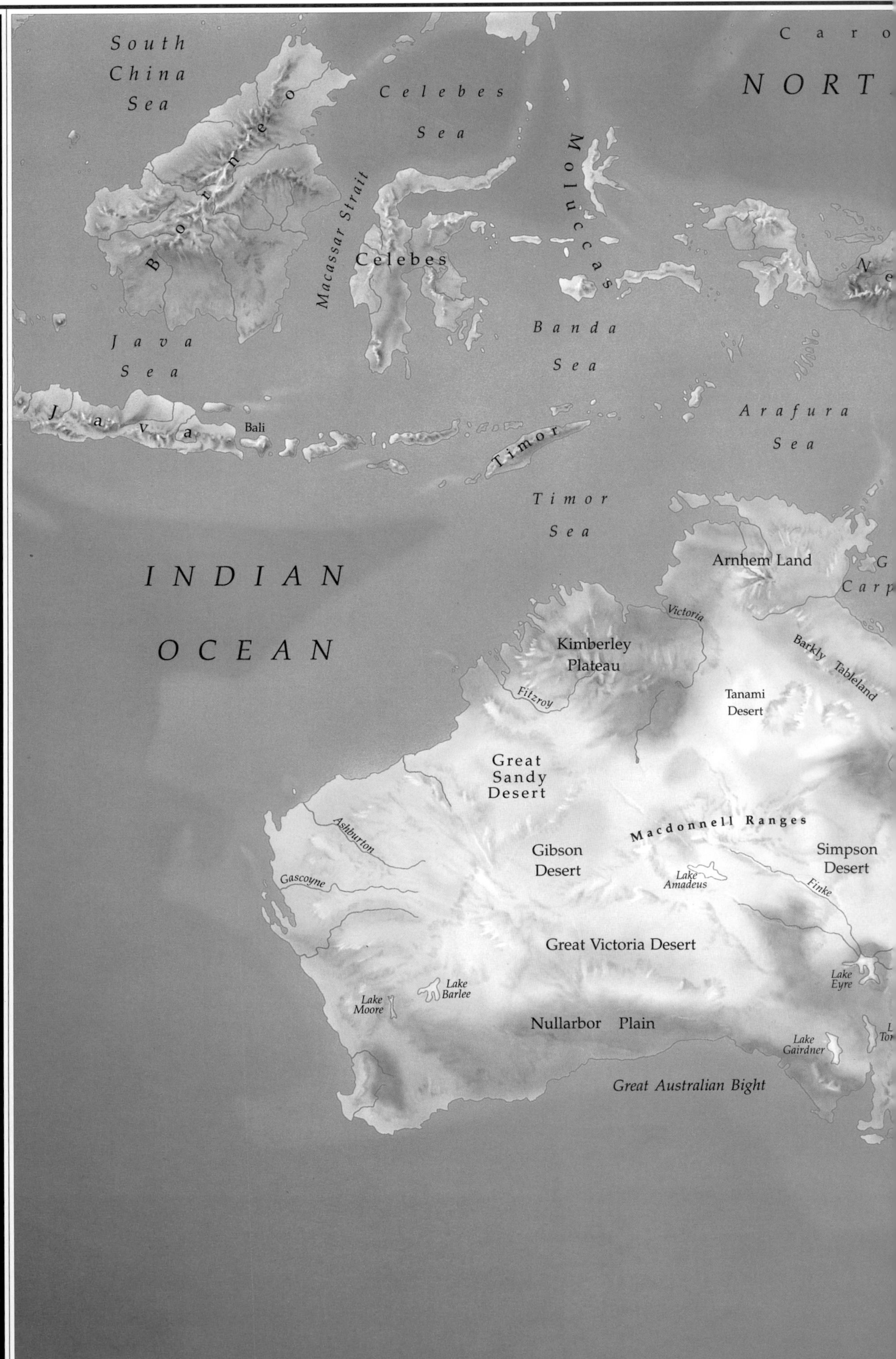

PACIFIC OCEAN
MICRONESIA
Pohnpei
Marshall Islands
MELANESIA
Admiralty Islands
New Ireland
Bismarck Sea
Mt Hagen
Mt Wilhelm
New Britain
Bougainville
Solomon Islands
Mt Victoria
Torres Strait
Nauru
Banaba
Kiribati
SOUTH PACIFIC OCEAN
POLYNESIA
Line Islands
Tokelau Islands
Tuvalu
Santa Cruz Islands
Cape York Peninsula
Coral Sea
Great Barrier Reef
Great Dividing Range
Flinders
Vanuatu
Samoan Islands
Fiji
Tahiti
Society Islands
Tonga
New Caledonia
Diamantina
Cooper Creek
Barwon
Darling
Lachlan
Murrumbidgee
Murray
Mt Kosciusko
Norfolk Island
Lord Howe Island
Kermadec Islands
Tasman Sea
North Island
New Zealand
Cook Strait
Mt Cook
South Island
Chatham Islands
Bass Strait
Tasmania
Bounty Islands
Antipodes Islands
Auckland Islands
Campbell Island
Macquarie Island
OCEAN

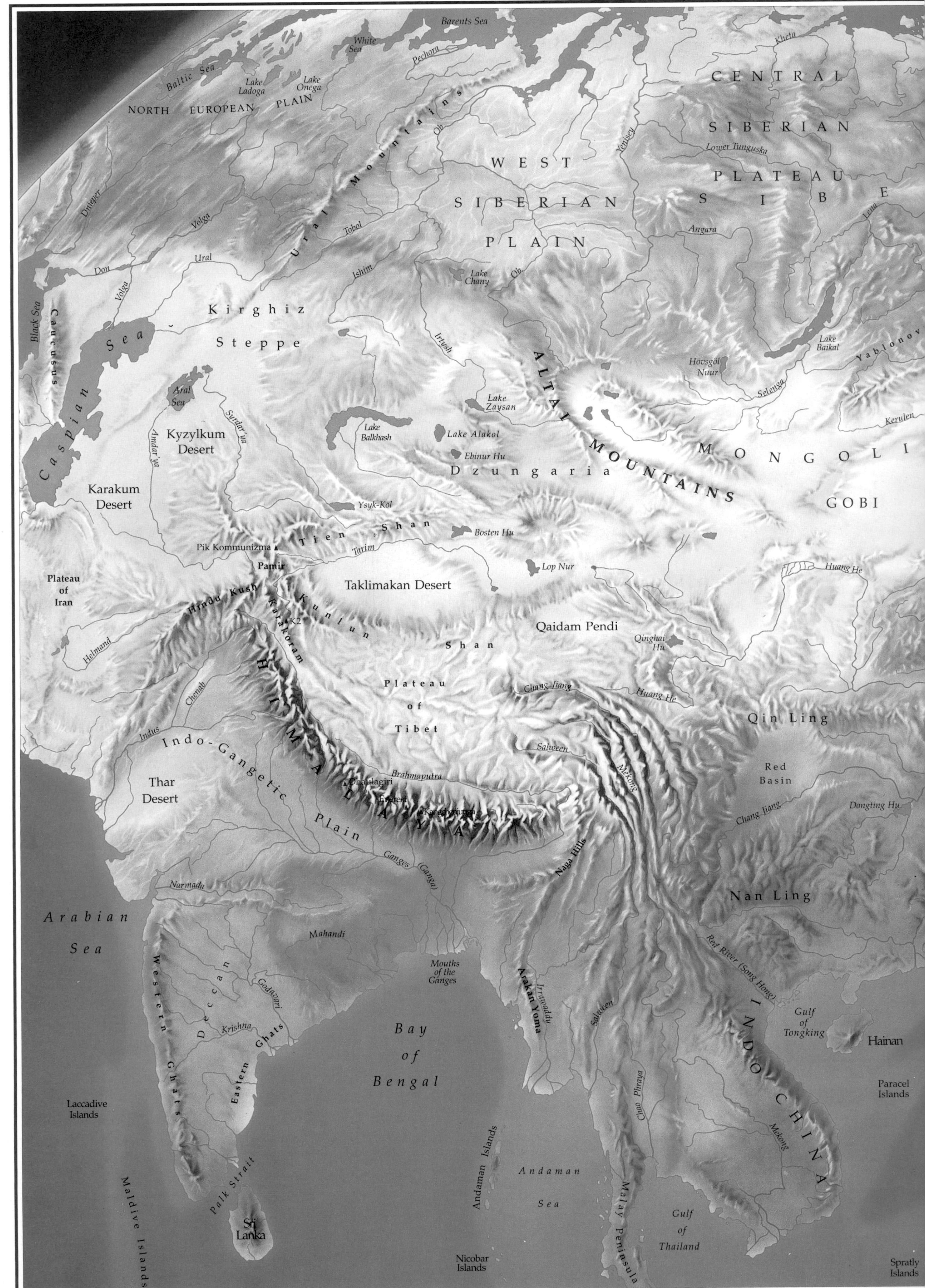
Barents Sea
White Sea
Baltic Sea
Lake Ladoga
Lake Onega
Pechora
Kheta
NORTH EUROPEAN PLAIN
CENTRAL SIBERIAN PLATEAU
Lower Tunguska
Yenisey
Ural Mountains
Ob
WEST SIBERIAN PLAIN
SIBE
Angara
Lena
Dnieper
Volga
Tobol
Ural
Don
Ishim
Lake Chany
Black Sea
Caucasus
Kirghiz Steppe
Caspian Sea
Irtysh
ALTAI MOUNTAINS
Lake Baikal
Yablonov
Hövsgöl Nuur
Selenga
Kerulen
Aral Sea
Syrdar'ya
Amdar'ya
Kyzylkum Desert
Lake Zaysan
Lake Balkhash
Lake Alakol
Ebinur Hu
Dzungaria
MONGOLI
GOBI
Karakum Desert
Ysyk-Köl
Tien Shan
Bosten Hu
Pik Kommunizma
Tarim
Lop Nur
Huang He
Pamir
Plateau of Iran
Taklimakan Desert
Hindu Kush
Karakoram
K2
Kunlun Shan
Qaidam Pendi
Qinghai Hu
Helmand
HIMALAYA
Plateau of Tibet
Chang Jiang
Huang He
Chenab
Qin Ling
Indus
Indo-Gangetic Plain
Salween
Red Basin
Thar Desert
Brahmaputra
Dhaulagiri
Everest
Kangchenjunga
Mekong
Chang Jiang
Dongting Hu
Naga Hills
Ganges
Ganga
Narmada
Nan Ling
Arabian Sea
Mahandi
Red River (Song Hong)
Western Ghats
Deccan
Godavari
Mouths of the Ganges
Arakan Yoma
Irrawaddy
Salween
Gulf of Tongking
Krishna
Ghats
Bay of Bengal
INDOCHINA
Hainan
Eastern
Laccadive Islands
Chao Phraya
Paracel Islands
Mekong
Andaman Islands
Andaman Sea
Maldive Islands
Palk Strait
Sri Lanka
Malay Peninsula
Gulf of Thailand
Nicobar Islands
Spratly Islands

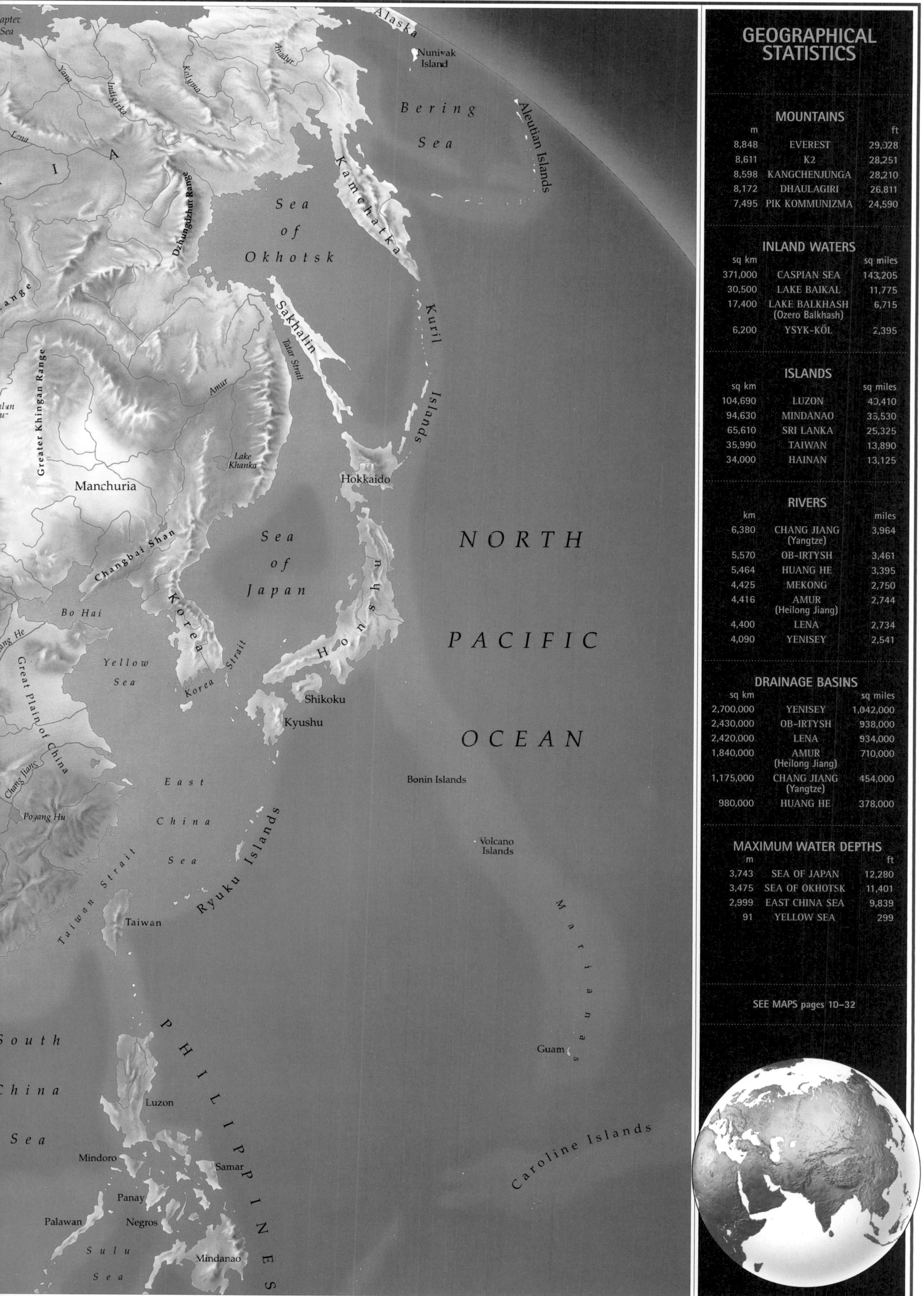

GEOGRAPHICAL STATISTICS

MOUNTAINS

m		ft
8,848	EVEREST	29,028
8,611	K2	28,251
8,598	KANGCHENJUNGA	28,210
8,172	DHAULAGIRI	26,811
7,495	PIK KOMMUNIZMA	24,590

INLAND WATERS

sq km		sq miles
371,000	CASPIAN SEA	143,205
30,500	LAKE BAIKAL	11,775
17,400	LAKE BALKHASH (Ozero Balkhash)	6,715
6,200	YSYK-KÖL	2,395

ISLANDS

sq km		sq miles
104,690	LUZON	40,410
94,630	MINDANAO	36,530
65,610	SRI LANKA	25,325
35,990	TAIWAN	13,890
34,000	HAINAN	13,125

RIVERS

km		miles
6,380	CHANG JIANG (Yangtze)	3,964
5,570	OB-IRTYSH	3,461
5,464	HUANG HE	3,395
4,425	MEKONG	2,750
4,416	AMUR (Heilong Jiang)	2,744
4,400	LENA	2,734
4,090	YENISEY	2,541

DRAINAGE BASINS

sq km		sq miles
2,700,000	YENISEY	1,042,000
2,430,000	OB-IRTYSH	938,000
2,420,000	LENA	934,000
1,840,000	AMUR (Heilong Jiang)	710,000
1,175,000	CHANG JIANG (Yangtze)	454,000
980,000	HUANG HE	378,000

MAXIMUM WATER DEPTHS

m		ft
3,743	SEA OF JAPAN	12,280
3,475	SEA OF OKHOTSK	11,401
2,999	EAST CHINA SEA	9,839
91	YELLOW SEA	299

SEE MAPS pages 10–32

NORTH POLE
ARCTIC
Ellesmere Island
Hudson Bay
Baffin Island
Davis Strait
Greenland
Greenland Sea
Svalbar
LABRADOR
Jan Mayen
North Cap
Denmark Strait
Norwegian Sea
Iceland
Faroe Islands
NORTH
ATLANTIC
OCEAN
British Isles
Grampians
North Sea
Vänern
Vättern
Ireland
Irish Sea
Great Britain
Severn
Thames
English Channel
Elbe
Odra
Vistula
Balti
Rhine
Seine
Loire
Danube
Hun
Bay of Biscay
Massif Central
Mt Blanc
Matterhorn
Po
Rhone
Garonne
Azores
Cantabrian Mts
Pyrenees
Ebro
Dinaric Alps
Adriatic Sea
Apennines
Corsica
Tagus
Balearic Islands
Sardinia
Guadalquivir
Mulhacén
Strait of Gibraltar
MEDITERR
Sicily
Malta
Madeira
ATLAS MOUNTAINS
Chott Melrhir
El Jerid
Gulf of Sirt
Canary Islands

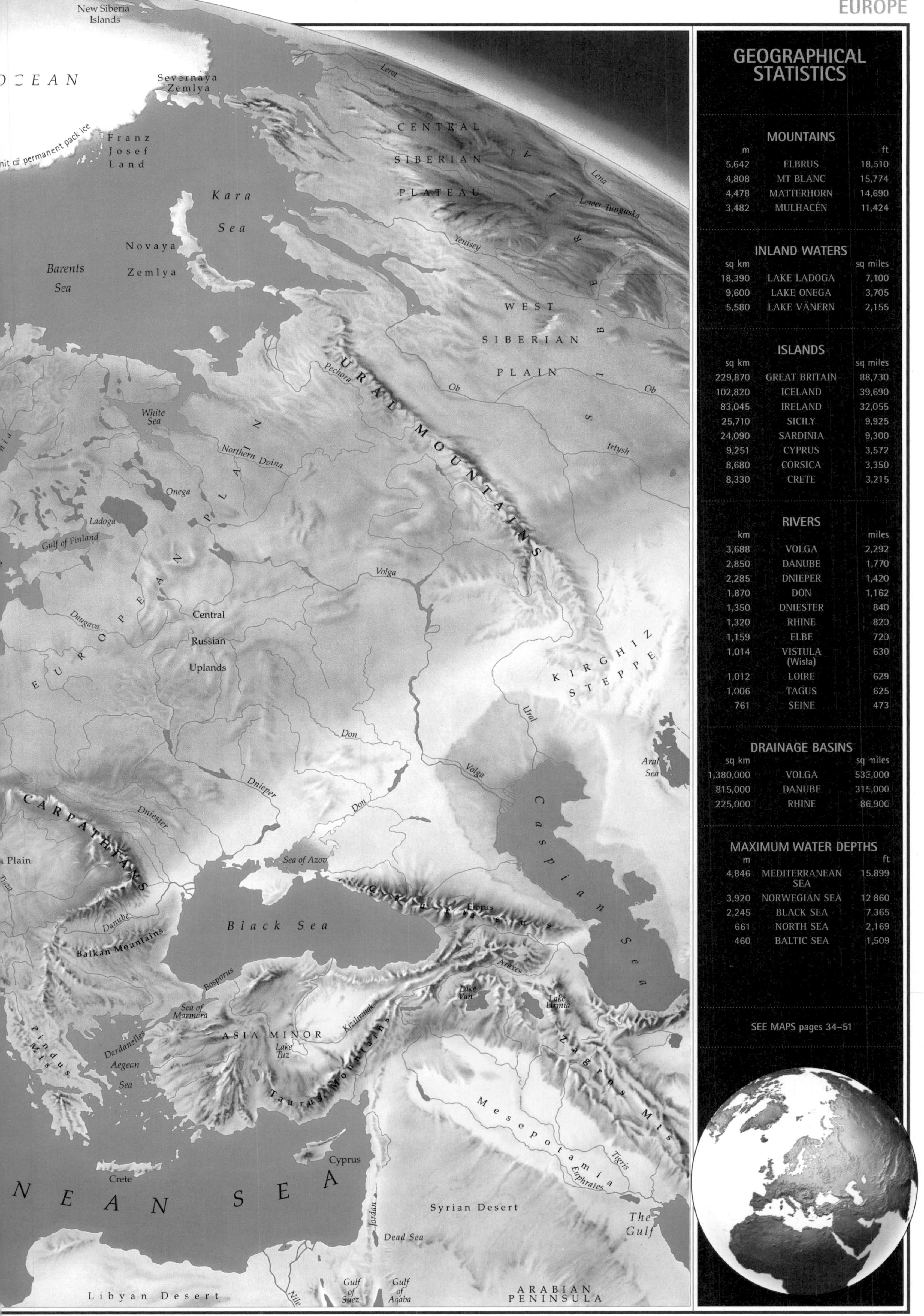

GEOGRAPHICAL STATISTICS

MOUNTAINS

m		ft
5,642	ELBRUS	18,510
4,808	MT BLANC	15,774
4,478	MATTERHORN	14,690
3,482	MULHACÉN	11,424

INLAND WATERS

sq km		sq miles
18,390	LAKE LADOGA	7,100
9,600	LAKE ONEGA	3,705
5,580	LAKE VÄNERN	2,155

ISLANDS

sq km		sq miles
229,870	GREAT BRITAIN	88,730
102,820	ICELAND	39,690
83,045	IRELAND	32,055
25,710	SICILY	9,925
24,090	SARDINIA	9,300
9,251	CYPRUS	3,572
8,680	CORSICA	3,350
8,330	CRETE	3,215

RIVERS

km		miles
3,688	VOLGA	2,292
2,850	DANUBE	1,770
2,285	DNIEPER	1,420
1,870	DON	1,162
1,350	DNIESTER	840
1,320	RHINE	820
1,159	ELBE	720
1,014	VISTULA (Wisła)	630
1,012	LOIRE	629
1,006	TAGUS	625
761	SEINE	473

DRAINAGE BASINS

sq km		sq miles
1,380,000	VOLGA	533,000
815,000	DANUBE	315,000
225,000	RHINE	86,900

MAXIMUM WATER DEPTHS

m		ft
4,846	MEDITERRANEAN SEA	15.899
3,920	NORWEGIAN SEA	12 860
2,245	BLACK SEA	7,365
661	NORTH SEA	2,169
460	BALTIC SEA	1,509

SEE MAPS pages 34–51

Iberian Peninsula
Strait of Gibraltar
Azores
Madeira
Canary Islands
ATLAS MOUNTAINS
Chott Melrhir
El Jerid
Malta
Crete
Gulf of Sirte
Mediterran
Libyan
S A H A R A
Hoggar
Tibesti
Lac Faguibine
Sénégal
Niger
Cape Verde Islands
Gambia
S A H E L
Lake Chad
Jebel Marra
Benue
Lake Volta
Grain Coast
Ivory Coast
Gold Coast
Bight of Benin
Mouths of the Niger
Mt Cameroun
Sanaga
Ubangi
Uele
Bioco
Gulf of Guinea
Príncipe
São Tomé
Congo(Zaïre)
St Paul Rocks
Annobón
Lac Mai-Ndome
Congo
Kasai
Cuango
Lake Upemba
SOUTH AMERICA
Ascension
S O U T H
Bié Plateau
St Helena
Cunene
Okavango
Etosha Pan
A T L A N T I C
Lake Ngami
Makgadikga Pan
Namib Desert
Kalahari Desert
O C E A N
Orange
Great Karoo
Cape of Good Hope

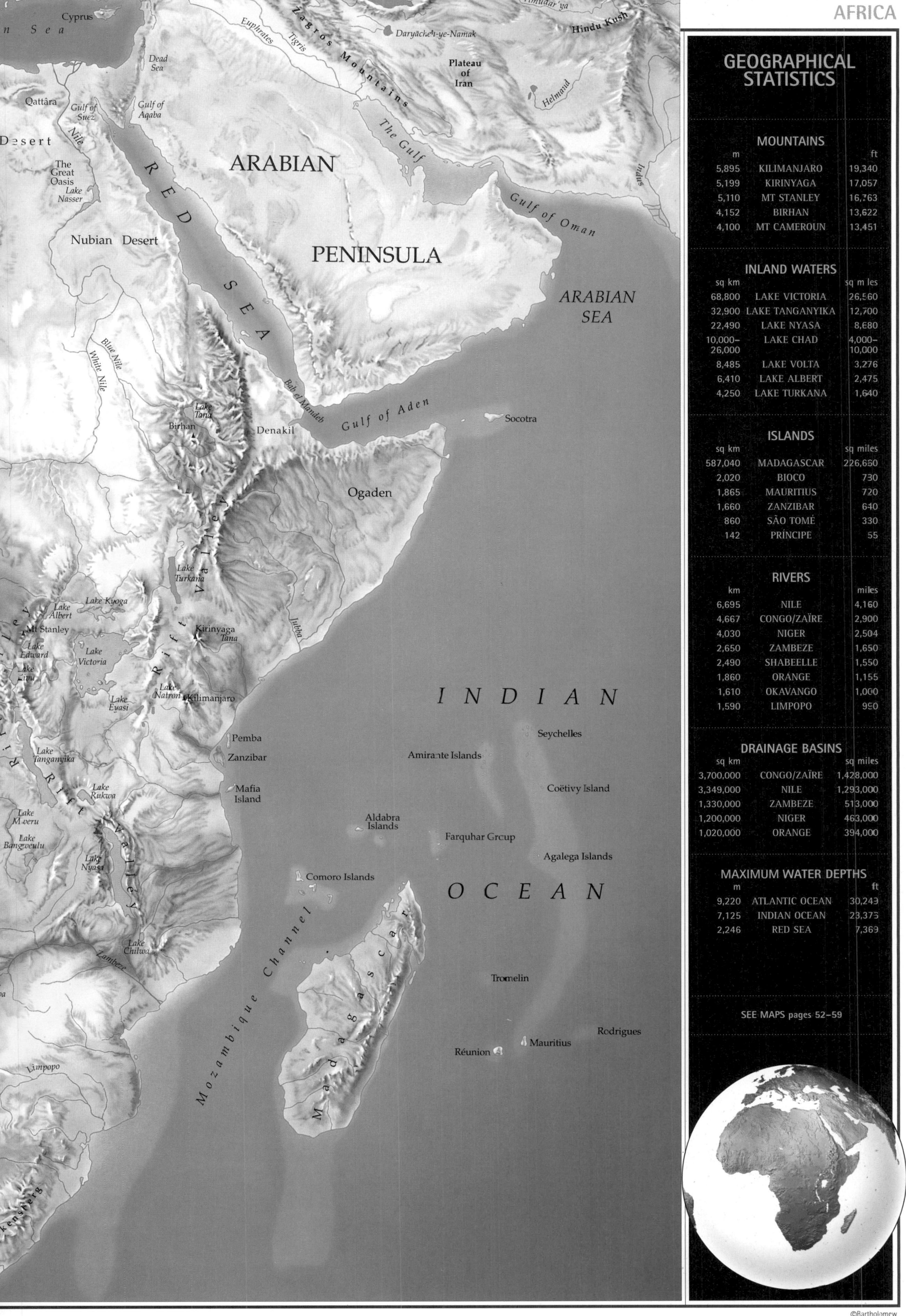

GEOGRAPHICAL STATISTICS

MOUNTAINS

m		ft
5,895	KILIMANJARO	19,340
5,199	KIRINYAGA	17,057
5,110	MT STANLEY	16,763
4,152	BIRHAN	13,622
4,100	MT CAMEROUN	13,451

INLAND WATERS

sq km		sq miles
68,800	LAKE VICTORIA	26,560
32,900	LAKE TANGANYIKA	12,700
22,490	LAKE NYASA	8,680
10,000–26,000	LAKE CHAD	4,000–10,000
8,485	LAKE VOLTA	3,276
6,410	LAKE ALBERT	2,475
4,250	LAKE TURKANA	1,640

ISLANDS

sq km		sq miles
587,040	MADAGASCAR	226,660
2,020	BIOCO	730
1,865	MAURITIUS	720
1,660	ZANZIBAR	640
860	SÃO TOMÉ	330
142	PRÍNCIPE	55

RIVERS

km		miles
6,695	NILE	4,160
4,667	CONGO/ZAÏRE	2,900
4,030	NIGER	2,504
2,650	ZAMBEZE	1,650
2,490	SHABEELLE	1,550
1,860	ORANGE	1,155
1,610	OKAVANGO	1,000
1,590	LIMPOPO	990

DRAINAGE BASINS

sq km		sq miles
3,700,000	CONGO/ZAÏRE	1,428,000
3,349,000	NILE	1,293,000
1,330,000	ZAMBEZE	513,000
1,200,000	NIGER	463,000
1,020,000	ORANGE	394,000

MAXIMUM WATER DEPTHS

m		ft
9,220	ATLANTIC OCEAN	30,243
7,125	INDIAN OCEAN	23,375
2,246	RED SEA	7,369

SEE MAPS pages 52–59

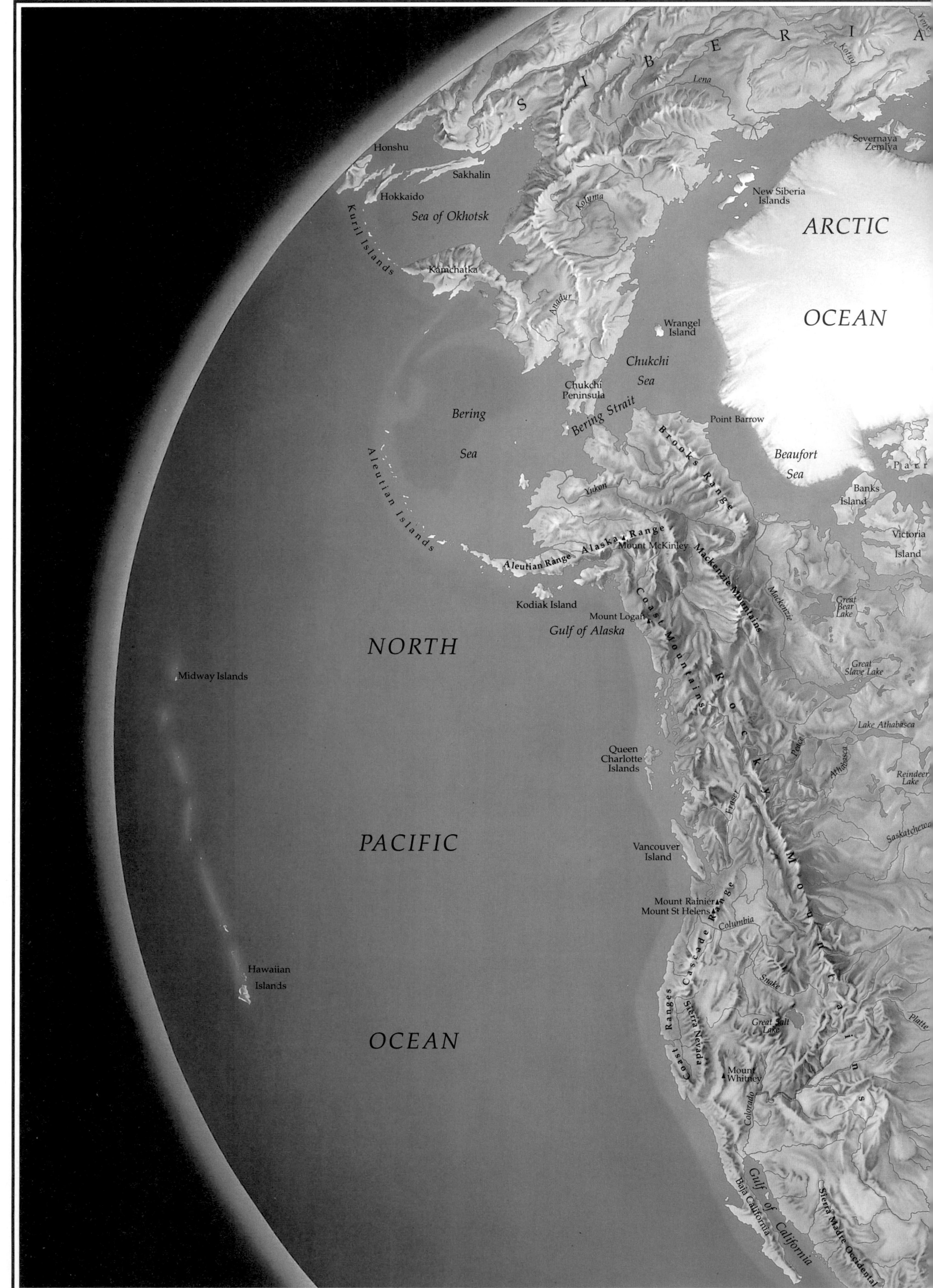

S I B E R I A
Lena
Kolyma
Honshu
Sakhalin
Hokkaido
Sea of Okhotsk
Kuril Islands
Kamchatka
Anadyr
Severnaya Zemlya
New Siberia Islands
ARCTIC
OCEAN
Wrangel Island
Chukchi Sea
Chukchi Peninsula
Bering Strait
Bering Sea
Point Barrow
Aleutian Islands
Brooks Range
Beaufort Sea
Banks Island
Victoria Island
Yukon
Alaska Range
Mount McKinley
Aleutian Range
Mackenzie Mountains
Mackenzie
Kodiak Island
Mount Logan
Gulf of Alaska
Coast Mountains
Great Bear Lake
Great Slave Lake
NORTH
Midway Islands
Lake Athabasca
Peace
Athabasca
Queen Charlotte Islands
Reindeer Lake
R o c k y M o u n t a i n s
Fraser
PACIFIC
Vancouver Island
Mount Rainier
Mount St Helens
Cascade Range
Columbia
Hawaiian Islands
Snake
Coast Ranges
Sierra Nevada
Great Salt Lake
OCEAN
Mount Whitney
Colorado
Platte
Gulf of California
Baja California
Sierra Madre Occidental

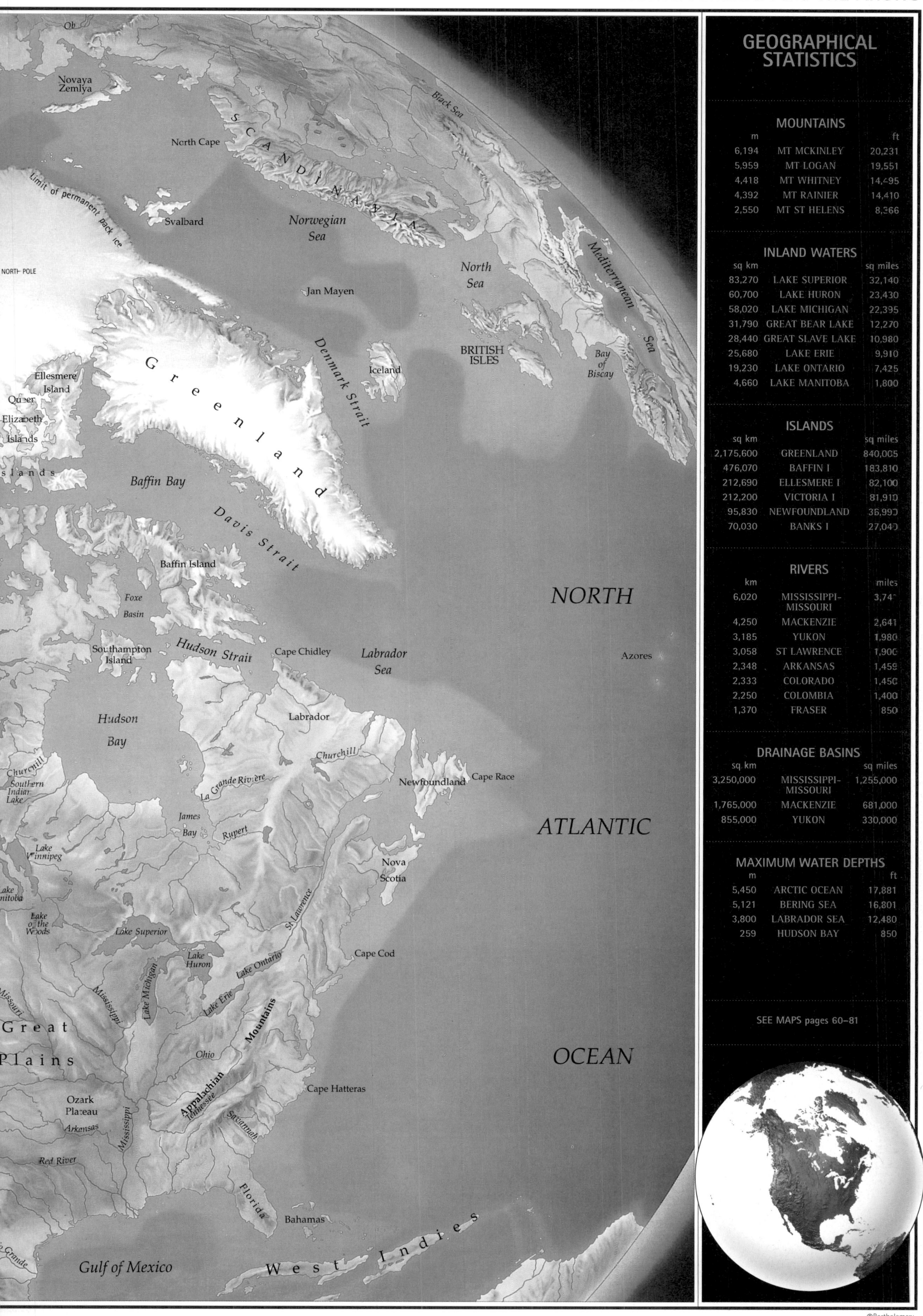

GEOGRAPHICAL STATISTICS

MOUNTAINS

m		ft
6,194	MT MCKINLEY	20,231
5,959	MT LOGAN	19,551
4,418	MT WHITNEY	14,495
4,392	MT RAINIER	14,410
2,550	MT ST HELENS	8,366

INLAND WATERS

sq km		sq miles
83,270	LAKE SUPERIOR	32,140
60,700	LAKE HURON	23,430
58,020	LAKE MICHIGAN	22,395
31,790	GREAT BEAR LAKE	12,270
28,440	GREAT SLAVE LAKE	10,980
25,680	LAKE ERIE	9,910
19,230	LAKE ONTARIO	7,425
4,660	LAKE MANITOBA	1,800

ISLANDS

sq km		sq miles
2,175,600	GREENLAND	840,005
476,070	BAFFIN I	183,810
212,690	ELLESMERE I	82,100
212,200	VICTORIA I	81,910
95,830	NEWFOUNDLAND	36,990
70,030	BANKS I	27,040

RIVERS

km		miles
6,020	MISSISSIPPI-MISSOURI	3,740
4,250	MACKENZIE	2,641
3,185	YUKON	1,980
3,058	ST LAWRENCE	1,900
2,348	ARKANSAS	1,459
2,333	COLORADO	1,450
2,250	COLOMBIA	1,400
1,370	FRASER	850

DRAINAGE BASINS

sq km		sq miles
3,250,000	MISSISSIPPI-MISSOURI	1,255,000
1,765,000	MACKENZIE	681,000
855,000	YUKON	330,000

MAXIMUM WATER DEPTHS

m		ft
5,450	ARCTIC OCEAN	17,881
5,121	BERING SEA	16,801
3,800	LABRADOR SEA	12,480
259	HUDSON BAY	850

SEE MAPS pages 60–81

GEOGRAPHICAL STATISTICS

MOUNTAINS

m		ft
6,768	HUASCARAN	22,205
6,388	ANCOHUMA	20,958
6,310	CHIMBORAZO	20,702
5,896	COTOPAXI	19,344
5,452	POPOCATÉPETL	17,887
2,810	RORAIMA	9,219

INLAND WATERS

sq km		sq miles
8,340	LAKE TITICACA	3,220
8,270	LAKE NICARAGUA	3,190
1,340	LAKE POOPO	520

ISLANDS

sq km		sq miles
114,525	CUBA	44,205
78,460	HISPANIOLA	30,285
10,990	JAMAICA	4,245
8,895	PUERTO RICO	3,435

RIVERS

km		miles
6,516	AMAZON	4,049
3,200	MADEIRA	1,990
3,000	PURUS	1,860
2,900	SÃO FRANCISCO	1,800
2,870	RIO GRANDE	1,785
2,500	ORINOCO	1,555
2,200	ARAGUAIA	1,370
2,100	XINGU	1,300
2,000	NEGRO	1,240
1,700	PARNAÍBA	1,060
1,609	MARAÑON	1,000
1,550	MAGDALENA	963
1,350	CAUCA	840

DRAINAGE BASINS

sq km		sq miles
7,050,000	AMAZON	2,721,000
1,000,000	NEGRO	386,000
945,000	ORINOCO	365,000
623,000	SÃO FRANCISCO	241,000
260,000	MAGDALENA	100,000

MAXIMUM WATER DEPTHS

m		ft
11,022	PACIFIC OCEAN	36,161
7,100	CARIBBEAN SEA	23,294
4,377	GULF OF MEXICO	14,360

SEE MAPS pages 82–87, 89–90

Gulf of California
Baja California
Sierra Madre Occidental
Rio Grande
Sierra Madre Oriental
GULF OF MEXICO
Florida
Gulf of Campeche
Yucatan
Popocatépetl
Sierra Madre del Sur
Gulf of Honduras
Lake Nicaragua
Isthmus of Pana
Gulf of Panama
PACIFIC
OCEAN
Isla del Coco
Isla de Malpelo
Galapagos Islands
Cotopaxi
Chimborazo
Jama
GREATE
W
C
CAR

NORTH
ATLANTIC
OCEAN
BAHAMAS
S T
I N D I E S
Hispaniola
Puerto
Rico
ANTILLES
BBEAN
EA
LESSER ANTILLES
Trinidad
Gulf of Darien
Lake Maracaibo
LLANOS
Orinoco
Cauca
Magdalena
Occidental
Cordillera Oriental
Roraima
Guiana Highlands
Branco
Mouths of the Amazon
Negro
Japurá
Putumayo
Amazon
Amazon
Marañon
Juruá
Purus
Madeira
Tapajós
Xingu
Tocantins
Parnaíba
Araguaia
São Francisco
Ucayali
Madre de Dios
MATO
GROSSO
Brazilian Highlands
Lake Titicaca
Ancohuma
Lake Poopó
Salar de Uyuni
Atacama Desert
GRAN CHACO
Paraguay
Paraná
Pilcomayo

GEOGRAPHICAL STATISTICS

MOUNTAINS

m		ft
6,960	ACONCAGUA	22,834
6,908	OJOS DEL SALADO	22,664
4,897	VINSON MASSIF	16,066
4,528	MT KIRKPATRICK	14,856
4,181	MT SIDLEY	13,718
3,794	MT EREBUS	12,447

ISLANDS

sq km		sq miles
47,000	TIERRA DEL FUEGO	18,140
12,175	FALKLAND IS	4,700
3,760	SOUTH GEORGIA	1,450

RIVERS

km		miles
4,500	PARANÁ	2,800
2,600	PARAGUAY	1,615
2,200	URUGUAY	1,370
1,500	SALADO	930
1,100	PILCOMAYO	680
810	CHUBUT	500

DRAINAGE BASINS

sq km		sq miles
3,100,000	PARANÁ	1,197,000
1,100,000	PARAGUAY	425,000
800,000	SALADO	309,000
307,000	URUGUAY	119,000

ANTARCTICA

The continental area is 13,340,000 sq km (5,149,000 sq miles).

Ice sheet permanently covers 98% of this, of which 87% lies on continental rock, whilst 11% is floating ice shelves.

The total volume of ice is 30,000,000 cu km (7,000,000 cu miles) with the greatest thickness being 4,700 m (15,420 ft) in east Antarctica.

SEE MAPS pages 88, 91–92

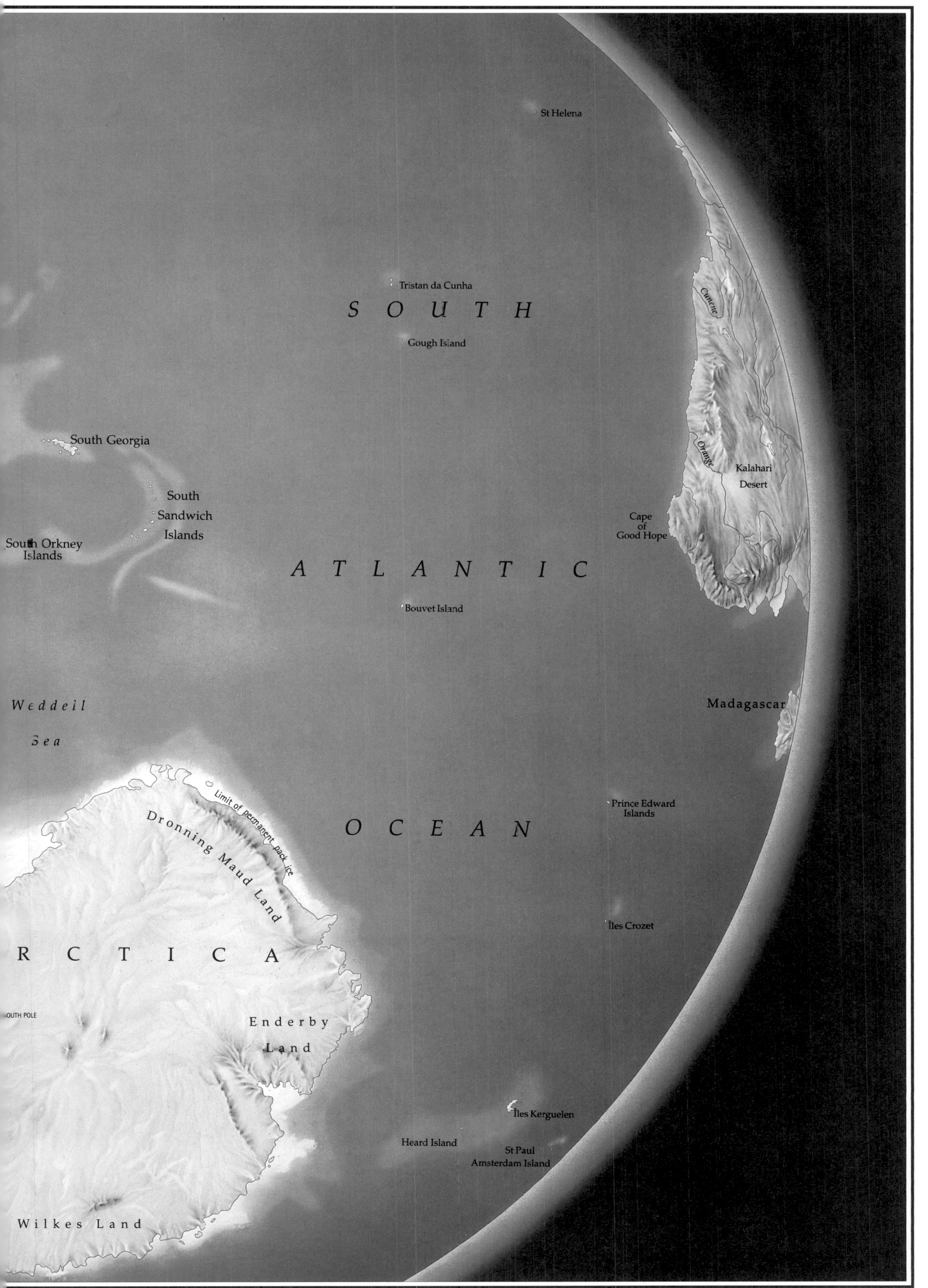
St Helena
Tristan da Cunha
SOUTH
Gough Island
South Georgia
South Sandwich Islands
South Orkney Islands
ATLANTIC
Bouvet Island
Cunene
Orange
Kalahari Desert
Cape of Good Hope
Weddell Sea
Madagascar
Limit of permanent pack ice
Dronning Maud Land
OCEAN
Prince Edward Islands
Îles Crozet
RCTICA
SOUTH POLE
Enderby Land
Îles Kerguelen
Heard Island
St Paul
Amsterdam Island
Wilkes Land

WORLD EXTREMES

	Highest Mountain	
8,848 m	Everest; Asia	*29,028 ft*
	Largest Inland Water Area	
371,000 sq km	Caspian Sea; Asia	*143,205 sq mls*
	Largest Island	
2,175,600 sq km	Greenland; North America	*839,780 sq mls*
	Longest River	
6,695 km	Nile; Africa	*4,160 mls*
	Largest Drainage Basin	
7,050,000 sq km	Amazon; South America	*2,721,000 sq mls*
	Deepest Water	
11,022 m	Marianas Trench; Pacific Ocean	*36,161 ft*

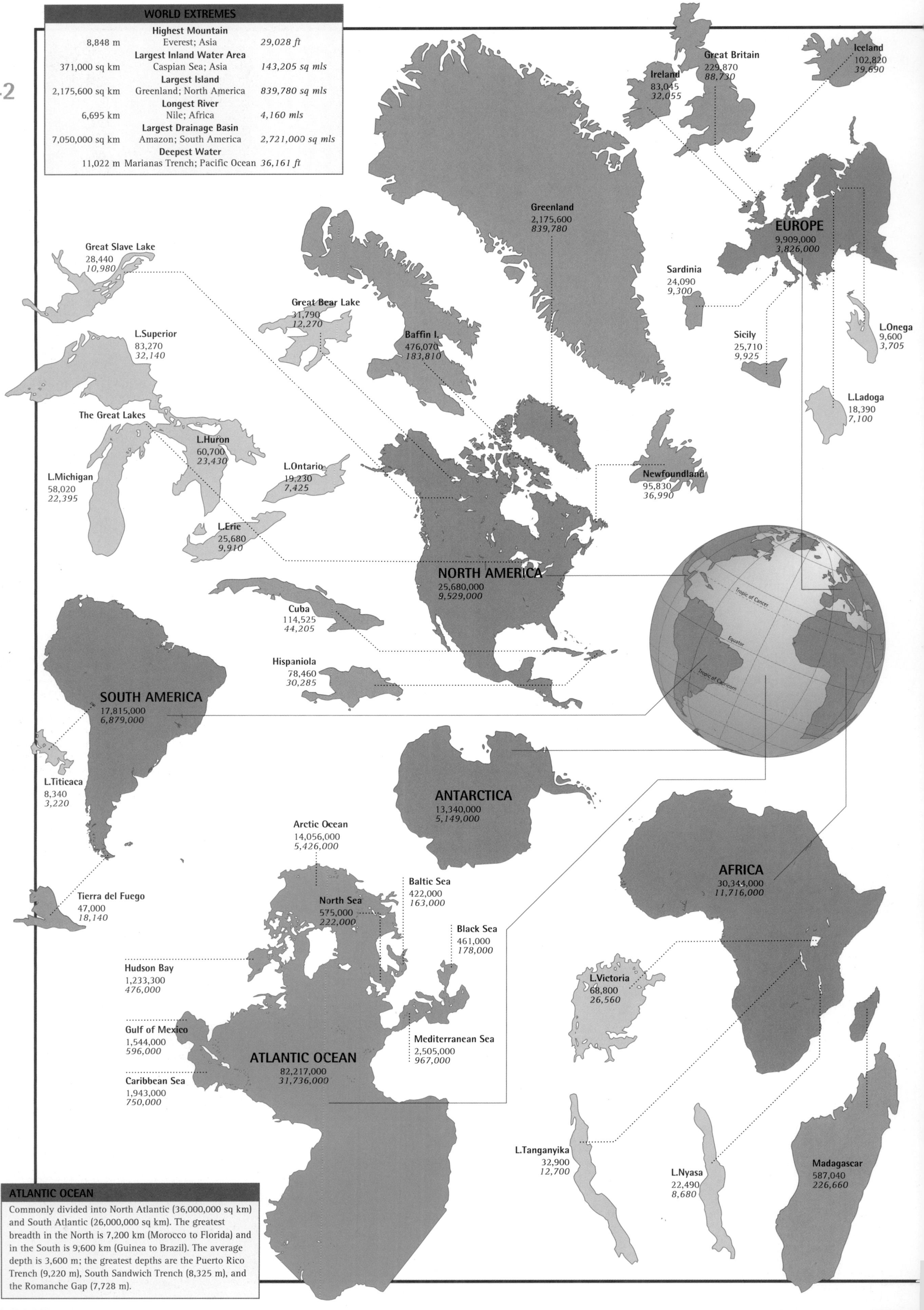

ATLANTIC OCEAN

Commonly divided into North Atlantic (36,000,000 sq km) and South Atlantic (26,000,000 sq km). The greatest breadth in the North is 7,200 km (Morocco to Florida) and in the South is 9,600 km (Guinea to Brazil). The average depth is 3,600 m; the greatest depths are the Puerto Rico Trench (9,220 m), South Sandwich Trench (8,325 m), and the Romanche Gap (7,728 m).

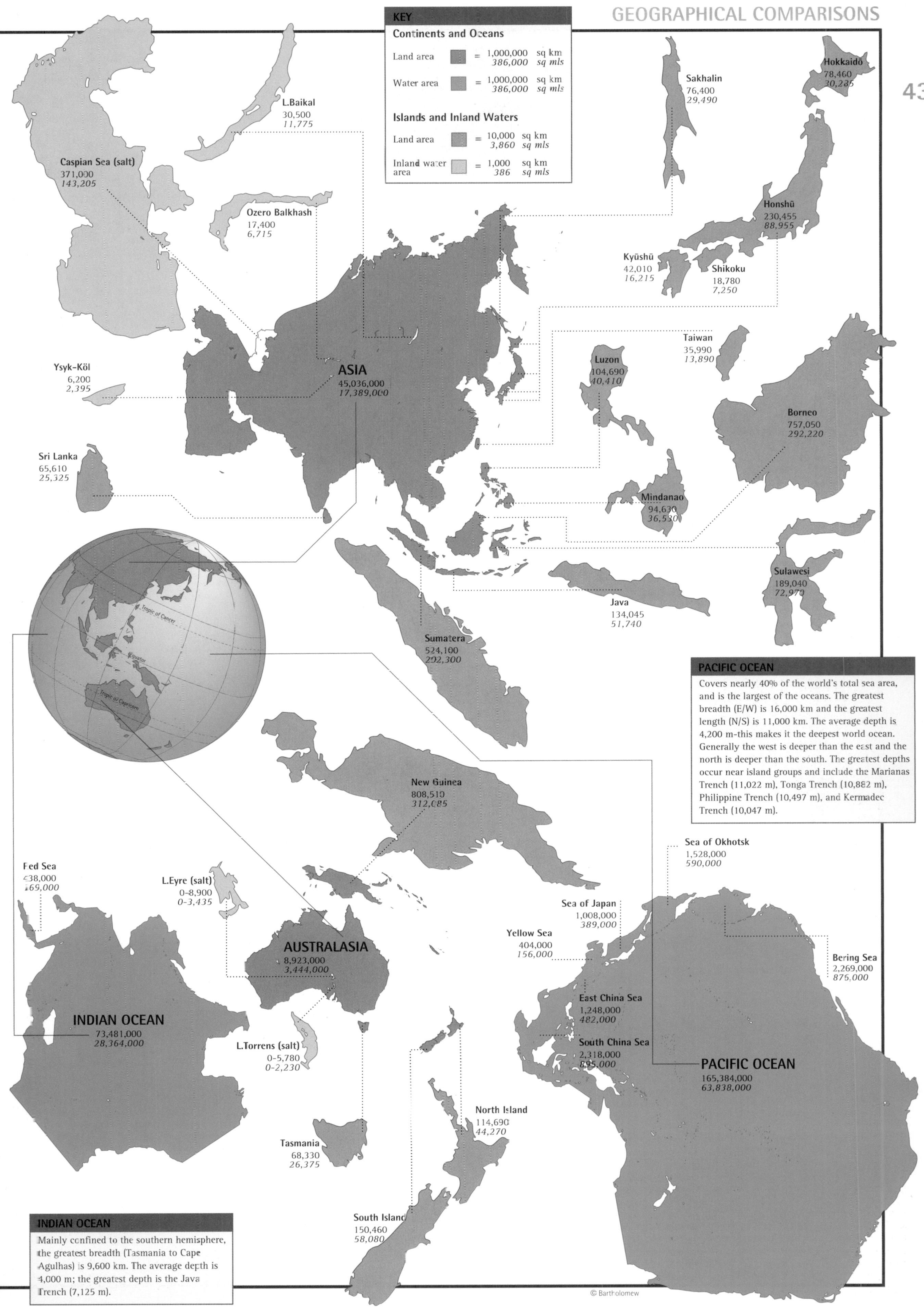

PACIFIC OCEAN

Covers nearly 40% of the world's total sea area, and is the largest of the oceans. The greatest breadth (E/W) is 16,000 km and the greatest length (N/S) is 11,000 km. The average depth is 4,200 m-this makes it the deepest world ocean. Generally the west is deeper than the east and the north is deeper than the south. The greatest depths occur near island groups and include the Marianas Trench (11,022 m), Tonga Trench (10,882 m), Philippine Trench (10,497 m), and Kermadec Trench (10,047 m).

INDIAN OCEAN

Mainly confined to the southern hemisphere, the greatest breadth (Tasmania to Cape Agulhas) is 9,600 km. The average depth is 4,000 m; the greatest depth is the Java Trench (7,125 m).

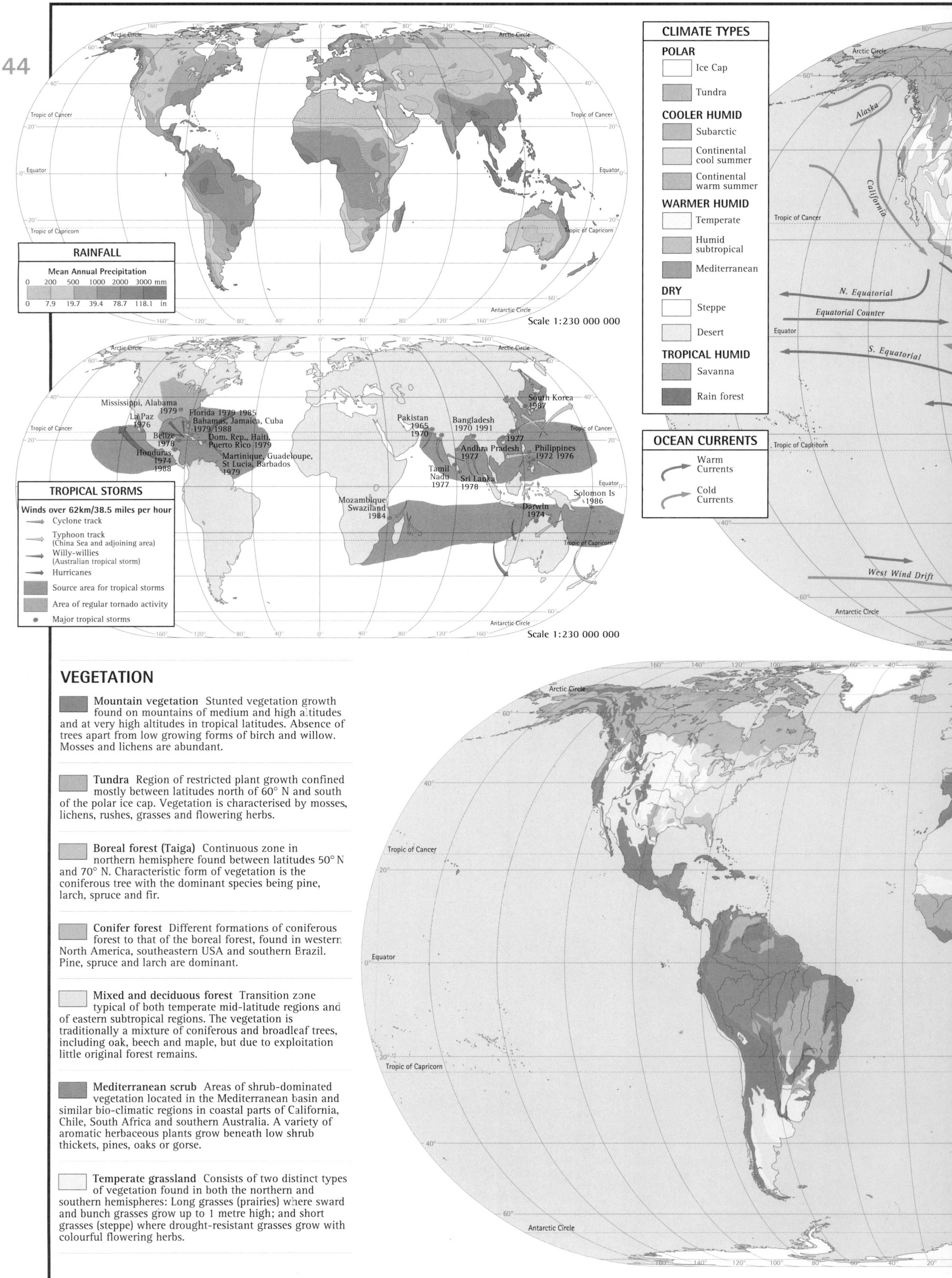
RAINFALL
Mean Annual Precipitation
0 200 500 1000 2000 3000 mm
0 7.9 19.7 39.4 78.7 118.1 in
Arctic Circle
Tropic of Cancer
Equator
Tropic of Capricorn
Antarctic Circle
Scale 1:230 000 000
TROPICAL STORMS
Winds over 62km/38.5 miles per hour
Cyclone track
Typhoon track
(China Sea and adjoining area)
Willy-willies
(Australian tropical storm)
Hurricanes
Source area for tropical storms
Area of regular tornado activity
Major tropical storms
Mississippi, Alabama 1979
La Paz 1976
Belize 1978
Honduras 1974 1988
Florida 1979 1985
Bahamas, Jamaica, Cuba 1979 1988
Dom. Rep., Haiti, Puerto Rico 1979
Martinique, Guadeloupe, St Lucia, Barbados 1979
Pakistan 1965 1970
Bangladesh 1970 1991
Andhra Pradesh 1977
Tamil Nadu 1977
Sri Lanka 1978
South Korea 1987
Philippines 1972 1976
Mozambique Swaziland 1984
Darwin 1974
Solomon Is 1986
Scale 1:230 000 000
CLIMATE TYPES
POLAR
Ice Cap
Tundra
COOLER HUMID
Subarctic
Continental cool summer
Continental warm summer
WARMER HUMID
Temperate
Humid subtropical
Mediterranean
DRY
Steppe
Desert
TROPICAL HUMID
Savanna
Rain forest
OCEAN CURRENTS
Warm Currents
Cold Currents
Alaska
California
N. Equatorial
Equatorial Counter
S. Equatorial
West Wind Drift
VEGETATION
Mountain vegetation Stunted vegetation growth found on mountains of medium and high altitudes and at very high altitudes in tropical latitudes. Absence of trees apart from low growing forms of birch and willow. Mosses and lichens are abundant.
Tundra Region of restricted plant growth confined mostly between latitudes north of 60° N and south of the polar ice cap. Vegetation is characterised by mosses, lichens, rushes, grasses and flowering herbs.
Boreal forest (Taiga) Continuous zone in northern hemisphere found between latitudes 50° N and 70° N. Characteristic form of vegetation is the coniferous tree with the dominant species being pine, larch, spruce and fir.
Conifer forest Different formations of coniferous forest to that of the boreal forest, found in western North America, southeastern USA and southern Brazil. Pine, spruce and larch are dominant.
Mixed and deciduous forest Transition zone typical of both temperate mid-latitude regions and of eastern subtropical regions. The vegetation is traditionally a mixture of coniferous and broadleaf trees, including oak, beech and maple, but due to exploitation little original forest remains.
Mediterranean scrub Areas of shrub-dominated vegetation located in the Mediterranean basin and similar bio-climatic regions in coastal parts of California, Chile, South Africa and southern Australia. A variety of aromatic herbaceous plants grow beneath low shrub thickets, pines, oaks or gorse.
Temperate grassland Consists of two distinct types of vegetation found in both the northern and southern hemispheres: Long grasses (prairies) where sward and bunch grasses grow up to 1 metre high; and short grasses (steppe) where drought-resistant grasses grow with colourful flowering herbs.
Arctic Circle
Tropic of Cancer
Equator
Tropic of Capricorn
Antarctic Circle
Eckert IV projection

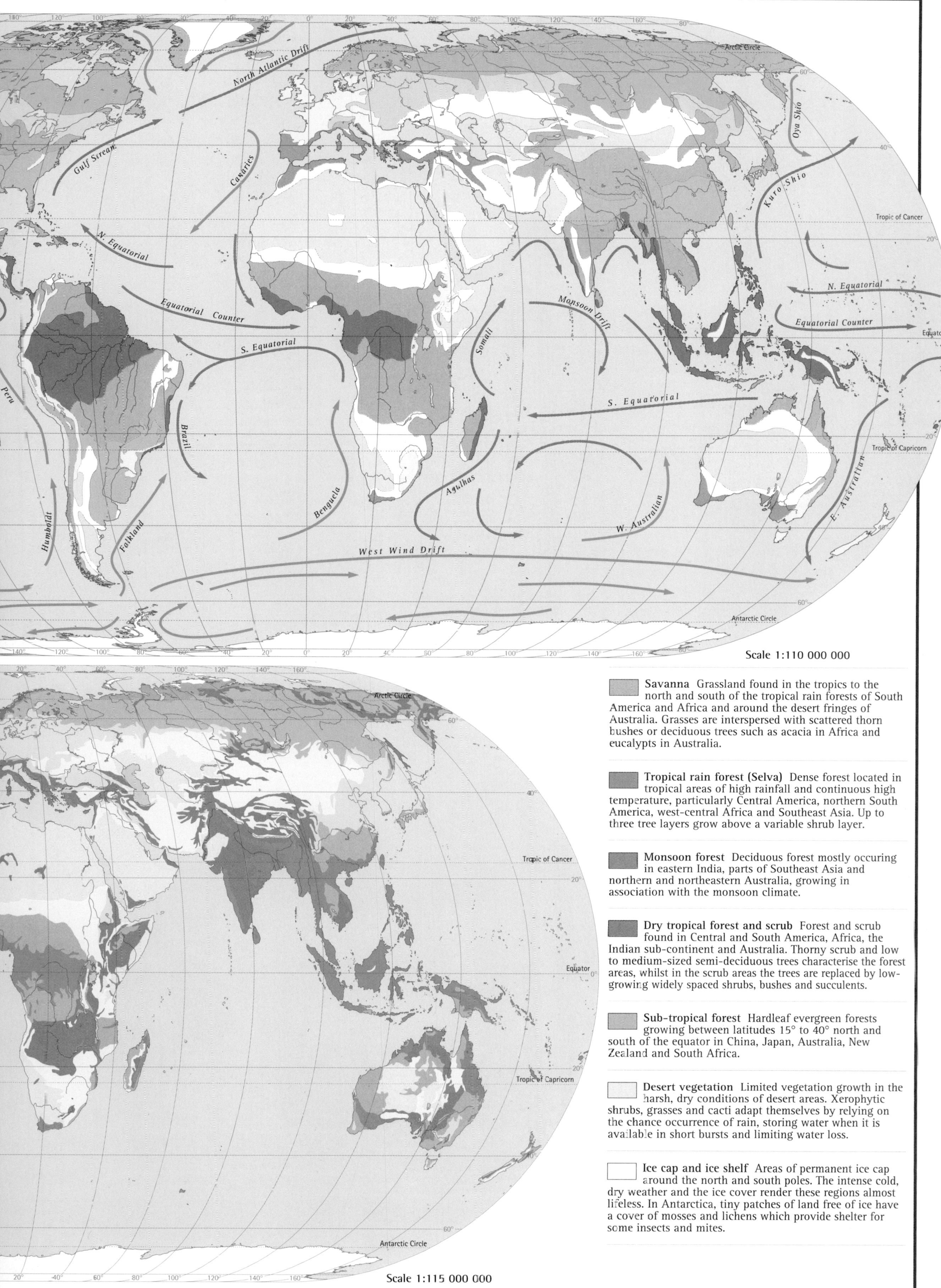

Savanna Grassland found in the tropics to the north and south of the tropical rain forests of South America and Africa and around the desert fringes of Australia. Grasses are interspersed with scattered thorn bushes or deciduous trees such as acacia in Africa and eucalypts in Australia.

Tropical rain forest (Selva) Dense forest located in tropical areas of high rainfall and continuous high temperature, particularly Central America, northern South America, west-central Africa and Southeast Asia. Up to three tree layers grow above a variable shrub layer.

Monsoon forest Deciduous forest mostly occuring in eastern India, parts of Southeast Asia and northern and northeastern Australia, growing in association with the monsoon climate.

Dry tropical forest and scrub Forest and scrub found in Central and South America, Africa, the Indian sub-continent and Australia. Thorny scrub and low to medium-sized semi-deciduous trees characterise the forest areas, whilst in the scrub areas the trees are replaced by low-growing widely spaced shrubs, bushes and succulents.

Sub-tropical forest Hardleaf evergreen forests growing between latitudes 15° to 40° north and south of the equator in China, Japan, Australia, New Zealand and South Africa.

Desert vegetation Limited vegetation growth in the harsh, dry conditions of desert areas. Xerophytic shrubs, grasses and cacti adapt themselves by relying on the chance occurrence of rain, storing water when it is available in short bursts and limiting water loss.

Ice cap and ice shelf Areas of permanent ice cap around the north and south poles. The intense cold, dry weather and the ice cover render these regions almost lifeless. In Antarctica, tiny patches of land free of ice have a cover of mosses and lichens which provide shelter for some insects and mites.

URBAN AGGLOMERATIONS

The populations given below are for selected urban agglomerations. These are defined as adjacent areas of settlement inhabited at urban levels of residential density, without regard to administrative boundaries.

Oceania
3,590,000 Sydney *Australia*
3,094,000 Melbourne *Australia*
1,450,000 Brisbane *Australia*
1,220,000 Perth *Australia*
1,039,000 Adelaide *Australia*
945,000 Auckland *New Zealand*

Asia
26,836,000 Tōkyō *Japan**
15,093,000 Bombay *India*
15,082,000 Shanghai *China*
12,362,000 Beijing *China*
11,673,000 Calcutta *India*
11,641,000 Seoul *S. Korea*
11,500,000 Jakarta *Indonesia*
10,687,000 Tianjin *China*
10,601,000 Ōsaka-Kōbe *Japan*
9,882,000 Delhi *India*
9,863,000 Karachi *Pakistan*
9,280,000 Manila-Quezon City *Philippines*
7,832,000 Dhaka *Bangladesh*
6,830,000 Tehrān *Iran*
6,566,000 Bangkok *Thailand*
5,906,000 Madras *India*
5,574,000 Hong Kong *China*
5,343,000 Hyderabad *India*
5,310,000 Shenyang *China*
5,085,000 Lahore *Pakistan*
4,749,000 Bangalore *India*
4,478,000 Baghdād *Iraq*
4,399,000 Wuhan *China*
4,082,000 Pusan *S. Korea*
4,056,000 Guangzhou *China*
3,851,000 Yangon *Myanmar*
3,688,000 Ahmadabad *India*
3,555,000 Hô Chi Minh *Vietnam*
3,525,000 Chongqing *China*
3,417,000 T'ai-pei *Taiwan*
3,401,000 Chengdu *China*
3,303,000 Harbin *China*
3,283,000 Xi'an *China*
3,196,000 Nagoya *Japan*
3,132,000 Dalian *China*
3,019,000 Jinan *China*
2,977,000 Bandung *Indonesia*
2,965,000 Nanjing *China*
2,940,000 Pune *India*
2,848,000 Singapore *Singapore*
2,826,000 Ankara *Turkey*
2,742,000 Surabaya *Indonesia*
2,704,000 Kita-Kyūshū *Japan*
2,576,000 Riyadh *Saudi Arabia*
2,523,000 Changchun *China*
2,502,000 Taiyuan *China*
2,470,000 P'yŏngyang *N. Korea*
2,432,000 Taegu *S. Korea*
2,356,000 Kanpur *India*
2,288,000 Tashkent *Uzbekistan*
2,222,000 Medan *Indonesia*
2,052,000 Damascus *Syria*
2,034,000 Kābul *Afghanistan*
2,031,000 İzmir *Turkey*
2,029,000 Lucknow *India*
2,011,000 Mashhad *Iran*
1,999,000 Zhengzhou *China*
1,942,000 Kunming *China*
1,921,000 Tel Aviv-Yafo *Israel*
1,875,000 Faisalabad *Pakistan*
1,855,000 Aleppo *Syria*
1,853,000 Baku *Azerbaijan*
1,792,000 Guiyang *China*
1,726,000 Kao-hsiung *Taiwan*
1,676,000 Peshawar *Pakistan*
1,643,000 Ürümqi *China*
1,581,000 Hangzhou *China*
1,563,000 Beirut *Lebanon*
1,498,000 Nanning *China*
1,469,000 Novosibirsk *Rus.Fed.*
1,353,000 T'bilisi *Georgia*
1,305,000 Yerevan *Armenia*
1,262,000 Almaty *Kazakstan*
1,247,000 Ha Nôi *Vietnam*
1,238,000 Kuala Lumpur *Malaysia*
1,187,000 'Ammān *Jordan*

Europe
9,469,000 Paris *France*
9,233,000 Moscow *Rus.Fed.*
7,817,000 İstanbul *Turkey*
7,335,000 London *U.K.*
6,481,000 Essen *Germany*
5,111,000 St Petersburg *Rus.Fed.*
4,251,000 Milan *Italy*
4,072,000 Madrid *Spain*
3,693,000 Athens *Greece*
3,606,000 Frankfurt am Main *Germany*
3,552,000 Katowice *Poland*
3,317,000 Berlin *Germany*
3,012,000 Naples *Italy*
2,984,000 Cologne *Germany*
2,931,000 Rome *Italy*
2,819,000 Barcelona *Spain*
2,809,000 Kiev *Ukraine*
2,625,000 Hamburg *Germany*
2,316,000 Warsaw *Poland*
2,302,000 Birmingham *U.K.*
2,277,000 Manchester *U.K.*
2,090,000 Bucharest *Romania*
2,060,000 Vienna *Austria*
2,017,000 Budapest *Hungary*
1,863,000 Lisbon *Portugal*
1,766,000 Minsk *Belarus*
1,680,000 Kharkiv *Ukraine*
1,545,000 Stockholm *Sweden*
1,454,000 Nizhniy Novgorod *Rus.Fed.*
1,413,000 Yekaterinburg *Rus.Fed.*
1,405,000 Belgrade *Yugoslavia*
1,384,000 Sofia *Bulgaria*
1,326,000 Copenhagen *Denmark*
1,311,000 Lyons *France*
1,230,000 Dnipropetrovs'k *Ukraine*
1,225,000 Prague *Czech Rep.*
1,109,000 Amsterdam *Netherlands*

Africa
10,287,000 Lagos *Nigeria*
9,656,000 Cairo *Egypt*
4,214,000 Kinshasa *Congo (Zaire)*
3,702,000 Algiers *Algeria*
3,577,000 Alexandria *Egypt*
3,289,000 Casablanca *Morocco*
3,272,000 Tripoli *Libya*
2,797,000 Abidjan *Côte d'Ivoire*
2,671,000 Cape Town *S. Africa*
2,429,000 Khartoum *Sudan*
2,227,000 Maputo *Mozambique*
2,209,000 Addis Ababa *Ethiopia*
2,207,000 Luanda *Angola*
2,079,000 Nairobi *Kenya*
2,037,000 Tunis *Tunisia*
1,986,000 Dakar *Senegal*
1,849,000 Johannesburg *S. Africa*
1,734,000 Dar es Salaam *Tanzania*
1,687,000 Accra *Ghana*
1,578,000 Rabat *Morocco*
1,322,000 Douala *Cameroon*
1,044,000 Harare *Zimbabwe*

North America
16,329,000 New York *U.S.A.*
15,643,000 México *Mexico*
12,410,000 Los Angeles *U.S.A.*
6,846,000 Chicago *U.S.A.*
4,483,000 Toronto *Canada*
4,304,000 Philadelphia *U.S.A.*
4,111,000 Washington D.C. *U.S.A.*
3,866,000 San Francisco *U.S.A.*
3,725,000 Detroit *U.S.A.*
3,612,000 Dallas *U.S.A.*
3,447,000 Miami-Fort Lauderdale *U.S.A.*
3,320,000 Montréal *Canada*
3,166,000 Houston *U.S.A.*
3,165,000 Guadalajara *Mexico*
2,842,000 Boston *U.S.A.*
2,806,000 Monterrey *Mexico*
2,716,000 San Diego *U.S.A.*
2,580,000 Santo Domingo *Dominican Republic*
2,464,000 Atlanta *U.S.A.*
2,353,000 Phoenix *U.S.A.*
2,241,000 Havana *Cuba*
2,239,000 Minneapolis *U.S.A.*
2,009,000 St Louis *U.S.A.*
1,969,000 Baltimore *U.S.A.*
1,939,000 Seattle *U.S.A.*
1,905,000 Tampa *U.S.A.*
1,823,000 Vancouver *Canada*
1,692,000 Cleveland *U.S.A.*
1,692,000 Pittsburg *U.S.A.*
1,682,000 Norfolk *U.S.A.*
1,611,000 Denver *U.S.A.*
1,266,000 Port-au-Prince *Haiti*
1,101,000 San Juan *Puerto Rico*
946,000 Guatemala *Guatemala*

South America
16,417,000 São Paulo *Brazil*
10,990,000 Buenos Aires *Argentina*
9,888,000 Rio de Janeiro *Brazil*
7,452,000 Lima *Peru*
5,614,000 Bogotá *Colombia*
5,065,000 Santiago *Chile*
3,899,000 Belo Horizonte *Brazil*
3,349,000 Porto Alegre *Brazil*
3,168,000 Recife *Brazil*
2,959,000 Caracas *Venezuela*
2,819,000 Salvador *Brazil*
2,660,000 Fortaleza *Brazil*
1,778,000 Brasília *Brazil*
1,769,000 Cali *Colombia*
1,717,000 Guayaquil *Ecuador*
1,607,000 Campinas *Brazil*
1,600,000 Maracaibo *Venezuela*
1,326,000 Montevideo *Uruguay*
1,294,000 Córdoba *Argentina*
1,246,000 La Paz *Bolivia*
1,244,000 Quito *Ecuador*

*includes Yokohama, Kawasaki, Chiba, and other adjacent towns and cities.

Source: United Nations. World urbanization prospects: the 1994 revision: estimates and projections of urban and rural populations and of urban agglomerations.

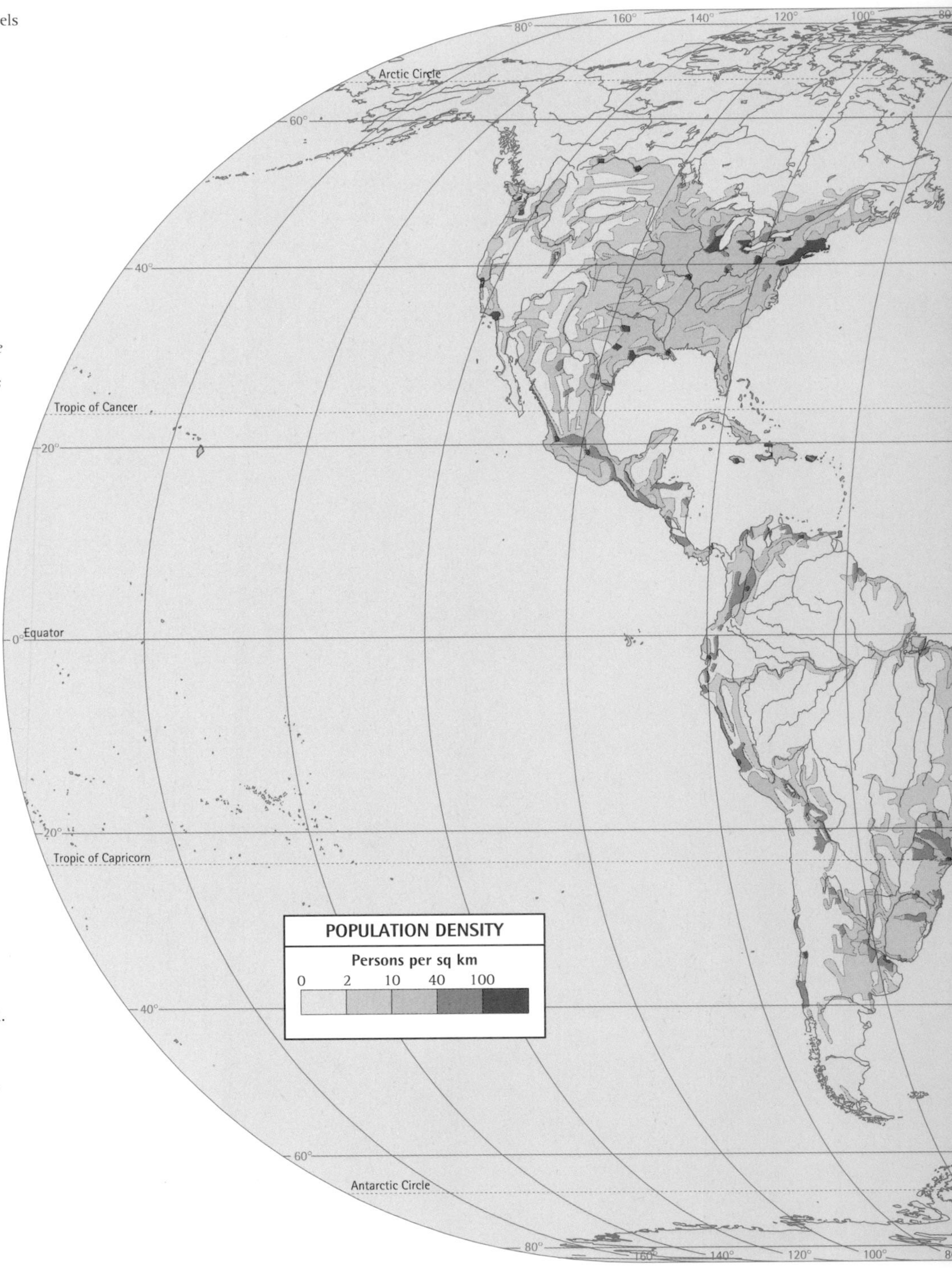

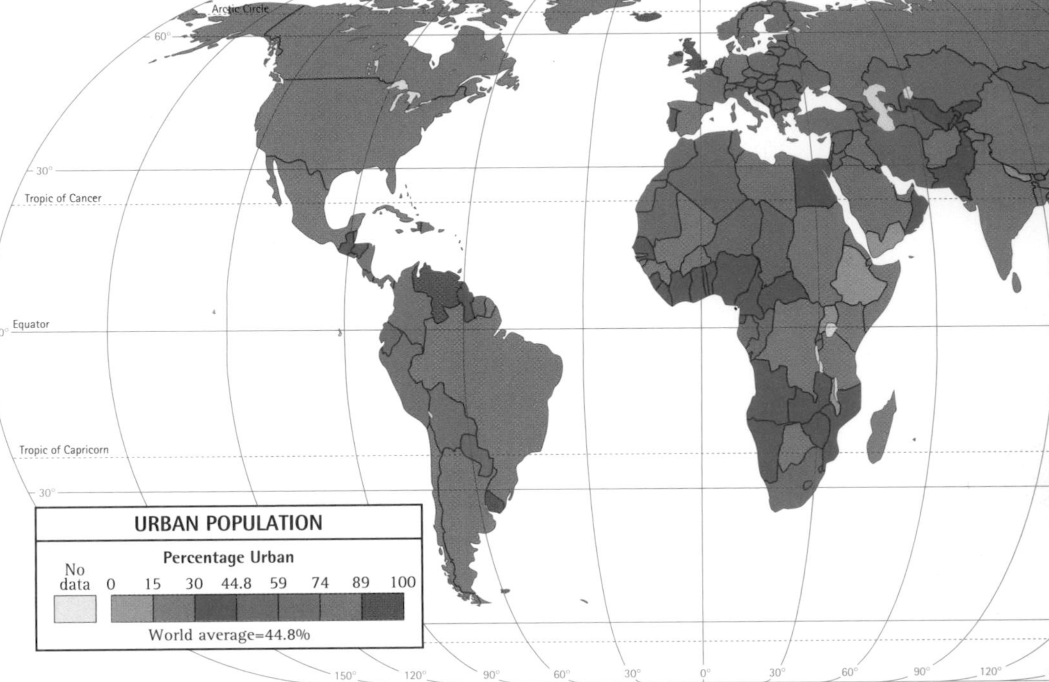

Scale 1:180 000 000

Eckert IV Projection

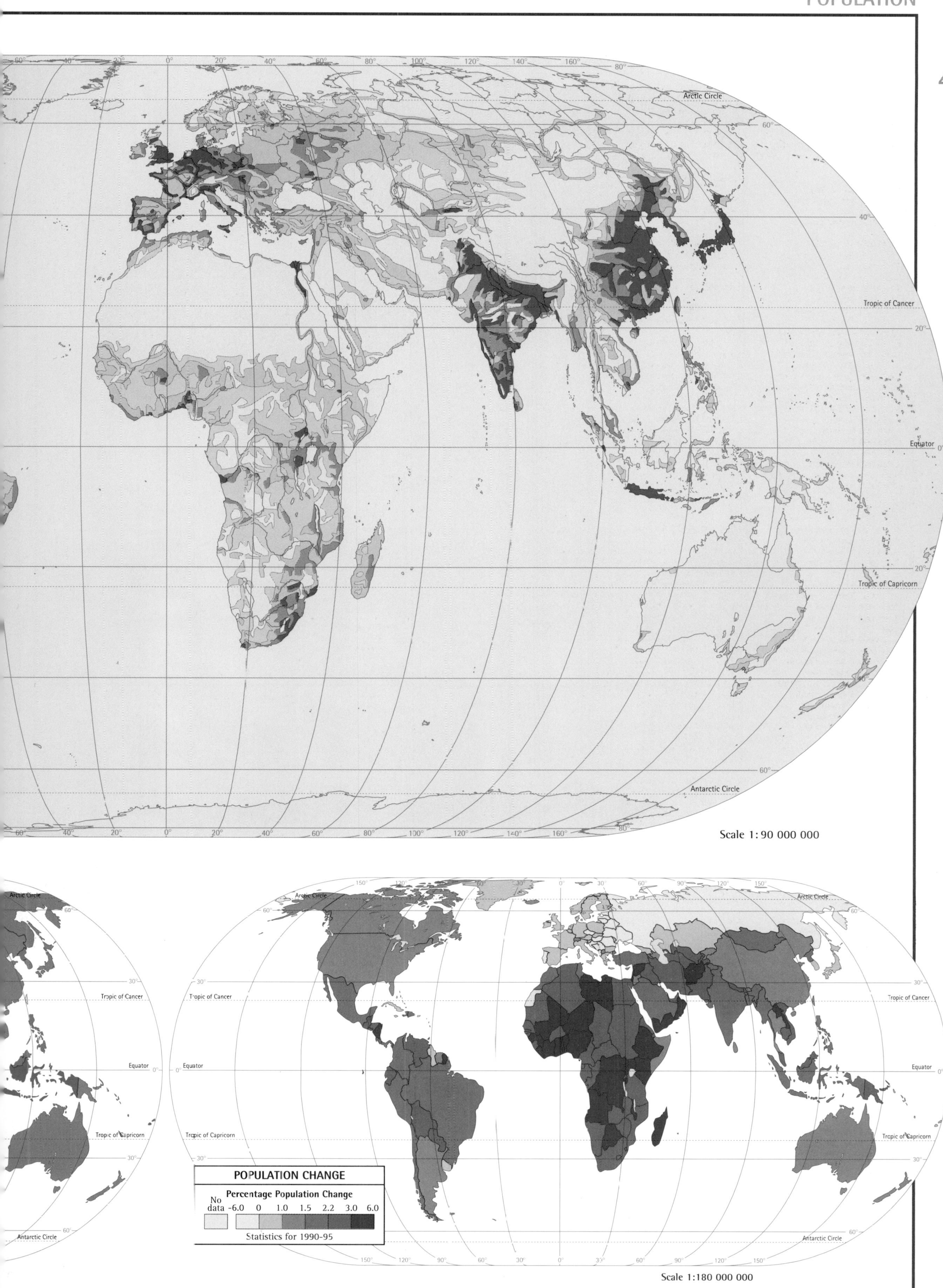
Arctic Circle
Tropic of Cancer
Equator
Tropic of Capricorn
Antarctic Circle
Scale 1: 90 000 000
POPULATION CHANGE
Percentage Population Change
No data
-6.0 0 1.0 1.5 2.2 3.0 6.0
Statistics for 1990-95
Scale 1:180 000 000

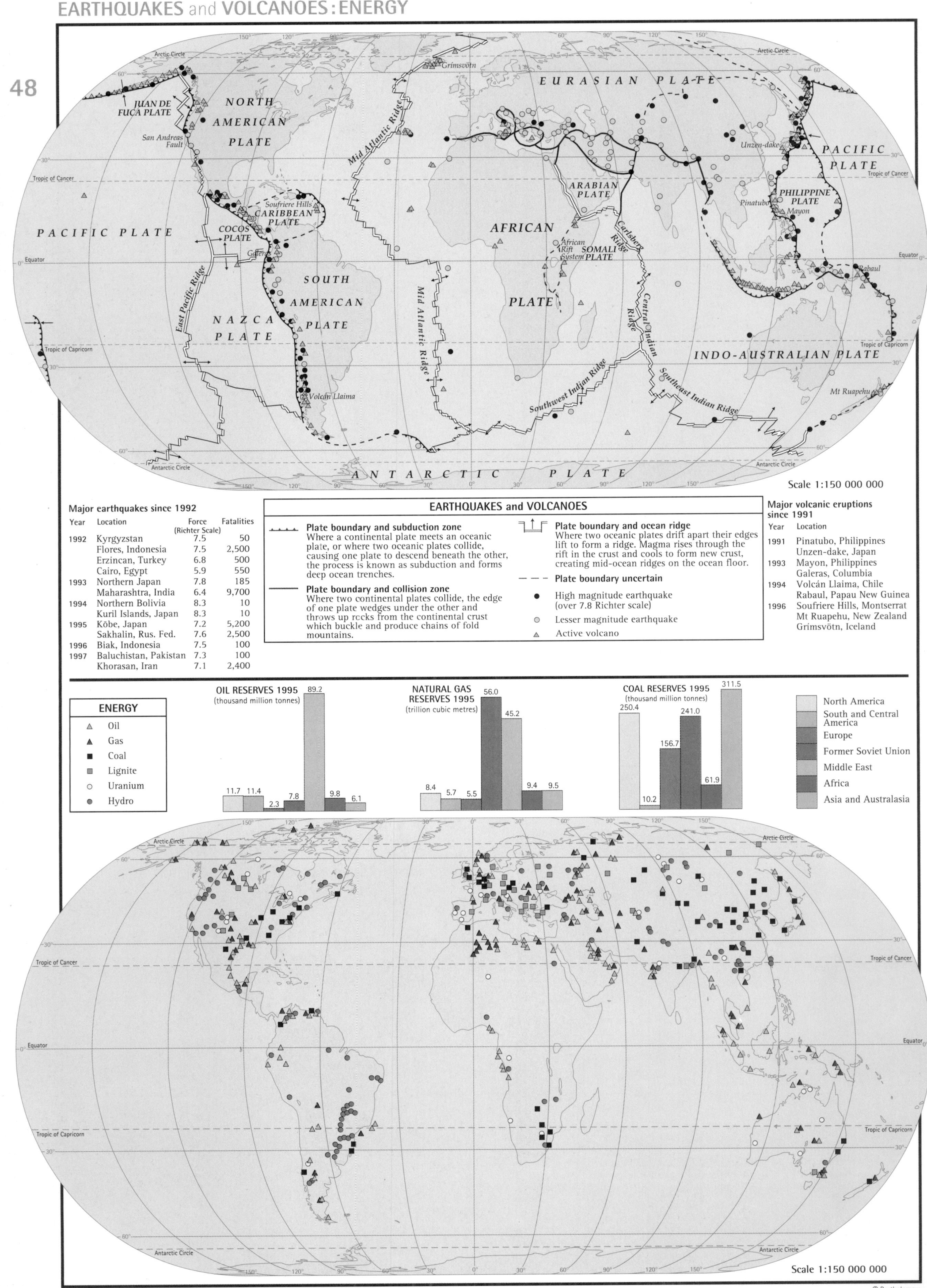

Major earthquakes since 1992

Year	Location	Force (Richter Scale)	Fatalities
1992	Kyrgyzstan	7.5	50
	Flores, Indonesia	7.5	2,500
	Erzincan, Turkey	6.8	500
	Cairo, Egypt	5.9	550
1993	Northern Japan	7.8	185
	Maharashtra, India	6.4	9,700
1994	Northern Bolivia	8.3	10
	Kuril Islands, Japan	8.3	10
1995	Kōbe, Japan	7.2	5,200
	Sakhalin, Rus. Fed.	7.6	2,500
1996	Biak, Indonesia	7.5	100
1997	Baluchistan, Pakistan	7.3	100
	Khorasan, Iran	7.1	2,400

Major volcanic eruptions since 1991

Year	Location
1991	Pinatubo, Philippines
	Unzen-dake, Japan
1993	Mayon, Philippines
	Galeras, Columbia
1994	Volcán Llaima, Chile
	Rabaul, Papau New Guinea
1996	Soufriere Hills, Montserrat
	Mt Ruapehu, New Zealand
	Grimsvötn, Iceland

Contents

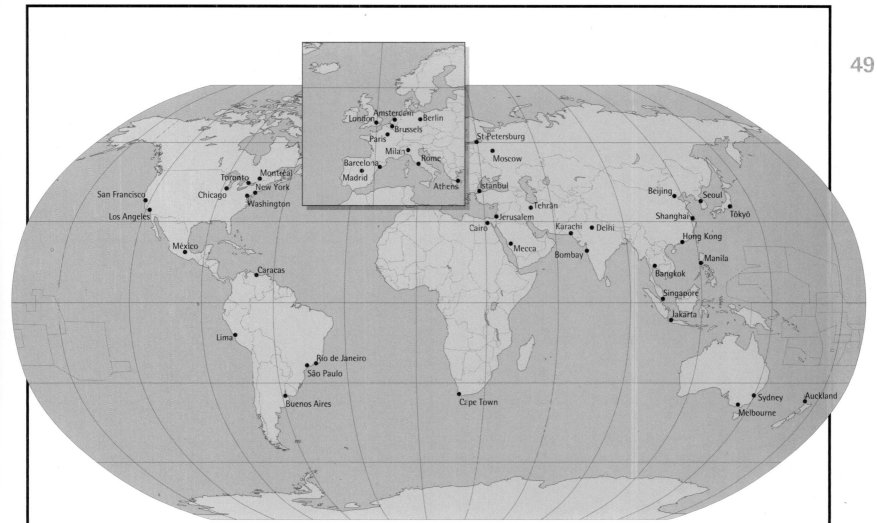

AMSTERDAM 55
ATHENS 55
AUCKLAND 50
BANGKOK 51
BARCELONA 60
BEIJING 51
BERLIN 55
BOMBAY 54
BRUSSELS 55
BUENOS AIRES 64
CAIRO 60
CAPE TOWN 60
CARACAS 64
CHICAGO 61
DELHI 54
HONG KONG 51
İSTANBUL 54
JAKARTA 50
JERUSALEM 54
KARACHI 51
LIMA 64
LONDON 56-57
LOS ANGELES 61
MADRID 60
MANILA 50
MECCA 54
MELBOURNE 50
MÉXICO 64
MILAN 60
MONTRÉAL 61
MOSCOW 55
NEW YORK 62-63
PARIS 58-59
RIO DE JANEIRO 64
ROME 60
ST PETERSBURG 55
SAN FRANCISCO 61
SÃO PAULO 64
SEOUL 51
SHANGHAI 51
SINGAPORE 50
SYDNEY 50
TEHRĀN 54
TŌKYŌ 52-53
TORONTO 61
WASHINGTON 61

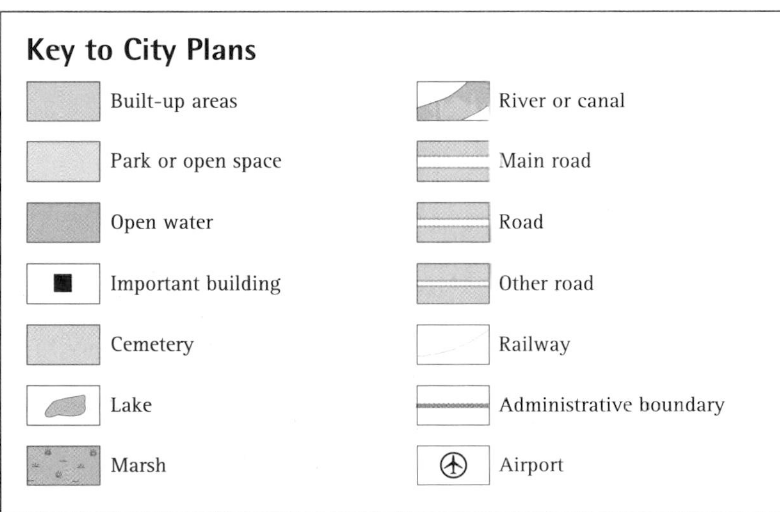

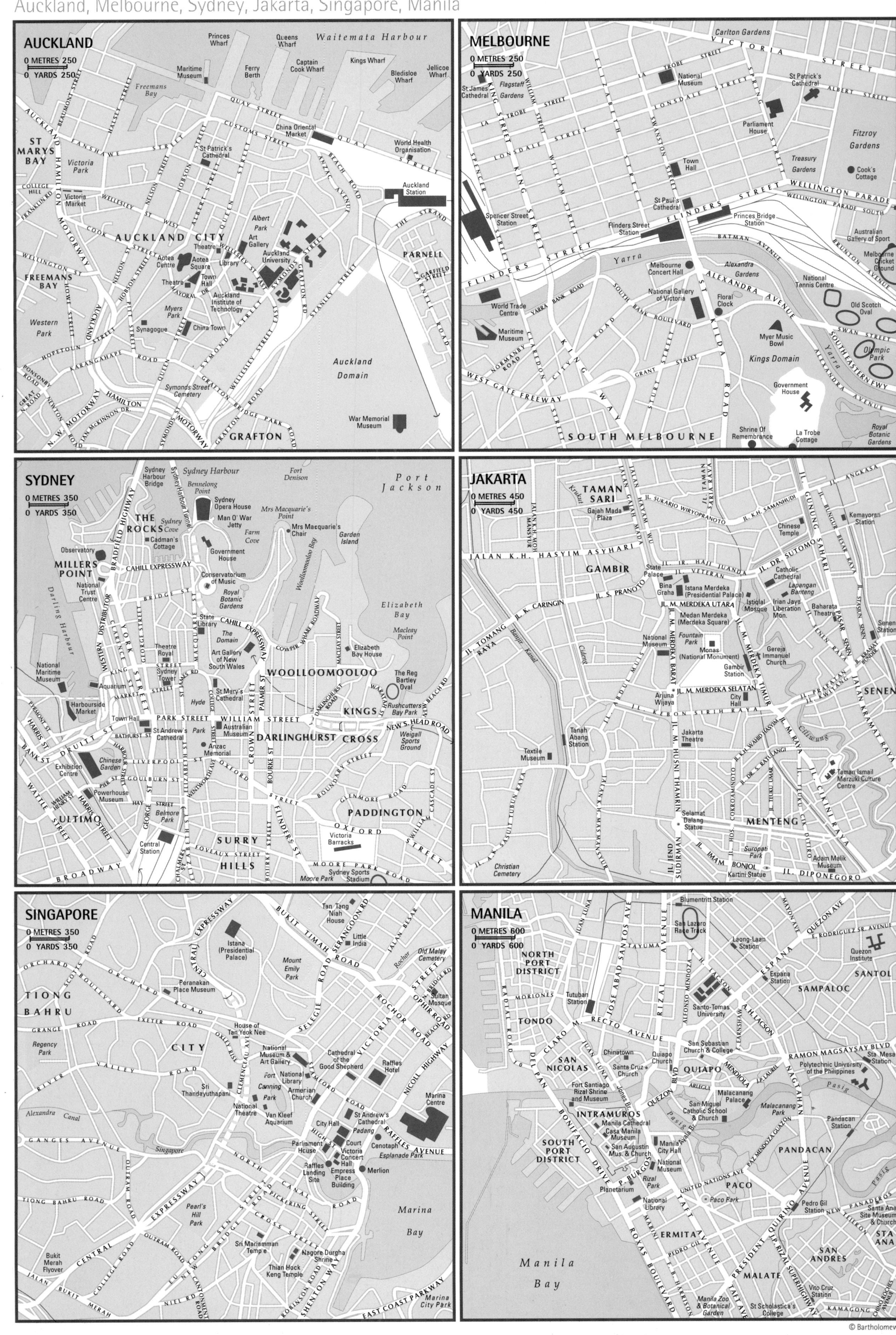
AUCKLAND
0 METRES 250
0 YARDS 250
Waitemata Harbour
Princes Wharf
Queens Wharf
Captain Cook Wharf
Kings Wharf
Ferry Berth
Maritime Museum
Bledisloe Wharf
Jellicoe Wharf
Freemans Bay
QUAY STREET
CUSTOMS STREET
China Oriental Market
World Health Organisation
ST MARYS BAY
Victoria Park
St Patrick's Cathedral
Auckland Station
COLLEGE HILL
Victoria Market
AUCKLAND CITY
Albert Park
Art Gallery
Auckland University
Theatre
Aotea Centre
Aotea Square
Library
Town Hall
Auckland Institute of Technology
PARNELL
FREEMANS BAY
Western Park
Myers Park
Synagogue
China Town
Auckland Domain
Symonds Street Cemetery
War Memorial Museum
GRAFTON
MELBOURNE
0 METRES 250
0 YARDS 250
Carlton Gardens
VICTORIA STREET
National Museum
St Patrick's Cathedral
Flagstaff Gardens
St James' Cathedral
LA TROBE STREET
LONSDALE STREET
Parliament House
Fitzroy Gardens
Treasury Gardens
Cook's Cottage
Town Hall
WELLINGTON PARADE
St Paul's Cathedral
Spencer Street Station
Flinders Street Station
Princes Bridge Station
FLINDERS STREET
Australian Gallery of Sport
Yarra
Melbourne Concert Hall
Alexandra Gardens
Melbourne Cricket Ground
National Gallery of Victoria
Floral Clock
ALEXANDRA AVENUE
National Tennis Centre
World Trade Centre
Maritime Museum
Old Scotch Oval
Myer Music Bowl
Kings Domain
Olympic Park
WEST GATE FREEWAY
Government House
Shrine Of Remembrance
La Trobe Cottage
Royal Botanic Gardens
SOUTH MELBOURNE
SYDNEY
0 METRES 350
0 YARDS 350
Sydney Harbour
Sydney Harbour Bridge
Sydney Harbour Tunnel
Bennelong Point
Fort Denison
Port Jackson
Sydney Opera House
Man O' War Jetty
Mrs Macquarie's Point
Mrs Macquarie's Chair
Garden Island
Farm Cove
THE ROCKS
Sydney Cove
Cadman's Cottage
Observatory
MILLERS POINT
CAHILL EXPRESSWAY
Government House
Conservatorium of Music
Woolloomooloo Bay
Royal Botanic Gardens
National Trust Centre
Darling Harbour
Elizabeth Bay
Macleay Point
State Library
The Domain
Art Gallery of New South Wales
Elizabeth Bay House
Theatre Royal
Sydney Tower
National Maritime Museum
Aquarium
WOOLLOOMOOLOO
The Reg Bartley Oval
St Mary's Cathedral
Hyde Park
Harbourside Market
KINGS CROSS
Rushcutters Bay Park
Town Hall
PARK STREET
WILLIAM STREET
St Andrew's Cathedral
Australian Museum
DARLINGHURST
NEW S. HEAD ROAD
Weigall Sports Ground
Anzac Memorial
Exhibition Centre
Chinese Garden
Powerhouse Museum
ULTIMO
Belmore Park
PADDINGTON
Central Station
SURRY HILLS
Victoria Barracks
BROADWAY
Moore Park
Sydney Sports Stadium
JAKARTA
0 METRES 450
0 YARDS 450
TAMAN SARI
Gajah Mada Plaza
Kemayoran Station
Chinese Temple
JALAN K.H. HASYIM ASYHARI
GAMBIR
State Palace
Catholic Cathedral
Lapangan Banteng
Bina Graha
Istana Merdeka (Presidential Palace)
Istiqlal Mosque
Irian Jaya Liberation Mon.
Baharata Theatre
JL. M. MERDEKA UTARA
Medan Merdeka (Merdeka Square)
Senen Station
National Museum
Fountain Park
Monas (National Monument)
Gereja Immanuel Church
Gambir Station
JL. M. MERDEKA SELATAN
Arjuna Wijaya
City Hall
SENEN
Tanah Abang Station
Jakarta Theatre
Textile Museum
Taman Ismail Marzuki Culture Centre
Selamat Datang Statue
MENTENG
Suropati Park
Adam Malik Museum
Christian Cemetery
Kartini Statue
JL. DIPONEGORO
SINGAPORE
0 METRES 350
0 YARDS 350
Tan Tang Niah House
Istana (Presidential Palace)
Little India
Mount Emily Park
Old Malay Cemetery
TIONG BAHRU
Peranakan Place Museum
Sultan Mosque
House of Tan Yeok Nee
Regency Park
CITY
National Museum & Art Gallery
Cathedral of the Good Shepherd
Raffles Hotel
Fort Canning Park
National Library
Armenian Church
Sri Thandayuthapani
Alexandra Canal
National Theatre
Van Kleef Aquarium
St Andrew's Cathedral
Marina Centre
City Hall
Padang
RAFFLES AVENUE
Parliament House
Court
Cenotaph
Victoria Concert Hall
Esplanade Park
Raffles Landing Site
Empress Place Building
Merlion
Singapore
Pearl's Hill Park
Marina Bay
Sri Mariamman Temple
Nagore Durgha Shrine
Bukit Merah Flyover
Thian Hock Keng Temple
EAST COAST PARKWAY
Marina City Park
MANILA
0 METRES 600
0 YARDS 600
Blumentritt Station
San Lazaro Race Track
Laong-Laan Station
Quezon Institute
NORTH PORT DISTRICT
SANTOL
España Station
SAMPALOC
Tutuban Station
Santo-Tomas University
TONDO
RECTO AVENUE
San Sebastian Church & College
RAMON MAGSAYSAY BLVD
Sta. Mesa Station
SAN NICOLAS
Chinatown
Quiapo Church
QUIAPO
Polytechnic University of the Philippines
Santa Cruz Church
Fort Santiago Rizal Shrine and Museum
Malacanang Palace
Malacanang Park
San Miguel Catholic School & Church
Pasig
INTRAMUROS
Manila Cathedral
Casa Manila Museum
San Augustin Mus. & Church
Manila City Hall
Pandacan Station
SOUTH PORT DISTRICT
PANDACAN
National Museum
Rizal Park
Planetarium
PACO
Paco Park
National Library
Pedro Gil Station
Santa Ana Site Museum & Church
STA ANA
ERMITA
SAN ANDRES
Manila Bay
MALATE
Vito Cruz Station
Manila Zoo & Botanical Garden
St Scholastica's College

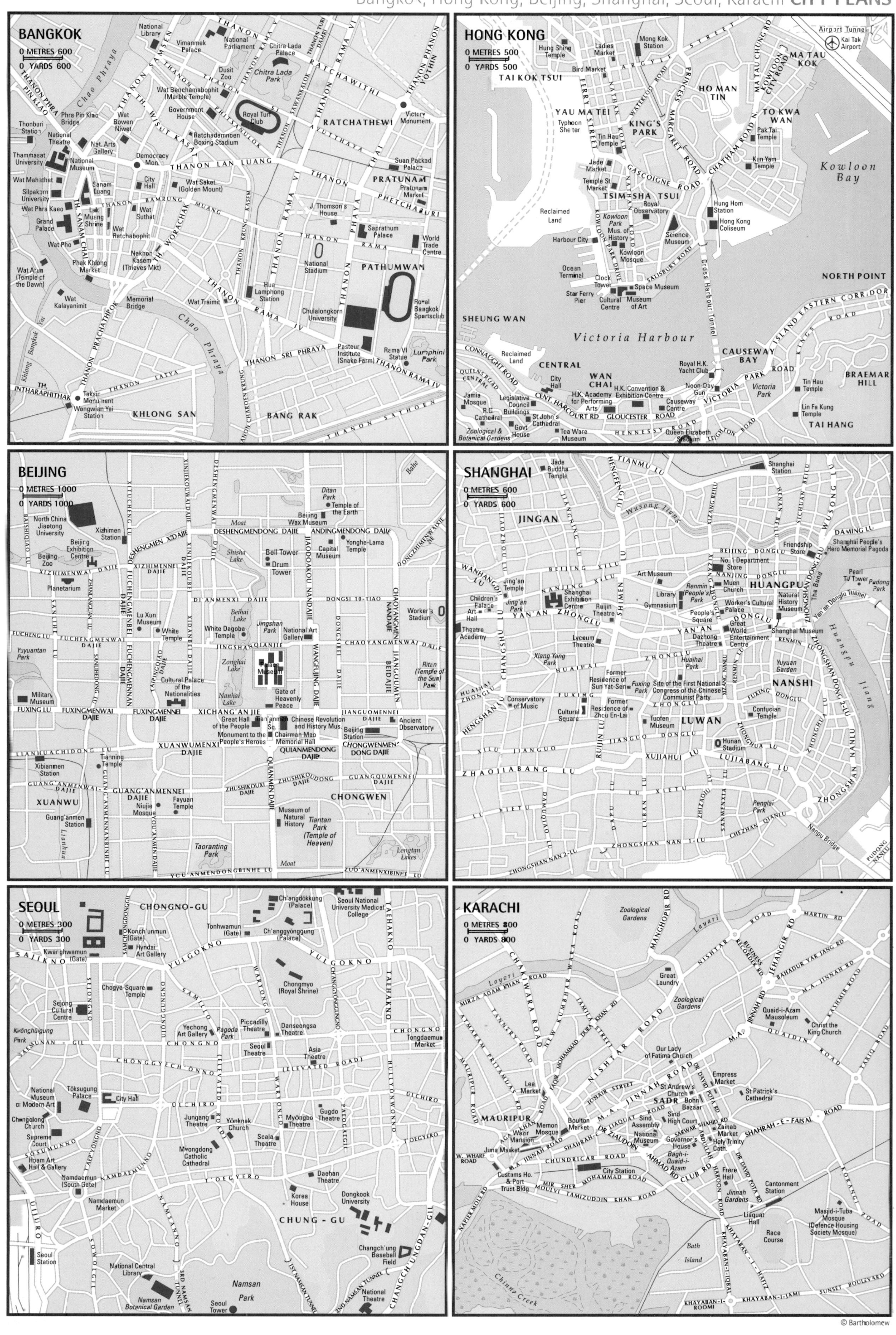
BANGKOK
0 METRES 600
0 YARDS 600
Chao Phraya
RATCHATHEWI
PRATUNAM
PATHUMWAN
KHLONG SAN
BANG RAK
Grand Palace
Wat Pho
National Museum
Democracy Mon.
Chulalongkorn University
Lumphini Park
Victory Monument
HONG KONG
0 METRES 500
0 YARDS 500
TAI KOK TSUI
YAU MA TEI
HO MAN TIN
TO KWA WAN
MA TAU KOK
Kowloon Bay
TSIM SHA TSUI
NORTH POINT
Victoria Harbour
SHEUNG WAN
CENTRAL
WAN CHAI
CAUSEWAY BAY
BRAEMAR HILL
TAI HANG
Kai Tak Airport
BEIJING
0 METRES 1000
0 YARDS 1000
XUANWU
CHONGWEN
Imperial Museum
Tian'anmen Sq.
Beihai Lake
Zhonghai Lake
Nanhai Lake
Tiantan Park (Temple of Heaven)
Beijing Station
SHANGHAI
0 METRES 600
0 YARDS 600
JINGAN
HUANGPU
NANSHI
LUWAN
Wusong Jiang
Huangpu Jiang
The Bund
Shanghai Station
SEOUL
0 METRES 300
0 YARDS 300
CHONGNO-GU
CHUNG-GU
Namsan Park
Seoul Station
Seoul Tower
City Hall
KARACHI
0 METRES 800
0 YARDS 800
Zoological Gardens
SADR
MAURIPUR
City Station
Chinna Creek
Bath Island
© Bartholomew

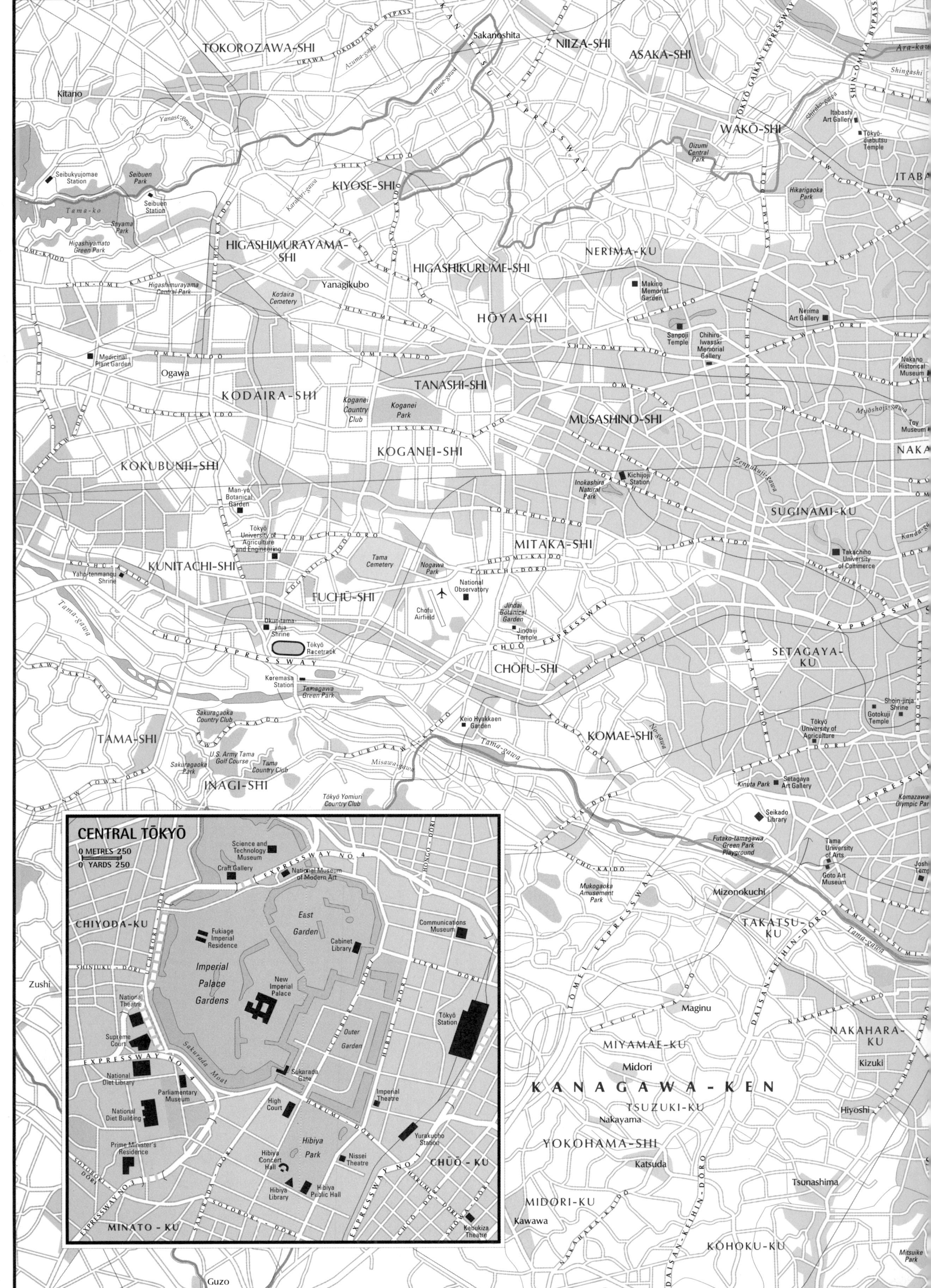
TOKOROZAWA-SHI
NIIZA-SHI
ASAKA-SHI
Kitano
WAKŌ-SHI
KIYOSE-SHI
HIGASHIMURAYAMA-SHI
NERIMA-KU
HIGASHIKURUME-SHI
Yanagikubo
HŌYA-SHI
Ogawa
KODAIRA-SHI
TANASHI-SHI
MUSASHINO-SHI
KOGANEI-SHI
KOKUBUNJI-SHI
SUGINAMI-KU
MITAKA-SHI
KUNITACHI-SHI
FUCHŪ-SHI
SETAGAYA-KU
CHŌFU-SHI
TAMA-SHI
KOMAE-SHI
INAGI-SHI
TAKATSU-KU
MIYAMAE-KU
NAKAHARA-KU
KANAGAWA-KEN
TSUZUKI-KU
YOKOHAMA-SHI
MIDORI-KU
KŌHOKU-KU
Zushi
Guzo
Mizonokuchi
Maginu
Midori
Nakayama
Katsuda
Kawawa
Tsunashima
Hiyoshi
Kizuki
CENTRAL TŌKYŌ
0 METRES 250
0 YARDS 250
CHIYODA-KU
Imperial Palace Gardens
East Garden
Outer Garden
Hibiya Park
Tōkyō Station
CHŪŌ-KU
MINATO-KU

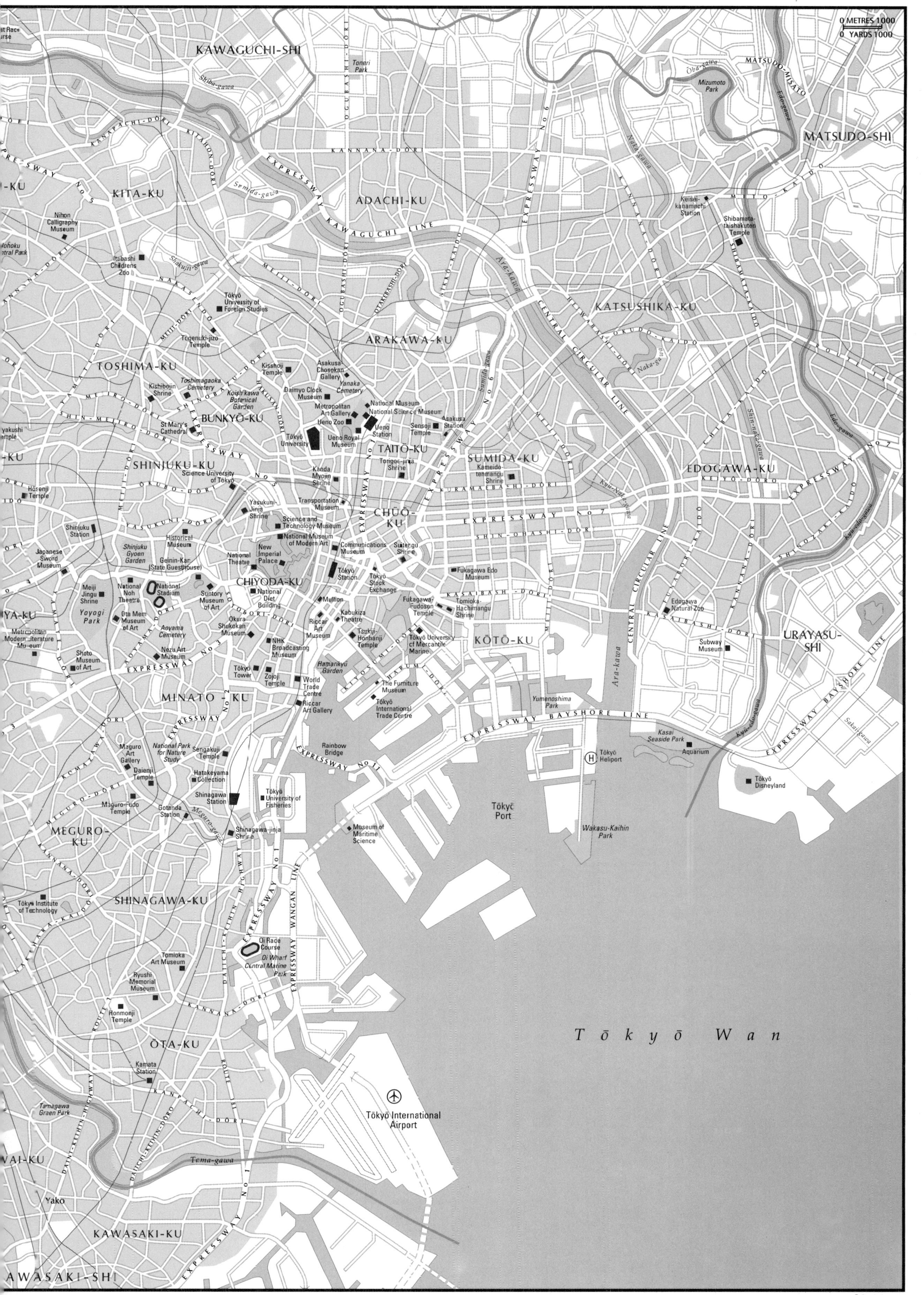
KAWAGUCHI-SHI
MATSUDO-SHI
KITA-KU
ADACHI-KU
KATSUSHIKA-KU
ARAKAWA-KU
TOSHIMA-KU
BUNKYŌ-KU
TAITŌ-KU
SUMIDA-KU
SHINJUKU-KU
EDOGAWA-KU
CHŪŌ-KU
CHIYODA-KU
KŌTŌ-KU
URAYASU-SHI
MINATO-KU
MEGURO-KU
SHINAGAWA-KU
ŌTA-KU
KAWASAKI-KU
Tōkyō Wan
Tōkyō Port
Tōkyō International Airport
Tōkyō Disneyland
Ueno Station
Shinjuku Station
Shinagawa Station
National Museum
National Science Museum
Ueno Zoo
Imperial Palace
Tōkyō Tower
Rainbow Bridge
Tōkyō Heliport
Tōkyō Stock Exchange
Meiji Jingu Shrine
Yoyogi Park
Shinjuku Gyoen Garden
Sensoji Temple
Hamarikyu Garden
Oi Race Course
Kasai Seaside Park
Aquarium
Yumenoshima Park
Wakasu-Kaihin Park
Museum of Maritime Science
EXPRESSWAY BAYSHORE LINE
CENTRAL CIRCULAR LINE
Ara-kawa
Sumida-gawa
Tama-gawa
0 METRES 1000
0 YARDS 1000

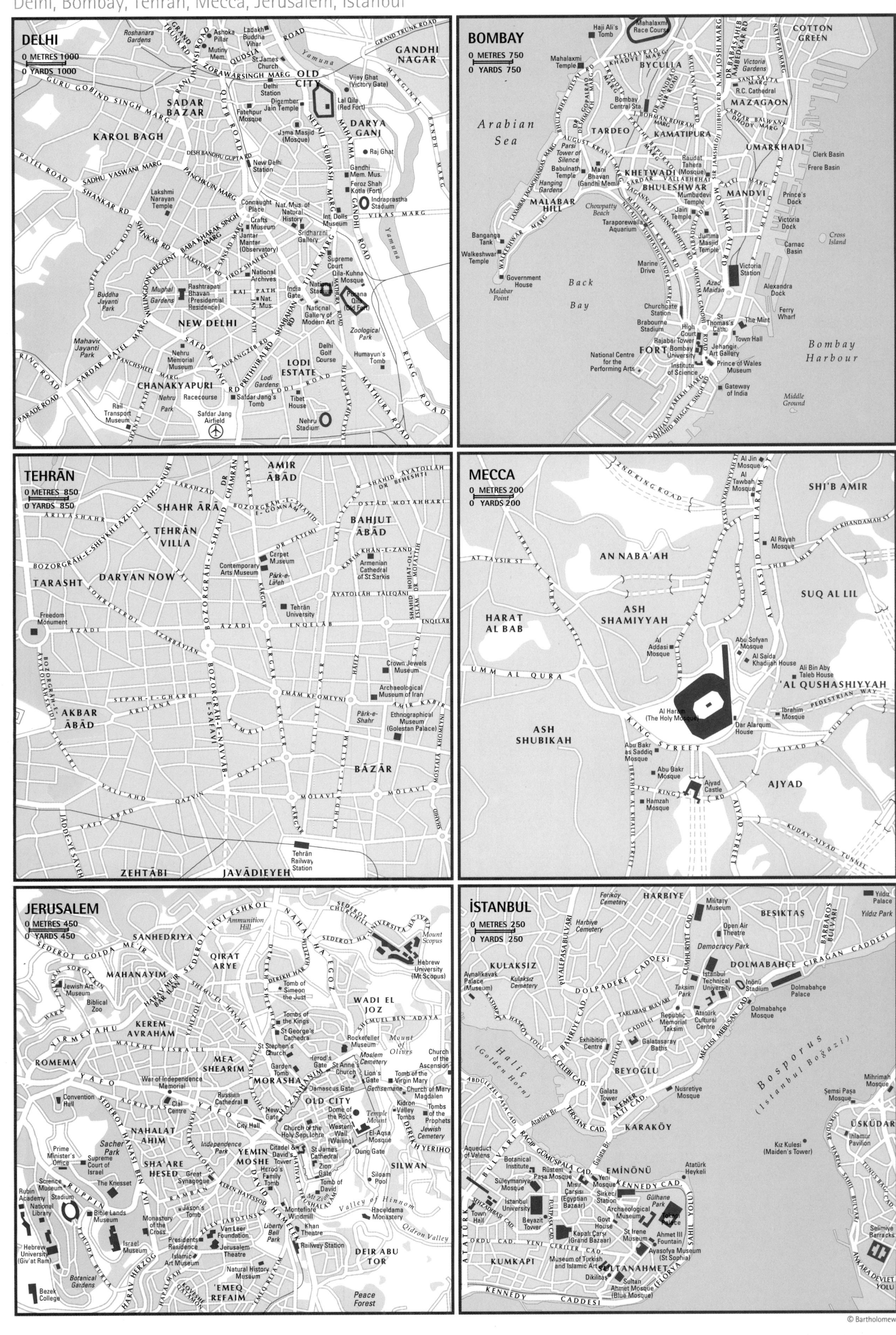
DELHI
0 METRES 1000
0 YARDS 1000
SADAR BAZAR
KAROL BAGH
OLD CITY
DARYA GANJ
GANDHI NAGAR
NEW DELHI
CHANAKYAPURI
LODI ESTATE
Roshanara Gardens
Ashoka Pillar
Ladakh Buddha Vihar
Mutiny Mem.
St James Church
Delhi Station
Digember Jain Temple
Fatehpur Mosque
Lal Qila (Red Fort)
Vijay Ghat (Victory Gate)
Jama Masjid (Mosque)
Raj Ghat
New Delhi Station
Gandhi Mem. Mus.
Feroz Shah Kotla (Fort)
Indraprastha Stadium
Lakshmi Narayan Temple
Connaught Place
Nat. Mus. of Natural History
Crafts Museum
Jantar Mantar (Observatory)
Sridharani Gallery
Int. Dolls Museum
Supreme Court
Qila-Kuhna Mosque
National Archives
Rashtrapati Bhavan (Presidential Residence)
Mughal Gardens
Buddha Jayanti Park
India Gate
Nat. Mus.
National Stadium
Purana Qila (Old Fort)
National Gallery of Modern Art
Zoological Park
Mahavir Jayanti Park
Nehru Memorial Museum
Delhi Golf Course
Humayun's Tomb
Lodi Gardens
Nehru Park
Racecourse
Safdar Jang's Tomb
Tibet House
Rail Transport Museum
Safdar Jang Airfield
Nehru Stadium
Yamuna
GRAND TRUNK ROAD
RING ROAD
MATHURA ROAD
BOMBAY
0 METRES 750
0 YARDS 750
Arabian Sea
Back Bay
Bombay Harbour
COTTON GREEN
BYCULLA
MAZAGAON
TARDEO
KAMATIPURA
UMARKHADI
KHETWADI
BHULESHWAR
MANDVI
MALABAR HILL
FORT
Haji Ali's Tomb
Mahalaxmi Race Course
Mahalaxmi Temple
Victoria Gardens
R.C. Cathedral
Bombay Central Sta.
Parsi Tower of Silence
Babulnath Temple
Hanging Gardens
Mani Bhavan (Gandhi Mem.)
Chowpatty Beach
Taraporewalla Aquarium
Raudat Tahera (Mosque)
Mumbadevi Temple
Jain Temple
Jumma Masjid
Banganga Tank
Walkeshwar Temple
Government House
Malabar Point
Marine Drive
Victoria Station
Azad Maidan
Churchgate Station
Brabourne Stadium
High Court
St Thomas's Cath.
The Mint
Town Hall
Rajabai Tower
Bombay University
Jehangir Art Gallery
National Centre for the Performing Arts
Institute of Science
Prince of Wales Museum
Gateway of India
Clerk Basin
Frere Basin
Prince's Dock
Victoria Dock
Carnac Basin
Cross Island
Alexandra Dock
Ferry Wharf
Middle Ground
TEHRĀN
0 METRES 850
0 YARDS 850
AMIR ĀBĀD
SHAHR ĀRĀ
TEHRĀN VILLA
BAHJUT ĀBĀD
TARASHT
DARYAN NOW
AKBAR ĀBĀD
BĀZĀR
ZEHTĀBI
JAVĀDIEYEH
Carpet Museum
Contemporary Arts Museum
Pārk-e-Lāleh
Armenian Cathedral of St Sarkis
Tehrān University
Freedom Monument
Crown Jewels Museum
Archaeological Museum of Iran
Pārk-e-Shahr
Ethnographical Museum (Golestan Palace)
Tehrān Railway Station
ĀZĀDI
ENQELĀB
MECCA
0 METRES 200
0 YARDS 200
AN NABA'AH
SHI'B AMIR
SUQ AL LIL
HARAT AL BAB
ASH SHAMIYYAH
'AL QUSHASHIYYAH
ASH SHUBIKAH
AJYAD
Al Jin Mosque
Al Tawbah Mosque
Al Rayah Mosque
Al Addasi Mosque
Abu Sofyan Mosque
Al Saida Khadijah House
Ali Bin Aby Taleb House
Al Haram (The Holy Mosque)
Dar Alarqum House
Ibrahim Mosque
Abu Bakr as Saddiq Mosque
Abu Bakr Mosque
Ajyad Castle
Hamzah Mosque
UMM AL QURA
KING STREET
JERUSALEM
0 METRES 450
0 YARDS 450
SANHEDRIYA
QIRAT ARYE
MAHANAYIM
KEREM AVRAHAM
ROMEMA
MEA SHEARIM
MORASHA
WADI EL JOZ
OLD CITY
NAHALAT AHIM
SHA'ARE HESED
YEMIN MOSHE
SILWAN
DEIR ABU TOR
'EMEQ REFAIM
Ammunition Hill
Mount Scopus
Hebrew University (Mt Scopus)
Jewish Art Museum
Biblical Zoo
Tomb of Simeon the Just
Tombs of the Kings
St George's Cathedral
Rockefeller Museum
Mount of Olives
Church of the Ascension
St Stephen's Church
Herod's Gate
St Anne's Church
Garden Tomb
Lion's Gate
Moslem Cemetery
Tomb of the Virgin Mary
Gethsemane
Church of Mary Magdalen
War of Independence Memorial
Convention Hall
Clal Centre
Russian Cathedral
Damascus Gate
Dome of the Rock
Temple Mount
New Gate
City Hall
Church of the Holy Sepulchre
Western Wall (Wailing)
El-Aqsa Mosque
Kidron Valley Tombs
Tombs of the Prophets
Jewish Cemetery
Dung Gate
Sacher Park
Independence Park
Citadel & David's Tower
St James Cathedral
Prime Minister's Office
Supreme Court of Israel
Great Synagogue
Zion Gate
Siloam Pool
Herod's Family Tomb
Tomb of David
Mt Zion
Science Museum
Rubin Academy
Stadium
The Knesset
National Library
Bible Lands Museum
Jason's Tomb
Monastery of the Cross
Montefiore Windmill
Haceldama Monastery
Van Leer Foundation
Liberty Bell Park
Khan Theatre
Railway Station
Hebrew University (Giv'at Ram)
Israel Museum
President's Residence
Jerusalem Theatre
Islamic Art Museum
Natural History Museum
Botanical Gardens
Bezek College
Peace Forest
Valley of Hinnom
Qidron Valley
İSTANBUL
0 METRES 250
0 YARDS 250
HARBIYE
BEŞIKTAŞ
KULAKSIZ
DOLMABAHÇE
BEYOĞLU
KARAKÖY
EMİNÖNÜ
KUMKAPI
SULTANAHMET
ÜSKÜDAR
Feriköy Cemetery
Harbiye Cemetery
Military Museum
Open Air Theatre
Democracy Park
Yıldız Palace
Yıldız Park
Aynalıkavak Palace (Museum)
Kulaksız Cemetery
İstanbul Technical University
İnönü Stadium
Dolmabahçe Palace
Dolmabahçe Mosque
Taksim Park
Republic Memorial Taksim
Atatürk Cultural Centre
Exhibition Centre
Galatasaray Baths
Haliç (Golden Horn)
Bosporus (İstanbul Boğazi)
Galata Tower
Nusretiye Mosque
Mihrimah Mosque
Şemsi Paşa Mosque
Ihlamur Pavilion
Kız Kulesi (Maiden's Tower)
Aqueduct of Valens
Botanical Institute
Süleymaniye Mosque
Rüstem Paşa Mosque
Yeni Mosque
Mısır Çarşısı (Egyptian Bazaar)
Sirkeci Station
Atatürk Heykeli
Gülhane Park
İstanbul University
Beyazit Tower
Archaeological Museum
Topkapı Palace
Town Hall
Kapalı Çarşı (Grand Bazaar)
Govt House
St Irene Museum
Ahmet III Fountain
Ayasofya Museum (St Sophia)
Museum of Turkish and Islamic Art
Dikilitaş
Sultan Ahmet Mosque (Blue Mosque)
Selimiye Barracks
KENNEDY CADDESİ
© Bartholomew

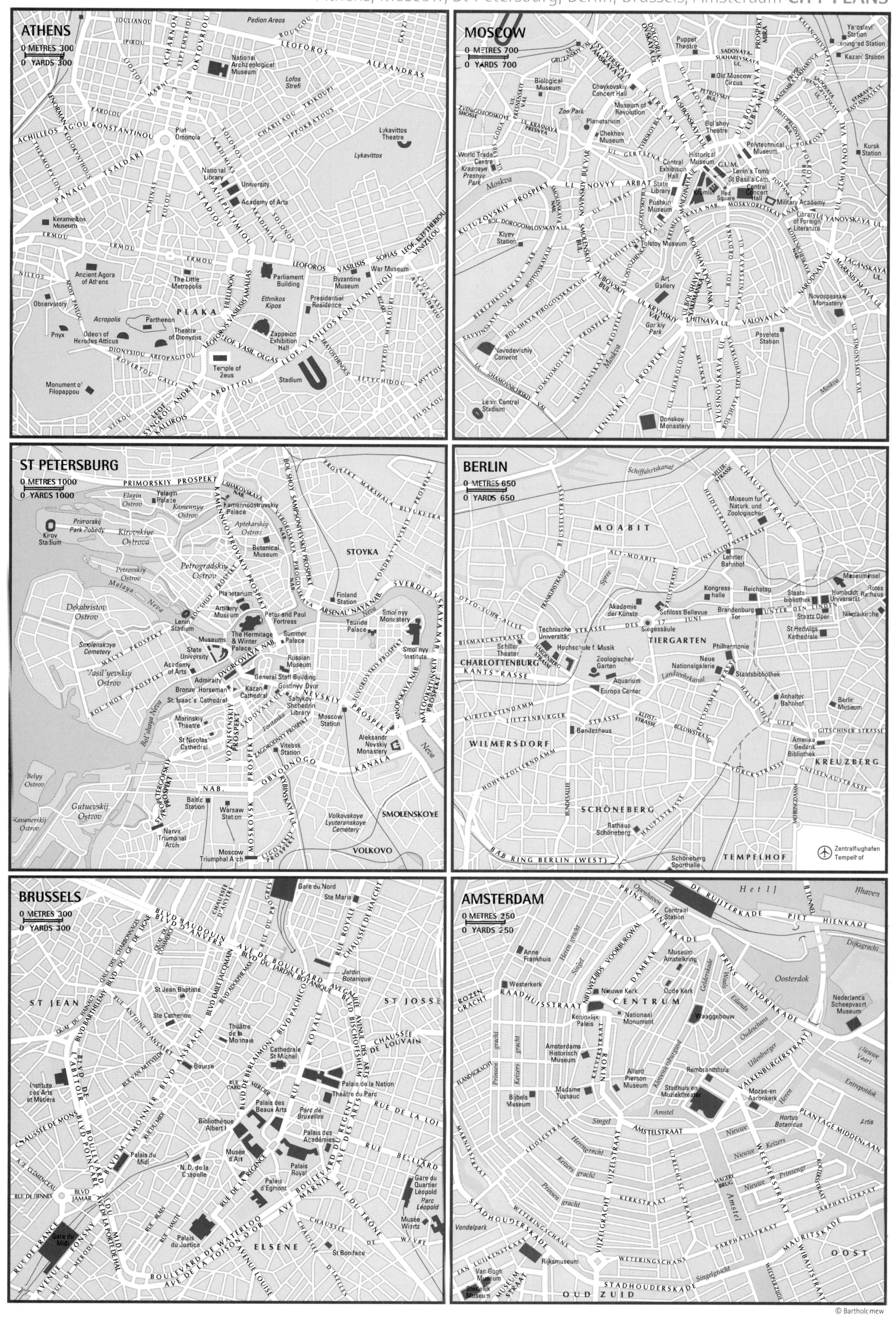
ATHENS
0 METRES 300
0 YARDS 300
Pedion Areos
National Archaeological Museum
Lofos Strefi
Lykavittos Theatre
Lykavittos
Plat. Omonoia
National Library
University
Academy of Arts
Kerameikos Museum
Ancient Agora of Athens
The Little Metropolis
Parliament Building
Byzantine Museum
War Museum
Presidential Residence
Ethnikos Kipos
Observatory
Acropolis
Parthenon
Pnyx
Odeon of Herodes Atticus
Theatre of Dionysus
Zappeion Exhibition Hall
Temple of Zeus
Stadium
Monument of Filopappou
PLAKA
MOSCOW
0 METRES 700
0 YARDS 700
Puppet Theatre
Yaroslavl' Station
Leningrad Station
Kazan' Station
Old Moscow Circus
Biological Museum
Chaykovskiy Concert Hall
Zoo Park
Museum of Revolution
Planetarium
Chekhov Museum
Bol'shoy Theatre
Historical Museum
Polytechnical Museum
Kursk Station
World Trade Centre
Krasnaya Presnya Park
Moskva
Central Exhibition Hall
G.U.M.
Lenin's Tomb
St Basil's Cath.
State Library
Kremlin
Red Square
Central Concert Hall
Military Academy
Pushkin Museum
Library of Foreign Literature
Kiyev Station
Tolstoy Museum
Art Gallery
Novospasskiy Monastery
Gor'kiy Park
Pavelets Station
Novodevichiy Convent
Lenin Central Stadium
Donskoy Monastery
ST PETERSBURG
0 METRES 1000
0 YARDS 1000
Elagin Ostrov
Yelagin Palace
Kamennyy Ostrov
Kamennoostrovskiy Palace
Primorskij Park Pobedy
Kirov Stadium
Kirovskiye Ostrova
Aptekarskiy Ostrov
Botanical Museum
STOYKA
Petrovskiy Ostrov
Petrogradskiy Ostrov
Planetarium
Finland Station
Dekabristov Ostrov
Artillery Museum
Peter and Paul Fortress
Smol'nyy Monastery
Lenin Stadium
Taurida Palace
Museums
The Hermitage & Winter Palace
Summer Palace
Smolenskoye Cemetery
State University
Smol'nyy Institute
Russian Museum
Academy of Arts
Vasil'yevskiy Ostrov
Admiralty
General Staff Building
Bronze Horseman
Kazan Cathedral
Gostinyy Dvor
St. Isaac's Cathedral
Saltykov-Shchedrin Library
Mariinskiy Theatre
Moscow Station
St Nicolas' Cathedral
Vitebsk Station
Aleksandr Nevskiy Monastery
Neva
Belyy Ostrov
Gutuevskij Ostrov
Baltic Station
Warsaw Station
Volkovskoye Lyuteranskoye Cemetery
SMOLENSKOYE
Narva Triumphal Arch
Moscow Triumphal Arch
VOLKOVO
BERLIN
0 METRES 650
0 YARDS 650
Schiffahrtskanal
Museum fur Naturk. und Zoologischer
MOABIT
Lehrter Bahnhof
Museumsinsel
Kongresshalle
Reichstag
Akademie der Künste
Schloss Bellevue
Brandenburg Tor
Staatsbibliothek
Humboldt Universität
Rotes Rathaus
Staats Oper
Nikolaikirche
Technische Universität
Siegessäule
TIERGARTEN
St Hedwigs Kathedrale
Schiller Theater
Hochschule f. Musik
Philharmonie
CHARLOTTENBURG
Zoologischer Garten
Neue Nationalgalerie
Staatsbibliothek
Aquarium
Europa Center
Landwehrkanal
Anhalter Bahnhof
Berlin Museum
Bandeshaus
WILMERSDORF
Amerika Gedenk Bibliothek
KREUZBERG
SCHÖNEBERG
Rathaus Schöneberg
Zentralflughafen Tempelhof
Schöneberg Sporthalle
TEMPELHOF
BRUSSELS
0 METRES 300
0 YARDS 300
Gare du Nord
Ste Marie
Jardin Botanique
ST JEAN
ST JOSSE
St Jean Baptiste
Ste Catherine
Théâtre de la Monnaie
Bourse
Cathedrale St Michel
Palais de la Nation
Théâtre du Parc
Institute des Arts et Métiers
Palais des Beaux Arts
Parc de Bruxelles
Bibliothèque Albert I
Palais des Académies
Musée d'Art
Palais du Midi
N. D. de la Chapelle
Palais Royal
Palais d'Egmont
Gare du Quartier Léopold
Parc Léopold
Musée Wiertz
Gare du Midi
Palais du Justice
ELSENE
St Boniface
AMSTERDAM
0 METRES 250
0 YARDS 250
Het IJ
Centraal Station
Anne Frankhuis
Museum Amstelkring
Westerkerk
Nieuwe Kerk
Oude Kerk
Oosterdok
Nederlands Scheepvaart Museum
CENTRUM
Koninklijk Paleis
National Monument
Waaggebouw
Amsterdams Historisch Museum
Allard Pierson Museum
Rembrandthuis
Madame Tussaud
Stadhuis en Muziektheater
Bijbels Museum
Mozes-en Aaronkerk
Hortus Botanicus
Amstel
Vondelpark
Rijksmuseum
Van Gogh Museum
Stedelijk Museum
OUD ZUID
OOST

CENTRAL LONDON
0 METRES 250
0 YARDS 250
The British Museum and British Library
HIGH HOLBORN
HOLBORN
Dominion Theatre
The Wigmore Hall
OXFORD STREET
REGENT STREET
CHARING CROSS ROAD
KINGSWAY
Lincoln's Inn Fields
Palladium
S O H O
Theatre Royal
Royal Courts of Justice
Royal Opera House
ALDWYCH
STRAND
NEW BOND STREET
SHAFTESBURY AVENUE
London Transport Museum
King's College
Somerset House
Royal Academy of Arts
PICCADILLY CIRCUS
HAYMARKET
National Gallery
M A Y F A I R
PICCADILLY
Charing Cross Sta.
TRAFALGAR SQUARE
Admiralty Arch
ST JAMES'S
Queen Elizabeth Hall and Purcell Room
Royal National Theatre
VICTORIA EMBANKMENT
Waterloo Br
Hungerford Bridge
Royal Festival Hall
WATERLOO RD
PALL MALL
Marlborough Ho.
St James's Palace
THE MALL
Government Buildings
WHITEHALL
Green Park
St James's Park
Thames
DOWNING
Treasury
PARLIAMENT STREET
CONSTITUTION HILL
Buckingham Palace
BIRDCAGE WALK
PARLIAMENT SQUARE
Westminster Br
Big Ben
Old County Hall
LAMBETH
WESTMINSTER BRIDGE ROAD
Houses of Parliament
GROSVENOR PLACE
W E S T M I N S T E R
Westminster Abbey
VICTORIA STREET
Lambeth Palace Gardens
Lambeth Palace
Victoria Station
Moor Park
South Oxley
WATFORD BYPASS
Darlands Lake Nature Reserve
Edgware
Stanmore
Canons Park
M1
WATFORD WAY
Finchley Golf Course
Finchley
Burnt Oak
Belmont
RAF Museums
A1 GREAT N WAY
Holders Hill
A406
Queensbury
EDGWARE ROAD
Kingsbury
Hendon
East Finchley
HENDON WAY
Golders Green
Fryent Country Park
Northwick Park
Wembley Park
Brent Res.
NORTH CIRCULAR ROAD
A41
Dollis Hill
Cricklewood
BRENT
Wembley Stadium
Gladstone Park
FINCHLEY ROAD
Wembley
Willesden
Sunbury Golf Course
Alperton
EALING ROAD
A406
Willesden Green
South Hampstead
Kilburn
Harlesden
Perivale
St. John's Wood
Lord's Cricket Ground
Park Royal
HARROW ROAD
Maida Vale
Ealing Golf Course
WESTERN AVENUE
NORTH ACTON
HANGER LANE
Wormwood Scrubs
WESTWAY
Hayes End
EALING
North Kensington
Paddington
Paddington Station
Ealing
A40(M)
Notting Hill
Bayswater
BAYSWATER
Hayes
Brent
Acton
East Acton
Shepherd's Bush
Kensington Palace
Kensington Gardens
Yiewsley
Southall
Hanwell
THE VALE
A40
Holland Park
Albert Hall
Grand Union Canal
Gunnersbury
HAMMERSMITH
Olympia
Nat. History Mus.
CROMWELL RD
West Drayton
Norwood Green
Gunnersbury Park
CHISWICK HIGH ROAD
AND FULHAM
M4
North Hyde
Osterley Park NT
Brentford
Chiswick
Chiswick House
Hammersmith Bridge
Earls Court
Earls Court Exhibition Centre
Colne
M25
Harmondsworth
Harlington
A4
Royal Botanic Gardens Kew
Castelnau
Football Stadium
FULHAM ROAD
KING'S RD
Heston
Osterley
Cranford
Syon House
Syon Park
KEW RD
A316
Barnes
Football Stadium
Heathrow Airport (London)
Hounslow West
Isleworth
Mortlake
Parsons Green
Putney Bridge
SOUTH CIRCULAR ROAD
A205
Hounslow
A30
ROEHAMPTON LANE
Wandsworth
HOUNSLOW
Richmond
Rugby Ground
Hounslow Heath
RICHMOND UPON
Putney
Putney Heath
WANDSWORTH
Southfields
Stanwell
East Bedfont
A316
Staines Reservoirs
Feltham
Crane
Twickenham
Thames
THAMES
Richmond Park
A3
A30
Tennis Courts
Wimbledon Park
KINGSTON
Wimbledon Common
Ashford
Hanworth
Staines
Teddington
Coombe Hill Golf Course
KINGSTON HILL
Wimbledon
A308
A316
Bushy Park
COOMBE LANE
KINGSTON ROAD
A24
Queen Mary Reservoir
Kempton Park Racecourse
Hampton
Norbiton
BYPASS
Sunbury
A308
Hampton Court
Kingston Upon Thames
New Malden
Morden
Bushy Mead
Molesey Reservoirs
West Molesey
East Molesey
Hampton Court Park
A307
KINGSTON UPON THAMES
West Barnes
Morden Park
A297
Queen Elizabeth II Reservoir
Island Barn Reservoir
M3
Shepperton
Thames Ditton
A309
Surbiton
Motspur Park
Chertsey
Chertsey Meads
Walton-on-Thames
Long Ditton
Old Malden
Tolworth
A3
S U R R E Y
Hinchley Wood
A309
Sandown Park Racecourse
North Cheam
A24
A217
SUTT
Mole
Addlestone
Weybridge
Esher
Burwood Park
Hersham
Worcester Park
Carshalton
Chessington
Wey
Nonsuch Park
Cheam
A232
M25
Claygate
A3
Horton Country Park
West Ewell
Sutton
Esher Common
East Ewell
St. Georges Hill
Ewell
A232
Belmont

0 METRES 1000
0 YARDS 1000
Chingford
Lord's Bushes
Chigwell
Hainault Forest Country Park
Palmers Green
Edmonton
Lee Valley Park
South Chingford
Chingford Hatch
Woodford Wells
Woodford Green
Grange Hill
Wood Green
Football Stadium
Banbury Res.
Hale End
Woodford
Woodford Bridge
REDBRIDGE
HARINGEY
Tottenham
Fullwell Cross
Alexandra Palace
Noel Park
Lockwood Res.
Higham Hill
Walthamstow
Fairlop Water
Muswell Hill
Alexandra Park
Epping Forest
Clayhall
Barkingside
Marks Gate
West Green
Snaresbrook
Hornsey
Harringay
WALTHAM FOREST
Hollow Pond
Chadwell Heath
Wanstead
Valentines Park
Seven Kings
Leytonstone
Wanstead Park
The Iveagh Bequest Kenwood House
Finsbury Park
East Reservoir
West Reservoir
Stamford Hill
Leyton
Central Park
Upper Clapton
Stoke Newington
Aldersbrook
Cranbrook
Finsbury Park
City of London Cemetery
Goodmayes
Beacontree
Hackney Marsh
Wanstead Flats
Football Stadium
Ilford
Shacklewell
Forest Gate
Manor Park
BARKING
Highbury
HACKNEY
Homerton
Stratford
Mayesbrook Park Sports Ground
Parsloes Park
CAMDEN
Dalston
London Fields
Barnsbury
Islington
ISLINGTON
Hoxton
Victoria Park
Upton
Barking
Dagenham
West Ham
London Zoo
Regent's Park
St Pancras Station
Kings Cross Station
Football Stadium
East Ham
Castle Green
Plaistow
Bethnal Green
Euston Station
Finsbury
St Pancras
Shoreditch
Mile End
NEWHAM
British Museum Library
Smithfield Market
Liverpool St Sta.
Bromley
Creekmouth
Thames
TOWER HAMLETS
St Paul's Cathedral
Holborn
WESTMINSTER
Blackfriars Sta.
Cannon St Sta.
Fenchurch St Station
Canning Town
Custom House
Hyde Park
Charing Cross Sta.
The Tower
Stepney
Whitechapel
Royal Victoria Dock
Royal Albert Dock
Thamesmead
Southwark
Wapping
Rotherhithe Tunnel
Poplar
Blackwall Tunnel
London City Airport
St. James's Palace
Green Park
Buckingham Palace
Westminster Abbey
Houses of Parliament
Waterloo Station
London Bridge Sta.
The Pool
Rotherhithe
Silvertown
Southmere
Erith Marshes
Thames Flood Barrier
Isle of Dogs
Victoria Station
Imperial War Museum
Newington
Bermondsey
Southwark Park
Greenland Dock
New Charlton
Woolwich
Abbey Wood
CHELSEA
Lambeth
Tate Gallery
Walworth
Lesnes Abbey Wood
Chelsea
Deptford
Plumstead
Plumstead Common
Bostall Heath
Chelsea Bridge
The Oval
Kennington
Burgess Park
Greenwich
National Maritime Mus.
Charlton
GREENWICH
Bostall Woods
West Heath
Battersea Park
Camberwell
Greenwich Park
Woolwich Common
Shrewsbury Park
South Lambeth
Peckham
Shooter's Hill
East Wickham Open Space
East Wickham
BATTERSEA
SOUTHWARK
New Cross
St John's
Blackheath
Kidbrooke
Eltham Common
Oxleas Wood
BEXLEY
Clapham Junction
Nunhead
Lewisham
Shepherdleas Wood
Welling
Ruskin Park
Danson Park
Bexleyheath
Clapham Common
Brixton
Peckham Rye
Brockley
LAMBETH
East Dulwich
Lee
Eltham
Avery Hill
Blackfen
Hither Green
Eltham Palace
Royal Blackheath Golf Course
Avery Hill Park
Bexley
Brockwell Park
Dulwich
Dulwich Park
Honor Oak Park
Bexley Park Wood
Balham
Catford
Mottingham
Lamorbey
LEWISHAM
New Eltham
Tooting Bec Common
West Norwood
Upper Sydenham
Forster Memorial Park
Grove Park
Longlands
Foots Cray Meadows
Streatham
Bellingham
Sidcup
Joyden's Wood
MERTON
Downham
Elmstead Wood
Tooting Graveney
Crystal Palace Park
Crystal Palace Athletics Stadium
Sundridge Park Golf Course
Foots Cray
Streatham Common
New Beckenham
Beckenham Place Park
Elmstead
Plaistow
Sundridge
Scadbury Park Nature Reserve
Upper Norwood
Penge
Chislehurst
Norbury Park
Beckenham
Park Wood
Streatham Vale
Norbury
Bromley
South Norwood
Bickley
St Pauls Cray
Elmers End
Petts Wood NT
Mitcham
South Norwood Country Park
Thornton Heath
Mitcham Common
Petts Wood
BROMLEY
Park Langley
Covet Wood
St Mary Cray
Upper Elmers End
Woodside
Langley Park Golf Course
Broad Green
Hayes
Reservoir
Bromley Common
Crofton Heath
Roundabout Wood
Orpington
Croydon
Addiscombe
Oddington
Waddon
Shirley
West Wickham
Hayes Common
Darrick Wood
Lloyd Park
Chelsfield
Wallington
Addington Hills
Addington
Keston
Farnborough
CROYDON
Croham Hurst
Littleheath Woods
New Addington
High Elms Golf Course
Carshalton on the Hill
Roundshaw Open Space
South Croydon
Pratt's Bottom
Sanderstead
Selsdon
Purley Downs Golf Course
Cuckoo Wood
© Bartholomew

Herblay
Conflans-Ste-Honorine
Maurecourt
Andrésy
Achères
Forêt de St-Germain
Maisons-Laffitte
Sartrouville
le Mesnil-le-Roi
Houilles
Montesson
Carrières-s.-Seine
le Vésinet
le Pecq
St-Germain-en-Laye
Chatou
Croissy-s.-Seine
Port-Marly
Mareil-Marly
Marly-le-Roi
L'Étang-la-Ville
Louveciennes
Bougival
La Celle-St-Cloud
Rueil-Malmaison
Nanterre
Suresnes
Puteaux
Courbevoie
La Garenne-Colombes
Colombes
Bois-Colombes
Bezons
Argenteuil
Cormeilles-en-Parisis
Montigny-lès-Cormeilles
Franconville
Ermont
Sannois
St-Gratien
Eaubonne
Soisy-sous-Montmorency
Montmorency
Andilly
Groslay
Montmagny
Deuil-la-Barre
Enghien-les-Bains
Epinay-sur-Seine
Villetaneuse
St-Denis
Villeneuve-la-Garenne
Gennevilliers
Asnières-s.-Seine
Clichy
St Ouen
Levallois-Perret
Neuilly-s.-Seine
Bois de Boulogne
Boulogne-Billancourt
St-Cloud
Garches
Vaucresson
Marnes-la-Coquette
Ville-d'Avray
Sèvres
Meudon
Issy-les-Moulineaux
Vanves
Malakoff
Montrouge
Gentilly
Le Kremlin-Bicêtre
Châtillon
Clamart
Bagneux
Arcueil
Cachan
Fontenay-aux-Roses
Le Plessis-Robinson
Bourg-la-Reine
L'Hay-les-Roses
Sceaux
Châtenay-Malabry
Antony
Fresnes
Chevilly-Larue
Wissous
Massy
Verrières-le-Buisson
Bièvres
Igny
Vauhallan
Saclay
Palaiseau
Villiers-le-Bâcle
Châteaufort
Magny-les-Hameaux
Milon-la-Chapelle
Toussus-le-Noble
Guyancourt
Buc
Les Loges-en-Josas
Jouy-en-Josas
Vélizy-Villacoublay
Viroflay
Chaville
Versailles
Le Chesnay
Rocquencourt
Bailly
Noisy-le-Roi
Fontenay-le-Fleury
St-Cyr-l'École
PARIS
VAL D'OISE
YVELINES
HAUTS-DE-SEINE
ESSONNE
Seine
Aéroport de Paris-Orly
A13
A14
A15
A86
A12

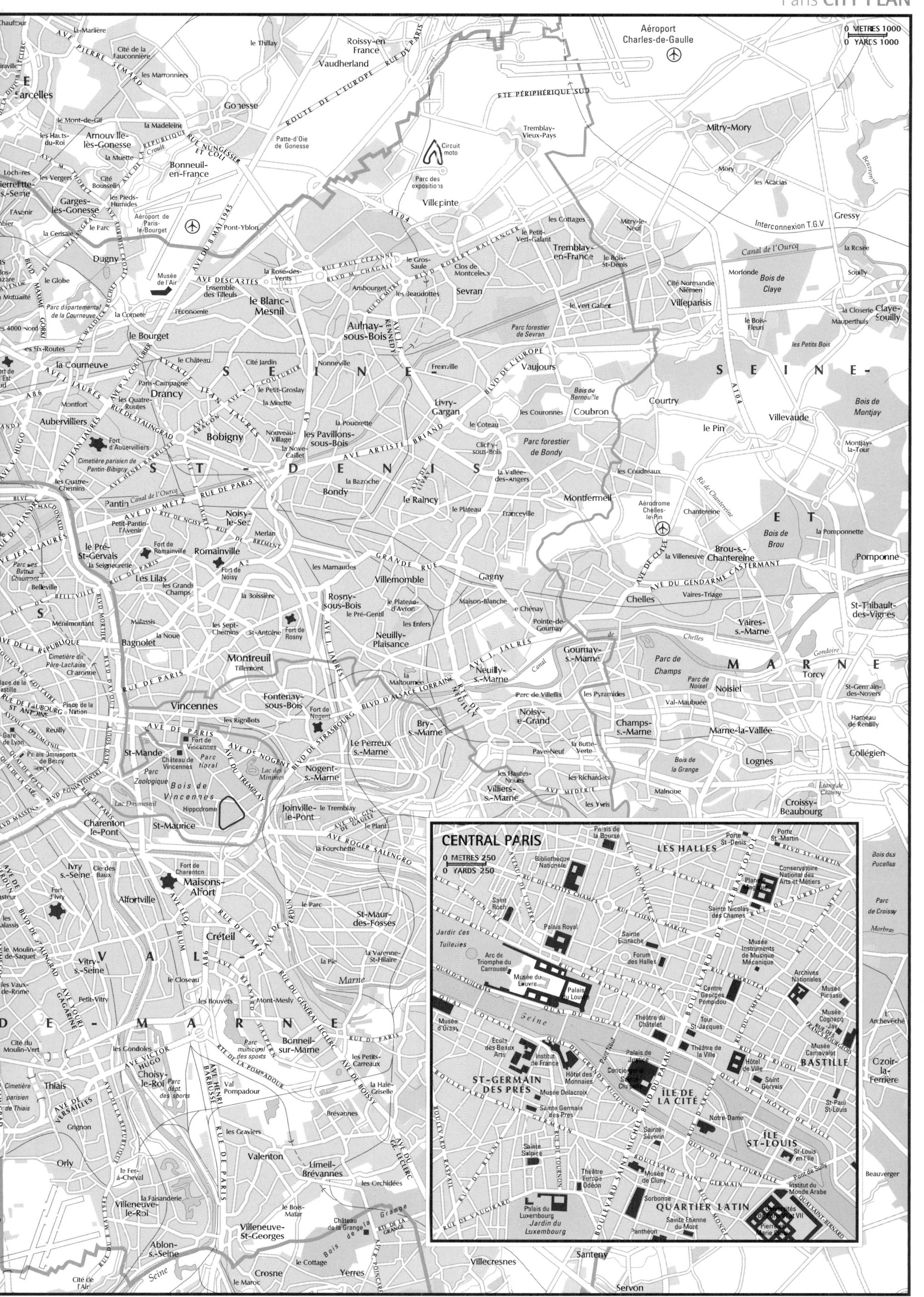
Aéroport Charles-de-Gaulle
0 METRES 1000
0 YARDS 1000
Roissy-en France
Vaudherland
le Thillay
Sarcelles
Gonesse
ROUTE DE L'EUROPE
RTE PÉRIPHÉRIQUE SUD
Tremblay-Vieux-Pays
Mitry-Mory
Arnouville-lès-Gonesse
Bonneuil-en-France
Patte-d'Oie de Gonesse
Circuit moto
Parc des expositions
Villepinte
Garges-lès-Gonesse
Aéroport de Paris-le-Bourget
Pont-Yblon
Dugny
Musée de l'Air
Mitry-le-Neuf
Gressy
Interconnexion T.G.V
Canal de l'Ourcq
Tremblay-en-France
Sevran
le Blanc-Mesnil
Aulnay-sous-Bois
Villeparisis
Claye-Souilly
Bois de Claye
le Bourget
Parc forestier de Sevran
Parc départemental de la Courneuve
la Courneuve
Vaujours
S E I N E -
S E I N E -
Drancy
Aubervilliers
Bobigny
Livry-Gargan
Coubron
Courtry
Villevaude
Bois de Montjay
les Pavillons-sous-Bois
Parc forestier de Bondy
le Pin
Fort d'Aubervilliers
Cimetière parisien de Pantin-Bibigny
S T - D E N I S
Bondy
le Raincy
Montfermeil
Aérodrome Chelles-le-Pin
E T
Pantin
Canal de l'Ourcq
Noisy-le-Sec
Romainville
le Pré-St-Gervais
Les Lilas
Bois de Brou
Brou-s.-Chantereine
Pomponne
Villemomble
Gagny
Chelles
St-Thibault-des-Vignes
Rosny-sous-Bois
Neuilly-Plaisance
Vaires-s.-Marne
Bagnolet
Montreuil
Cimetière du Père-Lachaise
Gournay-s.-Marne
Parc de Champs
M A R N E
Torcy
Noisiel
Vincennes
Fontenay-sous-Bois
Neuilly-s.-Marne
Noisy-le-Grand
Champs-s.-Marne
Marne-la-Vallée
St-Mandé
Bois de Vincennes
Parc Zoologique
Hippodrome
Le Perreux s.-Marne
Bry-s.-Marne
Nogent-s.-Marne
Lognes
Collégien
Charenton-le-Pont
St-Maurice
Joinville-le-Pont
Villiers-s.-Marne
Croissy-Beaubourg
Ivry s.-Seine
Maisons-Alfort
Alfortville
St-Maur-des-Fossés
Créteil
Vitry-s.-Seine
V A L -
D E - M A R N E
Bonneuil-sur-Marne
Thiais
Choisy-le-Roi
Orly
Valenton
Limeil-Brévannes
Villeneuve-le-Roi
Villeneuve-St-Georges
Ablon-s.-Seine
Crosne
Yerres
Villecresnes
Santeny
Servon
Ozoir-la-Ferrière
Seine
CENTRAL PARIS
0 METRES 250
0 YARDS 250
LES HALLES
Bibliothèque Nationale
Conservatoire National des Arts et Métiers
Palais Royal
Jardin des Tuileries
Arc de Triomphe du Carrousel
Musée du Louvre
Palais du Louvre
Forum des Halles
Centre Georges Pompidou
Musée Picasso
Musée d'Orsay
Institut de France
Palais de Justice
Sainte Chapelle
Hôtel de Ville
BASTILLE
ST-GERMAIN DES PRES
ÎLE DE LA CITÉ
Notre-Dame
ÎLE ST-LOUIS
Musée de Cluny
Sorbonne
QUARTIER LATIN
Palais du Luxembourg
Jardin du Luxembourg
Panthéon
Institut du Monde Arabe

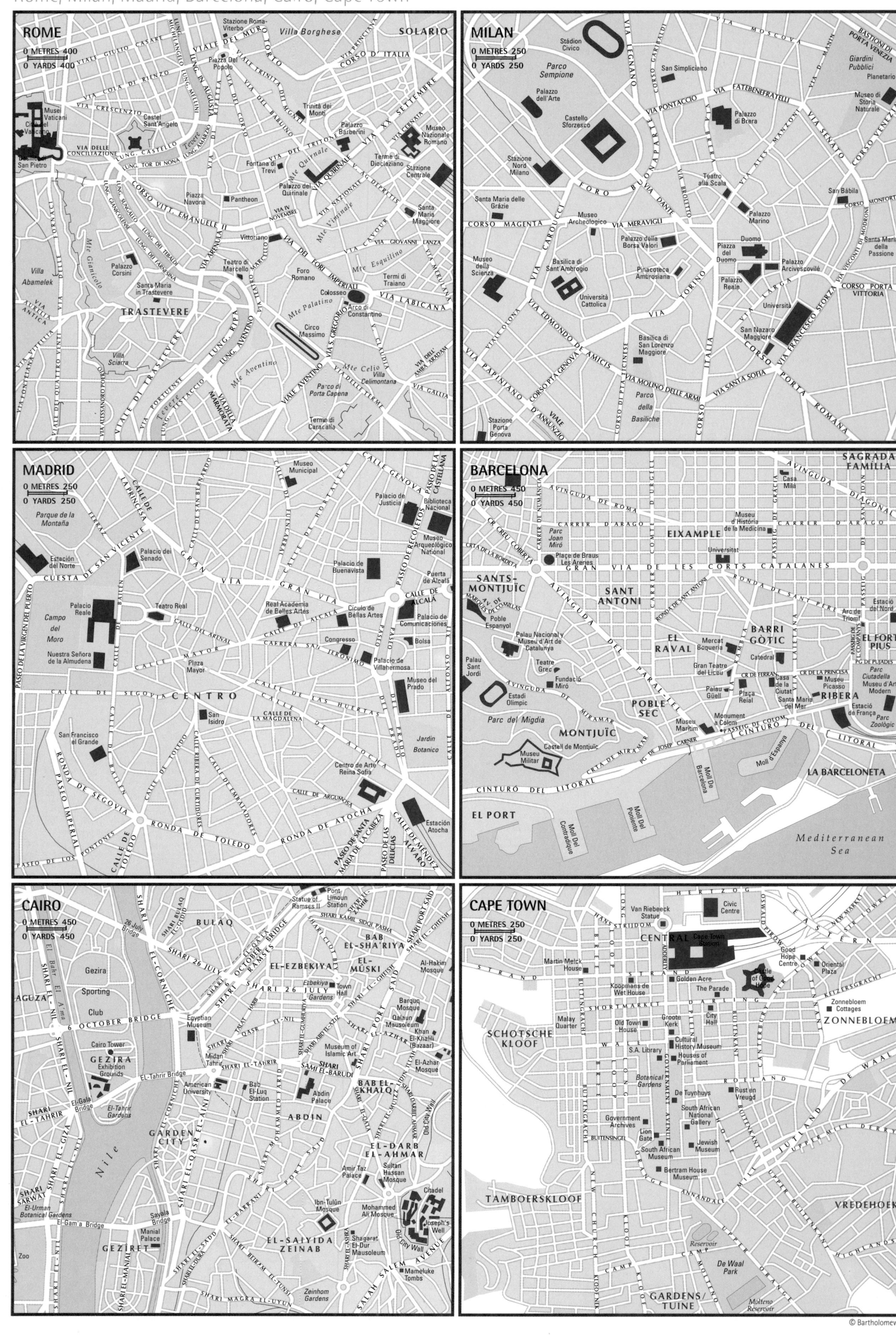
ROME
0 METRES 400
0 YARDS 400
Villa Borghese
SOLARIO
Piazza Del Popolo
Musei Vaticani
Castel Sant'Angelo
Basilica di San Pietro
Trinità dei Monti
Palazzo Barberini
Museo Nazionale Romano
Fontana di Trevi
Terme di Diocleziano
Stazione Centrale
Palazzo del Quirinale
Pantheon
Piazza Navona
Santa Maria Maggiore
Vittoriano
Teatro di Marcello
Foro Romano
Termi di Traiano
Colosseo
Arco di Constantino
Palazzo Corsini
Santa Maria in Trastevere
TRASTEVERE
Villa Abamelek
Circo Massimo
Villa Sciarra
Villa Celimontana
Parco di Porta Capena
Terme di Caracalla
MILAN
0 METRES 250
0 YARDS 250
Stàdion Civico
Parco Sempione
San Simpliciano
Giardini Pubblici
Planetario
Palazzo dell'Arte
Castello Sforzesco
Palazzo di Brera
Museo di Storia Naturale
Stazione Nord Milano
Teatro alla Scala
San Bàbila
Santa Maria delle Gràzie
Museo Archeologico
Palazzo Marino
Palazzo della Borsa Valori
Duomo
Piazza del Duomo
Santa Maria della Passione
Museo della Scienza
Basilica di Sant'Ambrogio
Pinacoteca Ambrosiana
Palazzo Arcivescovile
Palazzo Reale
Università Cattolica
Università
San Nazaro Maggiore
Basilica di San Lorenzo Maggiore
Parco della Basiliche
Stazione Porta Genova
MADRID
0 METRES 250
0 YARDS 250
Museo Municipal
Palacio de Justicia
Biblioteca Nacional
Parque de la Montaña
Museo Arqueológico National
Estación del Norte
Palacio del Senado
Palacio de Buenavista
Puerta de Alcalá
Palacio Reale
Teatro Real
Real Academia de Belles Artes
Circulo de Bellas Artes
Palacio de Comunicaciones
Campo del Moro
Congresso
Bolsa
Nuestra Señora de la Almudena
Plaza Mayor
Palacio de Villahermosa
Museo del Prado
CENTRO
San Isidro
San Francisco el Grande
Jardin Botanico
Centro de Arte Reina Sofia
Estación Atocha
BARCELONA
0 METRES 450
0 YARDS 450
SAGRADA FAMILIA
Casa Milà
Museu d'Història de la Medicina
EIXAMPLE
Parc Joan Miró
Plaçe de Braus Les Arenes
Universitat
SANTS-MONTJUÏC
SANT ANTONI
Estació del Nord
Arc de Triomf
Poble Espanyol
BARRI GÒTIC
EL FORT PIUS
Palau Nacional y Museu d'Art de Catalunya
Mercat Boqueria
EL RAVAL
Catedral
Palau Sant Jordi
Teatre Grec
Gran Teatre del Liceu
Parc Ciutadella
Museu Picasso
Museu d'Art Modern
Fundació Miró
Estadi Olimpic
Palau Güell
Plaça Reial
Casa de la Ciutat
RIBERA
Santa Maria del Mar
Estació de França
Parc Zoològic
POBLE SEC
Parc del Migdia
MONTJUÏC
Museu Marítim
Monument a Colom
Castell de Montjuïc
Museu Militar
Moll d'Espanya
LA BARCELONETA
Moll De Barcelona
EL PORT
Moll Del Contradique
Moll Del Poniente
Mediterranean Sea
CAIRO
0 METRES 450
0 YARDS 450
Pont Limoun Station
Statue of Ramses II
BULAQ
26 July Bridge
BAB EL-SHA'RIYA
Gezira
Sporting Club
EL-EZBEKIYA
EL-MÚSKI
Al-Hakim Mosque
Ezbekiya Gardens
Town Hall
AGUZA
6 OCTOBER BRIDGE
Egyptian Museum
Barquq Mosque
Qalaun Mausoleum
Khan El-Khalili (Bazaar)
Cairo Tower
GEZIRA
Exhibition Grounds
Midan Tahrir
Museum of Islamic Art
El-Azhar Mosque
El-Tahrir Bridge
American University
Bab El-Luq Station
Abdin Palace
BAB EL-KHALQ
El-Gala Bridge
El-Tahrir Gardens
ABDIN
GARDEN CITY
Nile
EL-DARB EL-AHMAR
Amir Taz Palace
Sultan Hassan Mosque
Citadel
Ibn-Tulûn Mosque
Mohammed Ali Mosque
Joseph's Well
El-Urman Botanical Gardens
El-Gam'a Bridge
Sayala Bridge
Manial Palace
GEZÎRET
EL-SAIYIDA ZEINAB
Shagarat El-Dur Mausoleum
Zoo
Mameluke Tombs
Zeinhom Gardens
CAPE TOWN
0 METRES 250
0 YARDS 250
Civic Centre
Van Riebeeck Statue
CENTRAL
Cape Town Station
Good Hope Centre
Martin Melck House
Oriental Plaza
Castle of Good Hope
Golden Acre
Koopmans de Wet House
The Parade
Zonnebloem Cottages
ZONNEBLOEM
Malay Quarter
Old Town House
Groote Kerk
City Hall
SCHOTSCHE KLOOF
Cultural History Museum
S.A. Library
Houses of Parliement
Botanical Gardens
De Tuynhuys
Rust en Vreugd
South African National Gallery
Government Archives
Lion Gate
Jewish Museum
South African Museum
Bertram House Museum
TAMBOERSKLOOF
VREDEHOEK
Reservoir
De Waal Park
GARDENS/TUINE
Molteno Reservoir

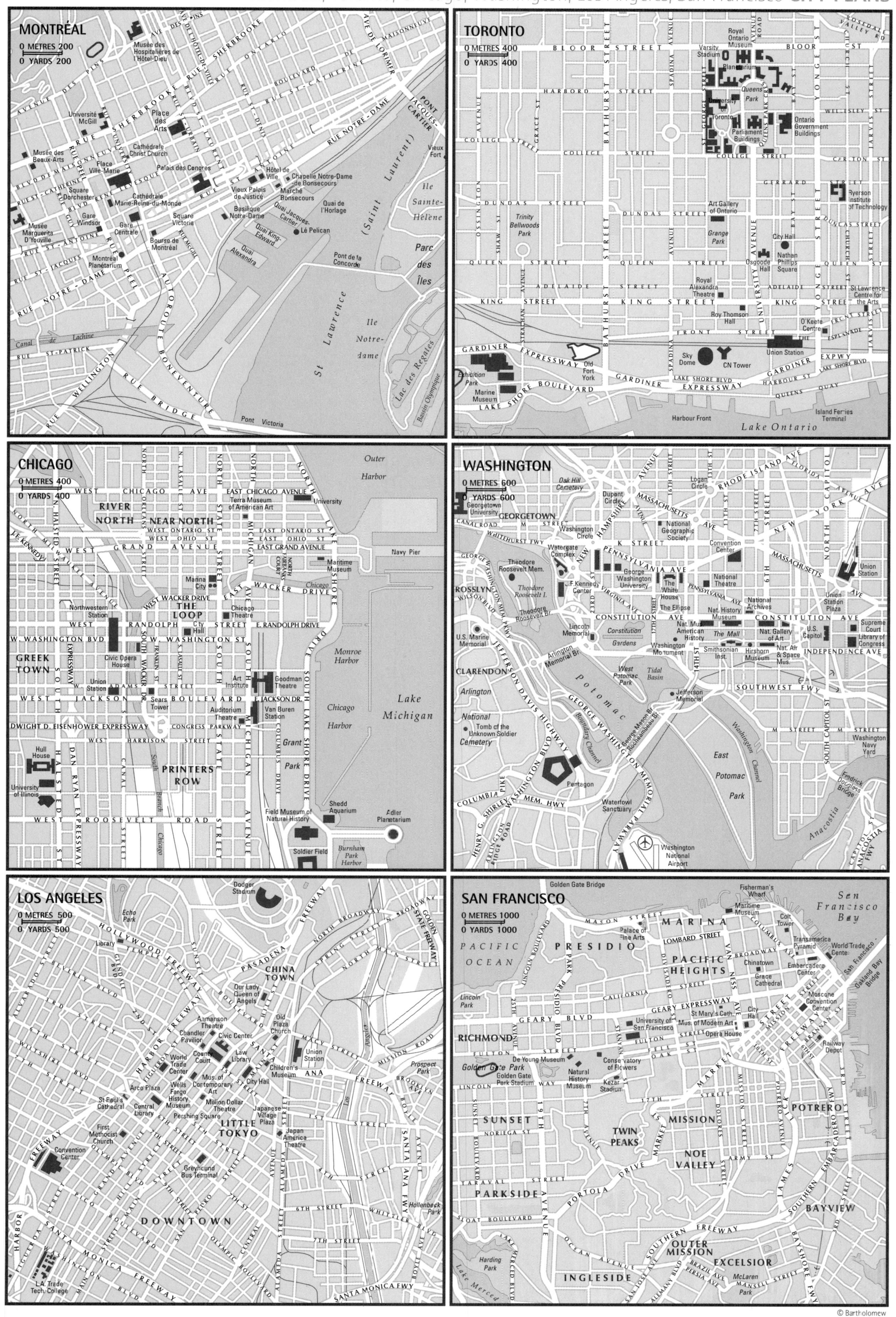
MONTRÉAL
0 METRES 200
0 YARDS 200
Musée des Hospitalières de l'Hôtel-Dieu
Université McGill
Place des Arts
Musée des Beaux-Arts
Cathédrale Christ Church
Place Ville-Marie
Palais des Congrès
Hôtel de Ville
Chapelle Notre-Dame de Bonsecours
Square Dorchester
Cathédrale Marie-Reine-du-Monde
Vieux Palais de Justice
Marché Bonsecours
Quai de l'Horloge
Basilique Notre-Dame
Gare Windsor
Gare Centrale
Square Victoria
Musée Marguerite D'Youville
Bourse de Montréal
Quai Jacques-Cartier
Quai King-Edward
Quai Alexandra
Le Pelican
Montréal Planétarium
Pont de la Concorde
Vieux Fort
Ile Sainte-Hélène
Parc des Îles
Ile Notre-dame
St Lawrence
(Saint Laurent)
Lac des Regates
Bassin Olympique
Canal de Lachine
Pont Jacques-Cartier
Pont Victoria
Rue Sherbrooke
Rue Ste-Catherine
Rue Notre-Dame
Rue St-Antoine
Rue St-Jacques
Rue St-Patrick
Rue Wellington
Rue Bridge
Autoroute Boneventure
Boulevard de Maisonneuve
Boulevard René-Lévesque
Rue Peel
Rue St-Denis
Rue St-Laurent
Rue St-Urbain
Avenue des Pins
Avenue de Lorimier
Rue Ontario
TORONTO
0 METRES 400
0 YARDS 400
Bloor Street
Harbord Street
College Street
Dundas Street
Queen Street
Adelaide Street
King Street
Front Street
Gerrard Street
Wellesley St
Carlton St
Bathurst Street
Spadina Avenue
University Avenue
Bay St
Yonge St
Jarvis Street
Church St
Ossington Avenue
Shaw St
Grace St
Strachan Avenue
Avenue Road
Queens Park Cres
St George St
Royal Ontario Museum
Varsity Stadium
Planetarium
Queens Park
University of Toronto
Parliament Buildings
Ontario Government Buildings
Ryerson Institute of Technology
Art Gallery of Ontario
Trinity Bellwoods Park
Grange Park
City Hall
Nathan Phillips Square
Osgoode Hall
Royal Alexandra Theatre
Roy Thomson Hall
O'Keefe Centre
St Lawrence Centre for the Arts
Union Station
Sky Dome
CN Tower
Gardiner Expressway
Old Fort York
Exhibition Park
Marine Museum
Lake Shore Boulevard
Harbour St
Queens Quay
Esplanade
Harbour Front
Island Ferries Terminal
Lake Ontario
Rosedale Valley Rd
CHICAGO
0 METRES 400
0 YARDS 400
West Chicago Ave
East Chicago Avenue
Terra Museum of American Art
University
RIVER NORTH
NEAR NORTH
West Ontario St
West Ohio St
East Ontario St
East Ohio St
West Grand Avenue
East Grand Avenue
Navy Pier
Maritime Museum
Marina City
Wacker Drive
West Wacker Drive
THE LOOP
Chicago Theatre
Northwestern Station
West Randolph Street
E. Randolph Drive
City Hall
W. Washington Bvd
W. Washington St
GREEK TOWN
Civic Opera House
Union Station
Adams Street
Art Institute
Goodman Theatre
West Jackson Boulevard
Jackson Dr.
Sears Tower
Auditorium Theatre
Van Buren Station
Dwight D. Eisenhower Expressway
Congress Parkway
West Harrison Street
Hull House
University of Illinois
PRINTERS ROW
Grant Park
Chicago Harbor
Monroe Harbor
Outer Harbor
Lake Michigan
Shedd Aquarium
Field Museum of Natural History
Adler Planetarium
Soldier Field
Burnham Park Harbor
West Roosevelt Road
Lake Shore Drive
North Lake Shore Drive
South Lake Shore Drive
Michigan Avenue
North State Street
South State Street
Halsted Street
Kennedy Expressway
Dan Ryan Expressway
Columbus Drive
Canal St
South Branch
Chicago River
WASHINGTON
0 METRES 600
0 YARDS 600
Georgetown University
GEORGETOWN
Oak Hill Cemetery
Dupont Circle
Logan Circle
Washington Circle
National Geographic Society
Convention Center
Watergate Complex
Theodore Roosevelt Mem.
Theodore Roosevelt I.
Theodore Roosevelt Br.
George Washington University
F Kennedy Center
The White House
The Ellipse
National Theatre
National Archives
Nat. History Museum
Nat. Mus. American History
Nat. Gallery of Art
The Mall
Constitution Gardens
Lincoln Memorial
Washington Monument
Smithsonian Inst.
Hirshhorn Museum
Nat. Air & Space Mus.
U.S. Capitol
Supreme Court
Library of Congress
Union Station
Union Station Plaza
Arlington Memorial Br.
U.S. Marine Memorial
ROSSLYN
CLARENDON
Arlington
National Cemetery
Tomb of the Unknown Soldier
West Potomac Park
Tidal Basin
Jefferson Memorial
Potomac
Boundary Channel
George Mason Br.
Rochambeau Br.
Pentagon
East Potomac Park
Washington Channel
Washington Navy Yard
Waterfowl Sanctuary
Washington National Airport
Anacostia
Fredrick Douglass Bridge
Massachusetts Ave
Rhode Island Ave
Florida Ave
New York Ave
New Hampshire Ave
Pennsylvania Ave
Virginia Ave
Constitution Ave
Independence Ave
K Street
M Street
Southwest Fwy
Jefferson Davis Highway
George Washington Memorial Parkway
Shirley Highway
Columbia Pike
Washington Mem. Hwy
Whitehurst Fwy
Canal Road
North Capitol St
South Capitol St
LOS ANGELES
0 METRES 500
0 YARDS 500
Dodger Stadium
Echo Park
Library
Hollywood Freeway
Temple St
Sunset Blvd
CHINA TOWN
Our Lady Queen of Angels
Old Plaza Church
Ahmanson Theatre
Chandler Pavilion
Civic Center
County Court
Law Library
City Hall
Union Station
Children's Museum
World Trade Center
Mus. of Contemporary Art
Arco Plaza
Wells Fargo History Museum
Million Dollar Theatre
St Paul's Cathedral
Central Library
Pershing Square
Japanese Village Plaza
LITTLE TOKYO
Japan America Theatre
First Methodist Church
Convention Center
Greyhound Bus Terminal
DOWNTOWN
LA Trade Tech. College
Harbor Freeway
Santa Monica Freeway
Santa Ana Freeway
Golden State Freeway
Pasadena Freeway
Prospect Park
Hollenbeck Park
Wilshire Blvd
Olympic Blvd
Alvarado St
Figueroa St
Grand Avenue
Broadway
Alameda Street
Mission Road
SAN FRANCISCO
0 METRES 1000
0 YARDS 1000
Golden Gate Bridge
Fisherman's Wharf
Maritime Museum
Coit Tower
San Francisco Bay
MARINA
Palace of Fine Arts
Lombard Street
PRESIDIO
PACIFIC OCEAN
PACIFIC HEIGHTS
Chinatown
Transamerica Pyramid
World Trade Center
Embarcadero Center
Grace Cathedral
San Francisco-Oakland Bay Bridge
Lincoln Park
Moscone Convention Center
Geary Expressway
St Mary's Cath.
City Hall
University of San Francisco
Mus. of Modern Art
Opera House
RICHMOND
Railway Depot
De Young Museum
Conservatory of Flowers
Golden Gate Park
Golden Gate Park Stadium
Natural History Museum
Kezar Stadium
Market Street
SUNSET
TWIN PEAKS
MISSION
POTRERO
NOE VALLEY
PARKSIDE
BAYVIEW
Harding Park
Lake Merced
OUTER MISSION
EXCELSIOR
INGLESIDE
McLaren Park
Southern Freeway
Bayshore Fwy
Portola Drive
Sloat Boulevard
Lincoln Way
19th Avenue
Van Ness Ave
Dolores St
Army St

CENTRAL MANHATTAN
0 METRES 250
0 YARDS 250
Central Park
Frick Collection
Columbus Circle
The Pond
Zoo
Carnegie Hall
THEATRE DISTRICT
Museum of Modern Art
Lever House
Seagram Building
Rockefeller Centre
St Patrick's Cathedral
St Bartholomew's Church
Bus Terminal
Times Square
Pan Am Building
GARMENT DISTRICT
Bryant Park
Grand Central Station
New York Public Library
Chrysler Building
United Nations Headquarters
MURRAY HILL
Madison Square Garden
Pennsylvania Station
Empire State Building
East River
Belmont I.
BROADWAY
PARK AVENUE
FRANKLIN D. ROOSEVELT DRIVE
Cedar Grove
Cedar Grove Reservoir
Wallington
Wood-Ridge
Teterboro Airport
Little Ferry
Ridgefield Park
Palisades Park
Fort Lee
Ridgefield
Edgewater
Palisade Amusement Park
Cliffside Park
Meadowlands Sports Complex
North Bergen
Fairview
General Grant Nat. Mem.
Columbia University
North Hudson Park
Secaucus
Guttenberg
Hudson
Central Park
Natural History Museum
Lincoln Centre
Museum of Art
W. New York
Union City
MANHATTAN
Weehawken
Lincoln Tunnel
Rockefeller Centre
Grand Central Station
Madison Square Garden
Empire State Building
United Nations Headquarters
Queens-Midtown Tunnel
Hackensack
Harrison
Passaic
Hoboken
Greenwich Village
Irvington
NEW JERSEY
Newark
Lincoln Park
Kearny Point
Jersey City
Holland Tunnel
China Town
East
World Trade Centre
Williamsburg Bridge
Manhattan Bridge
Brooklyn Bridge
Hillside
Newark International Airport
Liberty State Park
Ellis Island (N.Y.)
Castle Clinton
Governor's Island
Brooklyn Battery Tunnel
Liberty Island (N.Y.)
Statue of Liberty
Long Island University
Pratt Institute
Station
Elizabeth
Newark Bay
Buttermilk Channel
Red Hook
Crown
Brooklyn Museum
Botanical Garden
Zoo
Park Slope
Prospect Park
Warinanco Park
Bayonne
Upper Bay
Greenwood Cemetery
Shooters Island
Kill Van Kull
Bayonne Bridge
Linden
New Brighton
Port Richmond
Borough Park
Kensington
Zoo
Silver Lake Park
Westerleigh
Clove Lakes Park
Parkville
Brooklyn College
Bay Ridge
The Narrows
Shore Road Park
Linden Airport
Fox Hills
Dyker Beach Park
Fort Hamilton
New Utrecht
Bull's Head
STATEN ISLAND
Willow Brook Park
Verrazano Narrows Bridge
Fort Wadsworth
Grasmere
Rahway
Fresh Kills Park
Travis
Lower Bay
Gravesend Bay
Gravesend
Carteret
South Beach
LaTourette Park
Hoffman Island
Arthur Kill
Coney Island
Aquarium
Port Reading
New Dorp
Ocean View Cemetery
Swinburne Island
Rossville
Gateway National Recreation Area
Great Kills
Annadale
Woodrow
Great Kills Park
Clay Pit Ponds State Park Preserve
Great Kills Harbor
Rockaway Point
NEW JERSEY TURNPIKE
PULASKI SKYWAY
GARDEN STATE PARKWAY
VERRAZANO NARROWS BRIDGE

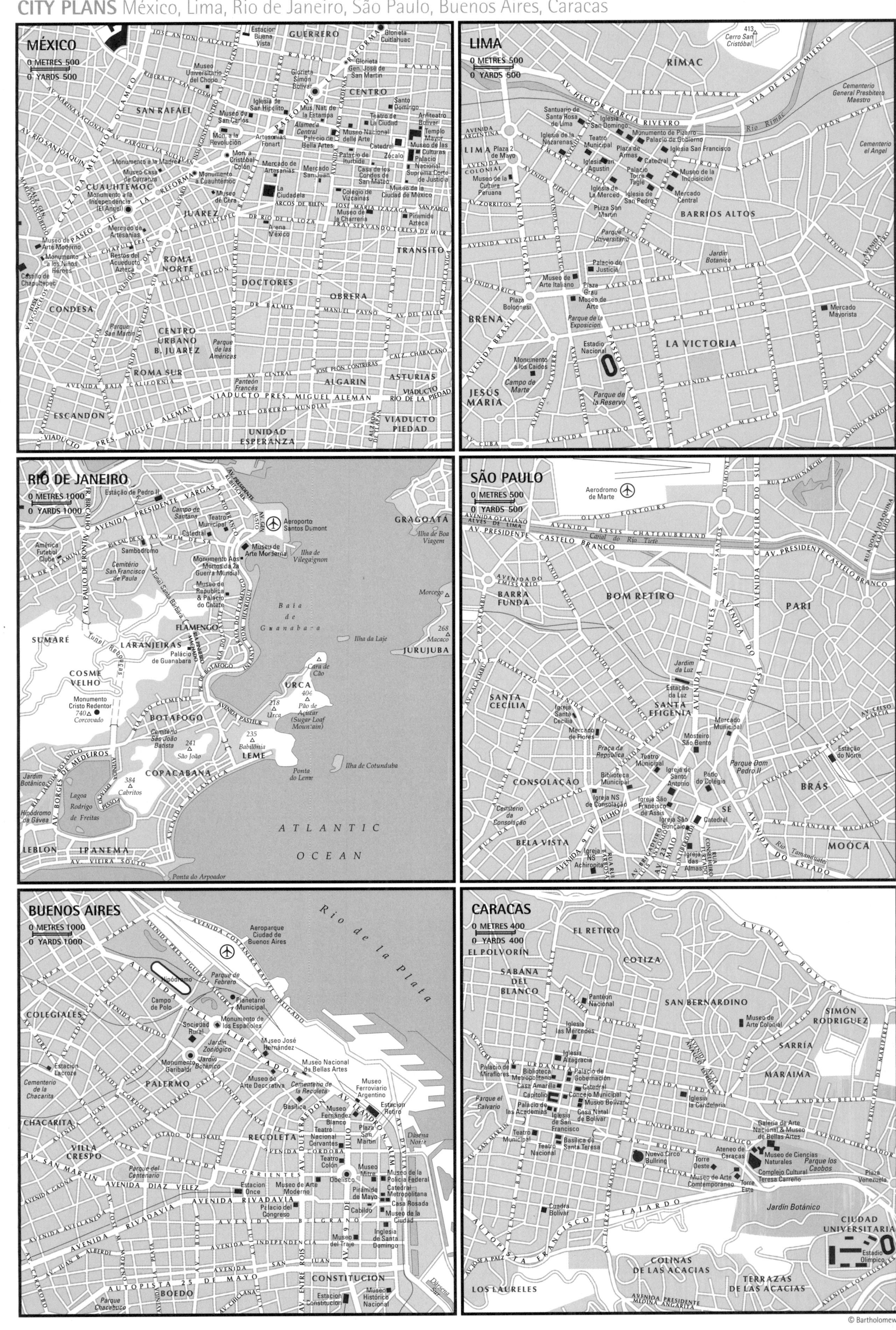
MÉXICO
0 METRES 500
0 YARDS 500
GUERRERO
SAN RAFAEL
CENTRO
CUAUHTEMOC
JUÁREZ
ROMA NORTE
DOCTORES
OBRERA
TRANSITO
CONDESA
CENTRO URBANO B. JUAREZ
ROMA SUR
ASTURIAS
ALGARIN
ESCANDON
UNIDAD ESPERANZA
VIADUCTO PIEDAD
Zócalo
Palacio de Bellas Artes
Monumento a la Revolución
Monumento a la Independencia (El Angel)
Castillo de Chapultepec
Catedral
Templo Mayor
Parque San Martín
Parque de las Américas
Panteón Francés
LIMA
0 METRES 500
0 YARDS 500
RÍMAC
Cerro San Cristóbal
BARRIOS ALTOS
BRENA
LA VICTORIA
JESÚS MARÍA
Plaza de Armas
Palacio de Gobierno
Catedral
Iglesia San Francisco
Plaza San Martín
Plaza 2 de Mayo
Palacio de Justicia
Museo de Arte
Parque de la Exposición
Estadio Nacional
Campo de Marte
Parque de la Reserva
Mercado Mayorista
Cementerio General Presbítero Maestro
Cementerio el Angel
Jardín Botánico
RIO DE JANEIRO
0 METRES 1000
0 YARDS 1000
Aeroporto Santos Dumont
Museu de Arte Moderna
Ilha de Vilegaignon
GRAGOATÁ
Baía de Guanabara
Ilha da Laje
JURUJUBA
SUMARÉ
FLAMENGO
LARANJEIRAS
COSME VELHO
Monumento Cristo Redentor
740 Corcovado
BOTAFOGO
URCA
Pão de Açúcar (Sugar Loaf Mountain)
LEME
COPACABANA
Lagoa Rodrigo de Freitas
Jardim Botânico
Hipódromo da Gávea
LEBLON
IPANEMA
Ilha de Cotunduba
ATLANTIC OCEAN
Ponta do Arpoador
SÃO PAULO
0 METRES 500
0 YARDS 500
Aerodromo de Marte
BARRA FUNDA
BOM RETIRO
PARI
SANTA CECÍLIA
SANTA EFIGÊNIA
Jardim da Luz
Estação da Luz
Mercado Municipal
Mosteiro São Bento
CONSOLAÇÃO
Teatro Municipal
Parque Dom Pedro II
BRÁS
Estação do Norte
SÉ
Catedral
BELA VISTA
MOÓCA
Cemitério da Consolação
BUENOS AIRES
0 METRES 1000
0 YARDS 1000
Rio de la Plata
Aeroparque Ciudad de Buenos Aires
Hipódromo
Campo de Polo
Planetario Municipal
COLEGIALES
PALERMO
Jardín Zoológico
Jardín Botánico
Museo Nacional de Bellas Artes
Cementerio de la Chacarita
CHACARITA
VILLA CRESPO
RECOLETA
Cementerio de la Recoleta
Estación Retiro
Teatro Colón
Obelisco
Casa Rosada
Catedral Metropolitana
Palacio del Congreso
Estación Once
BOEDO
CONSTITUCIÓN
Estación Constitución
CARACAS
0 METRES 400
0 YARDS 400
EL RETIRO
EL POLVORÍN
COTIZA
SABANA DEL BLANCO
Panteón Nacional
SAN BERNARDINO
SIMÓN RODRÍGUEZ
SARRÍA
MARAIMA
Palacio de Miraflores
Capitolio
Catedral
Museo de Bellas Artes
Museo de Ciencias Naturales
Complejo Cultural Teresa Carreño
Parque los Caobos
Plaza Venezuela
Jardín Botánico
CIUDAD UNIVERSITARIA
Estadio Olímpico
COLINAS DE LAS ACACIAS
TERRAZAS DE LAS ACACIAS
LOS LAURELES

SYMBOLS

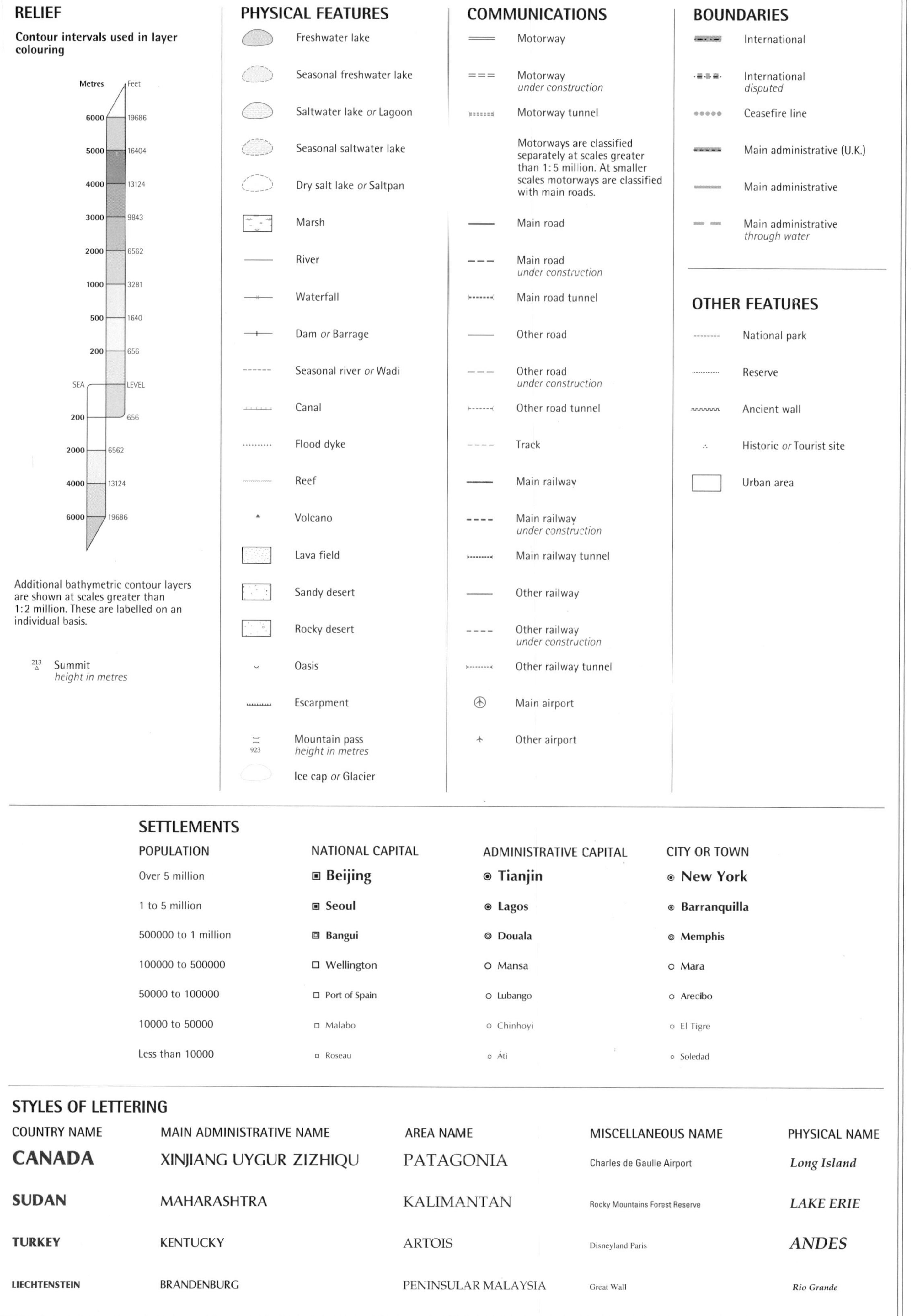
RELIEF
Contour intervals used in layer colouring
Metres
Feet
6000 19686
5000 16404
4000 13124
3000 9843
2000 6562
1000 3281
500 1640
200 656
SEA LEVEL
200 656
2000 6562
4000 13124
6000 19686
Additional bathymetric contour layers are shown at scales greater than 1:2 million. These are labelled on an individual basis.
213
Summit
height in metres
PHYSICAL FEATURES
Freshwater lake
Seasonal freshwater lake
Saltwater lake or Lagoon
Seasonal saltwater lake
Dry salt lake or Saltpan
Marsh
River
Waterfall
Dam or Barrage
Seasonal river or Wadi
Canal
Flood dyke
Reef
Volcano
Lava field
Sandy desert
Rocky desert
Oasis
Escarpment
923
Mountain pass
height in metres
Ice cap or Glacier
COMMUNICATIONS
Motorway
Motorway
under construction
Motorway tunnel
Motorways are classified separately at scales greater than 1:5 million. At smaller scales motorways are classified with main roads.
Main road
Main road
under construction
Main road tunnel
Other road
Other road
under construction
Other road tunnel
Track
Main railway
Main railway
under construction
Main railway tunnel
Other railway
Other railway
under construction
Other railway tunnel
Main airport
Other airport
BOUNDARIES
International
International
disputed
Ceasefire line
Main administrative (U.K.)
Main administrative
Main administrative
through water
OTHER FEATURES
National park
Reserve
Ancient wall
Historic or Tourist site
Urban area
SETTLEMENTS
POPULATION
NATIONAL CAPITAL
ADMINISTRATIVE CAPITAL
CITY OR TOWN
Over 5 million
Beijing
Tianjin
New York
1 to 5 million
Seoul
Lagos
Barranquilla
500000 to 1 million
Bangui
Douala
Memphis
100000 to 500000
Wellington
Mansa
Mara
50000 to 100000
Port of Spain
Lubango
Arecibo
10000 to 50000
Malabo
Chinhoyi
El Tigre
Less than 10000
Roseau
Ati
Soledad
STYLES OF LETTERING
COUNTRY NAME
MAIN ADMINISTRATIVE NAME
AREA NAME
MISCELLANEOUS NAME
PHYSICAL NAME
CANADA
XINJIANG UYGUR ZIZHIQU
PATAGONIA
Charles de Gaulle Airport
Long Island
SUDAN
MAHARASHTRA
KALIMANTAN
Rocky Mountains Forest Reserve
LAKE ERIE
TURKEY
KENTUCKY
ARTOIS
Disneyland Paris
ANDES
LIECHTENSTEIN
BRANDENBURG
PENINSULAR MALAYSIA
Great Wall
Rio Grande

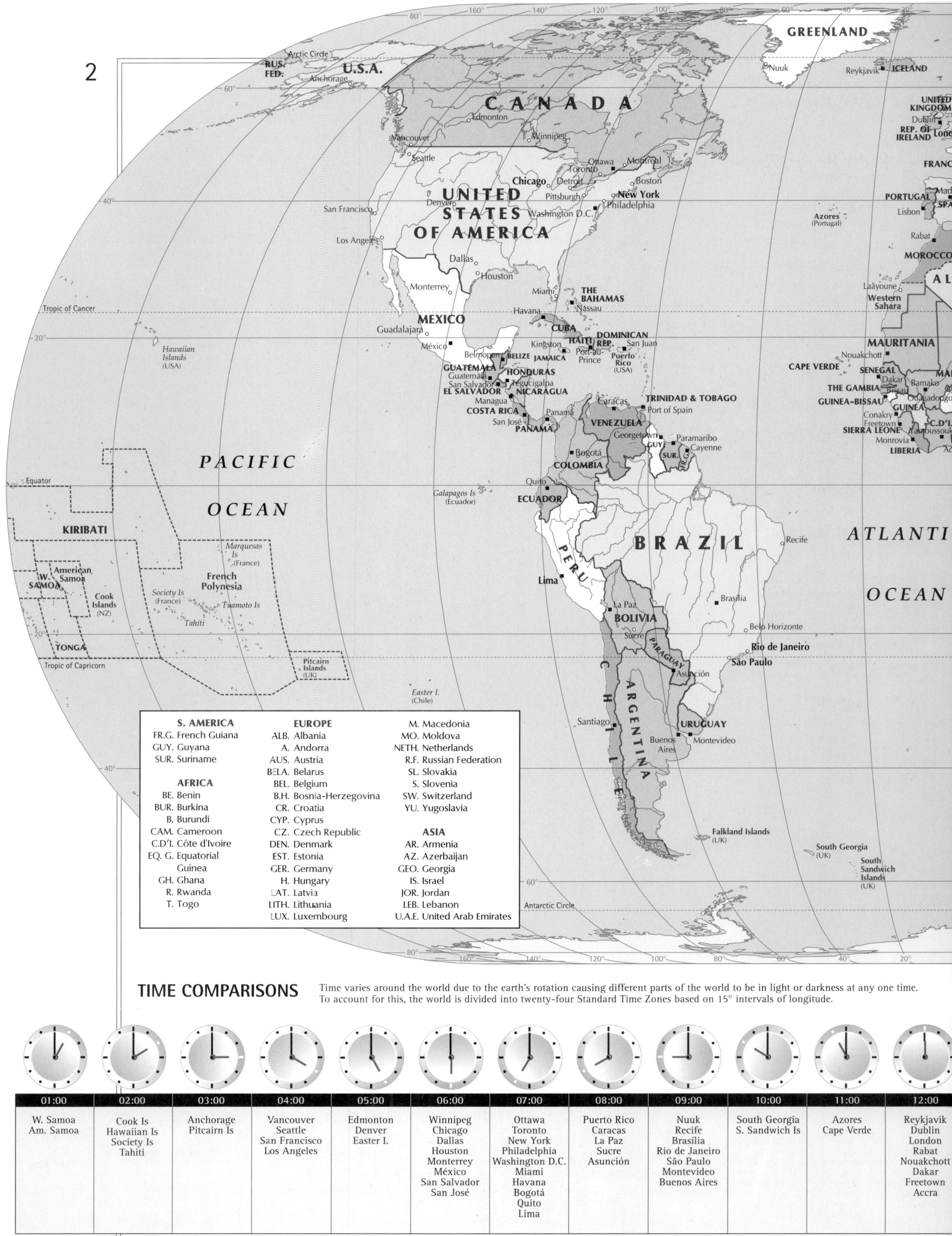

S. AMERICA		EUROPE			
FR.G.	French Guiana	ALB.	Albania	M.	Macedonia
GUY.	Guyana	A.	Andorra	MO.	Moldova
SUR.	Suriname	AUS.	Austria	NETH.	Netherlands
		BELA.	Belarus	R.F.	Russian Federation
AFRICA		BEL.	Belgium	SL.	Slovakia
BE.	Benin	B.H.	Bosnia-Herzegovina	S.	Slovenia
BUR.	Burkina	CR.	Croatia	SW.	Switzerland
B.	Burundi	CYP.	Cyprus	YU.	Yugoslavia
CAM.	Cameroon	CZ.	Czech Republic		**ASIA**
C.D'I.	Côte d'Ivoire	DEN.	Denmark	AR.	Armenia
EQ. G.	Equatorial Guinea	EST.	Estonia	AZ.	Azerbaijan
GH.	Ghana	GER.	Germany	GEO.	Georgia
R.	Rwanda	H.	Hungary	IS.	Israel
T.	Togo	LAT.	Latvia	JOR.	Jordan
		LITH.	Lithuania	LEB.	Lebanon
		LUX.	Luxembourg	U.A.E.	United Arab Emirates

TIME COMPARISONS

Time varies around the world due to the earth's rotation causing different parts of the world to be in light or darkness at any one time. To account for this, the world is divided into twenty-four Standard Time Zones based on 15° intervals of longitude.

01:00	02:00	03:00	04:00	05:00	06:00	07:00	08:00	09:00	10:00	11:00	12:00
W. Samoa Am. Samoa	Cook Is Hawaiian Is Society Is Tahiti	Anchorage Pitcairn Is	Vancouver Seattle San Francisco Los Angeles	Edmonton Denver Easter I.	Winnipeg Chicago Dallas Houston Monterrey México San Salvador San José	Ottawa Toronto New York Philadelphia Washington D.C. Miami Havana Bogotá Quito Lima	Puerto Rico Caracas La Paz Sucre Asunción	Nuuk Recife Brasília Rio de Janeiro São Paulo Montevideo Buenos Aires	South Georgia S. Sandwich Is	Azores Cape Verde	Reykjavik Dublin London Rabat Nouakchott Dakar Freetown Accra

Eckert IV Projection

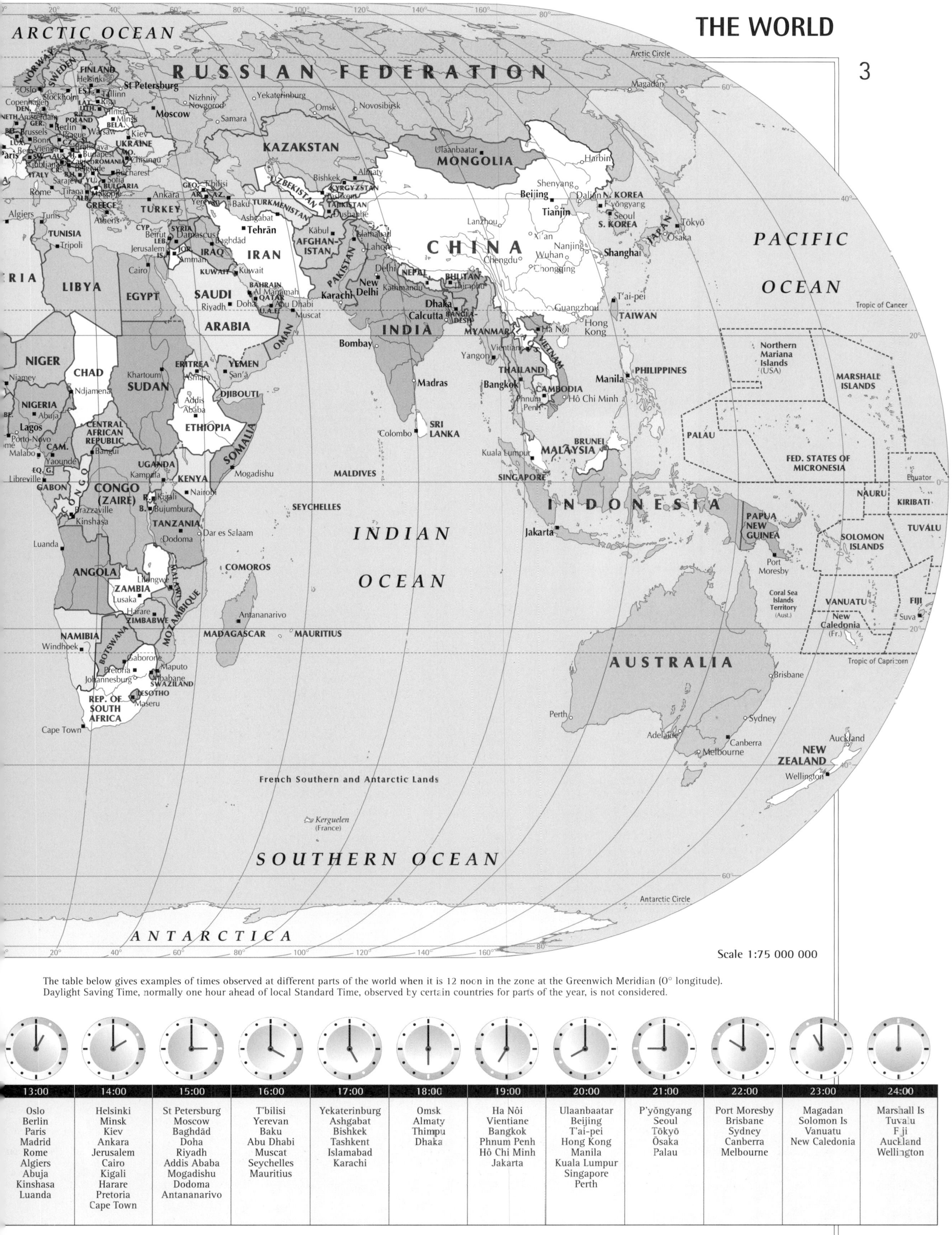

Scale 1:75 000 000

The table below gives examples of times observed at different parts of the world when it is 12 noon in the zone at the Greenwich Meridian (0° longitude). Daylight Saving Time, normally one hour ahead of local Standard Time, observed by certain countries for parts of the year, is not considered.

13:00	14:00	15:00	16:00	17:00	18:00	19:00	20:00	21:00	22:00	23:00	24:00
Oslo	Helsinki	St Petersburg	T'bilisi	Yekaterinburg	Omsk	Ha Nôi	Ulaanbaatar	P'yŏngyang	Port Moresby	Magadan	Marshall Is
Berlin	Minsk	Moscow	Yerevan	Ashgabat	Almaty	Vientiane	Beijing	Seoul	Brisbane	Solomon Is	Tuvalu
Paris	Kiev	Baghdād	Baku	Bishkek	Thimphu	Bangkok	T'ai-pei	Tōkyō	Sydney	Vanuatu	Fiji
Madrid	Ankara	Doha	Abu Dhabi	Tashkent	Dhaka	Phnum Penh	Hong Kong	Ōsaka	Canberra	New Caledonia	Auckland
Rome	Jerusalem	Riyadh	Muscat	Islamabad		Hô Chi Minh	Manila	Palau	Melbourne		Wellington
Algiers	Cairo	Addis Ababa	Seychelles	Karachi		Jakarta	Kuala Lumpur				
Abuja	Kigali	Mogadishu	Mauritius				Singapore				
Kinshasa	Harare	Dodoma					Perth				
Luanda	Pretoria	Antananarivo									
	Cape Town										

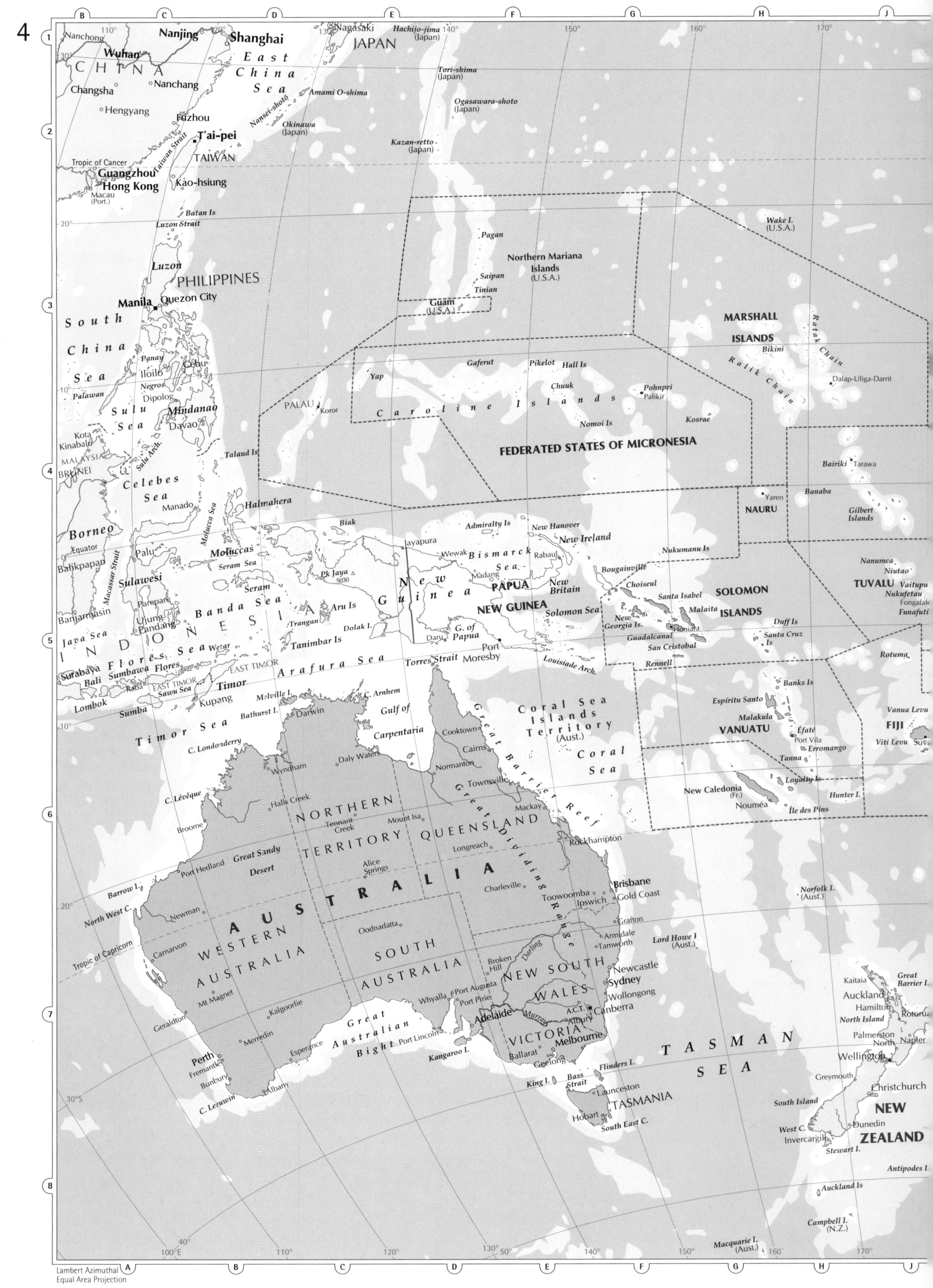

Metres | Feet
SEA LEVEL
200 — 656
3000 — 9843

Lambert Azimuthal Equal Area Projection

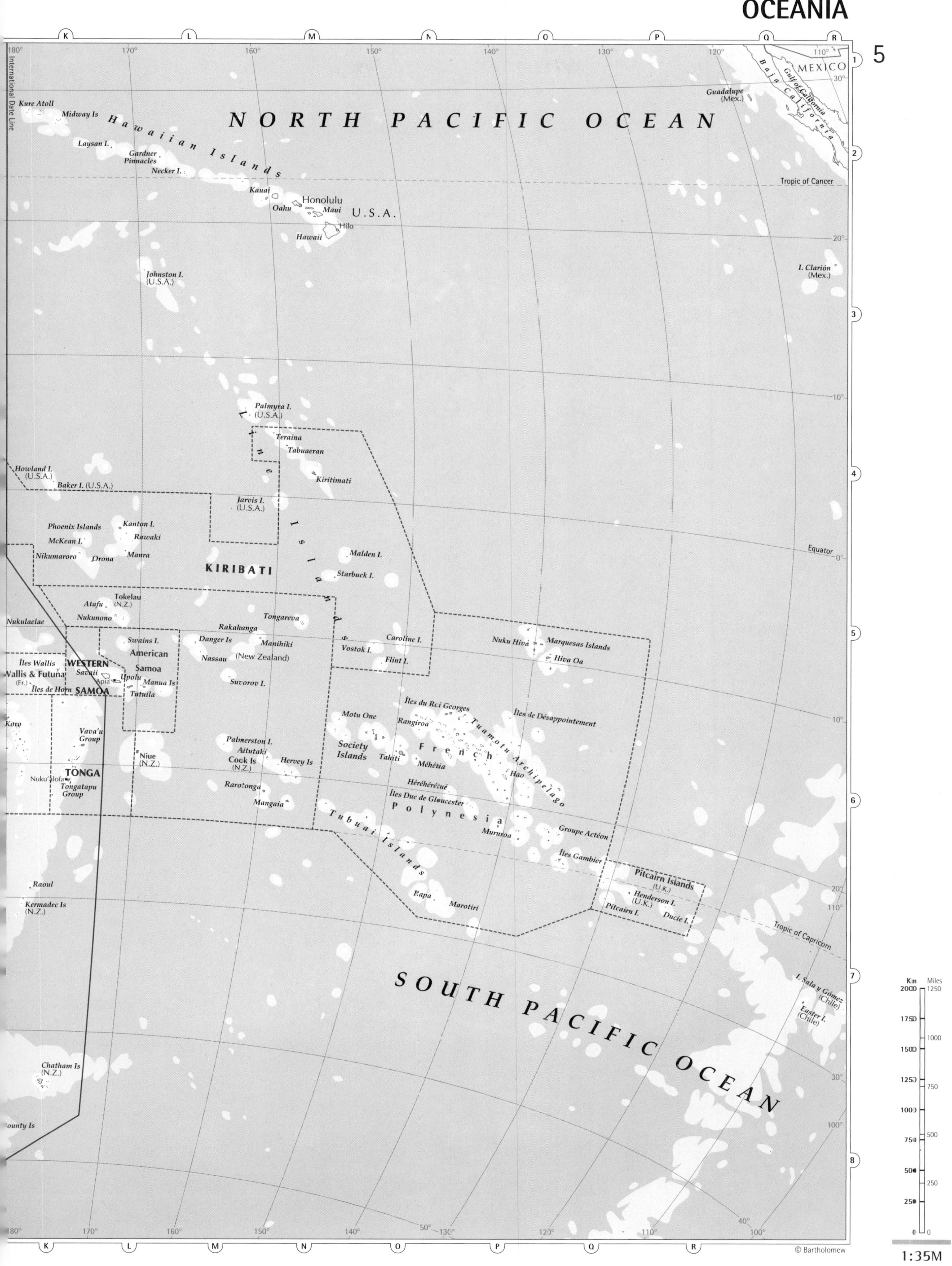

NORTH PACIFIC OCEAN
SOUTH PACIFIC OCEAN
International Date Line
Kure Atoll
Midway Is
Hawaiian Islands
Laysan I.
Gardner Pinnacles
Necker I.
Kauai
Oahu
Honolulu
Maui
U.S.A.
Hilo
Hawaii
Johnston I. (U.S.A.)
MEXICO
Baja California
Gulf of California
Guadalupe (Mex.)
Tropic of Cancer
I. Clarión (Mex.)
Equator
Palmyra I. (U.S.A.)
Line Islands
Teraina
Tabuaeran
Kiritimati
Howland I. (U.S.A.)
Baker I. (U.S.A.)
Jarvis I. (U.S.A.)
Phoenix Islands
Kanton I.
McKean I.
Rawaki
Nikumaroro
Orona
Manra
KIRIBATI
Malden I.
Starbuck I.
Atafu
Tokelau (N.Z.)
Nukunono
Nukulaelae
Tongareva
Rakahanga
Danger Is
Manihiki
Nassau
(New Zealand)
Swains I.
American Samoa
Îles Wallis
Wallis & Futuna (Fr.)
Îles de Horn
WESTERN SAMOA
Savaii
Apia
Upolu
Manua Is
Tutuila
Suvorov I.
Caroline I.
Vostok I.
Flint I.
Nuku Hiva
Marquesas Islands
Hiva Oa
Îles du Roi Georges
Îles de Désappointement
Motu One
Rangiroa
Tuamotu Archipelago
Society Islands
Tahiti
French Polynesia
Méhétia
Hao
Koro
Vava'u Group
Niue (N.Z.)
Palmerston I.
Aitutaki
Cook Is (N.Z.)
Hervey Is
TONGA
Nuku'alofa
Tongatapu Group
Rarotonga
Mangaia
Hérèhérètué
Îles Duc de Gloucester
Tubuai Islands
Mururoa
Groupe Actéon
Îles Gambier
Pitcairn Islands (U.K.)
Henderson I. (U.K.)
Pitcairn I.
Ducie I.
Rapa
Marotiri
Raoul
Kermadec Is (N.Z.)
Tropic of Capricorn
I. Sala y Gómez (Chile)
Easter I. (Chile)
Chatham Is (N.Z.)
Bounty Is
© Bartholomew
Km
Miles
2000
1750
1500
1250
1000
750
500
250
0
1250
1000
750
500
250
0
1:35M

INDONESIA
Celebes Sea
Banda Sea
Seram Sea
Arafura Sea
Flores Sea
Sawu Sea
Timor Sea
INDIAN OCEAN
SOUTHERN OCEAN
Great Australian Bight
Gulf of Carpentaria
Gulf of Papua
Bismarck Sea
Solomon
Coral Sea Islands Territory (Aust.)
Great Barrier Reef
Torres Strait
Bass Strait
IRIAN JAYA
NEW GUINEA
PAPUA NEW GUINEA
EAST TIMOR
Timor
Sulawesi (Celebes)
Halmahera
Seram
Ambon (Amboina)
Sumbawa
Sumba
Bismarck Archipelago
New Britain
New Ireland
Pegunungan Maoke
Pegunungan Van Rees
Cape York Peninsula
Arnhem Land
Kimberley Plateau
NORTHERN TERRITORY
WESTERN AUSTRALIA
SOUTH AUSTRALIA
QUEENSLAND
NEW SOUTH WALES
VICTORIA
TASMANIA
AUSTRALIA
GREAT SANDY DESERT
GREAT VICTORIA DESERT
Gibson Desert
Tanami Desert
Simpson Desert
Sturt Desert
Nullarbor Plain
Macdonnell Ranges
Hamersley Range
GREAT DIVIDING RANGE
Barkly Tableland
Buckland Tableland
Darling Downs
Lake Eyre (North)
Lake Eyre (South)
Lake Torrens
Lake Disappointment
Lake Carnegie
Kangaroo I.
King I.
Furneaux Group
Darwin
Perth
Adelaide
Melbourne
Sydney
Canberra
Hobart
Brisbane
Townsville
Cairns
Newcastle
Port Moresby
Kupang
Dili
Jayapura
Ujung Pandang
Manado
Lambert Azimuthal Equal Area Projection
Metres
Feet
SEA LEVEL

NAURU
Gilbert Islands (Kiribati)
KIRIBATI
Kingsmill Group
Phoenix Islands
SOLOMON ISLANDS
Bougainville Island
Choiseul
Santa Isabel
Malaita
Honiara
Guadalcanal
San Cristobal
Santa Cruz Islands (Solomon Is)
TUVALU
Funafuti
TOKELAU (N.Z.)
CORAL SEA
VANUATU
Espíritu Santo
Malakula
Port Vila
Erromango
Tanna
WALLIS AND FUTUNA (Fr.)
WESTERN SAMOA
Apia
Vanua Levu
Viti Levu
FIJI
Suva
NEW CALEDONIA (NOUVELLE CALÉDONIE) (Fr.)
Nouméa
Îs Loyauté (Loyalty Is) (Fr.)
TONGA
Nuku'alofa
NIUE (N.Z.)
Norfolk Island (Aust.)
Lord Howe Island (Aust.)
Brisbane
Gold Coast
SOUTH PACIFIC OCEAN
TASMAN SEA
Tropic of Capricorn
Equator
NORTH ISLAND
Auckland
Hamilton
Wellington
NEW ZEALAND
Christchurch
Canterbury Bight
SOUTH ISLAND
Dunedin
Invercargill
Stewart Island
Chatham Islands (N.Z.)
Bounty Islands
Auckland Is
© Bartholomew
1:20M

Metres | Feet
6000 | 19686
5000 | 16404
4000 | 13124
3000 | 9843
2000 | 6562
1000 | 3281
500 | 1640
200 | 656
SEA | LEVEL
200 | 656
2000 | 6562
4000 | 13124
6000 | 19686

Km | Miles
300
250 | 150
200
150 | 100
100
50 | 50
0 | 0

1:5M

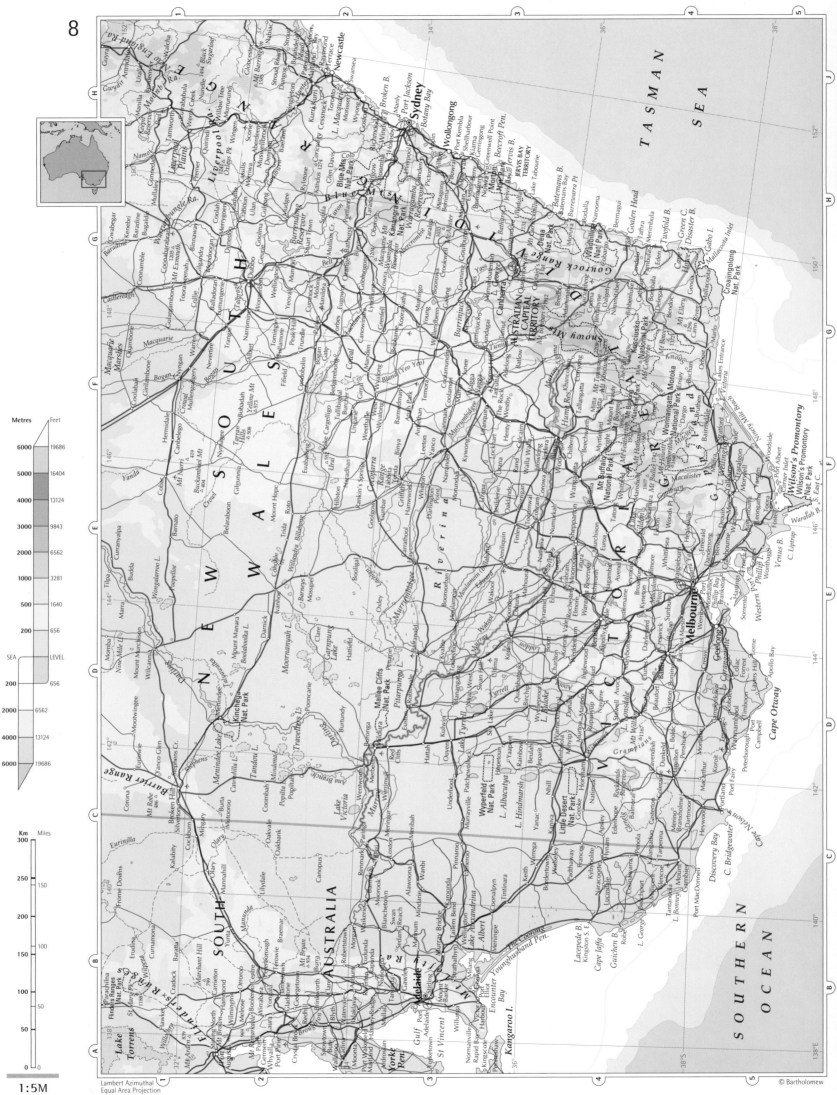

Lambert Azimuthal
Equal Area Projection

NEW ZEALAND

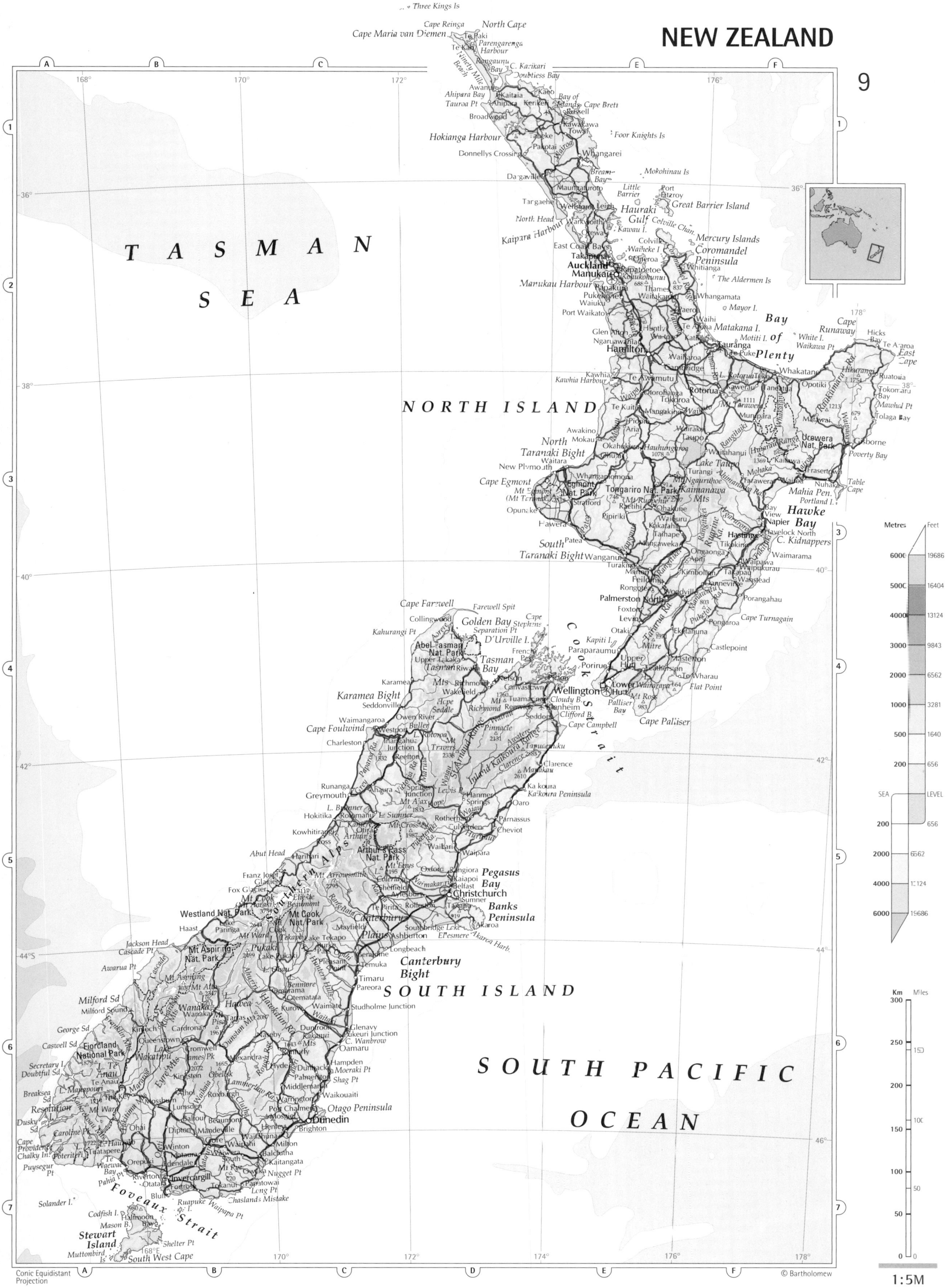

TASMAN SEA

NORTH ISLAND

SOUTH ISLAND

SOUTH PACIFIC OCEAN

Three Kings Is
North Cape
Cape Reinga
Cape Maria van Diemen
Hokianga Harbour
Whangarei
Great Barrier Island
Hauraki Gulf
Coromandel Peninsula
Auckland
Manukau
Hamilton
Tauranga
Bay of Plenty
East Cape
Rotorua
Gisborne
Lake Taupo
Tongariro Nat. Park
Egmont Nat. Park
Cape Egmont
New Plymouth
North Taranaki Bight
South Taranaki Bight
Wanganui
Napier
Hastings
Hawke Bay
Palmerston North
Wellington
Cook Strait
Cape Palliser
Cape Farewell
Golden Bay
Tasman Bay
Nelson
Blenheim
Karamea Bight
Cape Foulwind
Westport
Greymouth
Hokitika
Kaikoura Peninsula
Arthur's Pass Nat. Park
Christchurch
Pegasus Bay
Banks Peninsula
Canterbury Bight
Westland Nat. Park
Mt Cook Nat. Park
Mt Aspiring Nat. Park
Southern Alps
Timaru
Oamaru
Dunedin
Otago Peninsula
Milford Sd
Fiordland National Park
Te Anau
Queenstown
Invercargill
Foveaux Strait
Stewart Island
South West Cape

Metres / Feet
6000 – 19686
5000 – 16404
4000 – 13124
3000 – 9843
2000 – 6562
1000 – 3281
500 – 1640
200 – 656
SEA LEVEL
200 – 656
2000 – 6562
4000 – 13124
6000 – 19686

Km / Miles: 0–300 / 0–150

1:5M

Conic Equidistant Projection

ARCTIC OCEAN
Norwegian Sea
North Sea
Barents Sea
Kara Sea
Baltic Sea
Gulf of Bothnia
White Sea
Black Sea
Caspian Sea
Mediterranean Sea
Red Sea
Gulf of Aden
Gulf of Oman
The Gulf
ARABIAN SEA
BAY OF BENGAL
INDIAN OCEAN
Bay of Biscay
English Channel
Tyrrhenian Sea
Ionian Sea
Aegean Sea
Sea of Azov
Aral Sea
Ozero Balkhash
Spitsbergen
Svalbard (Nor.)
Franz Josef Land
O. Komsomolets
Severnaya Zemlya
O. Oktyabr'skoy Revolyutsii
O. Bol'shevik
Novaya Zemlya
Faroe Islands (Den.)
Nordkapp
Arctic Circle
North Pole
Ural Mountains
Caucasus
Altai Mts
Tien Shan
HIMALAYA
Mt Everest 8848
Rub' al Khālī
XINJIANG
XIZANG
Socotra (Yemen)
Laccadive Is (India)
Andaman Islands (India)
Nicobar Islands (India)
MALDIVES
Male
Gan
Addu Atoll
British Indian Ocean Terr.
Chagos Archipelago
SEYCHELLES
Mahé
Amirante Islands
Aldabra Is
COMOROS
Equator
Tropic of Cancer
RUSSIAN FEDERATION
(in Europe)
KAZAKSTAN
TURKMENISTAN
UZBEKISTAN
KYRGYZSTAN
TAJIKISTAN
AFGHANISTAN
PAKISTAN
INDIA
NEPAL
BHUTAN
BANGLADESH
MYANMAR (BURMA)
SRI LANKA
IRAN
IRAQ
SYRIA
TURKEY
CYPRUS
LEBANON
ISRAEL
JORDAN
KUWAIT
BAHRAIN
QATAR
U.A.E.
OMAN
SAUDI ARABIA
YEMEN
NORTH
SOUTH
EGYPT
LIBYA
SUDAN
ERITREA
DJIBOUTI
ETHIOPIA
SOMALIA
GEORGIA
ARMENIA
AZERBAIJAN
UKRAINE
BELARUS
MOLDOVA
ROMANIA
BULGARIA
GREECE
ALBANIA
MACEDONIA
YUGOSLAVIA
BOSNIA HERZEGOVINA
CROATIA
SLOVENIA
HUNGARY
SLOVAKIA
CZECH REP.
AUSTRIA
SWITZERLAND
ITALY
MALTA
GERMANY
POLAND
LITHUANIA
LATVIA
ESTONIA
FINLAND
SWEDEN
NORWAY
DENMARK
NETHERLANDS
BELGIUM
LUXEMBOURG
FRANCE
SPAIN
PORTUGAL
UNITED KINGDOM
REP. OF IRELAND
Madrid
Barcelona
Lyon
Paris
London
Dublin
Edinburgh
The Hague
Amsterdam
Brussels
Bonn
Hamburg
Berlin
Copenhagen
Oslo
Stockholm
Helsinki
Tallinn
Riga
Vilnius
Minsk
Warsaw
Prague
Vienna
Bratislava
Budapest
Ljubljana
Zagreb
Sarajevo
Belgrade
Skopje
Tirana
Sofia
Bucharest
Chişinău
Kiev
Odesa
Kharkiv
Moscow
St Petersburg
Archangel
Murmansk
Nizhniy Novgorod
Kazan
Perm
Saratov
Samara
Volgograd
Rostov-na-Donu
Astrakhan
Orenburg
Aktyubinsk
Yekaterinburg
Chelyabinsk
Omsk
Tomsk
Novosibirsk
Krasnoyarsk
Bratsk
Novokuznetsk
Barnaul
Pavlodar
Karaganda
Salekhard
Surgut
Norilsk
Yenisey
Ob'
Irtysh
Nizhnyaya Tunguska
Volga
Ural
Don
Danube
Rhine
Lake Ladoga
Lake Onega
München
Milan
Rome
Naples
Corsica
Sardinia
Sicily
Balearic Is
Tunis
Alps
Athens
Crete
Istanbul
Izmir
Ankara
Antalya
Samsun
Kayseri
Adana
Aleppo
Nicosia
Beirut
Damascus
Amman
Jerusalem
Port Said
Alexandria
Cairo
Nile
L. Nasser
Banghazi
Tbilisi
Yerevan
Baku
Tabrīz
Mosul
Baghdād
Tigris
Euphrates
Basra
Ahvāz
Tehrān
Mashhad
Esfahan
Shīrāz
Kermān
Zāhedān
Kuwait
Al Manāmah
Doha
Abu Dhabi
Dubai
Muscat
Riyadh
Medina
Jeddah
Mecca
Port Sudan
Asmara
San'a
Aden
Djibouti
Addis Ababa
Mogadishu
Ashgabat
Tashkent
Samarkand
Dushanbe
Bishkek
Almaty
Tacheng
Ürümqi
Kashi
Hotan
Yumen
K2
Herāt
Kābul
Kandahār
Quetta
Islamabad
Lahore
Ludhiana
Indus
Karachi
Hyderabad
Ahmadabad
Jaipur
Delhi
New Delhi
Kanpur
Jabalpur
Varanasi
Ganga
Kathmandu
Darjeeling
Thimphu
Shillong
Brahmaputra
Dhaka
Chittagong
Calcutta
Mandalay
Irrawaddy
Yangon
Nagpur
Bombay
Pune
Hyderabad
Vijayawada
Bangalore
Madras
Trivandrum
Colombo
30°
40°
50°
60°
70°
80°
90°
100°
110°
120°
130°
10°
0°
10°S
50°E

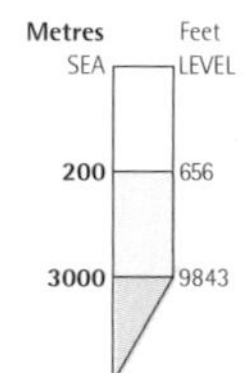

Two Point Equidistant Projection

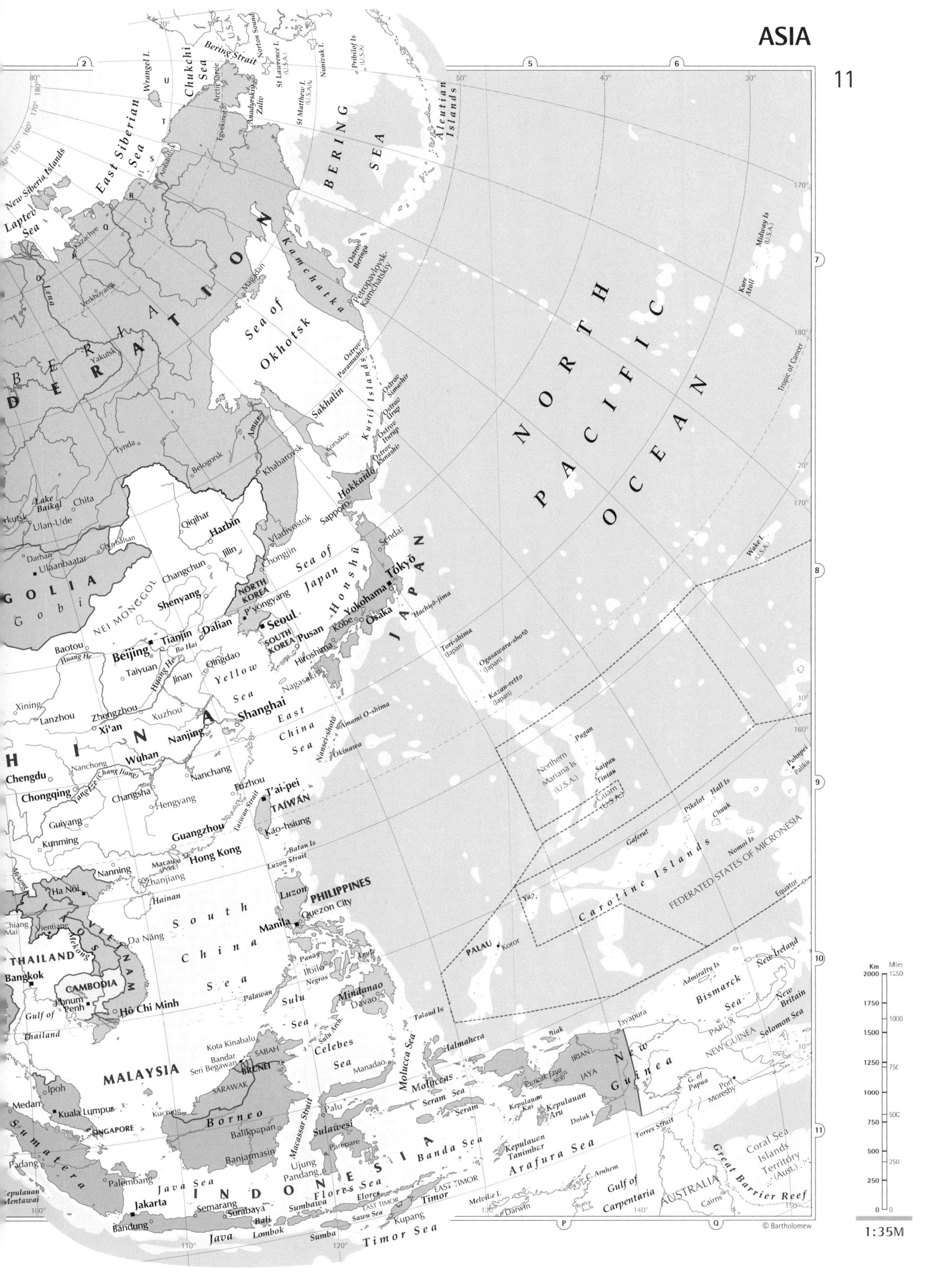
NORTH PACIFIC OCEAN
BERING SEA
Sea of Okhotsk
Sea of Japan
Yellow Sea
East China Sea
South China Sea
Sulu Sea
Celebes Sea
Molucca Sea
Banda Sea
Arafura Sea
Java Sea
Flores Sea
Timor Sea
Bismarck Sea
Solomon Sea
Coral Sea Islands Territory (Aust.)
CHINA
JAPAN
MONGOLIA
NORTH KOREA
SOUTH KOREA
TAIWAN
PHILIPPINES
MALAYSIA
INDONESIA
THAILAND
CAMBODIA
VIETNAM
BRUNEI
SINGAPORE
PALAU
FEDERATED STATES OF MICRONESIA
NEW GUINEA
AUSTRALIA
EAST TIMOR
Beijing
Tianjin
Dalian
Shanghai
Nanjing
Wuhan
Chengdu
Chongqing
Guangzhou
Hong Kong
Seoul
P'yongyang
Pusan
Tōkyō
Yokohama
Ōsaka
Kobe
Hiroshima
Sapporo
Sendai
T'ai-pei
Kao-hsiung
Manila
Quezon City
Hô Chi Minh
Ha Nôi
Bangkok
Phnum Penh
Kuala Lumpur
Jakarta
Bandung
Surabaya
Semarang
Harbin
Shenyang
Changchun
Jilin
Qiqihar
Vladivostok
Khabarovsk
Magadan
Yakutsk
Petropavlovsk-Kamchatskiy
Ulaanbaatar
Ulan-Ude
Chita
Kamchatka
Sakhalin
Kuril Islands
Hokkaidō
Honshū
Aleutian Islands
Bering Strait
Chukchi Sea
East Siberian Sea
Laptev Sea
New Siberia Islands
Wrangel I.
Lake Baikal
Gobi
Borneo
Sulawesi
Sumatera
Java
Mindanao
Luzon
Halmahera
Caroline Islands
Northern Mariana Is (U.S.A.)
Guam (U.S.A.)
Wake I. (U.S.A.)
Midway Is (U.S.A.)
Tropic of Cancer
Equator
Great Barrier Reef
Gulf of Carpentaria
Torres Strait
Port Moresby
Darwin
Cairns
Jayapura
© Bartholomew
1:35M

Metres | Feet
6000 | 19686
5000 | 16404
4000 | 13124
3000 | 9843
2000 | 6562
1000 | 3281
500 | 1640
200 | 656
SEA LEVEL
200 | 656
2000 | 6562
4000 | 13124
6000 | 19686

OCEAN
Chukchi Sea
Bering Strait
U.S.A.
St Lawrence I.
Nunivak I.
Pribilof Islands
Wrangell I.
Proliv Longa
East Siberian Sea
(Vostochno-Sibirskoye More)
Novosibirskiye Ostrova
(New Siberia Islands)
Laptev Sea
(More Laptevykh)
Severnaya Zemlya
O. Bolshevik
Poluostrov Taymyr
Khrebet Cherskogo
Verkhoyanskiy Khrebet
Koryakskiy Khrebet
Khrebet Kolymskiy
BERING SEA
Karaginskiy Zaliv
Anadyr'
Magadan
Kamchatka Peninsula
Petropavlovsk-Kamchatskiy
SEA OF OKHOTSK
(OKHOTSKOYE MORE)
Sakhalin
Kuril Islands
(Kuril'skiye Ostrova)
Yakutsk
SREDNE-SIBIRSKOYE PLOSKOGOR'YE
(CENTRAL SIBERIAN PLATEAU)
FEDERATION
Stanovoy Khrebet
Stanovoye Nagor'ye
Lake Baikal
(Ozero Baykal)
Irkutsk
Ulan-Ude
Chita
Bratsk
Angarsk
Blagoveshchensk
Khabarovsk
Komsomol'sk-na-Amure
Vladivostok
Nakhodka
Yuzhno-Sakhalinsk
Hokkaidō
Sapporo
Honshū
Sea of Japan
JAPAN
Tōkyō
Yokohama
Nagoya
Ōsaka
Kōbe
Kyōto
Hiroshima
Fukuoka
Kagoshima
Shikoku
NORTH KOREA
P'yŏngyang
SOUTH KOREA
Seoul
Pusan
Taegu
Yellow Sea
Bo Hai
Beijing
(Peking)
Tianjin
(Tientsin)
Shenyang
Harbin
Changchun
Dalian
Qiqihar
MONGOLIA
Ulaanbaatar
(Ulan Bator)
GOBI
CHINA
Baotou
Hohhot
Datong
Taiyuan
Zhangjiakou
Da Hinggan Ling
Km
Miles
1200
1000
800
600
400
200
0
600
450
300
150
0
© Bartholomew
1:21M

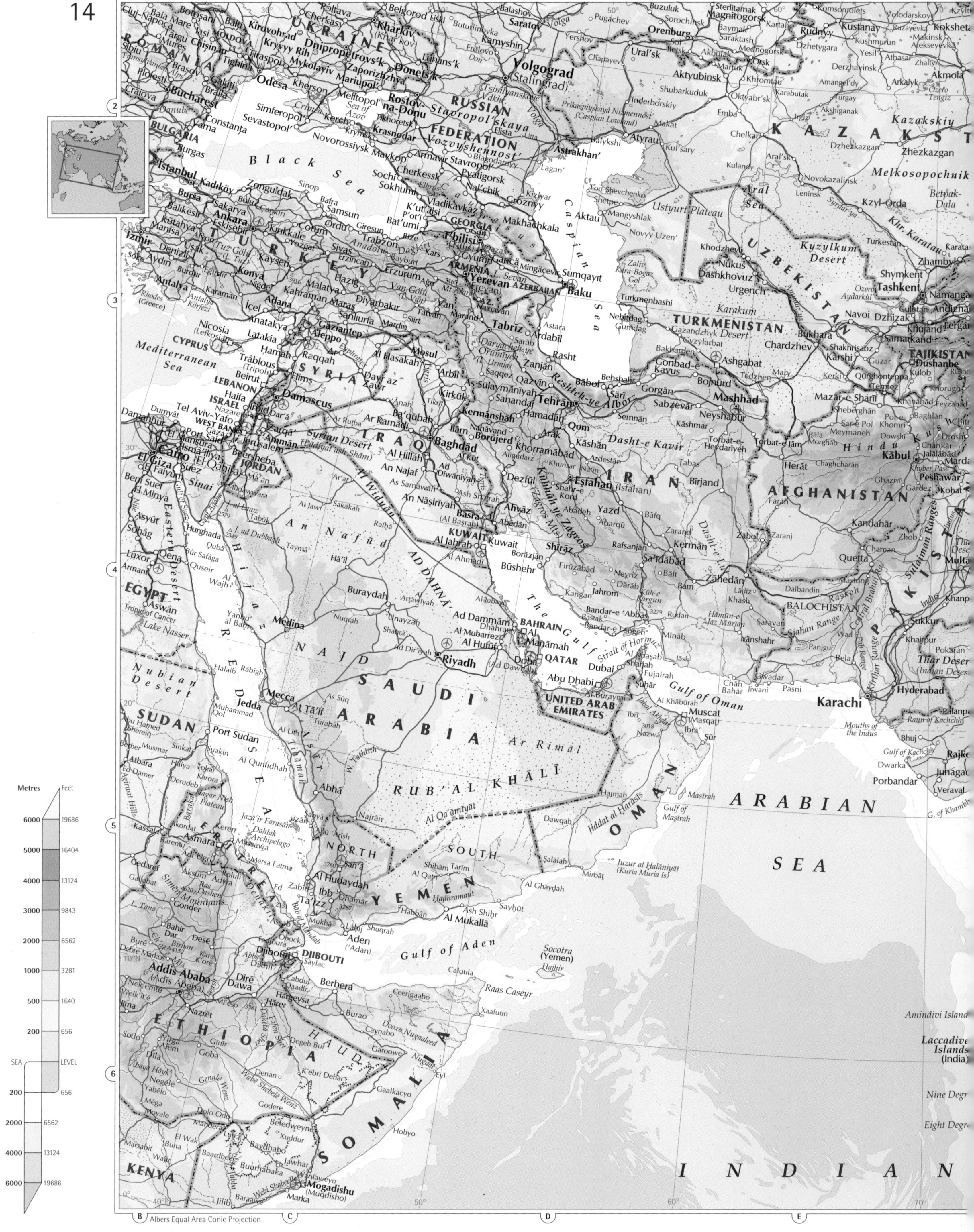
Metres
Feet
6000
19686
5000
16404
4000
13124
3000
9843
2000
6562
1000
3281
500
1640
200
656
SEA
LEVEL
200
656
2000
6562
4000
13124
6000
19686
Albers Equal Area Conic Projection
UKRAINE
RUSSIAN FEDERATION
KAZAKST
Black Sea
Caspian Sea
Aral Sea
TURKEY
GEORGIA
ARMENIA
AZERBAIJAN
UZBEKISTAN
TURKMENISTAN
TAJIKISTAN
CYPRUS
Mediterranean Sea
SYRIA
LEBANON
ISRAEL
WEST BANK
JORDAN
IRAQ
IRAN
AFGHANISTAN
PAKISTAN
KUWAIT
BAHRAIN
QATAR
UNITED ARAB EMIRATES
OMAN
SAUDI ARABIA
NORTH YEMEN
SOUTH YEMEN
EGYPT
SUDAN
ERITREA
DJIBOUTI
ETHIOPIA
SOMALIA
KENYA
RED SEA
The Gulf
Gulf of Oman
Gulf of Aden
ARABIAN SEA
INDIAN
An Nafūd
AD DAHNĀ'
NAJD
Rub' al Khālī
Syrian Desert
Dasht-e Kavir
Karakum
Kyzylkum Desert
Nubian Desert
Sinai
Volgograd (Stalingrad)
Bucharest
Odesa
İstanbul
Ankara
Tbilisi
Yerevan
Baku
Tehrān
Baghdād
Damascus
Beirut
Cairo
Jerusalem
'Ammān
Kuwait
Riyadh
Mecca
Jedda
Medina
Abu Dhabi
Dubai
Muscat (Masqat)
Aden
San'ā
Djibouti
Addis Ababa
Mogadishu (Muqdisho)
Karachi
Kābul
Ashgabat
Tashkent
Dushanbe
Mashhad
Esfahān
Shīrāz
Socotra (Yemen)
Laccadive Islands (India)

1:20M

BLACK (KARA
TURKEY
Sea of Marmara (Marmara Denizi)
İstanbul
Ankara
Bursa
Eskişehir
Konya
Antalya
Adana
Kayseri
Sivas
Malatya
Gaziantep
Samsun
Zonguldak
Tuz Gölü (L. Tuz)
Köroğlu Dağları
Toros Dağları
Bolkar Dağları
ANATOLIA
Rhodes (Rodos)
GREECE
Antalya Körfezi
CYPRUS
Nicosia
Limassol (Lemesos)
Larnaka
Aleppo (Halab)
Latakia (Al Lādhiqīyah)
Ḥamāh
Ḥimṣ (Homs)
Trâblous (Tripoli)
Beirut (Beyrouth)
LEBANON
Damascus (Dimashq)
Haifa
ISRAEL
WEST BANK
Tel Aviv-Yafo (Jaffa)
Jerusalem
GAZA
Amman
JORDAN
MEDITERRANEAN SEA
Alexandria (El Iskandarîya)
Port Said (Bûr Sa'îd)
El Mansûra
Tanta
Zagazig
Ismâ'ilîya
Cairo (El Qâhira)
El Gîza
Suez (El Suweis)
Helwân
EGYPT
SINAI
Gebel el Tîh
Metres
Feet
6000 19686
5000 16404
4000 13124
3000 9843
2000 6562
1000 3281
500 1640
200 656
SEA LEVEL
200 656
2000 6562
4000 13124
6000 19686
Conic Equidistant Projection

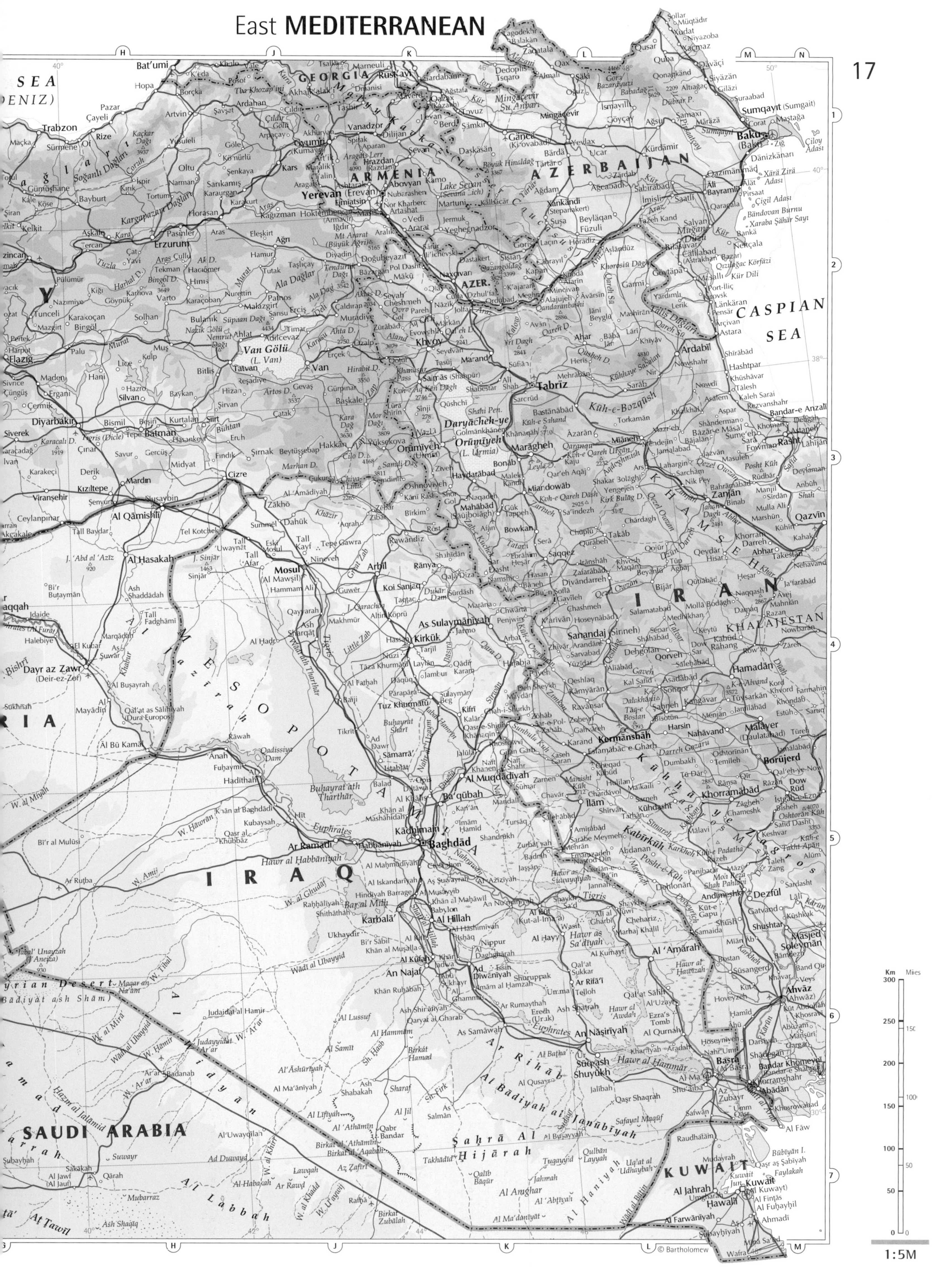
GEORGIA
ARMENIA
AZERBAIJAN
AZER.
IRAN
IRAQ
KUWAIT
SAUDI ARABIA
MESOPOTAMIA
CASPIAN SEA
Bat'umi
Trabzon
Rize
Erzurum
Kars
Gyumri
Yerevan (Erevan)
Ganca
Baku (Bakı)
Sumqayıt (Sumgait)
Naxçıvan
Tabrīz
Ardabīl
Rasht
Bandar-e Anzalī
Zanjān
Qazvīn
Hamadān
Borūjerd
Malāyer
Kermānshāh
Sanandaj (Sineh)
Khorramābād
Dezfūl
Ahvāz
Ābādān
Basra (Al Başrah)
Kuwait (Al Kuwayt)
Al Jahrah
Van Gölü (L. Van)
Daryācheh-ye Orūmīyeh (L. Urmia)
Orūmīyeh
Diyarbakır
Batman
Siirt
Mosul (Al Mawşil)
Arbīl
Kirkūk
As Sulaymānīyah
Baghdād
Ba'qūbah
Al Hillah
Karbalā'
An Najaf
Ad Dīwānīyah
Al Kūt
Al 'Amārah
An Nāşirīyah
Tikrīt
Sāmarrā'
Ar Ramādī
Dayr az Zawr (Deir-ez-Zor)
Al Hasakah
Al Qāmishlī
Euphrates
Tigris
Hawr al Hammār
Qadissiya Dam
Buhayrat ath Tharthār
Little Zab
Great Zab
Karkheh
Kārūn
Ṣaḥrā' Al Ḥijārah
Al Bādiyah al Janūbīyah
Wādī al Ubayyid
SEA
(DENIZ)
© Bartholomew
1:5M

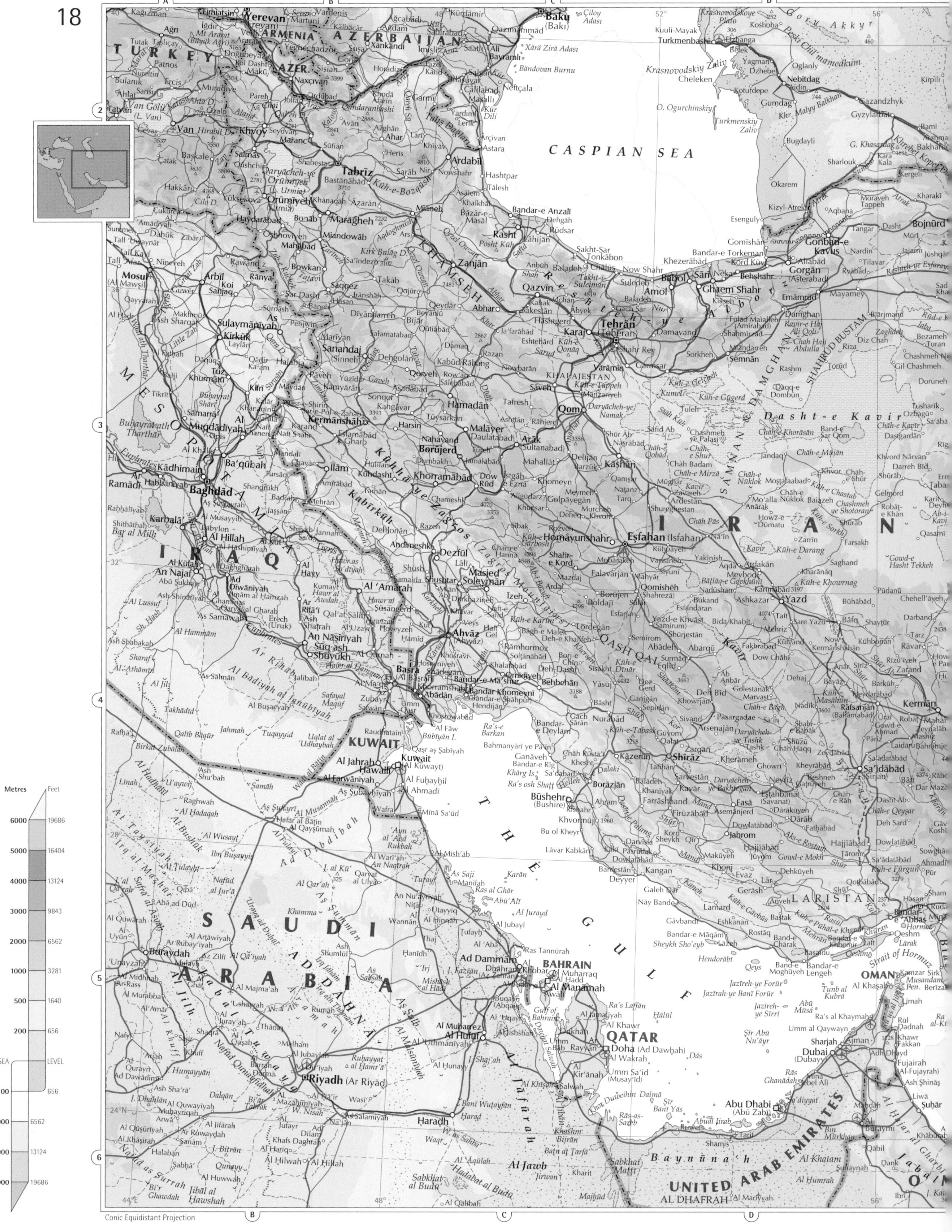

Conic Equidistant Projection

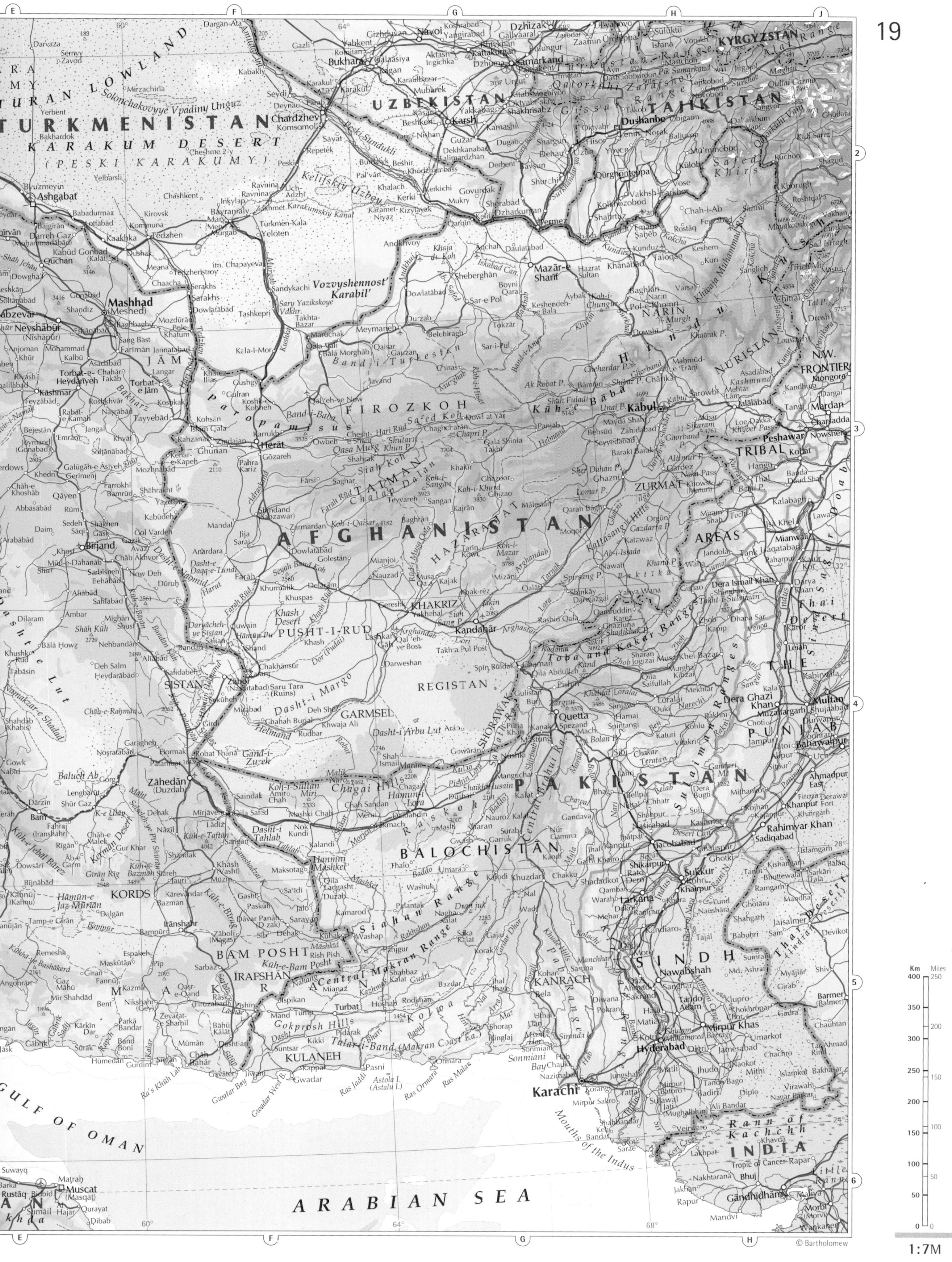
TURKMENISTAN
UZBEKISTAN
TAJIKISTAN
KYRGYZSTAN
AFGHANISTAN
PAKISTAN
INDIA
TURAN LOWLAND
KARAKUM DESERT
(PESKI KARAKUMY)
FIROZKOH
HAZARAJAT
PUSHT-I-RUD
REGISTAN
GARMSEL
SISTAN
BALOCHISTAN
MAKRAN
KULANEH
BAM POSHT
IRAFSHAN
KORDS
SINDH
PUNJAB
TRIBAL AREAS
N.W. FRONTIER
Hindu Kush
Paropamisus
Kūh-e Bābā
Rann of Kachchh
GULF OF OMAN
ARABIAN SEA
Ashgabat
Mashhad
Herāt
Kābul
Kandahār
Dushanbe
Samarkand
Bukhara
Quetta
Karachi
Hyderabad
Peshawar
Zāhedān
Muscat
Mouths of the Indus
Tropic of Cancer
Km
Miles
1:7M

ARABIAN PENINSULA

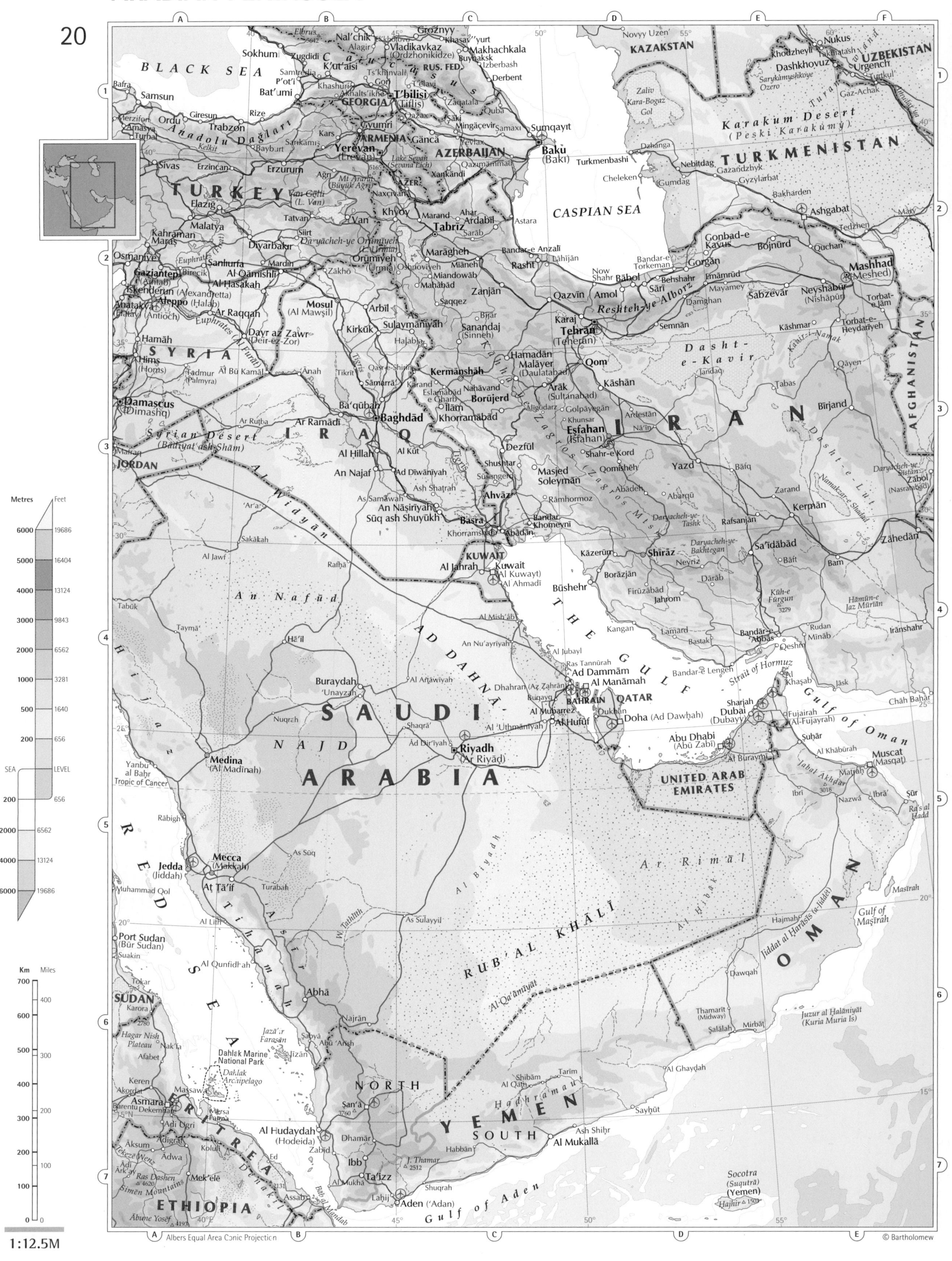

Albers Equal Area Conic Projection

MADHYA PRADESH
MAHARASHTRA
GUJARAT
ORISSA
BIHAR
ANDHRA PRADESH
KARNATAKA
KERALA
TAMIL NADU
GOA
INDIA
LAKSHADWEEP
MALDIVES
SRI LANKA
Ceylon
BAY OF BENGAL
Gulf of Mannar
Palk Strait
Palk Bay
Malabar Coast
Laccadive Islands
Bombay (Mumbai)
Pune (Poona)
Nagpur
Indore
Hyderabad
Secunderabad
Bangalore
Madras
Mysore
Coimbatore
Madurai
Cochin (Kochi)
Trivandrum (Thiruvananthapuram)
Vishakhapatnam (Vizagapatam)
Vijayawada
Colombo
Jaffna
Pondicherry (Puducherri)
Mouths of the Godavari
Mouths of the Krishna
Cape Comorin (Kanniya Kumari)
Nine Degree Channel
Eight Degree Channel
Minicoy
Indian states not named on map
1. DAMAN & DIU (A1)
2. DADRA & NAGAR HAVELI (A1)
Conic Equidistant Projection
© Bartholomew
Metres
Feet
6000 19686
5000 16404
4000 13124
3000 9843
2000 6562
1000 3281
500 1640
200 656
SEA LEVEL
200 656
2000 6562
4000 13124
6000 19686
Km
Miles
400 250
350
300 200
250 150
200
150 100
100
50 50
0 0

1:7M

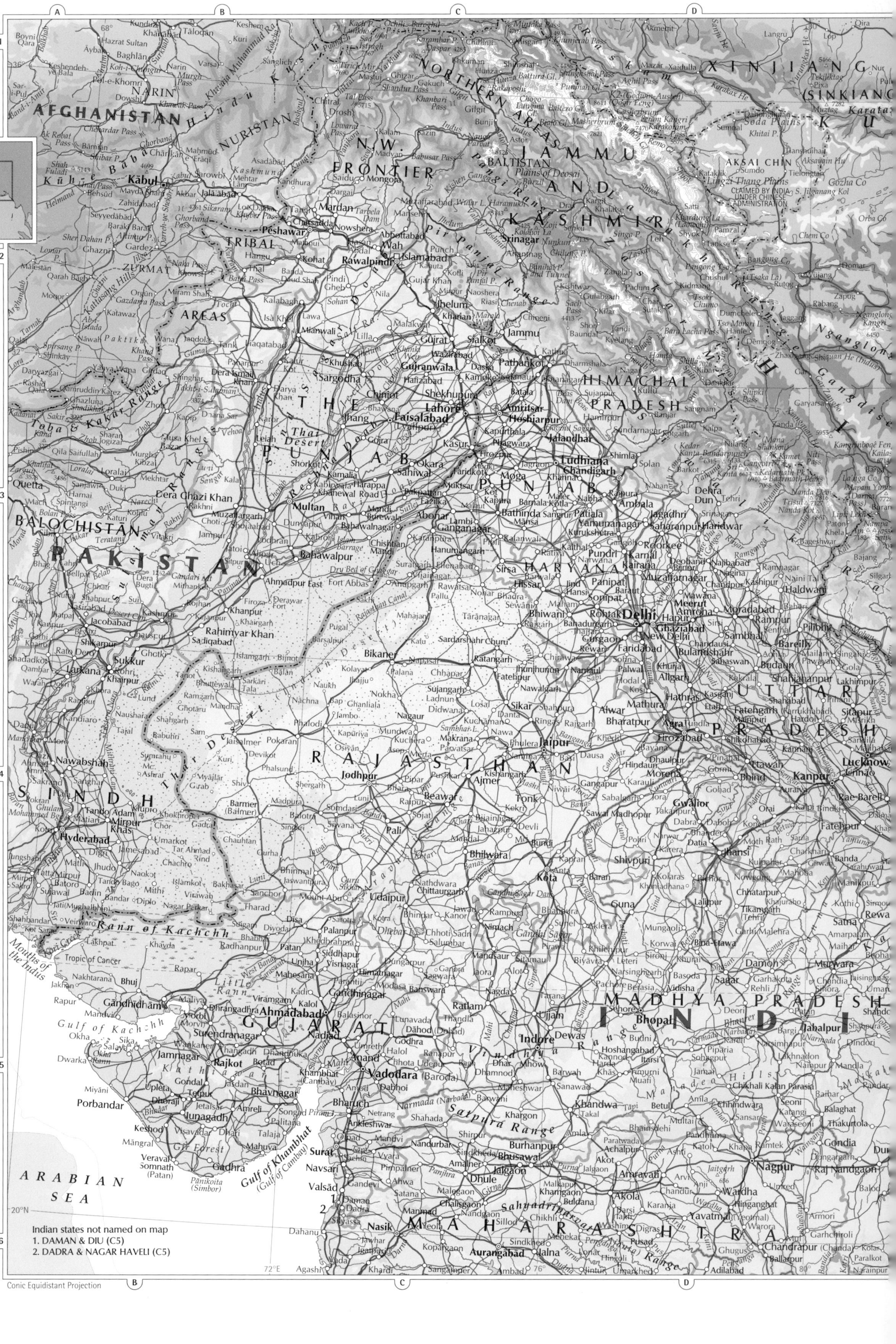

Metres	Feet
6000	19686
5000	16404
4000	13124
3000	9843
2000	6562
1000	3281
500	1640
200	656
SEA	LEVEL
200	656
2000	6562
4000	13124
6000	19686

Indian states not named on map
1. DAMAN & DIU (C5)
2. DADRA & NAGAR HAVELI (C5)

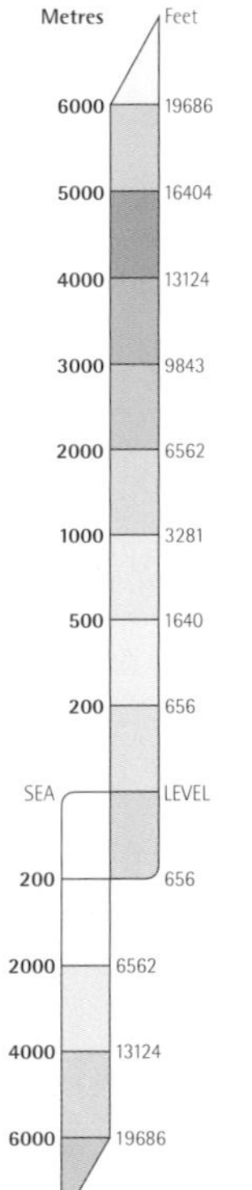

Conic Equidistant Projection

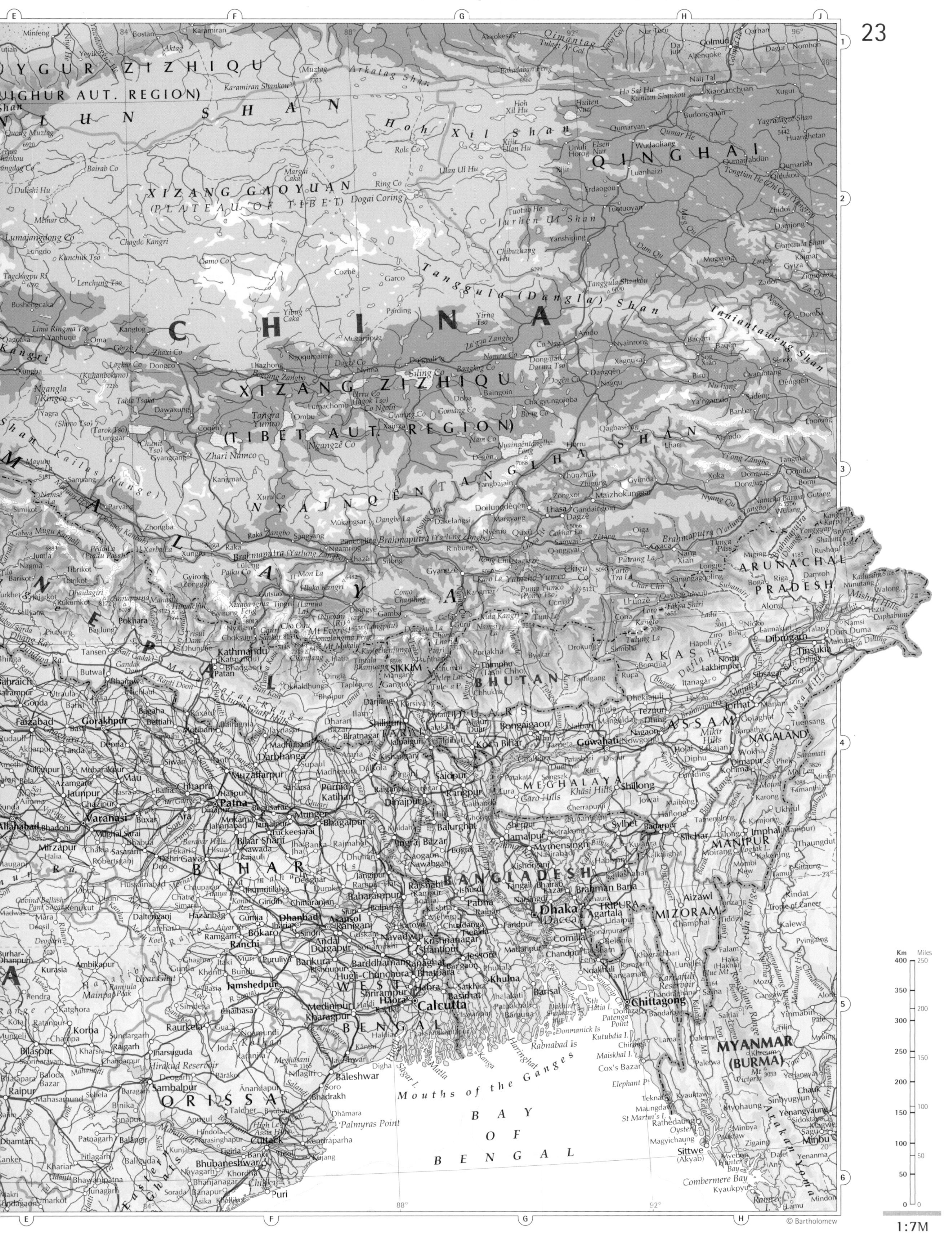
CHINA
XIZANG GAOYUAN
(PLATEAU OF TIBET)
XIZANG ZIZHIQU
(TIBET AUT. REGION)
QINGHAI
UIGHUR AUT. REGION)
Hoh Xil Shan
Tanggula (Dangla) Shan
Taniantaweng Shan
NYAINQÊNTANGLHA SHAN
HIMALAYA
NEPAL
Kathmandu
Mt Everest
SIKKIM
BHUTAN
Thimphu
ARUNACHAL PRADESH
ASSAM
NAGALAND
MEGHALAYA
MANIPUR
MIZORAM
TRIPURA
BANGLADESH
Dhaka
Chittagong
BIHAR
Patna
WEST BENGAL
Calcutta
ORISSA
Bhubaneshwar
MYANMAR (BURMA)
Mouths of the Ganges
BAY OF BENGAL
Lhasa
Brahmaputra (Yarlung Zangbo)
Km
Miles
1:7M
© Bartholomew

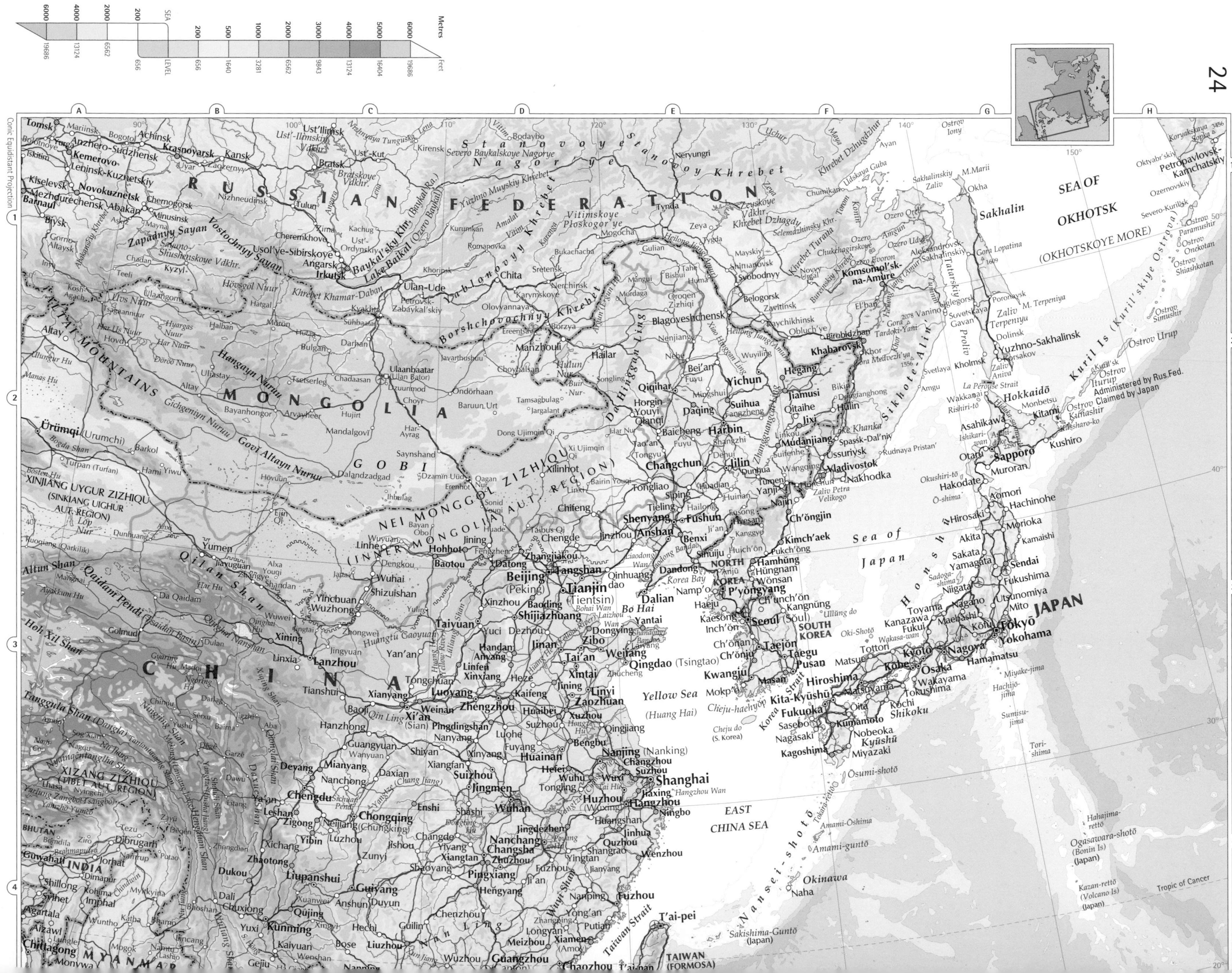
Metres
Feet
6000
19686
5000
16404
4000
13124
3000
9843
2000
6562
1000
3281
500
1640
200
656
SEA
LEVEL
200
656
2000
6562
4000
13124
6000
19686
Conic Equidistant Projection
SEA OF OKHOTSK
(OKHOTSKOYE MORE)
RUSSIAN FEDERATION
MONGOLIA
CHINA
JAPAN
NORTH KOREA
SOUTH KOREA
Sea of Japan
Yellow Sea
(Huang Hai)
EAST CHINA SEA
TAIWAN
(FORMOSA)
GOBI
NEI MONGGOL ZIZHIQU
(INNER MONGOLIA AUT. REGION)
XINJIANG UYGUR ZIZHIQU
(SINKIANG UIGHUR AUT. REGION)
XIZANG ZIZHIQU
(TIBET AUT. REGION)
ALTAI MOUNTAINS
Qaidam Pendi
Sakhalin
Hokkaidō
Honshu
Shikoku
Kyūshū
Okinawa
Kuril Is (Kuril'skiye Ostrova)
Tropic of Cancer
Beijing
(Peking)
Shanghai
Tianjin
(Tientsin)
Tōkyō
Seoul
(Sŏul)
P'yŏngyang
Vladivostok
Harbin
Irkutsk
Ulan-Ude
Ulaanbaatar
(Ulan Bator)
Ürümqi
(Urumchi)
Lanzhou
Xi'an
(Sian)
Wuhan
Chongqing
(Chungking)
Chengdu
Kunming
Guangzhou
Nanjing
(Nanking)
Hangzhou
Osaka
Kyōto
Nagoya
Yokohama
Sapporo
Fukuoka
Hiroshima
Pusan
Dalian
Shenyang
Changchun
Khabarovsk
Chita
Krasnoyarsk
Novokuznetsk
Tomsk
Petropavlovsk-Kamchatskiy
Naha
T'ai-pei
Fuzhou
Taiwan Strait
Korea Strait
Bo Hai
Korea Bay
INDIA
BHUTAN
MYANMAR

PACIFIC OCEAN
PHILIPPINE SEA
PHILIPPINES
SOUTH CHINA SEA
MALAYSIA
INDONESIA
BORNEO
INDIAN OCEAN
Java Sea
Banda Sea
Arafura Sea
Timor Sea
Celebes Sea
Sulu Sea
Flores Sea
Molucca Sea
Strait of Malacca
Gulf of Thailand
Andaman Sea
THAILAND
CAMBODIA
BURMA
PALAU
FEDERATED STATES OF MICRONESIA
NORTHERN MARIANA ISLANDS (U.S.A.)
IRIAN JAYA
NEW GUINEA
AUSTRALIA
EAST TIMOR
BRUNEI
SINGAPORE
SUMATERA
JAVA (JAWA)
Sulawesi (Celebes)
Mindanao
Luzon
Halmahera
Timor
Hainan (China)
Manila
Jakarta
Singapore
Kuala Lumpur
Bangkok
Ho Chi Minh (Saigon)
Hong Kong
Equator
© Bartholomew
Km
Miles

1:20M

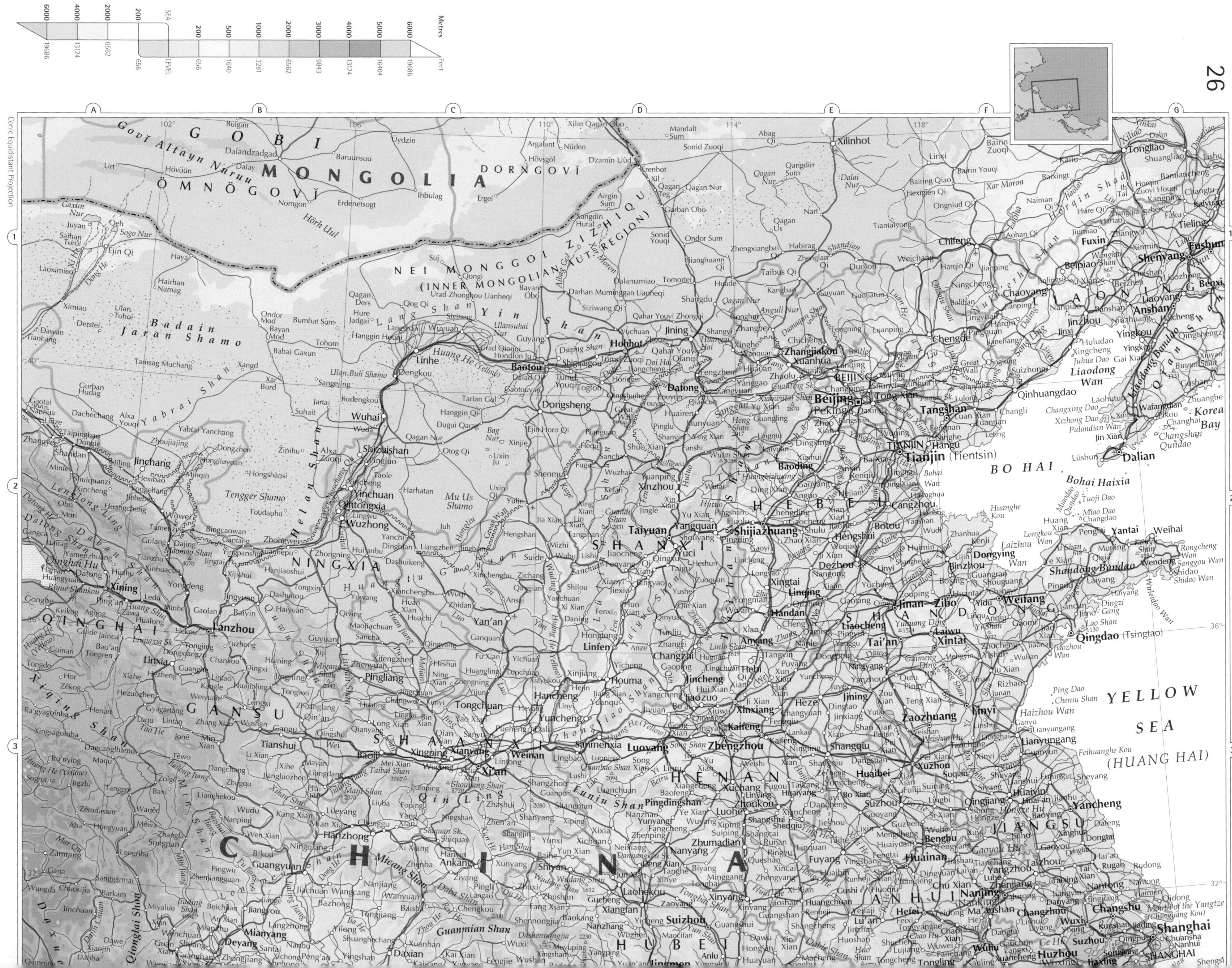

Conic Equidistant Projection

SOUTH CHINA SEA
LUZON STRAIT
GULF OF TONGKING
Taiwan Strait
TAIWAN (FORMOSA)
PHILIPPINES
SICHUAN
GUANGDONG
GUANGXI
JIANGXI
FUJIAN
ZHEJIANG
HUNAN
GUIZHOU
YUNNAN
HAINAN
VIETNAM
LAOS
THAILAND
Wuhan
Hangzhou
Ningbo
Shaoxing
Jinhua
Quzhou
Wenzhou
Jingdezhen
Nanchang
Changsha
Zhuzhou
Xiangtan
Hengyang
Fuzhou
Sanming
Quanzhou
Xiamen (Amoy)
Zhangzhou
Shantou
Chaozhou
Meizhou
Ganzhou
Chenzhou
Shaoguan
Guangzhou (Canton)
Foshan
Dongguan
Shenzhen
Zhongshan
Zhuhai
HONG KONG
Hong Kong
Macau (Port.)
Jiangmen
Zhaoqing
Maoming
Zhanjiang
Beihai
Qinzhou
Nanning
Wuzhou
Yulin
Guilin
Liuzhou
Hechi
Bose
Guiyang
Anshun
Duyun
Kaili
Zunyi
Liupanshui
Qujing
Kunming
Chuxiong
Gejiu
Kaiyuan
Zhaotong
Dongchuan
Xichang
Dukou
Yibin
Luzhou
Zigong
Neijiang
Leshan
Chongqing (Chungking)
Enshi
Yichang
Jingzhou
Shashi
Changde
Yueyang
Yiyang
Loudi
Shaoyang
Huaihua
Jishou
Pingxiang
Xinyu
Yichun
Ji'an
Jiujiang
Huangshi
Haikou
Sanya
Hà Nội (Hanoi)
Hải Phòng
Nam Định
Thái Bình
Thái Nguyên
Thanh Hoá
Vinh
Louangphrabang
Vientiane
Đồng Hới
T'ai-pei
Chi-lung
Hsin-chu
T'ai-chung
Chang-hua
Chia-i
T'ai-nan
Kao-hsiung
Hua-lien
T'ai-tung
Tropic of Cancer
Kowloon Peninsula
Lantau Island
Hong Kong Island
Mirs Bay
HONG KONG
1:750 000
Km
450
375
300
225
150
75
0
Miles
225
150
75
0

1:7.5M

SEA OF JAPAN
RUSSIAN FEDERATION
HOKKAIDŌ
La Pérouse Strait
Sakhalin
PRIMORSKIY KRAY
CHINA
HEILONGJIANG
JILIN
NORTH KOREA
Lake Khanka
Vladivostok
Nakhodka
Ussuriysk
Sapporo
Hakodate
Asahikawa
Kushiro
Obihiro
Muroran
Otaru
Aomori
Hachinohe
Akita
Morioka
Sendai
Jiamusi
Mudanjiang
Jixi
Qitaihe
Shuangyashan
Hegang
Ch'ŏngjin
Metres
Feet
6000
5000
4000
3000
2000
1000
500
200
SEA
LEVEL
19686
16404
13124
9843
6562
3281
1640
656
Conic Equidistant Projection

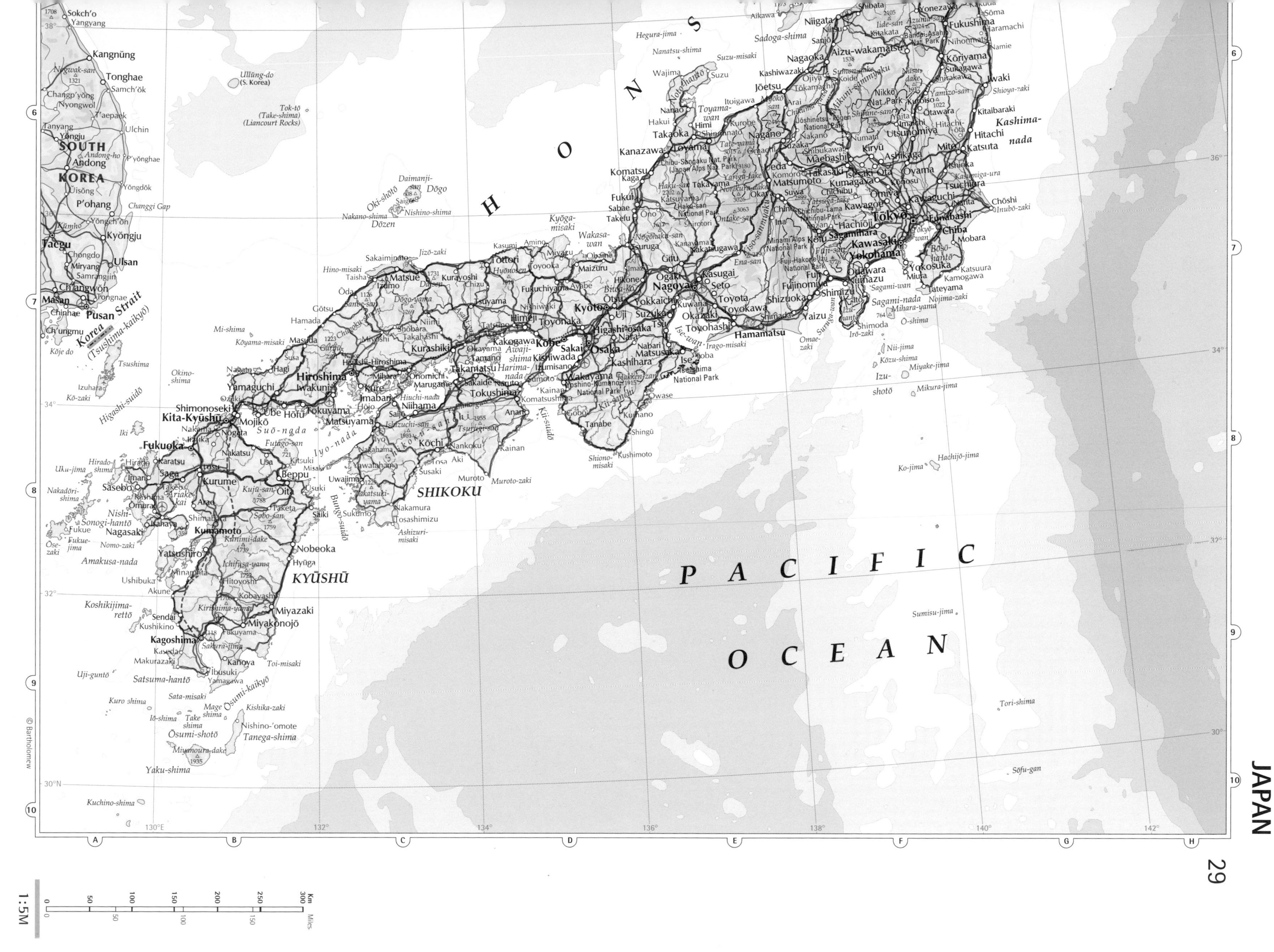

Km 300 250 200 150 100 50 0
Miles 150 100 50 0

1:5M

Northeast **CHINA, NORTH KOREA** and **SOUTH KOREA**

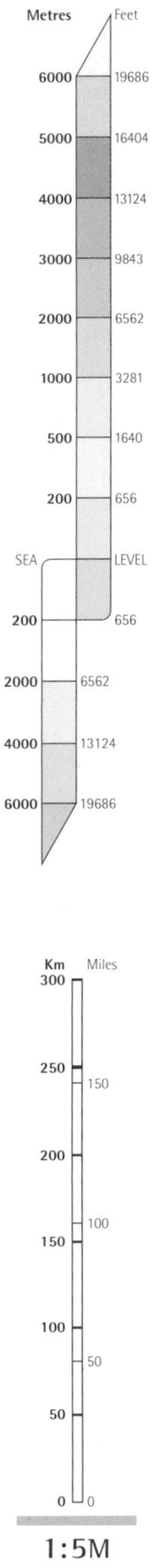

Metres	Feet
6000	19686
5000	16404
4000	13124
3000	9843
2000	6562
1000	3281
500	1640
200	656
SEA	LEVEL
200	656
2000	6562
4000	13124
6000	19686

Km	Miles
300	
250	150
200	
150	100
100	
50	50
0	0

1:5M

HEILONGJIANG
JILIN
CHINA
LIAONING
NEI MONGGOL ZIZHIQU
(INNER MONGOLIAN AUT. REGION)
SHANDONG
NORTH KOREA
SOUTH KOREA
JAPAN
RUS. FED.
SEA OF JAPAN
YELLOW SEA (HUANG HAI)
Korea Bay
Bohai Haixia
Liaodong Wan
Korea Strait (Tsushima-kaikyō)

Changchun, Jilin, Shenyang, Fushun, Anshan, Benxi, Dalian, Dandong, Siping, Tonghua, Vladivostok, Ussuriysk, Mudanjiang, Yanji, P'yŏngyang, Hamhŭng, Ch'ŏngjin, Wŏnsan, Kaesŏng, Seoul, Inch'ŏn, Taejŏn, Taegu, Kwangju, Pusan, Ulsan, Cheju, Fukuoka, Kita-Kyūshū, Shimonoseki

Conic Equidistant Projection

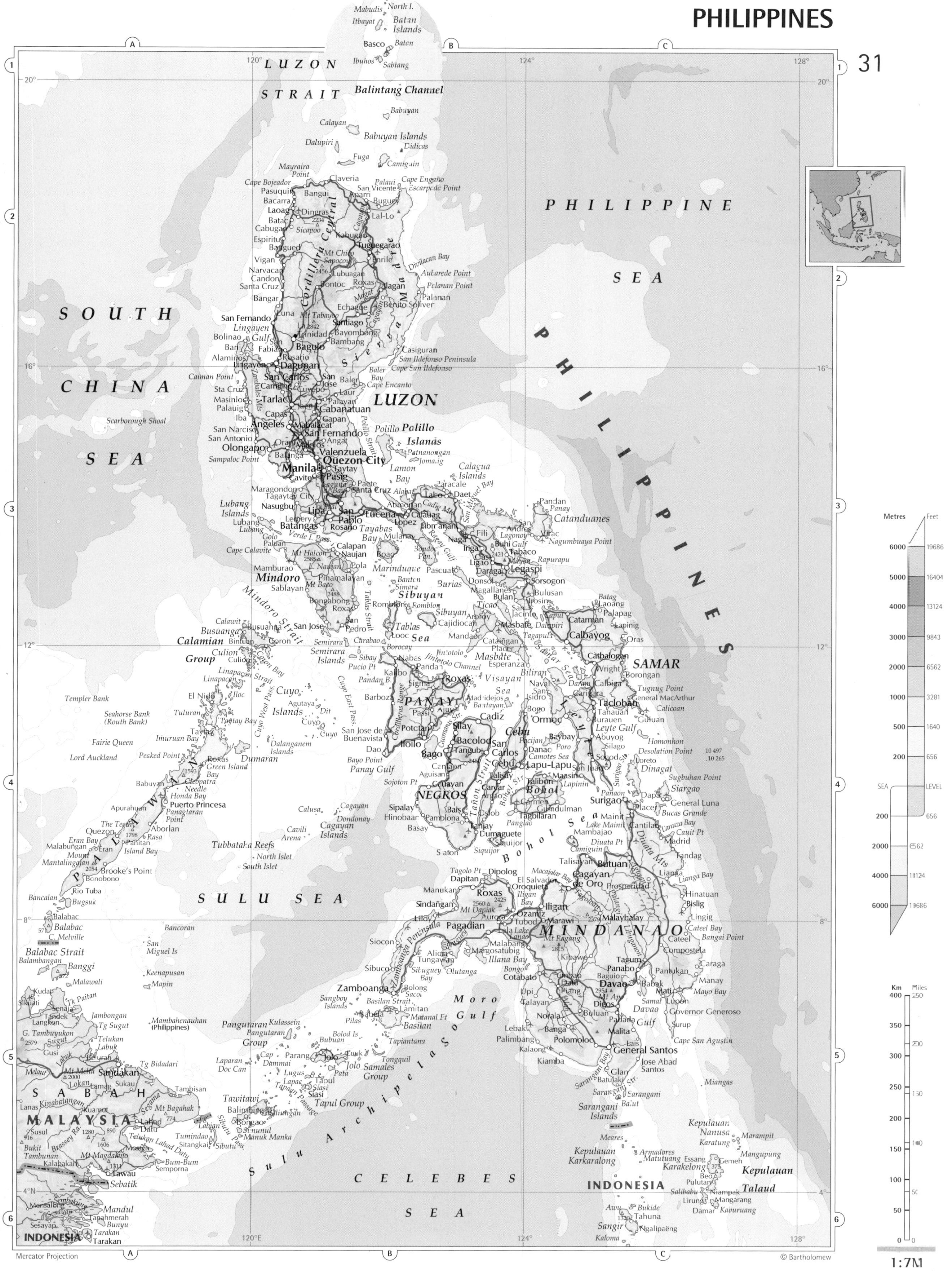
LUZON STRAIT
Balintang Channel
Batan Islands
Babuyan Islands
PHILIPPINE SEA
SOUTH CHINA SEA
PHILIPPINES
LUZON
Manila
Quezon City
Polillo Islands
Mindoro
Mindoro Strait
Calamian Group
Cuyo Islands
Sibuyan Sea
Tablas
Masbate
Visayan Sea
SAMAR
Leyte Gulf
PANAY
NEGROS
Cebu
Bohol
Bohol Sea
MINDANAO
Davao
Zamboanga
Moro Gulf
SULU SEA
Sulu Archipelago
CELEBES SEA
PALAWAN
Puerto Princesa
Balabac Strait
SABAH
MALAYSIA
INDONESIA
Kepulauan Talaud
Sarangani Islands
Tubbataha Reefs
Scarborough Shoal
Metres
Feet
SEA LEVEL
Km
Miles
Mercator Projection
© Bartholomew
1:7M

THAILAND, CAMBODIA and Peninsular MALAYSIA

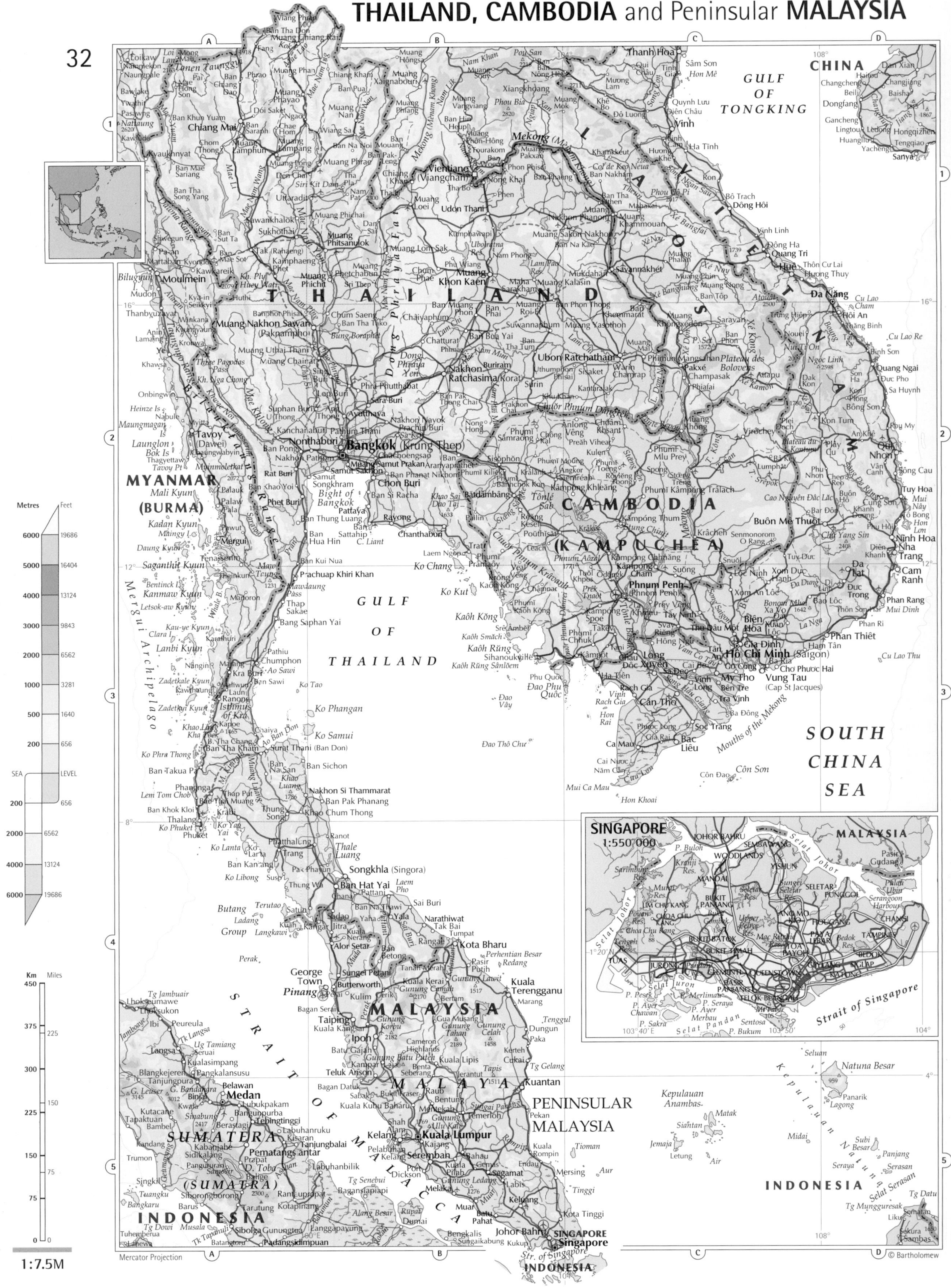

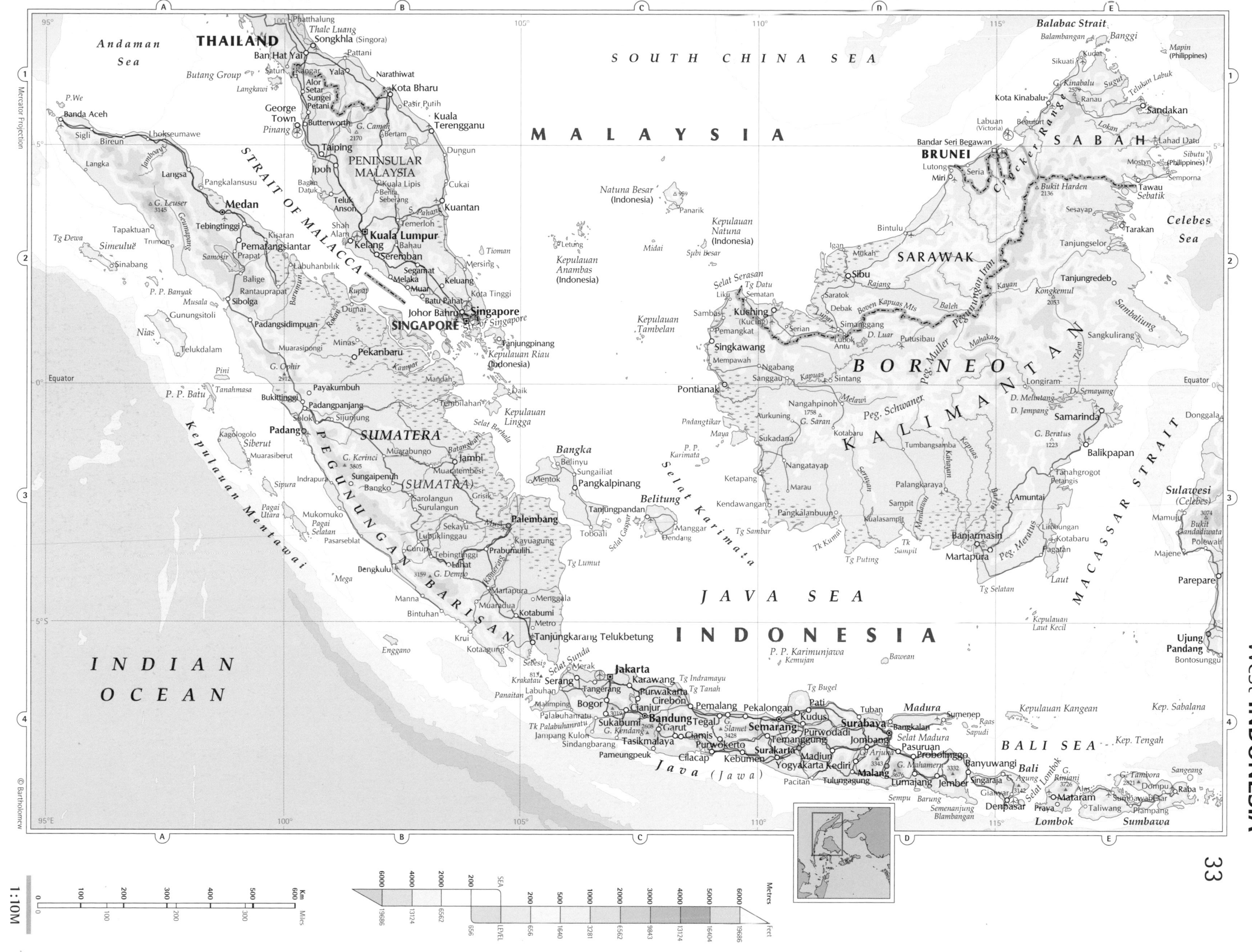
SOUTH CHINA SEA
MALAYSIA
INDONESIA
JAVA SEA
INDIAN OCEAN
MACASSAR STRAIT
STRAIT OF MALACCA
BALI SEA
Celebes Sea
Andaman Sea
THAILAND
BRUNEI
SINGAPORE
SABAH
SARAWAK
BORNEO
KALIMANTAN
SUMATERA
PENINSULAR MALAYSIA
PEGUNUNGAN BARISAN
Kepulauan Mentawai
Java (Jawa)
Bangka
Belitung
Madura
Bali
Lombok
Sumbawa
Sulawesi (Celebes)
Kuala Lumpur
Jakarta
Medan
Palembang
Pontianak
Kuching
Samarinda
Balikpapan
Banjarmasin
Surabaya
Semarang
Bandung
Padang
Pekanbaru
Jambi
Ujung Pandang
Kota Kinabalu
Sandakan
Bandar Seri Begawan
Banda Aceh
George Town
Equator
Mercator Projection
© Bartholomew
Metres
Feet
6000 19686
5000 16404
4000 13124
3000 9843
2000 6562
1000 3281
500 1640
200 656
SEA LEVEL
200 656
2000 6562
4000 13124
6000 19686
Km Miles
600
500 300
400
300 200
200 100
100
0 0
1:10M

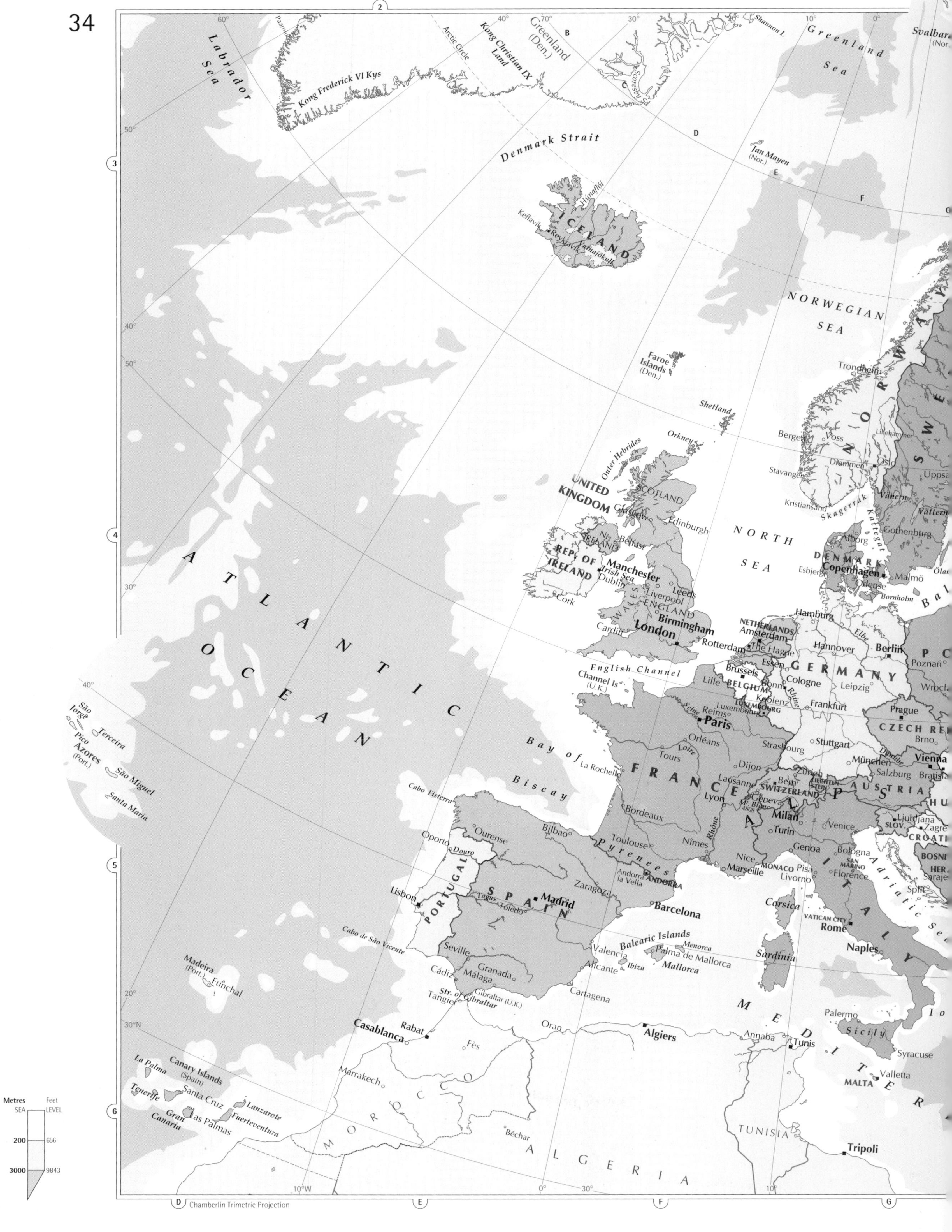
Labrador Sea
Kong Frederick VI Kys
Arctic Circle
Kong Christian IX Land
Greenland (Den.)
Scoresby Sd
Shannon I.
Greenland Sea
Svalbard (Nor.)
Denmark Strait
Jan Mayen (Nor.)
Húnaflói
ICELAND
Keflavík
Reykjavík
Vatnajökull
NORWEGIAN SEA
Faroe Islands (Den.)
Trondheim
Shetland
Orkney
Outer Hebrides
Bergen
Voss
Lillehammer
Oslo
Drammen
Stavanger
Kristiansand
Skagerrak
Kattegat
Uppsala
Vänern
Vättern
Gothenburg
NORWAY
SWEDEN
UNITED KINGDOM
SCOTLAND
Glasgow
Edinburgh
NORTH SEA
N. IRELAND
Belfast
REP. OF IRELAND
Manchester
Irish Sea
Dublin
Cork
Liverpool
Leeds
WALES
ENGLAND
Birmingham
Cardiff
London
Ålborg
DENMARK
Esbjerg
Copenhagen
Malmö
Odense
Bornholm
Öland
Hamburg
Elbe
NETHERLANDS
Amsterdam
The Hague
Rotterdam
Hannover
Berlin
Poznań
Essen
GERMANY
Wrocław
English Channel
Channel Is (U.K.)
Brussels
BELGIUM
Lille
Bonn
Cologne
Leipzig
LUXEMBOURG
Koblenz
Rhine
Luxembourg
Frankfurt
Prague
CZECH REP.
Brno
Seine
Reims
Paris
Orléans
Strasbourg
Stuttgart
Tours
Loire
Danube
München
Vienna
Dijon
Salzburg
Bratislava
La Rochelle
FRANCE
Zürich
LIECHTENSTEIN
Bern
SWITZERLAND
AUSTRIA
Lausanne
Geneva
Mt Blanc 4808
Lyon
Milan
Venice
Ljubljana
SLOV.
Zagreb
CROATIA
Bordeaux
Rhône
Turin
Genoa
Bologna
SAN MARINO
BOSNIA HERZ.
Sarajevo
Toulouse
Nîmes
Nice
MONACO
Pisa
Marseille
Livorno
Florence
Adriatic Sea
Split
Pyrenees
Andorra la Vella
ANDORRA
Corsica
VATICAN CITY
Rome
ITALY
Bay of Biscay
Cabo Fisterra
Bilbao
Oporto
Ourense
Douro
PORTUGAL
SPAIN
Zaragoza
Madrid
Tagus
Toledo
Lisbon
Barcelona
Balearic Islands
Menorca
Palma de Mallorca
Mallorca
Ibiza
Valencia
Alicante
Sardinia
Naples
Cabo de São Vicente
Seville
Granada
Cádiz
Málaga
Cartagena
Gibraltar (U.K.)
Str. of Gibraltar
Tangier
ATLANTIC OCEAN
São Jorge
Terceira
Pico
Azores (Port.)
São Miguel
Santa Maria
Madeira (Port.)
Funchal
MEDITERRANEAN
Palermo
Sicily
Ionian
Syracuse
Valletta
MALTA
Rabat
Casablanca
Fès
Oran
Algiers
Annaba
Tunis
Marrakech
MOROCCO
Béchar
ALGERIA
TUNISIA
Tripoli
La Palma
Canary Islands (Spain)
Santa Cruz
Tenerife
Lanzarote
Gran Canaria
Las Palmas
Fuerteventura
Chamberlin Trimetric Projection
Metres
SEA
200
3000
Feet
LEVEL
656
9843

Km / Miles
1050 / 600 / 900 / 750 / 450 / 600 / 300 / 450 / 300 / 150 / 150 / 0 / 0

1:18M

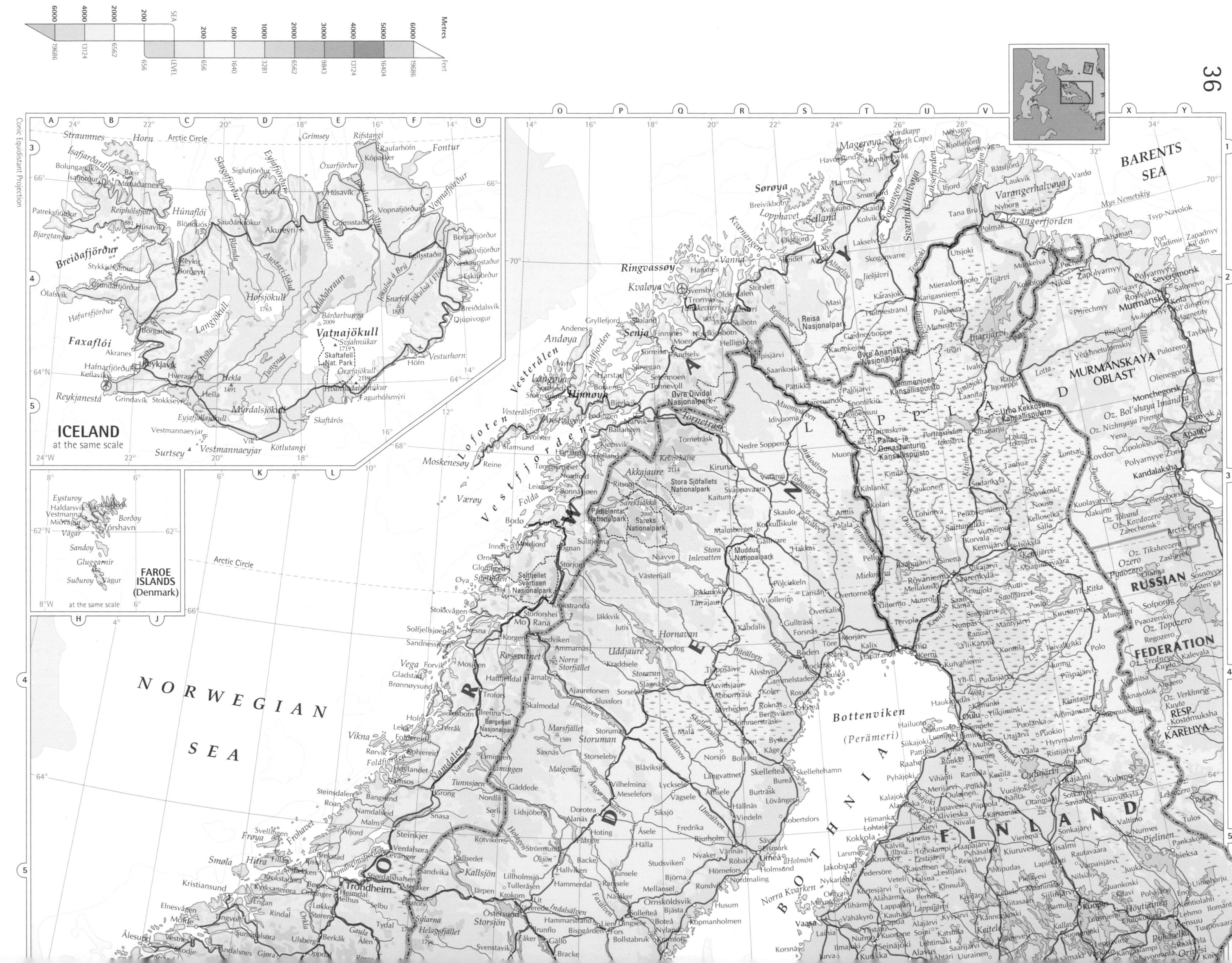

Conic Equidistant Projection

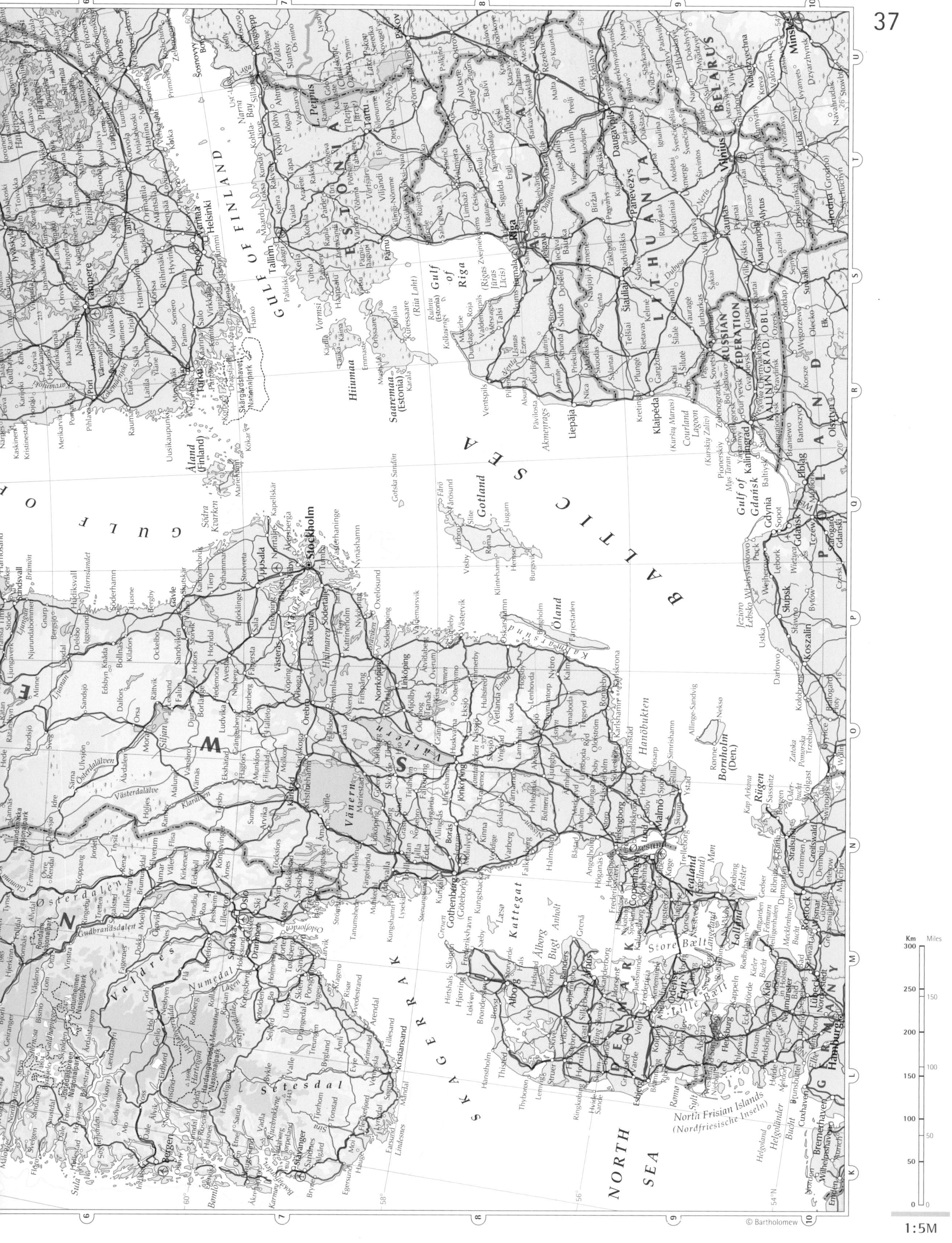

GULF OF FINLAND
BALTIC SEA
Gulf of Riga
SKAGERRAK
Kattegat
NORTH SEA
ESTONIA
LATVIA
LITHUANIA
BELARUS
RUSSIAN FEDERATION
KALININGRAD OBL.
POLAND
DENMARK
GERMANY
Helsinki
Tallinn
Riga
Vilnius
Minsk
Stockholm
Oslo
Copenhagen
Gotland
Öland
Bornholm (Den.)
Åland (Finland)
Saaremaa (Estonia)
Hiiumaa
Km
Miles
© Bartholomew

1:5M

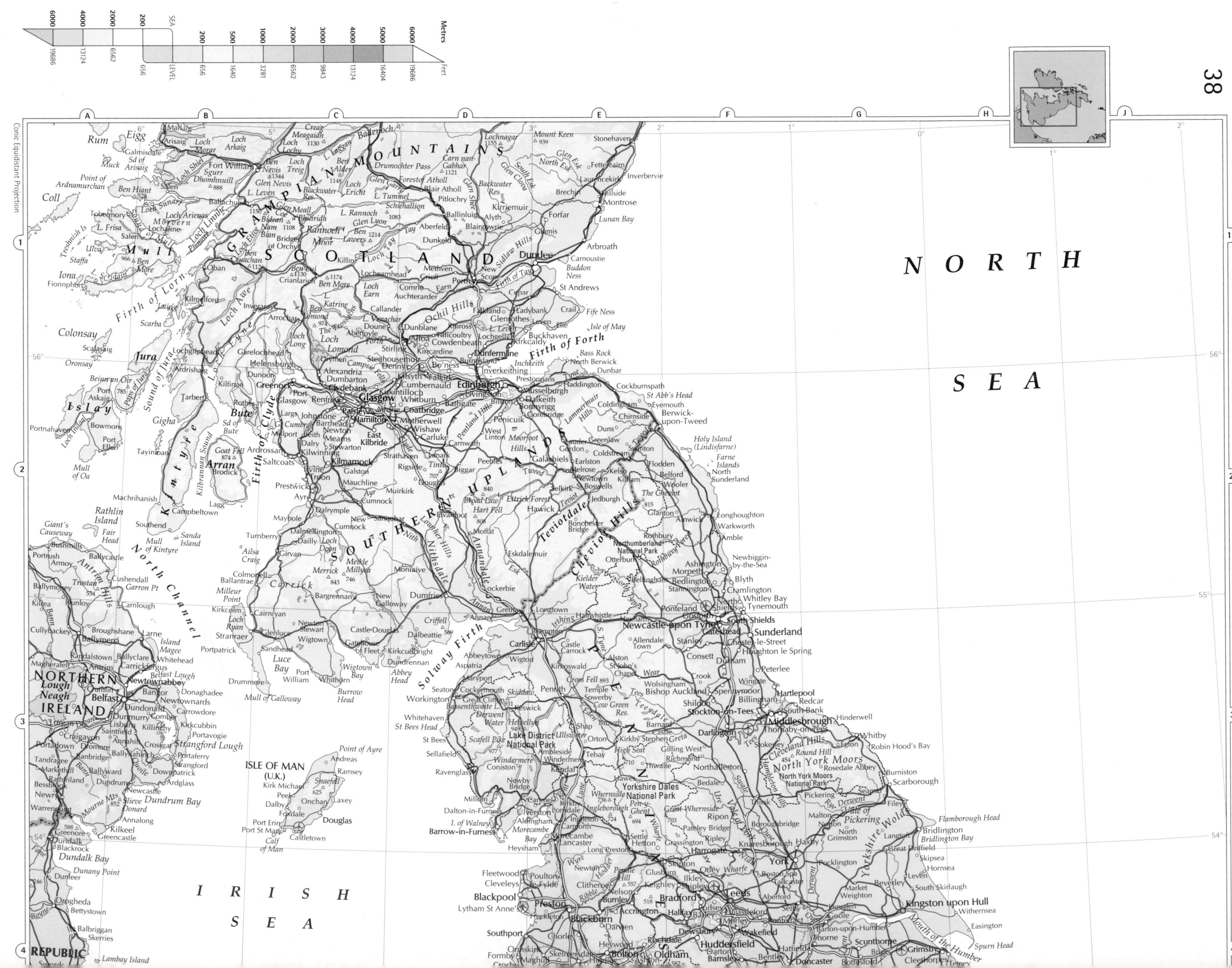

NORTH SEA
IRISH SEA
SCOTLAND
GRAMPIAN MOUNTAINS
SOUTHERN UPLANDS
PENNINES
NORTHERN IRELAND
ISLE OF MAN (U.K.)
Cheviot Hills
North York Moors
Firth of Forth
Firth of Clyde
Solway Firth
North Channel
Sound of Jura
Firth of Lorn
Edinburgh
Glasgow
Dundee
Newcastle upon Tyne
Sunderland
Middlesbrough
Leeds
Bradford
York
Kingston upon Hull
Belfast
Carlisle
Blackpool
Preston
Douglas
Arran
Islay
Jura
Mull
Metres
Feet
6000 19686
5000 16404
4000 13124
3000 9843
2000 6562
1000 3281
500 1640
200 656
SEA LEVEL
200 656
2000 6562
4000 13124
6000 19686
Conic Equidistant Projection

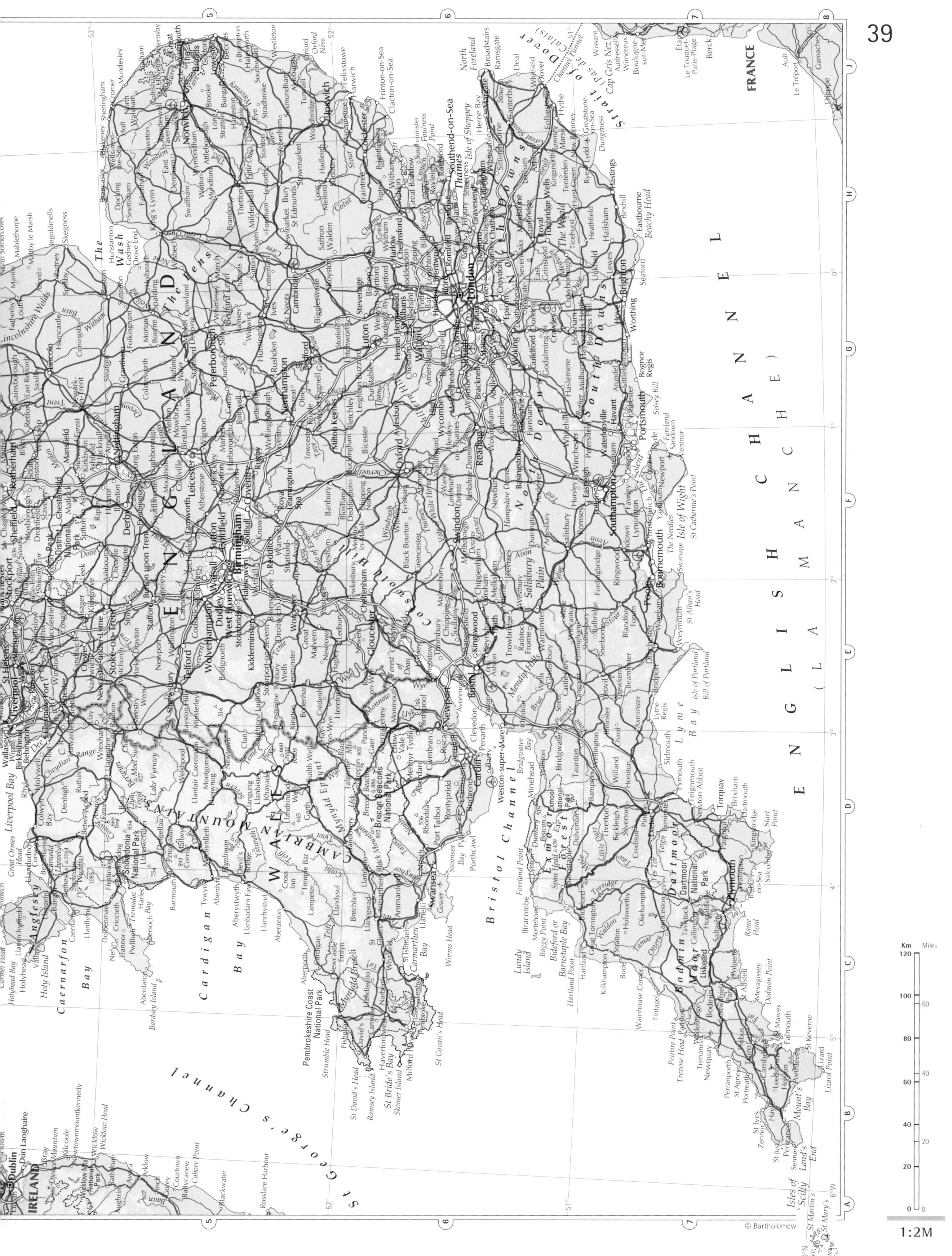
Km
Miles
1:2M
© Bartholomew

SCOTLAND

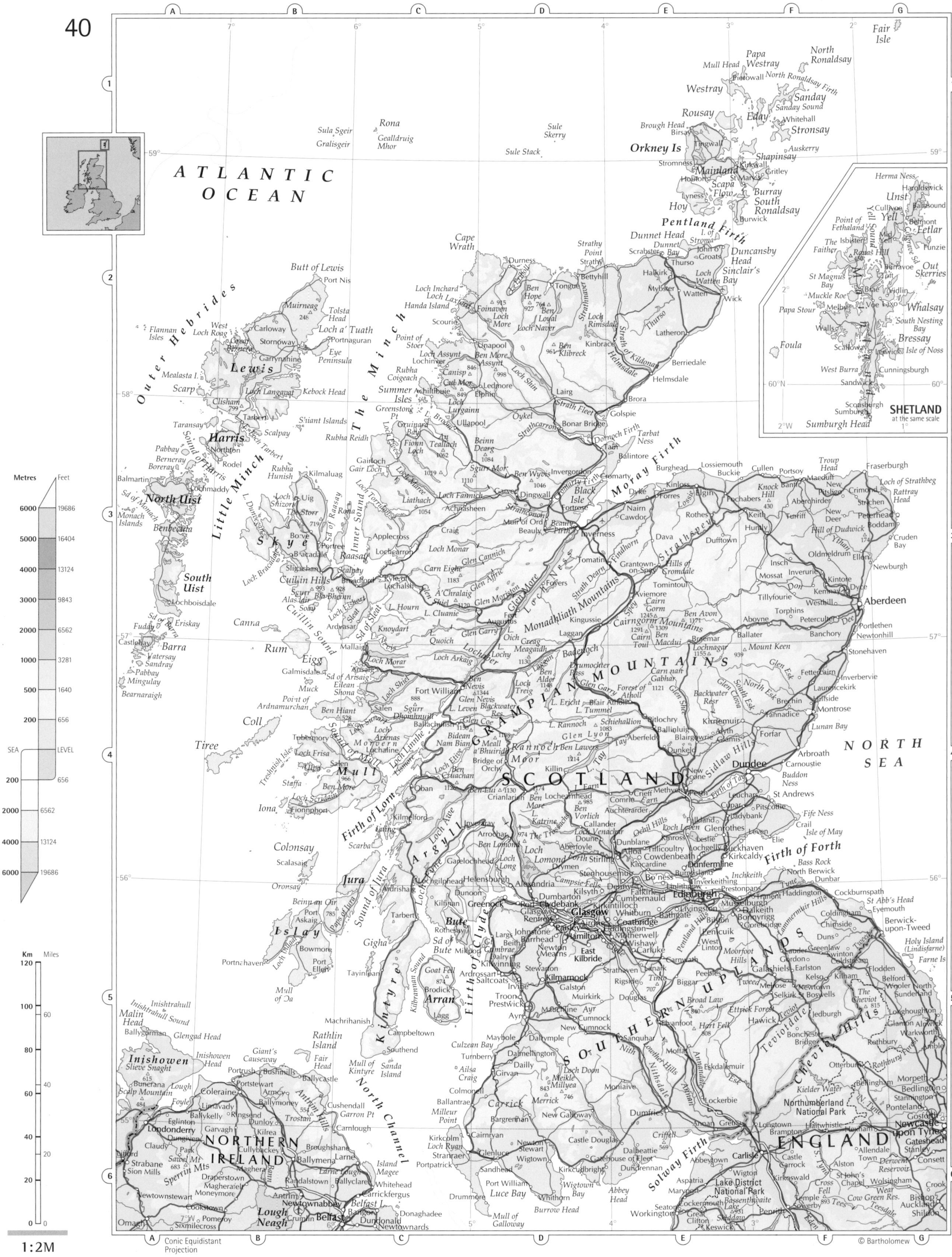

SHETLAND
at the same scale

Metres	Feet
6000	19686
5000	16404
4000	13124
3000	9843
2000	6562
1000	3281
500	1640
200	656
SEA	LEVEL
200	656
2000	6562
4000	13124
6000	19686

Km	Miles
120	
100	60
80	
60	40
40	
20	20
0	0

1:2M

Conic Equidistant
Projection

ATLANTIC OCEAN

NORTHERN IRELAND

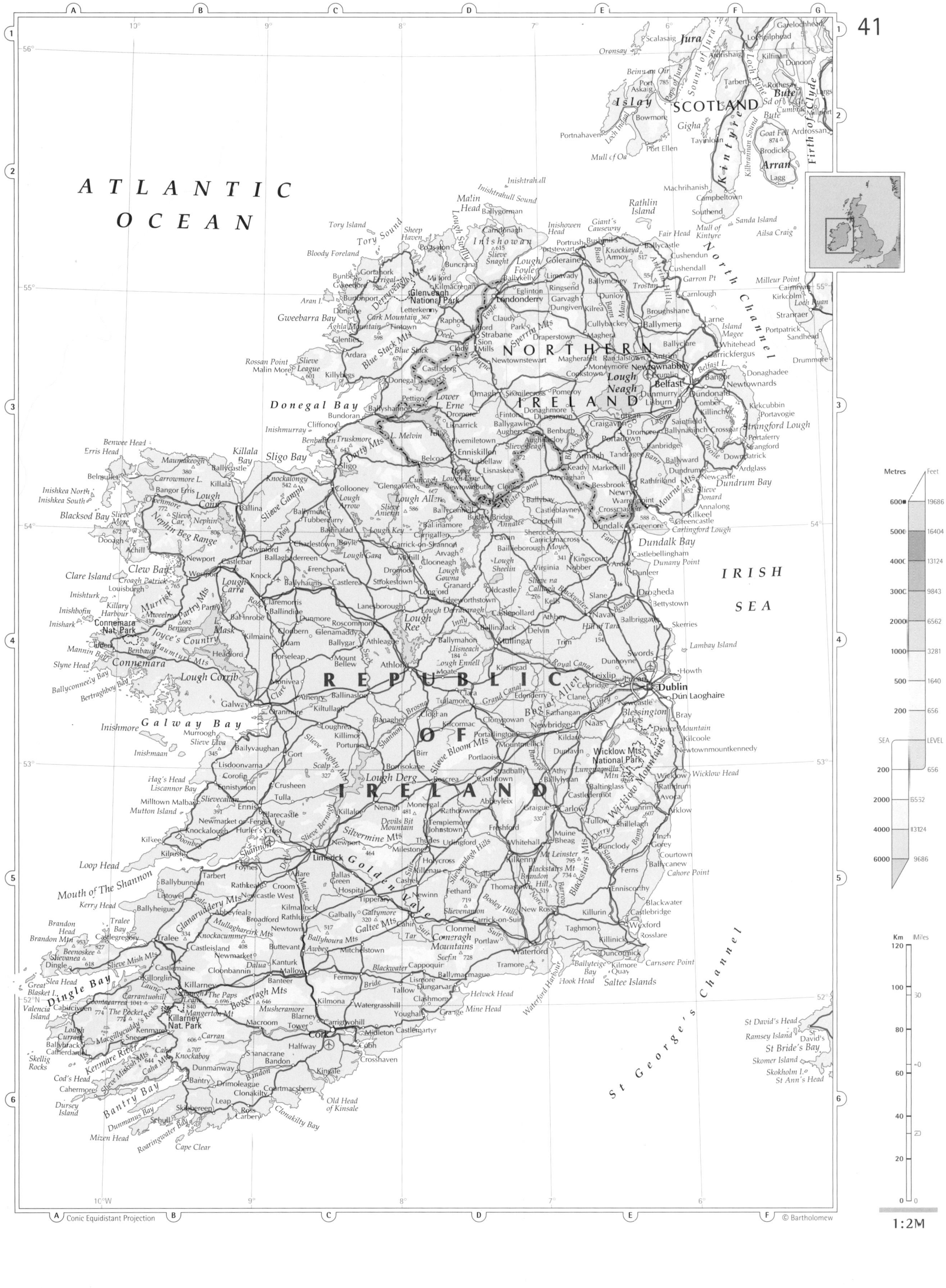

REPUBLIC OF IRELAND

IRISH SEA

SCOTLAND

Metres / Feet

600 — 19686
5000 — 16404
4000 — 13124
3000 — 9843
2000 — 6562
1000 — 3281
500 — 1640
200 — 656
SEA LEVEL
200 — 656
2000 — 6562
4000 — 13124
6000 — 19686

Km / Miles

1:2M

Conic Equidistant Projection

NORTH SEA
East Frisian Islands
(Ostfriesische Inseln)
Waddeneilanden
Waddenzee
IJsselmeer
(Zuider Zee)
Markermeer
Noordoost Polder
NETHERLANDS
BELGIUM
FRANCE
LUXEMBOURG
Amsterdam
The Hague
(Den Haag) ('s-Gravenhage)
Rotterdam
EUROPOORT
Utrecht
Groningen
Leeuwarden
Arnhem
Nijmegen
Eindhoven
Antwerp
Brussels
(Bruxelles)
Gent
Brugge
Ostend
(Oostende)
Dunkirk
(Dunkerque)
Lille
Liège
Namur
Charleroi
Maastricht
Aachen
Cologne
Düsseldorf
Duisburg
Essen
Dortmund
Münster
Trier
Saarbrücken
Metz
Reims
Amiens
Paris
ARDENNES
CHAMPAGNE
LORRAINE
PICARDIE
ARTOIS
FLANDRE
BORINAGE
HESBAYE
CONDROZ
FAMENNE
KEMPEN
HAGELAND
GAUME
VELUWE
TWENTE
NORDRHEIN
RHEINLAND
SAARLAND
Eifel
Hohe Venn
Metres
Feet
6000
19686
5000
16404
4000
13124
3000
9843
2000
6562
1000
3281
500
1640
200
656
SEA
LEVEL
200
656
2000
6562
4000
13124
6000
19686
Conic Equidistant
Projection

Km 0 20 40 60 80 100 120
Miles 0 20 40 60

1:2M

FRANCE

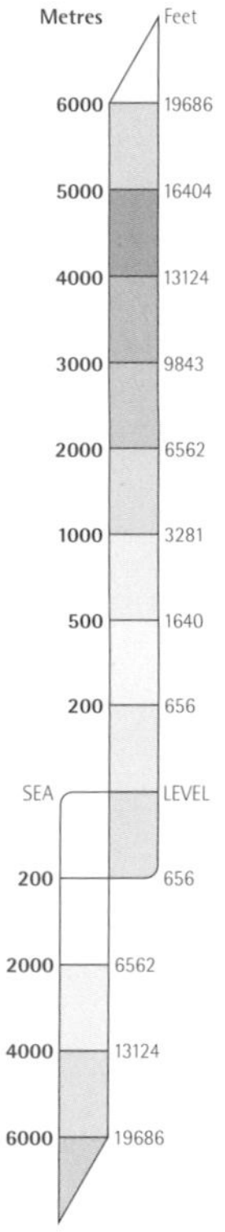

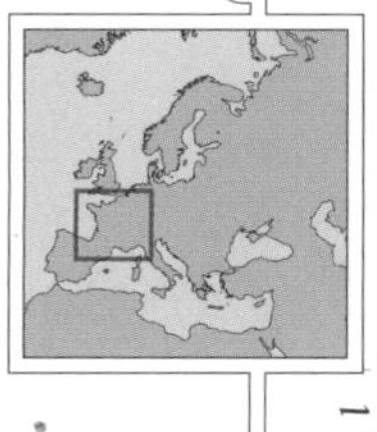

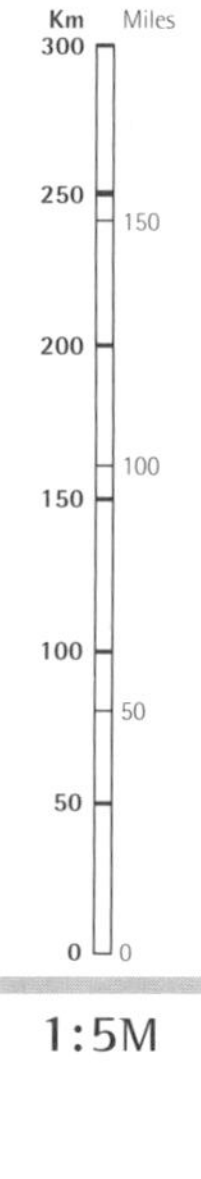

Metres	Feet
6000	19686
5000	16404
4000	13124
3000	9843
2000	6562
1000	3281
500	1640
200	656
SEA	LEVEL
200	656
2000	6562
4000	13124
6000	19686

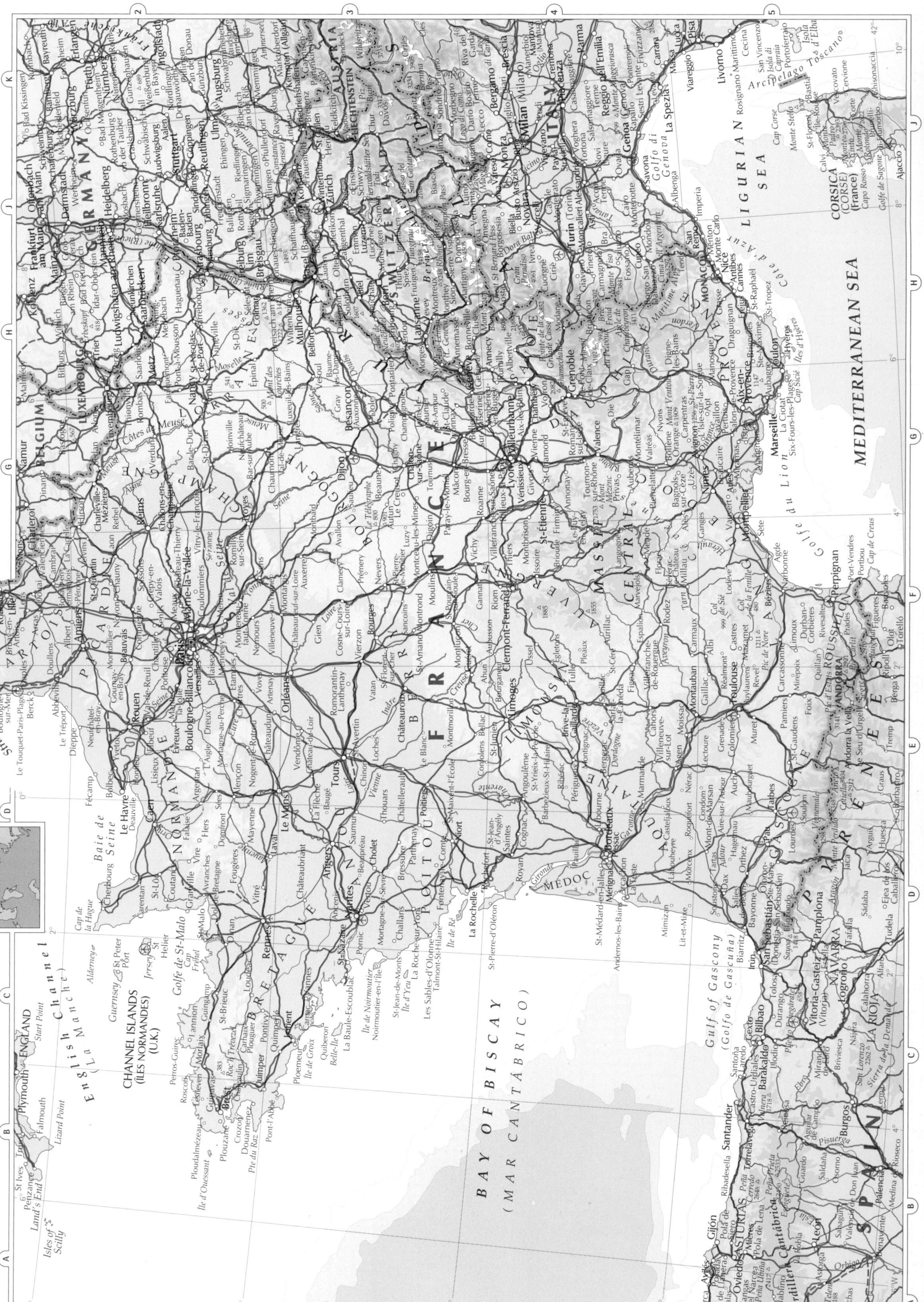

Km	Miles
300	
250	150
200	
150	100
100	
50	50
0	0

1:5M

Conic Equidistant Projection

BAY OF BISCAY
Gulf of Gascony (Golfo de Gascuña)
ATLANTIC OCEAN
MEDITERRANEAN SEA
Golfe du Lion
Costa Brava
Costa Blanca
Costa del Sol
Costa de la Luz
Golfo de Valencia
Golfo de Cádiz
Golfo de Almería
Strait of Gibraltar
Balearic Islands (Islas Baleares)
MENORCA (MINORCA)
MALLORCA (MAJORCA)
IBIZA (EIVISSA)
Formentera
FRANCE
SPAIN
PORTUGAL
ALGERIA
PYRENEES
Madrid
Lisbon (Lisboa)
Barcelona
Valencia
Zaragoza (Saragossa)
Bilbao
Sevilla
Málaga
Granada
Córdoba (Cordova)
Murcia
Alicante
Cartagena
Almería
Salamanca
Valladolid
Burgos
León
Oviedo
Gijón
Santander
San Sebastián (Donostia-San Sebastián)
Pamplona
Vitoria-Gasteiz
Logroño
A Coruña
Santiago de Compostela
Vigo
Ourense
Lugo
Oporto (Porto)
Coimbra
Braga
Badajoz
Cáceres
Mérida
Toledo
Cuenca
Teruel
Huelva
Cádiz
Jeréz de la Frontera
Jaén
Albacete
Gibraltar (U.K.)
Ceuta (Spain)
Tangier
Tétouan
Algiers (Alger)
Oran
Mostaganem
Palma de Mallorca
Marseille
Toulouse
Montpellier
Perpignan
Andorra la Vella
ANDORRA
Conic Equidistant Projection
© Bartholomew
Metres
Feet
6000
19686
5000
16404
4000
13124
3000
9843
2000
6562
1000
3281
500
1640
200
656
SEA
LEVEL
Km
Miles
300
250
200
150
100
50
0
1:5M

NORTH SEA
SKAGERRAK
Kattegat
BALTIC
NORWAY
SWEDEN
DENMARK
NETHERLANDS
BELGIUM
LUXEMBOURG
GERMANY
FRANCE
SWITZERLAND
LIECHTENSTEIN
AUSTRIA
CZECH REPUBLIC
POL
ALPS
Metres
Feet
6000
19686
5000
16404
4000
13124
3000
9843
2000
6562
1000
3281
500
1640
200
656
SEA
LEVEL
Conic Equidistant Projection

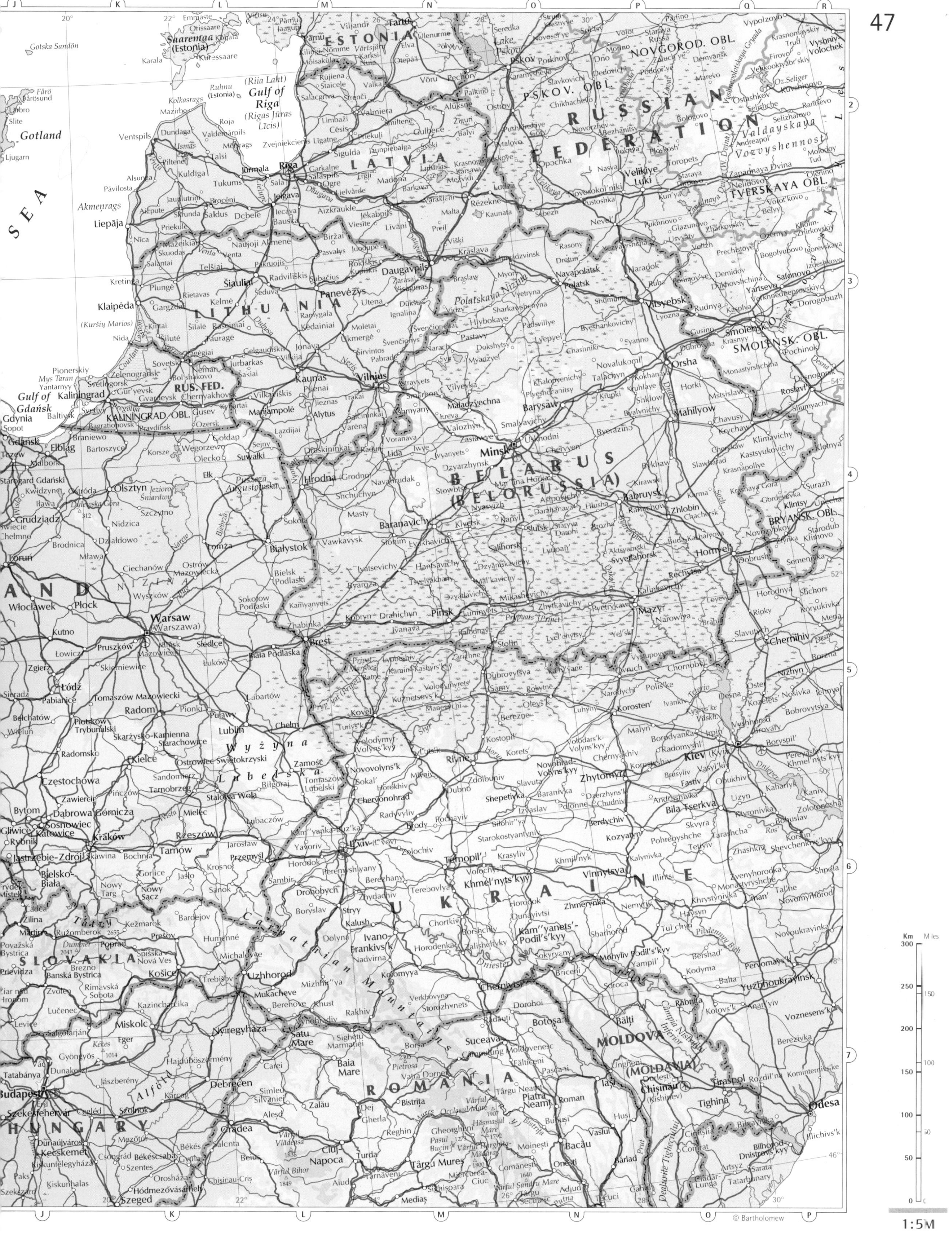
ESTONIA
LATVIA
LITHUANIA
RUSSIAN FEDERATION
RUS. FED.
KALININGRAD OBL.
BELARUS (BELORUSSIA)
UKRAINE
MOLDOVA (MOLDAVIA)
ROMANIA
HUNGARY
SLOVAKIA
PSKOV. OBL.
NOVGOROD. OBL.
TVERSKAYA OBL.
SMOLENSK. OBL.
BRYANSK. OBL.
Gotland
Gulf of Riga
Gulf of Gdańsk
Saaremaa (Estonia)
Riga
Vilnius
Minsk
Warsaw (Warszawa)
Kiev (Kyiv)
Chişinău (Kishinev)
Budapest
Odesa
Kaunas
Kaliningrad
Tartu
Pskov
Vitsyebsk
Mahilyow
Homyel'
Brest
Hrodna
Białystok
Lublin
Kraków
L'viv
Daugavpils
Šiauliai
Klaipėda
Liepāja
Carpathian Mountains
Km
Miles
1:5M
© Bartholomew

ITALY
SWITZERLAND
AUSTRIA
SLOVENIA
CROATIA
BOSNIA-HERZEGOVINA
FRANCE
PROVENCE
MONACO
SAN MARINO
VATICAN CITY
CORSICA (CORSE) (France)
SARDINIA (SARDEGNA) (Italy)
SICILY (SICILIA)
MALTA
ALGERIA
TUNISIA
Ligurian Sea
TYRRHENIAN SEA
ADRIATIC SEA
MEDITERRANEAN
IONIAN SEA
Golfo di Genova
Golfo di Venezia
Golfo di Taranto
Golfo di Manfredonia
Strait of Bonifacio
Sicilian Channel
Malta Channel
Isole Lipari
Arcipelago Toscano
Côte d'Azur
Alpen
Rome (Roma)
Milan (Milano)
Naples (Napoli)
Florence (Firenze)
Venice (Venezia)
Genoa (Genova)
Turin (Torino)
Palermo
Cagliari
Bari
Ancona
Pescara
Bologna
Trieste
Ljubljana
Zagreb
Rijeka
Split
Tunis
Nice
Marseille
Catania
Messina
Reggio di Calabria
Syracuse (Siracusa)
Taranto
Brindisi
Sassari
Ajaccio
Bastia
Metres
Feet
6000
19686
5000
16404
4000
13124
3000
9843
2000
6562
1000
3281
500
1640
200
656
SEA
LEVEL
Conic Equidistant Projection

1:5M

Metres
Feet
6000 19686
5000 16404
4000 13124
3000 9843
2000 6562
1000 3281
500 1640
200 656
SEA LEVEL
200 656
2000 6562
4000 13124
6000 19686
SWEDEN
FINLAND
ESTONIA
LATVIA
LITHUANIA
BELARUS (BELORUSSIA)
RUSSIAN FEDERATION
RESPUBLIKA KOMI
ARKHANGEL'SKAYA OBLAST'
RESPUBLIKA KARELIYA
LENINGRAD. OBLAST
VOLOGOD. OBLAST'
KOSTROM. OBLAST'
YAROSLAV. OBLAST
TVERSKAYA OBLAST'
NOVGOROD. OBL.
PSKOV. OBL.
SMOLENSK. OBLAST'
Gulf of Bothnia
Gulf of Finland
Gulf of Riga
BALTIC SEA
Lake Ladoga
Lake Onega
Lake Peipus
Onezhskaya Guba
Timanskiy Kryazh
Severnye Uvaly
Valdayskaya Vozvyshennost'
Smolenskaya Vozvyshennost'
Nyandomskiy Vozvyshennost'
Galichskaya Vozvyshennost'
Danilovskaya Vozvyshennost'
Privolzhskaya Vozvyshennost'
Moscow (Moskva)
St Petersburg (Leningrad)
Helsinki
Tallinn
Riga
Vilnius
Minsk
Stockholm
Warsaw
Kaliningrad
Archangel (Arkhangel'sk)
Severodvinsk
Syktyvkar
Ukhta
Kotlas
Vologda
Cherepovets
Yaroslavl'
Kostroma
Ivanovo
Nizhniy Novgorod (Gor'kiy)
Kazan'
Ul'yanovsk (Simbirsk)
Saransk
Penza
Ryazan'
Tula
Kaluga
Bryansk
Smolensk
Tver'
Novgorod
Pskov
Petrozavodsk
Vitsyebsk
Mahilyow
Homyel'
Hrodna
Kaunas
Daugavpils
Tartu
Turku
Tampere
Åland (Finland)
Gotland (Sweden)
Saaremaa (Estonia)
Hiiumaa
Courland Lagoon
Transverse Mercator Projection

Km 400 350 300 250 200 150 100 50 0
Miles 250 200 150 100 50 0

1:7M

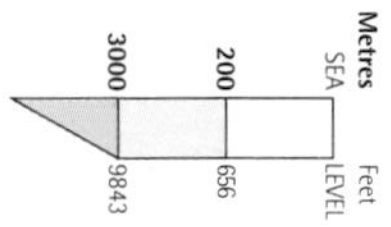

Metres SEA | Feet LEVEL
200 | 656
3000 | 9843

Oblated Stereographic Projection

A B C D E F G H J K L M
1 2 3 4

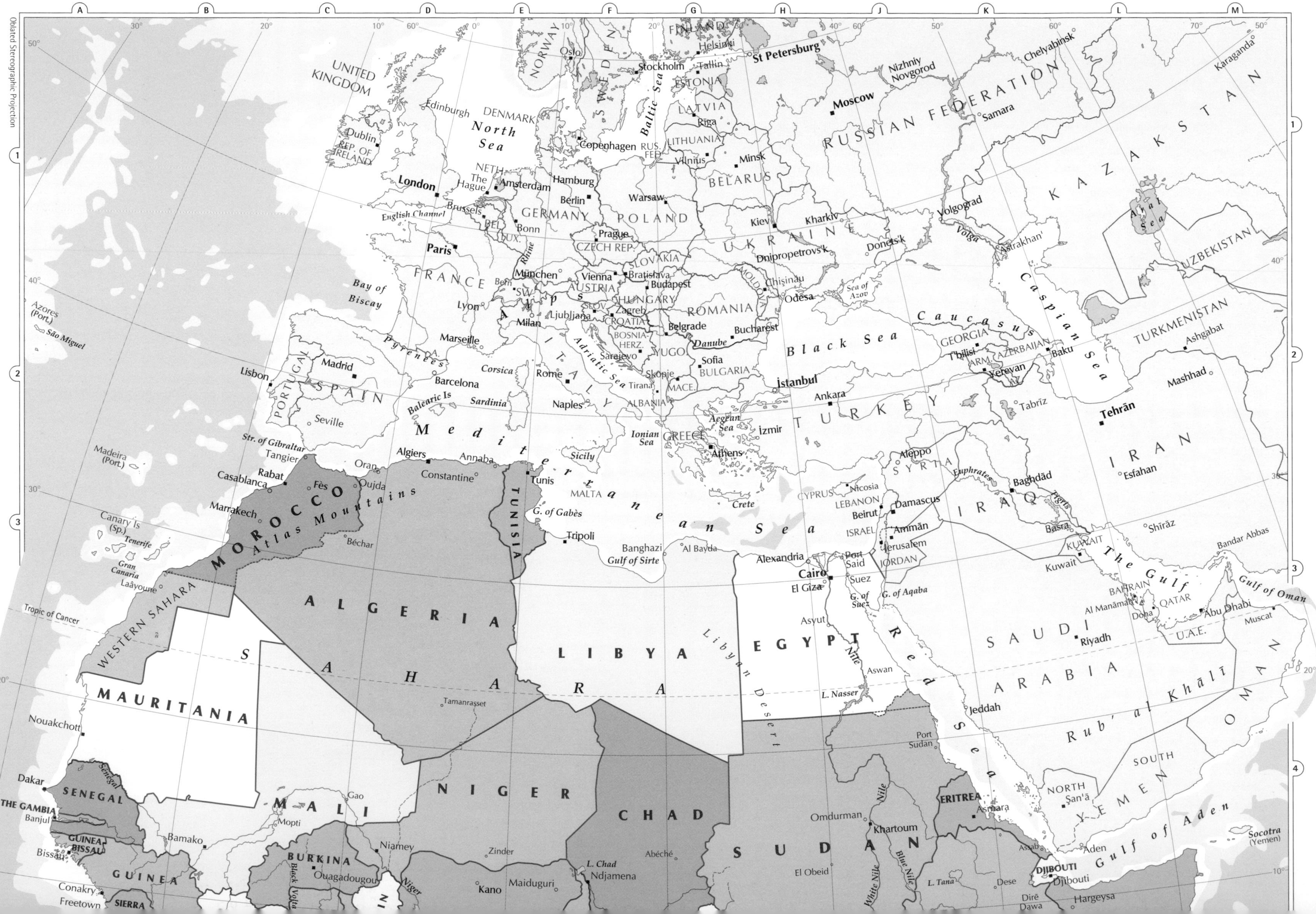

UNITED KINGDOM
REP. OF IRELAND
Dublin
Edinburgh
London
English Channel
North Sea
DENMARK
NORWAY
Oslo
SWEDEN
Stockholm
Baltic Sea
FINLAND
Helsinki
Tallinn
ESTONIA
LATVIA
Riga
LITHUANIA
Vilnius
RUS. FED.
BELARUS
Minsk
St Petersburg
Moscow
Nizhniy Novgorod
RUSSIAN FEDERATION
Samara
Chelyabinsk
Volgograd
Volga
Astrakhan'
Karaganda
KAZAKHSTAN
UZBEKISTAN
Aral Sea
TURKMENISTAN
Ashgabat
Mashhad
Caspian Sea
Baku
AZERBAIJAN
ARM.
Yerevan
GEORGIA
Tbilisi
Caucasus
Tabriz
Tehrān
IRAN
Esfahan
Shīrāz
Bandar Abbas
Gulf of Oman
Muscat
OMAN
U.A.E.
Abu Dhabi
QATAR
Doha
BAHRAIN
Al Manāmah
The Gulf
KUWAIT
Kuwait
Basra
Tigris
Baghdad
IRAQ
Euphrates
SYRIA
Aleppo
Damascus
LEBANON
Beirut
ISRAEL
Jerusalem
JORDAN
'Ammān
G. of Aqaba
SAUDI ARABIA
Riyadh
Rub' al Khālī
Jeddah
Red Sea
YEMEN
NORTH
SOUTH
San'a
Aden
Gulf of Aden
Socotra (Yemen)
DJIBOUTI
Djibouti
Hargeysa
Dirē Dawa
Dese
ERITREA
Asmara
Assab
L. Tana
Blue Nile
White Nile
Nile
Khartoum
Omdurman
El Obeid
Port Sudan
SUDAN
Abéché
CHAD
L. Chad
Ndjamena
Maiduguri
Kano
Zinder
NIGER
Niamey
Niger
Ouagadougou
BURKINA
Black Volta
Mopti
Gao
MALI
Bamako
GUINEA
Conakry
SIERRA
Freetown
GUINEA-BISSAU
Bissau
THE GAMBIA
Banjul
SENEGAL
Senegal
Dakar
Nouakchott
MAURITANIA
WESTERN SAHARA
Laâyoune
Canary Is (Sp.)
Tenerife
Gran Canaria
Madeira (Port.)
Azores (Port.)
São Miguel
Tropic of Cancer
SAHARA
MOROCCO
Atlas Mountains
Marrakech
Casablanca
Rabat
Fès
Tangier
Str. of Gibraltar
Oujda
Béchar
ALGERIA
Oran
Algiers
Constantine
Annaba
Tamanrasset
TUNISIA
Tunis
G. of Gabès
Tripoli
LIBYA
Gulf of Sirte
Banghazi
Al Bayda
Libyan Desert
EGYPT
Alexandria
Cairo
El Giza
Port Said
Suez
G. of Suez
Asyut
Aswan
L. Nasser
Mediterranean Sea
CYPRUS
Nicosia
Crete
MALTA
Sicily
Ionian Sea
Aegean Sea
Athens
GREECE
Izmir
TURKEY
Istanbul
Ankara
Black Sea
Sea of Azov
Donets'k
Kharkiv
UKRAINE
Kiev
Dnipropetrovs'k
Chişinău
MOLDOVA
ROMANIA
Bucharest
Danube
BULGARIA
Sofia
MACE.
Skopje
ALBANIA
Tiranë
YUGO.
Belgrade
BOSNIA-HERZ.
Sarajevo
CROATIA
Zagreb
SLOV.
Ljubljana
HUNGARY
Budapest
SLOVAKIA
Bratislava
AUSTRIA
Vienna
CZECH REP.
Prague
POLAND
Warsaw
GERMANY
Berlin
Hamburg
Copenhagen
Bonn
München
Rhine
NETH.
Amsterdam
The Hague
BEL.
Brussels
LUX.
FRANCE
Paris
Lyon
Marseille
SWITZ.
Alps
Bern
Milan
ITALY
Rome
Naples
Adriatic Sea
Corsica
Sardinia
Balearic Is
Pyrenees
Bay of Biscay
SPAIN
Madrid
Barcelona
Seville
PORTUGAL
Lisbon

10° 20° 30° 40° 50° 60° 70°

INDIAN OCEAN
SOUTH ATLANTIC OCEAN
ETHIOPIA
SOMALIA
KENYA
UGANDA
RWANDA
BURUNDI
TANZANIA
CENTRAL AFRICAN REPUBLIC
CONGO (ZAIRE)
CONGO
GABON
CAMEROON
NIGERIA
EQUAT. GUINEA
SÃO TOMÉ AND PRÍNCIPE
GHANA
TOGO
COTE D'IVOIRE
LIBERIA
ANGOLA
CABINDA (Ang.)
ZAMBIA
MALAWI
MOZAMBIQUE
ZIMBABWE
BOTSWANA
NAMIBIA
REPUBLIC OF SOUTH AFRICA
LESOTHO
SWAZILAND
MADAGASCAR
COMOROS
SEYCHELLES
MAURITIUS
Mozambique Channel
Gulf of Guinea
Bight of Benin
Kalahari Desert
Namib Desert
Addis Ababa
Mogadishu
Nairobi
Mombasa
Dar es Salaam
Zanzibar
Dodoma
Kampala
Kigali
Bujumbura
Kinshasa
Brazzaville
Bangui
Yaoundé
Douala
Libreville
Lagos
Ibadan
Abuja
Accra
Lomé
Abidjan
Yamoussoukro
Monrovia
Luanda
Lusaka
Harare
Lilongwe
Maputo
Gaborone
Windhoek
Pretoria
Johannesburg
Durban
Cape Town
Port Elizabeth
Bloemfontein
Maseru
Mbabane
Antananarivo
Lake Victoria
Lake Tanganyika
L. Nyasa
L. Turkana
L. Kariba
Kilimanjaro 5895
Kirinyaga 5199
Zambeze
Limpopo
Orange
Congo (Zaïre)
St Helena (U.K.)
Ascension I. (U.K.)
Tristan da Cunha (U.K.)
Cape of Good Hope
C. Agulhas
Tropic of Capricorn
Equator
© Bartholomew
Km Miles
1:28M

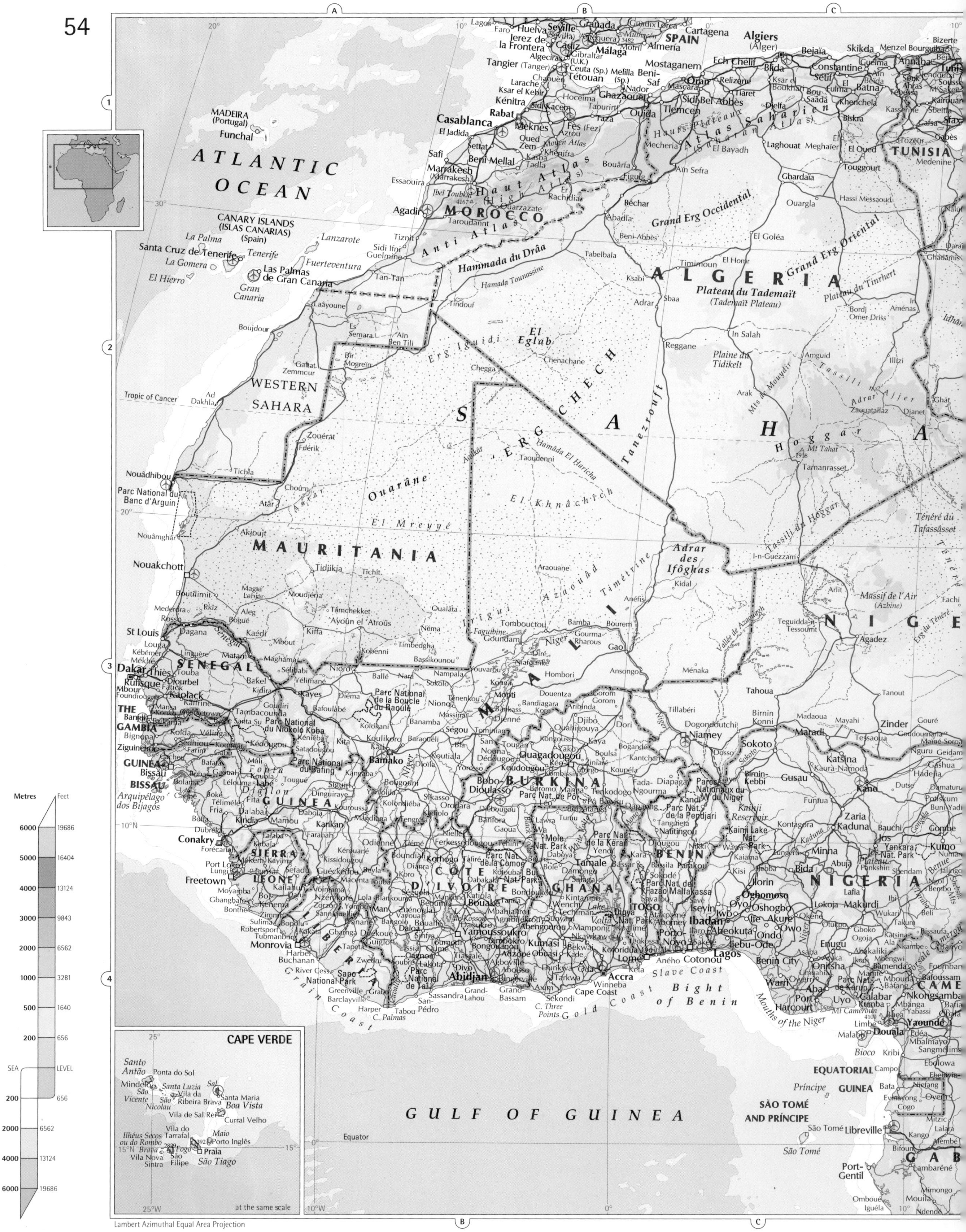

A B C

ATLANTIC OCEAN

MADEIRA (Portugal)
Funchal

CANARY ISLANDS (ISLAS CANARIAS) (Spain)
La Palma
Santa Cruz de Tenerife
Tenerife
La Gomera
El Hierro
Lanzarote
Fuerteventura
Las Palmas de Gran Canaria
Gran Canaria

Lagos
Faro
Huelva
Seville (Sevilla)
Granada
Jerez de la Frontera
Cádiz
Málaga
Algeciras
Gibraltar (U.K.)
Almería
Cartagena
SPAIN
Tangier (Tanger)
Ceuta (Sp.)
Melilla (Sp.)
Tétouan
Larache
Ksar el Kebir
Kénitra
Rabat
Casablanca
El Jadida
Meknès
Fès (Fez)
Safi
Marrakech (Marrakesh)
Essaouira
Agadir
Taroudannt
MOROCCO
Haut Atlas (High Atlas)
Anti Atlas
Jbel Toubkal 4167
Tiznit
Sidi Ifni
Guelmine
Tan-Tan
Hammada du Drâa
Tindouf
Laâyoune
Boujdour
Es Semara
WESTERN SAHARA
Ad Dakhla
Tropic of Cancer

Algiers (Alger)
Oran
Mostaganem
Tlemcen
Sidi Bel Abbès
Blida
Bejaïa
Skikda
Constantine
Annaba
Sétif
Batna
Biskra
Touggourt
Ouargla
Hassi Messaoud
Laghouat
Ghardaïa
Béchar
Ain Sefra
El Bayadh
Atlas Saharien (Saharan Atlas)
Hauts Plateaux
Grand Erg Occidental
Grand Erg Oriental
El Goléa
Timimoun
Adrar
Reggane
In Salah
Plateau du Tademaït (Tademaït Plateau)
Plaine du Tidikelt
ALGERIA
Tassili n Ajjer
Djanet
Hoggar
Mt Tahat 2918
Tamanrasset
Tassili du Hoggar
Bordj Omer Driss
Amguid
Illizi
In-Guezzam
El Eglab
Erg Iguidi
Erg Chech
Tanezrouft
SAHARA

Tunis
Bizerte
Sousse
Sfax
Gabès
Medenine
TUNISIA
Kairouan

Nouâdhibou
Parc National du Banc d'Arguin
Zouérat
Fdérik
Atâr
Ouarâne
El Mreyyé
Akjoujt
Nouâmghâr
Nouakchott
MAURITANIA
Tidjikja
Tichit
Boutilimit
Rosso
Kiffa
Ayoûn el 'Atroûs
Néma
Oualâta
Aleg
Kaédi

Taoudenni
El Khnâchîch
Adrar des Ifôghas
Kidal
Araouane
Azaouâd
Tombouctou
Gao
Bourem
Ménaka
MALI
Niger
Mopti
Ségou
Bamako
Kayes
Sikasso
Parc National de la Boucle du Baoulé

St Louis
Dakar
Thiès
Rufisque
Kaolack
Tambacounda
Ziguinchor
SENEGAL
THE GAMBIA
Banjul
GUINEA-BISSAU
Bissau
Arquipélago dos Bijagós
GUINEA
Conakry
Kankan
Labé
SIERRA LEONE
Freetown
LIBERIA
Monrovia
Buchanan
Harper
CÔTE D'IVOIRE
Yamoussoukro
Abidjan
Bouaké
San-Pédro
Grain Coast

BURKINA
Ouagadougou
Bobo-Dioulasso
GHANA
Kumasi
Tamale
Accra
Sekondi
Cape Coast
Gold Coast
TOGO
Lomé
BENIN
Porto-Novo
Cotonou
Slave Coast
Bight of Benin

NIGER
Niamey
Agadez
Zinder
Tahoua
Maradi
Arlit
Massif de l'Aïr (Azbine)
Ténéré du Tafassâsset

NIGERIA
Lagos
Ibadan
Ilorin
Kano
Kaduna
Zaria
Sokoto
Abuja
Jos
Enugu
Benin City
Onitsha
Port Harcourt
Calabar
Mouths of the Niger

CAMEROON
Yaoundé
Douala
Mt Cameroun 4100
EQUATORIAL GUINEA
Malabo
Bioco
Bata
Príncipe
SÃO TOMÉ AND PRÍNCIPE
São Tomé
Libreville
Port-Gentil
GABON

GULF OF GUINEA
Equator

CAPE VERDE

Santo Antão
Ponta do Sol
Mindelo
São Vicente
Santa Luzia
Sal
São Nicolau
Vila da Ribeira Brava
Santa Maria
Boa Vista
Vila de Sal Rei
Curral Velho
Ilhéus Secos ou do Rombo
Tarrafal
Vila do Maio
Maio
Porto Inglês
Brava
Fogo
Vila Nova Sintra
São Filipe
Praia
São Tiago
at the same scale

Metres	Feet
6000	19686
5000	16404
4000	13124
3000	9843
2000	6562
1000	3281
500	1640
200	656
SEA	LEVEL
200	656
2000	6562
4000	13124
6000	19686

Lambert Azimuthal Equal Area Projection

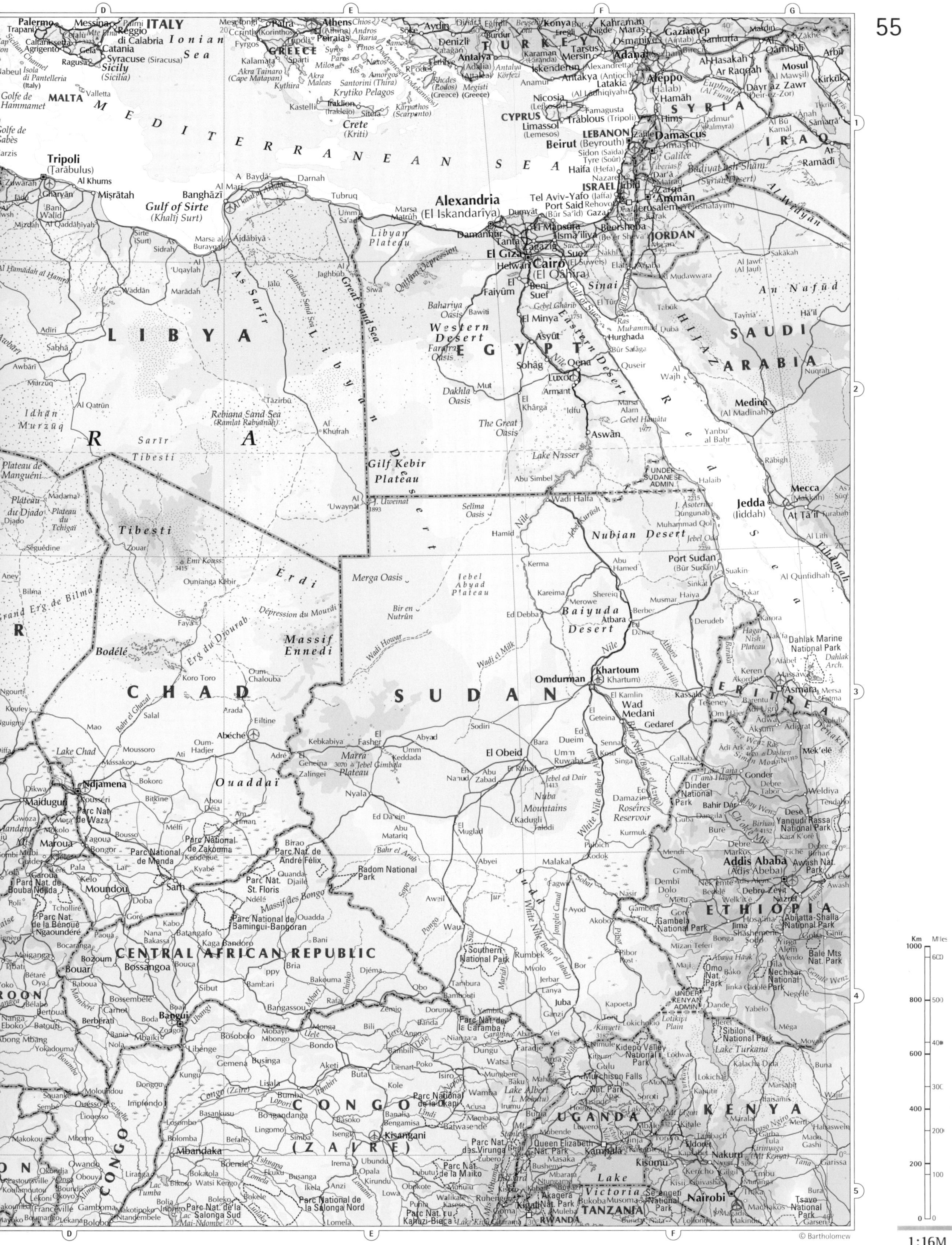
ITALY
Palermo
Messina
Reggio di Calabria
Catania
Syracuse (Siracusa)
Sicily (Sicilia)
Ionian Sea
Athens
GREECE
Crete (Kriti)
TURKEY
Antalya
Konya
Adana
Gaziantep
Aleppo (Halab)
SYRIA
Damascus
Mosul
IRAQ
CYPRUS
Nicosia
LEBANON
Beirut (Beyrouth)
ISRAEL
JORDAN
'Amman
Tel Aviv-Yafo (Jaffa)
Jerusalem
MALTA
Valletta
MEDITERRANEAN SEA
Tripoli (Tarabulus)
Gulf of Sirte (Khalij Surt)
Banghazi
Alexandria (El Iskandarîya)
Port Said
Cairo (El Qâhira)
El Giza
Suez
Sinai
Libyan Plateau
Great Sand Sea
LIBYA
EGYPT
Western Desert
Eastern Desert
Aswân
Luxor
Lake Nasser
Libyan Desert
SAHARA
Tibesti
Emi Koussi 3415
Gilf Kebir Plateau
Red Sea
SAUDI ARABIA
HIJAZ
An Nafud
Medina (Al Madinah)
Mecca (Makkah)
Jedda (Jiddah)
Nubian Desert
Port Sudan (Bûr Sudân)
Bayuda Desert
Atbara
Khartoum (El Khartum)
Omdurman
SUDAN
El Obeid
Wad Medani
Massif Ennedi
CHAD
Ndjamena
Lake Chad
Ouaddai
Abéché
ERITREA
Asmara
ETHIOPIA
Addis Ababa (Adis Abeba)
Lake Tana
CENTRAL AFRICAN REPUBLIC
Bangui
Bangassou
Juba
UGANDA
Kampala
Lake Albert
Lake Victoria
KENYA
Nairobi
Lake Turkana
CONGO (ZAIRE)
Kisangani
Mbandaka
CONGO
RWANDA
Kigali
TANZANIA
Km
Miles
1:16M
© Bartholomew

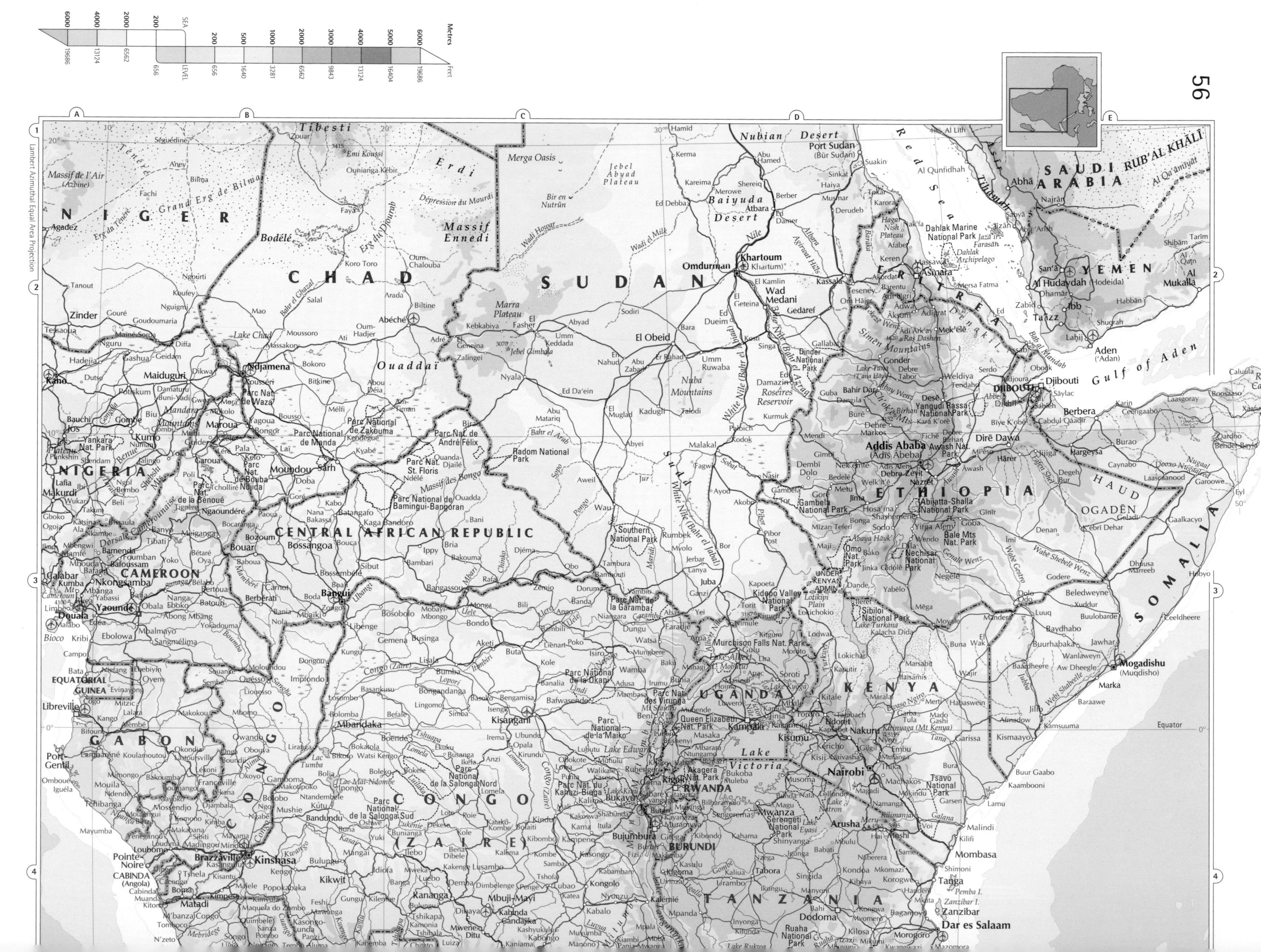
Metres
Feet
6000
19686
5000
16404
4000
13124
3000
9843
2000
6562
1000
3281
500
1640
200
656
SEA
LEVEL
656
200
2000
6562
4000
13124
6000
19686
Lambert Azimuthal Equal Area Projection
SAUDI ARABIA
RUB'AL KHĀLĪ
YEMEN
ERITREA
ETHIOPIA
SOMALIA
KENYA
UGANDA
RWANDA
BURUNDI
TANZANIA
SUDAN
CHAD
NIGER
NIGERIA
CAMEROON
CENTRAL AFRICAN REPUBLIC
GABON
CONGO
CONGO (ZAIRE)
EQUATORIAL GUINEA
CABINDA (Angola)
Red Sea
Gulf of Aden
Lake Victoria
Lake Chad
Nubian Desert
Baiyuda Desert
Tibesti
Massif Ennedi
Erdi
Ouaddai
Sudd
OGADĒN
HAUD
Khartoum
Omdurman
Addis Ababa
Mogadishu (Muqdisho)
Nairobi
Mombasa
Dar es Salaam
Kampala
Kigali
Bujumbura
Kinshasa
Brazzaville
Ndjamena
Bangui
Yaoundé
Douala
Libreville
Djibouti
Asmara
Aden
San'a
Port Sudan
El Obeid
Juba
Kisangani
Dodoma
Kano
Maiduguri
Zinder
Abéché
Wad Medani
Dirē Dawa
Berbera
Marka
Kismaayo
Tanga
Zanzibar
Arusha
Mwanza
Tabora
Matadi
Pointe-Noire
Equator

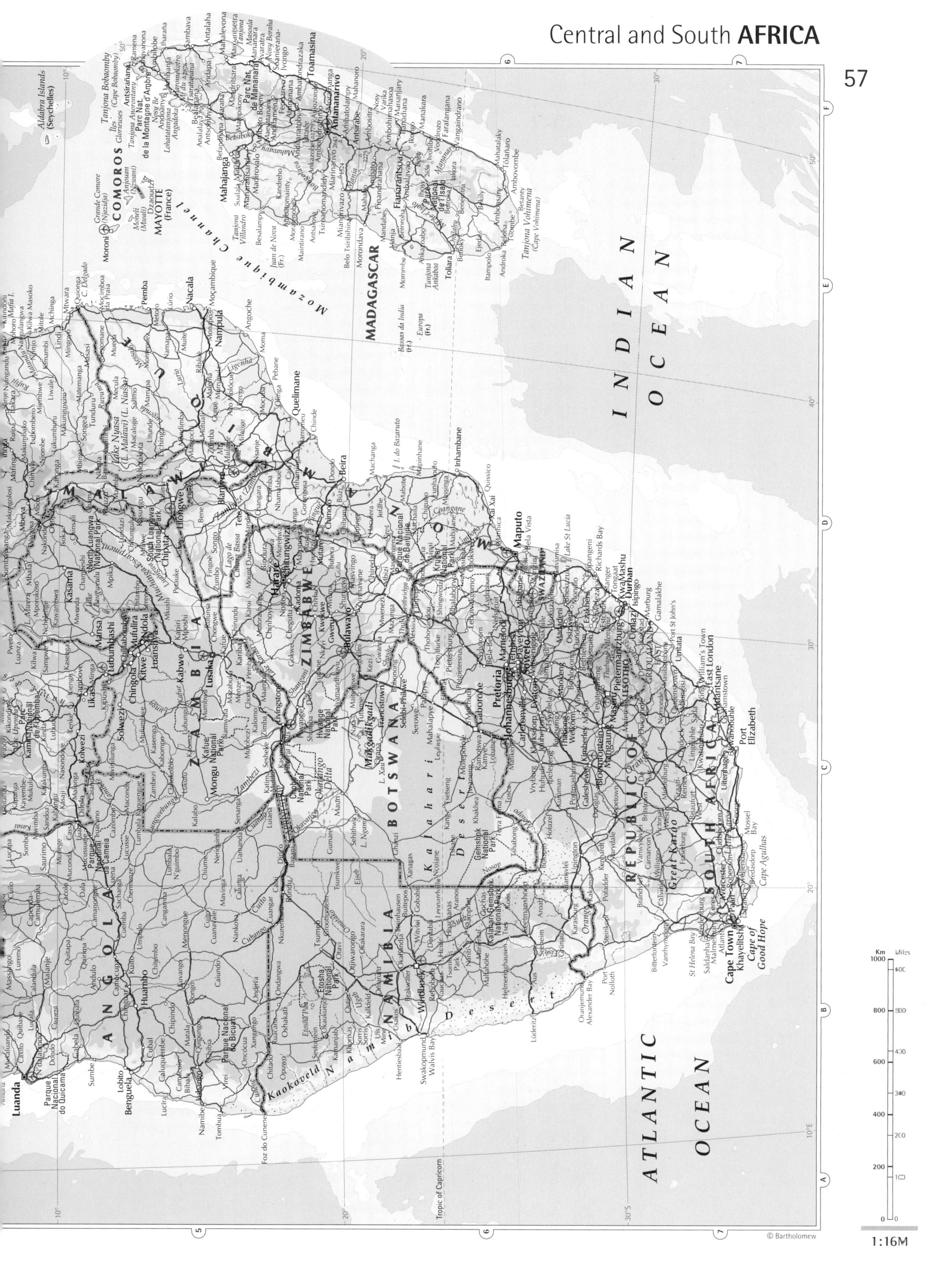
ATLANTIC OCEAN
INDIAN OCEAN
ANGOLA
ZAMBIA
MALAWI
MOZAMBIQUE
ZIMBABWE
BOTSWANA
NAMIBIA
REPUBLIC OF SOUTH AFRICA
LESOTHO
SWAZILAND
MADAGASCAR
COMOROS
MAYOTTE (France)
Mozambique Channel
Kalahari Desert
Namib Desert
Tropic of Capricorn
Luanda
Lusaka
Harare
Maputo
Pretoria
Johannesburg
Windhoek
Gaborone
Antananarivo
Cape Town
Durban
Bloemfontein
Port Elizabeth
East London
Cape of Good Hope
Km
Miles
1000
800
600
400
200
0
500
400
300
200
100
0
1:16M

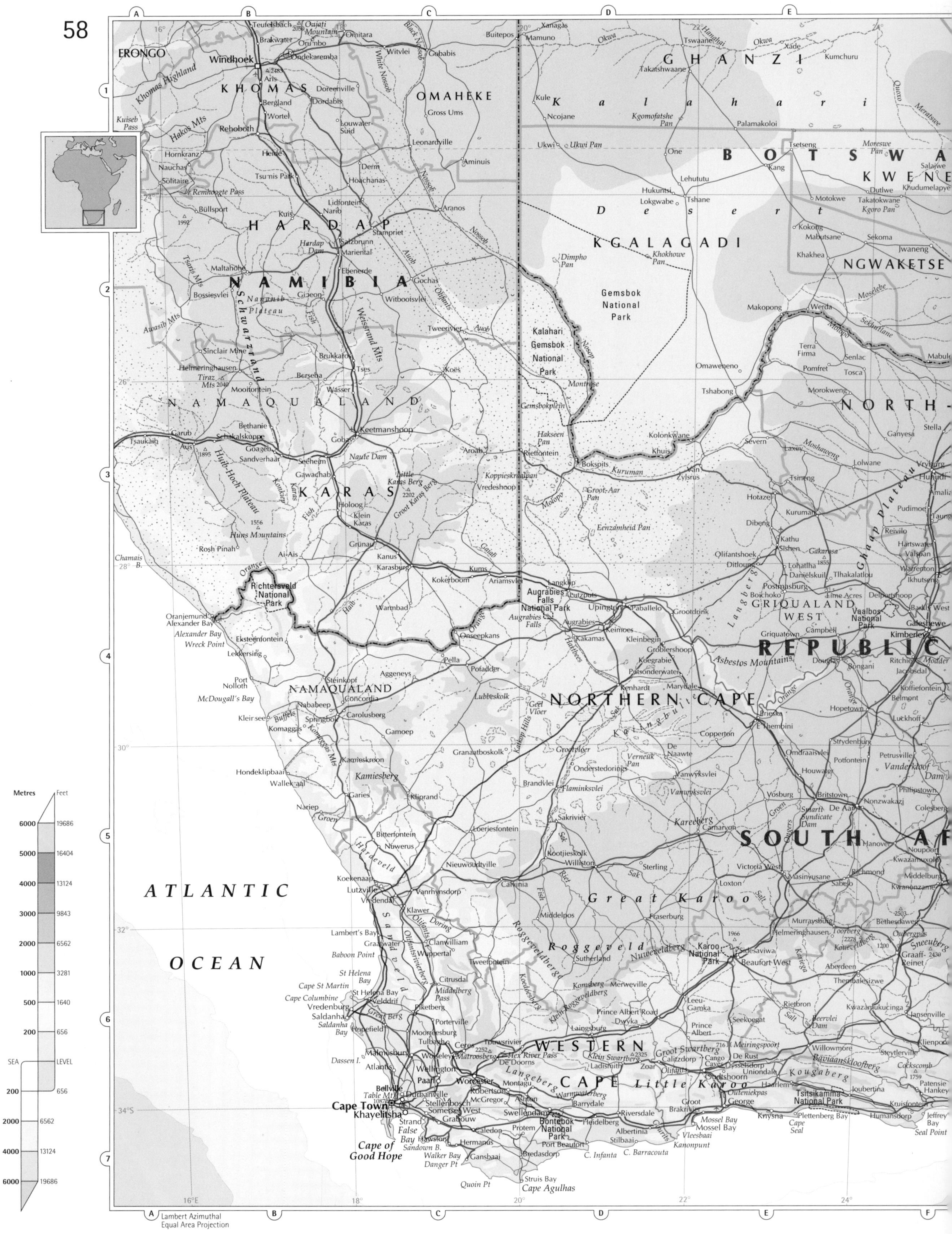

ERONGO
KHOMAS
OMAHEKE
HARDAP
NAMIBIA
KARAS
NAMAQUALAND
Windhoek
Rehoboth
Mariental
Keetmanshoop
Lüderitz
Aus
Karasburg
Gobabis
G H A N Z I
K a l a h a r i
D e s e r t
B O T S W A
KGALAGADI
KWENE
NGWAKETSE
Gemsbok National Park
Kalahari Gemsbok National Park
Richtersveld National Park
Augrabies Falls National Park
NORTHERN CAPE
GRIQUALAND WEST
REPUBLIC
SOUTH AF
NORTH-
WESTERN CAPE
Great Karoo
Little Karoo
Roggeveld
Karoo National Park
Bontebok National Park
Tsitsikamma National Park
Kimberley
Upington
Springbok
Calvinia
Beaufort West
Worcester
Paarl
Stellenbosch
George
Knysna
Oudtshoorn
Cape Town
Khayelitsha
Cape of Good Hope
Cape Agulhas
Saldanha Bay
Orange
ATLANTIC
OCEAN
Metres
Feet
6000
5000
4000
3000
2000
1000
500
200
SEA
LEVEL
19686
16404
13124
9843
6562
3281
1640
656
Lambert Azimuthal
Equal Area Projection

REPUBLIC OF SOUTH AFRICA

Km 300 250 200 150 100 50 0
Miles 150 100 50 0

1:5M

Metres SEA
Feet LEVEL
200
656
3000
9843
Bi-Polar Oblique Projection
NORTH PACIFIC OCEAN
Bering Sea
Aleutian Islands
Beaufort Sea
Chukchi Sea
Gulf of Alaska
Hudson Bay
James Bay
Davis Strait
Labrador Sea
Denmark Strait
Baffin Bay
Lincoln Sea
Wandel Sea
Foxe Basin
Hudson Strait
Gulf of Boothia
Amundsen Gulf
CANADA
U.S.A.
ALASKA
YUKON TERRITORY
NORTHWEST TERRITORIES
BRITISH COLUMBIA
ALBERTA
SASKATCHEWAN
MANITOBA
ONTARIO
QUEBEC
NEWFOUNDLAND
LABRADOR
Greenland (Denmark)
ICELAND
Reykjavík
Jan Mayen (Nor.)
Baffin Island
Victoria Island
Banks Island
Queen Elizabeth Islands
Ellesmere Island
Devon Island
Southampton I.
Coats I.
Mansel I.
Belcher Is
Vancouver Island
Queen Charlotte Islands
Kodiak I.
Nunivak I.
St Lawrence I. (U.S.A.)
St Matthew I. (U.S.A.)
Pribilof Is (U.S.A.)
Newfoundland
Anticosti I.
Mt McKinley 6194
Mt Logan
ROCKY MOUNTAINS
Anchorage
Fairbanks
Nome
Barrow
Pt Barrow
Point Hope
Arctic Circle
RUS. FED.
Bering Str.
Kotzebue Sd
Norton Sound
Bristol Bay
Dawson
Whitehorse
Inuvik
Yellowknife
Great Slave L.
Great Bear L.
Lake Athabasca
Edmonton
Calgary
Saskatoon
Regina
Winnipeg
Lake Winnipeg
Churchill
Thunder Bay
Lake Superior
L. Huron
Ottawa
Montréal
Quebec
Chicoutimi
St John's
Halifax
Vancouver
Victoria
Seattle
Portland
Salem
Sacramento
San Francisco
WASHINGTON
OREGON
IDAHO
MONTANA
WYOMING
NORTH DAKOTA
SOUTH DAKOTA
MINNESOTA
WISCONSIN
CALIFORNIA
NEVADA
MAINE
Minneapolis
St Paul
Duluth
Bismarck
Boise
Helena
Billings
Iqaluit
Cape Dorset
Resolute
Mackenzie
Yukon
Liard
Hecate Str.
Alexander Archipelago
Cook Inlet
Alaska Pen.
Kong Frederik VI Kyst
Kong Christian IX Land
Kong Christian X Land
Kong Frederik VIII Land

NORTH ATLANTIC OCEAN
Bermuda (U.K.)
UNITED STATES OF AMERICA
GULF OF MEXICO
CARIBBEAN SEA
MEXICO
CUBA
THE BAHAMAS
HAITI
DOMINICAN REP.
JAMAICA
BELIZE
GUATEMALA
HONDURAS
EL SALVADOR
NICARAGUA
COSTA RICA
PANAMA
VENEZUELA
COLOMBIA
ECUADOR
GUYANA
SURINAME
BRAZIL
TRINIDAD & TOBAGO
BARBADOS
ST VINCENT & THE GRENADINES
ST LUCIA
DOMINICA
ANTIGUA & BARBUDA
ST KITTS-NEVIS
GRENADA
Greater Antilles
Lesser Antilles
Gulf of California
Bahía de Campeche
Yucatan Channel
Str. of Florida
G. of Tehuantepec
G. of Darien
Tropic of Cancer
Equator
Galapagos Islands (Ecu.)
Clipperton I. (Fr.)
Revillagigedo Is. (Mex.)
Guadalupe (Mex.)
I. de Coco (C.R.)
I. de Malpelo (Col.)
Turks & Caicos Is (U.K.)
Cayman Is (U.K.)
New York
Washington D.C.
Chicago
Los Angeles
Houston
Dallas
Miami
New Orleans
México
Havana
Kingston
Port-au-Prince
Santo Domingo
Guatemala City
San Salvador
Tegucigalpa
Managua
San José
Panamá
Caracas
Bogotá
Quito
Georgetown
Km
Miles
1400
1200
1000
800
600
400
200
0
800
600
400
200
0
1:25M

Chamberlin Trimetric Projection

Km 1000 800 600 400 200 0

Miles 500 400 300 200 100 0

1:17M

Transverse Mercator Projection

1:7M

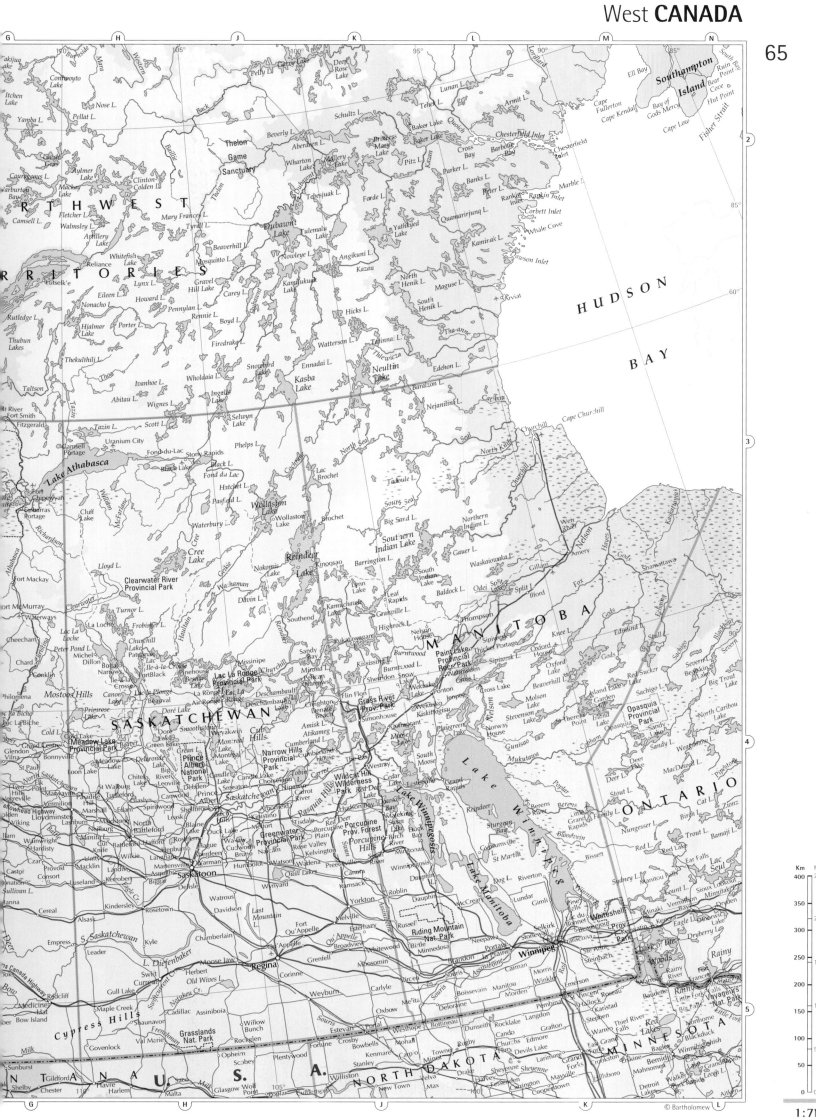

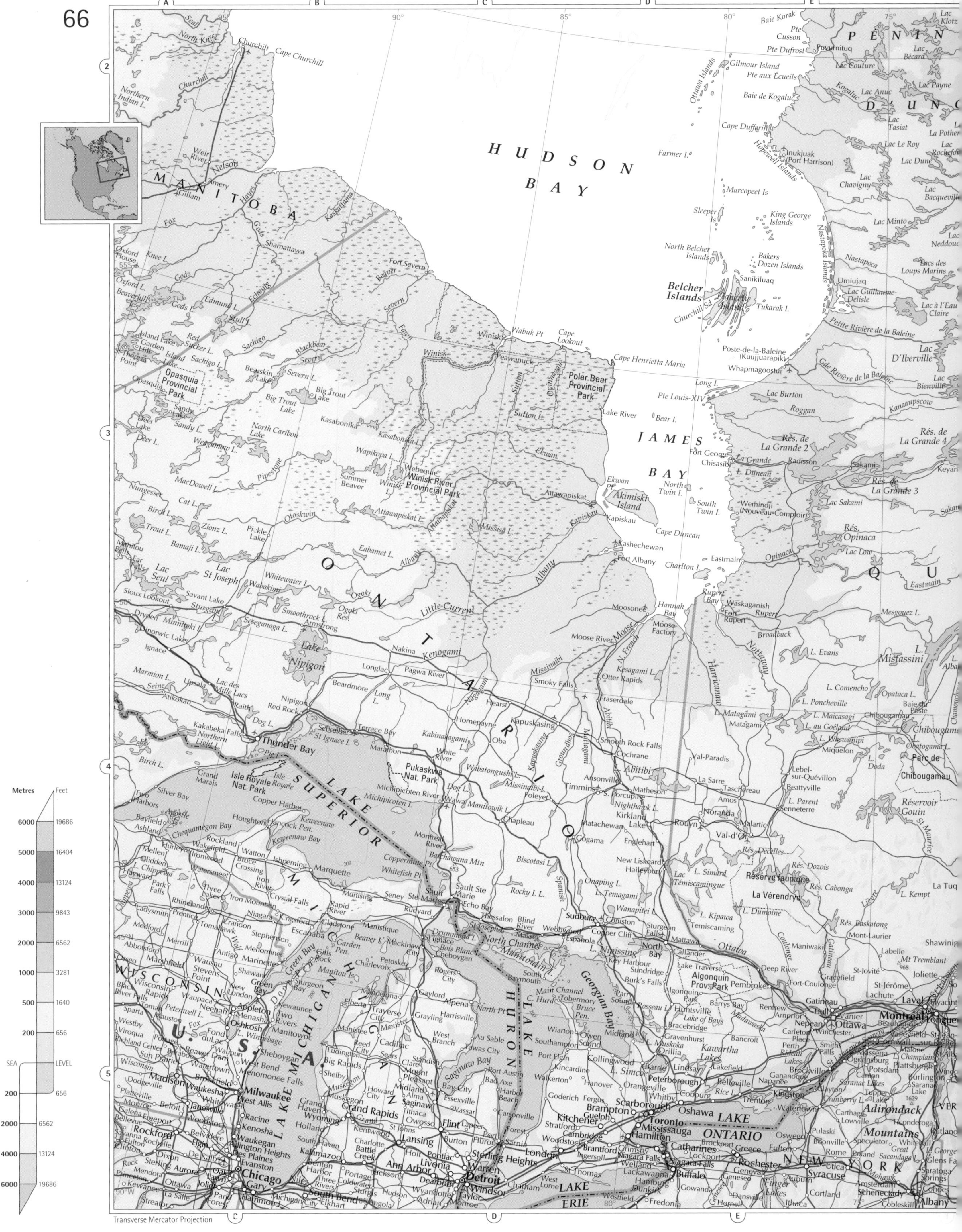

Transverse Mercator Projection

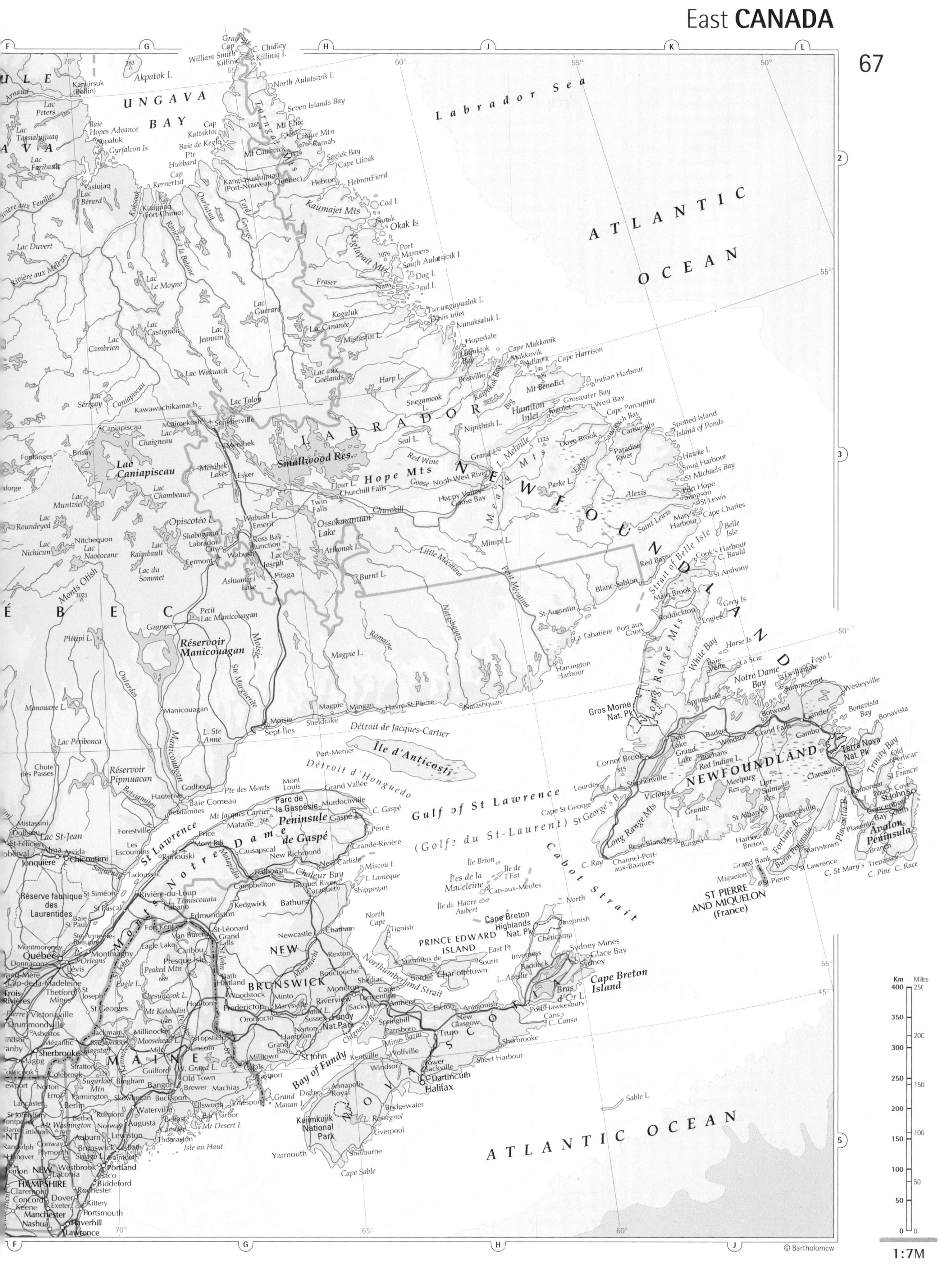
UNGAVA BAY
Labrador Sea
ATLANTIC OCEAN
LABRADOR
NEWFOUNDLAND
QUÉBEC
NEW BRUNSWICK
NOVA SCOTIA
MAINE
NEW HAMPSHIRE
PRINCE EDWARD ISLAND
ST PIERRE AND MIQUELON (France)
Gulf of St Lawrence
(Golfe du St-Laurent)
Cabot Strait
Strait of Belle Isle
Détroit de Jacques-Cartier
Détroit d'Honguedo
Île d'Anticosti
Northumberland Strait
Bay of Fundy
Chaleur Bay
Notre Dame Bay
Trinity Bay
Bonavista Bay
Akpatok I.
Kangirsuk (Bellin)
Kangiqsualujjuaq (Port-Nouveau-Québec)
Kuujjuaq (Fort-Chimo)
Torngat Mts
Mt Caubvick
Kaumajet Mts
Kiglapait Mts
Okak Is
Hebron
Nain
Hopedale
Makkovik
Cape Harrison
Indian Harbour
Postville
Hamilton Inlet
Groswater Bay
Cartwright
Mealy Mts
Hope Mts
Smallwood Res.
Churchill Falls
Goose Bay
Happy Valley
North West River
Lake Melville
Twin Falls
Ossokmanuan Lake
Wabush L.
Labrador City
Wabush
Fermont
Schefferville
Lac Caniapiscau
Réservoir Manicouagan
Gagnon
Monts Otish
Sept-Îles
Moisie
Havre-St-Pierre
Natashquan
Blanc-Sablon
Red Bay
St Anthony
Long Range Mts
Gros Morne Nat. Pk
Corner Brook
Deer Lake
Grand Falls
Gander
Botwood
Twillingate
Fogo I.
Terra Nova Nat. Pk
Clarenville
Stephenville
Port aux Basques
Channel-Port-aux-Basques
C. Ray
Burgeo
Marystown
Burin Peninsula
Placentia
Carbonear
St John's
Avalon Peninsula
C. Race
Fortune B.
Miquelon
St-Pierre
Îles de la Madeleine
Cap-aux-Meules
Cape Breton Island
Cape Breton Highlands Nat. Pk
Sydney
Sydney Mines
Glace Bay
Bras d'Or L.
Port Hawkesbury
Canso
C. Canso
Antigonish
New Glasgow
Truro
Pictou
Amherst
Springhill
Parrsboro
Minas Basin
Windsor
Kentville
Wolfville
Dartmouth
Halifax
Sheet Harbour
Sable I.
Bridgewater
Liverpool
Kejimkujik National Park
Digby
Annapolis Royal
Yarmouth
Shelburne
Cape Sable
Charlottetown
Summerside
Souris
East Pt
North Cape
Tignish
Moncton
Shediac
Sackville
Fundy Nat. Park
Saint John
Fredericton
Oromocto
Woodstock
Edmundston
Grand Falls
Bathurst
Campbellton
Dalhousie
Miramichi
Newcastle
Chatham
Caraquet
Shippegan
Gaspé
Percé
Peninsule de Gaspé
Parc de la Gaspésie
Matane
Rimouski
Mont Joli
Rivière-du-Loup
Baie Comeau
Forestville
Chicoutimi
Jonquière
Lac St-Jean
Réservoir Pipmuacan
Québec
Lévis
Thetford Mines
Drummondville
Victoriaville
Sherbrooke
Magog
St Georges
Bangor
Augusta
Portland
Bar Harbor
Mt Desert I.
Mt Katahdin
Presque Isle
Caribou
Moosehead L.
Concord
Manchester
Nashua
Portsmouth
Dover
Keene
Lawrence
Haverhill
Mt Washington
Berlin
Lewiston
Auburn
Km
Miles
1:7M
© Bartholomew

LAKE SUPERIOR
LAKE MICHIGAN
MINNESOTA
WISCONSIN
MICHIGAN
IOWA
ILLINOIS
INDIANA
MISSOURI
U. S.
Thunder Bay
Isle Royale
Isle Royale National Park
Pukaskwa National Park
Michipicoten Bay
Lake Superior Provincial Park
Quetico Provincial Park
Apostle Islands National Lakeshore
Pictured Rocks National Lakeshore
Sleeping Bear Dunes National Seashore
Keweenaw Bay
Keweenaw Peninsula
Sawtooth Mountains
Mesabi Range
Gogebic Range
Misquah Hills
Door Peninsula
Green Bay
Grand Traverse Bay
Little Traverse Bay
Duluth
Superior
St Paul
Marquette
Green Bay
Appleton
Oshkosh
Madison
Milwaukee
Racine
Kenosha
Waukegan
Rockford
Chicago
Gary
South Bend
Fort Wayne
Indianapolis
Grand Rapids
Lansing
Kalamazoo
Cedar Rapids
Davenport
Peoria
Springfield
Champaign
Bloomington
Muskegon
La Crosse
Eau Claire
Wausau
Rochester
Iowa City
Dubuque
Metres
Feet
6000
19686
5000
16404
4000
13124
3000
9843
2000
6562
1000
3281
500
1640
200
656
SEA
LEVEL
Lambert Conformal Conic Projection

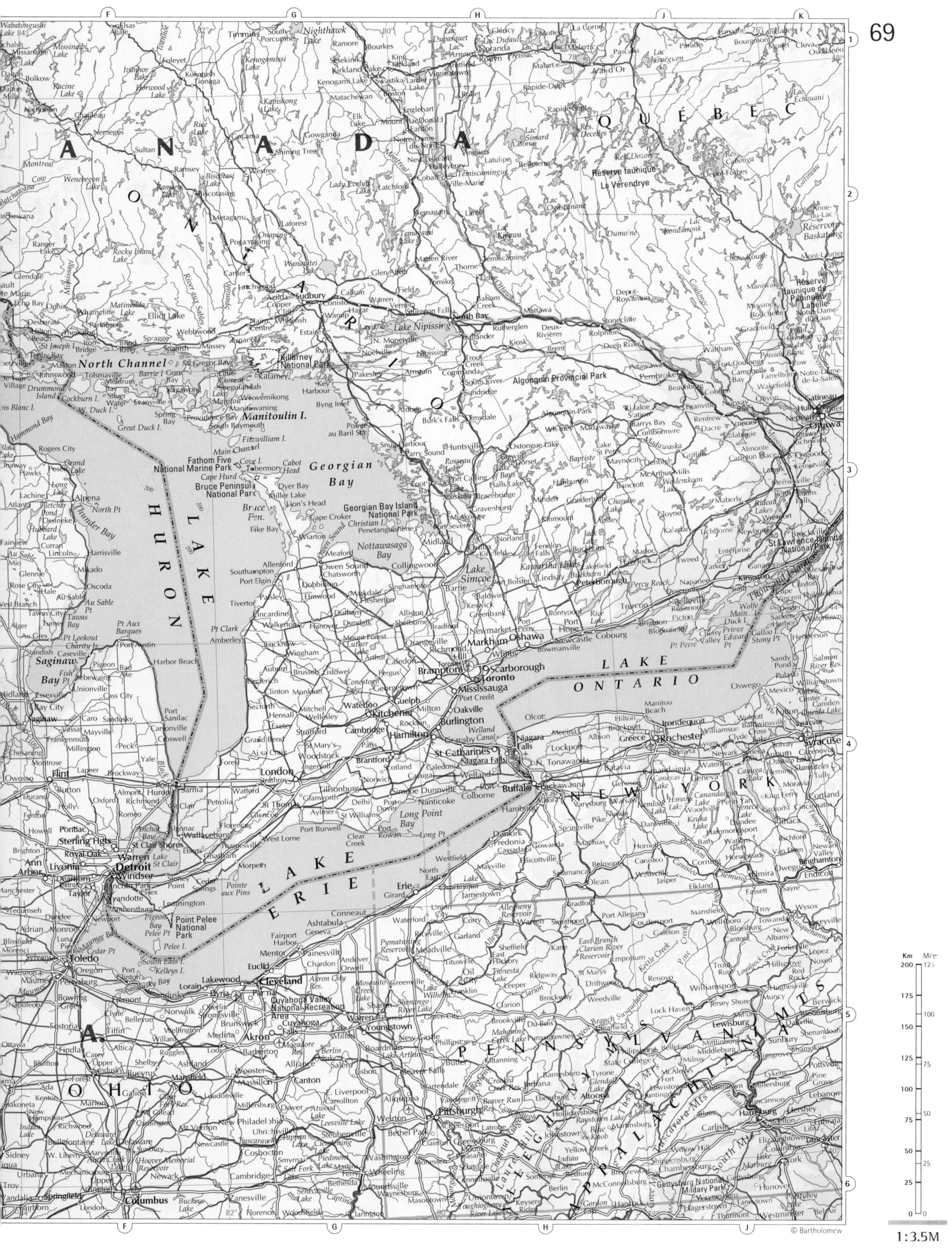
CANADA
ONTARIO
QUÉBEC
NEW YORK
PENNSYLVANIA
OHIO
LAKE HURON
LAKE ONTARIO
LAKE ERIE
Georgian Bay
North Channel
Manitoulin I.
Lake Nipissing
Lake Simcoe
Lake St Clair
Saginaw Bay
Algonquin Provincial Park
Réserve faunique La Vérendrye
Toronto
Ottawa
Hamilton
Mississauga
Buffalo
Rochester
Syracuse
Detroit
Windsor
Cleveland
Toledo
Pittsburgh
Columbus
Akron
Sudbury
North Bay
Kingston
London
Erie
ALLEGHENY MTS
APPALACHIAN MTS
Km
Miles
1:3.5M

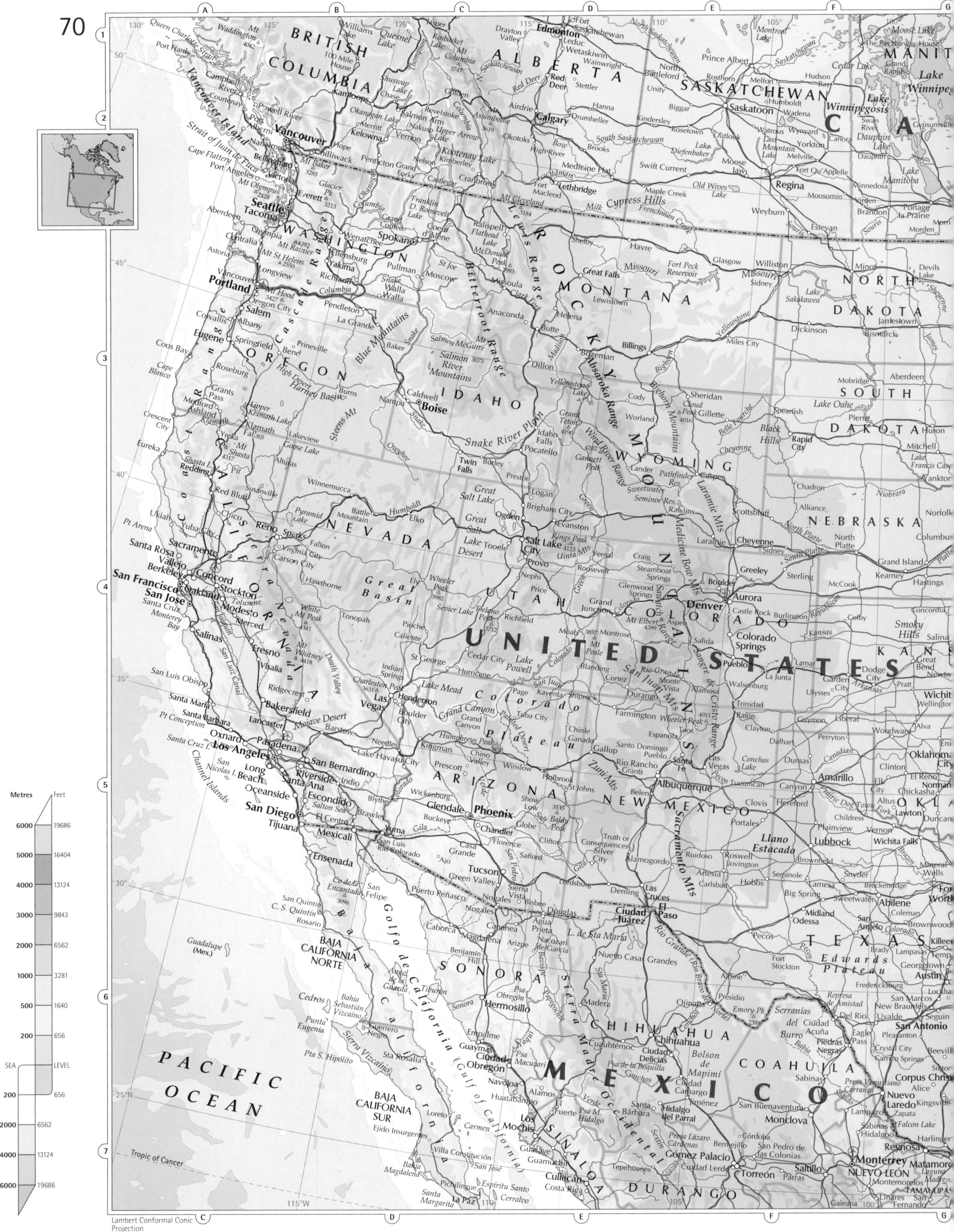

Metres | Feet

Metres	Feet
6000	19686
5000	16404
4000	13124
3000	9843
2000	6562
1000	3281
500	1640
200	656
SEA	LEVEL
200	656
2000	6562
4000	13124
6000	19686

Lambert Conformal Conic Projection

CANADA
ONTARIO
QUÉBEC
OF AMERICA
MINNESOTA
WISCONSIN
MICHIGAN
IOWA
ILLINOIS
INDIANA
OHIO
PENNSYLVANIA
NEW YORK
VERMONT
NEW HAMPSHIRE
MAINE
MASS.
CONN.
RHODE ISLAND
NEW JERSEY
DEL.
MARYLAND
WEST VIRGINIA
VIRGINIA
KENTUCKY
MISSOURI
TENNESSEE
NORTH CAROLINA
SOUTH CAROLINA
ARKANSAS
MISSISSIPPI
ALABAMA
GEORGIA
LOUISIANA
FLORIDA
NEW BRUNSWICK
Lake Superior
Lake Michigan
Lake Huron
Lake Ontario
Lake Erie
Georgian Bay
James Bay
Lake Nipigon
Appalachian Mountains
Allegheny Mountains
Blue Ridge
Cumberland Plateau
Ozark Plateau
Coastal Plain
ATLANTIC OCEAN
GULF OF MEXICO
THE BAHAMAS
Straits of Florida
Tropic of Cancer
New York
Philadelphia
Boston
Washington
Baltimore
Chicago
Detroit
Toronto
Montréal
Ottawa
Québec
Pittsburgh
Cleveland
Columbus
Cincinnati
Indianapolis
St Louis
Memphis
Nashville
Atlanta
Jacksonville
Miami
Tampa
New Orleans
Houston
Dallas
Milwaukee
Minneapolis
St Paul
Winnipeg
Thunder Bay
Kansas City
Nassau
1:12M

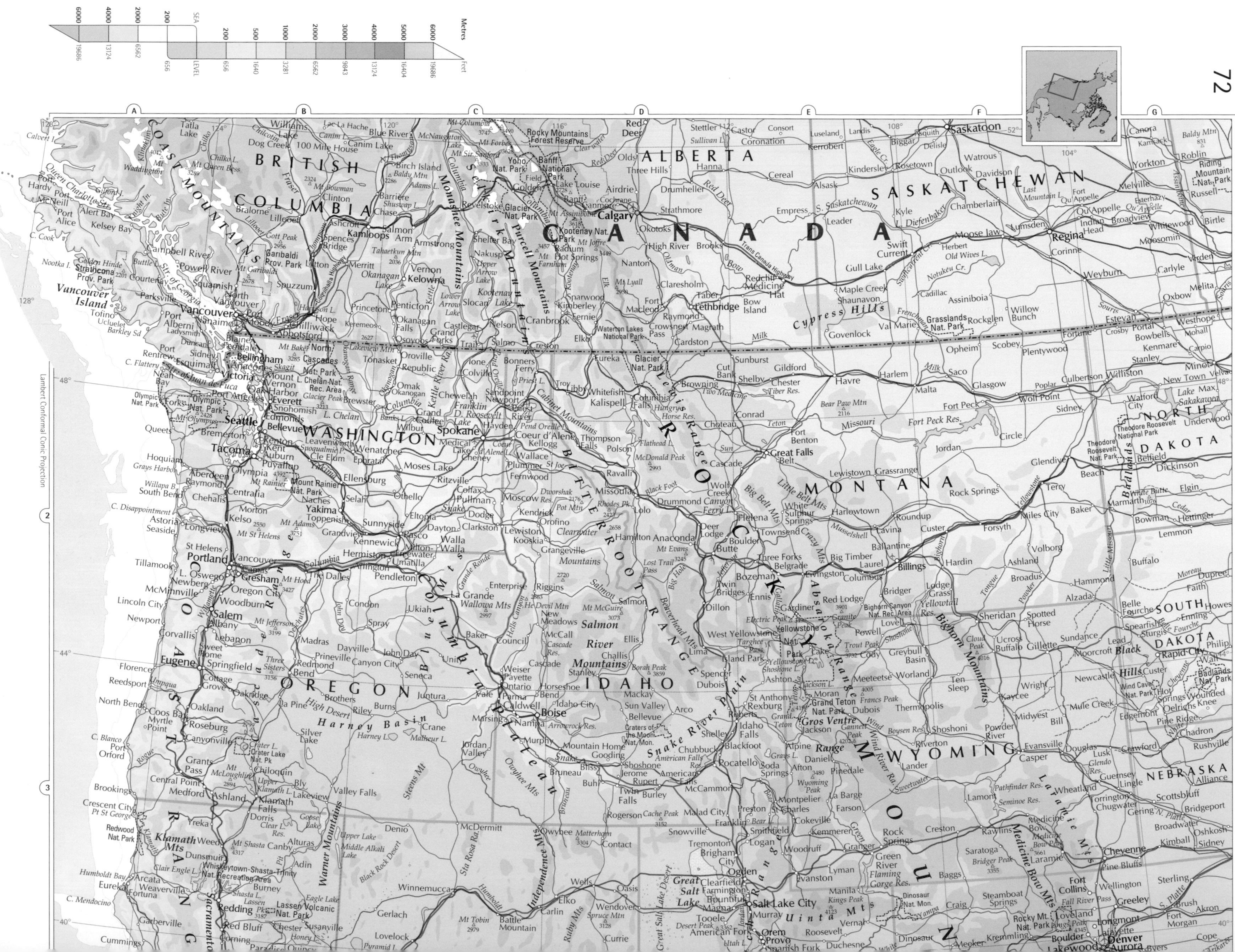

Metres
Feet
6000 19686
5000 16404
4000 13124
3000 9843
2000 6562
1000 3281
500 1640
200 656
SEA LEVEL
200 656
2000 6562
4000 13124
6000 19686
C A N A D A
BRITISH COLUMBIA
ALBERTA
SASKATCHEWAN
WASHINGTON
OREGON
IDAHO
MONTANA
WYOMING
NORTH DAKOTA
SOUTH DAKOTA
NEBRASKA
COAST MOUNTAINS
ROCKY MOUNTAINS
BITTERROOT RANGE
Lambert Conformal Conic Projection

COLORADO
UTAH
NEVADA
ARIZONA
NEW MEXICO
TEXAS
CALIFORNIA
MEXICO
SONORA
CHIHUAHUA
BAJA CALIFORNIA NORTE
PACIFIC OCEAN
GREAT BASIN
COLORADO PLATEAU
Golfo de California
Sierra Nevada
San Joaquin Valley
Mojave Desert
Sangre de Cristo Range
San Juan Mts
Sacramento Mountains
Llano Estacado
Channel Islands
Grand Canyon
Death Valley
Panamint Range
Black Mts
Sacramento
San Francisco
Oakland
San Jose
Fresno
Bakersfield
Los Angeles
Long Beach
San Diego
Tijuana
Mexicali
Las Vegas
Phoenix
Tucson
Albuquerque
Santa Fe
El Paso
Ciudad Juárez
Chihuahua
Hermosillo
Reno
Colorado Springs
Pueblo
Guaymas
Ensenada
Guadalupe (Mexico)
Km
400
350
300
250
200
150
100
50
0
Miles
250
200
150
100
50
0

1:7M

CALIFORNIA
NEVADA
SIERRA NEVADA
PACIFIC OCEAN
OAHU
(Hawaii)
1:1.5M
HAWAIIAN ISLANDS
(Main group)
(U.S.A.)
1:6M
PACIFIC
OCEAN
Metres
Feet
6000
19686
5000
16404
4000
13124
3000
9843
2000
6562
1000
3281
500
1640
200
656
SEA
LEVEL
200
656
2000
6562
4000
13124
6000
19686
San Francisco
Oakland
Berkeley
Concord
Daly City
Hayward
Sunnyvale
Santa Clara
San Jose
Sacramento
Stockton
Modesto
Merced
Fresno
Visalia
Bakersfield
Santa Rosa
Vallejo
Salinas
Monterey
Santa Cruz
Reno
Sparks
Carson City
Red Bluff
Chico
Oroville
Eureka
Lake Tahoe
Bishop
Death Valley
Santa Barbara
Oxnard
Ventura
Thousand Oaks
Simi Valley
Santa Clarita
Lancaster
Palmdale
Los Angeles
Pasadena
Glendale
Burbank
Long Beach
Torrance
Anaheim
Santa Ana
Irvine
Huntington Beach
Riverside
San Bernardino
Oceanside
Escondido
San Diego
Chula Vista
Tijuana
Ensenada
Mojave Desert
Channel Islands
Santa Barbara Channel
Gulf of Santa Catalina
Honolulu
Pearl City
Kailua
Kaneohe
Wahiawa
Kauai
Oahu
Molokai
Lanai
Maui
Kahoolawe
Hawaii
Hilo
Mauna Kea
Mauna Loa
Hawaii Volcanoes National Park
Lambert Conformal Conic Projection

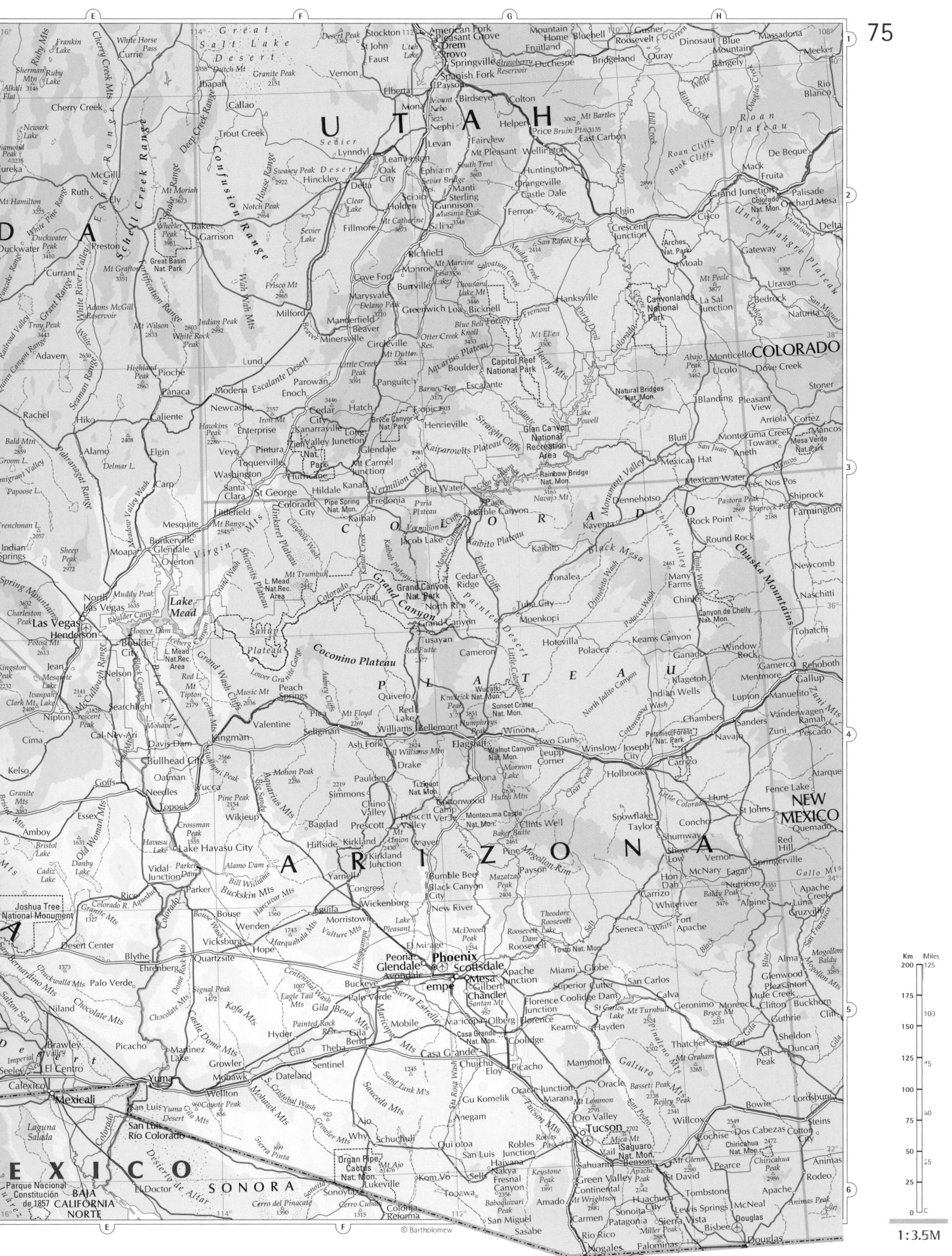
UTAH
ARIZONA
COLORADO
NEW MEXICO
MEXICO
SONORA
BAJA CALIFORNIA NORTE
COLORADO PLATEAU
Great Salt Lake Desert
Sevier Desert
Escalante Desert
Confusion Range
House Range
Schell Creek Range
Wah Wah Mts
Aquarius Plateau
Henry Mts
Kaiparowits Plateau
Coconino Plateau
Kaibab Plateau
Grand Canyon
Painted Desert
Black Mesa
Chuska Mountains
Mogollon Rim
Uncompahgre Plateau
Roan Plateau
Sonoran Desert
Gila Bend Mts
Kofa Mts
Lake Mead
Lake Powell
Provo
Spanish Fork
Price
Grand Junction
Moab
Richfield
Cedar City
St George
Kanab
Page
Monticello
Blanding
Cortez
Farmington
Shiprock
Gallup
Kayenta
Tuba City
Flagstaff
Williams
Sedona
Prescott
Kingman
Bullhead City
Lake Havasu City
Needles
Las Vegas
Henderson
Boulder City
Winslow
Holbrook
Show Low
Phoenix
Glendale
Scottsdale
Mesa
Tempe
Chandler
Casa Grande
Florence
Globe
Safford
Tucson
Nogales
Sierra Vista
Bisbee
Douglas
Benson
Willcox
Yuma
El Centro
Calexico
Mexicali
San Luis Río Colorado
Blythe
Parker
Wickenburg
Ajo
Canyonlands National Park
Capitol Reef National Park
Arches Nat. Park
Glen Canyon National Recreation Area
Zion Nat. Park
Bryce Canyon Nat. Park
Grand Canyon Nat. Park
Great Basin Nat. Park
Mesa Verde Nat. Park
Petrified Forest Nat. Park
Joshua Tree National Monument
Organ Pipe Cactus Nat. Mon.
Saguaro Nat. Mon.
© Bartholomew
Km
Miles
1:3.5M

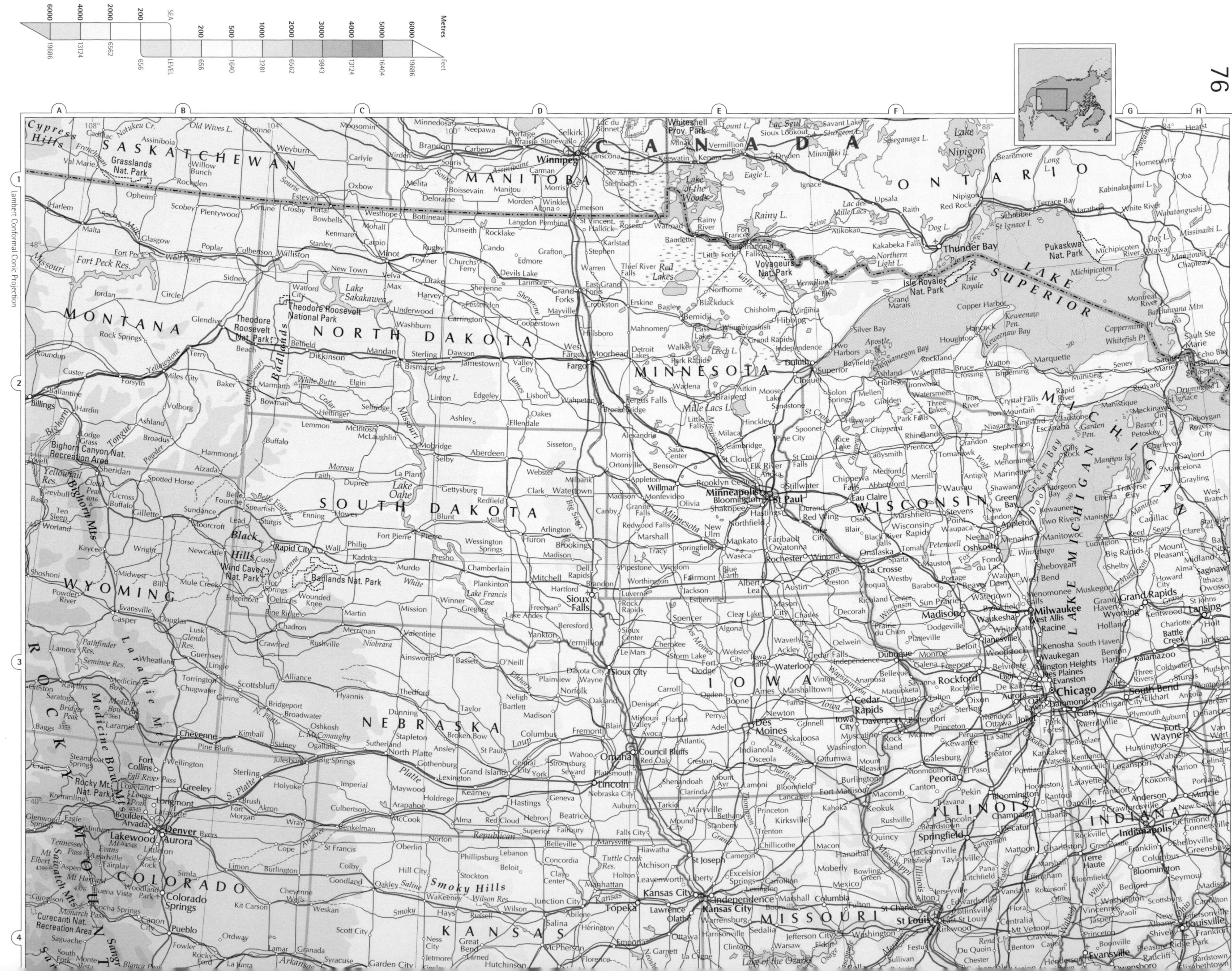

Metres
Feet
6000
19686
5000
16404
4000
13124
3000
9843
2000
6562
1000
3281
500
1640
200
656
SEA
LEVEL
200
656
2000
6562
4000
13124
6000
19686
Lambert Conformal Conic Projection
SASKATCHEWAN
MANITOBA
ONTARIO
CANADA
MONTANA
NORTH DAKOTA
SOUTH DAKOTA
MINNESOTA
WISCONSIN
MICHIGAN
IOWA
NEBRASKA
WYOMING
COLORADO
KANSAS
MISSOURI
ILLINOIS
INDIANA
LAKE SUPERIOR
LAKE MICHIGAN
ROCKY MOUNTAINS

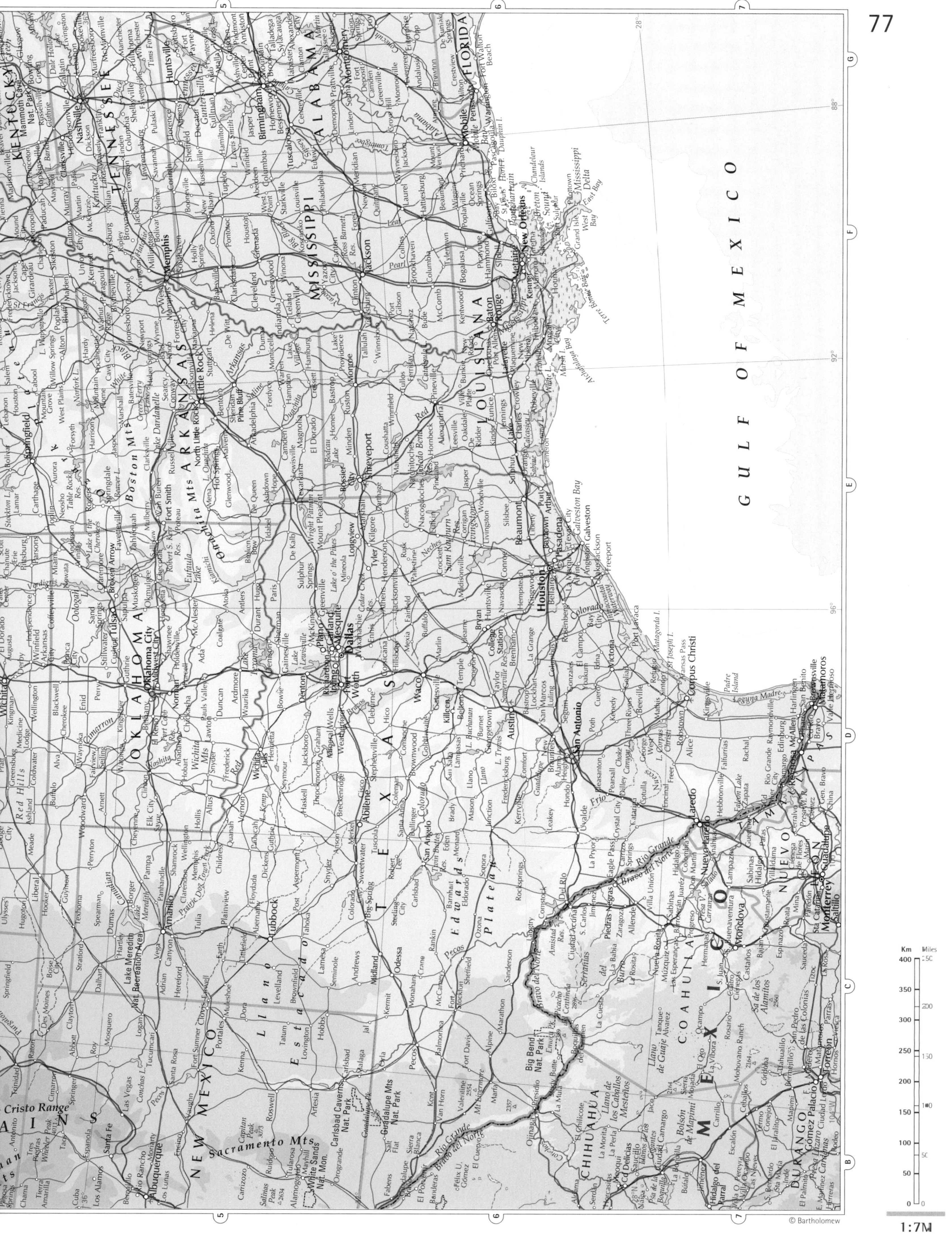
GULF OF MEXICO
KENTUCKY
TENNESSEE
ALABAMA
MISSISSIPPI
FLORIDA
ARKANSAS
LOUISIANA
OKLAHOMA
TEXAS
NEW MEXICO
COAHUILA
NUEVO LEON
TAMAULIPAS
CHIHUAHUA
DURANGO
MEXICO
Nashville
Huntsville
Birmingham
Montgomery
Mobile
Memphis
Jackson
New Orleans
Baton Rouge
Little Rock
Shreveport
Oklahoma City
Tulsa
Wichita
Dallas
Fort Worth
Houston
Galveston
San Antonio
Austin
Corpus Christi
Laredo
Nuevo Laredo
Monterrey
Saltillo
Torreón
Amarillo
Lubbock
Odessa
Midland
Albuquerque
Santa Fe
Ozark Plateau
Boston Mts
Ouachita Mts
Llano Estacado
Edwards Plateau
Sacramento Mts
Big Bend Nat. Park
Carlsbad Caverns Nat. Park
Guadalupe Mts Nat. Park
White Sands Nat. Mon.
Rio Grande
Mississippi Delta
Km
Miles
400
350
300
250
200
150
100
50
0
1:7M

Metres
Feet
6000 19686
5000 16404
4000 13124
3000 9843
2000 6562
1000 3281
500 1640
200 656
SEA LEVEL
200 656
2000 6562
4000 13124
6000 19686
C A N A D A
O N T A R I O
Q U É B E C
LAKE SUPERIOR
LAKE MICHIGAN
LAKE HURON
LAKE ERIE
LAKE ONTARIO
Georgian Bay
MINNESOTA
WISCONSIN
MICHIGAN
IOWA
ILLINOIS
INDIANA
OHIO
KENTUCKY
MISSOURI
WEST VIRGINIA
VIRGINIA
PENNSYLVANIA
NEW YORK
VERMONT
NEW HAMPSHIRE
MASSACHUSETTS
CONNECTICUT
RHODE ISLAND
NEW JERSEY
MAINE
NEW BRUNSWICK
MARYLAND
DELAWARE
Chicago
Detroit
Toronto
Montréal
Ottawa
Québec
Boston
New York
Philadelphia
Cleveland
Pittsburgh
Milwaukee
Indianapolis
Cincinnati
Columbus
Buffalo
Baltimore
Washington D.C.
Thunder Bay
Lambert Conformal Conic Projection

ATLANTIC
OCEAN
GULF
OF
MEXICO
THE BAHAMAS
TENNESSEE
NORTH CAROLINA
SOUTH CAROLINA
GEORGIA
ALABAMA
MISSISSIPPI
FLORIDA
COASTAL PLAIN
Memphis
Nashville
Knoxville
Chattanooga
Huntsville
Birmingham
Atlanta
Charlotte
Columbia
Charleston
Savannah
Jacksonville
Tallahassee
Mobile
Pensacola
New Orleans
Orlando
Tampa
St Petersburg
Miami
Fort Lauderdale
Hollywood
Nassau
Grand Bahama
Great Abaco
Eleuthera
Andros
Straits of Florida
Tongue of the Ocean
Cape Hatteras
Cape Canaveral
Tropic of Cancer
Km
Miles
1:7M
© Bartholomew

Metres / Feet

Metres	Feet
6000	19686
5000	16404
4000	13124
3000	9843
2000	6562
1000	3281
500	1640
200	656
SEA	LEVEL
200	656
2000	6562
4000	13124
6000	19686

Lambert Conformal Conic Projection

QUÉBEC
YORK
VERMONT
NEW HAMPSHIRE
MAINE
MASSACHUSETTS
CONNECTICUT
RHODE ISLAND
NEW JERSEY
DELAWARE
CANADA
NEW BRUNSWICK
ATLANTIC
OCEAN
Lake Champlain
Adirondack Mountains
Catskill Mountains
White Mountains
Green Mountains
Long Island Sound
Block Island Sound
Long Island
Massachusetts Bay
Cape Cod Bay
Cape Cod
Cape Cod National Seashore
Nantucket Sound
Nantucket Island
Martha's Vineyard
Block Island
Buzzards Bay
Delaware Bay
Chesapeake Bay
Fire Island National Seashore
Gateway National Recreational Area
Delaware Water Gap Nat. Rec. Area
Assateague Island National Seashore
Acadia Nat. Park
Mount Carleton Provincial Park
Albany
Syracuse
Binghamton
Boston
Providence
Hartford
Springfield
Worcester
New Haven
Bridgeport
Stamford
New York
Newark
Paterson
Yonkers
Philadelphia
Allentown
Trenton
Camden
Wilmington
Atlantic City
Ocean City
Portland
South Portland
Portsmouth
Concord
Manchester
Bangor
Augusta
Norfolk
Virginia Beach
Chesapeake
Hampton
Moosehead Lake
Chamberlain Lake
Mt Katahdin
continuation at the same scale
Km
Miles
1:3.5M
© Bartholomew

A
B
C
D
E
F
G
2
3
4
5
6
7
8
ARIZONA
NEW MEXICO
OKLAHOMA
ARKANSAS
TEXAS
LOUISIANA
MISSISSIPPI
ALABA
TENNESSE
U. S.
MEXICO
GUATEMALA
BELIZE
EL SALVADOR
HOND
GULF OF MEXIC
PACIFIC OCEAN
Golfo de California
Baja California
SIERRA MADRE OCCIDENTAL
Sierra Madre Oriental
Sierra Madre del Sur
Golfo de Tehuantepec
Bahía de Campeche
Yucatán
Llano Estacado
Edwards Plateau
Bolson de Mapimí
Albuquerque
Phoenix
Tucson
Glendale
Mexicali
Tijuana
Ensenada
El Paso
Ciudad Juárez
Oklahoma City
Tulsa
Amarillo
Lubbock
Dallas
Fort Worth
Abilene
Waco
Austin
San Antonio
Houston
Beaumont
Corpus Christi
Nuevo Laredo
Monterrey
Matamoros
Brownsville
Chihuahua
Hermosillo
Ciudad Obregón
Los Mochis
Culiacán
Mazatlán
Durango
Torreón
Saltillo
Zacatecas
San Luis Potosí
Aguascalientes
Guadalajara
León
Querétaro
Tampico
Ciudad Victoria
Poza Rica
México
Puebla
Veracruz
Oaxaca
Acapulco
Mérida
Campeche
Villahermosa
Coatzacoalcos
Tuxtla Gutiérrez
Guatemala
San Salvador
Tegucigalpa
Managua
Memphis
Little Rock
Shreveport
Jackson
Baton Rouge
New Orleans
Mobile
Nashville
Birmingham
Islas Revillagigedo (Mex.)
Clipperton Island (France)
I. de Coco (C.R.)
Islas Marías
110°W
105°
100°
95°
90°
30°
25°
20°
15°
10°
5°N
Metres
Feet
6000
19686
5000
16404
4000
13124
3000
9843
2000
6562
1000
3281
500
1640
200
656
SEA
LEVEL
200
656
2000
6562
4000
13124
6000
19686
Lambert Azimuthal
Equal Area Projection

ATLANTIC OCEAN
BERMUDA (U.K.)
Hamilton
Tropic of Cancer
THE BAHAMAS
Nassau
Andros
Great Bahama Bank
Straits of Florida
Grand Bahama
Freeport City
Little Abaco
Great Abaco
Eleuthera
Cat Island
San Salvador (Watling)
Exuma Sound
Rum Cay
Long Island
Crooked Island
Acklins Island
Mayaguana
Great Inagua
TURKS AND CAICOS ISLANDS (U.K.)
Cockburn Town
Turks Is
Caicos Is
NORTH CAROLINA
SOUTH CAROLINA
GEORGIA
FLORIDA
Raleigh
Durham
Charlotte
Wilmington
Charleston
Savannah
Atlanta
Macon
Columbus
Jacksonville
Tallahassee
Orlando
Tampa
St Petersburg
Fort Lauderdale
Hollywood
Miami
Key West
Cape Hatteras
Cape Lookout
Cape Fear
Cape Canaveral
Daytona Beach
Big Cypress Nat. Reserve
Everglades Nat. Park
Havana (Habana)
Matanzas
CUBA
Santa Clara
Cienfuegos
Camagüey
Holguín
Santiago de Cuba
Guantánamo
Pinar del Río
Isla de la Juventud
CAYMAN ISLANDS (U.K.)
Grand Cayman
JAMAICA
Kingston
Montego Bay
HISPANIOLA
HAITI
Port-au-Prince
DOMINICAN REPUBLIC
Santo Domingo
Santiago
Cap-Haïtien
Windward Pass.
Jamaica Channel
Mona Passage
PUERTO RICO (U.S.A.)
San Juan
Ponce
GREATER ANTILLES
LEEWARD ISLANDS
VIRGIN IS (U.K.)
VIRGIN IS (U.S.A.)
ANGUILLA (U.K.)
ANTIGUA AND BARBUDA
St John's
ST KITTS-NEVIS
Basseterre
MONTSERRAT (U.K.)
Plymouth
GUADELOUPE (Fr.)
Basse Terre
Pointe-à-Pitre
DOMINICA
Roseau
MARTINIQUE (Fr.)
Fort-de-France
ST LUCIA
Castries
ST VINCENT & THE GRENADINES
Kingstown
BARBADOS
Bridgetown
GRENADA
St George's
TRINIDAD AND TOBAGO
Port of Spain
WINDWARD ISLANDS
Lesser Antilles
NETHERLANDS ANTILLES
ARUBA (Neth.)
Willemstad
CARIBBEAN SEA
Swan Islands (Hond.)
Isla de Providencia (Col.)
Isla de San Andrés (Col.)
Cayos Miskitos (Nic.)
Puerto Cabezas
Bluefields
COSTA RICA
San José
Limón
PANAMA
Panamá
Colón
David
G. de Panamá
Golfo de Chiriquí
Golfo del Darién
COLOMBIA
Bogotá
Medellín
Cali
Barranquilla
Cartagena
Santa Marta
Cúcuta
Bucaramanga
Ibagué
Manizales
Pereira
Armenia
Popayán
Neiva
Buenaventura
Montería
Sincelejo
Valledupar
Riohacha
G. de Venezuela
VENEZUELA
Caracas
Maracaibo
Valencia
Barquisimeto
Maracay
Barcelona
Cumaná
Maturín
Ciudad Bolívar
Ciudad Guayana
San Cristóbal
Mérida
I. de Margarita
Serra Pacaraima
BRAZIL
I. de Malpelo (Col.)
Km
Miles
1:14M
© Bartholomew

Central **MEXICO**

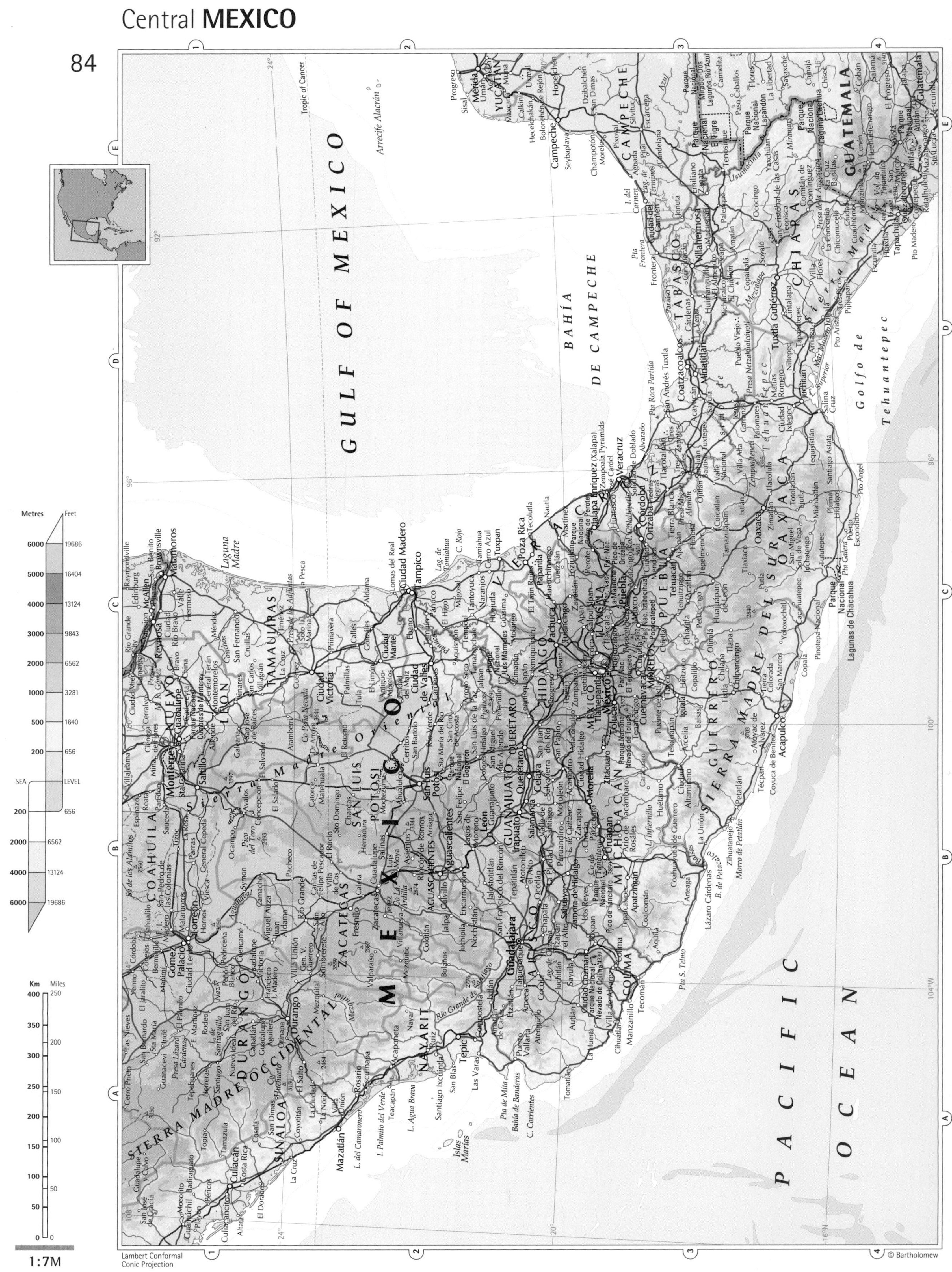

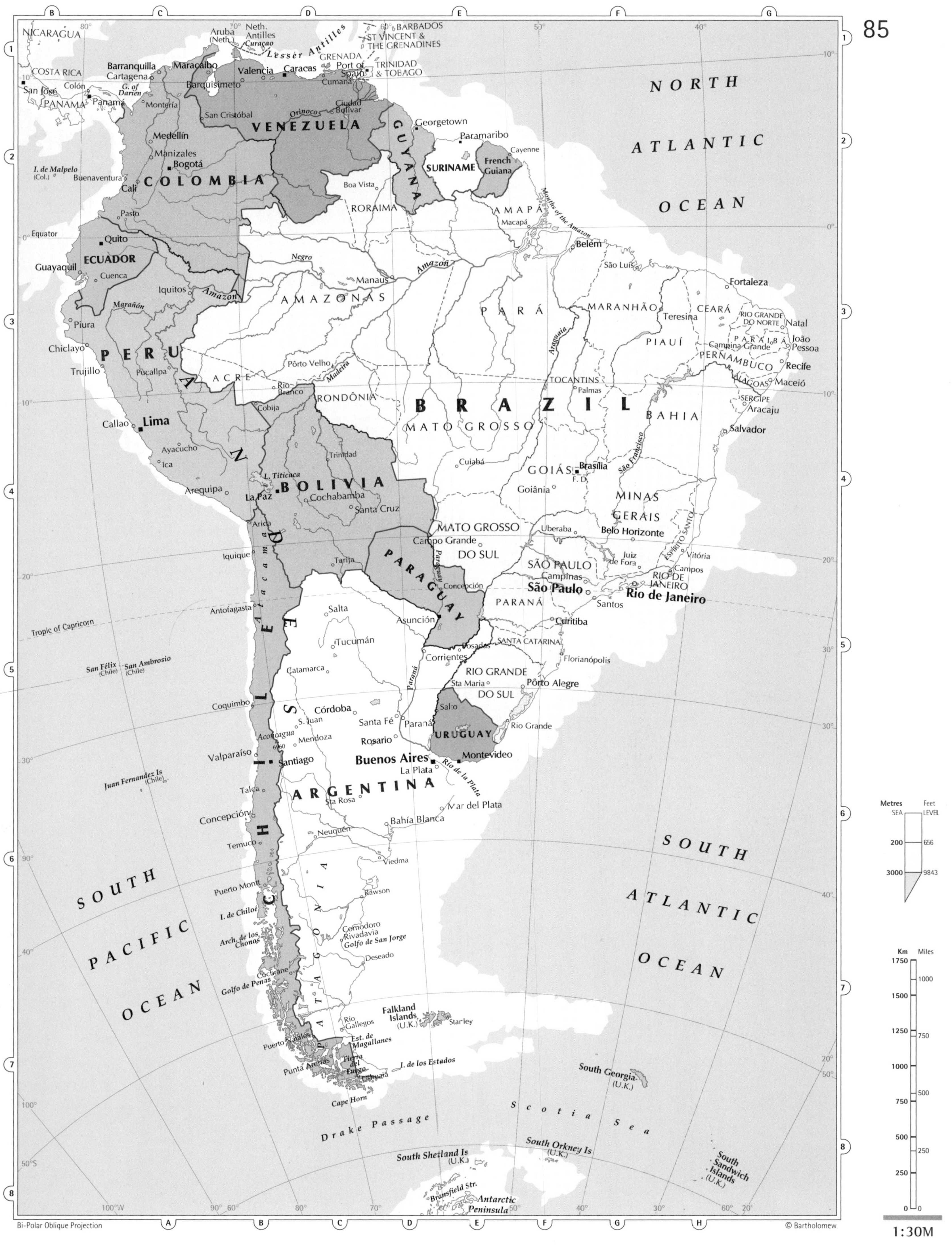
NORTH ATLANTIC OCEAN
SOUTH ATLANTIC OCEAN
SOUTH PACIFIC OCEAN
VENEZUELA
COLOMBIA
ECUADOR
PERU
BOLIVIA
BRAZIL
PARAGUAY
URUGUAY
ARGENTINA
CHILE
GUYANA
SURINAME
French Guiana
ANDES
PATAGONIA
Atacama
Caracas
Bogotá
Quito
Lima
La Paz
Brasília
Asunción
Montevideo
Buenos Aires
Santiago
Georgetown
Paramaribo
Cayenne
São Paulo
Rio de Janeiro
Belo Horizonte
Salvador
Recife
Fortaleza
Belém
Manaus
Amazon
Orinoco
Paraná
Paraguay
Río de la Plata
Tropic of Capricorn
Equator
Falkland Islands (U.K.)
South Georgia (U.K.)
South Orkney Is (U.K.)
South Shetland Is (U.K.)
South Sandwich Islands (U.K.)
Drake Passage
Scotia Sea
Cape Horn
Tierra del Fuego
Antarctic Peninsula
Lesser Antilles
Bi-Polar Oblique Projection
© Bartholomew
Metres Feet
SEA LEVEL
200 656
3000 9843
Km Miles
1750 1000
1500
1250 750
1000 500
750
500 250
250
0 0
1:30M

Lambert Azimuthal Equal Area Projection

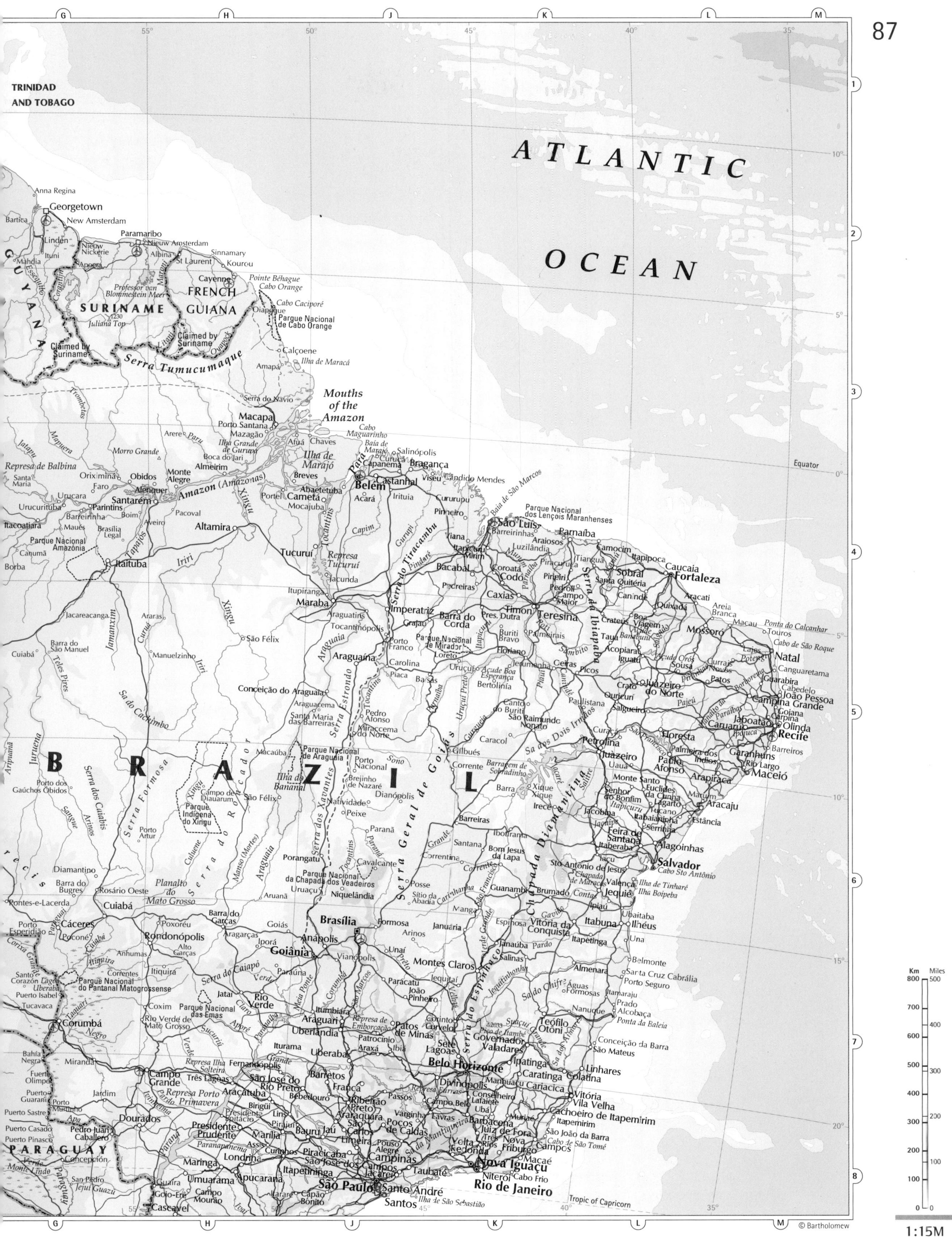

© Bartholomew

1:15M

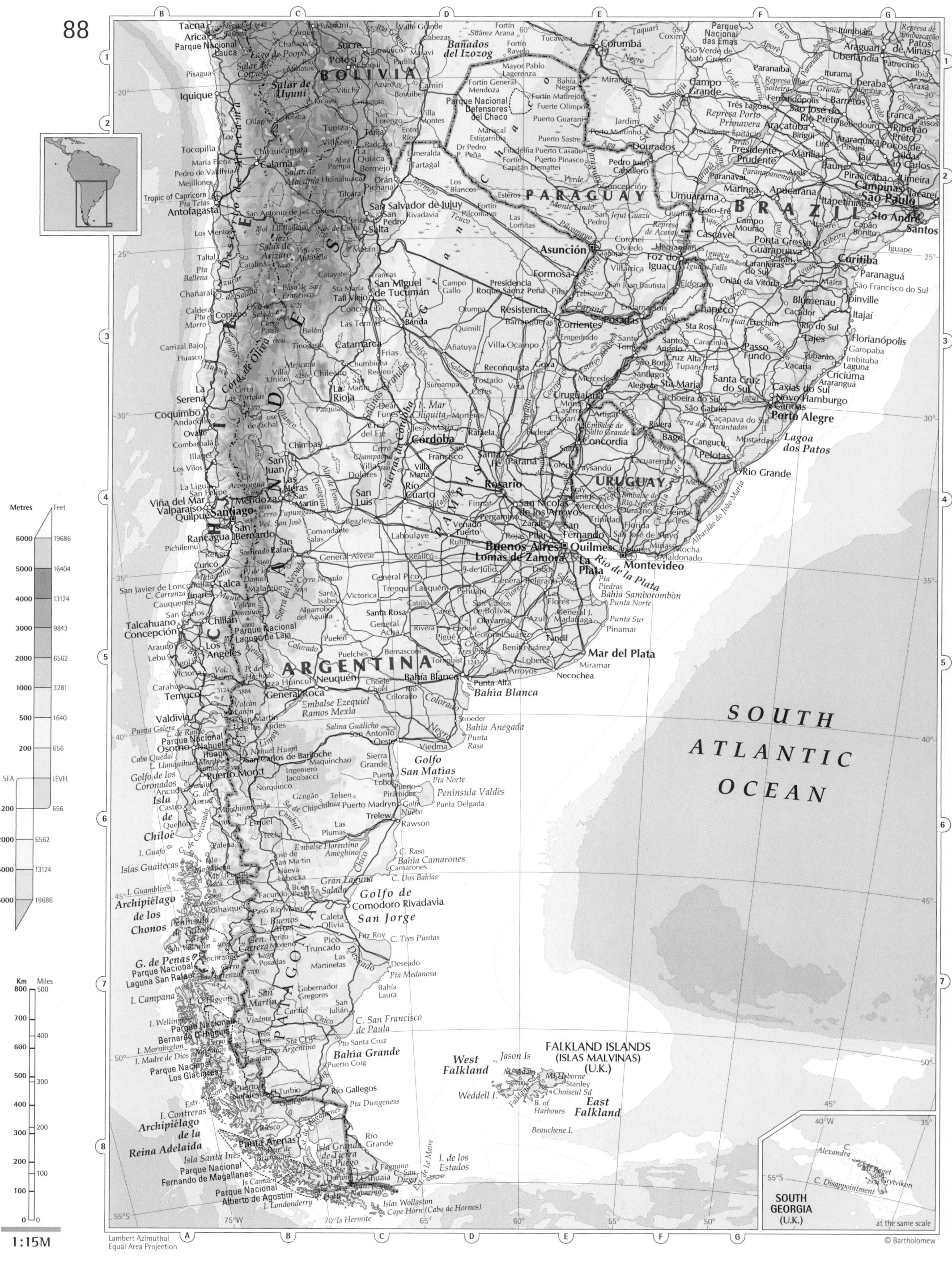
BOLIVIA
PARAGUAY
BRAZIL
URUGUAY
ARGENTINA
CHILE
PATAGONIA
PAMPAS
ANDES
SOUTH ATLANTIC OCEAN
FALKLAND ISLANDS (ISLAS MALVINAS) (U.K.)
West Falkland
East Falkland
Stanley
SOUTH GEORGIA (U.K.)
at the same scale
Asunción
Buenos Aires
Montevideo
Santiago
São Paulo
Curitiba
Porto Alegre
Córdoba
Rosario
Mendoza
La Plata
Mar del Plata
Bahía Blanca
Neuquén
Puerto Montt
Punta Arenas
Ushuaia
Río Gallegos
Comodoro Rivadavia
Antofagasta
Iquique
Arica
Tacna
Sucre
Potosí
Salar de Uyuni
Tropic of Capricorn
Río de la Plata
Golfo San Matías
Golfo de San Jorge
Bahía Grande
Península Valdés
Archipiélago de los Chonos
Isla de Chiloé
Tierra del Fuego
Cape Horn (Cabo de Hornos)
Metres
Feet
6000
5000
4000
3000
2000
1000
500
200
SEA
LEVEL
19686
16404
13124
9843
6562
3281
1640
656
Km
Miles
800
700
600
500
400
300
200
100
0
1:15M
Lambert Azimuthal
Equal Area Projection
© Bartholomew

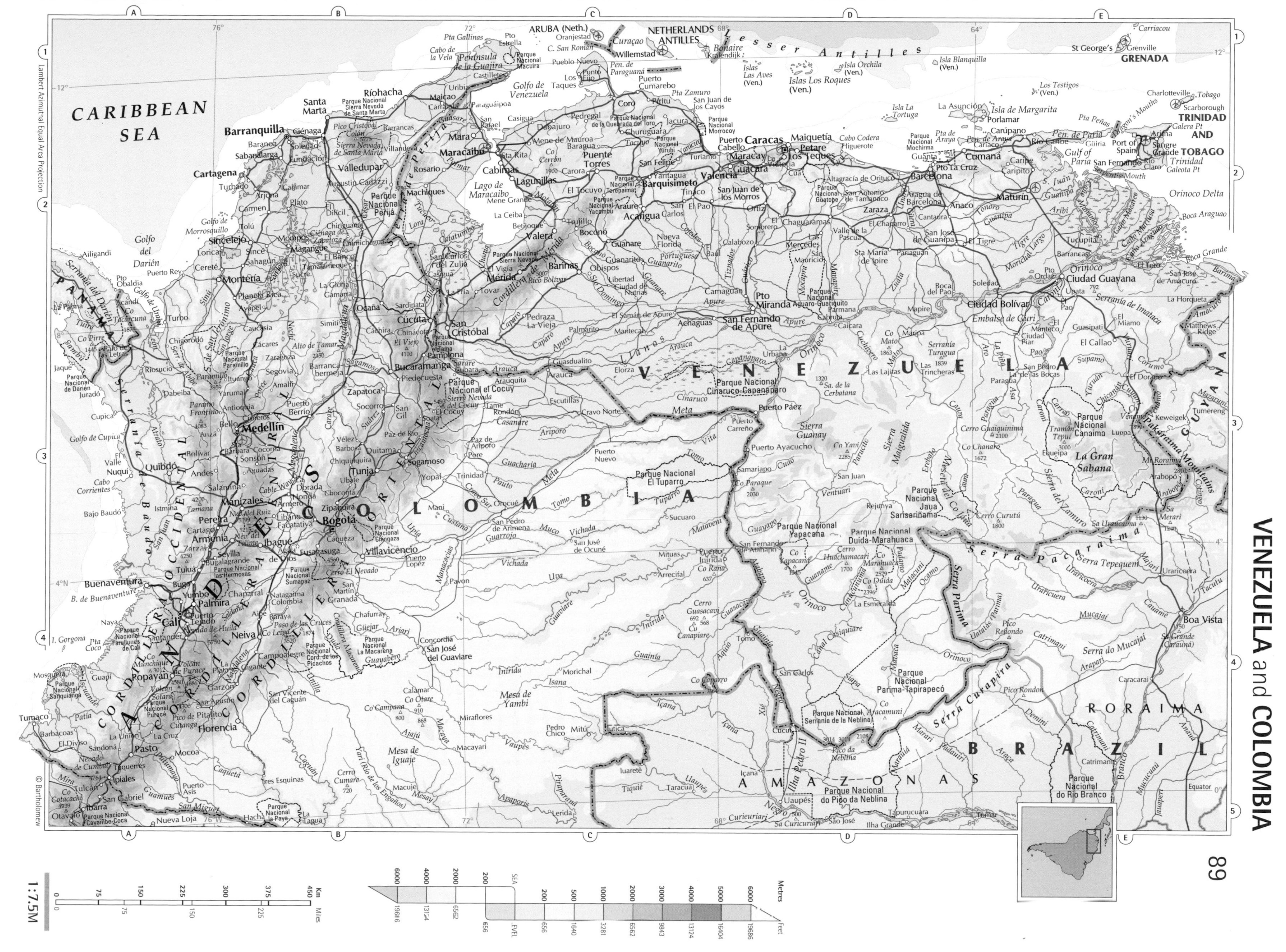

CARIBBEAN SEA
TRINIDAD AND TOBAGO
GRENADA
St George's
Port of Spain
San Fernando
Gulf of Paria
Lesser Antilles
Isla de Margarita
Isla La Tortuga
Isla La Orchila (Ven.)
Islas Los Roques (Ven.)
Islas Las Aves (Ven.)
NETHERLANDS ANTILLES
Bonaire
Curaçao
Willemstad
ARUBA (Neth.)
Oranjestad
Golfo de Venezuela
Península de la Guajira
Lago de Maracaibo
Maracaibo
Caracas
Valencia
Maracay
Barquisimeto
Barcelona
Cumaná
Maturín
Ciudad Guayana
Ciudad Bolívar
Orinoco Delta
Pakaraima Mountains
Parque Nacional Canaima
La Gran Sabana
Sierra Pacaraima
Serra Parima
Sierra Maigualida
Meseta del Cuao
San Fernando de Apure
Puerto Ayacucho
Mérida
San Cristóbal
Barinas
Cúcuta
Bucaramanga
Barranquilla
Cartagena
Santa Marta
Riohacha
Valledupar
Montería
Sincelejo
Medellín
Manizales
Pereira
Armenia
Ibagué
Bogotá
Tunja
Villavicencio
Neiva
Cali
Popayán
Pasto
Buenaventura
Quibdó
Florencia
Mocoa
Tumaco
Ibarra
Golfo de Urabá
Golfo del Darién
PANAMA
Serranía del Darién
Serranía de Baudó
CORDILLERA OCCIDENTAL
CORDILLERA CENTRAL
CORDILLERA ORIENTAL
Llanos
COLOMBIA
VENEZUELA
BRAZIL
RORAIMA
AMAZONAS
Boa Vista
Parque Nacional do Pico da Neblina
Parque Nacional do Rio Branco
Serra Curupira
Mesa de Yambi
Guaviare
Meta
Vichada
Apure
Arauca
Caquetá
Putumayo
Vaupés
Guainía
Negro
Magdalena
Cauca
Atrato
Caroní
Caura
Ventuari
Equator
Lambert Azimuthal Equal Area Projection
© Bartholomew
Metres
Feet
6000 19686
5000 16404
4000 13124
3000 9843
2000 6562
1000 3281
500 1640
200 656
SEA LEVEL
Km
Miles
450
375
300
225
150
75
0
1:7.5M

Southeast **BRAZIL**

Metres	Feet
6000	19686
5000	16404
4000	13124
3000	9843
2000	6562
1000	3281
500	1640
200	656
SEA	LEVEL
200	656
2000	6562
4000	13124
6000	19686

Km	Miles
450	
375	225
300	
225	150
150	
	75
75	
0	0

1:7.5M

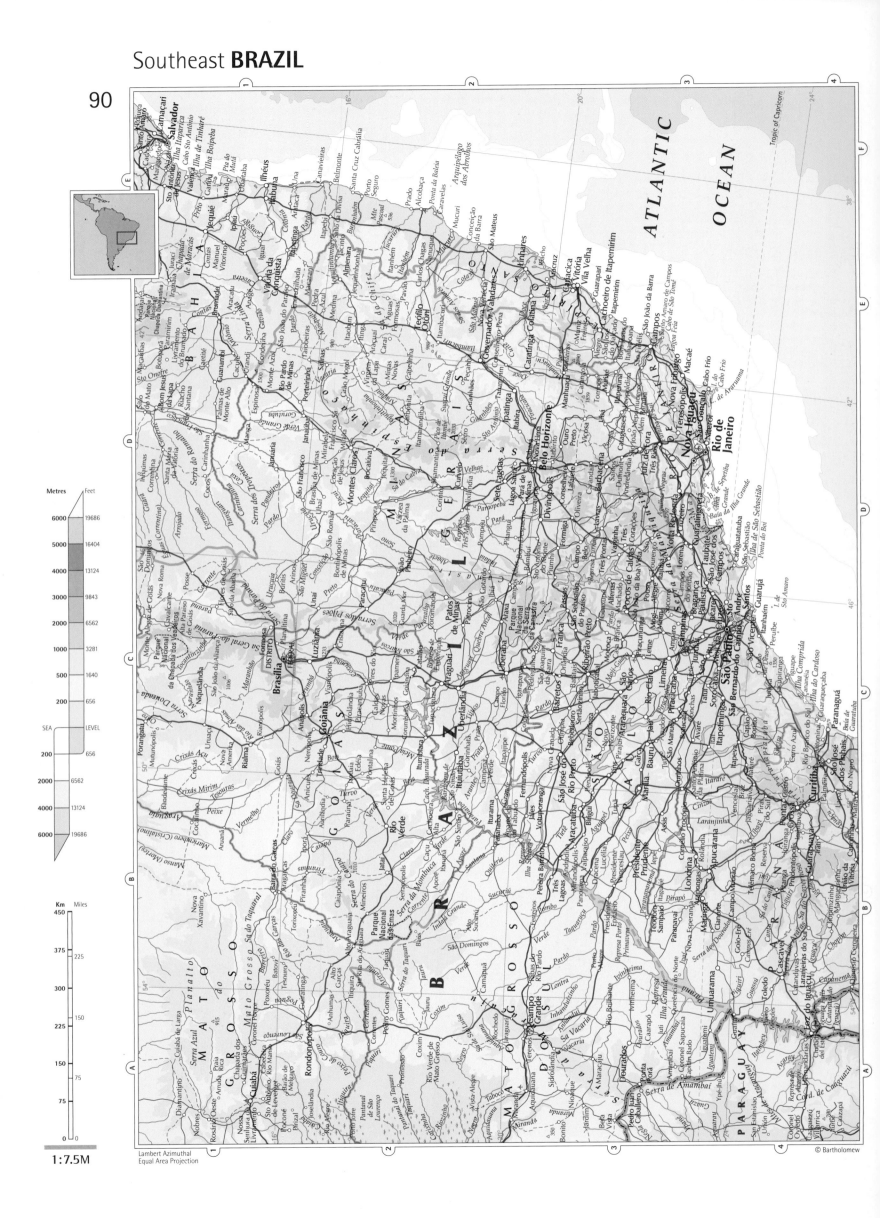

Lambert Azimuthal
Equal Area Projection

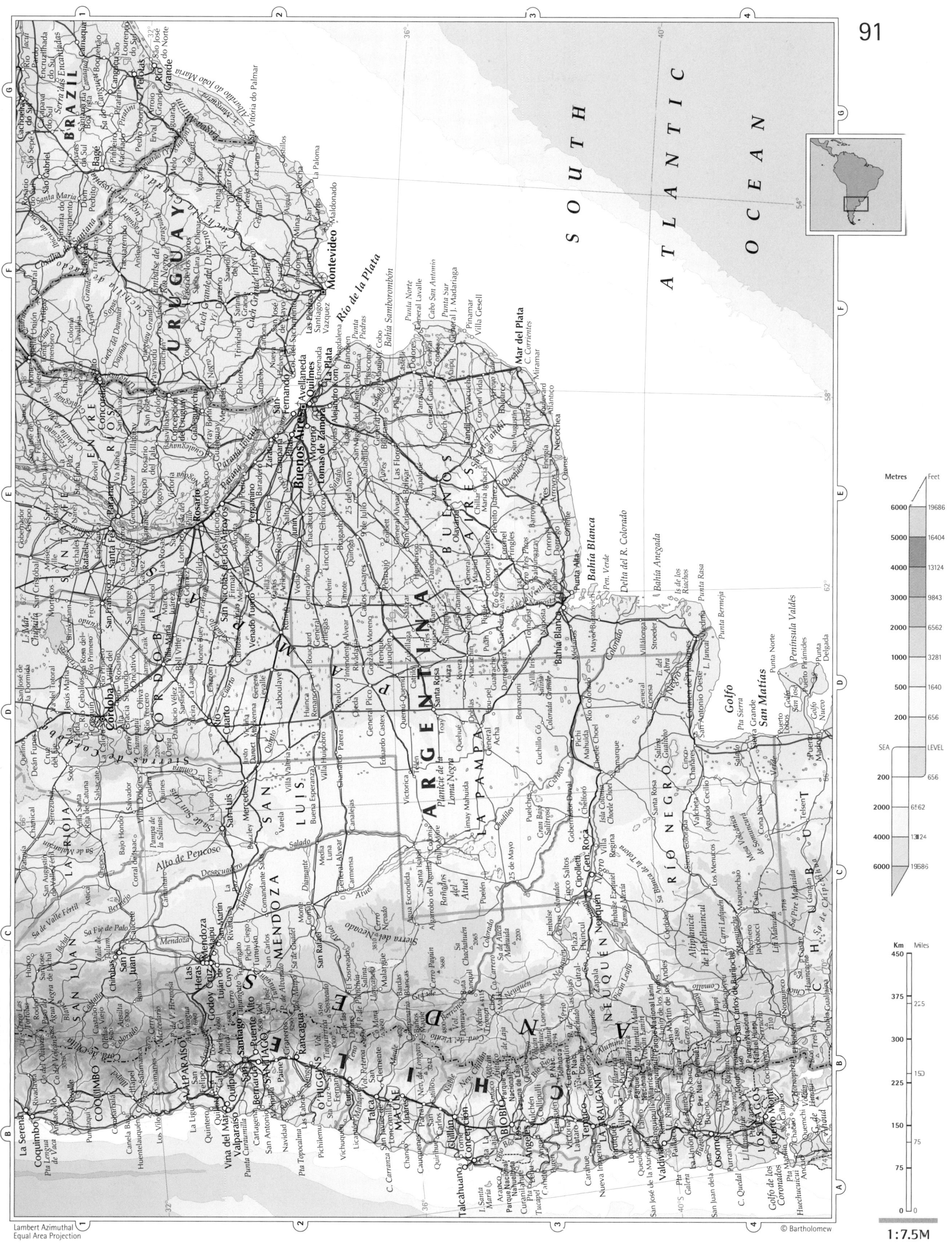

SOUTH ATLANTIC OCEAN
BRAZIL
URUGUAY
ARGENTINA
CHILE
BUENOS AIRES
LA PAMPA
CÓRDOBA
SAN LUIS
MENDOZA
SAN JUAN
LA RIOJA
NEUQUÉN
RÍO NEGRO
CHUBUT
ENTRE RÍOS
SANTA FE
Montevideo
Buenos Aires
La Plata
Río de la Plata
Mar del Plata
Bahía Blanca
Rosario
Córdoba
Mendoza
Santiago
Valparaíso
Concepción
Talcahuano
Temuco
Valdivia
Puerto Montt
Neuquén
Golfo San Matías
Península Valdés
Metres
Feet
6000
19686
5000
16404
4000
13124
3000
9843
2000
6562
1000
3281
500
1640
200
656
SEA
LEVEL
Km
Miles
450
375
300
225
150
75
0
Lambert Azimuthal
Equal Area Projection
© Bartholomew
1:7.5M

ANTARCTICA

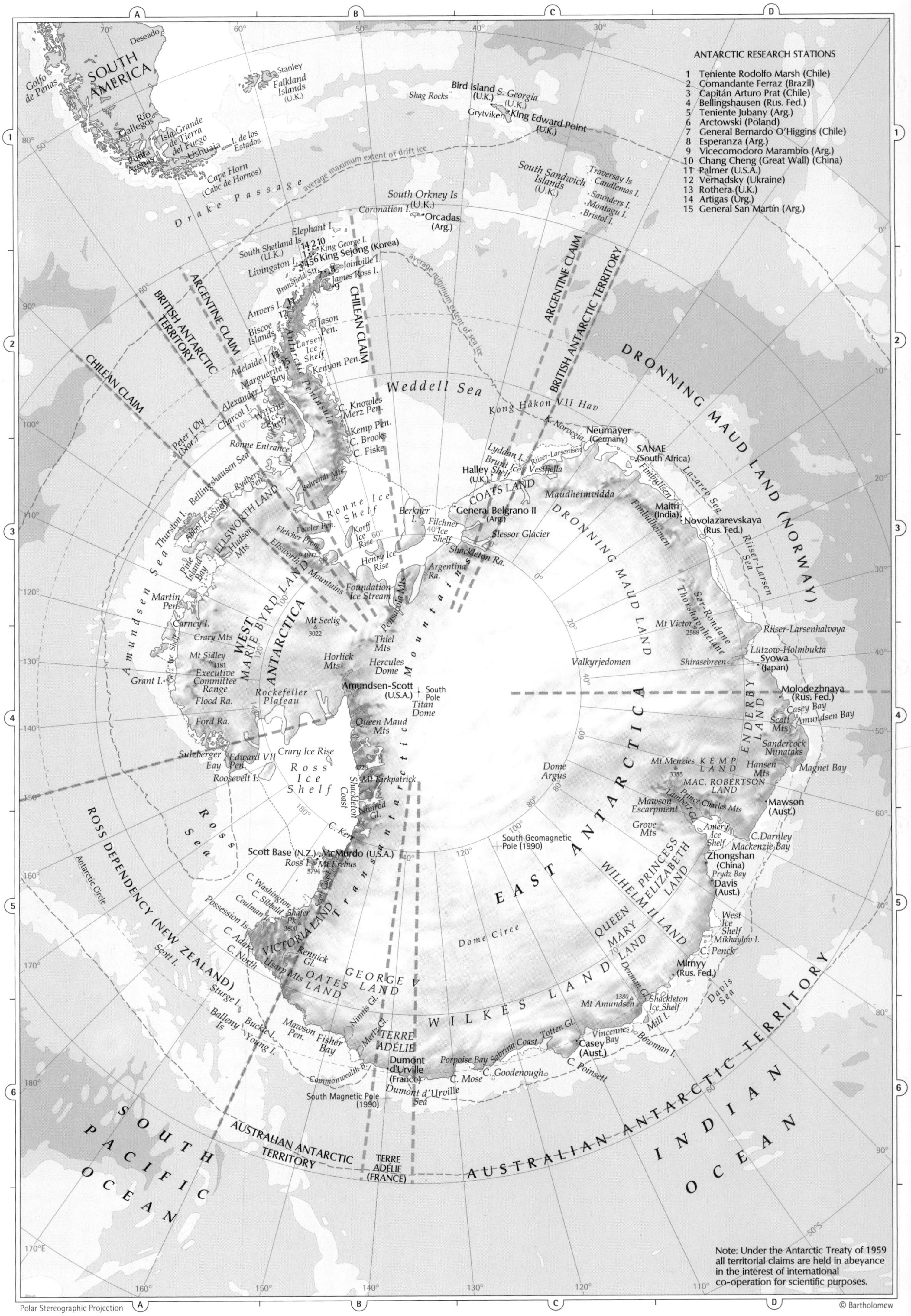

ANTARCTIC RESEARCH STATIONS

1 Teniente Rodolfo Marsh (Chile)
2 Comandante Ferraz (Brazil)
3 Capitán Arturo Prat (Chile)
4 Bellingshausen (Rus. Fed.)
5 Teniente Jubany (Arg.)
6 Arctowski (Poland)
7 General Bernardo O'Higgins (Chile)
8 Esperanza (Arg.)
9 Vicecomodoro Marambio (Arg.)
10 Chang Cheng (Great Wall) (China)
11 Palmer (U.S.A.)
12 Vernadsky (Ukraine)
13 Rothera (U.K.)
14 Artigas (Urg.)
15 General San Martín (Arg.)

Note: Under the Antarctic Treaty of 1959 all territorial claims are held in abeyance in the interest of international co-operation for scientific purposes.

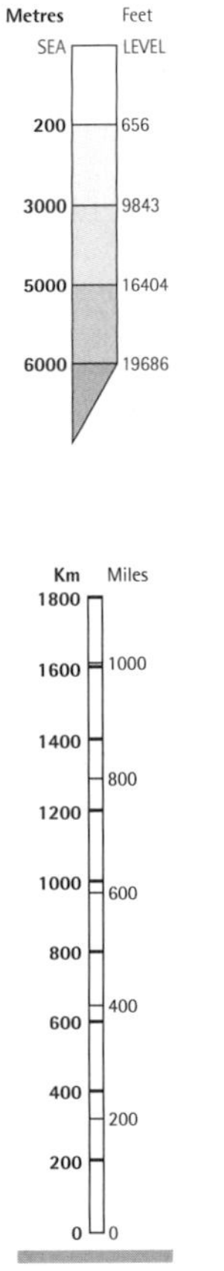

Metres	Feet
SEA	LEVEL
200	656
3000	9843
5000	16404
6000	19686

Km	Miles
1800	
1600	1000
1400	
	800
1200	
1000	600
800	
	400
600	
400	
	200
200	
0	0

1:32M

Polar Stereographic Projection

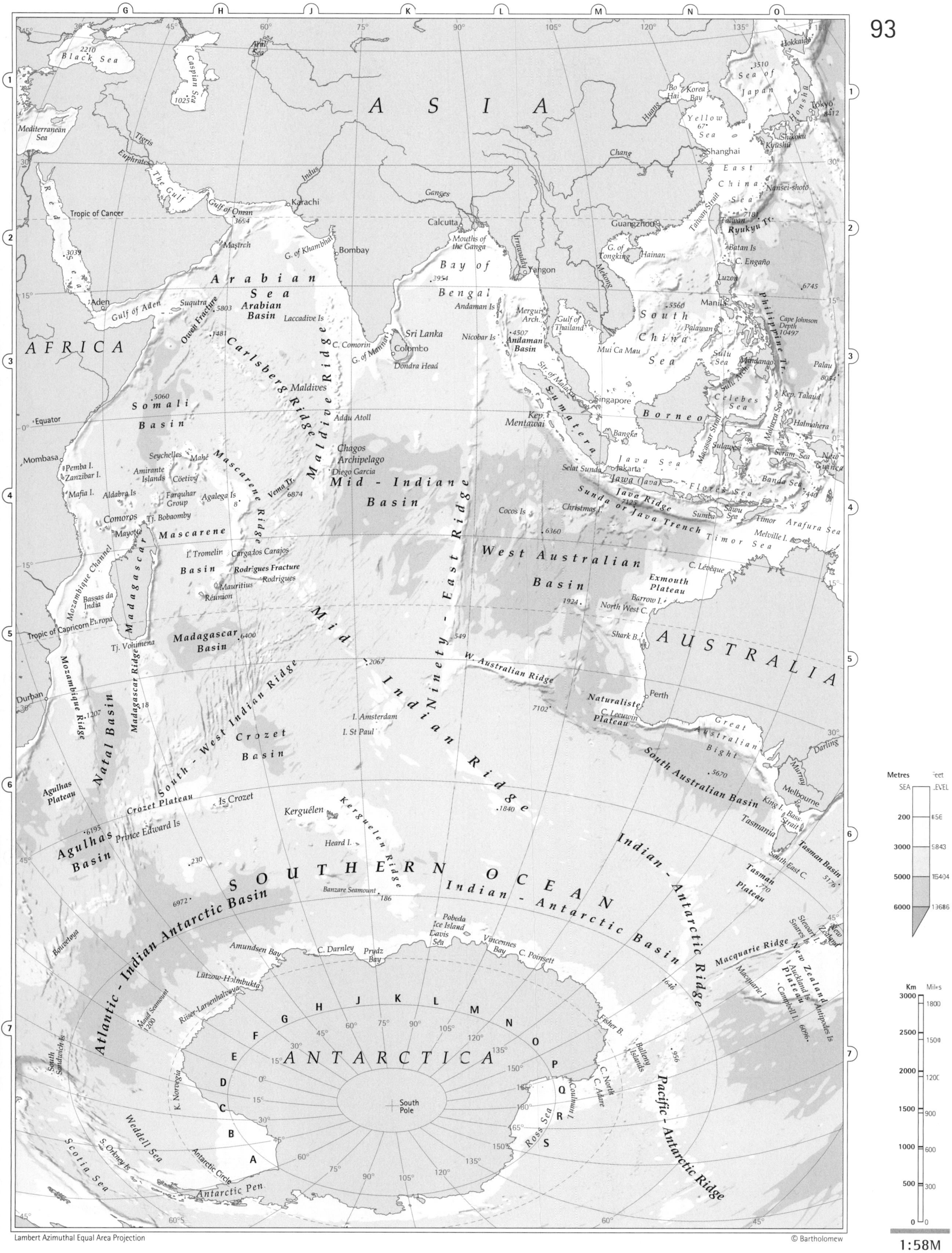

Metres / Feet
SEA LEVEL
200 | 656
3000 | 9843
5000 | 16404
6000 | 19686

Km / Miles
3000 | 1800
2500 | 1500
2000 | 1200
1500 | 900
1000 | 600
500 | 300
0 | 0

1:58M

Lambert Azimuthal Equal Area Projection

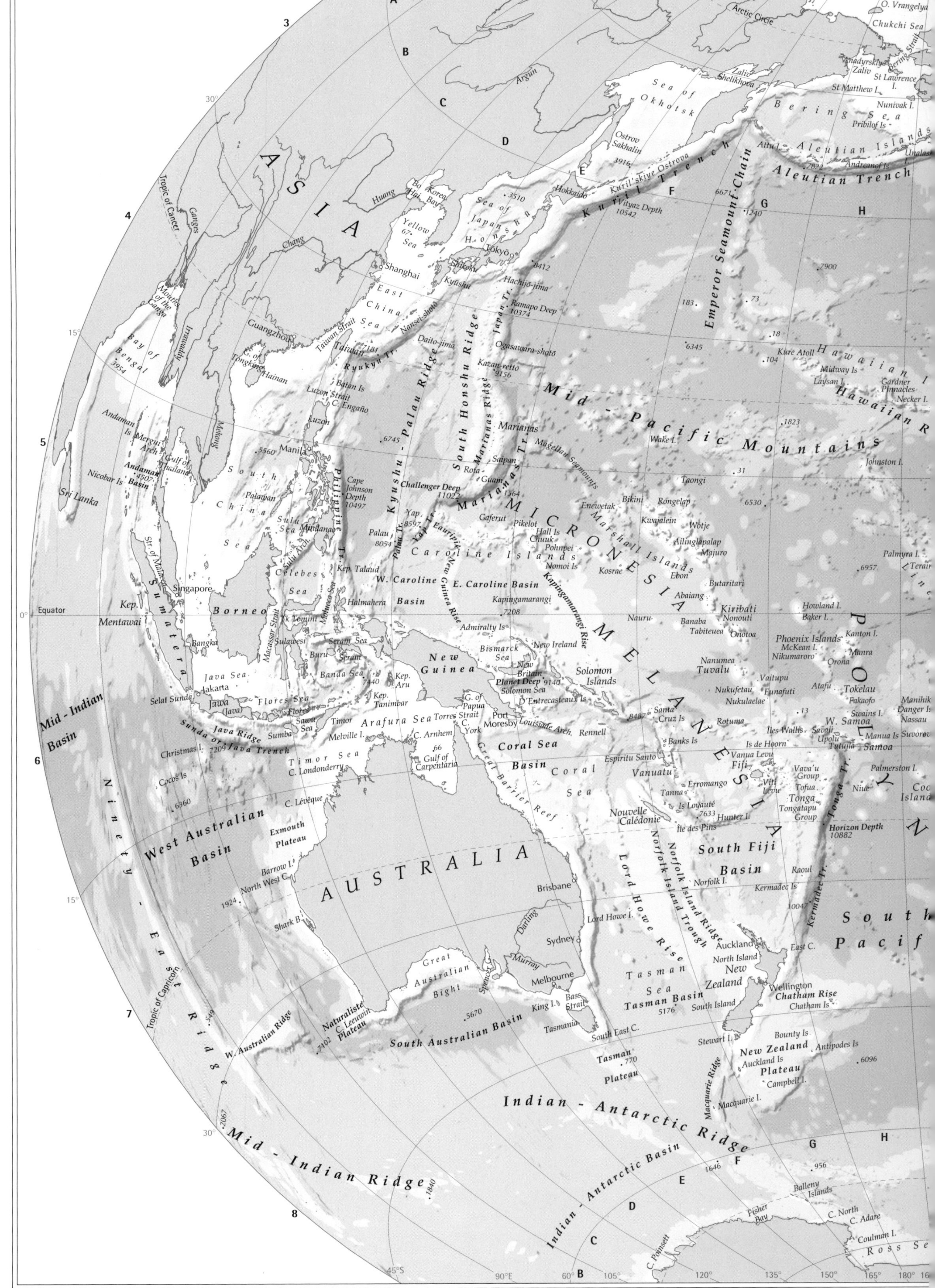

Lambert Azimuthal Equal Area Projection

Metres	Feet
SEA	LEVEL
200	656
3000	9843
5000	16404
6000	19686

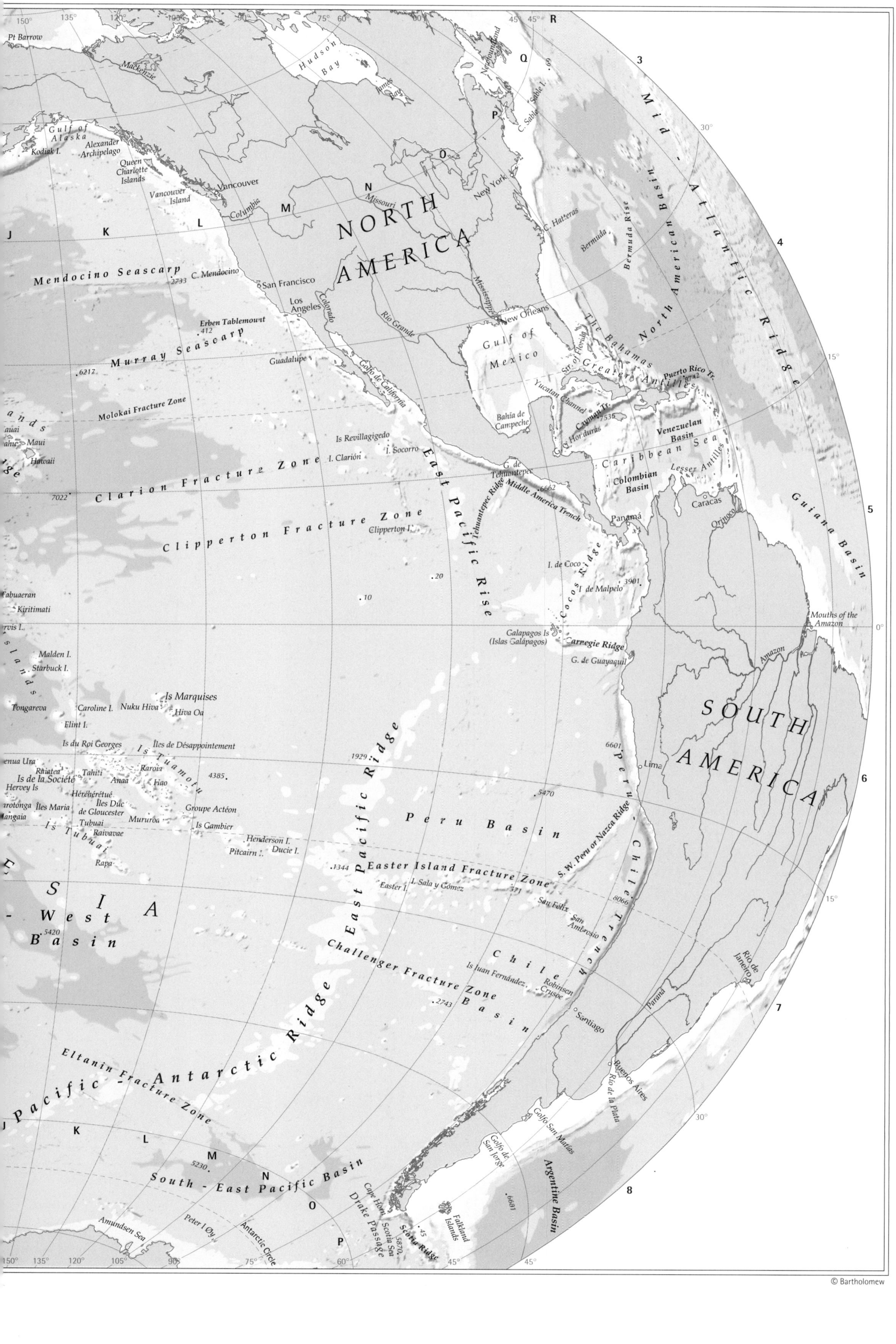

Pt Barrow
Mackenzie
Hudson Bay
James Bay
Newfoundland
C. Sable I.
Gulf of Alaska
Kodiak I.
Alexander Archipelago
Queen Charlotte Islands
Vancouver Island
Vancouver
Columbia
Missouri
New York
C. Hatteras
Bermuda
Bermuda Rise
North American Basin
Mid - Atlantic Ridge
NORTH AMERICA
Mendocino Seascarp
2733
C. Mendocino
San Francisco
Los Angeles
Colorado
Rio Grande
Mississippi
New Orleans
Erben Tablemount
412
Murray Seascarp
Guadalupe
6217
Gulf of Mexico
Str. of Florida
The Bahamas
Greater Antilles
Puerto Rico Tr.
8742
Golfo de California
Yucatan Channel
Cayman Tr.
7536
Bahía de Campeche
Honduras
Venezuelan Basin
Caribbean Sea
Lesser Antilles
Molokai Fracture Zone
Maui
Hawaii
Is Revillagigedo
I. Socorro
I. Clarión
G. de Tehuantepec
Tehuantepec Ridge
Middle America Trench
6662
Colombian Basin
Caracas
Orinoco
Guiana Basin
Clarion Fracture Zone
7022
Clipperton Fracture Zone
Clipperton I.
East Pacific Rise
Panamá
I. de Coco
Cocos Ridge
I. de Malpelo
3901
.20
.10
Tabuaeran
Kiritimati
Mouths of the Amazon
Galapagos Is (Islas Galápagos)
Carnegie Ridge
G. de Guayaquil
Amazon
Malden I.
Starbuck I.
Is Marquises
Nuku Hiva
Hiva Oa
Tongareva
Caroline I.
Flint I.
Is du Roi Georges
Îles de Désappointement
Is Tuamotu
SOUTH AMERICA
6601
Lima
Peru - Chile Trench
Is de la Société
Tahiti
Raiatea
Rarotonga
Anaa
Raroia
Hao
4385
1929
East Pacific Ridge
Hereheretue
Îles Duc de Gloucester
Îles Maria
Mururoa
Groupe Actéon
Is Gambier
Tubuai
Raivavae
Is Tubuai
Rapa
Hervey Is
Mangaia
5470
Peru Basin
S.W. Peru or Nazca Ridge
Henderson I.
Pitcairn I.
Ducie I.
1344
Easter Island Fracture Zone
Easter I.
I. Sala y Gómez
San Félix
San Ambrosio
8066
Challenger Fracture Zone
Chile Basin
Is Juan Fernández
Robinson Crusoe
2743
Santiago
Paraná
Rio de Janeiro
South - West Pacific Basin
5420
Pacific - Antarctic Ridge
Eltanin Fracture Zone
Buenos Aires
Río de la Plata
Golfo San Matías
Golfo de San Jorge
Argentine Basin
6681
5230
South - East Pacific Basin
Amundsen Sea
Peter I Øy
Antarctic Circle
Cape Horn
Drake Passage
Scotia Sea
5870
Scotia Ridge
Falkland Islands

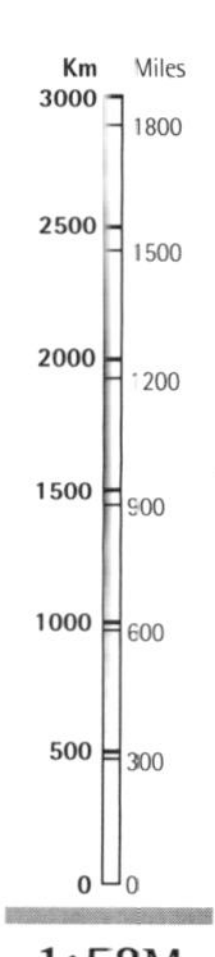

1:58M

ATLANTIC OCEAN

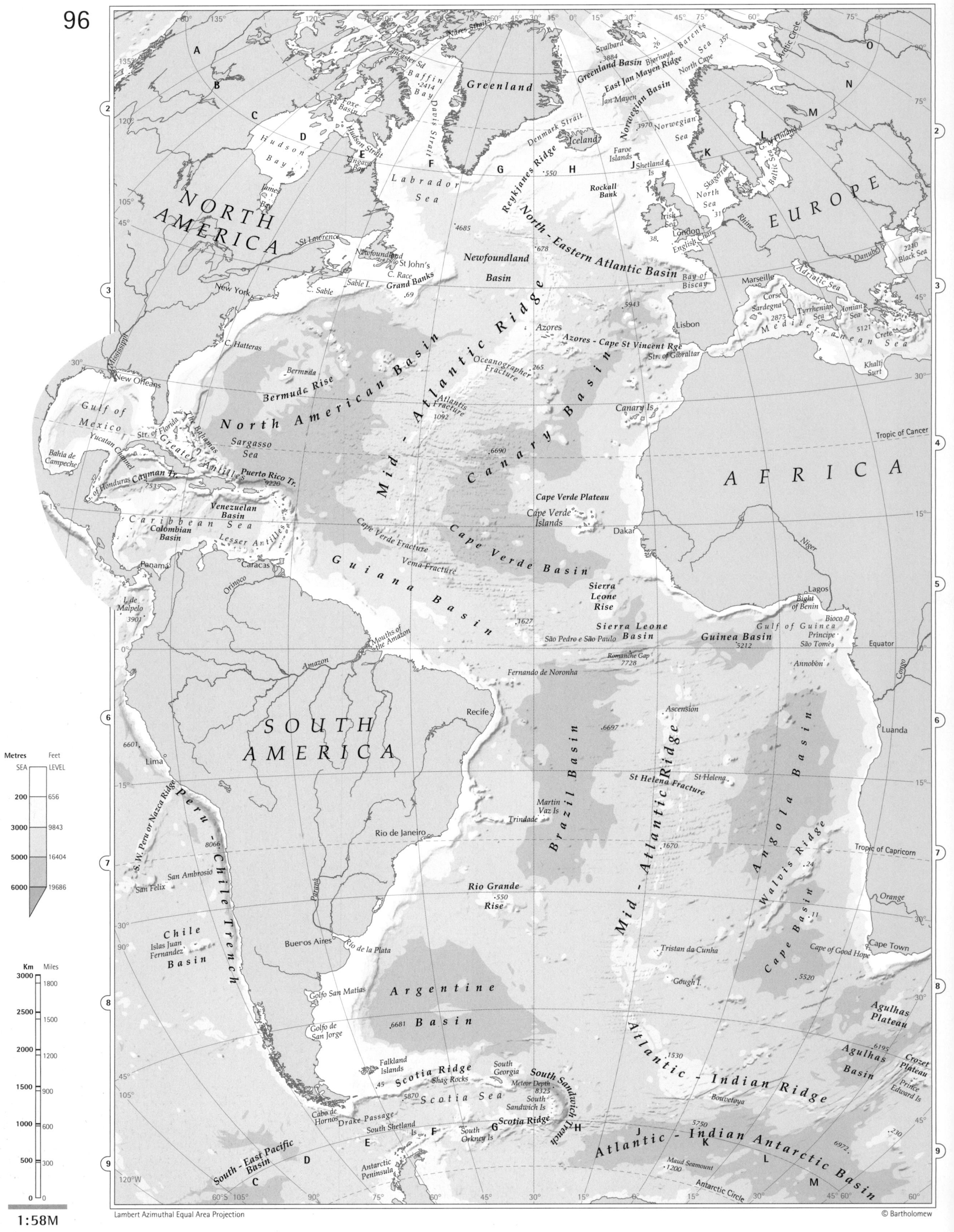

THE INDEX includes the names on the maps in the main map section of the ATLAS. The names are generally indexed to the largest scale map on which they appear, and can be located using the grid reference letters and numbers around the map frame. Names on insets have a symbol: □, followed by the inset number where more than one inset appears on the page.

Abbreviations used to describe features in the index are explained below.

Afgh. Afghanistan
AK Alaska
AL Alabama
Alg. Algeria
Alta Alberta
Ant. Antarctica
AR Arkansas
arch. archipelago
Arg. Argentina
Atl. Atlantic
Austr. Australia
AZ Arizona
Azer. Azerbaijan

b. bay
Bangl. Bangladesh
B.C. British Columbia
Bol. Bolivia
Bos.-Herz. Bosnia Herzegovina
Bulg. Bulgaria

c. cape
CA California
Can. Canada
C.A.R. Central African Republic
chan. channel
Co. County
CO Colorado
Col. Colombia
CT Connecticut

DC District of Colombia

DE Delaware
des. desert
div. division
Dom. Rep. Dominican Republic

Eng. England
escarp. escarpment
est. estuary
Eth. Ethiopia

Fin. Finland
FL Florida
Fr Guiana French Guiana

g. gulf
GA Georgia
gl. glacier
Ger. Germany

h. hill, hills
hd headland
HI Hawaii

i. island
IA Iowa
ID Idaho
IL Illinois
in. inlet
IN Indiana
Indon. Indonesia
is islands
Isr. Israel

isth. isthmus

Kazak. Kazakstan
KS Kansas
KY Kentucky
Kyrg. Kyrgyzstan

l. lake, lakes
LA Louisiana
lag. lagoon
Lith. Lithuania
Lux. Luxembourg

MA Massachusetts
Madag. Madagascar
Man. Manitoba
Maur. Mauritania
MD Maryland
ME Maine
Mex. Mexico
MI Michigan
MN Minnesota
MO Missouri
Moz. Mozambique
MS Mississippi
mt mountain
MT Montana
mts mountains

N. North, Northern
nat. national
N.B. New Brunswick
NC North Carolina
ND North Dakota
NE Nebraska
Neth. Netherlands
Neth. Ant. Netherlands Antilles
Nfld Newfoundland
NH New Hampshire
Nic. Nicaragua
NJ New Jersey
NM New Mexico

N.S. Nova Scotia
N.S.W. New South Wales
NV Nevada
N.W.T. Northwest Territories
NY New York
N.Z. New Zealand

OH Ohio
OK Oklahoma
Ont. Ontario
OR Oregon

PA Pennsylvania
Pac. Pacific
Pak. Pakistan
Para. Paraguay
P.E.I. Prince Edward Island
pen. peninsula
Phil. Philippines
plat. plateau
P.N.G. Papua New Guinea
Pol. Poland
Port. Portugal
pt point

Qld Queensland
Que. Quebec

r. river
reg. region
Rep. Republic
res. reserve
resr reservoir
rf reef
RI Rhode Island
Rus. Fed. Russian Federation

S. South
S.A. South Australia
Sask. Saskatchewan
S. Arabia Saudi Arabia
SC South Carolina

Scot. Scotland
SD South Dakota
Sing. Singapore
str. strait
Switz. Switzerland

Tajik. Tajikistan
Tanz. Tanzania
terr. territory
Thai. Thailand
TN Tennessee
Turk. Turkmenistan
TX Texas

U.A.E. United Arab Emirates
U.K. United Kingdom
Ukr. Ukraine
Uru. Uruguay
U.S.A. United States of America
UT Utah
Uzbek. Uzbekistan

v. valley
VA Virginia
Venez. Venezuela
Vic. Victoria
volc. volcano
VT Vermont

WA Washington
WV West Virginia
WY Wyoming

Y.T. Yukon Territory
Yugo. Yugoslavia

A

42 E4 **Aachen** Ger.
46 E6 **Aalen** Ger.
42 C4 **Aalst** Belgium
42 C4 **Aarschot** Belgium
26 A3 **Aba** China
56 D3 **Aba** Congo(Zaire)
54 C4 **Aba** Nigeria
18 B5 **Abā ad Dūd** S. Arabia
18 C4 **Ābādān** Iran
18 D4 **Ābādeh** Iran
54 B1 **Abadla** Alg.
90 D2 **Abaeté** *r.* Brazil
87 J4 **Abaetetuba** Brazil
26 E1 **Abag Qi** China
95 G5 **Abaiang** *i.* Pac. Oc.
73 E4 **Abajo Pk** *summit* U.S.A.
54 C4 **Abakaliki** Nigeria
24 B1 **Abakan** Rus. Fed.
24 A1 **Abakanskiy Khrebet** *mts* Rus. Fed.
51 E7 **Abana** Turkey
18 D4 **Āb Anbār** Iran
86 D6 **Abancay** Peru
18 D4 **Abarqū** Iran
28 J2 **Abashiri** Japan
28 J2 **Abashiri-wan** *b.* Japan
6 E3 **Abau** P.N.G.
56 D3 **Ābaya Hāyk'** *l.* Eth.
Ābay Wenz *r. see* **Blue Nile**
12 L4 **Abaza** Rus. Fed.
19 E3 **Abbāsābād** Iran
48 C4 **Abbasanta** *Sardinia* Italy
68 C2 **Abbaye, Pt** *pt* U.S.A.
56 E2 **Abbe, L.** *l.* Eth.
44 E1 **Abbeville** France
77 E6 **Abbeville** *LA* U.S.A.
79 D5 **Abbeville** *SC* U.S.A.
41 B5 **Abbeyfeale** Rep. of Ireland
40 E6 **Abbey Head** *hd* U.K.
41 D5 **Abbeyleix** Rep. of Ireland
38 D3 **Abbeytown** U.K.
36 Q4 **Abborrträsk** Sweden
92 A3 **Abbot Ice Shelf** *ice feature* Ant.
64 E5 **Abbotsford** Can.
68 B3 **Abbotsford** U.S.A.
73 F4 **Abbott** U.S.A.
22 C2 **Abbottabad** Pak.
17 H3 **'Abd al 'Azīz, J.** *h.* Syria
17 L5 **Abdanan** Iran
55 E3 **Abéché** Chad
19 E4 **Āb-e Garm** Iran
9 D4 **Abel Tasman National Park** N.Z.
54 B4 **Abengourou** Côte d'Ivoire
37 L9 **Åbenrå** Denmark
43 K6 **Abensberg** Ger.
54 C4 **Abeokuta** Nigeria
39 C5 **Aberaeron** U.K.
40 F3 **Aberchirder** U.K.
8 G2 **Abercrombie** *r.* Austr.
39 D6 **Aberdare** U.K.
39 C5 **Aberdaron** U.K.
8 H2 **Aberdeen** Austr.
65 H4 **Aberdeen** Can.
27 □ **Aberdeen** *H.K.* China
58 F6 **Aberdeen** S. Africa
40 F3 **Aberdeen** U.K.
81 E5 **Aberdeen** *MD* U.S.A.
77 F5 **Aberdeen** *MS* U.S.A.
76 D2 **Aberdeen** *SD* U.S.A.
72 B2 **Aberdeen** *WA* U.S.A.
65 J2 **Aberdeen Lake** *l.* Can.
39 C5 **Aberdyfi** U.K.
40 E4 **Aberfeldy** U.K.
38 F4 **Aberford** U.K.
40 D4 **Aberfoyle** U.K.
39 D6 **Abergavenny** U.K.
77 C5 **Abernathy** U.S.A.
39 C5 **Aberporth** U.K.
39 C5 **Abersoch** U.K.
39 C5 **Aberystwyth** U.K.
20 B6 **Abhā** S. Arabia
18 C2 **Abhar** Iran
18 C2 **Abhar** *r.* Iran
Abiad, Bahr el *r. see* **White Nile**
18 C3 **Ab-i Bazuft** *r.* Iran
89 A2 **Abibe, Serranía de** *mts* Col.
54 B4 **Abidjan** Côte d'Ivoire
19 H3 **Ab-i-Istada** *l.* Afgh.
56 D3 **Abijatta-Shalla National Park** Eth.
18 E3 **Ab-i-Kavir** *salt flat* Iran
76 D4 **Abilene** *KS* U.S.A.
77 D5 **Abilene** *TX* U.S.A.
39 F6 **Abingdon** U.K.
68 B5 **Abingdon** *IL* U.S.A.
80 C6 **Abingdon** *VA* U.S.A.
51 F6 **Abinsk** Rus. Fed.
19 G2 **Ab-i-Safed** *r.* Afgh.
86 C5 **Abiseo, Parque Nacional** *nat. park* Peru
65 H2 **Abitau Lake** *l.* Can.
66 D4 **Abitibi** *r.* Can.
66 E4 **Abitibi, Lake** *l.* Can.
54 B4 **Aboisso** Côte d'Ivoire
54 C4 **Abomey** Benin
22 C3 **Abonar** India
55 D4 **Abong Mbang** Cameroon
31 A4 **Aborlan** Phil.
55 D3 **Abou Déia** Chad
17 K1 **Abovyan** Armenia
40 F3 **Aboyne** U.K.
91 D4 **Abra, L. del** *l.* Arg.
45 B3 **Abrantes** Port.
88 C2 **Abra Pampa** Arg.
90 E2 **Abrolhos, Arquipélago dos** *is* Brazil
72 E2 **Absaroka Range** *mts* U.S.A.
43 H6 **Abtsgmünd** Ger.
18 C5 **Abū 'Alī** *i.* S. Arabia
18 D5 **Abual Jirab** *i.* U.A.E.
20 B6 **Abū 'Arīsh** S. Arabia
20 D5 **Abu Dhabi** U.A.E.
55 F3 **Abu Hamed** Sudan
54 C4 **Abuja** Nigeria
55 E3 **Abu Matariq** Sudan
18 D5 **Abū Mūsā** *i.* U.A.E.
86 E5 **Abunã** Brazil
86 E6 **Abunã** *r.* Bol.
20 A7 **Ābune Yosēf** *mt* Eth.
16 C6 **Abu Qir, Khalīg** *b.* Egypt
15 F4 **Abu Road** India
55 F2 **Abu Simbel** Egypt
17 K6 **Abū Şukhayr** Iraq
9 C5 **Abut Head** *hd* N.Z.
31 C4 **Abuyog** Phil.
55 E3 **Abu Zabad** Sudan
Abū Zabī *see* **Abu Dhabi**
17 M6 **Abūzam** Iran
55 E3 **Abyad** Sudan
55 E4 **Abyei** Sudan
18 C2 **Ābyek** Iran
81 J2 **Acadia Nat. Park** U.S.A.
84 B2 **Acambaro** Mex.
84 E2 **Acanceh** Mex.
89 A2 **Acandí** Col.
45 B1 **A Cañiza** Spain
84 A2 **Acaponeta** Mex.
84 C3 **Acapulco** Mex.
87 J4 **Acará** Brazil
87 K4 **Acaraú** *r.* Brazil
90 A4 **Acaray** *r.* Para.
88 E3 **Acaray, Represa de** *resr* Para.
89 C2 **Acarigua** Venez.
84 C3 **Acatlan** Mex.
84 C3 **Acatzingo** Mex.
84 D3 **Acayucán** Mex.
54 B4 **Accra** Ghana
38 E4 **Accrington** U.K.
89 C3 **Achaguas** Venez.
22 D5 **Achalpur** India
21 B2 **Achampet** India
13 T3 **Achayvayam** Rus. Fed.
30 D1 **Acheng** China
42 A4 **Achicourt** France
41 B4 **Achill** Rep. of Ireland
41 A4 **Achill Island** *i.* Rep. of Ireland
40 C2 **Achiltibuie** U.K.
43 H1 **Achim** Ger.
24 B1 **Achinsk** Rus. Fed.
40 C3 **Achnasheen** U.K.
40 C3 **A'Chralaig** *mt* U.K.
51 F6 **Achuyevo** Rus. Fed.
16 B3 **Acıgöl** *l.* Turkey
16 B3 **Acıpayam** Turkey
48 F6 **Acireale** *Sicily* Italy
76 E3 **Ackley** U.S.A.
83 K4 **Acklins Island** *i.* Bahamas
39 J5 **Acle** U.K.
91 B2 **Aconcagua** *r.* Chile
87 L5 **Acopiara** Brazil
45 B1 **A Coruña** Spain
48 C2 **Acqui Terme** Italy
16 E5 **Acre** Israel
48 G5 **Acri** Italy
46 J7 **Ács** Hungary
5 O7 **Actéon, Groupe** *is* Pac. Oc.
80 B4 **Ada** *OH* U.S.A.
77 D5 **Ada** *OK* U.S.A.
45 D2 **Adaja** *r.* Spain
8 G4 **Adaminaby** Austr.
88 E8 **Adam, Mt** *h.* Falkland Is
81 G3 **Adams** *MA* U.S.A.
68 C4 **Adams** *WV* U.S.A.
21 B4 **Adam's Bridge** *rf* India/Sri Lanka
64 F4 **Adams L.** *l.* Can.
75 E2 **Adams McGill Reservoir** U.S.A.
64 C3 **Adams, Mt** *mt* U.S.A.
72 B2 **Adams, Mt** *mt* U.S.A.
74 B2 **Adams Peak** *mt* U.S.A.
21 C5 **Adam's Pk** Sri Lanka
'Adan *see* **Aden**
16 E3 **Adana** Turkey
41 C5 **Adare** Rep. of Ireland
92 A5 **Adare, C.** *c.* Ant.
75 E2 **Adaven** U.S.A.
20 C5 **Ad Dahnā'** *des.* S. Arabia
54 A2 **Ad Dakhla** Western Sahara
20 D4 **Ad Dammām** S. Arabia
18 B5 **Ad Dawādimī** S. Arabia
Ad Dawḩah *see* **Doha**
17 J4 **Ad Dawr** Iraq
18 B5 **Ad Dibdibah** *plain* S. Arabia
18 B6 **Ad Dilam** S. Arabia
20 C5 **Ad Dir'īyah** S. Arabia
56 D3 **Addis Ababa** Eth.
81 K2 **Addison** U.S.A.
17 K6 **Ad Dīwānīyah** Iraq
39 G6 **Addlestone** U.K.
10 J10 **Addu Atoll** *atoll* Maldives
17 J6 **Ad Duwayd** *well* S. Arabia
79 D6 **Adel** *GA* U.S.A.
76 E3 **Adel** *IA* U.S.A.
8 B3 **Adelaide** Austr.
79 E7 **Adelaide** Bahamas
59 G6 **Adelaide** S. Africa
92 B2 **Adelaide I** *i.* Ant.
6 D3 **Adelaide River** Austr.
74 D4 **Adelanto** U.S.A.
8 G3 **Adelong** Austr.
20 C7 **Aden** Yemen
42 E4 **Adenau** Ger.
43 J1 **Adendorf** Ger.
20 C7 **Aden, Gulf of** *g.* Somalia/Yemen
18 D5 **Adh Dhayd** U.A.E.
25 F7 **Adi** *i.* Indon.
56 D2 **Ādī Ārk'ay** Eth.
56 D2 **Ādīgrat** Eth.
22 D6 **Adilabad** India
17 J2 **Adilcevaz** Turkey
72 B3 **Adin** U.S.A.
55 D2 **Adīrī** Libya
81 F2 **Adirondack Mountains** U.S.A.
Ādīs Ābeba *see* **Addis Ababa**
56 D3 **Ādīs Alem** Eth.
56 D2 **Adi Ugri** Eritrea
16 G3 **Adıyaman** Turkey
47 N7 **Adjud** Romania
84 C2 **Adjuntas, Presa de las** *resr* Mex.
67 J3 **Adlavik Islands** *is* Can.
6 C3 **Admiralty Gulf** *b.* Austr.
63 K2 **Admiralty Inlet** *in.* Can.
64 C3 **Admiralty Island** *i.* U.S.A.
64 C3 **Admiralty Island Nat. Monument** *res.* U.S.A.
6 E2 **Admiralty Islands** *is* P.N.G.
21 B3 **Adoni** India
43 L4 **Adorf** Ger.
43 G3 **Adorf (Diemelsee)** Ger.
44 D5 **Adour** *r.* France
45 E4 **Adra** Spain
48 F6 **Adrano** *Sicily* Italy
54 B2 **Adrar** Alg.
54 A2 **Adrar** *mts* Alg.
54 C3 **Adrar des Ifôghas** *reg.* Mali
54 A2 **Adrar Maur**
19 F3 **Adraskand** *r.* Afgh.
55 E3 **Adré** Chad
69 E5 **Adrian** *MI* U.S.A.
77 C5 **Adrian** *TX* U.S.A.
48 E2 **Adriatic Sea** *sea* Europe
21 B4 **Adur** India
56 C3 **Adusa** Congo(Zaire)
56 D2 **Ādwa** Eth.
13 P3 **Adycha** *r.* Rus. Fed.
51 F6 **Adygeya, Respublika** *div.* Rus. Fed.
51 F6 **Adygeysk** Rus. Fed.
51 H6 **Adyk** Rus. Fed.
54 B4 **Adzopé** Côte d'Ivoire
49 L5 **Aegean Sea** *sea* Greece/Turkey
43 H2 **Aerzen** Ger.
45 B1 **A Estrada** Spain
56 D2 **Afabet** Eritrea
17 K3 **Afan** Iran
10 H6 **Afghanistan** *country* Asia
36 M5 **Åfjord** Norway
56 E3 **Afmadow** Somalia
62 C4 **Afognak I.** *i.* U.S.A.
45 C1 **A Fonsagrada** Spain
16 F3 **Afrīn** *r.* Syria/Turkey
16 F2 **Afşin** Turkey
42 D2 **Afsluitdijk** *barrage* Neth.
72 E3 **Afton** U.S.A.
87 H4 **Afuá** Brazil
16 E5 **Afula** Israel
16 C2 **Afyon** Turkey
43 L4 **Aga** Ger.
54 C3 **Agadez** Niger
54 B1 **Agadir** Morocco
15 F2 **Agadyr'** Kazak.
53 K7 **Agalega Islands** *is* Mauritius
23 G5 **Agartala** India
22 C6 **Agashi** India
69 F2 **Agate** Can.
49 M6 **Agathonisi** *i.* Greece
54 B4 **Agboville** Côte d'Ivoire
17 L1 **Ağcabädi** Azer.
17 L2 **Ağdam** Azer.
44 F5 **Agde** France
44 E4 **Agen** France
58 C4 **Aggeneys** S. Africa
42 F4 **Agger** *r.* Ger.
22 D1 **Aghil Pass** China
41 C3 **Aghla Mountain** *h.* Rep. of Ireland
49 L7 **Agia Vervara** Greece
16 G2 **Ağın** Turkey
49 K6 **Agios Dimitrios** Greece
49 L5 **Agios Efstratios** *i.* Greece
49 M5 **Agios Fokas, Akra** *pt* Greece
49 K5 **Agios Konstantinos** Greece
49 L7 **Agios Nikolaos** Greece
49 K4 **Agiou Orous, Kolpos** *b.* Greece
55 F3 **Agirwat Hills** *h.* Sudan
59 F3 **Agisanang** S. Africa
54 B4 **Agnibilékrou** Côte d'Ivoire
49 L2 **Agnita** Romania
26 A2 **Agong** China
22 D4 **Agra** India
51 H7 **Agrakhanskiy Poluostrov** *pen.* Rus. Fed.
45 F2 **Agreda** Spain
17 J2 **Ağrı** Turkey
49 K7 **Agria Gramvousa** *i.* Greece
48 E6 **Agrigento** *Sicily* Italy
49 J5 **Agrinio** Greece
91 B3 **Agrio** *r.* Arg.
48 F4 **Agropoli** Italy
17 K1 **Ağstafa** Azer.
17 M1 **Ağsu** Azer.
84 A2 **Agua Brava, L.** *lag.* Mex.
84 E3 **Aguada** Mex.
89 B3 **Aguadas** Col.
89 B3 **Agua de Dios** Col.
83 L5 **Aguadilla** Puerto Rico
91 D4 **Aguado Cecilio** Arg.
83 H7 **Aguadulce** Panama
89 B3 **Agua Escondida** Arg.
84 B1 **Aguanaval** *r.* Mex.
91 C1 **Agua Negra, Paso del** *pass* Arg./Chile
90 B3 **Aguapeí** *r.* Brazil
82 C2 **Agua Prieta** Mex.
90 A3 **Aguaray Guazú** *r.* Para.
89 D2 **Aguaro-Guariquito, Parque Nacional** *nat. park* Venez.
84 B2 **Aguascalientes** Mex.
84 B2 **Aguascalientes** *div.* Mex.
90 E2 **Águas Formosas** Brazil
90 C3 **Agudos** Brazil
75 F5 **Aguila** U.S.A.
45 D1 **Aguilar de Campóo** Spain
45 F4 **Águilas** Spain
31 B4 **Aguisan** Phil.
93 F7 **Agulhas Basin** *sea feature* Ind. Ocean
58 D7 **Agulhas, Cape** *c.* S. Africa
90 D3 **Agulhas Negras** *mt* Brazil
93 F6 **Agulhas Plateau** *sea feature* Ind. Ocean
33 E4 **Agung, G.** *volc.* Indon.
31 C4 **Agusan** *r.* Phil.
31 B4 **Agutaya** Phil.
18 B2 **Ahar** Iran
9 C5 **Ahaura** N.Z.
42 F2 **Ahaus** Ger.
9 F3 **Ahimanawa Ra.** *mts* N.Z.
9 D1 **Ahipara** N.Z.
9 D1 **Ahipara Bay** *b.* N.Z.
62 B4 **Ahklun Mts** *mts* U.S.A.
17 J2 **Ahlat** Turkey
43 F3 **Ahlen** Ger.
22 C5 **Ahmadabad** India
18 E4 **Ahmadī** Iran
21 A2 **Ahmadnagar** India
22 B3 **Ahmadpur East** Pak.
43 J4 **Ahorn** Ger.
18 C4 **Ahram** Iran
43 J1 **Ahrensburg** Ger.
17 J2 **Ahta D.** *mt* Turkey
36 T5 **Ähtäri** Fin.
37 U7 **Ahtme** Estonia
17 M6 **Āhū** Iran
84 B2 **Ahualulco** Mex.
44 F3 **Ahun** France
9 B6 **Ahuriri** *r.* N.Z.
18 C4 **Ahvāz** Iran
22 C5 **Ahwa** India
Ahwāz *see* **Ahvāz**
30 C3 **Ai** *r.* China
58 B3 **Ai-Ais** Namibia
26 D1 **Aibag Gol** *r.* China
18 D2 **Aidin** Turkm.
74 □1 **Aiea** U.S.A.
15 E4 **Aigialousa** Cyprus
49 K6 **Aigina** *i.* Greece
49 K5 **Aigio** Greece
44 H4 **Aigle de Chambeyron** *mt* France
91 F2 **Aiguá** Uru.
29 F5 **Aikawa** Japan
79 D5 **Aiken** U.S.A.
89 A2 **Ailigandi** Panama
95 G5 **Ailinglapalap** *i.* Pac. Oc.
42 A5 **Ailly-sur-Noye** France
69 G4 **Ailsa Craig** Can.
40 C5 **Ailsa Craig** *i.* U.K.
90 E2 **Aimorés, Sa dos** *h.* Brazil
54 C1 **Aïn Beïda** Alg.
54 B2 **'Aïn Ben Tili** Maur.
45 H4 **Aïn Defla** Alg.
45 H5 **Aïn el Hadjel** Alg.
54 B1 **Aïn Sefra** Alg.
67 H4 **Ainslie, Lake** *l.* Can.
76 D3 **Ainsworth** U.S.A.
Aintab *see* **Gaziantep**
45 H4 **Aïn Taya** Alg.
45 G5 **Aïn Tédélès** Alg.
89 B4 **Aipe** Col.
32 C5 **Air** *i.* Indon.
64 G4 **Airdrie** Can.
40 E5 **Airdrie** U.K.
42 D6 **Aire** *r.* France
44 D5 **Aire-sur-l'Adour** France
63 L3 **Air Force I.** *i.* Can.
26 D1 **Airgin Sum** China
54 C3 **Aïr, Massif de l'** *mts* Niger
65 H3 **Air Ronge** Can.
88 B7 **Aisén, Pto** Chile
26 F2 **Ai Shan** *h.* China
64 B2 **Aishihik** Can.
64 B2 **Aishihik Lake** *l.* Can.
44 G2 **Aisne** *r.* France
45 F3 **Aitana** *mt* Spain
6 E2 **Aitape** P.N.G.
76 E2 **Aitken** U.S.A.
5 L6 **Aitutaki** *i.* Pac. Oc.
47 L7 **Aiud** Romania
44 G5 **Aix-en-Provence** France
44 G4 **Aix-les-Bains** France
64 D3 **Aiyansh** Can.
23 F5 **Aiyar Res.** *resr* India
23 H5 **Aizawl** India
37 T8 **Aizkraukle** Latvia
37 F8 **Aizpute** Latvia
29 F6 **Aizu-wakamatsu** Japan
48 C4 **Ajaccio** *Corsica* France
89 B4 **Ajajú** *r.* Col.
84 C3 **Ajalpán** Mex.
21 A1 **Ajanta** India
Ajanta Range *h. see* **Sahyadriparvat Range**
36 O4 **Ajaureforsen** Sweden
9 D5 **Ajax, Mt** *mt* N.Z.
55 E1 **Ajdābiyā** Libya
a-Jiddét *gravel area see* **Jiddat al Ḩarāsīs**
28 G4 **Ajigasawa** Japan
16 E5 **'Ajlūn** Jordan
18 D5 **Ajman** U.A.E.
22 C4 **Ajmer** India
75 F5 **Ajo** U.S.A.
75 F5 **Ajo, Mt** *mt* U.S.A.
31 B4 **Ajuy** Phil.
28 H3 **Akabira** Japan
56 D4 **Akagera National Park** Rwanda
21 B2 **Akalkot** India
28 J3 **Akan National Park** Japan
16 D4 **Akanthou** Cyprus
9 D5 **Akaroa** N.Z.
9 D5 **Akaroa Har** *in.* N.Z.
23 H4 **Akas** *reg.* India
19 H3 **Akbar** Afgh.
23 E4 **Akbarpur** India
45 J4 **Akbou** Alg.
12 G4 **Akbulak** Rus. Fed.
16 F2 **Akçadağ** Turkey
17 G3 **Akçakale** Turkey
16 C1 **Akçakoca** Turkey
16 D3 **Akçali D.** *mt* Turkey
16 C3 **Ak D.** *mt* Turkey
17 H2 **Ak D.** *mts* Turkey
16 C3 **Akdağ** *mt* Turkey
16 E2 **Akdağmadeni** Turkey
37 Q7 **Åkersberga** Sweden
42 C2 **Akersloot** Neth.
56 C3 **Aketi** Congo(Zaire)
17 J1 **Akhalk'alak'i** Georgia
51 G7 **Akhalts'ikhe** Georgia
23 G5 **Akhaura** Bangl.
20 E5 **Akhdar, Jabal** *mts* Oman
16 A2 **Akhisar** Turkey
16 F3 **Akhtarīn** Syria
51 H5 **Akhtubinsk** Rus. Fed.
17 J1 **Akhuryan** Armenia
29 C8 **Aki** Japan
66 D3 **Akimiski Island** *i.* Can.
16 E3 **Akıncı Burun** *pt* Turkey
16 G1 **Akıncılar** Turkey
28 G5 **Akita** Japan
54 A3 **Akjoujt** Maur.
36 P3 **Akkajaure** *l.* Sweden
28 J3 **Akkeshi** Japan
'Akko *see* **Acre**
16 F1 **Akkuş** Turkey
18 D1 **Akkyr, Gory** *h.* Turkm.
22 D4 **Aklera** India
37 R8 **Akmeņrags** *pt* Latvia
22 D1 **Akmeqit** China
14 F1 **Akmola** Kazak.
29 D7 **Akō** Japan
55 F4 **Akobo** Sudan
22 D5 **Akola** India
56 D2 **Akordat** Eritrea
16 D3 **Akören** Turkey
22 D5 **Akot** India
63 M3 **Akpatok Island** *i.* *Que.* Can.
67 G1 **Akpatok Island** *i.* Can.
36 B4 **Akranes** Iceland
51 C7 **Akrathos, Akra** *pt* Greece
37 J7 **Åkrehamne** Norway
19 G3 **Ak Robat Pass** Afgh.
72 G3 **Akron** *CO* U.S.A.
80 C4 **Akron** *OH* U.S.A.
80 C4 **Akron City Reservoir** U.S.A.
22 D2 **Aksai Chin** *terr.* China/India
16 E2 **Aksaray** Turkey
51 F6 **Aksay** Rus. Fed.
22 D2 **Aksayqin Hu** *l.* China/Jammu and Kashmir
16 C2 **Akşehir** Turkey
16 C2 **Akşehir Gölü** *l.* Turkey
16 C3 **Akseki** Turkey
18 D4 **Aks-e Rostam** *r.* Iran
14 E2 **Akshiganak** Kazak.
15 G2 **Aksu** China
16 C3 **Aksu** *r.* Turkey
56 D2 **Āksum** Eth.
23 F1 **Aktag** *mt* China
17 K2 **Aktas D.** *mt* Turkey
19 G2 **Aktash** Uzbek.
14 D2 **Aktau** Kazak.
15 F2 **Aktogay** Kazak.
47 O4 **Aktsyabrski** Belarus
14 D1 **Aktyubinsk** Kazak.
29 B8 **Akune** Japan
54 C4 **Akure** Nigeria
36 D4 **Akureyri** Iceland
23 G1 **Akxokesay** China
Akyab *see* **Sittwe**
16 G3 **Akziyaret** Turkey
37 L6 **Ål** Norway
18 C5 **Al 'Abā** S. Arabia
79 C5 **Alabama** *div.* U.S.A.
79 C6 **Alabama** *r.* U.S.A.
79 C5 **Alabaster** U.S.A.
31 B3 **Alabat** *i.* Phil.
17 K7 **Al 'Abţīyah** *well* Iraq
16 E1 **Alaca** Turkey
16 F2 **Alacahan** Turkey
16 E1 **Alaçam** Turkey
16 B2 **Alaçam Dağları** *mts* Turkey
84 E2 **Alacrán, Arrecife** *atoll* Mex.
17 J2 **Ala Dag** *mt* Turkey
17 J2 **Ala Dağlar** *mts* Turkey
16 E3 **Ala Dağlar** *mts* Turkey
51 H7 **Alagir** Rus. Fed.
87 L6 **Alagoinhas** Brazil
45 F2 **Alagón** Spain
31 C5 **Alah** *r.* Phil.
36 S5 **Alahärmä** Fin.
17 L7 **Al Ahmadī** Kuwait
19 H2 **Alai Range** *mts* Asia
36 S5 **Alajärvi** Fin.
83 H6 **Alajuela** Costa Rica
17 L2 **Alajujeh** Iran
22 D3 **Alaknanda** *r.* India
15 G2 **Alakol', Ozero** *l.* Kazak.
36 W3 **Alakurtti** Rus. Fed.
86 F4 **Alalaú** *r.* Brazil
17 J3 **Al 'Amādīyah** Iraq
18 B5 **Al'Amār** S. Arabia
17 L6 **Al 'Amārah** Iraq
23 H3 **Alamdo** China
17 K7 **Al Amghar** *waterhole* Iraq
31 A2 **Alaminos** Phil.
84 B1 **Alamitos, Sa de los** *mt* Mex.
75 E3 **Alamo** U.S.A.
75 F4 **Alamo Dam** *dam* U.S.A.
73 F5 **Alamogordo** U.S.A.
77 D6 **Alamo Heights** U.S.A.
73 E6 **Alamos** Mex.
70 E6 **Alamos** Mex.
73 F4 **Alamosa** U.S.A.
21 B3 **Alampur** India
36 O4 **Alanäs** Sweden
21 B2 **Aland** India
37 Q6 **Åland** *is* Fin.
43 K1 **Aland** *r.* Ger.
18 B2 **Aland** *r.* Iran
32 B5 **Alang Besar** *i.* Indon.
68 E3 **Alanson** U.S.A.
16 D3 **Alanya** Turkey
16 C1 **Alaplı** Turkey
Alappuzha *see* **Alleppey**
18 C6 **Al 'Āqūlah** *well* S. Arabia
45 E3 **Alarcón, Embalse de** *resr* Spain
20 C4 **Al Artāwīyah** S. Arabia
33 E4 **Alas** Indon.
16 B2 **Alaşehir** Turkey
17 J6 **Al 'Ashūrīyah** *well* Iraq
62 D3 **Alaska** *div.* U.S.A.
62 D4 **Alaska, Gulf of** *g.* U.S.A.
64 E3 **Alaska Highway** Can./U.S.A.
62 B4 **Alaska Peninsula** U.S.A.
62 D3 **Alaska Range** *mts* U.S.A.
17 M2 **Älät** Azer.
19 F2 **Alat** Uzbek.
17 J6 **Al 'Athāmīn** *h.* Iraq
50 H4 **Alatyr'** Rus. Fed.
50 H4 **Alatyr'** *r.* Rus. Fed.
86 C4 **Alausí** Ecuador
17 K1 **Alaverdi** Armenia
36 T4 **Alavieska** Fin.
36 S5 **Alavus** Fin.
8 C3 **Alawoona** Austr.
17 L1 **Alazani** *r.* Azer./Georgia
17 K5 **Al 'Azīzīyah** Iraq
48 C2 **Alba** Italy
16 F3 **Al Bāb** Syria
45 F3 **Albacete** Spain

8 C3 Albacutya, L. l. Austr.
17 K6 Al Bādiyah al Janūbīyah h. Iraq
49 K1 Alba Iulia Romania
66 F3 Albanel, L. l. Can.
35 G4 Albania country Europe
6 B5 Albany Austr.
79 C6 Albany GA U.S.A.
68 E5 Albany IN U.S.A.
78 C4 Albany KY U.S.A.
81 G3 Albany NY U.S.A.
72 B2 Albany OR U.S.A.
66 C3 Albany r. Can.
91 G2 Albardão do João Maria coastal area Brazil
18 B5 Al Barrah S. Arabia
Al Başrah see Basra
17 K6 Al Baţḩa' marsh Iraq
17 L7 Al Bāţin, Wādī watercourse Asia
6 E3 Albatross Bay b. Austr.
55 E1 Al Bayḑā' Libya
86 □ Albemarle, Pta pt Galapagos Is Ecuador
79 E5 Albemarle Sd chan. U.S.A.
48 C2 Albenga Italy
45 D3 Alberche r. Spain
6 D4 Alberga watercourse Austr.
45 B2 Albergaria-a-Velha Port.
8 F2 Albert Austr.
44 F2 Albert France
80 E6 Alberta U.S.A.
64 F4 Alberta div. Can.
64 F4 Alberta, Mt mt Can.
58 D7 Albertinia S. Africa
42 D4 Albert Kanaal canal Belgium
8 B3 Albert, Lake l. Austr.
56 D3 Albert, Lake l. Congo(Zaire)/Uganda
76 E3 Albert Lea U.S.A.
56 D3 Albert Nile r. Sudan/Uganda
88 B8 Alberto de Agostini, Parque Nacional nat. park Chile
59 H3 Alberton S. Africa
44 H4 Albertville France
42 E6 Albestroff France
44 F5 Albi France
87 H2 Albina Suriname
74 A2 Albion CA U.S.A.
81 J2 Albion ME U.S.A.
68 E4 Albion MI U.S.A.
80 D3 Albion NY U.S.A.
45 E5 Alborán, Isla de i. Spain
37 L8 Ålborg Denmark
37 M8 Ålborg Bugt b. Denmark
64 F4 Albreda Can.
18 C5 Al Budayyi Bahrain
18 C6 Al Budū', Sabkhat salt pan S. Arabia
45 B4 Albufeira Port.
17 H4 Āl Bū Kamāl Syria
73 F5 Albuquerque U.S.A.
20 E5 Al Buraymī Oman
45 C3 Alburquerque Spain
8 F4 Albury Austr.
17 H4 Al Buşayrah Syria
16 G7 Al Busayţā' plain S. Arabia
17 L6 Al Buşayyah Iraq
18 B4 Al Bushūk well S. Arabia
45 B3 Alcácer do Sal Port.
45 E2 Alcalá de Henares Spain
45 E4 Alcalá la Real Spain
48 E6 Alcamo Sicily Italy
45 F2 Alcañiz Spain
45 C3 Alcántara Spain
45 E3 Alcaraz Spain
45 D4 Alcaudete Spain
45 E3 Alcázar de San Juan Spain
51 F5 Alchevs'k Ukr.
91 D2 Alcira Arg.
90 E2 Alcobaça Brazil
45 F2 Alcora Spain
91 E2 Alcorta Arg.
45 F3 Alcoy Spain
45 H3 Alcúdia Spain
57 E4 Aldabra Islands is Seychelles
17 K5 Al Daghghārah Iraq
84 C2 Aldama Mex.
13 O4 Aldan Rus. Fed.
13 P3 Aldan r. Rus. Fed.
39 J5 Aldeburgh U.K.
9 F2 Aldermen Is, The is N.Z.
44 D2 Alderney i. Channel Is U.K.
74 B4 Alder Peak summit U.S.A.
39 G6 Aldershot U.K.
80 C6 Alderson U.S.A.
18 D6 Al Dhafrah reg. U.A.E.
38 D3 Aldingham U.K.
39 F5 Aldridge U.K.
68 B5 Aledo U.S.A.
54 A3 Aleg Maur.
90 E3 Alegre Brazil
88 E3 Alegrete Brazil
91 E2 Alejandro Korn Arg.
50 E2 Alekhovshchina Rus. Fed.
50 F3 Aleksandrov Rus. Fed.
51 J5 Aleksandrov Gay Rus. Fed.
51 H6 Aleksandrovskoye Rus. Fed.
13 Q4 Aleksandrovsk-Sakhalinskiy Rus. Fed.
14 F1 Alekseyevka Kazak.
51 F5 Alekseyevka Belgorod. Obl. Rus. Fed.
51 F5 Alekseyevka Belgorod. Obl. Rus. Fed.
51 G5 Alekseyevskaya Rus. Fed.
50 F4 Aleksin Rus. Fed.
49 J3 Aleksinac Yugo.
84 C3 Alemán, Presa Miguel resr Mex.
56 B4 Alèmbé Gabon
16 E1 Alembeyli Turkey
90 D3 Além Paraíba Brazil
36 M5 Ålen Norway
44 E2 Alençon France
87 H4 Alenquer Brazil
74 □2 Alenuihaha Channel U.S.A.
16 F3 Aleppo Syria
86 D6 Alerta Peru
64 D4 Alert Bay Can.
44 G4 Alès France
47 L7 Aleşd Romania
48 C2 Alessandria Italy
36 K5 Ålesund Norway
60 A4 Aleutian Islands is U.S.A.
62 C4 Aleutian Range mts U.S.A.
95 H2 Aleutian Trench sea feature Pac. Oc.
13 R4 Alevina, Mys c. Rus. Fed.
Alevişik see Samandağı
81 K2 Alexander U.S.A.
64 B3 Alexander Archipelago is U.S.A.
58 B4 Alexander Bay S. Africa
58 B4 Alexander Bay b. Namibia/S. Africa
79 C5 Alexander City U.S.A.
92 A2 Alexander I. i. Ant.
8 E4 Alexandra Austr.
9 B6 Alexandra N.Z.
88 □ Alexandra, C. c. Atl. Ocean
49 K4 Alexandreia Greece
Alexandretta see İskenderun
81 F2 Alexandria Can.
55 E1 Alexandria Egypt
49 L3 Alexandria Romania
59 G6 Alexandria S. Africa
40 D5 Alexandria U.K.
68 E5 Alexandria IN U.S.A.
77 E6 Alexandria LA U.S.A.
76 E2 Alexandria MN U.S.A.
80 E5 Alexandria VA U.S.A.
81 F2 Alexandria Bay U.S.A.
8 B3 Alexandrina, L. l. Austr.
49 L4 Alexandroupoli Greece
68 B5 Alexis U.S.A.
67 J3 Alexis r. Can.
64 E4 Alexis Creek Can.
12 K4 Aleysk Rus. Fed.
42 F4 Alf Ger.
45 F1 Alfaro Spain
17 L7 Al Farwānīyah Kuwait
17 J4 Al Fatḩah Iraq
17 M7 Al Fāw Iraq
43 H3 Alfeld (Leine) Ger.
90 D3 Alfenas Brazil
17 M7 Al Finţās Kuwait
47 K7 Alföld plain Hungary
39 H4 Alford U.K.
81 F2 Alfred Can.
81 H3 Alfred U.S.A.
17 M7 Al Fuḩayḩil Kuwait
Al-Fujayrah see Fujairah
18 B4 Al Fulayi watercourse S. Arabia
Al Furāt r. see Euphrates
37 J7 Algård Norway
91 C3 Algarrobo del Aguilla Arg.
45 B4 Algarve reg. Port.
50 G4 Algasovo Rus. Fed.
45 D4 Algeciras Spain
45 F3 Algemesí Spain
Alger see Algiers
69 E3 Alger U.S.A.
52 D3 Algeria country Africa
43 H2 Algermissen Ger.
17 K6 Al Ghammas Iraq
18 B5 Al Ghāţ S. Arabia
20 D6 Al Ghayḑah Yemen
48 C4 Alghero Sardinia Italy
54 C1 Algiers Alg.
59 F6 Algoa Bay b. S. Africa
68 D3 Algoma U.S.A.
76 E3 Algona U.S.A.
69 F4 Algonac U.S.A.
69 H3 Algonquin Park Can.
69 H3 Algonquin Provincial Park res. Can.
17 J7 Al Habakah well S. Arabia
18 B4 Al Ḩadaqah well S. Arabia
18 C5 Al Ḩadd Bahrain
18 A4 Al Hadhālīl plat. S. Arabia
17 J4 Al Hadīthah Iraq
17 J4 Al Ḩaḑr Iraq
16 F4 Al Ḩaffah Syria
18 B5 Al Ḩā'ir S. Arabia
19 E6 Al Hajar Oman
18 E5 Al Ḩajar al Gharbī mts Oman
17 G6 Al Hamad reg. Jordan/S. Arabia
55 D2 Al Ḩamādah al Ḩamrā' plat. Libya
45 F4 Alhama de Murcia Spain
17 J6 Al Hammām well Iraq
17 K7 Al Haniyah esc. Iraq
18 B6 Al Hariq S. Arabia
17 G6 Al Ḩarrah reg. S. Arabia
17 H3 Al Ḩasakah Syria
17 K5 Al Hāshimīyah Iraq
17 L5 Al Ḩayy Iraq
17 K5 Al Ḩillah Iraq
18 B6 Al Ḩillah S. Arabia
18 B6 Al Ḩilwah S. Arabia
18 C5 Al Ḩinnāh S. Arabia
54 B1 Al Hoceima Morocco
20 B7 Al Hudaydah Yemen
20 C4 Al Hufūf S. Arabia
18 D6 Al Ḩumrah reg. U.A.E.
18 C5 Al Ḩunayy S. Arabia
18 B6 Al Huwwah S. Arabia
18 D2 'Alīābād Iran
17 L4 'Alīābād Iran
19 E3 'Alīābād Iran
19 F4 'Alīābād Iran
49 M5 Aliağa Turkey
49 K4 Aliakmonas r. Greece
17 L5 'Alī al Gharbī Iraq
21 A2 Alībāg India
22 B4 Ali Bandar Pak.
17 M2 Äli Bayramlı Azer.
45 F3 Alicante Spain
59 G6 Alice S. Africa
77 D7 Alice U.S.A.
64 D3 Alice Arm Can.
6 D4 Alice Springs Austr.
79 E7 Alice Town Bahamas
31 B5 Alicia Phil.
22 D4 Aligarh India
18 C3 Alīgūdarz Iran
56 B4 Alima r. Congo
37 N8 Alingsås Sweden
16 B2 Aliova r. Turkey
22 B3 Alipur Pak.
23 G4 Alipur Duar India
80 C4 Aliquippa U.S.A.
56 E2 Ali Sabieh Djibouti
16 F6 'Al 'Īsāwīyah S. Arabia
17 K2 Alī Shah Iran
17 K5 Al Iskandarīyah Iraq
73 E6 Alisos r. Mex.
49 L5 Aliveri Greece
59 G5 Aliwal North S. Africa
64 G4 Alix Can.
55 E1 Al Jabal al Akhḑar mts Libya
18 C5 Al Jāfūrah des. S. Arabia
55 E2 Al Jaghbūb Libya
17 L7 Al Jahrah Kuwait
18 C5 Al Jamalīyah Qatar
18 C6 Al Jawb reg. S. Arabia
20 A4 Al Jawf S. Arabia
55 D1 Al Jawsh Libya
17 G3 Al Jazīrah reg. Iraq/Syria
45 B4 Aljezur Port.
18 C5 Al Jībān reg. S. Arabia
18 B6 Al Jifārah S. Arabia
17 J6 Al Jil well Iraq
18 B5 Al Jilh esc. S. Arabia
18 C5 Al Jishshah S. Arabia
16 E6 Al Jīzah Jordan
20 C4 Al Jubayl S. Arabia
18 B5 Al Jubaylah S. Arabia
18 B5 Al Jufayr S. Arabia
18 C5 Al Jurayd i. S. Arabia
18 B5 Al Jurayfah S. Arabia
45 B4 Aljustrel Port.
20 E5 Al Khābūrah Oman
17 K5 Al Khālis Iraq
20 E4 Al Khaşab Oman
18 A6 Al Khāşirah S. Arabia
18 D6 Al Khatam reg. U.A.E.
18 C5 Al Khawr Qatar
18 C5 Al Khīşah well S. Arabia
18 C5 Al Khobar S. Arabia
18 B5 Al Khuff reg. S. Arabia
55 E2 Al Khufrah Libya
55 D1 Al Khums Libya
17 K5 Al Kifl Iraq
18 C5 Al Kir'ānah Qatar
42 C2 Alkmaar Neth.
17 K5 Al Kūfah Iraq
17 L5 Al Kumayt Iraq
17 K5 Al Kūt Iraq
Al Kuwayt see Kuwait
17 H7 Al Labbah plain S. Arabia
Al Lādhiqīyah see Latakia
81 J1 Allagash ME U.S.A.
81 J1 Allagash r. ME U.S.A.
81 J1 Allagash Lake l. U.S.A.
23 E4 Allahabad India
16 F5 Al Lajā lava Syria
13 P3 Allakh-Yun' Rus. Fed.
59 G3 Allanridge S. Africa
59 H1 Alldays S. Africa
68 E4 Allegan U.S.A.
80 D4 Allegheny r. U.S.A.
80 C6 Allegheny Mountains U.S.A.
80 D4 Allegheny Reservoir U.S.A.
79 D5 Allendale U.S.A.
38 E3 Allendale Town U.K.
84 B1 Allende Mex.
43 G4 Allendorf (Lumda) Ger.
69 G3 Allenford Can.
41 C3 Allen, Lough l. Rep. of Ireland
81 F4 Allentown U.S.A.
21 B4 Alleppey India
43 J2 Aller r. Ger.
76 C3 Alliance NE U.S.A.
80 C4 Alliance OH U.S.A.
17 J6 Al Līfīyah well Iraq
37 O9 Allinge-Sandvig Denmark
69 H3 Alliston Can.
20 B5 Al Līth S. Arabia
40 E4 Alloa U.K.
21 C3 Allur India
21 C3 Alluru Kottapatnam India
17 J6 Al Lussuf well Iraq
67 F4 Alma Can.
68 E4 Alma MI U.S.A.
76 D3 Alma NE U.S.A.
75 H5 Alma NM U.S.A.
17 J6 Al Ma'ānīyah Iraq
45 B3 Almada Port.
17 K7 Al Ma'danīyāt well Iraq
45 D3 Almadén Spain
Al Madīnah see Medina
17 K5 Al Maḩmūdīyah Iraq
18 B5 Al Majma'ah S. Arabia
17 L1 Almalı Azer.
18 C5 Al Malsūnīyah reg. S. Arabia
18 C5 Al Manāmah Bahrain
74 B1 Almanor, Lake l. U.S.A.
45 F3 Almansa Spain
45 D2 Almanzor mt Spain
17 L6 Al Ma'qil Iraq
18 D6 Al Mariyyah U.A.E.
55 E1 Al Marj Libya
90 C1 Almas, Rio das r. Brazil
15 F2 Almaty Kazak.
Al Mawşil see Mosul
17 H4 Al Mayādīn Syria
18 B5 Al Mazāḩimīyah S. Arabia
45 E2 Almazán Spain
13 N3 Almaznyy Rus. Fed.
87 H4 Almeirim Brazil
45 B3 Almeirim Port.
42 E2 Almelo Neth.
90 E2 Almenara Brazil
45 C2 Almendra, Embalse de resr Spain
45 C3 Almendralejo Spain
42 D2 Almere Neth.
45 E4 Almería Spain
45 E4 Almería, Golfo de b. Spain
12 G4 Al'met'yevsk Rus. Fed.
37 O8 Älmhult Sweden
18 B5 Al Midhnab S. Arabia
45 D5 Almina, Pta pt Morocco
20 C4 Al Mish'āb S. Arabia
16 F5 Al Mismīyah Syria
45 B4 Almodôvar Port.
69 F4 Almont U.S.A.
69 J3 Almonte Can.
45 C4 Almonte Spain
20 C4 Al Mubarrez S. Arabia
16 E7 Al Mudawwara Jordan
18 C5 Al Muharraq Bahrain
20 C7 Al Mukallā Yemen
20 B7 Al Mukhā Yemen
45 E4 Almuñécar Spain
17 K5 Al Muqdādīyah Iraq
18 B5 Al Murabba S. Arabia
16 F1 Almus Turkey
18 B4 Al Musannāh ridge S. Arabia
17 K5 Al Musayyib Iraq
49 L7 Almyrou, Ormos b. Greece
74 □1 Alna Haina U.S.A.
38 F2 Alnwick U.K.
23 H5 Alon Myanmar
23 H3 Along India
49 K5 Alonnisos i. Greece
25 E7 Alor i. Indon.
25 E7 Alor, Kepulauan is Indon.
33 B1 Alor Setar Malaysia
Alost see Aalst
22 C5 Alot India
36 W4 Alozero Rus. Fed.
74 C4 Alpaugh U.S.A.
42 E3 Alpen Ger.
69 F3 Alpena U.S.A.
48 D1 Alpi Dolomitiche mts Italy
75 H5 Alpine AZ U.S.A.
77 C6 Alpine TX U.S.A.
72 E3 Alpine WY U.S.A.
34 F4 Alps mts Europe
20 C6 Al Qa'āmīyāt reg. S. Arabia
55 D1 Al Qaddāḩīyah Libya
16 F4 Al Qadmūs Syria
18 B5 Al Qā'īyah well S. Arabia
18 C6 Al Qalībah S. Arabia
17 H3 Al Qāmishlī Syria
18 B5 Al Qar'ah well S. Arabia
16 F4 Al Qaryatayn Syria
18 B5 Al Qaşab S. Arabia
20 C6 Al Qaţn Yemen
55 D2 Al Qaţrūn Libya
18 B4 Al Qayşūmah S. Arabia
16 E6 Al Qunayţirah Syria
20 B6 Al Qunfidhah S. Arabia
18 A5 Al Qurayn S. Arabia
17 L6 Al Qurnah Iraq
17 K6 Al Qusayr Iraq
18 B6 Al Qūşūrīyah S. Arabia
16 F5 Al Quţayfah Syria
18 A5 Al Quwārah S. Arabia
18 B5 Al Quwayīyah S. Arabia
44 H2 Alsace reg. France
39 E4 Alsager U.K.
17 J6 Al Samīt well Iraq
65 H4 Alsask Can.
43 H4 Alsfeld Ger.
43 K3 Alsleben (Saale) Ger.
38 E3 Alston U.K.
37 R8 Alsunga Latvia
36 S2 Alta Norway
36 S2 Altaelva r. Norway
91 D1 Alta Gracia Arg.
89 D2 Altagracia de Orituco Venez.
10 K5 Altai Mountains China/Mongolia
79 D6 Altamaha r. U.S.A.
87 H4 Altamira Brazil
9 B6 Alta, Mt mt N.Z.
48 G4 Altamura Italy
90 C1 Alta Paraiso de Goiás Brazil
84 A1 Altata Mex.
80 D6 Altavista U.S.A.
15 G2 Altay China
24 B2 Altay Mongolia
45 F3 Altea Spain
36 S1 Alteidet Norway
42 E4 Altenahr Ger.
42 F2 Altenberge Ger.
43 L4 Altenburg Ger.
42 F4 Altenkirchen (Westerwald) Ger.
23 H1 Altenqoke China
43 M1 Altentreptow Ger.
17 M1 Altıağaç Azer.
19 H3 Altimur Pass Afgh.
17 K4 Altin Köprü Iraq
49 M5 Altınoluk Turkey
16 C2 Altıntaş Turkey
86 E7 Altiplano plain Bol.
43 K2 Altmark reg. Ger.
43 J5 Altmühl r. Ger.
90 B2 Alto Araguaia Brazil
91 C2 Alto de Pencoso h. Arg.
89 B3 Alto de Tamar mt Col.
90 B2 Alto Garças Brazil
57 D5 Alto Molócuè Moz.
78 B4 Alton IL U.S.A.
77 F4 Alton MO U.S.A.
81 H3 Alton NH U.S.A.
76 D1 Altona Can.
80 D4 Altoona U.S.A.
90 B2 Alto Sucuriú Brazil
46 F6 Altötting Ger.
39 E4 Altrincham U.K.
43 L1 Alt Schwerin Ger.
24 A3 Altun Shan mts China
87 H3 Alturas U.S.A.
77 D5 Altus U.S.A.
16 G1 Alucra Turkey
37 U8 Alūksne Latvia
17 M5 Alūm Iran
80 B4 Alum Creek Lake l. U.S.A.
91 B3 Aluminé r. Arg.
91 B3 Aluminé, L. l. Arg.
51 E6 Alupka Ukr.
55 D1 Al 'Uqaylah Libya
18 C5 Al 'Uqayr S. Arabia
51 E6 Alushta Ukr.
17 K4 'Alut Iran
20 C4 Al 'Uthmānīyah S. Arabia
55 E2 Al 'Uwaynāt Libya
17 J6 Al 'Uwayqīlah S. Arabia
18 A5 Al 'Uyūn S. Arabia
17 L6 Al 'Uzayr Iraq
77 D4 Alva U.S.A.
84 D3 Alvarado Mex.
91 C2 Alvarado, P. de pass Chile
86 F4 Alvarães Brazil
37 M5 Alvdal Norway
37 O6 Älvdalen Sweden
37 O8 Alvesta Sweden
37 K6 Ålvik Norway
77 E6 Alvin U.S.A.
36 R4 Älvsbyn Sweden
14 B4 Al Wajh S. Arabia
18 C5 Al Wakrah Qatar
18 C5 Al Wannān S. Arabia
22 D4 Alwar India
18 B5 Al Wari'ah S. Arabia
21 B4 Alwaye India
17 H5 Al Widyān plat. Iraq/S. Arabia
18 B4 'Al Wusayţ well S. Arabia
26 A2 Alxa Youqi China
26 B2 Alxa Zuoqi China
6 D3 Alyangula Austr.
40 E4 Alyth U.K.
37 T9 Alytus Lith.
72 F2 Alzada U.S.A.
42 E5 Alzette r. Lux.
43 G5 Alzey Ger.
89 E3 Amacuro r. Guyana/Venez.
6 D4 Amadeus, Lake salt flat Austr.
63 L3 Amadjuak Lake l. Can.
75 G6 Amado U.S.A.
45 B3 Amadora Port.
29 A8 Amakusa-nada b. Japan
37 N7 Åmål Sweden
21 C2 Amalapuram India
24 D1 Amalat r. Rus. Fed.
89 B3 Amalfi Col.
58 F3 Amalia S. Africa
49 J6 Amaliada Greece
22 C5 Amalner India
25 F7 Amamapare Indon.
90 A3 Amambaí Brazil
90 A3 Amambaí r. Brazil
90 A3 Amambaí, Serra de h. Brazil/Para.
24 E4 Amami-guntō is Japan
24 E4 Amami-Ōshima i. Japan
14 E1 Amangel'dy Kazak.
48 G5 Amantea Italy
59 J5 Amanzimtoti S. Africa
87 H3 Amapá Brazil
45 C3 Amareleja Port.
74 D3 Amargosa Desert des. U.S.A.
74 D3 Amargosa Range mts U.S.A.
74 D3 Amargosa Valley U.S.A.
77 C5 Amarillo U.S.A.
48 F3 Amaro, Monte mt Italy
22 E4 Amarpatan India
16 E1 Amasya Turkey
84 D3 Amatán Mex.
84 A2 Amatlán de Cañas Mex.
42 D4 Amay Belgium
87 H4 Amazon r. S. America
89 D4 Amazonas div. Brazil
Amazonas r. see Amazon
87 G4 Amazónia, Parque Nacional nat. park Brazil
87 J3 Amazon, Mouths of the est. Brazil
22 C6 Ambad India
21 B2 Ambajogai India
22 D3 Ambala India
21 C5 Ambalangoda Sri Lanka
57 E6 Ambalavao Madag.
57 E5 Ambanja Madag.
19 E4 Ambar Iran
13 S3 Ambarchik Rus. Fed.
21 B4 Ambasamudram India
86 C4 Ambato Ecuador
57 E5 Ambato Boeny Madag.
57 E6 Ambato Finandrahana Madag.
57 E5 Ambatolampy Madag.
57 E5 Ambatomainty Madag.
57 E5 Ambatondrazaka Madag.
43 K5 Amberg Ger.
82 G5 Ambergris Cay i. Belize
44 G4 Ambérieu-en-Bugey France
69 G3 Amberley Can.
23 E5 Ambikapur India
57 E5 Ambilobe Madag.
64 C3 Ambition, Mt mt Can.
38 F2 Amble U.K.
38 E3 Ambleside U.K.
42 D4 Amblève r. Belgium
57 E6 Amboasary Madag.
57 E5 Ambohidratrimo Madag.
57 E6 Ambohimahasoa Madag.
25 E7 Ambon Indon.
25 E7 Ambon i. Indon.
57 E6 Ambositra Madag.
57 E6 Ambovombe Madag.
75 E4 Amboy CA U.S.A.
68 C5 Amboy IL U.S.A.
81 F3 Amboy Center U.S.A.
57 B4 Ambriz Angola
7 G3 Ambrym i. Vanuatu
21 B3 Ambur India
23 G2 Amdo China
84 A2 Ameca Mex.
42 D1 Ameland i. Neth.
80 E6 Amelia Court House U.S.A.
81 G4 Amenia U.S.A.
72 D3 American Falls U.S.A.
72 D3 American Falls Res. resr U.S.A.
75 G1 American Fork U.S.A.
5 K6 American Samoa terr. Pac. Oc.
79 C5 Americus U.S.A.
42 D2 Amersfoort Neth.
59 H3 Amersfoort S. Africa
39 G6 Amersham U.K.
65 L3 Amery Can.
92 D5 Amery Ice Shelf ice feature Ant.
76 E3 Ames U.S.A.
39 F6 Amesbury U.K.
81 H3 Amesbury U.S.A.
23 E4 Amethi India
49 K5 Amfissa Greece
13 P3 Amga Rus. Fed.
24 F2 Amgu Rus. Fed.
54 C2 Amguid Alg.
24 F1 Amgun' r. Rus. Fed.
67 H4 Amherst Can.
81 G3 Amherst MA U.S.A.
81 J2 Amherst ME U.S.A.
80 D6 Amherst VA U.S.A.
69 F4 Amherstburg Can.
48 D3 Amiata, Monte mt Italy
44 F2 Amiens France
17 H5 Amij, Wādī watercourse Iraq
21 A4 Amindivi Islands is India
29 D7 Amino Japan
58 C1 Aminuis Namibia
18 B3 Amīrābād Iran
Amirabad see Fūlād Maïalleh
53 K6 Amirante Islands is Seychelles
19 F4 Amir Chah Pak.
65 J4 Amisk L. l. Can.
77 C6 Amistad Res. resr Mex./U.S.A.
22 D5 Amla Madhya Pradesh India
37 L7 Åmli Norway
39 C4 Amlwch U.K.
16 E6 'Ammān Jordan
39 D6 Ammanford U.K.
36 V4 Ämmänsaari Fin.
36 P4 Ammarnäs Sweden
43 F1 Ammerland reg. Ger.
43 J3 Ammern Ger.
46 E7 Ammersee l. Ger.
Ammochostos see Famagusta
30 D4 Amnyong-dan hd N. Korea
22 C5 Amod India
27 B6 Amo Jiang r. China
18 D2 Amol Iran
43 H5 Amorbach Ger.
49 L6 Amorgos i. Greece
66 E4 Amos Can.
Amoy see Xiamen
21 C5 Amparai India
90 C3 Amparo Brazil
46 E6 Amper r. Ger.
45 G2 Amposta Spain
22 D5 Amravati India
22 B5 Amreli India
22 B4 Amri Pak.
16 E4 'Amrit Syria
22 C3 Amritsar India
22 D3 Amroha India
36 Q4 Åmsele Sweden
42 C2 Amstelveen Neth.
42 C2 Amsterdam Neth.
59 J3 Amsterdam S. Africa
81 F3 Amsterdam U.S.A.
93 K6 Amsterdam, Île i. Ind. Ocean
46 G6 Amstetten Austria
55 E3 Am Timan Chad
19 F1 Amudar'ya r. Turkm./Uzbek.
63 J2 Amund Ringnes I. Can.
92 D4 Amundsen Bay b. Ant.
92 B4 Amundsen Gl. gl. Ant.
62 F2 Amundsen Gulf g. Can.
92 C5 Amundsen, Mt mt Ant.
92 B4 Amundsen-Scott U.S.A. Base Ant.
92 A3 Amundsen Sea sea Ant.
33 E3 Amuntai Indon.
Amur r. see Heilong Jiang
13 P4 Amursk Rus. Fed.
51 F6 Amvrosiyivka Ukr.
68 E1 Amyot Can.
23 H6 An Myanmar
25 E7 Anabanua Indon.
13 N2 Anabar r. Rus. Fed.
13 N2 Anabarskiy Zaliv b. Rus. Fed.
8 C2 Ana Branch r. Austr.
74 C4 Anacapa Is is U.S.A.
89 D2 Anaco Venez.
72 D2 Anaconda U.S.A.
72 B1 Anacortes U.S.A.
77 D5 Anadarko U.S.A.
16 F1 Anadolu Dağları mts Turkey
13 T3 Anadyr' r. Rus. Fed.
13 U3 Anadyrskiy Zaliv b. Rus. Fed.
49 L6 Anafi i. Greece
90 E1 Anagé Brazil
17 H4 'Ānah Iraq
74 D5 Anaheim U.S.A.
64 D4 Anahim Lake Can.
77 C7 Anáhuac Mex.
21 B4 Anaimalai Hills mts India
21 B4 Anai Mudi Pk mt India
21 C2 Anakapalle India
57 E5 Analalava Madag.
86 F4 Anamã Brazil
33 C2 Anambas, Kepulauan is Indon.
68 B4 Anamosa U.S.A.
16 D3 Anamur Turkey
16 D3 Anamur Burnu pt Turkey
29 D8 Anan Japan
22 C5 Anand India
23 F5 Ānandapur India
23 F5 Anandpur r. India
21 B3 Anantapur India
22 C2 Anantnag Jammu and Kashmir
51 D6 Anan'yiv Ukr.
51 F6 Anapa Rus. Fed.
90 C2 Anápolis Brazil
18 D4 Anār Iran
18 D3 Anārak Iran
18 C3 Anarbar r. Iran
19 F3 Anardara Afgh.
16 D2 Anatolia reg. Turkey
7 G4 Anatom i. Vanuatu
88 D3 Añatuya Arg.
89 E4 Anauá r. Brazil
18 C2 Anbūh Iran
30 D4 Anbyon N. Korea
44 D3 Ancenis France
62 D3 Anchorage U.S.A.
69 F4 Anchor Bay b. U.S.A.
48 E3 Ancona Italy
88 B6 Ancud Chile
91 B4 Ancud, Golfo de g. Chile
91 B1 Andacollo Chile
23 F5 Andal India
36 K5 Åndalsnes Norway
45 D4 Andalucía div. Spain
77 G6 Andalusia U.S.A.
15 H6 Andaman and Nicobar Islands div. India
93 L3 Andaman Basin sea feature Ind. Ocean
15 H5 Andaman Islands Andaman and Nicobar Is
33 A1 Andaman Sea sea Asia
57 E5 Andapa Madag.
90 E1 Andaraí Brazil
36 P2 Andenes Norway
42 D4 Andenne Belgium
42 C4 Anderlecht Belgium
44 D4 Andernos-les-Bains France
62 D3 Anderson AK U.S.A.
68 E5 Anderson IN U.S.A.
77 E4 Anderson MO U.S.A.
79 D5 Anderson SC U.S.A.
62 F3 Anderson r. N.W.T. Can.
85 C3 Andes mts S. America
76 D3 Andes, Lake U.S.A.
36 P2 Andfjorden chan. Norway
21 B2 Andhra Pradesh div. India
57 E5 Andilamena Madag.
57 E5 Andilanatoby Madag.
18 C3 Andīmeshk Iran
16 F3 Andırın Turkey
51 H7 Andiyskoye Koysu r. Rus. Fed.
14 F2 Andizhan Uzbek.
19 G2 Andkhui r. Afgh.
19 G2 Andkhvoy Afgh.
57 E5 Andoany Madag.
86 C4 Andoas Peru
21 B2 Andol India
30 E5 Andong S. Korea
30 E5 Andong-ho l. S. Korea
34 F4 Andorra country Europe
45 G1 Andorra la Vella Andorra
39 F6 Andover U.K.
81 H2 Andover ME U.S.A.
80 C4 Andover OH U.S.A.
36 O2 Andøya i. Norway
90 B3 Andradina Brazil
50 E3 Andreapol' Rus. Fed.
38 C3 Andreas U.K.
56 C3 André Félix, Parc National de nat. park C.A.R.
90 D3 Andrelândia Brazil
77 C5 Andrews U.S.A.
48 G4 Andria Italy
57 E6 Androka Madag.
79 E7 Andros i. Bahamas
49 L6 Andros i. Greece
81 H2 Androscoggin r. U.S.A.
79 E7 Andros Town Bahamas
21 A4 Āndrott i. India
51 D5 Andrushivka Ukr.
36 Q2 Andselv Norway
45 D3 Andújar Spain
57 B5 Andulo Angola
54 C3 Anéfis Mali
83 M5 Anegada i. Virgin Is
91 D4 Anegada, Bahía b. Arg.
75 F5 Anegam U.S.A.
54 C4 Anécho Togo
'Aneiza, Jabal h. see 'Unayzah, Jabal
75 H3 Aneth U.S.A.
45 G1 Aneto mt Spain
55 D3 Aney Niger
27 E5 Anfu China
57 E5 Angadoka, Lohatanjona hd Madag.
24 B1 Angara r. Rus. Fed.
24 C1 Angarsk Rus. Fed.
31 B3 Angat Phil.
37 O5 Ånge Sweden
82 B3 Angel de la Guarda i. Mex.
31 B3 Angeles Phil.
37 N8 Ängelholm Sweden
74 B2 Angels Camp U.S.A.
36 P4 Ångermanälven r. Sweden
44 D3 Angers France
65 K2 Angikuni Lake l. Can.
32 B2 Angkor Cambodia
39 C4 Anglesey i. U.K.
77 E6 Angleton U.S.A.
69 H2 Angliers Can.
Angmagssalik see Tasiilaq
32 □ Ang Mo Kio Sing.
56 C3 Ango Congo(Zaire)
57 D5 Angoche Moz.
19 E5 Angohrān Iran
91 B3 Angol Chile
68 E5 Angola U.S.A.
53 F7 Angola country Africa
96 K7 Angola Basin sea feature Atl. Ocean
84 D3 Angostura, Presa de la resr Mex.
44 E4 Angoulême France
12 J5 Angren Uzbek.
32 B2 Ang Thong Thai.
61 M8 Anguilla terr. Caribbean Sea
26 E1 Anguli Nur l. China
26 E2 Anguo China
90 A3 Anhanduí r. Brazil
37 M8 Anholt i. Denmark
27 D4 Anhua China
26 E3 Anhui div. China
90 A2 Anhumas Brazil
30 D5 Anhŭng S. Korea
90 C2 Anicuns Brazil
50 G3 Anikovo Rus. Fed.
75 H6 Animas U.S.A.
75 H6 Animas Peak summit U.S.A.
32 A2 Anin Myanmar
28 H1 Aniva Rus. Fed.
28 H1 Aniva, Mys c. Rus. Fed.
24 G2 Aniva, Zaliv b. Rus. Fed.
7 G3 Aniwa i. Vanuatu
42 B5 Anizy-le-Château France
37 U6 Anjalankoski Fin.
21 B4 Anjengo India
27 F4 Anji China
22 D5 Anji India
19 E3 Anjoman Iran
44 D3 Anjou reg. France
57 E5 Anjouan i. Comoros
57 E5 Anjozorobe Madag.
30 C4 Anjŭ N. Korea
57 E6 Ankaboa, Tanjona pt Madag.
26 C3 Ankang China
16 D2 Ankara Turkey
57 E6 Ankazoabo Madag.
57 E5 Ankazobe Madag.
32 D2 An Khê Vietnam
22 C5 Ankleshwar India
27 B5 Anlong China
32 C2 Ânlong Vêng Cambodia
26 D4 Anlu China
30 D5 Anmyŏn Do i. S. Korea
51 G5 Anna Rus. Fed.
54 C1 Annaba Alg.
43 M4 Annaberg-Buchholtz Ger.
16 F4 An Nabk Syria
20 B4 An Nafūd des. S. Arabia
38 A3 Annahilt U.K.
17 K6 An Najaf Iraq
80 E5 Anna, Lake l. U.S.A.
41 D3 Annalee r. Rep. of Ireland
41 F3 Annalong U.K.
40 E6 Annan Scot. U.K.
40 E6 Annan r. U.K.
40 E5 Annandale v. U.K.
80 E5 Annapolis U.S.A.
67 G5 Annapolis Royal Can.
23 E3 Annapurna mt Nepal
18 C5 An Naqīrah well S. Arabia
69 F4 Ann Arbor U.S.A.
87 G2 Anna Regina Guyana
17 L6 An Nāşirīyah Iraq
81 H3 Ann, Cape hd U.S.A.
44 H4 Annecy France
44 H3 Annemasse France
42 E1 Annen Neth.
64 C4 Annette I. i. U.S.A.
27 B5 Anning China
79 C5 Anniston U.S.A.
53 E6 Annobón i. Equatorial Guinea
44 G4 Annonay France
20 C4 An Nu'ayrīyah S. Arabia
17 K5 An Nu'mānīyah Iraq
76 E2 Anoka U.S.A.
57 E5 Anorontany, Tanjona hd Madag.
49 L7 Ano Viannos Greece
27 D6 Anpu China
27 C6 Anpu Gang b. China
27 E4 Anqing China
26 F2 Anqiu China
27 D5 Anren China
42 D4 Ans Belgium
26 C2 Ansai China
16 F4 Ansariye, J. el mts Syria
43 J5 Ansbach Ger.
30 B3 Anshan China
27 B5 Anshun China
91 C1 Ansilta mt Arg.
91 F1 Ansina Uru.
76 D3 Ansley U.S.A.
77 D5 Anson U.S.A.
54 C3 Ansongo Mali
66 D4 Ansonville Can.
80 C5 Ansted U.S.A.
22 D4 Anta India
86 D6 Antabamba Peru
16 F3 Antakya Turkey
57 F5 Antalaha Madag.
16 C3 Antalya Turkey
16 C3 Antalya Körfezi g. Turkey
57 E5 Antananarivo Madag.
92 B2 Antarctic Peninsula Ant.
40 C3 An Teallach mt U.K.
74 D2 Antelope Range mts U.S.A.
45 D4 Antequera Spain
73 F5 Anthony U.S.A.
54 B2 Anti Atlas mts Morocco
44 H5 Antibes France
67 H4 Anticosti, Île d' i. Can.
68 C3 Antigo U.S.A.
67 H4 Antigonish Can.
82 F6 Antigua Guatemala
83 M5 Antigua i. Antigua
61 M8 Antigua and Barbuda country Caribbean Sea
84 C2 Antiguo-Morelos Mex.
49 K7 Antikythira i. Greece
49 K7 Antikythiro, Steno chan. Greece
Anti Lebanon mts see Sharqi, Jebel esh
Antioch see Antakya
74 B3 Antioch CA U.S.A.
68 C4 Antioch IL U.S.A.
89 B3 Antioquia Col.
4 J9 Antipodes Islands is N.Z.
49 L5 Antipsara i. Greece
77 E5 Antlers U.S.A.
88 B2 Antofagasta Chile
88 C3 Antofalla, Vol. volc. Arg.
42 B4 Antoing Belgium
90 C4 Antonina Brazil
90 E1 Antônio r. Brazil
74 B3 Antonio r. U.S.A.
73 F4 Antonito U.S.A.
41 E3 Antrim U.K.
41 E2 Antrim Hills h. U.K.
57 E5 Antsalova Madag.
57 E5 Antsirabe Madag.
57 E5 Antsirañana Madag.
57 E5 Antsohihy Madag.
36 S3 Anttis Sweden
37 U6 Anttola Fin.
30 E2 Antu China
91 B3 Antuco Chile
91 B3 Antuco, Volcán volc. Chile
81 F2 Antwerp U.S.A.

42 C3 Antwerpen Belgium
28 C3 Anuchino Rus. Fed.
66 E2 Anuc, Lac l. Can.
23 F5 Anugul India
30 D6 Anŭi S. Korea
22 C3 Anupgarh India
21 C4 Anuradhapura Sri Lanka
18 D5 Anveh Iran
Anvers see Antwerpen
92 B2 Anvers I. i. Ant.
27 F5 Anxi Fujian China
24 B2 Anxi Gansu China
26 B4 An Xian China
27 D4 Anxiang China
26 E2 Anxin China
6 D5 Anxious Bay b. Austr.
26 E2 Anyang China
30 D5 Anyang S. Korea
49 L6 Anydro i. Greece
24 B3 A'nyêmaqên Shan mts China
27 E4 Anyi China
27 E5 Anyuan China
27 B4 Anyue China
13 S3 Anyuysk Rus. Fed.
89 B3 Anzá Col.
26 D2 Anze China
24 A1 Anzhero-Sudzhensk Rus. Fed.
56 C4 Anzi Congo(Zaire)
48 E4 Anzio Italy
7 G3 Aoba i. Vanuatu
32 A3 Ao Ban Don b. Thai.
26 F1 Aohan Qi China
28 G4 Aomori Japan
22 D3 Aonla India
Aoraki, Mt mt see Cook, Mt
9 D4 Aorere r. N.Z.
32 A3 Ao Sawi b. Thai.
48 B2 Aosta Italy
54 B2 Aoukâr reg. Mali/Maur.
87 G8 Apa r. Brazil
56 D3 Apac Uganda
75 H6 Apache U.S.A.
75 H5 Apache Creek U.S.A.
75 G5 Apache Junction U.S.A.
75 G6 Apache Peak summit U.S.A.
79 C6 Apalachee Bay b. U.S.A.
79 C6 Apalachicola U.S.A.
84 C3 Apan Mex.
89 C4 Apaporis r. Col.
17 K1 Aparan Armenia
90 B3 Aparecida do Tabuado Brazil
31 B2 Aparri Phil.
36 X3 Apatity Rus. Fed.
84 B3 Apatzingán Mex.
37 U8 Ape Latvia
42 D2 Apeldoorn Neth.
43 H2 Apelern Ger.
43 H1 Apensen Ger.
22 E3 Api mt Nepal
7 J3 Apia Western Samoa
9 E3 Apiti N.Z.
87 G2 Apoera Suriname
43 K3 Apolda Ger.
8 D5 Apollo Bay Austr.
86 E6 Apolo Bol.
31 C5 Apo, Mt volc. Phil.
79 D6 Apopka, L. l. U.S.A.
90 B2 Aporé Brazil
90 B2 Aporé r. Brazil
78 B2 Apostle Islands is U.S.A.
68 B2 Apostle Islands National Lakeshore res. U.S.A.
16 E4 Apostolos Andreas, Cape c. Cyprus
80 B6 Appalachia U.S.A.
80 C6 Appalachian Mountains U.S.A.
48 E3 Appennino Abruzzese mts Italy
48 D2 Appennino Tosco-Emiliano mts Italy
48 E3 Appennino Umbro-Marchigiano mts Italy
8 H3 Appin Austr.
42 E1 Appingedam Neth.
40 C3 Applecross U.K.
76 D2 Appleton MN U.S.A.
68 C3 Appleton WI U.S.A.
74 D4 Apple Valley U.S.A.
80 D6 Appomattox U.S.A.
48 E4 Aprilia Italy
51 F6 Apsheronsk Rus. Fed.
8 C4 Apsley Austr.
69 H3 Apsley Can.
44 G5 Apt France
90 B3 Apucarana Brazil
31 A4 Apurahuan Phil.
89 D3 Apure r. Venez.
86 D6 Apurimac r. Peru
16 E7 'Aqaba Jordan
14 B4 Aqaba, Gulf of g. Asia
18 D2 Aqbana Iran
19 G2 Āqchah Afgh.
18 B2 Aq Chai r. Iran
18 D3 Āqdā Iran
18 B2 Aqdoghmish r. Iran
17 K3 Āq Kān Dāgh, Kūh-e mt Iran
17 J3 'Aqrah Iraq
75 F4 Aquarius Mts mts U.S.A.
75 G3 Aquarius Plateau plat. U.S.A.
48 G4 Aquaviva delle Fonti Italy
90 A3 Aquidauana Brazil
90 A2 Aquidauana r. Brazil
84 B3 Aquila Mex.
89 D4 Aquio r. Col.
84 C2 Aquismón Mex.
44 D4 Aquitaine reg. France
23 F4 Ara India
19 G4 Arab Afgh.
79 C5 Arab U.S.A.
19 E3 'Arabābād Iran
55 E3 Arab, Bahr el watercourse Sudan
93 J3 Arabian Basin sea feature Ind. Ocean
10 H8 Arabian Sea sea Ind. Ocean
89 E3 Arabopó Venez.
89 E3 Arabopó r. Venez.
16 D1 Araç Turkey
89 E4 Araça r. Brazil
87 L6 Aracaju Brazil
89 D4 Aracamuni, Co summit Venez.
90 A4 Aracanguy, Mtes de h. Para.
87 L4 Aracati Brazil
90 E1 Aracatu Brazil
90 B3 Araçatuba Brazil
45 C4 Aracena Spain
90 E2 Aracruz Brazil
90 D2 Araçuaí Brazil
90 D2 Araçuaí r. Brazil
49 J1 Arad Romania
55 E3 Arada Chad
17 L6 Arādah Iraq
6 D2 Arafura Sea sea Austr./Indon.
90 B1 Aragarças Brazil
17 J1 Aragats Armenia
17 K1 Aragats Lerr mt Armenia
45 F2 Aragón div. Spain
45 F1 Aragón r. Spain
87 J5 Araguacema Brazil
89 D2 Aragua de Barcelona Venez.
87 J5 Araguaia r. Brazil
87 H6 Araguaia, Parque Nacional de nat. park Brazil
87 J5 Araguaína Brazil
90 C2 Araguari Brazil
90 C2 Araguari r. Brazil
87 J5 Araguatins Brazil
51 H7 Aragvi r. Georgia
29 F6 Arai Japan
87 K4 Araiosos Brazil
54 C2 Arak Alg.
18 C3 Arāk Iran
23 H5 Arakan Yoma mts Myanmar
21 B3 Arakkonam India
17 K2 Aralık Turkey
14 E2 Aral Sea l. Kazak./Uzbek.
14 E2 Aral'sk Kazak.
51 J5 Aralsor, Ozero l. Kazak.
18 B5 Aramah plat. S. Arabia
84 C1 Aramberri Mex.
22 D6 Aran r. India
45 E2 Aranda de Duero Spain
17 L4 Arandān Iran
49 J2 Arandelovac Yugo.
21 B3 Arani India
41 C3 Aran Island i. Rep. of Ireland
41 B4 Aran Islands is Rep. of Ireland
45 E2 Aranjuez Spain
57 B6 Aranos Namibia
77 D7 Aransas Pass U.S.A.
90 B2 Arantes r. Brazil
7 H1 Aranuka i. Gilbert Is
29 B8 Arao Japan
54 B3 Araouane Mali
76 D3 Arapahoe U.S.A.
89 E4 Arapari r. Brazil
91 F1 Arapey Grande r. Uru.
87 L5 Arapiraca Brazil
49 L4 Arapis, Akra pt Greece
16 G2 Arapkir Turkey
90 B3 Arapongas Brazil
23 F4 A Rapti Doon r. Nepal
20 B3 'Ar'ar S. Arabia
88 G3 Araranguá Brazil
90 C3 Araraquara Brazil
87 H5 Araras Brazil
90 B4 Araras, Serra das mts Brazil
17 K2 Ararat Armenia
8 D4 Ararat Austr.
17 K2 Ararat, Mt mt Turkey
23 F4 Araria India
90 D3 Araruama, Lago de lag. Brazil
17 J6 'Ar'ar, W. watercourse Iraq/S. Arabia
17 J2 Aras Turkey
17 J1 Aras r. Turkey
90 E1 Arataca Brazil
89 C3 Arauca Col.
89 C3 Arauca r. Venez.
91 B3 Arauco Chile
89 C3 Arauquita Col.
89 C2 Araure Venez.
22 C4 Aravalli Range mts India
37 T7 Aravete Estonia
7 F2 Arawa P.N.G.
90 C2 Araxá Brazil
89 D2 Araya, Pen. de pen. Venez.
89 D2 Araya, Pta de pt Venez.
16 C2 Arayıt Dağı mt Turkey
17 M2 Araz r. Asia
17 K4 Arbat Iraq
50 J3 Arbazh Rus. Fed.
17 K3 Arbīl Iraq
37 O7 Arboga Sweden
65 J4 Arborfield Can.
40 F4 Arbroath U.K.
74 A2 Arbuckle U.S.A.
19 F4 Arbu Lut, Dasht-e des. Afgh.
44 D4 Arcachon France
79 D7 Arcadia U.S.A.
72 A3 Arcata U.S.A.
72 D4 Arc Dome summit U.S.A.
84 B3 Arcelia Mex.
50 G1 Archangel Rus. Fed.
6 E3 Archer r. Austr.
75 H2 Arches Nat. Park U.S.A.
18 E2 Archman Turkm.
17 M2 Ārçivan Azer.
72 D3 Arco U.S.A.
45 D4 Arcos de la Frontera Spain
63 K2 Arctic Bay Can.
3 Arctic Ocean ocean
62 C3 Arctic Plains U.S.A.
62 E3 Arctic Red r. Can.
92 B2 Arctowski Poland Base Ant.
18 C2 Ardabīl Iran
17 J1 Ardahan Turkey
18 D3 Ardakān Iran
18 C4 Ardal Iran
37 K6 Årdalstangen Norway
41 C3 Ardara Rep. of Ireland
49 L4 Ardas r. Bulg.
50 H4 Ardatov Mordov. Rus. Fed.
50 G4 Ardatov Nizheg. Rus. Fed.
69 G3 Ardbeg Can.
41 E4 Ardee Rep. of Ireland
8 A2 Arden, Mount h. Austr.
42 D5 Ardennes reg. Belgium
42 C5 Ardennes, Canal des canal France
18 D3 Ardestān Iran
41 F3 Ardglass U.K.
45 C3 Ardila r. Port.
84 B2 Ardilla, Cerro la mt Mex.
8 F3 Ardlethan Austr.
77 D5 Ardmore U.S.A.
40 B4 Ardnamurchan, Point of pt U.K.
40 C4 Ardrishaig U.K.
8 A3 Ardrossan Austr.
40 D5 Ardrossan U.K.
40 C3 Ardvasar U.K.
91 E2 Areco r. Arg.
87 L4 Areia Branca Brazil
42 E4 Aremberg h. Ger.
31 B4 Arena rf Phil.
74 A2 Arena, Pt pt U.S.A.
45 D2 Arenas de San Pedro Spain
37 L7 Arendal Norway
43 K2 Arendsee (Altmark) Ger.
39 D5 Arenig Fawr h. U.K.
49 K6 Areopoli Greece
86 D7 Arequipa Peru
87 H4 Arere Brazil
45 D2 Arévalo Spain
48 D3 Arezzo Italy
16 G6 'Arfajah well S. Arabia
26 D1 Argalant Mongolia
45 E2 Arganda Spain
31 B4 Argao Phil.
48 D2 Argenta Italy
44 D2 Argentan France
48 D3 Argentario, Monte h. Italy
48 B2 Argentera, Cima dell' mt Italy
42 F5 Argenthal Ger.
85 D6 Argentina country S. America
92 B3 Argentina Ra. mts Ant.
96 F8 Argentine Basin sea feature Atl. Ocean
88 B8 Argentino, Lago l. Arg.
49 L2 Argeș r. Romania
19 G4 Arghandab r. Afgh.
19 G4 Arghastan r. Afgh.
16 C2 Argıthanı Turkey
49 K6 Argolikos Kolpos b. Greece
49 K6 Argos Greece
49 J5 Argostoli Greece
45 F1 Arguís Spain
51 H7 Argun Rus. Fed.
24 E1 Argun' r. China/Rus. Fed.
74 D4 Argus Range mts U.S.A.
68 C4 Argyle U.S.A.
6 C3 Argyle, Lake l. Austr.
40 C4 Argyll reg. U.K.
37 M8 Århus Denmark
9 E3 Aria N.Z.
8 F3 Ariah Park Austr.
29 B8 Ariake-kai b. Japan
57 B6 Ariamsvlei Namibia
48 F4 Ariano Irpino Italy
89 B4 Ariari r. Col.
91 D2 Arias Arg.
15 F6 Ari Atoll Maldives
89 E2 Aribí r. Venez.
54 B3 Aribinda Burkina
88 B1 Arica Chile
40 C4 Arienas, Loch l. U.K.
16 F4 Arīḥā Syria
72 G4 Arikaree r. U.S.A.
89 E2 Arima Trinidad and Tobago
90 C1 Arinos Brazil
87 G6 Arinos r. Brazil
84 B3 Ario de Rosáles Mex.
89 C3 Ariporo r. Col.
86 F5 Aripuanã Brazil
86 F5 Aripuanã r. Brazil
86 F5 Ariquemes Brazil
90 B2 Ariranhá r. Brazil
58 B1 Aris Namibia
40 C4 Arisaig U.K.
40 C4 Arisaig, Sound of chan. U.K.
64 D4 Aristazabal I. i. Can.
75 G4 Arizona div. U.S.A.
70 D5 Arizpe Mex.
18 B5 'Arjah S. Arabia
36 P3 Arjeplog Sweden
89 B2 Arjona Col.
33 D4 Arjuna, G. volc. Indon.
51 G5 Arkadak Rus. Fed.
77 E5 Arkadelphia U.S.A.
40 C4 Arkaig, Loch l. U.K.
14 E1 Arkalyk Kazak.
77 E5 Arkansas div. U.S.A.
77 F5 Arkansas r. U.S.A.
77 D4 Arkansas City U.S.A.
23 G1 Arkatag Shan mts China
Arkhangel'sk see Archangel
50 G2 Arkhangel'skaya Oblast' div. Rus. Fed.
50 F4 Arkhangel'skoye Rus. Fed.
28 C3 Arkhipovka Rus. Fed.
41 E5 Arklow Rep. of Ireland
49 M6 Arkoi i. Greece
46 F3 Arkona, Kap hd Ger.
12 K2 Arkticheskogo Instituta, Ostrova is Rus. Fed.
81 F3 Arkville U.S.A.
44 G5 Arles France
59 G4 Arlington S. Africa
72 B2 Arlington OR U.S.A.
76 D2 Arlington SD U.S.A.
80 E5 Arlington VA U.S.A.
68 D4 Arlington Heights U.S.A.
54 C3 Arlit Niger
42 D5 Arlon Belgium
31 C5 Armadores i. Indon.
41 E3 Armagh U.K.
55 F2 Armant Egypt
51 G6 Armavir Rus. Fed.
89 B3 Armenia Col.
10 F5 Armenia country Asia
89 B3 Armero Col.
8 H1 Armidale Austr.
65 L2 Armit Lake l. Can.
22 E5 Armori India
84 B3 Armour, Mt mt Can./U.S.A.
41 E2 Armoy U.K.
64 F4 Armstrong B.C. Can.
66 C3 Armstrong Ont. Can.
28 E1 Armu r. Rus. Fed.
21 B2 Armur India
51 E6 Armyans'k Ukr.
16 D4 Arnaoutis, Cape c. Cyprus
67 F1 Arnaud r. Can.
37 M6 Årnes Norway
77 D4 Arnett U.S.A.
42 D3 Arnhem Neth.
6 D3 Arnhem Bay b. Austr.
6 D3 Arnhem, C. c. Austr.
6 D3 Arnhem Land reg. Austr.
48 D3 Arno r. Italy
39 F4 Arnold U.K.
68 D2 Arnold U.S.A.
69 H1 Arnoux, Lac l. Can.
69 J3 Arnprior Can.
43 G3 Arnsberg Ger.
43 J4 Arnstadt Ger.
69 H3 Arnstein Can.
43 H5 Arnstein Ger.
69 H1 Arntfield Can.
89 E3 Aro r. Venez.
57 B6 Aroab Namibia
43 H3 Arolsen Ger.
48 C2 Arona Italy
81 K1 Aroostook Can.
81 J1 Aroostook r. Can./U.S.A.
7 H2 Arorae i. Kiribati
31 B3 Aroroy Phil.
51 G7 Arpa r. Armenia/Turkey
17 J1 Arpaçay Turkey
19 G5 Arra r. Pak.
17 J5 Ar Ramādī Iraq
16 E7 Ar Ramlah Jordan
40 C5 Arran i. U.K.
17 G4 Ar Raqqah Syria
44 F1 Arras France
18 A5 Ar-Rass S. Arabia
16 F4 Ar Rastan Syria
17 J7 Ar Rawḍ well S. Arabia
18 C5 Ar Rayyān Qatar
89 C4 Arrecifal Col.
91 E2 Arrecifes Arg.
84 D3 Arriaga Chiapas Mex.
84 B2 Arriaga San Luis Potosí Mex.
91 E2 Arribeños Arg.
17 L6 Ar Rifā'ī Iraq
17 K6 Ar Riḥāb salt flat Iraq
20 D5 Ar Rimāl reg. S. Arabia
75 H3 Arriola U.S.A.
Ar Riyāḍ see Riyadh
40 C4 Arrochar U.K.
91 G2 Arroio Grande Brazil
90 C1 Arrojado r. Brazil
68 B1 Arrow Lake l. Can.
41 C3 Arrow, Lough l. Rep. of Ireland
72 D3 Arrowrock Res. resr U.S.A.
9 C5 Arrowsmith, Mt mt N.Z.
74 B4 Arroyo Grande U.S.A.
91 F3 Arroyo Grande r. Arg.
91 E2 Arroyo Seco Arg.
84 C2 Arroyo Seco Mex.
18 B5 Ar Rubay'iyah S. Arabia
90 A1 Arruda Brazil
17 K6 Ar Rumaythah Iraq
16 G4 Ar Ruṣāfah Syria
19 E6 Ar Rustāq Oman
17 H5 Ar Ruṭba Iraq
18 B6 Ar Ruwayḍah S. Arabia
37 L8 Års Denmark
18 B2 Ārs Iran
18 D4 Arsenajān Iran
28 C2 Arsen'yev Rus. Fed.
21 B3 Arsikere India
50 J3 Arsk Rus. Fed.
16 E3 Arslanköy Turkey
49 J5 Arta Greece
17 K2 Artashat Armenia
84 B3 Arteaga Mex.
28 C3 Artem Rus. Fed.
51 F5 Artemivs'k Ukr.
28 C3 Artemovskiy Rus. Fed.
44 E2 Artenay France
73 F5 Artesia U.S.A.
69 G4 Arthur Can.
80 C4 Arthur, Lake l. U.S.A.
6 F4 Arthur Pt pt Austr.
9 C5 Arthur's Pass N.Z.
9 C5 Arthur's Pass National Park N.Z.
79 F7 Arthur's Town Bahamas
91 F1 Artigas Uru.
92 B1 Artigas Uru. Base Ant.
17 J1 Art'ik Armenia
65 H2 Artillery Lake l. Can.
59 G2 Artisia Botswana
44 F1 Artois reg. France
42 A4 Artois, Collines d' h. France
17 J2 Artos D. mt Turkey
16 F1 Artova Turkey
51 D6 Artsyz Ukr.
15 F3 Artux China
17 H1 Artvin Turkey
56 D3 Arua Uganda
90 B1 Aruanã Brazil
61 L8 Aruba terr. Caribbean Sea
25 F7 Aru, Kepulauan is Indon.
86 F4 Arumã Brazil
23 F4 Arun r. Nepal
23 H3 Arunachal Pradesh div. India
39 G7 Arundel U.K.
56 D4 Arusha Tanz.
76 B4 Arvada U.S.A.
41 D4 Arvagh Rep. of Ireland
24 C2 Arvayheer Mongolia
22 D5 Arvi India
65 L2 Arviat Can.
67 F4 Arvida Can.
36 Q4 Arvidsjaur Sweden
37 N7 Arvika Sweden
74 C4 Arvin U.S.A.
18 B6 Arwā' S. Arabia
13 O2 Ary Rus. Fed.
50 G4 Arzamas Rus. Fed.
43 L4 Arzberg Ger.
45 F5 Arzew Alg.
51 H6 Arzgir Rus. Fed.
43 L4 Aš Czech Rep.
89 E3 Asa r. Venez.
54 C4 Asaba Nigeria
19 H3 Asadābād Afgh.
18 C3 Asadābād Iran
19 E3 Asadābād Iran
16 G3 Asad, Buḥayrat al resr Syria
32 A5 Asahan r. Indon.
28 H3 Asahi-dake volc. Japan
29 C7 Asahi-gawa r. Japan
28 H3 Asahikawa Japan
18 C2 Āsālem Iran
30 D5 Asan Man b. S. Korea
23 F5 Asansol India
42 F4 Asbach Ger.
67 F4 Asbestos Can.
58 E4 Asbestos Mountains S. Africa
81 F4 Asbury Park U.S.A.
48 F4 Ascea Italy
86 F7 Ascensión Bol.
82 G5 Ascensión, B. de la b. Mex.
53 C6 Ascension Island i. Atl. Ocean
43 H5 Aschaffenburg Ger.
42 F3 Ascheberg Ger.
43 K3 Aschersleben Ger.
48 E3 Ascoli Piceno Italy
37 O8 Åseda Sweden
36 P4 Åsele Sweden
18 D4 Āsemānjerd Iran
39 E6 Ashbourne U.K.
9 C5 Ashburton N.Z.
6 B4 Ashburton watercourse Austr.
63 D1 Ashburton Bay b. Can.
64 E4 Ashcroft Can.
16 E6 Ashdod Israel
77 E5 Ashdown U.S.A.
79 E5 Asheboro U.S.A.
79 D5 Asheville U.S.A.
39 H6 Ashford U.K.
75 F4 Ash Fork U.S.A.
19 E2 Ashgabat Turkm.
28 H3 Ashibetsu Japan
29 F6 Ashikaga Japan
38 F2 Ashington U.K.
50 J3 Ashit r. Rus. Fed.
29 C8 Ashizuri-misaki pt Japan
18 D4 Ashkazar Iran
77 D4 Ashland KS U.S.A.
80 B5 Ashland KY U.S.A.
81 J1 Ashland ME U.S.A.
72 F2 Ashland MT U.S.A.
81 H3 Ashland NH U.S.A.
80 B4 Ashland OH U.S.A.
72 B3 Ashland OR U.S.A.
80 E6 Ashland VA U.S.A.
68 B2 Ashland WI U.S.A.
76 D2 Ashley U.S.A.
50 C4 Ashmyany Belarus
75 H5 Ash Peak U.S.A.
16 E6 Ashqelon Israel
22 B4 Ashraf, Md. Pak.
17 J6 Ash Shabakah Iraq
17 H3 Ash Shaddādah Syria
17 H7 Ash Shaqīq well S. Arabia
18 B5 Ash Sha'rā' S. Arabia
17 J4 Ash Sharqāṭ Iraq
17 L6 Ash Shaṭrah Iraq
20 C7 Ash Shiḥr Yemen
17 K6 Ash Shināfīyah Iraq
18 E5 Ash Shināṣ Oman
18 B4 Ash Shu'bah S. Arabia
18 B5 Ash Shumlūl S. Arabia
80 C4 Ashtabula U.S.A.
17 K1 Ashtarak Armenia
22 D5 Ashti India
21 A2 Ashti India
18 C3 Ashtiān Iran
58 D6 Ashton S. Africa
72 E2 Ashton U.S.A.
38 E4 Ashton-under-Lyne U.K.
63 M4 Ashuanipi Lake l. Can.
79 C5 Ashville U.S.A.
84 B2 Asientos Mex.
21 B2 Asifabad India
23 F6 Āsika India
16 F4 'Āṣī, Nahr al r. Asia
48 C4 Asinara, Golfo dell' b. Sardinia Italy
12 K4 Asino Rus. Fed.
50 D4 Asipovichy Belarus
20 B5 'Asīr reg. S. Arabia
17 H2 Aşkale Turkey
37 M7 Asker Norway
37 O7 Askersund Sweden
37 M7 Askim Norway
24 B1 Askiz Rus. Fed.
17 L2 Aşlāndūz Iran
56 D2 Āsmara Eritrea
37 O8 Åsnen l. Sweden
49 L3 Asenovgrad Bulg.
22 C4 Asop India
17 M3 Aspar Iran
38 D3 Aspatria U.K.
73 F4 Aspen U.S.A.
43 H6 Asperg Ger.
77 C5 Aspermont U.S.A.
9 B6 Aspiring, Mt mt N.Z.
65 H4 Asquith Can.
16 F4 As Sa'an Syria
56 E2 Assab Eritrea
18 C5 As Sabsab well S. Arabia
16 F3 As Safīrah Syria
18 C5 As Saji well S. Arabia
18 B5 As Salamiyah S. Arabia
17 K6 As Salmān Iraq
23 H4 Assam div. India
17 K6 As Samāwah Iraq
16 F5 Aş Şanamayn Syria
55 E2 As Sarīr reg. Libya
81 F5 Assateague I. i. U.S.A.
81 F6 Assateague Island National Seashore res. U.S.A.
42 E1 Assen Neth.
42 B3 Assenede Belgium
42 D4 Assesse Belgium
23 F5 Assia Hills h. India
55 D1 As Sidrah Libya
65 H5 Assiniboia Can.
65 K5 Assiniboine r. Can.
64 F4 Assiniboine, Mt mt Can.
90 B3 Assis Brazil
48 E3 Assisi Italy
43 G4 Aßlar Ger.
17 L7 Aş Şubayḥīyah Kuwait
18 B4 Aş Şufayrī well S. Arabia
17 G4 As Sukhnah Syria
17 K4 As Sulaymānīyah Iraq
20 C5 As Sulayyil S. Arabia
18 C5 Aş Şulb reg. S. Arabia
18 B5 Aş Şummān plat. S. Arabia
20 B5 As Sūq S. Arabia
17 H4 Aş Şuwār Syria
16 F5 As Suwaydā' Syria
19 E6 As Suwayq Oman
17 K5 Aş Şuwayrah Iraq
40 C2 Assynt, Loch l. U.K.
49 M7 Astakida i. Greece
Astalu Island i. see Astola Island
17 M3 Astaneh Iran
17 M2 Astara Azer.
Asterabad see Gorgān
43 C2 Asti Italy
74 A2 Asti U.S.A.
91 C1 Astica Arg.
19 F5 Astola Island i. Pak.
22 C2 Astor Jammu and Kashmir
22 C2 Astor r. Pak.
45 C1 Astorga Spain
72 B2 Astoria U.S.A.
37 N8 Åstorp Sweden
14 C2 Astrakhan' Rus. Fed.
Astrakhan' Bazar see Cälilabad
51 H6 Astrakhanskaya Oblast' div. Rus. Fed.
50 C4 Astravyets Belarus
92 D3 Astrid Ridge sea feature Ant.
45 C1 Asturias div. Spain
49 M6 Astypalaia i. Greece
88 E3 Asunción Para.
55 F2 Aswān Egypt
55 F2 Asyūt Egypt
7 J4 Ata i. Tonga
89 D4 Atabapo r. Col./Venez.
88 C2 Atacama, Desierto de des. Chile
7 J2 Atafu i. Tokelau
54 C4 Atakpamé Togo
49 K5 Atalanti Greece
86 D6 Atalaya Peru
54 A2 Atâr Maur.
32 A1 Ataran r. Myanmar
75 H4 Atarque U.S.A.
74 B4 Atascadero U.S.A.
12 J5 Atasu Kazak.
25 E7 Atauro i. Indon.
55 F3 Atbara Sudan
55 F3 Atbara r. Sudan
14 E1 Atbasar Kazak.
77 F6 Atchafalaya Bay b. U.S.A.
76 E4 Atchison U.S.A.
84 A2 Atenguillo Mex.
48 E3 Aterno r. Italy
48 F3 Atessa Italy
42 B4 Ath Belgium
64 G4 Athabasca Can.
62 G4 Athabasca r. Can.
65 H3 Athabasca, Lake l. Can.
41 E4 Athboy Rep. of Ireland
41 C4 Athenry Rep. of Ireland
69 G3 Athens Can.
49 K6 Athens Greece
79 C5 Athens AL U.S.A.
79 D5 Athens GA U.S.A.
80 B5 Athens OH U.S.A.
79 C5 Athens TN U.S.A.
77 E5 Athens TX U.S.A.
39 F5 Atherstone U.K.
42 A5 Athies France
Athina see Athens
41 C4 Athleague Rep. of Ireland
41 D4 Athlone Rep. of Ireland
21 A2 Athni India
9 B6 Athol N.Z.
81 G3 Athol U.S.A.
40 E4 Atholl, Forest of reg. U.K.
49 L4 Athos mt Greece
17 J4 Ath Tharthār, Wādī r. Iraq
41 E5 Athy Rep. of Ireland
55 D3 Ati Chad
86 D7 Atico Peru
65 J4 Atikameg L. l. Can.
66 B4 Atikokan Can.
67 H3 Atikonak L. l. Can.
31 B3 Atimonan Phil.
21 B4 Atirampattinam India
84 E4 Atitlán Guatemala
84 E4 Atitlán, Parque Nacional nat. park Guatemala
13 R3 Atka Rus. Fed.
51 H5 Atkarsk Rus. Fed.
18 B5 'Atk, W. al watercourse S. Arabia
84 C3 Atlacomulco Mex.
79 C5 Atlanta GA U.S.A.
68 C5 Atlanta IL U.S.A.
69 E3 Atlanta MI U.S.A.
16 D2 Atlantı Turkey
76 E3 Atlantic U.S.A.
81 F5 Atlantic City U.S.A.
96 J9 Atlantic-Indian Antarctic Basin sea feature Atl. Ocean
96 J9 Atlantic-Indian Ridge sea feature Ind. Ocean
58 C6 Atlantis S. Africa
96 G3 Atlantis Fracture sea feature Atl. Ocean
52 D3 Atlas Mountains Alg./Morocco
54 C1 Atlas Saharien mts Alg.
64 C3 Atlin Can.
64 C3 Atlin Lake l. Can.
64 C3 Atlin Prov. Park Can.
16 E5 'Atlit Israel
84 C3 Atlixco Mex.
21 B3 Atmakur India
21 B3 Atmakur India
77 G6 Atmore U.S.A.
77 D5 Atoka U.S.A.
84 B2 Atotonilco el Alto Mex.
32 C1 Atouat mt Laos
84 B3 Atoyac de Alvarez Mex.
23 G4 Atrai r. India
18 E2 Atrak r. Iran
89 A3 Atrato r. Col.
18 D2 Atrek r. Iran/Turkm.
81 F5 Atsion U.S.A.
20 B5 Aṭ Ṭā'if S. Arabia
79 C5 Attalla U.S.A.
32 C2 Attapu Laos
49 M6 Attavyros mt Greece
66 D3 Attawapiskat Can.
66 C3 Attawapiskat r. Can.
66 C3 Attawapiskat L. l. Can.
17 G7 Aţ Ţawīl mts S. Arabia
18 A4 At Taysīyah plat. S. Arabia
43 F3 Attendorn Ger.
46 F7 Attersee l. Austria
68 D5 Attica IN U.S.A.
80 B4 Attica OH U.S.A.
42 C5 Attigny France
81 H3 Attleboro U.S.A.
39 J5 Attleborough U.K.
16 F7 Aţ Ţubayq reg. S. Arabia
94 G2 Attu Island i. U.S.A.
18 B5 Aţ Ţulayḥī well S. Arabia
21 B4 Attur India
40 B2 a' Tuath, Loch b. U.K.
91 C2 Atuel r. Arg.
37 O7 Åtvidaberg Sweden
80 C4 Atwood Lake l. U.S.A.
14 D2 Atyrau Kazak.
43 J5 Aub Ger.
44 G5 Aubagne France
42 D5 Aubange Belgium
31 B2 Aubarede Point pt Phil.
44 G4 Aubenas France
42 D5 Auboué France
75 F4 Aubrey Cliffs cliff U.S.A.
62 F3 Aubry Lake l. Can.
8 B3 Auburn Austr.
69 G4 Auburn Can.
79 C5 Auburn AL U.S.A.
74 B2 Auburn CA U.S.A.
68 E5 Auburn IN U.S.A.
81 H2 Auburn ME U.S.A.
76 E3 Auburn NE U.S.A.
80 E3 Auburn NY U.S.A.
72 B2 Auburn WA U.S.A.
44 F4 Aubusson France
91 C3 Auca Mahuida, Sa de mt Arg.
44 E5 Auch France
40 E4 Auchterarder U.K.
9 E2 Auckland N.Z.
7 G7 Auckland Islands is N.Z.
81 H2 Audet Can.
39 J7 Audresselles France
42 A4 Audruicq France
43 L4 Aue Ger.
43 G2 Aue r. Ger.
43 L4 Auerbach Ger.
43 K5 Auerbach in der Oberpfalz Ger.
43 L4 Auersberg mt Ger.
41 D3 Augher U.K.
41 E3 Aughnacloy U.K.
41 E5 Aughrim Rep. of Ireland
58 D4 Augrabies S. Africa
58 D4 Augrabies Falls waterfall S. Africa
58 D4 Augrabies Falls National Park S. Africa
69 F3 Au Gres U.S.A.
46 E6 Augsburg Ger.
48 F6 Augusta Sicily Italy
79 D5 Augusta GA U.S.A.
77 D4 Augusta KS U.S.A.
81 J2 Augusta ME U.S.A.
68 B3 Augusta WI U.S.A.
89 B2 Augustin Cadazzi Col.
6 B4 Augustus, Mt mt Austr.
42 B4 Aulnoye-Aymeries France
39 J7 Ault France
57 B6 Auob r. Namibia
67 G2 Aupaluk Can.
32 C5 Aur i. Malaysia
37 S6 Aura Fin.
22 D4 Auraiya India
22 C6 Aurangābād India
42 F1 Aurich Ger.
90 B2 Aurilândia Brazil
44 F4 Aurillac France
33 D3 Aurkuning Indon.
31 B5 Aurora Phil.
72 F4 Aurora CO U.S.A.
68 C5 Aurora IL U.S.A.
81 J2 Aurora ME U.S.A.
77 E4 Aurora MO U.S.A.
57 B6 Aus Namibia
69 F3 Au Sable U.S.A.
69 E3 Au Sable r. U.S.A.
81 G2 Ausable r. U.S.A.
81 G2 Ausable Forks U.S.A.
68 D2 Au Sable Pt pt MI U.S.A.
69 F3 Au Sable Pt pt MI U.S.A.
40 F1 Auskerry i. U.K.
36 D4 Austari-Jökulsá r. Iceland
76 E3 Austin MN U.S.A.
74 D2 Austin NV U.S.A.
77 D6 Austin TX U.S.A.
4 D7 Australia country Oceania
92 B6 Australian Antarctic Territory reg. Ant.
8 G3 Australian Capital Territory div. Austr.
34 G4 Austria country Europe
36 O2 Austvågøy i. Norway
84 A3 Autlán Mex.
36 U3 Autti Fin.
44 G3 Autun France
44 F4 Auvergne reg. France
44 F3 Auxerre France
42 A4 Auxi-le-Château France
44 G3 Auxonne France
81 F3 Ava U.S.A.
44 F3 Avallon France
74 C5 Avalon U.S.A.
67 K4 Avalon Peninsula Can.
84 B1 Avalos Mex.
18 B2 Avān Iran
16 E2 Avanos Turkey
90 C3 Avaré Brazil
17 L2 Āvārsīn Iran
74 D4 Avawatz Mts mts U.S.A.
19 F3 Avaz Iran
87 G4 Aveiro Brazil
45 B2 Aveiro Port.
45 B2 Aveiro, Ria de est. Port.
17 M4 Āvej Iran
91 E2 Avellaneda Arg.
48 F4 Avellino Italy
74 B3 Avenal U.S.A.
8 E4 Avenel Austr.
42 C2 Avenhorn Neth.
48 F4 Aversa Italy
42 B4 Avesnes-sur-Helpe France
37 P6 Avesta Sweden
44 F4 Aveyron r. France
48 E3 Avezzano Italy
40 E3 Aviemore U.K.
48 F4 Avigliano Italy
44 G5 Avignon France
45 D2 Ávila Spain
45 D1 Avilés Spain
42 A4 Avion France
21 C5 Avissawella Sri Lanka
50 H2 Avnyugskiy Rus. Fed.
8 D4 Avoca Vic. Austr.
41 E5 Avoca Rep. of Ireland
76 E3 Avoca U.S.A.
8 D4 Avoca r. Vic. Austr.
48 F6 Avola Sicily Italy
68 B5 Avon U.S.A.
39 F5 Avon r. Eng. U.K.
39 F7 Avon r. Eng. U.K.
39 E6 Avon r. Eng. U.K.
75 F5 Avondale U.S.A.
39 E6 Avonmouth U.K.
79 D7 Avon Park U.S.A.
44 D2 Avranches France
42 A5 Avre r. France
7 G2 Avuavu Solomon Is
29 D7 Awaji-shima i. Japan
9 E3 Awakino N.Z.
18 C5 Awālī Bahrain
9 D1 Awanui N.Z.
9 B6 Awarua Pt pt N.Z.
56 E3 Āwash Eth.
56 D3 Āwash r. Eth.
28 F5 Awa-shima i. Japan
56 D3 Awash National Park Eth.
58 A2 Awasib Mts mts Namibia
9 D4 Awatere r. N.Z.
55 D2 Awbārī Libya
41 C5 Awbeg r. Rep. of Ireland
17 L6 'Awdah, Hawr al l. Iraq
56 E3 Aw Dheegle Somalia
55 E4 Aweil Sudan
40 C4 Awe, Loch l. U.K.
54 C4 Awka Nigeria
31 C6 Awu mt Indon.
8 E4 Axedale Austr.
63 J2 Axel Heiberg I. Can.
54 B4 Axim Ghana
39 E7 Axminster U.K.
42 C5 Ay France
29 D7 Ayabe Japan
91 E3 Ayacucho Arg.
86 D6 Ayacucho Peru
15 G2 Ayaguz Kazak.
24 A3 Ayakkum Hu l. China
45 C4 Ayamonte Spain
24 F1 Ayan Rus. Fed.
51 E7 Ayancık Turkey
30 C4 Ayang N. Korea
89 B2 Ayapel Col.
16 D1 Ayaş Turkey
86 D6 Ayaviri Peru
19 H2 Āybak Afgh.
51 F5 Aydar r. Ukr.
14 E2 Aydarkul', Ozero l. Uzbek.
16 A3 Aydın Turkey
16 A2 Aydın Dağları mts Turkey
32 Ayer Chawan, P. i. Sing.
32 Ayer Merbau, P. i. Sing.
6 D4 Ayers Rock h. Austr.
13 N3 Aykhal Rus. Fed.
50 J2 Aykino Rus. Fed.
9 D5 Aylesbury N.Z.
39 G6 Aylesbury U.K.
80 E6 Aylett U.S.A.
45 E2 Ayllón Spain
69 G4 Aylmer Can.
65 H2 Aylmer Lake l. Can.
18 C4 'Ayn al 'Abd well S. Arabia
19 H2 Ayní Tajik.
16 G3 'Ayn 'Īsá Syria
55 F4 Ayod Sudan
13 S3 Ayon, O. i. Rus. Fed.
54 B3 'Ayoûn el 'Atroûs Maur.
6 E3 Ayr Austr.
40 D5 Ayr U.K.
40 D5 Ayr r. U.K.
16 D3 Ayrancı Turkey
38 C3 Ayre, Point of pt Isle of Man
49 M3 Aytos Bulg.
32 B2 Ayutthaya Thai.
49 M5 Ayvacık Turkey
16 F2 Ayvalı Turkey
49 M5 Ayvalık Turkey
23 E4 Azamgarh India
54 B3 Azaouâd reg. Mali
54 C3 Azaouagh, Vallée de watercourse Mali/Niger
18 B2 Āzarān Iran

Azbine *mts see* Aïr, Massif de l'
16 D1 Azdavay Turkey
10 F5 Azerbaijan *country* Asia
18 B2 Āzghān Iran
69 G2 Azilda Can.
81 H2 Aziscohos Lake *l.* U.S.A.
86 C4 Azogues Ecuador
12 F3 Azopol'ye Rus. Fed.
34 C5 Azores *terr.* Europe
96 H3 Azores - Cape St Vincent Ridge *sea feature* Atl. Ocean
51 F6 Azov Rus. Fed.
51 F6 Azov, Sea of *sea* Rus. Fed./Ukr.
54 B1 Azrou Morocco
73 F4 Aztec U.S.A.
45 D3 Azuaga Spain
88 B3 Azucar *r.* Chile
83 H7 Azuero, Península de *pen.* Panama
91 E3 Azul Arg.
84 E3 Azul *r.* Mex.
91 B4 Azul, Cerro *mt* Arg.
86 C5 Azul, Cordillera *mts* Peru
90 A1 Azul, Serra *h.* Brazil
29 G6 Azuma-san *volc.* Japan
86 F8 Azurduy Bol.
48 B6 Azzaba Alg.
16 F5 Az Zabadānī Syria
17 J6 Az Zafīrī *reg.* Iraq
Az Zahrān *see* Dhahran
18 B5 Az Zilfī S. Arabia
17 L6 Az Zubayr Iraq

B

16 E5 Ba'abda Lebanon
16 F4 Ba'albek Lebanon
56 E3 Baardheere Somalia
49 M5 Baba Burnu *pt* Turkey
49 N2 Babadag Romania
17 M1 Babadağ *mt* Azer.
19 E2 Babadurmaz Turkm.
51 C7 Babaeski Turkey
86 C4 Babahoyo Ecuador
21 B1 Babai India
23 E3 Babai *r.* Nepal
26 B1 Babai Gaxun China
17 L2 Bābā Jān Iran
31 C5 Babak Phil.
19 H3 Bābā, Kūh-e *mts* Afgh.
20 B7 Bāb al Mandab *str.* Africa/Asia
25 E7 Babar *i.* Indon.
56 D4 Babati Tanz.
50 E3 Babayevo Rus. Fed.
51 H7 Babayurt Rus. Fed.
68 B2 Babbitt U.S.A.
70 F6 Babia *r.* Mex.
62 F4 Babine *r.* Can.
64 D4 Babine Lake *l.* Can.
25 F7 Babo Indon.
18 D2 Bābol Iran
58 C6 Baboon Point *pt* S. Africa
75 G6 Baboquivari Peak *summit* U.S.A.
56 B3 Baboua C.A.R.
50 D4 Babruysk Belarus
22 B4 Babuhri India
22 C2 Babusar Pass Pak.
31 A4 Babuyan Phil.
31 B2 Babuyan *i.* Phil.
27 F7 Babuyan Channel Phil.
31 B2 Babuyan Islands *is* Phil.
17 K5 Babylon Iraq
87 K4 Bacabal Brazil
16 C1 Bacakliyayla T. *mt* Turkey
25 E7 Bacan *i.* Indon.
31 B2 Bacarra Phil.
47 N7 Bacău Romania
8 E4 Bacchus Marsh Austr.
27 C6 Bắc Giang Vietnam
73 F6 Bachiniva Mex.
15 F3 Bachu China
65 J1 Back *r.* Can.
49 H2 Bačka Palanka Yugo.
64 D2 Backbone Ranges *mts* Can.
36 P5 Backe Sweden
40 E4 Backwater Reservoir U.K.
27 B6 Bac Lac Vietnam
32 C3 Bac Liêu Vietnam
27 C6 Bắc Ninh Vietnam
31 B4 Bacolod Phil.
31 B3 Baco, Mt *mt* Phil.
27 B6 Bắc Quang Vietnam
66 F2 Bacqueville, Lac *l.* Can.
43 L6 Bad Abbach Ger.
21 A4 Badagara India
26 A1 Badain Jaran Shamo *des.* China
86 F4 Badajós, Lago *l.* Brazil
45 C3 Badajoz Spain
21 A3 Badami India
17 H6 Badanah S. Arabia
23 H4 Badarpur India
69 F4 Bad Axe U.S.A.
43 F5 Bad Bergzabern Ger.
43 G3 Bad Berleburg Ger.
43 J1 Bad Bevensen Ger.
43 K4 Bad Blankenburg Ger.
43 G4 Bad Camberg Ger.
67 H4 Baddeck Can.
19 G4 Baddo *r.* Pak.
43 H3 Bad Driburg Ger.
43 L3 Bad Düben Ger.
43 G5 Bad Dürkheim Ger.
43 J3 Bad Dürrenberg Ger.
16 C3 Bademli Geçidi *pass* Turkey
43 F4 Bad Ems Ger.
46 H6 Baden Austria
46 D7 Baden Switz.
46 D6 Baden-Baden Ger.
40 D4 Badenoch *reg.* U.K.
43 G5 Baden-Württemberg *div.* Ger.
43 G2 Bad Essen Ger.
67 J4 Badger Can.
43 J3 Bad Grund (Harz) Ger.
43 J3 Bad Harzburg Ger.
43 H4 Bad Hersfeld Ger.
46 F7 Bad Hofgastein Austria
43 G4 Bad Homburg vor der Höhe Ger.
48 D2 Badia Polesine Italy
22 B4 Badin Pak.
84 A1 Badiraguato Mex.
46 F7 Bad Ischl Austria
Bādiyat ash Shām *des. see* Syrian Desert
43 J4 Bad Kissingen Ger.
43 K3 Bad Kösen Ger.
43 F5 Bad Kreuznach Ger.
43 G4 Bad Laasphe Ger.
76 C2 Badlands *reg.* U.S.A.
76 C3 Badlands Nat. Park U.S.A.
43 J3 Bad Langensalza Ger.
43 J3 Bad Lauterberg im Harz Ger.
43 G3 Bad Lippspringe Ger.
43 F4 Bad Marienberg Ger.
43 H5 Bad Mergentheim Ger.
43 G4 Bad Nauheim Ger.
42 F4 Bad Neuenahr-Ahrweiler Ger.
43 J4 Bad Neustadt an der Saale Ger.
43 J1 Bad Oldesloe Ger.
26 D4 Badong China
32 C3 Ba Đông Vietnam
43 H3 Bad Pyrmont Ger.
17 K5 Badrah Iraq
46 F7 Bad Reichenhall Ger.
22 D3 Badrinath Peaks *mts* India
43 J3 Bad Sachsa Ger.
43 J2 Bad Salzdetfurth Ger.
43 G2 Bad Salzuflen Ger.
43 J4 Bad Salzungen Ger.
43 G4 Bad Schwalbach Ger.
43 J1 Bad Schwartau Ger.
46 E4 Bad Segeberg Ger.
6 E3 Badu I. *i.* Austr.
21 C5 Badulla Sri Lanka
43 G4 Bad Vilbel Ger.
43 K2 Bad Wilsnack Ger.
43 J5 Bad Windsheim Ger.
43 G1 Bad Zwischenahn Ger.
36 B3 Bæir Iceland
8 H2 Baerami Austr.
42 E4 Baesweiler Ger.
45 E4 Baeza Spain
54 D4 Bafang Cameroon
54 A3 Bafatá Guinea-Bissau
63 M2 Baffin Bay *b.* Can./Greenland
63 L2 Baffin Island *i.* Can.
54 D4 Bafia Cameroon
54 A3 Bafing, Parc National du *nat. park* Mali
54 A3 Bafoulabé Mali
54 D4 Bafoussam Cameroon
18 D4 Bāfq Iran
16 E1 Bafra Turkey
51 E7 Bafra Burnu *pt* Turkey
18 E4 Bāft Iran
56 C3 Bafwasende Congo(Zaire)
23 F4 Bagaha India
31 A5 Bagahak, Mt *h.* Malaysia
21 A2 Bagalkot India
56 D4 Bagamoyo Tanz.
33 B2 Bagan Datuk Malaysia
57 C5 Bagani Namibia
32 B4 Bagan Serai Malaysia
32 B5 Bagansiapiapi Indon.
75 F4 Bagdad U.S.A.
91 F1 Bagé Brazil
22 D3 Bageshwar India
72 F3 Baggs U.S.A.
39 C6 Baggy Point *pt* U.K.
22 C5 Bagh India
19 F2 Baghbaghū Iran
17 K5 Baghdād Iraq
18 C4 Bāgh-e Malek Iran
19 H2 Baghlān Afgh.
19 G3 Baghrān Afgh.
76 E2 Bagley U.S.A.
23 E3 Baglung Nepal
45 G1 Bagnères-de-Luchon France
44 G4 Bagnols-sur-Cèze France
23 F4 Bagnuiti *r.* Nepal
26 C2 Bag Nur *l.* China
Bago *see* Pegu
31 B4 Bago Phil.
47 K3 Bagrationovsk Rus. Fed.
31 C5 Baguio Phil.
31 B2 Baguio Phil.
22 D3 Bahadurgarh India
Bahāmabād *see* Rafsanjān
61 L7 Bahamas, The *country* Caribbean Sea
23 G4 Baharampur India
55 E2 Bahariya Oasis *oasis* Egypt
33 B2 Bahau Malaysia
22 C3 Bahawalnagar Pak.
22 B3 Bahawalpur Pak.
16 F3 Bahçe Turkey
26 C4 Ba He *r.* China
23 D3 Baheri India
56 D4 Bahi Tanz.
90 E1 Bahia *div.* Brazil
91 D3 Bahía Blanca Arg.
82 G5 Bahía, Islas de la *is* Honduras
88 C7 Bahía Laura Arg.
88 E2 Bahía Negra Para.
56 D2 Bahir Dar Eth.
18 C4 Bahmanyārī ye Pā'īn Iran
23 E4 Bahraich India
10 G7 Bahrain *country* Asia
18 C5 Bahrain, Gulf of *g.* Asia
17 M3 Bahrāmābād Iran
18 E4 Bahrāmjerd Iran
Bahr el Azraq *r. see* Blue Nile
19 F5 Bāhū Kālāt Iran
47 L7 Baia Mare Romania
18 D3 Baiazeh Iran
24 E2 Baicheng China
67 G4 Baie Comeau Can.
66 F3 Baie du Poste Can.
67 F4 Baie Saint Paul Can.
67 J4 Baie Verte Can.
26 E2 Baigou *r.* China
22 E5 Baihar India
26 D3 Baihe *Shaanxi* China
30 E2 Baihe China
17 J4 Baiji Iraq
24 C1 Baikal, Lake *l.* Rus. Fed.
49 K2 Băileşti Romania
49 K2 Băileştilor, Câmpia *plain* Romania
42 A4 Bailleul France
65 H2 Baillie *r.* Can.
41 E4 Baillieborough Rep. of Ireland
26 B3 Bailong Jiang *r.* China
24 C3 Baima China
39 G4 Bain *r.* U.K.
79 C6 Bainbridge *GA* U.S.A.
81 F3 Bainbridge *NY* U.S.A.
23 G3 Baingoin China
22 E2 Bairab Co *l.* China
23 F4 Bairagnia India
62 C3 Baird Mountains U.S.A.
4 J4 Bairiki *i.* Kiribati
26 F1 Bairing Qiao China
26 F1 Bairin Youqi China
26 F1 Bairin Zuoqi China
8 F4 Bairnsdale Austr.
16 F6 Bā'ir, Wādī *watercourse* Jordan
31 B4 Bais Phil.
27 C7 Baisha *Hainan* China
27 E5 Baisha *Jiangxi* China
26 C4 Baisha *Sichuan* China
30 D2 Baishan China
26 B3 Baishui Jiang *r.* China
27 B7 Bai Thương Vietnam
26 E1 Baitle *r.* China
30 A2 Baixingt China
26 B2 Baiyin China
55 F3 Baiyuda Desert *des.* Sudan
49 H1 Baja Hungary
82 A2 Baja California *pen.* Mex.
70 C6 Baja California Norte *div.* Mex.
70 D6 Baja California Sur *div.* Mex.
17 M3 Bājalān Iran
22 E3 Bajang Nepal
23 G5 Baj Baj India
19 E2 Bājgīrān Iran
89 A3 Bajo Baudó Col.
91 D1 Bajo Hondo Arg.
54 A3 Bakel Senegal
74 D4 Baker *CA* U.S.A.
72 F2 Baker *MT* U.S.A.
75 E2 Baker *NV* U.S.A.
72 C2 Baker *OR* U.S.A.
75 G4 Baker Butte *summit* U.S.A.
64 C3 Baker I. *i.* U.S.A.
7 J1 Baker Island *i.* Pac. Oc.
65 K2 Baker Lake Can.
65 K2 Baker Lake *l.* Can.
72 B1 Baker, Mt *volc.* U.S.A.
66 E2 Bakers Dozen Islands *is* Can.
74 C4 Bakersfield U.S.A.
32 C2 Bâ Kêv Cambodia
18 E2 Bakharden Turkm.
19 E2 Bakhardok Turkm.
19 F3 Bākharz *mts* Iran
22 B4 Bakhasar India
51 E6 Bakhchysaray Ukr.
51 E5 Bakhmach Ukr.
18 D4 Bakhtegan, Daryācheh-ye *l.* Iran
Bakı *see* Baku
16 B1 Bakırköy Turkey
56 D3 Bako Eth.
56 C3 Bakouma C.A.R.
56 B4 Bakoumba Gabon
51 G7 Baksan Rus. Fed.
17 M1 Baku Azer.
56 D3 Baku Congo(Zaire)
92 A4 Bakutis Coast *coastal area* Ant.
16 D2 Balâ Turkey
39 D5 Bala U.K.
31 A4 Balabac Phil.
31 A5 Balabac *i.* Phil.
33 E1 Balabac Strait *str.* Malaysia/Phil.
86 E6 Bala, Cerros de *mts* Bol.
17 K4 Balad Iraq
18 C2 Baladeh Iran
18 C4 Bāladeh Iran
18 C2 Baladeh Iran
22 E5 Balaghat India
21 A2 Balaghat Range *h.* India
19 E4 Bālā Ḥowz Iran
17 L1 Balakän Azer.
50 G3 Balakhna Rus. Fed.
8 B3 Balaklava Austr.
51 E6 Balaklava Ukr.
51 F5 Balakliya Ukr.
51 H4 Balakovo Rus. Fed.
33 E1 Balambangan *i.* Malaysia
19 F3 Bālā Morghāb Afgh.
22 B4 Bālān India
51 H5 Balanda *r.* Rus. Fed.
16 B3 Balan Dağı *mt* Turkey
31 B3 Balanga Phil.
23 E5 Balāngīr India
21 C5 Balangoda Sri Lanka
51 G5 Balashov Rus. Fed.
22 C5 Balasinor India
46 H7 Balaton *l.* Hungary
46 H7 Balatonboglár Hungary
46 H7 Balatonfüred Hungary
87 G4 Balbina, Represa de *resr* Brazil
41 E4 Balbriggan Rep. of Ireland
91 E3 Balcarce Arg.
49 N3 Balchik Bulg.
9 B7 Balclutha N.Z.
77 F5 Bald Knob U.S.A.
75 E3 Bald Mtn *mt* U.S.A.
65 K3 Baldock Lake *l.* Can.
69 H3 Baldwin Can.
79 D6 Baldwin *FL* U.S.A.
68 E4 Baldwin *MI* U.S.A.
68 A3 Baldwin *WI* U.S.A.
81 E3 Baldwinsville U.S.A.
75 H5 Baldy Peak *mt* U.S.A.
Baleares, Islas *is see* Balearic Islands
45 H3 Balearic Islands *is* Spain
33 D2 Baleh *r.* Malaysia
90 E2 Baleia, Ponta da *pt* Brazil
67 G2 Baleine, Rivière à la *r.* Can.
56 D3 Bale Mts National Park Eth.
31 B3 Baler Phil.
31 B3 Baler Bay *b.* Phil.
23 F5 Bāleshwar India
37 K6 Balestrand Norway
9 B6 Balfour N.Z.
33 E4 Bali *i.* Indon.
33 A2 Balige Indon.
23 E5 Baliguda India
26 F1 Balihan China
16 A2 Balıkesir Turkey
33 E3 Balikpapan Indon.
31 A5 Balimbing Phil.
21 C2 Balimila Reservoir India
6 E2 Balimo P.N.G.
46 D6 Balingen Ger.
31 B2 Balintang Channel *chan.* Phil.
40 E3 Balintore U.K.
33 E4 Bali Sea *g.* Indon.
31 B5 Baliungan *i.* Phil.
19 H2 Baljuvon Tajik.
42 D2 Balk Neth.
49 K3 Balkan Mountains Bulg./Yugo.
19 G2 Balkhab *r.* Afgh.
15 F2 Balkhash Kazak.
15 F2 Balkhash, Ozero *l.* Kazak.
51 H6 Balkuduk Kazak.
40 C4 Ballachulish U.K.
6 C5 Balladonia Austr.
8 G1 Balladoran Austr.
41 C4 Ballaghaderreen Rep. of Ireland
8 E4 Ballan Austr.
36 P2 Ballangen Norway
72 E2 Ballantine U.S.A.
40 D5 Ballantrae U.K.
8 D4 Ballarat Austr.
6 C4 Ballard, L. *salt flat* Austr.
22 C6 Ballarpur India
40 E3 Ballater U.K.
54 E3 Ballé Mali
88 B3 Ballena, Pta *pt* Chile
92 A6 Balleny Is *is* Ant.
23 F4 Ballia India
7 F4 Ballina Austr.
41 B3 Ballina Rep. of Ireland
41 C3 Ballinafad Rep. of Ireland
41 D4 Ballinalack Rep. of Ireland
41 D3 Ballinamore Rep. of Ireland
41 C4 Ballinasloe Rep. of Ireland
41 C4 Ballindine Rep. of Ireland
77 D6 Ballinger U.S.A.
40 E4 Ballinluig U.K.
41 B4 Ballinrobe Rep. of Ireland
81 G3 Ballston Spa U.S.A.
41 E3 Ballybay Rep. of Ireland
41 A6 Ballybrack Rep. of Ireland
41 B5 Ballybunnion Rep. of Ireland
41 E5 Ballycanew Rep. of Ireland
41 B3 Ballycastle Rep. of Ireland
41 E2 Ballycastle U.K.
41 F3 Ballyclare U.K.
41 A4 Ballyconneely Bay *b.* Rep. of Ireland
41 D3 Ballyconnell Rep. of Ireland
41 C4 Ballygar Rep. of Ireland
41 D3 Ballygawley U.K.
41 D2 Ballygorman Rep. of Ireland
41 C4 Ballyhaunis Rep. of Ireland
41 B5 Ballyheigue Rep. of Ireland
41 C5 Ballyhoura Mts *h.* Rep. of Ireland
41 D2 Ballykelly U.K.
41 D5 Ballylynan Rep. of Ireland
41 D5 Ballymacmague Rep. of Ireland
41 D4 Ballymahon Rep. of Ireland
41 E3 Ballymena U.K.
41 E2 Ballymoney U.K.
41 C3 Ballymote Rep. of Ireland
41 F3 Ballynahinch U.K.
41 C3 Ballyshannon Rep. of Ireland
41 E5 Ballyteige Bay *b.* Rep. of Ireland
41 B4 Ballyvaughan Rep. of Ireland
41 E3 Ballyward U.K.
40 A3 Balmartin U.K.
Balmer *see* Barmer
8 C4 Balmoral Austr.
77 C6 Balmorhea U.S.A.
19 G4 Balochistān *div.* Pak.
22 E5 Balod India
23 E5 Baloda Bazar India
6 E4 Balonne *r.* Austr.
22 C4 Balotra India
23 E4 Balrampur India
8 D3 Balranald Austr.
49 L2 Balş Romania
69 H2 Balsam Creek Can.
87 J5 Balsas Brazil
84 C3 Balsas Mex.
84 B3 Balsas *r.* Mex.
51 D6 Balta Ukr.
50 J3 Baltasi Rus. Fed.
40 □ Baltasound U.K.
22 D2 Baltero Gl. *gl.* Pak.
51 C6 Bălţi Moldova
12 C4 Baltic Sea *g.* Europe
16 C6 Balṭīm Egypt
59 H1 Baltimore S. Africa
80 E5 Baltimore U.S.A.
41 E5 Baltinglass Rep. of Ireland
22 C2 Baltistan *reg.* Jammu and Kashmir
47 J3 Baltiysk Rus. Fed.
19 E4 Baluch Ab *well* Iran
23 G4 Balurghat India
31 C5 Balut *i.* Phil.
43 F3 Balve Ger.
37 U8 Balvi Latvia
49 M5 Balya Turkey
14 D2 Balykshi Kazak.
19 E4 Bam Iran
19 E2 Bām Iran
27 C5 Bama China
6 E3 Bamaga Austr.
66 B3 Bamaji L. *l.* Can.
54 B3 Bamako Mali
54 B3 Bamba Mali
31 B2 Bambang Phil.
56 C3 Bambari C.A.R.
32 A5 Bambel Indon.
43 J5 Bamberg Ger.
79 D5 Bamberg U.S.A.
56 C3 Bambili Congo(Zaire)
59 G5 Bamboesberg *mts* S. Africa
56 C3 Bambouti C.A.R.
90 D3 Bambuí Brazil
17 M6 Bāmdezh Iran
54 D4 Bamenda Cameroon
18 E2 Bami Turkm.
19 G3 Bāmīān Afgh.
30 C2 Bamiancheng China
56 C3 Bamingui-Bangoran, Parc National de *nat. park* C.A.R.
19 F5 Bam Posht *reg.* Iran
19 F5 Bam Posht, Kūh-e *mts* Iran
39 D7 Bampton U.K.
19 F5 Bampūr Iran
19 E5 Bampūr *watercourse* Iran
19 F3 Bamrūd Iran
7 G2 Banaba *i.* Kiribati
87 L5 Banabuiu, Açude *resr* Brazil
91 C3 Bañados del Atuel *marsh* Arg.
86 F7 Bañados del Izozog *swamp* Bol.
41 D4 Banagher Rep. of Ireland
56 C3 Banalia Congo(Zaire)
59 K1 Banamana, Lagoa *l.* Moz.
54 B3 Banamba Mali
87 H6 Bananal, Ilha do *i.* Brazil
23 F6 Bānapur India
32 B2 Ban Aranyaprathet Thai.
22 D4 Banas *r.* India
16 B2 Banaz Turkey
32 B1 Ban Ban Laos
23 H3 Banbar China
32 B4 Ban Betong Thai.
41 E3 Banbridge U.K.
32 B2 Ban Bua Yai Thai.
39 F5 Banbury U.K.
31 A4 Bancalan *i.* Phil.
54 A2 Banc d'Arguin, Parc National du *nat. park* Maur.
32 A1 Ban Chiang Dao Thai.
40 F3 Banchory U.K.
82 G5 Banco Chinchorro *is* Mex.
31 A5 Bancoran *i.* Phil.
69 J3 Bancroft Can.
19 E3 Band Iran
56 C3 Banda Congo(Zaire)
22 E4 Banda India
33 A1 Banda Aceh Indon.
22 B2 Banda Daud Shah Pak.
32 A5 Bandahara, G. *mt* Indon.
29 F6 Bandai-Asahi National Park Japan
25 E7 Banda, Kepulauan *is* Indon.
19 F4 Bandān Iran
19 F4 Bandān Kūh *mts* Iran
Bandar *see* Machilipatnam
23 H5 Bandarban Bangl.
18 E5 Bandar-e 'Abbās Iran
18 C2 Bandar-e Anzalī Iran
18 C4 Bandar-e Deylam Iran
18 D5 Bandar-e Khoemir Iran
18 D5 Bandar-e Lengeh Iran
18 D5 Bandar-e Māqām Iran
18 C4 Bandar-e Ma'shur Iran
18 C4 Bandar-e Rīg Iran
Bandar-e Shāhpūr *see* Bandar Khomeynī
18 D2 Bandar-e Torkeman Iran
18 C4 Bandar Khomeynī Iran
22 D3 Bandarpunch *mt* India
33 D1 Bandar Seri Begawan Brunei
25 F7 Banda Sea Indon.
19 E5 Band Bonī Iran
18 D5 Band-e Chārak Iran
90 B1 Bandeirante Brazil
90 E3 Bandeiras, Pico de *mt* Brazil
59 H1 Bandelierkop S. Africa
18 D5 Band-e Moghūyeh Iran
84 A2 Banderas, Bahía de *b.* Mex.
18 D3 Band-e Sar Qom Iran
22 C4 Bandi *r. Rajasthan* India
22 E6 Bandia *r.* India
54 B3 Bandiagara Mali
19 G3 Band-i-Amir *r.* Afgh.
19 F3 Band-i-Baba *mts* Afgh.
16 A1 Bandırma Turkey
19 F3 Band-i-Turkestan *mts* Afgh.
41 C6 Bandon Rep. of Ireland
Ban Don *see* Surat Thani
41 C6 Bandon *r.* Rep. of Ireland
17 M2 Bāndovan Burnu *pt* Azer.
17 M6 Band Qīr Iran
56 B4 Bandundu Congo(Zaire)
33 C4 Bandung Indon.
18 B3 Bāneh Iran
83 J4 Banes Cuba
64 F4 Banff Can.
40 F3 Banff U.K.
64 F4 Banff National Park Can.
54 B3 Banfora Burkina
56 C4 Banga Congo(Zaire)
31 C5 Banga Phil.
31 C5 Bangai Point *pt* Phil.
21 B3 Bangalore India
22 D4 Banganga *r.* India
23 G5 Bangaon India
31 B2 Bangar Phil.
56 C3 Bangassou C.A.R.
23 E2 Bangdag Co *salt l.* China
32 C1 Bangfai, Xée *r.* Laos
6 C2 Banggai Indon.
25 E7 Banggai, Kepulauan *is* Indon.
33 E1 Banggi *i.* Malaysia
55 E1 Banghāzī Libya
32 C1 Banghiang, Xé *r.* Laos
33 C3 Bangka *i.* Indon.
33 D4 Bangkalan Indon.
32 A5 Bangkaru *i.* Indon.
33 B3 Bangko Indon.
23 G3 Bangkog Co *salt l.* China
32 B2 Bangkok Thai.
32 B2 Bangkok, Bight of *b.* Thai.
10 K7 Bangladesh *country* Asia
54 B4 Bangolo Côte d'Ivoire
22 D2 Bangong Co *l.* China
41 F3 Bangor *N. Ireland* U.K.
39 C4 Bangor *Wales* U.K.
81 J2 Bangor *ME* U.S.A.
68 D4 Bangor *MI* U.S.A.
81 F4 Bangor *PA* U.S.A.
41 B3 Bangor Erris Rep. of Ireland
32 A3 Bang Saphan Yai Thai.
75 F3 Bangs, Mt *mt* U.S.A.
36 M4 Bangsund Norway
31 B2 Bangued Phil.
56 B3 Bangui C.A.R.
31 B2 Bangui Phil.
32 A5 Bangunpurba Indon.
57 C5 Bangweulu, Lake *l.* Zambia
32 B4 Ban Hat Yai Thai.
57 D6 Banhine, Parque Nacional de *nat. park* Moz.
32 B1 Ban Hin Heup Laos
32 A2 Ban Hua Hin Thai.
56 C3 Bani C.A.R.
31 A2 Bani Phil.
56 B3 Bania C.A.R.
18 D5 Banī Forūr, Jazīrah-ye *i.* Iran
22 C2 Banihal Pass and Tunnel Jammu and Kashmir
80 D6 Banister *r.* U.S.A.
55 D1 Banī Walīd Libya
18 C5 Banī Wuṭayfān *well* S. Arabia
16 E4 Bāniyās Syria
16 E5 Bāniyās Syria
48 G2 Banja Luka Bos.-Herz.
22 D3 Banjar India
33 D3 Banjarmasin Indon.
54 A3 Banjul The Gambia
17 M2 Bankä Azer.
23 F4 Banka India
32 A4 Ban Kantang Thai.
21 A3 Bankapur India
54 B3 Bankass Mali
32 A2 Ban Khao Yoi Thai.
32 C1 Ban Khemmarat Thai.
32 A3 Ban Khok Kloi Thai.
32 A1 Ban Khun Yuam Thai.
23 F5 Banki India
62 F2 Banks Island *N.W.T.* Can.
62 E4 Banks Island *i. B.C.* Can.
7 G3 Banks Islands *is* Vanuatu
72 C2 Banks L. *l.* U.S.A.
65 L2 Banks Lake *l.* Can.
9 D5 Banks Peninsula *pen.* N.Z.
32 A2 Ban Kui Nua Thai.
23 F5 Bankura India
32 A1 Ban Mae Sariang Thai.
32 A1 Ban Mae Sot Thai.
32 B1 Ban Mouang Laos
32 B2 Ban Muang Phon Thai.
41 E5 Bann *r.* Rep. of Ireland
41 E3 Bann *r.* U.K.
32 C1 Ban Na Kae Thai.
32 C1 Ban Nakham Laos
32 B1 Ban Na Noi Thai.
32 A3 Ban Na San Thai.
32 B4 Ban Na Thawi Thai.
68 C5 Banner U.S.A.
79 E7 Bannerman Town Bahamas
74 D5 Banning U.S.A.
91 B3 Baños Maule Chile
32 B1 Ban Pak-Leng Laos
32 B3 Ban Pak Phanang Thai.
32 B2 Ban Pak Thong Chai Thai.
32 C1 Ban Phaeng Thai.
32 B1 Ban Phai Thai.
32 B2 Ban Phanat Nikhom Thai.
32 C2 Ban Phon Laos
32 B1 Ban Phon Thong Thai.
32 A2 Banphot Phisai Thai.
32 A2 Ban Pong Thai.
32 B1 Ban Pua Thai.
32 A1 Ban Saraphi Thai.
32 B2 Ban Sattahip Thai.
32 A3 Ban Sawi Thai.
23 E4 Bansi India
32 A3 Ban Sichon Thai.
32 B2 Ban Si Racha Thai.
47 J6 Banská Bystrica Slovakia
32 A1 Ban Sut Ta Thai.
21 B2 Banswada India
22 C5 Banswara India
32 A3 Ban Takua Pa Thai.
31 B4 Bantayan *i.* Phil.
41 C5 Banteer Rep. of Ireland
32 A3 Ban Tha Chang Thai.
32 A1 Ban Tha Don Thai.
32 A3 Ban Thai Muang Thai.
32 A3 Ban Tha Kham Thai.
32 A1 Ban Tha Song Yang Thai.
32 B2 Ban Tha Tako Thai.
32 B2 Ban Tha Tum Thai.
32 C1 Ban Tha Uthen Thai.
32 A2 Ban Thung Luang Thai.
31 B3 Banton *i.* Phil.
32 C1 Ban Tôp Laos
41 B6 Bantry Rep. of Ireland
41 B6 Bantry Bay *b.* Rep. of Ireland
21 A3 Bantval India
32 B1 Ban Woen Laos
33 A2 Banyak, Pulau Pulau *is* Indon.
54 D4 Banyo Cameroon
45 H1 Banyoles Spain
33 D4 Banyuwangi Indon.
92 C6 Banzare Coast *coastal area* Ant.
93 J7 Banzare Seamount *sea feature* Ind. Ocean
43 K1 Banzkow Ger.
26 B3 Bao'an China
26 E2 Baoding China
26 D3 Baofeng China
26 C3 Baoji China
27 C4 Baojing China
26 D4 Baokang China
30 E1 Baolin China
30 B2 Baolizhen China
32 C3 Bao Lôc Vietnam
28 C1 Baoqing China
24 B4 Baoshan China
26 D1 Baotou China
27 B4 Baoxing China
26 F3 Baoying China
22 C4 Bap India
21 C3 Bapatla India
42 A4 Bapaume France
69 H3 Baptiste Lake *l.* Can.
23 H2 Baqêm China
23 H3 Baqên China
17 K5 Ba'qūbah Iraq
86 □ Baquerizo Moreno *Galapagos Is* Ecuador
49 H3 Bar Yugo.
55 F3 Bara Sudan
56 E3 Baraawe Somalia
23 F4 Barabar Hills *h.* India
68 C4 Baraboo U.S.A.
68 B4 Baraboo *r.* U.S.A.
83 K4 Baracoa Cuba
91 E2 Baradero Arg.
8 G1 Baradine Austr.
8 G1 Baradine *r.* Austr.
68 C2 Baraga U.S.A.
23 E5 Baragarh India
89 C2 Baragua Venez.
83 K5 Barahona Dom. Rep.
23 H4 Barail Range *mts* India
23 H4 Barak *r.* India
56 D2 Baraka *watercourse* Eritrea/Sudan
45 E1 Barakaldo Spain
19 H3 Barakī Barak Afgh.
23 F5 Barākot India
22 D2 Bara Lacha Pass *pass* India
17 J5 Bar al Milḥ *l.* Iraq
65 K3 Baralzon Lake *l.* Can.
21 A2 Baramati India
22 D4 Baran India
22 B4 Baran *r.* Pak.
50 C4 Baranavichy Belarus
13 S3 Baranikha Rus. Fed.
51 C5 Baranivka Ukr.
19 F3 Bārān, Kūh-e *mts* Iran
89 B2 Baranoa Col.
64 B3 Baranof Island *i.* U.S.A.
90 A2 Barão de Melgaço Brazil
54 B3 Baraouéli Mali
42 D4 Baraque de Fraiture *h.* Belgium
25 E7 Barat Daya, Kepulauan *is* Indon.
8 B2 Baratta Austr.
22 D3 Baraut India
89 B4 Baraya Col.
90 D3 Barbacena Brazil
89 A4 Barbacoas Col.
61 N8 Barbados *country* Caribbean Sea
45 G1 Barbastro Spain
45 D4 Barbate de Franco Spain
74 □1 Barbers Pt *pt* U.S.A.
59 J2 Barberton S. Africa
80 C4 Barberton U.S.A.
44 D4 Barbezieux-St-Hilaire France
89 B3 Barbosa Col.
65 L2 Barbour Bay *b.* Can.
80 B6 Barbourville U.S.A.
31 B4 Barboza Phil.
83 M5 Barbuda *i.* Antigua
43 K3 Barby (Elbe) Ger.
6 E4 Barcaldine Austr.
45 H2 Barcelona Spain
89 D2 Barcelona Venez.
86 F4 Barcelos Brazil
43 J4 Barchfeld Ger.
54 B4 Barclayville Liberia
48 G2 Barcs Hungary
17 L1 Bärdä Azer.
36 E4 Bárðarbunga *mt* Iceland
91 C2 Bardas Blancas Arg.
23 F5 Barddhamān India
47 K6 Bardejov Slovakia
18 C5 Bardestān Iran
32 C2 Bar Đôn Vietnam
39 C5 Bardsey Island *i.* U.K.
78 C4 Bardstown U.S.A.
80 B5 Bardwell U.S.A.
22 D3 Bareilly India
12 C2 Barentsburg Svalbard
12 D2 Barentsøya *i.* Svalbard
12 F2 Barents Sea *sea* Arctic Ocean
56 D2 Barentu Eritrea
22 E3 Barga China
22 D5 Bargi India
40 D5 Bargrennan U.K.
43 J1 Bargteheide Ger.
23 G5 Barguna Bangl.
81 J2 Bar Harbor U.S.A.
48 G4 Bari Italy
32 C3 Ba Ria Vietnam
22 C3 Bari Doab *lowland* Pak.
23 E3 Barikot Nepal
89 E2 Barima *r.* Venez.
89 C2 Barinas Venez.
23 G5 Barisal Bangl.
33 B3 Barisan, Pegunungan *mts* Indon.
33 D3 Barito *r.* Indon.
86 F8 Baritu, Parque Nacional *nat. park* Arg.
19 E6 Barkā Oman
26 B4 Barkam China
18 C4 Barkan, Ra's-e *pt* Iran
37 U8 Barkava Latvia
64 E4 Barkerville Can.
78 C4 Barkley, L. *l.* U.S.A.
64 D5 Barkley Sd *in.* Can.
59 G5 Barkly East S. Africa
6 D3 Barkly Tableland *reg.* Austr.
58 F4 Barkly West S. Africa
24 B2 Barkol China
22 D3 Barkot India
18 E4 Barkūh Iran
47 N7 Bârlad Romania
44 G2 Bar-le-Duc France
6 B4 Barlee, L. *salt flat* Austr.
48 G4 Barletta Italy
8 F3 Barmedman Austr.
22 B4 Barmer India
8 C3 Barmera Austr.
39 C5 Barmouth U.K.
22 C3 Barnala India
38 F3 Barnard Castle U.K.
8 E1 Barnato Austr.
12 K4 Barnaul Rus. Fed.
81 F5 Barnegat U.S.A.
81 F5 Barnegat Bay *b.* U.S.A.
80 D4 Barnesboro U.S.A.
63 L2 Barnes Icecap *ice cap* Can.
42 D2 Barneveld Neth.
8 E2 Barneys Lake *l.* Austr.
75 G3 Barney Top *mt* U.S.A.
77 C6 Barnhart U.S.A.
38 F4 Barnsley U.K.
39 C6 Barnstaple U.K.
Barnstaple Bay *b. see* Bideford Bay
43 G2 Barnstorf Ger.
79 D5 Barnwell U.S.A.
Baroda *see* Vadodara
22 C1 Baroghil Pass Afgh.
23 H4 Barpathar India
23 G4 Barpeta India
68 D3 Barques, Pt Aux *pt MI* U.S.A.
69 F3 Barques, Pt Aux *pt MI* U.S.A.
89 C2 Barquisimeto Venez.
87 K6 Barra Brazil
40 A4 Barra *i.* U.K.
58 D7 Barracouta, Cape *hd* S. Africa
87 G6 Barra do Bugres Brazil
87 J5 Barra do Corda Brazil
90 B1 Barra do Garças Brazil
87 G5 Barra do São Manuel Brazil
86 C6 Barranca *Lima* Peru
86 C4 Barranca *Loreto* Peru
89 B3 Barranca-bermeja Col.
89 B2 Barrancas Col.
89 E2 Barrancas Venez.
91 B3 Barrancas *r. Mendoza/Neuquén* Arg.
88 E3 Barranqueras Arg.
89 B2 Barranquilla Col.
40 A3 Barra, Sound of *chan.* U.K.
81 G2 Barre U.S.A.
91 C1 Barreal Arg.
87 K6 Barreiras Brazil
87 G4 Barreirinha Brazil
87 K4 Barreirinhas Brazil
45 B3 Barreiro Port.
90 B1 Barreiro *r.* Brazil
87 L5 Barreiros Brazil
90 C3 Barretos Brazil
64 G4 Barrhead Can.
40 D5 Barrhead U.K.
69 H3 Barrie Can.
69 F3 Barrie I *i.* Can.
64 E4 Barrière Can.
8 C1 Barrier Range *h.* Austr.
65 J3 Barrington Lake *l.* Can.
8 H2 Barrington, Mt Austr.
68 B3 Barron U.S.A.
77 C7 Barroterán Mex.
91 E3 Barrow Arg.
62 C2 Barrow *AK* U.S.A.
41 E5 Barrow *r.* Rep. of Ireland
6 D4 Barrow Creek Austr.
6 B4 Barrow I. *i.* Austr.
38 D3 Barrow-in-Furness U.K.
62 C2 Barrow, Point *c.* U.S.A.
63 J2 Barrow Strait *str.* Can.
39 D6 Barry U.K.
58 D6 Barrydale S. Africa
69 J3 Barrys Bay Can.
22 C3 Barsalpur India
21 A2 Barsi India
22 D5 Barsi Takli India
43 H2 Barsinghausen Ger.
74 D4 Barstow U.S.A.
44 G2 Bar-sur-Aube France
46 F3 Barth Ger.
87 G2 Bartica Guyana
16 D1 Bartın Turkey
6 E3 Bartle Frere, Mt *mt* Austr.
75 G2 Bartles, Mt *mt* U.S.A.
71 G4 Bartlesville *OK* U.S.A.
76 D3 Bartlett *NE* U.S.A.
81 H2 Bartlett *NH* U.S.A.
64 F2 Bartlett Lake *l.* Can.
81 G2 Barton U.S.A.
38 G4 Barton-upon-Humber U.K.
47 K3 Bartoszyce Pol.
33 B2 Barumun *r.* Indon.
33 D4 Barung *i.* Indon.
32 A5 Barus Indon.
26 B1 Baruunsuu Mongolia
24 D2 Baruun Urt Mongolia
83 H7 Barú, Volcán *volc.* Panama
22 D5 Barwah India
22 C3 Barwala India
22 C5 Barwani India
6 E5 Barwon *r.* Austr.
50 D4 Barysaw Belarus
50 H4 Barysh Rus. Fed.
50 H4 Barysh *r.* Rus. Fed.
18 C3 Barzūk Iran
18 D5 Basaidu Iran
74 C2 Basalt U.S.A.
27 □ Basalt I. *i. H.K.* China
56 B3 Basankusu Congo(Zaire)
21 B2 Basar India

49 N2 Basarabi Romania
91 E2 Basavilbaso Arg.
31 B4 Basay Phil.
31 B1 Basco Phil.
46 C7 Basel Switz.
68 B1 Basewood Lake l. U.S.A.
19 E5 Bashākerd, Kūhhā-ye mts Iran
64 G4 Bashaw Can.
59 H6 Bashee r. S. Africa
19 H3 Bashgul r. Afgh.
50 G4 Bashmakovo Rus. Fed.
18 C4 Bāsht Iran
51 E6 Bashtanka Ukr.
22 D4 Basi India
23 F5 Basia India
31 B5 Basilan i. Phil.
31 B5 Basilan Strait chan. Phil.
39 H6 Basildon U.K.
72 E2 Basin U.S.A.
39 F6 Basingstoke U.K.
17 K4 Bāsīra r. Iraq
23 G5 Basirhat India
81 K2 Baskahegan Lake l. U.S.A.
17 K2 Başkale Turkey
69 K2 Baskatong, Réservoir resr Can.
51 H5 Baskunchak, Ozero l. Rus. Fed.
Basle see Basel
22 D5 Basoda India
56 C3 Basoko Congo(Zaire)
17 L6 Basra Iraq
48 D2 Bassano del Grappa Italy
54 C4 Bassar Togo
57 D6 Bassas da India i. Ind. Ocean
25 B5 Bassein Myanmar
38 D3 Bassenthwaite Lake l. U.K.
54 A3 Basse Santa Su The Gambia
83 M5 Basse Terre Guadeloupe
83 M5 Basseterre St Kitts-Nevis
76 D3 Bassett U.S.A.
75 G5 Bassett Peak summit U.S.A.
81 J2 Bass Harbor U.S.A.
54 B3 Bassikounou Maur.
54 C4 Bassila Benin
40 F4 Bass Rock i. U.K.
6 E5 Bass Strait str. Austr.
43 G2 Bassum Ger.
37 N8 Båstad Sweden
18 D5 Bastak Iran
18 B2 Bastānābād Iran
43 J4 Bastheim Ger.
23 E4 Basti India
48 C3 Bastia Corsica France
42 D4 Bastogne Belgium
77 F5 Bastrop LA U.S.A.
77 D6 Bastrop TX U.S.A.
19 G5 Basul r. Pak.
54 C4 Bata Equatorial Guinea
83 H4 Batabanó, Golfo de b. Cuba
31 B2 Batac Phil.
31 C3 Batag i. Phil.
13 P3 Batagay Rus. Fed.
22 B2 Batai Pass Pak.
22 C3 Batala India
45 B3 Batalha Port.
32 C5 Batam i. Indon.
13 O3 Batamay Rus. Fed.
31 B1 Batan i. Phil.
56 B3 Batangafo C.A.R.
31 B3 Batangas Phil.
33 B3 Batanghari r. Indon.
32 A5 Batangtoru Indon.
31 B1 Batan Islands is Phil.
90 C3 Batatais Brazil
68 C5 Batavia IL U.S.A.
80 D3 Batavia NY U.S.A.
51 F6 Bataysk Rus. Fed.
69 E2 Batchawana r. Can.
68 E2 Batchawana Bay Can.
66 D4 Batchawana Mtn h. Can.
6 D3 Batchelor Austr.
69 E2 Batchewana Can.
32 B2 Bătdâmbâng Cambodia
8 H3 Batemans B. b. Austr.
8 H3 Batemans Bay Austr.
77 F5 Batesville AR U.S.A.
77 F5 Batesville MS U.S.A.
50 D3 Batetskiy Rus. Fed.
67 G4 Bath N.B. Can.
69 J3 Bath Ont. Can.
39 E6 Bath U.K.
81 J3 Bath ME U.S.A.
80 E3 Bath NY U.S.A.
40 E5 Bathgate U.K.
22 C3 Bathinda India
8 G2 Bathurst Austr.
67 G4 Bathurst Can.
59 G6 Bathurst S. Africa
63 J2 Bathurst I. i. Can.
62 H3 Bathurst Inlet N.W.T. Can.
6 D3 Bathurst Island i. Austr.
8 G3 Bathurst, L. l. Austr.
18 D3 Bāṭlāq-e Gavkhūnī marsh Iran
38 F4 Batley U.K.
8 G3 Batlow Austr.
17 H3 Batman Turkey
54 C1 Batna Alg.
18 C6 Baṭn aṭ Ṭarfā' depression S. Arabia
77 F6 Baton Rouge U.S.A.
55 D4 Batouri Cameroon
90 B1 Batovi Brazil
16 E4 Batroûn Lebanon
36 V1 Båtsfjord Norway
21 C5 Batticaloa Sri Lanka
48 F4 Battipaglia Italy
65 G4 Battle r. Can.
68 E4 Battle Creek U.S.A.
65 H4 Battleford Can.
72 C3 Battle Mountain U.S.A.
22 C1 Battura Glacier gl. Jammu and Kashmir
32 B4 Batu Gajah Malaysia
31 C5 Batulaki Phil.
17 H1 Bat'umi Georgia
33 B2 Batu Pahat Malaysia
33 A3 Batu, Pulau Pulau is Indon.
32 B4 Batu Puteh, Gunung mt Malaysia
25 E7 Baubau Indon.
54 C3 Bauchi Nigeria
76 E1 Baudette U.S.A.
89 A3 Baudo, Serranía de mts Col.
44 D3 Baugé France
43 H5 Bauland reg. Ger.
67 K3 Bauld, C. hd Can.
44 H3 Baume-les-Dames France
22 C2 Baundal India
90 C3 Bauru Brazil
90 B2 Baús Brazil
42 E4 Bausendorf Ger.
37 T8 Bauska Latvia
46 G5 Bautzen Ger.
58 E6 Baviaanskloofberg mts S. Africa
70 E6 Bavispe r. Mex.
39 J5 Bawdeswell U.K.
33 D4 Bawean i. Indon.
42 F2 Bawinkel Ger.
55 E2 Bawiti Egypt
54 B3 Bawku Ghana
32 A1 Bawlake Myanmar
27 A4 Bawolung China
26 B3 Baxi China
26 E2 Ba Xian Hebei China
27 C4 Ba Xian Sichuan China
79 D6 Baxley U.S.A.
83 J4 Bayamo Cuba
22 D4 Bayana India
24 B3 Bayan Har Shan mts China
24 C2 Bayanhongor Mongolia
26 B1 Bayan Mod China
26 C1 Bayan Obo China
30 A1 Bayan Qagan China
18 D4 Bayāz Iran
31 C4 Baybay Phil.
17 H1 Bayburt Turkey
69 F4 Bay City MI U.S.A.
77 D6 Bay City TX U.S.A.
12 H3 Baydaratskaya Guba b. Rus. Fed.
56 E3 Baydhabo Somalia
43 L5 Bayerischer Wald mts Ger.
43 J5 Bayern div. Ger.
68 B2 Bayfield U.S.A.
49 M5 Bayındır Turkey
16 F6 Bāyir Jordan
Baykal, Ozero l. see Baikal, Lake
Baykal Range mts see Baykal'sky Khrebet
24 C1 Baykal'skiy Khrebet mts Rus. Fed.
17 H2 Baykan Turkey
31 B3 Bay, Laguna de lag. Phil.
12 G4 Baymak Rus. Fed.
16 D6 Baynūna'h reg. U.A.E.
31 B2 Bayombong Phil.
44 D5 Bayonne France
31 B4 Bayo Point pt Phil.
19 F2 Bayramaly Turkm.
49 M5 Bayramiç Turkey
43 K5 Bayreuth Ger.
77 F6 Bay St Louis U.S.A.
81 G4 Bay Shore U.S.A.
39 E5 Bayston Hill U.K.
19 G2 Baysun Uzbek.
19 G2 Baysuntau, Gory mts Uzbek.
77 E6 Baytown U.S.A.
9 F3 Bay View N.Z.
45 E4 Baza Spain
17 L1 Bazardyuzi, Gora mt Azer./Rus. Fed.
18 C2 Bāzār-e Māsāl Iran
17 K2 Bāzargān Iran
51 H4 Bazarnyy Karabulak Rus. Fed.
57 D6 Bazaruto, Ilha do i. Moz.
19 G5 Bazdar Pak.
26 C4 Bazhong China
19 F5 Bazman Iran
19 F4 Bazmān, Kūh-e mt Iran
32 C3 Be r. Vietnam
76 C2 Beach U.S.A.
69 J3 Beachburg Can.
81 F5 Beach Haven U.S.A.
8 C4 Beachport Austr.
81 F5 Beachwood U.S.A.
39 H7 Beachy Head hd U.K.
81 G4 Beacon U.S.A.
59 G6 Beacon Bay S. Africa
27 Beacon Hill h. H.K. China
39 G6 Beaconsfield U.K.
88 C8 Beagle, Canal chan. Arg.
6 C3 Beagle Gulf b. Austr.
57 E5 Bealanana Madag.
39 E7 Beaminster U.K.
72 E3 Bear r. U.S.A.
65 N2 Bear Cove b. Can.
66 C4 Beardmore Can.
92 B4 Beardmore Gl. gl. Ant.
68 B5 Beardstown U.S.A.
66 D3 Bear Island i. Can.
12 C2 Bear Island i. Svalbard
72 E3 Bear L. l. U.S.A.
64 D3 Bear Lake Can.
22 D4 Bearma r. India
40 A4 Bearnaraigh i. U.K.
72 E1 Bear Paw Mtn mt U.S.A.
92 A3 Bear Pen. pen. Ant.
66 B3 Bearskin Lake Can.
74 B2 Bear Valley U.S.A.
22 C3 Beas r. India
22 C3 Beas Dam dam India
83 K5 Beata, Cabo c. Dom. Rep.
83 K5 Beata, I. i. Dom. Rep.
76 D3 Beatrice U.S.A.
64 E3 Beatton r. Can.
64 E3 Beatton River Can.
74 D3 Beatty U.S.A.
66 E4 Beattyville Can.
44 G5 Beaucaire France
88 E8 Beauchene I. i. Falkland Is
8 D4 Beaufort Austr.
33 E1 Beaufort Malaysia
79 D5 Beaufort U.S.A.
62 D2 Beaufort Sea Can./U.S.A.
58 E6 Beaufort West S. Africa
66 F4 Beauharnois Can.
40 D3 Beauly U.K.
40 D3 Beauly Firth est. U.K.
39 C4 Beaumaris U.K.
42 C4 Beaumont Belgium
9 B6 Beaumont N.Z.
77 F6 Beaumont MS U.S.A.
80 B5 Beaumont OH U.S.A.
77 E6 Beaumont TX U.S.A.
44 G3 Beaune France
44 D3 Beaupréau France
42 A4 Beauquesne France
42 C4 Beauraing Belgium
65 K4 Beausejour Can.
44 F2 Beauvais France
65 H3 Beauval Can.
42 A4 Beauval France
75 F2 Beaver U.S.A.
62 H4 Beaver r. Alta. Can.
64 D2 Beaver r. B.C./Y.T. Can.
66 C2 Beaver r. Ont. Can.
75 F2 Beaver r. U.S.A.
64 A2 Beaver Creek Can.
78 C4 Beaver Dam KY U.S.A.
68 C4 Beaver Dam WV U.S.A.
80 C4 Beaver Falls U.S.A.
72 D2 Beaverhead Mts mts U.S.A.
65 K4 Beaverhill L. l. Man. Can.
65 J2 Beaverhill L. l. N.W.T. Can.
68 E3 Beaver Island i. U.S.A.
77 E4 Beaver L. resr U.S.A.
64 F3 Beaverlodge Can.
80 D4 Beaver Run Reservoir U.S.A.
22 C4 Beawar India
91 C2 Beazley Arg
90 C3 Bebedouro Brazil
39 D4 Bebington U.K.
43 H4 Bebra Ger.
66 F1 Bécard, Lac l. Can.
39 J5 Beccles U.K.
49 J2 Bečej Yugo.
45 C1 Becerreá Spain
54 B1 Béchar Alg.
43 J5 Bechhofen Ger.
80 C6 Beckley U.S.A.
43 G3 Beckum Ger.
43 L4 Bečov nad Teplou Czech Rep.
38 F3 Bedale U.K.
42 E4 Bedburg Ger.
81 J2 Beddington U.S.A.
56 D3 Bedelē Eth.
43 G1 Bederkesa Ger.
81 G2 Bedford Can.
59 J4 Bedford S. Africa
39 G5 Bedford U.K.
78 C4 Bedford IN U.S.A.
81 H3 Bedford MA U.S.A.
80 D4 Bedford PA U.S.A.
80 D6 Bedford VA U.S.A.
39 G5 Bedford Level lowland U.K.
8 F2 Bedgerebong Austr.
38 F2 Bedlington U.K.
32 Bedok Sing.
32 Bedok Res. resr Sing.
75 H2 Bedrock U.S.A.
42 E1 Bedum Neth.
39 F5 Bedworth U.K.
80 B5 Beech Fork Lake l. U.S.A.
68 C2 Beechwood U.S.A.
8 F4 Beechworth Austr.
8 H3 Beecroft Pen. pen. Austr.
43 L2 Beelitz Ger.
7 F4 Beenleigh Austr.
41 A5 Beenoskee h. Rep. of Ireland
42 B3 Beernem Belgium
16 E6 Beersheba Israel
Be'ér Sheva' see Beersheba
58 E6 Beervlei Dam dam S. Africa
43 L2 Beetzsee l. Ger.
77 D6 Beeville U.S.A.
56 C3 Befale Congo(Zaire)
57 E5 Befandriana Avaratra Madag.
8 G4 Bega Austr.
22 B3 Begari r. Pak.
45 H2 Begur, Cap de pt Spain
23 F4 Begusarai India
19 E3 Behābād Iran
87 H3 Béhague, Pointe pt Fr. Guiana
18 C4 Behbehān Iran
64 C3 Behm Canal in. U.S.A.
92 B3 Behrendt Mts mts Ant.
18 D2 Behshahr Iran
19 G3 Behsūd Afgh.
24 E2 Bei'an China
27 C4 Beibei China
26 B4 Beichuan China
27 C6 Beihai China
27 D6 Bei Jiang r. China
26 E2 Beijing China
26 E1 Beijing div. China
42 E2 Beilen Neth.
27 C7 Beili China
27 D6 Beiliu China
43 K5 Beilngries Ger.
40 C5 Beinn an Oir h. U.K.
40 D3 Beinn Dearg mt U.K.
30 A3 Beipiao China
57 D5 Beira Moz.
26 E3 Beiru r. China
16 E5 Beirut Lebanon
57 C6 Beitbridge Zimbabwe
40 D5 Beith U.K.
47 L7 Beiuş Romania
30 A3 Beizhen China
45 C3 Beja Port.
54 C1 Béja Tunisia
54 C1 Bejaïa Alg.
45 D2 Béjar Spain
19 E3 Bejestān Iran
22 B3 Beji r. Pak.
47 K7 Békés Hungary
47 K7 Békéscsaba Hungary
57 E6 Bekily Madag.
28 J3 Bekkai Japan
54 B4 Bekwai Ghana
23 E4 Bela India
19 G5 Bela Pak.
22 B3 Belab r. Pak.
59 H2 Bela-Bela S. Africa
55 D4 Bélabo Cameroon
49 J2 Bela Crkva Yugo.
81 E5 Bel Air U.S.A.
45 D3 Belalcázar Spain
43 L5 Bělá nad Radbuzou Czech Rep.
8 E2 Belaraboon Austr.
35 H3 Belarus country Europe
90 A3 Bela Vista Brazil
57 D6 Bela Vista Moz.
32 A5 Belawan Indon.
13 T3 Belaya r. Rus. Fed.
51 G6 Belaya Glina Rus. Fed.
51 G5 Belaya Kalitva Rus. Fed.
50 J3 Belaya Kholunitsa Rus. Fed.
47 J5 Bełchatów Pol.
80 B6 Belcher U.S.A.
63 K4 Belcher Islands is Can.
19 G3 Belchiragh Afgh.
16 F2 Belcik Turkey
41 D3 Belcoo U.K.
69 J1 Belcourt Can.
74 B1 Belden U.S.A.
56 E3 Beledweyne Somalia
18 D2 Belek Turkm.
87 J4 Belém Brazil
88 C3 Belén Arg.
16 F3 Belen Turkey
73 F5 Belen U.S.A.
7 G3 Bélep, Îles is New Caledonia
50 F4 Belev Rus. Fed.
9 D5 Belfast N.Z.
59 J2 Belfast S. Africa
41 F3 Belfast U.K.
81 J2 Belfast U.S.A.
41 F3 Belfast Lough in. U.K.
76 C2 Belfield U.S.A.
38 F2 Belford U.K.
44 H3 Belfort France
21 A3 Belgaum India
43 M3 Belgern Ger.
34 F3 Belgium country Europe
51 F5 Belgorod Rus. Fed.
51 F5 Belgorodskaya Oblast' div. Rus. Fed.
72 E2 Belgrade U.S.A.
49 J2 Belgrade Yugo.
54 D4 Beli Nigeria
48 E6 Belice r. Sicily Italy
50 G4 Belinskiy Rus. Fed.
33 C3 Belinyu Indon.
33 C3 Belitung i. Indon.
82 G5 Belize Belize
61 K8 Belize country Central America
28 E2 Belkina, Mys pt Rus. Fed.
13 F2 Bel'kovskiy, O. i. Rus. Fed.
8 G2 Bell r. Austr.
64 D4 Bella Bella Can.
44 E3 Bellac France
64 D4 Bella Coola Can.
77 E6 Bellaire U.S.A.
21 E3 Bellary India
91 F1 Bella Unión Uru.
80 E4 Bellefontaine U.S.A.
80 E4 Bellefonte U.S.A.
76 C2 Belle Fourche U.S.A.
76 C2 Belle Fourche r. U.S.A.
44 G3 Bellegarde-sur-Valserine France
79 D7 Belle Glade U.S.A.
44 C3 Belle-Île i. France
67 K3 Belle Isle i. Can.
63 M4 Belle Isle, Strait of Nfld Can.
67 J3 Belle Isle, Strait of str. Can.
75 G4 Bellemont U.S.A.
68 A5 Belle Plaine U.S.A.
69 H2 Belleterre Can.
69 J3 Belleville Can.
76 D4 Belleville U.S.A.
68 B4 Bellevue IA U.S.A.
72 D3 Bellevue ID U.S.A.
80 B4 Bellevue OH U.S.A.
72 B2 Bellevue WA U.S.A.
Bellin see Kangirsuk
38 E2 Bellingham U.K.
72 B1 Bellingham U.S.A.
92 B2 Bellingshausen Rus. Fed. Base Ant.
92 A3 Bellingshausen Sea sea Ant.
46 D7 Bellinzona Switz.
89 B3 Bello Col.
81 G3 Bellows Falls U.S.A.
22 B3 Bellpat Pak.
81 F5 Belltown U.S.A.
48 E1 Belluno Italy
21 B3 Belluru India
91 D2 Bell Ville Arg.
58 C6 Bellville S. Africa
43 G2 Belm Ger.
58 F4 Belmont S. Africa
40 Belmont U.K.
80 D3 Belmont U.S.A.
90 E1 Belmonte Brazil
82 G5 Belmopan Belize
41 B3 Belmullet Rep. of Ireland
42 B4 Belœil Belgium
81 G2 Beloeil Can.
24 E1 Belogorsk Rus. Fed.
57 E6 Beloha Madag.
90 D2 Belo Horizonte Brazil
76 D4 Beloit KS U.S.A.
68 C4 Beloit WV U.S.A.
50 E1 Belomorsk Rus. Fed.
23 G5 Belonia India
51 F6 Belorechensk Rus. Fed.
16 F3 Belören Turkey
12 G4 Beloretsk Rus. Fed.
Belorussia country see Belarus
57 E5 Belo Tsiribihina Madag.
50 F1 Beloye Rus. Fed.
Beloye More g. see White Sea
50 F2 Beloye, Ozero l. Rus. Fed.
50 F2 Belozersk Rus. Fed.
80 C5 Belpre U.S.A.
72 E2 Belt U.S.A.
74 D3 Belted Range mts U.S.A.
77 D6 Belton U.S.A.
21 A3 Belur India
31 A5 Beluran Malaysia
68 C4 Belvidere U.S.A.
50 H3 Belyshevo Rus. Fed.
50 E4 Belyy Rus. Fed.
12 J2 Belyy, O. i. Rus. Fed.
43 L2 Belzig Ger.
68 C6 Bement U.S.A.
76 E2 Bemidji U.S.A.
56 C4 Bena Dibele Congo(Zaire)
40 D4 Ben Alder mt U.K.
8 E4 Benalla Austr.
48 D6 Ben Arous Tunisia
45 D1 Benavente Spain
40 E3 Ben Avon mt U.K.
41 B4 Benbaun h. Rep. of Ireland
40 A3 Benbecula i. U.K.
41 C3 Benbulben h. Rep. of Ireland
41 E3 Benburb U.K.
40 C4 Ben Cruachan mt U.K.
72 B2 Bend U.S.A.
59 G5 Bendearg mt S. Africa
8 H1 Bendemeer Austr.
56 E3 Bender-Bayla Somalia
8 E4 Bendigo Austr.
8 G4 Bendoc Austr.
57 D5 Bene Moz.
81 J2 Benedicta U.S.A.
67 J3 Benedict, Mount h. Can.
57 E6 Benenitra Madag.
46 G6 Benešov Czech Rep.
42 E6 Bénestroff France
48 F4 Benevento Italy
26 F3 Beng r. China
10 K8 Bengal, Bay of sea Asia
56 C3 Bengamisa Congo(Zaire)
26 E3 Bengbu China
32 B5 Bengkalis Indon.
33 B3 Bengkulu Indon.
37 N7 Bengtsfors Sweden
57 B5 Benguela Angola
16 C6 Benha Egypt
40 B4 Ben Hiant h. U.K.
40 D2 Ben Hope mt U.K.
56 C3 Beni Congo(Zaire)
86 E6 Beni r. Bol.
54 B1 Beni-Abbès Alg.
45 F3 Benidorm Spain
54 B1 Beni Mellal Morocco
53 E5 Benin country Africa
54 C4 Benin, Bight of g. Africa
54 C4 Benin City Nigeria
54 B1 Beni-Saf Alg.
55 F2 Beni Suef Egypt
91 E3 Benito Juárez Arg.
31 B2 Benito Soliven Phil.
86 E6 Benjamim Constant Brazil
82 B2 Benjamín Hill Mex.
6 D2 Benjina Indon.
76 C3 Benkelman U.S.A.
40 D2 Ben Klibreck mt U.K.
40 D4 Ben Lawers mt U.K.
40 D4 Ben Lomond mt U.K.
40 D2 Ben Loyal h. U.K.
40 D4 Ben Lui mt U.K.
40 E3 Ben Macdui mt U.K.
40 C4 Ben More mt Scot. U.K.
40 B4 Ben More mt Scot. U.K.
40 D2 Ben More Assynt mt U.K.
9 C6 Benmore, L. l. N.Z.
13 Q2 Bennetta, O. i. Rus. Fed.
40 C4 Ben Nevis mt U.K.
81 G3 Bennington U.S.A.
59 H3 Benoni S. Africa
55 D4 Bénoué, Parc National de la nat. park Cameroon
43 G5 Bensheim Ger.
75 G6 Benson AZ U.S.A.
76 E2 Benson MN U.S.A.
19 E5 Bent Iran
33 B2 Benta Seberang Malaysia
80 D6 Bent Creek U.S.A.
25 E7 Benteng Indon.
6 D3 Bentinck I. i. Austr.
32 A3 Bentinck I. i. Myanmar
38 F4 Bentley U.K.
81 K2 Benton Can.
77 E5 Benton AR U.S.A.
74 C3 Benton CA U.S.A.
78 B4 Benton IL U.S.A.
68 D4 Benton Harbor U.S.A.
32 C3 Bên Tre Vietnam
32 B5 Bentung Malaysia
54 D4 Benue r. Nigeria
40 D4 Ben Vorlich mt U.K.
41 B4 Benwee h. Rep. of Ireland
41 B3 Benwee Head hd Rep. of Ireland
40 D3 Ben Wyvis mt U.K.
30 C3 Benxi Liaoning China
30 B3 Benxi Liaoning China
31 C5 Beo Indon.
Beograd see Belgrade
22 E5 Beohari India
54 B4 Béoumi Côte d'Ivoire
27 C5 Bepian Jiang r. China
29 B8 Beppu Japan
7 H3 Beqa i. Fiji
22 C4 Berach r. India
67 G2 Bérard, Lac l. Can.
22 D5 Berasia India
32 A5 Berastagi Indon.
49 H4 Berat Albania
33 E3 Beratus, Gunung mt Indon.
25 F7 Berau, Teluk b. Indon.
55 F3 Berber Sudan
56 E2 Berbera Somalia
56 B3 Berbérati C.A.R.
44 E1 Berck France
17 K1 Berd Armenia
13 O3 Berdigestyakh Rus. Fed.
24 A1 Berdsk Rus. Fed.
51 F6 Berdyans'k Ukr.
51 D5 Berdychiv Ukr.
80 A6 Berea U.S.A.
51 B5 Berehove Ukr.
6 E2 Bereina P.N.G.
65 K4 Berens r. Can.
65 K4 Berens River Can.
76 D3 Beresford U.S.A.
51 C5 Berezhany Ukr.
51 D6 Berezivka Ukr.
51 C5 Berezne Ukr.
50 G2 Bereznik Rus. Fed.
12 H3 Berezovo Rus. Fed.
43 K3 Berga Ger.
45 G1 Berga Spain
49 M5 Bergama Turkey
48 C2 Bergamo Italy
37 P6 Bergby Sweden
46 F3 Bergen Ger.
43 H2 Bergen Ger.
37 J6 Bergen Norway
42 C3 Bergen op Zoom Neth.
44 E4 Bergerac France
42 C6 Bergères-lès-Vertus France
42 E4 Bergheim Ger.
42 F4 Bergisches Land reg. Ger.
42 F4 Bergisch Gladbach Ger.
58 B1 Bergland Namibia
58 C2 Bergland U.S.A.
37 P6 Bergsjö Sweden
36 R4 Bergsviken Sweden
43 J5 Bergtheim Ger.
42 A4 Bergues France
42 E1 Bergum Neth.
59 H4 Bergville S. Africa
33 B3 Berhala, Selat chan. Indon.
13 S4 Beringa, O. i. Rus. Fed.
42 D3 Beringen Belgium
13 T3 Beringovskiy Rus. Fed.
13 T4 Bering Sea sea Pac. Oc.
62 B3 Bering Strait str. Rus. Fed./U.S.A.
18 E5 Berīzak Iran
36 M5 Berkåk Norway
42 E2 Berkel r. Neth.
74 A3 Berkeley U.S.A.
80 D5 Berkeley Springs U.S.A.
42 D2 Berkhout Neth.
92 B3 Berkner I. i. Ant.
49 K3 Berkovitsa Bulg.
39 F6 Berkshire Downs h. U.K.
42 C3 Berlare Belgium
36 V1 Berlevåg Norway
43 M2 Berlin Ger.
81 F5 Berlin MD U.S.A.
81 H2 Berlin NH U.S.A.
80 D5 Berlin PA U.S.A.
68 C4 Berlin WV U.S.A.
63 K2 Berlinguet Inlet in. Can.
80 C4 Berlin Lake l. U.S.A.
8 H4 Bermagui Austr.
91 D4 Bermeja, Pta pt Arg.
84 B1 Bermejillo Mex.
86 F8 Bermejo Bol.
91 C1 Bermejo r. San Juan Arg.
88 D2 Bermejo r. Chaco/Formosa Arg./Bol.
61 M6 Bermuda terr. Atl. Ocean
96 E3 Bermuda Rise sea feature Atl. Ocean
46 C7 Bern Switz.
73 F5 Bernalillo U.S.A.
88 A7 Bernardo O'Higgins, Parque Nacional nat. park Chile
91 D3 Bernasconi Arg.
43 K3 Bernburg (Saale) Ger.
43 G1 Berne Ger.
68 E5 Berne U.S.A.
46 C7 Berner Alpen mts Switz.
40 A3 Berneray i. U.K.
63 K2 Bernier Bay b. Can.
6 B4 Bernier I. i. Austr.
46 E7 Bernina Pass Switz.
42 F5 Bernkastel-Kues Ger.
57 E6 Beroroha Madag.
46 G6 Beroun Czech Rep.
46 F6 Berounka r. Czech Rep.
8 C3 Berri Austr.
40 E2 Berriedale U.K.
8 E3 Berrigan Austr.
8 H3 Berrima Austr.
45 H4 Berrouaghia Alg.
8 H3 Berry Austr.
44 E3 Berry reg. France
74 A2 Berryessa, Lake l. U.S.A.
79 E7 Berry Islands is Bahamas
58 B3 Berseba Namibia
43 F2 Bersenbrück Ger.
51 D5 Bershad' Ukr.
33 B1 Bertam Malaysia
87 K5 Bertolinia Brazil
55 D4 Bertoua Cameroon
41 B4 Bertraghboy Bay b. Rep. of Ireland
7 H2 Beru i. Kiribati
86 F4 Beruri Brazil
8 E5 Berwick Austr.
81 E4 Berwick U.S.A.
38 E2 Berwick-upon-Tweed U.K.
64 F3 Berwyn Can.
39 D5 Berwyn h. U.K.
51 E6 Beryslav Ukr.
57 E5 Besalampy Madag.
44 H3 Besançon France
19 G2 Beshir Turkm.
19 G2 Beshkent Uzbek.
18 D4 Beshneh Iran
17 H3 Beşiri Turkey
51 H7 Beslan Rus. Fed.
65 H3 Besnard Lake l. Can.
16 F3 Besni Turkey
41 E3 Bessbrook U.K.
79 C5 Bessemer AL U.S.A.
68 B2 Bessemer MI U.S.A.
57 E6 Betanty Madag.
45 B1 Betanzos Spain
55 D4 Bétaré Oya Cameroon
59 H3 Bethal S. Africa
58 B3 Bethanie Namibia
76 E3 Bethany MO U.S.A.
77 D5 Bethany OK U.S.A.
62 B3 Bethel AK U.S.A.
81 H2 Bethel ME U.S.A.
68 A6 Bethel MO U.S.A.
80 A5 Bethel OH U.S.A.
80 D4 Bethel Park U.S.A.
39 C4 Bethesda U.K.
80 E5 Bethesda MD U.S.A.
80 C4 Bethesda OH U.S.A.
58 F5 Bethesdaweg S. Africa
59 H4 Bethlehem S. Africa
81 F4 Bethlehem U.S.A.
16 E6 Bethlehem West Bank
59 F5 Bethulie S. Africa
42 A4 Béthune France
89 C2 Betijoque Venez.
57 E6 Betioky Madag.
14 F2 Betpak-Dala plain Kazak.
57 E6 Betroka Madag.
16 E5 Bet She'an Israel
67 G4 Betsiamites Can.
67 G4 Betsiamites r. Can.
57 E5 Betsiboka r. Madag.
68 D3 Betsie, Pt pt U.S.A.
68 E2 Betsy Lake l. U.S.A.
68 B5 Bettendorf U.S.A.
23 F4 Bettiah India
40 D2 Bettyhill U.K.
41 E4 Bettystown Rep. of Ireland
22 D5 Betul India
42 D3 Betuwe reg. Neth.
22 D4 Betwa r. India
39 D4 Betws-y-coed U.K.
43 F4 Betzdorf Ger.
8 D3 Beulah Austr.
68 D3 Beulah U.S.A.
39 H6 Beult r. U.K.
38 G4 Beverley U.K.
62 C4 Beverley, L. l. U.S.A.
81 H3 Beverly MA U.S.A.
80 C5 Beverly OH U.S.A.
74 C4 Beverly Hills U.S.A.
65 J2 Beverly Lake l. Can.
43 G1 Beverstedt Ger.
43 H3 Beverungen Ger.
42 C2 Beverwijk Neth.
42 F5 Bexbach Ger.
39 H7 Bexhill U.K.
18 B3 Beyānlū Iran
16 C3 Bey Dağları mts Turkey
16 B1 Beykoz Turkey
54 B4 Beyla Guinea
17 L2 Beyläqan Azer.
16 C1 Beypazarı Turkey
16 F2 Beypınarı Turkey
21 A4 Beypore India
Beyrouth see Beirut
16 C3 Beyşehir Turkey
16 C3 Beyşehir Gölü l. Turkey
51 F6 Beysug r. Rus. Fed.
17 J3 Beytüşşebap Turkey
18 E3 Bezameh Iran
50 J3 Bezbozhnik Rus. Fed.
50 D3 Bezhanitsy Rus. Fed.
50 F3 Bezhetsk Rus. Fed.
44 F5 Béziers France
Bezwada see Vijayawada
22 B4 Bhabhar India
23 E4 Bhabua India
22 B5 Bhadar r. India
23 F4 Bhadgaon Nepal
23 E4 Bhadohi India
22 C3 Bhadra India
21 C2 Bhadrachalam India
Bhadrachalam Road Sta. see Kottagudem
23 F5 Bhadrakh India
21 A3 Bhadra Reservoir India
21 A3 Bhadravati India
22 A3 Bhag Pak.
22 D2 Bhaga r. India
23 F4 Bhagalpur India
23 G5 Bhagirathi r. India
23 D5 Bhainsdehi India
23 G4 Bhairab Bazar Bangl.
23 E4 Bhairawa Nepal
21 B2 Bhalki India
24 B4 Bhamo Myanmar
21 C2 Bhamragarh India
22 D4 Bhander India
23 F6 Bhanjanagar India
22 C4 Bhanpura India
22 D5 Bhanrer Range h. India
22 D4 Bharatpur India
23 H4 Bhareli r. India
19 F5 Bhari r. Pak.
22 C5 Bharuch India
23 E5 Bhatapara India
21 A3 Bhatkal India
23 G5 Bhatpara India
21 B4 Bhavani India
21 B4 Bhavani r. India
22 C5 Bhavnagar India
22 C3 Bhawana Pak.
23 E6 Bhawanipatna India
59 J3 Bhekuzulu S. Africa
23 E3 Bheri r. Nepal
22 C4 Bhilwara India
21 B2 Bhima r. India
21 C2 Bhimavaram India
22 D4 Bhind India
22 C4 Bhindar India
23 E4 Bhinga India
22 C4 Bhinmal India
22 D3 Bhiwani India
23 F4 Bhojpur Nepal
21 B2 Bhongir India
59 H5 Bhongweni S. Africa
22 D5 Bhopal India
21 C2 Bhopalpatnam India
21 A2 Bhor India
23 F5 Bhuban India
23 F5 Bhubaneshwar India
22 B5 Bhuj India
22 C5 Bhusawal India
10 K7 Bhutan country Asia
22 B4 Bhuttewala India
18 E5 Bīābān mts Iran
22 C2 Biafo Gl. gl. Pak.
25 F7 Biak Indon.
25 F7 Biak i. Indon.
47 L4 Biała Podlaska Pol.
46 G4 Białogard Pol.
47 L4 Białystok Pol.
54 B4 Biankouma Côte d'Ivoire
30 B1 Bianzhao China
18 D2 Bīārjmand Iran
44 D5 Biarritz France
18 B5 Bi'ār Tabrāk well S. Arabia
46 D7 Biasca Switz.
28 G3 Bibai Japan
57 B5 Bibala Angola
8 G4 Bibbenluke Austr.
48 D3 Bibbiena Italy
46 D6 Biberach an der Riß Ger.
23 G4 Bibiyana r. Bangl.
43 G5 Biblis Ger.
16 C2 Biçer Turkey
39 F6 Bicester U.K.
65 G4 Biche, Lac La l. Can.
51 G7 Bichvint'a Georgia
6 D3 Bickerton I. i. Austr.
39 D7 Bickleigh U.K.
75 G2 Bicknell U.S.A.
57 B5 Bicuari, Parque Nacional do nat. park Angola
54 C4 Bida Nigeria
31 A5 Bidadari, Tg pt Malaysia
18 D4 Bida Khabit Iran
21 B2 Bidar India
19 E6 Bidbid Oman
81 H3 Biddeford U.S.A.
42 D2 Biddinghuizen Neth.
40 C4 Bidean Nam Bian mt U.K.
39 C6 Bideford U.K.
39 C6 Bideford Bay b. U.K.
47 L4 Biebrza r. Pol.
43 G4 Biedenkopf Ger.
46 C7 Biel Switz.
46 H5 Bielawa Pol.
43 G2 Bielefeld Ger.
48 C2 Biella Italy
47 J6 Bielsko-Biała Pol.
47 L4 Bielsk Podlaski Pol.
43 J1 Bienenbüttel Ger.
32 C3 Biên Hoa Vietnam
Bienne see Biel
66 F2 Bienville, Lac l. Can.
42 C3 Biesbosch, Nationaal Park de nat. park Neth.
59 F3 Biesiesvlei S. Africa
43 H6 Bietigheim-Bissingen Ger.
42 D5 Bièvre Belgium
56 B4 Bifoun Gabon
67 J3 Big r. Can.
74 A2 Big r. U.S.A.
51 C7 Biga Turkey
16 B2 Bigadiç Turkey
49 M5 Biga Yarımadası pen. Turkey
68 D2 Big Bay U.S.A.
68 D3 Big Bay de Noc b. U.S.A.
74 D4 Big Bear Lake U.S.A.
72 E2 Big Belt Mts mts U.S.A.
59 J3 Big Bend Swaziland
77 C6 Big Bend Nat. Park U.S.A.
77 F5 Big Black r. U.S.A.
39 D7 Bigbury-on-Sea U.K.
79 D7 Big Cypress Nat. Preserve res. U.S.A.
68 C3 Big Eau Pleine Reservoir U.S.A.
65 L5 Big Falls U.S.A.
65 H4 Biggar Can.
40 E5 Biggar U.K.
64 B3 Bigger, Mt mt Can.
39 G5 Biggleswade U.K.
72 D2 Big Hole r. U.S.A.
72 F2 Bighorn r. U.S.A.
72 E2 Bighorn Canyon Nat. Recreation Area res. U.S.A.
72 F2 Bighorn Mountains U.S.A.
79 F7 Bight, The Bahamas
63 L3 Big Island i. N.W.T. Can.
64 F2 Big Island i. Can.
81 K2 Big Lake l. U.S.A.
54 A3 Bignona Senegal
80 D6 Big Otter r. U.S.A.
74 C3 Big Pine U.S.A.
68 E4 Big Rapids U.S.A.
68 C3 Big Rib r. U.S.A.
65 H4 Big River Can.
68 D3 Big Sable Pt pt U.S.A.
64 C2 Big Salmon r. Can.
65 K3 Big Sand Lake l. Can.
75 F4 Big Sandy r. U.S.A.
76 D2 Big Sioux r. U.S.A.
74 D2 Big Smokey Valley v. U.S.A.
77 C5 Big Spring U.S.A.
76 C3 Big Springs U.S.A.
80 B6 Big Stone Gap U.S.A.
74 B3 Big Sur U.S.A.
72 E2 Big Timber U.S.A.
66 C3 Big Trout Lake Can.
66 C3 Big Trout Lake l. Can.
75 G3 Big Water U.S.A.
69 H3 Bigwin Can.
48 F2 Bihać Bos.-Herz.
23 F4 Bihar div. India
23 F4 Bihar Sharif India
28 J3 Bihoro Japan
47 L7 Bihor, Vârful mt Romania
54 A3 Bijagós, Arquipélago dos is Guinea-Bissau
22 C4 Bijainagar India
21 A2 Bijapur India
18 B3 Bījār Iran
21 C2 Bijārpur India
49 H2 Bijeljina Bos.-Herz.
49 H3 Bijelo Polje Yugo.
27 B5 Bijie China
19 E5 Bījnābād Iran
23 G4 Bijni India
22 D3 Bijnor India
22 B3 Bijnot Pak.
22 C3 Bikaner India
24 F2 Bikin Rus. Fed.
28 D1 Bikin r. Rus. Fed.
4 H4 Bikini i. Marshall Is
56 B4 Bikoro Congo(Zaire)
26 B3 Bikou China
22 C4 Bilara India

23 E5 Bilaspur India
17 M2 Biläsuvar Azer.
51 D5 Bila Tserkva Ukr.
32 A2 Bilauktaung Range mts Myanmar/Thai.
45 E1 Bilbao Spain
16 C6 Bilbeis Egypt
49 H3 Bileća Bos.-Herz.
16 B1 Bilecik Turkey
47 L5 Biłgoraj Pol.
56 D4 Bilharamulo Tanz.
51 D6 Bilhorod-Dnistrovs'kyy Ukr.
56 C3 Bili Congo(Zaire)
13 S3 Bilibino Rus. Fed.
31 C4 Biliran i. Phil.
30 B4 Biliu r. China
72 F3 Bill U.S.A.
39 H6 Billericay U.K.
38 F3 Billingham U.K.
72 E2 Billings U.S.A.
39 E7 Bill of Portland hd U.K.
75 F4 Bill Williams r. U.S.A.
75 F4 Bill Williams Mtn mt U.S.A.
55 D3 Bilma Niger
6 F4 Biloela Austr.
51 E6 Bilohirs'k Ukr.
47 N5 Bilohir"ya Ukr.
21 B2 Biloli India
51 F5 Bilolut's'k Ukr.
51 E5 Bilopillya Ukr.
51 F5 Bilovods'k Ukr.
79 B6 Biloxi U.S.A.
6 D4 Bilpa Morea Claypan salt flat Austr.
40 E5 Bilston U.K.
55 E3 Biltine Chad
32 A1 Bilugyun I. i. Myanmar
50 J4 Bilyarsk Rus. Fed.
51 D6 Bilyayivka Ukr.
42 D4 Bilzen Belgium
8 G3 Bimberi, Mt mt Austr.
79 E7 Bimini Is is Bahamas
17 M3 Binab Iran
22 D4 Bina-Etawa India
25 E7 Binaija, G. mt Indon.
16 F2 Binboğa Daği mt Turkey
22 E4 Bindki India
57 B4 Bindu Congo(Zaire)
57 D5 Bindura Zimbabwe
45 G2 Binefar Spain
26 B2 Bingcaowan China
43 F5 Bingen am Rhein Ger.
54 B4 Bingerville Côte d'Ivoire
81 J2 Bingham U.S.A.
81 F3 Binghamton U.S.A.
17 H2 Bingöl Turkey
17 H2 Bingol D. mt Turkey
27 C6 Binh Gia Vietnam
32 D2 Binh Sơn Vietnam
23 H4 Bini India
23 E5 Binika India
32 A5 Binjai Indon.
18 D5 Bin Mürkhan well U.A.E.
8 G1 Binnaway Austr.
32 C5 Bintan i. Indon.
31 B3 Bintuan Phil.
33 B3 Bintuhan Indon.
33 D2 Bintulu Malaysia
26 C3 Bin Xian China
8 F3 Binya Austr.
27 C6 Binyang China
26 F2 Binzhou China
91 B3 Biobío div. Chile
91 B3 Bio Bío r. Chile
54 C4 Bioco i. Equatorial Guinea
48 F3 Biograd na Moru Croatia
48 G3 Biokovo mts Croatia
21 A2 Bir India
19 F5 Bīrag, Kūh-e mts Iran
17 H5 Bi'r al Mulūsi Iraq
50 F2 Birandozero Rus. Fed.
56 C2 Birao C.A.R.
23 F4 Biratnagar Nepal
17 G3 Bi'r Buṭaymān Syria
64 G3 Birch r. Can.
65 H4 Birch Hills Can.
8 D3 Birchip Austr.
64 F4 Birch Island Can.
66 B3 Birch L. l. Can.
68 B2 Birch Lake l. U.S.A.
64 G3 Birch Mountains h. Can.
65 J4 Birch River Can.
42 D1 Birdaard Neth.
92 C1 Bird Island U.K. Base Ant.
75 G2 Birdseye U.S.A.
6 D4 Birdsville Austr.
16 F3 Birecik Turkey
55 E3 Bir en Nutrûn well Sudan
33 A1 Bireun Indon.
18 B6 Bi'r Ghawdah well S. Arabia
56 D2 Birhan mt Eth.
90 B3 Birigüi Brazil
19 E3 Bīrjand Iran
17 J6 Birkat al 'Aqabah well Iraq
17 J6 Birkat al 'Athāmīn well Iraq
17 K6 Birkāt Hamad well Iraq
18 A4 Birkat Zubālah waterhole S. Arabia
42 F5 Birkenfeld Ger.
39 D4 Birkenhead U.K.
16 C7 Birket Qârûn l. Egypt
17 K3 Birkim Iraq
48 F7 Birkirkara Malta
39 F5 Birmingham U.K.
79 C5 Birmingham U.S.A.
54 A2 Bîr Mogreïn Maur.
16 B6 Bîr Nâḩid oasis Egypt
54 C3 Birnin-Kebbi Nigeria
54 C3 Birnin Konni Niger
24 F2 Birobidzhan Rus. Fed.
41 D4 Birr Rep. of Ireland
17 J5 Bi'r Sābil Iraq
40 E1 Birsay U.K.
39 F5 Birstall U.K.
43 H4 Birstein Ger.
16 E7 Bîr Tâba Egypt
65 J4 Birtle Can.
23 H3 Biru China
21 A3 Birur India
37 T8 Biržai Lith.
75 H6 Bisbee U.S.A.
34 E4 Biscay, Bay of sea France/Spain
79 D7 Biscayne Nat. Park U.S.A.
46 F7 Bischofshofen Austria
92 B2 Biscoe Islands is Ant.
69 F2 Biscotasi Lake l. Can.
69 F2 Biscotasing Can.
27 C4 Bishan China
17 M5 Bīsheh Iran
15 F2 Bishkek Kyrg.
23 F5 Bishnupur India
59 G6 Bisho S. Africa
74 C3 Bishop U.S.A.
38 F3 Bishop Auckland U.K.
39 H6 Bishop's Stortford U.K.
17 G4 Bishrī, Jabal h. Syria
24 E1 Bishui China
54 C1 Biskra Alg.
31 C4 Bislig Phil.
76 C2 Bismarck U.S.A.
6 E2 Bismarck Archipelago is P.N.G.
6 E2 Bismarck Range mts P.N.G.
6 E2 Bismarck Sea sea P.N.G.
43 K2 Bismark (Altmark) Ger.
17 H3 Bismil Turkey
37 L6 Bismo Norway
17 L4 Bīsotūn Iran
36 P5 Bispgården Sweden
43 J1 Bispingen Ger.
45 G4 Bissa, Djebel mt Alg.
21 C2 Bissamcuttak India
54 A3 Bissau Guinea-Bissau
54 D4 Bissaula Nigeria
65 K4 Bissett Can.
64 F3 Bistcho Lake l. Can.
47 M7 Bistrița Romania
47 N7 Bistrița r. Romania
42 E5 Bitburg Ger.
42 F5 Bitche France
55 D3 Bitkine Chad
17 J2 Bitlis Turkey
49 J4 Bitola Macedonia
48 G4 Bitonto Italy
18 B6 Bitrān, J. h. S. Arabia
75 H2 Bitter Creek r. U.S.A.
43 L3 Bitterfeld Ger.
58 C5 Bitterfontein S. Africa
16 D6 Bitter Lakes l. Egypt
72 D2 Bitterroot Range mts U.S.A.
43 K2 Bittkau Ger.
51 G5 Bityug r. Rus. Fed.
55 D3 Biu Nigeria
29 D7 Biwa-ko l. Japan
26 D3 Biyang China
22 D5 Biyāvra India
56 E2 Bīye K'obē Eth.
12 K4 Biysk Rus. Fed.
59 H5 Bizana S. Africa
54 C1 Bizerte Tunisia
36 A4 Bjargtangar hd Iceland
36 Q5 Bjästa Sweden
48 G2 Bjelovar Croatia
36 P2 Bjerkvik Norway
37 L8 Bjerringbro Denmark
37 P6 Björklinge Sweden
37 L5 Bjorli Norway
36 Q5 Björna Sweden
Bjørnøya i. see Bear Island
36 Q5 Bjurholm Sweden
54 B3 Bla Mali
40 B3 Bla Bheinn mt U.K.
77 F5 Black r. AR U.S.A.
75 H5 Black r. AZ U.S.A.
69 F4 Black r. MI U.S.A.
68 B3 Black r. WI U.S.A.
6 E4 Blackall Austr.
68 C1 Black Bay b. Can.
66 B3 Blackbear r. Can.
39 F6 Black Bourton U.K.
38 E4 Blackburn U.K.
74 A2 Black Butte summit U.S.A.
74 A2 Black Butte L. l. U.S.A.
75 E4 Black Canyon U.S.A.
75 F4 Black Canyon City U.S.A.
76 E2 Blackduck U.S.A.
64 G4 Blackfalds Can.
72 D3 Blackfoot U.S.A.
72 D2 Black Foot r. U.S.A.
76 C2 Black Hills reg. U.S.A.
40 D3 Black Isle i. U.K.
65 H3 Black Lake Can.
65 H3 Black Lake l. Can.
69 E3 Black Lake l. U.S.A.
75 G3 Black Mesa plat. U.S.A.
39 D6 Black Mountain h. U.K.
74 D4 Black Mt mt U.S.A.
39 D6 Black Mts h. U.K.
75 E4 Black Mts mts AZ U.S.A.
58 C1 Black Nossob watercourse Namibia
27 □ Black Point pt H.K. China
38 D4 Blackpool U.K.
68 B3 Black River Falls U.S.A.
38 A4 Blackrock Rep. of Ireland
72 C3 Black Rock Desert U.S.A.
80 C6 Blacksburg U.S.A.
51 E7 Black Sea sea Asia/Europe
41 A3 Blacksod Bay b. Rep. of Ireland
41 E5 Blackstairs Mountain h. Rep. of Ireland
41 E5 Blackstairs Mountains h. Rep. of Ireland
80 E6 Blackstone U.S.A.
8 H1 Black Sugarloaf mt Austr.
54 B4 Black Volta r. Africa
41 E5 Blackwater Rep. of Ireland
41 E4 Blackwater r. Rep. of Ireland
41 D5 Blackwater r. Rep. of Ireland
41 E3 Blackwater r. Rep. of Ireland/U.K.
39 H6 Blackwater r. U.K.
80 E6 Blackwater r. U.S.A.
64 E2 Blackwater Lake l. Can.
40 D4 Blackwater Reservoir U.K.
77 D4 Blackwell U.S.A.
6 B5 Blackwood r. Austr.
51 G6 Blagodarnyy Rus. Fed.
28 D2 Blagodatnyy Rus. Fed.
49 K3 Blagoevgrad Bulg.
24 E1 Blagoveshchensk Rus. Fed.
80 E4 Blain U.S.A.
72 B1 Blaine U.S.A.
65 H4 Blaine Lake Can.
76 D3 Blair NE U.S.A.
68 B3 Blair WI U.S.A.
40 E4 Blair Atholl U.K.
40 E4 Blairgowrie U.K.
79 C6 Blakely U.S.A.
39 J5 Blakeney U.K.
68 C1 Blake Pt pt U.S.A.
91 E3 Blanca, Bahía b. Arg.
91 C3 Blanca de la Totora, Sa h. Arg.
73 F4 Blanca Peak summit U.S.A.
6 D4 Blanche, L. salt flat Austr.
80 B5 Blanchester U.S.A.
8 B3 Blanchetown Austr.
44 H4 Blanc, Mont mt France/Italy
91 C1 Blanco r. Arg.
86 F6 Blanco r. Bol.
72 A3 Blanco, C. c. U.S.A.
67 J3 Blanc-Sablon Can.
8 F2 Bland r. Austr.
36 D4 Blanda r. Iceland
39 E7 Blandford Forum U.K.
75 H3 Blanding U.S.A.
45 H2 Blanes Spain
68 E2 Blaney Park U.S.A.
32 A5 Blangkejeren Indon.
42 B3 Blankenberge Belgium
42 E4 Blankenheim Ger.
89 D2 Blanquilla, Isla i. Venez.
46 H6 Blansko Czech Rep.
57 D5 Blantyre Malawi
41 C6 Blarney Rep. of Ireland
43 H5 Blaufelden Ger.
36 Q4 Blåviksjön Sweden
8 G2 Blayney Austr.
43 J1 Bleckede Ger.
9 D4 Blenheim N.Z.
42 E3 Blerick Neth.
41 E4 Blessington Lakes l. Rep. of Ireland
39 G5 Bletchley U.K.
54 C1 Blida Alg.
42 F5 Blies r. Ger.
7 H3 Bligh Water b. Fiji
69 F2 Blind River Can.
72 D3 Bliss U.S.A.
69 F5 Blissfield U.S.A.
81 H4 Block I. i. U.S.A.
81 H4 Block Island Sound chan. U.S.A.
59 G4 Bloemfontein S. Africa
59 F3 Bloemhof S. Africa
59 F3 Bloemhof Dam dam S. Africa
43 H3 Blomberg Ger.
36 C4 Blönduós Iceland
81 E5 Bloodsworth I. i. U.S.A.
65 K4 Bloodvein r. Can.
41 C2 Bloody Foreland pt Rep. of Ireland
69 J4 Bloomfield Can.
68 A5 Bloomfield IA U.S.A.
78 C4 Bloomfield IN U.S.A.
73 E4 Bloomfield NM U.S.A.
68 C5 Bloomington IL U.S.A.
78 C4 Bloomington IN U.S.A.
76 E2 Bloomington MN U.S.A.
81 E4 Bloomsburg U.S.A.
80 E4 Blossburg U.S.A.
63 Q3 Blosseville Kyst Greenland
59 H1 Blouberg S. Africa
39 F5 Bloxham U.K.
75 H5 Blue r. U.S.A.
75 G1 Bluebell U.S.A.
75 G2 Blue Bell Knoll summit U.S.A.
76 E3 Blue Earth U.S.A.
80 C6 Bluefield U.S.A.
83 H6 Bluefields Nic.
81 J2 Blue Hill U.S.A.
69 H5 Blue Knob h. U.S.A.
75 H1 Blue Mountain U.S.A.
23 H5 Blue Mountain mt India
81 F3 Blue Mountain Lake U.S.A.
59 G4 Blue Mountain Pass Lesotho
8 G2 Blue Mountains Austr.
72 C2 Blue Mountains mts U.S.A.
8 H2 Blue Mountains Nat. Park Austr.
55 F3 Blue Nile r. Sudan
62 G3 Bluenose Lake l. Can.
79 C5 Blue Ridge U.S.A.
80 D6 Blue Ridge mts U.S.A.
64 F4 Blue River Can.
74 D2 Blue Springs U.S.A.
41 C3 Blue Stack mt Rep. of Ireland
41 C3 Blue Stack Mts h. Rep. of Ireland
80 C6 Bluestone Lake l. U.S.A.
9 B7 Bluff N.Z.
75 H3 Bluff U.S.A.
27 □ Bluff I. i. H.K. China
79 E7 Bluff, The Bahamas
68 E5 Bluffton IN U.S.A.
80 B4 Bluffton OH U.S.A.
88 G3 Blumenau Brazil
76 C2 Blunt U.S.A.
72 B3 Bly U.S.A.
8 B2 Blyth Austr.
38 F2 Blyth Eng. U.K.
39 F4 Blyth Eng. U.K.
75 E5 Blythe U.S.A.
77 F5 Blytheville U.S.A.
37 L7 Bø Norway
54 A4 Bo Sierra Leone
31 B3 Boac Phil.
87 K5 Boa Esperança, Açude resr Brazil
26 D3 Bo'ai Henan China
27 C6 Bo'ai Yunnan China
56 B3 Boali C.A.R.
59 K3 Boane Moz.
80 C4 Boardman U.S.A.
59 F1 Boatlaname Botswana
87 L5 Boa Viagem Brazil
89 E4 Boa Vista Brazil
54 □ Boa Vista i. Cape Verde
8 F2 Bobadah Austr.
27 D6 Bobai China
57 E5 Bobaomby, Tanjona c. Madag.
21 C2 Bobbili India
54 B3 Bobo-Dioulasso Burkina
57 C6 Bobonong Botswana
51 G5 Bobrov Rus. Fed.
51 D5 Bobrovytsya Ukr.
51 E5 Bobrynets' Ukr.
57 E6 Boby mt Madag.
89 E2 Boca Araguao est. Venez.
89 D2 Boca del Pao Venez.
83 M7 Boca de Macareo Venez.
86 E5 Boca do Acre Brazil
87 H4 Boca do Jari Brazil
89 E2 Boca Grande est. Venez.
90 D2 Bocaiúva Brazil
89 C2 Bocanó r. Venez.
56 B3 Bocaranga C.A.R.
79 D7 Boca Raton U.S.A.
83 H7 Bocas del Toro Panama
47 K6 Bochnia Pol.
42 E3 Bocholt Ger.
42 F3 Bochum Ger.
59 H1 Bochum S. Africa
43 J2 Bockenem Ger.
89 C2 Boconó Venez.
56 B3 Boda C.A.R.
8 H4 Bodalla Austr.
24 D1 Bodaybo Rus. Fed.
77 E5 Bodcau Lake l. U.S.A.
40 G3 Boddam U.K.
43 K3 Bode r. Ger.
74 A2 Bodega Head hd U.S.A.
55 D3 Bodélé reg. Chad
36 R4 Boden Sweden
39 E5 Bodenham U.K.
Bodensee l. see Constance, Lake
43 J2 Bodenteich Ger.
43 H3 Bodenwerder Ger.
21 B2 Bodhan India
21 B4 Bodinayakkanur India
39 C7 Bodmin U.K.
39 C7 Bodmin Moor reg. U.K.
36 O3 Bodø Norway
49 M6 Bodrum Turkey
42 C3 Boechout Belgium
56 C4 Boende Congo(Zaire)
54 A3 Boffa Guinea
23 H3 Boga India
77 F6 Bogalusa U.S.A.
8 F1 Bogan r. Austr.
54 B3 Bogandé Burkina
8 F2 Bogan Gate Austr.
50 J3 Bogatye Saby Rus. Fed.
16 E2 Boğazlıyan Turkey
23 F3 Bogcang Zangbo r. China
24 A2 Bogda Shan mts China
41 B5 Boggeragh Mts h. Rep. of Ireland
45 H5 Boghar Alg.
39 G7 Bognor Regis U.K.
31 C4 Bogo Phil.
41 D4 Bog of Allen reg. Rep. of Ireland
50 E4 Bogolyubovo Rus. Fed.
8 F4 Bogong, Mt mt Austr.
28 D2 Bogopol' Rus. Fed.
33 C4 Bogor Indon.
50 G3 Bogorodsk Rus. Fed.
50 J3 Bogorodskoye Rus. Fed.
89 B3 Bogotá Col.
24 A1 Bogotol Rus. Fed.
23 G4 Bogra Bangl.
13 L4 Boguchany Rus. Fed.
51 G5 Boguchar Rus. Fed.
54 A3 Bogué Maur.
26 F2 Bo Hai g. China
30 A4 Bohai Haixia chan. China
44 F2 Bohain-en-Vermandois France
26 E2 Bohai Wan b. China
43 L3 Böhlen Ger.
59 H4 Bohlokong S. Africa
43 L5 Böhmer Wald mts Ger.
43 G2 Bohmte Ger.
51 E5 Bohodukhiv Ukr.
31 C4 Bohol i. Phil.
31 C4 Bohol Sea sea Phil.
31 B4 Bohol Str. chan. Phil.
15 G2 Bohu China
51 D5 Bohuslav Ukr.
81 F4 Boiceville U.S.A.
58 E4 Boichoko S. Africa
59 G3 Boikhutso S. Africa
87 G4 Boim Brazil
23 H5 Boinu r. Myanmar
90 E1 Boipeba, Ilha i. Brazil
90 D4 Bois, Ponta do pt Brazil
90 C2 Bois r. Brazil
69 E3 Bois Blanc I. i. U.S.A.
42 C4 Bois de Chimay woodland Belgium
72 C3 Boise U.S.A.
77 C4 Boise City U.S.A.
65 J5 Boissevain Can.
59 F3 Boitumelong S. Africa
43 J1 Boizenburg Ger.
31 B2 Bojeador, Cape c. Phil.
18 E2 Bojnūrd Iran
23 G1 Bokadaban Feng mt China
23 H4 Bokajan India
23 F5 Bokaro India
56 B4 Bokatola Congo(Zaire)
54 A3 Boké Guinea
56 C4 Bokele Congo(Zaire)
37 J7 Boknafjorden chan. Norway
55 D3 Bokoro Chad
51 G5 Bokovskaya Rus. Fed.
50 E3 Boksitogorsk Rus. Fed.
58 D3 Bokspits Botswana
56 C4 Bolaiti Congo(Zaire)
54 A3 Bolama Guinea-Bissau
22 A3 Bolan r. Pak.
84 B2 Bolaños Mex.
22 A3 Bolan Pass pass Pak.
44 E2 Bolbec France
18 C4 Boldājī Iran
43 M1 Boldekow Ger.
15 G2 Bole China
54 B4 Bole Ghana
56 B4 Boleko Congo(Zaire)
54 B3 Bolgatanga Ghana
51 D6 Bolhrad Ukr.
28 B2 Boli China
56 B4 Bolia Congo(Zaire)
36 R4 Boliden Sweden
31 A2 Bolinao Phil.
49 L2 Bolintin-Vale Romania
89 A3 Bolívar Col.
86 C5 Bolívar Peru
77 E4 Bolivar MO U.S.A.
79 B5 Bolivar TN U.S.A.
85 D4 Bolivia country S. America
16 E3 Bolkar Dağları mts Turkey
50 F4 Bolkhov Rus. Fed.
69 F1 Bolkow Can.
44 G4 Bollène France
37 P6 Bollnäs Sweden
36 P5 Bollstabruk Sweden
37 N8 Bolmen l. Sweden
51 H7 Bolnisi Georgia
56 B4 Bolobo Congo(Zaire)
31 B5 Bolod Islands is Phil.
48 D2 Bologna Italy
47 P2 Bologovo Rus. Fed.
50 E3 Bologoye Rus. Fed.
59 F4 Bolokanang S. Africa
56 B3 Bolomba Congo(Zaire)
84 E2 Bolonchén de Rejón Mex.
31 B5 Bolong Phil.
12 K4 Bolotnoye Rus. Fed.
32 C2 Bolovens, Plateau des plat. Laos
23 F5 Bolpur India
48 D3 Bolsena, Lago di l. Italy
47 K3 Bol'shakovo Rus. Fed.
36 X3 Bol'shaya Imandra, Oz. l. Rus. Fed.
51 G6 Bol'shaya Martinovka Rus. Fed.
13 M2 Bol'shevik, O. i. Rus. Fed.
50 H2 Bol'shiye Chirki Rus. Fed.
13 S3 Bol'shoy Aluy r. Rus. Fed.
28 C3 Bol'shoy Kamen' Rus. Fed.
Bol'shoy Kavkaz mts see Caucasus
51 J5 Bol'shoy Uzen' r. Rus. Fed.
82 D3 Bolson de Mapimí des. Mex.
42 D1 Bolsward Neth.
38 E4 Bolton U.K.
80 B6 Bolton U.S.A.
16 C1 Bolu Turkey
36 B3 Bolungarvík Iceland
27 E6 Boluo China
16 C2 Bolvadin Turkey
48 D1 Bolzano Italy
56 B4 Boma Congo(Zaire)
8 H3 Bomaderry Austr.
8 G4 Bombala Austr.
21 A2 Bombay India
25 F7 Bomberai Peninsula Indon.
86 E5 Bom Comércio Brazil
90 D2 Bom Despacho Brazil
23 H4 Bomdila India
23 H3 Bomi China
90 D1 Bom Jesus da Lapa Brazil
90 E3 Bom Jesus do Itabapoana Brazil
37 J7 Bømlo i. Norway
18 B2 Bonāb Iran
80 E6 Bon Air U.S.A.
83 L6 Bonaire i. Neth. Ant.
83 H6 Bonanza Nic.
6 C3 Bonaparte Archipelago is Austr.
40 D3 Bonar Bridge U.K.
67 K4 Bonavista Can.
67 K4 Bonavista Bay b. Can.
55 D1 Bon, Cap c. Tunisia
40 F5 Bonchester Bridge U.K.
56 C3 Bondo Congo(Zaire)
31 B3 Bondoc Peninsula pen. Phil.
54 B4 Bondoukou Côte d'Ivoire
68 A3 Bone Lake l. U.S.A.
43 F3 Bönen Ger.
25 E7 Bonerate, Kepulauan is Indon.
40 E4 Bo'ness U.K.
25 E7 Bone, Teluk b. Indon.
90 D2 Bonfinópolis de Minas Brazil
56 D3 Bonga Eth.
31 B3 Bongabong Phil.
23 G4 Bongaigaon India
56 C3 Bongandanga Congo(Zaire)
58 H3 Bongani S. Africa
31 A5 Bongao Phil.
23 G3 Bong Co l. China
31 C5 Bongo i. Phil.
57 E5 Bongolava mts Madag.
56 C3 Bongo, Massif des mts C.A.R.
55 D3 Bongor Chad
54 B4 Bongouanou Côte d'Ivoire
32 D2 Bông Sơn Vietnam
42 C3 Bonheiden Belgium
48 C4 Bonifacio Corsica France
48 C4 Bonifacio, Strait of str. France/Italy
Bonin Is is see Ogasawara-shotō
90 A3 Bonito Brazil
42 F4 Bonn Ger.
36 O3 Bonnåsjøen Norway
72 C1 Bonners Ferry U.S.A.
44 H3 Bonneville France
8 C4 Bonney, L. l. Austr.
6 B5 Bonnie Rock Austr.
40 E5 Bonnyrigg U.K.
65 G4 Bonnyville Can.
31 A4 Bonobono Phil.
32 C3 Bonom Mhai mt Vietnam
48 C4 Bonorva Sardinia Italy
58 D7 Bontebok National Park S. Africa
54 A4 Bonthe Sierra Leone
31 B2 Bontoc Phil.
33 E4 Bontosunggu Indon.
59 F6 Bontrug S. Africa
59 G1 Bonwapitse Botswana
75 H2 Book Cliffs cliff U.S.A.
8 D2 Booleboolka L. l. Austr.
8 B2 Booleroo Centre Austr.
41 D5 Booley Hills h. Rep. of Ireland
8 E2 Booligal Austr.
76 E3 Boone IA U.S.A.
79 D4 Boone NC U.S.A.
80 B6 Boone Lake l. U.S.A.
80 B6 Booneville KY U.S.A.
77 F5 Booneville MS U.S.A.
74 A2 Boonville CA U.S.A.
78 C4 Boonville IN U.S.A.
76 E4 Boonville MO U.S.A.
81 F3 Boonville NY U.S.A.
8 E3 Booroorban Austr.
8 G3 Boorowa Austr.
8 D4 Boort Austr.
56 E2 Boosaaso Somalia
81 J3 Boothbay Harbor U.S.A.
63 J2 Boothia, Gulf of Can.
63 J2 Boothia Peninsula Can.
39 E4 Bootle U.K.
54 A4 Bopolu Liberia
42 F4 Boppard Ger.
91 G1 Boqueirão Brazil
70 E6 Boquilla, Presa de la resr Mex.
43 L5 Bor Czech Rep.
55 F4 Bor Sudan
16 E3 Bor Turkey
49 K2 Bor Yugo.
72 D2 Borah Peak summit U.S.A.
37 N8 Borås Sweden
18 C4 Borāzjān Iran
87 G4 Borba Brazil
87 L5 Borborema, Planalto da plat. Brazil
43 G3 Borchen Ger.
92 B5 Borchgrevink Coast coastal area Ant.
17 H1 Borçka Turkey
16 B3 Bor D. mt Turkey
44 D4 Bordeaux France
67 H4 Borden Can.
62 G2 Borden I. i. Can.
63 K2 Borden Peninsula pen. Can.
8 C4 Bordertown Austr.
36 C4 Borðeyri Iceland
45 J4 Bordj Bou Arréridj Alg.
45 G5 Bordj Bounaama Alg.
54 C2 Bordj Omer Driss Alg.
36 □ Borðoy i. Faroe Is
40 A3 Boreray i. U.K.
36 G4 Borgarfjörður Iceland
36 C4 Borgarnes Iceland
36 N4 Børgefjell Nasjonalpark nat. park Norway
77 C5 Borger U.S.A.
37 P8 Borgholm Sweden
48 B2 Borgo San Dalmazzo Italy
48 D3 Borgo San Lorenzo Italy
48 C2 Borgosesia Italy
42 B4 Borinage reg. Belgium
51 G5 Borisoglebsk Rus. Fed.
51 F5 Borisovka Rus. Fed.
50 F3 Borisovo-Sudskoye Rus. Fed.
18 C4 Borj-e Chīn Iran
51 G7 Borjomi Georgia
42 E3 Borken Ger.
36 P2 Borkenes Norway
42 E1 Borkum Ger.
42 E1 Borkum i. Ger.
37 O6 Borlänge Sweden
16 B2 Borlu Turkey
43 L3 Borna Ger.
42 D1 Borndiep chan. Neth.
42 E2 Borne Neth.
33 D2 Borneo i. Asia
37 O9 Bornholm i. Denmark
49 M5 Bornova Turkey
31 B4 Borocay i. Phil.
12 K3 Borodino Rus. Fed.
37 V6 Borodinskoye Rus. Fed.
51 D5 Borodyanka Ukr.
13 P3 Borogontsy Rus. Fed.
50 F3 Borok Rus. Fed.
54 B3 Boromo Burkina
31 C4 Borongan Phil.
38 F3 Boroughbridge U.K.
50 E3 Borovichi Rus. Fed.
50 J3 Borovoy Kirovsk. Rus. Fed.
50 K2 Borovoy Komi Rus. Fed.
50 E1 Borovoy Korel. Rus. Fed.
41 C5 Borrisokane Rep. of Ireland
6 D3 Borroloola Austr.
36 M5 Børsa Norway
47 M7 Borșa Romania
51 C5 Borshchiv Ukr.
24 C2 Borshchovochnyy Khrebet mts Rus. Fed.
18 C4 Borūjen Iran
18 C3 Borūjerd Iran
40 B3 Borve U.K.
51 B5 Boryslav Ukr.
51 D5 Boryspil' Ukr.
51 E5 Borzna Ukr.
24 D1 Borzya Rus. Fed.
48 G2 Bosanska Dubica Bos.-Herz.
48 G2 Bosanska Gradiška Bos.-Herz.
48 G2 Bosanska Krupa Bos.-Herz.
48 G2 Bosanski Novi Bos.-Herz.
48 G2 Bosansko Grahovo Bos.-Herz.
68 B4 Boscobel U.S.A.
27 C6 Bose China
59 F4 Boshof S. Africa
34 G4 Bosnia-Herzegovina country Europe
56 B3 Bosobolo Congo(Zaire)
29 G7 Bōsō-hantō pen. Japan
16 B1 Bosporus str. Turkey
56 B3 Bossangoa C.A.R.
56 B3 Bossembélé C.A.R.
77 E5 Bossier City U.S.A.
58 B2 Bossiesvlei Namibia
23 F1 Bostan China
17 L6 Bostan Iran
24 A2 Bosten Hu l. China
39 G5 Boston U.K.
81 H3 Boston U.S.A.
69 H1 Boston Creek Can.
81 H3 Boston-Logan International airport U.S.A.
77 E5 Boston Mts mts U.S.A.
38 F4 Boston Spa U.K.
68 D5 Boswell U.S.A.
22 B5 Botad India
8 H2 Botany Bay b. Austr.
36 P5 Boteå Sweden
49 L3 Botev mt Bulg.
49 K3 Botevgrad Bulg.
59 G3 Bothaville S. Africa
12 C3 Bothnia, Gulf of g. Fin./Sweden
51 H5 Botkul', Ozero l. Kazak./Rus. Fed.
47 N7 Botoșani Romania
26 E2 Botou China
32 C1 Bô Trach Vietnam
59 G4 Botshabelo S. Africa
53 G8 Botswana country Africa
48 G5 Botte Donato, Monte mt Italy
36 S4 Bottenviken g. Fin./Sweden
38 G4 Bottesford U.K.
76 C1 Bottineau U.S.A.
42 E3 Bottrop Ger.
90 C3 Botucatu Brazil
90 D1 Botuporã Brazil
67 K4 Botwood Can.
54 B4 Bouaflé Côte d'Ivoire
54 B4 Bouaké Côte d'Ivoire
56 B3 Bouar C.A.R.
54 B1 Bouârfa Morocco
55 D4 Bouba Ndjida, Parc National de nat. park Cameroon
56 B3 Bouca C.A.R.
42 B4 Bouchain France
91 D2 Bouchard, H. Arg.
81 G2 Boucherville Can.
69 K2 Bouchette Can.
54 B3 Boucle du Baoulé, Parc National de la nat. park Mali
67 H4 Bouctouche Can.
7 F2 Bougainville Island i. P.N.G.
54 B3 Bougouni Mali
42 D5 Bouillon Belgium
45 H4 Bouira Alg.
54 A2 Boujdour Western Sahara
72 F3 Boulder CO U.S.A.
72 D2 Boulder MT U.S.A.
75 G3 Boulder UT U.S.A.
75 E3 Boulder Canyon U.S.A.
75 E4 Boulder City U.S.A.
74 D5 Boulevard U.S.A.
91 E3 Boulevard Atlántico Arg.
6 D4 Boulia Austr.
44 F2 Boulogne-Billancourt France
44 E1 Boulogne-sur-Mer France
54 B3 Boulsa Burkina
56 B4 Boumango Gabon
55 D4 Boumba r. Cameroon
45 H4 Boumerdes Alg.
54 B4 Bouna Côte d'Ivoire
81 H2 Boundary Mountains U.S.A.
74 C3 Boundary Peak summit U.S.A.
54 B4 Boundiali Côte d'Ivoire
56 B4 Boundji Congo
32 D1 Boung r. Vietnam
27 A6 Boun Nua Laos
72 E3 Bountiful U.S.A.
7 H6 Bounty Islands is N.Z.
54 B3 Bourem Mali
44 E4 Bourganeuf France
44 G3 Bourg-en-Bresse France
44 F3 Bourges France
81 F2 Bourget Can.
69 K1 Bourgmont Can.
44 G3 Bourgogne reg. France
6 E5 Bourke Austr.
69 G1 Bourkes Can.
39 G5 Bourne U.K.
39 F7 Bournemouth U.K.
42 F2 Bourtanger Moor reg. Ger.
54 C1 Bou Saâda Alg.
48 C6 Bou Salem Tunisia
75 E5 Bouse U.S.A.
75 E5 Bouse Wash r. U.S.A.
55 D3 Bousso Chad
42 B4 Boussu Belgium
54 A3 Boutilimit Maur.
96 K9 Bouvetøya i. Atl. Ocean
42 C5 Bouy France
43 H3 Bovenden Ger.
33 D2 Boven Kapuas Mts mts Malaysia
91 E1 Bovril Arg.
65 G4 Bow r. Can.
76 C1 Bowbells U.S.A.
6 E4 Bowen Austr.
68 B5 Bowen U.S.A.
8 G4 Bowen, Mt mt Austr.
75 H5 Bowie AZ U.S.A.
77 D5 Bowie TX U.S.A.
65 G5 Bow Island Can.
18 B2 Bowkan Iran
78 C4 Bowling Green KY U.S.A.
76 F4 Bowling Green MO U.S.A.
80 B4 Bowling Green OH U.S.A.
80 E5 Bowling Green VA U.S.A.
76 C2 Bowman U.S.A.
92 C6 Bowman I. i. Ant.
64 E4 Bowman, Mt mt Can.
92 B3 Bowman Pen. pen. Ant.
69 H4 Bowmanville Can.
40 B5 Bowmore U.K.
8 H3 Bowral Austr.
64 E4 Bowron r. Can.
64 E4 Bowron Lake Provincial Park res. Can.
43 H5 Boxberg Ger.
26 E3 Bo Xian China
26 F2 Boxing China
42 D3 Boxtel Neth.
16 E1 Boyabat Turkey
27 E4 Boyang China
65 J2 Boyd Lake l. Can.
64 G4 Boyle Can.
41 C4 Boyle Rep. of Ireland
41 E4 Boyne r. Rep. of Ireland
19 G2 Boyni Qara Afgh.
79 D7 Boynton Beach U.S.A.
72 E3 Boysen Res. resr U.S.A.
86 F8 Boyuibe Bol.
17 K1 Böyük Hinaldağ mt Azer.
49 M5 Bozcaada i. Turkey
49 M5 Bozdağ mt Turkey
16 A2 Boz Dağları mts Turkey
16 B3 Bozdoğan Turkey
39 G5 Bozeat U.K.
72 E2 Bozeman U.S.A.
16 D3 Bozkır Turkey
56 B3 Bozoum C.A.R.
16 G3 Bozova Turkey
18 B2 Bozqūsh, Kūh-e mts Iran
16 C2 Bozüyük Turkey
48 B2 Bra Italy
92 B2 Brabant I. i. Ant.
48 G3 Brač i. Croatia
40 B3 Bracadale U.K.
40 B3 Bracadale, Loch b. U.K.
48 E3 Bracciano, Lago di l. Italy
69 H3 Bracebridge Can.
36 O5 Bracke Sweden
43 H5 Brackenheim Ger.
39 G6 Bracknell U.K.
48 G4 Bradano r. Italy
79 D7 Bradenton U.S.A.
69 H3 Bradford Can.
38 F4 Bradford U.K.
80 A4 Bradford OH U.S.A.
80 D4 Bradford PA U.S.A.
81 G3 Bradford VT U.S.A.
77 D6 Brady U.S.A.
64 B3 Brady Gl. gl. U.S.A.
40 □ Brae U.K.
8 B2 Braemar Austr.
40 E3 Braemar U.K.
45 B2 Braga Port.
91 E2 Bragado Arg.
87 J4 Bragança Brazil
45 C2 Bragança Port.
90 C3 Bragança Paulista Brazil
51 D5 Brahin Belarus
43 J1 Brahlstorf Ger.
23 G5 Brahmanbaria Bangl.
23 F5 Brahmani r. India
21 D2 Brahmapur India
23 G4 Brahmaputra r. Asia
49 M2 Brăila Romania
42 B5 Braine France
42 C4 Braine-le-Comte Belgium
76 E2 Brainerd U.S.A.
39 H6 Braintree U.K.
59 H1 Brak r. S. Africa
42 B4 Brakel Belgium
43 H3 Brakel Ger.
43 G1 Brake (Unterweser) Ger.
57 B6 Brakwater Namibia
64 E4 Bralorne Can.
37 L9 Bramming Denmark
37 P5 Brämön i. Sweden
69 H4 Brampton Can.
38 E3 Brampton Eng. U.K.
39 J5 Brampton Eng. U.K.
43 G2 Bramsche Ger.
39 H5 Brancaster U.K.
67 K4 Branch Can.
89 E4 Branco r. Brazil
37 M6 Brandbu Norway
37 L9 Brande Denmark
43 L2 Brandenburg Ger.
43 L2 Brandenburg div. Ger.
59 G4 Brandfort S. Africa
43 M3 Brandis Ger.
65 K5 Brandon Can.
39 H5 Brandon U.K.
76 D3 Brandon SD U.S.A.
81 G3 Brandon VT U.S.A.
41 A5 Brandon Head hd Rep. of Ireland
41 E5 Brandon Hill h. Rep. of Ireland
41 A5 Brandon Mountain mt Rep. of Ireland
58 D5 Brandvlei S. Africa
79 D6 Branford U.S.A.
47 J3 Braniewo Pol.
92 B2 Bransfield Str. str. Ant.
69 G4 Brantford Can.
8 C4 Branxholme Austr.
67 H4 Bras d'Or L. l. Can.
86 E6 Brasiléia Brazil
90 C1 Brasília Brazil
90 D2 Brasília de Minas Brazil
87 G4 Brasília Legal Brazil
47 N3 Braslaw Belarus
49 L2 Brașov Romania
31 A5 Brassey Range mts Malaysia
81 J2 Brassua Lake l. U.S.A.
46 H6 Bratislava Slovakia
24 C1 Bratsk Rus. Fed.
24 C1 Bratskoye Vdkhr. resr Rus. Fed.
81 G3 Brattleboro U.S.A.
46 F6 Braunau am Inn Austria
43 G4 Braunfels Ger.
43 J3 Braunlage Ger.
43 K3 Braunsbedra Ger.
43 J2 Braunschweig Ger.
54 □ Brava i. Cape Verde
37 P7 Bråviken in. Sweden
82 E3 Bravo del Norte, Río r. Mex./U.S.A.
75 E5 Brawley U.S.A.
41 E4 Bray Rep. of Ireland
64 F4 Brazeau Can.
64 F4 Brazeau r. Can.

85 E4 Brazil country S. America
96 H7 Brazil Basin sea feature Atl. Ocean
77 D5 Brazos r. U.S.A.
56 B4 Brazzaville Congo
49 H2 Brčko Bos.-Herz.
9 A6 Breaksea Sd in. N.Z.
9 E1 Bream Bay b. N.Z.
9 E1 Bream Head hd N.Z.
39 C6 Brechfa U.K.
40 F4 Brechin U.K.
42 C3 Brecht Belgium
76 D2 Breckenridge MN U.S.A.
77 D5 Breckenridge TX U.S.A.
46 H6 Břeclav Czech Rep.
39 D6 Brecon U.K.
39 D6 Brecon Beacons h. U.K.
39 D6 Brecon Beacons National Park U.K.
42 C3 Breda Neth.
58 D7 Bredasdorp S. Africa
8 G3 Bredbo Austr.
43 L2 Breddin Ger.
42 E3 Bredevoort Neth.
36 O3 Bredviken Norway
42 D3 Bree Belgium
80 D5 Breezewood U.S.A.
46 D7 Bregenz Austria
36 B4 Breiðafjörður b. Iceland
36 F4 Breiðdalsvík Iceland
43 G4 Breidenbach Ger.
46 C6 Breisach am Rhein Ger.
43 J1 Breitenfelde Ger.
43 J5 Breitengüßbach Ger.
36 S1 Breivikbotn Norway
87 J6 Brejinho de Nazaré Brazil
36 L5 Brekstad Norway
43 G1 Bremen Ger.
79 C5 Bremen GA U.S.A.
68 D5 Bremen IN U.S.A.
43 G1 Bremerhaven Ger.
72 B2 Bremerton U.S.A.
43 H1 Bremervörde Ger.
42 F4 Bremm Ger.
77 D6 Brenham U.S.A.
36 N4 Brenna Norway
46 E7 Brenner Pass Austria/Italy
69 H2 Brent Can.
48 D2 Brenta r. Italy
39 H6 Brentwood U.K.
74 B3 Brentwood CA U.S.A.
81 G4 Brentwood NY U.S.A.
48 D2 Brescia Italy
48 D1 Bressanone Italy
40 □ Bressay i. U.K.
44 D3 Bressuire France
51 B4 Brest Belarus
44 B2 Brest France
44 C2 Bretagne reg. France
42 A5 Breteuil France
77 F6 Breton Sound b. U.S.A.
9 E1 Brett, Cape c. N.Z.
43 G5 Bretten Ger.
39 E4 Bretton U.K.
79 D5 Brevard U.S.A.
87 H4 Breves Brazil
68 E2 Brevort U.S.A.
6 E4 Brewarrina Austr.
81 J2 Brewer U.S.A.
72 C1 Brewster U.S.A.
77 G6 Brewton U.S.A.
59 H3 Breyten S. Africa
Brezhnev see Naberezhnyye Chelny
47 J6 Brezno Slovakia
48 G2 Brezovo Polje h. Croatia
56 C3 Bria C.A.R.
44 H4 Briançon France
8 F3 Bribbaree Austr.
51 C5 Briceni Moldova
44 H4 Bric Froid mt France/Italy
41 C5 Bride r. Rep. of Ireland
75 G1 Bridgeland U.S.A.
39 D6 Bridgend U.K.
40 D4 Bridge of Orchy U.K.
74 C2 Bridgeport CA U.S.A.
81 G4 Bridgeport CT U.S.A.
76 C3 Bridgeport NE U.S.A.
72 E2 Bridger U.S.A.
72 F3 Bridger Peak summit U.S.A.
81 F5 Bridgeton U.S.A.
83 N6 Bridgetown Barbados
67 H5 Bridgewater Can.
81 K1 Bridgewater U.S.A.
8 C5 Bridgewater, C. hd Austr.
39 E5 Bridgnorth U.K.
81 H2 Bridgton U.S.A.
39 D6 Bridgwater U.K.
39 D6 Bridgwater Bay b. U.K.
38 G3 Bridlington U.K.
38 G3 Bridlington Bay b. U.K.
39 E7 Bridport U.K.
46 C7 Brig Switz.
38 G4 Brigg U.K.
72 D3 Brigham City U.S.A.
8 F4 Bright Austr.
39 J6 Brightlingsea U.K.
69 J3 Brighton Can.
9 C6 Brighton N.Z.
39 G7 Brighton U.K.
69 F4 Brighton U.S.A.
44 H5 Brignoles France
54 A3 Brikama The Gambia
43 G3 Brilon Ger.
48 G4 Brindisi Italy
91 D1 Brinkmann Arg.
8 B2 Brinkworth Austr.
67 H4 Brion, Île i. Can.
44 F4 Brioude France
67 F3 Brisay Can.
7 F4 Brisbane Austr.
81 K1 Bristol Can.
39 E6 Bristol U.K.
81 G4 Bristol CT U.S.A.
81 F4 Bristol PA U.S.A.
80 B6 Bristol TN U.S.A.
62 B4 Bristol Bay b. U.S.A.
39 C6 Bristol Channel est. U.K.
92 C1 Bristol I. i. Atl. Ocean
75 E4 Bristol Lake l. U.S.A.
75 E4 Bristol Mts mts U.S.A.
92 A2 British Antarctic Territory reg. Ant.
64 D3 British Columbia div. Can.
63 K1 British Empire Range mts Can.
10 J10 British Ind. Ocean Territory terr. Ind. Ocean
59 G2 Brits S. Africa
58 E5 Britstown S. Africa
Brittany reg. see Bretagne
44 E4 Brive-la-Gaillarde France
45 E1 Briviesca Spain
39 D7 Brixham U.K.
46 H6 Brno Czech Rep.
79 D5 Broad r. U.S.A.
81 F3 Broadalbin U.S.A.
66 E3 Broadback r. Can.
8 E4 Broadford Austr.
41 C5 Broadford Rep. of Ireland
40 C3 Broadford U.K.
40 E5 Broad Law h. U.K.
39 J6 Broadstairs U.K.
72 F2 Broadus U.S.A.
65 J4 Broadview Can.
76 C3 Broadwater U.S.A.
9 D1 Broadwood N.Z.
37 S8 Brocēni Latvia
65 J3 Brochet Can.
65 J3 Brochet, Lac l. Can.
43 J3 Brocken mt Ger.
62 G2 Brock I. i. Can.
80 E3 Brockport U.S.A.
81 H3 Brockton U.S.A.
69 K3 Brockville Can.
69 F4 Brockway MI U.S.A.
80 D4 Brockway PA U.S.A.
63 K2 Brodeur Peninsula pen. Can.
68 C4 Brodhead U.S.A.
40 C5 Brodick U.K.
47 J4 Brodnica Pol.
51 C5 Brody Ukr.
77 E4 Broken Arrow U.S.A.
8 H2 Broken B. b. Austr.
76 D3 Broken Bow NE U.S.A.
77 E5 Broken Bow OK U.S.A.
8 C1 Broken Hill Austr
43 J2 Brome Ger.
39 G6 Bromley U.K.
39 E5 Bromsgrove U.K.
37 L8 Brønderslev Denmark
59 H2 Bronkhorstspruit S. Africa
36 N4 Brønnøysund Norway
68 E5 Bronson U.S.A.
39 J5 Brooke U.K.
31 A4 Brooke's Point Phil.
68 C4 Brookfield U.S.A.
77 F6 Brookhaven U.S.A.
72 A3 Brookings OR U.S.A.
76 D2 Brookings SD U.S.A.
81 H3 Brookline U.S.A.
68 A5 Brooklyn IA U.S.A.
68 B5 Brooklyn IL U.S.A.
76 E2 Brooklyn Center U.S.A.
80 D6 Brookneal U.S.A.
65 G4 Brooks Can.
74 A2 Brooks CA U.S.A.
81 J2 Brooks ME U.S.A.
92 B3 Brooks, C. c. Ant.
62 D3 Brooks Range mts U.S.A.
79 D6 Brooksville U.S.A.
80 D4 Brookville U.S.A.
6 C3 Broome Austr.
40 C3 Broom, Loch in. U.K.
40 E2 Brora U.K.
37 O9 Brösarp Sweden
41 D4 Brosna r. Rep. of Ireland
72 B3 Brothers U.S.A.
27 □ Brothers, The is H.K. China
38 E3 Brough U.K.
40 E1 Brough Head hd U.K.
41 E3 Broughshane U.K.
8 B2 Broughton r. Austr.
63 M3 Broughton Island Can.
47 P5 Brovary Ukr.
37 L8 Brovst Denmark
77 C5 Brownfield U.S.A.
72 D1 Browning U.S.A.
8 B2 Brown, Mt mt Austr.
68 D6 Brownsburg U.S.A.
81 F5 Browns Mills U.S.A.
79 B5 Brownsville TN U.S.A.
77 D7 Brownsville TX U.S.A.
81 J2 Brownville U.S.A.
81 J2 Brownville Junction U.S.A.
77 D6 Brownwood U.S.A.
47 O4 Brozha Belarus
44 F1 Bruay-en-Artois France
68 C2 Bruce Crossing U.S.A.
66 D4 Bruce Pen. pen. Can.
69 G3 Bruce Peninsula National Park Can.
43 G5 Bruchsal Ger.
43 L2 Brück Ger.
46 G7 Bruck an der Mur Austria
39 E6 Brue r. U.K.
42 B3 Bruges Belgium
Brugge see Bruges
43 G5 Brühl Baden-Württemberg Ger.
42 E4 Brühl Nordrhein-Westfalen Ger.
75 G2 Bruin Pt summit U.S.A.
23 J3 Bruint India
58 C2 Brukkaros Namibia
68 B2 Brule U.S.A.
42 C5 Brûly Belgium
90 E1 Brumado Brazil
37 M6 Brumunddal Norway
43 K2 Brunau Ger.
72 D3 Bruneau U.S.A.
72 D3 Bruneau r. U.S.A.
11 N9 Brunei country Asia
36 O5 Brunflo Sweden
48 D1 Brunico Italy
9 C5 Brunner, L. l. N.Z.
65 H4 Bruno Can.
46 D4 Brunsbüttel Ger.
79 D6 Brunswick GA U.S.A.
81 J3 Brunswick ME U.S.A.
80 C4 Brunswick OH U.S.A.
88 B8 Brunswick, Peninsula de pen. Chile
46 H6 Bruntál Czech Rep.
92 C3 Brunt Ice Shelf ice feature Ant.
59 J4 Bruntville S. Africa
6 E6 Bruny I. i. Austr.
72 G3 Brush U.S.A.
42 C4 Brussels Belgium
69 G4 Brussels Can.
68 D3 Brussels U.S.A.
47 O5 Brusyliv Ukr.
8 F4 Bruthen Austr.
Bruxelles see Brussels
80 A4 Bryan OH U.S.A.
77 D6 Bryan TX U.S.A.
92 A3 Bryan Coast coastal area Ant.
8 B2 Bryan, Mt h. Austr.
50 E4 Bryansk Rus. Fed.
50 E4 Bryanskaya Oblast' div. Rus. Fed.
51 H6 Bryanskoye Rus. Fed.
75 F3 Bryce Canyon Nat. Park U.S.A.
75 H5 Bryce Mt mt U.S.A.
37 J7 Bryne Norway
51 F6 Bryukhovetskaya Rus. Fed.
46 H5 Brzeg Pol.
7 F2 Buala Solomon Is
54 A3 Buba Guinea-Bissau
17 M7 Būbīyān I. i. Kuwait
31 B5 Bubuan i. Phil.
16 C3 Bucak Turkey
89 B3 Bucaramanga Col.
31 C4 Bucas Grande i. Phil.
8 G4 Buchan Austr.
54 A4 Buchanan Liberia
68 D5 Buchanan MI U.S.A.
80 D6 Buchanan VA U.S.A.
77 D6 Buchanan, L. l. U.S.A.
63 L2 Buchan Gulf b. Can.
67 J4 Buchans Can.
49 M2 Bucharest Romania
43 J1 Büchen Ger.
43 H5 Buchen (Odenwald) Ger.
43 L1 Buchholz Ger.
43 H1 Bucholz in der Nordheide Ger.
74 B4 Buchon, Point pt U.S.A.
47 M7 Bucin, Pasul pass Romania
8 E1 Buckambool Mt h. Austr.
43 H2 Bückeburg Ger.
43 H2 Bücken Ger.
75 F5 Buckeye U.S.A.
80 B5 Buckeye Lake l. U.S.A.
80 C5 Buckhannon U.S.A.
80 C5 Buckhannon r. U.S.A.
40 E4 Buckhaven U.K.
69 H3 Buckhorn Can.
75 H5 Buckhorn U.S.A.
69 H3 Buckhorn Lake l. Can.
80 B6 Buckhorn Lake l. U.S.A.
40 F3 Buckie U.K.
69 K3 Buckingham Can.
39 G5 Buckingham U.K.
80 D6 Buckingham U.S.A.
6 D3 Buckingham Bay b. Austr.
6 E4 Buckland Tableland reg. Austr.
92 A6 Buckle I. i. Ant.
75 F4 Buckskin Mts mts U.S.A.
74 B2 Bucks Mt mt U.S.A.
81 J2 Bucksport U.S.A.
43 L2 Bückwitz Ger.
București see Bucharest
80 B4 Bucyrus U.S.A.
47 P4 Buda-Kashalyova Belarus
47 J7 Budapest Hungary
22 D3 Budaun India
8 E1 Budda Austr.
92 C6 Budd Coast coastal area Ant.
40 F4 Buddon Ness pt U.K.
48 C4 Buddusò Sardinia Italy
39 C7 Bude U.K.
77 F6 Bude U.S.A.
51 H6 Budennovsk Rus. Fed.
43 H4 Büdingen Ger.
22 D5 Budni India
50 E3 Budogoshch' Rus. Fed.
23 H2 Budongquan China
48 C4 Budoni Sardinia Italy
54 C4 Buea Cameroon
74 B4 Buellton U.S.A.
91 D2 Buena Esperanza Arg.
89 A4 Buenaventura Col.
82 C3 Buenaventura Mex.
89 A4 Buenaventure, B. de b. Col.
73 F4 Buena Vista CO U.S.A.
80 D6 Buena Vista VA U.S.A.
45 E2 Buendia, Embalse de resr Spain
91 B4 Bueno r. Chile
91 E2 Buenos Aires Arg.
91 E3 Buenos Aires div. Arg.
88 B7 Buenos Aires, L. l. Arg./Chile
88 C7 Buen Pasto Arg.
80 D3 Buffalo NY U.S.A.
77 D4 Buffalo OK U.S.A.
76 C2 Buffalo SD U.S.A.
77 D6 Buffalo TX U.S.A.
68 B3 Buffalo WI U.S.A.
72 F2 Buffalo WY U.S.A.
64 G3 Buffalo r. Can.
68 B3 Buffalo r. U.S.A.
64 F3 Buffalo Head Hills h. Can.
64 F2 Buffalo Lake l. Can.
8 F4 Buffalo, Mt mt Austr.
65 H3 Buffalo Narrows Can.
58 B4 Buffels watercourse S. Africa
59 G1 Buffels Drift S. Africa
79 D5 Buford U.S.A.
49 L2 Buftea Romania
47 K4 Bug r. Pol.
89 A4 Buga Col.
89 A3 Bugalagrande Col.
8 G1 Bugaldie Austr.
18 D2 Bugdayli Turkm.
33 D4 Bugel, Tanjung pt Indon.
42 C3 Buggenhout Belgium
48 G2 Bugojno Bos.-Herz.
31 A4 Bugsuk i. Phil.
31 B2 Buguey Phil.
18 D4 Būhābād Iran
17 J5 Buḩayrat ath Tharthār l. Iraq
17 K4 Buḩayrat Shārī l. Iraq
57 D5 Buhera Zimbabwe
31 B3 Buhi Phil.
72 D3 Buhl ID U.S.A.
68 A2 Buhl MN U.S.A.
17 J3 Bühtan r. Turkey
47 N7 Buhuşi Romania
39 D5 Builth Wells U.K.
54 B4 Bui National Park Ghana
50 J4 Buinsk Rus. Fed.
17 L4 Bu'in Soflā Iran
24 D2 Buir Nur l. Mongolia
57 B6 Buitepos Namibia
49 J3 Bujanovac Yugo.
56 C4 Bujumbura Burundi
24 D1 Bukachacha Rus. Fed.
7 F2 Buka I. i. P.N.G.
18 D4 Būkand Iran
56 C4 Bukavu Congo(Zaire)
19 G2 Bukhara Uzbek.
31 C6 Bukide i. Indon.
32 □ Bukit Batok Sing.
32 B5 Bukit Fraser Malaysia
32 □ Bukit Panjang Sing.
32 □ Bukit Timah Sing.
33 B3 Bukittinggi Indon.
56 D4 Bukoba Tanz.
32 □ Bukom, P. i. Sing.
25 F7 Bula Indon.
50 J4 Bula r. Rus. Fed.
46 D7 Bülach Switz.
8 J2 Bulahdelal Austr.
31 B3 Bulan Phil.
16 G1 Bulancak Turkey
22 D3 Bulandshahr India
17 J2 Bulanık Turkey
57 C6 Bulawayo Zimbabwe
16 F3 Bulbul Syria
16 B2 Buldan Turkey
22 D5 Buldana India
59 J2 Bulembu Swaziland
26 B1 Bulgan Mongolia
24 C2 Bulgan Mongolia
35 H4 Bulgaria country Europe
9 D4 Buller r. N.Z.
8 F4 Buller, Mt mt Austr.
75 E4 Bullhead City U.S.A.
74 D4 Bullion Mts mts U.S.A.
58 E2 Büllsport Namibia
32 □ Buloh, P. i. Sing.
8 D4 Buloke, Lake l. Austr.
59 G4 Bultfontein S. Africa
31 C5 Buluan Phil.
6 C2 Bulukumba Indon.
13 O2 Bulun Rus. Fed.
56 B4 Bulungu Bandundu Congo(Zaire)
56 C4 Bulungu Kasai-Occidental Congo(Zaire)
19 G2 Bulungur Uzbek.
31 C3 Bulusan Phil.
56 C3 Bumba Congo(Zaire)
26 B1 Bumbat Sum China
75 F4 Bumble Bee U.S.A.
31 A5 Bum-Bum i. Malaysia
56 B4 Buna Congo(Zaire)
56 D3 Buna Kenya
56 C4 Bunazi Tanz.
41 C2 Bunbeg Rep. of Ireland
6 B5 Bunbury Austr.
41 E5 Bunclody Rep. of Ireland
41 D2 Buncrana Rep. of Ireland
56 C4 Bunda Tanz.
6 F4 Bundaberg Austr.
22 C4 Bundi India
41 C3 Bundoran Rep. of Ireland
23 F5 Bundu India
39 J5 Bungay U.K.
32 B2 Bung Boraphet l. Thai.
8 G3 Bungendore Austr.
92 C5 Bunger Hills h. Ant.
29 C8 Bungo-suidō chan. Japan
56 D3 Bunia Congo(Zaire)
56 C4 Bunianga Congo(Zaire)
8 D4 Buninyong Austr.
54 D3 Buni-Yadi Nigeria
22 C2 Bunji Jammu and Kashmir
75 E3 Bunkerville U.S.A.
77 E6 Bunkie U.S.A.
79 D6 Bunnell U.S.A.
16 E2 Bünyan Turkey
31 A3 Bunyu i. Indon.
18 C4 Bu ol Kheyr Iran
32 D2 Buôn Hô Vietnam
32 D2 Buôn Mê Thuột Vietnam
13 P2 Buorkhaya, Guba b. Rus. Fed.
20 C4 Buqayq S. Arabia
56 D4 Bura Kenya
22 E3 Burang China
90 E2 Buranhaém r. Brazil
56 E3 Burao Somalia
31 C4 Burauen Phil.
20 B4 Buraydah S. Arabia
43 G4 Burbach Ger.
74 C4 Burbank U.S.A.
8 F2 Burcher Austr.
19 G2 Burdalyk Turkm.
16 C3 Burdur Turkey
56 D2 Burē Eth.
39 J5 Bure r. U.K.
36 R4 Bureå Sweden
24 F1 Bureinskiy Khrebet mts Rus. Fed.
16 D6 Bûr Fu'ad Egypt
49 M3 Burgas Bulg.
79 E5 Burgaw U.S.A.
43 K2 Burg bei Magdeburg Ger.
43 J5 Burgbernheim Ger.
43 J2 Burgdorf Ger.
67 J4 Burgeo Can.
59 G5 Burgersdorp S. Africa
59 J2 Burgersfort S. Africa
39 G7 Burgess Hill U.K.
43 H4 Burghaun Ger.
46 F6 Burghausen Ger.
40 E3 Burghead U.K.
42 B3 Burgh-Haamstede Neth.
48 E6 Burgio, Serra di h. Sicily Italy
43 L5 Burglengenfeld Ger.
45 E1 Burgos Spain
43 L4 Burgstädt Ger.
37 Q8 Burgsvik Sweden
Burgundy reg. see Bourgogne
24 B3 Burhan Budai Shan mts China
49 M5 Burhaniye Turkey
22 D5 Burhanpur India
23 E5 Burhar-Dhanpuri India
23 F4 Burhi Gandak r. India
31 B3 Burias i. Phil.
23 H4 Buri Dihing r. India
23 E4 Buri Gandak r. Nepal
67 J4 Burin Peninsula pen. Can.
32 B2 Buriram Thai.
87 K5 Buriti Bravo Brazil
90 C1 Buritis Brazil
19 G4 Burj Pak.
92 A3 Burke I. i. Ant.
9 C6 Burke Pass N.Z.
6 D3 Burketown Austr.
52 D4 Burkina country Africa
69 H3 Burk's Falls Can.
72 D3 Burley U.S.A.
69 H4 Burlington Can.
76 C4 Burlington CO U.S.A.
68 B5 Burlington IA U.S.A.
68 D5 Burlington IN U.S.A.
81 J2 Burlington ME U.S.A.
81 G2 Burlington VT U.S.A.
68 C4 Burlington WI U.S.A.
Burma country see Myanmar
77 D6 Burnet U.S.A.
72 B3 Burney U.S.A.
81 J2 Burnham U.S.A.
6 E6 Burnie Austr.
38 G3 Burniston U.K.
38 E4 Burnley U.K.
72 C3 Burns U.S.A.
65 H1 Burnside r. Can.
62 F4 Burns Lake Can.
80 C5 Burnsville Lake l. U.S.A.
79 F7 Burnt Ground Bahamas
40 E4 Burntisland U.K.
67 H3 Burnt Lake l. Can.
65 K3 Burntwood r. Can.
65 J3 Burnt Wood Lake l. Can.
8 D3 Buronga Austr.
12 K5 Burqin China
16 G5 Burqu' Jordan
8 B2 Burra Austr.
40 □ Burravoe U.K.
40 F2 Burray i. U.K.
49 J4 Burrel Albania
8 G2 Burrendong Reservoir Austr.
8 H3 Burrewarra Pt pt Austr.
45 F3 Burriana Spain
8 G3 Burrinjuck Austr.
8 G3 Burrinjuck Reservoir Austr.
80 B5 Burr Oak Reservoir U.S.A.
82 D3 Burro, Serranías del mts Mex.
40 D6 Burrow Head hd U.K.
75 G2 Burrville U.S.A.
16 B1 Bursa Turkey
55 F2 Bûr Safâga Egypt
Bûr Sa'îd see Port Said
43 G5 Bürstadt Ger.
Bûr Sudan see Port Sudan
8 C2 Burta Austr.
68 E3 Burt Lake l. U.S.A.
69 F4 Burton U.S.A.
66 E3 Burton, Lac l. Can.
41 C3 Burtonport Rep. of Ireland
39 F5 Burton upon Trent U.K.
36 R4 Burträsk Sweden
81 K1 Burtts Corner Can.
8 D2 Burtundy Austr.
25 E7 Buru i. Indon
16 C6 Burullus, Bahra el lag. Egypt
53 G6 Burundi country Africa
56 C4 Bururi Burundi
64 B2 Burwash Landing Can.
40 F2 Burwick U.K.
51 E5 Buryn' Ukr.
39 H5 Bury St Edmunds U.K.
22 C2 Burzil Pass Jammu and Kashmir
56 C4 Busanga Congo(Zaire)
41 E2 Bush r. U.K.
18 C4 Būshehr Iran
23 E2 Bushêngcaka China
56 D4 Bushenyi Uganda
Bushire see Būshehr
41 E2 Bushmills U.K.
68 B5 Bushnell U.S.A.
56 C3 Businga Congo(Zaire)
32 □ Busing, P. i. Sing.
16 F5 Buşrá ash Shām Syria
6 B5 Busselton Austr.
42 D2 Bussum Neth.
77 C7 Bustamante Mex.
48 C2 Busto Arsizio Italy
31 A3 Busuanga Phil.
31 A3 Busuanga i. Phil.
56 C3 Buta Congo(Zaire)
32 A4 Butang Group is Thai.
91 C3 Buta Ranquil Arg.
56 C4 Butare Rwanda
95 G5 Butaritari i. Pac. Oc.
8 A2 Bute Austr.
40 C5 Bute i. U.K.
64 D4 Butedale Can.
64 D4 Bute In. in. Can.
40 C5 Bute, Sound of chan. U.K.
59 H4 Butha Buthe Lesotho
43 G1 Butjadingen reg. Ger.
68 E5 Butler IN U.S.A.
80 D4 Butler PA U.S.A.
41 D3 Butlers Bridge Rep. of Ireland
25 E7 Buton i. Indon.
43 L1 Bütow Ger.
72 D2 Butte U.S.A.
43 K3 Buttelstedt Ger.
74 B1 Butte Meadows U.S.A.
33 B1 Butterworth Malaysia
59 H6 Butterworth S. Africa
41 C5 Buttevant Rep. of Ireland
64 D5 Buttle L. l. Can.
40 B2 Butt of Lewis hd U.K.
63 J4 Button Bay b. Can.
74 C4 Buttonwillow U.S.A.
31 C4 Butuan Phil.
27 B5 Butuo China
51 G5 Buturlinovka Rus. Fed.
23 E4 Butwal Nepal
43 G4 Butzbach Ger.
56 E3 Buulobarde Somalia
56 E4 Buur Gaabo Somalia
56 E3 Buurhabaka Somalia
23 F4 Buxar India
43 H1 Buxtehude Ger.
39 F4 Buxton U.K.
50 G3 Buy Rus. Fed.
68 A1 Buyck U.S.A.
51 H7 Buynaksk Rus. Fed.
Büyük Ağrı mt see Ararat, Mt
16 A3 Büyükmenderes r. Turkey
30 B3 Buyun Shan mt China
42 C5 Buzancy France
49 M2 Buzău Romania
57 D5 Búzi Moz.
12 G4 Buzuluk Rus. Fed.
51 G5 Buzuluk r. Rus. Fed.
81 H4 Buzzards Bay b. U.S.A.
23 G4 Byakar Bhutan
49 L3 Byala Bulg.
49 K3 Byala Slatina Bulg.
47 O4 Byalynichy Belarus
62 H2 Byam Martin I. i. Can.
50 D4 Byarezina r. Belarus
50 C4 Byaroza Belarus
16 E4 Byblos Lebanon
46 J4 Bydgoszcz Pol.
50 D4 Byerazino Belarus
72 F4 Byers U.S.A.
47 O3 Byeshankovichy Belarus
37 K7 Bygland Norway
50 D4 Bykhaw Belarus
37 K7 Bykle Norway
63 L2 Bylot Island i. Can.
69 G3 Byng Inlet Can.
92 B5 Byrd Gl. gl. Ant.
37 K6 Byrkjelo Norway
68 C4 Byron IL U.S.A.
81 H2 Byron ME U.S.A.
7 F4 Byron Bay Austr.
13 M2 Byrranga, Gory mts Rus. Fed.
36 R4 Byske Sweden
13 P3 Bytantay r. Rus. Fed.
47 J5 Bytom Pol.
46 H3 Bytów Pol.
19 E2 Byuzmeyin Turkm.

C

88 E3 Caacupé Para.
90 A4 Caaguazú, Cordillera de h. Para.
90 A4 Caaguazú Para.
90 A3 Caarapó Brazil
90 A4 Caazapá Para.
86 C6 Caballas Peru
86 D4 Caballococha Peru
31 B3 Cabanatuan Phil.
67 G4 Cabano Can.
56 E2 Cabdul Qaadir Somalia
90 A1 Cabeceira Rio Manso Brazil
87 M5 Cabedelo Brazil
45 D3 Cabeza del Buey Spain
86 F7 Cabezas Bol.
91 E3 Cabildo Arg.
89 C2 Cabimas Venez.
56 B4 Cabinda Angola
56 B4 Cabinda div. Angola
72 C1 Cabinet Mts mts U.S.A.
89 B3 Cable Way pass Col.
90 D3 Cabo Frio Brazil
90 E3 Cabo Frio, Ilha do i. Brazil
66 E4 Cabonga, Réservoir resr Can.
77 E4 Cabool U.S.A.
7 F4 Caboolture Austr.
87 H3 Cabo Orange, Parque Nacional de nat. park Brazil
86 C4 Cabo Pantoja Peru
82 B2 Caborca Mex.
69 G3 Cabot Head pt Can.
67 J4 Cabot Strait str. Can.
90 D2 Cabral, Serra do mts Brazil
17 L2 Cäbrayıl Azer.
45 H3 Cabrera i. Spain
45 C1 Cabrera, Sierra de la mts Spain
45 F3 Cabriel r. Spain
89 D3 Cabruta Venez.
31 B2 Cabugao Phil.
88 F3 Caçador Brazil
84 C3 Cacahuatepec Mex.
49 J3 Čačak Yugo.
91 G1 Caçapava do Sul Brazil
80 D5 Cacapon r. U.S.A.
89 B3 Cácares Col.
48 C4 Caccia, Capo pt Sardinia Italy
87 G7 Cáceres Brazil
45 C3 Cáceres Spain
72 D3 Cache Peak summit U.S.A.
54 A3 Cacheu Guinea-Bissau
88 C3 Cachi r. Arg.
87 H5 Cachimbo, Serra do h. Brazil
89 B3 Cáchira Col.
90 E1 Cachoeira Brazil
90 B2 Cachoeira Alta Brazil
91 G1 Cachoeira do Sul Brazil
90 E3 Cachoeiro de Itapemirim Brazil
54 A3 Cacine Guinea-Bissau
87 H3 Caciporé, Cabo pt Brazil
57 B5 Cacolo Angola
56 B4 Cacongo Angola
74 D3 Cactus Range mts U.S.A.
90 B2 Caçu Brazil
90 D1 Caculé Brazil
47 J6 Čadca Slovakia
43 H1 Cadenberge Ger.
84 B1 Cadereyta Mex.
31 B3 Cadig Mountains Phil.
69 H1 Cadillac Que. Can.
65 H5 Cadillac Sask. Can.
68 E3 Cadillac U.S.A.
31 B4 Cadiz Phil.
45 C4 Cádiz Spain
45 C4 Cádiz, Golfo de g. Spain
75 E4 Cadiz Lake l. U.S.A.
44 D2 Caen France
39 C4 Caernarfon U.K.
39 C4 Caernarfon Bay b. U.K.
39 D6 Caerphilly U.K.
80 B5 Caesar Creek Lake l. U.S.A.
16 E5 Caesarea Israel
90 D1 Caetité Brazil
88 C3 Cafayate Arg.
31 B4 Cagayan i. Phil.
31 B2 Cagayan r. Phil.
31 C4 Cagayan de Oro Phil.
31 B4 Cagayan Islands is Phil.
48 E3 Cagli Italy
48 C5 Cagliari Sardinia Italy
48 C5 Cagliari, Golfo di b. Sardinia Italy
89 B4 Caguán r. Col.
41 B6 Caha h. Rep. of Ireland
79 C5 Cahaba r. U.S.A.
41 B6 Caha Mts h. Rep. of Ireland
41 A6 Cahermore Rep. of Ireland
41 D5 Cahir Rep. of Ireland
41 A6 Cahirciveen Rep. of Ireland
57 D5 Cahora Bassa, Lago de resr Moz.
41 E5 Cahore Point pt Rep. of Ireland
44 E4 Cahors France
86 C5 Cahuapanas Peru
51 D6 Cahul Moldova
57 D5 Caia Moz.
87 G6 Caiabis, Serra dos h. Brazil
57 C5 Caianda Angola
90 B2 Caiapó r. Brazil
90 B2 Caiapônia Brazil
90 B2 Caiapó, Serra do mts Brazil
83 J4 Caibarién Cuba
32 C3 Cai Be Vietnam
89 D3 Caicara Venez.
83 K4 Caicos Is is Turks and Caicos Is
91 B1 Caimanes Chile
31 A3 Caiman Point pt Phil.
45 F2 Caimodorro mt Spain
32 C3 Cai Nuoc Vietnam
40 E3 Cairn Gorm mt U.K.
40 E3 Cairngorm Mountains U.K.
40 C6 Cairnryan U.K.
6 E3 Cairns Austr.
40 E3 Cairn Toul mt U.K.
55 F1 Cairo Egypt
79 C6 Cairo U.S.A.
48 C2 Cairo Montenotte Italy
57 B5 Caiundo Angola
86 C5 Cajamarca Peru
31 B3 Cajidiocan Phil.
48 G1 Čakovec Croatia
16 B2 Çal Turkey
59 G5 Cala S. Africa
54 C4 Calabar Nigeria
69 J3 Calabogie Can.
89 D2 Calabozo Venez.
49 K3 Calafat Romania
88 B8 Calafate Arg.
31 B3 Calagua Islands is Phil.
45 F1 Calahorra Spain
57 B5 Calai Angola
44 E1 Calais France
81 K2 Calais U.S.A.
86 F5 Calama Brazil
88 C2 Calama Chile
89 B2 Calamar Bolívar Col.
89 B4 Calamar Guaviare Col.
31 A4 Calamian Group is Phil.
45 F2 Calamocha Spain
57 B4 Calandula Angola
55 E2 Calanscio Sand Sea des. Libya
31 B3 Calapan Phil.
49 M2 Călărași Romania
45 F2 Calatayud Spain
31 B3 Calauag Phil.
31 B3 Calavite, Cape pt Phil.
31 A3 Calawit i. Phil.
31 B2 Calayan i. Phil.
31 C3 Calbayog Phil.
43 K3 Calbe (Saale) Ger.
31 C4 Calbiga Phil.
91 B4 Calbuco Chile
87 L5 Calcanhar, Ponta do pt Brazil
77 E6 Calcasieu L. l. U.S.A.
87 H3 Calçoene Brazil
23 G5 Calcutta India
45 B3 Caldas da Rainha Port.
90 C2 Caldas Novas Brazil
43 H3 Calden Ger.
88 B3 Caldera Chile
17 J2 Çaldıran Turkey
72 C3 Caldwell U.S.A.
80 D3 Caledon Can.
58 C7 Caledon S. Africa
59 G5 Caledon r. Lesotho/S. Africa
69 H4 Caledonia Can.
68 B4 Caledonia U.S.A.
84 B2 Calera Mex.
88 C7 Caleta Olivia Arg.
75 E5 Calexico U.S.A.
38 C3 Calf of Man i. U.K.
64 G4 Calgary Can.
79 C5 Calhoun U.S.A.
89 A4 Cali Col.
31 C4 Calicoan i. Phil.
21 A4 Calicut India
74 C4 Caliente CA U.S.A.
75 E3 Caliente NV U.S.A.
74 B3 California div. U.S.A.
74 B3 California Aqueduct canal U.S.A.
82 B2 California, Golfo de g. Mex.
74 C4 California Hot Springs U.S.A.
17 M2 Cälilabad Azer.
73 D5 Calipatria U.S.A.
74 A2 Calistoga U.S.A.
58 D6 Calitzdorp S. Africa
84 E2 Calkiní Mex.
74 D2 Callaghan, Mt mt U.S.A.
79 D6 Callahan U.S.A.
41 D5 Callan Rep. of Ireland
69 H2 Callander Can.
40 D4 Callander U.K.
86 C6 Callao Peru
75 F2 Callao U.S.A.
84 C2 Calles Mex.
81 F4 Callicoon U.S.A.
39 C7 Callington U.K.
69 G2 Callum Can.
64 G4 Calmar Can.
68 B4 Calmar U.S.A.
75 E4 Cal-Nev-Ari U.S.A.
79 D7 Caloosahatchee r. U.S.A.
74 B2 Calpine U.S.A.
84 C3 Calpulálpan Mex.
48 F6 Caltanissetta Sicily Italy
68 C2 Calumet U.S.A.
57 B5 Calunga Angola
57 B5 Caluquembe Angola
31 B4 Calusa i. Phil.
56 F2 Caluula Somalia
75 G5 Calva U.S.A.
64 D4 Calvert I. i. Can.
48 C3 Calvi Corsica France
45 H3 Calvià Spain
84 B2 Calvillo Mex.
58 C5 Calvinia S. Africa
48 F4 Calvo, Monte mt Italy
39 H5 Cam r. U.K.
90 E1 Camaçari Brazil
74 B2 Camache Reservoir U.S.A.
84 B1 Camacho Mex.
57 B5 Camacuio Angola
57 B5 Camacupa Angola
89 D2 Camaguán Venez.
83 J4 Camagüey Cuba
83 J4 Camagüey, Arch. de is Cuba
33 B1 Camah, Gunung mt Malaysia
Çamalan see Gülek
86 D7 Camana Peru
57 C5 Camanongue Angola
90 B2 Camapuã Brazil
91 G1 Camaquã Brazil
91 G1 Camaquã r. Brazil
16 E3 Çamardı Turkey
84 C1 Camargo Mex.
84 A2 Camaronero, L. del lag. Mex.
88 C6 Camarones Arg.
88 C6 Camarones, Bahía b. Arg.
72 B2 Camas U.S.A.
32 C3 Ca Mau Vietnam
Cambay see Khambhat
Cambay, Gulf of g. see Khambhat, Gulf of
39 G6 Camberley U.K.
11 M8 Cambodia country Asia
39 B7 Camborne U.K.
44 F1 Cambrai France
74 B4 Cambria U.S.A.
39 D5 Cambrian Mountains reg. U.K.
69 G4 Cambridge Can.
9 E2 Cambridge N.Z.
39 H5 Cambridge U.K.
68 B5 Cambridge IL U.S.A.
81 H3 Cambridge MA U.S.A.
81 E5 Cambridge MD U.S.A.
76 E2 Cambridge MN U.S.A.
81 G3 Cambridge NY U.S.A.
80 C4 Cambridge OH U.S.A.
67 G2 Cambrien, Lac l. Can.
8 H3 Camden Austr.
79 C5 Camden AL U.S.A.
77 E5 Camden AR U.S.A.
81 J2 Camden ME U.S.A.
81 F5 Camden NJ U.S.A.
81 F3 Camden NY U.S.A.
79 D5 Camden SC U.S.A.
88 B8 Camden, Isla i. Chile
57 C5 Cameia, Parque Nacional da nat. park Angola
75 G4 Cameron AZ U.S.A.
77 E6 Cameron LA U.S.A.
76 E4 Cameron MO U.S.A.
77 D6 Cameron TX U.S.A.
68 B3 Cameron WI U.S.A.
32 B4 Cameron Highlands Malaysia
64 F3 Cameron Hills h. Can.
74 B2 Cameron Park U.S.A.
53 F5 Cameroon country Africa
54 C4 Cameroun, Mt mt Cameroon
87 J4 Cametá Brazil
31 B2 Camiguin i. Phil.
31 C4 Camiguin i. Phil.
31 B3 Camiling Phil.
79 C6 Camilla U.S.A.
86 F8 Camiri Bol.
87 K4 Camocim Brazil
6 D3 Camooweal Austr.
31 C4 Camotes Sea g. Phil.
91 E2 Campana Arg.
89 B4 Campana, Co h. Col.
88 A7 Campana, I. i. Chile
91 B2 Campanario mt Arg./Chile
64 D4 Campania I. i. Can.
58 E4 Campbell S. Africa

9 E4 Campbell, Cape c. N.Z.
4 H10 Campbell Island i. N.Z.
64 D4 Campbell River Can.
69 J3 Campbells Bay Can.
78 C4 Campbellsville U.S.A.
67 G4 Campbellton Can.
40 C5 Campbeltown U.K.
84 E3 Campeche Mex.
84 E3 Campeche div. Mex.
84 D3 Campeche, Bahía de g. Mex.
8 D5 Camperdown Austr.
49 L2 Câmpina Romania
87 L5 Campina Grande Brazil
90 C3 Campinas Brazil
90 C2 Campina Verde Brazil
54 C4 Campo Cameroon
89 B4 Campoalegre Col.
48 F4 Campobasso Italy
90 D3 Campo Belo Brazil
87 H6 Campo de Diauarum Brazil
90 C2 Campo Florido Brazil
88 D3 Campo Gallo Arg.
90 A3 Campo Grande Brazil
87 K4 Campo Maior Brazil
45 C3 Campo Maior Port.
90 B4 Campo Mourão Brazil
90 E3 Campos Brazil
90 C2 Campos Altos Brazil
90 D3 Campos do Jordão Brazil
90 B4 Campos Erê reg. Brazil
40 D4 Campsie Fells h. U.K.
80 B6 Campton KY U.S.A.
81 H3 Campton NH U.S.A.
49 L2 Câmpulung Romania
47 M7 Câmpulung Moldovenesc Romania
75 G4 Camp Verde U.S.A.
32 D3 Cam Ranh Vietnam
64 G4 Camrose Can.
39 B6 Camrose U.K.
65 G2 Camsell Lake l. Can.
65 H3 Camsell Portage Can.
51 C7 Çan Turkey
81 G3 Canaan U.S.A.
60 G4 Canada country N. America
91 E2 Cañada de Gómez Arg.
81 H2 Canada Falls Lake l. U.S.A.
77 C5 Canadian r. U.S.A.
89 E3 Canaima, Parque Nacional nat. park Venez.
81 F3 Canajoharie U.S.A.
51 C7 Çanakkale Turkey
Çanakkale Boğazı str. see Dardanelles
91 C2 Canalejas Arg.
80 E3 Canandaigua U.S.A.
80 E3 Canandaigua Lake l. U.S.A.
82 B2 Cananea Mex.
67 H2 Canapée, Lac l. Can.
90 C4 Cananéia Brazil
89 C4 Canapiare, Co h. Col.
86 C4 Cañar Ecuador
Canarias, Islas is see Canary Islands
96 G4 Canary Basin sea feature Atl. Ocean
34 D6 Canary Islands div. Spain
81 F3 Canastota U.S.A.
90 C2 Canastra, Serra da mts Brazil
84 A1 Canatlán Mex.
79 D6 Canaveral, Cape c. U.S.A.
45 E2 Cañaveras Spain
90 E1 Canavieiras Brazil
8 F1 Canbelego Austr.
8 G3 Canberra Austr.
72 B3 Canby CA U.S.A.
76 D2 Canby MN U.S.A.
82 G4 Cancún Mex.
73 F6 Candelaria Chihuahua Mex.
84 E3 Candelaria Mex.
45 D2 Candeleda Spain
8 G4 Candelo Austr.
87 J4 Cândido Mendes Brazil
16 D1 Çandır Turkey
65 H4 Candle Lake Can.
65 H4 Candle Lake l. Can.
92 C1 Candlemas I. i. Atl. Ocean
81 G4 Candlewood, Lake l. U.S.A.
76 D1 Cando U.S.A.
31 B2 Candon Phil.
91 B1 Canela Baja Chile
91 F2 Canelones Uru.
91 B3 Cañete Chile
45 F2 Cañete Spain
86 D6 Cangallo Peru
57 B5 Cangamba Angola
45 C1 Cangas del Narcea Spain
58 E6 Cango Caves caves S. Africa
87 L5 Canguaretama Brazil
91 G1 Canguçu Brazil
91 G1 Canguçu, Sa do h. Brazil
27 D6 Cangwu China
26 E2 Cangzhou China
67 G3 Caniapiscau Can.
67 G2 Caniapiscau r. Can.
63 L4 Caniapiscau, Lac l. Can.
67 G3 Caniapiscau, Rés. resr Can.
48 E6 Canicattì Sicily Italy
64 E4 Canim Lake Can.
64 E4 Canim Lake l. Can.
87 L4 Canindé Brazil
87 K5 Canindé r. Brazil
40 C2 Canisp h. U.K.
80 E3 Canisteo U.S.A.
80 E3 Canisteo r. U.S.A.
84 B2 Cañitas de Felipe Pescador Mex.
16 D1 Çankırı Turkey
31 B4 Canlaon Phil.
64 F4 Canmore Can.
40 B3 Canna i. U.K.
21 A4 Cannanore India
21 A4 Cannanore Islands is India
44 H5 Cannes France
39 E5 Cannock U.K.
8 G4 Cann River Austr.
89 E2 Caño Araguao r. Venez.
88 F3 Canoas Brazil
65 H3 Canoe L. l. Can.
90 B4 Canoinhas Brazil
89 E2 Caño Macareo r. Venez.
89 E2 Caño Manamo r. Venez.
89 E2 Caño Mariusa r. Venez.
73 F4 Canon City U.S.A.
8 C2 Canopus Austr.
65 J4 Canora Can.
8 G2 Canowindra Austr.
67 H4 Canso, C. hd Can.
45 D1 Cantábrica, Cordillera mts Spain
91 C2 Cantantal Arg.
89 D2 Cantaura Venez.
81 K2 Canterbury Can.
39 J6 Canterbury U.K.
9 C6 Canterbury Bight b. N.Z.
9 C5 Canterbury Plains plain N.Z.
32 C3 Cân Thơ Vietnam
31 C4 Cantilan Phil.
87 K5 Canto do Buriti Brazil
Canton see Guangzhou
68 B5 Canton IL U.S.A.
81 H2 Canton ME U.S.A.
68 B5 Canton MO U.S.A.
77 F5 Canton MS U.S.A.
81 F2 Canton NY U.S.A.
80 C4 Canton OH U.S.A.
80 E4 Canton PA U.S.A.
90 B4 Cantu r. Brazil
90 B4 Cantu, Serra do h. Brazil
91 E2 Cañuelas Arg.
87 G4 Canumã Brazil
86 F5 Canutama Brazil
9 D4 Canvastown N.Z.
39 H6 Canvey Island U.K.
77 C5 Canyon U.S.A.
72 C2 Canyon City U.S.A.
75 H3 Canyon de Chelly National Monument res. U.S.A.
72 D2 Canyon Ferry L. l. U.S.A.
75 H2 Canyonlands National Park U.S.A.
64 D2 Canyon Ranges mts Can.
72 B3 Canyonville U.S.A.
30 C3 Cao r. China
27 C6 Cao Băng Vietnam
32 D2 Cao Nguyên Đăc Lăc plat. Vietnam
30 C2 Caoshi China
26 E3 Cao Xian China
31 B5 Cap i. Phil.
89 D3 Capanaparo r. Venez.
87 J4 Capanema Brazil
90 B4 Capanema r. Brazil
90 C4 Capão Bonito Brazil
89 C3 Caparo r. Venez.
89 C4 Caparro, Co h. Brazil
31 B3 Capas Phil.
67 H4 Cap-aux-Meules Can.
67 F4 Cap-de-la-Madeleine Can.
6 E6 Cape Barren Island i. Austr
96 K8 Cape Basin sea feature Atl. Ocean
67 H4 Cape Breton Highlands Nat. Park Can.
67 H4 Cape Breton Island i. Can.
67 J3 Cape Charles Can.
81 E6 Cape Charles U.S.A.
54 B4 Cape Coast Ghana
81 H4 Cape Cod Bay b. U.S.A.
81 J4 Cape Cod National Seashore res. U.S.A.
79 D7 Cape Coral U.S.A.
69 G3 Cape Croker Can.
63 L3 Cape Dorset Can.
79 E5 Cape Fear r. U.S.A.
77 F4 Cape Girardeau U.S.A.
94 D5 Cape Johnson Depth depth Pac. Oc.
90 D2 Capelinha Brazil
42 C3 Capelle aan de IJssel Neth.
81 F5 Cape May U.S.A.
81 F5 Cape May Court House U.S.A.
81 F5 Cape May Pt pt U.S.A.
57 B4 Capenda-Camulemba Angola
63 M5 Cape Sable c. Can.
67 J4 Cape St George Can.
67 H4 Cape Tormentine Can.
58 C6 Cape Town S. Africa
96 G5 Cape Verde Basin sea feature Atl. Ocean
96 F5 Cape Verde Fracture sea feature Atl. Ocean
96 H4 Cape Verde Plateau sea feature Atl. Ocean
81 E2 Cape Vincent U.S.A.
6 E3 Cape York Peninsula Austr.
83 K5 Cap-Haïtien Haiti
87 J4 Capim r. Brazil
92 B2 Capitán Arturo Prat Chile Base Ant.
90 A3 Capitán Bado Para.
73 F5 Capitan Peak mt U.S.A.
75 G2 Capitol Reef National Park U.S.A.
48 G3 Čapljina Bos.-Herz.
48 F5 Capo d'Orlando Sicily Italy
41 D5 Cappoquin Rep. of Ireland
48 C3 Capraia, Isola di i. Italy
6 F4 Capricorn Channel chan. Austr.
48 F4 Capri, Isola di i. Italy
57 C5 Caprivi Strip reg. Namibia
Cap St Jacques see Vung Tau
74 □2 Captain Cook U.S.A.
8 G3 Captain's Flat Austr.
80 C5 Captina r. U.S.A.
31 C3 Capul i. Phil.
86 C3 Caquetá r. Col.
89 B3 Cáqueza Col.
31 B3 Carabao i. Phil.
49 L2 Caracal Romania
89 E4 Caracarai Brazil
89 D2 Caracas Venez.
87 K5 Caracol Brazil
84 B3 Carácuaro Mex.
31 C5 Caraga Phil.
91 F2 Caraguatá r. Uru.
90 D3 Caraguatatuba Brazil
91 B3 Carahue Chile
90 E2 Caraí Brazil
90 D3 Carandaí Brazil
90 D3 Carangola Brazil
49 K2 Caransebeş Romania
67 H4 Caraquet Can.
89 B3 Carare r. Col.
83 H5 Caratasca, Laguna lag. Honduras
90 D2 Caratinga Brazil
86 E4 Carauari Brazil
Carauná mt see Grande, Serra
45 F3 Caravaca de la Cruz Spain
90 E2 Caravelas Brazil
88 F3 Carazinho Brazil
76 D1 Carbery Can.
48 C5 Carbonara, Capo pt Sardinia Italy
78 B4 Carbondale IL U.S.A.
81 F4 Carbondale PA U.S.A.
67 K4 Carbonear Can.
48 C5 Carbonia Sardinia Italy
90 D2 Carbonita Brazil
45 F3 Carcaixent Spain
31 B4 Carcar Phil.
91 E2 Carcaraña r. Arg.
44 F5 Carcassonne France
64 C2 Carcross Can.
6 B4 Cardabia Austr.
21 B4 Cardamon Hills mts India
84 C2 Cárdenas San Luis Potosí Mex.
84 D3 Cárdenas Tabasco Mex.
88 B7 Cardiel, L. l. Arg.
39 D6 Cardiff U.K.
39 C5 Cardigan U.K.
39 C5 Cardigan Bay b. U.K.
81 F2 Cardinal Can.
80 B4 Cardington U.S.A.
91 F2 Cardona Uru.
90 C4 Cardoso, Ilha do i. Brazil
9 B6 Cardrona N.Z.
64 G5 Cardston Can.
47 L7 Carei Romania
44 D2 Carentan France
80 B4 Carey U.S.A.
6 C4 Carey, L. salt flat Austr.
65 J2 Carey Lake l. Can.
93 J5 Cargados Carajos is Mauritius
44 C2 Carhaix-Plouguer France
91 D3 Carhué Arg.
90 E3 Cariacica Brazil
89 E2 Cariaco Venez.
61 L8 Caribbean Sea sea Atl. Ocean
64 E4 Cariboo Mts mts Can.
81 K1 Caribou U.S.A.
65 K3 Caribou r. Man. Can.
64 D2 Caribou r. N.W.T. Can.
68 E2 Caribou I. i. Can.
63 K4 Caribou Lake l. Can.
64 F3 Caribou Mountains Can.
31 C4 Carigara Phil.
42 D5 Carignan France
45 F2 Cariñena Spain
90 D1 Carinhanha Brazil
90 D1 Carinhanha r. Brazil
89 E2 Caripe Venez.
89 E2 Caripito Venez.
41 D3 Cark Mountain h. Rep. of Ireland
69 J3 Carleton Place Can.
59 G3 Carletonville S. Africa
72 C3 Carlin U.S.A.
41 E3 Carlingford Lough in. Rep. of Ireland/U.K.
38 E3 Carlisle U.K.
80 A5 Carlisle KY U.S.A.
80 E4 Carlisle PA U.S.A.
44 E5 Carlit, Pic mt France
91 E2 Carlos Casares Arg.
90 E2 Carlos Chagas Brazil
41 E5 Carlow Rep. of Ireland
40 B2 Carloway U.K.
74 D5 Carlsbad CA U.S.A.
73 F5 Carlsbad NM U.S.A.
77 C6 Carlsbad TX U.S.A.
73 F5 Carlsbad Caverns Nat. Park U.S.A.
93 J3 Carlsberg Ridge sea feature Ind. Ocean
92 B3 Carlson In. in Ant.
40 E5 Carluke U.K.
65 J5 Carlyle Can.
64 B2 Carmacks Can.
48 B2 Carmagnola Italy
65 K5 Carman Can.
39 C6 Carmarthen U.K.
39 C6 Carmarthen Bay b. U.K.
44 F4 Carmaux France
81 J2 Carmel U.S.A.
39 C4 Carmel Head hd U.K.
84 E3 Carmelita Guatemala
91 E2 Carmelo Uru.
89 B2 Carmen Col.
31 C4 Carmen Phil.
75 G6 Carmen U.S.A.
82 B3 Carmen i. Mex.
91 D4 Carmen de Patagones Arg.
84 E3 Carmen, Isla del i. Mex.
91 C2 Carmensa Arg.
78 B4 Carmi U.S.A.
74 B2 Carmichael U.S.A.
45 D4 Carmona Spain
44 C3 Carnac France
58 E5 Carnarvon S. Africa
41 D2 Carndonagh Rep. of Ireland
39 D4 Carnedd Llywelyn mt U.K.
6 C4 Carnegie, L. salt flat Austr.
95 O6 Carnegie Ridge sea feature Pac. Oc.
40 C3 Carn Eighe mt U.K.
68 D3 Carney U.S.A.
92 A3 Carney I. i. Ant.
38 E3 Carnforth U.K.
41 F3 Carnlough U.K.
40 E4 Carn nan Gabhar mt U.K.
56 B3 Carnot C.A.R.
6 D5 Carnot, C. hd Austr.
40 F4 Carnoustie U.K.
41 E5 Carnsore Point pt Rep. of Ireland
40 E5 Carnwath U.K.
65 H4 Carnwood Can.
69 F4 Caro U.S.A.
79 D7 Carol City U.S.A.
87 J5 Carolina Brazil
59 J3 Carolina S. Africa
5 M5 Caroline I. i. Kiribati
4 F4 Caroline Islands is Pac. Oc.
9 A6 Caroline Pk summit N.Z.
58 B4 Carolusberg S. Africa
89 E2 Caroní r. Venez.
89 C2 Carora Venez.
75 E3 Carp U.S.A.
47 L6 Carpathian Mountains Romania/Ukraine
6 D3 Carpentaria, Gulf of g. Austr.
44 G4 Carpentras France
48 D2 Carpi Italy
87 L5 Carpina Brazil
74 C4 Carpinteria U.S.A.
65 J5 Carpio U.S.A.
64 E4 Carp Lake Prov. Park res. Can.
81 H2 Carrabassett Valley U.S.A.
79 C6 Carrabelle U.S.A.
89 B2 Carraipía Col.
41 B4 Carra, Lough l. Rep. of Ireland
41 B6 Carran h. Rep. of Ireland
41 B6 Carrantuohill mt Rep. of Ireland
91 B2 Carranza, C. pt Chile
82 D3 Carranza, Presa V. l. Mex.
89 E3 Carrao r. Venez.
48 D2 Carrara Italy
8 E3 Carrathool Austr.
91 C3 Carrero, Co mt Arg.
89 E1 Carriacou i. Grenada
40 D5 Carrick reg. U.K.
41 F3 Carrickfergus U.K.
41 E4 Carrickmacross Rep. of Ireland
41 C4 Carrick-on-Shannon Rep. of Ireland
41 D5 Carrick-on-Suir Rep. of Ireland
8 B2 Carrieton Austr.
41 D4 Carrigallen Rep. of Ireland
41 C6 Carrigtwohill Rep. of Ireland
91 C4 Carri Lafquén, L. l. Arg.
76 D2 Carrington U.S.A.
88 B3 Carrizal Bajo Chile
75 H4 Carrizo AZ U.S.A.
75 G4 Carrizo AZ U.S.A.
74 D5 Carrizo Cr. r. U.S.A.
77 D6 Carrizo Springs U.S.A.
73 F5 Carrizozo U.S.A.
76 E3 Carroll U.S.A.
79 C5 Carrollton GA U.S.A.
78 C4 Carrollton KY U.S.A.
76 E4 Carrollton MO U.S.A.
80 C4 Carrollton OH U.S.A.
65 J4 Carrot r. Can.
65 J4 Carrot River Can.
38 B3 Carrowdore U.K.
41 B3 Carrowmore Lake l. Rep. of Ireland
81 F2 Carry Falls Reservoir U.S.A.
16 F1 Çarşamba Turkey
68 E4 Carson City MI U.S.A.
74 C2 Carson City NV U.S.A.
74 C2 Carson Lake l. U.S.A.
74 C2 Carson Sink l. U.S.A.
69 F4 Carsonville U.S.A.
91 B2 Cartagena Chile
89 B2 Cartagena Col.
45 F4 Cartagena Spain
89 B3 Cartago Col.
83 H7 Cartago Costa Rica
79 C5 Cartersville U.S.A.
68 B5 Carthage IL U.S.A.
77 E4 Carthage MO U.S.A.
81 F2 Carthage NY U.S.A.
77 E5 Carthage TX U.S.A.
69 G2 Cartier Can.
38 E3 Cartmel U.K.
67 J3 Cartwright Can.
87 L5 Caruarú Brazil
89 E2 Carúpano Venez.
74 D2 Carvers U.S.A.
42 A4 Carvin France
79 E5 Cary U.S.A.
54 B1 Casablanca Morocco
90 C3 Casa Branca Brazil
73 E6 Casa de Janos Mex.
75 G5 Casa Grande U.S.A.
75 G5 Casa Grande National Monument res. U.S.A.
48 C2 Casale Monferrato Italy
48 D2 Casalmaggiore Italy
89 C3 Casanare r. Col.
49 H4 Casarano Italy
68 B4 Cascade IA U.S.A.
72 C2 Cascade ID U.S.A.
72 E2 Cascade MT U.S.A.
9 B6 Cascade r. N.Z.
9 B6 Cascade Pt pt N.Z.
72 B3 Cascade Range mts U.S.A.
72 D2 Cascade Res. resr U.S.A.
45 B3 Cascais Port.
90 B4 Cascavel Brazil
81 J3 Casco Bay b. U.S.A.
48 F4 Caserta Italy
69 F4 Caseville U.S.A.
92 C6 Casey Austr. Base Ant.
92 D4 Casey Bay b. Ant.
41 D5 Cashel Rep. of Ireland
68 B4 Cashton U.S.A.
89 C2 Casigua Falcón Venez.
89 B2 Casigua Zulia Venez.
31 B2 Casiguran Phil.
91 E2 Casilda Arg.
7 F4 Casino Austr.
89 D4 Casiquiare, Canal r. Venez.
86 C5 Casma Peru
68 E4 Casnovia U.S.A.
74 A2 Caspar U.S.A.
45 F2 Caspe Spain
72 F3 Casper U.S.A.
Caspian Lowland lowland see Prikaspiyskaya Nizmennost'
10 F5 Caspian Sea sea Asia/Europe
80 D5 Cass U.S.A.
69 F4 Cass r. U.S.A.
80 D3 Cassadaga U.S.A.
57 C5 Cassai Angola
69 F4 Cass City U.S.A.
42 A4 Cassel France
81 F2 Casselman Can.
64 D3 Cassiar Can.
64 C3 Cassiar Mountains Can.
8 G2 Cassilis Austr.
48 E4 Cassino Italy
76 E2 Cass Lake U.S.A.
87 J4 Castanhal Brazil
91 C1 Castaño r. Arg.
77 C7 Castaños Mex.
91 C1 Castaño Viejo Arg.
48 D2 Castelfranco Veneto Italy
44 E4 Casteljaloux France
48 F4 Castellammare di Stabia Italy
91 F3 Castelli Arg.
45 F3 Castelló de la Plana Spain
45 C3 Castelo Branco Port.
45 C3 Castelo de Vide Port.
48 C4 Castelsardo Sardinia Italy
48 E6 Casteltermini Sicily Italy
48 E6 Castelvetrano Sicily Italy
8 C4 Casterton Austr.
67 G2 Castignon, Lac l. Can.
45 E3 Castilla - La Mancha div. Spain
45 D2 Castilla y León div. Spain
89 C2 Castilletes Col.
91 G2 Castillos Uru.
41 B4 Castlebar Rep. of Ireland
40 A4 Castlebay U.K.
41 E4 Castlebellingham Rep. of Ireland
41 E3 Castleblayney Rep. of Ireland
41 E5 Castlebridge Rep. of Ireland
38 E3 Castle Carrock U.K.
39 E6 Castle Cary U.K.
75 G2 Castle Dale U.S.A.
41 D3 Castlederg U.K.
41 E5 Castledermot Rep. of Ireland
75 E5 Castle Dome Mts mts U.S.A.
39 F5 Castle Donnington U.K.
40 E6 Castle Douglas U.K.
38 F4 Castleford U.K.
64 F5 Castlegar Can.
41 A5 Castlegregory Rep. of Ireland
41 B5 Castleisland Rep. of Ireland
8 E4 Castlemaine Austr.
41 B5 Castlemaine Rep. of Ireland
41 C6 Castlemartyr Rep. of Ireland
74 B4 Castle Mt mt U.S.A.
27 □ Castle Peak h. H.K. China
27 □ Castle Peak Bay b. H.K. China
9 F4 Castlepoint N.Z.
41 D4 Castlepollard Rep. of Ireland
41 C4 Castlerea Rep. of Ireland
8 G1 Castlereagh r. Austr.
73 F4 Castle Rock U.S.A.
68 B4 Castle Rock Lake l. U.S.A.
38 C3 Castletown Isle of Man
41 D5 Castletown Rep. of Ireland
65 G4 Castor Can.
44 F5 Castres France
42 C2 Castricum Neth.
83 M6 Castries St Lucia
90 C4 Castro Brazil
88 B6 Castro Chile
45 D4 Castro del Río Spain
45 E1 Castro-Urdiales Spain
45 B4 Castro Verde Port.
48 G5 Castrovillari Italy
74 B3 Castroville U.S.A.
9 A6 Caswell Sd in. N.Z.
17 H2 Çat Turkey
86 B5 Catacaos Peru
90 D3 Cataguases Brazil
77 E6 Catahoula L. l. U.S.A.
31 B3 Cataiñgan Phil.
17 J3 Çatak Turkey
90 C2 Catalão Brazil
45 G2 Cataluña div. Spain
88 C3 Catamarca Arg.
31 C3 Catanduanes i. Phil.
90 B4 Catanduvas Brazil
48 F6 Catania Sicily Italy
48 G5 Catanzaro Italy
77 D6 Catarina U.S.A.
31 C3 Catarman Phil.
45 F3 Catarroja Spain
89 B2 Catatumbo r. Venez.
31 C4 Catbalogan Phil.
79 E7 Cat Cays is Bahamas
31 C5 Cateel Phil.
31 C5 Cateel Bay b. Phil.
59 K3 Catembe Moz.
8 G4 Cathcart Austr.
59 G6 Cathcart S. Africa
59 H4 Cathedral Peak mt S. Africa
41 A6 Catherdaniel Rep. of Ireland
75 F2 Catherine, Mt mt U.S.A.
91 B3 Catillo Chile
79 E7 Cat Island i. Bahamas
66 B3 Cat L. l. Can.
82 G4 Catoche, C. c. Mex.
80 E5 Catonsville U.S.A.
84 B2 Catorce Mex.
91 D3 Catriló Arg.
89 E4 Catrimani Brazil
89 E4 Catrimani r. Brazil
81 G3 Catskill U.S.A.
81 F4 Catskill Mts mts U.S.A.
42 A4 Cats, Mont des h. France
59 K3 Catuane Moz.
89 E4 Cauamé r. Brazil
31 B4 Cauayan Phil.
67 H2 Caubvick, Mount mt Can.
89 B3 Cauca r. Col.
87 L4 Caucaia Brazil
89 B3 Caucasia Col.
35 K4 Caucasus mts Asia/Europe
91 C1 Caucete Arg.
81 J1 Caucomgomoc Lake l. U.S.A.
42 B4 Caudry France
31 C4 Cauit Point pt Phil.
91 B2 Cauquenes Chile
89 D3 Caura r. Venez.
67 G4 Causapscal Can.
44 G5 Cavaillon France
90 C1 Cavalcante Brazil
54 B4 Cavally r. Côte d'Ivoire
41 D4 Cavan Rep. of Ireland
77 F4 Cave City U.S.A.
90 E1 Caveira r. Brazil
8 D4 Cavendish Austr.
90 B4 Cavernoso, Serra do mts Brazil
80 B5 Cave Run Lake l. U.S.A.
31 B4 Cavili rf Phil.
31 B3 Cavite Phil.
40 E3 Cawdor U.K.
8 C2 Cawndilla Lake l. Austr.
39 J5 Cawston U.K.
87 K4 Caxias Brazil
88 F3 Caxias do Sul Brazil
57 B4 Caxito Angola
16 C2 Çay Turkey
79 D5 Cayce U.S.A.
16 D1 Çaycuma Turkey
17 H1 Çayeli Turkey
87 H3 Cayenne Fr. Guiana
16 E3 Çayhan Turkey
16 C1 Çayırhan Turkey
83 J5 Cayman Brac i. Cayman Is
61 K8 Cayman Islands terr. Caribbean Sea
96 D4 Cayman Trench sea feature Atl. Ocean
56 E3 Caynabo Somalia
69 H4 Cayuga Can.
80 E3 Cayuga Lake l. U.S.A.
81 F3 Cazenovia U.S.A.
57 C5 Cazombo Angola
91 F2 Cebollatí r. Uru.
31 B4 Cebu Phil.
31 B4 Cebu i. Phil.
68 C3 Cecil U.S.A.
48 D3 Cecina Italy
68 A4 Cedar r. IA U.S.A.
76 C2 Cedar r. ND U.S.A.
68 D4 Cedarburg U.S.A.
75 F3 Cedar City U.S.A.
77 D5 Cedar Creek Res. resr U.S.A.
68 A4 Cedar Falls U.S.A.
68 D4 Cedar Grove WI U.S.A.
80 C5 Cedar Grove WV U.S.A.
81 F6 Cedar I. i. U.S.A.
65 J4 Cedar L. l. Can.
68 D5 Cedar Lake l. U.S.A.
80 B4 Cedar Pt pt U.S.A.
68 B5 Cedar Rapids U.S.A.
75 G3 Cedar Ridge U.S.A.
81 F5 Cedar Run U.S.A.
69 F4 Cedar Springs Can.
68 E4 Cedar Springs U.S.A.
79 C5 Cedartown U.S.A.
59 H5 Cedarville S. Africa
68 E3 Cedarville U.S.A.
82 A3 Cedros i. Mex.
6 D5 Ceduna Austr.
56 E3 Ceeldheere Somalia
56 E2 Ceerigaabo Somalia
48 F5 Cefalù Sicily Italy
47 J7 Cegléd Hungary
27 B5 Cêheng China
16 E1 Çekerek Turkey
32 B4 Celah, Gunung mt Malaysia
84 B2 Celaya Mex.
41 E4 Celbridge Rep. of Ireland
Celebes i. see Sulawesi
33 E2 Celebes Sea sea Indon./Phil.
80 A4 Celina U.S.A.
48 F1 Celje Slovenia
43 J2 Celle Ger.
16 E1 Cemilbey Turkey
16 G2 Çemişgezek Turkey
25 F7 Cenderawasih, Teluk b. Indon.
27 C5 Cengong China
75 F5 Centennial Wash r. U.S.A.
77 E6 Center U.S.A.
81 G4 Centereach U.S.A.
79 C5 Center Point U.S.A.
80 B5 Centerville U.S.A.
59 G1 Central div. Botswana
53 F5 Central African Republic country Africa
19 G4 Central Brahui Range mts Pak.
68 B4 Central City IA U.S.A.
76 D3 Central City NE U.S.A.
89 A4 Central, Cordillera mts Col.
86 C5 Central, Cordillera mts Peru
31 B2 Central, Cordillera mts Phil.
27 □ Central District H.K. China
78 B4 Centralia IL U.S.A.
72 B2 Centralia WA U.S.A.
68 A2 Central Lakes U.S.A.
19 G5 Central Makran Range mts Pak.
72 B3 Central Point U.S.A.
6 E2 Central Ra. mts P.N.G.
79 C5 Centreville U.S.A.
27 D6 Cenxi China
Cephalonia i. see Kefallonia
89 D3 Cerbatana, Sa de la mt Venez.
75 E4 Cerbat Mts mts U.S.A.
65 G4 Cereal Can.
88 D3 Ceres Arg.
58 C6 Ceres S. Africa
89 B2 Cereté Col.
45 E2 Cerezo de Abajo Spain
48 F4 Cerignola Italy
16 D2 Çerikli Turkey
16 D1 Çerkeş Turkey
16 G3 Çermelik r. Syria
17 G2 Çermik Turkey
49 N2 Cernavodă Romania
84 C1 Cerralvo Mex.
82 C4 Cerralvo i. Mex.
49 H4 Cërrik Albania
84 B2 Cerritos Mex.
90 C4 Cerro Azul Brazil
84 C2 Cerro Azul Mex.
86 B4 Cerro de Amotape, Parque Nacional nat. park Peru
86 C6 Cerro de Pasco Peru
89 D3 Cerro Jáua, Meseta del plat. Venez.
89 C2 Cerrón, Co mt Venez.
84 A1 Cerro Prieto Mex.
91 C3 Cerros Colorados, Embalse resr Arg.
48 F4 Cervati, Monte mt Italy
48 C3 Cervione Corsica France
45 C1 Cervo Spain
89 B2 César r. Col.
48 E2 Cesena Italy
37 T8 Cēsis Latvia
46 G6 České Budějovice Czech Rep.
46 G6 Český Krumlov Czech Rep.
43 L5 Český Les mts Czech Rep./Ger.
49 M5 Çeşme Turkey
8 H2 Cessnock Austr.
49 H3 Cetinje Yugo.
48 F5 Cetraro Italy
45 D5 Ceuta Spain
44 F4 Cévennes mts France
16 E3 Ceyhan Turkey
16 E3 Ceyhan r. Turkey
17 H3 Ceylanpınar Turkey
19 F2 Chaacha Turkm.
42 A5 Chaalis, Abbaye de France
91 E2 Chacabuco Arg.
91 B4 Chacao Chile
91 C3 Chachahuén, Sa mt Arg.
86 C5 Chachapoyas Peru
50 D4 Chachersk Belarus
32 B2 Chachoengsao Thai.
22 B4 Chachro Pak.
64 C4 Chacon, C. c. U.S.A.
52 F4 Chad country Africa
15 H1 Chadan Rus. Fed.
59 G1 Chadibe Botswana
91 C3 Chadileo r. Arg.
55 D3 Chad, Lake l. Africa
76 C3 Chadron U.S.A.
32 A1 Chae Hom Thai.
30 C4 Chaeryŏng N. Korea
89 B4 Chafurray Col.
19 G4 Chagai Pak.
19 F4 Chagai Hills mts Afgh./Pak.
23 F2 Chagdo Kangri reg. China
19 G3 Chaghcharān Afgh.
44 G3 Chagny France
10 J10 Chagos Archipelago is British Ind. Ocean Terr.
50 J4 Chagra r. Rus. Fed.
89 D2 Chaguaramas Venez.
23 G3 Cha'gyüngoinba China
19 F4 Chahah Burjal Afgh.
19 E3 Chāh Ākhvor Iran
19 E3 Chahār Takāb Iran
18 D3 Chāh Badam Iran
19 F5 Chāh Bahār Iran
18 D4 Chāh-e Bāgh well Iran
18 E3 Chāh-e Kavīr well Iran
18 D3 Chāh-e Khorāsān well Iran
19 E3 Chāh-e Khoshāb Iran
19 E4 Chāh-e Malek Iran
18 D3 Chāh-e Mīrzā well Iran
18 D3 Chāh-e Mūjān well Iran
18 D3 Chāh-e Nūklok Iran
18 D3 Chāh-e Nūklok well Iran
18 D4 Chāh-e Qeyşar well Iran
18 D3 Chāh-e Qobād well Iran
18 D4 Chāh-e Rāh Iran
19 E4 Chāh-e Raḩmān well Iran
18 D3 Chāh-e Shūr Iran
18 D3 Chāh-e Shur well Iran
18 D3 Chah Haji Abdulla well Iran
18 D4 Chāh Ḩaqq Iran
19 H2 Chah-i-Ab Afgh.
17 K4 Chah-i-Shurkh Iraq
18 D3 Chāh Pās well Iran
18 C4 Chāh Rūstā'ī Iran
19 F4 Chah Sandan Pak.
30 C2 Chai r. China
23 F5 Chāībāsa India
67 G3 Chaigneau, Lac l. Can.
32 B2 Chai Si r. Thai.
27 □ Chai Wan H.K. China
32 A3 Chaiya Thai.
32 B2 Chaiyaphum Thai.
91 F1 Chajarí Arg.
22 B3 Chakar r. Pak.
23 H5 Chakaria Bangl.
19 F4 Chakhānsūr Afgh.
23 E4 Chakia India
19 G5 Chakku Pak.
86 D7 Chala Peru
19 G3 Chalap Dalan mts Afgh.
82 G6 Chalatenango El Salvador
67 G4 Chaleur Bay in. Can.
27 D5 Chaling China
22 C5 Chalisgaon India
49 K5 Chalkida Greece
9 A7 Chalky Inlet in. N.Z.
44 D3 Challans France
86 E7 Challapata Bol.
94 E5 Challenger Deep depth Pac. Oc.
95 M8 Challenger Fracture Zone sea feature Pac. Oc.
72 D2 Challis U.S.A.
44 G2 Châlons-en-Champagne France
44 G3 Chalon-sur-Saône France
30 C2 Chaluhe China
18 C2 Chālūs Iran
43 L5 Cham Ger.
73 F4 Chama U.S.A.
57 D5 Chama Zambia
89 C2 Chama r. Venez.
91 D2 Chamaico Arg.
58 A3 Chamais Bay b. Namibia
19 G4 Chaman Pak.
22 D4 Chambal r. India
67 G3 Chambeaux, Lac l. Can.
65 H4 Chamberlain Can.
76 D3 Chamberlain U.S.A.
81 J1 Chamberlain Lake l. U.S.A.
75 H4 Chambers U.S.A.
80 E5 Chambersburg U.S.A.
44 G4 Chambéry France
57 D5 Chambeshi Zambia
48 C7 Chambi, Jebel mt Tunisia
44 G4 Chamechaude mt France
18 C3 Cham-e Ḩannā Iran
18 C3 Chameshk Iran
91 C1 Chamical Arg.
23 F4 Chamlang mt Nepal
32 B3 Châmnar Cambodia
66 F4 Chamouchouane r. Can.
23 E5 Champa India
64 B2 Champagne Can.
44 G2 Champagne reg. France
59 H4 Champagne Castle mt S. Africa
44 G3 Champagnole France
68 C5 Champaign U.S.A.
91 D1 Champaqui, Cerro mt Arg.
32 C2 Champasak Laos
23 H5 Champhai India
68 D2 Champion U.S.A.
81 G2 Champlain U.S.A.
81 G2 Champlain, L. l. Can./U.S.A.
84 E3 Champotón Mex.
21 B4 Chamrajnagar India
50 H4 Chamzinka Rus. Fed.
32 B4 Chana Thai.
88 B3 Chañaral Chile
89 E3 Chanaro, Co mt Venez.
91 B2 Chanco Chile
Chanda see Chandrapur
62 D3 Chandalar r. U.S.A.
23 E5 Chandarpur India
22 D3 Chandausi India
77 F6 Chandeleur Islands is U.S.A.
22 E5 Chandia India
22 D3 Chandigarh India
75 G5 Chandler U.S.A.
69 J3 Chandos Lake l. Can.
23 G5 Chandpur Bangl.
22 D3 Chandpur India
23 H5 Chandraghona Bangl.
22 D6 Chandrapur India
22 D5 Chandur India
57 D6 Changane r. Moz.
57 D5 Changara Moz.
30 E3 Changbai China
30 D3 Changbai Shan mts China/N. Korea
27 C7 Changcheng China
92 B1 Chang Cheng (Great Wall) China Base Ant.
30 C2 Changchun China
30 C1 Changchunling China
26 F2 Changdao China
27 D4 Changde China
30 D4 Changdo N. Korea
26 E3 Changfeng China
30 E5 Changgi Gap pt S. Korea
30 B4 Changhai China
30 D6 Changhang S. Korea
30 D5 Changhowan S. Korea
27 F5 Chang-hua Taiwan
32 D1 Changhua Jiang r. China
30 D6 Changhung S. Korea
32 □ Changi Sing.
27 C7 Changjiang China
Chang Jiang r. see Yangtze
Changjiang Kou est. see Yangtze, Mouth of the
30 D3 Changjin N. Korea
30 D3 Changjin Reservoir N. Korea
27 F5 Changle China
26 F2 Changli China
30 B1 Changling China
27 D5 Changning China
30 C4 Changnyŏn N. Korea
26 E1 Changping China
30 E5 Changp'yŏng S. Korea
30 C4 Changsan-got pt N. Korea
27 D4 Changsha China
27 F4 Changshan China
30 B4 Changshan Qundao is China
27 C4 Changshou China
27 D4 Changshoujie China
26 F4 Changshu China
27 C5 Changshun China
30 D6 Changsŏng S. Korea
27 E5 Changtai China
27 E5 Changting Fujian China
30 E1 Changting Heilongjiang China
30 C2 Changtu China
30 E6 Ch'angwŏn S. Korea
26 C3 Changwu China
30 A4 Changxing Dao i. China
27 D4 Changyang China
26 F2 Changyi China
30 C4 Changyŏn N. Korea
26 E3 Changyuan China
26 D2 Changzhi China
26 F4 Changzhou China
49 L7 Chania Greece
30 D3 Chanjin r. N. Korea
26 B3 Chankou China
21 B3 Channapatna India
74 C5 Channel Islands is U.S.A.
34 E4 Channel Islands terr. English Channel
74 B5 Channel Is Nat. Park U.S.A.
67 J4 Channel-Port-aux-Basques Can.
39 J6 Channel Tunnel tunnel France/U.K.
68 C2 Channing U.S.A.
45 C1 Chantada Spain

32 B2 Chanthaburi Thai.
44 F2 Chantilly France
77 E4 Chanute U.S.A.
12 J4 Chany, Ozero salt l. Rus. Fed.
26 E2 Chaobai Xinhe r. China
26 E4 Chao Hu l. China
32 B2 Chao Phraya r. Thai.
54 B1 Chaouèn Morocco
23 H2 Chaowula Shan mts China
26 E4 Chao Xian China
27 E6 Chaoyang Guangdong China
26 F1 Chaoyang Liaoning China
27 E6 Chaozhou China
90 E1 Chapada Diamantina, Parque Nacional nat. park Brazil
90 A1 Chapada dos Guimarães Brazil
90 C1 Chapada dos Veadeiros, Parque Nacional da nat. park Brazil
84 B2 Chapala Mex.
84 B2 Chapala, L. de l. Mex.
89 B4 Chaparral Col.
14 D1 Chapayev Kazak.
50 J4 Chapayevsk Rus. Fed.
88 F3 Chapecó Brazil
88 F3 Chapecó r. Brazil
39 F4 Chapel-en-le-Frith U.K.
79 E5 Chapel Hill U.S.A.
42 C4 Chapelle-lez-Herlaimont Belgium
39 F4 Chapeltown U.K.
68 D5 Chapin, Lake l. U.S.A.
69 F2 Chapleau Can.
50 F4 Chaplygin Rus. Fed.
51 E6 Chaplynka Ukr.
80 B6 Chapmanville U.S.A.
19 G3 Chapri Pass pass Afgh.
86 E7 Chaqui Bol.
22 D2 Char Jammu and Kashmir
84 B2 Charcas Mex.
23 H3 Char Chu r. China
92 A2 Charcot I. i. Ant.
65 G3 Chard Can.
39 E7 Chard U.K.
17 L3 Chārdagh Iran
17 L5 Chardāvol Iran
80 C4 Chardon U.S.A.
19 F2 Chardzhev Turkm.
44 E3 Charente r. France
19 H3 Chārīkār Afgh.
76 E3 Chariton r. U.S.A.
69 F3 Charity Is i. U.S.A.
12 G3 Charkayuvom Rus. Fed.
22 D4 Charkhari India
42 C4 Charleroi Belgium
71 L4 Charles, Cape pt VA U.S.A.
68 A4 Charles City U.S.A.
42 A5 Charles de Gaulle airport France
77 E6 Charles, Lake U.S.A.
9 C4 Charleston N.Z.
78 B4 Charleston IL U.S.A.
81 J2 Charleston ME U.S.A.
77 F4 Charleston MO U.S.A.
79 E5 Charleston SC U.S.A.
80 C5 Charleston WV U.S.A.
75 E3 Charleston Peak summit U.S.A.
41 C4 Charlestown Rep. of Ireland
81 G3 Charlestown NH U.S.A.
81 H4 Charlestown RI U.S.A.
80 E5 Charles Town U.S.A.
6 E4 Charleville Austr.
44 G2 Charleville-Mézières France
68 E3 Charlevoix U.S.A.
64 E3 Charlie Lake Can.
68 E4 Charlotte MI U.S.A.
79 D5 Charlotte NC U.S.A.
79 D7 Charlotte Harbor b. U.S.A.
80 D5 Charlottesville U.S.A.
67 H4 Charlottetown Can.
89 E2 Charlotteville Trinidad and Tobago
8 D4 Charlton Austr.
66 E3 Charlton I. i. Can.
50 F2 Charozero Rus. Fed.
22 B2 Charsadda Pak.
6 E4 Charters Towers Austr.
44 E2 Chartres France
91 E2 Chascomús Arg.
64 F4 Chase Can.
19 F2 Chashkent Turkm.
17 L4 Chashmeh Iran
18 E3 Chashmeh Nūrī Iran
18 D3 Chashmeh ye Palasi Iran
18 D3 Chashmeh ye Shotoran well Iran
50 D4 Chashniki Belarus
9 B7 Chaslands Mistake c. N.Z.
30 D3 Chasŏng N. Korea
18 D3 Chastab, Kūh-e mts Iran
44 D3 Châteaubriant France
44 E3 Château-du-Loir France
44 E2 Châteaudun France
81 F2 Chateaugay U.S.A.
81 G2 Châteauguay Can.
44 B2 Châteaulin France
44 F3 Châteauneuf-sur-Loire France
44 E3 Châteauroux France
42 E6 Château-Salins France
44 F2 Château-Thierry France
42 C4 Châtelet Belgium
44 E3 Châtellerault France
68 A4 Chatfield U.S.A.
67 G4 Chatham N.B. Can.
69 F4 Chatham Ont. Can.
39 H6 Chatham U.K.
81 H4 Chatham MA U.S.A.
81 G3 Chatham NY U.S.A.
80 D6 Chatham VA U.S.A.
7 J6 Chatham Islands is N.Z.
94 G8 Chatham Rise sea feature Pac. Oc.
64 C4 Chatham Sd chan. Can.
64 C3 Chatham Strait chan. U.S.A.
23 F4 Chatra India
69 G3 Chatsworth Can.
68 C5 Chatsworth U.S.A.
79 C5 Chattanooga U.S.A.
39 H5 Chatteris U.K.
32 B2 Chatturat Thai.
32 C3 Châu Đôc Vietnam
22 B4 Chauhtan India
23 H5 Chauk Myanmar
22 E4 Chauka r. India
44 G2 Chaumont France
32 A2 Chaungwabyin Myanmar
13 S3 Chaunskaya Guba b. Rus. Fed.
44 F2 Chauny France
23 F4 Chauparan India
80 D3 Chautauqua, Lake l. U.S.A.
21 C4 Chavakachcheri Sri Lanka
18 B3 Chavār Iran
87 J4 Chaves Brazil
45 C2 Chaves Port.
66 E2 Chavigny, Lac l. Can.
50 D4 Chavusy Belarus
22 A3 Chawal r. Pak.
27 B6 Chây r. Vietnam
Chāyul see Qayü
91 D2 Chazón Arg.
81 G2 Chazy U.S.A.
39 F5 Cheadle U.K.
80 D5 Cheat r. U.S.A.
46 F5 Cheb Czech Rep.
48 D7 Chebba Tunisia
50 H3 Cheboksary Rus. Fed.
68 E3 Cheboygan U.S.A.
51 H7 Chechen', Ostrov i. Rus. Fed.
51 H7 Chechenskaya Respublika div. Rus. Fed.
30 E5 Chech'ŏn S. Korea
77 E5 Checotah U.S.A.
30 A5 Chedao China
39 E6 Cheddar U.K.
65 G3 Cheecham Can.
92 B5 Cheetham, C. c. Ant.
62 B3 Chefornak AK U.S.A.
59 K1 Chefu Moz.
54 B2 Chegga Maur.
57 D5 Chegutu Zimbabwe
72 B2 Chehalis U.S.A.
19 H3 Chehardar Pass Afgh.
17 L5 Chehariz Iraq
18 E4 Chehell'āyeh Iran
30 D7 Cheju S. Korea
30 D7 Cheju-do i. S. Korea
30 D7 Cheju-haehyŏp chan. S. Korea
50 F4 Chekhov Rus. Fed.
72 B2 Chelan, L. l. U.S.A.
18 D2 Cheleken Turkm.
91 C3 Chelforó Arg.
45 G4 Chélif r. Alg.
14 D2 Chelkar Kazak.
47 L5 Chełm Pol.
39 H6 Chelmer r. U.K.
47 J4 Chełmno Pol.
39 H6 Chelmsford U.K.
81 H3 Chelmsford U.S.A.
39 E6 Cheltenham U.K.
45 F3 Chelva Spain
12 H4 Chelyabinsk Rus. Fed.
57 D5 Chemba Moz.
22 D2 Chem Co l. China
43 L4 Chemnitz Ger.
80 E3 Chemung r. U.S.A.
22 B3 Chenab r. Pak.
54 B2 Chenachane Alg.
81 F3 Chenango r. U.S.A.
72 C2 Cheney U.S.A.
77 D4 Cheney Res. resr U.S.A.
21 C3 Chengalpattu India
26 E2 Cheng'an China
27 D5 Chengbu China
26 E1 Chengde China
27 B4 Chengdu China
26 C3 Chenggu China
27 E6 Chenghai China
26 C4 Chengkou China
25 D5 Chengmai China
30 B4 Chengzitan China
26 F3 Cheniu Shan i. China
68 C5 Chenoa U.S.A.
27 D5 Chenxi China
27 D5 Chenzhou China
32 D2 Cheo Reo Vietnam
86 C5 Chepén Peru
91 C1 Chepes Arg.
39 E6 Chepstow U.K.
50 J3 Cheptsa r. Rus. Fed.
17 L5 Cheqad Kabūd Iran
68 B2 Chequamegon Bay b. U.S.A.
44 F3 Cher r. France
84 B3 Cherán Mex.
79 E5 Cheraw U.S.A.
44 D2 Cherbourg France
45 H4 Cherchell Alg.
50 J4 Cherdakly Rus. Fed.
24 C1 Cheremkhovo Rus. Fed.
28 D2 Cheremshany Rus. Fed.
50 F3 Cherepovets Rus. Fed.
50 H2 Cherevkovo Rus. Fed.
48 B7 Chéria Alg.
51 E5 Cherkasy Ukr.
51 G6 Cherkessk Rus. Fed.
21 C2 Cherla India
57 C5 Chermenze Angola
12 K2 Chernaya Rus. Fed.
50 J3 Chernaya Kholunitsa Rus. Fed.
28 C2 Chernigovka Rus. Fed.
51 D5 Chernihiv Ukr.
51 F6 Cherninivka Ukr.
51 C5 Chernivtsi Ukr.
24 B1 Chernogorsk Rus. Fed.
50 H3 Chernovskoye Rus. Fed.
51 D5 Chernyakhiv Ukr.
47 K3 Chernyakhovsk Rus. Fed.
51 F5 Chernyanka Rus. Fed.
13 N3 Chernyshevskiy Rus. Fed.
51 H6 Chernyye Zemli reg. Rus. Fed.
51 H5 Chernyy Yar Rus. Fed.
76 E3 Cherokee IA U.S.A.
77 D4 Cherokee OK U.S.A.
77 E4 Cherokees, Lake o' the l. U.S.A.
79 E7 Cherokee Sound Bahamas
91 B3 Cherquenco Chile
23 G4 Cherrapunji India
75 E2 Cherry Creek U.S.A.
75 E1 Cherry Creek Mts mts U.S.A.
81 K2 Cherryfield U.S.A.
7 G3 Cherry Island i. Solomon Is
69 J4 Cherry Valley Can.
81 F3 Cherry Valley U.S.A.
13 Q3 Cherskogo, Khrebet mts Rus. Fed.
51 G5 Chertkovo Rus. Fed.
50 J2 Cherva Rus. Fed.
49 L3 Cherven Bryag Bulg.
51 C5 Chervonohrad Ukr.
51 E5 Chervonozavods'ke Ukr.
50 D4 Chervyen' Belarus
39 F6 Cherwell r. U.K.
50 D4 Cherykaw Belarus
69 F4 Chesaning U.S.A.
81 E6 Chesapeake U.S.A.
81 E5 Chesapeake Bay b. U.S.A.
39 G6 Chesham U.K.
81 G3 Cheshire U.S.A.
39 E4 Cheshire Plain lowland U.K.
19 F2 Cheshme 2-y Turkm.
12 F3 Cheshskaya Guba b. Rus. Fed.
19 F3 Chesht-e Sharīf Afgh.
39 G6 Cheshunt U.K.
39 E4 Chester U.K.
74 B1 Chester CA U.S.A.
78 B4 Chester IL U.S.A.
72 E1 Chester MT U.S.A.
81 F5 Chester PA U.S.A.
79 D5 Chester SC U.S.A.
81 E5 Chester r. U.S.A.
39 F4 Chesterfield U.K.
7 F3 Chesterfield, Îles is New Caledonia
63 J3 Chesterfield Inlet N.W.T. Can.
65 L2 Chesterfield Inlet Can.
65 L2 Chesterfield Inlet in. Can.
38 F3 Chester-le-Street U.K.
81 E5 Chestertown MD U.S.A.
81 G3 Chestertown NY U.S.A.
81 F2 Chesterville Can.
80 D4 Chestnut Ridge ridge U.S.A.
81 J1 Chesuncook U.S.A.
81 J1 Chesuncook Lake l. U.S.A.
48 B6 Chetaïbi Alg.
67 H4 Chéticamp Can.
21 A4 Chetlat i. India
82 G5 Chetumal Mex.
64 E3 Chetwynd Can.
27 □ Cheung Chau H.K. China
27 □ Cheung Chau i. H.K. China
9 D5 Cheviot N.Z.
38 E2 Cheviot Hills h. U.K.
38 E2 Cheviot, The h. U.K.
72 C1 Chewelah U.S.A.
77 D5 Cheyenne OK U.S.A.
72 F3 Cheyenne WY U.S.A.
76 C3 Cheyenne r. U.S.A.
76 C4 Cheyenne Wells U.S.A.
64 E4 Chezacut Can.
22 C4 Chhapar India
23 F4 Chhapra India
22 D4 Chhatarpur India
22 B3 Chhatr Pak.
22 D5 Chhindwara India
22 C5 Chhota Udepur India
22 C4 Chhoti Sadri India
23 G4 Chhukha Bhutan
27 F6 Chia-i Taiwan
32 B1 Chiang Kham Thai.
32 B1 Chiang Khan Thai.
32 A1 Chiang Mai Thai.
84 D3 Chiapas div. Mex.
48 C2 Chiari Italy
84 C3 Chiautla Mex.
48 E2 Chioggia Italy
29 G7 Chiba Japan
57 B5 Chibia Angola
57 D6 Chiboma Moz.
66 F4 Chibougamau Can.
66 F4 Chibougamau L. l. Can.
66 F4 Chibougamau, Parc de res. Can.
29 E6 Chibu-Sangaku Nat. Park Japan
59 K2 Chibuto Moz.
23 G2 Chibuzhang Hu l. China
Chicacole see Srikakulam
68 D5 Chicago U.S.A.
68 D5 Chicago Heights U.S.A.
68 C5 Chicago Ship Canal canal U.S.A.
89 B3 Chicamocha r. Col.
89 E3 Chicanán r. Venez.
64 B3 Chichagof U.S.A.
64 B3 Chichagof Island i. U.S.A.
26 E1 Chicheng China
39 G7 Chichester U.K.
6 B4 Chichester Range mts Austr.
29 F7 Chichibu Japan
29 F7 Chichibu-Tama National Park Japan
80 E6 Chickahominy r. U.S.A.
79 C5 Chickamauga L. l. U.S.A.
77 D5 Chickasha U.S.A.
45 C4 Chiclana de la Frontera Spain
86 C5 Chiclayo Peru
74 B2 Chico U.S.A.
88 C6 Chico r. Chubut Arg.
91 B4 Chico r. Chubut/Rio Negro Arg.
88 C7 Chico r. Santa Cruz Arg.
59 L2 Chicomo Moz.
84 D4 Chicomucelo Mex.
81 G3 Chicopee U.S.A.
31 B2 Chico Sapocoy, Mt mt Phil.
67 F4 Chicoutimi Can.
59 J1 Chicualacuala Moz.
21 B4 Chidambaram India
59 L2 Chidenguele Moz.
67 H1 Chidley, C. c. Can.
30 D6 Chido S. Korea
59 L2 Chiducuane Moz.
79 D6 Chiefland U.S.A.
46 F7 Chiemsee l. Ger.
42 D5 Chiers r. France
48 F3 Chieti Italy
84 C3 Chietla Mex.
26 F1 Chifeng China
90 E2 Chifre, Serra do mts Brazil
12 J5 Chiganak Kazak.
67 G4 Chignecto B. b. Can.
89 A3 Chigorodó Col.
57 D6 Chigubo Moz.
23 G3 Chigu Co l. China
82 C3 Chihuahua Mex.
27 D6 Chikan China
21 B3 Chik Ballapur India
50 D3 Chikhachevo Rus. Fed.
22 D5 Chikhali Kalan Parasia India
22 D5 Chikhli India
21 A3 Chikmagalur India
29 F6 Chikuma-gawa r. Japan
64 E4 Chilanko Forks Can.
84 C3 Chilapa Mex.
15 F3 Chilas Jammu and Kashmir
21 B5 Chilaw Sri Lanka
74 B2 Chilcoot U.S.A.
64 E4 Chilcotin r. Can.
77 C5 Childress U.S.A.
85 C7 Chile country S. America
95 O8 Chile Basin sea feature Pac. Oc.
88 C3 Chilecito Arg.
51 H6 Chilgir Rus. Fed.
23 F6 Chilika Lake l. India
57 C5 Chililabombwe Zambia
64 E4 Chilko r. Can.
64 E4 Chilko L. l. Can.
91 B3 Chillán Chile
91 B3 Chillán, Nevado mts Chile
91 E3 Chillar Arg.
76 E4 Chillicothe MO U.S.A.
80 B5 Chillicothe OH U.S.A.
68 C5 Chillicothe U.S.A.
22 C1 Chillinji Pak.
64 E5 Chilliwack Can.
18 D1 Chil'mamedkum, Peski des. Turkm.
88 B6 Chiloé, Isla de i. Chile
72 B3 Chiloquin U.S.A.
84 C3 Chilpancingo Mex.
8 F4 Chiltern Austr.
39 G6 Chiltern Hills h. U.K.
68 C3 Chilton U.S.A.
27 F5 Chi-lung Taiwan
22 D2 Chilung Pass pass India
57 D4 Chimala Tanz.
42 C4 Chimay Belgium
91 C1 Chimbas Arg.
85 C4 Chimborazo mt Ecuador
85 C5 Chimbote Peru
83 B2 Chimichaguá Col.
57 D5 Chimoio Moz.
84 C1 China Mex.
10 L6 China country Asia
83 B3 Chinácota Col.
84 E3 Chinajá Guatemala
74 D4 China Lake l. CA U.S.A.
81 J2 China Lake l. ME U.S.A.
82 G6 Chinandega Nic.
74 C5 China Pt pt U.S.A.
83 C6 Chincha Alta Peru
64 F3 Chinchaga r. Can.
81 F6 Chincoteague B. b. U.S.A.
57 D5 Chinde Moz.
30 D6 Chindo S. Korea
30 D6 Chin-do i. S. Korea
24 B3 Chindu China
23 H5 Chindwin r. Myanmar
22 C2 Chineni Jammu and Kashmir
89 B3 Chingaza, Parque Nacional nat. park Col.
30 C4 Chinghwa N. Korea
57 C5 Chingola Zambia
57 B5 Chinguar Angola
30 E6 Chinhae S. Korea
57 D5 Chinhoyi Zimbabwe
22 C3 Chiniot Pak.
30 E6 Chinju S. Korea
56 C3 Chinko r. C.A.R.
75 H3 Chinle U.S.A.
75 H3 Chinle Valley v. U.S.A.
75 H3 Chinle Wash r. U.S.A.
27 F5 Chinmen Taiwan
27 F5 Chinmen Tao i. Taiwan
21 A3 Chinnur India
29 F7 Chino Japan
44 E3 Chinon France
75 F4 Chino Valley U.S.A.
57 D5 Chinsali Zambia
21 E3 Chintamani India
48 E2 Chioggia Italy
45 M5 Chios Greece
49 L5 Chios i. Greece
57 D5 Chipata Zambia
91 C4 Chipchihua, Sa de mts Arg.
57 E5 Chipindo Angola
57 D6 Chipinge Zimbabwe
21 A2 Chiplun India
39 E6 Chippenham U.K.
68 B3 Chippewa r. U.S.A.
68 B3 Chippewa Falls U.S.A.
68 B3 Chippewa, Lake l. U.S.A.
39 F6 Chipping Norton U.K.
39 E6 Chipping Sodbury U.K.
81 K2 Chiputneticook Lakes l. U.S.A.
82 G6 Chiquimula Guatemala
89 B3 Chiquinquira Col.
51 G5 Chir r. Rus. Fed.
21 C3 Chirada India
21 A4 Chirakkal India
21 C3 Chirala India
19 G3 Chiras Afgh.
22 C3 Chirāwa India
57 C6 Chiredzi Zimbabwe
75 H5 Chiricahua National Monument res. U.S.A.
75 H6 Chiricahua Peak summit U.S.A.
89 B2 Chiriguaná Col.
62 C4 Chirikof I. i. U.S.A.
83 H7 Chiriquí, Golfo de b. Panama
39 D5 Chirk U.K.
40 F5 Chirnside U.K.
49 L3 Chirpan Bulg.
83 H7 Chirripo mt Costa Rica
57 C5 Chirundu Zambia
66 E3 Chisasibi Can.
84 E4 Chisec Guatemala
68 A2 Chisholm U.S.A.
22 C3 Chishtian Mandi Pak.
27 B4 Chishur China
51 D6 Chişinău Moldova
47 K7 Chişineu-Criş Romania
50 J4 Chistopol' Rus. Fed.
24 D1 Chita Rus. Fed.
57 B5 Chitado Angola
57 D5 Chitambo Zambia
56 C4 Chitato Angola
65 H4 Chitek Lake Can.
57 B5 Chitembo Angola
57 D4 Chitipa Malawi
57 C5 Chitokoloki Zambia
28 G3 Chitose Japan
21 B3 Chitradurga India
22 B2 Chitral Pak.
22 B2 Chitral r. Pak.
83 H7 Chitré Panama
23 G5 Chittagong Bangl.
23 F5 Chittaranjan India
22 C4 Chittaurgarh India
21 B3 Chittoor India
21 B4 Chittur India
57 D5 Chitungulu Zambia
57 D5 Chitungwiza Zimbabwe
57 C5 Chiume Angola
57 D5 Chivhu Zimbabwe
91 E2 Chivilcoy Arg.
27 D6 Chixi China
17 J3 Chiya-e Linik h. Iraq
29 D7 Chizu Japan
50 G3 Chkalovsk Rus. Fed.
28 C2 Chkalovskoye Rus. Fed.
30 D5 Ch'o i. S. Korea
32 □ Choa Chu Kang Sing.
32 □ Choa Chu Kang h. Sing.
32 C2 Chŏâm Khsant Cambodia
91 B1 Choapa r. Chile
57 C5 Chobe National Park Botswana
30 D3 Choch'iwŏn S. Korea
75 E5 Chocolate Mts mts U.S.A.
89 B3 Chocontá Col.
30 C4 Cho Do i. N. Korea
43 L4 Chodov Czech Rep.
91 D3 Choele Choel Arg.
22 C2 Chogo Lungma Gl. gl. Pak.
51 H6 Chograyskoye Vdkhr. resr Rus. Fed.
65 J4 Choiceland Can.
7 F2 Choiseul i. Solomon Is
88 E8 Choiseul Sound chan. Falkland Is
46 H4 Chojnice Pol.
28 G5 Chōkai-san volc. Japan
77 D6 Choke Canyon L. l. U.S.A.
56 D2 Ch'ok'ē Mts mts Eth.
23 F3 Choksum China
13 Q2 Chokurdakh Rus. Fed.
57 D6 Chókwé Moz.
44 D3 Cholet France
91 B4 Cholila Arg.
82 G6 Choluteca Honduras
57 C5 Choma Zambia
30 E5 Chŏmch'ŏr S. Korea
23 G4 Chomo Lhari mt Bhutan
32 A1 Chom Thong Thai.
46 F5 Chomutov Czech Rep.
13 M3 Chona r. Rus. Fed.
30 D5 Ch'ŏnan S. Korea
32 B2 Chon Buri Thai.
30 D3 Ch'ŏnch'ŏn N. Korea
86 B4 Chone Ecuador
27 F5 Chong'an China
30 C4 Chongchon r. N. Korea
30 E6 Chongdo S. Korea
30 E3 Ch'ŏngjin N. Korea
30 C4 Chŏngju N. Korea
30 D6 Chŏngju S. Korea
30 D5 Ch'ŏngju S. Korea
32 B2 Chŏng Kal Cambodia
30 D4 Chŏngp'yŏng N. Korea
27 C4 Chongqing China
27 E5 Chongren China
59 K2 Chonguene Moz.
57 C5 Chongwe Zambia
27 D4 Chongyang China
27 F5 Chongyang Xi r. China
27 E5 Chongyi China
27 C6 Chongzuo China
30 D6 Chŏnju S. Korea
23 F3 Cho Oyu mt China
32 C3 Cho Phuoc Hai Vietnam
90 B4 Chopim r. Brazil
90 B4 Chopimzinho Brazil
81 F5 Choptank r. U.S.A.
22 B4 Chor Pak.
38 E4 Chorley U.K.
51 D5 Chornobyl' Ukr.
51 E6 Chornomors'ke Ukr.
51 C5 Chortkiv Ukr.
30 D4 Ch'ŏrwŏn S. Korea
30 C3 Ch'osan N. Korea
29 G7 Chōshi Japan
91 B3 Chos Malal Arg.
46 G4 Choszczno Pol.
86 C5 Chota Peru
72 D2 Choteau U.S.A.
22 B3 Choti Pak.
54 A2 Choûm Maur.
74 B3 Chowchilla U.S.A.
64 F4 Chown, Mt mt Can.
24 D2 Choybalsan Mongolia
24 C2 Choyr Mongolia
46 H6 Chřiby h. Czech Rep.
68 D6 Chrisman U.S.A.
59 J3 Chrissiesmeer S. Africa
9 D5 Christchurch N.Z.
39 F7 Christchurch U.K.
59 F3 Christiana S. Africa
63 M2 Christian, C. pt Can.
69 G3 Christian I. i. Can.
Christiansåb see Qasigiannguit
80 C6 Christiansburg U.S.A.
64 C3 Christian Sound chan. U.S.A.
65 G3 Christina r. Can.
7 G6 Christina, Mt mt N.Z.
Christmas Island i. see Kiritimati
25 C8 Christmas Island terr. Ind. Ocean
46 G6 Chrudim Czech Rep.
49 L7 Chrysi i. Greece
15 F2 Chu Kazak.
12 H5 Chu r. Kazak.
23 G5 Chuadanga Bangl.
59 K2 Chuali, L. l. Moz.
26 F4 Chuansha China
72 D3 Chubbuck U.S.A.
91 C4 Chubut div. Arg.
88 C6 Chubut r. Arg.
75 E5 Chuckwalla Mts mts U.S.A.
51 D5 Chudniv Ukr.
50 D3 Chudovo Rus. Fed.
Chudskoye Ozero l. see Peipus, Lake
62 C4 Chugach Mountains mts U.S.A.
29 C7 Chūgoku-sanchi mts Japan
28 C2 Chuguyevka Rus. Fed.
72 F3 Chugwater U.S.A.
51 F5 Chuhuyiv Ukr.
75 G5 Chuichu U.S.A.
24 F1 Chukchagirskoye, Ozero l. Rus. Fed.
13 V3 Chukchi Sea sea Rus. Fed./U.S.A.
50 G3 Chukhloma Rus. Fed.
13 U3 Chukotskiy Poluostrov pen. Rus. Fed.
50 H1 Chulasa Rus. Fed.
74 D5 Chula Vista U.S.A.
12 K4 Chulym Rus. Fed.
23 G4 Chumbi China
88 C3 Chumbicha Arg.
24 F1 Chumikan Rus. Fed.
32 B1 Chum Phae Thai.
32 A3 Chumphon Thai.
32 B2 Chum Saeng Thai.
13 L4 Chuna r. Rus. Fed.
27 F4 Chun'an China
30 D5 Ch'unch'ŏn S. Korea
30 D5 Ch'ungju S. Korea
Chungking see Chongqing
30 E6 Ch'ungmu S. Korea
30 C4 Chŭngsan N. Korea
19 H3 Chungur, Koh-i- h. Afgh.
30 F2 Chunhua China
23 F3 Chunit Tso salt l. China
13 M3 Chunya r. Rus. Fed.
32 C3 Chuŏr Phnum Dâmrei mts Cambodia
32 C2 Chuŏr Phnum Dângrĕk mts Cambodia/Thai.
32 B2 Chuŏr Phnum Krâvanh mts Cambodia
26 A4 Chuosijia China
17 L3 Chūplū Iran
86 D7 Chuquibamba Peru
88 C2 Chuquicamata Chile
46 D7 Chur Switz.
13 P3 Churapcha Rus. Fed.
65 L3 Churchill Can.
65 K3 Churchill r. Man./Sask. Can.
67 H3 Churchill r. Nfld Can.
63 J4 Churchill r. Sask. Can.
65 L3 Churchill, Cape c. Can.
67 H3 Churchill Falls Can.
65 H3 Churchill Lake l. Can.
64 D3 Churchill Peak summit Can.
66 E2 Churchill Sound chan. Can.
76 D1 Churchs Ferry U.S.A.
80 D5 Churchville U.S.A.
23 F4 Churia Ghati Hills mts Nepal
50 H3 Churov Rus. Fed.
22 C3 Churu India
89 C2 Churuguara Venez.
22 D2 Chushul Jammu and Kashmir
75 H3 Chuska Mountains mts U.S.A.
67 F4 Chute-des-Passes Can.
69 J2 Chute-Rouge Can.
69 K2 Chute-St-Philippe Can.
27 F5 Chu-tung Taiwan
4 G4 Chuuk i. Micronesia
50 H4 Chuvashskaya Respublika div. Rus. Fed.
26 F3 Chu Xian China
27 A5 Chuxiong China
32 D2 Chư Yang Sin mt Vietnam
17 K4 Chwārtā Iraq
51 D6 Ciadâr-Lunga Moldova
33 C4 Ciamis Indon.
33 C4 Cianjur Indon.
90 B3 Cianorte Brazil
73 E6 Cibuta Mex.
48 F2 Čićarija mts Croatia
16 E2 Çiçekdağı Turkey
51 E7 Cide Turkey
47 K4 Ciechanów Pol.
83 J4 Ciego de Avila Cuba
89 B2 Ciénaga Col.
89 B2 Ciénaga de Zapatoza l. Col.
84 B1 Ciénega de Flores Mex.
73 E6 Cieneguita Mex.
83 H4 Cienfuegos Cuba
45 F3 Cieza Spain
45 E2 Cifuentes Spain
17 M2 Çigil Adası i. Azer.
45 E3 Cigüela r. Spain
16 D2 Cihanbeyli Turkey
84 A3 Cihuatlán Mex.
45 D3 Cijara, Embalse de resr Spain
33 C4 Cilacap Indon.
17 J1 Çıldır Turkey
17 J1 Çıldır Gölü l. Turkey
27 D4 Cili China
17 K3 Cilo D. mt Turkey
17 N1 Çiloy Adası i. Azer.
75 E4 Cima U.S.A.
73 F4 Cimarron U.S.A.
77 D4 Cimarron r. U.S.A.
42 D5 Cimetière d'Ossuaire France
51 D6 Cimişlia Moldova
48 D2 Cimone, Monte mt Italy
17 H3 Çınar Turkey
89 C3 Cinaruco r. Venez.
89 D3 Cinaruco-Capanaparo, Parque Nacional nat. park Venez.
45 G2 Cinca r. Spain
80 A5 Cincinnati U.S.A.
81 F3 Cincinnatus U.S.A.
91 D4 Cinco Chañares Arg.
91 C3 Cinco Saltos Arg.
39 E6 Cinderford U.K.
16 B3 Çine Turkey
42 D4 Ciney Belgium
84 D3 Cintalapa Mex.
44 J5 Cinto, Monte mt France
90 B3 Cinzas r. Brazil
91 C3 Cipolletti Arg.
62 D3 Circle AK U.S.A.
72 F2 Circle U.S.A.
80 B5 Circleville OH U.S.A.
75 F2 Circleville UT U.S.A.
33 C4 Cirebon Indon.
39 F6 Cirencester U.K.
48 B2 Ciriè Italy
48 G5 Cirò Marina Italy
67 H2 Cirque Mtn mt Can.
68 C6 Cisco IL U.S.A.
77 D5 Cisco TX U.S.A.
75 H2 Cisco UT U.S.A.
89 B3 Cisneros Col.
84 C3 Citlaltépetl, Vol. volc. Mex.
48 G3 Čitluk Bos.-Herz.
58 C6 Citrusdal S. Africa
48 E3 Città di Castello Italy
49 L2 Ciucaş, Vârful mt Romania
82 D3 Ciudad Acuña Mex.
84 B3 Ciudad Altamirano Mex.
89 E3 Ciudad Bolívar Venez.
82 C3 Ciudad Camargo Mex.
84 E4 Ciudad Cuauhtémoc Mex.
84 E3 Ciudad del Carmen Mex.
90 A4 Ciudad del Este Para.
82 C3 Ciudad Delicias Mex.
84 C2 Ciudad del Maíz Mex.
89 C2 Ciudad de Nutrias Venez.
84 C2 Ciudad de Valles Mex.
89 E2 Ciudad Guayana Venez.
84 B3 Ciudad Guzmán Mex.
84 B3 Ciudad Hidalgo Mex.
84 D3 Ciudad Ixtepec Mex.
82 C2 Ciudad Juárez Mex.
84 B1 Ciudad Lerdo Mex.
84 C2 Ciudad Madero Mex.
84 C2 Ciudad Mante Mex.
84 C3 Ciudad Mendoza Mex.
84 C1 Ciudad Mier Mex.
82 C3 Ciudad Obregón Mex.
89 E3 Ciudad Piar Venez.
45 E3 Ciudad Real Spain
84 C1 Ciudad Río Bravo Mex.
45 C2 Ciudad Rodrigo Spain
84 C2 Ciudad Victoria Mex.
45 H2 Ciutadella de Menorca Spain
16 F1 Civa Burnu pt Turkey
16 B2 Civan Dağ mt Turkey
48 E1 Cividale del Friuli Italy
48 E3 Civita Castellana Italy
48 E3 Civitanova Marche Italy
48 D3 Civitavecchia Italy
16 B2 Çivril Turkey
27 F4 Cixi China
26 E2 Ci Xian China
17 J3 Cizre Turkey
39 J6 Clacton-on-Sea U.K.
41 D3 Clady U.K.
65 G3 Claire, Lake l. Can.
72 B3 Clair Engle L. resr U.S.A.
80 D4 Clairton U.S.A.
44 F3 Clamecy France
72 D2 Clan Alpine Mts mts U.S.A.
41 E4 Clane Rep. of Ireland
79 C5 Clanton U.S.A.
58 C6 Clanwilliam S. Africa
41 D4 Clara Rep. of Ireland
32 A3 Clara I. i. Myanmar
8 D2 Clare N.S.W. Austr.
8 B2 Clare S.A. Austr.
68 E4 Clare U.S.A.
41 C4 Clare r. Rep. of Ireland
41 C5 Clarecastle Rep. of Ireland
41 A4 Clare Island i. Rep. of Ireland
81 G3 Claremont U.S.A.
77 E4 Claremore U.S.A.
41 C4 Claremorris Rep. of Ireland
9 D5 Clarence N.Z.
92 B1 Clarence I. i. Ant.
64 C3 Clarence Str. chan. U.S.A.
79 F7 Clarence Town Bahamas
77 C5 Clarendon U.S.A.
67 K4 Clarenville Can.
64 G5 Claresholm Can.
76 E3 Clarinda U.S.A.
80 C5 Clarington U.S.A.
80 D4 Clarion U.S.A.
80 D4 Clarion r. U.S.A.
95 L4 Clarion Fracture Zone sea feature Pac. Oc.
61 G8 Clarión, Isla i. Mex.
76 D2 Clark U.S.A.
59 H5 Clarkebury S. Africa
6 E6 Clarke I. i. Austr.
70 D2 Clark Fork r. MT U.S.A.
79 D5 Clark Hill Res. resr U.S.A.
75 E4 Clark Mt mt U.S.A.
69 G3 Clark, Pt pt Can.
80 C5 Clarksburg U.S.A.
77 F5 Clarksdale U.S.A.
81 F4 Clarks Summit U.S.A.
72 C2 Clarkston U.S.A.
77 E5 Clarksville AR U.S.A.
68 A4 Clarksville IA U.S.A.
79 C4 Clarksville TN U.S.A.
90 B1 Claro r. Goiás Brazil
90 B2 Claro r. Goiás Brazil
41 D5 Clashmore Rep. of Ireland
41 D3 Claudy U.K.
31 B2 Claveria Phil.
42 D4 Clavier Belgium
81 G2 Clayburg U.S.A.
76 D4 Clay Center U.S.A.
75 F3 Clayhole Wash r. U.S.A.
79 D5 Clayton GA U.S.A.
73 G4 Clayton NM U.S.A.
81 E2 Clayton NY U.S.A.
81 J1 Clayton Lake U.S.A.
80 C6 Claytor Lake l. U.S.A.
41 B6 Clear, Cape c. Rep. of Ireland
69 G4 Clear Creek Can.
75 G4 Clear Creek r. U.S.A.
62 D4 Cleare, C. c. U.S.A.
80 D4 Clearfield PA U.S.A.
72 E3 Clearfield UT U.S.A.
80 B4 Clear Fork Reservoir U.S.A.
64 F3 Clear Hills mts Can.
76 E3 Clear Lake IA U.S.A.
68 A3 Clear Lake WV U.S.A.
74 A2 Clear Lake l. CA U.S.A.
75 F2 Clear Lake l. UT U.S.A.
72 B3 Clear L. Res. resr U.S.A.
79 D7 Clearwater U.S.A.
64 F4 Clearwater r. Alta. Can.
65 H3 Clearwater r. Sask. Can.
27 □ Clear Water Bay b. H.K. China
72 D2 Clearwater Mountains U.S.A.
65 H3 Clearwater River Provincial Park res. Can.
77 D5 Cleburne U.S.A.
72 B2 Cle Elum U.S.A.
38 G4 Cleethorpes U.K.
32 □ Clementi Sing.
80 C5 Clendenin U.S.A.
80 C4 Clendening Lake l. U.S.A.
31 A4 Cleopatra Needle mt Phil.
69 H1 Cléricy Can.
6 E4 Clermont Austr.
42 A5 Clermont France
79 D6 Clermont U.S.A.
42 D5 Clermont-en-Argonne France
44 F4 Clermont-Ferrand France
42 E4 Clervaux Lux.
48 D1 Cles Italy
39 E6 Clevedon U.K.
77 F5 Cleveland MS U.S.A.
80 C4 Cleveland OH U.S.A.
79 C5 Cleveland TN U.S.A.
68 D2 Cleveland Cliffs Basin l. U.S.A.
38 F3 Cleveland Hills h. U.K.
64 G5 Cleveland, Mt mt U.S.A.
38 D4 Cleveleys U.K.
41 B4 Clew Bay b. Rep. of Ireland
79 D7 Clewiston U.S.A.
41 A4 Clifden Rep. of Ireland
75 H5 Cliff U.S.A.
41 C3 Cliffoney Rep. of Ireland
9 E4 Clifford Bay b. N.Z.
75 H5 Clifton U.S.A.
80 D6 Clifton Forge U.S.A.
80 B6 Clinch r. U.S.A.
80 B6 Clinch Mountain U.S.A.
64 E4 Clinton B.C. Can.
69 G4 Clinton Ont. Can.
81 G4 Clinton CT U.S.A.
68 B5 Clinton IA U.S.A.
68 C5 Clinton IL U.S.A.
81 H3 Clinton MA U.S.A.
81 J2 Clinton ME U.S.A.
76 E4 Clinton MO U.S.A.
77 F5 Clinton MS U.S.A.
79 E5 Clinton NC U.S.A.
77 D5 Clinton OK U.S.A.
65 H2 Clinton-Colden Lake l. Can.
68 C5 Clinton Lake l. U.S.A.
68 C3 Clintonville U.S.A.
75 G4 Clints Well U.S.A.
95 L5 Clipperton Fracture Zone sea feature Pac. Oc.
82 C6 Clipperton Island terr. Pac. Oc.
40 B3 Clisham h. U.K.
38 E4 Clitheroe U.K.
59 G4 Clocolan S. Africa
41 D4 Cloghan Rep. of Ireland
41 C6 Clonakilty Rep. of Ireland
41 C6 Clonakilty Bay b. Rep. of Ireland
41 C4 Clonbern Rep. of Ireland
6 E4 Cloncurry Austr.
41 D3 Clones Rep. of Ireland
41 D5 Clonmel Rep. of Ireland
41 D4 Clonygowan Rep. of Ireland
41 B5 Cloonbannin Rep. of Ireland
41 D4 Clooneagh Rep. of Ireland
43 G2 Cloppenburg Ger.
68 A2 Cloquet U.S.A.
72 F2 Cloud Peak summit U.S.A.
9 E4 Cloudy Bay b. N.Z.
27 □ Cloudy Hill h. H.K. China
69 K1 Clova Can.
74 A2 Cloverdale U.S.A.
77 C5 Clovis U.S.A.
69 J3 Cloyne Can.
40 C3 Cluanie, Loch l. U.K.
65 H3 Cluff Lake Can.
47 L7 Cluj-Napoca Romania
39 D5 Clun U.K.
8 D4 Clunes Austr.
44 H3 Cluses France
39 D4 Clwydian Range h. U.K.
64 G4 Clyde Can.
80 E3 Clyde NY U.S.A.
80 B4 Clyde OH U.S.A.
40 D5 Clyde r. U.K.
40 D5 Clydebank U.K.
40 D5 Clyde, Firth of est. U.K.

63 M2 **Clyde River** Can.
73 C5 **Coachella** U.S.A.
91 B2 **Co Aconcagua** *mt* Arg.
84 B3 **Coahuayutla de Guerrero** Mex.
84 B1 **Coahuila** *div.* Mex.
64 D2 **Coal** *r.* Can.
68 C5 **Coal City** U.S.A.
84 B3 **Coalcomán** Mex.
74 D3 **Coaldale** U.S.A.
77 D5 **Coalgate** U.S.A.
74 B3 **Coalinga** U.S.A.
64 D3 **Coal River** Can.
39 F5 **Coalville** U.K.
86 F4 **Coari** Brazil
86 F5 **Coari** *r.* Brazil
79 C6 **Coastal Plain** *plain* U.S.A.
64 D4 **Coast Mountains** *mts* Can.
72 B2 **Coast Range** *mts* U.S.A.
74 B3 **Coast Ranges** *mts* U.S.A.
40 E5 **Coatbridge** U.K.
84 E4 **Coatepeque** Guatemala
81 F5 **Coatesville** U.S.A.
67 F4 **Coaticook** Can.
63 K3 **Coats Island** *i.* Can.
92 C3 **Coats Land** *coastal area* Ant.
84 D3 **Coatzacoalcos** Mex.
69 H2 **Cobalt** Can.
82 F5 **Cobán** Guatemala
8 E1 **Cobar** Austr.
8 G4 **Cobargo** Austr.
8 G4 **Cobberas, Mt** *mt* Austr.
8 D5 **Cobden** Austr.
69 J3 **Cobden** Can.
41 C6 **Cóbh** Rep. of Ireland
65 K4 **Cobham** *r.* Can.
86 E6 **Cobija** Bol.
81 F3 **Cobleskill** U.S.A.
69 H4 **Cobourg** Can.
6 D3 **Cobourg Penina** *pen.* Austr.
8 E3 **Cobram** Austr.
43 J4 **Coburg** Ger.
45 D2 **Coca** Spain
90 B1 **Cocalinho** Brazil
Cocanada *see* **Kākināda**
86 E7 **Cochabamba** Bol.
91 B4 **Cochamó** Chile
42 F4 **Cochem** Ger.
21 B4 **Cochin** India
75 H5 **Cochise** U.S.A.
64 G4 **Cochrane** *Alta.* Can.
66 D4 **Cochrane** *Ont.* Can.
88 B7 **Cochrane** Chile
65 J3 **Cochrane** *r.* Can.
8 C2 **Cockburn** Austr.
69 F3 **Cockburn I.** *i.* Can.
40 F5 **Cockburnspath** U.K.
79 F7 **Cockburn Town** Bahamas
83 K4 **Cockburn Town** Turks and Caicos Is
38 D3 **Cockermouth** U.K.
58 F6 **Cockscomb** *summit* S. Africa
83 H6 **Coco** *r.* Honduras/Nic.
82 G7 **Coco, Isla de** *i.* Col.
75 F4 **Coconino Plateau** U.S.A.
8 F2 **Cocoparra Range** *h.* Austr.
89 A4 **Coco, Pta** *pt* Col.
89 B3 **Cocorná** Col.
90 D1 **Cocos** Brazil
93 L4 **Cocos Is** *is* Ind. Ocean
95 O5 **Cocos Ridge** *sea feature* Pac. Oc.
84 B2 **Cocula** Mex.
89 B3 **Cocuy, Parque Nacional el** *nat. park* Col.
89 B3 **Cocuy, Sierra Nevada del** *mt* Col.
86 F4 **Codajás** Brazil
81 H4 **Cod, Cape** *c.* U.S.A.
89 D2 **Codera, C.** *pt* Venez.
9 A7 **Codfish I.** *i.* N.Z.
48 E2 **Codigoro** Italy
67 H2 **Cod Island** *i.* Can.
49 L2 **Codlea** Romania
87 K4 **Codó** Brazil
39 E5 **Codsall** U.K.
41 A6 **Cod's Head** *hd* Rep. of Ireland
72 E2 **Cody** U.S.A.
6 E3 **Coen** Austr.
42 F3 **Coesfeld** Ger.
53 K6 **Coëtivy** *i.* Seychelles
72 C2 **Coeur d'Alene** U.S.A.
72 C2 **Coeur d'Alene L.** *l.* U.S.A.
42 E2 **Coevorden** Neth.
59 H5 **Coffee Bay** S. Africa
77 E4 **Coffeyville** U.S.A.
7 F5 **Coffs Harbour** Austr.
59 G6 **Cofimvaba** S. Africa
84 C3 **Cofre de Perote, Parque Nacional** *nat. park* Mex.
68 B4 **Coggon** U.S.A.
44 D4 **Cognac** France
54 C4 **Cogo** Equatorial Guinea
80 E3 **Cohocton** *r.* U.S.A.
81 G3 **Cohoes** U.S.A.
8 E3 **Cohuna** Austr.
83 H7 **Coiba, Isla** *i.* Panama
88 C8 **Coig** *r.* Arg.
88 B7 **Coihaique** Chile
21 B4 **Coimbatore** India
45 B2 **Coimbra** Port.
45 D4 **Coín** Spain
86 E7 **Coipasa, Salar de** *salt flat* Bol.
89 C2 **Cojedes** *r.* Venez.
72 E3 **Cokeville** U.S.A.
8 D5 **Colac** Austr.
Colair L. *l.* *see* **Kolleru L.**
90 E2 **Colatina** Brazil
43 K2 **Colbitz** Ger.
76 C4 **Colby** U.S.A.
86 D7 **Colca** *r.* Peru
39 H6 **Colchester** U.K.
68 B5 **Colchester** U.S.A.
40 F5 **Coldingham** U.K.
43 L3 **Colditz** Ger.
65 G4 **Cold L.** *l.* Can.
65 G4 **Cold Lake** Can.
40 F5 **Coldstream** U.K.
77 D4 **Coldwater** *KS* U.S.A.
68 E5 **Coldwater** *MI* U.S.A.
68 D1 **Coldwell** Can.
81 H2 **Colebrook** U.S.A.
68 E4 **Coleman** *MI* U.S.A.
77 D6 **Coleman** *TX* U.S.A.
59 H4 **Colenso** S. Africa
8 C4 **Coleraine** Austr.
41 E2 **Coleraine** U.K.
9 C5 **Coleridge, L.** *l.* N.Z.
21 B4 **Coleroon** *r.* India
58 F5 **Colesberg** S. Africa
74 B2 **Colfax** *CA* U.S.A.
72 C2 **Colfax** *WA* U.S.A.
40 □ **Colgrave Sound** *chan.* U.K.
59 G3 **Coligny** S. Africa
84 B3 **Colima** Mex.
84 B3 **Colima** *div.* Mex.
40 B4 **Coll** *i.* U.K.
45 E2 **Collado Villalba** Spain
79 C5 **College Park** U.S.A.
77 D6 **College Station** U.S.A.
8 G1 **Collie** Austr.
6 C3 **Collier Bay** *b.* Austr.
69 G3 **Collingwood** Can.
9 D4 **Collingwood** N.Z.
77 F6 **Collins** U.S.A.
78 B4 **Collinsville** U.S.A.
91 B3 **Collipulli** Chile
41 C3 **Collooney** Rep. of Ireland
44 H2 **Colmar** France
45 E2 **Colmenar Viejo** Spain
40 D5 **Colmonell** U.K.
39 H6 **Colne** *r.* U.K.
8 H2 **Colo** *r.* Austr.
42 F4 **Cologne** Ger.
68 C3 **Coloma** U.S.A.
90 C3 **Colômbia** Brazil
77 D7 **Colombia** Mex.
85 C2 **Colombia** *country* S. America
96 D5 **Colombian Basin** *sea feature* Atl. Ocean
21 B5 **Colombo** Sri Lanka
44 E5 **Colomiers** France
91 E2 **Colón** *Buenos Aires* Arg.
91 E2 **Colón** *Entre Ríos* Arg.
83 H4 **Colón** Cuba
83 J7 **Colón** Panama
73 C6 **Colonet, C.** *c.* Mex.
90 E1 **Colônia** *r.* Brazil
91 D3 **Colonia Choele Choel, Isla** *i.* Arg.
91 F2 **Colonia del Sacramento** Uru.
91 C3 **Colonia Emilio Mitre** Arg.
91 F1 **Colonia Lavalleja** Uru.
80 E6 **Colonial Heights** U.S.A.
75 F6 **Colonia Reforma** Mex.
48 G5 **Colonna, Capo** *pt* Italy
40 B4 **Colonsay** *i.* U.K.
91 D3 **Colorada Grande, Salina** *l.* Arg.
73 F4 **Colorado** *div.* U.S.A.
91 D3 **Colorado** *r.* *La Pampa/Río Negro* Arg.
91 C1 **Colorado** *r.* *San Juan* Arg.
75 E5 **Colorado** *r.* Mex./U.S.A.
77 D6 **Colorado** *r.* U.S.A.
75 F3 **Colorado City** *AZ* U.S.A.
77 C5 **Colorado City** *TX* U.S.A.
91 D3 **Colorado, Delta del Río** *delta* Arg.
74 D5 **Colorado Desert** U.S.A.
75 H2 **Colorado National Monument** *res.* U.S.A.
75 G3 **Colorado Plateau** U.S.A.
75 E4 **Colorado River Aqueduct** *canal* U.S.A.
73 F4 **Colorado Springs** U.S.A.
84 B2 **Colotlán** Mex.
43 M1 **Cölpin** Ger.
39 G5 **Colsterworth** U.K.
39 J5 **Coltishall** U.K.
74 D4 **Colton** *CA* U.S.A.
81 F2 **Colton** *NY* U.S.A.
75 G2 **Colton** *UT* U.S.A.
80 E5 **Columbia** *MD* U.S.A.
76 E4 **Columbia** *MO* U.S.A.
77 F6 **Columbia** *MS* U.S.A.
80 E4 **Columbia** *PA* U.S.A.
79 D5 **Columbia** *SC* U.S.A.
79 C5 **Columbia** *TN* U.S.A.
72 B2 **Columbia** *r.* Can./U.S.A.
63 L1 **Columbia, C.** *c.* Can.
68 E5 **Columbia City** U.S.A.
80 E5 **Columbia, District of** *div.* U.S.A.
81 K2 **Columbia Falls** *ME* U.S.A.
72 D1 **Columbia Falls** *MT* U.S.A.
64 F4 **Columbia Mountains** Can.
64 F4 **Columbia, Mt** *mt* Can.
72 C2 **Columbia Plateau** *plat.* U.S.A.
58 B6 **Columbine, Cape** *pt* S. Africa
79 C5 **Columbus** *GA* U.S.A.
78 C4 **Columbus** *IN* U.S.A.
77 F5 **Columbus** *MS* U.S.A.
72 E2 **Columbus** *MT* U.S.A.
76 D3 **Columbus** *NE* U.S.A.
73 F6 **Columbus** *NM* U.S.A.
80 B5 **Columbus** *OH* U.S.A.
77 D6 **Columbus** *TX* U.S.A.
68 C4 **Columbus** *WV* U.S.A.
68 B5 **Columbus Jct** U.S.A.
79 F7 **Columbus Pt** *pt* Bahamas
74 D2 **Columbus Salt Marsh** *salt marsh* U.S.A.
74 A2 **Colusa** U.S.A.
9 E2 **Colville** N.Z.
72 C1 **Colville** U.S.A.
62 C3 **Colville** *r.* *AK* U.S.A.
9 E2 **Colville Channel** *chan.* N.Z.
62 F3 **Colville Lake** Can.
39 D4 **Colwyn Bay** U.K.
48 E2 **Comacchio** Italy
48 E2 **Comacchio, Valli di** *lag.* Italy
23 G3 **Comai** China
91 B4 **Comallo** *r.* Arg.
77 D6 **Comanche** U.S.A.
92 B1 **Comandante Ferraz** *Brazil Base* Ant.
91 C2 **Comandante Salas** Arg.
47 N7 **Comănești** Romania
91 B1 **Combarbalá** Chile
41 F3 **Comber** U.K.
69 J3 **Combermere** Can.
23 H6 **Combermere Bay** *b.* Myanmar
42 A4 **Combles** France
59 K1 **Combomune** Moz.
66 E3 **Comencho, L.** *l.* Can.
41 D5 **Comeragh Mountains** *h.* Rep. of Ireland
77 D6 **Comfort** U.S.A.
23 G5 **Comilla** Bangl.
42 A4 **Comines** Belgium
48 C4 **Comino, Capo** *pt* *Sardinia* Italy
84 D3 **Comitán de Domínguez** Mex.
81 G4 **Commack** U.S.A.
69 H3 **Commanda** Can.
63 K3 **Committee Bay** *b.* Can.
92 B6 **Commonwealth B.** *b.* Ant.
48 C2 **Como** Italy
23 G3 **Como Chamling** *l.* China
88 C7 **Comodoro Rivadavia** Arg.
54 B4 **Comoé, Parc National de la** *nat. park* Côte d'Ivoire
48 C2 **Como, Lago di** *l.* Italy
21 B4 **Comorin, Cape** *c.* India
53 J7 **Comoros** *country* Africa
44 F2 **Compiègne** France
84 A2 **Compostela** Mex.
31 C5 **Compostela** Phil.
90 C4 **Comprida, Ilha** *i.* Brazil
68 C5 **Compton** U.S.A.
51 D6 **Comrat** Moldova
40 E4 **Comrie** U.K.
77 C6 **Comstock** U.S.A.
23 H4 **Cona** China
54 A4 **Conakry** Guinea
91 C4 **Cona Niyeo** Arg.
90 C2 **Conceição** *r.* Brazil
90 E2 **Conceição da Barra** Brazil
87 J5 **Conceição do Araguaia** Brazil
88 C3 **Concepción** Arg.
86 F7 **Concepción** Bol.
91 B3 **Concepción** Chile
84 B1 **Concepción** Mex.
83 H7 **Concepción** Panama
88 E2 **Concepción** Para.
91 E2 **Concepción del Uruguay** Arg.
67 K4 **Conception Bay South** Can.
79 F7 **Conception I.** *i.* Bahamas
74 B4 **Conception, Pt** *pt* U.S.A.
90 C3 **Conchas** Brazil
73 F5 **Conchas L.** *l.* U.S.A.
75 H4 **Concho** U.S.A.
82 D3 **Conchos** *r.* *Chihuahua* Mex.
84 C1 **Conchos** *r.* *Tamaulipas* Mex.
74 A3 **Concord** *CA* U.S.A.
79 D5 **Concord** *NC* U.S.A.
81 H3 **Concord** *NH* U.S.A.
91 F1 **Concordia** Arg.
89 B4 **Concordia** Col.
58 B4 **Concordia** S. Africa
76 D4 **Concordia** U.S.A.
23 C3 **Côn Đao** Vietnam
90 E1 **Condeúba** Brazil
8 F2 **Condobolin** Austr.
44 E5 **Condom** France
72 B2 **Condon** U.S.A.
42 D4 **Condroz** *reg.* Belgium
79 C6 **Conecuh** *r.* U.S.A.
48 E2 **Conegliano** Italy
84 B1 **Conejos** Mex.
80 D4 **Conemaugh** *r.* U.S.A.
69 G4 **Conestogo Lake** *l.* Can.
80 E3 **Conesus Lake** *l.* U.S.A.
81 G4 **Coney I.** *i.* U.S.A.
6 F3 **Conflict Group** *is* P.N.G.
44 E3 **Confolens** France
75 F2 **Confusion Range** *mts* U.S.A.
27 D6 **Conghua** China
27 C5 **Congjiang** China
39 E4 **Congleton** U.K.
53 F5 **Congo** *country* Africa
53 G6 **Congo** *country* Africa
56 B4 **Congo** *r.* Africa
75 F4 **Congress** U.S.A.
91 B3 **Conguillo, Parque Nacional** *nat. park* Chile
39 G4 **Coningsby** U.K.
66 D4 **Coniston** Can.
38 D3 **Coniston** U.K.
65 G3 **Conklin** Can.
91 D2 **Conlara** Arg.
91 D2 **Conlara** *r.* Arg.
80 C4 **Conneaut** U.S.A.
81 G4 **Connecticut** *div.* U.S.A.
78 F3 **Connecticut** *r.* U.S.A.
80 D4 **Connellsville** U.S.A.
41 B4 **Connemara** *reg.* Rep. of Ireland
81 J1 **Conners** Can.
78 C4 **Connersville** U.S.A.
41 B3 **Conn, Lough** *l.* Rep. of Ireland
8 E2 **Conoble** Austr.
27 B6 **Co Nôi** Vietnam
81 E5 **Conowingo** U.S.A.
72 E1 **Conrad** U.S.A.
77 E6 **Conroe** U.S.A.
90 D3 **Conselheiro Lafaiete** Brazil
90 E2 **Conselheiro Pena** Brazil
38 F3 **Consett** U.K.
32 C3 **Côn Sơn** *i.* Vietnam
65 G4 **Consort** Can.
46 D7 **Constance, Lake** *l.* Ger./Switz.
86 F5 **Constância dos Baetas** Brazil
49 N2 **Constanța** Romania
45 D4 **Constantina** Spain
54 C1 **Constantine** Alg.
68 E5 **Constantine** U.S.A.
75 E6 **Constitución de 1857, Parque Nacional** *nat. park* Mex.
72 D3 **Contact** U.S.A.
86 C5 **Contamana** Peru
90 E1 **Contas** *r.* Brazil
75 G6 **Continental** U.S.A.
81 H3 **Contoocook** *r.* U.S.A.
88 B8 **Contreras, I.** *i.* Chile
65 G1 **Contwoyto Lake** *l.* Can.
77 E5 **Conway** *AR* U.S.A.
81 H3 **Conway** *NH* U.S.A.
79 E5 **Conway** *SC* U.S.A.
7 H4 **Conway Reef** *rf* Fiji
39 D4 **Conwy** U.K.
39 D4 **Conwy** *r.* U.K.
6 D4 **Coober Pedy** Austr.
62 A4 **Cook** U.S.A.
64 D4 **Cook, C.** *c.* Can.
79 C4 **Cookeville** U.S.A.
59 F6 **Cookhouse** S. Africa
62 C3 **Cook Inlet** *chan.* U.S.A.
5 L6 **Cook Islands** *terr.* Pac. Oc.
9 C5 **Cook, Mt** *mt* N.Z.
81 F3 **Cooksburg** U.S.A.
67 J3 **Cook's Harbour** Can.
41 E3 **Cookstown** U.K.
9 E4 **Cook Strait** *str.* N.Z.
6 E3 **Cooktown** Austr.
8 F1 **Coolabah** Austr.
8 G1 **Coolah** Austr.
8 F3 **Coolamon** Austr.
6 C5 **Coolgardie** Austr.
75 G5 **Coolidge** U.S.A.
75 G5 **Coolidge Dam** U.S.A.
8 G4 **Cooma** Austr.
41 A6 **Coomacarrea** *h.* Rep. of Ireland
8 C2 **Coombah** Austr.
8 B3 **Coonalpyn** Austr.
8 G1 **Coonamble** Austr.
8 C4 **Coonawarra** Austr.
8 G1 **Coonbarabran** Austr.
Coondapoor *see* **Kundāpura**
6 D4 **Cooper Creek** *watercourse* Austr.
81 J2 **Coopers Mills** U.S.A.
79 E7 **Coopers Town** Bahamas
76 D2 **Cooperstown** *ND* U.S.A.
81 F3 **Cooperstown** *NY* U.S.A.
8 B3 **Coorong, The** *in.* Austr.
72 A3 **Coos Bay** U.S.A.
8 G3 **Cootamundra** Austr.
41 D3 **Cootehill** Rep. of Ireland
91 B3 **Copahue, Volcán** *mt* Chile
84 D3 **Copainalá** Mex.
84 C3 **Copala** Mex.
84 C3 **Copalillo** Mex.
72 G4 **Cope** U.S.A.
37 N9 **Copenhagen** Denmark
88 B3 **Copiapo** Chile
88 B3 **Copiapo** *r.* Chile
48 D2 **Copparo** Italy
69 G2 **Copper Cliff** Can.
68 D2 **Copper Harbor** U.S.A.
62 G3 **Coppermine** *N.W.T.* Can.
62 G3 **Coppermine** *r.* *N.W.T.* Can.
68 E2 **Coppermine Pt** *pt* Can.
58 E4 **Copperton** S. Africa
23 F3 **Coqên** China
91 B1 **Coquimbo** Chile
91 B1 **Coquimbo** *div.* Chile
49 L3 **Corabia** Romania
90 D2 **Coração de Jesus** Brazil
Coracesium *see* **Alanya**
86 D7 **Coracora** Peru
79 D7 **Coral Gables** U.S.A.
63 K3 **Coral Harbour** Can.
7 F3 **Coral Sea** *sea* Coral Sea Is Terr.
94 E6 **Coral Sea Basin** *sea feature* Pac. Oc.
4 F6 **Coral Sea Islands Territory** *terr.* Pac. Oc.
68 B5 **Coralville Reservoir** U.S.A.
8 D5 **Corangamite, L.** *l.* Austr.
87 G3 **Corantijn** *r.* Suriname
17 M1 **Corat** Azer.
42 B5 **Corbeny** France
91 E2 **Corbett** Arg.
65 L2 **Corbett Inlet** *in.* Can.
42 A5 **Corbie** France
80 A6 **Corbin** U.S.A.
39 G5 **Corby** U.K.
74 C3 **Corcoran** U.S.A.
88 B6 **Corcovado, G. de** *b.* Chile
79 D6 **Cordele** U.S.A.
89 B4 **Cordillera de los Picachos, Parque Nacional** *nat. park* Col.
31 B4 **Cordilleras Range** *mts* Phil.
91 C4 **Córdoba** *Río Negro* Arg.
91 D1 **Córdoba** Arg.
84 B1 **Córdoba** *Durango* Mex.
84 C3 **Córdoba** *Veracruz* Mex.
45 D4 **Córdoba** Spain
91 D2 **Córdoba** *div.* Arg.
91 D2 **Córdoba, Sierras de** *mts* Arg.
Cordova *see* **Córdoba**
62 D3 **Cordova** *AK* U.S.A.
64 C4 **Cordova Bay** *b.* U.S.A.
81 K2 **Corea** U.S.A.
49 H5 **Corfu** *i.* Greece
45 C3 **Coria** Spain
8 H2 **Coricudgy** *mt* Austr.
48 G5 **Corigliano Calabro** Italy
81 J2 **Corinna** U.S.A.
65 J4 **Corinne** Can.
77 F5 **Corinth** *MS* U.S.A.
81 G3 **Corinth** *NY* U.S.A.
90 D2 **Corinto** Brazil
87 G7 **Corixa Grande** *r.* Bol./Brazil
90 A2 **Corixinha** *r.* Brazil
41 C6 **Cork** Rep. of Ireland
48 E6 **Corleone** *Sicily* Italy
16 A1 **Çorlu** Turkey
65 J4 **Cormorant** Can.
59 H3 **Cornelia** S. Africa
90 B3 **Cornélio Procópio** Brazil
68 B3 **Cornell** U.S.A.
67 J4 **Corner Brook** Can.
8 F5 **Corner Inlet** *b.* Austr.
42 C5 **Cornillet, Mont** *h.* France
74 A2 **Corning** *CA* U.S.A.
80 E3 **Corning** *NY* U.S.A.
Corn Islands *is* *see* **Maíz, Islas del**
48 E3 **Corno, Monte** *mt* Italy
66 F4 **Cornwall** Can.
63 J2 **Cornwallis I.** *i.* Can.
89 C2 **Coro** Venez.
87 K4 **Coroatá** Brazil
86 E7 **Corocoro** Bol.
41 B5 **Corofin** Rep. of Ireland
86 E7 **Coroico** Bol.
90 C2 **Coromandel** Brazil
9 E2 **Coromandel Peninsula** N.Z.
9 E2 **Coromandel Range** *h.* N.Z.
31 B3 **Coron** Phil.
8 C1 **Corona** Austr.
74 D5 **Corona** U.S.A.
74 D5 **Coronado** U.S.A.
83 H7 **Coronado, Baiá de** *b.* Costa Rica
91 B4 **Coronados, Golfo de los** *b.* Chile
65 G4 **Coronation** Can.
62 G3 **Coronation Gulf** Can.
92 B1 **Coronation I.** *i.* Atl. Ocean
64 C3 **Coronation Island** *i.* U.S.A.
31 B4 **Coron Bay** *b.* Phil.
91 E1 **Coronda** Arg.
91 E2 **Coronel Brandsen** Arg.
91 E3 **Coronel Dorrego** Arg.
88 E3 **Coronel Oviedo** Para.
90 A1 **Coronel Ponce** Brazil
91 E3 **Coronel Pringles** Arg.
90 A3 **Coronel Sapucaia** Brazil
91 E3 **Coronel Suárez** Arg.
91 F3 **Coronel Vidal** Arg.
49 J4 **Çorovodë** Albania
8 F3 **Corowa** Austr.
77 D7 **Corpus Christi** U.S.A.
77 D6 **Corpus Christi, L.** *l.* U.S.A.
86 E7 **Corque** Bol.
45 D3 **Corral de Cantos** *mt* Spain
91 C1 **Corral de Isaac** Arg.
87 J6 **Corrente** Brazil
90 D1 **Corrente** *r.* *Bahia* Brazil
90 B2 **Corrente** *r.* *Goiás* Brazil
90 C1 **Correntina** *r.* Brazil
90 A2 **Correntes** Brazil
90 A2 **Correntes** *r.* Brazil
90 D1 **Correntina** Brazil
Correntina *r.* *see* **Éguas**
41 B4 **Corrib, Lough** *l.* Rep. of Ireland
88 E3 **Corrientes** Arg.
88 E3 **Corrientes** *r.* Arg.
84 A2 **Corrientes, C.** *c.* Mex.
91 F3 **Corrientes, C.** *hd* Arg.
89 A3 **Corrientes, Cabo** *hd* Col.
77 E6 **Corrigan** U.S.A.
39 D5 **Corris** U.K.
80 D4 **Corry** U.S.A.
8 F4 **Corryong** Austr.
Corse *i.* *see* **Corsica**
48 C3 **Corse, Cap** *hd* *Corsica* France
39 E6 **Corsham** U.K.
44 J5 **Corsica** *i.* France
77 D5 **Corsicana** U.S.A.
Cort Adelzier, Kap *hd* *see* **Kangeq**
48 C3 **Corte** *Corsica* France
45 C4 **Cortegana** Spain
75 H3 **Cortez** U.S.A.
74 D1 **Cortez Mts** *mts* U.S.A.
48 E1 **Cortina d'Ampezzo** Italy
81 E3 **Cortland** U.S.A.
39 J5 **Corton** U.K.
48 D3 **Cortona** Italy
45 B3 **Coruche** Port.
17 H1 **Çoruh** *r.* Turkey
16 E1 **Çorum** Turkey
87 G7 **Corumbá** Brazil
90 C2 **Corumbá** *r.* Brazil
90 C2 **Corumbaíba** Brazil
89 E3 **Corumo** *r.* Venez.
72 B2 **Corvallis** U.S.A.
39 D5 **Corwen** U.K.
84 A1 **Cosalá** Mex.
48 G5 **Cosenza** Italy
80 C4 **Coshocton** U.S.A.
44 F3 **Cosne-Cours-sur-Loire** France
91 D1 **Cosquín** Arg.
45 F3 **Costa Blanca** *coastal area* Spain
45 H2 **Costa Brava** *coastal area* France/Spain
45 C4 **Costa de la Luz** *coastal area* Spain
45 D4 **Costa del Sol** *coastal area* Spain
83 H6 **Costa de Mosquitos** *coastal area* Nic.
84 A1 **Costa Rica** Mex.
61 K8 **Costa Rica** *country* Central America
49 L2 **Costești** Romania
81 J2 **Costigan** U.S.A.
43 L3 **Coswig** Ger.
31 C5 **Cotabato** Phil.
89 A4 **Cotacachi, Co** *mt* Ecuador
86 E8 **Cotagaita** Bol.
90 E2 **Cotaxé** *r.* Brazil
44 H5 **Côte d'Azur** *coastal area* France
53 D5 **Côte d'Ivoire** *country* Africa
64 C3 **Cote, Mt** *mt* U.S.A.
44 G2 **Côtes de Meuse** *ridge* France
39 D5 **Cothi** *r.* U.K.
45 G1 **Cotiella** *mt* Spain
89 E3 **Cotingo** *r.* Brazil
54 C4 **Cotonou** Benin
86 C4 **Cotopaxi, Volcán** *volc.* Ecuador
39 E6 **Cotswold Hills** *h.* U.K.
72 B3 **Cottage Grove** U.S.A.
46 G5 **Cottbus** Ger.
21 B3 **Cotteliar** *r.* India
39 H5 **Cottenham** U.K.
75 H5 **Cotton City** U.S.A.
75 F4 **Cottonwood** U.S.A.
75 G4 **Cottonwood Wash** *r.* U.S.A.
77 D6 **Cotulla** U.S.A.
80 D4 **Coudersport** U.S.A.
92 B5 **Coulman I.** *i.* Ant.
44 F2 **Coulommiers** France
69 J2 **Coulonge** *r.* Can.
74 B3 **Coulterville** U.S.A.
72 C2 **Council** U.S.A.
76 E3 **Council Bluffs** U.S.A.
65 G2 **Courageous Lake** *l.* Can.
37 R9 **Courland Lagoon** *lag.* Lith./Rus. Fed.
64 E5 **Courtenay** Can.
41 C6 **Courtmacsherry** Rep. of Ireland
41 E5 **Courtown** Rep. of Ireland
Courtrai *see* **Kortrijk**
77 E5 **Coushatta** U.S.A.
44 D2 **Coutances** France
66 E2 **Couture, Lac** *l.* Can.
42 C4 **Couvin** Belgium
75 F2 **Cove Fort** U.S.A.
69 G3 **Cove I.** *i.* Can.
80 E5 **Cove Mts** *h.* U.S.A.
39 F5 **Coventry** U.K.
81 E5 **Cove Point** U.S.A.
45 C2 **Covilhã** Port.
79 D5 **Covington** *GA* U.S.A.
68 D5 **Covington** *IN* U.S.A.
80 A5 **Covington** *KY* U.S.A.
79 B5 **Covington** *TN* U.S.A.
80 D6 **Covington** *VA* U.S.A.
69 F2 **Cow** *r.* Can.
8 F2 **Cowal, L.** *l.* Austr.
6 C5 **Cowan, L.** *salt flat* Austr.
81 G2 **Cowansville** Can.
40 E4 **Cowdenbeath** U.K.
8 E5 **Cowes** Austr.
39 F7 **Cowes** U.K.
38 E3 **Cow Green Reservoir** U.K.
80 D5 **Cowpasture** *r.* U.S.A.
8 G2 **Cowra** Austr.
90 D1 **Coxá** *r.* Brazil
91 F1 **Coxilha de Santana** *h.* Brazil/Uru.
90 A2 **Coxim** Brazil
90 A2 **Coxim** *r.* Brazil
81 G3 **Coxsackie** U.S.A.
23 H5 **Cox's Bazar** Bangl.
74 D4 **Coyote Lake** *l.* U.S.A.
75 E5 **Coyote Peak** *summit* *AZ* U.S.A.
74 C3 **Coyote Peak** *summit* *CA* U.S.A.
84 A2 **Coyotitán** Mex.
84 B3 **Coyuca de Benítez** Mex.
23 F2 **Cozhê** China
49 L2 **Cozia, Vârful** *mt* Romania
73 D6 **Cozón, Co** *mt* Mex.
82 G4 **Cozumel** Mex.
82 G4 **Cozumel, I. de** *i.* Mex.
8 G2 **Craboon** Austr.
8 B1 **Cradock** Austr.
59 F6 **Cradock** S. Africa
40 C3 **Craig** U.K.
64 C3 **Craig** *AK* U.S.A.
72 F3 **Craig** *CO* U.S.A.
41 E3 **Craigavon** U.K.
8 E4 **Craigieburn** Austr.
80 D5 **Craigsville** U.S.A.
40 F4 **Crail** U.K.
43 J5 **Crailsheim** Ger.
49 K2 **Craiova** Romania
38 F2 **Cramlington** U.K.
81 F2 **Cranberry L.** *l.* U.S.A.
81 F2 **Cranberry Lake** U.S.A.
8 E5 **Cranbourne** Austr.
64 F5 **Cranbrook** Can.
68 C3 **Crandon** U.S.A.
72 C3 **Crane** *OR* U.S.A.
77 C6 **Crane** *TX* U.S.A.
68 A1 **Crane Lake** U.S.A.
81 H4 **Cranston** U.S.A.
92 B4 **Crary Ice Rise** *ice feature* Ant.
92 A4 **Crary Mts** *mts* Ant.
72 B3 **Crater L.** *l.* U.S.A.
72 B3 **Crater Lake Nat. Pk** U.S.A.
72 D3 **Craters of the Moon Nat. Mon.** *res.* U.S.A.
87 K5 **Crateús** Brazil
87 L5 **Crato** Brazil
89 C3 **Cravo Norte** Col.
89 C3 **Cravo Sur** *r.* Col.
76 C3 **Crawford** U.S.A.
68 D5 **Crawfordsville** U.S.A.
79 C6 **Crawfordville** U.S.A.
39 G6 **Crawley** U.K.
72 E2 **Crazy Mts** *mts* U.S.A.
40 D4 **Creag Meagaidh** *mt* U.K.
65 H4 **Crean L.** *l.* Can.
39 E5 **Credenhill** U.K.
39 D7 **Crediton** U.K.
65 H3 **Cree** *r.* Can.
65 H3 **Cree Lake** *l.* Can.
65 J4 **Creighton** Can.
42 A5 **Creil** France
42 D2 **Creil** Neth.
43 J2 **Cremlingen** Ger.
48 D2 **Cremona** Italy
44 F2 **Crépy-en-Valois** France
48 F2 **Cres** *i.* Croatia
72 A3 **Crescent City** U.S.A.
27 □ **Crescent I.** *i.* *H.K.* China
75 H2 **Crescent Junction** U.S.A.
74 B1 **Crescent Mills** U.S.A.
75 E4 **Crescent Peak** *summit* U.S.A.
68 A4 **Cresco** U.S.A.
91 E2 **Crespo** Arg.
8 D5 **Cressy** Austr.
64 F5 **Creston** Can.
76 E3 **Creston** *IA* U.S.A.
72 F3 **Creston** *WY* U.S.A.
79 C6 **Crestview** U.S.A.
81 F5 **Crestwood Village** U.S.A.
8 D4 **Creswick** Austr.
49 L7 **Crete** *i.* Greece
45 H1 **Creus, Cap de** *pt* Spain
44 E3 **Creuse** *r.* France
43 K5 **Creußen** Ger.
42 E5 **Creutzwald** France
43 J3 **Creuzburg** Ger.
39 E4 **Crewe** U.K.
80 D6 **Crewe** U.S.A.
39 E7 **Crewkerne** U.K.
40 D4 **Crianlarich** U.K.
39 C5 **Criccieth** U.K.
88 G3 **Criciúma** Brazil
40 E4 **Crieff** U.K.
40 E6 **Criffell** *h.* U.K.
48 F2 **Crikvenica** Croatia
51 E6 **Crimea** *pen.* Ukr.
43 L4 **Crimmitschau** Ger.
40 G3 **Crimond** U.K.
81 F6 **Crisfield** U.S.A.
90 C2 **Cristalina** Brazil
Cristalino *r.* *see* **Mariembero**
89 B2 **Cristóbal Colón, Pico** *mt* Col.
90 C1 **Crixás** Brazil
90 C1 **Crixás Açu** *r.* Brazil
90 B1 **Crixás Mirim** *r.* Brazil
Crna Gora *div.* *see* **Montenegro**
48 F2 **Črnomelj** Slovenia
41 B4 **Croagh Patrick** *h.* Rep. of Ireland
8 G4 **Croajingolong Nat. Park** Austr.
34 G4 **Croatia** *country* Europe
33 E2 **Crocker Range** *mts* Malaysia
77 E6 **Crockett** U.S.A.
81 F3 **Croghan** U.S.A.
42 A4 **Croisilles** France
6 D3 **Croker I.** *i.* Austr.
40 D3 **Cromarty** U.K.
40 D3 **Cromarty Firth** *est.* U.K.
40 E3 **Cromdale, Hills of** *h.* U.K.
39 J5 **Cromer** U.K.
9 B6 **Cromwell** N.Z.
38 F3 **Crook** U.K.
80 D4 **Crooked Creek Reservoir** U.S.A.
27 □ **Crooked I.** *i.* *H.K.* China
83 K4 **Crooked I. Passage** *chan.* Bahamas
83 K4 **Crooked Island** *i.* Bahamas
68 B1 **Crooked Lake** *l.* Can./U.S.A.
76 D2 **Crookston** U.S.A.
8 G3 **Crookwell** Austr.
41 C5 **Croom** Rep. of Ireland
38 D4 **Crosby** U.K.
65 J5 **Crosby** U.S.A.
65 L2 **Cross Bay** *b.* Can.
79 D6 **Cross City** U.S.A.
81 K1 **Cross Creek** Can.
77 E5 **Crossett** U.S.A.
38 E3 **Cross Fell** *h.* U.K.
41 F3 **Crossgar** U.K.
41 C6 **Crosshaven** Rep. of Ireland
39 C5 **Cross Inn** U.K.
65 K4 **Cross Lake** Can.
65 K4 **Cross Lake** *l.* Can.
80 E3 **Cross Lake** *l.* U.S.A.
9 D5 **Crossley, Mt** *mt* N.Z.
41 E3 **Crossmaglen** U.K.
75 E4 **Crossman Peak** *summit* U.S.A.
64 B3 **Cross Sound** *chan.* U.S.A.
68 E3 **Cross Village** U.S.A.
79 C5 **Crossville** U.S.A.
69 F4 **Croswell** U.S.A.
48 G5 **Crotone** Italy
39 H6 **Crouch** *r.* U.K.
8 F1 **Crowal** *r.* Austr.
39 H6 **Crowborough** U.K.
8 E2 **Crowl** *r.* Austr.
39 G5 **Crowland** U.K.
77 E6 **Crowley** U.S.A.
74 C3 **Crowley, Lake** *l.* U.S.A.
68 D5 **Crown Point** *IN* U.S.A.
81 G3 **Crown Point** *NY* U.S.A.
92 C3 **Crown Princess Martha Coast** *coastal area* Ant.
64 G5 **Crowsnest Pass** Can.
39 G6 **Croydon** U.K.
93 H6 **Crozet Basin** *sea feature* Ind. Ocean
93 H7 **Crozet, Îles** *is* Ind. Ocean
93 G6 **Crozet Plateau** *sea feature* Ind. Ocean
62 G2 **Crozier Chan.** *chan.* Can.
44 B2 **Crozon** France
40 G3 **Cruden Bay** U.K.
84 C1 **Cruillas** Mex.
41 E3 **Crumlin** U.K.
41 C5 **Crusheen** Rep. of Ireland
88 F3 **Cruz Alta** Brazil
83 J5 **Cruz, Cabo** *c.* Cuba
91 D1 **Cruz del Eje** Arg.
90 D3 **Cruzeiro** Brazil
86 D5 **Cruzeiro do Sul** Brazil
75 H5 **Cruzville** U.S.A.
64 E3 **Crysdale, Mt** *mt* Can.
8 B2 **Crystal Brook** Austr.
77 D6 **Crystal City** U.S.A.
68 C2 **Crystal Falls** U.S.A.
68 C4 **Crystal Lake** U.S.A.
47 K7 **Csongrád** Hungary
17 K5 **Ctesiphon** Iraq
89 D2 **Cúa** Venez.
32 C3 **Cửa Lớn** *r.* Vietnam
57 C5 **Cuando** *r.* Angola/Zambia
57 B5 **Cuangar** Angola
56 B4 **Cuango** *r.* Angola/Congo(Zaire)
57 B4 **Cuanza** *r.* Angola
89 D3 **Cuao** *r.* Venez.
91 F1 **Cuaro** *r.* Uru.
91 D2 **Cuarto** *r.* Arg.
82 C3 **Cuauhtémoc** Mex.
84 C3 **Cuautla** Mex.
68 B5 **Cuba** *IL* U.S.A.
73 F4 **Cuba** *NM* U.S.A.
61 K7 **Cuba** *country* Caribbean Sea
75 F6 **Cubabi, Cerro** *summit* Mex.
57 B5 **Cubal** Angola
57 B5 **Cubango** *r.* Angola/Namibia
89 B3 **Cubara** Col.
65 J4 **Cub Hills** *h.* Can.
16 D1 **Çubuk** Turkey
91 F1 **Cuchilla Grande Inferior** *h.* Uru.
91 D3 **Cuchillo-Có** Arg.
89 D3 **Cuchivero** *r.* Venez.
80 E6 **Cuckoo** U.S.A.
89 D4 **Cucuí** Brazil
89 B3 **Cúcuta** Col.
21 B4 **Cuddalore** India
21 B3 **Cuddapah** India
65 H4 **Cudworth** Can.
45 D2 **Cuéllar** Spain
57 B5 **Cuemba** Angola
86 C4 **Cuenca** Ecuador
45 E2 **Cuenca** Spain
84 B1 **Cuencamé** Mex.
45 E2 **Cuenca, Serranía de** *mts* Spain
84 C3 **Cuernavaca** Mex.
77 D6 **Cuero** U.S.A.
74 B4 **Cuesta Pass** *pass* U.S.A.
84 C2 **Cuetzalán** Mex.
49 K2 **Cugir** Romania
87 G5 **Cuiabá** *Amazonas* Brazil
90 A1 **Cuiabá** *Moto Grosso* Brazil
90 A2 **Cuiabá** *r.* Brazil
90 A1 **Cuiabá de Larga** Brazil
84 C3 **Cuicatlan** Mex.
42 D3 **Cuijk** Neth.
40 B3 **Cuillin Hills** *mts* U.K.
40 B3 **Cuillin Sound** *chan.* U.K.
57 B4 **Cuilo** Angola
90 E2 **Cuité** *r.* Brazil
57 B5 **Cuito** *r.* Angola
57 B5 **Cuito Cuanavale** Angola
84 B3 **Cuitzeo, L. de** *l.* Mex.
33 B2 **Cukai** Malaysia
17 J3 **Çukurca** Turkey
32 D2 **Cu Lao Cham** *i.* Vietnam
32 D2 **Cu Lao Re** *i.* Vietnam
32 D3 **Cu Lao Thu** *i.* Vietnam
72 F1 **Culbertson** *MT* U.S.A.
76 C3 **Culbertson** *NE* U.S.A.
8 F3 **Culcairn** Austr.
45 C2 **Culebra, Sierra de la** *mts* Spain
17 K2 **Culfa** Azer.
84 A1 **Culiacán** Mex.
84 A1 **Culiacancito** Mex.
31 A4 **Culion** Phil.
31 A4 **Culion** *i.* Phil.
40 F3 **Cullen** U.K.
45 F3 **Cullera** Spain
40 □ **Cullivoe** U.K.
79 C5 **Cullman** U.S.A.
17 H2 **Çullu** Turkey
41 E3 **Cullybackey** U.K.
40 C2 **Cul Mor** *h.* U.K.
80 D5 **Culpeper** U.S.A.
86 □ **Culpepper, Isla** *i.* *Galapagos Is* Ecuador
87 H6 **Culuene** *r.* Brazil
9 D5 **Culverden** N.Z.
40 D5 **Culzean Bay** *b.* U.K.
89 D2 **Cumaná** Venez.
89 B4 **Cumare, Cerro** *h.* Col.
89 A4 **Cumbal, Nevado de** *mt* Col.
80 D5 **Cumberland** *MD* U.S.A.
68 A3 **Cumberland** *WV* U.S.A.
78 C4 **Cumberland** *r.* U.S.A.
65 J4 **Cumberland House** Can.
65 J4 **Cumberland Lake** *l.* Can.
80 B6 **Cumberland Mtn** *mts* U.S.A.
63 M3 **Cumberland Peninsula** Can.
78 C4 **Cumberland Plateau** *plat.* U.S.A.
68 C2 **Cumberland Pt** *pt* U.S.A.
63 M3 **Cumberland Sound** *chan.* Can.
40 E5 **Cumbernauld** U.K.
84 B1 **Cumbres de Monterey, Parque Nacional** *nat. park* Mex.
43 K1 **Cumlosen** Ger.
74 A2 **Cummings** U.S.A.
8 G2 **Cumnock** Austr.
40 D5 **Cumnock** U.K.
16 D3 **Çumra** Turkey
41 D3 **Cuncagh** *h.* Rep. of Ireland/U.K.
84 D3 **Cunduacán** Mex.
84 E4 **Cunén** Guatemala
57 B5 **Cunene** *r.* Angola
48 B2 **Cuneo** Italy
32 D2 **Cung Sơn** Vietnam
17 G2 **Çüngüş** Turkey
6 E4 **Cunnamulla** Austr.
40 □ **Cunningsburgh** U.K.
89 D4 **Cunucunuma** *r.* Venez.
48 B2 **Cuorgnè** Italy
40 E4 **Cupar** U.K.
89 A3 **Cupica** Col.
89 A3 **Cupica, Golfo de** *b.* Col.
87 L5 **Curaçá** Brazil
83 L6 **Curaçao** *i.* Neth. Ant.
91 B3 **Curacautín** Chile
91 D3 **Curacó** *r.* Arg.
91 B3 **Curanilahue** Chile
89 D4 **Curapira, Serra** *mts* Brazil/Venez.
86 D4 **Curaray** *r.* Ecuador
91 B2 **Curaumilla, Punta** *pt* Chile
73 F4 **Curecanti Nat. Rec. Area** *res.* U.S.A.
91 B2 **Curicó** Chile
89 D5 **Curicuriari, Sa.** *h.* Brazil
89 D5 **Curieuriari** *r.* Brazil
90 C4 **Curitiba** Brazil
8 B1 **Curnamona** Austr.
8 H1 **Currabubula** Austr.
87 L5 **Currais Novos** Brazil
54 □ **Curral Velho** Cape Verde
69 F3 **Curran** U.S.A.
41 A6 **Currane, Lough** *l.* Rep. of Ireland

75 E2 Currant U.S.A.
8 E1 Curranyalpa Austr.
79 E7 Current Bahamas
6 E5 Currie Austr.
75 E1 Currie U.S.A.
8 H3 Currockbilly, Mt Austr.
6 F4 Curtis I. *i.* Austr.
87 H5 Curuá *r.* Brazil
87 J4 Curuçá Brazil
33 B3 Curup Indon.
87 K4 Cururupu Brazil
89 E3 Curutú, Cerro *mt* Venez.
90 D2 Curvelo Brazil
86 D6 Cusco Peru
41 E2 Cushendall U.K.
41 E2 Cushendun U.K.
77 D4 Cushing U.S.A.
89 C3 Cusiana *r.* Col.
79 C5 Cusseta U.S.A.
68 A1 Cusson U.S.A.
66 E1 Cusson, Pte *pt* Can.
72 F2 Custer *MT* U.S.A.
76 C3 Custer *SD* U.S.A.
89 A4 Cutanga, Pico de *mt* Col.
72 D1 Cut Bank U.S.A.
79 C6 Cuthbert U.S.A.
65 H4 Cut Knife Can.
81 K2 Cutler U.S.A.
79 D7 Cutler Ridge U.S.A.
91 C3 Cutral-Co Arg.
23 F5 Cuttack India
75 G5 Cutter U.S.A.
43 G1 Cuxhaven Ger.
80 C4 Cuyahoga Falls U.S.A.
80 C4 Cuyahoga Valley National Recreation Area *res.* U.S.A.
74 C4 Cuyama *r.* U.S.A.
31 B3 Cuyapo Phil.
31 B4 Cuyo Phil.
31 B4 Cuyo *i.* Phil.
31 B4 Cuyo East Pass. *chan.* Phil.
31 B4 Cuyo Islands *is* Phil.
31 B4 Cuyo West Pass. *chan.* Phil.
89 E3 Cuyuni *r.* Guyana
Cuzco *see* Cusco
39 D6 Cwmbran U.K.
56 C4 Cyangugu Rwanda
49 L6 Cyclades *is* Greece
80 A5 Cynthiana U.S.A.
65 G5 Cypress Hills *mts* Can.
10 E6 Cyprus *country* Asia
65 G4 Czar Can.
34 G4 Czech Republic *country* Europe
46 H4 Czersk Pol.
47 J5 Częstochowa Pol.

D

30 C1 Da'an China
16 F6 Dab'a Jordan
89 C2 Dabajuro Venez.
54 B4 Dabakala Côte d'Ivoire
26 A2 Daban Shan *mts* China
26 C3 Daba Shan *mts* China
89 A3 Dabeiba Col.
43 K1 Dabel Ger.
22 C5 Dabhoi India
21 A2 Dabhol India
26 E4 Dabie Shan *mts* China
22 D4 Daboh India
54 A3 Dabola Guinea
54 B4 Daboya Ghana
22 D4 Dabra India
47 J5 Dąbrowa Górnicza Pol.
27 E5 Dabu China
30 B1 Dabusu Pao *l.* China
Dacca *see* Dhaka
46 E6 Dachau Ger.
26 A2 Dachechang China
21 B2 Dachepalle India
69 J3 Dacre Can.
16 D1 Daday Turkey
79 D6 Dade City U.S.A.
22 C5 Dadra India
22 C5 Dadra and Nagar Haveli *div.* India
22 A4 Dadu Pak.
27 B4 Dadu He *r.* China
32 C3 Đa Dung *r.* Vietnam
31 B3 Daet Phil.
27 B5 Dafang China
26 F3 Dafeng China
30 D2 Dafengman China
23 H4 Dafla Hills *mts* India
54 A3 Dagana Senegal
26 B3 Dagcanglhamo China
51 H7 Dagestan, Respublika *div.* Rus. Fed.
26 F2 Dagu *r.* China
27 B5 Daguan China
27 □ D'Aguilar Peak *h.* *H.K.* China
31 B2 Dagupan Phil.
23 H1 Dagur China
23 G3 Dagzê China
23 F3 Dagzê Co *salt l.* China
22 C6 Dahanu India
26 D1 Dahei *r.* China
30 C2 Dahei Shan *mts* China
28 C1 Dahezhen China
24 D2 Da Hinggan Ling *mts* China
56 E2 Dahlak Archipelago *is* Eritrea
56 E2 Dahlak Marine National Park Eritrea
42 E4 Dahlem Ger.
43 J1 Dahlenburg Ger.
48 C7 Dahmani Tunisia
43 F5 Dahn Ger.
22 C5 Dāhod India
22 D2 Dahongliutan China/Jammu and Kashmir
43 J2 Dähre Ger.
17 J3 Dahūk Iraq
30 C3 Dahuofang Shuiku *resr* China
30 B3 Dahushan China
26 D1 Dai Hai *l.* China
33 B3 Daik Indon.
40 D5 Dailly U.K.
19 E3 Daim Iran
29 C6 Daimanji-san *h.* Japan
45 E3 Daimiel Spain
91 E3 Daireaux Arg.
68 A2 Dairyland U.S.A.
29 C7 Daisen *volc.* Japan
27 G4 Daishan China
27 F5 Daiyun Shan *mts* China
6 D4 Dajarra Austr.
26 A4 Dajin Chuan *r.* China
26 B2 Dajing China
23 H1 Da Juh China
54 A3 Dakar Senegal
23 G3 Dakelangsi China
23 G5 Dakhin Shahbaz-pur I. *i.* Bangl.
55 E2 Dakhla Oasis *oasis* Egypt
32 C2 Dak Kon Vietnam
50 D4 Dakol'ka *r.* Belarus
76 D3 Dakota City U.S.A.
49 J3 Đakovica Yugo.
49 H2 Đakovo Croatia
57 C5 Dala Angola
54 A3 Dalaba Guinea
26 D1 Dalad Qi China
26 E1 Dalai Nur *l.* China
18 C4 Dalaki, Rud-e *r.* Iran
26 D1 Dalamamiao China
16 B3 Dalaman Turkey
16 B3 Dalaman *r.* Turkey
24 C2 Dalandzadgad Mongolia
31 B4 Dalanganem Islands *is* Phil.
4 J4 Dalap-Uliga-Darrit Marshall Is
32 D3 Đa Lat Vietnam
26 B1 Dalay Mongolia
19 G4 Dalbandin Pak.
40 E6 Dalbeattie U.K.
6 F4 Dalby Austr.
38 C3 Dalby U.K.
37 J6 Dale *Hordaland* Norway
37 J6 Dale *Sogn og Fjordane* Norway
80 E5 Dale City U.S.A.
77 G4 Dale Hollow Lake *l.* U.S.A.
42 E2 Dalen Neth.
23 H6 Dalet Myanmar
23 H5 Daletme Myanmar
37 O6 Dalfors Sweden
19 E5 Dalgān Iran
8 G4 Dalgety Austr.
77 C4 Dalhart U.S.A.
67 G4 Dalhousie Can.
26 D3 Dali *Shaanxi* China
24 C4 Dali *Yunnan* China
30 A4 Dalian China
27 B4 Daliang Shan *mts* China
30 B2 Dalin China
26 F1 Daling *r.* China
30 D3 Dalizi China
40 E5 Dalkeith U.K.
23 F4 Dālkola India
81 F4 Dallas *PA* U.S.A.
77 D5 Dallas *TX* U.S.A.
68 B5 Dallas City U.S.A.
72 B2 Dalles, The U.S.A.
64 C4 Dall I. *i.* U.S.A.
18 D5 Dalmā *i.* U.A.E.
91 D2 Dalmacio Vélez Sarsfield Arg.
22 E4 Dalman India
48 G3 Dalmatia *reg.* Croatia
40 D5 Dalmellington U.K.
28 D2 Dal'negorsk Rus. Fed.
28 C2 Dal'nerechensk Rus. Fed.
54 B4 Daloa Côte d'Ivoire
27 C5 Dalou Shan *mts* China
18 B5 Dalqān *well* S. Arabia
40 D5 Dalry U.K.
40 D5 Dalrymple U.K.
6 E4 Dalrymple, L. *l.* Austr.
6 E4 Dalrymple, Mt *mt* Austr.
23 F4 Daltenganj India
69 E1 Dalton Can.
59 J4 Dalton S. Africa
79 C5 Dalton *GA* U.S.A.
81 G3 Dalton *MA* U.S.A.
38 D3 Dalton-in-Furness U.K.
69 E1 Dalton Mills Can.
41 C5 Dalua *r.* Rep. of Ireland
31 B2 Dalupiri *i.* Phil.
31 C3 Dalupiri *i.* Phil.
36 D4 Dalvik Iceland
6 D3 Daly *r.* Austr.
74 A3 Daly City U.S.A.
6 D3 Daly Waters Austr.
22 C5 Daman India
22 C5 Daman and Diu *div.* India
55 F1 Damanhûr Egypt
18 C3 Damaq Iran
26 E1 Damaqun Shan *mts* China
31 C6 Damar Indon.
25 E7 Damar *i.* Indon.
16 F5 Damascus Syria
91 B2 Damas, P. de las *pass* Arg./Chile
54 D3 Damaturu Nigeria
18 D3 Damavand Iran
21 C5 Dambulla Sri Lanka
18 D2 Damghan Iran
26 E2 Daming China
27 C6 Daming Shan *mt* China
18 D2 Damjong China
31 B5 Dammai *i.* Phil.
42 B3 Damme Belgium
43 G2 Damme Ger.
22 D5 Damoh India
54 B4 Damongo Ghana
6 E2 Dampier Strait *chan.* P.N.G.
25 F7 Dampir, Selat *chan.* Indon.
Damqoq Kanbab *r* see Maquan He
23 H2 Dam Qu *r.* China
23 H3 Damroh India
42 E1 Damwoude Neth.
54 B4 Danané Côte d'Ivoire
32 D1 Đa Năng Vietnam
31 C4 Danao Phil.
26 A4 Danba China
81 G4 Danbury *CT* U.S.A.
81 H3 Danbury *NH* U.S.A.
81 G3 Danby U.S.A.
75 E4 Danby Lake *l.* U.S.A.
26 E3 Dancheng China
56 D3 Dande Eth.
21 A3 Dandeli India
8 E4 Dandenong Austr.
30 C3 Dandong China
39 E4 Dane *r.* U.K.
63 Q2 Daneborg Greenland
81 K2 Danforth U.S.A.
27 E6 Dangan Liedao *is* China
23 G3 Dangbe La *pass* China
28 B2 Dangbizhen Rus. Fed.
26 B3 Dangchang China
5 P5 Danger Islands *is* Pac. Oc.
58 C7 Danger Pt *pt* S. Africa
56 D2 Dangila Eth.
Dangla *mts see* Tanggula Shan
23 G3 Dangqên China
82 G5 Dangriga Belize
26 E3 Dangshan China
26 F4 Dangtu China
27 D4 Dangyang China
72 E3 Daniel U.S.A.
58 E4 Daniëlskuil S. Africa
50 G3 Danilov Rus. Fed.
51 H5 Danilovka Rus. Fed.
50 G3 Danilovskaya Vozvyshennost' *reg.* Rus. Fed.
26 D2 Daning China
17 M1 Dänizkänarı Azer.
26 D3 Danjiangkou Sk. *resr* China
18 E6 Dank Oman
22 D2 Dankhar India
50 F4 Dankov Rus. Fed.
27 B4 Danleng China
82 G6 Danlí Honduras
Dannebrogsø *i. see* Qillak
81 G2 Dannemora U.S.A.
43 K1 Dannenberg (Elbe) Ger.
43 M1 Dannenwalde Ger.
9 F4 Dannevirke N.Z.
59 J4 Dannhauser S. Africa
32 B1 Dan Sai Thai.
80 E3 Dansville U.S.A.
22 C4 Danta India
21 C2 Dantewara India
49 M3 Danube *r.* Europe
68 D5 Danville *IL* U.S.A.
68 D6 Danville *IN* U.S.A.
78 C4 Danville *KY* U.S.A.
69 J5 Danville *PA* U.S.A.
80 D6 Danville *VA* U.S.A.
27 C7 Dan Xian China
26 F4 Danyang China
27 C5 Danzhai China
31 B4 Dao Phil.
27 C6 Đao Bach Long Vi *i.* Vietnam
27 C6 Đao Cai Bâu *i.* Vietnam
27 C6 Đao Cat Ba *i.* Vietnam
32 B3 Đao Phu Quôc *i.* Vietnam
32 B3 Đao Thô Chu' *i.* Vietnam
54 B4 Daoukro Côte d'Ivoire
32 B3 Đao Vây *i.* Vietnam
27 D5 Dao Xian China
27 C4 Daozhen China
31 C4 Dapa Phil.
54 C3 Dapaong Togo
23 J4 Daphabum *mt* India
31 B4 Dapiak, Mt *mt* Phil.
31 B4 Dapitan Phil.
15 H3 Da Qaidam China
24 E2 Daqing China
18 D3 Daqq-e Dombūn Iran
19 F3 Daqq-e-Tundi, Dasht-e *l.* Afgh.
26 D1 Daquing Shan *mts* China
17 K4 Dāqūq Iraq
27 G4 Daqu Shan *i.* China
16 F5 Dar'ā Syria
18 D4 Dārāb Iran
31 B3 Daraga Phil.
47 O4 Darahanava Belarus
54 D1 Daraj Libya
18 D4 Dārākūyeh Iran
31 C4 Daram *i.* Phil.
18 D3 Darang, Kūh-e *h.* Iran
13 N4 Darasun Rus. Fed.
18 E4 Darband Iran
23 F4 Darbhanga India
74 C2 Dardanelle U.S.A.
77 E5 Dardanelle, Lake *l.* U.S.A.
49 M4 Dardanelles *str.* Turkey
43 J3 Dardesheim Ger.
16 F2 Darende Turkey
56 D4 Dar es Salaam Tanz.
48 D2 Darfo Boario Terme Italy
22 B2 Dargai Pak.
19 F1 Dargan-Ata Turkm.
9 D1 Dargaville N.Z.
8 F4 Dargo Austr.
24 C2 Darhan Mongolia
26 D1 Darhan Muminggan Lianheqi China
79 D6 Darien U.S.A.
89 A2 Darién, Golfo del *g.* Col.
83 J7 Darién, Parque Nacional de *nat. park* Panama
89 A2 Darién, Serranía del *mts* Panama
23 G4 Dārjiling India
18 C4 Darkhazīneh Iran
24 B3 Darlag China
8 D2 Darling *r.* Austr.
6 E4 Darling Downs *reg.* Austr.
6 B5 Darling Range *h.* Austr.
38 F3 Darlington U.K.
68 B4 Darlington U.S.A.
8 F3 Darlington Point Austr.
46 H3 Darłowo Pol.
18 B5 Darmā S. Arabia
22 E3 Darma Pass China/India
21 B2 Darmaraopet India
18 E4 Dar Mazār Iran
43 G5 Darmstadt Ger.
22 C5 Darna *r.* India
55 E1 Darnah Libya
59 J4 Darnall S. Africa
8 D2 Darnick Austr.
62 F3 Darnley Bay *b.* Can.
92 D5 Darnley, C. *c.* Ant.
45 F2 Daroca Spain
50 G3 Darovka Rus. Fed.
50 H3 Darovskoy Rus. Fed.
91 D3 Darregueira Arg.
18 E3 Darreh Bīd Iran
19 E2 Darreh Gaz Iran
17 L4 Darreh Gozaru *r.* Iran
19 H3 Darreh-ye Shekārī *r.* Afgh.
21 B3 Darsi India
17 M6 Darsīyeh Iran
39 D7 Dart *r.* U.K.
39 H6 Dartford U.K.
8 C4 Dartmoor Austr.
39 C7 Dartmoor *reg.* U.K.
39 D7 Dartmoor National Park U.K.
67 H5 Dartmouth Can.
39 D7 Dartmouth U.K.
38 F4 Darton U.K.
41 C3 Darty Mts *h.* Rep. of Ireland
6 E2 Daru P.N.G.
54 A4 Daru Sierra Leone
23 G3 Darum Tso *l.* China
48 G2 Daruvar Croatia
19 E1 Darvaza Turkm.
18 C4 Darvīsla Iran
19 G4 Darwazgai Afgh.
38 E4 Darwen U.K.
19 G4 Darweshan Afgh.
6 D3 Darwin Austr.
88 C8 Darwin, Mte *mt* Chile
22 B3 Darya Khan Pak.
19 E4 Dārzīn Iran
18 D5 Dās *i.* U.A.E.
26 D4 Dashennongjia *mt* China
20 E1 Dashkhovuz Turkm.
18 E2 Dasht Iran
19 F5 Dasht *r.* Pak.
18 E4 Dasht Āb Iran
18 C4 Dasht-e Palang *r.* Iran
19 F5 Dashtiari Iran
19 H2 Dashtiobburdon Tajik.
26 C2 Dashuikeng China
26 B2 Dashuitou China
22 C2 Daska Pak.
17 L1 Daşkäsän Azer.
22 C1 Daspar *mt* Pak.
43 H3 Dassel Ger.
58 C6 Dassen Island *i.* S. Africa
17 L2 Dastakert Armenia
18 E3 Dastgardān Iran
30 F2 Da Suifen *r.* China
49 M6 Datça Turkey
28 G3 Date Japan
75 F5 Dateland U.S.A.
22 D4 Datia India
27 E5 Datian China
26 A2 Datong *Cinghai* China
26 D1 Datong *Shanxi* China
26 B2 Datong He *r.* China
26 A2 Datong Shan *mts* China
31 C5 Datu Piang Phil.
33 C2 Datu, Tanjung *c.* Indon./Malaysia
50 C3 Daugava *r.* Belarus/Latvia
37 U9 Daugavpils Latvia
19 G2 Daulatabad Afgh.
22 C6 Daulatabad India
Daulatabad *see* Malāyer
42 E4 Daun Ger.
21 A2 Daund India
32 A2 Daung Kyun *i.* Myanmar
65 J4 Dauphin Can.
44 G4 Dauphiné *reg.* France
77 F6 Dauphin I. *i.* U.S.A.
65 K4 Dauphin L. *l.* Can.
22 D4 Dausa India
40 E3 Dava U.K.
17 M1 Däväçi Azer.
21 A3 Davangere India
31 C5 Davao Phil.
31 C5 Davao Gulf *b.* Phil.
19 F5 Dāvar Panāh Iran
59 H2 Davel S. Africa
74 A3 Davenport *CA* U.S.A.
68 E5 Davenport *IA* U.S.A.
39 F5 Daventry U.K.
59 H3 Daveyton S. Africa
83 H7 David Panama
65 H4 Davidson Can.
65 J3 Davin Lake *l.* Can.
74 B2 Davis U.S.A.
92 C5 Davis *Austr. Base* Ant.
75 E4 Davis Dam U.S.A.
67 H2 Davis Inlet Can.
92 C5 Davis Sea *sea* Ant.
63 N3 Davis Strait *str.* Can./Greenland
46 C7 Davos Switz.
30 B3 Dawa China
26 A1 Dawan China
23 F3 Dawaxung China
26 B4 Dawe China
Dawei *see* Tavoy
26 E3 Dawen *r.* China
18 C5 Dawhat Salwah *b.* Qatar/S. Arabia
32 A1 Dawna Range *mts* Myanmar/Thai.
20 D6 Dawqah Oman
62 E3 Dawson *Y.T.* Can.
79 C3 Dawson *GA* U.S.A.
76 D2 Dawson *ND* U.S.A.
65 J4 Dawson Bay *b.* Can.
64 E3 Dawson Creek Can.
65 L2 Dawson Inlet *in.* Can.
64 B2 Dawson Range *mts* Can.
26 E4 Dawu *Hubei* China
24 C3 Dawu *Sichuan* China
44 D5 Dax France
26 C4 Daxian China
27 C6 Daxin China
26 E2 Daxing China
27 A4 Daxue Shan *mts* China
30 B4 Dayang *r.* China
23 H4 Dayang *r.* India
27 D6 Dayao Shan *mts* China
27 E4 Daye China
27 B4 Dayi China
8 E4 Daylesford Austr.
74 D3 Daylight Pass U.S.A.
91 F1 Daymán *r.* Uru.
91 F1 Daymán, Cuchilla del *h.* Uru.
27 D4 Dayong China
17 H4 Dayr az Zawr Syria
80 A5 Dayton *OH* U.S.A.
79 C5 Dayton *TN* U.S.A.
72 C2 Dayton *WA* U.S.A.
79 D6 Daytona Beach U.S.A.
27 E5 Dayu China
27 D5 Dayu Ling *mts* China
26 F3 Da Yunhe *r.* China
72 C3 Dayville U.S.A.
27 D7 Dazhou Dao *i.* China
27 C4 Dazhu China
27 B4 Dazu China
58 F5 De Aar S. Africa
68 D2 Dead *r.* U.S.A.
79 F7 Deadman's Cay Bahamas
75 E4 Dead Mts *mts* U.S.A.
81 H2 Dead River *r.* U.S.A.
16 E6 Dead Sea *salt l.* Asia
39 J6 Deal U.K.
59 F4 Dealesville S. Africa
27 E4 De'an China
64 D4 Dean *r.* Can.
39 E6 Dean, Forest of *forest* U.K.
91 D1 Deán Funes Arg.
69 F4 Dearborn U.S.A.
64 D3 Dease *r.* Can.
64 C3 Dease Lake Can.
62 H3 Dease Strait *chan.* Can.
74 D3 Death Valley *v.* U.S.A.
74 D3 Death Valley Junction U.S.A.
74 D3 Death Valley National Monument *res.* U.S.A.
44 E2 Deauville France
33 D2 Debak Malaysia
27 C6 Debao China
49 J4 Debar Macedonia
65 H4 Debden Can.
39 J5 Debenham U.K.
75 H2 De Beque U.S.A.
81 J2 Deblois U.S.A.
56 D3 Debre Birhan Eth.
47 K7 Debrecen Hungary
56 D2 Debre Markos Eth.
56 D2 Debre Tabor Eth.
56 D3 Debre Zeyit Eth.
79 C5 Decatur *AL* U.S.A.
79 C5 Decatur *GA* U.S.A.
68 C6 Decatur *IL* U.S.A.
68 E5 Decatur *IN* U.S.A.
68 E4 Decatur *MI* U.S.A.
21 B2 Deccan *plat.* India
69 H2 Decelles, Réservoir *resr* Can.
46 G5 Děčín Czech Rep.
68 B4 Decorah U.S.A.
39 F6 Deddington U.K.
43 J2 Dedeleben Ger.
43 J2 Dedelstorf Ger.
42 E2 Dedemsvaart Neth.
90 C4 Dedo de Deus *mt* Brazil
58 C6 De Doorns S. Africa
17 L1 Dedoplis Tsqaro Georgia
54 B3 Dédougou Burkina
50 D3 Dedovichi Rus. Fed.
57 D5 Dedza Malawi
39 D4 Dee *est. Wales* U.K.
39 E4 Dee *r. Eng./Wales* U.K.
40 F3 Dee *r. Scot.* U.K.
41 C5 Deel *r.* Rep. of Ireland
41 D3 Deele *r.* Rep. of Ireland
27 □ Deep Bay *b.* *H.K.* China
80 D5 Deep Creek Lake *l.* U.S.A.
75 F2 Deep Creek Range *mts* U.S.A.
69 J2 Deep River Can.
81 G4 Deep River U.S.A.
65 K1 Deep Rose Lake *l.* Can.
74 D3 Deep Springs U.S.A.
80 B5 Deer Creek Lake *l.* U.S.A.
81 K2 Deer I. *i.* Can.
81 J2 Deer I. *i.* U.S.A.
81 J2 Deer Isle U.S.A.
66 B3 Deer L. *l.* Can.
67 J4 Deer Lake *Nfld* Can.
66 B3 Deer Lake *Ont.* Can.
72 D2 Deer Lodge U.S.A.
88 D2 Defensores del Chaco, Parque Nacional *nat. park* Para.
80 A4 Defiance U.S.A.
79 C6 De Funiak Springs U.S.A.
24 B3 Dêgê China
56 E3 Degeh Bur Eth.
23 G3 Dêgên China
43 L6 Deggendorf Ger.
22 C3 Degh *r.* Pak.
42 B3 De Haan Belgium
18 D4 Dehaj Iran
19 F4 Dehak Iran
19 F5 Dehak Iran
18 D4 Deh Bīd Iran
18 C4 Deh-Dasht Iran
18 C4 Deh-e Khalīfeh Iran
18 C3 Deheq Iran
18 C2 Dehgāh Iran
18 B3 Dehgolān Iran
21 B5 Dehiwala-Mount Lavinia Sri Lanka
18 D5 Dehkūyeh Iran
18 B3 Dehlonān Iran
22 D3 Dehra Dun India
23 F4 Dehri India
19 E4 Deh Salm Iran
18 E4 Deh Sard Iran
17 K4 Deh Sheykh Iran
19 F4 Deh Shū Afgh.
27 F5 Dehua China
30 C1 Dehui China
42 B4 Deinze Belgium
16 E5 Deir el Qamer Lebanon
Deir-ez-Zor *see* Dayr az Zawr
47 L7 Dej Romania
27 C4 Dejiang China
68 C5 De Kalb *IL* U.S.A.
77 E5 De Kalb *TX* U.S.A.
81 F2 De Kalb Junction U.S.A.
20 A6 Dekemhare Eritrea
56 C4 Dekese Congo(Zaire)
19 G2 Dekhkanabad Uzbek.
42 C1 De Koog Neth.
42 C2 De Kooy Neth.
74 C4 Delano U.S.A.
75 F2 Delano Peak *summit* U.S.A.
19 F3 Delārām Afgh.
59 F3 Delareyville S. Africa
65 H4 Delaronde Lake *l.* Can.
68 C5 Delavan *IL* U.S.A.
68 C4 Delavan *WV* U.S.A.
80 B4 Delaware U.S.A.
81 F5 Delaware *div.* U.S.A.
81 F4 Delaware *r.* U.S.A.
81 F5 Delaware Bay *b.* U.S.A.
80 B4 Delaware Lake *l.* U.S.A.
81 F4 Delaware Water Gap National Recreational Area *res.* U.S.A.
43 G3 Delbrück Ger.
8 G4 Delegate Austr.
46 C7 Delémont Switz.
42 C2 Delft Neth.
21 B4 Delft I. *i.* Sri Lanka
42 E1 Delfzijl Neth.
57 E5 Delgado, Cabo *pt* Moz.
69 G4 Delhi Can.
22 D3 Delhi India
73 F4 Delhi *CO* U.S.A.
81 F3 Delhi *NY* U.S.A.
17 J2 Deli *r.* Turkey
16 E2 Delice Turkey
16 E1 Delice *r.* Turkey
18 C3 Delījān Iran
64 E1 Déljne Can.
24 B3 Delingha China
65 H4 Delisle Can.
43 L3 Delitzsch Ger.
43 H3 Delligsen Ger.
76 D3 Dell Rapids U.S.A.
45 H4 Dellys Alg.
74 D5 Del Mar U.S.A.
75 E3 Delmar L. *l.* U.S.A.
43 G1 Delmenhorst Ger.
13 R2 De-Longa, O-va *is* Rus. Fed.
62 B3 De Long Mts *mts* U.S.A.
65 J5 Deloraine Can.
68 D5 Delphi U.S.A.
80 A4 Delphos U.S.A.
58 F4 Delportshoop S. Africa
79 D7 Delray Beach U.S.A.
73 E6 Del Río Mex.
77 C6 Del Rio U.S.A.
37 P6 Delsbo Sweden
75 H2 Delta *CO* U.S.A.
68 A5 Delta *IA* U.S.A.
75 F2 Delta *UT* U.S.A.
62 D3 Delta Junction U.S.A.
81 F3 Delta Reservoir *resr* U.S.A.
79 D6 Deltona U.S.A.
41 D4 Delvin Rep. of Ireland
49 J5 Delvinë Albania
45 E1 Demanda, Sierra de la *mts* Spain
56 C4 Demba Congo(Zaire)
56 D3 Dembī Dolo Eth.
50 D4 Demidov Rus. Fed.
73 F5 Deming U.S.A.
89 E4 Demini *r.* Brazil
16 B2 Demirci Turkey
49 M4 Demirköy Turkey
46 F4 Demmin Ger.
79 C5 Demopolis U.S.A.
68 D5 Demotte U.S.A.
33 B3 Dempo, G. *volc.* Indon.
22 D2 Dêmqog China/India
50 H2 Dem'yanovo Rus. Fed.
47 Q2 Demyansk Rus. Fed.
58 D5 De Naawte S. Africa
56 E2 Denakil *reg.* Eritrea
56 E3 Denan Eth.
65 J4 Denare Beach Can.
19 G2 Denau Uzbek.
69 J3 Denbigh Can.
39 D4 Denbigh U.K.
42 C1 Den Burg Neth.
32 B1 Den Chai Thai.
33 C3 Dendang Indon.
42 C3 Dendermonde Belgium
59 H1 Dendron S. Africa
26 C1 Dengkou China
23 H3 Dêngqên China
26 D3 Deng Xian China
Den Haag *see* The Hague
6 B4 Denham Austr.
42 E2 Den Ham Neth.
42 C2 Den Helder Neth.
45 G3 Denia Spain
8 E3 Deniliquin Austr.
72 C3 Denio U.S.A.
76 E3 Denison *IA* U.S.A.
77 D5 Denison *TX* U.S.A.
16 B3 Denizli Turkey
8 H2 Denman Austr.
92 C5 Denman Glacier *gl.* Ant.
6 B5 Denmark Austr.
34 F3 Denmark *country* Europe
34 C2 Denmark Strait *str.* Greenland/Iceland
75 H3 Dennehotso U.S.A.
81 H4 Dennis Port U.S.A.
40 E4 Denny U.K.
81 K2 Dennysville U.S.A.
33 E4 Denpasar Indon.
81 F5 Denton *MD* U.S.A.
77 D5 Denton *TX* U.S.A.
6 F2 D'Entrecasteaux Islands *is* P.N.G.
6 B5 d'Entrecasteaux, Pt *pt* Austr.
7 G3 d'Entrecasteaux, Récifs *rf* New Caledonia
72 F4 Denver U.S.A.
23 F4 Deo India
22 D3 Deoband India
23 F5 Deogarh India
23 E5 Deogarh *mt* India
23 F4 Deoghar India
22 D5 Deori India
23 E4 Deoria India
22 C2 Deosai, Plains of *plain* Pak.
23 E5 Deosil India
42 A3 De Panne Belgium
42 D3 De Peel *reg.* Neth.
68 C3 De Pere U.S.A.
81 F3 Deposit U.S.A.
69 J2 Depot-Forbes Can.
69 J2 Depot-Rowanton Can.
68 C5 Depue U.S.A.
13 P3 Deputatskiy Rus. Fed.
24 B4 Dêqên China
27 D6 Deqing *Guangdong* China
27 F4 Deqing *Zhejiang* China
27 F5 Deqiu China
77 E5 De Queen U.S.A.
22 B3 Dera Bugti Pak.
22 B3 Dera Ghazi Khan Pak.
22 B3 Dera Ismail Khan Pak.
22 B3 Derawar Fort Pak.
51 J7 Derbent Rus. Fed.
19 G2 Derbent Uzbek.
6 C3 Derby Austr.
39 F5 Derby U.K.
81 G4 Derby *CT* U.S.A.
77 D4 Derby *KS* U.S.A.
41 D3 Derg *r.* Rep. of Ireland/U.K.
51 J5 Dergachi Rus. Fed.
41 C5 Derg, Lough *l.* Rep. of Ireland
51 F5 Derhachi Ukr.
77 E6 De Ridder U.S.A.
17 H3 Derik Turkey
16 E2 Derinkuyu Turkey
51 F5 Derkul *r.* Rus. Fed./Ukr.
58 C1 Derm Namibia
41 D4 Derravaragh, Lough *l.* Rep. of Ireland
81 H3 Derry U.S.A.
41 E5 Derry *r.* Rep. of Ireland
41 C3 Derryveagh Mts *h.* Rep. of Ireland
26 A1 Derstei China
55 F3 Derudeb Sudan
58 E6 De Rust S. Africa
48 G2 Derventa Bos.-Herz.
6 E6 Derwent *r.* Austr.
38 G4 Derwent *r.* U.K.
40 G6 Derwent Reservoir *resr* U.K.
38 D3 Derwent Water *l.* U.K.
14 E1 Derzhavinsk Kazak.
91 C2 Desaguadero *r.* Arg.
86 E7 Desaguadero *r.* Bol.
5 N6 Désappointement, Îles du *is* Pac. Oc.
74 D2 Desatoya Mts *mts* U.S.A.
69 F2 Desbarats Can.
62 F3 Des Bois, Lac *l.* Can.
65 J3 Deschambault L. *l.* Can.
65 J4 Deschambault Lake Can.
72 B2 Deschutes *r.* U.S.A.
56 D2 Desē Eth.
88 C7 Deseado Arg.
88 C7 Deseado *r.* Arg.
69 J3 Deseronto Can.
22 B3 Desert Canal *canal* Pak.
75 E5 Desert Center U.S.A.
75 F1 Desert Peak *summit* U.S.A.
64 G3 Desmarais Can.
76 E3 Des Moines *IA* U.S.A.
73 G4 Des Moines *NM* U.S.A.
68 A5 Des Moines *r.* *IA* U.S.A.
51 D5 Desna Ukr.
50 E5 Desna *r.* Rus. Fed.
50 E4 Desnogorsk Rus. Fed.
31 C4 Desolation Point *pt* Phil.
68 D4 Des Plaines U.S.A.
53 K6 Desroches *i.* Seychelles
43 L3 Dessau Ger.
42 B3 Destelbergen Belgium
69 H1 Destor Can.
64 B2 Destruction Bay Can.
49 J2 Deta Romania
64 G2 Detah Can.
57 C5 Dete Zimbabwe
43 G3 Detmold Ger.
68 D3 Detour, Pt *pt* U.S.A.
69 F3 De Tour Village U.S.A.
69 F4 Detroit U.S.A.
76 E2 Detroit Lakes U.S.A.
8 G3 Deua Nat. Park Austr.
43 L3 Deuben Ger.
42 D3 Deurne Neth.
48 F1 Deutschlandsberg Austria
43 L3 Deutzen Ger.
69 H2 Deux-Rivières Can.
49 K2 Deva Romania
21 B2 Devarkonda India
16 E2 Develi Turkey
42 E2 Deventer Neth.
46 H6 Devét Skal *h.* Czech Rep.
22 B4 Devikot India
41 D5 Devils Bit Mountain *h.* Rep. of Ireland
39 D5 Devil's Bridge U.K.
74 C4 Devils Den U.S.A.
74 C2 Devils Gate *pass* U.S.A.
68 B2 Devils I. *i.* U.S.A.
76 D1 Devils Lake U.S.A.
74 C3 Devils Peak *summit* U.S.A.
74 C3 Devils Postpile National Monument *res.* U.S.A.
79 F7 Devil's Pt Bahamas
39 F6 Devizes U.K.
22 C4 Devli India
49 M3 Devnya Bulg.
64 G4 Devon Can.
39 G5 Devon *r.* U.K.
63 J2 Devon Island *i.* Can.
6 E6 Devonport Austr.
16 C1 Devrek Turkey
16 D1 Devrekâni Turkey
16 E1 Devrez *r.* Turkey
21 A2 Devrukh India
22 D5 Dewas India
33 A2 Dewa, Tanjung *pt* Indon.
59 G4 Dewetsdorp S. Africa
80 B6 Dewey Lake *l.* U.S.A.
77 F5 De Witt *AR* U.S.A.
68 B5 De Witt *IA* U.S.A.
38 F4 Dewsbury U.K.
27 E4 Dexing China
81 J2 Dexter *ME* U.S.A.
77 F4 Dexter *MO* U.S.A.
81 E2 Dexter *NY* U.S.A.
26 B4 Deyang China
18 E3 Deyhuk Iran
17 M3 Deylaman Iran
19 F2 Deynau Turkm.
6 D2 Deyong, Tg *pt* Indon.
18 C5 Deyyer Iran
17 M6 Dez *r.* Iran
18 C3 Dezfūl Iran
18 C4 Dez Gerd Iran
26 E2 Dezhou China
18 B5 Dhahlān, J. *h.* S. Arabia
20 D4 Dhahran S. Arabia
23 G5 Dhaka Bangl.
23 G5 Dhaleswari *r.* Bangl.
23 H4 Dhaleswari *r.* India
20 B7 Dhamār Yemen
23 F5 Dhāmara India
22 C5 Dhamnod India
23 E5 Dhamtari India
22 B3 Dhana Sar Pak.
23 F5 Dhanbad India
22 C5 Dhandhuka India
23 E3 Dhang Ra. *mts* Nepal
22 C5 Dhar India
23 F4 Dharan Bazar Nepal
21 B4 Dharapuram India
22 B5 Dhari India
21 B3 Dharmapuri India
21 B3 Dharmavaram India
22 D2 Dharmshala India
21 A3 Dhārwād India
22 D4 Dhasan *r.* India
23 E3 Dhaulagiri *mt* Nepal
22 D4 Dhaulpur India
22 C4 Dhebar L. *l.* India
23 H4 Dhekiajuli India
16 E6 Dhībān Jordan
23 H4 Dhing India
21 B3 Dhone India
22 B5 Dhoraji India
22 B5 Dhrangadhra India
22 C5 Dhule India
23 F4 Dhulian India
23 F4 Dhunche Nepal
22 D4 Dhund *r.* India
56 E3 Dhuusa Marreeb Somalia
49 L7 Dia *i.* Greece
74 B3 Diablo, Mt *mt* U.S.A.
74 B3 Diablo Range *mts* U.S.A.
91 E2 Diamante Arg.
91 C2 Diamante *r.* Arg.
90 D2 Diamantina Brazil
6 D4 Diamantina *watercourse* Austr.
87 K6 Diamantina, Chapada *plat.* Brazil
90 A1 Diamantino Brazil
74 □ Diamond Head *hd* U.S.A.
75 E2 Diamond Peak *summit* U.S.A.
27 D6 Dianbai China
27 B5 Dian Chi *l.* China
27 C4 Dianjiang China
87 J6 Dianópolis Brazil
54 B4 Dianra Côte d'Ivoire
28 B2 Diaoling China
54 C3 Diapaga Burkina
19 E6 Dibab Oman
23 H4 Dibang *r.* India
56 C4 Dibaya Congo(Zaire)
58 E3 Dibeng S. Africa
66 F2 D'Iberville, Lac *l.* Can.
59 G1 Dibete Botswana
23 H4 Dibrugarh India
77 C5 Dickens U.S.A.
81 J1 Dickey U.S.A.
76 C2 Dickinson U.S.A.
79 C4 Dickson U.S.A.
81 F4 Dickson City U.S.A.
Dicle *r. see* Tigris
31 B2 Didicas *i.* Phil.
22 C4 Didwana India
49 M4 Didymoteicho Greece
44 G4 Die France
42 F4 Dieblich Ger.
54 B3 Diébougou Burkina
43 G5 Dieburg Ger.
65 H4 Diefenbaker, L. *l.* Can.
93 J4 Diego Garcia *i.* British Ind. Ocean Terr.
42 E5 Diekirch Lux.
54 B3 Diéma Mali
43 H3 Diemel *r.* Ger.
27 B6 Điên Biên Vietnam
32 C1 Điên Châu Vietnam
32 D2 Điên Khanh Vietnam
43 G2 Diepholz Ger.
44 E2 Dieppe France
26 C2 Di'er Nonchang Qu *r.* China
30 C1 Di'er Songhua Jiang *r.* China
42 D3 Diessen Neth.
42 D4 Diest Belgium
46 D7 Dietikon Switz.
43 G4 Diez Ger.
55 D3 Diffa Niger
21 D2 Digapahandi India
67 G5 Digby Can.
23 F5 Digha India
44 H4 Digne-les-Bains France
44 F3 Digoin France
31 C5 Digos Phil.
22 D5 Digras India
22 B4 Digri Pak.
25 F7 Digul *r.* Indon.

54 B4 Digya National Park Ghana
44 G3 Dijon France
56 E2 Dikhil Djibouti
49 M5 Dikili Turkey
42 A3 Diksmuide Belgium
12 K2 Dikson Rus. Fed.
55 D3 Dikwa Nigeria
56 D3 Dīla Eth.
19 E4 Dilaram Iran
6 C2 Dili Indon.
17 K1 Dilijan Armenia
32 D3 Di Linh Vietnam
43 G4 Dillenburg Ger.
77 D6 Dilley U.S.A.
46 E6 Dillingen an der Donau Ger.
42 E5 Dillingen (Saar) Ger.
62 C4 Dillingham U.S.A.
65 H3 Dillon Can.
72 D2 Dillon MT U.S.A.
79 E5 Dillon SC U.S.A.
57 C5 Dilolo Congo(Zaire)
42 D3 Dilsen Belgium
17 K5 Diltāwa Iraq
23 H4 Dimapur India
16 F5 Dimashq Syria
56 C4 Dimbelenge Congo(Zaire)
54 B4 Dimbokro Côte d'Ivoire
8 D4 Dimboola Austr.
49 L3 Dimitrovgrad Bulg.
50 J4 Dimitrovgrad Rus. Fed.
16 E6 Dīmona Israel
58 D2 Dimpho Pan salt pan Botswana
31 C4 Dinagat i. Phil.
23 G4 Dinajpur Bangl.
44 C2 Dinan France
22 C2 Dinanagar India
42 C4 Dinant Belgium
23 F4 Dinapur India
16 C2 Dinar Turkey
48 G2 Dinara mts Croatia
18 C4 Dīnār, Kūh-e mt Iran
55 F3 Dinder National Park Sudan
21 B4 Dindigul India
59 K1 Dindiza Moz.
22 E5 Dindori India
16 D3 Dinek Turkey
26 C2 Dingbian China
56 B4 Dinge Angola
43 J3 Dingelstädt Ger.
27 G4 Dinghai China
23 F4 Dingla Nepal
41 A5 Dingle Rep. of Ireland
41 A5 Dingle Bay b. Rep. of Ireland
27 E5 Dingnan China
31 B2 Dingras Phil.
26 E3 Dingtao China
54 A3 Dinguiraye Guinea
40 D3 Dingwall U.K.
26 B3 Dingxi China
26 E2 Ding Xian China
26 E2 Dingxing China
26 E3 Dingyuan China
26 F2 Dingzi Gang harbour China
27 C6 Dinh Lập Vietnam
43 J5 Dinkelsbühl Ger.
75 G3 Dinnebito Wash r. U.S.A.
23 F3 Dinngyê China
59 G1 Dinokwe Botswana
65 L5 Dinorwic Lake U.S.A.
75 H1 Dinosaur U.S.A.
72 E3 Dinosaur Nat. Mon. res. U.S.A.
42 E3 Dinslaken Ger.
54 B3 Dioïla Mali
90 B4 Dionísio Cerqueira Brazil
54 A3 Diourbel Senegal
23 H4 Diphu India
22 B4 Diplo Pak.
31 B4 Dipolog Phil.
9 B6 Dipton N.Z.
16 F2 Dirckli Turkey
54 B3 Diré Mali
6 E3 Direction, C. c. Austr.
56 E3 Dirē Dawa Eth.
57 C5 Dirico Angola
6 B4 Dirk Hartog I. i. Austr.
6 E4 Dirranbandi Austr.
75 G2 Dirty Devil r. U.S.A.
22 C4 Dīsa India
88 □ Disappointment, C. c. Atl. Ocean
72 A2 Disappointment, C. c. U.S.A.
6 C4 Disappointment, L. salt flat Austr.
8 G4 Disaster B. b. Austr.
8 C5 Discovery Bay b. Austr.
27 □ Discovery Bay b. H.K. China
Disko i. see Qeqertarsuatsiaq
Disko Bugt b. see Qeqertarsuup Tunua
81 E6 Dismal Swamp swamp U.S.A.
42 A6 Disneyland Paris France
23 G4 Dispur India
39 J5 Diss U.K.
90 C1 Distrito Federal div. Brazil
16 C6 Disūq Egypt
31 B4 Dit i. Phil.
58 E4 Ditloung S. Africa
48 F6 Dittaino r. Sicily Italy
31 C4 Diuata Mountains mts Phil.
31 C4 Diuata Pt pt Phil.
18 B3 Dīvāndarreh Iran
50 G4 Diveyevo Rus. Fed.
31 B2 Divilacan Bay b. Phil.
90 D3 Divinópolis Brazil
51 G6 Divnoye Rus. Fed.
54 B4 Divo Côte d'Ivoire
16 G2 Divriği Turkey
19 G5 Diwana Pak.
81 H2 Dixfield U.S.A.
81 J2 Dixmont U.S.A.
74 B2 Dixon CA U.S.A.
68 C5 Dixon IL U.S.A.
64 C4 Dixon Entrance chan. Can./U.S.A.
64 F3 Dixonville Can.
81 H2 Dixville Can.
17 J2 Diyadin Turkey
17 K5 Diyālā r. Iraq
17 H3 Diyarbakır Turkey
22 B4 Diyodar India
Dizak see Dāvar Panāh
18 D3 Diz Chah Iran
55 D2 Djado Niger
55 D2 Djado, Plateau du plat. Niger
56 B4 Djambala Congo
54 C2 Djanet Alg.
54 C1 Djelfa Alg.
56 C3 Djéma C.A.R.
54 B3 Djenné Mali
54 B3 Djibo Burkina
56 E2 Djibouti Djibouti
52 J4 Djibouti country Africa
41 E4 Djouce Mountain h. Rep. of Ireland
54 C4 Djougou Benin
36 F4 Djúpivogur Iceland
37 O6 Djurås Sweden
17 K1 Dmanisi Georgia
13 Q2 Dmitriya Lapteva, Proliv chan. Rus. Fed.
28 C2 Dmitriyevka Primorskiy Kray Rus. Fed.
50 G4 Dmitriyevka Tambov. Rus. Fed.
51 E4 Dmitriyev-L'govskiy Rus. Fed.
50 F3 Dmitrov Rus. Fed.
47 P5 Dnieper r. Europe
47 N6 Dniester r. Ukr.
47 Q7 Dnipro r. Ukr.
51 E5 Dniprodzerzhyns'k Ukr.
51 E5 Dnipropetrovs'k Ukr.
51 E6 Dniprorudne Ukr.
50 D3 Dno Rus. Fed.
Dnyapro r. see Dnieper
55 D4 Doba Chad
23 G3 Doba China
69 G3 Dobbinton Can.
37 S8 Dobele Latvia
43 M3 Döbeln Ger.
25 F7 Doberai, Jazirah Indon.
91 D3 Doblas Arg.
25 F7 Dobo Indon.
49 H2 Doboj Bos.-Herz.
43 K4 Döbra-berg h. Ger.
49 M3 Dobrich Bulg.
51 G4 Dobrinka Rus. Fed.
51 D4 Dobrush Belarus
31 A5 Doc Can rf Phil.
90 E2 Doce r. Brazil
39 H5 Docking U.K.
84 B2 Doctor Arroyo Mex.
73 F6 Doctor B. Domínguez Mex.
21 B3 Dod Ballapur India
49 M6 Dodecanese is Greece
Dodekanisos is see Dodecanese
72 C2 Dodge U.S.A.
68 A3 Dodge Center U.S.A.
77 C4 Dodge City U.S.A.
68 B4 Dodgeville U.S.A.
39 C7 Dodman Point pt U.K.
56 D4 Dodoma Tanz.
42 E3 Doetinchem Neth.
25 E7 Dofa Indon.
23 G2 Dogai Coring salt l. China
16 F2 Doğanşehir Turkey
64 E4 Dog Creek Can.
23 G3 Dogên Co l. China
67 H2 Dog Island i. Can.
65 K4 Dog L. l. Can.
69 E1 Dog Lake l. Can.
29 C6 Dōgo i. Japan
54 C3 Dogondoutchi Niger
29 C7 Dōgo-yama mt Japan
17 K2 Doğubeyazıt Turkey
23 G3 Do'gyaling China
18 C5 Doha Qatar
Dohad see Dāhod
23 H5 Dohazar Bangl.
23 G3 Doilungdêqên China
32 A1 Doi Saket Thai.
87 K5 Dois Irmãos, Serra dos h. Brazil
49 K4 Dojran, Lake l. Greece/Macedonia
37 M6 Dokka Norway
42 E1 Dokkum Neth.
22 B4 Dokri Pak.
47 N3 Dokshytsy Belarus
51 F6 Dokuchayevs'k Ukr.
25 F7 Dolak, Pulau i. Indon.
67 F4 Dolbeau Can.
39 C5 Dolbenmaen U.K.
44 D2 Dol-de-Bretagne France
44 G3 Dole France
39 D5 Dolgellau U.K.
43 M1 Dolgen Ger.
81 F3 Dolgeville U.S.A.
51 F4 Dolgorukovo Rus. Fed.
51 F4 Dolgoye Rus. Fed.
48 C5 Dolianova Sardinia Italy
24 G2 Dolinsk Rus. Fed.
92 B2 Dolleman I. i. Ant.
43 K6 Dollnstein Ger.
56 E3 Dolo Odo Eth.
91 F3 Dolores Arg.
91 E2 Dolores Uru.
75 H2 Dolores r. U.S.A.
84 B2 Dolores Hidalgo Mex.
62 G3 Dolphin and Union Str. Can.
27 B7 Đô Lương Vietnam
51 B5 Dolyna Ukr.
16 B2 Domaniç Turkey
22 E2 Domar China
46 F6 Domažlice Czech Rep.
23 H2 Domba China
37 L5 Dombås Norway
46 J7 Dombóvár Hungary
92 C4 Dome Argus ice feature Ant.
92 C5 Dome Circle ice feature Ant.
64 E4 Dome Creek Can.
64 D2 Dome Pk summit Can.
75 E5 Dome Rock Mts mts U.S.A.
44 D2 Domfront France
61 M8 Dominica country Caribbean Sea
61 L8 Dominican Republic country Caribbean Sea
43 K1 Dömitz Ger.
32 C2 Dom Noi, L. r. Thai.
48 C1 Domodossola Italy
49 K5 Domokos Greece
91 F1 Dom Pedrito Brazil
33 E4 Dompu Indon.
91 B3 Domuyo, Volcán volc. Arg.
21 B2 Don r. India
51 G5 Don r. Rus. Fed.
40 F3 Don r. U.K.
41 F3 Donaghadee U.K.
41 E3 Donaghmore U.K.
8 D4 Donald Austr.
Donau r. Austria/Ger. see Danube
46 D7 Donaueschingen Ger.
46 E6 Donauwörth Ger.
45 D3 Don Benito Spain
38 F4 Doncaster U.K.
57 B4 Dondo Angola
57 D5 Dondo Moz.
31 B4 Dondonay i. Phil.
21 C5 Dondra Head c. Sri Lanka
41 C3 Donegal Rep. of Ireland
41 C3 Donegal Bay g. Rep. of Ireland
51 F6 Donets'k Ukr.
51 F5 Donets'kyy Kryazh h. Rus. Fed./Ukr.
27 D5 Dong'an China
6 B4 Dongara Austr.
22 E5 Dongargarh India
27 B5 Dongchuan China
23 F2 Dongco China
27 C7 Dongfang China
28 C1 Dongfanghong China
30 C2 Dongfeng China
33 E3 Donggala Indon.
30 C4 Donggou China
27 E5 Donggu China
27 D6 Dongguan China
32 C1 Đông Hà Vietnam
26 F3 Donghai China
27 D6 Donghai Dao i. China
26 C3 Dong He r. Sichuan China
26 A1 Dong He watercourse Nei Monggol China
32 C1 Đông Hôi Vietnam
30 E1 Dongjingcheng China
23 H3 Dongjug Xizang China
23 H3 Dongjug Xizang China
27 D5 Dongkou China
23 G4 Dongkya La pass India
27 C5 Donglan China
26 A2 Dongle China
30 C2 Dongliao r. China
30 B1 Dongminzhutun China
30 F2 Dongning China
57 B5 Dongo Angola
56 B3 Dongou Congo
32 B1 Dong Phraya Fai mts Thai.
32 B2 Dong Phraya Yen esc. Thai.
27 D6 Dongping Guangdong China
26 E3 Dongping Shandong China
23 G3 Dongqiao China
27 E6 Dongshan China
27 F6 Dongshan Dao i. China
26 D2 Dongsheng China
26 F3 Dongtai Jiangsu China
26 F3 Dongtai r. China
27 D4 Dongting Hu l. China
27 F5 Dongtou China
24 D2 Dong Ujimqin Qi China
27 E4 Dongxiang China
26 B3 Dongxiangzu China
27 F4 Dongyang China
26 F2 Dongying China
26 B2 Dongzhen China
27 E4 Dongzhi China
64 B2 Donjek r. Can.
42 E1 Donkerbroek Neth.
23 G5 Donmanick Islands is Bangl.
77 C7 Don Martín Mex.
67 F4 Donnacona Can.
64 F3 Donnelly Can.
9 D1 Donnellys Crossing N.Z.
74 B2 Donner Pass U.S.A.
Donostia-San Sebastián see San Sebastián
49 L6 Donoussa i. Greece
50 F4 Donskoy Rus. Fed.
51 G6 Donskoye Rus. Fed.
31 B3 Donsol Phil.
32 C2 Don, Xé r. Laos
41 A4 Dooagh Rep. of Ireland
41 B5 Doonbeg r. Rep. of Ireland
40 D5 Doon, Loch l. U.K.
42 D2 Doorn Neth.
68 D3 Door Peninsula pen. U.S.A.
42 D3 Doorwerth Neth.
56 E3 Dooxo Nugaaleed v. Somalia
19 F4 Dor watercourse Afgh.
77 C5 Dora U.S.A.
48 C2 Dora Baltea r. Italy
39 E7 Dorchester U.K.
57 B6 Dordabis Namibia
44 E4 Dordogne r. France
42 C3 Dordrecht Neth.
59 G5 Dordrecht S. Africa
58 C1 Doreenville Namibia
65 H4 Doré L. l. Can.
65 H4 Doré Lake Can.
48 C4 Dorgali Sardinia Italy
54 B3 Dori Burkina
19 G4 Dori r. Afgh.
58 C5 Doring r. S. Africa
39 G6 Dorking U.K.
42 E3 Dormagen Ger.
42 B5 Dormans France
26 C1 Dorngovĭ div. Mongolia
40 D3 Dornoch Firth est. U.K.
42 F1 Dornum Ger.
50 E4 Dorogobuzh Rus. Fed.
47 N7 Dorohoi Romania
24 B2 Döröö Nuur l. Mongolia
36 P4 Dorotea Sweden
6 B4 Dorre I. i. Austr.
72 B3 Dorris U.S.A.
54 D4 Dorsale Camerounaise slope Cameroon/Nigeria
69 H3 Dorset Can.
42 F3 Dortmund Ger.
80 B6 Dorton U.S.A.
16 F3 Dörtyol Turkey
43 G1 Dorum Ger.
56 C3 Doruma Congo(Zaire)
18 E3 Dorūneh Iran
81 G2 Dorval Can.
43 H2 Dörverden Ger.
88 C6 Dos Bahías, C. pt Arg.
75 H5 Dos Cabezas U.S.A.
86 C5 Dos de Mayo Peru
27 C6 Đo Son Vietnam
74 B3 Dos Palos U.S.A.
43 L2 Dosse r. Ger.
54 C3 Dosso Niger
79 C6 Dothan U.S.A.
44 F1 Douai France
54 C4 Douala Cameroon
44 B2 Douarnenez France
27 □ Double I. i. H.K. China
74 C4 Double Peak summit U.S.A.
44 H3 Doubs r. France
9 A6 Doubtful Sound in. N.Z.
9 D1 Doubtless Bay b. N.Z.
54 B3 Douentza Mali
38 C3 Douglas Isle of Man
58 E4 Douglas S. Africa
40 E5 Douglas Scot. U.K.
64 C3 Douglas AK U.S.A.
75 H6 Douglas AZ U.S.A.
79 D6 Douglas GA U.S.A.
72 F3 Douglas WY U.S.A.
64 D4 Douglas Chan. chan. Can.
75 H2 Douglas Creek r. U.S.A.
44 F1 Doullens France
40 D4 Doune U.K.
90 C2 Dourada, Cach. waterfall Brazil
90 B2 Dourada, Serra h. Brazil
90 C1 Dourada, Serra mts Brazil
90 A3 Dourados Brazil
90 A3 Dourados r. Brazil
90 B3 Dourados, Serra dos h. Brazil
45 C2 Douro r. Port.
42 D5 Douzy France
39 F4 Dove r. Eng. U.K.
39 J5 Dove r. Eng. U.K.
67 J3 Dove Brook Can.
75 H3 Dove Creek U.S.A.
39 J6 Dover U.K.
81 F5 Dover DE U.S.A.
81 H3 Dover NH U.S.A.
81 F4 Dover NJ U.S.A.
80 C4 Dover OH U.S.A.
81 J2 Dover-Foxcroft U.S.A.
39 J7 Dover, Strait of str. France/U.K.
17 L5 Doveyrīch r. Iran/Iraq
68 D5 Dowagiac U.S.A.
18 D4 Dow Chāhī Iran
19 E2 Dowgha'ī Iran
32 A5 Dowi, Tg pt Indon.
19 F3 Dowlatābād Afgh.
19 G2 Dowlatābād Afgh.
18 D4 Dowlatābād Iran
18 E4 Dowlatābād Iran
19 F2 Dowlatābād Iran
19 G3 Dowl at Yār Afgh.
74 B2 Downieville U.S.A.
41 F3 Downpatrick U.K.
81 F3 Downsville U.S.A.
18 C3 Dow Rūd Iran
17 L4 Dow Sar Iran
19 E4 Dowsārī Iran
19 H3 Dowshī Afgh.
74 B1 Doyle U.S.A.
81 F4 Doylestown U.S.A.
29 C6 Dōzen is Japan
69 J2 Dozois, Réservoir resr Can.
90 B3 Dracena Brazil
42 E1 Drachten Neth.
49 L2 Drăgănești-Olt Romania
49 L2 Drăgășani Romania
89 E2 Dragon's Mouths str. Trinidad/Venez.
37 S6 Dragsfjärd Fin.
44 H5 Draguignan France
51 C4 Drahichyn Belarus
75 F4 Drake AZ U.S.A.
65 J5 Drake ND U.S.A.
59 H5 Drakensberg mts Lesotho/S. Africa
59 J2 Drakensberg mts S. Africa
85 C8 Drake Passage str. Ant.
49 L4 Drama Greece
37 M7 Drammen Norway
37 L7 Drangedal Norway
19 G5 Dran juk h. Pak.
43 H3 Dransfeld Ger.
41 E3 Draperstown U.K.
22 C2 Dras Jammu and Kashmir
46 F7 Drau r. Austria
64 G4 Drayton Valley Can.
48 B6 Dréan Alg.
43 H4 Dreistelz-berge h. Ger.
46 F5 Dresden Ger.
50 D4 Dretun' Belarus
44 E2 Dreux France
37 N6 Drevsjø Norway
80 D4 Driftwood U.S.A.
41 B6 Drimoleague Rep. of Ireland
48 G3 Drniš Croatia
49 K2 Drobeta-Turnu Severin Romania
43 H1 Drochtersen Ger.
41 E4 Drogheda Rep. of Ireland
51 B5 Drohobych Ukr.
Droichead Átha see Drogheda
39 E5 Droitwich U.K.
23 G4 Drokung India
43 J2 Drömling reg. Ger.
41 D4 Dromod Rep. of Ireland
41 E3 Dromore Co. Down U.K.
41 D3 Dromore Co. Tyrone U.K.
39 F4 Dronfield U.K.
63 Q2 Dronning Louise Land reg. Greenland
92 C3 Dronning Maud Land reg. Ant.
42 D2 Dronten Neth.
22 B2 Drosh Pak.
51 F4 Droskovo Rus. Fed.
8 E5 Drouin Austr.
88 D2 Dr Pedro P. Peña Para.
64 G4 Drumheller Can.
72 D2 Drummond MT U.S.A.
68 B2 Drummond WI U.S.A.
69 F3 Drummond Island i. U.S.A.
67 F4 Drummondville Can.
40 D6 Drummore U.K.
40 D4 Drumochter Pass U.K.
37 T10 Druskininkai Lith.
13 Q3 Druzhina Rus. Fed.
49 L3 Dryanovo Bulg.
64 B3 Dry Bay b. U.S.A.
65 L5 Dryberry L. l. Can.
68 E2 Dryburg U.S.A.
66 B4 Dryden Can.
92 D5 Drygalski I. i. Ant.
92 B5 Drygalski Ice Tongue ice feature Ant.
74 D2 Dry Lake l. U.S.A.
40 D4 Drymen U.K.
6 C3 Drysdale r. Austr.
18 C3 Dūāb r. Iran
27 C6 Du'an China
81 F2 Duane U.S.A.
23 G4 Duars reg. India
14 B4 Ḍubā S. Arabia
20 E4 Dubai U.A.E.
65 J2 Dubawnt r. Can.
62 H3 Dubawnt Lake l. N.W.T. Can.
65 J2 Dubawnt Lake l. Can.
Dubayy see Dubai
14 B4 Dubbagh, J. ad mt S. Arabia
8 G2 Dubbo Austr.
68 D1 Dublin Can.
41 E4 Dublin Rep. of Ireland
79 D5 Dublin U.S.A.
50 F3 Dubna Rus. Fed.
51 C5 Dubno Ukr.
72 D2 Dubois ID U.S.A.
72 E3 Dubois WY U.S.A.
80 D4 Du Bois U.S.A.
51 H5 Dubovka Rus. Fed.
51 G6 Dubovskoye Rus. Fed.
17 M1 Dübrar P. pass Azer.
54 A4 Dubréka Guinea
49 H3 Dubrovnik Croatia
51 C5 Dubrovytsya Ukr.
50 D4 Dubrowna Belarus
68 B4 Dubuque U.S.A.
37 S9 Dubysa r. Lith.
5 N7 Duc de Gloucester, Îles is Pac. Oc.
27 E4 Duchang China
75 G1 Duchesne U.S.A.
5 P7 Ducie Island i. Pac. Oc.
79 C5 Duck r. U.S.A.
65 J4 Duck Bay Can.
65 H4 Duck Lake Can.
68 E4 Duck Lake U.S.A.
75 E2 Duckwater U.S.A.
75 E2 Duckwater Peak summit U.S.A.
32 D2 Đức Phô Vietnam
32 D3 Đức Trong Vietnam
89 B4 Duda r. Col.
42 E5 Dudelange Lux.
43 J3 Duderstadt Ger.
23 E4 Dudhi India
23 G4 Dudhnai India
12 K3 Dudinka Rus. Fed.
39 E5 Dudley U.K.
22 D6 Dudna r. India
40 F3 Dudwick, Hill of h. U.K.
54 B4 Duékoué Côte d'Ivoire
45 C2 Duero r. Spain
69 H1 Dufault, Lac l. Can.
92 B4 Dufek Coast coastal area Ant.
42 C3 Duffel Belgium
66 E2 Dufferin, Cape hd Can.
80 B6 Duffield U.S.A.
7 G2 Duff Is is Solomon Is
40 E3 Dufftown U.K.
66 E1 Dufrost, Pte pt Can.
19 G2 Dugab Uzbek.
48 F3 Dugi Otok i. Croatia
26 C2 Dugui Qarag China
26 D3 Du He r. China
89 D4 Duida, Co mt Venez.
86 E3 Duida-Marahuaca, Parque Nacional nat. park Venez.
42 E3 Duisburg Ger.
89 B3 Duitama Col.
59 J1 Duiwelskloof S. Africa
17 K4 Dukān Dam dam Iraq
59 G5 Dukathole S. Africa
64 C4 Duke I. i. U.S.A.
18 C5 Dukhān Qatar
47 Q3 Dukhovshchina Rus. Fed.
22 B3 Duki Pak.
27 A5 Dukou China
37 U9 Dūkštas Lith.
24 B3 Dulan China
88 D3 Dulce r. Arg.
23 E2 Dulishi Hu salt l. China
59 J2 Dullstroom S. Africa
42 F3 Dülmen Ger.
49 M3 Dulovo Bulg.
68 A2 Duluth U.S.A.
68 A2 Duluth/Superior airport U.S.A.
39 D6 Dulverton U.K.
16 F5 Dūmā Syria
31 B4 Dumaguete Phil.
33 B2 Dumai Indon.
31 B4 Dumaran i. Phil.
77 F5 Dumas AR U.S.A.
77 C5 Dumas TX U.S.A.
16 F5 Ḍumayr Syria
38 F3 Dumbakh Iran
40 D5 Dumbarton U.K.
59 J3 Dumbe S. Africa
47 J6 Ďumbier mt Slovakia
22 D2 Dumchele Jammu and Kashmir
23 H4 Dum Duma India
40 E5 Dumfries U.K.
23 F4 Dumka India
43 G2 Dümmer l. Ger.
66 E4 Dumoine, L. l. Can.
92 B6 Dumont d'Urville France base Ant.
92 B6 Dumont d'Urville Sea sea Ant.
42 F4 Dümpelfeld Ger.
55 F1 Dumyât Egypt
43 J3 Dün ridge Ger.
Duna r. Hungary see Danube
46 H7 Dunajská Streda Slovakia
47 J7 Dunakeszi Hungary
41 E4 Dunany Point pt Rep. of Ireland
Dunărea r. Romania see Danube
49 N2 Dunării, Delta delta Romania
47 J7 Dunaújváros Hungary
Dunav r. Yugo. see Danube
51 C5 Dunayivtsi Ukr.
9 C6 Dunback N.Z.
40 F4 Dunbar U.K.
40 E4 Dunblane U.K.
41 E4 Dunboyne Rep. of Ireland
64 E5 Duncan Can.
75 H5 Duncan AZ U.S.A.
77 D5 Duncan OK U.S.A.
66 D3 Duncan, Cape c. Can.
66 E3 Duncan, L. l. Can.
80 E4 Duncannon U.S.A.
40 E2 Duncansby Head hd U.K.
68 B5 Duncans Mills U.S.A.
41 E5 Duncormick Rep. of Ireland
37 S8 Dundaga Latvia
69 G3 Dundalk Can.
41 E3 Dundalk Rep. of Ireland
80 E5 Dundalk U.S.A.
41 E4 Dundalk Bay b. Rep. of Ireland
Dundas see Uummannaq
64 C4 Dundas I. i. Can.
Dun Dealgan see Dundalk
59 J4 Dundee S. Africa
40 F4 Dundee U.K.
69 F5 Dundee MI U.S.A.
80 E3 Dundee NY U.S.A.
41 F3 Dundonald U.K.
40 E6 Dundrennan U.K.
41 F3 Dundrum U.K.
41 F3 Dundrum Bay b. U.K.
23 E4 Dundwa Range mts India/Nepal
9 C6 Dunedin N.Z.
79 D6 Dunedin U.S.A.
8 G2 Dunedoo Austr.
66 F2 Dune, Lac l. Can.
40 E4 Dunfermline U.K.
41 E3 Dungannon U.K.
22 C5 Dungarpur India
41 D5 Dungarvan Rep. of Ireland
39 H7 Dungeness hd U.K.
88 C8 Dungeness, Pta pt Arg.
42 F4 Düngenheim Ger.
41 E3 Dungiven U.K.
41 C3 Dungloe Rep. of Ireland
8 H2 Dungog Austr.
56 C3 Dungu Congo(Zaire)
33 B2 Dungun Malaysia
55 F2 Dungunab Sudan
30 E2 Dunhua China
24 B2 Dunhuang China
8 D4 Dunkeld Austr.
40 E4 Dunkeld U.K.
Dunkerque see Dunkirk
39 D6 Dunkery Beacon h. U.K.
44 F1 Dunkirk France
80 D3 Dunkirk U.S.A.
54 B4 Dunkwa Ghana
41 E4 Dún Laoghaire Rep. of Ireland
41 E4 Dunlavin Rep. of Ireland
41 E4 Dunleer Rep. of Ireland
41 E2 Dunloy U.K.
41 B6 Dunmanus Bay b. Rep. of Ireland
41 B6 Dunmanway Rep. of Ireland
41 C4 Dunmore Rep. of Ireland
79 E7 Dunmore Town Bahamas
74 D3 Dunmovin U.S.A.
41 F3 Dunmurry U.K.
79 E5 Dunn U.S.A.
40 E2 Dunnet Bay b. U.K.
40 E2 Dunnet Head hd U.K.
74 B2 Dunnigan U.S.A.
76 C3 Dunning U.S.A.
69 H4 Dunnville Can.
8 D4 Dunolly Austr.
40 D5 Dunoon U.K.
40 F5 Duns U.K.
76 C1 Dunseith U.S.A.
72 B3 Dunsmuir U.S.A.
39 G6 Dunstable U.K.
9 B6 Dunstan Mts mts N.Z.
42 D5 Dun-sur-Meuse France
9 C6 Duntroon N.Z.
40 B3 Dunvegan, Loch in. U.K.
22 B3 Dunyapur Pak.
26 E1 Duolun China
27 D5 Dupang Ling mts China
69 H1 Duparquet, Lac l. Can.
76 C2 Dupree U.S.A.
78 B4 Du Quoin U.S.A.
6 C3 Durack r. Austr.
Dura Europos see Qal'at as Sālihīyah
16 E1 Durağan Turkey
44 G5 Durance r. France
69 F4 Durand MI U.S.A.
68 B3 Durand WI U.S.A.
84 A1 Durango Mex.
45 E1 Durango Spain
73 F4 Durango U.S.A.
84 A1 Durango div. Mex.
77 D5 Durant U.S.A.
91 F2 Durazno Uru.
91 F1 Durazno, Cuchilla Grande del h. Uru.
59 J4 Durban S. Africa
44 F5 Durban-Corbières France
58 C6 Durbanville S. Africa
80 D5 Durbin U.S.A.
42 D4 Durbuy Belgium
42 E4 Düren Ger.
22 E5 Durg India
23 F5 Durgapur India
69 G3 Durham Can.
38 F3 Durham U.K.
74 B2 Durham CA U.S.A.
79 E4 Durham NC U.S.A.
81 H3 Durham NH U.S.A.
51 D6 Durleşti Moldova
43 G6 Durmersheim Ger.
49 H3 Durmitor mt Yugo.
40 D2 Durness U.K.
49 H4 Durrës Albania
39 F6 Durrington U.K.
41 A6 Dursey Island i. Rep. of Ireland
16 B2 Dursunbey Turkey
19 F3 Dūrūḥ Iran
16 F5 Durūz, Jabal ad mt Syria
9 D4 D'Urville Island i. N.Z.
6 D2 d'Urville, Tanjung pt Indon.
19 G3 Durzab Afgh.
19 G4 Dushai Pak.
19 E2 Dushak Turkm.
27 C5 Dushan China
19 H2 Dushanbe Tajik.
51 H7 Dushet'i Georgia
9 A6 Dusky Sound in. N.Z.
42 E3 Düsseldorf Ger.
75 F1 Dutch Mt mt U.S.A.
58 E1 Dutlwe Botswana
54 C3 Dutse Nigeria
75 F2 Dutton, Mt mt U.S.A.
50 H3 Duvannoye Rus. Fed.
67 F2 Duvert, Lac l. Can.
27 C5 Duyun China
19 F5 Duzab Pak.
16 C1 Düzce Turkey
Duzdab see Zāhedān
50 D4 Dvina, Western r. Rus. Fed.
51 F5 Dvorichna Ukr.
28 B2 Dvoryanka Rus. Fed.
22 B5 Dwarka India
59 G2 Dwarsberg S. Africa
68 C5 Dwight U.S.A.
42 E2 Dwingelderveld, Nationaal Park nat. park Neth.
72 C2 Dworshak Res. resr U.S.A.
58 D6 Dwyka S. Africa
50 E4 Dyat'kovo Rus. Fed.
40 F3 Dyce U.K.
68 D5 Dyer IN U.S.A.
74 C3 Dyer NV U.S.A.
69 G3 Dyer Bay Can.
63 M3 Dyer, C. c. Can.
79 B4 Dyersburg U.S.A.
68 B4 Dyersville U.S.A.
39 D5 Dyfi r. U.K.
40 E3 Dyke U.K.
51 G7 Dykh Tau mt Georgia/Rus. Fed.
43 L5 Dyleň h. Czech Rep.
47 J4 Dylewska Góra h. Pol.
59 H5 Dyoki S. Africa
68 A4 Dysart U.S.A.
58 E6 Dysselsdorp S. Africa
24 D2 Dzamïn Üüd Mongolia
57 E5 Dzaoudzi Mayotte Africa
50 G3 Dzerzhinsk Rus. Fed.
47 N5 Dzerzhyns'k Ukr.
18 D1 Dzhanga Turkm.
51 E6 Dzhankoy Ukr.
51 H5 Dzhanybek Rus. Fed.
19 G2 Dzharkurgan Uzbek.
18 D2 Dzhebel Turkm.
14 E1 Dzhetygara Kazak.
14 E2 Dzhezkazgan Kazak.
13 R3 Dzhigudzhak Rus. Fed.
19 G1 Dzhizak Uzbek.
24 F1 Dzhugdzhur, Khrebet mts Rus. Fed.
Dzhul'fa see Culfa
19 G2 Dzhuma Uzbek.
15 F2 Dzhungarskiy Alatau, Khr. mts China/Kazak.
12 H5 Dzhusaly Kazak.
47 K4 Działdowo Pol.
84 E3 Dzibalchén Mex.
24 C2 Dzuunmod Mongolia
50 C4 Dzyaniskavichy Belarus
50 C4 Dzyarzhynsk Belarus
47 N4 Dzyatlavichy Belarus

E

66 C3 Eabamet L. l. Can.
75 H4 Eagar U.S.A.
73 F4 Eagle U.S.A.
67 J3 Eagle r. Can.
81 F3 Eagle Bay U.S.A.
65 H4 Eagle Cr. r. Can.
74 D4 Eagle Crags summit U.S.A.
65 L5 Eagle L. l. Can.
72 B3 Eagle L. l. CA U.S.A.
81 J1 Eagle Lake ME U.S.A.
81 J1 Eagle Lake l. ME U.S.A.
68 B2 Eagle Mtn h. U.S.A.
77 C6 Eagle Pass U.S.A.
62 D3 Eagle Plain plain Can.
68 C2 Eagle River MI U.S.A.
68 C3 Eagle River WV U.S.A.
64 F3 Eaglesham Can.
75 F5 Eagle Tail Mts mts U.S.A.
66 B3 Ear Falls Can.
74 C4 Earlimart U.S.A.
40 F5 Earlston U.K.
69 H2 Earlton Can.
40 E4 Earn r. U.K.
40 D4 Earn, L. l. U.K.
77 C5 Earth U.S.A.
38 H4 Easington U.K.
79 D5 Easley U.S.A.
92 C5 East Antarctica reg. Ant.
81 F4 East Ararat U.S.A.
80 D3 East Aurora U.S.A.
77 F6 East Bay b. U.S.A.
81 G2 East Berkshire U.S.A.
39 H7 Eastbourne U.K.
80 D4 East Branch Clarion River Reservoir U.S.A.
81 H4 East Brooklyn U.S.A.
9 G2 East Cape c. N.Z.
75 G2 East Carbon U.S.A.
94 E5 East Caroline Basin sea feature Pac. Oc.
68 D5 East Chicago U.S.A.
24 E3 East China Sea Asia
9 E2 East Coast Bays N.Z.
81 G2 East Corinth U.S.A.
39 H5 East Dereham U.K.
5 R7 Easter Island i. Pac. Oc.
95 M7 Easter Island Fracture Zone sea feature Pac. Oc.
59 G5 Eastern Cape div. S. Africa
55 F2 Eastern Desert des. Egypt
23 E6 Eastern Ghats mts India
22 B4 Eastern Nara canal Pak.
Eastern Transvaal div. see Mpumalanga
65 K4 Easterville Can.
88 E8 East Falkland i. Falkland Is
81 H4 East Falmouth U.S.A.
42 E1 East Frisian Islands is Ger.
74 D2 Eastgate U.S.A.
76 D2 East Grand Forks U.S.A.
39 G6 East Grinstead U.K.
81 G3 Easthampton U.S.A.
81 G4 East Hampton U.S.A.
80 D4 East Hickory U.S.A.
81 G3 East Jamaica U.S.A.
96 K1 East Jan Mayen Ridge sea feature Atl. Ocean
68 E3 East Jordan U.S.A.
40 D5 East Kilbride U.K.
68 D3 Eastlake U.S.A.
27 □ East Lamma Channel H.K. China
39 F7 Eastleigh U.K.
80 C4 East Liverpool U.S.A.
40 B3 East Loch Tarbert b. U.K.
59 G6 East London S. Africa
80 B5 East Lynn Lake l. U.S.A.
66 E3 Eastmain Que. Can.
66 F3 Eastmain r. Que. Can.
81 G2 Eastman Can.
79 D5 Eastman U.S.A.
81 J2 East Millinocket U.S.A.
68 B5 East Moline U.S.A.
68 C5 Easton IL U.S.A.
81 E5 Easton MD U.S.A.
81 F4 Easton PA U.S.A.
95 M8 East Pacific Ridge sea feature Pac. Oc.
95 N5 East Pacific Rise sea feature Pac. Oc.
74 A2 East Park Res. resr U.S.A.
79 C5 East Point U.S.A.
67 H4 East Point pt P.E.I. Can.
81 K2 Eastport ME U.S.A.
68 E3 Eastport MI U.S.A.
74 D1 East Range mts U.S.A.
East Retford see Retford
78 B4 East St Louis U.S.A.
13 R2 East Siberian Sea sea Rus. Fed.
11 O10 East Timor reg. Asia
23 F4 East Tons r. India
68 C4 East Troy U.S.A.
81 F6 Eastville U.S.A.
74 C2 East Walker r. U.S.A.
81 G3 East Wallingford U.S.A.
79 D5 Eatonton U.S.A.
68 B3 Eau Claire U.S.A.
68 B3 Eau Claire r. U.S.A.
66 F2 Eau Claire, Lac à l' l. Can.
25 G6 Eauripik Atoll Micronesia
94 E5 Eauripik - New Guinea Rise sea feature Pac. Oc.
84 C2 Ebano Mex.
39 D6 Ebbw Vale U.K.
54 D4 Ebebiyin Equatorial Guinea
58 B2 Ebenerde Namibia
80 D4 Ebensburg U.S.A.
16 C2 Eber Gölü l. Turkey
43 J3 Ebergötzen Ger.
46 F4 Eberswalde-Finow Ger.
69 F4 Eberts Can.
28 G3 Ebetsu Japan
27 B4 Ebian China
48 F4 Eboli Italy
54 D4 Ebolowa Cameroon
95 G5 Ebon i. Pac. Oc.
17 K3 Ebrāhim Ḥeṣār Iran
45 G2 Ebro r. Spain
43 J1 Ebstorf Ger.
49 M4 Eceabat Turkey
31 B2 Echague Phil.
45 E1 Echarri-Aranaz Spain
54 C1 Ech Chélif Alg.
45 E1 Echegárate, Puerto pass Spain
27 E4 Echeng China
64 F1 Echo Bay N.W.T. Can.
69 E2 Echo Bay Ont. Can.
75 G3 Echo Cliffs cliff U.S.A.
66 B3 Echoing r. Can.
69 K2 Échouani, Lac l. Can.
42 D3 Echt Neth.
42 E5 Echternach Lux.
8 E4 Echuca Austr.
43 G4 Echzell Ger.
45 D4 Écija Spain
43 K5 Eckental Ger.
68 E2 Eckerman U.S.A.

46 D3 Eckernförde Ger.
63 L2 Eclipse Sound chan. Can.
85 C3 Ecuador country S. America
66 E2 Écueils, Pte aux pt Can.
56 E2 Ed Eritrea
37 M7 Ed Sweden
65 H4 Edam Can.
42 D2 Edam Neth.
40 F1 Eday i. U.K.
55 E3 Ed Da'ein Sudan
55 F3 Ed Damazin Sudan
55 F3 Ed Damer Sudan
55 F3 Ed Debba Sudan
55 F3 Ed Dueim Sudan
6 E6 Eddystone Pt pt Austr.
42 D2 Ede Neth.
54 D4 Edéa Cameroon
65 K2 Edehon Lake l. Can.
90 C2 Edéia Brazil
8 G4 Eden Austr.
77 D6 Eden TX U.S.A.
38 E3 Eden r. U.K.
59 F4 Edenburg S. Africa
9 B7 Edendale N.Z.
41 D4 Edenderry Rep. of Ireland
8 C4 Edenhope Austr.
79 E4 Edenton U.S.A.
59 G3 Edenville S. Africa
49 K4 Edessa Greece
43 F1 Edewecht Ger.
81 H4 Edgartown U.S.A.
76 D2 Edgeley U.S.A.
76 C3 Edgemont U.S.A.
68 C4 Edgerton U.S.A.
41 D4 Edgeworthstown Rep. of Ireland
68 A5 Edina U.S.A.
77 D7 Edinburg U.S.A.
40 E5 Edinburgh U.K.
51 C7 Edirne Turkey
64 F4 Edith Cavell, Mt mt Can.
72 B2 Edmonds U.S.A.
64 G4 Edmonton Can.
65 K5 Edmore U.S.A.
68 B4 Edmund U.S.A.
65 L4 Edmund L. l. Can.
67 G4 Edmundston Can.
77 D6 Edna U.S.A.
64 C3 Edna Bay U.S.A.
49 M5 Edremit Turkey
37 O6 Edsbyn Sweden
64 F4 Edson Can.
91 D2 Eduardo Castex Arg.
8 E3 Edward r. Austr.
68 C1 Edward I. i. Can.
56 C4 Edward, Lake l. Congo(Zaire)/Uganda
81 F2 Edwards U.S.A.
77 C6 Edwards Plateau plat. U.S.A.
78 B4 Edwardsville U.S.A.
92 D4 Edward VIII Ice Shelf ice feature Ant.
92 A4 Edward VII Pen. pen. Ant.
64 C3 Edziza Pk mt Can.
42 B3 Eeklo Belgium
74 A1 Eel r. U.S.A.
42 E1 Eemshaven pt Neth.
42 E1 Eenrum Neth.
58 D3 Eenzamheid Pan salt pan S. Africa
7 G3 Éfaté i. Vanuatu
78 B4 Effingham U.S.A.
16 D1 Eflâni Turkey
75 E2 Egan Range mts U.S.A.
69 J3 Eganville Can.
47 K7 Eger Hungary
37 K7 Egersund Norway
43 G3 Eggegebirge h. Ger.
43 K5 Eggolsheim Ger.
42 C4 Eghezée Belgium
36 F4 Egilsstaðir Iceland
16 C3 Eğirdir Turkey
16 C3 Eğirdir Gölü l. Turkey
44 F4 Égletons France
41 D2 Eglinton U.K.
62 F2 Eglinton I. i. Can.
42 C2 Egmond aan Zee Neth.
9 D3 Egmont, Cape c. N.Z.
9 E3 Egmont, Mt volc. N.Z.
9 E3 Egmont National Park N.Z.
16 B2 Eğriğöz Dağı mts Turkey
38 G3 Egton U.K.
90 D1 Éguas r. Brazil
13 V3 Egvekinot Rus. Fed.
52 G3 Egypt country Africa
46 D6 Ehingen (Donau) Ger.
43 J2 Ehra-Lessien Ger.
75 E5 Ehrenberg U.S.A.
43 J5 Eibelstadt Ger.
42 E2 Eibergen Neth.
43 H4 Eichenzell Ger.
43 K6 Eichstätt Ger.
37 K6 Eidfjord Norway
37 M6 Eidsvoll Norway
42 E4 Eifel reg. Ger.
40 B4 Eigg i. U.K.
21 A4 Eight Degree Chan. India/Maldives
92 A3 Eights Coast coastal area Ant.
6 C3 Eighty Mile Beach beach Austr.
8 E4 Eildon Austr.
8 F4 Eildon, Lake l. Austr.
40 C4 Eilean Shona i. U.K.
65 H2 Eileen Lake l. Can.
43 L3 Eilenburg Ger.
43 J2 Eimke Ger.
43 H3 Einbeck Ger.
42 D3 Eindhoven Neth.
46 D7 Einsiedeln Switz.
86 E5 Eirunepé Brazil
43 H3 Eisberg h. Ger.
57 C5 Eiseb watercourse Namibia
43 J4 Eisenach Ger.
43 K4 Eisenberg Ger.
46 G4 Eisenhüttenstadt Ger.
46 H7 Eisenstadt Austria
43 J4 Eisfeld Ger.
40 C3 Eishort, Loch in. U.K.
43 K3 Eisleben Lutherstadt Ger.
43 H4 Eiterfeld Ger.
Eivissa see Ibiza
Eivissa i. see Ibiza
45 F1 Ejea de los Caballeros Spain
57 E6 Ejeda Madag.
82 B3 Ejido Insurgentes Mex.
26 C2 Ejin Horo Qi China
26 A1 Ejin Qi China
17 K1 Ejmiatsin Armenia
84 C3 Ejutla Mex.
37 S7 Ekenäs Fin.
42 C3 Ekeren Belgium
9 E4 Eketahuna N.Z.
15 F1 Ekibastuz Kazak.
13 M3 Ekonda Rus. Fed.
37 N6 Ekshärad Sweden
37 O8 Eksjö Sweden
58 B4 Eksteenfontein S. Africa
56 C4 Ekuku Congo(Zaire)
66 D3 Ekwan r. Can.
66 D3 Ekwan Point pt Can.
49 K6 Elafonisou, Steno chan. Greece
16 B6 El 'Alamein Egypt
84 D3 El Almendro Mex.
16 B6 El 'Amirîya Egypt
59 H2 Elands r. S. Africa
59 H2 Elandsdoorn S. Africa
48 B7 El Aouinet Alg.
16 B6 El 'Arab, Khalîg b. Egypt
16 D6 El 'Arîsh Egypt
49 K5 Elassona Greece
16 E7 Elat Israel
17 G2 Elazığ Turkey
48 D3 Elba, Isola d' i. Italy
24 F1 El'ban Rus. Fed.
89 B2 El Banco Col.
16 D6 El Bardawîl, Sabkhet lag. Egypt
49 J4 Elbasan Albania
16 E2 Elbaşı Turkey
89 C2 El Baúl Venez.
54 C1 El Bayadh Alg.
43 J1 Elbe r. Ger.
68 D3 Elberta MI U.S.A.
75 G2 Elberta UT U.S.A.
73 F4 Elbert, Mount mt U.S.A.
79 D5 Elberton U.S.A.
44 E2 Elbeuf France
16 F2 Elbistan Turkey
47 J3 Elbląg Pol.
91 B4 El Bolsón Arg.
79 E7 Elbow Cay i. Bahamas
51 G7 Elbrus mt Rus. Fed.
42 D2 Elburg Neth.
45 E2 El Burgo de Osma Spain
91 C2 El Cain Arg.
74 D5 El Cajon U.S.A.
89 E3 El Callao Venez.
77 D6 El Campo U.S.A.
75 E5 El Centro U.S.A.
86 F7 El Cerro Bol.
89 D2 El Chaparro Venez.
45 F3 Elche Spain
84 D3 El Chichón volc. Mex.
6 D3 Elcho I. i. Austr.
89 B3 El Cocuy Col.
45 F3 Elda Spain
43 K1 Elde r. Ger.
69 H2 Eldee Can.
74 D5 El Descanso Mex.
89 B2 El Difícil Col.
13 P3 El'dikan Rus. Fed.
89 A4 El Diviso Col.
75 E6 El Doctor Mex.
68 A5 Eldon IA U.S.A.
76 E4 Eldon MO U.S.A.
88 F3 Eldorado Arg.
84 A1 El Dorado Mex.
77 E5 El Dorado AR U.S.A.
77 D4 El Dorado KS U.S.A.
77 C6 Eldorado U.S.A.
89 E3 El Dorado Venez.
56 D3 Eldoret Kenya
72 E2 Electric Peak summit U.S.A.
54 B2 El Eglab plat. Alg.
45 E4 El Ejido Spain
50 F4 Elektrostal' Rus. Fed.
86 D4 El Encanto Col.
43 J3 Elend Ger.
73 F5 Elephant Butte Res. resr U.S.A.
92 B1 Elephant I. i. Ant.
23 H5 Elephant Point pt Bangl.
17 J2 Eleşkirt Turkey
54 C1 El Eulma Alg.
79 E7 Eleuthera i. Bahamas
48 C6 El Fahs Tunisia
55 F2 El Faiyûm Egypt
55 E3 El Fasher Sudan
43 H4 Elfershausen Ger.
70 E6 El Fuerte Mex.
55 E3 El Geneina Sudan
55 F3 El Geteina Sudan
40 E3 Elgin U.K.
68 C4 Elgin IL U.S.A.
76 C2 Elgin ND U.S.A.
75 E3 Elgin NV U.S.A.
75 G2 Elgin UT U.S.A.
13 Q3 El'ginskiy Rus. Fed.
55 F2 El Gîza Egypt
84 B2 El Gogorrón, Parque Nacional nat. park Mex.
54 C1 El Goléa Alg.
55 F4 Elgon, Mount mt Uganda
48 B6 El Hadjar Alg.
16 B6 El Hammâm Egypt
16 F6 El Hazim Jordan
54 A2 El Hierro i. Canary Is
84 C2 El Higo Mex.
54 C2 El Homr Alg.
40 F4 Elie U.K.
9 C5 Elie de Beaumont mt N.Z.
62 B3 Elim AK U.S.A.
47 H2 Eliot, Mount mt Can.
45 F1 Elizondo Spain
El Iskandarîya see Alexandria
51 H6 Elista Rus. Fed.
68 B4 Elizabeth IL U.S.A.
81 F4 Elizabeth NJ U.S.A.
80 C5 Elizabeth WV U.S.A.
79 E4 Elizabeth City U.S.A.
81 H4 Elizabeth Is is U.S.A.
79 D4 Elizabethton U.S.A.
78 C4 Elizabethtown KY U.S.A.
79 E5 Elizabethtown NC U.S.A.
81 G2 Elizabethtown NY U.S.A.
80 E4 Elizabethtown PA U.S.A.
54 B1 El Jadida Morocco
16 F6 El Jafr Jordan
84 A1 El Jaralito Mex.
48 D7 El Jem Tunisia
47 L4 Ełk Pol.
74 A2 Elk U.S.A.
64 G4 Elk r. Can.
80 C5 Elk r. U.S.A.
16 F4 El Kaa Lebanon
48 C6 El Kala Alg.
55 F3 El Kamlin Sudan
77 D5 Elk City U.S.A.
74 A2 Elk Creek U.S.A.
74 B2 Elk Grove U.S.A.
55 F2 El Khârga Egypt
68 E5 Elkhart U.S.A.
El Khartum see Khartoum
54 B2 El Khnâchîch esc. Mali
68 C4 Elkhorn U.S.A.
76 D3 Elkhorn r. U.S.A.
49 M3 Elkhovo Bulg.
80 D5 Elkins U.S.A.
64 G4 Elk Island Nat. Park Can.
69 G2 Elk Lake Can.
68 E3 Elk Lake l. U.S.A.
80 E4 Elkland U.S.A.
64 F5 Elko Can.
72 D3 Elko U.S.A.
65 G4 Elk Point Can.
76 E2 Elk River U.S.A.
81 F5 Elkton MD U.S.A.
80 D5 Elkton VA U.S.A.
17 G4 El Kubar Syria
65 M2 Ell Bay b. Can.
63 H2 Ellef Ringnes I. i. Can.
22 C3 Ellenabad India
76 D2 Ellendale U.S.A.
75 G2 Ellen, Mt mt U.S.A.
72 B2 Ellensburg U.S.A.
81 F4 Ellenville U.S.A.
8 G4 Ellery, Mt mt Austr.
63 K2 Ellesmere Island i. Can.
9 D5 Ellesmere, Lake l. N.Z.
39 E4 Ellesmere Port U.K.
62 H3 Ellice r. Can.
80 D3 Ellicottville U.S.A.
84 C2 El Limón Mex.
43 J5 Ellingen Ger.
59 G5 Elliot S. Africa
59 H5 Elliotdale S. Africa
69 F2 Elliot Lake Can.
72 D2 Ellis U.S.A.
59 G1 Ellisras S. Africa
40 F3 Ellon U.K.
81 J2 Ellsworth ME U.S.A.
68 A3 Ellsworth WI U.S.A.
92 A3 Ellsworth Land reg. Ant.
92 B3 Ellsworth Mountains Ant.
43 J6 Ellwangen (Jagst) Ger.
16 B3 Elmalı Turkey
74 D6 El Maneadero Mex.
55 F1 El Mansûra Egypt
89 E3 El Manteco Venez.
54 C1 El Meghaïer Alg.
89 E3 El Miamo Venez.
16 E4 El Mina Lebanon
55 F2 El Minya Egypt
68 E3 Elmira MI U.S.A.
80 E3 Elmira NY U.S.A.
75 F5 El Mirage U.S.A.
45 E4 El Moral Spain
8 E4 Elmore Austr.
91 D2 El Morro mt Arg.
54 B2 El Mreyyé reg. Maur.
43 H1 Elmshorn Ger.
55 E3 El Muglad Sudan
69 G3 Elmwood Can.
68 C5 Elmwood IL U.S.A.
68 A3 Elmwood WI U.S.A.
36 K5 Elnesvågen Norway
89 B3 El Nevado, Cerro mt Col.
31 A4 El Nido Phil.
55 F3 El Obeid Sudan
89 C3 Elorza Venez.
54 C1 El Oued Alg.
75 G5 Eloy U.S.A.
84 A1 El Palmito Mex.
89 E2 El Pao Bolívar Venez.
89 C2 El Pao Cojedes Venez.
68 C5 El Paso IL U.S.A.
73 F6 El Paso TX U.S.A.
40 C2 Elphin U.K.
74 C3 El Portal U.S.A.
45 H2 El Prat de Llobregat Spain
84 E4 El Progreso Guatemala
45 C4 El Puerto de Santa María Spain
El Qâhira see Cairo
16 D6 El Qantara Egypt
16 E7 El Quweira Jordan
77 D5 El Reno U.S.A.
84 B2 El Retorno Mex.
68 B4 Elroy U.S.A.
84 B2 El Rucio Mex.
64 B2 Elsa Can.
16 C7 El Saff Egypt
84 B1 El Salado Mex.
16 D6 El Sâlhîya Egypt
84 A2 El Salto Mex.
84 B1 El Salvador Mex.
31 C4 El Salvador Phil.
61 K8 El Salvador country Central America
89 C3 El Samán de Apure Venez.
69 F1 Elsas Can.
43 G2 Else r. Ger.
23 H2 Elsen Nur l. China
16 D7 El Shatt Egypt
89 D2 El Sombrero Venez.
91 C2 El Sosneado Arg.
El Suweis see Suez
84 C2 El Tajin Ruins Mex.
95 L9 Eltanin Fracture Zone sea feature Pac. Oc.
48 C6 El Tarf Alg.
45 C1 El Teleno mt Spain
84 C3 El Tepozteco, Parque Nacional nat. park Mex.
16 E7 El Thamad Egypt
89 D2 El Tigre Venez.
84 E3 El Tigre, Parque Nacional nat. park Guatemala
43 J5 Eltmann Ger.
89 C2 El Tocuyo Venez.
51 H5 El'ton Rus. Fed.
51 H5 El'ton, Ozero l. Rus. Fed.
72 C2 Eltopia U.S.A.
89 E2 El Toro Venez.
91 E2 El Trébol Arg.
89 C3 El Tuparro, Parque Nacional nat. park Col.
55 F2 El Tur Egypt
88 B8 El Turbio Chile
21 C2 Eluru India
37 U7 Elva Estonia
89 A3 El Valle Col.
40 E5 Elvanfoot U.K.
45 C3 Elvas Port.
37 M6 Elverum Norway
89 B3 El Viejo mt Col.
89 C2 El Vigía Venez.
86 D5 Elvira Brazil
56 E3 El Wak Kenya
68 E5 Elwood U.S.A.
43 J3 Elxleben Ger.
39 H5 Ely U.K.
68 B2 Ely MN U.S.A.
75 E2 Ely NV U.S.A.
80 B4 Elyria U.S.A.
43 G4 Elz Ger.
43 H2 Elze Ger.
7 G3 Émaé i. Vanuatu
18 D2 Emāmrūd Iran
19 H2 Emām Şaḩeb Afgh.
17 L5 Emāmzadeh Naşrod Dīn Iran
37 O8 Emån r. Sweden
90 B2 Emas, Parque Nacional das nat. park Brazil
14 D2 Emba Kazak.
59 H3 Embalenhle S. Africa
65 G3 Embarras Portage Can.
90 C2 Emborcação, Represa de resr Brazil
81 F2 Embrun Can.
56 D4 Embu Kenya
42 F1 Emden Ger.
27 B4 Emei China
27 B4 Emei Shan mt China
8 E4 Emerald Vic. Austr.
6 E4 Emerald Austr.
67 G3 Emeril Can.
65 K5 Emerson Can.
16 B2 Emet Turkey
59 J2 Emgwenya S. Africa
75 E3 Emigrant Valley v. U.S.A.
59 J2 Emijindini S. Africa
55 D3 Emi Koussi mt Chad
84 E3 Emiliano Zapata Mex.
49 M3 Eminska Planina h. Bulg.
16 C2 Emir D. mt Turkey
16 C2 Emirdağ Turkey
37 O8 Emmaboda Sweden
37 S7 Emmaste Estonia
42 D2 Emmeloord Neth.
42 F4 Emmelshausen Ger.
42 E2 Emmen Neth.
46 D7 Emmen Switz.
42 E3 Emmerich Ger.
21 E3 Emmiganuru India
77 C6 Emory Pk summit U.S.A.
82 E3 Empalme Mex.
59 J4 Empangeni S. Africa
88 E3 Empedrado Arg.
94 E3 Emperor Seamount Chain sea feature Pac. Oc.
48 E3 Empoli Italy
76 E4 Emporia KS U.S.A.
80 E6 Emporia VA U.S.A.
80 E4 Emporium U.S.A.
65 G4 Empress Can.
19 E3 'Emrānī Iran
42 F2 Ems r. Ger.
69 H3 Emsdale Can.
42 F2 Emsdetten Ger.
42 F1 Ems-Jade-Kanal canal Ger.
42 F2 Emsland reg. Ger.
59 H3 Emzinoni S. Africa
36 N5 Enafors Sweden
25 F7 Enarotali Indon.
29 E7 Ena-san mt Japan
82 A2 Encantada, Co de la mt Mex.
91 G1 Encantadas, Serra das h. Brazil
31 B3 Encanto, Cape pt Phil.
84 B2 Encarnación Mex.
88 E3 Encarnación Para.
77 D6 Encinal U.S.A.
74 D5 Encinitas U.S.A.
73 F5 Encino U.S.A.
8 B3 Encounter Bay b. Austr.
90 E1 Encruzilhada Brazil
91 G1 Encruzilhada do Sul Brazil
64 D4 Endako Can.
32 B5 Endau Malaysia
6 E3 Endeavour Strait chan. Austr.
25 E7 Endeh Indon.
92 D4 Enderby Land reg. Ant.
81 E3 Endicott U.S.A.
64 C3 Endicott Arm in. U.S.A.
62 C3 Endicott Mts mts U.S.A.
91 E3 Energía Arg.
51 E6 Enerhodar Ukr.
94 F5 Enewetak i. Pac. Oc.
48 D6 Enfidaville Tunisia
81 G3 Enfield U.S.A.
68 E2 Engadine U.S.A.
36 L5 Engan Norway
31 B2 Engaño, Cape c. Phil.
Engaños, Río de los r. see Yari
28 H2 Engaru Japan
59 G5 Engcobo S. Africa
51 H5 Engel's Rus. Fed.
42 C1 Engelschmangat chan. Neth.
33 B4 Enggano i. Indon.
42 C4 Enghien Belgium
34 E3 England div. U.K.
67 J3 Englee Can.
79 E5 Englehard U.S.A.
69 H2 Englehart Can.
39 D7 English Channel str. France/U.K.
51 G7 Enguri r. Georgia
59 J4 Enhlalakahle S. Africa
77 D4 Enid U.S.A.
28 G3 Eniwa Japan
42 D2 Enkhuizen Neth.
37 P7 Enköping Sweden
48 F6 Enna Sicily Italy
65 J2 Ennadai Lake l. Can.
55 E3 En Nahud Sudan
55 E3 Ennedi, Massif mts Chad
41 D4 Ennell, Lough l. Rep. of Ireland
76 C2 Enning U.S.A.
41 C5 Ennis Rep. of Ireland
72 E2 Ennis MT U.S.A.
77 D5 Ennis TX U.S.A.
41 E5 Enniscorthy Rep. of Ireland
41 D3 Enniskillen U.K.
41 B5 Ennistymon Rep. of Ireland
46 G7 Enns r. Austria
36 W5 Eno Fin.
75 F3 Enoch U.S.A.
36 S2 Enontekiö Fin.
27 D6 Enping China
31 B2 Enrile Phil.
42 D2 Ens Neth.
8 F4 Ensay Austr.
42 E2 Enschede Neth.
43 G3 Ense Ger.
91 F2 Ensenada Arg.
82 A2 Ensenada Mex.
27 C4 Enshi China
64 F2 Enterprise N.W.T. Can.
69 J3 Enterprise Ont. Can.
79 C6 Enterprise AL U.S.A.
72 C2 Enterprise OR U.S.A.
75 F3 Enterprise UT U.S.A.
64 F4 Entrance Can.
86 F8 Entre Ríos Bol.
91 E2 Entre Ríos div. Arg.
45 B3 Entroncamento Port.
54 C4 Enugu Nigeria
13 V3 Enurmino Rus. Fed.
86 D5 Envira Brazil
86 D5 Envira r. Brazil
9 C5 Enys, Mt mt N.Z.
29 F7 Enzan Japan
42 D2 Epe Neth.
44 H2 Épernay France
75 G2 Ephraim U.S.A.
81 E4 Ephrata PA U.S.A.
72 C2 Ephrata WA U.S.A.
7 G3 Épi i. Vanuatu
44 H2 Épinal France
16 D4 Episkopi Cyprus
48 E4 Epomeo, Monte h. Italy
39 H6 Epping U.K.
43 G4 Eppstein Ger.
39 G6 Epsom U.K.
91 D3 Epu-pel Arg.
18 D4 Eqlīd Iran
53 E5 Equatorial Guinea country Africa
89 E3 Equeipa Venez.
31 A4 Eran Phil.
31 A4 Eran Bay b. Phil.
16 F1 Erbaa Turkey
43 L5 Erbendorf Ger.
95 L3 Erben Tablemount depth Pac. Oc.
42 F5 Erbeskopf h. Ger.
17 J2 Erçek Turkey
17 J2 Erciş Turkey
16 E2 Erciyes Dağı mt Turkey
47 J7 Érd Hungary
23 H2 Erdaogou China
30 D2 Erdao Jiang r. China
16 A1 Erdek Turkey
16 E3 Erdemli Turkey
26 C1 Erdenetsogt Mongolia
55 E3 Erdi reg. Chad
51 H6 Erdniyevskiy Rus. Fed.
89 D3 Erebato r. Venez.
92 B5 Erebus, Mt mt Ant.
17 K6 Erech Iraq
88 F3 Erechim Brazil
24 D2 Ereentsav Mongolia
16 E3 Ereğli Konya Turkey
16 C1 Ereğli Zonguldak Turkey
48 F6 Erei, Monti mts Sicily Italy
26 D1 Erenhot China
18 E3 Eresk Iran
45 D2 Eresma r. Spain
49 K5 Eretria Greece
Erevan see Yerevan
43 K4 Erfurt Ger.
17 G2 Ergani Turkey
54 B2 'Erg Chech sand dunes Alg./Mali
55 D3 Erg du Djourab sand dunes Chad
54 D3 Erg du Ténéré des. Niger
26 C1 Ergel Mongolia
49 M4 Ergene r. Turkey
54 B2 Erg Iguidi sand dunes Alg./Maur.
37 T8 Ērgļi Latvia
28 A1 Ergu China
Ergun He r. see Argun'
30 C3 Erhulai China
40 D2 Eriboll, Loch in. U.K.
40 D4 Ericht, Loch l. U.K.
68 B5 Erie IL U.S.A.
77 E4 Erie KS U.S.A.
80 C3 Erie PA U.S.A.
69 G4 Erie, Lake l. Can./U.S.A.
28 H3 Erimo Japan
28 H4 Erimo-misaki c. Japan
40 A3 Eriskay i. U.K.
52 H4 Eritrea country Africa
16 E2 Erkilet Turkey
43 K5 Erlangen Ger.
6 D4 Erldunda Austr.
30 E2 Erlong Shan mt China
30 C2 Erlongshan Sk. resr China
42 D2 Ermelo Neth.
59 H3 Ermelo S. Africa
16 D3 Ermenek Turkey
49 L6 Ermoupoli Greece
21 B4 Ernakulam India
21 B4 Erode India
58 A1 Erongo div. Namibia
42 D3 Erp Neth.
54 B1 Er Rachidia Morocco
55 F3 Er Rahad Sudan
57 D5 Errego Moz.
48 D7 Er Remla Tunisia
41 C2 Errigal h. Rep. of Ireland
41 A3 Erris Head hd Rep. of Ireland
81 H2 Errol U.S.A.
7 G3 Erromango i. Vanuatu
49 J4 Ersekë Albania
76 D2 Erskine U.S.A.
36 R5 Ersmark Sweden
51 G5 Ertil' Rus. Fed.
8 B1 Erudina Austr.
17 J3 Eruh Turkey
91 G2 Erval Brazil
80 D5 Erwin U.S.A.
43 G3 Erwitte Ger.
43 K2 Erxleben Sachsen-Anhalt Ger.
43 K2 Erxleben Sachsen-Anhalt Ger.
43 L4 Erzgebirge mts Czech Rep./Ger.
16 F3 Erzin Turkey
17 G2 Erzincan Turkey
17 H2 Erzurum Turkey
28 G4 Esan-misaki pt Japan
28 G4 Esashi Japan
28 H2 Esashi Japan
37 L9 Esbjerg Denmark
75 G3 Escalante U.S.A.
75 G3 Escalante r. U.S.A.
75 F3 Escalante Desert des. U.S.A.
68 D3 Escanaba U.S.A.
84 E3 Escárcega Mex.
31 B2 Escarpada Point pt Phil.
45 F2 Escatrón Spain
42 B4 Escaut r. Belgium
42 D3 Esch Neth.
42 E2 Esche Ger.
43 J2 Eschede Ger.
42 D5 Esch-sur-Alzette Lux.
43 J3 Eschwege Ger.
42 E4 Eschweiler Ger.
74 D5 Escondido U.S.A.
84 A2 Escuinapa Mex.
84 E4 Escuintla Guatemala
84 D4 Escuintla Mex.
89 C3 Escutillas Col.
16 B3 Eşen Turkey
18 D2 Esenguly Turkm.
42 F1 Esens Ger.
18 C3 Eşfahan Iran
18 D4 Esfandāran Iran
18 C4 Esfarjan Iran
19 E3 Eshāqābād Iran
18 D5 Eshkanān Iran
59 J4 Eshowe S. Africa
16 E6 Esh Sharā mts Jordan
18 C3 Eshtehārd Iran
57 C6 Esigodini Zimbabwe
59 K4 Esikhawini S. Africa
38 D2 Esk r. U.K.
40 E5 Eskdalemuir U.K.
67 G3 Esker Can.
36 F4 Eskifjörður Iceland
37 P7 Eskilstuna Sweden
62 E3 Eskimo Lakes l. Can.
17 J3 Eski Mosul Iraq
16 D1 Eskipazar Turkey
16 C2 Eskişehir Turkey
45 D1 Esla r. Spain
18 B3 Eslāmābād e Gharb Iran
16 B3 Esler D. mt Turkey
43 G3 Eslohe (Sauerland) Ger.
37 N9 Eslöv Sweden
16 B2 Eşme Turkey
86 C3 Esmeraldas Ecuador
68 E1 Esnagi Lake l. Can.
42 B4 Esnes France
19 F5 Espakeh Iran
44 F4 Espalion France
69 G2 Espanola Can.
73 F4 Espanola U.S.A.
86 □ Española, Isla i. Galapagos Is Ecuador
74 A2 Esparto U.S.A.
43 G2 Espelkamp Ger.
6 C5 Esperance Austr.
91 E1 Esperanza Arg.
82 C3 Esperanza Mex.
31 C4 Esperanza Phil.
92 B2 Esperanza Arg. Base Ant.
45 B3 Espichel, Cabo hd Port.
45 D1 Espigüete mt Spain
84 B1 Espinazo Mex.
90 D2 Espinhaço, Serra do mts Brazil
90 D1 Espinosa Brazil
90 E2 Espírito Santo div. Brazil
31 B2 Espiritu Phil.
70 D7 Espíritu Santo i. Mex.
7 G3 Espiritu Santo i. Vanuatu
37 T6 Espoo Fin.
45 F4 Espuña mt Spain
88 B6 Esquel Arg.
64 E5 Esquimalt Can.
31 C5 Essang Indon.
54 B1 Essaouira Morocco
54 A2 Es Semara Western Sahara
42 C3 Essen Belgium
42 F3 Essen Ger.
42 F2 Essen (Oldenburg) Ger.
87 G3 Essequibo r. Guyana
69 F4 Essex Can.
75 E4 Essex U.S.A.
81 G2 Essex Junction U.S.A.
69 F4 Essexville U.S.A.
13 R4 Esso Rus. Fed.
88 D8 Estados, I. de los i. Arg.
18 D4 Eşţahbānāt Iran
69 G2 Estaire Can.
87 L6 Estância Brazil
45 G1 Estats, Pic d' mt France/Spain
59 H4 Estcourt S. Africa
43 H1 Este r. Ger.
45 E1 Estella Spain
45 D4 Estepa Spain
45 D4 Estepona Spain
65 J4 Esterhazy Can.
74 B4 Estero Bay b. U.S.A.
88 D2 Esteros Para.
88 E3 Esteros del Iberá marsh Arg.
65 J5 Estevan Can.
76 E3 Estherville U.S.A.
67 H4 Est, Île de l' i. Can.
79 D5 Estill U.S.A.
81 J1 Est, Lac de l' l. Can.
35 H3 Estonia country Europe
42 A5 Estrées-St-Denis France
45 C2 Estrela, Serra da mts Port.
45 E3 Estrella mt Spain
45 C3 Estremoz Port.
87 J5 Estrondo, Serra h. Brazil
17 M4 Estūh Iran
22 D4 Etah India
42 D5 Étain France
44 F2 Étampes France
44 E1 Étaples France
22 D4 Etawah India
59 J3 eThandakukhanya S. Africa
58 E4 E'Thembini S. Africa
53 H5 Ethiopia country Africa
16 D2 Etimesğut Turkey
40 C4 Etive, Loch in. U.K.
48 F6 Etna, Monte volc. Sicily Italy
37 J7 Etne Norway
64 C3 Etolin I. i. U.S.A.
57 B5 Etosha National Park Namibia
57 B5 Etosha Pan salt pan Namibia
49 L3 Etropole Bulg.
21 B4 Ettaiyapuram India
42 E5 Ettelbruck Lux.
42 C3 Etten-Leur Neth.
43 G6 Ettlingen Ger.
40 E5 Ettrick Forest reg. U.K.
84 A2 Etzatlán Mex.
8 F2 Euabalong Austr.
Euboea i. see Evvoia
6 C5 Eucla Austr.
80 C4 Euclid U.S.A.
87 L6 Euclides da Cunha Brazil
8 G4 Eucumbene, L. l. Austr.
8 B3 Eudunda Austr.
79 C6 Eufaula U.S.A.
77 E5 Eufaula Lake resr U.S.A.
72 B2 Eugene U.S.A.
82 A3 Eugenia, Pta c. Mex.
8 G2 Eugowra Austr.
8 G1 Eumungerie Austr.
77 E6 Eunice U.S.A.
42 E4 Eupen Belgium
17 K6 Euphrates r. Asia
37 S6 Eura Fin.
44 E2 Eure r. France
72 A3 Eureka CA U.S.A.
72 D1 Eureka MT U.S.A.
75 E2 Eureka NV U.S.A.
8 C1 Eurinilla r. Austr.
8 C1 Euriowie Austr.
8 E4 Euroa Austr.
57 E6 Europa, Île i. Ind. Ocean
45 D4 Europa Point pt Gibraltar
42 C3 Europoort reg. Neth.
42 E4 Euskirchen Ger.
8 D3 Euston Austr.
64 D4 Eutsuk Lake l. Can.
79 C5 Eutaw U.S.A.
43 L3 Eutzsch Ger.
59 H3 Evander S. Africa
64 F4 Evansburg Can.
92 B3 Evans Ice Stream ice feature Ant.
66 E3 Evans, L. l. Can.
73 F4 Evans, Mt mt CO U.S.A.
72 D2 Evans, Mt mt MT U.S.A.
63 K3 Evans Strait Can.
68 D4 Evanston IL U.S.A.
72 E3 Evanston WY U.S.A.
69 F3 Evansville Can.
78 C4 Evansville IN U.S.A.
68 C4 Evansville WI U.S.A.
72 F3 Evansville WY U.S.A.
68 E4 Evart U.S.A.
59 G3 Evaton S. Africa
18 D5 Evaz Iran
68 A2 Eveleth U.S.A.
13 R3 Evensk Rus. Fed.
6 D4 Everard Range h. Austr.
42 D3 Everdingen Neth.
23 F4 Everest, Mt mt China
81 K1 Everett Can.
72 B1 Everett U.S.A.
42 B3 Evergem Belgium
79 D7 Everglades Nat. Park U.S.A.
79 D7 Everglades, The swamp U.S.A.
77 G6 Evergreen U.S.A.
39 F5 Evesham U.K.
39 F5 Evesham, Vale of reg. U.K.
36 S5 Evijärvi Fin.
54 D4 Evinayong Equatorial Guinea
37 K7 Evje Norway
45 C3 Évora Port.
24 F1 Evoron, Ozero l. Rus. Fed.
17 K2 Evowghlī Iran
44 E2 Évreux France
49 K6 Evrotas r. Greece
16 D4 Evrychou Cyprus
49 L5 Evvoia i. Greece
74 □1 Ewa Beach U.S.A.
56 D3 Ewaso Ngiro r. Kenya
40 C3 Ewe, Loch in. U.K.
92 B2 Ewing I. i. Ant.
86 E6 Exaltación Bol.
59 G4 Excelsior S. Africa
74 C2 Excelsior Mtn mt U.S.A.
74 C2 Excelsior Mts mts U.S.A.
76 E4 Excelsior Springs U.S.A.
39 D6 Exe r. U.K.
92 A4 Executive Committee Range mts Ant.
8 H3 Exeter Austr.
69 G4 Exeter Can.
39 D7 Exeter U.K.
74 C3 Exeter CA U.S.A.
81 H3 Exeter NH U.S.A.
42 E2 Exloo Neth.
39 D7 Exminster U.K.
39 D6 Exmoor Forest reg. U.K.
39 D6 Exmoor National Park U.K.
81 F6 Exmore U.S.A.
39 D7 Exmouth U.K.
6 B4 Exmouth Gulf b. Austr.
8 G1 Exmouth, Mt mt Austr.
93 M5 Exmouth Plateau sea feature Ind. Ocean
45 D3 Extremadura div. Spain
79 E7 Exuma Sound chan. Bahamas
56 D4 Eyasi, Lake salt l. Tanz.
39 J5 Eye U.K.
40 F5 Eyemouth U.K.
40 B2 Eye Peninsula pen. U.K.
36 D5 Eyjafjallajökull ice cap Iceland
36 D3 Eyjafjörður in. Iceland
56 E3 Eyl Somalia
39 F6 Eynsham U.K.
6 D4 Eyre, Lake (North) salt flat Austr.
6 D4 Eyre, Lake (South) salt flat Austr.
9 B6 Eyre Mountains mts N.Z.
6 D5 Eyre Peninsula pen. Austr.
43 H2 Eystrup Ger.
36 □ Eysturoy i. Faroe Is
59 J4 Ezakheni S. Africa
59 H3 Ezenzeleni S. Africa
91 C3 Ezequiel Ramos Mexía, Embalse resr Arg.
50 J2 Ezhva Rus. Fed.
49 M5 Ezine Turkey
16 F1 Ezinepazar Turkey
17 L6 Ezra's Tomb Iraq

F

21 A5 Faadhippolhu Atoll Maldives
77 B6 Fabens U.S.A.
64 F2 Faber Lake l. Can.
32 □ Faber, Mt h. Sing.
37 M9 Fåborg Denmark
48 E3 Fabriano Italy
89 B3 Facatativá Col.
42 B4 Faches-Thumesnil France
54 D3 Fachi Niger
81 F4 Factoryville U.S.A.
88 B7 Facundo Arg.
54 C3 Fada-Ngourma Burkina
48 D2 Faenza Italy
Faeroes terr. see Faroe Islands
25 F7 Fafanlap Indon.
56 E3 Fafen Shet' watercourse Eth.
49 L2 Făgăraş Romania
37 L6 Fagernes Norway
37 O7 Fagersta Sweden
88 C8 Fagnano, L. l. Arg./Chile
42 C4 Fagne reg. Belgium
54 B3 Faguibine, Lac l. Mali
36 E5 Fagurhólsmýri Iceland
55 F4 Fagwir Sudan
19 E4 Fahraj Iran
62 D3 Fairbanks U.S.A.
80 B5 Fairborn U.S.A.
76 D3 Fairbury U.S.A.
80 E5 Fairfax U.S.A.
74 A2 Fairfield CA U.S.A.
68 B5 Fairfield IA U.S.A.
78 C4 Fairfield OH U.S.A.
77 D6 Fairfield TX U.S.A.
81 G3 Fair Haven U.S.A.
41 E2 Fair Head hd U.K.
31 A4 Fairie Queen sand bank Phil.
40 G1 Fair Isle i. U.K.
76 E3 Fairmont MN U.S.A.
80 C5 Fairmont WV U.S.A.
73 F4 Fairplay U.S.A.
68 D3 Fairport U.S.A.
80 C4 Fairport Harbor U.S.A.
64 F3 Fairview Can.
69 E3 Fairview MI U.S.A.
77 D4 Fairview OK U.S.A.
75 G2 Fairview UT U.S.A.
27 □ Fairview Park H.K. China
64 B3 Fairweather, Cape c. U.S.A.
64 B3 Fairweather, Mt mt Can./U.S.A.
25 G6 Fais i. Micronesia
22 C3 Faisalabad Pak.
42 C5 Faissault France
76 C2 Faith U.S.A.
40 □ Faither, The pt U.K.
23 E4 Faizabad India
7 J2 Fakaofo i. Tokelau
39 H5 Fakenham U.K.
36 O5 Fåker Sweden
25 F7 Fakfak Indon.

18 D4 Fakhrabad Iran
30 B2 Faku China
39 C7 Fal r. U.K.
54 A4 Falaba Sierra Leone
44 D2 Falaise France
23 G4 Falakata India
23 H5 Falam Myanmar
18 C3 Falavarjan Iran
77 D7 Falcon Lake l. Mex./U.S.A.
77 D7 Falfurrias U.S.A.
64 F3 Falher Can.
43 M3 Falkenberg Ger.
37 N8 Falkenberg Sweden
43 L1 Falkenhagen Ger.
43 L3 Falkenhain Ger.
43 M2 Falkensee Ger.
43 L5 Falkenstein Ger.
40 E5 Falkirk U.K.
40 E4 Falkland U.K.
85 D8 Falkland Islands terr. Atl. Ocean
88 D8 Falkland Sound chan. Falkland Is
37 N7 Falköping Sweden
74 D5 Fallbrook U.S.A.
43 H2 Fallingbostel Ger.
74 C2 Fallon U.S.A.
81 H4 Fall River U.S.A.
72 F3 Fall River Pass U.S.A.
76 E3 Falls City U.S.A.
39 B7 Falmouth U.K.
80 A5 Falmouth KY U.S.A.
81 H3 Falmouth ME U.S.A.
68 E3 Falmouth MI U.S.A.
58 C7 False Bay b. S. Africa
37 M9 Falster i. Denmark
47 N7 Fălticeni Romania
37 O6 Falun Sweden
16 D4 Famagusta Cyprus
42 E5 Fameck France
42 D4 Famenne v. Belgium
65 K4 Family L. l. Can.
26 F4 Fanchang China
41 E4 Fane r. Rep. of Ireland
32 A1 Fang Thai.
26 D3 Fangcheng China
27 C4 Fangdou Shan mts China
27 F6 Fang-liao Taiwan
26 E2 Fangshan Beijing China
26 D2 Fangshan Shanxi China
27 F6 Fangshan Taiwan
26 D3 Fang Xian China
28 A2 Fangzheng China
27 □ Fanling H.K. China
40 C3 Fannich, Loch l. U.K.
19 E5 Fannūj Iran
48 E3 Fano Italy
27 F5 Fanshan China
26 D2 Fanshi China
27 B6 Fan Si Pan mt Vietnam
19 F2 Farab Turkm.
56 C3 Faradje Congo(Zaire)
57 E6 Farafangana Madag.
55 E2 Farafra Oasis oasis Egypt
19 F3 Farāh Afgh.
19 F4 Farah Rūd r. Afgh.
89 A4 Farallones de Cali, Parque Nacional nat. park Col.
54 A3 Faranah Guinea
25 G6 Faraulep Atoll Micronesia
39 F7 Fareham U.K.
9 D4 Farewell, Cape c. N.Z.
9 D4 Farewell Spit spit N.Z.
37 N7 Färgelanda Sweden
76 D2 Fargo U.S.A.
76 E2 Faribault U.S.A.
67 F2 Faribault, Lac l. Can.
22 D3 Faridabad India
22 C3 Faridkot India
23 G5 Faridpur Bangl.
54 A3 Farim Guinea-Bissau
19 E3 Farīmān Iran
37 P8 Färjestaden Sweden
19 H2 Farkhor Tajik.
17 M4 Farmahin Iran
68 C5 Farmer City U.S.A.
66 D2 Farmer Island i. Can.
64 E3 Farmington Can.
68 B5 Farmington IA U.S.A.
68 B5 Farmington IL U.S.A.
81 H2 Farmington ME U.S.A.
81 H3 Farmington NH U.S.A.
75 H3 Farmington NM U.S.A.
72 E3 Farmington UT U.S.A.
64 D4 Far Mt. mt Can.
80 D6 Farmville U.S.A.
39 G6 Farnborough U.K.
38 F2 Farne Islands is U.K.
39 G6 Farnham U.K.
64 F4 Farnham, Mt mt Can.
87 G4 Faro Brazil
64 C2 Faro Can.
45 C4 Faro Port.
37 Q8 Fårö i. Sweden
34 E2 Faroe Islands terr. Atl. Ocean
37 Q8 Fårösund Sweden
53 K7 Farquhar Group is Seychelles
18 D4 Farrāshband Iran
80 C4 Farrell U.S.A.
69 K3 Farrellton Can.
19 E3 Farrokhī Iran
Farrukhabad see Fatehgarh
18 D3 Farsakh Iran
49 K5 Farsala Greece
19 F3 Fārsī Afgh.
72 E3 Farson U.S.A.
37 K7 Farsund Norway
Farvel, Kap c. see Uummannarsuaq
77 C5 Farwell U.S.A.
18 D4 Fasā Iran
48 G4 Fasano Italy
43 J2 Faßberg Ger.
80 E4 Fassett U.S.A.
51 D5 Fastiv Ukr.
22 D4 Fatehgarh India
22 C4 Fatehpur Rajasthan India
22 E4 Fatehpur Uttar Pradesh India
18 D4 Fathābād Iran
69 G3 Fathom Five National Marine Park Can.
54 A3 Fatick Senegal
44 H2 Faulquemont France
59 F4 Fauresmith S. Africa
36 O3 Fauske Norway
75 F1 Faust U.S.A.
48 E6 Favignana, Isola i. Sicily Italy
64 G4 Fawcett Can.
39 F7 Fawley U.K.
66 C3 Fawn r. Can.
36 B4 Faxaflói b. Iceland
36 P5 Faxälven r. Sweden
27 B5 Faxian Hu l. China
55 D3 Faya Chad
68 D3 Fayette U.S.A.
77 E4 Fayetteville AR U.S.A.
79 E5 Fayetteville NC U.S.A.
79 C5 Fayetteville TN U.S.A.
16 D6 Fâyid Egypt
17 M7 Faylakah i. Kuwait
54 C4 Fazao Malfakassa, Parc National de nat. park Togo
22 C3 Fazilka India
18 C5 Fazrān, J. h. S. Arabia
54 A2 Fdérik Maur.
41 B5 Feale r. Rep. of Ireland
79 E5 Fear, Cape c. U.S.A.
74 B2 Feather Falls U.S.A.
9 E4 Featherston N.Z.
8 F4 Featherston, Mt Austr.
44 E2 Fécamp France
91 F1 Federación Arg.
88 E4 Federal Arg.
46 E3 Fehmarn i. Ger.
43 L2 Fehrbellin Ger.
90 E3 Feia, Lagoa lag. Brazil
26 E4 Feidong China
26 F3 Feihuanghe Kou est. China
86 D5 Feijó Brazil
9 E4 Feilding N.Z.
87 L6 Feira de Santana Brazil
26 E4 Feixi China
16 E3 Feke Turkey
45 H3 Felanitx Spain
68 D3 Felch U.S.A.
43 M1 Feldberg Ger.
46 D7 Feldberg mt Ger.
46 D7 Feldkirch Austria
46 G7 Feldkirchen in Kärnten Austria
91 E1 Feliciano r. Arg.
90 D2 Felixlândia Brazil
39 J6 Felixstowe U.K.
48 D1 Feltre Italy
37 M5 Femunden l. Norway
37 N5 Femundsmarka Nasjonalpark nat. park Norway
26 D2 Fen r. China
48 D3 Fenaio, Punta del pt Italy
75 H4 Fence Lake U.S.A.
69 H3 Fenelon Falls Can.
49 L4 Fengari mt Greece
27 E4 Fengcheng Jiangxi China
30 C3 Fengcheng Liaoning China
27 C4 Fengdu China
27 C5 Fenggang China
30 D1 Fengguang China
27 F6 Fenghua China
27 C5 Fenghuang China
26 C4 Fengjie China
27 D6 Fengkai China
27 F6 Fenglin Taiwan
26 F2 Fengnan China
26 E1 Fengning China
26 E3 Fengqiu China
27 C5 Fengshan China
27 E6 Fengshun China
26 E3 Fengtai China
27 E4 Fengxin China
26 E3 Fengyang China
26 D1 Fengzhen China
23 G5 Feni Bangl.
7 F2 Feni Is is P.N.G.
44 F5 Fenille, Col de la pass France
68 B4 Fennimore U.S.A.
57 E5 Fenoarivo Atsinanana Madag.
39 G5 Fens, The reg. U.K.
69 F4 Fenton U.S.A.
26 D2 Fenxi China
26 D2 Fenyang China
27 E5 Fenyi China
51 E6 Feodosiya Ukr.
48 B6 Fer, Cap de hd Alg.
19 E3 Ferdows Iran
14 F2 Fergana Uzbek.
69 G4 Fergus Can.
76 D2 Fergus Falls U.S.A.
6 F2 Fergusson I. i. P.N.G.
48 C7 Fériana Tunisia
54 B4 Ferkessédougou Côte d'Ivoire
48 E3 Fermo Italy
67 G3 Fermont Can.
45 C2 Fermoselle Spain
41 C5 Fermoy Rep. of Ireland
79 D6 Fernandina Beach U.S.A.
86 □ Fernandina, Isla i. Galapagos Is Ecuador
88 B8 Fernando de Magallanes, Parque Nacional nat. park Chile
96 G6 Fernando de Noronha i. Atl. Ocean
90 B3 Fernandópolis Brazil
72 B1 Ferndale U.S.A.
39 F7 Ferndown U.K.
64 F5 Fernie Can.
74 C2 Fernley U.S.A.
81 F4 Fernridge U.S.A.
41 E5 Ferns Rep. of Ireland
72 C2 Fernwood U.S.A.
48 D2 Ferrara Italy
90 B3 Ferreiros Brazil
77 F6 Ferriday U.S.A.
48 C4 Ferro, Capo pt Sardinia Italy
45 B1 Ferrol Spain
75 G2 Ferron U.S.A.
42 D1 Ferwerd Neth.
54 B1 Fès Morocco
56 B4 Feshi Congo(Zaire)
65 K5 Fessenden U.S.A.
76 F4 Festus U.S.A.
40 □ Fethaland, Point of pt U.K.
41 D5 Fethard Rep. of Ireland
16 B3 Fethiye Turkey
40 □ Fetlar i. U.K.
40 F4 Fettercairn U.K.
43 K5 Feucht Ger.
43 J5 Feuchtwangen Ger.
67 F2 Feuilles, Rivière aux r. Can.
16 F3 Fevzipaşa Turkey
19 H2 Feyzābād Afgh.
19 E3 Feyzābād Iran
Fez see Fès
39 D5 Ffestiniog U.K.
57 E6 Fianarantsoa Madag.
56 D3 Fichē Eth.
43 L4 Fichtelgebirge reg. Ger.
59 G4 Ficksburg S. Africa
64 F4 Field B.C. Can.
69 G2 Field Ont. Can.
49 H4 Fier Albania
68 E3 Fife Lake U.S.A.
40 F4 Fife Ness pt U.K.
8 F2 Fifield Austr.
68 B3 Fifield U.S.A.
44 F4 Figeac France
45 B2 Figueira da Foz Port.
45 H1 Figueres Spain
54 B1 Figuig Morocco
4 J6 Fiji country Pac. Oc.
88 D2 Filadélfia Para.
92 B3 Filchner Ice Shelf ice feature Ant.
38 G3 Filey U.K.
49 J5 Filippiada Greece
37 O7 Filipstad Sweden
36 L5 Fillan Norway
74 C4 Fillmore CA U.S.A.
75 F2 Fillmore UT U.S.A.
92 C3 Fimbulheimen mts Ant.
92 C3 Fimbulisen ice feature Ant.
81 F2 Finch Can.
40 E3 Findhorn r. U.K.
17 H3 Fındık Turkey
80 B4 Findlay U.S.A.
6 E6 Fingal Austr.
66 E5 Finger Lakes l. U.S.A.
57 D5 Fingoè Moz.
16 C3 Finike Turkey
16 C3 Finike Körfezi b. Turkey
Finisterre, Cape c. see Fisterra, Cabo
35 H2 Finland country Europe
37 S7 Finland, Gulf of g. Europe
64 D3 Finlay r. Can.
64 D3 Finlay, Mt mt Can.
8 E3 Finley Austr.
43 K3 Finne ridge Ger.
36 P2 Finnsnes Norway
37 O7 Finspång Sweden
41 D3 Fintona U.K.
41 C3 Fintown Rep. of Ireland
40 C3 Fionn Loch l. U.K.
40 B4 Fionnphort U.K.
9 A6 Fiordland National Park N.Z.
Firat r. see Euphrates
74 B3 Firebaugh U.S.A.
65 J2 Firedrake Lake l. Can.
81 G4 Fire Island National Seashore res. U.S.A.
Firenze see Florence
17 K6 Firk, Sha'īb watercourse Iraq
88 E2 Firmat Arg.
44 G4 Firminy France
43 J6 Firngrund reg. Ger.
47 Q2 Firovo Rus. Fed.
22 B3 Firoza Pak.
22 D4 Firozabad India
19 G3 Firozkoh reg. Afgh.
22 C3 Firozpur India
81 H2 First Connecticut L. l. U.S.A.
18 D4 Fīrūzābād Iran
Firuzabad see Rāsk
42 F5 Fischbach Ger.
57 B6 Fish r. Namibia
58 D5 Fish r. S. Africa
92 B6 Fisher Bay b. Ant.
81 F6 Fisherman I. i. U.S.A.
81 H4 Fishers I. i. U.S.A.
65 N2 Fisher Strait chan. Can.
39 C6 Fishguard U.K.
64 E2 Fish Lake l. Can.
68 A2 Fish Lake l. MN U.S.A.
75 G2 Fish Lake l. UT U.S.A.
27 □ Fish Ponds l. H.K. China
69 F4 Fish Pt pt U.S.A.
92 B3 Fiske, C. c. Ant.
Fiskenæsset see Qeqertarsuatsiaat
42 B5 Fismes France
45 B1 Fisterra Spain
45 B1 Fisterra, Cabo c. Spain
81 H3 Fitchburg U.S.A.
65 G3 Fitzgerald Can.
79 D6 Fitzgerald U.S.A.
88 C7 Fitz Roy Arg.
6 C3 Fitzroy Crossing Austr.
69 G3 Fitzwilliam I. i. Can.
41 D3 Fivemiletown U.K.
48 D2 Fivizzano Italy
56 C4 Fizi Congo(Zaire)
37 L6 Flå Norway
59 H5 Flagstaff S. Africa
75 G4 Flagstaff U.S.A.
81 H2 Flagstaff Lake l. U.S.A.
66 E2 Flaherty Island i. Can.
68 B3 Flambeau r. U.S.A.
38 G3 Flamborough Head hd U.K.
43 L2 Fläming h. Ger.
72 E3 Flaming Gorge Res. l. U.S.A.
58 D5 Flaminksvlei salt pan S. Africa
42 A4 Flandre reg. France
40 A2 Flannan Isles is U.K.
36 O4 Flåsjön l. Sweden
68 E4 Flat r. U.S.A.
72 D2 Flathead L. l. U.S.A.
72 D2 Flathead Lake l. U.S.A.
9 E4 Flat Point pt N.Z.
72 A1 Flattery, C. c. U.S.A.
6 E3 Flattery, C. pt Austr.
43 K2 Fleetmark Ger.
38 D4 Fleetwood U.K.
81 F4 Fleetwood U.S.A.
37 K7 Flekkefjord Norway
80 E3 Fleming U.S.A.
80 B5 Flemingsburg U.S.A.
37 P7 Flen Sweden
46 D3 Flensburg Ger.
44 D2 Flers France
69 G3 Flesherton Can.
65 H2 Fletcher Lake l. Can.
69 F3 Fletcher Pond l. U.S.A.
92 B3 Fletcher Prom. hd Ant.
6 E3 Flinders r. Austr.
6 B5 Flinders Bay b. Austr.
6 E5 Flinders I. i. Austr.
8 A2 Flinders Ranges mts Austr.
8 B1 Flinders Ranges Nat. Park Austr.
65 J4 Flin Flon Can.
39 D4 Flint U.K.
69 F4 Flint U.S.A.
79 C6 Flint r. GA U.S.A.
69 F4 Flint r. MI U.S.A.
5 M6 Flint I. i. Kiribati
37 N6 Flisa Norway
38 E2 Flodden U.K.
43 M4 Flöha Ger.
43 M4 Flöha r. Ger.
92 A4 Flood Ra. mts Ant.
68 A2 Floodwood U.S.A.
78 B4 Flora U.S.A.
44 F4 Florac France
42 E5 Florange France
69 F4 Florence Can.
48 D3 Florence Italy
79 C5 Florence AL U.S.A.
75 G5 Florence AZ U.S.A.
76 D4 Florence KS U.S.A.
80 C5 Florence OH U.S.A.
72 A3 Florence OR U.S.A.
79 E5 Florence SC U.S.A.
75 G5 Florence Junction U.S.A.
81 K1 Florenceville Can.
89 B4 Florencia Col.
42 C4 Florennes Belgium
88 C6 Florentino Ameghino, Embalse resr Arg.
82 G5 Flores Guatemala
25 E7 Flores i. Indon.
91 E2 Flores r. Arg.
90 C1 Flores de Goiás Brazil
25 D7 Flores Sea Indon.
87 L5 Floresta Brazil
87 K5 Floriano Brazil
88 G3 Florianópolis Brazil
91 F2 Florida Uru.
79 D6 Florida div. U.S.A.
79 D7 Florida Bay b. U.S.A.
79 D7 Florida City U.S.A.
7 G2 Florida Is is Solomon Is
71 K7 Florida Keys is FL U.S.A.
83 H4 Florida, Straits of str. Bahamas/U.S.A.
49 J4 Florina Greece
37 J6 Florø Norway
67 H3 Flour Lake l. Can.
68 A4 Floyd IA U.S.A.
80 C6 Floyd VA U.S.A.
77 C5 Floydada U.S.A.
75 F4 Floyd, Mt mt U.S.A.
42 D2 Fluessen l. Neth.
80 C5 Fly U.S.A.
6 E2 Fly r. P.N.G.
49 H3 Foča Bos.-Herz.
40 E3 Fochabers U.K.
59 G3 Fochville S. Africa
49 M2 Focşani Romania
27 D6 Fogang China
48 F4 Foggia Italy
54 □ Fogo i. Cape Verde
67 K4 Fogo I. i. Can.
40 D2 Foinaven h. U.K.
44 E5 Foix France
36 O3 Folda chan. Norway
36 N4 Foldereid Norway
36 M4 Foldfjorden chan. Norway
49 L6 Folegandros i. Greece
69 F1 Foleyet Can.
48 E3 Foligno Italy
39 J6 Folkestone U.K.
39 G5 Folkingham U.K.
79 D6 Folkston U.S.A.
37 M5 Folldal Norway
48 D3 Follonica Italy
74 B2 Folsom Lake l. U.S.A.
51 G6 Fomin Rus. Fed.
50 J2 Fominskiy Rus. Fed.
65 H3 Fond-du-Lac Can.
68 C4 Fond du Lac U.S.A.
65 J3 Fond du Lac r. Can.
45 B2 Fondevila Spain
48 E4 Fondi Italy
7 H2 Fongafale Tuvalu
48 C4 Fonni Sardinia Italy
82 G6 Fonseca, G. de b. Central America
67 F3 Fontanges Can.
64 E3 Fontas Can.
64 E3 Fontas r. Can.
86 E4 Fonte Boa Brazil
44 D3 Fontenay-le-Comte France
36 F3 Fontur pt Iceland
69 H3 Foot's Bay Can.
26 C3 Foping China
8 G2 Forbes Austr.
72 C1 Forbes, Mt mt Can.
43 K5 Forchheim Ger.
67 G2 Ford r. Can.
68 D2 Ford r. U.S.A.
37 J6 Førde Norway
65 K2 Forde Lake l. Can.
39 H5 Fordham U.K.
39 F7 Fordingbridge U.K.
92 A4 Ford Ra. mts Ant.
77 E5 Fordyce U.S.A.
54 A4 Forécariah Guinea
39 F7 Foreland hd U.K.
39 D6 Foreland Point pt U.K.
64 D4 Foresight Mtn mt Can.
69 G4 Forest Can.
77 F5 Forest MS U.S.A.
80 B4 Forest OH U.S.A.
81 G3 Forest Dale U.S.A.
8 F3 Forest Hill Austr.
74 B2 Foresthill U.S.A.
68 A3 Forest Lake U.S.A.
79 C5 Forest Park U.S.A.
67 G4 Forestville Can.
40 F4 Forfar U.K.
72 A2 Forks U.S.A.
81 J2 Forks, The U.S.A.
80 E4 Forksville U.S.A.
48 E2 Forlì Italy
38 D4 Formby U.K.
45 G3 Formentera i. Spain
45 H3 Formentor, Cap de pt Spain
90 D3 Formiga Brazil
88 E3 Formosa Arg.
90 C1 Formosa Brazil
87 G6 Formosa, Serra h. Brazil
90 D1 Formoso r. Brazil
40 E3 Forres U.K.
8 D5 Forrest Vic. Austr.
68 C5 Forrest U.S.A.
77 F5 Forrest City U.S.A.
68 C4 Forreston U.S.A.
36 P5 Fors Sweden
6 E3 Forsayth Austr.
36 S3 Forsnäs Sweden
37 S6 Forssa Fin.
77 E4 Forsyth MO U.S.A.
72 F2 Forsyth MT U.S.A.
69 J1 Forsythe Can.
22 C3 Fort Abbas Pak.
66 D3 Fort Albany Can.
87 L4 Fortaleza Brazil
75 H5 Fort Apache U.S.A.
64 G4 Fort Assiniboine Can.
68 C4 Fort Atkinson U.S.A.
40 D3 Fort Augustus U.K.
59 G6 Fort Beaufort S. Africa
72 E2 Fort Benton U.S.A.
65 H3 Fort Black Can.
74 A2 Fort Bragg U.S.A.
Fort-Chimo see Kuujjuaq
65 G3 Fort Chipewyan Can.
77 D5 Fort Cobb Res. resr U.S.A.
72 F3 Fort Collins U.S.A.
69 J3 Fort-Coulonge Can.
81 F2 Fort Covington U.S.A.
77 C6 Fort Davis U.S.A.
83 M6 Fort-de-France Martinique
79 C5 Fort Deposit U.S.A.
76 E3 Fort Dodge U.S.A.
76 E1 Fort Frances U.S.A.
66 E3 Fort George Can.
62 F3 Fort Good Hope Can.
40 D4 Forth r. U.K.
40 F4 Forth, Firth of est. U.K.
75 E2 Fortification Range mts U.S.A.
88 D2 Fortín Capitán Demattei Para.
88 D2 Fortín General Mendoza Para.
88 E2 Fortín Madrejón Para.
88 D2 Fortín Pilcomayo Arg.
86 F7 Fortín Ravelo Bol.
86 F7 Fortín Suárez Arana Bol.
81 J1 Fort Kent U.S.A.
79 D7 Fort Lauderdale U.S.A.
64 E2 Fort Liard Can.
68 B3 Fort McCoy U.S.A.
65 G3 Fort Mackay Can.
64 G5 Fort Macleod Can.
65 G3 Fort McMurray Can.
62 E3 Fort McPherson Can.
68 B5 Fort Madison U.S.A.
72 G3 Fort Morgan U.S.A.
79 D7 Fort Myers U.S.A.
64 E3 Fort Nelson Can.
64 E3 Fort Nelson r. Can.
64 D2 Fort Norman Can.
79 C5 Fort Payne U.S.A.
72 F1 Fort Peck U.S.A.
72 F2 Fort Peck Res. resr U.S.A.
79 D7 Fort Pierce U.S.A.
76 C2 Fort Pierre U.S.A.
64 F2 Fort Providence Can.
65 J4 Fort Qu'Appelle Can.
64 G2 Fort Resolution Can.
9 B7 Fortrose N.Z.
40 D3 Fortrose U.K.
74 A2 Fort Ross U.S.A.
66 E3 Fort Rupert Can.
64 E4 Fort St James Can.
64 E3 Fort St John Can.
64 G4 Fort Saskatchewan Can.
77 E4 Fort Scott U.S.A.
66 C2 Fort Severn Can.
14 D2 Fort-Shevchenko Rus. Fed.
64 E2 Fort Simpson Can.
65 G2 Fort Smith Can.
77 E5 Fort Smith U.S.A.
77 C6 Fort Stockton U.S.A.
73 F5 Fort Sumner U.S.A.
72 A3 Fortuna U.S.A.
76 C1 Fortune U.S.A.
67 J4 Fortune B. b. Can.
64 F3 Fort Vermilion Can.
79 C6 Fort Walton Beach U.S.A.
68 E5 Fort Wayne U.S.A.
40 C4 Fort William U.K.
77 D5 Fort Worth U.S.A.
62 D3 Fort Yukon U.S.A.
18 D5 Forūr, Jazīreh-ye i. Iran
36 N4 Forvik Norway
27 D6 Foshan China
48 B2 Fossano Italy
8 F5 Foster Austr.
63 Q2 Foster B. b. Greenland
64 B3 Foster, Mt mt Can./U.S.A.
80 B4 Fostoria U.S.A.
39 G4 Fotherby U.K.
44 D2 Fougères France
40 □ Foula i. U.K.
39 H6 Foulness Point pt U.K.
21 C4 Foul Pt pt Sri Lanka
9 C4 Foulwind, Cape c. N.Z.
54 D4 Foumban Cameroon
92 B3 Foundation Ice Stream ice feature Ant.
54 A3 Foundiougne Senegal
68 A4 Fountain U.S.A.
44 G2 Fourches, Mont des h. France
74 D4 Four Corners U.S.A.
59 H4 Fouriesburg S. Africa
42 C4 Fourmies France
49 M6 Fournoi i. Greece
68 C2 Fourteen Mile Pt pt U.S.A.
54 A3 Fouta Djallon reg. Guinea
9 A7 Foveaux Strait str. N.Z.
79 E7 Fowl Cay i. Bahamas
73 F4 Fowler CO U.S.A.
68 D5 Fowler IN U.S.A.
68 E4 Fowler MI U.S.A.
92 B3 Fowler Pen. pen. Ant.
6 D5 Fowlers Bay Austr.
17 M3 Fowman Iran
65 L3 Fox r. Can.
68 C4 Fox r. U.S.A.
64 F4 Fox Creek Can.
38 C3 Foxdale U.K.
63 K3 Foxe Basin g. Can.
63 K3 Foxe Channel str. Can.
63 L3 Foxe Peninsula Can.
9 C5 Fox Glacier N.Z.
64 G3 Fox Lake Can.
68 C4 Fox Lake U.S.A.
9 E4 Foxton N.Z.
40 D3 Foyers U.K.
41 D3 Foyle r. Rep. of Ireland/U.K.
41 D2 Foyle, Lough b. Rep. of Ireland/U.K.
41 B5 Foynes Rep. of Ireland
57 B5 Foz do Cunene Angola
90 A4 Foz do Iguaçu Brazil
45 G2 Fraga Spain
92 D4 Framnes Mts mts Ant.
90 C3 Franca Brazil
7 G3 Français, Récif des rf New Caledonia
34 E4 France country Europe
8 C4 Frances Austr.
64 D2 Frances r. Can.
64 D2 Frances Lake Can.
64 D2 Frances Lake l. Can.
68 D5 Francesville U.S.A.
56 B4 Franceville Gabon
76 D3 Francis Case, Lake l. U.S.A.
84 B1 Francisco I. Madero Coahuila Mex.
84 A1 Francisco I. Madero Durango Mex.
90 D2 Francisco Sá Brazil
81 H2 Francis, Lake l. U.S.A.
57 C6 Francistown Botswana
64 D4 François Lake l. Can.
72 E3 Francs Peak summit U.S.A.
42 D1 Franeker Neth.
43 M4 Frankenberg Ger.
43 G3 Frankenberg (Eder) Ger.
69 F4 Frankenmuth U.S.A.
43 G5 Frankenthal (Pfalz) Ger.
43 K4 Frankenwald forest Ger.
59 H3 Frankfort S. Africa
68 D5 Frankfort IN U.S.A.
78 C4 Frankfort KY U.S.A.
68 D3 Frankfort MI U.S.A.
43 G4 Frankfurt am Main Ger.
46 G4 Frankfurt an der Oder Ger.
75 E1 Frankin Lake l. U.S.A.
43 K5 Fränkische Alb reg. Ger.
43 K5 Fränkische Schweiz reg. Ger.
72 E3 Franklin ID U.S.A.
78 C4 Franklin IN U.S.A.
77 F6 Franklin LA U.S.A.
81 H3 Franklin MA U.S.A.
79 D5 Franklin NC U.S.A.
81 H3 Franklin NH U.S.A.
81 F4 Franklin NJ U.S.A.
80 D4 Franklin PA U.S.A.
79 C5 Franklin TN U.S.A.
80 E6 Franklin VA U.S.A.
80 D5 Franklin WV U.S.A.
62 F3 Franklin Bay b. Can.
72 C1 Franklin D. Roosevelt Lake l. U.S.A.
92 B5 Franklin I. i. Ant.
64 E2 Franklin Mountains Can.
9 A6 Franklin Mts mts N.Z.
63 J2 Franklin Str. Can.
8 E5 Frankston Austr.
37 P5 Fränsta Sweden
68 E1 Franz Can.
9 C5 Franz Josef Glacier N.Z.
12 G2 Franz Josef Land is Rus. Fed.
48 C5 Frasca, Capo della pt Sardinia Italy
48 E4 Frascati Italy
64 E4 Fraser r. B.C. Can.
67 H2 Fraser r. Nfld Can.
58 D5 Fraserburg S. Africa
40 F3 Fraserburgh U.K.
66 D4 Fraserdale Can.
7 F4 Fraser Island i. Austr.
64 E4 Fraser Lake Can.
64 E4 Fraser Plateau plat. Can.
9 F3 Frasertown N.Z.
68 E2 Frater Can.
46 D7 Frauenfeld Switz.
91 E2 Fray Bentos Uru.
42 E4 Frechen Ger.
38 E4 Freckleton U.K.
68 E3 Frederic MI U.S.A.
68 A3 Frederic WI U.S.A.
37 L9 Fredericia Denmark
80 E5 Frederick MD U.S.A.
77 D5 Frederick OK U.S.A.
77 D6 Fredericksburg TX U.S.A.
80 E5 Fredericksburg VA U.S.A.
64 C3 Frederick Sound chan. U.S.A.
77 F4 Fredericktown U.S.A.
67 G4 Fredericton Can.
Frederikshåb see Paamiut
37 M8 Frederikshavn Denmark
37 N9 Frederiksværk Denmark
75 F3 Fredonia AZ U.S.A.
80 D3 Fredonia NY U.S.A.
36 Q4 Fredrika Sweden
37 M7 Fredrikstad Norway
81 F4 Freehold U.S.A.
81 F4 Freeland U.S.A.
74 C2 Freel Peak summit U.S.A.
76 D3 Freeman U.S.A.
68 D5 Freeman, Lake l. U.S.A.
68 C4 Freeport IL U.S.A.
81 H3 Freeport ME U.S.A.
81 G4 Freeport NY U.S.A.
77 E6 Freeport TX U.S.A.
79 E7 Freeport City Bahamas
77 D7 Freer U.S.A.
59 G4 Free State div. S. Africa
54 A4 Freetown Sierra Leone
45 C3 Fregenal de la Sierra Spain
44 C2 Fréhel, Cap pt France
46 C6 Freiburg im Breisgau Ger.
42 F5 Freisen Ger.
46 E6 Freising Ger.
46 G6 Freistadt Austria
44 H5 Fréjus France
6 B5 Fremantle Austr.
68 E4 Fremont MI U.S.A.
76 D3 Fremont NE U.S.A.
80 B4 Fremont OH U.S.A.
75 G2 Fremont r. U.S.A.
80 B6 Frenchburg U.S.A.
80 C4 French Creek r. U.S.A.
85 E2 French Guiana terr. S. America
8 E5 French I. i. Austr.
74 C2 Frenchman U.S.A.
65 H5 Frenchman r. Can./U.S.A.
74 B2 Frenchman L. l. CA U.S.A.
75 E3 Frenchman L. l. NV U.S.A.
41 C4 Frenchpark Rep. of Ireland
9 D4 French Pass N.Z.
5 N6 French Polynesia terr. Pac. Oc.
3 □ French Southern and Antarctic Lands terr. Southern Ocean
81 J1 Frenchville U.S.A.
42 F2 Freren Ger.
41 D5 Freshford Rep. of Ireland
75 G6 Fresnal Canyon U.S.A.
84 B2 Fresnillo Mex.
74 C3 Fresno U.S.A.
74 C3 Fresno r. U.S.A.
45 H3 Freu, Cap des pt Spain
43 F4 Freudenberg Ger.
46 D6 Freudenstadt Ger.
42 A4 Frévent France
43 L1 Freyenstein Ger.
44 H2 Freyming-Merlebach France
91 D1 Freyre Arg.
54 A3 Fria Guinea
74 C3 Friant U.S.A.
88 C3 Frias Arg.
46 C7 Fribourg Switz.
43 F1 Friedeburg Ger.
43 M1 Friedland Ger.
46 D7 Friedrichshafen Ger.
81 J3 Friendship U.S.A.
43 L2 Friesack Ger.
42 D1 Friese Wad tidal flats Neth.
43 F1 Friesoythe Ger.
39 J6 Frinton-on-Sea U.K.
77 D6 Frio r. U.S.A.
40 B4 Frisa, Loch l. U.K.
75 F2 Frisco Mt mt U.S.A.
43 H3 Fritzlar Ger.
63 M3 Frobisher Bay b. Can.
65 H3 Frobisher Lake l. Can.
36 L5 Frohavet b. Norway
43 L3 Frohburg Ger.
42 A5 Froissy France
51 G5 Frolovo Rus. Fed.
50 K2 Frolovskaya Rus. Fed.
39 E6 Frome U.K.
8 B1 Frome Downs Austr.
6 D5 Frome, Lake salt flat Austr.
43 F3 Fröndenberg Ger.
84 D3 Frontera Mex.
84 D3 Frontera, Pta pt Mex.
80 D5 Front Royal U.S.A.
48 E4 Frosinone Italy
80 D5 Frostburg U.S.A.
36 L5 Frøya i. Norway
42 A4 Fruges France
75 H2 Fruita U.S.A.
75 G1 Fruitland U.S.A.
46 C7 Frutigen Switz.
47 J6 Frýdek-Místek Czech Rep.
81 H2 Fryeburg U.S.A.
27 F5 Fu'an China
27 D5 Fuchuan China
27 F4 Fuchun Jiang r. China
40 A3 Fuday i. U.K.
27 E5 Fude China
27 F5 Fuding China
45 E2 Fuenlabrada Spain
45 D3 Fuente Obejuna Spain
88 E2 Fuerte Olimpo Para.
54 A2 Fuerteventura i. Canary Is
31 B2 Fuga i. Phil.
26 E3 Fugou China
26 D2 Fugu China
17 J4 Fuḩaymī Iraq
20 E4 Fujairah U.A.E.
29 F7 Fuji Japan
27 E5 Fujian div. China
26 C4 Fu Jiang r. China
29 F7 Fuji-Hakone-Izu National Park Japan
28 B1 Fujin China
29 F7 Fujinomiya Japan
29 F7 Fuji-san volc. Japan
28 H3 Fukagawa Japan
29 D7 Fukuchiyama Japan
29 A8 Fukue Japan
29 A8 Fukue-jima i. Japan
29 E6 Fukui Japan
29 B8 Fukuoka Japan
29 G6 Fukushima Japan
29 B9 Fukuyama Japan
18 D2 Fūlād Maïalleh Iran
43 H4 Fulda Ger.
43 H3 Fulda r. Ger.
39 G6 Fulham U.K.
26 E3 Fuliji China
27 C4 Fuling China
65 M2 Fullerton, Cape hd Can.
68 B5 Fulton IL U.S.A.
78 B4 Fulton KY U.S.A.
76 F4 Fulton MO U.S.A.
81 E3 Fulton NY U.S.A.
59 K2 Fumane Moz.
42 C5 Fumay France
29 F7 Funabashi Japan
7 H2 Funafuti i. Tuvalu
54 A1 Funchal Port.
89 B2 Fundación Col.
45 C2 Fundão Port.
67 G5 Fundy, Bay of g. Can.
67 G4 Fundy Nat. Park Can.
74 D3 Funeral Peak summit U.S.A.
57 D6 Funhalouro Moz.
26 F3 Funing Jiangsu China
27 B6 Funing Yunnan China
26 D3 Funiu Shan mts China
54 C3 Funtua Nigeria
40 □ Funzie U.K.
27 F5 Fuqing China
30 D2 Fur r. China
28 H3 Furano Japan
18 E5 Fürgun, Kūh-e mt Iran
50 G3 Furmanov Rus. Fed.
28 D3 Furmanovo Rus. Fed.
74 D3 Furnace Creek U.S.A.
90 C3 Furnas, Represa resr Brazil
6 E6 Furneaux Group is Austr.
43 F2 Fürstenau Ger.
43 M1 Fürstenberg Ger.
46 G4 Fürstenwalde Ger.
43 J5 Fürth Ger.
43 L5 Furth im Wald Ger.
28 G3 Furubira Japan
28 G5 Furukawa Japan
63 K3 Fury and Hecla Strait str. Can.
89 B3 Fusagasugá Col.
27 C7 Fushan Hainan China
30 A5 Fushan Shandong China
30 B3 Fushun Liaoning China
30 B3 Fushun Liaoning China
27 B4 Fushun Sichuan China
30 B3 Fushuncheng China
30 D2 Fusong China
27 C6 Fusui China
29 B8 Futago-san volc. Japan
7 H3 Futuna i. Vanuatu
27 E5 Futun Xi r. China
26 C3 Fu Xian China
30 A2 Fuxin Liaoning China
30 A2 Fuxin Liaoning China
28 F5 Fuya Japan
26 E3 Fuyang Anhui China
27 F4 Fuyang Zhejiang China
26 E2 Fuyang r. China
24 E2 Fuyu Heilongjiang China
30 C1 Fuyu China
27 B5 Fuyuan China
27 F5 Fuzhou Fujian China
27 E5 Fuzhou Jiangxi China
30 A4 Fuzhou Wan b. China
17 L2 Füzuli Azer.
37 M9 Fyn i. Denmark
40 C5 Fyne, Loch in. U.K.
F.Y.R.O.M. country see Macedonia

G

48 C6 Gaâfour Tunisia
56 E3 Gaalkacyo Somalia
59 F2 Gabane Botswana
74 D2 Gabbs U.S.A.
74 C2 Gabbs Valley Range mts U.S.A.
57 B5 Gabela Angola
54 D1 Gabès Tunisia
55 D1 Gabès, Golfe de g. Tunisia
8 G4 Gabo I. i. Austr.
53 F6 Gabon country Africa
57 C6 Gaborone Botswana
19 E5 Gābrīk Iran
19 E5 Gābrīk watercourse Iran
49 L3 Gabrovo Bulg.
54 A3 Gabú Guinea-Bissau
18 C2 Gach Sār Iran
18 C4 Gach Sārān Iran
21 A3 Gadag India
36 O4 Gäddede Sweden
43 K1 Gadebusch Ger.
22 B5 Gadhra India
22 B4 Gadra Pak.
79 C5 Gadsden U.S.A.
21 B2 Gadwal India
36 S2 Gædnovuoppe Norway
39 D6 Gaer U.K.
49 L2 Găeşti Romania
48 E4 Gaeta Italy
48 E4 Gaeta, Golfo di g. Italy
4 F4 Gaferut i. Micronesia
79 D5 Gaffney U.S.A.
54 C1 Gafsa Tunisia
50 E4 Gagarin Rus. Fed.
50 H4 Gagino Rus. Fed.
54 B4 Gagnoa Côte d'Ivoire
67 G3 Gagnon Can.
51 G7 Gagra Georgia
17 L4 Gahvāreh Iran
58 C3 Gaiab watercourse Namibia
23 G4 Gaibandha Bangl.
43 H6 Gaildorf Ger.
44 E5 Gaillac France

79 D6 Gainesville FL U.S.A.
79 D5 Gainesville GA U.S.A.
77 D5 Gainesville TX U.S.A.
39 G4 Gainsborough U.K.
6 D5 Gairdner, Lake salt flat Austr.
40 C3 Gairloch U.K.
40 C3 Gair Loch in. U.K.
30 B3 Gai Xian China
21 C2 Gajapatinagaram India
19 G5 Gajar Pak.
58 E3 Gakarosa mt S. Africa
22 C1 Gakuch Jammu and Kashmir
23 G3 Gala China
19 G2 Galaasiya Uzbek.
16 C7 Galâla el Baharîya, G. el plat. Egypt
56 D4 Galana r. Kenya
40 F5 Galashiels U.K.
49 N2 Galați Romania
49 H4 Galatina Italy
80 C6 Galax U.S.A.
41 C5 Galbally Rep. of Ireland
37 L6 Galdhøpiggen summit Norway
84 B1 Galeana Mex.
18 D5 Galeh Dār Iran
68 B4 Galena U.S.A.
89 E2 Galeota Pt pt Trinidad and Tobago
89 E2 Galera Pt pt Trinidad and Tobago
84 C4 Galera, Pta pt Mex.
91 B4 Galera, Punta pt Chile
68 B5 Galesburg U.S.A.
58 F4 Galeshewe S. Africa
68 B3 Galesville U.S.A.
80 E4 Galeton U.S.A.
51 G7 Gali Georgia
50 G3 Galich Rus. Fed.
50 G2 Galichskaya Vozvyshennost' reg. Rus. Fed.
45 C1 Galicia div. Spain
16 E5 Galilee, Sea of l. Israel
80 B4 Galion U.S.A.
48 C6 Galite, Canal de la chan. Tunisia
75 G5 Galiuro Mts mts U.S.A.
55 F3 Gallabat Sudan
79 C4 Gallatin U.S.A.
72 E2 Gallatin r. U.S.A.
21 C5 Galle Sri Lanka
88 B8 Gallegos r. Arg.
89 C1 Gallinas, Pta pt Col.
48 H4 Gallipoli Italy
80 B5 Gallipolis U.S.A.
36 R3 Gällivare Sweden
36 O5 Gällö Sweden
81 E3 Gallo I. i. U.S.A.
75 H4 Gallo Mts mts U.S.A.
40 D6 Galloway, Mull of c. U.K.
75 H4 Gallup U.S.A.
19 G1 Gallyaaral Uzbek.
40 B4 Galmisdale U.K.
8 G3 Galong Austr.
21 C4 Galoya Sri Lanka
21 C5 Gal Oya r. Sri Lanka
40 D5 Galston U.K.
74 B2 Galt U.S.A.
54 A2 Galtat Zemmour Western Sahara
41 C5 Galtee Mountains h. Rep. of Ireland
41 C5 Galtymore h. Rep. of Ireland
19 E3 Galūgāh-e Āsīyeh Iran
68 B5 Galva U.S.A.
77 E6 Galveston U.S.A.
77 E6 Galveston Bay b. U.S.A.
91 E2 Galvez Arg.
23 E3 Galwa Nepal
41 B4 Galway Rep. of Ireland
41 B4 Galway Bay g. Rep. of Ireland
27 B6 Gâm r. Vietnam
39 J8 Gamaches France
59 J5 Gamalakhe S. Africa
89 B2 Gamarra Col.
23 G3 Gamba China
56 D3 Gambēla Eth.
56 D3 Gambela National Park Eth.
62 A3 Gambell U.S.A.
22 D4 Gambhir r. India
52 C4 Gambia, The country Africa
5 O7 Gambier, Îles is Pac. Oc.
67 K4 Gambo Can.
56 B4 Gamboma Congo
75 H4 Gamerco U.S.A.
37 P8 Gamleby Sweden
36 S4 Gammelstaden Sweden
58 C4 Gamoep S. Africa
28 B3 Gamova, Mys pt Rus. Fed.
21 C5 Gampola Sri Lanka
19 F4 Gamshadzai K. mts Iran
10 J10 Gan Maldives
26 A3 Gana China
75 H4 Ganado U.S.A.
69 J3 Gananoque Can.
18 C4 Ganāveh Iran
17 L1 Gäncä Azer.
27 C7 Gancheng China
Gand see Gent
33 E3 Gandadiwata, Bukit mt Indon.
23 G3 Gandaingoin China
56 C4 Gandajika Congo(Zaire)
23 E4 Gandak Dam dam Nepal
22 B3 Gandari Mountain mt Pak.
22 A3 Gandava Pak.
67 K4 Gander Can.
43 G1 Ganderkesee Ger.
45 G2 Gandesa Spain
22 C5 Gandevi India
22 B5 Gāndhīdhām India
22 C5 Gandhinagar India
22 C4 Gāndhi Sāgar resr India
22 C4 Gāndhi Sāgar Dam dam India
45 F3 Gandía Spain
19 F4 Gand-i-Zureh plain Afgh.
90 E1 Gandu Brazil
21 C5 Ganga r. Sri Lanka
91 C4 Gangán Arg.
22 C3 Ganganagar India
22 D4 Gangapur India
23 H5 Gangaw Myanmar
21 B3 Gangawati India
26 A2 Gangca China
22 E3 Gangdisê Shan mts China
44 F5 Ganges France
23 G5 Ganges, Mouths of the est. Bangl./India
22 D3 Gangoh India
22 D3 Gangotri mt India
23 G4 Gangtok India
26 B3 Gangu China
21 D2 Ganjam India
18 C4 Ganjgūn Iran
27 E4 Gan Jiang r. China
27 B4 Ganluo China
8 F3 Ganmain Austr.
44 F3 Gannat France
72 E3 Gannett Peak summit U.S.A.
22 C5 Ganora India
26 C2 Ganquan China
58 C7 Gansbaai S. Africa
26 B3 Gansu div. China
26 B2 Gantang China
51 G7 Gant'iadi Georgia
27 E5 Gan Xian China
58 F3 Ganyesa S. Africa
26 F3 Ganyu China
27 E5 Ganzhou China
55 F4 Ganzi Sudan
54 B3 Gao Mali
27 E4 Gao'an China
26 E2 Gaocheng China
26 F4 Gaochun China
27 E4 Gaohebu China
26 B2 Gaolan China
26 F2 Gaomi China
27 D5 Gaomutang China
26 D3 Gaoping China
26 A2 Gaotai China
26 E2 Gaotang China
26 C2 Gaotouyao China
54 B3 Gaoua Burkina
54 A3 Gaoual Guinea
27 B4 Gao Xian China
26 E2 Gaoyang China
26 E2 Gaoyi China
26 F3 Gaoyou China
26 F3 Gaoyou Hu l. China
27 D6 Gaozhou China
44 H4 Gap France
31 B3 Gapan Phil.
45 F5 Gap Carbon hd Alg.
22 E2 Gar China
19 F4 Garagheh Iran
41 C4 Gara, Lough l. Rep. of Ireland
56 C3 Garamba r. Congo(Zaire)
56 C3 Garamba, Parc National de la nat. park Congo(Zaire)
87 L5 Garanhuns Brazil
59 G2 Ga-Rankuwa S. Africa
56 D3 Garba Tula Kenya
74 A1 Garberville U.S.A.
18 C3 Garbosh, Kūh-e mt Iran
43 H2 Garbsen Ger.
90 C3 Garça Brazil
90 B1 Garças, Rio das r. Brazil
23 G2 Garco China
17 K1 Gardabani Georgia
48 D2 Garda, Lago di l. Italy
48 B6 Garde, Cap de hd Alg.
43 K2 Gardelegen Ger.
76 C4 Garden City U.S.A.
68 D3 Garden Corners U.S.A.
74 C5 Garden Grove U.S.A.
65 L4 Garden Hill Can.
68 E3 Garden I. i. U.S.A.
78 C2 Garden Pen. pen. U.S.A.
19 H3 Gardez Afgh.
81 J2 Gardiner ME U.S.A.
72 E2 Gardiner MT U.S.A.
81 G4 Gardiners I. i. U.S.A.
68 C5 Gardner U.S.A.
81 K2 Gardner Lake l. U.S.A.
5 L2 Gardner Pinnacles is HI U.S.A.
74 C2 Gardnerville U.S.A.
40 D4 Garelochhead U.K.
68 E2 Gargantua, Cape c. Can.
17 M6 Gargar Iran
37 R9 Gargždai Lith.
22 D5 Garhakota India
22 E5 Garhchiroli India
22 A3 Garhi Khairo Pak.
22 D4 Garhi Malehra India
64 E5 Garibaldi, Mt mt Can.
64 E5 Garibaldi Prov. Park nat. park Can.
59 F5 Gariep Dam resr S. Africa
58 B5 Garies S. Africa
48 E4 Garigliano r. Italy
56 D4 Garissa Kenya
37 T8 Garkalne Latvia
80 D4 Garland PA U.S.A.
77 D5 Garland TX U.S.A.
18 C2 Garmī Iran
47 E7 Garmisch-Partenkirchen Ger.
18 D3 Garmsar Iran
19 F4 Garmsel reg. Afgh.
76 E4 Garnett U.S.A.
8 D2 Garnpung Lake l. Austr.
23 G4 Gāro Hills h. India
44 D4 Garonne r. France
56 E3 Garoowe Somalia
88 G3 Garopaba Brazil
54 D4 Garoua Cameroon
91 D3 Garré Arg.
75 E2 Garrison U.S.A.
41 F2 Garron Point pt U.K.
19 G4 Garruk Pak.
65 J1 Garry Lake l. Can.
40 D4 Garry, Loch l. U.K.
40 B2 Garrynahine U.K.
56 E4 Garsen Kenya
39 D5 Garth U.K.
43 K1 Gartow Ger.
58 B3 Garub Namibia
33 C4 Garut Indon.
41 E3 Garvagh U.K.
40 D3 Garve U.K.
68 D5 Gary U.S.A.
23 E3 Garyarsa China
29 C7 Garyū-zan mt Japan
22 D2 Gar Zangbo r. China
24 B3 Garzê China
89 B4 Garzón Col.
44 D5 Gascogne reg. France
76 E4 Gasconade r. U.S.A.
44 C5 Gascony, Gulf of g. France/Spain
6 B4 Gascoyne r. Austr.
Gascuña, Golfo de g. see Gascony, Gulf of
22 D2 Gasherbrum mt China/Jammu and Kashmir
19 F5 Gasht Iran
54 D3 Gashua Nigeria
19 E3 Gask Iran
33 C3 Gaspar, Selat chan. Indon.
67 H4 Gaspé Can.
67 H4 Gaspé, C. c. Can.
67 G4 Gaspé, Péninsule de pen. Can.
67 G4 Gaspésie, Parc de la nat. park Can.
42 E2 Gasselte Neth.
79 D5 Gastonia U.S.A.
91 C4 Gastre Arg.
45 E4 Gata, Cabo de c. Spain
16 D4 Gata, Cape c. Cyprus
50 D3 Gatchina Rus. Fed.
80 B6 Gate City U.S.A.
40 D6 Gatehouse of Fleet U.K.
38 F3 Gateshead U.K.
77 D6 Gatesville U.S.A.
75 H2 Gateway U.S.A.
81 F4 Gateway National Recreational Area res. U.S.A.
69 K3 Gatineau Can.
69 K2 Gatineau r. Can.
18 D4 Gatrūyeh Iran
17 M5 Gatvand Iran
7 H3 Gau i. Fiji
65 K3 Gauer Lake l. Can.
36 M5 Gaula r. Norway
80 C5 Gauley Bridge U.S.A.
42 D5 Gaume reg. Belgium
23 F4 Gauri Sankar mt China
59 G3 Gauteng div. S. Africa
19 G3 Gauzan Afgh.
19 F5 Gavāter Iran
18 D5 Gāvbandī Iran
18 D5 Gāvbūs, Kūh-e mts Iran
49 L7 Gavdos i. Greece
18 B3 Gaveh r. Iran
90 E1 Gavião r. Brazil
17 L4 Gavīleh Iran
74 B4 Gaviota U.S.A.
18 E4 Gav Koshī Iran
37 P6 Gävle Sweden
50 F3 Gavrilov-Yam Rus. Fed.
58 B3 Gawachab Namibia
8 B3 Gawler Austr.
26 A1 Gaxun Nur salt l. China
23 F4 Gaya India
54 C3 Gaya Niger
30 E2 Gaya r. China
68 E3 Gaylord U.S.A.
16 E6 Gaza Gaza
59 K1 Gaza div. Moz.
16 E6 Gaza terr. Asia
20 F1 Gaz-Achak Turkm.
18 D2 Gazandzhyk Turkm.
19 H3 Gazdarra Pass Afgh.
16 F3 Gaziantep Turkey
19 F3 Gazīk Iran
16 D3 Gazipaşa Turkey
19 F1 Gazli Uzbek.
19 E5 Gaz Māhū Iran
19 E4 Gaz Şāleḩ Iran
54 A4 Gbangbatok Sierra Leone
54 B4 Gbarnga Liberia
54 C4 Gboko Nigeria
47 J3 Gdańsk Pol.
47 J3 Gdańsk, Gulf of g. Pol./Rus. Fed.
50 C3 Gdov Rus. Fed.
47 J3 Gdynia Pol.
40 C1 Gealldruig Mhor i. U.K.
43 J3 Gebesee Ger.
55 F3 Gedaref Sudan
43 H4 Gedern Ger.
42 C5 Gedinne Belgium
16 B2 Gediz Turkey
16 A2 Gediz r. Turkey
39 H5 Gedney Drove End U.K.
37 M9 Gedser Denmark
42 D3 Geel Belgium
8 E5 Geelong Austr.
58 D4 Geel Vloer salt pan S. Africa
42 F2 Geeste Ger.
43 J1 Geesthacht Ger.
26 F4 Ge Hu l. China
54 D3 Geidam Nigeria
43 H5 Geiersberg h. Ger.
65 J3 Geikie r. Can.
42 E4 Geilenkirchen Ger.
37 L6 Geilo Norway
37 K5 Geiranger Norway
68 E6 Geist Reservoir U.S.A.
43 L3 Geithain Ger.
27 B6 Gejiu China
48 F6 Gela Sicily Italy
56 E3 Geladī Eth.
32 B4 Gelang, Tanjung pt Malaysia
42 E3 Geldern Ger.
51 F6 Gelendzhik Rus. Fed.
47 L3 Gelgaudiškis Lith.
51 C7 Gelibolu Turkey
16 C2 Gelincik Dağı mt Turkey
18 E3 Gelmord Iran
43 H4 Gelnhausen Ger.
42 F3 Gelsenkirchen Ger.
32 B5 Gemas Malaysia
31 C5 Gemeh Indon.
56 B3 Gemena Congo(Zaire)
16 F2 Gemerek Turkey
16 B1 Gemlik Turkey
48 E1 Gemona del Friuli Italy
57 C6 Gemsbok National Park Botswana
58 D3 Gemsbokplein well S. Africa
56 E3 Genalē Wenz r. Eth.
42 C4 Genappe Belgium
91 D3 General Acha Arg.
91 E3 General Alvear Buenos Aires Arg.
91 E1 General Alvear Entre Rios Arg.
91 C2 General Alvear Mendoza Arg.
91 E2 General Belgrano Arg.
92 B3 General Belgrano II Arg. Base Ant.
92 B2 General Bernardo O'Higgins Chile Base Ant.
84 C1 General Bravo Mex.
88 B7 General Carrera, L. l. Chile
84 B1 General Cepeda Mex.
91 F3 General Conesa Buenos Aires Arg.
91 D4 General Conesa Rio Negro Arg.
91 F3 General Guido Arg.
91 F3 General J. Madariaga Arg.
91 E3 General La Madrid Arg.
91 F3 General Lavalle Arg.
91 D2 General Levalle Arg.
31 C4 General Luna Phil.
31 C4 General MacArthur Phil.
91 D2 General Pico Arg.
91 E2 General Pinto Arg.
91 C3 General Roca Arg.
92 B2 General San Martín Arg. Base Ant.
31 C5 General Santos Phil.
84 C1 General Terán Mex.
84 B2 General Vicente Guerrero Mex.
91 D2 General Villegas Arg.
80 D3 Genesee r. U.S.A.
68 B5 Geneseo IL U.S.A.
80 E3 Geneseo NY U.S.A.
59 G3 Geneva S. Africa
Geneva see Genève
68 C5 Geneva IL U.S.A.
76 D3 Geneva NE U.S.A.
80 E3 Geneva NY U.S.A.
80 C4 Geneva OH U.S.A.
Geneva, Lake l. see Léman, Lac
68 C4 Geneva, Lake l. U.S.A.
46 C7 Genève Switz.
45 D4 Genil r. Spain
42 D4 Genk Belgium
42 D3 Gennep Neth.
8 G4 Genoa Austr.
48 C2 Genoa Italy
Genova see Genoa
48 C2 Genova, Golfo di g. Italy
42 B3 Gent Belgium
43 L2 Genthin Ger.
6 B5 Geographe Bay b. Austr.
58 E6 George S. Africa
67 G2 George r. Can.
8 G3 George, L. l. N.S.W. Austr.
8 B4 George, L. l. S.A. Austr.
79 D6 George, L. l. U.S.A.
81 G3 George, Lake l. U.S.A.
9 A6 George Sd in. N.Z.
8 B2 Georgetown S.A. Austr.
79 F7 George Town Bahamas
69 H4 Georgetown Can.
87 G2 Georgetown Guyana
33 B1 George Town Malaysia
54 A3 Georgetown The Gambia
81 F5 Georgetown DE U.S.A.
68 D6 Georgetown IL U.S.A.
78 C4 Georgetown KY U.S.A.
80 B5 Georgetown OH U.S.A.
79 E5 Georgetown SC U.S.A.
77 D6 Georgetown TX U.S.A.
92 B2 George VI Sd chan. Ant.
92 B5 George V Land reg. Ant.
77 D6 George West U.S.A.
10 F5 Georgia country Asia
79 D5 Georgia div. U.S.A.
69 G3 Georgian Bay l. Can.
69 G3 Georgian Bay Island National Park Can.
64 E5 Georgia, Strait of chan. Can.
6 D4 Georgina watercourse Austr.
15 J2 Georgiyevka Kazak.
51 G6 Georgiyevsk Rus. Fed.
50 H3 Georgiyevskoye Rus. Fed.
43 L4 Gera Ger.
42 B4 Geraardsbergen Belgium
87 J6 Geral de Goiás, Serra h. Brazil
9 C6 Geraldine N.Z.
90 C1 Geral do Paraná, Serra h. Brazil
6 B4 Geraldton Austr.
19 E5 Gerāsh Iran
17 H3 Gercüş Turkey
16 D1 Gerede Turkey
16 D1 Gerede r. Turkey
19 G4 Gereshk Afgh.
32 B4 Gerik Malaysia
19 E3 Gerīmenj Iran
76 C3 Gering U.S.A.
72 C3 Gerlach U.S.A.
64 E3 Germansen Landing Can.
80 E5 Germantown U.S.A.
34 F3 Germany country Europe
43 G5 Germersheim Ger.
59 H3 Germiston S. Africa
43 G5 Gernsheim Ger.
42 E4 Gerolstein Ger.
43 J5 Gerolzhofen Ger.
75 G5 Geronimo U.S.A.
8 H3 Gerringong Austr.
43 H4 Gersfeld Ger.
43 J4 Gerstungen Ger.
43 K2 Gerwisch Ger.
23 F2 Gêrzê China
51 E7 Gerze Turkey
42 F3 Gescher Ger.
18 B3 Getcheh, Kūh-e h. Iran
42 D4 Gete r. Belgium
80 E5 Gettysburg PA U.S.A.
76 D2 Gettysburg SD U.S.A.
80 E5 Gettysburg National Military Park res. U.S.A.
27 C5 Getu He r. China
92 A4 Getz Ice Shelf ice feature Ant.
33 A2 Geumapang r. Indon.
8 G2 Geurie Austr.
17 J2 Gevaş Turkey
49 K4 Gevgelija Macedonia
45 E1 Gexto Spain
Gey see Nikshahr
32 □ Geylang Sing.
59 F3 Geysdorp S. Africa
16 C1 Geyve Turkey
58 F2 Ghaap Plateau S. Africa
54 C1 Ghadāmis Libya
18 D2 Ghaem Shahr Iran
22 C3 Ghaggar, Dry Bed of watercourse Pak.
22 E4 Ghaghara r. India
23 F5 Ghaghra India
53 D5 Ghana country Africa
18 D5 Ghanādah, Rās pt U.A.E.
22 C4 Ghanliala India
57 C6 Ghanzi Botswana
58 E1 Ghanzi div. Botswana
16 E6 Gharandal Jordan
54 C1 Ghardaïa Alg.
19 H2 Gharm Tajik.
18 C5 Ghār, Ras al pt S. Arabia
55 D1 Gharyān Libya
54 D2 Ghāt Libya
22 B3 Ghauspur Pak.
55 D3 Ghazal, Bahr el watercourse Chad
54 B1 Ghazaouet Alg.
22 D3 Ghaziabad India
23 E4 Ghazipur India
22 A3 Ghazluna Pak.
19 H3 Ghaznī Afgh.
19 H3 Ghazni r. Afgh.
19 G3 Ghazoor Afgh.
Ghent see Gent
47 M7 Gheorgheni Romania
47 L7 Gherla Romania
48 C3 Ghisonaccia Corsica France
19 G3 Ghizao Afgh.
22 C1 Ghizar Pak.
21 A2 Ghod r. India
23 G4 Ghoraghat Bangl.
19 H3 Ghorband r. Afgh.
19 H3 Ghorband Pass Afgh.
22 B4 Ghotāru India
22 B4 Ghotki Pak.
18 D4 Ghōwrī Iran
23 F4 Ghuari r. India
17 J5 Ghudāf, Wādī al watercourse Iraq
19 J2 Ghūdara Tajik.
22 C6 Ghugus India
22 B4 Ghulam Mohammed Barrage barrage Pak.
19 F3 Ghurian Afgh.
42 A3 Ghyvelde France
32 C3 Gia Đinh Vietnam
51 G6 Giaginskaya Rus. Fed.
49 K4 Giannitsa Greece
59 H4 Giant's Castle mt S. Africa
41 E2 Giant's Causeway U.K.
33 E4 Gianyar Indon.
32 C3 Gia Rai Vietnam
48 F6 Giarre Sicily Italy
48 B2 Giaveno Italy
58 B2 Gibeon Namibia
34 E5 Gibraltar terr. Europe
45 C5 Gibraltar, Strait of str. Morocco/Spain
68 C5 Gibson City U.S.A.
6 C4 Gibson Desert Austr.
24 B2 Gichgeniyn Nuruu mts Mongolia
21 B3 Giddalur India
16 D6 Giddi, G. el h. Egypt
56 D3 Gīdolē Eth.
44 F3 Gien France
43 G4 Gießen Ger.
43 J2 Gifhorn Ger.
64 F3 Gift Lake Can.
29 E7 Gifu Japan
89 B4 Gigante Col.
77 B7 Gigantes, Llanos de los plain Mex.
40 C5 Gigha i. U.K.
45 D1 Gijón Spain
75 F5 Gila r. U.S.A.
75 F5 Gila Bend U.S.A.
75 F5 Gila Bend Mts mts U.S.A.
75 E5 Gila Mts mts U.S.A.
17 K4 Gīlān Garb Iran
17 M1 Giläzi Azer.
75 G5 Gilbert AZ U.S.A.
80 C6 Gilbert WV U.S.A.
6 E3 Gilbert r. Austr.
7 H2 Gilbert Islands is Kiribati
87 J5 Gilbués Brazil
18 E3 Gil Chashmeh Iran
72 E1 Gildford U.S.A.
55 E2 Gilf Kebir Plateau plat. Egypt
64 D4 Gilford I. i. Can.
8 G1 Gilgandra Austr.
56 D4 Gilgil Kenya
22 C2 Gilgit Jammu and Kashmir
22 C2 Gilgit r. Jammu and Kashmir
8 F2 Gilgunnia Austr.
64 D4 Gil Island i. Can.
65 L3 Gillam Can.
68 C3 Gillett U.S.A.
72 F2 Gillette U.S.A.
39 H6 Gillingham Eng. U.K.
39 E6 Gillingham Eng. U.K.
38 F3 Gilling West U.K.
92 D5 Gillock I. i. Ant.
68 D3 Gills Rock U.S.A.
68 D5 Gilman IL U.S.A.
68 B3 Gilman WI U.S.A.
66 E2 Gilmour Island i. Can.
74 B3 Gilroy U.S.A.
81 G3 Gilsum U.S.A.
55 E3 Gimbala, Jebel mt Sudan
56 D3 Gīmbī Eth.
65 K4 Gimli Can.
21 C5 Gin Ganga r. Sri Lanka
21 B3 Gingee India
56 E3 Gīnīr Eth.
48 G4 Ginosa Italy
48 G4 Gioia del Colle Italy
8 E5 Gippsland reg. Austr.
22 B4 Girab India
19 E5 Girān Iran
19 E4 Gīrān Rīg mt Iran
80 C3 Girard U.S.A.
22 B3 Girdao Pak.
19 G5 Girdar Dhor r. Pak.
19 F4 Girdi Iran
16 G1 Giresun Turkey
22 B5 Gir Forest forest India
23 F4 Girīdīh India
8 F1 Girilambone Austr.
22 C5 Girna r. India
45 H2 Girona Spain
44 D4 Gironde est. France
8 F2 Girral Austr.
40 D5 Girvan U.K.
50 E2 Girvas Rus. Fed.
22 E4 Girwan India
9 G3 Gisborne N.Z.
64 E4 Giscome Can.
37 N8 Gislaved Sweden
19 G2 Gissar Range mts Tajik./Uzbek.
56 C4 Gitarama Rwanda
56 C4 Gitega Burundi
48 E3 Giulianova Italy
49 L3 Giurgiu Romania
49 L2 Giuvala, Pasul pass Romania
42 C4 Givet France
44 G4 Givors France
42 C6 Givry-en-Argonne France
59 J1 Giyani S. Africa
16 C7 Giza Pyramids Egypt
19 G1 Gizhduvan Uzbek.
13 S3 Gizhiga Rus. Fed.
49 J4 Gjirokastër Albania
63 J3 Gjoa Haven Can.
36 L5 Gjøra Norway
37 M6 Gjøvik Norway
67 J4 Glace Bay Can.
64 B3 Glacier B. b. U.S.A.
64 B3 Glacier Bay National Park and Preserve U.S.A.
64 F4 Glacier Nat. Park Can.
72 D1 Glacier Nat. Park U.S.A.
72 B1 Glacier Peak volc. U.S.A.
36 M4 Gladstad Norway
8 B2 Gladstone S.A. Austr.
6 F4 Gladstone Austr.
68 D3 Gladstone U.S.A.
68 E4 Gladwin U.S.A.
40 E4 Glamis U.K.
31 C5 Glan Phil.
42 F5 Glan r. Ger.
41 B5 Glanaruddery Mts h. Rep. of Ireland
43 G2 Glandorf Ger.
38 F2 Glanton U.K.
69 G4 Glanworth Can.
40 D5 Glasgow U.K.
78 C4 Glasgow KY U.S.A.
72 F1 Glasgow MT U.S.A.
80 D6 Glasgow VA U.S.A.
65 H4 Glaslyn Can.
74 C3 Glass Mt mt U.S.A.
39 E6 Glastonbury U.K.
43 L4 Glauchau Ger.
12 G4 Glazov Rus. Fed.
51 F4 Glazunovka Rus. Fed.
47 P3 Glazunovo Rus. Fed.
81 H2 Glen U.S.A.
40 C3 Glen Affric v. U.K.
69 G2 Glen Afton Can.
9 E2 Glen Afton N.Z.
62 D3 Glenallen U.S.A.
59 H1 Glen Alpine Dam dam S. Africa
41 C4 Glenamaddy Rep. of Ireland
68 E3 Glen Arbor U.S.A.
9 C6 Glenavy N.Z.
40 C3 Glen Cannich v. U.K.
73 E4 Glen Canyon gorge U.S.A.
75 G3 Glen Canyon National Recreation Area res. U.S.A.
40 E4 Glen Clova v. U.K.
8 C4 Glencoe Austr.
69 G4 Glencoe Can.
59 J4 Glencoe S. Africa
40 C4 Glen Coe v. U.K.
69 E2 Glendale Can.
75 F5 Glendale AZ U.S.A.
74 C4 Glendale CA U.S.A.
75 E3 Glendale NV U.S.A.
75 F3 Glendale UT U.S.A.
80 D4 Glendale Lake l. U.S.A.
8 H2 Glen Davis Austr.
72 F2 Glendive U.S.A.
65 G4 Glendon Can.
72 F3 Glendo Res. l. U.S.A.
8 C4 Glenelg r. Austr.
40 F4 Glen Esk v. U.K.
40 A5 Glengad Head hd Rep. of Ireland
40 C3 Glen Garry v. Scot. U.K.
40 D4 Glen Garry v. Scot. U.K.
41 D3 Glengavlen Rep. of Ireland
6 F4 Glen Innes Austr.
40 D6 Glenluce U.K.
40 D4 Glen Lyon v. U.K.
40 D3 Glen More v. U.K.
40 D3 Glen Moriston v. U.K.
40 C4 Glen Nevis v. U.K.
69 F3 Glennie U.S.A.
75 G6 Glenn, Mt mt U.S.A.
80 E6 Glenns U.S.A.
64 C3 Glenora Can.
81 F2 Glen Robertson Can.
40 E4 Glenrothes U.K.
81 G3 Glens Falls U.S.A.
40 E4 Glen Shee v. U.K.
40 C3 Glen Shiel v. U.K.
41 C3 Glenties Rep. of Ireland
41 D2 Glenveagh National Park Rep. of Ireland
80 C5 Glenville U.S.A.
77 E5 Glenwood AR U.S.A.
75 H5 Glenwood NM U.S.A.
73 F4 Glenwood Springs U.S.A.
68 B2 Glidden U.S.A.
43 J1 Glinde Ger.
47 J5 Gliwice Pol.
75 G5 Globe U.S.A.
46 H5 Głogów Pol.
36 N3 Glomfjord Norway
37 M5 Glomma r. Norway
57 E5 Glorieuses, Îles is Ind. Ocean
8 H1 Gloucester Austr.
39 E6 Gloucester U.K.
81 H3 Gloucester MA U.S.A.
80 E6 Gloucester VA U.S.A.
81 F3 Gloversville U.S.A.
43 L2 Glöwen Ger.
28 D1 Glubinnoye Rus. Fed.
51 G6 Glubokiy Rus. Fed.
15 G1 Glubokoye Kazak.
43 H1 Glückstadt Ger.
36 □ Gluggarnir h. Faroe Is
38 F4 Glusburn U.K.
51 H5 Gmelinka Rus. Fed.
46 G6 Gmünd Austria
46 F7 Gmunden Austria
37 P5 Gnarp Sweden
43 H1 Gnarrenburg Ger.
46 H4 Gniezno Pol.
49 J3 Gnjilane Yugo.
21 A3 Goa India
21 A3 Goa div. India
58 B3 Goageb Namibia
8 H4 Goalen Head hd Austr.
23 G4 Goalpara India
40 C5 Goat Fell h. U.K.
56 E3 Goba Eth.
57 B6 Gobabis Namibia
58 C3 Gobas Namibia
91 E1 Gobernador Crespo Arg.
91 C3 Gobernador Duval Arg.
88 B7 Gobernador Gregores Arg.
11 M5 Gobi des. Mongolia
29 D8 Gobō Japan
42 E3 Goch Ger.
57 B6 Gochas Namibia
32 C3 Go Công Vietnam
39 G6 Godalming U.K.
21 C2 Godavari r. India
21 C2 Godavari, Mouths of the river mouth India
67 G4 Godbout Can.
74 C3 Goddard, Mt mt U.S.A.
56 E3 Godere Eth.
69 G4 Goderich Can.
22 C5 Godhra India
91 C2 Godoy Cruz Arg.
65 L3 Gods r. Can.
65 L4 Gods Lake l. Can.
65 M2 Gods Mercy, Bay of b. Can.
Godwin Austen mt see K2
42 B3 Goedereede Neth.
66 E4 Goéland, Lac au l. Can.
67 H2 Goélands, Lac aux l. Can.
42 B3 Goes Neth.
69 E2 Goetzville U.S.A.
75 E4 Goffs U.S.A.
69 G2 Gogama Can.
68 C2 Gogebic, Lake l. U.S.A.
68 C2 Gogebic Range h. U.S.A.
Gogra r. see Ghaghara
22 D4 Gohad India
87 M5 Goiana Brazil
90 C2 Goiandira Brazil
90 C2 Goiânia Brazil
90 B1 Goiás Brazil
90 B2 Goiás div. Brazil
90 B4 Goio-Erê Brazil
22 C3 Gojra Pak.
21 A2 Gokak India
51 C7 Gökçeada i. Turkey
16 B2 Gökçedağ Turkey
23 G3 Gokhar La pass China
16 E1 Gökirmak r. Turkey
19 F5 Gokprosh Hills mts Pak.
16 F2 Göksun Turkey
16 E3 Göksu Nehri r. Turkey
57 C5 Gokwe Zimbabwe
37 L6 Gol Norway
22 E3 Gola India
23 H4 Golaghat India
16 F3 Gölbaşı Turkey
12 K2 Gol'chikha Rus. Fed.
16 B1 Gölcük Turkey
47 L3 Gołdap Pol.
43 L1 Goldberg Ger.
7 F4 Gold Coast Austr.
54 B4 Gold Coast coastal area Ghana
64 F4 Golden Can.
9 D4 Golden Bay b. N.Z.
43 J3 Goldene Aue reg. Ger.
74 A3 Golden Gate National Recreation Area res. U.S.A.
64 D5 Golden Hinde mt Can.
43 G2 Goldenstedt Ger.
41 C5 Golden Vale lowland Rep. of Ireland
74 D3 Goldfield U.S.A.
74 D3 Gold Point U.S.A.
79 E5 Goldsboro U.S.A.
77 D6 Goldthwaite U.S.A.
17 J1 Göle Turkey
19 F3 Golestān Afgh.
18 D4 Golestānak Iran
74 C4 Goleta U.S.A.
77 D6 Goliad U.S.A.
30 A1 Golin Baixing China
16 F1 Gölköy Turkey
43 L2 Golm Ger.
17 K3 Golmānkhānen Iran
24 B3 Golmud China
23 H1 Golmud He r. China
31 B3 Golo i. Phil.
28 J3 Golovnino Rus. Fed.
18 C3 Golpāyegān Iran
16 C1 Gölpazarı Turkey
40 E3 Golspie U.K.
19 F3 Gol Vardeh Iran
49 L4 Golyama Syutkya mt Bulg.
49 L4 Golyam Persenk mt Bulg.
43 L2 Golzow Ger.
56 C4 Goma Congo(Zaire)
23 G3 Gomang Co salt l. China
22 E4 Gomati r. India
32 □ Gombak, Bukit h. Sing.
54 D3 Gombe Nigeria
56 D4 Gombe r. Tanz.
55 D3 Gombi Nigeria
54 A2 Gomera, La i. Canary Is
84 B1 Gómez Palacio Mex.
84 C1 Gómez, Presa M. R. resr Mex.
18 D2 Gomīshān Iran
43 K2 Gommern Ger.
23 F2 Gomo Co salt l. China
19 E2 Gonābād Iran
Gonabad see Jūymand
83 K5 Gonaïves Haiti
59 J1 Gonarezhou National Park Zimbabwe
83 K5 Gonâve, Île de la i. Haiti
18 D2 Gonbad-e Kavus Iran
23 E4 Gonda India
22 B5 Gondal India
56 D2 Gonder Eth.
22 E5 Gondia India
16 A1 Gönen Turkey
27 D4 Gong'an China
27 D5 Gongcheng China
27 A4 Gongga Shan mt China
26 A2 Gonghe China
26 E1 Gonghui China
90 E1 Gongogi r. Brazil
54 D3 Gongola r. Nigeria
27 B5 Gongwang Shan mts China
26 D3 Gong Xian Henan China
27 B4 Gong Xian Sichuan China
59 H6 Gonubie S. Africa
84 C2 Gonzáles Mex.
74 B3 Gonzales CA U.S.A.
77 D6 Gonzales TX U.S.A.
91 D2 González Moreno Arg.
80 E6 Goochland U.S.A.
92 C6 Goodenough, C. c. Ant.
6 F2 Goodenough I. i. P.N.G.
69 H3 Gooderham Can.
68 E3 Good Harbor Bay b. U.S.A.
58 C7 Good Hope, Cape of c. S. Africa
72 D3 Gooding U.S.A.
76 C4 Goodland U.S.A.
38 G4 Goole U.K.
8 E3 Goolgowi Austr.
8 G2 Goolma Austr.
8 G2 Gooloogong Austr.
8 B3 Goolwa Austr.
6 F4 Goondiwindi Austr.
67 H3 Goose r. Can.
72 B3 Goose L. l. U.S.A.
21 B3 Gooty India
46 D6 Göppingen Ger.
22 E4 Gorakhpur India
49 H3 Goražde Bos.-Herz.
50 G3 Gorchukha Rus. Fed.
79 E7 Gorda Cay i. Bahamas
16 B2 Gördes Turkey
47 P4 Gordeyevka Rus. Fed.
40 F5 Gordon U.K.
6 E6 Gordon, L. l. Austr.
64 G2 Gordon Lake l. Can.
80 D5 Gordon Lake l. U.S.A.
80 D5 Gordonsville U.S.A.
55 D4 Goré Chad
56 D3 Gorē Eth.
9 B7 Gore N.Z.
69 F3 Gore Bay Can.
40 E5 Gorebridge U.K.
41 E5 Gorey Rep. of Ireland
19 E4 Gorg Iran
18 D2 Gorgān Iran
89 A4 Gorgona, I. i. Col.
81 H2 Gorham U.S.A.
51 H7 Gori Georgia
42 C3 Gorinchem Neth.
17 L2 Goris Armenia
48 E2 Gorizia Italy
Gor'kiy see Nizhniy Novgorod
51 H5 Gor'ko-Solenoye, Ozero l. Rus. Fed.
50 G3 Gor'kovskoye Vdkhr. resr Rus. Fed.
47 K6 Gorlice Pol.
46 G5 Görlitz Ger.
22 D4 Gormi India
49 L3 Gorna Oryakhovitsa Bulg.
49 J2 Gornji Milanovac Yugo.
48 G3 Gornji Vakuf Bos.-Herz.
24 A1 Gorno-Altaysk Rus. Fed.
28 G1 Gornozavodsk Rus. Fed.
12 K4 Gornyak Rus. Fed.
28 C2 Gornye Klyuchi Rus. Fed.
28 C2 Gornyy Primorskiy Kray Rus. Fed.
51 J5 Gornyy Saratov. Obl. Rus. Fed.
51 H5 Gornyy Balykley Rus. Fed.
50 G3 Gorodets Rus. Fed.
51 H5 Gorodishche Rus. Fed.
51 G6 Gorodovikovsk Rus. Fed.
6 E2 Goroka P.N.G.
8 C4 Goroke Austr.
50 G3 Gorokhovets Rus. Fed.
54 B3 Gorom Gorom Burkina
57 D5 Gorongosa Moz.

25 E6 Gorontalo Indon.
51 F5 Gorshechnoye Rus. Fed.
41 C4 Gort Rep. of Ireland
41 C2 Gortahork Rep. of Ireland
90 D1 Gorutuba r. Brazil
51 F6 Goryachiy Klyuch Rus. Fed.
43 L2 Görzke Ger.
46 G4 Gorzów Wielkopolski Pol.
8 H2 Gosford Austr.
38 F2 Gosforth U.K.
68 E5 Goshen IN U.S.A.
81 F4 Goshen NY U.S.A.
28 G4 Goshogawara Japan
43 J3 Goslar Ger.
48 F2 Gospić Croatia
39 F7 Gosport U.K.
49 J4 Gostivar Macedonia
Göteborg see Gothenburg
37 N7 Götene Sweden
43 J4 Gotha Ger.
37 M8 Gothenburg Sweden
76 C3 Gothenburg U.S.A.
37 Q8 Gotland i. Sweden
49 K4 Gotse Delchev Bulg.
37 Q7 Gotska Sandön i. Sweden
29 C7 Gōtsu Japan
43 H3 Göttingen Ger.
64 E4 Gott Peak summit Can.
Gottwaldow see Zlín
30 A3 Goubangzi China
42 C2 Gouda Neth.
54 A3 Goudiri Senegal
53 D3 Goudoumaria Niger
68 E1 Goudreau Can.
96 J8 Gough Island i. Atl. Ocean
66 F4 Gouin, Réservoir resr Can.
68 E2 Goulais River Can.
8 G3 Goulburn Austr.
8 H2 Goulburn r. N.S.W. Austr.
8 E4 Goulburn r. Vic. Austr.
6 D3 Goulburn Is is Austr.
68 E2 Gould City U.S.A.
92 B4 Gould Coast coastal area Ant.
54 B3 Goundam Mali
45 G4 Gouraya Alg.
54 D3 Gouré Niger
58 D7 Gourits r. S. Africa
54 B3 Gourma-Rharous Mali
44 E2 Gournay-en-Bray France
8 G4 Gourock Range mts Austr.
42 A5 Goussainville France
81 F2 Gouverneur U.S.A.
65 H5 Govenlock Can.
90 E2 Governador Valadares Brazil
31 C5 Governor Generoso Phil.
79 E7 Governor's Harbour Bahamas
24 B2 Govĭ Altayn Nuruu mts Mongolia
23 E4 Govind Ballash Pant Sāgar resr India
22 D3 Govind Sagar resr India
19 G2 Govurdak Turkm.
80 D3 Gowanda U.S.A.
19 G4 Gowārān Afgh.
18 D4 Gowd-e Aḥmad Iran
18 E3 Gowd-e Hasht Tekkeh waterhole Iran
18 D4 Gowd-e Mokh l. Iran
39 C6 Gower pen. U.K.
69 G2 Gowganda Can.
19 E4 Gowk Iran
41 D4 Gowna, Lough l. Rep. of Ireland
88 E3 Goya Arg.
17 L1 Göyçay Azer.
17 H2 Göynük Turkey
28 G5 Goyō-zan mt Japan
17 M2 Göytäpä Azer.
19 F3 Gōzareh Afgh.
16 G2 Gözene Turkey
22 E2 Gozha Co salt l. China
48 F6 Gozo i. Malta
58 F6 Graaff-Reinet S. Africa
58 C6 Graafwater S. Africa
43 J4 Grabfeld plain Ger.
54 B4 Grabo Côte d'Ivoire
58 C7 Grabouw S. Africa
43 K1 Grabow Ger.
48 F2 Gračac Croatia
69 J2 Gracefield Can.
43 L3 Gräfenhainichen Ger.
43 K5 Grafenwöhr Ger.
7 F4 Grafton Austr.
76 D1 Grafton ND U.S.A.
68 D4 Grafton WI U.S.A.
80 C5 Grafton WV U.S.A.
75 E2 Grafton, Mt mt U.S.A.
77 D5 Graham U.S.A.
Graham Bell Island i. see Greem-Bell, Ostrov
63 J2 Graham I. i. Can.
64 C4 Graham Island i. Can.
81 J2 Graham Lake l. U.S.A.
92 B2 Graham Land reg. Ant.
75 H5 Graham, Mt mt U.S.A.
59 G6 Grahamstown S. Africa
41 E5 Graigue Rep. of Ireland
54 A4 Grain Coast coastal area Liberia
87 J5 Grajaú Brazil
40 B1 Gralisgeir i. U.K.
49 J4 Grámmos mt Greece
40 D4 Grampian Mountains U.K.
8 D4 Grampians mts Austr.
58 C5 Granaatboskolk S. Africa
89 B4 Granada Col.
83 G6 Granada Nic.
45 E4 Granada Spain
76 C4 Granada U.S.A.
41 D4 Granard Rep. of Ireland
91 C3 Gran Bajo Salitroso salt flat Arg.
66 F4 Granby Can.
54 A2 Gran Canaria i. Canary Is
88 D3 Gran Chaco reg. Arg./Para.
78 C3 Grand r. MI U.S.A.
76 E3 Grand r. MO U.S.A.
79 E7 Grand Bahama i. Bahamas
67 J4 Grand Bank Can.
96 F2 Grand Banks sea feature Atl. Ocean
54 B4 Grand-Bassam Côte d'Ivoire
67 G4 Grand Bay Can.
69 G4 Grand Bend Can.
41 D4 Grand Canal canal Rep. of Ireland
75 F3 Grand Canyon U.S.A.
75 F3 Grand Canyon gorge U.S.A.
75 F3 Grand Canyon Nat. Park U.S.A.
83 H5 Grand Cayman i. Cayman Is
65 G4 Grand Centre Can.
72 C2 Grand Coulee U.S.A.
91 C3 Grande r. Arg.
87 J6 Grande r. Bahia Brazil
90 B2 Grande r. São Paulo Brazil
88 C8 Grande, Bahía b. Arg.
64 F4 Grande Cache Can.
44 H4 Grande Casse, Pointe de la mt France
57 E5 Grande Comore i. Comoros
91 F1 Grande, Cuchilla h. Uru.
90 D3 Grande, Ilha i. Brazil
64 F3 Grande Prairie Can.
55 D3 Grand Erg de Bilma sand dunes Niger
54 B1 Grand Erg Occidental des. Alg.
54 C2 Grand Erg Oriental des. Alg.
67 H4 Grande-Rivière Can.
66 F3 Grande Rivière de la Baleine r. Can.
72 C2 Grande Ronde r. U.S.A.
89 E4 Grande, Serra mt Brazil
67 G4 Grand Falls N.B. Can.
67 J4 Grand Falls Nfld Can.
64 F5 Grand Forks Can.
76 D2 Grand Forks U.S.A.
81 F3 Grand Gorge U.S.A.
81 K2 Grand Harbour Can.
68 D4 Grand Haven U.S.A.
64 F2 Grandin, Lac l. Can.
76 D3 Grand Island U.S.A.
68 D2 Grand Island i. U.S.A.
77 F6 Grand Isle LA U.S.A.
81 J1 Grand Isle ME U.S.A.
75 H2 Grand Junction U.S.A.
54 B4 Grand-Lahou Côte d'Ivoire
67 G4 Grand Lake l. N.B. Can.
67 J4 Grand Lake l. Nfld Can.
67 H3 Grand Lake l. Nfld Can.
77 E6 Grand Lake l. LA U.S.A.
81 K2 Grand Lake l. ME U.S.A.
69 F3 Grand Lake l. MI U.S.A.
81 J1 Grand Lake Matagamon l. U.S.A.
80 A4 Grand Lake St Marys l. U.S.A.
81 J1 Grand Lake Seboeis l. U.S.A.
81 K2 Grand Lake Stream U.S.A.
68 E4 Grand Ledge U.S.A.
67 G5 Grand Manan I. i. Can.
68 E2 Grand Marais MI U.S.A.
68 B2 Grand Marais MN U.S.A.
67 F4 Grand-Mère Can.
45 B3 Grândola Port.
7 G3 Grand Passage chan. New Caledonia
68 C2 Grand Portage U.S.A.
65 K4 Grand Rapids Can.
68 E4 Grand Rapids MI U.S.A.
76 E2 Grand Rapids MN U.S.A.
7 G3 Grand Récif de Cook rf New Caledonia
7 G4 Grand Récif du Sud rf New Caledonia
72 E3 Grand Teton mt U.S.A.
72 E3 Grand Teton Nat. Park U.S.A.
68 E3 Grand Traverse Bay b. U.S.A.
67 G4 Grand Vallée Can.
72 C2 Grandview U.S.A.
75 F3 Grand Wash r. U.S.A.
75 E4 Grand Wash Cliffs cliff U.S.A.
91 B2 Graneros Chile
41 D6 Grange Rep. of Ireland
72 E3 Granger U.S.A.
37 O6 Grängesberg Sweden
72 C2 Grangeville U.S.A.
64 D3 Granisle Can.
76 E2 Granite Falls U.S.A.
67 J4 Granite Lake l. Can.
75 E4 Granite Mts mts U.S.A.
72 E2 Granite Peak summit MT U.S.A.
75 F1 Granite Peak summit UT U.S.A.
48 E6 Granitola, Capo c. Sicily Italy
88 C6 Gran Laguna Salada l. Arg.
37 O7 Gränna Sweden
48 B2 Gran Paradiso mt Italy
46 E7 Gran Pilastro mt Austria/Italy
43 L3 Granschütz Ger.
43 M1 Gransee Ger.
39 G5 Grantham U.K.
92 A4 Grant I. i. Ant.
74 D2 Grant, Mt mt NV U.S.A.
74 C2 Grant, Mt mt NV U.S.A.
40 E3 Grantown-on-Spey U.K.
75 E2 Grant Range mts U.S.A.
73 F5 Grants U.S.A.
72 B3 Grants Pass U.S.A.
44 D2 Granville France
68 C5 Granville IL U.S.A.
81 G3 Granville NY U.S.A.
65 J3 Granville Lake l. Can.
90 D2 Grão Mogol Brazil
74 C4 Grapevine U.S.A.
74 D3 Grapevine Mts mts U.S.A.
81 G3 Graphite U.S.A.
59 J2 Graskop S. Africa
65 G2 Gras, Lac de l. Can.
81 F2 Grass r. U.S.A.
44 H5 Grasse France
38 F3 Grassington U.K.
65 H5 Grasslands Nat. Park Can.
72 E2 Grassrange U.S.A.
65 J4 Grass River Prov. Park res. Can.
74 B2 Grass Valley U.S.A.
79 E7 Grassy Cr. r. Bahamas
37 N7 Grästorp Sweden
68 B4 Gratiot U.S.A.
45 G1 Graus Spain
65 J2 Gravel Hill Lake l. Can.
42 A4 Gravelines France
59 J1 Gravelotte S. Africa
69 H3 Gravenhurst Can.
39 H6 Gravesend U.K.
48 G4 Gravina in Puglia Italy
68 E3 Grawn U.S.A.
44 G3 Gray France
81 H3 Gray U.S.A.
68 E3 Grayling U.S.A.
39 H6 Grays U.K.
72 A2 Grays Harbor in. U.S.A.
72 E3 Grays L. l. U.S.A.
80 B5 Grayson U.S.A.
67 H1 Gray Strait chan. Can.
78 B4 Grayville U.S.A.
46 G7 Graz Austria
79 E7 Great Abaco i. Bahamas
6 C5 Great Australian Bight g. Austr.
39 H6 Great Baddow U.K.
83 J3 Great Bahama Bank sea feature Bahamas
9 E2 Great Barrier Island i. N.Z.
6 E3 Great Barrier Reef rf Austr.
81 G3 Great Barrington U.S.A.
73 C4 Great Basin basin U.S.A.
75 E2 Great Basin Nat. Park U.S.A.
81 F5 Great Bay b. U.S.A.
64 E1 Great Bear r. Can.
64 E1 Great Bear Lake l. Can.
76 D4 Great Bend U.S.A.
58 C6 Great Berg r. S. Africa
40 B2 Great Bernera i. U.K.
41 A5 Great Blasket I. i. Rep. of Ireland
38 D3 Great Clifton U.K.
40 D5 Great Cumbrae i. U.K.
8 F4 Great Dividing Range mts Austr.
38 G3 Great Driffield U.K.
69 F3 Great Duck I. i. Can.
81 F5 Great Egg Harbor in. U.S.A.
83 H4 Greater Antilles is Caribbean Sea
83 J4 Great Exuma i. Bahamas
72 E2 Great Falls U.S.A.
59 G6 Great Fish r. S. Africa
59 G6 Great Fish Point pt S. Africa
23 F4 Great Gandak r. India
79 E7 Great Guana Cay i. Bahamas
79 E7 Great Harbour Cay i. Bahamas
83 K4 Great Inagua i. Bahamas
58 D5 Great Karoo plat. S. Africa
59 H6 Great Kei r. S. Africa
6 E6 Great Lake l. Austr.
39 E5 Great Malvern U.K.
80 A5 Great Miami r. U.S.A.
52 E2 Great Oasis, The oasis Egypt
39 D4 Great Ormes Head hd U.K.
39 H5 Great Ouse r. U.K.
81 G4 Great Peconic Bay b. U.S.A.
81 H4 Great Pt pt U.S.A.
39 D5 Great Rhos h. U.K.
56 D4 Great Ruaha r. Tanz.
81 F3 Great Sacandaga L. l. U.S.A.
48 B2 Great St Bernard Pass Italy/Switz.
79 E7 Great Sale Cay i. Bahamas
72 D3 Great Salt Lake l. U.S.A.
72 D3 Great Salt Lake Desert U.S.A.
55 E2 Great Sand Sea des. Egypt/Libya
6 C4 Great Sandy Desert Austr.
7 H3 Great Sea Reef rf Fiji
62 G3 Great Slave Lake N.W.T. Can.
64 G2 Great Slave Lake l. Can.
79 D5 Great Smoky Mts mts U.S.A.
79 D5 Great Smoky Mts Nat. Park U.S.A.
64 E3 Great Snow Mtn mt Can.
81 G4 Great South Bay b. U.S.A.
39 H7 Greatstone-on-Sea U.K.
39 J6 Great Stour r. U.K.
39 C7 Great Torrington U.K.
6 C4 Great Victoria Desert Austr.
26 F1 Great Wall China
39 H6 Great Waltham U.K.
81 K2 Great Wass I. i. U.S.A.
38 F3 Great Whernside h. U.K.
39 J5 Great Yarmouth U.K.
17 J3 Great Zab r. Iraq
48 E4 Greco, Monte mt Italy
45 D2 Gredos, Sa de mts Spain
35 H5 Greece country Europe
72 F3 Greeley U.S.A.
63 K1 Greely Fiord in. Can.
12 H1 Greem-Bell, Ostrov i. Rus. Fed.
78 C4 Green r. KY U.S.A.
75 H2 Green r. UT/WY U.S.A.
69 H3 Greenbank Can.
68 C3 Green Bay U.S.A.
68 D3 Green Bay b. U.S.A.
8 H4 Green C. hd Austr.
41 E3 Greencastle U.K.
78 C4 Greencastle U.S.A.
79 E7 Green Cay i. Bahamas
79 D6 Green Cove Springs U.S.A.
68 A4 Greene IA U.S.A.
81 F3 Greene NY U.S.A.
79 D4 Greeneville U.S.A.
74 B3 Greenfield CA U.S.A.
68 E6 Greenfield IN U.S.A.
81 G3 Greenfield MA U.S.A.
80 B5 Greenfield OH U.S.A.
68 C4 Greenfield WI U.S.A.
31 A4 Green Island Bay b. Phil.
65 H4 Green Lake Can.
68 C4 Green Lake l. U.S.A.
60 N2 Greenland terr. Arctic Ocean
96 J1 Greenland Basin sea feature Arctic Ocean
34 E1 Greenland Sea sea Arctic Ocean
40 F5 Greenlaw U.K.
81 G2 Green Mountains U.S.A.
40 D5 Greenock U.K.
41 E3 Greenore Rep. of Ireland
81 G4 Greenport U.S.A.
73 E4 Green River UT U.S.A.
72 E3 Green River WY U.S.A.
79 E4 Greensboro U.S.A.
78 C4 Greensburg IN U.S.A.
77 D4 Greensburg KS U.S.A.
80 D4 Greensburg PA U.S.A.
40 C3 Greenstone Point pt U.K.
71 L5 Green Swamp swamp NC U.S.A.
80 B5 Greenup U.S.A.
81 F2 Green Valley Can.
75 G6 Green Valley U.S.A.
68 C5 Greenview U.S.A.
54 B4 Greenville Liberia
79 C6 Greenville AL U.S.A.
74 B1 Greenville CA U.S.A.
79 D6 Greenville FL U.S.A.
81 J2 Greenville ME U.S.A.
68 E4 Greenville MI U.S.A.
77 F5 Greenville MS U.S.A.
79 E5 Greenville NC U.S.A.
81 H3 Greenville NH U.S.A.
80 A4 Greenville OH U.S.A.
80 C4 Greenville PA U.S.A.
79 D5 Greenville SC U.S.A.
77 D5 Greenville TX U.S.A.
65 J4 Greenwater Provincial Park res. Can.
8 H3 Greenwell Point Austr.
81 G4 Greenwich CT U.S.A.
81 G3 Greenwich NY U.S.A.
75 G2 Greenwich UT U.S.A.
77 F5 Greenwood MS U.S.A.
79 D5 Greenwood SC U.S.A.
77 E5 Greers Ferry Lake l. U.S.A.
76 D3 Gregory U.S.A.
6 C4 Gregory Lake salt flat Austr.
6 E3 Gregory Range h. Austr.
46 F3 Greifswald Ger.
43 L4 Greiz Ger.
16 E4 Greko, Cape c. Cyprus
37 M8 Grenå Denmark
77 F5 Grenada U.S.A.
61 M8 Grenada country Caribbean Sea
44 E5 Grenade France
37 M8 Grenen spit Denmark
8 G2 Grenfell Austr.
65 J4 Grenfell Can.
44 G4 Grenoble France
89 E1 Grenville Grenada
6 E3 Grenville, C. hd Austr.
72 B2 Gresham U.S.A.
38 F3 Greta r. U.K.
40 E6 Gretna U.K.
77 F6 Gretna U.S.A.
43 J3 Greußen Ger.
42 B3 Grevelingen chan. Neth.
42 F2 Greven Ger.
49 J4 Grevena Greece
42 D3 Grevenbicht Neth.
42 E3 Grevenbroich Ger.
42 E5 Grevenmacher Lux.
46 E4 Grevesmühlen Ger.
9 C5 Grey r. N.Z.
72 E2 Greybull U.S.A.
64 B2 Grey Hunter Pk summit Can.
67 J3 Grey Is is Can.
9 C5 Greymouth N.Z.
6 E4 Grey Range h. Austr.
59 J4 Greytown S. Africa
42 C4 Grez-Doiceau Belgium
51 G5 Gribanovskiy Rus. Fed.
74 B2 Gridley CA U.S.A.
68 C5 Gridley IL U.S.A.
79 C5 Griffin U.S.A.
8 F3 Griffith Austr.
69 J3 Griffith Can.
62 F2 Griffiths Point pt Can.
43 L3 Grimma Ger.
46 F3 Grimmen Ger.
69 H4 Grimsby Can.
38 G4 Grimsby U.K.
36 E3 Grímsey i. Iceland
64 F3 Grimshaw Can.
36 E4 Grímsstaðir Iceland
37 L7 Grimstad Norway
36 B5 Grindavík Iceland
37 L9 Grindsted Denmark
49 N2 Grindul Chituc spit Romania
76 E3 Grinnell U.S.A.
59 H5 Griqualand East reg. S. Africa
58 E4 Griqualand West reg. S. Africa
58 E4 Griquatown S. Africa
63 K2 Grise Fiord Can.
33 B3 Grisik Indon.
39 J7 Gris Nez, Cap pt France
40 F2 Gritley U.K.
48 G2 Grmeč mts Bos.-Herz.
42 C3 Grobbendonk Belgium
59 H2 Groblersdal S. Africa
58 E4 Groblershoop S. Africa
28 B2 Grodekovo Rus. Fed.
Grodno see Hrodna
58 B5 Groen watercourse Northern Cape S. Africa
58 E5 Groen watercourse Northern Cape S. Africa
44 C3 Groix, Île de i. France
48 D6 Grombalia Tunisia
42 F2 Gronau (Westfalen) Ger.
36 N4 Grong Norway
42 E1 Groningen Neth.
42 E1 Groninger Wad tidal flats Neth.
75 E3 Groom L. l. U.S.A.
58 D3 Groot-Aar Pan salt pan S. Africa
58 E7 Groot Brakrivier S. Africa
59 H3 Grootdraaidam dam S. Africa
58 D4 Grootdrink S. Africa
6 D3 Groote Eylandt i. Austr.
57 B5 Grootfontein Namibia
58 C3 Groot Karas Berg plat. Namibia
59 J1 Groot Letaba r. S. Africa
59 G2 Groot Marico S. Africa
58 D6 Groot Swartberg mts S. Africa
58 D5 Grootvloer salt pan S. Africa
59 G6 Groot Winterberg mt S. Africa
68 E3 Gros Cap U.S.A.
67 J4 Gros Morne Nat. Pk Can.
43 J3 Großengottern Ger.
43 G2 Großenkneten Ger.
43 H4 Großenlüder Ger.
43 J4 Großer Beerberg h. Ger.
43 J4 Großer Gleichberg h. Ger.
46 G7 Grosser Speikkogel mt Austria
48 D3 Grosseto Italy
43 G5 Groß-Gerau Ger.
48 E1 Großglockner mt Austria
43 J2 Groß Oesingen Ger.
43 K3 Großrudestedt Ger.
43 M2 Groß Schönebeck Ger.
58 C1 Gross Ums Namibia
72 E3 Gros Ventre Range mts U.S.A.
67 J3 Groswater Bay b. Can.
81 E3 Groton U.S.A.
80 D5 Grottoes U.S.A.
64 F3 Grouard Can.
66 D4 Groundhog r. Can.
42 D1 Grouw Neth.
80 C4 Grove City U.S.A.
79 C6 Grove Hill U.S.A.
74 B3 Groveland U.S.A.
92 D5 Grove Mts mts Ant.
74 B4 Grover Beach U.S.A.
81 H2 Groveton U.S.A.
75 F5 Growler U.S.A.
75 F5 Growler Mts mts U.S.A.
51 H7 Groznyy Rus. Fed.
49 M3 Grudovo Bulg.
47 J4 Grudziądz Pol.
40 C3 Gruinard Bay b. U.K.
57 B6 Grünau Namibia
36 B4 Grundarfjörður Iceland
80 B6 Grundy U.S.A.
43 G5 Grünstadt Ger.
51 F4 Gryazi Rus. Fed.
50 G3 Gryazovets Rus. Fed.
46 G4 Gryfice Pol.
46 G4 Gryfino Pol.
46 G5 Gryfów Śląski Pol.
36 P2 Gryllefjord Norway
88 □ Grytviken Atl. Ocean
23 F5 Gua India
83 J4 Guacanayabo, Golfo de b. Cuba
89 D2 Guacara Venez.
89 C3 Guacharía r. Col.
45 D4 Guadajoz r. Spain
84 B2 Guadalajara Mex.
45 E2 Guadalajara Spain
45 F2 Guadalaviar r. Spain
7 G2 Guadalcanal i. Solomon Is
45 C4 Guadalete r. Spain
45 F2 Guadalope r. Spain
45 D4 Guadalquivir r. Spain
84 B1 Guadalupe Nuevo León Mex.
84 B2 Guadalupe Zacatecas Mex.
74 B4 Guadalupe U.S.A.
70 C6 Guadalupe i. Mex.
77 D6 Guadalupe r. U.S.A.
84 A1 Guadalupe Aguilera Mex.
77 B6 Guadalupe Mts Nat. Park U.S.A.
77 B6 Guadalupe Pk mt U.S.A.
45 D3 Guadalupe, Sierra de mts Spain
84 A1 Guadalupe Victoria Mex.
84 A1 Guadalupe y Calvo Mex.
45 D2 Guadarrama, Sierra de mts Spain
61 M8 Guadeloupe terr. Caribbean Sea
91 C2 Guadel, Sa de mts Arg.
45 C4 Guadiana r. Port./Spain
45 E4 Guadix Spain
88 B6 Guafo, I. i. Chile
89 D4 Guainía r. Col./Venez.
89 E3 Guaiquinima, Cerro mt Venez.
90 A4 Guaíra Brazil
88 B6 Guaitecas, Islas is Chile
89 C1 Guajira, Península de pen. Col.
86 C4 Gualaceo Ecuador
74 A2 Gualala U.S.A.
91 E2 Gualeguay Arg.
91 E2 Gualeguay r. Arg.
91 E2 Gualeguaychu Arg.
91 B4 Gualjaina Arg.
4 F3 Guam terr. Pac. Oc.
88 A6 Guamblin, I. i. Chile
91 D3 Guaminí Arg.
84 A1 Guamúchil Mex.
89 A4 Guamués r. Col.
32 B4 Gua Musang Malaysia
84 A1 Guanacevi Mex.
91 D3 Guanaco, Co h. Arg.
84 B2 Guanajuato Mex.
84 B2 Guanajuato div. Mex.
90 D1 Guanambi Brazil
89 D4 Guaname r. Venez.
89 C2 Guanare Venez.
89 C2 Guanare r. Venez.
89 C2 Guanarito Venez.
89 C2 Guanarito r. Venez.
89 D3 Guanay, Sierra mts Venez.
26 D2 Guandi Shan mt China
83 H4 Guane Cuba
27 C4 Guang'an China
27 D6 Guangdong div. China
27 F4 Guangfeng China
27 D6 Guanghai China
26 B4 Guanghan China
27 E5 Guangchang China
26 B3 Guanghe China
27 E4 Guangji China
26 E2 Guangling China
30 B4 Guanglu Dao i. China
27 B5 Guangnan China
27 D6 Guangning China
26 F2 Guangrao China
26 E4 Guangshan China
26 D4 Guangshui China
27 C6 Guangxi div. China
26 B3 Guangyuan China
27 E5 Guangze China
27 D6 Guangzhou China
90 D2 Guanhães Brazil
90 D2 Guanhães r. Brazil
89 E2 Guanipa r. Venez.
27 B5 Guanling China
26 C4 Guanmian Shan mts China
26 D3 Guanpo China
30 C3 Guanshui China
89 D2 Guanta Venez.
83 J4 Guantánamo Cuba
26 E1 Guanting Sk. resr China
26 B4 Guan Xian China
27 D5 Guanyang China
27 G3 Guanyun China
89 A4 Guapí Col.
86 F6 Guaporé r. Bol./Brazil
86 E7 Guaqui Bol.
90 D1 Guará r. Brazil
87 L5 Guarabira Brazil
90 E3 Guarapari Brazil
90 B4 Guarapuava Brazil
90 C4 Guaraqueçaba Brazil
90 D3 Guaratinguetá Brazil
90 C4 Guaratuba, Baía de b. Brazil
45 C2 Guarda Port.
90 C2 Guarda Mor Brazil
45 D1 Guardo Spain
89 D2 Guárico r. Venez.
89 C3 Guarrojo r. Col.
90 C4 Guarujá Brazil
89 D4 Guasacavi r. Col.
89 C4 Guasacavi, Cerro h. Col.
89 B2 Guasare r. Venez.
82 C3 Guasave Mex.
89 C3 Guasdualito Venez.
84 C2 Guasima Mex.
89 E3 Guasipati Venez.
90 B4 Guassú r. Brazil
82 F6 Guatemala Guatemala
61 J8 Guatemala country Central America
89 D2 Guatope, Parque Nacional nat. park Venez.
91 D3 Guatrache Arg.
89 C4 Guaviare r. Col.
90 C3 Guaxupé Brazil
89 B4 Guayabero r. Col.
89 D3 Guayapo r. Venez.
86 C4 Guayaquil Ecuador
86 B4 Guayaquil, Golfo de g. Ecuador
86 E6 Guayaramerín Bol.
82 B3 Guaymas Mex.
56 D2 Guba Eth.
21 B3 Gubbi India
48 E3 Gubbio Italy
51 F5 Gubkin Rus. Fed.
26 D3 Gucheng China
51 G7 Gudaut'a Georgia
37 M6 Gudbrandsdalen v. Norway
51 H7 Gudermes Rus. Fed.
21 C2 Gudivada India
21 B3 Gudiyattam India
30 E2 Gudong r. China
19 G5 Gudri r. Pak.
16 D1 Güdül Turkey
21 B3 Gudur Andhra Pradesh India
37 K6 Gudvangen Norway
54 A4 Guéckédou Guinea
69 J1 Guéguen, Lac l. Can.
89 B4 Güejar r. Col.
54 C1 Guelma Alg.
54 A2 Guelmine Morocco
69 G4 Guelph Can.
84 C2 Guémez Mex.
42 E5 Guénange France
89 D2 Güera r. Venez.
67 G2 Guerard, Lac l. Can.
44 E3 Guéret France
72 F3 Guernsey U.S.A.
44 C2 Guernsey i. Channel Is U.K.
84 B3 Guerrero div. Mex.
82 B3 Guerrero Negro Mex.
63 M4 Guers, Lac l. Can.
18 D3 Gūgerd, Kūh-e mts Iran
96 F5 Guiana Basin sea feature Atl. Ocean
8 B4 Guichen B. b. Austr.
27 E4 Guichi China
91 F2 Guichón Uru.
26 A3 Guide China
55 D4 Guider Cameroon
27 C5 Guiding China
48 E4 Guidonia-Montecelio Italy
54 B4 Guiglo Côte d'Ivoire
42 B5 Guignicourt France
59 K2 Guija Moz.
27 D6 Gui Jiang r. China
27 F4 Guiji Shan mts China
39 G6 Guildford U.K.
81 J2 Guilford U.S.A.
27 D5 Guilin China
66 E2 Guillaume-Delisle, Lac l. Can.
45 B2 Guimarães Port.
31 B4 Guimaras Str. chan. Phil.
26 E3 Guimeng Ding mt China
26 A3 Guinan China
74 A2 Guinda U.S.A.
31 C4 Guindulman Phil.
52 C4 Guinea country Africa
96 J5 Guinea Basin sea feature Atl. Ocean
52 C4 Guinea-Bissau country Africa
53 D5 Guinea, Gulf of g. Africa
83 H4 Güines Cuba
44 C2 Guingamp France
44 B2 Guipavas France
27 D6 Guiping China
90 B2 Guiratinga Brazil
89 E2 Güiria Venez.
42 B5 Guiscard France
42 B5 Guise France
31 C4 Guiuan Phil.
27 E4 Guixi China
27 C6 Gui Xian China
27 C5 Guiyang Guizhou China
27 D5 Guiyang Hunan China
27 C5 Guizhou div. China
22 B5 Gujarat div. India
22 C2 Gujar Khan Pak.
22 C2 Gujranwala Pak.
22 C2 Gujrat Pak.
75 G5 Gu Komelik U.S.A.
51 F5 Gukovo Rus. Fed.
17 K3 Gük Tappeh Iran
22 D2 Gulabgarh Jammu and Kashmir
26 B2 Gulang China
8 G1 Gulargambone Austr.
21 B2 Gulbarga India
37 U8 Gulbene Latvia
16 E3 Gülek Turkey
77 F6 Gulfport U.S.A.
18 C4 Gulf, The g. Asia
8 G2 Gulgong Austr.
24 E1 Gulian China
27 B5 Gulin China
19 G4 Gulistan Pak.
14 E2 Gulistan Uzbek.
43 K1 Gülitz Ger.
68 E3 Gull I. i. U.S.A.
65 H4 Gull Lake Can.
36 R3 Gullträsk Sweden
16 D3 Gülnar Turkey
19 F3 Gulran Afgh.
51 G7 Gulrip'shi Georgia
16 E2 Gülşehir Turkey
56 D3 Gulu Uganda
22 B3 Gumal r. Pak.
57 C5 Gumare Botswana
18 D2 Gumdag Turkm.
23 F5 Gumia India
23 F5 Gumla India
42 F3 Gummersbach Ger.
16 E1 Gümüşhacıköy Turkey
17 G1 Gümüşhane Turkey
22 D4 Guna India
8 E3 Gunbar Austr.
8 G3 Gundagai Austr.
43 H5 Gundelsheim Ger.
16 D3 Gündoğmuş Turkey
16 B2 Güney Turkey
56 B4 Gungu Congo(Zaire)
51 H7 Gunib Rus. Fed.
65 K4 Gunisao r. Can.
8 H1 Gunnedah Austr.
92 D3 Gunnerus Ridge sea feature Ant.
8 G3 Gunning Austr.
73 F4 Gunnison CO U.S.A.
75 G2 Gunnison UT U.S.A.
73 E4 Gunnison r. U.S.A.
21 B3 Guntakal India
43 J3 Güntersberge Ger.
79 C5 Guntersville U.S.A.
79 C5 Guntersville L. l. U.S.A.
21 C2 Guntur India
33 A2 Gunungsitoli Indon.
32 A5 Gunungtua Indon.
21 C2 Gunupur India
46 E6 Günzburg Ger.
43 J5 Gunzenhausen Ger.
26 E1 Guojiatun China
26 E3 Guoyang China
26 A2 Gurban Hudag China
26 D1 Gurban Obo China
19 F5 Gurdim Iran
16 B2 Güre Turkey
22 D3 Gurgaon India
87 K5 Gurgueia r. Brazil
22 B4 Gurha India
89 E3 Guri, Embalse de resr Venez.
90 C2 Gurinhatã Brazil
51 H7 Gurjaani Georgia
19 E4 Gur Khar Iran
17 J2 Gürpınar Turkey
23 G3 Guru China
57 D5 Guruè Moz.
16 F2 Gürün Turkey
87 J4 Gurupi r. Brazil
22 C4 Guru Sikhar mt India
50 B4 Gur'yevsk Rus. Fed.
54 C3 Gusau Nigeria
43 K2 Güsen Ger.
50 B4 Gusev Rus. Fed.
30 B4 Gushan China
75 H1 Gusher U.S.A.
19 F3 Gushgy Turkm.
26 E3 Gushi China
31 A5 Gusi Malaysia
13 M2 Gusikha Rus. Fed.
50 D4 Gusino Rus. Fed.
13 M4 Gusinoozersk Rus. Fed.
23 F5 Guskara India
50 G4 Gus'-Khrustal'nyy Rus. Fed.
48 C5 Guspini Sardinia Italy
43 K3 Güsten Ger.
74 B3 Gustine U.S.A.
43 L1 Güstrow Ger.
23 H3 Gutang China
43 M2 Güterfelde Ger.
43 G3 Gütersloh Ger.
75 H5 Guthrie AZ U.S.A.
78 C4 Guthrie KY U.S.A.
77 D5 Guthrie OK U.S.A.
77 C5 Guthrie TX U.S.A.
27 E5 Gutian Fujian China
27 F5 Gutian Fujian China
42 E5 Gutland reg. Ger./Lux.
23 F3 Gutsuo China
68 B4 Guttenberg U.S.A.
57 D5 Gutu Zimbabwe
23 G4 Guwahati India
17 J3 Guwēr Iraq
43 H3 Guxhagen Ger.
85 E2 Guyana country S. America
26 D1 Guyang China
77 C4 Guymon U.S.A.
18 D4 Gūyom Iran
8 H1 Guyra Austr.
26 E1 Guyuan Hebei China
26 C3 Guyuan Ningxia China
19 G2 Guzar Uzbek.
27 C4 Guzhang China
26 E3 Guzhen China
47 K3 Gvardeysk Rus. Fed.
8 G1 Gwabegar Austr.
19 F5 Gwadar Pak.
19 F5 Gwadar West Bay b. Pak.
22 D4 Gwalior India
57 C6 Gwanda Zimbabwe
19 G4 Gwash Pak.
19 F5 Gwatar Bay b. Pak.
41 C3 Gweebarra Bay b. Rep. of Ireland
41 C2 Gweedore Rep. of Ireland
57 C5 Gweru Zimbabwe
68 D2 Gwinn U.S.A.
55 D3 Gwoza Nigeria
8 H1 Gwydir r. Austr.
23 H3 Gyaca China
26 B3 Gyagartang China
23 F3 Gyangrang China
23 G3 Gyangzê China
23 G3 Gyaring Co l. China
24 B3 Gyaring Hu l. China
49 L6 Gyaros i. Greece
23 H3 Gyarubtang China
12 J2 Gydanskiy Poluostrov pen. Rus. Fed.
23 H3 Gyimda China
23 F3 Gyirong Xizang China
23 F3 Gyirong Xizang China
23 H2 Gyiza China
63 O3 Gyldenløves Fjord in. Greenland
7 F4 Gympie Austr.
47 J7 Gyöngyös Hungary
46 H7 Győr Hungary
65 K4 Gypsumville Can.
67 G2 Gyrfalcon Is i. Can.
49 K6 Gytheio Greece
47 K7 Gyula Hungary
17 J1 Gyumri Armenia
18 E2 Gyzylarbat Turkm.

H

36 T5 Haapajärvi Fin.
36 T4 Haapavesi Fin.
37 S7 Haapsalu Estonia
42 C2 Haarlem Neth.
58 E6 Haarlem S. Africa
43 G3 Haarstrang ridge Ger.
9 B5 Haast N.Z.
19 G5 Hab r. Pak.
Habana see Havana
21 C4 Habarane Sri Lanka
56 D3 Habaswein Kenya
64 F3 Habay Can.
20 C7 Ḥabbān Yemen
17 J5 Ḥabbānīyah Iraq
17 J5 Ḥabbānīyah, Hawr al l. Iraq
19 G5 Hab Chauki Pak.
23 G4 Habiganj Bangl.
26 E1 Habirag China
23 G5 Habra India
89 B5 Hacha Col.
91 B3 Hachado, P. de pass Arg./Chile
29 F8 Hachijō-jima i. Japan
28 G4 Hachinohe Japan
29 F7 Hachiōji Japan
16 F2 Hacıbektaş Turkey
17 H2 Hacıömer Turkey
57 D6 Hacufera Moz.
18 C6 Hadabat al Budū plain S. Arabia
21 A3 Hadagalli India
40 F5 Haddington U.K.
54 D3 Hadejia Nigeria
16 E5 Hadera Israel
37 L9 Haderslev Denmark
20 C6 Ḥaḍhramaut reg. Yemen
16 D3 Hadım Turkey
39 H5 Hadleigh U.K.
62 H2 Hadley Bay b. Can.
30 D6 Hadong S. Korea
16 F6 Ḥadraj, Wādī watercourse S. Arabia
37 M8 Hadsund Denmark
51 E5 Hadyach Ukr.
91 F1 Haedo, Cuchilla de h. Uru.
30 C4 Haeju N. Korea
30 C5 Haeju-man b. N. Korea
30 D6 Haenam S. Korea
59 H1 Haenertsburg S. Africa
18 B4 Hafar al Bāṭin S. Arabia
65 H4 Hafford Can.
16 F2 Hafik Turkey
22 C2 Hafizabad Pak.
23 H4 Hāflong India
36 C4 Hafnarfjörður Iceland
18 C4 Haft Gel Iran
36 B4 Hafursfjörður b. Iceland
69 G2 Hagar Can.
21 B3 Hagari r. India
56 D2 Hagar Nish Plateau plat. Eritrea
42 C4 Hageland reg. Belgium
42 F3 Hagen Ger.
6 E2 Hagen, Mount mt P.N.G.
43 K1 Hagenow Ger.
80 E5 Hagerstown U.S.A.
44 D5 Hagetmau France

37 N6 Hagfors Sweden
29 B7 Hagi Japan
27 B6 Ha Giang Vietnam
39 E5 Hagley U.K.
41 B5 Hag's Head *hd* Rep. of Ireland
65 H4 Hague Can.
44 D2 Hague, Cap de la *pt* France
44 H2 Haguenau France
24 G4 Hahajima-rettō *is* Japan
56 D4 Hai Tanz.
26 E2 Hai *r.* China
26 F3 Hai'an China
58 B4 Haib *watercourse* Namibia
30 B3 Haicheng China
43 K5 Haidenaab *r.* Ger.
27 C6 Hai Dương Vietnam
16 E5 Haifa Israel
16 E5 Haifa, Bay of *b.* Israel
27 E6 Haifeng China
43 G4 Haiger Ger.
27 D6 Haikang China
27 D6 Haikou China
20 B4 Hā'il S. Arabia
24 D2 Hailar China
69 H2 Haileybury Can.
30 E1 Hailin China
30 C2 Hailong China
39 H7 Hailsham U.K.
36 T4 Hailuoto Fin.
26 F4 Haimen China
27 C7 Hainan *div.* China
27 D7 Hainan *i.* China
64 B3 Haines U.S.A.
64 B2 Haines Junction Can.
43 J3 Hainich *ridge* Ger.
43 M4 Hainichen Ger.
43 J3 Hainleite *ridge* Ger.
27 C6 Hai Phong Vietnam
26 A2 Hairag China
26 B1 Hairhan Namag China
27 F5 Haitan Dao *i.* China
61 L8 Haiti *country* Caribbean Sea
27 C7 Haitou China
75 G5 Haivana Nakya U.S.A.
74 D3 Haiwee Reservoir U.S.A.
26 E2 Haixing China
55 F3 Haiya Sudan
26 A2 Haiyan *Qinghai* China
27 F4 Haiyan *Zhejiang* China
30 A5 Haiyang China
30 B4 Haiyang Dao *i.* China
26 B2 Haiyuan China
26 F3 Haizhou Wan *b.* China
47 K7 Hajdúböszörmény Hungary
48 C7 Hajeb El Ayoun Tunisia
20 D7 Ḥajhir *mt* Yemen
28 F5 Hajiki-zaki *pt* Japan
23 F4 Hajipur India
18 D4 Ḥajjīābād Iran
18 D4 Ḥajjīābād Iran
20 E6 Hajmah Oman
23 H5 Haka Myanmar
74 □2 Hakalau U.S.A.
91 C4 Hakelhuincul, Altiplanicie de *plat.* Arg.
Hakha *see* Haka
17 J3 Hakkârı Turkey
36 R3 Hakkas Sweden
29 D7 Hakken-zan *mt* Japan
28 H2 Hako-dake *mt* Japan
28 G4 Hakodate Japan
58 B1 Hakos Mts *mts* Namibia
58 D3 Hakseen Pan *salt pan* S. Africa
29 E6 Hakui Japan
29 E6 Haku-san *volc.* Japan
29 E6 Haku-san National Park Japan
22 B4 Hala Pak.
Ḥalab *see* Aleppo
18 B6 Halabān S. Arabia
17 K4 Ḥalabja Iraq
30 C1 Halaha China
30 C1 Halahai China
55 F2 Halaib Sudan
20 E6 Ḥalāniyāt, Juzur al *is* Oman
74 □2 Halawa U.S.A.
16 F4 Halba Lebanon
24 B2 Halban Mongolia
43 K3 Halberstadt Ger.
31 B3 Halcon, Mt *mt* Phil.
36 □ Haldarsvik Faroe Is
37 M7 Halden Norway
43 K2 Haldensleben Ger.
23 G5 Haldi *r.* India
23 G5 Haldia India
23 G4 Haldibari India
22 D3 Haldwani India
69 F3 Hale U.S.A.
17 G4 Halebiye Syria
74 □1 Haleiwa U.S.A.
39 E5 Halesowen U.K.
39 J5 Halesworth U.K.
16 F3 Halfeti Turkey
9 B7 Halfmoon Bay N.Z.
41 C6 Halfway Rep. of Ireland
64 E3 Halfway *r.* Can.
42 C2 Halfweg Neth.
23 E4 Halia India
69 H3 Haliburton Can.
67 H5 Halifax Can.
38 F4 Halifax U.K.
80 D6 Halifax U.S.A.
40 E2 Halkirk U.K.
36 P5 Hälla Sweden
30 D7 Halla-san *mt* S. Korea
63 K3 Hall Beach Can.
42 C4 Halle Belgium
42 E3 Halle Neth.
37 O7 Hällefors Sweden
46 F7 Hallein Austria
43 K3 Halle-Neustadt Ger.
43 K3 Halle (Saale) Ger.
92 A5 Hallett, C. *c.* Ant.
92 C3 Halley *U.K. Base* Ant.
4 G4 Hall Islands *is* Micronesia
36 O4 Hällnäs Sweden
76 D1 Hallock U.S.A.
63 M3 Hall Peninsula *pen.* Can.
37 O7 Hallsberg Sweden
6 C3 Halls Creek Austr.
69 H3 Halls Lake Can.
42 B4 Halluin France
36 O5 Hallviken Sweden
25 E6 Halmahera *i.* Indon.
37 N8 Halmstad Sweden
22 C5 Halol India
37 M8 Hals Denmark
36 T5 Halsua Fin.
42 F3 Haltern Ger.
38 E3 Haltwhistle U.K.
18 D5 Ḥālūl *i.* Qatar
42 F3 Halver Ger.
42 B5 Ham France
29 C7 Hamada Japan
54 B2 Ḥamâda El Ḥaricha *des.* Mali
18 C3 Hamadān Iran
54 B2 Hamada Tounassine *des.* Alg.
16 F4 Ḥamāh Syria
28 G3 Hamamasu Japan
29 E7 Hamamatsu Japan
37 M6 Hamar Norway
36 O2 Hamarøy Norway
28 H2 Hamatonbetsu Japan
21 C5 Hambantota Sri Lanka
43 G1 Hambergen Ger.
38 F3 Hambleton Hills *h.* U.K.
43 H1 Hamburg Ger.
59 G6 Hamburg S. Africa
77 F5 Hamburg *AR* U.S.A.
80 D3 Hamburg *NY* U.S.A.
81 F4 Hamburg *PA* U.S.A.
43 G1 Hamburgisches Wattenmeer, Nationalpark *nat. park* Ger.
81 G4 Hamden U.S.A.
37 T6 Hämeenlinna Fin.
43 H2 Hameln Ger.
6 B4 Hamersley Range *mts* Austr.
30 D4 Hamhŭng N. Korea
24 B2 Hami China
18 C4 Ḥamīd Iran
55 F2 Hamīd Sudan
8 D4 Hamilton Austr.
83 M2 Hamilton Bermuda
69 H4 Hamilton Can.
9 E2 Hamilton N.Z.
40 D5 Hamilton U.K.
79 C5 Hamilton *AL* U.S.A.
68 B5 Hamilton *IL* U.S.A.
72 D2 Hamilton *MT* U.S.A.
81 F3 Hamilton *NY* U.S.A.
80 A5 Hamilton *OH* U.S.A.
74 A2 Hamilton City U.S.A.
74 B3 Hamilton, Mt *mt CA* U.S.A.
75 E2 Hamilton, Mt *mt NV* U.S.A.
37 U6 Hamina Fin.
22 D3 Hamirpur India
17 H6 Ḥāmir, W. *watercourse* S. Arabia
67 J3 Hamiton Inlet *in.* Can.
30 D4 Hamju N. Korea
8 B3 Hamley Bridge Austr.
68 D3 Hamlin Lake *l.* U.S.A.
43 F3 Hamm Ger.
54 B2 Hammada du Drâa *plat.* Alg.
17 J3 Ḥammām Ali Iraq
48 D6 Hammamet Tunisia
55 D1 Hammamet, Golfe de *b.* Tunisia
17 L6 Ḥammār, Hawr al *l.* Iraq
36 P5 Hammarstrand Sweden
43 H4 Hammelburg Ger.
36 O5 Hammerdal Sweden
36 S1 Hammerfest Norway
42 E3 Hamminkeln Ger.
8 B2 Hammond Austr.
68 D5 Hammond *IN* U.S.A.
77 F6 Hammond *LA* U.S.A.
72 F2 Hammond *MT* U.S.A.
69 E3 Hammond Bay *b.* U.S.A.
80 E3 Hammondsport U.S.A.
81 F5 Hammonton U.S.A.
42 D4 Hamoir Belgium
9 C6 Hampden N.Z.
39 F6 Hampshire Downs *h.* U.K.
67 G4 Hampton Can.
77 E5 Hampton *AR* U.S.A.
81 H3 Hampton *NH* U.S.A.
81 E6 Hampton *VA* U.S.A.
17 K4 Ḥamrīn, Jabal *h.* Iraq
32 C3 Ham Tân Vietnam
22 D2 Hamta Pass *pass* India
19 E5 Hāmūn-e Jaz Mūrīān *salt marsh* Iran
19 F4 Hāmūn Helmand *salt flat* Afgh./Iran
19 G4 Hamun-i-Lora *l.* Pak.
19 F4 Hāmūn Pu *marsh* Afgh.
17 J2 Hamur Turkey
74 □2 Hana U.S.A.
58 E1 Hanahai *watercourse* Botswana/Namibia
74 □2 Hanalei U.S.A.
28 G5 Hanamaki Japan
43 G4 Hanau Ger.
26 D3 Hancheng China
80 D5 Hancock *MD* U.S.A.
68 C2 Hancock *MI* U.S.A.
81 F4 Hancock *NY* U.S.A.
40 C2 Handa Island *i.* U.K.
26 E2 Handan China
56 D4 Handeni Tanz.
74 C3 Hanford U.S.A.
21 A3 Hangal India
24 B2 Hangayn Nuruu *mts* Mongolia
26 C1 Hanggin Houqi China
26 C2 Hanggin Qi China
42 D4 Han, Grotte de Belgium
26 E2 Hangu China
22 B2 Hangu Pak.
27 D5 Hanguang China
27 F4 Hangzhou China
27 F4 Hangzhou Wan *b.* China
17 H2 Hani Turkey
18 C5 Ḥanīdh S. Arabia
26 B2 Hanjiaoshui China
43 J2 Hankensbüttel Ger.
58 F6 Hankey S. Africa
37 S7 Hanko Fin.
75 G2 Hanksville U.S.A.
22 D2 Hanle Jammu and Kashmir
9 D5 Hanmer Springs N.Z.
19 F4 Hanmni Mashkel *salt flat* Pak.
65 G4 Hanna Can.
66 D3 Hannah Bay *b.* Can.
68 B6 Hannibal U.S.A.
43 H2 Hannover Ger.
43 H3 Hannoversch Münden Ger.
42 D4 Hannut Belgium
37 O9 Hanöbukten *b.* Sweden
27 B6 Ha Nôi Vietnam
Hanoi *see* Ha Nôi
69 G3 Hanover Can.
58 F5 Hanover S. Africa
81 G3 Hanover *NH* U.S.A.
80 E5 Hanover *PA* U.S.A.
92 D4 Hansen Mts *mts* Ant.
27 D4 Hanshou China
26 E4 Han Shui *r.* China
22 D3 Hansi India
36 Q2 Hansnes Norway
80 B6 Hansonville U.S.A.
37 L8 Hanstholm Denmark
42 E6 Han-sur-Nied France
50 C4 Hantsavichy Belarus
22 C3 Hanumangarh India
8 F3 Hanwood Austr.
27 E4 Hanyang China
26 C3 Hanyin China
27 B4 Hanyuan China
26 C3 Hanzhong China
5 N6 Hao *i.* Pac. Oc.
23 G5 Hāora India
36 T4 Haparanda Sweden
23 H4 Hāpoli India
67 H3 Happy Valley-Goose Bay Can.
30 E3 Hapsu N. Korea
22 D3 Hapur India
21 C5 Haputale Sri Lanka
18 C5 Ḥaraḍ *well* S. Arabia
18 C5 Ḥaraḍh S. Arabia
50 D4 Haradok Belarus
29 G6 Haramachi Japan
22 C2 Haramukh *mt* India
22 C3 Harappa Road Pak.
57 D5 Harare Zimbabwe
24 C2 Har-Ayrag Mongolia
54 A4 Harbel Liberia
24 E2 Harbin China
69 F4 Harbor Beach U.S.A.
68 E3 Harbor Springs U.S.A.
67 J4 Harbour Breton Can.
88 E8 Harbours, B. of *b.* Falkland Is
75 F5 Harcuvar Mts *mts* U.S.A.
22 D5 Harda Khās India
37 K6 Hardangervidda *plat.* Norway
37 K6 Hardangervidda Nasjonalpark *nat. park* Norway
58 B2 Hardap *div.* Namibia
58 B2 Hardap Dam *dam* Namibia
42 E2 Hardenberg Neth.
33 E2 Harden, Bukit *mt* Indon.
42 D2 Harderwijk Neth.
58 C5 Hardeveld *mts* S. Africa
43 H5 Hardheim Ger.
72 F2 Hardin U.S.A.
59 H5 Harding S. Africa
65 G4 Hardisty Can.
64 F2 Hardisty Lake *l.* Can.
22 E4 Hardoi India
81 G2 Hardwick U.S.A.
77 F4 Hardy U.S.A.
68 E4 Hardy Reservoir *resr* U.S.A.
16 D6 Hareidīn, W. *watercourse* Egypt
42 B4 Harelbeke Belgium
42 E1 Haren Neth.
42 F2 Haren (Ems) Ger.
56 E3 Hārer Eth.
81 F4 Harford U.S.A.
56 E3 Hargeysa Somalia
47 M7 Harghita-Mădăraş, Vârful *mt* Romania
17 H2 Harhal D. *mts* Turkey
26 C2 Harhatan China
24 B3 Har Hu *l.* China
22 D3 Haridwar India
21 A3 Harihar India
9 C5 Harihari N.Z.
29 D7 Harima-nada *b.* Japan
23 G5 Haringhat *r.* Bangl.
42 C3 Haringvliet *est.* Neth.
19 G3 Hari Rūd *r.* Afgh./Iran
37 S6 Harjavalta Fin.
76 E3 Harlan *IA* U.S.A.
80 B6 Harlan *KY* U.S.A.
39 C5 Harlech U.K.
72 E1 Harlem U.S.A.
39 J5 Harleston U.K.
42 D1 Harlingen Neth.
77 D7 Harlingen U.S.A.
39 H6 Harlow U.K.
72 E2 Harlowtown U.S.A.
42 B5 Harly France
81 J2 Harmony *ME* U.S.A.
68 A4 Harmony *MN* U.S.A.
43 J1 Harmsdorf Ger.
22 A3 Harnai Pak.
42 A4 Harnes France
72 B3 Harney Basin *basin* U.S.A.
72 C3 Harney L. *l.* U.S.A.
37 P5 Härnösand Sweden
24 E2 Har Nur China
24 B2 Har Nuur *l.* Mongolia
40 □ Haroldswick U.K.
54 B4 Harper Liberia
74 D4 Harper Lake *l.* U.S.A.
80 E5 Harpers Ferry U.S.A.
67 H2 Harp Lake *l.* Can.
43 G2 Harpstedt Ger.
17 G2 Harput Turkey
26 F1 Harqin China
26 F1 Harqin Qi China
75 F5 Harquahala Mts *mts* U.S.A.
17 G3 Harran Turkey
16 F5 Harrat er Rujeila *lava* Jordan
66 E3 Harricanaw *r.* Can.
79 C5 Harriman U.S.A.
81 G3 Harriman Reservoir U.S.A.
81 F5 Harrington U.S.A.
67 J3 Harrington Harbour Can.
40 B3 Harris U.K.
78 B4 Harrisburg *IL* U.S.A.
80 E4 Harrisburg *PA* U.S.A.
59 H4 Harrismith S. Africa
77 E4 Harrison *AR* U.S.A.
68 E3 Harrison *MI* U.S.A.
62 C2 Harrison Bay *b.* U.S.A.
80 D5 Harrisonburg U.S.A.
67 J3 Harrison, Cape *c.* Can.
64 E5 Harrison L. *l.* Can.
76 E4 Harrisonville U.S.A.
40 A3 Harris, Sound of *chan.* U.K.
69 F3 Harrisville *MI* U.S.A.
81 F2 Harrisville *NY* U.S.A.
80 C5 Harrisville *WV* U.S.A.
38 F4 Harrogate U.K.
43 H1 Harsefeld Ger.
18 B3 Harsin Iran
16 G1 Harşit *r.* Turkey
49 M2 Hârşova Romania
36 P2 Harstad Norway
43 H2 Harsum Ger.
68 D4 Hart U.S.A.
30 B2 Hartao China
58 D4 Hartbees *watercourse* S. Africa
46 G7 Hartberg Austria
37 K6 Harteigan *mt* Norway
40 E5 Hart Fell *h.* U.K.
81 G4 Hartford *CT* U.S.A.
68 D4 Hartford *MI* U.S.A.
76 D3 Hartford *SD* U.S.A.
68 C4 Hartford *WV* U.S.A.
64 E3 Hart Highway Can.
67 G4 Hartland Can.
39 C7 Hartland U.K.
81 J2 Hartland U.S.A.
39 C6 Hartland Point *pt* U.K.
38 F3 Hartlepool U.K.
77 C5 Hartley U.S.A.
64 D4 Hartley Bay Can.
37 U6 Hartola Fin.
64 E4 Hart Ranges *mts* Can.
46 E6 Härtsfeld *h.* Ger.
58 F3 Hartswater S. Africa
79 D5 Hartwell Res. *resr* U.S.A.
24 B2 Har Us Nuur *l.* Mongolia
19 F3 Harut *watercourse* Afgh.
68 C4 Harvard U.S.A.
73 F4 Harvard, Mt *mt* U.S.A.
81 K2 Harvey Can.
68 D2 Harvey *MI* U.S.A.
76 C2 Harvey *ND* U.S.A.
39 J6 Harwich U.K.
22 C3 Haryana *div.* India
16 F6 Ḥaşāh, Wādī al *watercourse* Jordan
18 B2 Hasan Iran
22 C2 Hasan Abdal Pak.
16 E2 Hasan Dağı *mts* Turkey
17 H2 Hasankeyf Turkey
18 E5 Ḥasan Langī Iran
21 B2 Hasanparti India
16 E5 Hasbani *r.* Lebanon
16 E2 Hasbek Turkey
17 K6 Ḥasb, Sha'īb *watercourse* Iraq
23 E5 Hasdo *r.* India
43 F2 Hase *r.* Ger.
42 F2 Haselünne Ger.
43 J4 Hasenkopf *h.* Ger.
18 C3 Hashtgerd Iran
18 C2 Hashtpar Iran
77 D5 Haskell U.S.A.
39 G6 Haslemere U.K.
47 M7 Hăşmaşul Mare *mt* Romania
21 B3 Hassan India
17 K4 Hassan Iraq
75 F5 Hassayampa *r.* U.S.A.
43 J4 Haßberge *reg.* Ger.
42 D4 Hasselt Belgium
42 E2 Hasselt Neth.
54 C1 Hassi Messaoud Alg.
37 N8 Hässleholm Sweden
8 E5 Hastings Austr.
9 F3 Hastings N.Z.
39 H7 Hastings U.K.
68 E4 Hastings *MI* U.S.A.
68 A3 Hastings *MN* U.S.A.
76 D3 Hastings *NE* U.S.A.
Hatay *see* Antakya
75 F3 Hatch U.S.A.
79 E7 Hatchet Bay Bahamas
65 J3 Hatchet Lake *l.* Can.
79 B5 Hatchie *r.* U.S.A.
8 D2 Hatfield Austr.
38 G4 Hatfield U.K.
24 C1 Hatgal Mongolia
22 D4 Hathras India
23 F4 Hatia Nepal
32 C3 Ha Tiên Vietnam
32 C1 Ha Tĩnh Vietnam
8 D3 Hattah Austr.
79 F5 Hatteras, Cape *c.* U.S.A.
36 N4 Hattfjelldal Norway
23 E6 Hatti *r.* India
79 B6 Hattiesburg U.S.A.
42 F3 Hattingen Ger.
56 E3 Haud *reg.* Eth.
37 K7 Hauge Norway
37 J7 Haugesund Norway
9 E3 Hauhungaroa *mt* N.Z.
37 K7 Haukeligrend Norway
36 T4 Haukipudas Fin.
37 V5 Haukivesi *l.* Fin.
65 H3 Haultain *r.* Can.
9 E2 Hauraki Gulf *g.* N.Z.
9 A7 Hauroko, L. *l.* N.Z.
54 B1 Haut Atlas *mts* Morocco
67 G4 Hauterive Can.
81 J3 Haut, Isle au *i.* U.S.A.
54 B1 Hauts Plateaux *plat.* Alg.
74 □1 Hauula U.S.A.
83 H4 Havana Cuba
68 B5 Havana U.S.A.
39 G7 Havant U.K.
75 E4 Havasu Lake *l.* U.S.A.
43 L2 Havel *r.* Ger.
42 D4 Havelange Belgium
43 L2 Havelberg Ger.
43 L2 Havelländisches Luch *marsh* Ger.
69 J3 Havelock Can.
79 E5 Havelock U.S.A.
9 F3 Havelock North N.Z.
39 C6 Haverfordwest U.K.
81 H3 Haverhill U.S.A.
21 A3 Haveri India
42 D4 Haversin Belgium
42 F3 Havixbeck Ger.
46 G6 Havlíčkův Brod Czech Rep.
36 T1 Havøysund Norway
49 M5 Havran Turkey
72 E1 Havre U.S.A.
67 H4 Havre Aubert, Île du *i.* Can.
81 E5 Havre de Grace U.S.A.
67 H3 Havre-St-Pierre Can.
49 M4 Havsa Turkey
16 E1 Havza Turkey
74 □2 Hawaii *i.* U.S.A.
5 K2 Hawaiian Islands *is* Pac. Oc.
94 H4 Hawaiian Ridge *sea feature* Pac. Oc.
74 □2 Hawaii Volcanoes National Park U.S.A.
17 L7 Ḥawallī Kuwait
39 D4 Hawarden U.K.
9 B6 Hawea, L. *l.* N.Z.
9 E3 Hawera N.Z.
38 E3 Hawes U.K.
74 □2 Hawi U.S.A.
40 F5 Hawick U.K.
17 L6 Hawīzah, Hawr al *l.* Iraq
9 B6 Hawkdun Range *mts* N.Z.
9 F3 Hawke Bay *b.* N.Z.
67 J3 Hawke Island *i.* Can.
8 B1 Hawker Austr.
81 F2 Hawkesbury Can.
75 F3 Hawkins Peak *summit* U.S.A.
69 F3 Hawks U.S.A.
81 K2 Hawkshaw Can.
81 F4 Hawley U.S.A.
17 J5 Ḥawrān, Wādī *watercourse* Iraq
58 C7 Hawston S. Africa
74 C2 Hawthorne U.S.A.
30 C1 Haxat China
38 F3 Haxby U.K.
8 E3 Hay Austr.
64 F2 Hay *r.* Can.
68 B3 Hay *r.* U.S.A.
26 B1 Haya China
28 G5 Hayachine-san *mt* Japan
18 B2 Haydarābād Iran
75 G5 Hayden *AZ* U.S.A.
72 C2 Hayden *ID* U.S.A.
65 L3 Hayes *r.* Can.
63 M2 Hayes Halvø *pen.* Greenland
39 B7 Hayle U.K.
16 D2 Haymana Turkey
80 E5 Haymarket U.S.A.
63 J3 Haynes *r.* Can.
81 J2 Haynesville U.S.A.
39 D5 Hay-on-Wye U.K.
51 C7 Hayrabolu Turkey
64 F2 Hay River Can.
76 D4 Hays U.S.A.
51 D5 Haysyn Ukr.
74 A3 Hayward *CA* U.S.A.
68 B2 Hayward *WI* U.S.A.
39 G7 Haywards Heath U.K.
19 G3 Hazarajat *reg.* Afgh.
80 B6 Hazard U.S.A.
23 F5 Hazārībāg India
23 E5 Hazaribagh Range *mts* India
42 A4 Hazebrouck France
64 D3 Hazelton Can.
81 F4 Hazelton U.S.A.
62 G2 Hazen Strait *chan.* Can.
42 C2 Hazerswoude-Rijndijk Neth.
17 G6 Ḥazm al Jalāmid *ridge* S. Arabia
19 G2 Hazrat Sultan Afgh.
17 H2 Hazro Turkey
41 B4 Headford Rep. of Ireland
74 A2 Healdsburg U.S.A.
8 E4 Healesville Austr.
39 F4 Heanor U.K.
93 J7 Heard Island *i.* Ind. Ocean
77 D6 Hearne U.S.A.
66 D4 Hearst Can.
92 B2 Hearst I. *i.* Ant.
39 H7 Heathfield U.K
81 E6 Heathsville U.S.A.
77 D7 Hebbronville U.S.A.
26 E2 Hebei *div.* China
75 F2 Heber Springs U.S.A.
26 E3 Hebi China
67 H2 Hebron Can.
68 D5 Hebron *IN* U.S.A.
76 D3 Hebron *NE* U.S.A.
81 G3 Hebron *NY* U.S.A.
16 E6 Hebron West Bank
67 H2 Hebron Fiord *in.* Can.
62 E4 Hecate Strait *B.C.* Can.
64 C4 Hecate Strait *chan.* Can.
84 E2 Hecelchakán Mex.
64 C3 Heceta I. *i.* U.S.A.
27 C5 Hechi China
27 C4 Hechuan China
37 N5 Hede Sweden
37 O6 Hedemora Sweden
27 D6 Hede Sk. *resr* China
72 C2 He Devil Mt. *mt* U.S.A.
68 A5 Hedrick U.S.A.
42 D2 Heeg Neth.
42 F2 Heek Ger.
42 C4 Heer Belgium
42 E2 Heerde Neth.
42 D2 Heerenveen Neth.
42 C2 Heerhugowaard Neth.
42 D4 Heerlen Neth.
Hefa *see* Haifa
26 E4 Hefei China
27 D4 Hefeng China
28 B1 Hegang China
29 E6 Hegura-jima *i.* Japan
43 K3 Heidberg *h.* Ger.
46 D3 Heide Ger.
57 B6 Heide Namibia
43 G5 Heidelberg Ger.
59 H3 Heidelberg *Gauteng* S. Africa
58 D7 Heidelberg *Western Cape* S. Africa
59 G3 Heilbron S. Africa
43 H5 Heilbronn Ger.
46 E3 Heiligenhafen Ger.
27 □ Hei Ling Chau *i. H.K.* China
30 E1 Heilongjiang *div.* China
24 E2 Heilong Jiang *r.* China/Rus. Fed.
43 J5 Heilsbronn Ger.
36 M5 Heimdal Norway
37 U6 Heinola Fin.
32 A2 Heinze Is *is* Myanmar
30 B3 Heishan China
23 C3 Heist-op-den-Berg Belgium
26 E2 Hejian China
27 B4 Hejiang China
27 D6 He Jiang *r.* China
26 D3 Hejin China
16 F2 Hekimhan Turkey
36 D5 Hekla *volc.* Iceland
26 B2 Hekou *Gansu* China
27 B6 Hekou *Yunnan* China
36 N5 Helagsfjället *mt* Sweden
26 B2 Helan Shan *mts* China
43 K3 Helbra Ger.
23 H4 Helem India
77 F5 Helena *AR* U.S.A.
72 E2 Helena *MT* U.S.A.
74 D3 Helen, Mt *mt* U.S.A.
40 D4 Helensburgh U.K.
16 E6 Ḥelez Israel
46 C3 Helgoland *i.* Ger.
46 D3 Helgoländer Bucht *b.* Ger.
36 C5 Hella Iceland
36 P2 Helland Norway
13 C4 Helleh *r.* Iran
42 C3 Hellevoetsluis Neth.
36 R2 Helligskogen Norway
45 F3 Hellín Spain
72 C2 Hells Canyon *gorge* U.S.A.
19 F4 Helmand *r.* Afgh.
43 K4 Helmbrechts Ger.
43 J3 Helme *r.* Ger.
57 B6 Helmeringhausen Namibia
58 E6 Helmeringhausen S. Africa
42 D3 Helmond Neth.
40 E2 Helmsdale U.K.
40 E2 Helmsdale *r.* U.K.
43 K2 Helmstedt Ger.
30 E2 Helong China
75 G2 Helper U.S.A.
37 N8 Helsingborg Sweden
37 N8 Helsingør Denmark
37 T6 Helsinki Fin.
39 B7 Helston U.K.
38 D3 Helvellyn *mt* U.K.
41 D5 Helvick Head *hd* Rep. of Ireland
55 F2 Helwân Egypt
39 G6 Hemel Hempstead U.K.
74 D5 Hemet U.S.A.
80 E3 Hemlock Lake *l.* U.S.A.
43 H2 Hemmingen Ger.
81 G2 Hemmingford Can.
43 H1 Hemmoor Ger.
77 D6 Hempstead U.S.A.
39 J5 Hemsby U.K.
37 Q8 Hemse Sweden
26 A3 Henan *Qinghai* China
26 D3 Henan *div.* China
45 E2 Henares *r.* Spain
28 F4 Henashi-zaki *pt* Japan
16 C1 Hendek Turkey
91 E3 Henderson Arg.
78 C4 Henderson *KY* U.S.A.
79 E4 Henderson *NC* U.S.A.
75 E3 Henderson *NV* U.S.A.
81 E3 Henderson *NY* U.S.A.
77 E5 Henderson *TX* U.S.A.
5 P7 Henderson Island *i.* Pac. Oc.
79 D5 Hendersonville *NC* U.S.A.
79 C4 Hendersonville *TN* U.S.A.
18 C4 Hendījān Iran
39 G6 Hendon U.K.
18 D5 Hendorābī *i.* Iran
24 B4 Hengduan Shan *mts* China
42 E2 Hengelo Neth.
27 D5 Hengshan *Hunan* China
26 C2 Hengshan *Shaanxi* China
30 F1 Hengshan China
27 D5 Heng Shan *mt Hunan* China
26 D2 Heng Shan *mt* China
26 E2 Hengshui China
27 C6 Heng Xian China
27 D5 Hengyang *Hunan* China
51 E6 Heniches'k Ukr.
9 C6 Henley N.Z.
39 G6 Henley-on-Thames U.K.
81 F5 Henlopen, Cape *pt* U.S.A.
42 F4 Hennef (Sieg) Ger.
59 G3 Hennenman S. Africa
43 M2 Hennigsdorf Berlin Ger.
81 H3 Henniker U.S.A.
77 D5 Henrietta U.S.A.
66 D2 Henrietta Maria, Cape *c.* Can.
75 G3 Henrieville U.S.A.
68 C5 Henry U.S.A.
92 B3 Henry Ice Rise *ice feature* Ant.
63 M3 Henry Kater, C. *hd* Can.
75 G2 Henry Mts *mts* U.S.A.
69 G4 Hensall Can.
43 H1 Henstedt-Ulzburg Ger.
57 B6 Hentiesbaai Namibia
8 F3 Henty Austr.
25 B5 Henzada Myanmar
65 H4 Hepburn Can.
27 E5 Heping China
27 C6 Hepu China
26 D2 Hequ China
19 F3 Herāt Afgh.
44 F5 Hérault *r.* France
65 H4 Herbert Can.
43 G4 Herborn Ger.
43 H4 Herbstein Ger.
92 B4 Hercules Dome *ice feature* Ant.
42 F3 Herdecke Ger.
43 F4 Herdorf Ger.
39 E5 Hereford U.K.
77 C5 Hereford U.S.A.
5 N6 Héréhérétué *i.* Pac. Oc.
42 C4 Herent Belgium
43 G2 Herford Ger.
43 J4 Heringen (Werra) Ger.
76 D4 Herington U.S.A.
18 B2 Herīs Iran
46 D7 Herisau Switz.
92 B3 Heritage Ra. *mts* Ant.
81 F3 Herkimer U.S.A.
43 J3 Herleshausen Ger.
40 □ Herma Ness *hd* U.K.
43 J2 Hermannsburg Ger.
58 C7 Hermanus S. Africa
59 H5 Hermes, Cape *pt* S. Africa
8 F1 Hermidale Austr.
72 C2 Hermiston U.S.A.
88 C9 Hermite, Is *i.* Chile
6 E2 Hermit Is *is* P.N.G.
Hermon, Mount *mt see* Sheikh, Jebel esh
91 B2 Hermosa, P. de V. *pass* Chile
89 B4 Hermosas, Parque Nacional las *nat. park* Col.
82 B3 Hermosillo Mex.
88 F3 Hernandarias Para.
42 F3 Herne Ger.
39 J6 Herne Bay U.K.
37 L8 Herning Denmark
68 D1 Heron Bay Can.
84 B2 Herradura Mex.
45 D3 Herrera del Duque Spain
84 A1 Herreras Mex.
43 J5 Herrieden Ger.
80 E4 Hershey U.S.A.
39 G6 Hertford U.K.
59 F4 Hertzogville S. Africa
42 D4 Herve Belgium
7 F4 Hervey Bay *b.* Austr.
5 M6 Hervey Islands *is* Pac. Oc.
43 L2 Herzberg *Brandenburg* Ger.
43 M3 Herzberg *Brandenburg* Ger.
42 F2 Herzlake Ger.
43 J5 Herzogenaurach Ger.
43 L1 Herzsprung Ger.
17 M4 Ḥeşar Iran
42 C4 Hesbaye *reg.* Belgium
42 F1 Hesel Ger.
27 C6 Heshan China
26 C3 Heshui China
26 D2 Heshun China
74 D4 Hesperia U.S.A.
64 C2 Hess *r.* Can.
43 J5 Heßdorf Ger.
43 J5 Hesselberg *h.* Ger.
43 H4 Hessen *div.* Ger.
43 H3 Hessisch Lichtenau Ger.
27 B6 Het *r.* Laos
74 B3 Hetch Hetchy Aqueduct *canal* U.S.A.
42 D3 Heteren Neth.
76 C2 Hettinger U.S.A.
38 E3 Hetton U.K.
43 K3 Hettstedt Ger.
38 E3 Hexham U.K.
26 F4 He Xian *Anhui* China
27 D5 He Xian *Guangxi* China
26 B2 Hexibao China
26 E1 Hexigten Qi China
58 C6 Hex River Pass S. Africa
26 D3 Heyang China
18 D4 Ḥeydarābād Iran
19 F4 Ḥeydarābād Iran
38 E3 Heysham U.K.
27 E6 Heyuan China
8 C5 Heywood Austr.
38 E4 Heywood U.K.
68 C5 Heyworth U.S.A.
26 E3 Heze China
27 B5 Hezhang China
26 B3 Hezheng China
26 B3 Hezuozhen China
79 D7 Hialeah U.S.A.
76 E4 Hiawatha U.S.A.
68 A2 Hibbing U.S.A.
79 D5 Hickory U.S.A.
9 G2 Hicks Bay N.Z.
65 K2 Hicks L. *l.* Can.
80 A4 Hicksville U.S.A.
77 D5 Hico U.S.A.
28 H3 Hidaka-sanmyaku *mts* Japan
84 C2 Hidalgo *div.* Mex.
82 C3 Hidalgo del Parral Mex.
82 C3 Hidalgo, Psa M. *resr* Mex.
90 C2 Hidrolândia Brazil
29 C7 Higashi-Hiroshima Japan
28 G5 Higashine Japan
29 D7 Higashi-ōsaka Japan
29 A8 Higashi-suidō *chan.* Japan
81 F3 Higgins Bay U.S.A.
68 E3 Higgins Lake *l.* U.S.A.
High Atlas *mts see* Haut Atlas
72 B3 High Desert U.S.A.
68 C3 High Falls Reservoir U.S.A.
68 E3 High I. *i.* U.S.A.
27 □ High Island Res. *H.K.* China
68 D4 Highland Park U.S.A.
74 C2 Highland Peak *summit CA* U.S.A.
75 E3 Highland Peak *summit NV* U.S.A.
64 F3 High Level Can.
23 F5 High Level Canal *canal* India
79 E5 High Point U.S.A.
64 F3 High Prairie Can.
64 G4 High River Can.
79 E7 High Rock Bahamas
65 J3 Highrock Lake *l.* Can.
38 E3 High Seat *h.* U.K.
81 F4 Hightstown U.S.A.
39 G6 High Wycombe U.K.
89 D2 Higuerote Venez.
37 S7 Hiiumaa *i.* Estonia
20 A4 Hijaz *reg.* S. Arabia
75 E3 Hiko U.S.A.
29 E7 Hikone Japan
9 G2 Hikurangi *mt* N.Z.
75 F3 Hildale U.S.A.
43 J4 Hildburghausen Ger.
43 J4 Hilders Ger.
43 H2 Hildesheim Ger.
23 G4 Hili Bangl.
92 B5 Hillary Coast *coastal area* Ant.
76 D4 Hill City U.S.A.
75 H2 Hill Creek *r.* U.S.A.
42 C2 Hillegom Neth.
37 N9 Hillerød Denmark
76 D2 Hillsboro *ND* U.S.A.
81 H3 Hillsboro *NH* U.S.A.
80 B5 Hillsboro *OH* U.S.A.
77 D5 Hillsboro *TX* U.S.A.
68 B4 Hillsboro *WV* U.S.A.
80 C5 Hillsboro *WV* U.S.A.
68 E5 Hillsdale *MI* U.S.A.
81 G3 Hillsdale *NY* U.S.A.
80 E4 Hillsgrove U.S.A.
40 F4 Hillside U.K.
75 F4 Hillside U.S.A.
8 E2 Hillston Austr.
80 C6 Hillsville U.S.A.
8 H3 Hilltop Austr.
74 □2 Hilo U.S.A.
59 J4 Hilton S. Africa
80 E3 Hilton U.S.A.
69 F2 Hilton Beach Can.
79 D5 Hilton Head Island U.S.A.
17 G3 Hilvan Turkey
42 D2 Hilversum Neth.
22 D3 Himachal Pradesh *div.* India
10 J6 Himalaya *mts* Asia
23 F3 Himalchul *mt* Nepal
36 S4 Himanka Fin.
49 H4 Himarë Albania
22 C5 Himatnagar India
29 D7 Himeji Japan
28 G5 Himekami-dake *mt* Japan
59 H4 Himeville S. Africa
29 E6 Himi Japan
16 F4 Ḥimş Syria
16 F4 Ḥimş, Baḥrat *resr* Syria
31 C4 Hinatuan Phil.
6 E3 Hinchinbrook I. *i.* Austr.
39 F5 Hinckley U.K.
68 A2 Hinckley *MN* U.S.A.
75 F2 Hinckley *UT* U.S.A.
81 F3 Hinckley Reservoir U.S.A.
22 D3 Hindan *r.* India
22 D4 Hindaun India
38 G3 Hinderwell U.K.
17 K5 Hindīyah Barrage Iraq
38 E4 Hindley U.K.
80 B6 Hindman U.S.A.
8 C4 Hindmarsh, L. *l.* Austr.
23 F5 Hindola India
19 G3 Hindu Kush *mts* Afgh./Pak.
21 B3 Hindupur India
64 F3 Hines Creek Can.
79 D6 Hinesville U.S.A.
22 D5 Hinganghat India
19 G5 Hinglaj Pak.
19 G5 Hingol *r.* Pak.
22 D6 Hingoli India
17 H2 Hınıs Turkey
74 D4 Hinkley U.S.A.
36 O2 Hinnøya *i.* Norway
31 B4 Hinobaan Phil.
45 D3 Hinojosa del Duque Spain
29 C7 Hino-misaki *pt* Japan
81 G3 Hinsdale U.S.A.
42 F1 Hinte Ger.
64 F4 Hinton Can.
80 C6 Hinton U.S.A.
42 C2 Hippolytushoef Neth.
17 K2 Hirabit Dağ *mt* Turkey
29 A8 Hirado Japan
29 A8 Hirado-shima *i.* Japan
23 E5 Hirakud Reservoir India
28 H3 Hiroo Japan
28 G4 Hirosaki Japan
29 C7 Hiroshima Japan
43 K5 Hirschaid Ger.
43 K4 Hirschberg Ger.
46 E7 Hirschberg *mt* Ger.
44 G2 Hirson France
37 L8 Hirtshals Denmark
17 M3 Hisar Iran
19 G3 Hisar, Koh-i- *mts* Afgh.
16 D1 Hisarönü Turkey
16 E6 Hisban Jordan
19 H2 Hisor Tajik.
83 K4 Hispaniola *i.* Caribbean Sea
22 C3 Hissar India
23 F4 Hisua India
17 J5 Hīt Iraq
29 G6 Hitachi Japan
29 G6 Hitachi-ōta Japan
29 B8 Hitoyoshi Japan
36 L5 Hitra *i.* Norway
43 K1 Hitzacker Ger.
29 C7 Hiuchi-nada *b.* Japan
5 O5 Hiva Oa *i.* Pac. Oc.
64 E4 Hixon Can.
17 J2 Hizan Turkey
37 O7 Hjälmaren *l.* Sweden
65 H2 Hjalmar Lake *l.* Can.
37 L5 Hjerkinn Norway
37 O7 Hjo Sweden
37 M8 Hjørring Denmark
59 J4 Hlabisa S. Africa
23 F3 Hlako Kangri *mt* China

59 J3 Hlatikulu Swaziland
51 E5 Hlobyne Ukr.
59 G4 Hlohlowane S. Africa
59 H4 Hlotse Lesotho
59 K4 Hluhluwe S. Africa
51 E5 Hlukhiv Ukr.
47 O4 Hlusha Belarus
50 C4 Hlybokaye Belarus
54 C4 Ho Ghana
57 B6 Hoachanas Namibia
6 E6 Hobart Austr.
77 D5 Hobart U.S.A.
77 C5 Hobbs U.S.A.
92 A4 Hobbs Coast *coastal area* Ant.
79 D7 Hobe Sound U.S.A.
37 L8 Hobro Denmark
56 E3 Hobyo Somalia
43 H5 Höchberg Ger.
32 C3 Hô Chi Minh Vietnam
46 G7 Hochschwab *mt* Austria
43 G5 Hockenheim Ger.
80 B5 Hocking *r.* U.S.A.
22 D4 Hodal India
38 E4 Hodder *r.* U.K.
39 G6 Hoddesdon U.K.
Hodeida *see* Al Hudaydah
81 K1 Hodgdon U.S.A.
47 K7 Hódmezővásárhely Hungary
45 J5 Hodna, Chott el *salt l.* Alg.
30 D4 Hodo dan *pt* N. Korea
42 C3 Hoek van Holland Neth.
42 D4 Hoensbroek Neth.
30 E2 Hoeryŏng N. Korea
30 D4 Hoeyang N. Korea
43 K4 Hof Ger.
43 J4 Hofheim in Unterfranken Ger.
59 F5 Hofmeyr S. Africa
36 F4 Höfn Iceland
37 P6 Hofors Sweden
36 D4 Hofsjökull *ice cap* Iceland
29 B7 Hōfu Japan
37 N8 Höganäs Sweden
54 C2 Hoggar *plat.* Alg.
81 F6 Hog I. *i.* U.S.A.
37 P8 Högsby Sweden
43 H5 Hohenloher Ebene *plain* Ger.
43 L3 Hohenmölsen Ger.
43 L2 Hohennauen Ger.
43 K4 Hohenwarte-talsperre *resr* Ger.
43 H4 Hohe Rhön *mts* Ger.
46 F7 Hohe Tauern *mts* Austria
42 E4 Hohe Venn *moorland* Belgium
26 D1 Hohhot China
23 G2 Hoh Xil Hu *salt l.* China
23 G2 Hoh Xil Shan *mts* China
32 D2 Hôi An Vietnam
56 D3 Hoima Uganda
27 B6 Hôi Xuân Vietnam
23 H4 Hojai India
29 C8 Hōjo Japan
9 D1 Hokianga Harbour *in.* N.Z.
9 C5 Hokitika N.Z.
28 H3 Hokkaidō *i.* Japan
37 L7 Hokksund Norway
17 K1 Hoktemberyan Armenia
37 L6 Hol Norway
21 B3 Holalkere India
37 M9 Holbæk Denmark
39 H5 Holbeach U.K.
75 G4 Holbrook U.S.A.
68 B3 Holcombe Flowage *resr* U.S.A.
65 G4 Holden Can.
75 F2 Holden U.S.A.
77 D5 Holdenville U.S.A.
76 D3 Holdrege U.S.A.
21 B3 Hole Narsipur India
83 J4 Holguín Cuba
37 N6 Höljes Sweden
68 D4 Holland U.S.A.
80 D4 Hollidaysburg U.S.A.
64 C3 Hollis *AK* U.S.A.
77 D5 Hollis *OK* U.S.A.
74 B3 Hollister U.S.A.
69 F4 Holly U.S.A.
77 F5 Holly Springs U.S.A.
79 D7 Hollywood U.S.A.
36 N4 Holm Norway
62 G2 Holman Can.
36 T2 Holmestrand *Finnmark* Norway
37 M7 Holmestrand *Vestfold* Norway
36 R5 Holmön *i.* Sweden
63 M2 Holms Ø *i.* Greenland
36 R5 Holmsund Sweden
58 B3 Holoog Namibia
37 L8 Holstebro Denmark
79 D4 Holston *r.* U.S.A.
80 C6 Holston Lake *l.* U.S.A.
39 C7 Holsworthy U.K.
39 J5 Holt U.K.
68 E4 Holt U.S.A.
76 E4 Holton U.S.A.
42 D1 Holwerd Neth.
41 D5 Holycross Rep. of Ireland
39 C4 Holyhead U.K.
39 C4 Holyhead Bay *b.* U.K.
38 F2 Holy Island *i.* *Eng.* U.K.
39 C4 Holy Island *i.* *Wales* U.K.
81 G3 Holyoke U.S.A.
39 D4 Holywell U.K.
43 L3 Holzhausen Ger.
46 E7 Holzkirchen Ger.
43 H3 Holzminden Ger.
18 C3 Homāyunshahr Iran
43 H3 Homberg (Efze) Ger.
54 B3 Hombori Mali
42 F5 Homburg Ger.
63 M3 Home Bay *b.* Can.
42 D5 Homécourt France
77 E5 Homer U.S.A.
79 D6 Homerville U.S.A.
79 D7 Homestead U.S.A.
79 C5 Homewood U.S.A.
21 B2 Homnabad India
31 C4 Homonhon *pt* Phil.
Homs *see* Ḥimṣ
51 D4 Homyel' Belarus
21 A3 Honavar India
89 B3 Honda Col.
31 A4 Honda Bay *b.* Phil.
75 H4 Hon Dah U.S.A.
58 B5 Hondeklipbaai S. Africa
26 C1 Hondlon Ju China
77 D6 Hondo U.S.A.
42 E1 Hondsrug *reg.* Neth.
61 K8 Honduras *country* Central America
37 M6 Hønefoss Norway
81 F4 Honesdale U.S.A.
74 B1 Honey Lake *l.* U.S.A.
81 E3 Honeyoye Lake *l.* U.S.A.
44 E2 Honfleur France
26 E4 Hong'an China
30 D5 Hongch'ŏn S. Korea
27 C6 Hông Gai Vietnam
27 E6 Honghai Wan *b.* China
27 B6 Honghe China
26 E3 Hong He *r.* China
27 D4 Honghu China
27 C5 Hongjiang China
27 E6 Hong Kong China
27 E6 Hong Kong *div.* China
27 □ Hong Kong Island *i.* *H.K.* China
26 C2 Hongliu *r.* China
26 B2 Hongliuyuan China
32 C3 Hông Ngư Vietnam
27 C6 Hong or Red River, Mouths of the *est.* Vietnam
27 C7 Hongqizhen China
26 B2 Hongshansi China
30 D2 Hongshi China
27 D6 Hongshui He *r.* China
27 C6 Hông, Sông *r.* Vietnam
26 D2 Hongtong China
67 G4 Honguedo, Détroit d' *chan.* Can.
30 D3 Hongwŏn N. Korea
30 B1 Hongxing China
26 B3 Hongyuan China
26 F3 Hongze China
26 F3 Hongze Hu *l.* China
7 F2 Honiara Solomon Is
39 D7 Honiton U.K.
28 G5 Honjō Japan
37 S6 Honkajoki Fin.
32 C3 Hon Khoai *i.* Vietnam
32 D2 Hon Lon *i.* Vietnam
32 C1 Hon Mê *i.* Vietnam
21 A3 Honnali India
36 T1 Honningsvåg Norway
74 □2 Honokaa U.S.A.
74 □1 Honolulu U.S.A.
32 C3 Hon Rai *i.* Vietnam
29 C7 Honshū *i.* Japan
72 B2 Hood, Mt *volc.* U.S.A.
6 B5 Hood Pt *pt* Austr.
42 E2 Hoogeveen Neth.
42 E1 Hoogezand-Sappemeer Neth.
77 C4 Hooker U.S.A.
41 E5 Hook Head *hd* Rep. of Ireland
Hook of Holland *see* Hoek van Holland
64 B3 Hoonah U.S.A.
62 B3 Hooper Bay *AK* U.S.A.
81 E5 Hooper I. *i.* U.S.A.
68 D5 Hoopeston U.S.A.
59 F3 Hoopstad S. Africa
37 N9 Höör Sweden
42 D2 Hoorn Neth.
81 G3 Hoosick U.S.A.
75 E3 Hoover Dam *dam* U.S.A.
80 B4 Hoover Memorial Reservoir U.S.A.
17 H1 Hopa Turkey
81 F4 Hop Bottom U.S.A.
64 E5 Hope *B.C.* Can.
77 E5 Hope *AR* U.S.A.
75 F5 Hope *AZ* U.S.A.
9 D5 Hope *r.* N.Z.
67 J2 Hopedale Can.
58 C6 Hopefield S. Africa
84 E3 Hopelchén Mex.
67 H3 Hope Mountains Can.
12 D2 Hopen *i.* Svalbard
62 B3 Hope, Point *c.* U.S.A.
9 D4 Hope Saddle *pass* N.Z.
67 G2 Hopes Advance, Baie *b.* Can.
8 D3 Hopetoun Austr.
58 F4 Hopetown S. Africa
80 E6 Hopewell U.S.A.
67 G2 Hopewell Islands *is* Can.
6 C4 Hopkins, L. *salt flat* Austr.
78 C4 Hopkinsville U.S.A.
74 A2 Hopland U.S.A.
72 B2 Hoquiam U.S.A.
26 A3 Hor China
17 L2 Horadiz Azer.
17 J1 Horasan Turkey
37 N9 Hörby Sweden
68 C4 Horeb, Mount U.S.A.
26 H1 Hörh Uul *mts* Mongolia
68 C4 Horicon U.S.A.
26 D1 Horinger China
94 H6 Horizon Depth *depth* Pac. Oc.
50 D4 Horki Belarus
92 B4 Horlick Mts *mts* Ant.
51 F5 Horlivka Ukr.
19 F4 Hormak Iran
18 E5 Hormoz *i.* Iran
18 E5 Hormuz, Strait of *str.* Iran/Oman
46 G6 Horn Austria
36 B3 Horn *c.* Iceland
64 F2 Horn *r.* Can.
36 P3 Hornavan *l.* Sweden
77 E6 Hornbeck U.S.A.
43 J2 Hornburg Ger.
88 C9 Horn, Cape *c.* Chile
39 G4 Horncastle U.K.
37 P6 Horndal Sweden
43 H1 Horneburg Ger.
36 Q5 Hörnefors Sweden
80 E3 Hornell U.S.A.
66 D4 Hornepayne Can.
79 B6 Horn I. *i.* U.S.A.
46 D6 Hornisgrinde *mt* Ger.
7 J3 Horn, Îles de *is* Wallis and Futuna Is
58 B1 Hornkranz Namibia
91 B4 Hornopiren, V. *volc.* Chile
84 B1 Hornos Mex.
Hornos, Cabo de *c.* *see* Horn, Cape
8 H2 Hornsby Austr.
38 G4 Hornsea U.K.
37 P6 Hornslandet *pen.* Sweden
47 M6 Horodenka Ukr.
51 D5 Horodnya Ukr.
51 C5 Horodok *Khmel'nyts'kyy* Ukr.
51 B5 Horodok *L'viv* Ukr.
28 H2 Horokanai Japan
47 M5 Horokhiv Ukr.
28 H3 Horoshiri-dake *mt* Japan
30 A2 Horqin Shadi *reg.* China
24 E2 Horqin Youyi Qianqi China
30 A1 Horqin Youyi Zhongqi China
30 B2 Horqin Zuoyi Houqi China
30 B1 Horqin Zuoyi Zhongqi China
39 C7 Horrabridge U.K.
23 G3 Horru China
64 E4 Horsefly Can.
80 E3 Horseheads U.S.A.
67 J3 Horse Is *is* Can.
41 C4 Horseleap Rep. of Ireland
37 L9 Horsens Denmark
72 C3 Horseshoe Bend U.S.A.
8 D4 Horsham Austr.
39 G6 Horsham U.K.
43 L5 Horšovský Týn Czech Rep.
43 H4 Horst *h.* Ger.
42 F2 Hörstel Ger.
37 M7 Horten Norway
62 F3 Horton *r.* Can.
69 F1 Horwood Lake *l.* Can.
47 N5 Horyn' *r.* Ukr.
23 H2 Ho Sai Hu *l.* China
56 D3 Hosa'ina Eth.
43 H4 Hösbach Ger.
21 B3 Hosdurga India
17 L4 Hoseynābād Iran
18 C4 Ḥoseynīyeh Iran
19 F5 Hoshab Pak.
22 D5 Hoshangabad India
22 C3 Hoshiarpur India
21 B3 Hospet India
41 C5 Hospital Rep. of Ireland
91 F1 Hospital, Cuchilla del *h.* Uru.
88 C9 Hoste, I. *i.* Chile
36 O5 Hotagen *l.* Sweden
15 G3 Hotan China
58 E3 Hotazel S. Africa
75 G4 Hotevilla U.S.A.
8 F4 Hotham, Mt *mt* Austr.
36 P4 Hoting Sweden
77 E5 Hot Springs *AR* U.S.A.
76 C3 Hot Springs *SD* U.S.A.
64 F1 Hottah Lake *l.* Can.
83 K5 Hotte, Massif de la *mts* Haiti
42 D4 Houffalize Belgium
32 □ Hougang Sing.
68 C2 Houghton U.S.A.
68 E3 Houghton Lake U.S.A.
68 E3 Houghton Lake *l.* U.S.A.
38 F3 Houghton le Spring U.K.
81 K1 Houlton U.S.A.
26 D3 Houma China
77 F6 Houma U.S.A.
40 C3 Hourn, Loch *in.* U.K.
81 G3 Housatonic U.S.A.
75 F2 House Range *mts* U.S.A.
64 D4 Houston Can.
77 F4 Houston *MO* U.S.A.
77 F5 Houston *MS* U.S.A.
77 E6 Houston *TX* U.S.A.
59 H1 Hout *r.* S. Africa
6 B4 Houtman Abrolhos *is* Austr.
40 E2 Houton U.K.
58 E5 Houwater S. Africa
24 B2 Hovd Mongolia
39 G7 Hove U.K.
39 J5 Hoveton U.K.
18 C4 Hoveyzeh Iran
37 O8 Hovmantorp Sweden
26 C1 Hövsgöl Mongolia
24 C1 Hövsgöl Nuur *l.* Mongolia
24 C2 Hövüün Mongolia
68 E4 Howard City U.S.A.
65 H2 Howard Lake *l.* Can.
38 G4 Howden U.K.
8 G4 Howe, C. *hd* Austr.
69 F4 Howell U.S.A.
76 C2 Howes U.S.A.
81 G2 Howick Can.
59 J4 Howick S. Africa
8 F4 Howitt, Mt *mt* Austr.
81 J2 Howland U.S.A.
7 J1 Howland Island *i.* Pac. Oc.
8 F3 Howlong Austr.
41 E4 Howth Rep. of Ireland
18 D3 Ḥowz-e Dūmatu Iran
18 E4 Ḥowz-e Panj Iran
43 H3 Höxter Ger.
40 E2 Hoy *i.* U.K.
43 H2 Hoya Ger.
37 K6 Høyanger Norway
46 G5 Hoyerswerda Ger.
36 N4 Høylandet Norway
43 K3 Hoym Ger.
36 V5 Höytiäinen *l.* Fin.
17 G2 Hozat Turkey
46 G5 Hradec Králové Czech Rep.
43 M4 Hradiště *h.* Czech Rep.
49 H3 Hrasnica Bos.-Herz.
17 K1 Hrazdan Armenia
51 E5 Hrebinka Ukr.
50 B4 Hrodna Belarus
27 F6 Hsi-hsu-p'ing Hsü *i.* Taiwan
27 F5 Hsin-chu Taiwan
27 F5 Hsueh Shan *mt* Taiwan
27 E5 Hua'an China
89 D4 Huachamacari, Cerro *mt* Venez.
26 C2 Huachi China
86 C6 Huacho Peru
28 B1 Huachuan China
75 G6 Huachuca City U.S.A.
91 C1 Huaco Arg.
26 D1 Huade China
30 D2 Huadian China
26 E1 Huai'an *Hebei* China
26 F3 Huai'an *Jiangsu* China
26 E3 Huaibei China
26 E3 Huaibin China
30 C2 Huaide China
30 C2 Huaidezhen China
26 F3 Huai He *r.* China
27 C5 Huaihua China
27 D6 Huaiji China
26 E1 Huailai China
27 B7 Huai Luang *r.* Thai.
26 E3 Huainan China
27 E4 Huaining China
26 D2 Huairen China
26 E3 Huaiyang China
26 F3 Huaiyin China
26 E3 Huaiyuan *Anhui* China
27 C5 Huaiyuan *Guangxi* China
26 B3 Huajialing China
84 C3 Huajuápan de León Mex.
25 E7 Huaki Indon.
75 F4 Hualapai Peak *summit* U.S.A.
27 F5 Hua-lien Taiwan
86 C5 Huallaga *r.* Peru
26 B2 Hualong China
57 B5 Huambo Angola
28 B1 Huanan China
91 C4 Huancache, Sa *mts* Arg.
86 C6 Huancayo Peru
26 E2 Huangbizhuang Sk. *resr* China
26 A2 Huangcheng China
26 E3 Huangchuan China
27 E4 Huanggang China
Huang Hai *sea see* Yellow Sea
26 E2 Huang He *r.* China
26 F2 Huanghe Kou *est.* China
23 H2 Huanghetan China
26 E2 Huanghua China
26 C3 Huangling China
27 C7 Huangliu China
27 E4 Huangmei China
30 C2 Huangnihe China
27 E4 Huangpi China
27 C5 Huangping China
26 D1 Huangqi Hai *l.* China
27 F4 Huangshan China
27 F4 Huang Shan *mt* China
27 E4 Huangshi China
26 B2 Huang Shui *r.* China
26 C2 Huangtu Gaoyuan *plat.* China
26 F2 Huang Xian China
27 F4 Huangyan China
26 A2 Huangyuan China
27 C5 Huanjiang China
26 C2 Huan Jiang *r.* China
30 C3 Huanren China
26 F2 Huantai China
86 C5 Huanuco Peru
86 E7 Huanuni Bol.
26 C2 Huan Xian China
27 G5 Hua-p'ing Hsü *i.* Taiwan
86 C5 Huaráz Peru
86 C6 Huarmey Peru
27 D4 Huarong China
86 C5 Huascaran, Nevado de *mt* Peru
88 B3 Huasco Chile
88 B3 Huasco *r.* Chile
30 D2 Huashulinzi China
82 C3 Huatabampo Mex.
26 C3 Huating China
30 A3 Huatong China
84 C3 Huatusco Mex.
84 C2 Huauchinango Mex.
84 C3 Huautla Mex.
27 D6 Hua Xian *Guangdong* China
26 E3 Hua Xian *Henan* China
26 D4 Huayuan *Hubei* China
27 C4 Huayuan *Hunan* China
27 C4 Huayun China
27 D6 Huazhou China
69 F3 Hubbard Lake *l.* U.S.A.
64 B2 Hubbard, Mt *mt* Can./U.S.A.
67 G2 Hubbard, Pointe *hd* Can.
26 D4 Hubei *div.* China
21 A3 Hubli India
30 D3 Huch'ang N. Korea
42 E3 Hückelhoven Ger.
39 F4 Hucknall U.K.
38 F4 Huddersfield U.K.
80 B6 Huddy U.S.A.
37 P6 Hudiksvall Sweden
68 E5 Hudson *MI* U.S.A.
81 G3 Hudson *NY* U.S.A.
68 A3 Hudson *WI* U.S.A.
78 F3 Hudson *r.* U.S.A.
65 J4 Hudson Bay *Sask.* Can.
63 K4 Hudson Bay *b.* Can.
81 G3 Hudson Falls U.S.A.
63 Q2 Hudson Land *reg.* Greenland
92 A3 Hudson Mts *mts* Ant.
64 E3 Hudson's Hope Can.
63 L3 Hudson Strait *str.* Can.
32 C1 Huê Vietnam
91 A4 Huechucuicui, Pta *pt* Chile
82 F5 Huehuetenango Guatemala
84 A1 Huehueto, Cerro *mt* Mex.
84 C3 Huejotzingo Mex.
84 C2 Huejutla Mex.
45 C4 Huelva Spain
91 B1 Huentelauquén Chile
91 B4 Huequi, Volcán *volc.* Chile
45 F4 Huércal-Overa Spain
45 F1 Huesca Spain
45 E4 Huéscar Spain
84 B3 Huétamo Mex.
80 E4 Hughesville U.S.A.
23 F5 Hugli *est.* India
23 G5 Hugli-Chunchura India
77 E5 Hugo U.S.A.
77 C4 Hugoton U.S.A.
26 D2 Huguan China
58 F3 Huhudi S. Africa
27 F5 Hui'an China
26 C2 Hui'anbu China
9 F3 Huiarau Range *mts* N.Z.
58 B3 Huib-Hoch Plateau *plat.* Namibia
27 E5 Huichang China
30 D3 Huich'ŏn N. Korea
27 E6 Huidong *Guangdong* China
27 B5 Huidong *Sichuan* China
30 D2 Huifa *r.* China
42 C3 Huijbergen Neth.
26 E3 Huiji *r.* China
27 E6 Huilai China
89 B4 Huila, Nevado de *mt* Col.
27 B5 Huili China
84 D3 Huimanguillo Mex.
26 E2 Huimin China
88 C2 Huinahuaca Arg.
30 D2 Huinan China
91 D2 Huinca Renancó Arg.
26 B3 Huining China
27 C5 Huishui China
23 G2 Huiten Nur *l.* China
27 C5 Huitong China
37 S6 Huittinen Fin.
84 C3 Huitzuco Mex.
26 C3 Hui Xian *Gansu* China
26 D3 Hui Xian *Henan* China
84 D4 Huixtla Mex.
27 B5 Huize China
27 E6 Huizhou China
24 C2 Hujirt Mongolia
27 F4 Hukou China
58 D1 Hukuntsi Botswana
82 E2 Hulbert Lake *l.* U.S.A.
18 B3 Hulilan Iran
28 C2 Hulin China
69 K3 Hull Can.
37 O8 Hultsfred Sweden
30 A3 Huludao China
24 D2 Hulun Nur *l.* China
51 F6 Hulyaypole Ukr.
24 E1 Huma China
86 F5 Humaitá Brazil
58 F7 Humansdorp S. Africa
18 B5 Humayyān, J. *h.* S. Arabia
38 H4 Humber, Mouth of the *est.* U.K.
65 H4 Humboldt Can.
72 C3 Humboldt *r.* U.S.A.
72 A3 Humboldt Bay *b.* U.S.A.
74 C1 Humboldt Lake *l.* U.S.A.
74 C1 Humboldt Range *mts* U.S.A.
74 D2 Humbolt Salt Marsh *marsh* U.S.A.
19 E5 Hūmedān Iran
27 D7 Hu Men *chan.* China
47 K6 Humenné Slovakia
8 F3 Hume Reservoir *resr* Austr.
73 C4 Humphreys, Mt *mt* U.S.A.
75 G4 Humphreys Peak *summit* U.S.A.
30 B3 Hun *r.* China
36 C4 Húnaflói *b.* Iceland
27 D5 Hunan *div.* China
30 F2 Hunchun China
30 F2 Hunchun *r.* China
43 L3 Hundeluft Ger.
37 M9 Hundested Denmark
49 K2 Hunedoara Romania
43 H4 Hünfeld Ger.
34 G4 Hungary *country* Europe
6 E4 Hungerford Austr.
30 D4 Hŭngnam N. Korea
72 D1 Hungry Horse Res. *resr* U.S.A.
27 □ Hung Shui Kiu *H.K.* China
27 C6 Hưng Yên Vietnam
30 D3 Hunjiang China
30 C3 Hun Jiang *r.* China
58 B3 Huns Mountains Namibia
42 F5 Hunsrück *reg.* Ger.
39 H5 Hunstanton U.K.
21 B3 Hunsur India
75 H4 Hunt U.S.A.
43 G2 Hunte *r.* Ger.
81 F3 Hunter U.S.A.
8 H2 Hunter *r.* Austr.
64 D4 Hunter I. *i.* Can.
7 H4 Hunter I. *i.* New Caledonia
6 E6 Hunter Is *is* Austr.
23 H6 Hunter's Bay *b.* Myanmar
9 C6 Hunters Hills, The *h.* N.Z.
81 F2 Huntingdon Can.
39 G5 Huntingdon U.K.
80 E4 Huntingdon U.S.A.
68 E5 Huntington *IN* U.S.A.
75 G2 Huntington *UT* U.S.A.
80 B5 Huntington *WV* U.S.A.
74 D5 Huntington Beach U.S.A.
9 E2 Huntly N.Z.
40 F3 Huntly U.K.
69 H3 Huntsville Can.
79 C5 Huntsville *AL* U.S.A.
77 E6 Huntsville *TX* U.S.A.
26 D2 Hunyuan China
22 C1 Hunza Pak.
22 C2 Hunza *r.* Pak.
30 B1 Huolin *r.* China
26 E2 Huolu China
32 C1 Hương Khê Vietnam
32 C1 Hương Thuy Vietnam
6 E2 Huon Peninsula *pen.* P.N.G.
26 E3 Huoqiu China
26 E4 Huoshan China
26 E4 Huo Shan *mt* China
27 F6 Huo-shao Tao *i.* Taiwan
26 D2 Huo Xian China
18 E4 Hūr Iran
69 G3 Hurd, Cape *hd* Can.
26 C1 Hure Jadgai China
30 A2 Hure Qi China
55 F2 Hurghada Egypt
68 C1 Hurkett Can.
41 C5 Hurler's Cross Rep. of Ireland
68 B2 Hurley U.S.A.
76 D2 Huron U.S.A.
68 C2 Huron Bay *b.* U.S.A.
69 F3 Huron, Lake *l.* Can./U.S.A.
68 D2 Huron Mts *h.* U.S.A.
75 F3 Hurricane U.S.A.
39 F6 Hursley U.K.
39 H6 Hurst Green U.K.
9 D5 Hurunui *r.* N.Z.
36 E3 Húsavík *Norðurland eystra* Iceland
36 C4 Húsavík *Vestfirðir* Iceland
47 O7 Huşi Romania
37 O8 Huskvarna Sweden
62 C3 Huslia U.S.A.
37 J7 Husnes Norway
23 F4 Hussainabad India
46 D3 Husum Ger.
36 Q5 Husum Sweden
24 C2 Hutag Mongolia
76 D4 Hutchinson U.S.A.
75 G4 Hutch Mtn *mt* U.S.A.
32 A1 Huthi Myanmar
28 C2 Hutou China
65 N2 Hut Point *pt* Can.
80 D5 Huttonsville U.S.A.
26 D2 Hutuo *r.* China
16 G3 Hüvek Turkey
26 C3 Hu Xian China
26 F4 Huzhou China
26 A2 Huzhu China
36 E4 Hvannadalshnúkur *mt* Iceland
48 G3 Hvar *i.* Croatia
51 E6 Hvardiys'ke Ukr.
36 C4 Hveragerði Iceland
37 L8 Hvide Sande Denmark
36 C4 Hvíta *r.* Iceland
30 E3 Hwadae N. Korea
57 C5 Hwange Zimbabwe
57 C5 Hwange National Park Zimbabwe
30 C4 Hwangju N. Korea
57 D5 Hwedza Zimbabwe
81 H4 Hyannis *MA* U.S.A.
76 C3 Hyannis *NE* U.S.A.
24 B2 Hyargas Nuur *l.* Mongolia
64 C3 Hydaburg U.S.A.
9 C6 Hyde N.Z.
6 B5 Hyden Austr.
80 B6 Hyden U.S.A.
81 G4 Hyde Park U.S.A.
75 F5 Hyder U.S.A.
21 B2 Hyderabad India
22 B4 Hyderabad Pak.
44 H5 Hyères France
44 H5 Hyères, Îles d' *is* France
30 E3 Hyesan N. Korea
64 D2 Hyland *r.* Can.
37 J6 Hyllestad Norway
37 N8 Hyltebruk Sweden
8 C4 Hynam Austr.
29 D7 Hyōnosen *mt* Japan
36 V4 Hyrynsalmi Fin.
64 F3 Hythe Can.
39 J6 Hythe U.K.
29 B8 Hyūga Japan
37 T6 Hyvinkää Fin.

I

86 E6 Iaco *r.* Brazil
87 K6 Iaçu Brazil
57 E6 Iakora Madag.
49 M2 Ialomiţa *r.* Romania
49 M2 Ianca Romania
47 N7 Iaşi Romania
31 A3 Iba Phil.
54 C4 Ibadan Nigeria
89 B3 Ibagué Col.
75 F1 Ibapah U.S.A.
86 C3 Ibarra Ecuador
20 B7 Ibb Yemen
43 F2 Ibbenbüren Ger.
32 A4 Ibi Indon.
54 C4 Ibi Nigeria
90 C2 Ibiá Brazil
87 K4 Ibiapaba, Serra da *h.* Brazil
91 F1 Ibicuí da Cruz *r.* Brazil
90 E2 Ibiraçu Brazil
45 G3 Ibiza Spain
45 G3 Ibiza *i.* *Balearic Is* Spain
48 F6 Iblei, Monti *mts* *Sicily* Italy
18 B5 Ibn Buşayyiş *well* S. Arabia
87 K6 Ibotirama Brazil
20 E5 Ibrā' Oman
20 E5 Ibrī Oman
31 B1 Ibuhos *i.* Phil.
29 B9 Ibusuki Japan
86 C6 Ica Peru
89 D4 Içana Brazil
89 D4 Içana *r.* Brazil
75 E3 Iceberg Canyon U.S.A.
16 E3 İçel Turkey
34 C2 Iceland *country* Europe
21 A2 Ichalkaranji India
21 D2 Ichchapuram India
29 B8 Ichifusa-yama *mt* Japan
28 G5 Ichinoseki Japan
13 R4 Ichinskaya Sopka *mt* Rus. Fed.
51 E5 Ichnya Ukr.
30 D4 Ich'ŏn N. Korea
30 D5 Ich'ŏn S. Korea
42 B3 Ichtegem Belgium
43 J4 Ichtershausen Ger.
64 B3 Icy Pt *pt* U.S.A.
64 B3 Icy Strait *chan.* U.S.A.
77 E5 Idabel U.S.A.
72 D2 Idaho *div.* U.S.A.
72 D3 Idaho City U.S.A.
72 D3 Idaho Falls U.S.A.
42 F5 Idar-Oberstein Ger.
55 F2 Idfu Egypt
54 D2 Idhān Awbārī *des.* Libya
55 D2 Idhān Murzūq *des.* Libya
56 B4 Idiofa Congo(Zaire)
62 C3 Iditarod U.S.A.
36 S2 Idivuoma Sweden
16 C6 Idku Egypt
16 F4 Idlib Syria
37 N6 Idre Sweden
43 G4 Idstein Ger.
59 H6 Idutywa S. Africa
37 T8 Iecava Latvia
90 B3 Iepê Brazil
42 A4 Ieper Belgium
49 L7 Ierapetra Greece
57 D4 Ifakara Tanz.
57 E6 Ifanadiana Madag.
54 C4 Ife Nigeria
36 U1 Ifjord Norway
33 D2 Igan Malaysia
90 C3 Igarapava Brazil
12 K3 Igarka Rus. Fed.
22 C6 Igatpuri India
17 K2 Iğdır Turkey
37 P6 Iggesund Sweden
48 C5 Iglesias *Sardinia* Italy
63 K3 Igloolik Can.
66 B4 Ignace Can.
37 U9 Ignalina Lith.
51 C7 İğneada Turkey
49 N4 İğneada Burnu *pt* Turkey
47 Q3 Igorevskaya Rus. Fed.
49 J5 Igoumenitsa Greece
12 H3 Igrim Rus. Fed.
90 B4 Iguaçu *r.* Brazil
90 A4 Iguaçu Falls *waterfall* Arg./Brazil
90 E1 Iguaí Brazil
89 B4 Iguaje, Mesa de *h.* Col.
84 C3 Iguala Mex.
45 G2 Igualada Spain
90 C4 Iguape Brazil
90 D3 Iguarapé Brazil
90 A3 Iguatemi Brazil
90 A3 Iguatemi *r.* Brazil
87 L5 Iguatu Brazil
Iguazú, Cataratas do *waterfall see* Iguaçu Falls
56 A4 Iguéla Gabon
56 D4 Igunga Tanz.
57 E5 Iharaña Madag.
24 C2 Ihbulag Mongolia
57 E6 Ihosy Madag.
30 B2 Ih Tal China
29 F6 Iide-san *mt* Japan
36 U2 Iijärvi *l.* Fin.
36 T4 Iijoki *r.* Fin.
36 U5 Iisalmi Fin.
29 B8 Iizuka Japan
54 C4 Ijebu-Ode Nigeria
17 K1 Ijevan Armenia
42 C2 IJmuiden Neth.
42 D2 IJssel *r.* Neth.
42 D2 IJsselmeer *l.* Neth.
37 S6 Ikaalinen Fin.
59 G2 Ikageleng S. Africa
59 G3 Ikageng S. Africa
49 M6 Ikaria *i.* Greece
37 L8 Ikast Denmark
28 H3 Ikeda Japan
56 C4 Ikela Congo(Zaire)
49 K3 Ikhtiman Bulg.
58 F4 Ikhutseng S. Africa
29 A8 Iki *i.* Japan
51 H6 Iki-Burul Rus. Fed.
54 C4 Ikom Nigeria
57 E6 Ikongo Madag.
51 H6 Ikryanoye Rus. Fed.
56 D4 Ikungu Tanz.
31 B2 Ilagan Phil.
56 D3 Ilaisamis Kenya
18 B3 Īlām Iran
23 F4 Ilam Nepal
54 C4 Ilaro Nigeria
47 J4 Iława Pol.
65 H3 Île-à-la-Crosse Can.
65 H3 Île-à-la-Crosse, Lac *l.* Can.
56 C4 Ilebo Congo(Zaire)
56 D3 Ileret Kenya
50 G2 Ileza Rus. Fed.
65 K3 Ilford Can.
39 H6 Ilford U.K.
39 C6 Ilfracombe U.K.
16 D1 Ilgaz Turkey
16 D1 Ilgaz D. *mts* Turkey
16 C2 Ilgın Turkey
89 D5 Ilha Grande Brazil
90 D3 Ilha Grande, Baía da *b.* Brazil
90 B3 Ilha Grande, Represa *resr* Brazil
90 B3 Ilha Solteira, Represa *resr* Brazil
45 B2 Ílhavo Port.
90 E1 Ilhéus Brazil
54 □ Ilhéus Secos ou do Rombo *i.* Cape Verde
62 C4 Iliamna Lake *l.* U.S.A.
16 G2 İliç Turkey
31 C4 Iligan Phil.
31 C4 Iligan Bay *b.* Phil.
50 H2 Il'insko-Podomskoye Rus. Fed.
81 F3 Ilion U.S.A.
21 B3 Ilkal India
39 F5 Ilkeston U.K.
38 F4 Ilkley U.K.
31 B5 Illana Bay *b.* Phil.
91 B1 Illapel Chile
91 B1 Illapel *r.* Chile
46 E7 Iller *r.* Ger.
51 D6 Illichivs'k Ukr.
86 E7 Illimani, Nevado de *mt* Bol.
68 C5 Illinois *div.* U.S.A.
68 C5 Illinois *r.* U.S.A.
68 B5 Illinois and Mississippi Canal *canal* U.S.A.
51 D5 Illintsi Ukr.
54 C2 Illizi Alg.
43 K4 Ilm *r.* Ger.
36 S5 Ilmajoki Fin.
43 J4 Ilmenau Ger.
43 J1 Ilmenau *r.* Ger.
50 D3 Il'men', Ozero *l.* Rus. Fed.
39 E7 Ilminster U.K.
86 D7 Ilo Peru
31 A4 Iloc *i.* Phil.
31 B4 Iloilo Phil.
36 W5 Ilomantsi Fin.
54 C4 Ilorin Nigeria
51 F6 Ilovays'k Ukr.
51 G5 Ilovlya Rus. Fed.
51 H5 Ilovlya *r.* Rus. Fed.
43 J2 Ilsede Ger.
63 N3 Ilulissat Greenland
29 C7 Imabari Japan
29 F6 Imaichi Japan
17 K6 Imām al Ḥamzah Iraq
16 E3 İmamoğlu Turkey
17 K5 Imām Ḥamīd Iraq
28 D2 Iman *r.* Rus. Fed.
29 A8 Imari Japan
89 E3 Imataca, Serranía de *mts* Venez.
37 V6 Imatra Fin.
29 E7 Imazu Japan
88 G3 Imbituba Brazil
90 B4 Imbituva Brazil
50 G3 Imeni Babushkina Rus. Fed.
19 F2 Imeni Chapayeva Turkm.
56 E3 Īmī Eth.
17 M2 İmişli Azer.
30 D6 Imja-do *i.* S. Korea
30 D4 Imjin *r.* N. Korea
48 D2 Imola Italy
59 H4 Impendle S. Africa
87 J5 Imperatriz Brazil
48 C3 Imperia Italy
76 C3 Imperial U.S.A.
74 D5 Imperial Beach U.S.A.
75 E5 Imperial Valley *v.* U.S.A.
56 B3 Impfondo Congo
23 H4 Imphal India
49 L4 İmroz Turkey
16 F5 Imtān Syria
31 A4 Imuruan Bay *b.* Phil.
29 E7 Ina Japan
86 E6 Inambari *r.* Peru
54 C2 In Aménas Alg.
9 C4 Inangahua Junction N.Z.
25 F7 Inanwatan Indon.
36 U2 Inari Fin.
36 U2 Inarijärvi *l.* Fin.
36 T2 Inarijoki *r.* Fin./Norway
45 H3 Inca Spain
51 C7 İnce Burnu *pt* Turkey
51 E7 İnce Burnu *pt* Turkey
16 D3 İncekum Burnu *pt* Turkey
16 E2 İncesu Turkey
41 E5 Inch Rep. of Ireland
40 C2 Inchard, Loch *b.* U.K.
40 E4 Inchkeith *i.* U.K.
30 D5 Inch'ŏn S. Korea
59 K2 Incomati *r.* Moz.
40 B5 Indaal, Loch *in.* U.K.
90 D2 Indaiá *r.* Brazil
90 B2 Indaiá Grande *r.* Brazil
36 P5 Indalsälven *r.* Sweden
37 J6 Indalstø Norway
84 A1 Indé Mex.
74 C3 Independence *CA* U.S.A.
68 B4 Independence *IA* U.S.A.
77 E4 Independence *KS* U.S.A.
68 A2 Independence *MN* U.S.A.
76 E4 Independence *MO* U.S.A.
80 C6 Independence *VA* U.S.A.
68 B3 Independence *WI* U.S.A.
72 C3 Independence Mts U.S.A.
14 D2 Inderborskiy Kazak.
21 B2 Indi India
10 J7 India *country* Asia
68 D2 Indian *r.* U.S.A.
80 D4 Indiana U.S.A.
68 D5 Indiana *div.* U.S.A.
68 D5 Indiana Dunes National Lakeshore *res.* U.S.A.
93 M7 Indian-Antarctic Basin *sea feature* Ind. Ocean
93 O7 Indian-Antarctic Ridge *sea feature* Pac. Oc.
68 D6 Indianapolis U.S.A.
Indian Desert *see* Thar Desert
67 J3 Indian Harbour Can.
81 F3 Indian Lake *NY* U.S.A.
68 D3 Indian Lake *l.* *MI* U.S.A.
80 B4 Indian Lake *l.* *OH* U.S.A.
80 D4 Indian Lake *l.* *PA* U.S.A.
76 E3 Indianola *IA* U.S.A.
77 F5 Indianola *MS* U.S.A.
75 F2 Indian Peak *summit* U.S.A.
68 E3 Indian River U.S.A.
75 E3 Indian Springs U.S.A.
75 G4 Indian Wells U.S.A.
13 Q2 Indigirka *r.* Rus. Fed.
49 J2 Indija Yugo.
64 F2 Indin Lake *l.* Can.
74 D5 Indio U.S.A.
7 G3 Indispensable Reefs *rf* Solomon Is
11 N10 Indonesia *country* Asia
22 C5 Indore India
33 C4 Indramayu, Tanjung *pt* Indon.
33 B3 Indrapura Indon.
21 C2 Indravati *r.* India
44 E3 Indre *r.* France
Indur *see* Nizamabad
22 B4 Indus *r.* Pak.
22 A5 Indus, Mouths of the *est.* Pak.
59 G5 Indwe S. Africa
51 E7 İnebolu Turkey
16 B1 İnegöl Turkey
80 B6 Inez U.S.A.
58 D7 Infanta, Cape *hd* S. Africa
84 B3 Infiernillo, L. *l.* Mex.
68 D3 Ingalls U.S.A.
65 J2 Ingalls Lake *l.* Can.

74 B2 Ingalls, Mt mt U.S.A.
42 B4 Ingelmunster Belgium
91 C4 Ingeniero Jacobacci Arg.
69 G4 Ingersoll Can.
19 G2 Ingichka Uzbek.
38 E3 Ingleborough h. U.K.
63 L2 Inglefield Land reg. Greenland
38 E3 Ingleton U.K.
8 D4 Inglewood Austr.
39 H4 Ingoldmells U.K.
46 E6 Ingolstadt Ger.
67 H4 Ingonish Can.
23 G4 Ingrāj Bāzār India
64 F2 Ingray Lake l. Can.
92 D5 Ingrid Christensen Coast coastal area Ant.
51 H7 Ingushskaya Respublika div. Rus. Fed.
59 K3 Ingwavuma S. Africa
59 K2 Inhaca Moz.
59 K2 Inhaca e dos Portugueses, Ilhas da S. Africa
59 K3 Inhaca, Península pen. Moz.
57 D6 Inhambane Moz.
59 K1 Inhambane div. Moz.
57 D5 Inhaminga Moz.
90 A3 Inhanduízinho r. Brazil
90 D1 Inhaúmas Brazil
89 C4 Inírida r. Col.
41 A4 Inishark i. Rep. of Ireland
41 A4 Inishbofin i. Rep. of Ireland
41 A3 Inishkea North i. Rep. of Ireland
41 A3 Inishkea South i. Rep. of Ireland
41 B4 Inishmaan i. Rep. of Ireland
41 B4 Inishmore i. Rep. of Ireland
41 C3 Inishmurray i. Rep. of Ireland
41 D2 Inishowen pen. Rep. of Ireland
41 E2 Inishowen Head hd Rep. of Ireland
41 D2 Inishtrahull i. Rep. of Ireland
41 D2 Inishtrahull Sound chan. Rep. of Ireland
41 A4 Inishturk i. Rep. of Ireland
19 F2 Inkylap Turkm.
9 D5 Inland Kaikoura Range mts N.Z.
36 O3 Inndyr Norway
Inner Mongolian Aut. Region div. see Nei Monggol Zizhiqu
40 C3 Inner Sound chan. U.K.
6 E3 Innisfail Austr.
46 E7 Innsbruck Austria
41 D4 Inny r. Rep. of Ireland
56 B4 Inongo Congo(Zaire)
46 J4 Inowrocław Pol.
54 C2 In Salah Alg.
50 H4 Insar Rus. Fed.
40 F3 Insch U.K.
30 D6 Insil S. Korea
12 H3 Inta Rus. Fed.
91 D2 Intendente Alvear Arg.
46 C7 Interlaken Switz.
76 E1 International Falls U.S.A.
29 G7 Inubō-zaki pt Japan
66 E2 Inukjuak Can.
62 E3 Inuvik Can.
40 C4 Inveraray U.K.
40 F4 Inverbervie U.K.
9 B7 Invercargill N.Z.
6 F4 Inverell Austr.
40 D3 Invergordon U.K.
40 E4 Inverkeithing U.K.
67 H4 Inverness Can.
40 D3 Inverness U.K.
79 D6 Inverness U.S.A.
40 F3 Inverurie U.K.
6 D5 Investigator Strait chan. Austr.
15 G1 Inya Rus. Fed.
73 C5 Inyokern U.S.A.
74 C3 Inyo Mts mts U.S.A.
56 D4 Inyonga Tanz.
50 H4 Inza Rus. Fed.
51 G4 Inzhavino Rus. Fed.
49 J5 Ioannina Greece
77 E4 Iola U.S.A.
40 B4 Iona i. U.K.
72 C1 Ione U.S.A.
68 E4 Ionia U.S.A.
49 H5 Ionian Islands is Greece
48 G6 Ionian Sea sea Greece/Italy
Ionioi Nisoi is see Ionian Islands
24 G1 Iony, Ostrov i. Rus. Fed.
17 L1 Iori r. Georgia
49 L6 Ios i. Greece
29 B9 Iō-shima i. Japan
68 A4 Iowa div. U.S.A.
68 B5 Iowa r. U.S.A.
68 B5 Iowa City U.S.A.
76 E3 Iowa Falls U.S.A.
90 C2 Ipameri Brazil
86 D5 Iparía Peru
90 D2 Ipatinga Brazil
51 G6 Ipatovo Rus. Fed.
59 F3 Ipelegeng S. Africa
89 A4 Ipiales Col.
90 E1 Ipiaú Brazil
90 B4 Ipiranga Brazil
33 B2 Ipoh Malaysia
87 L5 Ipojuca r. Brazil
90 B2 Iporá Brazil
56 C3 Ippy C.A.R.
49 M4 Ipsala Turkey
39 J5 Ipswich U.K.
63 M3 Iqaluit Can.
88 B2 Iquique Chile
86 D4 Iquitos Peru
19 F5 Īrafshān reg. Iran
29 E7 Irago-misaki pt Japan
49 L6 Irakleia i. Greece
Irakleio see Iraklion
49 L7 Iraklion Greece
90 E1 Iramaia Brazil
10 G6 Iran country Asia
33 D2 Iran, Pegunungan mts Indon.
18 B2 Irānshāh Iran
19 F5 Irānshahr Iran
Iranshahr see Fahraj
84 B2 Irapuato Mex.
10 F6 Iraq country Asia
81 G2 Irasville U.S.A.
90 B4 Irati Brazil
16 E5 Irbid Jordan
12 H4 Irbit Rus. Fed.
87 K6 Irecê Brazil
34 E3 Ireland, Republic of country Europe
56 C4 Irema Congo(Zaire)
14 E2 Irgiz Kazak.
30 D6 Iri S. Korea
25 F7 Irian Jaya reg. Indon.
17 L2 Īrī Dagh mt Iran
31 B3 Iriga Phil.
54 B3 Irîgui reg. Mali/Maur.
57 D4 Iringa Tanz.
21 B4 Irinjalakuda India
87 H4 Iriri r. Brazil
38 B4 Irish Sea sea Rep. of Ireland
87 J4 Irituia Brazil
18 C5 'Irj well S. Arabia
24 C1 Irkutsk Rus. Fed.
16 D2 Irmak Turkey
69 F2 Iron Bridge Can.
80 E3 Irondequoit U.S.A.
68 C3 Iron Mountain MI U.S.A.
75 F3 Iron Mountain mt UT U.S.A.
68 C2 Iron River U.S.A.
77 F4 Ironton MO U.S.A.
80 B5 Ironton OH U.S.A.
68 B2 Ironwood U.S.A.
81 F2 Iroquois Can.
68 D5 Iroquois r. U.S.A.
31 C3 Irosin Phil.
29 F7 Irō-zaki pt Japan
51 D5 Irpin' Ukr.
18 A5 Irq al Mazhūr sand dunes S. Arabia
18 B5 'Irq ath Thāmām sand dunes S. Arabia
18 B5 Irq Jahām sand dunes S. Arabia
23 H Irrawaddy r. China/Myanmar
25 B5 Irrawaddy, Mouths of the est. Myanmar
22 C1 Irshad Pass Afgh./Pak.
50 J2 Irta Rus. Fed.
38 E3 Irthing r. U.K.
15 F1 Irtysh r. Kazak./Rus. Fed.
56 C3 Irumu Congo(Zaire)
45 F1 Irún Spain
40 D5 Irvine U.K.
74 D5 Irvine CA U.S.A.
80 B6 Irvine KY U.S.A.
77 D5 Irving U.S.A.
31 B5 Isabela Phil.
86 □ Isabela, Isla i. Galapagos Is Ecuador
83 G6 Isabelia, Cordillera mts Nic.
68 B2 Isabella U.S.A.
74 C4 Isabella Lake l. U.S.A.
68 D2 Isabelle, Pt pt U.S.A.
36 B3 Ísafjarðardjúp est. Iceland
36 B3 Ísafjörður Iceland
29 B8 Isahaya Japan
22 B2 Isà Khel Pak.
50 G1 Isakogorka Rus. Fed.
57 E6 Isalo, Massif de l' mts Madag.
57 E6 Isalo, Parc National de l' nat. park Madag.
89 C4 Isana r. Col.
40 □ Isbister U.K.
48 E4 Ischia, Isola d' i. Italy
89 A4 Iscuande r. Col.
29 E7 Ise Japan
56 C3 Isengi Congo(Zaire)
44 H4 Isère r. France
43 F3 Iserlohn Ger.
43 H2 Isernhagen Ger.
48 F4 Isernia Italy
29 F6 Isesaki Japan
29 E7 Ise-shima National Park Japan
29 E7 Ise-wan b. Japan
54 C4 Iseyin Nigeria
Isfahan see Eşfahan
19 H2 Isfana Kyrg.
17 K5 Ishāq Iraq
50 J4 Isheyevka Rus. Fed.
28 G3 Ishikari-gawa r. Japan
28 G3 Ishikari-wan b. Japan
28 G5 Ishinomaki Japan
28 G5 Ishinomaki-wan b. Japan
29 G6 Ishioka Japan
29 C8 Ishizuchi-san mt Japan
22 C1 Ishkuman Pak.
68 D2 Ishpeming U.S.A.
19 G2 Ishtykhan Uzbek.
23 G4 Ishurdi Bangl.
86 E7 Isiboro Sécure, Parque Nacional nat. park Bol.
16 B2 Işıklı Turkey
16 B2 Işıklı Barajı resr Turkey
12 J4 Isil'kul' Rus. Fed.
59 J4 Isipingo S. Africa
56 C3 Isiro Congo(Zaire)
12 H3 Iskabad Canal canal Afgh.
16 F3 İskenderun Turkey
16 E1 İskilip Turkey
24 A1 Iskitim Rus. Fed.
49 L3 Iskŭr r. Bulg.
64 C3 Iskut Can.
64 C3 Iskut r. Can.
16 F3 İslahiye Turkey
22 C2 Islamabad Pak.
22 C3 Islam Barrage barrage Pak.
22 B4 Islamgarh Pak.
22 B4 Islamkot Pak.
79 D7 Islamorada U.S.A.
19 F3 Islam Qala Afgh.
31 A4 Island Bay b. Phil.
81 J1 Island Falls U.S.A.
65 L4 Island L. l. Can.
6 D5 Island Lagoon salt flat Austr.
65 L4 Island Lake Can.
68 A2 Island Lake l. U.S.A.
41 F3 Island Magee pen. U.K.
74 A1 Island Mountain U.S.A.
72 E2 Island Park U.S.A.
81 H2 Island Pond U.S.A.
9 E1 Islands, Bay of b. N.Z.
40 B5 Islay i. U.K.
80 E6 Isle of Wight U.S.A.
68 C2 Isle Royale National Park U.S.A.
55 F1 Ismā'īlīya Egypt
17 M1 İsmayıllı Azer.
37 R5 Isojoki Fin.
57 D5 Isoka Zambia
36 U3 Isokylä Fin.
48 G5 Isola di Capo Rizzuto Italy
16 C3 Isparta Turkey
49 M3 Isperikh Bulg.
19 F5 Ispikan Pak.
17 H1 İspir Turkey
10 E6 Israel country Asia
50 H4 Issa Rus. Fed.
42 E3 Isselburg Ger.
54 B4 Issia Côte d'Ivoire
17 K6 Issin Iraq
44 F4 Issoire France
17 J4 Iştablāt Iraq
16 B1 İstanbul Turkey
İstanbul Boğazı str. see Bosporus
18 C3 Istgāh-e Eznā Iran
49 K5 Istiaia Greece
89 A3 Istmina Col.
79 D7 Istokpoga, L. l. U.S.A.
48 E2 Istra pen. Croatia
44 G5 Istres France
Istria pen. see Istra
23 G5 Iswaripur Bangl.
87 L6 Itabaianinha Brazil
87 L6 Itaberaba Brazil
90 D2 Itabira Brazil
90 D3 Itabirito Brazil
90 E1 Itabuna Brazil
87 G4 Itacoatiara Brazil
90 B3 Itaguajé Brazil
90 C3 Itaí Brazil
90 A4 Itaimbey r. Para.
87 G4 Itaituba Brazil
88 G3 Itajaí Brazil
90 D3 Itajubá Brazil
23 F5 Itaki India
34 G4 Italy country Europe
87 L7 Itamaraju Brazil
90 D2 Itamarandiba Brazil
90 E2 Itambacuri Brazil
90 E2 Itambacuri r. Brazil
90 D2 Itambé, Pico de mt Brazil
57 E6 Itampolo Madag.
23 H4 Itanagar India
90 D1 Itanguari r. Brazil
90 C4 Itanhaém Brazil
90 E2 Itanhém Brazil
90 E2 Itanhém r. Brazil
90 E2 Itaobim Brazil
90 C2 Itapajipe Brazil
90 E1 Itaparica, Ilha i. Brazil
90 E1 Itapebi Brazil
90 E3 Itapemirim Brazil
90 E3 Itaperuna Brazil
90 E1 Itapetinga Brazil
90 C3 Itapetininga Brazil
90 C3 Itapeva Brazil
87 L6 Itapicuru r. Bahia Brazil
87 K5 Itapicuru r. Maranhão Brazil
87 K4 Itapicuru Mirim Brazil
87 L4 Itapipoca Brazil
90 C4 Itararé Brazil
90 C3 Itararé r. Brazil
22 D5 Itarsi India
90 B2 Itarumã Brazil
31 B1 Itbayat i. Phil.
64 G1 Itchen Lake l. Can.
49 K5 Itea Greece
68 E4 Ithaca MI U.S.A.
80 E3 Ithaca NY U.S.A.
43 H2 Ith Hils ridge Ger.
16 F6 Ithrah S. Arabia
56 C3 Itimbiri r. Congo(Zaire)
90 E2 Itinga Brazil
90 A2 Itiquira Brazil
90 A2 Itiquira r. Brazil
29 F7 Itō Japan
29 E6 Itoigawa Japan
48 C4 Ittiri Sardinia Italy
90 C3 Itu Brazil
89 B3 Ituango Col.
86 D5 Ituí r. Brazil
90 C2 Ituiutaba Brazil
56 C4 Itula Congo(Zaire)
90 C2 Itumbiara Brazil
87 G2 Ituni Guyana
87 J5 Itupiranga Brazil
90 B2 Iturama Brazil
90 A4 Iturbe Para.
24 G2 Iturup, Ostrov i. Rus. Fed.
86 E5 Ituxi r. Brazil
46 D4 Itzehoe Ger.
13 V3 Iultin Rus. Fed.
90 B3 Ivaí r. Brazil
36 U2 Ivalo Fin.
36 U2 Ivalojoki r. Fin.
51 C4 Ivanava Belarus
49 H3 Ivangrad Yugo.
8 E2 Ivanhoe Austr.
69 F1 Ivanhoe r. Can.
65 H2 Ivanhoe Lake l. N.W.T. Can.
69 F1 Ivanhoe Lake l. Ont. Can.
47 O5 Ivankiv Ukr.
51 C5 Ivano-Frankivs'k Ukr.
50 G3 Ivanovo Rus. Fed.
50 G3 Ivanovskaya Oblast' div. Rus. Fed.
75 E4 Ivanpah Lake l. U.S.A.
50 J4 Ivanteyevka Rus. Fed.
50 C4 Ivatsevichy Belarus
49 M4 Ivaylovgrad Bulg.
12 H3 Ivdel' Rus. Fed.
90 B3 Ivinheima Brazil
90 B3 Ivinheima r. Brazil
63 O3 Ivittuut Greenland
57 E6 Ivohibe Madag.
48 B2 Ivrea Italy
49 M5 İvrindi Turkey
51 H7 Ivris Ugheltekhili pass Georgia
63 L3 Ivujivik Can.
47 N4 Ivyanyets Belarus
28 G5 Iwaizumi Japan
29 G6 Iwaki Japan
28 G4 Iwaki-san volc. Japan
29 C7 Iwakuni Japan
28 G3 Iwamizawa Japan
28 G5 Iwate-san volc. Japan
54 C4 Iwo Nigeria
50 C4 Iwye Belarus
42 C4 Ixelles Belgium
84 C2 Ixmiquilpán Mex.
59 J5 Ixopo S. Africa
84 A2 Ixtlán Nayarit Mex.
84 C3 Ixtlán Oaxaca Mex.
39 H5 Ixworth U.K.
29 C8 Iyo Japan
29 C8 Iyo-nada b. Japan
82 G5 Izabal, L. de l. Guatemala
84 C4 Izapa Mex.
28 G3 Izari-dake mt Japan
56 D4 Izazi Tanz.
51 H7 Izberbash Rus. Fed.
47 O3 Izdeshkovo Rus. Fed.
42 B4 Izegem Belgium
18 C4 Īzeh Iran
12 G4 Izhevsk Rus. Fed.
12 G3 Izhma Rus. Fed.
50 K1 Izhma r. Rus. Fed.
51 F4 Izmalkovo Rus. Fed.
51 D6 Izmayil Ukr.
49 M5 İzmir Turkey
49 M5 İzmir Körfezi g. Turkey
16 B1 İznik Gölü l. Turkey
51 G6 Izobil'nyy Rus. Fed.
84 C3 Iztaccihuatl-Popocatépetl, Parque Nacional nat. park Mex.
29 F7 Izu-hantō pen. Japan
29 A7 Izuhara Japan
29 D7 Izumisano Japan
29 C7 Izumo Japan
29 F7 Izu-shotō is Japan
51 C5 Izyaslav Ukr.
51 F5 Izyum Ukr.

J

18 E3 Jaba watercourse Iran
Jabal, Bahr el r. see White Nile
45 E3 Jabalón r. Spain
22 D5 Jabalpur India
16 F3 Jabbūl Syria
6 D3 Jabiru Austr.
16 E4 Jablah Syria
48 G3 Jablanica Bos.-Herz.
87 M5 Jaboatão Brazil
90 C3 Jaboticabal Brazil
45 F1 Jaca Spain
87 K6 Jacaré r. Brazil
87 G5 Jacareacanga Brazil
90 C3 Jacareí Brazil
91 C1 Jáchal r. Arg.
43 L4 Jáchymov Czech Rep.
90 E2 Jacinto Brazil
86 F5 Jaciparaná r. Brazil
68 D1 Jackfish Can.
69 H3 Jack Lake l. Can.
81 H2 Jackman U.S.A.
77 D5 Jacksboro U.S.A.
77 J6 Jackson AL U.S.A.
74 B2 Jackson CA U.S.A.
80 B6 Jackson KY U.S.A.
68 E4 Jackson MI U.S.A.
76 E3 Jackson MN U.S.A.
77 F4 Jackson MO U.S.A.
77 F5 Jackson MS U.S.A.
80 B5 Jackson OH U.S.A.
79 B5 Jackson TN U.S.A.
72 E3 Jackson WY U.S.A.
9 B5 Jackson Head hd N.Z.
72 E2 Jackson L. l. U.S.A.
77 E6 Jackson, Lake U.S.A.
68 D3 Jacksonport U.S.A.
77 E5 Jacksonville AR U.S.A.
79 D6 Jacksonville FL U.S.A.
68 B6 Jacksonville IL U.S.A.
79 E5 Jacksonville NC U.S.A.
77 E6 Jacksonville TX U.S.A.
79 D6 Jacksonville Beach U.S.A.
83 K5 Jacmel Haiti
22 E3 Jacobabad Pak.
87 K6 Jacobina Brazil
75 F3 Jacob Lake U.S.A.
58 F4 Jacobsdal S. Africa
Jacobshavn see Ilulissat
67 H4 Jacques-Cartier, Détroit de chan. Can.
67 G4 Jacques Cartier, Mt mt Can.
67 G4 Jacquet River Can.
91 G1 Jacuí r. Brazil
37 L6 Jacuípe r. Brazil
87 J4 Jacunda Brazil
90 C4 Jacupiranga Brazil
89 C2 Jacura Venez.
21 B2 Jadcherla India
19 F5 Jaddi, Ras pt Pak.
43 G1 Jadebusen b. Ger.
48 G2 Jadovnik mt Bos.-Herz.
55 D1 Jādū Libya
86 C5 Jaén Peru
31 B3 Jaen Phil.
45 E4 Jaén Spain
18 C3 Ja'farābād Iran
Jaffa see Tel Aviv-Yafo
8 B4 Jaffa, C. pt Austr.
21 B4 Jaffna Sri Lanka
81 G3 Jaffrey U.S.A.
22 D3 Jagadhri India
21 B3 Jagalur India
21 C2 Jagdalpur India
59 F4 Jagersfontein S. Africa
22 D2 Jaggang China
19 E5 Jagin watercourse Iran
Jagok Tso salt l. see Urru Co
22 C3 Jagraon India
43 H5 Jagst r. Ger.
21 B2 Jagtial India
91 G2 Jaguarão Brazil
91 G2 Jaguarão r. Brazil/Uru.
90 C4 Jaguariaíva Brazil
23 F4 Jahanabad India
17 M3 Jahan Dagh mt Iran
22 C4 Jahazpur India
17 K7 Jahmah well Iraq
18 D4 Jahrom Iran
25 B3 Jainca China
22 C4 Jaipur India
22 B4 Jaisalmer India
22 E5 Jaisinghnagar India
22 D5 Jaitgarh mt India
23 E3 Jajarkot Nepal
18 E2 Jajarm Iran
48 G2 Jajce Bos.-Herz.
33 C4 Jakarta Indon.
64 C2 Jakes Corner Can.
22 B5 Jakhan India
19 G4 Jakin mt Afgh.
36 P3 Jäkkvik Sweden
36 S5 Jakobstad Fin.
77 C5 Jal U.S.A.
19 H3 Jalālābād Afgh.
15 F2 Jalal-Abad Kyrg.
22 C3 Jalandhar India
84 E4 Jalapa Guatemala
84 C3 Jalapa Enríquez Mex.
37 S5 Jalasjärvi Fin.
23 G4 Jaldhaka r. Bangl.
21 B2 Jaldrug India
90 B3 Jales Brazil
23 F5 Jaleshwar India
22 D5 Jalgaon Maharashtra India
22 C5 Jalgaon Maharashtra India
17 L6 Jalībah Iraq
54 D4 Jalingo Nigeria
84 B2 Jalisco div. Mex.
22 C6 Jalna India
19 F5 Jālo Iran
45 F2 Jalón r. Spain
84 B2 Jalostotitlán Mex.
84 B2 Jalpa Mex.
23 G4 Jalpaiguri India
84 C2 Jalpan Mex.
55 E2 Jālū Libya
17 K4 Jalūlā Iraq
19 F3 Jām r. Iran
19 F3 Jām reg. Iran
22 D5 Jamai India
61 L8 Jamaica country Caribbean Sea
83 J5 Jamaica Channel chan. Haiti/Jamaica
18 C3 Jamālābād Iran
17 L3 Jamalabad Iran
23 G4 Jamalpur Bangl.
23 F4 Jamalpur India
87 G5 Jamanxim r. Brazil
33 B3 Jambi Indon.
22 C4 Jambo India
33 A2 Jamboaye r. Indon.
31 A5 Jambongan i. Malaysia
32 A4 Jambuair, Tg pt Indon.
17 K4 Jambur Iraq
21 A1 Jambusar India
76 D2 James r. ND U.S.A.
80 D6 James r. VA U.S.A.
22 B4 Jamesabad Pak.
66 D3 James Bay b. Can.
91 D2 James Craik Arg.
63 Q2 Jameson Land reg. Greenland
9 B6 James Pk mt N.Z.
92 B2 James Ross I. i. Ant.
63 J3 James Ross Strait chan. Can.
8 B2 Jamestown Austr.
59 G5 Jamestown S. Africa
76 D2 Jamestown ND U.S.A.
80 D3 Jamestown NY U.S.A.
18 C4 Jamīlābād Iran
21 A2 Jamkhandi India
21 A2 Jamkhed India
21 B3 Jammalamadugu India
22 C2 Jammu Jammu and Kashmir
22 C2 Jammu and Kashmir terr. Asia
22 B5 Jamnagar India
22 D4 Jamni r. India
33 C4 Jampang Kulon Indon.
22 B3 Jampur Pak.
37 T6 Jämsä Fin.
37 T6 Jämsänkoski Fin.
23 F5 Jamshedpur India
23 G5 Jamuna r. Bangl.
90 D1 Janaúba Brazil
90 B2 Jandaia Brazil
18 D3 Jandaq Iran
22 B2 Jandola Pak.
74 B1 Janesville CA U.S.A.
68 C4 Janesville WI U.S.A.
19 E3 Jangal Iran
23 G4 Jangipur India
17 L2 Jānī Beyglū Iran
43 M2 Jänickendorf Ger.
34 E1 Jan Mayen terr. Norway
17 L5 Jannah Iraq
19 F3 Jannatabad Iran
58 F6 Jansenville S. Africa
90 D1 Januária Brazil
22 C5 Jaora India
11 P6 Japan country Asia
Japan Alps Nat. Park nat. park see Chibu-Sangaku Nat. Park
28 C5 Japan, Sea of sea Pac. Oc.
94 E4 Japan Tr. sea feature Pac. Oc.
86 E4 Japurá r. Brazil
23 H4 Japvo Mount mt India
89 A3 Jaqué Panama
16 G3 Jarābulus Syria
90 A3 Jaraguari Brazil
16 E5 Jarash Jordan
90 A3 Jardim Brazil
83 J4 Jardines de la Reina, Archipiélago de los is Cuba
30 B2 Jargalang China
24 D2 Jargalant Mongolia
17 K4 Jarmo Iraq
37 P7 Järna Sweden
46 H5 Jarocin Pol.
47 L5 Jarosław Pol.
36 N5 Järpen Sweden
16 C4 Jarrāhi watercourse Iran
26 B2 Jartai China
86 F6 Jarú Brazil
30 A1 Jarud Qi China
37 T7 Järvakandi Estonia
37 T6 Järvenpää Fin.
5 L5 Jarvis I. i. Pac. Oc.
22 B5 Jasdan India
19 E5 Jāsk Iran
47 K6 Jasło Pol.
88 D8 Jason Is is Falkland Is
92 B2 Jason Pen. pen. Ant.
64 F4 Jasper Can.
79 C5 Jasper AL U.S.A.
77 E4 Jasper AR U.S.A.
79 D6 Jasper FL U.S.A.
78 C4 Jasper IN U.S.A.
80 E3 Jasper NY U.S.A.
80 B5 Jasper OH U.S.A.
77 E6 Jasper TX U.S.A.
64 F4 Jasper Nat. Park Can.
17 K5 Jaşşān Iraq
47 J6 Jastrzębie-Zdrój Pol.
22 C4 Jaswantpura India
47 J7 Jászberény Hungary
90 B2 Jataí Brazil
87 G4 Jatapu r. Brazil
21 A2 Jath India
22 B4 Jati Pak.
22 B3 Jatoi Pak.
90 C3 Jaú Brazil
86 F4 Jaú r. Brazil
89 E5 Jauaperi r. Brazil
89 D3 Jaua Sarisariñama, Parque Nacional nat. park Venez.
37 S8 Jaunlutriņi Latvia
37 U8 Jaunpiebalga Latvia
23 E4 Jaunpur India
86 F4 Jaú, Parque Nacional do nat. park Brazil
19 F4 Jauri Iran
90 A2 Jauru Brazil
90 B2 Jauru r. Brazil
51 G7 Java Georgia
33 C4 Java i. Indon.
21 B3 Javadi Hills mts India
19 G3 Javand Afgh.
93 M4 Java Ridge sea feature Ind. Ocean
24 D2 Javarthushuu Mongolia
33 D3 Java Sea sea Indon.
Java Trench sea feature see Sunda Trench
43 K2 Jävenitz Ger.
Jawa i. see Java
22 C4 Jawad India
22 B4 Jawai r. India
16 F3 Jawbān Bayk Syria
22 C6 Jawhar India
56 E3 Jawhar Somalia
46 H5 Jawor Pol.
25 F7 Jaya, Pk mt Indon.
25 G7 Jayapura Indon.
23 F4 Jaynagar India
16 F5 Jayrūd Syria
20 B6 Jazā'ir Farasān is S. Arabia
17 M3 Jazvān Iran
17 G4 Jdaide Syria
75 E4 Jean U.S.A.
64 E2 Jean Marie River Can.
67 G2 Jeannin, Lac l. Can.
19 E4 Jebāl Bārez, Kūh-e mts Iran
54 C4 Jebba Nigeria
55 E3 Jebel Abyad Plateau plat. Sudan
22 C3 Jech Doab lowland Pak.
40 F5 Jedburgh U.K.
20 A5 Jedda S. Arabia
48 C6 Jedeida Tunisia
43 K1 Jeetze r. Ger.
81 F3 Jefferson NY U.S.A.
68 C4 Jefferson WI U.S.A.
72 D2 Jefferson r. U.S.A.
76 E4 Jefferson City U.S.A.
74 D2 Jefferson, Mt mt NV U.S.A.
72 B2 Jefferson, Mt volc. OR U.S.A.
78 C4 Jeffersonville U.S.A.
58 F7 Jeffrey's Bay S. Africa
88 E2 Jejuí Guazú r. Para.
37 T8 Jēkabpils Latvia
46 G5 Jelenia Góra Pol.
23 G4 Jelep La pass China
37 S8 Jelgava Latvia
80 A6 Jellico U.S.A.
32 C5 Jemaja i. Indon.
33 D4 Jember Indon.
33 E3 Jempang, Danau l. Indon.
43 K4 Jena Ger.
54 C1 Jendouba Tunisia
16 E5 Jenin West Bank
80 B6 Jenkins U.S.A.
74 A2 Jenner U.S.A.
77 E6 Jennings U.S.A.
65 K4 Jenpeg Can.
8 D4 Jeparit Austr.
90 E1 Jequié Brazil
90 D2 Jequitaí Brazil
90 D2 Jequitaí r. Brazil
90 E2 Jequitinhonha Brazil
90 E2 Jequitinhonha r. Brazil
32 B5 Jerantut Malaysia
55 F4 Jerbar Sudan
83 K5 Jérémie Haiti
84 B2 Jerez Mex.
45 C4 Jerez de la Frontera Spain
45 C3 Jerez de los Caballeros Spain
49 J5 Jergucat Albania
16 E6 Jericho West Bank
43 L2 Jerichow Ger.
8 E3 Jerilderie Austr.
17 K2 Jermuk Armenia
72 D3 Jerome U.S.A.
44 C2 Jersey i. Channel Is U.K.
81 F4 Jersey City U.S.A.
80 E4 Jersey Shore U.S.A.
78 B4 Jerseyville U.S.A.
87 K5 Jerumenha Brazil
16 E6 Jerusalem Israel/West Bank
8 H3 Jervis B. b. Austr.
8 H3 Jervis Bay Austr.
8 H3 Jervis Bay Terr. Austr.
48 F1 Jesenice Slovenia
48 E3 Jesi Italy
43 L3 Jessen Ger.
37 M6 Jessheim Norway
23 G5 Jessore Bangl.
43 H1 Jesteburg Ger.
79 D6 Jesup U.S.A.
84 D3 Jesús Carranza Mex.
91 D1 Jesús María Arg.
22 B5 Jetalsar India
76 D4 Jetmore U.S.A.
43 F1 Jever Ger.
23 F4 Jha Jha India
22 D3 Jhajjar India
22 C4 Jhajju India
22 A3 Jhal Pak.
23 G5 Jhalakati Bangl.
19 G5 Jhal Jhao Pak.
22 C3 Jhang Pak.
22 D4 Jhansi India
23 F5 Jharia India
23 F5 Jharsuguda India
22 B3 Jhatpat Pak.
22 C2 Jhelum Pak.
22 C2 Jhelum r. Pak.
23 G5 Jhenida Bangl.
22 B4 Jhudo Pak.
23 F4 Jhumritilaiya India
22 C3 Jhunjhunūn India
26 C3 Jiachuan China
26 F4 Jiading China
27 D5 Jiahe China
27 B4 Jiajiang China
26 B3 Jialing Jiang r. China
28 B1 Jiamusi China
27 E5 Ji'an Jiangxi China
30 D3 Ji'an China
26 F1 Jianchang China
27 F4 Jiande China
27 B4 Jiang'an China
27 C4 Jiangbei China
27 A6 Jiangcheng China
27 B5 Jiangchuan China
26 B4 Jiange China
27 D5 Jianghua China
27 C4 Jiangjin China
27 C5 Jiangkou China
27 E5 Jiangle China
27 D4 Jiangling China
26 B3 Jiangluozhen China
27 D6 Jiangmen China
27 F4 Jiangshan China
26 F3 Jiangsu div. China
27 E5 Jiangxi div. China
26 D3 Jiang Xian China
26 F4 Jiangyan China
27 D5 Jiangyong China
26 B4 Jiangyou China
26 F3 Jianhu China
27 D6 Jian Jiang r. China
27 D4 Jianli China
27 E5 Jianning China
27 F5 Jian'ou China
26 F1 Jianping Liaoning China
26 F1 Jianping Liaoning China
27 C4 Jianshi China
27 B6 Jianshui China
27 F5 Jianyang Fujian China
27 B4 Jianyang Sichuan China
26 D2 Jiaocheng China
26 E2 Jiaohe Hebei China
30 D2 Jiaohe China
27 F4 Jiaojiang China
30 A2 Jiaolai r. Nei Monggol China
26 F2 Jiaolai r. Shandong China
27 E5 Jiaoling China
26 F3 Jiaonan China
26 E2 Jiao Xian China
26 F2 Jiaozhou Wan b. China
26 D3 Jiaozuo China
30 D2 Jiapigou China
26 F3 Jiashan China
26 D2 Jia Xian China
26 F4 Jiaxing China
27 D4 Jiayu China
24 B3 Jiayuguan China
27 E6 Jiazi China
18 B6 Jibāl al Ḩawshah mts S. Arabia
Jiddah see Jedda
20 E6 Jiddat al Ḩarāsīs gravel area Oman
30 F1 Jidong China
26 B2 Jiehebe China
36 Q2 Jiehkkevarri mt Norway
27 E6 Jieshi China
27 E6 Jieshi Wan b. China
26 E3 Jieshou China
36 T2 Iešjávri l. Norway
27 E6 Jiexi China
26 D2 Jiexiu China
27 E6 Jieyang China
37 T9 Jieznas Lith.
26 A3 Jigzhi China
46 G6 Jihlava Czech Rep.
19 F3 Jija Sarai Afgh.
56 E3 Jijiga Eth.
27 A4 Jiju China
19 H3 Jilga r. Afgh.
22 D2 Jilganang Kol, S. salt l. China/Jammu and Kashmir
56 E3 Jilib Somalia
30 D2 Jilin China
30 C2 Jilin div. China
26 A2 Jiling China
30 C2 Jilin Handa Ling mts China
56 D3 Jīma Eth.
82 D3 Jiménez Chihuahua Mex.
84 C1 Jiménez Mex.
26 F2 Jimo China
81 F4 Jim Thorpe U.S.A.
26 E2 Jinan China
26 B2 Jinchang China
26 D3 Jincheng China
26 B4 Jinchuan China
22 D3 Jind India
8 G4 Jindabyne Austr.
8 F3 Jindera Austr.
46 G6 Jindřichův Hradec Czech Rep.
26 C3 Jing r. China
27 E4 Jing'an China
26 C2 Jingbian China
26 C3 Jingchuan China
27 F4 Jingde China
27 E4 Jingdezhen China
27 E5 Jinggangshan China
27 E4 Jinggongqiao China
26 E2 Jinghai China
25 C4 Jinghong China
26 F3 Jingjiang China
26 D2 Jingle China
26 D4 Jingmen China
26 B3 Jingning China
30 E2 Jingpo China
30 E2 Jingpo Hu resr China
26 B2 Jingtai China
27 C6 Jingxi China
27 F4 Jing Xian Anhui China
27 C5 Jing Xian Hunan China
30 D2 Jingyu China
26 B2 Jingyuan China
26 F3 Jinhu China
27 F4 Jinhua China
26 D1 Jining Nei Monggol China
26 E3 Jining Shandong China
56 D3 Jinja Uganda
27 F5 Jinjiang China
27 E4 Jin Jiang r. China
56 D3 Jinka Eth.
30 A3 Jinlingsi China
27 C7 Jinmu Jiao pt China
82 G6 Jinotepe Nic.
27 C5 Jinping Guizhou China
27 B6 Jinping Yunnan China
27 A5 Jinping Shan mts China
27 C5 Jinsha China
Jinsha Jiang r. see Yangtze
26 F4 Jinshan China
27 D4 Jinshi China
26 B4 Jintang China
31 B4 Jintotolo i. Phil.
31 B4 Jintotolo Channel chan. Phil.
22 D6 Jintur India
27 E5 Jinxi Jiangxi China
30 A3 Jinxi China
30 A3 Jin Xian Liaoning China
30 A4 Jin Xian Liaoning China
27 E4 Jinxian China
26 E3 Jinxiang Shandong China
27 F5 Jinxiang Zhejiang China
27 B5 Jinyang China
27 F4 Jinyun China
26 E4 Jinzhai China
30 A3 Jinzhou China
30 A4 Jinzhou Wan b. China
86 F5 Jiparaná r. Brazil
86 B4 Jipijapa Ecuador
19 H2 Jirgatol Tajik.
19 E4 Jīroft Iran
18 C6 Jirwan well S. Arabia
27 C4 Jishou China
27 E5 Jishui China
16 F4 Jisr ash Shughūr Syria
32 B4 Jitra Malaysia
26 C2 Jiudengkou China
26 B4 Jiuding Shan mt China
26 C3 Jiufoping China
27 E4 Jiujiang Jiangxi China
27 E4 Jiujiang Jiangxi China
27 E4 Jiuling Shan mts China
27 A4 Jiulong China
30 A2 Jiumiao China
30 B5 Jiurongcheng China
30 C1 Jiutai China
27 C5 Jiuxu China
19 F5 Jiwani Pak.
27 F4 Jixi Anhui China
30 F1 Jixi China
26 E2 Ji Xian Hebei China
26 E3 Ji Xian Henan China
28 B1 Jixian China
26 D3 Jiyuan China
20 B6 Jīzān S. Arabia
29 C7 Jizō-zaki pt Japan
87 M5 João Pessoa Brazil
90 C2 João Pinheiro Brazil
74 C2 Job Peak summit U.S.A.
43 L4 Jocketa Ger.
23 F5 Joda India
22 C4 Jodhpur India
36 V5 Joensuu Fin.
29 F6 Jōetsu Japan
57 D6 Jofane Moz.
64 F4 Joffre, Mt mt Can.
37 U7 Jõgeva Estonia
37 U7 Jõgua Estonia
59 G3 Johannesburg S. Africa
74 D4 Johannesburg U.S.A.
22 E5 Johilla r. India
72 C2 John Day U.S.A.
72 B2 John Day r. U.S.A.
64 F3 John d'Or Prairie Can.
80 D6 John H. Kerr Res. resr U.S.A.

40 E2 **John o'Groats** U.K.
79 D4 **Johnson City** U.S.A.
64 C2 **Johnson's Crossing** Can.
79 D5 **Johnston** U.S.A.
40 D5 **Johnstone** U.K.
5 L3 **Johnston I.** *i.* Pac. Oc.
41 D5 **Johnstown** Rep. of Ireland
81 F3 **Johnstown** *NY* U.S.A.
80 D4 **Johnstown** *PA* U.S.A.
69 F3 **Johnswood** U.S.A.
33 B2 **Johor Bahru** Malaysia
37 U7 **Jõhvi** Estonia
88 G3 **Joinville** Brazil
44 G2 **Joinville** France
92 B2 **Joinville I.** *i.* Ant.
36 Q3 **Jokkmokk** Sweden
36 F4 **Jökulsá á Brú** *r.* Iceland
36 E3 **Jökulsá á Fjöllum** *r.* Iceland
36 F4 **Jökulsá í Fljótsdal** *r.* Iceland
18 B2 **Jolfa** Iran
68 C5 **Joliet** U.S.A.
66 F4 **Joliette** Can.
31 B5 **Jolo** Phil.
31 B5 **Jolo** *i.* Phil.
31 B3 **Jomalig** *i.* Phil.
33 D4 **Jombang** Indon.
37 T9 **Jonava** Lith.
26 B3 **Jonê** China
77 F5 **Jonesboro** *AR* U.S.A.
81 K2 **Jonesboro** *ME* U.S.A.
92 A3 **Jones Mts** *mts* Ant.
81 K2 **Jonesport** U.S.A.
63 K2 **Jones Sound** *chan.* Can.
80 B6 **Jonesville** U.S.A.
55 F4 **Jonglei Canal** *canal* Sudan
23 E5 **Jonk** *r.* India
37 O8 **Jönköping** Sweden
67 F4 **Jonquière** Can.
84 D3 **Jonuta** Mex.
77 E4 **Joplin** U.S.A.
81 E5 **Joppatowne** U.S.A.
22 D4 **Jora** India
72 F2 **Jordan** U.S.A.
10 E6 **Jordan** *country* Asia
16 E6 **Jordan** *r.* Asia
72 E3 **Jordan** *r.* U.S.A.
72 C3 **Jordan Valley** U.S.A.
90 B4 **Jordão** *r.* Brazil
37 N6 **Jordet** Norway
23 H4 **Jorhat** India
43 H1 **Jork** Ger.
36 R4 **Jörn** Sweden
37 U5 **Joroinen** Fin.
37 K7 **Jørpeland** Norway
54 C4 **Jos** Nigeria
31 C5 **Jose Abad Santos** Phil.
84 C3 **José Cardel** Mex.
88 B6 **José de San Martin** Arg.
90 A2 **Joselândia** Brazil
91 F2 **José Pedro Varela** Uru.
6 C3 **Joseph Bonaparte Gulf** *g.* Austr.
75 G4 **Joseph City** U.S.A.
67 G3 **Joseph, Lac** *l.* Can.
63 M4 **Joseph, Lake** *l.* Can.
29 F6 **Jöshinetsu-kōgen National Park** Japan
75 E5 **Joshua Tree National Monument** *res.* U.S.A.
54 C4 **Jos Plateau** *plat.* Nigeria
37 K6 **Jostedalsbreen Nasjonalpark** *nat. park* Norway
37 L6 **Jotunheimen Nasjonalpark** *nat. park* Norway
58 E6 **Joubertina** S. Africa
59 G3 **Jouberton** S. Africa
42 D2 **Joure** Neth.
37 U6 **Joutsa** Fin.
37 V6 **Joutseno** Fin.
42 E5 **Jouy-aux-Arches** France
23 H4 **Jowai** India
41 B4 **Joyce's Country** *reg.* Rep. of Ireland
84 B1 **Juan Aldama** Mex.
72 A1 **Juan de Fuca, Str. of** *chan.* U.S.A.
57 E5 **Juan de Nova** *i.* Ind. Ocean
85 C6 **Juan Fernández, Islas** *is* Chile
36 V5 **Juankoski** Fin.
87 K5 **Juàzeiro** Brazil
87 L5 **Juàzeiro do Norte** Brazil
55 F4 **Juba** Sudan
56 E3 **Jubba** *r.* Somalia
74 D4 **Jubilee Pass** *pass* U.S.A.
45 F3 **Júcar** *r.* Spain
84 C3 **Juchatengo** Mex.
84 B2 **Juchipila** Mex.
84 D3 **Juchitán** Mex.
84 A2 **Juchitlán** Mex.
90 E2 **Jucuruçu** *r.* Brazil
37 J7 **Judaberg** Norway
17 H6 **Judaidat al Hamir** Iraq
17 H6 **Judayyidat 'Ar'ar** *well* Iraq
46 G7 **Judenburg** Austria
37 M9 **Juelsminde** Denmark
26 C2 **Juh** China
26 F1 **Juhua Dao** *i.* China
83 G6 **Juigalpa** Nic.
42 F1 **Juist** *i.* Ger.
90 D3 **Juiz de Fora** Brazil
86 E8 **Julaca** Bol.
76 C3 **Julesburg** U.S.A.
86 D7 **Juliaca** Peru
42 C2 **Julianadorp** Neth.
87 G3 **Juliana Top** *summit* Suriname
42 E4 **Jülich** Ger.
48 E1 **Julijske Alpe** *mts* Slovenia
91 E2 **Julio, 9 de** Arg.
86 C5 **Jumbilla** Peru
45 F3 **Jumilla** Spain
23 E3 **Jumla** Nepal
22 B5 **Junagadh** India
23 E6 **Junagarh** India
26 F3 **Junan** China
91 B2 **Juncal** *mt* Chile
91 D4 **Juncal, L.** *l.* Arg.
77 D6 **Junction** *TX* U.S.A.
73 D4 **Junction** *UT* U.S.A.
76 D4 **Junction City** U.S.A.
90 C3 **Jundiaí** Brazil
64 C3 **Juneau** U.S.A.
8 F3 **Junee** Austr.
46 C7 **Jungfrau** *mt* Switz.
24 A2 **Junggar Pendi** *basin* China
22 A4 **Jungshahi** Pak.
80 E4 **Juniata** *r.* U.S.A.
91 E2 **Junín** Arg.
91 B3 **Junín de los Andes** Arg.
81 K1 **Juniper** Can.
74 B3 **Junipero Serro Peak** *summit* U.S.A.
27 B4 **Junlian** China
21 A2 **Junnar** India
36 P5 **Junsele** Sweden
72 C3 **Juntura** U.S.A.
26 D3 **Jun Xian** China
37 T8 **Juodupė** Lith.
90 C4 **Juquiá** Brazil
55 E4 **Jur** *r.* Sudan
40 C4 **Jura** *i.* U.K.
44 H3 **Jura** *mts* France/Switz.
90 E1 **Jurací** Brazil
89 A3 **Juradó** Col.
40 C5 **Jura, Sound of** *chan.* U.K.
37 S9 **Jurbarkas** Lith.
16 E6 **Jurf ed Darāwīsh** Jordan
43 L1 **Jürgenstorf** Ger.
30 A1 **Jurh** China
30 A1 **Jurhe** China
23 G2 **Jurhen Ul Shan** *mts* China
37 S8 **Jūrmala** Latvia
36 U4 **Jurmu** Fin.
26 F4 **Jurong** China
32 □ **Jurong** Sing.
86 E4 **Juruá** *r.* Brazil
87 G6 **Juruena** *r.* Brazil
36 R5 **Jurva** Fin.
18 E2 **Jūshqān** Iran
91 D2 **Justo Daract** Arg.
86 E4 **Jutaí** *r.* Brazil
43 M3 **Jüterbog** Ger.
90 A3 **Juti** Brazil
82 G6 **Jutiapa** Guatemala
82 G6 **Juticalpa** Honduras
36 P3 **Jutis** Sweden
36 V5 **Juuka** Fin.
37 U6 **Juva** Fin.
83 H4 **Juventud, Isla de la** *i.* Cuba
19 F4 **Juwain** Afgh.
26 F3 **Ju Xian** China
26 A1 **Juyan** China
26 E3 **Juye** China
19 E3 **Jūymand** Iran
18 D4 **Jūyom** Iran
57 C6 **Jwaneng** Botswana
37 T5 **Jyväskylä** Fin.

K

22 D2 **K2** *mt* China/Jammu and Kashmir
30 C4 **Ka** *i.* N. Korea
19 E2 **Kaakhka** Turkm.
74 □1 **Kaala** *mt* U.S.A.
56 E4 **Kaambooni** Kenya
37 S6 **Kaarina** Fin.
43 K1 **Kaarßen** Ger.
42 E3 **Kaarst** Ger.
36 V5 **Kaavi** Fin.
19 F2 **Kabakly** Turkm.
54 A4 **Kabala** Sierra Leone
56 C4 **Kabale** Uganda
56 C4 **Kabalo** Congo(Zaire)
56 C4 **Kabambare** Congo(Zaire)
57 C5 **Kabangu** Congo(Zaire)
32 A5 **Kabanjahe** Indon.
51 G7 **Kabardino-Balkarskaya Respublika** *div.* Rus. Fed.
56 C4 **Kabare** Congo(Zaire)
36 R3 **Kåbdalis** Sweden
68 E1 **Kabenung Lake** *l.* Can.
66 D4 **Kabinakagami Lake** *l.* Can.
56 C4 **Kabinda** Congo(Zaire)
18 B3 **Kabīrkūh** *mts* Iran
22 B3 **Kabirwala** Pak.
58 B3 **Kabo** C.A.R.
57 C5 **Kabompo** Zambia
56 C4 **Kabongo** Congo(Zaire)
19 F3 **Kabūdeh** Iran
19 E2 **Kabūd Gonbad** Iran
18 C3 **Kabūd Rāhang** Iran
31 B2 **Kabugao** Phil.
19 H3 **Kābul** Afgh.
19 H3 **Kabul** *r.* Afgh.
31 C6 **Kaburuang** *i.* Indon.
57 C5 **Kabwe** Zambia
19 F4 **Kacha Kuh** *mts* Iran/Pak.
51 H5 **Kachalinskaya** Rus. Fed.
22 B5 **Kachchh, Gulf of** *g.* India
22 C1 **Kach Pass** *pass* Afgh.
24 C1 **Kachug** Rus. Fed.
17 H1 **Kaçkar Dağı** *mt* Turkey
21 B4 **Kadaiyanallur** India
22 A3 **Kadanai** *r.* Afgh./Pak.
32 A2 **Kadan Kyun** *i.* Myanmar
7 H3 **Kadavu** *i.* Fiji
7 H3 **Kadavu Passage** *chan.* Fiji
54 B4 **Kade** Ghana
17 K5 **Kādhimain** Iraq
22 C5 **Kadi** India
16 B1 **Kadıköy** Turkey
8 A2 **Kadina** Austr.
16 D2 **Kadınhanı** Turkey
54 B3 **Kadiolo** Mali
21 B3 **Kadiri** India
16 F3 **Kadirli** Turkey
21 A4 **Kadmat** *i.* India
76 C3 **Kadoka** U.S.A.
57 C5 **Kadoma** Zimbabwe
55 E3 **Kadugli** Sudan
54 C3 **Kaduna** Nigeria
54 C3 **Kaduna** *r.* Nigeria
23 J3 **Kadusam** *mt* China
50 F3 **Kaduy** Rus. Fed.
21 A2 **Kadwa** *r.* India
50 G3 **Kadyy** Rus. Fed.
12 G3 **Kadzherom** Rus. Fed.
30 C4 **Kaechon** N. Korea
54 A3 **Kaédi** Maur.
55 D3 **Kaélé** Cameroon
74 □1 **Kaena Pt** *pt* U.S.A.
9 D1 **Kaeo** N.Z.
30 D5 **Kaesŏng** N. Korea
16 F6 **Kāf** S. Arabia
57 C4 **Kafakumba** Congo(Zaire)
54 C3 **Kaffrine** Senegal
49 L5 **Kafireas, Akra** *pt* Greece
16 C6 **Kafr el Sheik** Egypt
57 C5 **Kafue** Zambia
57 C5 **Kafue** *r.* Zambia
57 C5 **Kafue National Park** Zambia
29 E6 **Kaga** Japan
56 B3 **Kaga Bandoro** C.A.R.
51 G6 **Kagal'nitskaya** Rus. Fed.
19 G2 **Kagan** Uzbek.
69 F3 **Kagawong** Can.
36 R4 **Kåge** Sweden
17 J1 **Kağızman** Turkey
33 A3 **Kagologolo** Indon.
29 B9 **Kagoshima** Japan
18 C2 **Kahak** Iran
74 □1 **Kahaluu** U.S.A.
56 D4 **Kahama** Tanz.
74 □1 **Kahana** U.S.A.
51 D5 **Kaharlyk** Ukr.
33 D3 **Kahayan** *r.* Indon.
56 B4 **Kahemba** Congo(Zaire)
9 A6 **Kaherekoau Mts** *mts* N.Z.
43 K4 **Kahla** Ger.
Kahnu *see* **Kahnūj**
19 E5 **Kahnūj** Iran
68 B5 **Kahoka** U.S.A.
74 □2 **Kahoolawe** *i.* U.S.A.
16 F3 **Kahraman Maraş** Turkey
22 B3 **Kahror** Pak.
16 G3 **Kâhta** Turkey
74 □1 **Kahuku** U.S.A.
74 □1 **Kahuku Pt** *pt* U.S.A.
74 □2 **Kahului** U.S.A.
9 D4 **Kahurangi Point** *pt* N.Z.
22 C2 **Kahuta** Pak.
56 C4 **Kahuzi-Biega, Parc National du** *nat. park* Congo(Zaire)
54 C4 **Kaiama** Nigeria
9 D5 **Kaiapoi** N.Z.
75 F3 **Kaibab** U.S.A.
73 D4 **Kaibab Plat.** *plat.* U.S.A.
25 F7 **Kai Besar** *i.* Indon.
75 G3 **Kaibito** U.S.A.
75 G3 **Kaibito Plateau** *plat.* U.S.A.
26 E3 **Kaifeng** *Henan* China
26 E3 **Kaifeng** *Henan* China
27 F4 **Kaihua** China
58 D4 **Kaiingveld** *reg.* S. Africa
26 C4 **Kaijiang** China
25 F7 **Kai Kecil** *i.* Indon.
25 F7 **Kai, Kepulauan** *is* Indon.
9 D5 **Kaikoura** N.Z.
9 D5 **Kaikoura Peninsula** *pen.* N.Z.
27 □ **Kai Kung Leng** *h. H.K.* China
54 A4 **Kailahun** Sierra Leone
Kailas *mt see* **Kangrinboqê Feng**
23 G4 **Kailāshahar** India
Kailas Range *mts see* **Gangdisê Shan**
27 C5 **Kaili** China
30 A2 **Kailu** China
74 □1 **Kailua** U.S.A.
74 □2 **Kailua Kona** U.S.A.
9 E2 **Kaimai Range** *h.* N.Z.
6 D2 **Kaimana** Indon.
9 E3 **Kaimanawa Mountains** N.Z.
23 H2 **Kaimar** China
22 E4 **Kaimur Range** *h.* India
37 S7 **Käina** Estonia
29 D8 **Kainan** Japan
29 D7 **Kainan** Japan
54 C3 **Kainji Lake National Park** Nigeria
54 C3 **Kainji Reservoir** Nigeria
9 E2 **Kaipara Harbour** *in.* N.Z.
75 G3 **Kaiparowits Plateau** *plat.* U.S.A.
27 D6 **Kaiping** China
67 J3 **Kaipokok Bay** *in.* Can.
22 D3 **Kairana** India
54 D1 **Kairouan** Tunisia
43 F5 **Kaiserslautern** Ger.
30 E2 **Kaishantun** China
9 D1 **Kaitaia** N.Z.
9 B7 **Kaitangata** N.Z.
9 F3 **Kaitawa** N.Z.
22 D3 **Kaithal** India
36 R3 **Kaitum** Sweden
6 C2 **Kaiwatu** Indon.
74 □2 **Kaiwi Channel** U.S.A.
26 C4 **Kai Xian** China
27 C5 **Kaiyang** China
27 B6 **Kaiyuan** *Yunnan* China
30 C2 **Kaiyuan** China
36 U4 **Kajaani** Fin.
6 E4 **Kajabbi** Austr.
19 G3 **Kajaki** Afgh.
32 B5 **Kajang** Malaysia
22 B3 **Kajanpur** Pak.
17 L2 **K'ajaran** Armenia
19 G3 **Kajrān** Afgh.
17 L3 **Kaju** Iran
66 C4 **Kakabeka Falls** Can.
58 D4 **Kakamas** S. Africa
56 D3 **Kakamega** Kenya
9 C6 **Kakanui Mts** *mts* N.Z.
54 A4 **Kakata** Liberia
9 E3 **Kakatahi** N.Z.
23 H4 **Kakching** India
29 C7 **Kake** Japan
64 C3 **Kake** U.S.A.
56 C4 **Kakenge** Congo(Zaire)
43 K2 **Kakerbeck** Ger.
51 E6 **Kakhovka** Ukr.
51 E6 **Kakhovs'ke Vodoskhovyshche** *resr* Ukr.
18 C4 **Kākī** Iran
21 C2 **Kākināda** India
64 F2 **Kakisa** Can.
64 F2 **Kakisa** *r.* Can.
64 F2 **Kakisa Lake** *l.* Can.
29 D7 **Kakogawa** Japan
56 C4 **Kakoswa** Congo(Zaire)
22 D4 **Kakrala** India
62 D2 **Kaktovik** U.S.A.
29 G6 **Kakuda** Japan
64 F4 **Kakwa** *r.* Can.
22 B3 **Kala** Pak.
48 D7 **Kalaâ Kebira** Tunisia
22 B2 **Kalabagh** Pak.
25 E7 **Kalabahi** Indon.
31 A5 **Kalabakan** Malaysia
8 C1 **Kalabity** Austr.
57 C5 **Kalabo** Zambia
51 G5 **Kalach** Rus. Fed.
56 D3 **Kalacha Dida** Kenya
51 G5 **Kalach-na-Donu** Rus. Fed.
23 H5 **Kaladan** *r.* India/Myanmar
69 J3 **Kaladar** Can.
74 □2 **Ka Lae** *c.* U.S.A.
53 G8 **Kalahari Desert** *des.* Africa
57 B6 **Kalahari Gemsbok National Park** S. Africa
19 F3 **Kala-I-Mor** Turkm.
36 S4 **Kalajoki** Fin.
36 T4 **Kalajoki** *r.* Fin.
22 C2 **Kalam** Pak.
59 C1 **Kalamare** Botswana
49 K4 **Kalamaria** Greece
49 K6 **Kalamata** Greece
68 E4 **Kalamazoo** U.S.A.
68 D4 **Kalamazoo** *r.* U.S.A.
49 J5 **Kalampaka** Greece
22 C3 **Kalanaur** India
51 E6 **Kalanchak** Ukr.
19 F4 **Kalandi** Pak.
8 C4 **Kalangadoo** Austr.
22 C3 **Kalanwali** India
31 C5 **Kalaong** Phil.
21 C4 **Kala Oya** *r.* Sri Lanka
17 K4 **Kalār** Iraq
19 F5 **Kalar** *watercourse* Iran
Kalāt *see* **Kabūd Gonbad**
19 G4 **Kalat** Pak.
74 □2 **Kalaupapa** U.S.A.
51 G6 **Kalaus** *r.* Rus. Fed.
17 L1 **Kälbäcär** Azer.
6 B4 **Kalbarri** Austr.
43 K2 **Kalbe (Milde)** Ger.
19 E3 **Kalbū** Iran
16 B3 **Kale** *Denizli* Turkey
17 G1 **Kale** Turkey
16 D1 **Kalecik** Turkey
43 J3 **Kalefeld** Ger.
17 M3 **Kaleh Sarai** Iran
56 C4 **Kalema** Congo(Zaire)
56 C4 **Kalémié** Congo(Zaire)
68 D3 **Kaleva** U.S.A.
36 W4 **Kalevala** Rus. Fed.
23 H5 **Kalewa** Myanmar
6 C5 **Kalgoorlie** Austr.
48 F2 **Kali** Croatia
22 E3 **Kali** *r.* India/Nepal
31 B4 **Kalibo** Phil.
23 F4 **Kali Gadaki** *r.* Nepal
56 C4 **Kalima** Congo(Zaire)
33 D3 **Kalimantan** *reg.* Indon.
22 E4 **Kali Nadi** *r.* India
21 A3 **Kalinadi** *r.* India
50 B4 **Kaliningrad** Rus. Fed.
50 B4 **Kaliningradskaya Oblast'** *div.* Rus. Fed.
50 G3 **Kalinino** Rus. Fed.
51 H5 **Kalininsk** Rus. Fed.
51 F6 **Kalininskaya** Rus. Fed.
51 D4 **Kalinkavichy** Belarus
22 D4 **Kali Sindh** *r.* India
72 D1 **Kalispell** U.S.A.
46 J5 **Kalisz** Pol.
51 G5 **Kalitva** *r.* Rus. Fed.
56 D4 **Kaliua** Tanz.
36 S4 **Kalix** Sweden
36 S3 **Kalixälven** *r.* Sweden
23 H4 **Kalkalighat** India
16 B3 **Kalkan** Turkey
68 E3 **Kalkaska** U.S.A.
57 B6 **Kalkfeld** Namibia
59 F4 **Kalkfonteindam** *dam* S. Africa
42 E4 **Kall** Ger.
32 □ **Kallang** Sing.
37 U7 **Kallaste** Estonia
36 U5 **Kallavesi** *l.* Fin.
36 N5 **Kallsedet** Sweden
36 N5 **Kallsjön** *l.* Sweden
37 P8 **Kalmar** Sweden
37 P8 **Kalmarsund** *chan.* Sweden
43 G5 **Kalmit** *h.* Ger.
51 F6 **Kal'mius** *r.* Ukr.
21 C5 **Kalmunai** Sri Lanka
51 H6 **Kalmykiya, Respublika** *div.* Rus. Fed.
23 G4 **Kalni** *r.* Bangl.
47 N5 **Kalodnaye** Belarus
22 C5 **Kalol** India
31 C6 **Kaloma** *i.* Indon.
57 C5 **Kalomo** Zambia
64 D4 **Kalone Pk** *summit* Can.
18 B2 **Kalow** *r.* Iran
22 D3 **Kalpa** India
21 A4 **Kalpeni** *i.* India
22 D4 **Kalpi** India
17 L4 **Kal Safīd** Iran
62 C3 **Kaltag** U.S.A.
43 H1 **Kaltenkirchen** Ger.
43 J4 **Kaltensundheim** Ger.
22 C3 **Kalu** India
50 F4 **Kaluga** Rus. Fed.
37 M9 **Kalundborg** Denmark
22 B2 **Kalur Kot** Pak.
51 C5 **Kalush** Ukr.
21 B5 **Kalutara** Sri Lanka
50 E4 **Kaluzhskaya Oblast'** *div.* Rus. Fed.
36 S5 **Kälviä** Fin.
21 A2 **Kalyan** India
50 F3 **Kalyazin** Rus. Fed.
49 M6 **Kalymnos** *i.* Greece
47 M6 **Kalynivka** Ukr.
56 C4 **Kama** Congo(Zaire)
28 G5 **Kamaishi** Japan
22 C3 **Kamalia** Pak.
16 D2 **Kaman** Turkey
57 B5 **Kamanjab** Namibia
21 B2 **Kamareddi** India
19 F5 **Kamarod** Pak.
19 G2 **Kamashi** Uzbek.
6 C5 **Kambalda** Austr.
21 B4 **Kambam** India
30 E3 **Kambo Ho** *mt* N. Korea
57 C5 **Kambove** Congo(Zaire)
13 S4 **Kamchatka** *r.* Rus. Fed.
13 R4 **Kamchatka Peninsula** Rus. Fed.
49 M3 **Kamchiya** *r.* Bulg.
43 F3 **Kamen** Ger.
49 K4 **Kamenitsa** *mt* Bulg.
50 H4 **Kamenka** *Penzen.* Rus. Fed.
28 E2 **Kamenka** *Primorskiy Kray* Rus. Fed.
12 K4 **Kamen'-na-Obi** Rus. Fed.
50 F3 **Kamenniki** Rus. Fed.
50 D2 **Kamennogorsk** Rus. Fed.
51 G6 **Kamennomostskiy** Rus. Fed.
51 G6 **Kamenolomni** Rus. Fed.
28 C2 **Kamen'-Rybolov** Rus. Fed.
13 S3 **Kamenskoye** Rus. Fed.
51 G5 **Kamensk-Shakhtinskiy** Rus. Fed.
12 H4 **Kamensk-Ural'skiy** Rus. Fed.
50 G3 **Kameshkovo** Rus. Fed.
22 D3 **Kamet** *mt* China
58 C5 **Kamiesberge** *mts* S. Africa
58 B5 **Kamieskroon** S. Africa
65 J2 **Kamilukuak Lake** *l.* Can.
57 C4 **Kamina** Congo(Zaire)
65 L2 **Kaminak Lake** *l.* Can.
47 M5 **Kamin'-Kashyrs'kyy** Ukr.
28 H3 **Kamishihoro** Japan
23 H4 **Kamjong** India
23 F4 **Kamla** *r.* India
64 E4 **Kamloops** Can.
17 K1 **Kamo** Armenia
29 G7 **Kamogawa** Japan
22 C3 **Kamoke** Pak.
56 C4 **Kamonia** Congo(Zaire)
32 C2 **Kamon, Xé** *r.* Laos
56 D3 **Kampala** Uganda
32 B4 **Kampar** Malaysia
33 B2 **Kampar** *r.* Indon.
42 D2 **Kampen** Neth.
56 C4 **Kampene** Congo(Zaire)
32 A1 **Kamphaeng Phet** Thai.
21 B3 **Kampli** India
32 C3 **Kâmpóng Cham** Cambodia
32 C2 **Kâmpóng Chhnăng** Cambodia
32 C2 **Kâmpóng Khleăng** Cambodia
32 C3 **Kâmpóng Spoe** Cambodia
32 C2 **Kâmpóng Thum** Cambodia
32 C3 **Kâmpôt** Cambodia
Kampuchea *country see* **Cambodia**
25 F7 **Kamrau, Teluk** *b.* Indon.
65 J4 **Kamsack** Can.
12 G4 **Kamskoye Vdkhr.** *resr* Rus. Fed.
56 E3 **Kamsuuma** Somalia
65 J3 **Kamuchawie Lake** *l.* Can.
56 D3 **Kamuli** Uganda
51 C5 **Kam"yane** Ukr.
51 C5 **Kam"yanets'-Podil's'kyy** Ukr.
51 C5 **Kam"yanka-Buz'ka** Ukr.
47 L4 **Kamyanyets** Belarus
18 B3 **Kāmyārān** Iran
51 F6 **Kamyshevatskaya** Rus. Fed.
51 H5 **Kamyshin** Rus. Fed.
51 J6 **Kamyzyak** Rus. Fed.
18 E5 **Kamzar** Oman
66 F3 **Kanaaupscow** *r.* Can.
75 F3 **Kanab** U.S.A.
75 F3 **Kanab Creek** *r.* U.S.A.
19 G4 **Kanak** Pak.
17 K5 **Kan'ān** Iraq
56 C4 **Kananga** Congo(Zaire)
8 H2 **Kanangra Nat. Park** Austr.
75 F3 **Kanarraville** U.S.A.
50 H4 **Kanash** Rus. Fed.
80 C5 **Kanawha** *r.* U.S.A.
29 E7 **Kanayama** Japan
29 E6 **Kanazawa** Japan
32 A2 **Kanchanaburi** Thai.
21 B3 **Kanchipuram** India
22 A3 **Kand** *mt* Pak.
19 G4 **Kandahār** Afgh.
36 X3 **Kandalaksha** Rus. Fed.
32 A5 **Kandang** Indon.
22 B2 **Kandhura** Pak.
54 C3 **Kandi** Benin
19 G4 **Kandi** Pak.
22 B4 **Kandiaro** Pak.
16 C1 **Kandıra** Turkey
8 G2 **Kandos** Austr.
57 E5 **Kandreho** Madag.
21 B3 **Kandukur** India
21 C5 **Kandy** Sri Lanka
80 D4 **Kane** U.S.A.
63 M2 **Kane Basin** *b.* Can./Greenland
18 D5 **Kaneh** *watercourse* Iran
74 □1 **Kaneohe** U.S.A.
74 □1 **Kaneohe Bay** *b.* U.S.A.
51 F6 **Kanevskaya** Rus. Fed.
57 C6 **Kang** Botswana
23 G5 **Kanga** *r.* Bangl.
63 N3 **Kangaatsiaq** Greenland
54 B3 **Kangaba** Mali
16 F2 **Kangal** Turkey
18 D5 **Kangan** Iran
19 E5 **Kangān** Iran
33 B1 **Kangar** Malaysia
8 A3 **Kangaroo I.** *i.* Austr.
36 V5 **Kangaslampi** Fin.
37 U6 **Kangasniemi** Fin.
18 B3 **Kangāvar** Iran
26 E1 **Kangbao** China
23 G4 **Kangchenjunga** *mt* Nepal
27 A4 **Kangding** China
30 D4 **Kangdong** N. Korea
63 M3 **Kangeak Pt** *pt* Can.
33 E4 **Kangean, Kepulauan** *is* Indon.
63 O3 **Kangeq** *hd* Greenland
63 O4 **Kangerlussuaq** *in.* Greenland
63 N2 **Kangersuatsiaq** Greenland
63 P3 **Kangertittivatsiaq** *in.* Greenland
30 D3 **Kanggye** N. Korea
30 D5 **Kanghwa** S. Korea
30 D5 **Kanghwa Do** *i.* S. Korea
67 G2 **Kangiqsualujjuaq** Can.
63 L3 **Kangiqsujuaq** Can.
67 G1 **Kangirsuk** Can.
26 B3 **Kangle** China
23 F3 **Kangmar** *Xizang* China
23 G3 **Kangmar** *Xizang* China
30 E5 **Kangnŭng** S. Korea
56 B3 **Kango** Gabon
30 B2 **Kangping** China
23 J3 **Kangri Karpo Pass** India
22 E3 **Kangrinboqê Feng** *mt* China
23 H4 **Kangto** *mt* China
23 F2 **Kangtog** China
26 B3 **Kang Xian** China
22 D5 **Kanhan** *r.* India
23 E4 **Kanhar** *r.* India
56 C4 **Kaniama** Congo(Zaire)
9 C5 **Kaniere, L.** *l.* N.Z.
21 B3 **Kanigiri** India
12 F3 **Kanin, Poluostrov** *pen.* Rus. Fed.
17 K3 **Kānī Rash** Iraq
51 D5 **Kaniv** Ukr.
8 C4 **Kaniva** Austr.
37 S6 **Kankaanpää** Fin.
68 D5 **Kankakee** U.S.A.
68 C5 **Kankakee** *r.* U.S.A.
54 B3 **Kankan** Guinea
23 E5 **Kanker** India
21 C4 **Kankesanturai** Sri Lanka
32 A3 **Kanmaw Kyun** *i.* Myanmar
22 D4 **Kannanj** India
79 D5 **Kannapolis** U.S.A.
21 B4 **Kanniyakumari** India
Kanniya Kumari *c. see* **Comorin, Cape**
22 D5 **Kannod** India
36 T5 **Kannonkoski** Fin.
Kannur *see* **Cannanore**
36 S5 **Kannus** Fin.
54 C3 **Kano** Nigeria
58 D7 **Kanonpunt** *pt* S. Africa
22 C4 **Kanor** India
29 B9 **Kanoya** Japan
22 E4 **Kanpur** India
22 B3 **Kanpur** Pak.
19 G5 **Kanrach** *reg.* Pak.
76 D4 **Kansas** *div.* U.S.A.
76 D4 **Kansas** *r.* U.S.A.
76 E4 **Kansas City** *KS* U.S.A.
76 E4 **Kansas City** *MO* U.S.A.
24 B1 **Kansk** Rus. Fed.
30 E4 **Kansŏng** S. Korea
23 G4 **Kantanagar** Bangl.
32 C2 **Kantaralak** Thai.
54 C3 **Kantchari** Burkina
51 F5 **Kantemirovka** Rus. Fed.
23 F5 **Kānthi** India
23 F4 **Kanti** India
22 C3 **Kantli** *r.* India
7 J2 **Kanton Island** *i.* Kiribati
41 C5 **Kanturk** Rep. of Ireland
58 C3 **Kanus** Namibia
59 J2 **KaNyamazane** S. Africa
57 C6 **Kanye** Botswana
32 B3 **Kaôh Kông** *i.* Cambodia
32 B3 **Kaôh Rŭng** *i.* Cambodia
32 B3 **Kaôh Rŭng Sânlŏem** *i.* Cambodia
27 F6 **Kao-hsiung** Taiwan
32 B3 **Kaôh Smăch** *i.* Cambodia
57 B5 **Kaokoveld** *plat.* Namibia
54 A3 **Kaolack** Senegal
57 C5 **Kaoma** Zambia
74 □2 **Kapaa** U.S.A.
74 □2 **Kapaau** U.S.A.
17 L2 **Kapan** Armenia
57 C4 **Kapanga** Congo(Zaire)
15 F2 **Kapchagay** Kazak.
42 C3 **Kapellen** Belgium
49 K6 **Kapello, Akra** *pt* Greece
37 Q7 **Kapellskär** Sweden
16 A1 **Kapıdağı Yarımadası** *pen.* Turkey
23 G4 **Kapili** *r.* India
94 F5 **Kapingamarangi Rise** *sea feature* Pac. Oc.
94 F5 **Kapingamarangi** *i.* Pac. Oc.
22 B3 **Kapip** Pak.
57 C5 **Kapiri Mposhi** Zambia
63 N3 **Kapisigdlit** Greenland
66 D3 **Kapiskau** Can.
66 D3 **Kapiskau** *r.* Can.
69 G2 **Kapiskong Lake** *l.* Can.
9 E4 **Kapiti I.** *i.* N.Z.
32 A3 **Kapoe** Thai.
55 F4 **Kapoeta** Sudan
46 H7 **Kaposvár** Hungary
19 F5 **Kappar** Pak.
42 F5 **Kappel** Ger.
46 D3 **Kappeln** Ger.
22 D4 **Kapran** India
56 D3 **Kapsabet** Kenya
30 E3 **Kapsan** N. Korea
33 D3 **Kapuas** *r.* Indon.
33 D2 **Kapuas** *r.* Indon.
8 B3 **Kapunda** Austr.
22 C4 **Kapūriya** India
22 C3 **Kapurthala** India
66 D4 **Kapuskasing** Can.
66 D4 **Kapuskasing** *r.* Can.
51 H5 **Kapustin Yar** Rus. Fed.
56 D3 **Kaputir** Kenya
46 H7 **Kapuvár** Hungary
50 C4 **Kapyl'** Belarus
30 D5 **Kap'yŏng** S. Korea
54 C4 **Kara** Togo
17 H2 **Kara** *r.* Turkey
49 M5 **Kara Ada** *i.* Turkey
16 D2 **Karaali** Turkey
19 F2 **Karabil', Vozvyshennost'** *reg.* Turkm.
20 D1 **Kara-Bogaz Gol, Zaliv** *b.* Turkm.
16 D1 **Karabük** Turkey
14 E2 **Karabutak** Kazak.
16 B1 **Karacabey** Turkey
17 G3 **Karacadağ** Turkey
16 D3 **Karacadağ** *mts* Turkey
16 B3 **Karacaköy** Turkey
17 G3 **Karacalı Dağ** *mt* Turkey
16 B3 **Karacasu** Turkey
16 C3 **Karaca Yarımadası** *pen.* Turkey
51 G7 **Karachayevo-Cherkesskaya Respublika** *div.* Rus. Fed.
51 G7 **Karachayevsk** Rus. Fed.
50 E4 **Karachev** Rus. Fed.
19 G5 **Karachi** Pak.
17 J2 **Karaçoban** Turkey
21 A2 **Karad** India
16 D3 **Kara Dağ** *mt* Turkey
17 J3 **Kara Dağ** *mt* Turkey
Kara Deniz *sea see* **Black Sea**
15 F2 **Karaganda** Kazak.
15 F2 **Karagayly** Kazak.
13 S4 **Karaginskiy Zaliv** *b.* Rus. Fed.
16 B2 **Karahallı** Turkey
16 E2 **Karahasanlı** Turkey
21 B4 **Kāraikāl** India
21 B4 **Karaikkudi** India
16 E3 **Karaisalı** Turkey
18 C3 **Karaj** Iran
18 C3 **Karaj** *r.* Iran
16 E6 **Karak** Jordan
18 E2 **Kara Kala** Turkm.
22 E1 **Karakax He** *r.* China
17 G3 **Karakeçi** Turkey
16 D2 **Karakeçili** Turkey
25 E6 **Karakelong** *i.* Indon.
17 H2 **Karakoçan** Turkey
12 J5 **Kara-Köl** Kyrg.
15 F2 **Karakol** Kyrg.
22 D2 **Karakoram Pass** China/Jammu and Kashmir
15 F3 **Karakoram Range** *mts* Asia
56 D2 **Kara K'orē** Eth.
19 F2 **Karakul'** Uzbek.
19 F2 **Karakul'** Uzbek.
19 F2 **Karakum Desert** Turkm.
14 D2 **Karakum, Peski** *des.* Kazak.
19 F2 **Karakumskiy Kanal** *canal* Turkm.
19 E2 **Kara Kumy** *reg.* Turkm.
Karakumy, Peski *des. see* **Karakum Desert**
17 J1 **Karakurt** Turkey
37 R7 **Karala** Estonia
16 D3 **Karaman** Turkey
16 B3 **Karamanlı** Turkey
15 G2 **Karamay** China
22 C1 **Karambar Pass** Afgh./Pak.
9 D4 **Karamea** N.Z.
9 C4 **Karamea Bight** *b.* N.Z.
19 G2 **Karamet-Niyaz** Turkm.
23 F1 **Karamiran** China
23 F1 **Karamiran Shankou** *pass* China
16 B1 **Karamürsel** Turkey
50 D3 **Karamyshevo** Rus. Fed.
18 C5 **Karān** *i.* S. Arabia
18 B3 **Karand** Iran
22 D5 **Karanja** India
21 B2 **Karanja** *r.* India
23 F5 **Karanjia** India
22 C3 **Karanpura** India
16 D3 **Karapınar** Turkey
58 B3 **Karas** *div.* Namibia
58 B3 **Karas** *watercourse* Namibia
57 B6 **Karasburg** Namibia
12 J2 **Kara Sea** *sea* Rus. Fed.
36 T2 **Karasjok** Norway
16 C1 **Karasu** Turkey
17 J2 **Karasu** *r.* Turkey
12 J4 **Karasuk** Rus. Fed.
16 E3 **Karataş** Turkey
16 E3 **Karataş Burun** *pt* Turkey
14 F2 **Karatau** Kazak.
14 E2 **Karatau, Khr.** *mts* Kazak.
22 E2 **Karatax Shan** *mts* China
32 A3 **Karathuri** Myanmar
21 B4 **Karativu** *i.* Sri Lanka
23 G4 **Karatoya** *r.* Bangl.
29 A8 **Karatsu** Japan
31 C5 **Karatung** *i.* Indon.
19 G2 **Karaulbazar** Uzbek.
22 D4 **Karauli** India
17 J1 **Karaurgan** Turkey
33 C4 **Karawang** Indon.
17 K5 **Karbalā'** Iraq
43 G4 **Karben** Ger.
47 K7 **Karcag** Hungary
42 F4 **Karden** Ger.
49 J5 **Karditsa** Greece
37 S7 **Kärdla** Estonia
59 G4 **Karee** S. Africa
58 D5 **Kareeberge** *mts* S. Africa
55 F3 **Kareima** Sudan
51 G7 **K'areli** Georgia
22 D5 **Kareli** India
50 E2 **Kareliya, Respublika** *div.* Rus. Fed.
24 D1 **Karenga** *r.* Rus. Fed.
22 D4 **Karera** India
36 S2 **Karesuando** Sweden
19 F5 **Kārevāndar** Iran
51 H7 **Kargalinskaya** Rus. Fed.
17 H2 **Kargapazarı Dağları** *mts* Turkey
16 E1 **Kargı** Turkey
22 D2 **Kargil** Jammu and Kashmir
50 F2 **Kargopol'** Rus. Fed.
37 P6 **Karholmsbruk** Sweden
57 C5 **Kariba** Zimbabwe
57 C5 **Kariba, Lake** *resr* Zambia/Zimbabwe
28 F3 **Kariba-yama** *volc.* Japan
58 E6 **Kariega** *r.* S. Africa
36 T2 **Karigasniemi** Fin.
37 R5 **Karijoki** Fin.
9 D1 **Karikari, Cape** *c.* N.Z.
18 D3 **Karīmābād** Iran
33 C3 **Karimata, Pulau Pulau** *is* Indon.
33 C3 **Karimata, Selat** *str.* Indon.
21 B2 **Karimnagar** India
33 D4 **Karimunjawa, Pulau Pulau** *is* Indon.
56 E2 **Karin** Somalia
18 E3 **Karit** Iran
21 A2 **Karjat** India
23 F5 **Karkai** *r.* India
21 A3 **Karkal** India
31 C5 **Karkaralong, Kepulauan** *is* Indon.
6 E2 **Karkar I.** *i.* P.N.G.
18 C4 **Karkheh** *r.* Iran
19 E5 **Kārkīn Dar** Iran
51 E6 **Karkinits'ka Zatoka** *g.* Ukr.
37 T6 **Kärkölä** Fin.
37 T7 **Karksi-Nuia** Estonia
17 H2 **Karlıova** Turkey
51 E5 **Karlivka** Ukr.
Karl-Marx-Stadt *see* **Chemnitz**
48 F2 **Karlovac** Croatia
49 L3 **Karlovo** Bulg.
46 F5 **Karlovy Vary** Czech Rep.
43 G6 **Karlsbad** Ger.
37 O7 **Karlsborg** Sweden
37 O8 **Karlshamn** Sweden
37 O7 **Karlskoga** Sweden
37 O8 **Karlskrona** Sweden
43 G5 **Karlsruhe** Ger.
37 N7 **Karlstad** Sweden
76 D1 **Karlstad** U.S.A.
43 H5 **Karlstadt** Ger.
50 D4 **Karma** Belarus
21 A2 **Karmala** India
37 J7 **Karmøy** *i.* Norway
23 H5 **Karnafuli Reservoir** Bangl.
22 D3 **Karnal** India
23 E3 **Karnali** *r.* Nepal
21 A3 **Karnataka** *div.* India
49 M3 **Karnobat** Bulg.
19 G5 **Karodi** Pak.
57 C5 **Karoi** Zimbabwe
23 G3 **Karo La** *pass* China
23 H4 **Karong** India
57 D4 **Karonga** Malawi
58 E6 **Karoo National Park** S. Africa
8 B3 **Karoonda** Austr.
22 B3 **Karor** Pak.
56 D2 **Karora** Eritrea
43 L1 **Karow** Ger.
49 M7 **Karpathos** *i.* Greece
49 M6 **Karpathou, Steno** *chan.* Greece
Karpaty *mts see* **Carpathian Mountains**
49 J5 **Karpenisi** Greece
50 H1 **Karpogory** Rus. Fed.
6 B4 **Karratha** Austr.
19 F3 **Karrukh** Afgh.
17 J1 **Kars** Turkey
36 T5 **Kärsämäki** Fin.
37 U8 **Kārsava** Latvia
19 G2 **Karshi** Uzbek.
23 G4 **Kārsiyāng** India
12 G3 **Karskiye Vorota, Proliv** *str.* Rus. Fed.
Karskoye More *sea see* **Kara Sea**
43 K1 **Karstädt** Ger.
36 T5 **Karstula** Fin.
16 B1 **Kartal** Turkey
12 H4 **Kartaly** Rus. Fed.
36 U5 **Karttula** Fin.
18 C4 **Kārūn** *r.* Iran
18 C4 **Karun, Kūh-e** *h.* Iran
21 B4 **Karur** India
37 S5 **Karvia** Fin.
37 S6 **Karvianjoki** *r.* Fin.
21 A3 **Karwar** India
24 D1 **Karymskoye** Rus. Fed.
49 L5 **Karystos** Greece
16 B3 **Kaş** Turkey
66 C3 **Kasabonika** Can.
66 C3 **Kasabonika Lake** *l.* Can.
56 B4 **Kasai** *r.* Congo(Zaire)
57 C5 **Kasaji** Congo(Zaire)
57 D5 **Kasama** Zambia
19 G2 **Kasan** Uzbek.
57 C5 **Kasane** Botswana
56 B4 **Kasangulu** Congo(Zaire)
21 A3 **Kasaragod** India
65 J2 **Kasba Lake** *l.* Can.
54 B1 **Kasba Tadla** Morocco
29 B9 **Kaseda** Japan
17 L4 **Kaseh Garan** Iran
57 C5 **Kasempa** Zambia
57 C5 **Kasenga** Congo(Zaire)
56 C4 **Kasese** Congo(Zaire)
56 D3 **Kasese** Uganda
22 D4 **Kasganj** India
18 C3 **Kāshān** Iran
66 D3 **Kashechewan** Can.
Kashgar *see* **Kashi**
15 F3 **Kashi** China
29 D7 **Kashihara** Japan
29 B8 **Kashima** Japan
29 G6 **Kashima-nada** *b.* Japan
50 F3 **Kashin** Rus. Fed.
22 D3 **Kashipur** India
29 F6 **Kashiwazaki** Japan
17 L5 **Kashkan** *r.* Iran
19 E3 **Kāshmar** Iran
22 C2 **Kashmir, Vale of** *v.* India
22 B3 **Kashmor** Pak.
19 H3 **Kashmund** *reg.* Afgh.

56 C4 **Kashyukulu** Congo(Zaire)
50 G4 **Kasimov** Rus. Fed.
78 B4 **Kaskaskia** *r.* U.S.A.
65 L3 **Kaskattama** *r.* Can.
37 R5 **Kaskinen** Fin.
56 C4 **Kasongo** Congo(Zaire)
56 B4 **Kasongo-Lunda** Congo(Zaire)
49 M7 **Kasos** *i.* Greece
49 M7 **Kasou, Steno** *chan.* Greece
51 H7 **Kaspi** Georgia
51 H7 **Kaspiysk** Rus. Fed.
Kaspiyskoye More *sea see* **Caspian Sea**
47 P3 **Kasplya** Rus. Fed.
55 F3 **Kassala** Sudan
49 K4 **Kassandra** *pen.* Greece
49 K4 **Kassandras, Kolpos** *b.* Greece
43 H3 **Kassel** Ger.
54 C1 **Kasserine** Tunisia
68 A3 **Kasson** U.S.A.
16 D1 **Kastamonu** Turkey
42 F4 **Kastellaun** Ger.
49 K7 **Kastelli** Greece
42 C3 **Kasterlee** Belgium
49 J4 **Kastoria** Greece
50 E4 **Kastsyukovichy** Belarus
29 E7 **Kasugai** Japan
56 D4 **Kasulu** Tanz.
29 D7 **Kasumi** Japan
29 G6 **Kasumiga-ura** *l.* Japan
51 J7 **Kasumkent** Rus. Fed.
57 D5 **Kasungu** Malawi
22 C3 **Kasur** Pak.
81 J2 **Katahdin, Mt** *mt* U.S.A.
22 D2 **Kataklik** Jammu and Kashmir
56 C4 **Katako-Kombe** Congo(Zaire)
22 D5 **Katangi** India
6 B5 **Katanning** Austr.
19 H3 **Katawaz** Afgh.
56 C4 **Katea** Congo(Zaire)
49 K4 **Katerini** Greece
64 C3 **Kate's Needle** *mt* Can./U.S.A.
57 D5 **Katete** Zambia
23 E5 **Katghora** India
24 B4 **Katha** Myanmar
6 D3 **Katherine** *r.* Austr.
22 B5 **Kathiawar** *pen.* India
16 D6 **Kathib el Henu** *sand dunes* Egypt
21 C4 **Kathiraveli** Sri Lanka
59 H3 **Kathlehong** S. Africa
23 F4 **Kathmandu** Nepal
58 E3 **Kathu** S. Africa
22 C2 **Kathua** Jammu and Kashmir
54 B3 **Kati** Mali
23 F4 **Katihar** India
9 E2 **Katikati** N.Z.
59 G6 **Kati-Kati** S. Africa
57 C5 **Katima Mulilo** Namibia
54 B4 **Katiola** Côte d'Ivoire
58 D4 **Katkop Hills** *reg.* S. Africa
Katmandu *see* **Kathmandu**
49 J5 **Kato Achaïa** Greece
22 D5 **Katol** India
32 □ **Katong** Sing.
8 H2 **Katoomba** Austr.
47 J5 **Katowice** Pol.
23 G5 **Katoya** India
37 P7 **Katrineholm** Sweden
40 D4 **Katrine, Loch** *l.* U.K.
54 C3 **Katsina** Nigeria
54 C4 **Katsina-Ala** Nigeria
29 G6 **Katsuta** Japan
29 G7 **Katsuura** Japan
29 E6 **Katsuyama** Japan
67 G2 **Kattaktoc, Cap** *hd* Can.
19 G2 **Kattakurgan** Uzbek.
19 G3 **Kattasang Hills** *mts* Afgh.
37 M8 **Kattegat** *str.* Denmark/Sweden
22 B3 **Katuri** Pak.
42 C2 **Katwijk aan Zee** Neth.
43 H5 **Katzenbuckel** *h.* Ger.
74 □2 **Kauai** *i.* U.S.A.
74 □2 **Kauai Channel** U.S.A.
43 F4 **Kaub** Ger.
43 H3 **Kaufungen** Ger.
37 S5 **Kauhajoki** Fin.
36 S5 **Kauhava** Fin.
36 T3 **Kaukonen** Fin.
74 □2 **Kaula** *i.* U.S.A.
74 □2 **Kaulakahi Channel** U.S.A.
67 H2 **Kaumajet Mts** *mts* Can.
74 □2 **Kaunakakai** U.S.A.
37 S9 **Kaunas** Lith.
37 U8 **Kaunata** Latvia
54 C3 **Kaura-Namoda** Nigeria
27 □ **Kau Sai Chau** *i. H.K.* China
36 S5 **Kaustinen** Fin.
36 S2 **Kautokeino** Norway
32 A3 **Kau-ye Kyun** *i.* Myanmar
49 K4 **Kavadarci** Macedonia
16 F1 **Kavak** Turkey
49 L4 **Kavala** Greece
28 D2 **Kavalerovo** Rus. Fed.
21 C3 **Kavali** India
18 D4 **Kavār** Iran
21 A4 **Kavaratti** *i.* India
49 N3 **Kavarna** Bulg.
21 B4 **Kāveri** *r.* India
18 D4 **Kavīr** *des.* Iran
18 D3 **Kavir** *salt flat* Iran
18 D3 **Kavir** *salt flat* Iran
18 D3 **Kavir, Dasht-e** *des.* Iran
18 D3 **Kavīr-e Hāj Ali Qoli** *salt l.* Iran
19 E3 **Kavir-i-Namak** *salt flat* Iran
29 F7 **Kawagoe** Japan
29 F7 **Kawaguchi** Japan
74 □2 **Kawaihae** U.S.A.
9 E1 **Kawakawa** N.Z.
57 C4 **Kawambwa** Zambia
66 E5 **Kawartha Lakes** *l.* Can.
29 F7 **Kawasaki** Japan
9 E2 **Kawau I.** *i.* N.Z.
67 G2 **Kawawachikamach** Can.
9 F3 **Kawerau** N.Z.
9 E3 **Kawhia** N.Z.
9 E3 **Kawhia Harbour** *in.* N.Z.
74 D3 **Kawich Range** *mts* U.S.A.
32 A1 **Kawkareik** Myanmar
32 A1 **Kawludo** Myanmar
18 E6 **Kawr, J.** *mt* Oman
32 A3 **Kawthaung** Myanmar
54 B3 **Kaya** Burkina
16 F2 **Kayadibi** Turkey
13 M2 **Kayak** Rus. Fed.
33 E2 **Kayan** *r.* Indon.
56 C4 **Kayanaza** Burundi
21 B4 **Kayankulam** India
72 F3 **Kaycee** U.S.A.
57 C4 **Kayembe-Mukulu** Congo(Zaire)
75 G3 **Kayenta** U.S.A.
54 A3 **Kayes** Mali
54 A4 **Kayima** Sierra Leone
15 F2 **Kaynar** Kazak.
16 F2 **Kaynar** Turkey
16 F3 **Kaypak** Turkey
51 H5 **Kaysatskoye** Rus. Fed.
16 E2 **Kayseri** Turkey
33 B3 **Kayuagung** Indon.
12 K3 **Kayyerkan** Rus. Fed.
13 P2 **Kazach'ye** Rus. Fed.
Kazakh *see* **Qazax**
14 F1 **Kazakhskiy Melkosopochnik** *reg.* Kazak.
10 G5 **Kazakstan** *country* Asia
50 J4 **Kazan'** Rus. Fed.
65 K2 **Kazan** *r.* Can.
16 D3 **Kazancı** Turkey
50 J4 **Kazanka** *r.* Rus. Fed.
49 L3 **Kazanlŭk** Bulg.
24 G4 **Kazan-rettō** *is* Japan
51 G5 **Kazanskaya** Rus. Fed.
51 H7 **Kazbek** *mt* Georgia/Rus. Fed.
49 M5 **Kaz Dağı** *mts* Turkey
18 C4 **Kāzerūn** Iran
50 J2 **Kazhim** Rus. Fed.
19 F5 **Kazhmak** *r.* Pak.
47 K6 **Kazincbarcika** Hungary
19 F5 **Kazmīr** Iran
51 H7 **Kazret'i** Georgia
51 J5 **Kaztalovka** Kazak.
28 G4 **Kazuno** Japan
12 H3 **Kazymskiy Mys** Rus. Fed.
49 L6 **Kea** *i.* Greece
41 E3 **Keady** U.K.
74 □2 **Kealakekua Bay** *b.* U.S.A.
17 M4 **K-e-Alvand** *mt* Iran
75 G4 **Keams Canyon** U.S.A.
76 D3 **Kearney** U.S.A.
75 G5 **Kearny** U.S.A.
16 G2 **Keban** Turkey
16 G2 **Keban Barajı** *resr* Turkey
54 A3 **Kébémèr** Senegal
16 F4 **Kebir** *r.* Lebanon/Syria
55 E3 **Kebkabiya** Sudan
36 Q3 **Kebnekaise** *mt* Sweden
40 B2 **Kebock Head** *hd* U.K.
56 E3 **K'ebrī Dehar** Eth.
33 C4 **Kebumen** Indon.
64 D3 **Kechika** *r.* Can.
16 C3 **Keçiborlu** Turkey
47 J7 **Kecskemét** Hungary
17 H1 **K'eda** Georgia
37 S9 **Kėdainiai** Lith.
17 L4 **K-e Dalakhāni** *h.* Iraq
22 D3 **Kedar Kanta** *mt* India
22 D3 **Kedarnath Peak** *mt* India
67 G4 **Kedgwick** Can.
33 D4 **Kediri** Indon.
54 A3 **Kédougou** Senegal
64 D2 **Keele** *r.* Can.
64 C2 **Keele Pk** *summit* Can.
73 C4 **Keeler** U.S.A.
31 A5 **Keenapusan** *i.* Phil
81 G3 **Keene** U.S.A.
40 F4 **Keen, Mount** *mt* U.K.
8 H1 **Keepit Reservoir** Austr.
42 C3 **Keerbergen** Belgium
57 B6 **Keetmanshoop** Namibia
65 L6 **Keewatin** Can.
65 L5 **Keewatin** U.S.A.
49 J5 **Kefallonia** *i.* Greece
25 E7 **Kefamenanu** Indon.
36 B4 **Keflavik** Iceland
21 C5 **Kegalla** Sri Lanka
15 F2 **Kegen** Kazak.
67 G2 **Keglo, Baie de** *b.* Can.
51 H6 **Kegul'ta** Rus. Fed.
37 T7 **Kehra** Estonia
38 F4 **Keighley** U.K.
37 T7 **Keila** Estonia
58 D4 **Keimoes** S. Africa
36 U5 **Keitele** Fin.
36 T5 **Keitele** *l.* Fin.
8 C4 **Keith** Austr.
40 F3 **Keith** U.K.
64 E1 **Keith Arm** *b.* Can.
67 G5 **Kejimkujik National Park** Can.
74 □2 **Kekaha** U.S.A.
47 K7 **Kékes** *mt* Hungary
22 C4 **Kekri** India
15 F6 **Kelai** *i.* Maldives
26 D2 **Kelan** China
33 B2 **Kelang** Malaysia
32 B4 **Kelantan** *r.* Malaysia
42 E4 **Kelberg** Ger.
43 K6 **Kelheim** Ger.
48 D6 **Kelibia** Tunisia
19 G2 **Kelif** Turkm.
19 F2 **Kelifskiy Uzboy** *marsh* Turkm.
43 G4 **Kelkheim (Taunus)** Ger.
17 G1 **Kelkit** Turkey
16 F1 **Kelkit** *r.* Turkey
64 E2 **Keller Lake** *l.* Can.
80 B4 **Kelleys I.** *i.* U.S.A.
72 C2 **Kellogg** U.S.A.
36 V3 **Kelloselkä** Fin.
41 E4 **Kells** Rep. of Ireland
37 S9 **Kelmė** Lith.
42 E4 **Kelmis** Belgium
55 D4 **Kelo** Chad
64 F5 **Kelowna** Can.
64 D4 **Kelsey Bay** Can.
74 A2 **Kelseyville** U.S.A.
40 F5 **Kelso** U.K.
75 E4 **Kelso** *CA* U.S.A.
72 B2 **Kelso** *WA* U.S.A.
33 B2 **Keluang** Malaysia
65 J4 **Kelvington** Can.
50 E1 **Kem'** Rus. Fed.
50 E1 **Kem'** *r.* Rus. Fed.
17 G2 **Kemah** Turkey
16 G2 **Kemaliye** Turkey
49 M5 **Kemalpaşa** Turkey
64 D4 **Kemano** Can.
16 C3 **Kemer** *Antalya* Turkey
16 B3 **Kemer** *Muğla* Turkey
16 B3 **Kemer Barajı** *resr* Turkey
24 A1 **Kemerovo** Rus. Fed.
36 T4 **Kemi** Fin.
36 U3 **Kemijärvi** Fin.
36 U3 **Kemijärvi** *l.* Fin.
36 T3 **Kemijoki** *r.* Fin.
72 E3 **Kemmerer** U.S.A.
43 K5 **Kemnath** Ger.
40 F3 **Kemnay** U.K.
36 T4 **Kempele** Fin
42 E3 **Kempen** Ger.
42 C3 **Kempen** *reg.* Belgium
77 D5 **Kemp, L.** *l.* U.S.A.
92 D4 **Kemp Land** *reg.* Ant.
92 B2 **Kemp Pen.** *pen.* Ant.
79 E7 **Kemp's Bay** Bahamas
46 E7 **Kempten (Allgäu)** Ger.
66 F4 **Kempt, L.** *l.* Can.
59 H3 **Kempton Park** S. Africa
69 K3 **Kemptville** Can.
33 D4 **Kemujan** *i.* Indon.
22 E4 **Ken** *r.* India
62 C3 **Kenai** U.S.A.
62 C4 **Kenai Mts** *mts* U.S.A.
19 F3 **Kenar-e-Kapeh** Afgh.
38 E3 **Kendal** U.K.
65 M2 **Kendall, Cape** *hd* Can.
68 E5 **Kendallville** U.S.A.
33 C4 **Kendang, Gunung** *volc.* Indon.
25 E7 **Kendari** Indon.
33 D3 **Kendawangan** Indon.
55 D3 **Kendégué** Chad
23 F5 **Kendrāparha** India
72 C2 **Kendrick** U.S.A.
75 G4 **Kendrick Peak** *summit* U.S.A.
8 G1 **Kenebri** Austr.
77 D6 **Kenedy** U.S.A.
54 A4 **Kenema** Sierra Leone
56 B4 **Kenge** Congo(Zaire)
25 B4 **Kengtung** Myanmar
58 D4 **Kenhardt** S. Africa
54 A3 **Kéniéba** Mali
54 B1 **Kénitra** Morocco
26 F2 **Kenli** China
41 B6 **Kenmare** Rep. of Ireland
76 C1 **Kenmare** U.S.A.
41 A6 **Kenmare River** *in.* Rep. of Ireland
42 E5 **Kenn** Ger.
73 G5 **Kenna** U.S.A.
81 J2 **Kennebec** *r.* U.S.A.
81 H3 **Kennebunk** U.S.A.
81 H3 **Kennebunkport** U.S.A.
77 F6 **Kenner** U.S.A.
39 F6 **Kennet** *r.* U.K.
77 F4 **Kennett** U.S.A.
72 C2 **Kennewick** U.S.A.
69 G1 **Kenogami Lake** Can.
69 G1 **Kenogamissi Lake** *l.* Can.
64 B2 **Keno Hill** Can.
65 L5 **Kenora** Can.
68 D4 **Kenosha** U.S.A.
50 F2 **Kenozero, Ozero** *l.* Rus. Fed.
81 G4 **Kent** *CT* U.S.A.
77 B6 **Kent** *TX* U.S.A.
72 B2 **Kent** *WA* U.S.A.
38 E3 **Kent** *r.* U.K.
59 H6 **Kentani** S. Africa
68 D5 **Kentland** U.S.A.
80 B4 **Kenton** U.S.A.
80 A6 **Kentucky** *div.* U.S.A.
71 K4 **Kentucky** *r. KY* U.S.A.
79 B4 **Kentucky Lake** *l.* U.S.A.
67 H4 **Kentville** Can.
77 F6 **Kentwood** *LA* U.S.A.
68 E4 **Kentwood** *MI* U.S.A.
53 H5 **Kenya** *country* Africa
Kenya, Mount *mt see* **Kirinyaga**
68 A3 **Kenyon** U.S.A.
92 B2 **Kenyon Pen.** *pen.* Ant.
74 □2 **Keokea** U.S.A.
68 B5 **Keokuk** U.S.A.
32 C1 **Keo Neua, Col de** *pass* Laos/Vietnam
68 B5 **Keosauqua** U.S.A.
6 F4 **Keppel Bay** *b.* Austr.
32 □ **Keppel Harbour** *chan.* Sing.
16 B2 **Kepsut** Turkey
19 E4 **Kerāh** Iran
21 A4 **Kerala** *div.* India
8 D3 **Kerang** Austr.
54 C4 **Kéran, Parc National de la** *nat. park* Togo
37 T6 **Kerava** Fin.
45 G4 **Kerba** Alg.
51 F6 **Kerch** Ukr.
6 E2 **Kerema** P.N.G.
64 F5 **Keremeos** Can.
51 E7 **Kerempe Burun** *pt* Turkey
56 D2 **Keren** Eritrea
18 E2 **Kergeli** Turkm.
93 J7 **Kerguélen** *i.* Ind. Ocean
93 J7 **Kerguelen Ridge** *sea feature* Ind. Ocean
56 D4 **Kericho** Kenya
9 D1 **Kerikeri** N.Z.
37 V6 **Kerimäki** Fin.
33 B3 **Kerinci, G.** *volc.* Indon.
23 E2 **Keriya Shankou** *pass* China
42 E3 **Kerken** Ger.
19 G2 **Kerki** Turkm.
19 G2 **Kerkichi** Turkm.
49 K4 **Kerkinitis, Limni** *l.* Greece
49 H5 **Kerkyra** Greece
Kerkyra *i. see* **Corfu**
55 F3 **Kerma** Sudan
5 K8 **Kermadec Islands** *is* N.Z.
94 H8 **Kermadec Tr.** *sea feature* Pac. Oc.
18 E4 **Kermān** Iran
74 B3 **Kerman** U.S.A.
19 E4 **Kermān Desert** *des.* Iran
18 B3 **Kermānshāh** Iran
18 D4 **Kermānshāhān** Iran
77 C6 **Kermit** U.S.A.
73 C5 **Kern** *r.* U.S.A.
67 G2 **Kernertut, Cap** *pt* Can.
74 C4 **Kernville** U.S.A.
50 K2 **Keros** Rus. Fed.
49 L6 **Keros** *i.* Greece
54 B4 **Kérouané** Guinea
42 E4 **Kerpen** Ger.
92 B5 **Kerr, C.** *c.* Ant.
65 H4 **Kerrobert** Can.
77 D6 **Kerrville** U.S.A.
41 B5 **Kerry Head** *hd* Rep. of Ireland
32 B4 **Kerteh** Malaysia
37 M9 **Kerteminde** Denmark
16 D4 **Keryneia** Cyprus
50 H3 **Kerzhenets** *r.* Rus. Fed.
66 D3 **Kesagami Lake** *l.* Can.
37 V6 **Kesälahti** Fin.
51 C7 **Keşan** Turkey
16 G1 **Keşap** Turkey
28 G5 **Kesennuma** Japan
19 H2 **Keshem** Afgh.
19 G2 **Keshendeh-ye Bala** Afgh.
22 B5 **Keshod** India
17 M5 **Keshvar** Iran
16 D2 **Keskin** Turkey
50 E2 **Keskozero** Rus. Fed.
42 E3 **Kessel** Neth.
59 H4 **Kestell** S. Africa
36 W4 **Kesten'ga** Rus. Fed.
36 U4 **Kestilä** Fin.
69 H3 **Keswick** Can.
38 D3 **Keswick** U.K.
46 H7 **Keszthely** Hungary
12 K4 **Ket'** *r.* Rus. Fed.
54 C4 **Keta** Ghana
32 □ **Ketam, P.** *i.* Sing.
33 D3 **Ketapang** Indon.
64 C3 **Ketchikan** U.S.A.
42 D2 **Ketelmeer** *l.* Neth.
19 G5 **Keti Bandar** Pak.
39 G5 **Kettering** U.K.
80 A5 **Kettering** U.S.A.
64 F5 **Kettle** *r.* Can.
68 A2 **Kettle** *r.* U.S.A.
80 E4 **Kettle Creek** *r.* U.S.A.
74 C3 **Kettleman City** U.S.A.
72 C1 **Kettle River Ra.** *mts* U.S.A.
80 E3 **Keuka Lake** *l.* U.S.A.
37 T5 **Keuruu** Fin.
68 C5 **Kewanee** U.S.A.
68 C3 **Kewaunee** U.S.A.
68 C2 **Keweenaw Bay** *b.* U.S.A.
68 C2 **Keweenaw Peninsula** U.S.A.
68 C2 **Keweenaw Pt** *pt* U.S.A.
89 E3 **Keweigek** Guyana
68 F3 **Keyano** Can.
69 G3 **Key Harbour** Can.
79 D7 **Key Largo** U.S.A.
41 C3 **Key, Lough** *l.* Rep. of Ireland
39 E5 **Keynsham** U.K.
80 D5 **Keyser** U.S.A.
80 D5 **Keysers Ridge** U.S.A.
75 G5 **Keystone Peak** *summit* U.S.A.
80 D6 **Keysville** U.S.A.
9 A3 **Key, The** N.Z.
17 M4 **Keytū** Iran
79 D7 **Key West** *FL* U.S.A.
68 B4 **Key West** *IA* U.S.A.
81 H3 **Kezar Falls** U.S.A.
57 C6 **Kezi** Zimbabwe
47 K6 **Kežmarok** Slovakia
58 D2 **Kgalagadi** *div.* Botswana
59 G2 **Kgatleng** *div.* Botswana
58 D **Kgomofatshe Pan** *salt pan* Botswana
58 F2 **Kgoro Pan** *salt pan* Botswana
59 G3 **Kgotsong** S. Africa
24 F2 **Khabarovsk** Rus. Fed.
Khabis *see* **Shahdāb**
17 H4 **Khabur** *r.* Syria
17 J7 **Khadd, W. al** *watercourse* S. Arabia
18 B6 **Khafs Daghrah** S. Arabia
22 E4 **Khaga** India
23 G5 **Khagrachari** Bangl.
22 B3 **Khairgarh** Pak.
22 B4 **Khairpur** Pak.
19 G2 **Khaja du Koh** *h.* Afgh.
22 D4 **Khajurāho** India
57 C6 **Khakhea** Botswana
19 G3 **Khakīr** Afgh.
19 G4 **Khak-rēz** Afgh.
19 G4 **Khakriz** *reg.* Afgh.
19 G2 **Khalach** Turkm.
18 C4 **Khalafabād** Iran
18 C3 **Khalajestan** *reg.* Iran
22 D2 **Khalatse** Jammu and Kashmir
22 A3 **Khalifat** *mt* Pak.
19 E3 **Khalilabad** Iran
18 C2 **Khalkhāl** Iran
23 F6 **Khallikot** India
50 D4 **Khalopyenichy** Belarus
24 C1 **Khamar-Daban, Khrebet** *mts* Rus. Fed.
22 C5 **Khambhat** India
22 B5 **Khambhat, Gulf of** *g.* India
22 D5 **Khamgaon** India
32 C1 **Khamkkeut** Laos
18 B5 **Khamma** *well* S. Arabia
21 C2 **Khammam** India
13 N3 **Khamra** Rus. Fed.
18 C3 **Khamseh** *reg.* Iran
19 H2 **Khānābād** Afgh.
17 J5 **Khān al Baghdādī** Iraq
17 K5 **Khān al Maḥāwīl** Iraq
17 K5 **Khān al Mashāhidah** Iraq
17 K5 **Khān al Muṣalla** Iraq
21 A3 **Khanapur** India
18 B2 **Khānaqāh** Iran
17 K4 **Khānaqīn** Iraq
17 K2 **Khanasur Pass** Iran/Turkey
16 F6 **Khān az Zabīb** Jordan
22 C2 **Khanbari Pass** *pass* Jammu and Kashmir
8 G4 **Khancoban** Austr.
22 B2 **Khand Pass** Afgh./Pak.
22 D5 **Khandwa** India
13 P3 **Khandyga** Rus. Fed.
22 B3 **Khanewal** Pak.
32 D2 **Khanh Dương** Vietnam
22 D4 **Khaniadhana** India
18 D4 **Khanīyak** Iran
17 K5 **Khān Jadwal** Iraq
28 C2 **Khanka, Lake** *l.* China/Rus. Fed.
Khanka, Ozero *l. see* **Khanka, Lake**
22 C2 **Khanki Weir** *barrage* Pak.
22 D3 **Khanna** India
22 B3 **Khanpur** Pak.
17 K6 **Khān Ruḥābah** Iraq
16 F4 **Khān Shaykhūn** Syria
15 F2 **Khantau** Kazak.
12 L3 **Khantayskoye, Ozero** *l.* Rus. Fed.
12 H3 **Khanty-Mansiysk** Rus. Fed.
16 E6 **Khān Yūnis** Gaza
32 A3 **Khao Chum Thong** Thai.
22 D5 **Khapa** India
18 C3 **Khar** *r.* Iran
51 H6 **Kharabali** Rus. Fed.
23 F5 **Kharagpur** India
18 E2 **Kharakī** Iran
19 G4 **Kharan** Pak.
18 E5 **Khārān** *r.* Iran
18 D3 **Kharānaq** Iran
22 B2 **Kharbin Pass** Afgh.
22 C6 **Khardi** India
22 D2 **Khardung La** *pass* India
19 F3 **Kharez Ilias** Afgh.
17 L6 **Kharfiyah** Iraq
18 C4 **Khārg Islands** *is* Iran
22 C5 **Khargon** India
22 C4 **Khari** *r. Rajasthan* India
22 C2 **Kharian** Pak.
23 E5 **Khariar** India
18 C6 **Kharit** S. Arabia
51 F5 **Kharkiv** Ukr.
Khar'kov *see* **Kharkiv**
49 L4 **Kharmanli** Bulg.
50 G3 **Kharovsk** Rus. Fed.
23 E5 **Kharsia** India
55 F3 **Khartoum** Sudan
13 E2 **Khasardag, Gora** *mt* Turkm.
51 H7 **Khasav'yurt** Rus. Fed.
19 F4 **Khash** Afgh.
19 F4 **Khāsh** Iran
19 F4 **Khash Desert** *des.* Afgh.
18 C5 **Khashm Bijrān** *h.* S. Arabia
19 F4 **Khash Rūd** *r.* Afgh.
51 G7 **Khashuri** Georgia
23 G4 **Khāsi Hills** *h.* India
49 L4 **Khaskovo** Bulg.
13 M2 **Khatanga** Rus. Fed.
13 M2 **Khatanga, Gulf of** *b.* Rus. Fed.
16 D6 **Khatmia Pass** Egypt
13 T3 **Khatyrka** Rus. Fed.
18 C4 **Khāvar** Iran
22 B5 **Khavda** India
19 H3 **Khawak Pass** Afgh.
18 E5 **Khawr Fakkan** U.A.E.
32 A2 **Khawsa** Myanmar
59 F5 **Khayamnandi** S. Africa
58 C7 **Khayelitsha** S. Africa
17 J3 **Khāzir** *r.* Iraq
32 C1 **Khê Bo** Vietnam
21 A2 **Khed** India
22 C4 **Khedbrahma** India
19 E3 **Khedrī** Iran
22 E3 **Khela** India
45 H4 **Khemis Miliana** Alg.
54 C1 **Khenchela** Alg.
54 B1 **Khenifra** Morocco
18 D4 **Kherāmeh** Iran
22 D4 **Kherli** India
18 C4 **Khersan** *r.* Iran
51 E6 **Kherson** Ukr.
18 C4 **Khesht** Iran
13 L2 **Kheta** *r.* Rus. Fed.
18 D4 **Kheyrābād** Iran
18 D2 **Khezerābād** Iran
22 D4 **Khilchipur** India
16 F4 **Khirbat Isrīyah** Syria
17 J6 **Khirr, Wādī al** *watercourse* S. Arabia
22 D2 **Khitai P.** *pass* China/Jammu and Kashmir
18 B2 **Khīyāv** Iran
37 V6 **Khiytola** Rus. Fed.
51 C5 **Khmel'nyts'kyy** Ukr.
51 C5 **Khmil'nyk** Ukr.
18 B2 **Khodā Āfarīn** Iran
19 G2 **Khodzhambass** Turkm.
14 D2 **Khodzheyli** Uzbek.
58 D2 **Khokhowe Pan** *salt pan* Botswana
22 B4 **Khokhropar** Pak.
50 G1 **Kholmogory** Rus. Fed.
24 G2 **Kholmsk** Rus. Fed.
47 Q3 **Kholm-Zhirkovskiy** Rus. Fed.
17 M3 **Khoman** Iran
58 B1 **Khomas** *div.* Namibia
58 A1 **Khomas Highland** *reg.* Namibia
18 C3 **Khomeyn** Iran
17 M4 **Khondāb** Iran
51 G7 **Khoni** Georgia
19 E3 **Khonj** Iran
13 Q3 **Khonu** Rus. Fed.
51 G5 **Khoper** *r.* Rus. Fed.
24 F2 **Khor** Rus. Fed.
24 F2 **Khor** *r.* Rus. Fed.
22 B4 **Khora** Pak.
23 F5 **Khordha** India
18 C5 **Khor Duweihin** *b.* S. Arabia/U.A.E.
24 C1 **Khorinsk** Rus. Fed.
57 B6 **Khorixas** Namibia
28 C2 **Khorol** Rus. Fed.
51 E5 **Khorol** Ukr.
17 L2 **Khoroslū Dāgh** *h.* Iran
18 C3 **Khorramābād** Iran
17 M3 **Khorram Darreh** Iran
18 C4 **Khorramshahr** Iran
19 H2 **Khorugh** Tajik.
19 E3 **Khosf** Iran
51 H6 **Khosheutovo** Rus. Fed.
18 C4 **Khosravī** Iran
18 C4 **Khosrowabad** Iran
17 K4 **Khosrowvī** Iran
18 D4 **Khowrjān** Iran
18 D3 **Khowrnag, Kūh-e** *mt* Iran
19 H3 **Khowst** Afgh.
24 E1 **Khrebet Dzhagdy** *mts* Rus. Fed.
23 H5 **Khreum** Myanmar
23 G4 **Khri** *r.* India
50 H2 **Khristoforovo** Rus. Fed.
13 Q2 **Khroma** *r.* Rus. Fed.
14 D1 **Khromtau** Kazak.
28 D2 **Khrustalnyy** Rus. Fed.
47 O6 **Khrystynivka** Ukr.
19 G5 **Khude Hills** *mts* Pak.
58 F1 **Khudumelapye** Botswana
18 B5 **Khuff** S. Arabia
19 F5 **Khūh Lab, Ra's** *pt* Iran
58 D3 **Khuis** Botswana
14 E2 **Khūjand** Tajik.
32 C2 **Khu Khan** Thai.
19 G3 **Khulm** *r.* Afgh.
23 G5 **Khulna** Bangl.
17 J1 **Khulo** Georgia
59 G3 **Khuma** S. Africa
22 C2 **Khunjerab Pass** China/Jammu and Kashmir
18 C3 **Khunsar** Iran
23 F5 **Khunti** India
19 E3 **Khūr** Iran
22 D4 **Khurai** India
18 D5 **Khūran** *chan.* Iran
19 G3 **Khurd, Koh-i-** *mt* Afgh.
22 D3 **Khurja** India
19 F3 **Khurmalik** Afgh.
22 C2 **Khushab** Pak.
17 M3 **Khūshāvar** Iran
19 E4 **Khushk Rud** Iran
19 F3 **Khuspas** Afgh.
51 B5 **Khust** Ukr.
59 G3 **Khutsong** S. Africa
19 G5 **Khuzdar** Pak.
19 F3 **Khvāf** Iran
50 J4 **Khvalynsk** Rus. Fed.
18 D3 **Khvor** Iran
18 E3 **Khvord Nārvan** Iran
18 C4 **Khvormūj** Iran
17 L3 **Khvosh Maqām** Iran
18 B2 **Khvoy** Iran
50 E3 **Khvoynaya** Rus. Fed.
32 A2 **Khwae Noi** *r.* Thai.
19 F4 **Khwaja Ali** Afgh.
19 H2 **Khwaja Muhammad Range** *mts* Afgh.
22 B2 **Khyber Pass** Afgh./Pak.
8 H3 **Kiama** Austr.
31 C5 **Kiamba** Phil.
56 C4 **Kiambi** Congo(Zaire)
77 E5 **Kiamichi** *r.* U.S.A.
36 V4 **Kiantajärvi** *l.* Fin.
18 D2 **Kīāseh** Iran
22 D2 **Kibar** India
31 C5 **Kibawe** Phil.
56 D4 **Kibaya** Tanz.
57 D4 **Kibiti** Tanz.
56 C4 **Kibombo** Congo(Zaire)
56 D4 **Kibondo** Tanz.
49 J4 **Kičevo** Macedonia
50 H3 **Kichmengskiy Gorodok** Rus. Fed.
54 C3 **Kidal** Mali
39 E5 **Kidderminster** U.K.
56 D3 **Kidepo Valley National Park** Uganda
54 A3 **Kidira** Senegal
22 D2 **Kidmang** Jammu and Kashmir
9 F3 **Kidnappers, Cape** *c.* N.Z.
39 E4 **Kidsgrove** U.K.
46 E3 **Kiel** Ger.
68 C4 **Kiel** U.S.A.
47 K5 **Kielce** Pol.
38 E2 **Kielder Water** *resr* U.K.
46 E3 **Kieler Bucht** *b.* Ger.
57 C5 **Kienge** Congo(Zaire)
42 F3 **Kierspe** Ger.
51 D5 **Kiev** Ukr.
54 A3 **Kiffa** Maur.
49 K5 **Kifisia** Greece
17 K4 **Kifrī** Iraq
56 D4 **Kigali** Rwanda
17 H2 **Kiğı** Turkey
67 H2 **Kiglapait Mts** *mts* Can.
56 C4 **Kigoma** Tanz.
36 S3 **Kihlanki** Fin.
37 S5 **Kihniö** Fin.
36 T4 **Kiiminki** Fin.
29 D8 **Kii-sanchi** *mts* Japan
29 D8 **Kii-suidō** *chan.* Japan
49 J2 **Kikinda** Yugo.
19 F5 **Kikki** Pak.
50 H3 **Kiknur** Rus. Fed.
28 G4 **Kikonai** Japan
57 C4 **Kikondja** Congo(Zaire)
6 E2 **Kikori** P.N.G.
6 E2 **Kikori** *r.* P.N.G.
56 B4 **Kikwit** Congo(Zaire)
37 P6 **Kilafors** Sweden
21 B4 **Kilakkarai** India
22 D2 **Kilar** India
74 □2 **Kilauea** U.S.A.
74 □2 **Kilauea Crater** *crater* U.S.A.
40 C5 **Kilbrannan Sound** *chan.* U.K.
30 E3 **Kilchu** N. Korea
41 E4 **Kilcoole** Rep. of Ireland
41 D4 **Kilcormac** Rep. of Ireland
41 E4 **Kildare** Rep. of Ireland
36 X2 **Kil'dinstroy** Rus. Fed.
56 B4 **Kilembe** Congo(Zaire)
40 C5 **Kilfinan** U.K.
77 E5 **Kilgore** U.S.A.
38 E2 **Kilham** U.K.
56 D4 **Kilifi** Kenya
56 D4 **Kilimanjaro** *mt* Tanz.
7 F2 **Kilinailau Is** *is* P.N.G.
57 D4 **Kilindoni** Tanz.
37 T7 **Kilingi-Nõmme** Estonia
16 F3 **Kilis** Turkey
51 D6 **Kiliya** Ukr.
41 B5 **Kilkee** Rep. of Ireland
41 F3 **Kilkeel** U.K.
41 D5 **Kilkenny** Rep. of Ireland
39 C7 **Kilkhampton** U.K.
49 K4 **Kilkis** Greece
41 B3 **Killala** Rep. of Ireland
41 B3 **Killala Bay** *b.* Rep. of Ireland
41 C5 **Killaloe** Rep. of Ireland
69 J3 **Killaloe Station** Can.
65 G4 **Killam** Can.
69 G3 **Killarney** Can.
41 B5 **Killarney** Rep. of Ireland
69 G2 **Killarney National Park** Can.
41 B6 **Killarney National Park** Rep. of Ireland
41 B4 **Killary Harbour** *b.* Rep. of Ireland
77 D6 **Killeen** U.S.A.
41 D5 **Killenaule** Rep. of Ireland
41 C4 **Killimor** Rep. of Ireland
40 D4 **Killin** U.K.
41 F3 **Killinchy** U.K.
41 E5 **Killinick** Rep. of Ireland
67 H1 **Killiniq** Can.
67 H1 **Killiniq Island** *i.* Can.
41 B5 **Killorglin** Rep. of Ireland
41 E5 **Killurin** Rep. of Ireland
41 C3 **Killybegs** Rep. of Ireland
41 D2 **Kilmacrenan** Rep. of Ireland
41 B4 **Kilmaine** Rep. of Ireland
41 C5 **Kilmallock** Rep. of Ireland
40 B3 **Kilmaluag** U.K.
40 D5 **Kilmarnock** U.K.
40 C4 **Kilmelford** U.K.
50 J3 **Kil'mez'** Rus. Fed.
50 J3 **Kil'mez'** *r.* Rus. Fed.
41 C6 **Kilmona** Rep. of Ireland
8 E4 **Kilmore** Austr.
41 E5 **Kilmore Quay** Rep. of Ireland
56 D4 **Kilosa** Tanz.
36 R2 **Kilpisjärvi** Fin.
36 X2 **Kilp"yavr** Rus. Fed.
41 E3 **Kilrea** U.K.
41 B5 **Kilrush** Rep. of Ireland
40 D5 **Kilsyth** U.K.
21 A4 **Kiltān** *i.* India
41 C4 **Kiltullagh** Rep. of Ireland
57 C4 **Kilwa** Congo(Zaire)
57 D4 **Kilwa Masoko** Tanz.
40 D5 **Kilwinning** U.K.
57 D4 **Kimambi** Tanz.
56 B4 **Kimba** Congo
76 C3 **Kimball** U.S.A.
6 F2 **Kimbe** P.N.G.
64 F5 **Kimberley** Can.
58 F4 **Kimberley** S. Africa
6 C3 **Kimberley Plateau** *plat.* Austr.
9 E4 **Kimbolton** N.Z.
30 E3 **Kimch'aek** N. Korea
30 E5 **Kimch'ŏn** S. Korea
37 S6 **Kimito** Fin.
30 D6 **Kimje** S. Korea
49 L6 **Kimolos** *i.* Greece
50 F4 **Kimovsk** Rus. Fed.
56 B4 **Kimpese** Congo(Zaire)
29 F5 **Kimpoku-san** *mt* Japan
50 F3 **Kimry** Rus. Fed.
56 B4 **Kimvula** Congo(Zaire)
33 E1 **Kinabalu, Gunung** *mt* Malaysia
31 A5 **Kinabatangan** *r.* Malaysia
49 M6 **Kinaros** *i.* Greece
40 E2 **Kinbrace** U.K.
69 G3 **Kincardine** Can.
40 E4 **Kincardine** U.K.
8 D2 **Kinchega National Park** Austr.
64 D3 **Kincolith** Can.
57 C4 **Kinda** Congo(Zaire)
23 H5 **Kindat** Myanmar
77 E6 **Kinder** U.S.A.
39 F4 **Kinder Scout** *h.* U.K.
65 H4 **Kindersley** Can.
54 A3 **Kindia** Guinea
56 C4 **Kindu** Congo(Zaire)
50 G3 **Kineshma** Rus. Fed.
6 F4 **Kingaroy** Austr.
74 B3 **King City** U.S.A.
92 C1 **King Edward Point** *U.K. Base* Ant.
80 E3 **King Ferry** U.S.A.
81 H2 **Kingfield** U.S.A.
77 D5 **Kingfisher** U.S.A.
92 B1 **King George I.** *i.* Ant.
66 E2 **King George Islands** *is* Can.
64 D4 **King I.** *i.* Can.
50 D3 **Kingisepp** Rus. Fed.
6 E5 **King Island** *i.* Austr.
69 H1 **King Kirkland** Can.
92 D5 **King Leopold and Queen Astrid Coast** *coastal area* Ant.
6 C3 **King Leopold Ranges** *h.* Austr.
75 E4 **Kingman** *AZ* U.S.A.
77 D4 **Kingman** *KS* U.S.A.
81 J2 **Kingman** *ME* U.S.A.
64 D3 **King Mtn** *mt* Can.
92 A3 **King Pen.** *pen.* Ant.
41 D5 **Kings** *r.* Rep. of Ireland
74 C3 **Kings** *r.* U.S.A.
39 D7 **Kingsbridge** U.K.
74 C3 **Kingsburg** U.S.A.
81 J2 **Kingsbury** U.S.A.
74 C3 **Kings Canyon National Park** U.S.A.
8 A3 **Kingscote** Austr.
41 E4 **Kingscourt** Rep. of Ireland
92 B2 **King Sejong** *Korea Base* Ant.
68 C3 **Kingsford** U.S.A.
79 D6 **Kingsland** *GA* U.S.A.
68 E5 **Kingsland** *IN* U.S.A.
39 H5 **King's Lynn** U.K.
7 H2 **Kingsmill Group** *is* Kiribati
39 H6 **Kingsnorth** U.K.
6 C3 **King Sound** *b.* Austr.
72 E3 **Kings Peak** *summit* U.S.A.
80 B6 **Kingsport** U.S.A.
69 J3 **Kingston** Can.
83 J5 **Kingston** Jamaica
9 B6 **Kingston** N.Z.
68 B6 **Kingston** *IL* U.S.A.
81 F4 **Kingston** *NY* U.S.A.
75 E4 **Kingston Peak** *summit* U.S.A.
8 B4 **Kingston South East** Austr.
38 G4 **Kingston upon Hull** U.K.
83 M6 **Kingstown** St Vincent
77 D7 **Kingsville** U.S.A.
39 E6 **Kingswood** U.K.
39 D5 **Kington** U.K.
40 D3 **Kingussie** U.K.
63 J3 **King William I.** *i.* Can.
59 G6 **King William's Town** S. Africa
77 E6 **Kingwood** *TX* U.S.A.
80 D5 **Kingwood** *WV* U.S.A.
65 J4 **Kinistino** Can.
28 G5 **Kinka-san** *i.* Japan
9 B6 **Kinloch** N.Z.
40 E3 **Kinloss** U.K.
69 H3 **Kinmount** Can.
37 N8 **Kinna** Sweden
41 D4 **Kinnegad** Rep. of Ireland
21 C4 **Kinniyai** Sri Lanka
36 T5 **Kinnula** Fin.
65 J3 **Kinoosao** Can.
40 E4 **Kinross** U.K.
41 C6 **Kinsale** Rep. of Ireland
56 B4 **Kinshasa** Congo(Zaire)
76 D4 **Kinsley** U.S.A.
79 E5 **Kinston** U.S.A.
37 R9 **Kintai** Lith.
54 B4 **Kintampo** Ghana
40 F3 **Kintore** U.K.
40 C5 **Kintyre** *pen.* U.K.
40 C5 **Kintyre, Mull of** *hd* U.K.
64 F3 **Kinuso** Can.
55 F4 **Kinyeti** *mt* Sudan
43 H4 **Kinzig** *r.* Ger.
69 H2 **Kiosk** Can.
66 E4 **Kipawa, Lac** *l.* Can.
81 F6 **Kiptopeke** U.S.A.
57 C5 **Kipushi** Congo(Zaire)
7 G3 **Kirakira** Solomon Is
21 C2 **Kirandul** India
50 D4 **Kirawsk** Belarus
43 G2 **Kirchdorf** Ger.
43 G5 **Kirchheim-Bolanden** Ger.
24 C1 **Kirensk** Rus. Fed.
5 L5 **Kiribati** *country* Pac. Oc.
17 H1 **Kırık** Turkey
16 F3 **Kırıkhan** Turkey
16 D2 **Kırıkkale** Turkey
50 F3 **Kirillov** Rus. Fed.
56 D3 **Kirinyaga** *mt* Kenya
50 E3 **Kirishi** Rus. Fed.
29 B9 **Kirishima-yama** *volc.* Japan
5 M4 **Kiritimati** *i.* Kiribati
16 A2 **Kırkağaç** Turkey
18 B2 **Kirk Bulāg D.** *mt* Iran
39 E4 **Kirkby** U.K.
39 F4 **Kirkby in Ashfield** U.K.
38 E3 **Kirkby Lonsdale** U.K.
38 E3 **Kirkby Stephen** U.K.
40 E4 **Kirkcaldy** U.K.
40 C6 **Kirkcolm** U.K.
40 D6 **Kirkcudbright** U.K.
37 N6 **Kirkenær** Norway
36 W2 **Kirkenes** Norway
69 H3 **Kirkfield** Can.
40 D5 **Kirkintilloch** U.K.
37 T6 **Kirkkonummi** Fin.
75 F4 **Kirkland** U.S.A.
75 F4 **Kirkland Junction** U.S.A.
69 G1 **Kirkland Lake** Can.
51 C7 **Kırklareli** Turkey
38 C3 **Kirk Michael** U.K.
38 E3 **Kirkoswald** U.K.
76 E3 **Kirksville** U.S.A.
17 K4 **Kirkūk** Iraq
40 F2 **Kirkwall** U.K.
59 F6 **Kirkwood** S. Africa
74 B2 **Kirkwood** *CA* U.S.A.
76 F4 **Kirkwood** *MO* U.S.A.
16 C1 **Kırmır** *r.* Turkey
42 F5 **Kirn** Ger.
50 E4 **Kirov** *Kaluzh. Obl.* Rus. Fed.
Kirov *see* **Vyatka**
Kirovabad *see* **Gäncä**
50 J3 **Kirovo-Chepetsk** Rus. Fed.
51 E5 **Kirovohrad** Ukr.
17 M2 **Kirovsk** Azer.
50 D3 **Kirovsk** *Leningrad.* Rus. Fed.
36 X3 **Kirovsk** *Murmansk.* Rus. Fed.
19 F2 **Kirovsk** Turkm.
50 J3 **Kirovskaya Oblast'** *div.* Rus. Fed.
28 C2 **Kirovskiy** Rus. Fed.
92 B4 **Kirpatrick, Mt** *mt* Ant.
18 E2 **Kirpili** Turkm.
40 E4 **Kirriemuir** U.K.
50 K3 **Kirs** Rus. Fed.
50 G4 **Kirsanov** Rus. Fed.
16 E2 **Kırşehir** Turkey
19 G5 **Kirthar Range** *mts* Pak.
43 H4 **Kirtorf** Ger.
36 R3 **Kiruna** Sweden
56 C4 **Kirundu** Congo(Zaire)
50 H4 **Kirya** Rus. Fed.
29 F6 **Kiryū** Japan
37 O8 **Kisa** Sweden
56 C3 **Kisangani** Congo(Zaire)

56 B4 Kisantu Congo(Zaire)
33 A2 Kisaran Indon.
24 A1 Kiselevsk Rus. Fed.
23 F4 Kishanganj India
22 B4 Kishangarh Rajasthan India
22 C4 Kishangarh Rajasthan India
22 C2 Kishen Ganga r. India/Pak.
29 B9 Kishika-zaki pt Japan
Kishinev see Chişinău
29 D7 Kishiwada Japan
23 G4 Kishorganj Bangl.
22 C2 Kishtwar Jammu and Kashmir
54 C4 Kisi Nigeria
56 D4 Kisii Kenya
65 K4 Kiskittogisu L. l. Can.
47 J7 Kiskunfélegyháza Hungary
47 J7 Kiskunhalas Hungary
51 G7 Kislovodsk Rus. Fed.
56 E4 Kismaayo Somalia
56 C4 Kisoro Uganda
29 E7 Kiso-sanmyaku mts Japan
54 A4 Kissidougou Guinea
79 D6 Kissimmee U.S.A.
79 D7 Kissimmee, L. l. U.S.A.
65 J3 Kississing L. l. Can.
Kistna r. see Krishna
56 D4 Kisumu Kenya
54 B3 Kita Mali
19 G2 Kitab Uzbek.
29 G6 Kitaibaraki Japan
28 G5 Kitakami Japan
28 G5 Kitakami-gawa r. Japan
29 F6 Kitakata Japan
29 B8 Kita-Kyūshū Japan
56 D3 Kitale Kenya
13 Q5 Kitami Japan
73 G4 Kit Carson U.S.A.
69 G4 Kitchener Can.
36 W5 Kitee Fin.
56 D3 Kitgum Uganda
64 D4 Kitimat Can.
36 U3 Kitinen r. Fin.
56 B4 Kitona Congo(Zaire)
29 B8 Kitsuki Japan
80 D4 Kittanning U.S.A.
81 F4 Kittatinny Mts h. U.S.A.
81 H3 Kittery U.S.A.
36 T3 Kittilä Fin.
79 F4 Kitty Hawk U.S.A.
56 D4 Kitunda Tanz.
64 D3 Kitwanga Can.
57 C5 Kitwe Zambia
46 F7 Kitzbüheler Alpen mts Austria
43 J5 Kitzingen Ger.
43 L3 Kitzscher Ger.
36 U5 Kiuruvesi Fin.
36 T5 Kivijärvi Fin.
37 U7 Kiviõli Estonia
56 C4 Kivu, Lake l. Congo(Zaire)/Rwanda
28 C3 Kiyevka Rus. Fed.
49 N4 Kıyıköy Turkey
12 G4 Kizel Rus. Fed.
50 H2 Kizema Rus. Fed.
16 B3 Kızılca D. mt Turkey
16 D1 Kızılcahamam Turkey
16 G2 Kızıl D. mt Turkey
16 D1 Kızılırmak Turkey
16 D2 Kızılırmak r. Turkey
16 C3 Kızılkaya Turkey
16 D3 Kızılören Turkey
17 H3 Kızıltepe Turkey
51 H7 Kizil"yurt Rus. Fed.
51 H7 Kizlyar Rus. Fed.
18 D2 Kizyl-Atrek Turkm.
19 G2 Kizylayak Turkm.
36 U1 Kjøllefjord Norway
36 P2 Kjøpsvik Norway
46 G5 Kladno Czech Rep.
46 G7 Klagenfurt Austria
75 H4 Klagetoh U.S.A.
37 R9 Klaipėda Lith.
36 □ Klaksvík Faroe Is
72 B3 Klamath r. U.S.A.
72 B3 Klamath Falls U.S.A.
72 B3 Klamath Mts mts U.S.A.
37 N6 Klarälven r. Sweden
46 F6 Klatovy Czech Rep.
58 C5 Klawer S. Africa
64 C3 Klawock U.S.A.
42 E2 Klazienaveen Neth.
64 E4 Kleena Kleene Can.
58 D4 Kleinbegin S. Africa
58 C3 Klein Karas Namibia
58 D6 Klein Roggeveldberg mts S. Africa
58 B4 Kleinsee S. Africa
58 D6 Klein Swartberg mts S. Africa
64 D4 Klemtu Can.
59 G3 Klerksdorp S. Africa
50 E4 Kletnya Rus. Fed.
51 G5 Kletskiy Rus. Fed.
42 E3 Kleve Ger.
58 F6 Klienpoort S. Africa
50 D4 Klimavichy Belarus
51 E4 Klimovo Rus. Fed.
50 F4 Klimovsk Rus. Fed.
50 F3 Klin Rus. Fed.
64 D4 Klinaklini r. Can.
43 H5 Klingenberg am Main Ger.
43 L4 Klingenthal Ger.
43 L1 Klink Ger.
46 F5 Klínovec mt Czech Rep.
37 Q8 Klintehamn Sweden
51 J5 Klintsovka Rus. Fed.
50 E4 Klintsy Rus. Fed.
58 C5 Kliprand S. Africa
48 G2 Ključ Bos.-Herz.
46 H5 Kłodzko Pol.
64 C3 Klondike Gold Rush National History Park U.S.A.
42 E2 Kloosterhaar Neth.
46 H6 Klosterneuburg Austria
43 K2 Klötze (Altmark) Ger.
66 F1 Klotz, Lac l. Can.
64 A2 Kluane Game Sanctuary res. Can.
64 B2 Kluane Lake l. Can.
64 B2 Kluane National Park Can.
46 J5 Kluczbork Pol.
22 B4 Klupro Pak.
50 C4 Klyetsk Belarus
13 S4 Klyuchevskaya Sopka volc. Rus. Fed.
37 O6 Knåda Sweden
38 F3 Knaresborough U.K.
65 L3 Knee Lake l. Can.
43 J5 Knetzgau Ger.
68 B1 Knife Lake l. Can./U.S.A.
64 D4 Knight In. in. Can.
39 D5 Knighton U.K.
68 E6 Knightstown U.S.A.
48 G2 Knin Croatia
46 G7 Knittelfeld Austria
49 K3 Knjaževac Yugo.
41 C4 Knock Rep. of Ireland
41 B6 Knockaboy h. Rep. of Ireland
41 B5 Knockacummer h. Rep. of Ireland
41 C3 Knockalongy h. Rep. of Ireland
41 B5 Knockalough Rep. of Ireland
40 F3 Knock Hill h. U.K.
41 E2 Knocklayd h. U.K.
42 B3 Knokke-Heist Belgium
43 M1 Knorrendorf Ger.
39 F5 Knowle U.K.
92 B2 Knowles, C. c. Ant.
81 J1 Knowles Corner U.S.A.
81 G2 Knowlton Can.
68 D5 Knox U.S.A.
64 C4 Knox, C. c. Can.
92 C6 Knox Coast Ant.
74 A2 Knoxville CA U.S.A.
68 B5 Knoxville IL U.S.A.
79 D4 Knoxville TN U.S.A.
40 C3 Knoydart reg. U.K.
63 N1 Knud Rasmussen Land reg. Greenland
58 E7 Knysna S. Africa
29 B9 Kobayashi Japan
36 V2 Kobbfoss Norway
29 D7 Kōbe Japan
København see Copenhagen
54 B3 Kobenni Maur.
42 F4 Koblenz Ger.
50 J3 Kobra Rus. Fed.
25 F7 Kobroör i. Indon.
50 C4 Kobryn Belarus
51 G7 K'obulet'i Georgia
49 K4 Kočani Macedonia
16 B1 Kocasu r. Turkey
48 F2 Kočevje Slovenia
32 A3 Ko Chan i. Thai.
30 D6 Kōch'ang S. Korea
30 D6 Koch'ang S. Korea
32 B2 Ko Chang i. Thai.
23 G4 Koch Bihār India
43 H5 Kocher r. Ger.
Kochi see Cochin
29 C8 Kōchi Japan
50 H4 Kochkurovo Rus. Fed.
51 H6 Kochubey Rus. Fed.
51 G6 Kochubeyevskoye Rus. Fed.
21 B4 Kodaikanal India
21 D2 Kodala India
62 C4 Kodiak U.S.A.
62 C4 Kodiak Island i. U.S.A.
59 G1 Kodibeleng Botswana
50 F2 Kodino Rus. Fed.
55 F4 Kodok Sudan
51 G7 Kodori r. Georgia
51 D5 Kodyma Ukr.
49 L4 Kodzhaele mt Bulg./Greece
58 D6 Koedoesberg mts S. Africa
58 D4 Koegrabie S. Africa
58 C5 Koekenaap S. Africa
23 E4 Koel r. India
42 D3 Koersel Belgium
57 B6 Koës Namibia
75 F5 Kofa Mts mts U.S.A.
58 F4 Koffiefontein S. Africa
54 B4 Koforidua Ghana
29 F7 Kōfu Japan
66 E2 Kogaluc r. Can.
66 E2 Kogaluc, Baie de b. Can.
67 H2 Kogaluk r. Can.
37 N9 Køge Denmark
19 G5 Kohan Pak.
22 B2 Kohat Pak.
37 T7 Kohila Estonia
23 H4 Kohima India
22 B3 Kohlu Pak.
19 F3 Kohsan Afgh.
37 U7 Kohtla-Järve Estonia
9 E2 Kohukohunui h. N.Z.
30 D6 Kohŭng S. Korea
29 F6 Koide Japan
64 A2 Koidern Can.
21 B3 Koilkuntla India
30 D3 Koindong N. Korea
17 K3 Koi Sanjaq Iraq
30 E6 Kōje do i. S. Korea
28 F4 Ko-jima i. Japan
29 F8 Ko-jima i. Japan
32 A1 Kok r. Thai.
81 J2 Kokadjo U.S.A.
14 E3 Kokand Uzbek.
37 R7 Kökar Fin.
19 H2 Kokcha r. Afgh.
37 R6 Kokemäenjoki r. Fin.
58 C4 Kokerboom Namibia
47 O3 Kokhanava Belarus
50 G3 Kokhma Rus. Fed.
21 C4 Kokkilai Sri Lanka
36 S5 Kokkola Fin.
74 □1 Koko Hd hd U.S.A.
68 D5 Kokomo U.S.A.
58 E2 Kokong Botswana
59 G3 Kokosi S. Africa
15 G2 Kokpekty Kazak.
30 D4 Koksan N. Korea
50 H3 Koksharka Rus. Fed.
14 E1 Kokshetau Kazak.
67 G2 Koksoak r. Can.
59 H5 Kokstad S. Africa
32 B3 Ko Kut i. Thai.
36 X2 Kola Rus. Fed.
Kolab r. see Sābari
19 G5 Kolachi r. Pak.
22 C2 Kolahoi mt India
25 E7 Kolaka Indon.
32 A4 Ko Lanta Thai.
32 A4 Ko Lanta i. Thai.
12 E3 Kola Peninsula pen. Rus. Fed.
21 B3 Kolar Karnataka India
22 E6 Kolar Madhya Pradesh India
22 D4 Kolaras India
21 B3 Kolar Gold Fields India
36 S3 Kolari Fin.
22 C4 Kolayat India
50 F3 Kol'chugino Rus. Fed.
54 A3 Kolda Senegal
37 L9 Kolding Denmark
56 C3 Kole Haute-Zaïre Congo(Zaire)
56 C4 Kole Kasai-Oriental Congo(Zaire)
45 H4 Koléa Alg.
36 R4 Koler Sweden
12 F3 Kolguyev, O. i. Rus. Fed.
22 F5 Kolhan reg. India
21 A2 Kolhapur India
32 A4 Ko Libong i. Thai.
37 S7 Kõljala Estonia
37 S8 Kolkasrags pt Latvia
19 H2 Kolkhozobod Tajik.
Kollam see Quilon
21 B3 Kollegal India
21 C2 Kolleru L. l. India
42 E1 Kollum Neth.
Köln see Cologne
46 G3 Kołobrzeg Pol.
50 H3 Kologriv Rus. Fed.
54 B3 Kolokani Mali
7 F2 Kolombangara i. Solomon Is
50 F4 Kolomna Rus. Fed.
51 C5 Kolomyya Ukr.
54 B3 Kolondiéba Mali
6 C2 Kolonedale Indon.
58 D3 Kolonkwane Botswana
12 K4 Kolpashevo Rus. Fed.
51 F4 Kolpny Rus. Fed.
Kol'skiy Poluostrov pen. see Kola Peninsula
20 B7 Koluli Eritrea
21 A2 Kolvan India
36 M4 Kolvereid Norway
36 T1 Kolvik Norway
19 G5 Kolwa reg. Pak.
57 C5 Kolwezi Congo(Zaire)
13 R3 Kolyma r. Rus. Fed.
13 R3 Kolymskaya Nizmennost' lowland Rus. Fed.
13 R3 Kolymskiy, Khrebet mts Rus. Fed.
50 H4 Kolyshley Rus. Fed.
49 K3 Kom mt Bulg.
28 G3 Komaga-take volc. Japan
58 B4 Komaggas S. Africa
58 B4 Komaggas Mts mts S. Africa
13 S4 Komandorskiye Ostrova is Rus. Fed.
46 J7 Komárno Slovakia
59 J2 Komatipoort S. Africa
29 E6 Komatsu Japan
29 D7 Komatsushima Japan
56 C4 Kombe Congo(Zaire)
54 B3 Kombissiri Burkina
33 B3 Komering r. Indon.
59 G6 Komga S. Africa
51 D6 Kominternivs'ke Ukr.
50 J2 Komi, Respublika div. Rus. Fed.
48 G3 Komiža Croatia
49 H1 Komló Hungary
19 F2 Kommuna Turkm.
56 B4 Komono Congo
29 F6 Komoro Japan
49 L4 Komotini Greece
58 D6 Komsberg mts S. Africa
14 E1 Komsomolets Kazak.
13 L1 Komsomolets, O. i. Rus. Fed.
50 G3 Komsomol'sk Rus. Fed.
19 F2 Komsomol'sk Turkm.
51 E5 Komsomol's'k Ukr.
51 H6 Komsomol'skiy Kalmykiya Rus. Fed.
50 H4 Komsomol'skiy Mordov. Rus. Fed.
24 F1 Komsomol'sk-na-Amure Rus. Fed.
12 H3 Komsomol'skiy Rus. Fed.
17 J1 Kömürlü Turkey
75 F6 Kom Vo U.S.A.
50 F3 Konakovo Rus. Fed.
23 F5 Konar Res. resr India
22 D4 Konch India
23 E6 Kondagaon India
69 J2 Kondiaronk, Lac l. Can.
56 D4 Kondoa Tanz.
50 E2 Kondopoga Rus. Fed.
50 E4 Kondrovo Rus. Fed.
63 P3 Kong Christian IX Land reg. Greenland
60 P2 Kong Christian X Land reg. Greenland
63 O3 Kong Frederik VI Kyst reg. Greenland
60 Q2 Kong Frederik VIII Land reg. Greenland
92 C2 Kong Håkon VII Hav sea Ant.
30 D5 Kongju S. Korea
12 D2 Kong Karl's Land is Svalbard
33 E2 Kongkemul mt Indon.
56 C4 Kongolo Congo(Zaire)
63 Q2 Kong Oscar Fjord in. Greenland
54 B3 Kongoussi Burkina
37 L7 Kongsberg Norway
37 N6 Kongsvinger Norway
32 C2 Kông, T. r. Cambodia
56 D4 Kongwa Tanz.
63 Q2 Kong Wilhelm Land reg. Greenland
32 C2 Kong, Xé r. Laos
43 K4 Königsee Ger.
42 F4 Königswinter Ger.
46 J4 Konin Pol.
24 F1 Konin r. Rus. Fed.
49 G3 Konjic Bos.-Herz.
58 B3 Konkiep watercourse Namibia
54 B3 Konna Mali
43 K3 Könnern Ger.
36 U5 Konnevesi Fin.
50 G2 Konosha Rus. Fed.
29 F6 Kōnosu Japan
51 E5 Konotop Ukr.
32 D2 Kon Plong Vietnam
43 L5 Konstantinovy Lázně Czech Rep.
46 D7 Konstanz Ger.
54 C3 Kontagora Nigeria
36 V5 Kontiolahti Fin.
36 U4 Konttila Fin.
32 C2 Kon Tum Vietnam
32 D2 Kontum, Plateau du plat. Vietnam
16 D3 Konya Turkey
42 E5 Konz Ger.
74 □1 Koolau Range mts U.S.A.
8 E3 Koondrook Austr.
80 D5 Koon Lake l. U.S.A.
8 G3 Koorawatha Austr.
72 C2 Kooskia U.S.A.
64 F5 Kootenay r. Can./U.S.A.
64 F5 Kootenay L. l. Can.
64 F4 Kootenay Nat. Park Can.
58 D5 Kootjieskolk S. Africa
51 H5 Kopanovka Rus. Fed.
22 C6 Kopargaon India
36 E3 Kópasker Iceland
48 E2 Koper Slovenia
18 E2 Kopet Dag, Khrebet mts Turkm.
32 B3 Ko Phangan i. Thai.
32 A3 Ko Phra Thong i. Thai.
32 A4 Ko Phuket i. Thai.
37 P7 Köping Sweden
36 Q5 Köpmanholmen Sweden
59 F2 Kopong Botswana
21 B3 Koppal India
37 M6 Koppang Norway
37 O7 Kopparberg Sweden
59 G3 Koppies S. Africa
58 E3 Koppieskraalpan salt pan S. Africa
48 G1 Koprivnica Croatia
16 C3 Köprü r. Turkey
18 D4 Kor watercourse Iran
50 G4 Korablino Rus. Fed.
19 G5 Korak Pak.
66 E1 Korak, Baie b. Can.
21 B2 Korangal India
19 G5 Korangi Pak.
21 C2 Koraput India
Korat see Nakhon Ratchasima
23 E5 Korba India
48 D6 Korba Tunisia
43 G3 Korbach Ger.
32 B4 Korbu, Gunung mt Malaysia
49 J4 Korçë Albania
48 G3 Korčula Croatia
48 G3 Korčula i. Croatia
48 G3 Korčulanski Kanal chan. Croatia
17 M4 Kord Khvord Iran
18 D2 Kord Küv Iran
19 F5 Kords reg. Iran
18 D4 Kord Sheykh Iran
30 B4 Korea Bay g. China/N. Korea
11 O5 Korea, North country Asia
11 O6 Korea, South country Asia
29 A7 Korea Strait str. Japan/S. Korea
21 A2 Koregaon India
51 F6 Korenovsk Rus. Fed.
51 C5 Korets' Ukr.
16 B1 Körfez Turkey
92 B3 Korff Ice Rise ice feature Ant.
36 N3 Korgen Norway
54 B4 Korhogo Côte d'Ivoire
22 B5 Kori Creek in. India
49 K5 Korinthiakos Kolpos chan. Greece
49 K6 Korinthos Greece
46 H7 Kőris-hegy mt Hungary
49 J4 Koritnik mt Albania
29 G6 Kōriyama Japan
16 C3 Korkuteli Turkey
16 D4 Kormakitis, Cape c. Cyprus
46 H7 Körmend Hungary
54 B4 Koro Côte d'Ivoire
54 B3 Koro Mali
7 H3 Koro i. Fiji
51 F5 Korocha Rus. Fed.
16 D1 Köroğlu Dağları mts Turkey
16 D1 Köroğlu Tepesi mt Turkey
56 D4 Korogwe Tanz.
8 D5 Koroit Austr.
8 D4 Korong Vale Austr.
49 K4 Koronia, L. l. Greece
7 H3 Koro Sea b. Fiji
51 D5 Korosten' Ukr.
51 D5 Korostyshiv Ukr.
55 D3 Koro Toro Chad
37 T5 Korpilahti Fin.
37 R6 Korpo Fin.
24 G2 Korsakov Rus. Fed.
50 J3 Korshik Rus. Fed.
36 R5 Korsnäs Fin.
37 M9 Korsør Denmark
51 D5 Korsun'-Shevchenkivs'kyy Ukr.
47 K3 Korsze Pol.
36 S5 Kortesjärvi Fin.
50 J2 Kortkeros Rus. Fed.
42 B4 Kortrijk Belgium
50 G3 Kortsovo Rus. Fed.
8 E5 Korumburra Austr.
54 D4 Korup, Parc National de nat. park Cameroon
36 U3 Korvala Fin.
22 D4 Korwai India
24 H1 Koryakskaya Sopka volc. Rus. Fed.
13 S3 Koryakskiy Khrebet mts Rus. Fed.
50 H2 Koryazhma Rus. Fed.
30 E6 Koryŏng S. Korea
51 E5 Koryukivka Ukr.
49 M6 Kos i. Greece
32 B3 Ko Samui i. Thai.
30 D4 Kosan N. Korea
46 H4 Kościan Pol.
77 F5 Kosciusko U.S.A.
64 C3 Kosciusko I. i. U.S.A.
8 G4 Kosciusko, Mt mt Austr.
8 G4 Kosciusko National Park Austr.
17 G1 Köse Turkey
16 F1 Köse Dağı mt Turkey
21 B2 Kosgi India
15 G2 Kosh-Agach Rus. Fed.
29 A9 Koshikijima-rettō is Japan
19 F3 Koshkak Iran
19 F3 Koshk-e-Kohneh Afgh.
68 C4 Koshkoning, Lake l. U.S.A.
18 D1 Koshoba Turkm.
19 G1 Koshrabad Uzbek.
22 D4 Kosi India
22 D3 Kosi r. India
59 K3 Kosi Bay b. S. Africa
47 K6 Košice Slovakia
21 B3 Kosigi India
36 R3 Koskullskule Sweden
50 J2 Koslan Rus. Fed.
30 E4 Kosŏng N. Korea
30 E3 Kosŏng-ni N. Korea
49 J3 Kosovo div. Yugo.
49 J3 Kosovska Mitrovica Yugo.
4 H4 Kosrae i. Micronesia
43 K5 Kösseine h. Ger.
54 B4 Kossou, Lac de l. Côte d'Ivoire
49 K3 Kostenets Bulg.
59 G2 Koster S. Africa
55 F3 Kosti Sudan
49 K3 Kostinbrod Bulg.
12 K3 Kostino Rus. Fed.
50 D1 Kostomuksha Rus. Fed.
51 C5 Kostopil' Ukr.
50 G3 Kostroma Rus. Fed.
50 G3 Kostroma r. Rus. Fed.
50 G3 Kostromskaya Oblast' div. Rus. Fed.
46 G4 Kostrzyn Pol.
51 F5 Kostyantynivka Ukr.
46 H3 Koszalin Pol.
46 H7 Kőszeg Hungary
23 E5 Kota Madhya Pradesh India
22 C4 Kota Rajasthan India
32 B4 Kotaagung Indon.
22 C4 Kota Barrage barrage India
33 D3 Kotabaru Indon.
33 E3 Kotabaru Indon.
32 B3 Kota Bharu Malaysia
33 B3 Kotabumi Indon.
22 C4 Kota Dam dam India
33 E1 Kota Kinabalu Malaysia
32 A3 Ko Tao i. Thai.
21 C2 Kotapārh India
32 B5 Kotapinang Indon.
22 C4 Kotari r. India
33 B2 Kota Tinggi Malaysia
50 J3 Kotel'nich Rus. Fed.
51 G6 Kotel'nikovo Rus. Fed.
13 P2 Kotel'nyy, O. i. Rus. Fed.
22 D3 Kotgarh India
43 K3 Köthen (Anhalt) Ger.
22 E4 Kothi India
37 U6 Kotka Fin.
22 C3 Kot Kapura India
50 H2 Kotlas Rus. Fed.
22 C2 Kotli Pak.
62 B3 Kotlik AK U.S.A.
36 D5 Kötlutangi pt Iceland
37 V7 Kotly Rus. Fed.
48 G2 Kotor Varoš Bos.-Herz.
54 B4 Kotouba Côte d'Ivoire
51 H5 Kotovo Rus. Fed.
51 G4 Kotovsk Rus. Fed.
51 D6 Kotovs'k Ukr.
22 C4 Kotra India
22 B4 Kotri Pak.
22 E6 Kotri r. India
22 A5 Kot Sarae Pak.
21 C2 Kottagudem India
21 B4 Kottarakara India
21 B4 Kottayam India
21 B5 Kotte Sri Lanka
21 B3 Kotturu India
18 D2 Koturdepe Turkm.
13 M2 Kotuy r. Rus. Fed.
62 B3 Kotzebue U.S.A.
62 B3 Kotzebue Sound b. U.S.A.
43 L5 Kötzting Ger.
54 A3 Koubia Guinea
54 B3 Koudougou Burkina
58 E6 Koueveldberg mts S. Africa
55 D3 Koufey Niger
49 M7 Koufonisi i. Greece
58 E6 Kougaberg mts S. Africa
16 D4 Kouklia Cyprus
56 B4 Koulamoutou Gabon
54 B3 Koulikoro Mali
7 G4 Koumac New Caledonia
54 A3 Koundâra Guinea
54 B3 Koupéla Burkina
87 H2 Kourou Fr. Guiana
54 B3 Kouroussa Guinea
55 D3 Kousséri Cameroon
54 B3 Koutiala Mali
37 U6 Kouvola Fin.
36 W3 Kovdor Rus. Fed.
36 W3 Kovdozero, Oz. l. Rus. Fed.
51 C5 Kovel' Ukr.
50 G3 Kovernino Rus. Fed.
21 B4 Kovilpatti India
50 G3 Kovrov Rus. Fed.
50 G4 Kovylkino Rus. Fed.
50 F2 Kovzhskoye, Ozero l. Rus. Fed.
9 C5 Kowhitirangi N.Z.
27 □ Kowloon Peninsula H.K. China
27 □ Kowloon Pk h. H.K. China
30 D4 Kowŏn N. Korea
29 B7 Koyama-misaki pt Japan
32 A3 Ko Yao Yai i. Thai.
16 B3 Köyceğiz Turkey
50 J2 Koygorodok Rus. Fed.
21 A2 Koyna Res. resr India
50 H1 Koynas Rus. Fed.
62 C3 Koyukuk r. U.S.A.
16 F1 Koyulhisar Turkey
50 F3 Koza Rus. Fed.
29 A7 Kō-zaki pt Japan
16 E3 Kozan Turkey
49 J4 Kozani Greece
48 G2 Kozara mts Bos.-Herz.
51 D5 Kozelets' Ukr.
50 E4 Kozel'sk Rus. Fed.
Kozhikode see Calicut
16 C1 Kozlu Turkey
50 H3 Koz'modem'yansk Rus. Fed.
49 K4 Kožuf mts Greece/Macedonia
29 F7 Kōzu-shima i. Japan
51 D5 Kozyatyn Ukr.
54 C4 Kpalimé Togo
32 A3 Krabi Thai.
32 A3 Kra Buri Thai.
32 C2 Krâcheh Cambodia
36 P4 Kraddsele Sweden
37 L7 Kragerø Norway
42 D2 Kraggenburg Neth.
49 J2 Kragujevac Yugo.
43 G5 Kraichgau reg. Ger.
32 A3 Kra, Isthmus of isth. Thai.
33 C4 Krakatau i. Indon.
32 C2 Krâkôr Cambodia
47 J5 Kraków Pol.
43 L1 Krakower See l. Ger.
32 B2 Krâlănh Cambodia
89 C1 Kralendijk Neth. Ant.
51 F5 Kramators'k Ukr.
36 P5 Kramfors Sweden
42 C3 Krammer est. Neth.
49 K6 Kranidi Greece
48 F1 Kranj Slovenia
32 □ Kranji Res. resr Sing.
59 J4 Kranskop S. Africa
50 H2 Krasavino Rus. Fed.
12 G2 Krasino Rus. Fed.
28 B3 Kraskino Rus. Fed.
37 U9 Krāslava Latvia
43 L4 Kraslice Czech Rep.
47 P4 Krasnapollye Belarus
50 D4 Krasnaya Gora Rus. Fed.
51 H5 Krasnoarmeysk Rus. Fed.
51 F6 Krasnoarmeyskaya Rus. Fed.
51 F5 Krasnoarmiys'k Ukr.
50 H2 Krasnoborsk Rus. Fed.
51 F6 Krasnodar Rus. Fed.
51 F6 Krasnodarskiy Kray div. Rus. Fed.
51 F5 Krasnodon Ukr.
50 D3 Krasnogorodskoye Rus. Fed.
51 G6 Krasnogvardeyskoye Rus. Fed.
51 E5 Krasnohrad Ukr.
51 E6 Krasnohvardiys'ke Ukr.
47 R2 Krasnomayskiy Rus. Fed.
51 E6 Krasnoperekops'k Ukr.
28 D2 Krasnorechenskiy Rus. Fed.
37 V6 Krasnosel'skoye Rus. Fed.
50 G4 Krasnoslobodsk Rus. Fed.
18 D2 Krasnovodskiy Zaliv b. Turkm.
18 D1 Krasnovodskoye Plato plat. Turkm.
24 B1 Krasnoyarsk Rus. Fed.
47 P3 Krasnyy Rus. Fed.
50 H3 Krasnyye Baki Rus. Fed.
51 H6 Krasnyye Barrikady Rus. Fed.
50 F3 Krasnyy Kholm Rus. Fed.
51 H5 Krasnyy Kut Rus. Fed.
50 D3 Krasnyy Luch Rus. Fed.
51 F5 Krasnyy Lyman Ukr.
51 J6 Krasnyy Yar Astrak. Rus. Fed.
51 H5 Krasnyy Yar Volgograd. Rus. Fed.
51 C5 Krasyliv Ukr.
51 H7 Kraynovka Rus. Fed.
42 E3 Krefeld Ger.
51 E5 Kremenchuk Ukr.
51 E5 Kremenchuts'ka Vodoskhovshche resr Ukr.
51 G5 Kremenskaya Rus. Fed.
46 G6 Křemešník h. Czech Rep.
72 F3 Kremmling U.S.A.
46 G6 Krems an der Donau Austria
13 U3 Kresta, Zaliv b. Rus. Fed.
50 E3 Kresttsy Rus. Fed.
37 R9 Kretinga Lith.
42 E4 Kreuzau Ger.
43 F4 Kreuztal Ger.
47 N3 Kreva Belarus
54 C4 Kribi Cameroon
59 H3 Kriel S. Africa
49 J5 Krikellos Greece
28 H2 Kril'on, Mys c. Rus. Fed.
15 F5 Krishna r. India
21 B3 Krishnagiri India
21 C3 Krishna, Mouths of the river mouth India
23 G5 Krishnanagar India
21 B3 Krishnaraja Sagara l. India
37 K7 Kristiansand Norway
37 O8 Kristianstad Sweden
36 K5 Kristiansund Norway
37 O7 Kristinehamn Sweden
37 R5 Kristinestad Fin.
Kriti i. see Crete
Krivoy Rog see Kryvyy Rih
48 G1 Križevci Croatia
48 F2 Krk i. Croatia
36 O5 Krokom Sweden
36 L5 Krokstadøra Norway
36 O3 Krokstranda Norway
51 E5 Krolevets' Ukr.
43 K4 Kronach Ger.
32 B3 Krŏng Kaôh Kŏng Cambodia
36 S5 Kronoby Fin.
63 P3 Kronprins Frederik Bjerge mt Greenland
32 A2 Kronwa Myanmar
59 G3 Kroonstad S. Africa
51 G6 Kropotkin Rus. Fed.
43 L3 Kropstädt Ger.
47 K6 Krosno Pol.
46 H5 Krotoszyn Pol.
59 J2 Kruger National Park S. Africa
47 O3 Kruhlaye Belarus
33 B4 Krui Indon.
58 F7 Kruisfontein S. Africa
49 H4 Krujë Albania
49 L4 Krumovgrad Bulg.
Krungkao see Ayutthaya
Krung Thep see Bangkok
47 O3 Krupki Belarus
49 J3 Kruševac Yugo.
43 L4 Krušné Hory mts Czech Rep.
64 B3 Kruzof I. i. U.S.A.
50 D4 Krychaw Belarus
51 F6 Krymsk Rus. Fed.
49 L6 Krytiko Pelagos sea Greece
51 E6 Kryvyy Rih Ukr.
54 B2 Ksabi Alg.
54 C1 Ksar el Boukhari Alg.
54 B1 Ksar el Kebir Morocco
51 F5 Kshenskiy Rus. Fed.
48 D7 Ksour Essaf Tunisia
50 H3 Kstovo Rus. Fed.
32 A4 Kuah Malaysia
32 B4 Kuala Kangsar Malaysia
32 B4 Kuala Kerai Malaysia
32 B5 Kuala Kubu Baharu Malaysia
33 B2 Kuala Lipis Malaysia
33 B2 Kuala Lumpur Malaysia
32 B4 Kuala Nerang Malaysia
32 B5 Kuala Pilah Malaysia
32 B5 Kuala Rompin Malaysia
33 D3 Kualasampit Indon.
32 A4 Kualasimpang Indon.
33 B1 Kuala Terengganu Malaysia
31 A5 Kuamut Malaysia
30 C3 Kuandian China
27 F6 Kuanshan Taiwan
33 B2 Kuantan Malaysia
51 G6 Kuban' r. Rus. Fed.
17 J5 Kubaysah Iraq
50 F3 Kubenskoye, Ozero l. Rus. Fed.
50 H4 Kubnya r. Rus. Fed.
49 M3 Kubrat Bulg.
22 C4 Kuchaman India
22 C4 Kuchera India
33 D2 Kuching Malaysia
29 A10 Kuchino-shima i. Japan
Kucing see Kuching
49 H4 Kuçovë Albania
21 A3 Kudal India
33 E1 Kudat Malaysia
21 B3 Kudligi India
21 A3 Kudremukh mt India
33 D4 Kudus Indon.
46 F7 Kufstein Austria
50 H3 Kugesi Rus. Fed.
62 E3 Kugmallit Bay b. Can.
19 F5 Kūhak Iran
23 E3 Kuhanbokano mt China
43 L1 Kuhbier Ger.
18 E4 Kūhbonān Iran
18 B3 Kūhdasht Iran
17 L2 Kūhhaye Sabalan mts Iran
17 M3 Kūhīn Iran
36 V4 Kuhmo Fin.
37 T6 Kuhmoinen Fin.
18 D3 Kūhpāyeh Iran
18 E5 Kūh, Ra's-al pt Iran
43 L3 Kühren Ger.
58 B2 Kuis Namibia
58 A1 Kuiseb Pass Namibia
57 B5 Kuito Angola
64 C3 Kuiu Island i. U.S.A.
36 T4 Kuivaniemi Fin.
18 B5 Kū', J. al h. S. Arabia
23 F5 Kujang India
30 C4 Kujang-dong N. Korea
28 G4 Kuji Japan
29 B8 Kujū-san volc. Japan
69 F1 Kukatush Can.
49 J3 Kukës Albania
50 J3 Kukmor Rus. Fed.
32 B5 Kukup Malaysia
18 D5 Kūl r. Iran
16 B2 Kula Turkey
23 G3 Kula Kangri mt Bhutan
14 D2 Kulandy Kazak.
19 F5 Kulaneh reg. Pak.
19 G4 Kulao r. Pak.
13 P2 Kular Rus. Fed.
31 B5 Kulassein i. Phil.
23 H4 Kulaura Bangl.
37 R8 Kuldīga Latvia
58 D1 Kule Botswana
50 G4 Kulebaki Rus. Fed.
32 C2 Kulen Cambodia
50 H2 Kulikovo Rus. Fed.
32 B4 Kulim Malaysia
19 J2 Kuli Sarez l. Tajik.
22 D3 Kullu India
43 K4 Kulmbach Ger.
19 H2 Kŭlob Tajik.
17 H2 Kulp Turkey
22 D4 Kulpahar India
81 F4 Kulpsville U.S.A.
14 D2 Kul'sary Kazak.
43 H5 Külsheim Ger.
16 D2 Kulu Turkey
16 C3 Kulübe Tepe mt Turkey
12 J4 Kulunda Rus. Fed.
12 J4 Kulundinskoye, Ozero salt l. Rus. Fed.
18 D4 Kūlvand Iran
8 D3 Kulwin Austr.
30 D5 Kŭm r. S. Korea
51 H6 Kuma r. Rus. Fed.
29 F6 Kumagaya Japan
28 F3 Kumaishi Japan
33 D3 Kumai, Teluk b. Indon.
29 B8 Kumamoto Japan
29 E8 Kumano Japan
49 J3 Kumanovo Macedonia
54 B4 Kumasi Ghana
Kumayri see Gyumri
54 C4 Kumba Cameroon
21 B4 Kumbakonam India
16 C2 Kümbet Turkey
58 E1 Kumchuru Botswana
18 D3 Kumel well Iran
12 G4 Kumertau Rus. Fed.
30 E4 Kumgang-san mt N. Korea
30 E6 Kŭmho r. S. Korea
30 D4 Kumhwa S. Korea
30 E5 Kumi S. Korea
37 O7 Kumla Sweden
43 M2 Kummersdorf-Alexanderdorf Ger.
54 D3 Kumo Nigeria
30 D6 Kŭmō-do i. S. Korea
32 B1 Kumphawapi Thai.
58 C4 Kums Namibia
21 A3 Kumta India
51 H7 Kumukh Rus. Fed.
19 H3 Kunar r. Afgh.
24 G2 Kunashir, Ostrov i. Rus. Fed.
23 E2 Kunchuk Tso salt l. China
37 U7 Kunda Estonia
23 E4 Kunda India
21 A3 Kundāpura India
22 B2 Kundar r. Afgh./Pak.
19 H2 Kunduz Afgh.
19 H2 Kunduz r. Afgh.
37 M8 Kungälv Sweden
15 F2 Kungei Alatau mts Kazak./Kyrg.
64 C4 Kunghit I. i. Can.
37 N8 Kungsbacka Sweden
37 M7 Kungshamn Sweden
56 B3 Kungu Congo(Zaire)
22 D6 Kuni r. India
29 B8 Kunimi-dake mt Japan
23 F5 Kunjabar India
23 G4 Kunlui r. India/Nepal
15 F3 Kunlun Shan mts China
23 H2 Kunlun Shankou pass China
27 B5 Kunming China
22 D4 Kuno r. India
30 D6 Kunsan S. Korea
26 F4 Kunshan China
6 C3 Kununurra Austr.
22 D4 Kunwari r. India
50 D3 Kun'ya Rus. Fed.
30 A5 Kunyu Shan h. China
43 H5 Künzelsau Ger.
43 K3 Künzels-Berg h. Ger.
27 F4 Kuocang Shan mts China
37 T6 Kuohijärvi l. Fin.
36 V3 Kuolayarvi Rus. Fed.
36 U5 Kuopio Fin.
36 S5 Kuortane Fin.
48 2 Kupa r. Croatia/Slovenia
25 E8 Kupang Indon.
37 T9 Kupiškis Lith.
64 C3 Kupreanof Island i. U.S.A.
51 F5 Kup"yans'k Ukr.
15 G2 Kuqa China
17 M2 Kür r. Azer.
17 K1 Kura r. Azer./Georgia
51 G7 Kura r. Georgia/Rus. Fed.
51 H7 Kurakh Rus. Fed.
29 C7 Kurashiki Japan
23 E5 Kurasia India
29 C7 Kurayoshi Japan
16 B1 Kurban Dağı mt Turkey
51 E5 Kurchatov Rus. Fed.
17 M1 Kürdämir Azer.
17 M2 Kür Dili pt Azer.
21 A2 Kurduvadi India
49 L4 Kŭrdzhali Bulg.
29 C7 Kure Japan
16 D1 Küre Turkey
5 K2 Kure Atoll atoll HI U.S.A.
37 S7 Kuressaare Estonia
12 H4 Kurgan Rus. Fed.
51 G6 Kurganinsk Rus. Fed.
19 H2 Kuri Afgh.
22 B4 Kuri India
Kuria Muria Islands is see Ḥalāniyāt, Juzur al
36 S5 Kurikka Fin.
28 G5 Kurikoma-yama volc. Japan
24 G2 Kuril Islands is Rus. Fed.
24 G2 Kuril'sk Japan
Kuril'skiye Ostrova is see Kuril Islands
94 F2 Kuril Trench sea feature Pac. Oc.
55 F3 Kurmuk Sudan
21 B3 Kurnool India
16 E6 Kurnub Israel
29 E6 Kurobe Japan
28 G4 Kuroishi Japan
29 G6 Kuroiso Japan
43 J4 Kurort Schmalkalden Ger.
29 A9 Kuro-shima i. Japan
50 F4 Kurovskoye Rus. Fed.
9 C6 Kurow N.Z.
22 B2 Kurram r. Afgh./Pak.
8 H2 Kurri Kurri Austr.
Kuršių Marios lag. see Courland Lagoon
51 F5 Kursk Rus. Fed.
51 H6 Kurskaya Rus. Fed.
51 F5 Kurskaya Oblast' div. Rus. Fed.
Kurskiy Zaliv lag. see Courland Lagoon
16 D1 Kurşunlu Turkey
17 H3 Kurtalan Turkey
23 G4 Kuru r. Bhutan
16 G2 Kuruçay Turkey
22 D3 Kurukshetra India
24 A2 Kuruktag mts China
58 E3 Kuruman S. Africa
58 D3 Kuruman watercourse S. Africa

29 B8 Kurume Japan
24 D1 Kurumkan Rus. Fed.
21 C5 Kurunegala Sri Lanka
55 F2 Kurūsh, Jebel reg. Sudan
49 M6 Kuşadası Turkey
49 M6 Kuşadası Körfezi b. Turkey
64 B2 Kusawa Lake l. Can.
42 F5 Kusel Ger.
16 A1 Kuş Gölü l. Turkey
51 F6 Kushchevskaya Rus. Fed.
29 B9 Kushikino Japan
29 D8 Kushimoto Japan
28 J3 Kushiro Japan
28 J3 Kushiro-Shitsugen National Park Japan
19 F3 Kushka r. Turkm.
17 M5 Kūshkak Iran
14 E1 Kushmurun Kazak.
21 B3 Kushtagi India
23 G5 Kushtia Bangl.
26 C2 Kushui r. China
62 C3 Kuskokwim r. U.S.A.
62 B4 Kuskokwim Bay b. U.S.A.
62 C3 Kuskokwim Mts U.S.A.
30 C4 Kusŏng N. Korea
28 J3 Kussharo-ko l. Japan
14 E1 Kustanay Kazak.
43 F1 Küstenkanal canal Ger.
18 C4 Kut Iran
17 M6 Kūt Abdollāh Iran
32 A5 Kutacane Indon.
16 B2 Kütahya Turkey
51 G7 K'ut'aisi Georgia
Kut-al-Imara see Al Kūt
51 H6 Kutan Rus. Fed.
28 G3 Kutchan Japan
17 M5 Kūt-e Gapu Iran
48 G2 Kutina Croatia
48 G2 Kutjevo Croatia
47 J4 Kutno Pol.
56 B4 Kutu Congo(Zaire)
23 G5 Kutubdia I. i. Bangl.
62 G2 Kuujjua r. Can.
67 G2 Kuujjuaq Can.
Kuujjuarapik see Poste-de-la-Baleine
18 D1 Kuuli-Mayak Turkm.
36 V4 Kuusamo Fin.
37 U6 Kuusankoski Fin.
57 B5 Kuvango Angola
50 E3 Kuvshinovo Rus. Fed.
17 L7 Kuwait Kuwait
10 F7 Kuwait country Asia
17 L7 Kuwait Jun b. Kuwait
29 E7 Kuwana Japan
50 G1 Kuya Rus. Fed.
12 J4 Kuybyshev Novosibirsk Rus. Fed.
Kuybyshev see Samara
50 J4 Kuybyshevskoye Vdkhr. resr Rus. Fed.
26 D2 Kuye r. China
15 G2 Kuytun China
49 N6 Kuyucak Turkey
37 V6 Kuznechnoye Rus. Fed.
50 H4 Kuznetsk Rus. Fed.
28 F1 Kuznetsovo Rus. Fed.
51 C5 Kuznetsovs'k Ukr.
36 R1 Kvænangen chan. Norway
36 Q2 Kvaløya i. Norway
36 S1 Kvalsund Norway
Kvareli see Qvareli
48 F2 Kvarnerić chan. Croatia
62 C4 Kvichak Bay b. U.S.A.
64 D3 Kwadacha Wilderness Prov. Park res. Can.
27 □ Kwai Tau Leng h. H.K. China
95 G5 Kwajalein i. Pac. Oc.
32 A5 Kwala Indon.
59 J4 KwaMashu S. Africa
59 H2 KwaMhlanga S. Africa
30 D5 Kwangch'ŏn S. Korea
30 D6 Kwangju S. Korea
56 B4 Kwango r. Congo(Zaire)
56 D4 Kwangwazi Tanz.
30 D6 Kwangyang S. Korea
59 F6 Kwanobuhle S. Africa
59 F6 KwaNojoli S. Africa
59 G6 Kwanonqubela S. Africa
58 F5 Kwanonzame S. Africa
59 G6 Kwatinidubu S. Africa
59 H3 KwaZamokhule S. Africa
58 F6 Kwazamukucinga S. Africa
58 F5 Kwazamuxolo S. Africa
59 H3 KwaZanele S. Africa
59 J4 Kwazulu-Natal div. S. Africa
57 C5 Kwekwe Zimbabwe
58 F1 Kweneng div. Botswana
56 B4 Kwenge r. Congo(Zaire)
59 G5 Kwezi-Naledi S. Africa
47 J4 Kwidzyn Pol.
62 B4 Kwigillingok AK U.S.A.
6 E2 Kwikila P.N.G.
56 B4 Kwilu r. Angola/Congo(Zaire)
25 F7 Kwoka mt Indon.
27 □ Kwun Tong H.K. China
55 D4 Kyabé Chad
8 E4 Kyabram Austr.
32 A1 Kya-in Seikkyi Myanmar
24 C1 Kyakhta Rus. Fed.
8 D3 Kyalite Austr.
6 D5 Kyancutta Austr.
50 F1 Kyanda Rus. Fed.
32 A1 Kyaukhnyat Myanmar
23 H6 Kyaukpyu Myanmar
23 H5 Kyauktaw Myanmar
37 S9 Kybartai Lith.
8 C4 Kybybolite Austr.
22 D2 Kyelang India
26 A2 Kyikug China
Kyiv see Kiev
Kyklades is see Cyclades
65 H4 Kyle Can.
40 C3 Kyle of Lochalsh U.K.
42 E5 Kyll r. Ger.
49 K6 Kyllini mt Greece
8 E4 Kyneton Austr.
56 D3 Kyoga, Lake l. Uganda
29 D7 Kyōga-misaki pt Japan
32 A1 Kyondo Myanmar
30 E6 Kyŏngju S. Korea
29 D7 Kyōto Japan
49 J6 Kyparissia Greece
49 J6 Kyparissiakos Kolpos b. Greece
12 H4 Kypshak, Ozero salt l. Kazak.
49 L5 Kyra Panagia i. Greece
10 J5 Kyrgyzstan country Asia
43 L2 Kyritz Ger.
36 L5 Kyrksæterøra Norway
12 G3 Kyrta Rus. Fed.
50 H1 Kyssa Rus. Fed.
13 P3 Kytalyktakh Rus. Fed.
49 K6 Kythira i. Greece
49 L6 Kythnos i. Greece
32 A2 Kyungyaung Myanmar
29 B8 Kyūshū i. Japan
94 D5 Kyushu - Palau Ridge sea feature Pac. Oc.
49 K3 Kyustendil Bulg.
8 F3 Kywong Austr.
51 D5 Kyyivs'ke Vdskh. resr Ukr.
36 T5 Kyyjärvi Fin.
24 B1 Kyzyl Rus. Fed.
14 E2 Kyzylkum Desert Uzbek.
15 H1 Kyzyl-Mazhalyk Rus. Fed.
14 E2 Kzyl-Orda Kazak.
14 F1 Kzyltu Kazak.

L

42 F4 Laacher See l. Ger.
37 T7 Laagri Estonia
36 U2 Laanila Fin.
91 B3 La Araucania div. Chile
56 E3 Laascaanood Somalia
56 E2 Laasgoray Somalia
89 E2 La Asunción Venez.
54 A2 Laâyoune Western Sahara
51 G6 Laba r. Rus. Fed.
77 C6 La Babia Mex.
88 D3 La Banda Arg.
72 E3 La Barge U.S.A.
7 H3 Labasa Fiji
44 C3 La Baule-Escoublac France
54 A3 Labé Guinea
66 F4 Labelle Can.
68 B5 La Belle U.S.A.
64 B2 Laberge, Lake l. Can.
31 A5 Labian, Tg pt Malaysia
64 E2 La Biche r. Can.
51 G6 Labinsk Rus. Fed.
32 B5 Labis Malaysia
31 B3 Labo Phil.
16 F4 Laboué Lebanon
44 D4 Labouheyre France
91 D2 Laboulaye Arg.
67 H3 Labrador Can.
67 G3 Labrador City Can.
63 N3 Labrador Sea Can./Greenland
86 F5 Lábrea Brazil
33 E1 Labuan Malaysia
33 C4 Labuhan Indon.
33 B2 Labuhanbilik Indon.
32 A5 Labuhanruku Indon.
31 A5 Labuk r. Malaysia
33 E1 Labuk, Telukan b. Malaysia
25 E7 Labuna Indon.
12 H3 Labytnangi Rus. Fed.
49 H4 Laç Albania
91 D1 La Calera Arg.
91 B2 La Calera Chile
84 E3 Lacandón, Parque Nacional nat. park Guatemala
44 F2 La Capelle France
91 B4 Lacar, L. l. Arg.
91 D2 La Carlota Arg.
45 E3 La Carolina Spain
49 M2 Lăcăuţi, Vârful mt Romania
81 J1 Lac-Baker Can.
14 F5 Laccadive Islands India
65 K4 Lac du Bonnet Can.
82 G5 La Ceiba Honduras
89 C2 La Ceiba Venez.
8 B4 Lacepede B. b. Austr.
81 E4 Laceyville U.S.A.
81 H1 Lac Frontière Can.
50 F2 Lacha, Ozero l. Rus. Fed.
43 J2 Lachendorf Ger.
69 F3 Lachine U.S.A.
8 E3 Lachlan r. Austr.
83 J7 La Chorrera Panama
66 F4 Lachute Can.
17 L2 Laçın Azer.
44 G5 La Ciotat France
84 A2 La Ciudad Mex.
80 D3 Lackawanna U.S.A.
65 G4 Lac La Biche Can.
64 E4 Lac La Hache Can.
64 F2 Lac la Martre Can.
65 H3 Lac La Ronge Provincial Park res. Can.
67 F4 Lac Mégantic Can.
81 G2 Lacolle Can.
73 E6 La Colorada Mex.
64 G4 Lacombe Can.
84 D3 La Concordia Mex.
48 C5 Laconi Sardinia Italy
81 H3 Laconia U.S.A.
69 J1 La Corne Can.
68 B4 La Crescent U.S.A.
68 B4 La Crosse U.S.A.
89 A4 La Cruz Col.
84 A2 La Cruz Sinaloa Mex.
84 C1 La Cruz Tamaulipas Mex.
76 E4 La Cygne U.S.A.
22 D2 Ladakh Range mts India
32 A4 Ladang i. Thai.
16 E1 Lâdik Turkey
58 D6 Ladismith S. Africa
19 F4 Lādīz Iran
22 C4 Ladnun India
89 B3 La Dorada Col.
Ladozhskoye Ozero l. see Lagoda, Lake
23 H4 Ladu mt India
50 E2 Ladva Rus. Fed.
50 E2 Ladva-Vetka Rus. Fed.
63 K2 Lady Ann Strait chan. Can.
40 E4 Ladybank U.K.
59 G4 Ladybrand S. Africa
69 G2 Lady Evelyn Lake l. Can.
59 G5 Lady Frere S. Africa
59 G5 Lady Grey S. Africa
64 E5 Ladysmith Can.
59 H4 Ladysmith S. Africa
68 B3 Ladysmith U.S.A.
6 E2 Lae P.N.G.
32 B2 Laem Ngop Thai.
32 B4 Laem Pho pt Thai.
37 K6 Lærdalsøyri Norway
86 F8 La Esmeralda Bol.
89 D4 La Esmeralda Venez.
37 M8 Læsø i. Denmark
30 D2 Lafa China
91 D1 La Falda Arg.
72 F4 Lafayette CO U.S.A.
68 D5 Lafayette IN U.S.A.
77 E6 Lafayette LA U.S.A.
79 C5 La Fayette U.S.A.
42 B5 La Fère France
42 B5 La Ferté-Milon France
42 B6 La Ferté-sous-Jouarre France
18 C5 Laffān, Ra's pt Qatar
54 C4 Lafia Nigeria
44 D3 La Flèche France
80 A6 La Follette U.S.A.
69 H2 Laforce Can.
69 G2 Laforest Can.
67 F3 Laforge Can.
89 B2 La Fría Venez.
18 D5 Laft Iran
48 C6 La Galite i. Tunisia
51 H6 Lagan' Rus. Fed.
41 E3 Lagan r. U.K.
87 L6 Lagarto Brazil
43 G3 Lage Ger.
37 L7 Lågen r. Norway
40 C5 Lagg U.K.
40 D3 Laggan U.K.
40 D4 Laggan, Loch l. U.K.
54 C1 Laghouat Alg.
23 F2 Lagkor Co salt l. China
89 B2 La Gloria Col.
90 D2 Lagoa Santa Brazil
50 D2 Lagoda, Lake l. Rus. Fed.
17 L1 Lagodekhi Georgia
32 D5 Lagong i. Indon.
31 B3 Lagonoy Gulf b. Phil.
88 B7 Lago Posadas Arg.
91 B4 Lago Ranco Chile
54 C4 Lagos Nigeria
45 B4 Lagos Port.
84 B2 Lagos de Moreno Mex.
72 C2 La Grande U.S.A.
66 E3 La Grande r. Can.
66 E3 La Grande 2, Réservoir de resr Can.
66 E3 La Grande 3, Réservoir de resr Can.
66 F3 La Grande 4, Réservoir de resr Can.
6 C3 Lagrange Austr.
79 C5 La Grange GA U.S.A.
81 J2 La Grange ME U.S.A.
68 D5 La Grange MI U.S.A.
68 B5 La Grange MO U.S.A.
77 D6 La Grange TX U.S.A.
68 E5 Lagrange U.S.A.
89 E3 La Gran Sabana plat. Venez.
88 G3 Laguna Brazil
74 D5 Laguna Beach U.S.A.
91 B3 Laguna de Laja, Parque Nacional nat. park Chile
84 E4 Laguna Lachua, Parque Nacional nat. park Guatemala
74 D5 Laguna Mts mts U.S.A.
86 C5 Lagunas Peru
88 A7 Laguna San Rafael, Parque Nacional nat. park Chile
84 C3 Lagunas de Chacahua, Parque Nacional nat. park Mex.
89 C2 Lagunillas Venez.
33 E1 Lahad Datu Malaysia
31 A5 Lahad Datu, Telukan b. Malaysia
74 □2 Lahaina U.S.A.
17 M3 Lahargin Iran
33 B3 Lahat Indon.
32 A5 Lahewa Indon.
20 B7 Lahij Yemen
18 C2 Lāhījān Iran
74 □1 Lahilahi Pt pt U.S.A.
43 F4 Lahn r. Ger.
42 F4 Lahnstein Ger.
37 N8 Laholm Sweden
74 C2 Lahontan Res. resr U.S.A.
22 C3 Lahore Pak.
89 E3 La Horqueta Venez.
22 B3 Lahri Pak.
37 T6 Lahti Fin.
84 A3 La Huerta Mex.
55 D4 Laï Chad
26 F3 Lai'an China
27 C6 Laibin China
18 E4 Laidāru Iran
74 □1 Laie U.S.A.
74 □1 Laie Pt pt U.S.A.
27 C4 Laifeng China
44 E2 L'Aigle France
36 S5 Laihia Fin.
23 H4 Laimakuri India
58 D6 Laingsburg S. Africa
36 S3 Lainioälven r. Sweden
40 D2 Lairg U.K.
31 C5 Lais Phil.
37 R6 Laitila Fin.
48 D1 Laives Italy
26 E2 Laiwu China
26 F2 Laiyang China
26 E2 Laiyuan China
26 F2 Laizhou Wan b. China
91 B3 Laja r. Chile
91 B3 Laja, Lago de l. Chile
6 D3 Lajamanu Austr.
87 L5 Lajes Rio Grande do Norte Brazil
88 F3 Lajes Santa Catarina Brazil
73 G4 La Junta U.S.A.
72 E2 Lake U.S.A.
7 J3 Lakeba i. Fiji
16 D6 Lake Bardawīl Reserve Egypt
8 D4 Lake Bolac Austr.
8 F2 Lake Cargelligo Austr.
72 B1 Lake Chelan Nat. Recreation Area res. U.S.A.
79 D6 Lake City FL U.S.A.
68 E3 Lake City MI U.S.A.
68 A3 Lake City MN U.S.A.
79 E5 Lake City SC U.S.A.
38 D3 Lake District Nat. Park U.K.
74 D5 Lake Elsinore U.S.A.
69 H3 Lakefield Can.
68 C4 Lake Geneva U.S.A.
63 M3 Lake Harbour Can.
75 E4 Lake Havasu City U.S.A.
74 C4 Lake Isabella U.S.A.
79 D6 Lakeland U.S.A.
68 C2 Lake Linden U.S.A.
64 F4 Lake Louise Can.
75 E4 Lake Mead National Recreation Area res. U.S.A.
81 J2 Lake Moxie U.S.A.
72 B2 Lake Oswego U.S.A.
9 B5 Lake Paringa N.Z.
81 G2 Lake Placid U.S.A.
74 A2 Lakeport U.S.A.
9 C6 Lake Pukaki N.Z.
66 D3 Lake River Can.
69 H3 Lake St Peter Can.
8 G4 Lakes Entrance Austr.
68 E2 Lake Superior National Park Can.
8 H3 Lake Tabourie Austr.
9 C6 Lake Tekapo N.Z.
66 E4 Lake Traverse Can.
72 B3 Lakeview U.S.A.
72 F4 Lakewood CO U.S.A.
81 F4 Lakewood NJ U.S.A.
80 C4 Lakewood OH U.S.A.
79 D7 Lake Worth U.S.A.
50 D2 Lakhdenpokh'ya Rus. Fed.
22 E4 Lakhimpur India
22 D5 Lakhnadon India
22 B5 Lakhpat India
49 K6 Lakonikos Kolpos b. Greece
54 B4 Lakota Côte d'Ivoire
36 U1 Laksefjorden chan. Norway
36 T1 Lakselv Norway
14 F5 Lakshadweep div. India
23 G5 Laksham Bangl.
21 E2 Lakshettipet India
23 G5 Lakshmikantapur India
31 E5 Lala Phil.
91 D2 La Laguna Arg.
91 E3 La Laja Chile
56 E3 Lalara Gabon
43 L1 Lalendorf Ger.
18 C3 Lālī Iran
84 E3 La Libertad Guatemala
91 E2 La Ligua Chile
30 D1 Lalin China
45 E1 Lalín Spain
30 C1 Lalin r. China
45 D4 La Línea de la Concepción Spain
22 D4 Lalitpur India
31 E2 Lal-Lo Phil.
65 H3 La Loche Can.
65 H3 La Loche, Lac l. Can.
42 C4 La Louvière Belgium
50 H2 Lal'sk Rus. Fed.
23 H5 Lama Bangl.
48 C4 La Maddalena Sardinia Italy
31 A5 Lamag Malaysia
32 A2 Lamaing Myanmar
La Manche str. see English Channel
76 C4 Lamar CO U.S.A.
77 E4 Lamar MO U.S.A.
18 D5 Lamard Iran
48 C5 La Marmora, Punta mt Sardinia Italy
91 D3 Lamarque Arg.
77 E6 La Marque U.S.A.
64 F2 La Martre, Lac l. Can.
56 B4 Lambaréné Gabon
86 C5 Lambayeque Peru
41 F4 Lambay Island i. Rep. of Ireland
92 D4 Lambert Gl. gl. Ant.
58 C6 Lambert's Bay S. Africa
22 C3 Lambi India
39 F6 Lambourn Downs h. U.K.
32 C2 Lam Chi r. Thai.
45 C2 Lamego Port.
67 H4 Lamèque, I. i. Can.
86 C6 La Merced Peru
8 C3 Lameroo Austr.
77 C5 Lamesa U.S.A.
74 D5 La Mesa U.S.A.
49 K5 Lamia Greece
73 E6 La Misa Mex.
74 D5 La Misión Mex.
31 B5 Lamitan Phil.
27 □ Lamma I. i. H.K. China
9 B6 Lammerlaw Ra. mts N.Z.
40 F5 Lammermuir Hills h. U.K.
37 O8 Lammhult Sweden
37 T6 Lammi Fin.
68 C5 La Moille U.S.A.
81 G2 Lamoille r. U.S.A.
68 B5 La Moine r. U.S.A.
31 B3 Lamon Bay b. Phil.
76 E3 Lamoni U.S.A.
72 F3 Lamont U.S.A.
77 B6 La Morita Mex.
69 H1 La Motte Can.
32 B1 Lam Pao Res. resr Thai.
77 D6 Lampasas U.S.A.
70 F6 Lampazos Mex.
48 E7 Lampedusa, Isola di i. Sicily Italy
39 C5 Lampeter U.K.
32 B2 Lam Plai Mat r. Thai.
50 F4 Lamskoye Rus. Fed.
27 □ Lam Tin H.K. China
56 E4 Lamu Kenya
23 H6 Lamu Myanmar
74 □2 Lanai i. U.S.A.
74 □2 Lanai City U.S.A.
31 C5 Lanao, Lake l. Phil.
69 J3 Lanark Can.
40 E5 Lanark U.K.
68 C4 Lanark U.S.A.
31 A5 Lanas Malaysia
32 A3 Lanbi Kyun i. Myanmar
Lancang Jiang r. see Mekong
81 F2 Lancaster Can.
38 E3 Lancaster U.K.
74 C4 Lancaster CA U.S.A.
68 A5 Lancaster MO U.S.A.
81 H2 Lancaster NH U.S.A.
80 B5 Lancaster OH U.S.A.
81 E4 Lancaster PA U.S.A.
79 D5 Lancaster SC U.S.A.
68 B4 Lancaster WV U.S.A.
38 E4 Lancaster Canal canal U.K.
63 K2 Lancaster Sound str. Can.
48 F3 Lanciano Italy
91 B3 Lanco Chile
26 F2 Lancun China
46 F6 Landau an der Isar Ger.
43 G5 Landau in der Pfalz Ger.
46 E7 Landeck Austria
72 E3 Lander U.S.A.
43 H2 Landesbergen Ger.
65 H4 Landis Can.
46 E6 Landsberg am Lech Ger.
39 B7 Land's End pt U.K.
46 F6 Landshut Ger.
37 N9 Landskrona Sweden
42 F5 Landstuhl Ger.
43 G1 Land Wursten reg. Ger.
41 D4 Lanesborough Rep. of Ireland
32 C3 La Nga r. Vietnam
22 E3 La'nga Co l. China
26 C3 Langao China
19 F3 Langar Iran
40 B2 Langavat, Loch l. U.K.
58 E4 Langberg mts S. Africa
76 D1 Langdon U.S.A.
58 C6 Langeberg mts S. Africa
37 M9 Langeland i. Denmark
37 T6 Längelmäki Fin.
37 T6 Längelmävesi l. Fin.
43 J3 Langelsheim Ger.
43 G1 Langen Ger.
43 H3 Langenhagen Ger.
43 F4 Langenhahn Ger.
43 F5 Langenlonsheim Ger.
46 C7 Langenthal Switz.
43 K2 Langenweddingen Ger.
42 F1 Langeoog Ger.
42 F1 Langeoog i. Ger.
37 L7 Langesund Norway
32 B5 Langgapayung Indon.
43 G4 Langgöns Ger.
65 H4 Langham Can.
36 C4 Langjökull ice cap Iceland
33 A2 Langka Indon.
33 A1 Langkawi i. Malaysia
32 A3 Lang Kha Toek, Khao mt Thai.
58 D4 Langklip S. Africa
31 A5 Langkon Malaysia
69 K1 Langlade Can.
68 C3 Langlade U.S.A.
44 F4 Langogne France
36 O2 Langøya i. Norway
23 F3 Langphu mt China
39 E6 Langport U.K.
27 F5 Langqi China
44 G3 Langres France
22 D1 Langru China
33 A2 Langsa Indon.
32 A4 Langsa, Teluk b. Indon.
36 P5 Långsele Sweden
26 C1 Langshan China
26 C1 Lang Shan mts China
27 C6 Lang Sơn Vietnam
38 G3 Langtoft U.K.
77 C6 Langtry U.S.A.
44 F5 Languedoc reg. France
36 R4 Långvattnet Sweden
43 H2 Langwedel Ger.
26 F4 Langxi China
26 C4 Langzhong China
69 H2 Laniel Can.
65 H4 Lanigan Can.
74 □1 Lanikai U.S.A.
91 B3 Lanín, Parque Nacional nat. park Arg.
91 B3 Lanín, Volcán volc. Arg.
26 E3 Lankao China
17 M2 Länkäran Azer.
42 C2 Lannion France
84 A2 La Noria Mex.
36 S3 Lansån Sweden
68 C2 L'Anse U.S.A.
68 B4 Lansing IA U.S.A.
68 E4 Lansing MI U.S.A.
64 C2 Lansing r. Can.
27 D6 Lantau I. i. H.K. China
27 □ Lantau Island i. H.K. China
27 □ Lantau Peak h. H.K. China
31 C4 Lanuza Bay b. Phil.
27 F4 Lanxi China
55 F4 Lanya Sudan
27 F6 Lan Yü i. Taiwan
54 A2 Lanzarote i. Canary Is
26 B2 Lanzhou China
30 B1 Lanzijing China
31 B2 Laoag Phil.
31 C3 Laoang Phil.
27 B6 Lao Cai Vietnam
26 F1 Laoha r. China
26 D3 Laohekou China
30 A4 Laohutun China
30 D3 Laoling China
30 D3 Lao Ling mts China
44 F2 Laon France
68 C3 Laona U.S.A.
11 M7 Laos country Asia
26 F2 Lao Shan mt China
30 E2 Laotougou China
30 C3 Laotuding Shan h. China
Laowohi pass see Khardung La
26 A1 Laoximiao China
30 E2 Laoye Ling mts China
90 C4 Lapa Brazil
31 B5 Lapac i. Phil.
83 J7 La Palma Panama
45 C4 La Palma del Condado Spain
91 F2 La Paloma Uru.
91 D3 La Pampa div. Arg.
74 B4 La Panza Range mts U.S.A.
89 E3 La Paragua Venez.
31 A5 Laparan i. Phil.
91 E1 La Paz Entre Ríos Arg.
91 C2 La Paz Mendoza Arg.
86 E7 La Paz Bol.
82 B4 La Paz Mex.
68 D5 Lapaz U.S.A.
86 E4 La Pedrera Col.
69 F4 Lapeer U.S.A.
28 G2 La Pérouse Strait str. Japan/Rus. Fed.
84 C2 La Pesca Mex.
84 B2 La Piedad Mex.
89 E3 La Piña r. Venez.
72 B3 La Pine U.S.A.
31 C3 Lapinig Phil.
31 C4 Lapinin i. Phil.
36 U5 Lapinlahti Fin.
16 D4 Lapithos Cyprus
77 F6 Laplace U.S.A.
76 C2 La Plant U.S.A.
91 F2 La Plata Arg.
89 B4 La Plata Col.
50 G1 Lapominka Rus. Fed.
68 D5 La Porte U.S.A.
68 A4 La Porte City U.S.A.
36 S5 Lappajärvi Fin.
36 S5 Lappajärvi l. Fin.
37 V6 Lappeenranta Fin.
43 L5 Lappersdorf Ger.
36 S2 Lappland reg. Europe
81 G2 La Prairie Can.
77 D6 La Pryor U.S.A.
49 M4 Lâpseki Turkey
Laptevykh, More sea see Laptev Sea
13 N2 Laptev Sea sea Rus. Fed.
36 S5 Lapua Fin.
31 B4 Lapu-Lapu Phil.
88 C2 La Quiaca Arg.
48 E3 L'Aquila Italy
74 D5 La Quinta U.S.A.
18 D5 Lār Iran
54 B1 Larache Morocco
18 E5 Lārak i. Iran
72 F3 Laramie U.S.A.
72 F3 Laramie Mts mts U.S.A.
Laranda see Karaman
90 B4 Laranjeiras do Sul Brazil
90 B3 Laranjinha r. Brazil
25 E7 Larantuka Indon.
25 F7 Larat i. Indon.
45 H4 Larba Alg.
37 O8 Lärbro Sweden
69 G2 Larchwood Can.
69 H1 Larder Lake Can.
45 E1 Laredo Spain
77 D7 Laredo U.S.A.
79 D7 Largo U.S.A.
40 D5 Largs U.K.
18 B2 Lārī Iran
48 D6 L'Ariana Tunisia
65 K5 Larimore U.S.A.
88 C3 La Rioja Arg.
91 C1 La Rioja div. Arg.
45 E1 La Rioja div. Spain
49 K5 Larisa Greece
18 E5 Laristan reg. Iran
22 B4 Larkana Pak.
46 C7 Larmont mt France/Switz.
16 D4 Larnaka Cyprus
41 F3 Larne U.K.
76 D4 Larned U.S.A.
40 C6 Larne Lough in U.K.
45 D1 La Robla Spain
42 D4 La Roche-en-Ardenne Belgium
44 D3 La Rochelle France
44 D3 La Roche-sur-Yon France
45 E3 La Roda Spain
83 L5 La Romana Dom. Rep.
65 H3 La Ronge Can.
84 B1 La Rosa Mex.
6 D3 Larrimah Austr.
92 B2 Larsen Ice Shelf ice feature Ant.
36 S5 Larsmo Fin.
37 M7 Larvik Norway
75 H2 La Sal Junction U.S.A.
81 G2 La Salle Can.
68 C5 La Salle U.S.A.
66 E4 La Sarre Can.
89 D2 Las Aves, Islas is Venez.
91 B2 Las Cabras Chile
67 J4 La Scie Can.
73 F5 Las Cruces U.S.A.
83 K5 La Selle mt Haiti
91 B1 La Serena Chile
77 C7 Las Esperanças Mex.
91 E3 Las Flores Arg.
19 F5 Lāshār r. Iran
65 H4 Lashburn Can.
91 C2 Las Heras Arg.
24 B4 Lashio Myanmar
19 G4 Lashkar Gāh Afgh.
91 B3 Las Lajas Arg.
89 D3 Las Lajitas Venez.
88 D2 Las Lomitas Arg.
45 C4 Las Marismas marsh Spain
88 C7 Las Martinetas Arg.
89 D2 Las Mercedes Venez.
84 A1 Las Nieves Mex.
74 D5 Las Palmas r. Mex.
54 A2 Las Palmas de Gran Canaria Canary Is
48 C2 La Spezia Italy
91 F2 Las Piedras Uru.
88 C6 Las Plumas Arg.
91 E2 Las Rosas Arg.
72 B3 Lassen Pk volc. U.S.A.
72 B3 Lassen Volcanic Nat. Park U.S.A.
92 B2 Lassiter Coast coastal area Ant.
83 H7 Las Tablas Panama
88 D3 Las Termas Arg.
65 H4 Last Mountain L. l. Can.
56 B4 Lastoursville Gabon
48 G3 Lastovo i. Croatia
89 D3 Las Trincheras Venez.
43 F2 Lastrup Ger.
73 F6 Las Varas Chihuahua Mex.
84 A2 Las Varas Mex.
91 D1 Las Varillas Arg.
73 F5 Las Vegas NM U.S.A.
75 E3 Las Vegas NV U.S.A.
45 D3 Las Villuercas mt Spain
67 J3 La Tabatière Can.
86 C4 Latacunga Ecuador
92 A2 Latady I. i. Ant.
89 B5 La Tagua Col.
16 E4 Latakia Syria
69 H2 Latchford Can.
23 F5 Latehar India
44 D4 La Teste France
42 F2 Lathen Ger.
40 E2 Latheron U.K.
48 E4 Latina Italy
91 D2 La Toma Arg.
89 D2 La Tortuga, Isla i. Venez.
80 D4 Latrobe U.S.A.
42 E2 Lattrop Neth.
69 H2 Latulipe Can.
66 F4 La Tuque Can.
21 B2 Latur India
35 H3 Latvia country Europe
88 C1 Lauca, Parque Nacional nat. park Chile
46 F5 Lauchhammer Ger.
40 F5 Lauder U.K.
43 H1 Lauenbrück Ger.
43 J1 Lauenburg (Elbe) Ger.
43 K5 Lauf an der Pegnitz Ger.
44 H3 Laufen Switz.
68 D2 Laughing Fish Pt pt U.S.A.
37 S7 Lauka Estonia
36 V1 Laukvik Norway
28 D2 Laulyu Rus. Fed.
32 A3 Laun Thai.
6 E6 Launceston Austr.
39 C7 Launceston U.K.
41 B5 Laune r. Rep. of Ireland
32 A2 Launglon Bok Is is Myanmar
91 B4 La Unión Chile
89 A4 La Unión Col.
82 G6 La Unión El Salvador
84 B3 La Unión Mex.
31 B3 Laur Phil.
8 B2 Laura S.A. Austr.
6 E3 Laura Austr.
89 D3 La Urbana Venez.
81 F5 Laurel DE U.S.A.
77 F6 Laurel MS U.S.A.
72 E2 Laurel MT U.S.A.
80 D4 Laurel Hill h. U.S.A.
80 A6 Laurel River Lake l. U.S.A.
40 F4 Laurencekirk U.K.
67 F4 Laurentides, Réserve faunique des res. Can.
48 F4 Lauria Italy
79 E5 Laurinburg U.S.A.
68 C2 Laurium U.S.A.
46 C7 Lausanne Switz.
33 E3 Laut i. Indon.
91 B3 Lautaro Chile
43 H4 Lautersbach (Hessen) Ger.
33 E3 Laut Kecil, Kepulauan is Indon.
7 H3 Lautoka Fiji
36 V5 Lauvuskylä Fin.
66 F4 Laval Can.
44 D2 Laval France
48 F1 Lavant r. Austria/Slovenia
88 B5 Lavapié, Pta pt Chile
18 C4 Lāvar Kabkān Iran
84 D3 La Venta Mex.
6 C4 Laverton Austr.
89 D2 La Victoria Venez.
69 G2 Lavigne Can.
72 E2 Lavina U.S.A.
90 D3 Lavras Brazil
91 G1 Lavras do Sul Brazil
59 J3 Lavumisa Swaziland
22 B2 Lawa Pak.
92 C6 Law Dome ice feature Ant.
32 B4 Lawit, Gunung mt Malaysia
17 J7 Lawqah waterhole S. Arabia
54 B3 Lawra Ghana
76 E4 Lawrence KS U.S.A.
81 H3 Lawrence MA U.S.A.
79 C5 Lawrenceburg U.S.A.
81 K2 Lawrence Station Can.
80 E6 Lawrenceville U.S.A.
77 D5 Lawton U.S.A.
14 B4 Lawz, J. al mt S. Arabia
37 O7 Laxå Sweden
58 E3 Laxey S. Africa
38 C3 Laxey U.K.
40 C2 Laxford, Loch in. U.K.
40 □ Laxo U.K.
8 D5 Layers Hill Austr.
17 K4 Laylān Iraq
5 K2 Laysan Island i. HI U.S.A.
74 A2 Laytonville U.S.A.
49 J2 Lazarevac Yugo.
92 D3 Lazarev Sea sea Ant
51 F7 Lazarevskoye Rus. Fed.
73 D6 Lázaro Cárdenas Baja California Mex.
84 B3 Lázaro Cárdenas Mex.
84 A1 Lázaro Cárdenas, Presa resr Mex.
91 F2 Lazcano Uru.
37 S9 Lazdijai Lith.
18 D5 Lāzeh Iran
13 P3 Lazo Rus. Fed.
28 C3 Lazo Rus. Fed.
32 B2 Leach Cambodia
68 E2 Leach I. i. Can.
76 C2 Lead U.S.A.
65 H4 Leader Can.
8 G2 Leadville Austr.
73 F4 Leadville U.S.A.
77 F6 Leaf r. U.S.A.
65 J3 Leaf Rapids Can.
77 D6 Leakey U.S.A.
69 F4 Leamington Can.
75 F2 Leamington U.S.A.
39 F5 Leamington Spa, Royal U.K.
27 E5 Le'an China
41 B5 Leane, Lough l. Rep. of Ireland
41 B6 Leap Rep. of Ireland
65 H4 Leask Can.
39 G6 Leatherhead U.K.
76 E4 Leavenworth KS U.S.A.
72 B2 Leavenworth WA U.S.A.
74 C2 Leavitt Peak summit U.S.A.
42 E5 Lebach Ger.
31 C5 Lebak Phil.
68 D5 Lebanon IN U.S.A.
76 D4 Lebanon KS U.S.A.
77 E4 Lebanon MO U.S.A.
81 G3 Lebanon NH U.S.A.
81 F4 Lebanon NJ U.S.A.
80 A5 Lebanon OH U.S.A.
72 B2 Lebanon OR U.S.A.
81 E4 Lebanon PA U.S.A.
79 C4 Lebanon TN U.S.A.
10 E6 Lebanon country Asia
42 C3 Lebbeke Belgium
50 F4 Lebedyan' Rus. Fed.
51 E5 Lebedyn Ukr.
44 E3 Le Blanc France
46 H3 Lębork Pol.
59 H2 Lebowakgomo S. Africa
45 C4 Lebrija Spain
46 H3 Łebsko, Jezioro lag. Pol.
91 B3 Lebu Chile
42 B4 Le Cateau-Cambrésis France
42 B4 Le Catelet France
49 H4 Lecce Italy
48 C2 Lecco Italy
46 E7 Lech r. Austria/Ger.
49 J6 Lechaina Greece
27 D5 Lechang China
42 C5 Le Chesne France
46 E7 Lechtaler Alpen mts Austria
46 D3 Leck Ger.
44 G3 Le Creusot France
44 E5 Lectoure France
32 B5 Ledang, Gunung mt Malaysia
39 E5 Ledbury U.K.
45 D2 Ledesma Spain
40 D2 Ledmore U.K.
50 E1 Ledmozero Rus. Fed.
27 C7 Ledong China
26 B2 Ledu China
64 G4 Leduc Can.
81 G3 Lee U.S.A.
76 E2 Leech L. l. U.S.A.
38 F4 Leeds U.K.
81 H2 Leeds Junction U.S.A.
39 B7 Leedstown U.K.
42 E1 Leek Neth.
39 E4 Leek U.K.
42 D3 Leende Neth.
80 D4 Leeper U.S.A.
42 F1 Leer (Ostfriesland) Ger.
79 D6 Leesburg FL U.S.A.
80 E5 Leesburg VA U.S.A.
43 H2 Leese Ger.
77 E6 Leesville U.S.A.
80 C4 Leesville Lake l. U.S.A.
8 F3 Leeton Austr.
58 D6 Leeu-Gamka S. Africa
42 D1 Leeuwarden Neth.
6 B5 Leeuwin, C. c. Austr.
74 C3 Lee Vining U.S.A.
83 M5 Leeward Islands is Caribbean Sea
16 D4 Lefka Cyprus
49 J5 Lefkada Greece
49 J5 Lefkada i. Greece
16 D4 Lefkara Cyprus
49 J5 Lefkimmi Greece
Lefkosia see Nicosia
31 B3 Legaspi Phil.
42 F2 Legden Ger.
74 A2 Leggett U.S.A.
48 D2 Legnago Italy
46 H5 Legnica Pol.
22 D2 Leh Jammu and Kashmir
44 E2 Le Havre France
81 F4 Lehighton U.S.A.
36 V5 Lehmo Fin.
43 L2 Lehnin Ger.
43 J2 Lehre Ger.
43 H2 Lehrte Ger.
36 S5 Lehtimäki Fin.
58 D1 Lehututu Botswana
22 B3 Leiah Pak.
46 G7 Leibnitz Austria
39 F5 Leicester U.K.
6 D3 Leichhardt r. Austr.
42 C2 Leiden Neth.
9 E2 Leigh N.Z.
38 E4 Leigh U.K.
39 G6 Leighton Buzzard U.K.
43 G5 Leimen Ger.
43 H2 Leine r. Ger.
43 J3 Leinefelde Ger.
41 E5 Leinster, Mount h. Rep. of Ireland
49 M6 Leipsoi i. Greece
43 L3 Leipzig Ger.
36 O3 Leiranger Norway
45 B3 Leiria Port.

27 C5 Leishan China
27 D5 Lei Shui r. China
43 L3 Leisnig Ger.
78 C4 Leitchfield U.S.A.
89 B4 Leiva, Co mt Col.
41 E4 Leixlip Rep. of Ireland
27 D5 Leiyang China
27 C6 Leizhou Bandao pen. China
27 D6 Leizhou Wan b. China
36 M4 Leka Norway
56 B4 Lékana Congo
48 C6 Le Kef Tunisia
58 B4 Lekkersing S. Africa
56 B4 Lékoni Gabon
37 O6 Leksand Sweden
36 W5 Leksozero, Oz. l. Rus. Fed.
68 E3 Leland MI U.S.A.
77 F5 Leland MS U.S.A.
54 A3 Lélouma Guinea
42 D2 Lelystad Neth.
88 C9 Le Maire, Estrecho de chan. Arg.
44 H3 Léman, Lac l. France/Switz.
44 E2 Le Mans France
76 D3 Le Mars U.S.A.
42 F5 Lemberg France
43 G2 Lembruch Ger.
90 C3 Leme Brazil
42 E2 Lemele Neth.
31 B3 Lemery Phil.
Lemesos see Limassol
43 G2 Lemgo Ger.
37 U6 Lemi Fin.
63 M3 Lemieux Islands is Can.
36 T2 Lemmenjoen Kansallispuisto nat. park Fin.
42 D2 Lemmer Neth.
76 C2 Lemmon U.S.A.
75 G5 Lemmon, Mt mt U.S.A.
74 C3 Lemoore U.S.A.
23 H5 Lemro r. Myanmar
32 A3 Lem Tom Chob pt Thai.
48 G4 Le Murge reg. Italy
37 L8 Lemvig Denmark
68 C4 Lena U.S.A.
24 C1 Lena r. Rus. Fed.
23 E2 Lenchung Tso salt l. China
87 K4 Lençóis Maranhenses, Parque Nacional dos nat. park Brazil
19 E4 Lengbarüt Iran
43 F2 Lengerich Ger.
26 A2 Lenglong Ling mts China
27 D5 Lengshuijiang China
27 D5 Lengshuitan China
91 B1 Lengua de Vaca, Pta hd Chile
39 H6 Lenham U.K.
37 O8 Lenhovda Sweden
19 H2 Lenin Tajik.
51 H7 Lenina, Kanal canal Rus. Fed.
Leningrad see St Petersburg
51 F6 Leningradskaya Rus. Fed.
50 E3 Leningradskaya Oblast' div. Rus. Fed.
13 T3 Leningradskiy Rus. Fed.
28 D2 Lenino Rus. Fed.
14 E2 Leninsk Kazak.
51 H5 Leninsk Rus. Fed.
50 F4 Leninskiy Rus. Fed.
24 A1 Leninsk-Kuznetskiy Rus. Fed.
50 H3 Leninskoye Rus. Fed.
43 F3 Lenne r. Ger.
79 D5 Lenoir U.S.A.
81 G3 Lenox U.S.A.
44 F1 Lens France
13 N3 Lensk Rus. Fed.
51 G7 Lentekhi Georgia
46 H7 Lenti Hungary
48 F6 Lentini Sicily Italy
43 K1 Lenzen Ger.
54 B3 Léo Burkina
46 G7 Leoben Austria
39 E5 Leominster U.K.
81 H3 Leominster U.S.A.
84 B2 León Mex.
82 G6 León Nic.
45 D1 León Spain
89 A3 León r. Col.
57 B6 Leonardville Namibia
16 E4 Leonarisson Cyprus
8 E5 Leongatha Austr.
6 C4 Leonora Austr.
90 D3 Leopoldina Brazil
65 H4 Leoville Can.
59 G1 Lephalala r. S. Africa
57 C6 Lephepe Botswana
59 F5 Lephoi S. Africa
27 E4 Leping China
44 G4 Le Pont-de-Claix France
36 U5 Leppävirta Fin.
44 F4 Le-Puy-en-Velay France
42 B4 Le Quesnoy France
59 G1 Lerala Botswana
59 G4 Leratswana S. Africa
55 D4 Léré Chad
89 C5 Lerida Col.
Lérida see Lleida
17 M2 Lerik Azer.
45 E1 Lerma Spain
51 G6 Lermontov Rus. Fed.
28 D1 Lermontovka Rus. Fed.
49 M6 Leros i. Greece
68 C5 Le Roy U.S.A.
37 N8 Lerum Sweden
40 □ Lerwick U.K.
49 L5 Lesbos i. Greece
83 K5 Les Cayes Haiti
67 G4 Les Escoumins Can.
81 J1 Les Étroits Can.
45 G1 Le Seu d'Urgell Spain
27 B4 Leshan China
49 J3 Leskovac Yugo.
40 E4 Leslie U.K.
44 B2 Lesneven France
50 K3 Lesnoy Rus. Fed.
28 D1 Lesopil'noye Rus. Fed.
12 L4 Lesosibirsk Rus. Fed.
53 G8 Lesotho country Africa
28 C2 Lesozavodsk Rus. Fed.
44 D3 Les Sables-d'Olonne France
42 D4 Lesse r. Belgium
83 L6 Lesser Antilles is Caribbean Sea
Lesser Caucasus mts see Malyy Kavkaz
64 G3 Lesser Slave Lake l. Can.
64 G3 Lesser Slave Lake Provincial Park res. Can.
42 B4 Lessines Belgium
36 T5 Lestijärvi Fin.
36 T5 Lestijärvi l. Fin.
Lesvos i. see Lesbos
46 H5 Leszno Pol.
59 J1 Letaba S. Africa
39 G6 Letchworth U.K.
22 D4 Leteri India
23 H5 Letha Range mts Myanmar
64 G5 Lethbridge Can.
86 G3 Lethem Guyana
86 E4 Leticia Col.
25 E7 Leti, Kepulauan is Indon.
26 F2 Leting China
59 F2 Letlhakeng Botswana
39 J7 Le Touquet-Paris-Plage France
44 E1 Le Tréport France
59 J1 Letsitele S. Africa
32 A3 Letsok-aw Kyun i. Myanmar
59 F3 Letsopa S. Africa
41 D3 Letterkenny Rep. of Ireland
33 C2 Letung Indon.
43 K2 Letzlingen Ger.
40 F4 Leuchars U.K.
50 G1 Leunovo Rus. Fed.
75 G4 Leupp Corner U.S.A.
42 D2 Leusden Neth.
32 A2 Leuser, G. mt Indon.
43 J5 Leutershausen Ger.
42 C4 Leuven Belgium
49 K5 Levadeia Greece
75 G2 Levan U.S.A.
36 M5 Levanger Norway
48 C2 Levanto Italy
48 E5 Levanzo, Isola di i. Sicily Italy
51 H7 Levashi Rus. Fed.
77 C5 Levelland U.S.A.
38 G4 Leven Eng. U.K.
40 F4 Leven Scot. U.K.
40 C4 Leven, Loch in. U.K.
40 E4 Leven, Loch l. U.K.
6 C3 Lévêque, C. c. Austr.
68 E3 Levering U.S.A.
42 E3 Leverkusen Ger.
47 J6 Levice Slovakia
9 E4 Levin N.Z.
67 F4 Lévis Can.
49 M6 Levitha i. Greece
81 G4 Levittown NY U.S.A.
81 F4 Levittown PA U.S.A.
49 L3 Levski Bulg.
39 H7 Lewes U.K.
81 F5 Lewes U.S.A.
40 B2 Lewis i. U.K.
80 E4 Lewisburg PA U.S.A.
80 C6 Lewisburg WV U.S.A.
9 D5 Lewis Pass pass N.Z.
72 D1 Lewis Range mts U.S.A.
79 C5 Lewis Smith, L. l. U.S.A.
75 G6 Lewis Springs U.S.A.
72 C2 Lewiston ID U.S.A.
81 H2 Lewiston ME U.S.A.
68 B4 Lewiston MN U.S.A.
68 B5 Lewistown IL U.S.A.
72 E2 Lewistown MT U.S.A.
80 E4 Lewistown PA U.S.A.
77 E5 Lewisville U.S.A.
77 D5 Lewisville, Lake l. U.S.A.
68 C5 Lexington IL U.S.A.
78 C4 Lexington KY U.S.A.
76 E4 Lexington MO U.S.A.
79 D5 Lexington NC U.S.A.
76 D3 Lexington NE U.S.A.
79 B5 Lexington TN U.S.A.
80 D6 Lexington VA U.S.A.
80 E5 Lexington Park U.S.A.
59 J1 Leydsdorp S. Africa
27 C5 Leye China
17 L3 Leyla D. h. Iran
31 C4 Leyte i. Phil.
31 C4 Leyte Gulf g. Phil.
49 H4 Lezhë Albania
27 B4 Lezhi China
51 E5 L'gov Rus. Fed.
23 H3 Lhari China
23 G3 Lhasa China
23 G3 Lhasa He r. China
23 F3 Lhazê China
23 F3 Lhazhong China
33 A1 Lhokseumawe Indon.
32 A4 Lhoksukon Indon.
23 H3 Lhorong China
23 H3 Lhünzê China
23 G3 Lhünzhub China
27 E5 Liancheng China
42 A5 Liancourt France
Liancourt Rocks i. see Tok-tō
31 C4 Lianga Phil.
31 C4 Lianga Bay b. Phil.
27 E4 Liangaz Hu l. China
26 D1 Liangcheng China
26 C3 Liangdang China
26 B3 Lianghekou China
27 C4 Liangping China
27 B5 Liangwang Shan mts China
26 C2 Liangzhen China
27 D5 Lianhua China
27 E6 Lianhua Shan mts China
27 F5 Lianjiang Fujian China
27 D6 Lianjiang Guangdong China
27 D5 Liannan China
27 E5 Lianping China
27 D5 Lianshan China
26 F3 Lianshui China
32 B2 Liant, C. pt Thai.
27 D5 Lian Xian China
27 D5 Lianyuan China
26 F3 Lianyungang Jiangsu China
30 F1 Lianzhushan China
30 B2 Liao r. China
26 E2 Liaocheng China
30 B3 Liaodong Bandao pen. China
30 A3 Liaodong Wan b. China
30 B3 Liaohe Kou river mouth China
30 B3 Liaoning div. China
30 B3 Liaoyang China
30 C2 Liaoyuan China
30 B3 Liaozhong China
49 H5 Liapades Greece
22 B2 Liaqatabad Pak.
64 E2 Liard r. Can.
64 D3 Liard River Can.
19 G5 Liari Pak.
40 C3 Liathach mt U.K.
16 F4 Liban, Jebel mts Lebanon
89 B3 Libano Col.
72 D1 Libby U.S.A.
56 B3 Libenge Congo(Zaire)
77 C4 Liberal U.S.A.
46 G5 Liberec Czech Rep.
83 G6 Liberia Costa Rica
53 D5 Liberia country Africa
89 C2 Libertad Venez.
89 C2 Libertad Venez.
68 B6 Liberty IL U.S.A.
81 J2 Liberty ME U.S.A.
76 E4 Liberty MO U.S.A.
81 F4 Liberty NY U.S.A.
77 E6 Liberty TX U.S.A.
42 D5 Libin Belgium
31 B3 Libmanan Phil.
27 C5 Libo China
59 H5 Libode S. Africa
44 D4 Libourne France
56 A3 Libreville Gabon
31 C5 Libuganon r. Phil.
52 F3 Libya country Africa
52 G3 Libyan Desert. Egypt/Libya
55 E1 Libyan Plateau plat. Egypt
91 B2 Licantén Chile
48 E6 Licata Sicily Italy
17 H2 Lice Turkey
43 G4 Lich Ger.
39 F5 Lichfield U.K.
57 D5 Lichinga Moz.
43 K4 Lichte Ger.
43 G3 Lichtenau Ger.
59 G3 Lichtenburg S. Africa
43 K4 Lichtenfels Ger.
42 E3 Lichtenvoorde Neth.
27 C4 Lichuan Hubei China
27 E5 Lichuan Jiangxi China
80 B5 Licking r. U.S.A.
50 C4 Lida Belarus
74 D3 Lida U.S.A.
58 C2 Lidfontein Namibia
37 N7 Lidköping Sweden
36 O4 Lidsjöberg Sweden
43 H2 Liebenau Ger.
43 J2 Liebenburg Ger.
43 M2 Liebenwalde Ger.
6 D4 Liebig, Mt mt Austr.
34 F4 Liechtenstein country Europe
42 D4 Liège Belgium
36 W5 Lieksa Fin.
47 M2 Lielupe r. Latvia
37 T8 Lielvārde Latvia
36 P5 Lien Sweden
56 C3 Lienart Congo(Zaire)
46 F7 Lienz Austria
37 R8 Liepāja Latvia
42 C3 Lier Belgium
37 J7 Liervik Norway
42 D3 Lieshout Neth.
42 A4 Liévin France
69 K2 Lièvre r. Can.
46 G7 Liezen Austria
41 E4 Liffey r. Rep. of Ireland
41 D3 Lifford Rep. of Ireland
91 C4 Lifi Mahuida mt Arg.
7 G4 Lifou i. New Caledonia
31 B3 Ligao Phil.
37 T8 Līgatne Latvia
57 D5 Ligonha r. Moz.
68 E5 Ligonier U.S.A.
Ligure, Mar sea see Ligurian Sea
44 J5 Ligurian Sea sea France/Italy
6 F2 Lihir Group is P.N.G.
74 □2 Lihue U.S.A.
27 D5 Li Jiang r. China
26 F2 Lijin China
57 C5 Likasi Congo(Zaire)
64 E4 Likely Can.
50 E3 Likhoslavl' Rus. Fed.
33 C2 Liku Indon.
50 G3 Likurga Rus. Fed.
48 C3 L'Île-Rousse Corsica France
43 G1 Lilienthal Ger.
27 D5 Liling China
22 C2 Lilla Pak.
37 N7 Lilla Edet Sweden
42 C3 Lille Belgium
44 F1 Lille France
37 L9 Lille Bælt chan. Denmark
37 M6 Lillehammer Norway
42 A4 Lillers France
37 L7 Lillesand Norway
37 M7 Lillestrom Norway
68 E4 Lilley U.S.A.
36 O5 Lillholmsjö Sweden
64 E4 Lillooet Can.
64 E4 Lillooet r. Can.
23 H4 Lilong India
57 D5 Lilongwe Malawi
31 B4 Liloy Phil.
8 B2 Lilydale Austr.
86 C6 Lima Peru
72 D2 Lima MT U.S.A.
80 A4 Lima OH U.S.A.
18 E5 Limah Oman
51 H6 Liman Rus. Fed.
91 B1 Limari r. Chile
23 E2 Lima Ringma Tso salt l. China
16 D4 Limassol Cyprus
41 E2 Limavady U.K.
91 C3 Limay r. Arg.
91 C3 Limay Mahuida Arg.
37 T8 Limbaži Latvia
54 C4 Limbe Cameroon
33 E3 Limbungan Indon.
43 G4 Limburg an der Lahn Ger.
32 □ Lim Chu Kang Sing.
32 □ Lim Chu Kang h. Sing.
58 E4 Lime Acres S. Africa
90 C3 Limeira Brazil
41 C5 Limerick Rep. of Ireland
68 A4 Lime Springs U.S.A.
81 K1 Limestone U.S.A.
36 N4 Limingen Norway
36 N4 Limingen l. Norway
81 H3 Limington U.S.A.
36 T4 Liminka Fin.
49 L5 Limnos i. Greece
81 F2 Limoges Can.
44 E4 Limoges France
83 H6 Limón Costa Rica
73 G4 Limon U.S.A.
16 E3 Limonlu Turkey
44 E4 Limousin reg. France
44 F5 Limoux France
59 K1 Limpopo r. Africa
18 A4 Līnah S. Arabia
36 W2 Linakhamari Rus. Fed.
27 F4 Lin'an China
31 A4 Linapacan i. Phil.
31 A4 Linapacan Strait chan. Phil.
91 B2 Linares Chile
84 C1 Linares Mex.
45 E3 Linares Spain
24 C4 Lincang China
26 E2 Lincheng China
27 E5 Linchuan China
91 E2 Lincoln Arg.
39 G4 Lincoln U.K.
74 B2 Lincoln CA U.S.A.
68 C5 Lincoln IL U.S.A.
81 J2 Lincoln ME U.S.A.
69 F3 Lincoln MI U.S.A.
76 D3 Lincoln NE U.S.A.
81 H2 Lincoln NH U.S.A.
72 A2 Lincoln City U.S.A.
69 F4 Lincoln Park U.S.A.
60 M1 Lincoln Sea sea Can./Greenland
39 G4 Lincolnshire Wolds reg. U.K.
81 J2 Lincolnville U.S.A.
90 E1 Linda, Sa h. Brazil
43 L2 Lindau Ger.
46 D7 Lindau (Bodensee) Ger.
43 G4 Linden Ger.
87 G2 Linden Guyana
79 C5 Linden AL U.S.A.
79 C5 Linden TN U.S.A.
68 A2 Linden Grove U.S.A.
63 O3 Lindenow Fjord in. Greenland
43 F2 Lindern (Oldenburg) Ger.
37 K7 Lindesnes c. Norway
57 D4 Lindi Tanz.
56 C3 Lindi r. Congo(Zaire)
Lindisfarne i. see Holy Island
59 G3 Lindley S. Africa
49 N6 Lindos, Akra pt Greece
81 K1 Lindsay N.B. Can.
69 H3 Lindsay Ont. Can.
74 C3 Lindsay U.S.A.
5 L4 Line Islands is Pac. Oc.
26 D2 Linfen China
21 A3 Linganamakki Reservoir India
31 B2 Lingayen Phil.
31 B2 Lingayen Gulf b. Phil.
26 D3 Lingbao China
26 E3 Lingbi China
27 D5 Lingchuan Guangxi China
26 D3 Lingchuan Shanxi China
59 G6 Lingelethu S. Africa
59 F6 Lingelihle S. Africa
42 F2 Lingen (Ems) Ger.
33 B3 Lingga, Kepulauan is Indon.
31 C5 Lingig Phil.
72 F3 Lingle U.S.A.
56 C3 Lingomo Congo(Zaire)
26 E2 Lingqiu China
27 C6 Lingshan China
27 C7 Lingshui China
21 B2 Lingsugur India
26 C3 Lingtai China
27 C7 Lingtou China
54 A3 Linguère Senegal
27 D5 Lingui China
26 C2 Lingwu China
27 D5 Ling Xian China
26 F1 Lingyuan China
27 C5 Lingyun China
22 D2 Lingzi Thang Plains l. China/Jammu and Kashmir
27 F4 Linhai China
90 E2 Linhares Brazil
32 C1 Linh Cam Vietnam
26 C1 Linhe China
81 H1 Linière Can.
30 D3 Linjiang China
37 O7 Linköping Sweden
30 F1 Linkou China
27 D4 Linli China
40 E5 Linlithgow U.K.
26 D2 Linlü Shan mt China
40 C4 Linnhe, Loch in. U.K.
42 E4 Linnich Ger.
74 A1 Linn, Mt mt U.S.A.
26 E2 Linqing China
26 F2 Linqu China
26 E3 Linquan China
26 D3 Linru China
90 C3 Lins Brazil
26 F3 Linshu China
27 C4 Linshui China
26 B3 Lintan China
26 B3 Lintao China
76 C2 Linton U.S.A.
26 C3 Lintong China
26 F1 Linxi China
26 B3 Linxia China
26 D2 Lin Xian China
27 D4 Linxiang China
26 E2 Linyi Shandong China
26 F3 Linyi Shandong China
26 D3 Linyi Shanxi China
26 E3 Linying China
46 G6 Linz Austria
26 A2 Linze China
44 F5 Lion, Golfe du g. France
69 G3 Lion's Head Can.
81 F4 Lionville U.S.A.
56 B3 Liouesso Congo
31 B3 Lipa Phil.
48 F5 Lipari Italy
48 F5 Lipari, Isola i. Italy
48 F5 Lipari, Isole is Italy
51 F4 Lipetsk Rus. Fed.
51 F4 Lipetskaya Oblast' div. Rus. Fed.
50 F2 Lipin Bor Rus. Fed.
27 C5 Liping China
49 J1 Lipova Romania
28 B2 Lipovtsy Rus. Fed.
43 E3 Lippe r. Ger.
43 G3 Lippstadt Ger.
22 E3 Lipti Lekh pass Nepal
8 E5 Liptrap, C. hd Austr.
27 D5 Lipu China
56 D3 Lira Uganda
56 B4 Liranga Congo
31 C6 Lirung Indon.
56 C3 Lisala Congo(Zaire)
41 D3 Lisbellaw U.K.
Lisboa see Lisbon
45 B3 Lisbon Port.
68 C5 Lisbon IL U.S.A.
81 H2 Lisbon ME U.S.A.
76 D2 Lisbon ND U.S.A.
81 H2 Lisbon NH U.S.A.
80 C4 Lisbon OH U.S.A.
41 E3 Lisburn U.K.
41 B5 Liscannor Bay b. Rep. of Ireland
41 B4 Lisdoonvarna Rep. of Ireland
27 F5 Li-shan Taiwan
26 D2 Lishi China
30 C2 Lishu China
26 F4 Lishui Jiangsu China
27 F4 Lishui Zhejiang China
27 D4 Li Shui r. China
44 E2 Lisieux France
39 C7 Liskeard U.K.
51 F5 Liski Rus. Fed.
42 A5 L'Isle-Adam France
44 G5 L'Isle-sur-la-Sorgue France
41 D5 Lismore Rep. of Ireland
40 C4 Lismore i. U.K.
41 D3 Lisnarrick U.K.
41 D3 Lisnaskea U.K.
69 G4 Listowel Can.
41 B5 Listowel Rep. of Ireland
36 O5 Lit Sweden
27 C6 Litang Guangxi China
24 C3 Litang Sichuan China
87 H3 Litani r. Fr. Guiana/Suriname
16 E5 Līṭānī r. Lebanon
74 B1 Litchfield CA U.S.A.
78 B4 Litchfield IL U.S.A.
71 H2 Litchfield MN U.S.A.
44 D4 Lit-et-Mixe France
8 H2 Lithgow Austr.
35 H3 Lithuania country Europe
81 E4 Lititz U.S.A.
46 G5 Litoměřice Czech Rep.
79 E7 Little Abaco i. Bahamas
79 E7 Little Bahama Bank sand bank Bahamas
9 E2 Little Barrier i. N.Z.
68 D3 Little Bay de Noc b. U.S.A.
72 E2 Little Belt Mts mts U.S.A.
83 H5 Little Cayman i. Cayman Is
75 H4 Little Colorado r. U.S.A.
75 F3 Little Creek Peak summit U.S.A.
69 G3 Little Current Can.
66 C3 Little Current r. Can.
39 D7 Little Dart r. U.K.
8 C4 Little Desert Nat. Park Austr.
81 F5 Little Egg Harbor in. U.S.A.
79 F7 Little Exuma i. Bahamas
76 E2 Little Falls MN U.S.A.
81 F3 Little Falls NY U.S.A.
75 F3 Littlefield AZ U.S.A.
77 C5 Littlefield TX U.S.A.
76 E1 Little Fork U.S.A.
68 A1 Little Fork r. U.S.A.
23 F4 Little Gandak r. India
65 K4 Little Grand Rapids Can.
39 G7 Littlehampton U.K.
80 C5 Little Kanawha r. U.S.A.
58 C3 Little Karas Berg plat. Namibia
58 D6 Little Karoo plat. S. Africa
68 D2 Little Lake U.S.A.
67 H3 Little Mecatina r. Can.
80 A5 Little Miami r. U.S.A.
40 B3 Little Minch str. U.K.
76 C2 Little Missouri r. U.S.A.
39 H5 Little Ouse r. U.K.
68 D1 Little Pic r. Can.
22 B5 Little Rann marsh India
77 E5 Little Rock U.S.A.
68 D4 Little Sable Pt pt U.S.A.
79 F7 Little San Salvador i. Bahamas
64 F4 Little Smoky r. Can.
73 F4 Littleton CO U.S.A.
81 H2 Littleton NH U.S.A.
80 C5 Littleton WV U.S.A.
68 E3 Little Traverse Bay b. U.S.A.
17 J4 Little Zab r. Iraq
57 D5 Litunde Moz.
64 B3 Lituya Bay b. U.S.A.
30 B2 Liu r. China
26 C3 Liuba China
27 F6 Liuchiu Yü i. Taiwan
27 C5 Liuchong He r. China
30 B5 Liugong Dao i. China
26 F1 Liugu r. China
30 C2 Liuhe China
27 D4 Liujiachang China
27 C5 Liujiang China
26 B3 Liujiaxia Sk. resr China
26 C3 Liupan Shan mts China
27 B5 Liupanshui China
27 D4 Liuyang China
27 C5 Liuzhou China
28 C3 Livadiya Rus. Fed.
37 U8 Līvāni Latvia
74 B2 Live Oak CA U.S.A.
79 D6 Live Oak FL U.S.A.
6 C3 Liveringa Austr.
74 B3 Livermore U.S.A.
81 H2 Livermore Falls U.S.A.
77 B6 Livermore, Mt mt U.S.A.
8 H2 Liverpool Austr.
67 H5 Liverpool Can.
39 E4 Liverpool U.K.
39 D4 Liverpool Bay U.K.
62 E3 Liverpool Bay b. Can.
63 L2 Liverpool, C. c. Can.
8 H1 Liverpool Plains Austr.
8 H1 Liverpool Ra. mts Austr.
40 E5 Livingston U.K.
74 B3 Livingston CA U.S.A.
72 E2 Livingston MT U.S.A.
79 C4 Livingston TN U.S.A.
77 E6 Livingston TX U.S.A.
57 C5 Livingstone Zambia
92 B2 Livingston I. i. Ant.
77 E6 Livingston, L. l. U.S.A.
48 G3 Livno Bos.-Herz.
51 F4 Livny Rus. Fed.
36 U4 Livojoki r. Fin.
69 F4 Livonia U.S.A.
48 D3 Livorno Italy
90 E1 Livramento do Brumado Brazil
18 E5 Liwā Oman
57 D4 Liwale Tanz.
26 B3 Li Xian Gansu China
27 D4 Li Xian Hunan China
26 B4 Li Xian Sichuan China
26 E3 Lixin China
26 F4 Liyang China
39 B8 Lizard U.K.
39 B8 Lizard Point pt U.K.
42 B5 Lizy-sur-Ourcq France
48 F1 Ljubljana Slovenia
37 Q8 Ljugarn Sweden
37 P5 Ljungan r. Sweden
37 P5 Ljungaverk Sweden
37 N8 Ljungby Sweden
37 P6 Ljusdal Sweden
37 O6 Ljusnan r. Sweden
37 P6 Ljusne Sweden
88 B5 Llaima, Volcán volc. Chile
39 C5 Llanbadarn Fawr U.K.
39 D5 Llanbister U.K.
39 D6 Llandeilo U.K.
39 C6 Llandissilio U.K.
39 D6 Llandovery U.K.
39 D5 Llandrindod Wells U.K.
39 D4 Llandudno U.K.
39 C5 Llandysul U.K.
39 C6 Llanegwad U.K.
39 C6 Llanelli U.K.
39 C4 Llanerchymedd U.K.
39 D5 Llanfair Caereinion U.K.
39 C4 Llangefni U.K.
39 D5 Llangollen U.K.
39 D5 Llangurig U.K.
39 C4 Llanllyfni U.K.
39 C5 Llannor U.K.
77 D6 Llano U.S.A.
77 D6 Llano r. U.S.A.
77 C5 Llano Estacado plain U.S.A.
89 C3 Llanos reg. Col./Venez.
91 B4 Llanquihue, L. l. Chile
39 C5 Llanrhystud U.K.
39 D6 Llantrisant U.K.
39 D5 Llanuwchllyn U.K.
39 D5 Llanwnog U.K.
39 D4 Llay U.K.
45 G2 Lleida Spain
45 C3 Llerena Spain
45 F3 Llíria Spain
45 E1 Llodio Spain
62 F4 Lloyd George, Mt Can.
65 H3 Lloyd Lake l. Can.
65 G4 Lloydminster Can.
45 H3 Llucmajor Spain
88 C2 Llullaillaco, Vol. volc. Chile
27 B6 Lô r. China/Vietnam
75 G2 Loa U.S.A.
88 C2 Loa r. Chile
50 J3 Loban' r. Rus. Fed.
45 D4 Lobatejo mt Spain
57 C6 Lobatse Botswana
43 K3 Löbejün Ger.
43 L3 Löbenberg h. Ger.
91 E3 Loberia Arg.
57 B5 Lobito Angola
91 E2 Lobos Arg.
43 L2 Loburg Ger.
40 D4 Lochaber reg. U.K.
40 C4 Lochaline U.K.
69 E1 Lochalsh Can.
40 A3 Lochboisdale U.K.
40 C3 Lochcarron U.K.
38 C1 Lochearnhead U.K.
42 E2 Lochem Neth.
44 E3 Loches France
40 E4 Lochgelly U.K.
40 C4 Lochgilphead U.K.
40 C2 Lochinver U.K.
40 A3 Lochmaddy U.K.
40 E4 Lochnagar mt U.K.
80 E5 Loch Raven Reservoir U.S.A.
40 D4 Lochy, Loch l. U.K.
40 E5 Lockerbie U.K.
8 F3 Lockhart Austr.
77 D6 Lockhart U.S.A.
80 E4 Lock Haven U.S.A.
80 D3 Lockport U.S.A.
32 C3 Lôc Ninh Vietnam
80 B5 Locust Grove U.S.A.
16 E6 Lod Israel
8 D3 Loddon r. Austr.
44 F5 Lodève France
50 E2 Lodeynoye Pole Rus. Fed.
72 F2 Lodge Grass U.S.A.
22 B3 Lodhran Pak.
48 C2 Lodi Italy
74 B2 Lodi CA U.S.A.
80 B4 Lodi OH U.S.A.
36 O2 Lødingen Norway
56 D3 Lodwar Kenya
47 J5 Łódź Pol.
19 H3 Loe Dakka Afgh.
58 C5 Loeriesfontein S. Africa
36 N2 Lofoten is Norway
51 G5 Log Rus. Fed.
73 G5 Logan NM U.S.A.
80 B5 Logan OH U.S.A.
72 E3 Logan UT U.S.A.
80 C6 Logan WV U.S.A.
64 D2 Logan Mountains mts Can.
64 A2 Logan, Mt mt Can.
62 D3 Logan, Mt mt Can.
68 D5 Logansport U.S.A.
48 F2 Logatec Slovenia
45 E1 Logroño Spain
23 H4 Logtak L. l. India
58 E4 Lohatlha S. Africa
43 H3 Lohfelden Ger.
36 T3 Lohiniva Fin.
37 S6 Lohjanjärvi l. Fin.
43 G2 Löhne Ger.
43 G2 Lohne (Oldenburg) Ger.
36 S4 Lohtaja Fin.
32 A1 Loikaw Myanmar
32 A1 Loi Lan mt Myanmar/Thai.
37 S6 Loimaa Fin.
44 E3 Loire r. France
86 C4 Loja Ecuador
45 D4 Loja Spain
33 E1 Lokan r. Malaysia
36 U3 Lokan tekojärvi l. Fin.
42 C3 Lokeren Belgium
58 D2 Lokgwabe Botswana
56 D3 Lokichar Kenya
56 D3 Lokichokio Kenya
37 L8 Løkken Denmark
36 L5 Løkken Norway
47 P2 Loknya Rus. Fed.
54 C4 Lokoja Nigeria
54 C4 Lokossa Benin
51 E4 Lokot' Rus. Fed.
37 T7 Loksa Estonia
63 M3 Loks Land i. Can.
54 B4 Lola Guinea
74 B2 Lola, Mt mt U.S.A.
37 M9 Lolland i. Denmark
56 D4 Lollondo Tanz.
72 D2 Lolo U.S.A.
58 E3 Lolwane S. Africa
49 K3 Lom Bulg.
37 L6 Lom Norway
56 C4 Lomami r. Congo(Zaire)
91 D3 Loma Negra, Planicie de la plain Arg.
19 G3 Lomar Pass pass Afgh.
84 C2 Lomas del Real Mex.
91 E2 Lomas de Zamora Arg.
33 E4 Lombok i. Indon.
33 E4 Lombok, Selat chan. Indon.
54 C4 Lomé Togo
56 C4 Lomela Congo(Zaire)
56 C4 Lomela r. Congo(Zaire)
42 A4 Lomme France
42 D3 Lommel Belgium
40 D4 Lomond, Loch l. U.K.
50 G1 Lomovoye Rus. Fed.
25 D7 Lompobattang, Gunung mt Indon.
74 B4 Lompoc U.S.A.
47 L4 Łomża Pol.
22 D6 Lonar India
91 B3 Loncoche Chile
91 B3 Loncopue Arg.
69 G4 London Can.
39 G6 London U.K.
80 A6 London KY U.S.A.
80 B5 London OH U.S.A.
41 D3 Londonderry U.K.
81 G3 Londonderry U.S.A.
6 C3 Londonderry, C. c. Austr.
88 B9 Londonderry, I. i. Chile
90 B3 Londrina Brazil
74 C3 Lone Pine U.S.A.
27 C6 Long'an China
13 T2 Longa, Proliv chan. Rus. Fed.
39 E6 Long Ashton U.K.
91 B3 Longaví, Nev. de mt Chile
79 E5 Long Bay b. U.S.A.
9 C6 Longbeach N.Z.
74 C5 Long Beach CA U.S.A.
81 G4 Long Beach NY U.S.A.
81 F4 Long Branch U.S.A.
68 A6 Long Branch Lake l. U.S.A.
27 B4 Longchang China
27 E5 Longchuan China
39 F5 Long Eaton U.K.
30 D1 Longfengshan Sk. resr China
41 D4 Longford Rep. of Ireland
27 E5 Longhai China
27 □ Long Harbour in. H.K. China
38 F2 Longhoughton U.K.
33 E3 Longiram Indon.
83 J4 Long Island i. Bahamas
66 E3 Long Island i. Can.
6 E2 Long Island i. P.N.G.
81 G4 Long Island i. U.S.A.
81 G4 Long Island Sound chan. U.S.A.
27 C5 Long Jiang r. China
23 H3 Longju China
26 F2 Longkou Wan b. China
66 C4 Longlac Can.
81 F3 Long Lake NY U.S.A.
66 C4 Long Lake l. Can.
81 J1 Long Lake l. ME U.S.A.
68 E3 Long Lake l. MI U.S.A.
69 F3 Long Lake l. MI U.S.A.
76 C2 Long Lake l. ND U.S.A.
81 F2 Long Lake l. NY U.S.A.
27 C5 Longli China
27 B5 Longlin China
40 D4 Long, Loch in. U.K.
39 H5 Long Melford U.K.
27 E6 Longmen China
26 B3 Longmen Shan mts China
72 F3 Longmont U.S.A.
27 E5 Longnan China
69 G4 Long Point pt Can.
9 B7 Long Point pt N.Z.
69 G4 Long Point Bay b. Can.
38 E3 Long Preston U.K.
27 F4 Longquan China
27 F4 Longquan Xi r. China
63 N5 Long Range Mountains Can.
67 J4 Long Range Mts h. Can.
6 E4 Longreach Austr.
26 B3 Longriba China
27 C4 Longshan China
27 D5 Longsheng China
72 F3 Longs Peak summit U.S.A.
39 J5 Long Stratton U.K.
27 D4 Longtian China
38 E2 Longtown U.K.
66 F4 Longueuil Can.
42 D5 Longuyon France
74 A2 Longvale U.S.A.
75 F3 Long Valley Junction U.S.A.
77 E5 Longview TX U.S.A.
72 B2 Longview WA U.S.A.
28 C2 Longwangmiao Rus. Fed.
26 B3 Longxi China
26 C3 Long Xian China
27 E5 Longxi Shan mt China
32 C3 Long Xuyên Vietnam
27 E5 Longyan China
26 E2 Longyao China
27 C6 Longzhou China
43 F2 Löningen Ger.
37 O8 Lönsboda Sweden
8 D4 Lonsdale, Lake l. Austr.
44 G3 Lons-le-Saunier France
90 B3 Lontra r. Brazil
31 B3 Looc Phil.
68 E4 Looking Glass r. U.S.A.
81 F4 Lookout U.S.A.
66 D2 Lookout, Cape c. Can.
79 E5 Lookout, Cape c. U.S.A.
74 C3 Lookout Mt mt U.S.A.
69 F3 Lookout, Pt pt U.S.A.
68 C1 Loon Can.
64 F3 Loon r. Can.
65 H4 Loon Lake Can.
81 J1 Loon Lake l. U.S.A.
41 B5 Loop Head hd Rep. of Ireland
22 E1 Lop China
24 G1 Lopatina, Gora mt Rus. Fed.
50 H4 Lopatino Rus. Fed.
32 B2 Lop Buri Thai.
31 B3 Lopez Phil.
81 E4 Lopez U.S.A.
24 B2 Lop Nur l. China
56 C3 Lopori r. Congo(Zaire)
36 R1 Lopphavet b. Norway
50 J2 Loptyuga Rus. Fed.
19 G4 Lora r. Afgh.
89 B2 Lora r. Venez.
45 D4 Lora del Río Spain
80 B4 Lorain U.S.A.
22 B3 Loralai Pak.
22 B3 Loralai r. Pak.
80 A4 Loramie, Lake l. U.S.A.
45 F4 Lorca Spain
43 F4 Lorch Ger.
31 A4 Lord Auckland sand bank Phil.
18 C4 Lordegān Iran
7 F5 Lord Howe Island i. Pac. Oc.
94 F8 Lord Howe Rise sea feature Pac. Oc.
75 H5 Lordsburg U.S.A.
43 F4 Loreley Ger.
90 D3 Lorena Brazil
25 F7 Lorentz r. Indon.
86 F7 Loreto Bol.
87 J5 Loreto Brazil
82 B3 Loreto Mex.
31 C4 Loreto Phil.
89 B2 Lorica Col.
44 C3 Lorient France
65 L1 Lorillard r. Can.
8 D5 Lorne Austr.
40 C4 Lorn, Firth of est. U.K.
23 H3 Loro r. China
44 G2 Lorraine reg. France
43 G5 Lorsch Ger.
43 F2 Lorup Ger.
22 C4 Losal India
73 F5 Los Alamos U.S.A.
91 B2 Los Andes Chile
91 B3 Los Angeles Chile
74 C5 Los Angeles CA U.S.A.
74 C4 Los Angeles Aqueduct canal U.S.A.
74 B3 Los Banos U.S.A.
88 D2 Los Blancos Arg.
88 B7 Los Chonos, Archipiélago de is Chile
74 D5 Los Coronados is Mex.
74 B3 Los Gatos U.S.A.
88 B8 Los Glaciares, Parque Nacional nat. park Arg.
42 E5 Losheim Ger.
48 F2 Lošinj i. Croatia
59 H2 Loskop Dam dam S. Africa
91 B4 Los Lagos div. Chile
73 F5 Los Lunas U.S.A.
84 C2 Los Mármoles, Parque Nacional nat. park Mex.
91 C4 Los Menucos Arg.
82 C3 Los Mochis Mex.
74 A1 Los Molinos U.S.A.
56 B3 Losombo Congo(Zaire)
84 B3 Los Reyes Mex.
89 D2 Los Roques, Islas is Venez.
42 E2 Losser Neth.
40 E3 Lossie r. U.K.
40 E3 Lossiemouth U.K.

43 L4 Lößnitz Ger.
89 C2 Los Taques Venez.
89 D2 Los Teques Venez.
89 E2 Los Testigos is Venez.
74 C4 Lost Hills U.S.A.
72 D2 Lost Trail Pass pass U.S.A.
39 C7 Lostwithiel U.K.
88 C2 Los Vientos Chile
91 B1 Los Vilos Chile
91 B3 Lota Chile
19 E2 Lotfābād Iran
59 J3 Lothair S. Africa
56 D3 Lotikipi Plain plain Kenya
56 C4 Loto Congo(Zaire)
50 E3 Lotoshino Rus. Fed.
59 G1 Lotsane r. Botswana
36 V2 Lotta r. Fin./Rus. Fed.
43 F2 Lotte Ger.
25 C4 Louang Namtha Laos
25 C5 Louangphrabang Laos
56 B4 Loubomo Congo
44 C2 Loudéac France
27 D5 Loudi China
56 B4 Loudima Congo
80 B4 Loudonville U.S.A.
54 A3 Louga Senegal
39 F5 Loughborough U.K.
39 C6 Loughor r. U.K.
41 C4 Loughrea Rep. of Ireland
39 H6 Loughton U.K.
80 B5 Louisa KY U.S.A.
80 E5 Louisa VA U.S.A.
41 B4 Louisburgh Rep. of Ireland
64 C4 Louise I. i. Can.
7 F3 Louisiade Archipelago is P.N.G.
77 E6 Louisiana div. U.S.A.
59 H1 Louis Trichardt S. Africa
79 D5 Louisville GA U.S.A.
78 C4 Louisville KY U.S.A.
77 F5 Louisville MS U.S.A.
66 E3 Louis-XIV, Pointe c. Can.
12 E3 Loukhi Rus. Fed.
45 B4 Loulé Port.
65 L4 Lount L. l. Can.
46 F5 Louny Czech Rep.
76 D3 Loup r. U.S.A.
66 F2 Loups Marins, Lacs des l. Can.
67 J4 Lourdes Can.
44 D5 Lourdes France
45 B2 Lousã Port.
30 E1 Loushan China
39 G4 Louth U.K.
49 K5 Loutra Aidipsou Greece
Louvain see Leuven
58 B1 Louwater-Suid Namibia
59 J3 Louwsburg S. Africa
36 R4 Lövånger Sweden
50 D3 Lovat' r. Rus. Fed.
49 L3 Lovech Bulg.
72 F3 Loveland U.S.A.
72 E2 Lovell U.S.A.
74 C1 Lovelock U.S.A.
42 B3 Lovendegem Belgium
37 U6 Loviisa Fin.
80 D6 Lovingston U.S.A.
68 C6 Lovington IL U.S.A.
77 C5 Lovington NM U.S.A.
69 K3 Low Can.
56 C4 Lowa Congo(Zaire)
22 B2 Lowarai Pass pass Pak.
65 M2 Low, Cape c. Can.
81 H3 Lowell MA U.S.A.
68 E4 Lowell MI U.S.A.
81 G2 Lowell VT U.S.A.
64 F5 Lower Arrow L. l. Can.
75 F4 Lower Granite Gorge gorge U.S.A.
9 E4 Lower Hutt N.Z.
74 A2 Lower Lake U.S.A.
41 D3 Lower Lough Erne l. U.K.
32 □ Lower Peirce Res. resr Sing.
64 D3 Lower Post Can.
67 H5 Lower Sackville Can.
39 J5 Lowestoft U.K.
47 J4 Łowicz Pol.
66 E3 Low, Lac l. Can.
40 E5 Lowther Hills h. U.K.
81 F3 Lowville U.S.A.
43 G1 Loxstedt Ger.
8 C3 Loxton Austr.
58 E5 Loxton S. Africa
80 E4 Loyalsock Creek r. U.S.A.
74 B2 Loyalton U.S.A.
Loyalty Is is see Loyauté, Îs
7 G4 Loyauté, Îs is New Caledonia
51 D5 Loyew Belarus
49 H2 Loznica Yugo.
51 F5 Lozova Ukr.
55 C5 Luacano Angola
26 E4 Lu'an China
26 D3 Luanchuan China
57 B4 Luanda Angola
32 A3 Luang, Khao mt Thai.
57 D5 Luangwa r. Zambia
23 H2 Luanhaizi China
26 F1 Luan He r. China
26 F2 Luannan China
26 E1 Luanping China
57 C5 Luanshya Zambia
26 F2 Luan Xian China
57 C4 Luanza Congo(Zaire)
45 C1 Luarca Spain
33 D2 Luar, Danau l. Indon.
57 C5 Luau Angola
47 L5 Lubaczów Pol.
37 U8 Lubānas l. Latvia
31 B3 Lubang Phil.
31 B3 Lubang i. Phil.
31 A3 Lubang Islands is Phil.
57 B5 Lubango Angola
56 C4 Lubao Congo(Zaire)
47 L5 Lubartów Pol.
43 G2 Lübbecke Ger.
58 C4 Lubbeskolk salt pan S. Africa
77 C5 Lubbock U.S.A.
43 K2 Lübbow Ger.
43 J1 Lübeck Ger.
47 L5 Lubelska, Wyżyna reg. Pol.
56 C4 Lubero Congo(Zaire)
46 H5 Lubin Pol.
47 L5 Lublin Pol.
51 E5 Lubny Ukr.
33 D2 Lubok Antu Malaysia
43 K1 Lübstorf Ger.
43 K1 Lübtheen Ger.
31 B2 Lubuagan Phil.
57 C4 Lubudi Congo(Zaire)
33 B3 Lubuklinggau Indon.
32 A5 Lubukpakam Indon.
57 C5 Lubumbashi Congo(Zaire)
57 C5 Lubungu Zambia
56 C4 Lubutu Congo(Zaire)
43 L1 Lübz Ger.
57 B4 Lucala Angola
41 E4 Lucan Rep. of Ireland
64 A2 Lucania, Mt mt Can.
57 C4 Lucapa Angola
79 E7 Lucaya Bahamas
48 D3 Lucca Italy
40 D6 Luce Bay b. U.K.
90 B3 Lucélia Brazil
31 B3 Lucena Phil.
45 D4 Lucena Spain
47 J6 Lučenec Slovakia
48 F4 Lucera Italy
Lucerne see Luzern
28 D1 Luchegorsk Rus. Fed.
27 D6 Luchuan China
27 B6 Lüchun China
8 C4 Lucindale Austr.
57 B5 Lucira Angola
23 F4 Luckeesarai India
43 M2 Luckenwalde Ger.
58 F4 Luckhoff S. Africa
69 G4 Lucknow Can.
22 E4 Lucknow India
57 C5 Lucusse Angola
50 F1 Luda Rus. Fed.
42 F3 Lüdenscheid Ger.
57 B6 Lüderitz Namibia
43 J1 Lüdersdorf Ger.
22 C3 Ludhiana India
27 B5 Ludian China
68 D4 Ludington U.S.A.
39 E5 Ludlow U.K.
74 D4 Ludlow CA U.S.A.
81 J1 Ludlow ME U.S.A.
81 G3 Ludlow VT U.S.A.
49 M3 Ludogorie reg. Bulg.
37 O6 Ludvika Sweden
43 H6 Ludwigsburg Ger.
43 M2 Ludwigsfelde Ger.
43 G5 Ludwigshafen am Rhein Ger.
43 K1 Ludwigslust Ger
37 U8 Ludza Latvia
56 C4 Luebo Congo(Zaire)
57 B5 Luena Angola
89 E3 Luepa Venez.
26 C3 Lüeyang China
27 E6 Lufeng China
77 E6 Lufkin U.S.A.
50 D3 Luga Rus. Fed.
50 D3 Luga r. Rus. Fed.
48 C1 Lugano Switz.
43 L4 Lugau Ger.
43 H3 Lügde Ger.
57 D5 Lugenda r. Moz.
39 D5 Lugg r. U.K.
48 D2 Lugo Italy
45 C1 Lugo Spain
49 J2 Lugoj Romania
31 B5 Lugus i. Phil.
51 F5 Luhans'k Ukr.
26 F3 Luhe China
43 J1 Luhe r. Ger.
23 H4 Luhit r. India
57 D4 Luhombero Tanz.
51 D5 Luhyny Ukr.
57 C5 Luiana Angola
Luik see Liège
56 C4 Luilaka r. Congo(Zaire)
40 C4 Luing i. U.K.
48 C2 Luino Italy
36 U3 Luiro r. Fin.
84 B2 Luis Moya Mex.
56 C4 Luiza Congo(Zaire)
91 E2 Lujan r. Arg.
91 C2 Luján de Cuyo Arg.
26 E4 Lujiang China
49 H2 Lukavac Bos.-Herz.
56 C4 Lukenie r. Congo(Zaire)
75 F6 Lukeville U.S.A.
50 G3 Lukh r. Rus. Fed.
50 F4 Lukhovitsy Rus. Fed.
49 L3 Lukovit Bulg.
47 L5 Łuków Pol.
50 H4 Lukoyanov Rus. Fed.
57 C5 Lukulu Zambia
57 D4 Lukumburu Tanz.
36 S4 Luleå Sweden
36 R4 Luleälven r. Sweden
16 A1 Lüleburgaz Turkey
27 B5 Luliang China
26 D2 Lüliang Shan mts China
77 D6 Luling U.S.A.
26 F2 Lulong China
23 F3 Lülung China
23 F3 Lumachomo China
33 D4 Lumajang Indon.
23 E2 Lumajangdong Co salt l. China
57 C5 Lumbala Kaquengue Angola
57 C5 Lumbala N'guimbo Angola
79 E5 Lumberton U.S.A.
45 C2 Lumbrales Spain
23 H4 Lumding India
36 T4 Lumijoki Fin.
32 C2 Lumphăt Cambodia
9 B6 Lumsden N.Z.
33 C3 Lumut, Tanjung pt Indon.
31 B2 Luna Phil.
75 H5 Luna U.S.A.
40 F4 Lunan Bay b. U.K.
65 L2 Lunan Lake l. Can.
69 F5 Luna Pier U.S.A.
22 C5 Lunavada India
22 B4 Lund Pak.
37 N9 Lund Sweden
72 E4 Lund U.S.A.
65 K4 Lundar Can.
57 D5 Lundazi Zambia
39 C6 Lundy Island i. U.K.
38 E3 Lune r. U.K.
43 J1 Lüneburg Ger.
43 J1 Lüneburger Heide reg. Ger.
42 F3 Lünen Ger.
44 H2 Lunéville France
57 C5 Lunga r. Zambia
23 E2 Lungdo China
23 E3 Lunggar China
54 A4 Lungi Sierra Leone
27 □ Lung Kwu Chau h. H.K. China
23 H5 Lunglei India
41 E5 Lungnaquilla Mountain mt Rep. of Ireland
57 C5 Lungwebungu r. Zambia
22 C4 Luni India
22 C4 Luni r. India
22 B3 Luni r. Pak.
74 C2 Luning U.S.A.
50 H4 Lunino Rus. Fed.
51 C4 Luninyets Belarus
22 C1 Lunkho mt Afgh./Pak.
42 F2 Lünne Ger.
54 A4 Lunsar Sierra Leone
59 H2 Lunsklip S. Africa
15 G2 Luntai China
26 D3 Luo r. Henan China
26 C3 Luo r. Shaanxi China
27 C5 Luocheng China
26 C3 Luochuan China
27 C5 Luodian China
27 D6 Luoding China
27 D6 Luodou Sha i. China
26 E3 Luohe China
26 D3 Luoning China
27 B5 Luoping China
26 E3 Luoshan China
27 E4 Luotian China
26 D3 Luoyang China
27 F5 Luoyuan China
30 F2 Luozigou China
57 C5 Lupane Zimbabwe
33 D2 Lupar r. Malaysia
49 K2 Lupeni Romania
57 D5 Lupilichi Moz.
31 C5 Lupon Phil.
75 H4 Lupton U.S.A.
26 B3 Luqu China
27 B5 Luquan China
17 K3 Lūrā Shīrīn Iran
57 B4 Luremo Angola
40 C2 Lurgainn, Loch l. U.K.
41 E3 Lurgan U.K.
57 E5 Lúrio Moz.
57 D5 Lurio r. Moz.
57 C5 Lusaka Zambia
56 C4 Lusambo Congo(Zaire)
6 F2 Lusancay Islands and Reefs is P.N.G.
64 F4 Luscar Can.
65 H4 Luseland Can.
26 D3 Lushi China
49 H4 Lushnjë Albania
30 D2 Lushuihe China
30 A4 Lüshun China
59 H5 Lusikisiki S. Africa
72 F3 Lusk U.S.A.
18 E4 Lut, Dasht-e des. Iran
69 G4 Luther Lake l. Can.
43 L3 Lutherstadt Wittenberg Ger.
39 G6 Luton U.K.
33 D2 Lutong Malaysia
65 G2 Łutselk'e Can.
51 C5 Luts'k Ukr.
42 D2 Luttelgeest Neth.
42 E2 Luttenberg Neth.
43 H5 Lützelbach Ger.
92 D4 Lützow-Holmbukta b. Ant.
58 D4 Lutzputs S. Africa
58 C5 Lutzville S. Africa
31 B5 Luuk Phil.
37 U6 Luumäki Fin.
56 E3 Luuq Somalia
76 D3 Luverne U.S.A.
56 C4 Luvua r. Congo(Zaire)
59 J1 Luvuvhu r. S. Africa
56 D3 Luwero Uganda
42 E5 Luxembourg Lux.
34 F4 Luxembourg country Europe
44 H3 Luxeuil-les-Bains France
27 D4 Luxi Hunan China
27 B5 Luxi Yunnan China
59 F5 Luxolweni S. Africa
55 F2 Luxor Egypt
26 E3 Luyi China
42 D3 Luyksgestel Neth.
50 H2 Luza Rus. Fed.
50 J2 Luza r. Rus. Fed.
46 D7 Luzern Switz.
27 C5 Luzhai China
27 B5 Luzhi China
27 B4 Luzhou China
90 C2 Luziânia Brazil
87 K4 Luzilândia Brazil
31 B3 Luzon i. Phil.
31 B1 Luzon Strait str. Phil.
44 F3 Luzy France
51 C5 L'viv Ukr.
L'vov see L'viv
50 D3 Lyady Rus. Fed.
50 C4 Lyakhavichy Belarus
64 G5 Lyall, Mt mt Can.
Lyallpur see Faisalabad
36 Q4 Lycksele Sweden
39 H7 Lydd U.K.
92 C3 Lyddan I. i. Ant.
59 J2 Lydenburg S. Africa
39 E6 Lydney U.K.
51 D5 Lyel'chytsy Belarus
64 C4 Lyell I. i. Can.
74 C3 Lyell, Mt mt U.S.A.
50 D4 Lyepyel' Belarus
80 E4 Lykens U.S.A.
72 E3 Lyman U.S.A.
39 E7 Lyme Bay b. U.K.
39 E7 Lyme Regis U.K.
39 F7 Lymington U.K.
80 D6 Lynchburg U.S.A.
81 H2 Lynchville U.S.A.
8 G2 Lyndhurst Austr.
81 G2 Lyndonville U.S.A.
40 E2 Lyness U.K.
37 K7 Lyngdal Norway
81 H3 Lynn U.S.A.
64 B3 Lynn Canal chan. U.S.A.
75 F2 Lynndyl U.S.A.
65 J3 Lynn Lake Can.
39 D6 Lynton U.K.
65 H2 Lynx Lake l. Can.
44 G4 Lyon France
81 G2 Lyon Mountain U.S.A.
79 D5 Lyons GA U.S.A.
80 E3 Lyons NY U.S.A.
81 F3 Lyons Falls U.S.A.
50 D4 Lyozna Belarus
7 F2 Lyra Reef rf P.N.G.
37 M7 Lysekil Sweden
50 H3 Lyskovo Rus. Fed.
12 G4 Lys'va Rus. Fed.
51 F5 Lysychans'k Ukr.
38 D4 Lytham St Anne's U.K.
64 E4 Lytton Can.
50 D4 Lyuban' Belarus
51 C5 Lyubeshiv Ukr.
50 E4 Lyudinovo Rus. Fed.
50 H3 Lyunda r. Rus. Fed.

M

57 C5 Maamba Zambia
16 E6 Ma'an Jordan
36 U5 Maaninka Fin.
36 V3 Maaninkavaara Fin.
26 F4 Ma'anshan China
37 T7 Maardu Estonia
16 F4 Ma'arrat an Nu'mān Syria
42 D2 Maarssen Neth.
42 E3 Maas r. Neth.
42 D3 Maaseik Belgium
31 C4 Maasin Phil.
42 D4 Maasmechelen Belgium
42 D4 Maastricht Neth.
59 H1 Maastroom S. Africa
31 B3 Mabalacat Phil.
57 D6 Mabalane Moz.
86 G2 Mabaruma Guyana
69 J3 Maberly Can.
27 B4 Mabian China
39 H4 Mablethorpe U.K.
59 H2 Mabopane S. Africa
57 D6 Mabote Moz.
31 B1 Mabudis i. Phil.
58 F2 Mabule Botswana
58 E2 Mabutsane Botswana
91 D3 Macachín Arg.
81 K2 McAdam Can.
90 E3 Macaé Brazil
31 C4 Macajalar Bay b. Phil.
77 E5 McAlester U.S.A.
80 E4 McAlevys Fort U.S.A.
8 G3 McAlister mt Austr.
8 F4 Macalister r. Austr.
77 D7 McAllen U.S.A.
57 D5 Macaloge Moz.
62 H3 MacAlpine Lake l. Can.
88 B7 Macá, Mt mt Chile
59 K1 Macandze Moz.
87 H3 Macapá Brazil
86 C4 Macará Ecuador
90 E1 Macarani Brazil
89 B4 Macarena, Cordillera mts Col.
89 B4 Macarena, Parque Nacional La nat. park Col.
8 D5 Macarthur Austr.
80 B5 McArthur U.S.A.
69 J3 McArthur Mills Can.
64 B2 McArthur Wildlife Sanctuary res. Can.
86 C4 Macas Ecuador
33 E3 Macassar Strait str. Indon.
87 L5 Macau Brazil
27 D6 Macau Macau
87 H6 Macaúba Brazil
90 D1 Macaúbas Brazil
89 B4 Macaya r. Col.
89 B4 Macayari Col.
64 E4 McBride Can.
72 C2 McCall U.S.A.
77 C6 McCamey U.S.A.
72 D3 McCammon U.S.A.
59 K2 Maccaretane Moz.
64 C4 McCauley I. i. Can.
39 E4 Macclesfield U.K.
62 H2 McClintock Chan. Can.
74 B3 McClure, L. l. U.S.A.
62 F2 McClure Strait Can.
77 F6 McComb U.S.A.
76 C3 McConaughy, L. l. U.S.A.
80 E5 McConnellsburg U.S.A.
80 C5 McConnelsville U.S.A.
76 C3 McCook U.S.A.
65 K4 McCreary Can.
75 E4 McCullough Range mts U.S.A.
64 D3 McDame Can.
72 C3 McDermitt U.S.A.
6 C4 Macdonald, L. salt flat Austr.
72 D2 McDonald Peak summit U.S.A.
6 D4 Macdonnell Ranges mts Austr.
58 B4 McDougall's Bay b. S. Africa
66 B3 MacDowell L. l. Can.
75 G5 McDowell Peak summit U.S.A.
40 F3 Macduff U.K.
45 C2 Macedo de Cavaleiros Port.
8 E4 Macedon mt Austr.
35 H4 Macedonia country Europe
87 L5 Maceió Brazil
54 B4 Macenta Guinea
48 E3 Macerata Italy
74 C4 McFarland U.S.A.
65 H3 McFarlane r. Can.
6 D5 Macfarlane, L. salt flat Austr.
75 E2 McGill U.S.A.
41 B6 Macgillycuddy's Reeks mts Rep. of Ireland
62 C3 McGrath U.S.A.
58 C6 McGregor S. Africa
68 A2 McGregor U.S.A.
64 E4 McGregor r. Can.
69 G2 McGregor Bay Can.
72 D2 McGuire, Mt mt U.S.A.
22 A3 Mach Pak.
86 C4 Machachi Ecuador
90 D3 Machado Brazil
57 D6 Machaila Moz.
56 D4 Machakos Kenya
86 C4 Machala Ecuador
57 D6 Machanga Moz.
59 E2 Machatuine Moz.
42 C5 Machault France
26 E4 Macheng China
21 B2 Macherla India
21 C2 Māchhakund Dam dam India
81 K2 Machias ME U.S.A.
80 D3 Machias NY U.S.A.
81 J1 Machias r. U.S.A.
21 C2 Machilipatnam India
89 B2 Machiques Venez.
40 C5 Machrihanish U.K.
39 D5 Machynlleth U.K.
59 K2 Macia Moz.
49 N2 Măcin Romania
81 G2 McIndoe Falls U.S.A.
76 C2 McIntosh U.S.A.
75 H2 Mack U.S.A.
17 G1 Maçka Turkey
6 E4 Mackay Austr.
72 D2 Mackay U.S.A.
65 G2 Mackay Lake l. Can.
6 C4 Mackay, Lake salt flat Austr.
7 J2 McKean Island i. Kiribati
80 A6 McKee U.S.A.
80 D4 McKeesport U.S.A.
81 F3 McKeever U.S.A.
64 E3 Mackenzie B.C. Can.
68 C1 Mackenzie Ont. Can.
79 E4 McKenzie U.S.A.
62 E3 Mackenzie r. Can.
92 D5 Mackenzie Bay b. Ant.
62 E3 Mackenzie Bay b. Y.T. Can.
64 F2 Mackenzie Bison Sanctuary res. Can.
62 G2 Mackenzie King I. Can.
64 C2 Mackenzie Mountains mts Can.
62 E3 Mackenzie Mts Can.
68 E3 Mackinac I. i. U.S.A.
68 E3 Mackinac, Straits of chan. U.S.A.
68 C5 Mackinaw r. U.S.A.
68 E3 Mackinaw City U.S.A.
62 C3 McKinley, Mt U.S.A.
77 C5 McKinney U.S.A.
92 B2 Mackintosh, C. c. Ant.
74 C4 McKittrick U.S.A.
65 H4 Macklin Can.
7 F5 Macksville Austr.
76 C2 McLaughlin U.S.A.
59 H5 Maclear S. Africa
64 F3 McLennan Can.
64 F4 McLeod r. Can.
64 E3 McLeod Lake Can.
6 B4 Macleod, Lake l. Austr.
72 B3 McLoughlin, Mt mt U.S.A.
68 E2 McMillan U.S.A.
64 C2 Macmillan r. Can.
72 B2 McMinnville OR U.S.A.
79 C5 McMinnville TN U.S.A.
92 B5 McMurdo U.S.A. Base Ant.
75 H4 McNary U.S.A.
64 F4 McNaughton Lake l. Can.
75 H6 McNeal U.S.A.
68 B5 Macomb U.S.A.
48 C4 Macomer Sardinia Italy
44 G3 Mâcon France
79 D5 Macon GA U.S.A.
76 E4 Macon MO U.S.A.
57 C5 Macondo Angola
76 D4 McPherson U.S.A.
8 F1 Macquarie r. Austr.
6 E6 Macquarie Harbour in. Austr.
4 G10 Macquarie Island i. Austr.
8 H2 Macquarie, L. b. Austr.
8 F1 Macquarie Marshes marsh Austr.
8 G2 Macquarie Mt mt Austr.
94 F9 Macquarie Ridge sea feature Pac. Oc.
64 B2 McQuesten r. Can.
79 D5 McRae U.S.A.
32 □ MacRitchie Res. resr Sing.
92 D4 Mac. Robertson Land reg. Ant.
41 C6 Macroom Rep. of Ireland
89 C1 Macuira, Parque Nacional nat. park Col.
89 B4 Macuje Col.
6 D4 Macumba watercourse Austr.
86 D6 Macusani Peru
84 D3 Macuspana Mex.
70 E6 Macuzari, Presa resr Mex.
64 E1 McVicar Arm b. Can.
81 J2 Macwahoc U.S.A.
16 E6 Mādabā Jordan
59 J3 Madadeni S. Africa
53 J8 Madagascar country Africa
93 H5 Madagascar Basin sea feature Ind. Ocean
93 G6 Madagascar Ridge sea feature Ind. Ocean
21 B3 Madakasira India
55 D2 Madama Niger
49 L4 Madan Bulg.
21 B3 Madanapalle India
6 E2 Madang P.N.G.
54 C3 Madaoua Niger
23 G5 Madaripur Bangl.
69 J3 Madawaska Can.
81 J1 Madawaska U.S.A.
69 J3 Madawaska r. Can.
86 F5 Madeira r. Brazil
34 D5 Madeira terr. Port.
67 H4 Madeleine, Îles de la is Can.
68 B2 Madeline I. i. U.S.A.
17 G2 Maden Turkey
82 C3 Madera Mex.
74 B3 Madera U.S.A.
21 A3 Madgaon India
23 F4 Madhepura India
21 C2 Madhira India
23 F4 Madhubani India
22 D5 Madhya Pradesh div. India
59 F3 Madibogo S. Africa
21 A3 Madikeri India
56 B4 Madingou Congo
86 E6 Madini r. Bol.
57 E5 Madirovalo Madag.
78 C4 Madison IN U.S.A.
81 J2 Madison ME U.S.A.
76 D2 Madison MN U.S.A.
76 D3 Madison NE U.S.A.
76 D2 Madison SD U.S.A.
68 C4 Madison WI U.S.A.
80 C5 Madison WV U.S.A.
70 D2 Madison r. MT U.S.A.
78 C4 Madisonville KY U.S.A.
77 E6 Madisonville TX U.S.A.
33 D4 Madiun Indon.
69 J3 Madoc Can.
56 D3 Mado Gashi Kenya
24 B3 Madoi China
37 U8 Madona Latvia
22 B4 Madpura India
49 M5 Madra Dağı mts Turkey
21 C3 Madras India
72 B2 Madras U.S.A.
86 D6 Madre de Dios r. Peru
88 A8 Madre de Dios, I. i. Chile
84 B3 Madre del Sur, Sierra mts Mex.
84 C1 Madre, Laguna lag. Mex.
77 D7 Madre, Laguna lag. U.S.A.
84 A1 Madre Occidental, Sierra mts Mex.
84 B1 Madre Oriental, Sierra mts Mex.
31 B2 Madre, Sierra mt Phil.
84 D3 Madre, Sierra mts Mex.
31 C4 Madrid Phil.
45 E2 Madrid Spain
31 B4 Madridejos Phil.
45 E3 Madridejos Spain
21 C2 Madugula India
33 D4 Madura i. Indon.
21 B4 Madurai India
33 D4 Madura, Selat chan. Indon.
23 E4 Madwas India
22 C2 Madyan Pak.
51 H7 Madzhalis Rus. Fed.
29 F6 Maebashi Japan
32 A1 Mae Hong Son Thai.
32 A1 Mae Khlong r. Thai.
32 A1 Mae Lao r. Thai.
32 A1 Mae Li r. Thai.
32 B1 Mae Nam Ing r. Thai.
32 C2 Mae Nam Mun r. Thai.
32 B2 Mae Nam Nan r. Thai.
32 B2 Mae Nam Pa Sak r. Thai.
32 B2 Mae Nam Ping r. Thai.
32 A1 Mae Nam Wang r. Thai.
32 B2 Mae Nam Yom r. Thai.
83 J5 Maestra, Sierra mts Cuba
57 E5 Maevatanana Madag.
7 G3 Maéwo i. Vanuatu
32 A1 Mae Yuam r. Myanmar/Thai.
65 J4 Mafeking Can.
59 G4 Mafeteng Lesotho
8 F4 Maffra Austr.
57 D4 Mafia I. i. Tanz.
59 F2 Mafikeng S. Africa
57 D4 Mafinga Tanz.
90 C4 Mafra Brazil
16 F5 Mafraq Jordan
59 J5 Magabeni S. Africa
13 R4 Magadan Rus. Fed.
56 D4 Magadi Kenya
59 K1 Magaiza Moz.
31 B3 Magallanes Phil.
88 B8 Magallanes, Estrecho de chan. Chile
89 B2 Magangue Col.
16 D3 Mağara Turkey
Magas see Zābolī
31 B2 Magat r. Phil.
91 F2 Magdalena Arg.
86 F6 Magdalena Bol.
82 B2 Magdalena Mex.
73 F5 Magdalena U.S.A.
89 B3 Magdalena r. Col.
70 D7 Magdalena, Bahía b. Mex.
88 B6 Magdalena, Isla i. Chile
31 A5 Magdaleno, Mt mt Malaysia
43 K2 Magdeburg Ger.
94 F4 Magellan Seamounts sea feature Pac. Oc.
36 T1 Magerøya i. Norway
29 B9 Mage-shima i. Japan
48 C2 Maggiorasca, Monte mt Italy
48 C2 Maggiore, Lago l. Italy
54 A3 Maghama Maur.
41 E3 Maghera U.K.
41 E3 Magherafelt U.K.
38 E4 Maghull U.K.
72 D3 Magna U.S.A.
48 F6 Magna Grande mt Sicily Italy
92 D4 Magnet Bay b. Ant.
6 E3 Magnetic I. i. Austr.
36 X2 Magnetity Rus. Fed.
12 G4 Magnitogorsk Rus. Fed.
77 E5 Magnolia U.S.A.
67 F4 Magog Can.
84 C2 Magosal Mex.
67 H3 Magpie Can.
68 E1 Magpie r. Can.
67 H3 Magpie L. l. Can.
68 E1 Magpie Lake l. Can.
64 G5 Magrath Can.
74 D3 Magruder Mt mt U.S.A.
54 A3 Magta' Lahjar Maur.
56 D4 Magu Tanz.
27 B6 Maguan China
87 J4 Maguarinho, Cabo pt Brazil
59 K2 Magude Moz.
81 K2 Magundy Can.
65 K2 Maguse Lake l. Can.
23 H5 Magwe Myanmar
23 H5 Magyichaung Myanmar
18 B2 Mahābād Iran
21 A2 Mahabaleshwar India
Mahabalipuram see Māmallapuram
23 F4 Mahabharat Range mts Nepal
57 E6 Mahabo Madag.
21 A2 Mahad India
22 D5 Mahadeo Hills h. India
56 D3 Mahagi Congo(Zaire)
22 C3 Mahajan India
57 E5 Mahajanga Madag.
33 D2 Mahakam r. Indon.
57 C6 Mahalapye Botswana
57 E5 Mahalevona Madag.
18 C3 Mahallāt Iran
22 D3 Maham India
33 D4 Mahameru, Gunung volc. Indon.
18 E4 Mahān Iran
23 F5 Mahanadi r. India
57 E5 Mahanoro Madag.
22 C6 Maharashtra div. India
23 E5 Mahasamund India
32 B1 Maha Sarakham Thai.
57 E6 Mahatalaky Madag.
57 E5 Mahavanona Madag.
57 E5 Mahavavy r. Madag.
21 C5 Mahaweli Ganga r. Sri Lanka
32 C1 Mahaxai Laos
21 C2 Mahbubabad India
21 B2 Mahbubnagar India
18 D5 Maḩḑah Oman
87 G2 Mahdia Guyana
48 D7 Mahdia Tunisia
53 K6 Mahé i. Seychelles
21 D2 Mahendragiri mt India
22 C5 Mahesāna India
22 C5 Maheshwar India
22 C5 Mahi r. India
19 E4 Māhī watercourse Iran
9 F3 Mahia Peninsula pen. N.Z.
50 D4 Mahilyow Belarus
21 C5 Mahiyangana Sri Lanka
59 J4 Mahlabatini S. Africa
43 K2 Mahlsdorf Ger.
19 H3 Maḩmūd-e 'Erāqī Afgh.
17 M4 Mahnīān Iran
76 D2 Mahnomen U.S.A.
22 D4 Mahoba India
45 J3 Mahón Spain
80 D4 Mahoning Creek Lake l. U.S.A.
23 H5 Mahudaung Hgts mts Myanmar
22 B5 Mahuva India
49 M4 Mahya Dağı mt Turkey
18 C3 Mahyār Iran
23 H4 Maibang India
89 B2 Maicao Col.
66 E4 Maicasagi, Lac l. Can.
27 C6 Maichen China
39 G6 Maidenhead U.K.
65 H4 Maidstone Can.
39 H6 Maidstone U.K.
55 D3 Maiduguri Nigeria
89 D3 Maigualida, Sierra mts Venez.
41 C5 Maigue r. Rep. of Ireland
22 E4 Maihar India
26 C3 Maiji Shan mt China
22 E5 Maikala Range h. India
56 C4 Maiko, Parc National de la nat. park Congo(Zaire)
22 E3 Mailani India
43 H5 Main r. Ger.
41 E3 Main r. U.K.
67 J3 Main Brook Can.
69 F3 Main Channel Can.
56 B4 Mai-Ndombe, Lac l. Congo(Zaire)
43 K5 Main-Donau-Kanal canal Ger.
69 J4 Main Duck I. i. Can.
81 J2 Maine div. U.S.A.
54 D3 Maïné-Soroa Niger
32 A2 Maingy I. i. Myanmar
43 H5 Mainhardt Ger.
31 C4 Mainit Phil.
31 C4 Mainit, Lake l. Phil.
40 E1 Mainland i. Orkney U.K.
40 □ Mainland i. Shetland U.K.
43 K4 Mainleus Ger.
23 E5 Mainpat reg. India
22 D4 Mainpuri India
57 E5 Maintirano Madag.
43 G4 Mainz Ger.
54 □ Maio i. Cape Verde
91 C2 Maipó, Vol. volc. Chile
91 F3 Maipú Buenos Aires Arg.
91 C2 Maipú Mendoza Arg.
89 D2 Maiquetía Venez.
23 G5 Maiskhal I. i. Bang.
57 C6 Maitengwe Botswana
8 H2 Maitland N.S.W. Austr.
8 A3 Maitland S.A. Austr.
92 D3 Maitri India Base Ant.
23 G3 Maizhokunggar China
83 H6 Maíz, Islas del is Nic.
29 D7 Maizuru Japan
49 H3 Maja Jezercë mt Albania
21 B2 Majalgaon India
89 E4 Majari r. Brazil
33 E3 Majene Indon.
18 C6 Majhūd well S. Arabia
56 D3 Majī Eth.
26 E2 Majia r. China
27 D6 Majiang China
Majorca i. see Mallorca
23 H4 Majuli I. i. India
95 G5 Majuro i. Pac. Oc.
59 G4 Majwemasweu S. Africa
56 B4 Makabana Congo
74 □ Makaha U.S.A.
25 D7 Makale Indon.
23 F4 Makalu, Mt mt China
56 C4 Makamba Burundi
15 G2 Makanchi Kazak.
74 □ Makapuu Hd hd U.S.A.
50 J2 Makar-Ib Rus. Fed.
48 G3 Makarska Croatia
14 D2 Makat Kazak.
59 K3 Makatini Flats lowland S. Africa
54 A4 Makeni Sierra Leone
57 C6 Makgadikgadi salt pan Botswana
51 H7 Makhachkala Rus. Fed.
16 G4 Makhfar al Ḩammām Syria
17 J4 Makhmūr Iraq
56 D4 Makindu Kenya
14 F1 Makinsk Kazak.
51 F5 Makiyivka Ukr.
Makkah see Mecca
67 J2 Makkovik Can.
67 J2 Makkovik, Cape c. Can.
42 D1 Makkum Neth.
49 J1 Makó Hungary
56 B3 Makokou Gabon
57 D4 Makongolosi Tanz.
58 E2 Makopong Botswana
56 B4 Makotipoko Congo
19 F5 Makran reg. Iran/Pak.
22 C4 Makrana India
Makran Coast Range mts see Talar-i-Band
23 E6 Makri India
49 L6 Makronisi i. Greece
50 E3 Maksatikha Rus. Fed.
28 E1 Maksimovka Rus. Fed.
19 F4 Maksotag Iran
18 B2 Mākū Iran
23 H4 Makum India
57 D4 Makumbako Tanz.
57 D5 Makunguwiro Tanz.
29 B9 Makurazaki Japan
54 C4 Makurdi Nigeria
18 D4 Makūyeh Iran
59 F3 Makwassie S. Africa
36 Q4 Malå Sweden
31 C5 Malabang Phil.
21 A3 Malabar Coast coastal area India
54 C4 Malabo Equatorial Guinea
31 A4 Malabuñgan Phil.
33 A2 Malacca, Strait of str. Indon./Malaysia
72 D3 Malad City U.S.A.
50 C4 Maladzyechna Belarus
45 D4 Málaga Spain
81 F5 Malaga NJ U.S.A.
73 F5 Malaga NM U.S.A.
7 G2 Malaita i. Solomon Is
55 F4 Malakal Sudan
21 C2 Malakanagiri India
7 G3 Malakula i. Vanuatu
22 C2 Malakwal Pak.
25 E7 Malamala Indon.
33 D4 Malang Indon.
57 B4 Malanje Angola
19 G5 Malan, Ras pt Pak.
91 C1 Malanzán, Sa de mts Arg.
21 B4 Malappuram India
83 H7 Mala, Pta pt Panama
37 P7 Mälaren l. Sweden
91 C2 Malargüe Arg.
69 H1 Malartic Can.
69 H1 Malartic, Lac l. Can
64 A3 Malaspina Glacier gl. U.S.A.
16 G2 Malatya Turkey
22 C3 Malaut India
17 L5 Malāvi Iran
31 A5 Malawali i. Malaysia
53 H6 Malawi country Africa
Malawi, Lake l. see Nyasa, Lake
50 E3 Malaya Vishera Rus. Fed.
31 C4 Malaybalay Phil.
18 C3 Malāyer Iran
11 M9 Malaysia country Asia
17 J2 Malazgirt Turkey
47 J3 Malbork Pol.
42 E5 Malborn Ger.
43 L1 Malchin Ger.
43 L1 Malchiner See l. Ger.
23 G4 Māldah India
42 B3 Maldegem Belgium
77 F4 Malden U.S.A.
5 M5 Malden I. i. Kiribati
93 J4 Maldive Ridge sea feature Ind. Ocean
10 J9 Maldives country Ind. Ocean
39 H6 Maldon U.K.
91 F2 Maldonado Uru.
10 J9 Male Maldives
49 K6 Maleas, Akra i. Greece
15 F6 Male Atoll Maldives
59 F4 Malebogo S. Africa
21 B2 Malegaon India
22 C5 Malegaon India
46 H6 Malé Karpaty h. Slovakia
17 L3 Malek Kandī Iran
56 B4 Malele Congo(Zaire)
57 D5 Malema Moz.
22 C3 Maler Kotla India
19 G3 Mālestān Afgh.
51 H7 Malgobek Rus. Fed.
36 P4 Malgomaj l. Sweden
18 B5 Malham S. Arabia
72 C3 Malheur L. l. U.S.A.

56 C4 Mali Congo(Zaire)
54 A3 Mali Guinea
52 D4 Mali country Africa
26 C3 Malian r. China
22 E4 Malihabad India
19 F4 Malik Naro mt Pak.
32 A2 Mali Kyun i. Myanmar
25 E7 Malili Indon.
33 C4 Malimping Indon.
84 C3 Malinche, Parque Nacional La nat. park Mex.
56 E4 Malindi Kenya
41 D2 Malin Head hd Rep. of Ireland
41 C3 Malin More Rep. of Ireland
28 D2 Malinovka r. Rus. Fed.
27 B6 Malipo China
48 F2 Mali Raginac mt Croatia
31 C5 Malita Phil.
32 A3 Maliwun Myanmar
22 B5 Maliya India
17 L5 Malkaili Iran
22 D5 Malkapur India
51 C7 Malkara Turkey
47 N4 Mal'kavichy Belarus
49 M4 Malko Tŭrnovo Bulg.
8 G4 Mallacoota Austr.
8 G4 Mallacoota Inlet Austr.
40 C4 Mallaig U.K.
8 B3 Mallala Austr.
8 D3 Mallee Cliffs Nat. Park Austr.
65 K2 Mallery Lake l. Can.
45 H3 Mallorca i. Spain
41 C5 Mallow Rep. of Ireland
39 D5 Mallwyd U.K.
36 M4 Malm Norway
36 R3 Malmberget Sweden
42 E4 Malmédy Belgium
58 C6 Malmesbury S. Africa
39 E6 Malmesbury U.K.
37 N9 Malmö Sweden
50 J3 Malmyzh Rus. Fed.
7 G3 Malo i. Vanuatu
31 B3 Malolos Phil.
81 F2 Malone U.S.A.
27 B5 Malong China
57 C5 Malonga Congo(Zaire)
50 F2 Maloshuyka Rus. Fed.
37 J6 Måløy Norway
50 F4 Maloyaroslavets Rus. Fed.
86 B3 Malpelo, Isla de i. Col.
21 A3 Malprabha r. India
37 U8 Malta Latvia
72 F1 Malta U.S.A.
34 G5 Malta country Europe
48 F6 Malta Channel Italy/Malta
57 B6 Maltahöhe Namibia
39 F4 Maltby U.K.
39 H4 Maltby le Marsh U.K.
38 G3 Malton U.K.
25 E7 Maluku is Indon.
37 N6 Malung Sweden
59 H4 Maluti Mountains mts Lesotho
7 G2 Malu'u Solomon Is
21 A2 Malvan India
77 E5 Malvern U.S.A.
Malvinas, Islas terr. see Falkland Islands
51 D5 Malyn Ukr.
13 S3 Malyy Anyuy r. Rus. Fed.
18 D2 Malyy Balkhan, Khrebet h. Turkm.
51 H6 Malyye Derbety Rus. Fed.
51 G7 Malyy Kavkaz mts Asia
13 Q2 Malyy Lyakhovskiy, Ostrov i. Rus. Fed.
51 J5 Malyy Uzen' r. Kazak./Rus. Fed.
13 Q3 Mama r. Rus. Fed.
59 H3 Mamafubedu S. Africa
21 C3 Māmallapuram India
31 A5 Mambahenauhan i. Phil.
31 C4 Mambajao Phil.
56 C3 Mambasa Congo(Zaire)
56 B3 Mambéré r. C.A.R.
31 B3 Mamburao Phil.
59 H2 Mamelodi S. Africa
54 C4 Mamfé Cameroon
75 G5 Mammoth U.S.A.
78 C4 Mammoth Cave Nat. Park U.S.A.
74 C3 Mammoth Lakes U.S.A.
86 E6 Mamoré r. Bol./Brazil
54 A3 Mamou Guinea
57 E5 Mampikony Madag.
54 B4 Mampong Ghana
91 B3 Mamuil Malal, P. pass Arg./Chile
33 E3 Mamuju Indon.
58 D1 Mamuno Botswana
54 B4 Man Côte d'Ivoire
89 B3 Manacacias r. Col.
86 F4 Manacapuru Brazil
45 H3 Manacor Spain
25 E6 Manadao Indon.
82 G6 Managua Nic.
82 G6 Managua, L. de l. Nic.
57 E6 Manakara Madag.
9 D5 Manakau mt N.Z.
6 E2 Manam I. i. P.N.G.
74 □1 Manana i. U.S.A.
57 E6 Mananara r. Madag.
57 E5 Mananara Avaratra Madag.
57 E5 Mananara, Parc National de nat. park Madag.
8 D3 Manangatang Austr.
57 E6 Mananjary Madag.
21 B4 Mānantavādi India
89 D2 Manapire r. Venez.
9 A6 Manapouri, L. l. N.Z.
57 E5 Manarantsandry Madag.
23 G4 Manas r. Bhutan
22 D3 Mana Shankou pass India
24 A2 Manas Hu l. China
23 F3 Manaslu mt Nepal
80 E5 Manassas U.S.A.
25 E7 Manatuto Indon.
86 F4 Manaus Brazil
16 C3 Manavgat Turkey
9 E4 Manawatu r. N.Z.
31 C5 Manay Phil.
16 F3 Manbij Syria
39 H4 Manby U.K.
68 E3 Mancelona U.S.A.
39 E4 Manchester U.K.
74 A2 Manchester CA U.S.A.
81 G4 Manchester CT U.S.A.
68 B4 Manchester IA U.S.A.
80 B6 Manchester KY U.S.A.
69 E4 Manchester MI U.S.A.
81 H3 Manchester NH U.S.A.
80 B5 Manchester OH U.S.A.
79 C5 Manchester TN U.S.A.
81 G3 Manchester VT U.S.A.
22 A4 Manchhar L. l. Pak.
16 F2 Mancılık Turkey
75 H3 Mancos U.S.A.
75 H3 Mancos r. U.S.A.
19 F5 Mand Pak.
18 D4 Mand r. Iran
57 E6 Mandabe Madag.
33 B2 Mandah Indon.
32 □ Mandai Sing.
19 F3 Mandal Afgh.
22 C4 Mandal India
37 K7 Mandal Norway
25 G7 Mandala, Pk mt Indon.
25 B4 Mandalay Myanmar
24 C2 Mandalgovĭ Mongolia
17 K5 Mandalī Iraq
26 D1 Mandalt Sum China
76 C2 Mandan U.S.A.
31 B3 Mandaon Phil.
55 D4 Manda, Parc National de nat. park Chad
55 D3 Mandara Mountains Cameroon/Nigeria
48 C5 Mandas Sardinia Italy
56 E3 Mandera Kenya
75 F2 Manderfield U.S.A.
42 E4 Manderscheid Ger.
83 J5 Mandeville Jamaica
9 B6 Mandeville N.Z.
22 B4 Mandha India
54 B3 Mandiana Guinea
22 C3 Mandi Burewala Pak.
57 D5 Mandié Moz.
57 D5 Mandimba Moz.
59 J4 Mandini S. Africa
23 F5 Mandira Dam dam India
22 E5 Mandla India
57 E5 Mandritsara Madag.
22 C4 Mandsaur India
31 A6 Mandul i. Indon.
6 B5 Mandurah Austr.
48 G4 Manduria Italy
22 B5 Mandvi Gujarat India
22 C5 Mandvi Gujarat India
21 B3 Mandya India
21 B2 Maner r. India
48 D2 Manerbio Italy
47 M5 Manevychi Ukr.
48 F4 Manfredonia Italy
48 G4 Manfredonia, Golfo di g. Italy
90 D1 Manga Brazil
54 B3 Manga Burkina
56 B4 Mangai Congo(Zaire)
5 M7 Mangaia i. Pac. Oc.
9 E3 Mangakino N.Z.
21 C2 Mangalagiri India
23 H4 Mangaldai India
49 N3 Mangalia Romania
21 A3 Mangalore India
21 A2 Mangalvedha India
23 G4 Mangan India
21 C2 Mangapet India
31 C6 Mangarang Indon.
59 G4 Mangaung S. Africa
9 E3 Mangaweka N.Z.
23 G4 Mangde r. Bhutan
41 B6 Mangerton Mt h. Rep. of Ireland
33 C3 Manggar Indon.
24 B3 Mangnai China
57 D5 Mangochi Malawi
25 E7 Mangole i. Indon.
39 E6 Mangotsfield U.K.
22 B5 Māngral India
79 E7 Mangrove Cay Bahamas
45 C2 Mangualde Port.
19 G4 Manguchar Pak.
91 G2 Mangueira, L. l. Brazil
90 B4 Mangueirinha Brazil
55 D2 Manguéni, Plateau du plat. Niger
24 E1 Mangui China
31 C5 Mangupung i. Indon.
14 D2 Mangyshlak Kazak.
76 D4 Manhattan KS U.S.A.
74 D2 Manhattan NV U.S.A.
57 D6 Manhica Moz.
59 K3 Manhoca Moz.
90 D3 Manhuaçu Brazil
90 E2 Manhuaçu r. Brazil
89 B3 Mani Col.
57 E5 Mania r. Madag.
48 E1 Maniago Italy
86 F5 Manicoré Brazil
67 G3 Manicouagan Can.
67 G3 Manicouagan r. Can.
67 G3 Manicouagan, Réservoir Can.
18 C5 Manīfah S. Arabia
5 L6 Manihiki i. Pac. Oc.
Manikgarh see Rajura
22 E4 Manikpur India
31 B3 Manila Phil.
72 E3 Manila U.S.A.
8 G2 Manildra Austr.
8 H1 Manilla Austr.
Manipur see Imphal
23 H4 Manipur div. India
49 M5 Manisa Turkey
17 L5 Manisht Kūh mt Iran
38 C3 Man, Isle of terr. Europe
68 D3 Manistee U.S.A.
68 E3 Manistee r. U.S.A.
68 D3 Manistique U.S.A.
68 E2 Manistique Lake l. U.S.A.
66 B2 Manitoba div. Can.
65 K4 Manitoba, Lake l. Can.
65 H4 Manito L. l. Can.
65 K5 Manitou Can.
80 E3 Manitou Beach U.S.A.
66 B3 Manitou Falls Can.
68 D2 Manitou Island i. U.S.A.
78 C2 Manitou Islands is U.S.A.
69 G3 Manitou, Lake l. Can.
69 F3 Manitoulin I. i. Can.
69 G3 Manitowaning Can.
66 D4 Manitowik Lake l. Can.
68 D3 Manitowoc U.S.A.
69 K2 Maniwaki Can.
89 B3 Manizales Col.
57 E6 Manja Madag.
59 K2 Manjacaze Moz.
21 B4 Manjeri India
30 D3 Man Jiang r. China
17 M3 Manjil Iran
21 B2 Manjra r. India
76 E2 Mankato U.S.A.
59 J3 Mankayane Swaziland
54 B4 Mankono Côte d'Ivoire
21 C4 Mankulam Sri Lanka
8 H2 Manly Austr.
22 C5 Manmad India
33 B3 Manna Indon.
8 B2 Mannahill Austr.
21 B4 Mannar Sri Lanka
15 F6 Mannar, Gulf of India/Sri Lanka
21 B4 Mannar, Gulf of g. India/Sri Lanka
21 B3 Manneru r. India
43 G5 Mannheim Ger.
41 A4 Mannin Bay b. Rep. of Ireland
64 F3 Manning Can.
79 D5 Manning U.S.A.
39 J6 Manningtree U.K.
48 C4 Mannu, Capo pt Sardinia Italy
8 B3 Mannum Austr.
25 F7 Manokwari Indon.
56 C4 Manono Congo(Zaire)
32 A3 Manoron Myanmar
44 G5 Manosque France
63 L4 Manouane Lake l. Can.
30 D3 Manp'o N. Korea
7 J2 Manra i. Kiribati
45 G2 Manresa Spain
22 C3 Mansa India
57 C5 Mansa Zambia
54 A3 Mansa Konko The Gambia
22 C2 Mansehra Pak.
63 L3 Mansel Island i. Can.
8 F4 Mansfield Austr.
39 F4 Mansfield U.K.
77 E5 Mansfield LA U.S.A.
80 B4 Mansfield OH U.S.A.
80 E4 Mansfield PA U.S.A.
87 H6 Manso r. Brazil
64 E3 Manson Creek Can.
17 M6 Manşūrī Iran
16 E3 Mansurlu Turkey
86 B4 Manta Ecuador
86 B4 Manta, B. de b. Ecuador
31 A4 Mantalingajan, Mount mt Phil.
30 E3 Mantapsan mt N. Korea
74 B3 Manteca U.S.A.
89 C3 Mantecal Venez.
43 L5 Mantel Ger.
79 F5 Manteo U.S.A.
44 E2 Mantes-la-Jolie France
21 B2 Manthani India
75 G2 Manti U.S.A.
90 D3 Mantiqueira, Serra da mts Brazil
68 E3 Manton U.S.A.
48 D2 Mantova Italy
37 T6 Mäntsälä Fin.
37 T5 Mänttä Fin.
Mantua see Mantova
50 H3 Manturovo Rus. Fed.
37 U6 Mäntyharju Fin.
36 U3 Mäntyjärvi Fin.
5 L6 Manua Islands is Pac. Oc.
75 H4 Manuelito U.S.A.
91 F2 Manuel J. Cobo Arg.
90 E1 Manuel Vitorino Brazil
87 H5 Manuelzinho Brazil
25 E7 Manui i. Indon.
19 E5 Manūjān Iran
31 B4 Manukan Phil.
9 E2 Manukau N.Z.
9 E2 Manukau Harbour in. N.Z.
31 A5 Manuk Manka i. Phil.
8 B2 Manunda r. Austr.
86 D6 Manu, Parque Nacional nat. park Peru
6 E2 Manus I. i. P.N.G.
21 B3 Manvi India
59 F2 Manyana Botswana
51 G6 Manych-Gudilo, Ozero l. Rus. Fed.
75 H3 Many Farms U.S.A.
56 D4 Manyoni Tanz.
16 D6 Manzala, Bahra el l. Egypt
45 E3 Manzanares Spain
83 J4 Manzanillo Cuba
84 A3 Manzanillo Mex.
18 C3 Manzariyeh Iran
24 D2 Manzhouli China
59 J3 Manzini Swaziland
55 D3 Mao Chad
Maó see Mahón
26 D4 Maocifan China
26 C2 Maojiachuan China
59 G3 Maokeng S. Africa
25 F7 Maoke, Pegunungan mts Indon.
30 B3 Maokui Shan h. China
30 B2 Maolin China
26 B2 Maomao Shan mt China
27 D6 Maoming China
27 □ Ma On Shan h. H.K. China
57 D6 Mapai Moz.
22 E3 Mapam Yumco l. China
59 F5 Maphodi S. Africa
84 B1 Mapimí Mex.
31 A5 Mapin i. Phil.
57 D6 Mapinhane Moz.
89 D3 Mapire Venez.
68 E4 Maple r. U.S.A.
65 H5 Maple Creek Can.
59 G4 Mapoteng Lesotho
87 G4 Mapuera r. Brazil
59 K2 Mapulanguene Moz.
57 D6 Maputo Moz.
59 K2 Maputo div. Moz.
59 K3 Maputo r. Moz.
59 G4 Maputsoe Lesotho
17 H6 Maqar an Na'am well Iraq
26 B3 Maqu China
23 E3 Maquan He r. China
56 B4 Maquela do Zombo Angola
91 C4 Maquinchao Arg.
91 C4 Maquinchao r. Arg.
68 B4 Maquoketa U.S.A.
68 B4 Maquoketa r. U.S.A.
19 G5 Mar r. Pak.
23 E5 Māra India
59 H1 Mara S. Africa
89 C2 Mara Venez.
65 H1 Mara r. Can.
86 E4 Maraã Brazil
87 J5 Maraba Brazil
89 C2 Maracaibo Venez.
89 C2 Maracaibo, Lago de l. Venez.
87 H3 Maracá, Ilha de i. Brazil
90 A3 Maracaju Brazil
90 A3 Maracaju, Serra de h. Brazil
90 E1 Maracás, Chapada de reg. Brazil
89 D2 Maracay Venez.
55 D2 Marādah Libya
54 C3 Maradi Niger
18 B2 Marāgheh Iran
90 E1 Maragogipe Brazil
31 B3 Maragondon Phil.
89 D4 Marahuaca, Co mt Venez.
87 J4 Marajó, Baía de est. Brazil
87 J3 Marajó, Ilha de i. Brazil
21 B3 Marakkanam India
56 D3 Maralal Kenya
22 C2 Marala Weir barrage Pak.
17 J1 Maralik Armenia
6 D5 Maralinga Austr.
7 G2 Maramasike i. Solomon Is
31 C5 Marampit i. Indon.
19 G4 Maran mt Pak.
17 K4 Marāna Iraq
75 G5 Marana U.S.A.
18 B2 Marand Iran
32 B4 Marang Malaysia
32 A3 Marang Myanmar
90 C1 Maranhão r. Brazil
86 D4 Marañón r. Peru
59 L2 Marão Moz.
45 C2 Marão mt Port.
89 D4 Marari r. Brazil
9 A6 Mararoa r. N.Z.
68 D1 Marathon Can.
79 D7 Marathon FL U.S.A.
77 C6 Marathon TX U.S.A.
90 E1 Maraú Brazil
33 D3 Marau Indon.
89 D4 Marauiá r. Brazil
31 C4 Marawi Phil.
17 M1 Märäzä Azer.
45 D4 Marbella Spain
6 B4 Marble Bar Austr.
75 G3 Marble Canyon U.S.A.
75 G3 Marble Canyon gorge U.S.A.
59 H2 Marble Hall S. Africa
81 H3 Marblehead U.S.A.
65 L2 Marble I. i. Can.
59 J5 Marburg S. Africa
43 G4 Marburg an der Lahn Ger.
80 E5 Marburg, Lake l. U.S.A.
46 H7 Marcali Hungary
39 H5 March U.K.
8 B2 Marchant Hill h. Austr.
42 D4 Marche-en-Famenne Belgium
45 D4 Marchena Spain
86 □ Marchena, Isla i. Galapagos Is Ecuador
91 D1 Mar Chiquita, L. l. Arg.
46 G6 Marchtrenk Austria
79 D7 Marco U.S.A.
42 B4 Marcoing France
66 E2 Marcopeet Islands is Can.
91 D2 Marcos Juárez Arg.
81 G2 Marcy, Mt mt U.S.A.
22 C2 Mardan Pak.
91 F3 Mar del Plata Arg.
17 H3 Mardin Turkey
7 G4 Maré i. New Caledonia
40 C3 Maree, Loch l. U.K.
68 A5 Marengo IA U.S.A.
68 C4 Marengo IL U.S.A.
48 E6 Marettimo, Isola i. Sicily Italy
50 E3 Marevo Rus. Fed.
77 B6 Marfa U.S.A.
23 F2 Margai Caka salt l. China
6 B5 Margaret River Austr.
89 E2 Margarita, Isla de i. Venez.
28 D3 Margaritovo Rus. Fed.
59 J5 Margate S. Africa
39 J6 Margate U.K.
19 F4 Margo, Dasht-i des. Afgh.
31 B5 Margosatubig Phil.
42 D4 Margraten Neth.
68 E3 Margrethe, Lake l. U.S.A.
64 E4 Marguerite Can.
92 B2 Marguerite Bay b. Ant.
23 G3 Margyang China
17 L5 Marhaj Khalīl Iraq
17 J3 Marhan D. h. Iraq
51 E6 Marhanets' Ukr.
88 C2 María Elena Chile
6 D3 Maria I. i. Austr.
91 E3 María Ignacia Arg.
95 J7 Maria, Îles is Pac. Oc.
94 E4 Marianas Ridge sea feature Pac. Oc.
94 E5 Marianas Tr. sea feature Pac. Oc.
23 H4 Mariani India
64 F2 Marian Lake l. Can.
77 F5 Marianna AR U.S.A.
79 C6 Marianna FL U.S.A.
46 F6 Mariánské Lázně Czech Rep.
84 A2 Marías, Islas is Mex.
83 H7 Mariato, Pta pt Panama
9 D1 Maria van Diemen, Cape c. N.Z.
48 F1 Maribor Slovenia
75 F5 Maricopa AZ U.S.A.
74 C4 Maricopa CA U.S.A.
75 F5 Maricopa Mts mts U.S.A.
55 E4 Maridi watercourse Sudan
92 A4 Marie Byrd Land reg. Ant.
83 M5 Marie Galante i. Guadeloupe
37 Q6 Mariehamn Fin.
90 B1 Mariembero r. Brazil
43 M4 Marienberg Ger.
42 F1 Marienhafe Ger.
57 B6 Mariental Namibia
37 N7 Mariestad Sweden
79 C5 Marietta GA U.S.A.
80 C5 Marietta OH U.S.A.
44 G5 Marignane France
24 G1 Marii, Mys pt Rus. Fed.
24 A1 Mariinsk Rus. Fed.
37 S9 Marijampolė Lith.
90 C3 Marília Brazil
77 C7 Marin Mex.
45 B1 Marín Spain
48 G5 Marina di Gioiosa Ionica Italy
50 D4 Mar"ina Horka Belarus
31 B3 Marinduque i. Phil.
68 D3 Marinette U.S.A.
90 B3 Maringá Brazil
45 B3 Marinha Grande Port.
78 B4 Marion IL U.S.A.
68 E5 Marion IN U.S.A.
81 K2 Marion ME U.S.A.
80 B4 Marion OH U.S.A.
79 E5 Marion SC U.S.A.
80 C6 Marion VA U.S.A.
79 D5 Marion, L. l. U.S.A.
89 D3 Maripa Venez.
74 C3 Mariposa U.S.A.
88 D2 Mariscal Estigarribia Para.
44 H4 Maritime Alps mts France/Italy
49 L3 Maritsa r. Bulg.
50 J3 Mari-Turek Rus. Fed.
51 F6 Mariupol' Ukr.
18 B3 Marīvān Iran
50 J3 Mariy El, Respublika div. Rus. Fed.
56 E3 Marka Somalia
17 K2 Mārkān Iran
21 B3 Markapur India
37 N8 Markaryd Sweden
69 G3 Markdale Can.
59 H1 Marken S. Africa
42 D2 Markermeer l. Neth.
39 G5 Market Deeping U.K.
39 E5 Market Drayton U.K.
39 G5 Market Harborough U.K.
41 E3 Markethill U.K.
38 G4 Market Weighton U.K.
13 N3 Markha r. Rus. Fed.
69 H4 Markham Can.
92 B4 Markham, Mt mt Ant.
51 F5 Markivka Ukr.
43 L3 Markkleeberg Ger.
43 H2 Marklohe Ger.
13 T3 Markovo Rus. Fed.
43 L3 Markranstädt Ger.
51 H5 Marks Rus. Fed.
43 H5 Marktheidenfeld Ger.
46 E7 Marktoberdorf Ger.
43 L4 Marktredwitz Ger.
68 B6 Mark Twain Lake l. U.S.A.
42 F3 Marl Ger.
81 H3 Marlborough U.S.A.
39 F6 Marlborough Downs h. U.K.
42 B5 Marle France
77 D6 Marlin U.S.A.
80 C5 Marlinton U.S.A.
8 G4 Marlo Austr.
44 E4 Marmande France
Marmara Denizi g. see Marmara, Sea of
16 B2 Marmara Gölü l. Turkey
16 B1 Marmara, Sea of g. Turkey
16 B3 Marmaris Turkey
76 C2 Marmarth U.S.A.
80 C5 Marmet U.S.A.
66 B4 Marmion L. l. Can.
48 D1 Marmolada mt Italy
44 F2 Marne-la-Vallée France
17 K1 Marneuli Georgia
43 K1 Marnitz Ger.
8 D4 Marnoo Austr.
57 E5 Maroantsetra Madag.
43 J4 Maroldsweisach Ger.
57 E5 Maromokotro mt Madag.
57 D5 Marondera Zimbabwe
87 H2 Maroni r. Fr. Guiana
5 N7 Marotiri i. Pac. Oc.
55 D3 Maroua Cameroon
57 E5 Marovoay Madag.
17 H4 Marqādah Syria
26 A3 Mar Qu r. China
59 G4 Marquard S. Africa
5 O5 Marquesas Islands is Pac. Oc.
79 D7 Marquesas Keys is U.S.A.
68 D2 Marquette U.S.A.
42 B4 Marquion France
8 D1 Marra Austr.
59 K2 Marracuene Moz.
54 B1 Marrakech Morocco
Marrakesh see Marrakech
59 L2 Marrangua, Lagoa l. Moz.
55 E3 Marra Plateau plat. Sudan
8 F3 Marrar Austr.
77 F6 Marrero U.S.A.
57 D5 Marromeu Moz.
57 D5 Marrupa Moz.
55 F2 Marsa Alam Egypt
55 D1 Marsa al Burayqah Libya
56 D3 Marsabit Kenya
48 E6 Marsala Sicily Italy
55 E1 Marsa Maṭrūḥ Egypt
43 G3 Marsberg Ger.
48 E3 Marsciano Italy
8 F2 Marsden Austr.
42 C2 Marsdiep chan. Neth.
44 G5 Marseille France
68 C5 Marseilles U.S.A.
90 D3 Mar, Serra do mts Brazil
36 O4 Marsfjället mt Sweden
65 H4 Marshall Can.
77 E5 Marshall AR U.S.A.
78 C4 Marshall IL U.S.A.
68 E4 Marshall MI U.S.A.
76 E2 Marshall MN U.S.A.
76 E4 Marshall MO U.S.A.
77 E5 Marshall TX U.S.A.
4 H3 Marshall Islands country Pac. Oc.
76 E3 Marshalltown U.S.A.
68 B3 Marshfield U.S.A.
79 E7 Marsh Harbour Bahamas
81 K1 Mars Hill U.S.A.
77 F6 Marsh Island i. U.S.A.
64 C2 Marsh Lake l. Can.
17 M3 Marshūn Iran
72 C3 Marsing U.S.A.
37 P7 Märsta Sweden
23 F4 Marsyangdi r. Nepal
32 A1 Martaban Myanmar
25 B5 Martaban, Gulf of Myanmar
33 D3 Martapura Kalimantan Indon.
33 B3 Martapura Sumatera Indon.
69 H2 Marten River Can.
65 H4 Martensville Can.
81 H4 Martha's Vineyard i. U.S.A.
46 C7 Martigny Switz.
47 J6 Martin Slovakia
76 C3 Martin SD U.S.A.
79 B4 Martin TN U.S.A.
84 C2 Martínez Mex.
84 A1 Martínez, E. Mex.
75 E5 Martinez Lake U.S.A.
61 M8 Martinique terr. Caribbean Sea
79 C5 Martin, L. l. U.S.A.
92 A3 Martin Pen. pen. Ant.
80 D4 Martinsburg PA U.S.A.
80 E5 Martinsburg WV U.S.A.
80 C4 Martins Ferry U.S.A.
80 D6 Martinsville U.S.A.
96 H7 Martin Vas, Is is Atl. Ocean
9 E4 Marton N.Z.
45 G2 Martorell Spain
45 E4 Martos Spain
14 D1 Martuk Kazak.
17 K1 Martuni Armenia
19 F3 Maruchak Afgh.
29 C7 Marugame Japan
9 D5 Maruia r. N.Z.
87 L6 Maruim Brazil
51 G7 Marukhis Ugheltekhili pass Georgia/Rus. Fed.
8 G3 Marulan Austr.
18 D4 Marvast Iran
44 F4 Marvejols France
75 G2 Marvine, Mt mt U.S.A.
65 G4 Marwayne Can.
19 F2 Mary Turkm.
8 D4 Maryborough Vic. Austr.
7 F4 Maryborough Austr.
58 H3 Marydale S. Africa
50 J4 Mar'yevka Rus. Fed.
65 H2 Mary Frances Lake l. Can.
81 E5 Maryland div. U.S.A.
38 D3 Maryport U.K.
67 J3 Mary's Harbour Can.
67 K4 Marystown Can.
75 F2 Marysvale U.S.A.
67 G4 Marysville Can.
74 B2 Marysville CA U.S.A.
76 D4 Marysville KS U.S.A.
80 B4 Marysville OH U.S.A.
79 C5 Maryville U.S.A.
76 E3 Maryville U.S.A.
43 L2 Marzahna Ger.
18 D4 Masāhūn, Kūh-e mt Iran
56 D4 Masaka Uganda
59 G5 Masakhane S. Africa
17 M2 Masallı Azer.
6 C2 Masamba Indon.
30 E6 Masan S. Korea
81 J1 Masardis U.S.A.
57 D5 Masasi Tanz.
86 F7 Masaví Bol.
31 B3 Masbate Phil.
31 B4 Masbate i. Phil.
54 C1 Mascara Alg.
93 H4 Mascarene Basin sea feature Ind. Ocean
93 J4 Mascarene Ridge sea feature Ind. Ocean
81 G2 Mascouche Can.
59 G4 Maseru Lesotho
59 H4 Mashai Lesotho
27 C6 Mashan China
22 D2 Masherbrum mt Pak.
19 E2 Mashhad Iran
22 C4 Mashi r. India
17 L2 Mashīrān Iran
18 E4 Mashīz Iran
19 F5 Mashket r. Pak.
19 F4 Mashki Chah Pak.
19 F5 Māshkīd r. Iran
36 S2 Masi Norway
59 G5 Masibambane S. Africa
59 G4 Masilo S. Africa
56 D3 Masindi Uganda
31 A3 Masinloc Phil.
58 E5 Masinyusane S. Africa
20 E5 Maṣīrah i. Oman
20 E6 Maṣīrah, Gulf of b. Oman
17 K1 Masis Armenia
18 C4 Masjed Soleymān Iran
16 G3 Maskanah Syria
41 B4 Mask, Lough l. Rep. of Ireland
19 E5 Maskūtān Iran
19 G4 Maslti Pak.
57 F5 Masoala, Tanjona c. Madag.
68 E4 Mason MI U.S.A.
74 C2 Mason NV U.S.A.
77 D6 Mason TX U.S.A.
9 A7 Mason Bay b. N.Z.
76 E3 Mason City IA U.S.A.
68 C5 Mason City IL U.S.A.
80 D5 Masontown U.S.A.
Masqaṭ see Muscat
48 D2 Massa Italy
81 G3 Massachusetts div. U.S.A.
81 H3 Massachusetts Bay b. U.S.A.
75 H1 Massadona U.S.A.
48 G4 Massafra Italy
55 D3 Massakory Chad
48 D3 Massa Marittimo Italy
57 D6 Massangena Moz.
57 B4 Massango Angola
56 D2 Massawa Eritrea
81 G2 Massawippi, Lac l. Can.
81 F2 Massena U.S.A.
64 C4 Masset Can.
69 F2 Massey Can.
44 F4 Massif Central mts France
80 C4 Massillon U.S.A.
54 B3 Massina Mali
57 D6 Massinga Moz.
57 D6 Massingir Moz.
59 K1 Massingir, Barragem de resr Moz.
59 K2 Massintonto r. Moz./S. Africa
92 D3 Massivet mts Ant.
69 K3 Masson Can.
92 D5 Masson I. i. Ant.
17 M1 Maştağa Azer.
19 H2 Mastchoh Tajik.
9 E4 Masterton N.Z.
49 M5 Masticho, Akra pt Greece
79 E7 Mastic Point Bahamas
22 C1 Mastuj Pak.
19 G4 Mastung Pak.
50 C4 Masty Belarus
29 B7 Masuda Japan
17 M3 Masuleh Iran
Masulipatam see Machilipatnam
57 D6 Masvingo Zimbabwe
16 F4 Maşyāf Syria
69 G2 Matachewan Can.
73 F6 Matachic Mex.
89 D4 Matacuni r. Venez.
56 B4 Matadi Congo(Zaire)
83 G6 Matagalpa Nic.
66 E4 Matagami Can.
66 E4 Matagami, Lac l. Can.
77 D6 Matagorda I. i. U.S.A.
32 C5 Matak i. Indon.
9 F2 Matakana Island i. N.Z.
57 B5 Matala Angola
21 C5 Matale Sri Lanka
54 A3 Matam Senegal
84 B1 Matamoros Coahuila Mex.
84 C1 Matamoros Tamaulipas Mex.
31 B5 Matanal Point pt Phil.
57 D4 Matandu r. Tanz.
67 G4 Matane Can.
22 B2 Matanui Pak.
83 H4 Matanzas Cuba
Matapan, Cape pt see Tainaro, Akra
67 G4 Matapédia r. Can.
91 B2 Mataquito r. Chile
21 C5 Matara Sri Lanka
33 E4 Mataram Indon.
86 D7 Matarani Peru
6 D3 Mataranka Austr.
45 H2 Mataró Spain
59 H5 Matatiele S. Africa
9 B7 Mataura N.Z.
9 B7 Mataura r. N.Z.
89 C3 Mataveni r. Col.
9 F3 Matawai N.Z.
86 F6 Mategua Bol.
84 B2 Matehuala Mex.
57 D5 Matemanga Tanz.
48 G4 Matera Italy
48 C6 Mateur Tunisia
66 D4 Matheson Can.
77 D6 Mathis U.S.A.
8 E3 Mathoura Austr.
22 D4 Mathura India
31 C5 Mati Phil.
23 G4 Matiali India
27 D5 Matianxu China
22 B4 Matiari Pak.
84 D3 Matías Romero Mex.
67 G3 Matimekosh Can.
69 F2 Matinenda Lake l. Can.
81 J3 Matinicus I. i. U.S.A.
23 G5 Matla r. India
59 G2 Matlabas S. Africa
59 G2 Matlabas r. S. Africa
22 B4 Matli Pak.
39 F4 Matlock U.K.
89 D3 Mato r. Venez.
89 D3 Mato, Co mt Venez.
86 G7 Mato Grosso Brazil
90 A1 Mato Grosso div. Brazil
90 A3 Mato Grosso do Sul div. Brazil
90 A1 Mato Grosso, Planalto do plat. Brazil
59 K2 Matola Moz.
45 B2 Matosinhos Port.
20 E5 Maṭraḥ Oman
58 C6 Matroosberg mt S. Africa
29 C7 Matsue Japan
28 G4 Matsumae Japan
29 E6 Matsumoto Japan
29 E7 Matsusaka Japan
27 F5 Matsu Tao i. Taiwan
29 C8 Matsuyama Japan
66 D4 Mattagami r. Can.
69 H2 Mattawa Can.
81 J2 Mattawamkeag U.S.A.
46 C7 Matterhorn mt Italy/Switz.
72 D3 Matterhorn mt U.S.A.
89 E3 Matthews Ridge Guyana
83 K4 Matthew Town Bahamas
18 D6 Maṭṭī, Sabkhat salt pan S. Arabia
78 B4 Mattoon U.S.A.
Matturai see Matara
21 C5 Matugama Sri Lanka
7 H3 Matuku i. Fiji
Matun see Khowst
89 E2 Maturín Venez.
31 C5 Matutuang i. Indon.
59 G4 Matwabeng S. Africa
22 E4 Mau Uttar Pradesh India
23 E4 Mau Uttar Pradesh India
23 E4 Mau Aimma India
42 B4 Maubeuge France
44 E5 Maubourguet France
40 D5 Mauchline U.K.
92 C3 Maudheimvidda mts Ant.
93 E7 Maud Seamount depth Ind. Ocean
87 G4 Maués Brazil
23 E4 Mauganj India
74 □2 Maui i. U.S.A.
95 J7 Mauke i. Pac. Oc.
43 G6 Maulbronn Ger.
91 B2 Maule div. Chile
91 B2 Maule r. Chile
91 B4 Maullín Chile
41 B3 Maumakeogh h. Rep. of Ireland
80 B4 Maumee U.S.A.
80 B4 Maumee r. U.S.A.
69 F5 Maumee Bay b. U.S.A.
41 B4 Maumturk Mts h. Rep. of Ireland
57 C5 Maun Botswana
74 □2 Mauna Kea volc. U.S.A.
74 □2 Mauna Loa volc. U.S.A.
74 □1 Maunalua B. b. U.S.A.
59 G1 Maunatlala Botswana
9 E2 Maungaturoto N.Z.
23 H5 Maungdaw Myanmar
32 A2 Maungmagan Is is Myanmar
62 F3 Maunoir, Lac l. Can.
6 D4 Maurice, L. salt flat Austr.
42 D3 Maurik Neth.
52 C3 Mauritania country Africa
53 K7 Mauritius country Ind. Ocean
68 B4 Mauston U.S.A.
89 D4 Mavaca r. Venez.
57 C5 Mavinga Angola
59 G5 Mavuya S. Africa
22 D3 Mawana India
56 B4 Mawanga Congo(Zaire)
27 D4 Ma Wang Dui China
32 A3 Mawdaung Pass Myanmar/Thai.
9 G3 Mawhai Pt pt N.Z.
92 D4 Mawson Austr. Base Ant.
92 D5 Mawson Coast coastal area Ant.
92 D4 Mawson Escarpment esc. Ant.
92 B6 Mawson Pen. pen. Ant.
32 A3 Maw Taung mt Myanmar
76 C2 Max U.S.A.
84 E2 Maxcanú Mex.
48 C5 Maxia, Punta mt Sardinia Italy
68 D5 Maxinkuckee, Lake l. U.S.A.
36 S5 Maxmo Fin.
69 F2 Maxton U.S.A.
74 A2 Maxwell U.S.A.
33 C3 Maya i. Indon.
24 F1 Maya r. Rus. Fed.
83 K4 Mayaguana i. Bahamas
83 L5 Mayagüez Puerto Rico
54 C3 Mayahi Niger
19 H2 Mayakovskogo mt Tajik.
56 B4 Mayama Congo
18 D2 Mayamey Iran
82 G5 Maya Mountains mts Belize/Guatemala
26 B3 Mayan China
27 C5 Mayang China
28 F5 Maya-san mt Japan
40 D5 Maybole U.K.
17 K4 Maydān Iraq
19 H3 Maydā Shahr Afgh.
42 F4 Mayen Ger.
44 D2 Mayenne France
44 D2 Mayenne r. France
75 F4 Mayer U.S.A.
64 F4 Mayerthorpe Can.
9 C5 Mayfield N.Z.
78 B4 Mayfield U.S.A.
73 F5 Mayhill U.S.A.
30 E1 Mayi r. China
40 F4 May, Isle of i. U.K.
51 G6 Maykop Rus. Fed.
24 B4 Maymyo Myanmar
24 B1 Mayna Rus. Fed.
21 A2 Mayni India
69 J3 Maynooth Can.
64 B2 Mayo Can.
91 E2 Mayo, 25 de Buenos Aires Arg.
91 C3 Mayo, 25 de La Pampa Arg.
31 C5 Mayo Bay b. Phil.
56 B4 Mayoko Congo
64 B2 Mayo Lake l. Can.
31 B3 Mayon volc. Phil.
91 D3 Mayor Buratovich Arg.
9 F2 Mayor I. i. N.Z.
88 D1 Mayor Pablo Lagerenza Para.
53 J7 Mayotte terr. Africa
31 B2 Mayraira Point pt Phil.
24 E1 Mayskiy Rus. Fed.
80 B5 Maysville U.S.A.
56 B4 Mayumba Gabon
23 E3 Mayum La pass China
21 B4 Mayuram India

69 F4 Mayville MI U.S.A.
76 D2 Mayville ND U.S.A.
80 D3 Mayville NY U.S.A.
68 C4 Mayville WI U.S.A.
76 C3 Maywood U.S.A.
91 D3 Maza Arg.
50 F3 Maza Rus. Fed.
57 C5 Mazabuka Zambia
87 H4 Mazagão Brazil
44 F5 Mazamet France
22 D1 Mazar China
48 E6 Mazara del Vallo *Sicily* Italy
19 G2 Mazār-e Sharīf Afgh.
19 G3 Mazar, Koh-i- *mt* Afgh.
89 E3 Mazaruni *r.* Guyana
82 F6 Mazatenango Guatemala
84 A2 Mazatlán Mex.
75 G4 Mazatzal Peak *summit* U.S.A.
18 C3 Mazdaj Iran
37 S8 Mažeikiai Lith.
17 G2 Mazgirt Turkey
37 S8 Mazirbe Latvia
56 D4 Mazomora Tanz.
17 M3 Mazr'eh Iran
17 M5 Māzū Iran
57 C6 Mazunga Zimbabwe
51 D4 Mazyr Belarus
59 J3 Mbabane Swaziland
54 B4 Mbahiakro Côte d'Ivoire
56 B3 Mbaïki C.A.R.
57 D4 Mbala Zambia
56 D3 Mbale Uganda
54 D4 Mbalmayo Cameroon
56 B4 Mbandaka Congo(Zaire)
54 C4 Mbanga Cameroon
56 B4 M'banza Congo Angola
56 D4 Mbarara Uganda
56 C3 Mbari *r.* C.A.R.
59 K3 Mbaswana S. Africa
54 D4 Mbengwi Cameroon
57 D4 Mbeya Tanz.
57 D5 Mbinga Tanz.
57 D6 Mbizi Zimbabwe
56 B3 Mbomo Congo
54 D4 Mbouda Cameroon
54 A3 Mbour Senegal
54 A3 Mbout Maur.
57 D4 Mbozi Tanz.
56 C4 Mbuji-Mayi Congo(Zaire)
56 D4 Mbulu Tanz.
56 D4 Mbuyuni Tanz.
57 D4 Mchinga Tanz.
59 G6 Mdantsane S. Africa
48 B6 M'Daourouch Alg.
77 C4 Meade U.S.A.
75 E3 Mead, Lake *l.* U.S.A.
65 H4 Meadow Lake Can.
65 H4 Meadow Lake Provincial Park *res.* Can.
75 E3 Meadow Valley Wash *r.* U.S.A.
80 C4 Meadville U.S.A.
69 G3 Meaford Can.
28 J3 Meaken-dake *volc.* Japan
40 A2 Mealasta Island *i.* U.K.
45 B2 Mealhada Port.
40 D4 Meall a'Bhuiridh *mt* U.K.
67 J3 Mealy Mountains Can.
19 F2 Meana Turkm.
64 F3 Meander River Can.
31 C5 Meares *i.* Indon.
44 F2 Meaux France
56 B4 Mebridege *r.* Angola
20 A5 Mecca S. Arabia
81 H2 Mechanic Falls U.S.A.
80 B4 Mechanicsburg U.S.A.
68 B5 Mechanicsville U.S.A.
42 C3 Mechelen Belgium
42 D4 Mechelen Neth.
54 B1 Mecheria Alg.
42 E4 Mechernich Ger.
16 E1 Mecitözü Turkey
42 F4 Meckenheim Ger.
46 E3 Mecklenburger Bucht *b.* Ger.
43 K1 Mecklenburgische Seenplatte *reg.* Ger.
43 L1 Mecklenburg-Vorpommern *div.* Ger.
57 D5 Mecula Moz.
45 C2 Meda Port.
21 B2 Medak India
33 A2 Medan Indon.
91 D3 Médanos Arg.
88 C7 Medanosa, Pta *pt* Arg.
21 C4 Medawachchiya Sri Lanka
21 B2 Medchal India
81 K2 Meddybemps L. *l.* U.S.A.
45 H4 Médéa Alg.
43 G3 Medebach Ger.
89 B3 Medellín Col.
39 F4 Meden *r.* U.K.
54 D1 Medenine Tunisia
54 A3 Mederdra Maur.
72 B3 Medford OR U.S.A.
68 B3 Medford WI U.S.A.
81 F5 Medford Farms U.S.A.
49 N2 Medgidia Romania
17 L4 Medhīkhan Iran
68 B5 Media U.S.A.
91 C2 Media Luna Arg.
47 M7 Mediaş Romania
72 C2 Medical Lake U.S.A.
72 F3 Medicine Bow U.S.A.
72 F3 Medicine Bow Mts *mts* U.S.A.
72 F3 Medicine Bow Peak *summit* U.S.A.
65 G4 Medicine Hat Can.
77 D4 Medicine Lodge U.S.A.
90 E2 Medina Brazil
20 A5 Medina S. Arabia
80 D3 Medina NY U.S.A.
80 C4 Medina OH U.S.A.
45 E2 Medinaceli Spain
45 D2 Medina del Campo Spain
45 D2 Medina de Rioseco Spain
23 F5 Medinīpur India
34 F5 Mediterranean Sea *sea* Africa/Europe
48 B6 Medjerda, Monts de la *mts* Alg.
12 G4 Mednogorsk Rus. Fed.
94 G2 Mednyy, Ostrov *i.* Rus. Fed.
44 D4 Médoc *reg.* France
50 H3 Medvedevo Rus. Fed.
51 H5 Medveditsa *r.* Rus. Fed.
48 F2 Medvednica *mts* Croatia
13 S2 Medvezh'i, O-va *is* Rus. Fed.
24 F2 Medvezh'ya, Gora *mt* China/Rus. Fed.
50 E2 Medvezh'yegorsk Rus. Fed.
39 H6 Medway *r.* U.K.
6 B4 Meekatharra Austr.
75 H1 Meeker U.S.A.
74 B2 Meeks Bay U.S.A.
67 J4 Meelpaeg Res. *resr* Can.
43 L4 Meerane Ger.
42 E3 Meerlo Neth.
22 D3 Meerut India
72 E2 Meeteetse U.S.A.
56 D3 Mēga Eth.
33 B3 Mega *i.* Indon.
23 G4 Meghalaya *div.* India
23 F5 Meghāsani *mt* India
23 G5 Meghna *r.* Bangl.
17 L2 Meghri Armenia
16 B3 Megisti *i.* Greece
36 U1 Mehamn Norway
19 G5 Mehar Pak.
6 B4 Meharry, Mt *mt* Austr.
22 D5 Mehekar India
23 G5 Meherpur Bangl.
80 E6 Meherrin *r.* U.S.A.
5 N6 Méhétia *i.* Pac. Oc.
17 L2 Mehrābān Iran
17 L5 Mehrān Iraq
18 D5 Mehrān *watercourse* Iran
42 E4 Mehren Ger.
18 D4 Mehriz Iran
19 H3 Mehtar Lām Afgh.
90 C2 Meia Ponte *r.* Brazil
55 D4 Meiganga Cameroon
27 B4 Meigu China
27 E5 Mei Jiang *r.* China
42 D3 Meijnweg, Nationaal Park De *nat. park* Neth.
40 D5 Meikle Millyea *h.* U.K.
25 B4 Meiktila Myanmar
43 J2 Meine Ger.
43 J2 Meinersen Ger.
43 J4 Meiningen Ger.
58 E6 Meiringspoort *pass* S. Africa
27 B4 Meishan China
46 F5 Meißen Ger.
27 C5 Meitan China
26 C3 Mei Xian China
27 E5 Meizhou China
22 D4 Mej *r.* India
88 C3 Mejicana *mt* Arg.
88 B2 Mejillones Chile
56 D2 Mek'elē Eth.
54 A3 Mékhé Senegal
22 B3 Mekhtar Pak.
48 C7 Meknassy Tunisia
54 B1 Meknès Morocco
32 C2 Mekong *r.* Asia
24 B3 Mekong *r.* China
32 C3 Mekong, Mouths of the *est.* Vietnam
33 B2 Melaka Malaysia
94 G6 Melanesia *is* Pac Oc.
31 A5 Melaut *r.* Malaysia
33 D3 Melawi *r.* Indon.
8 E4 Melbourne Austr.
79 D6 Melbourne U.S.A.
40 □ Melby U.K.
46 D3 Meldorf Ger.
69 F3 Meldrum Bay Can.
16 E2 Melendiz Dağı *mt* Turkey
50 G4 Melenki Rus. Fed.
67 F2 Mélèzes, Rivière aux *r.* Can.
55 D3 Mélfi Chad
48 F4 Melfi Italy
65 J4 Melfort Can.
36 M5 Melhus Norway
45 C1 Melide Spain
54 B1 Melilla Spain
91 E2 Melincué Arg.
33 E3 Melintang, Danau *l.* Indon.
91 B2 Melipilla Chile
42 B3 Meliskerke Neth.
65 J5 Melita Can.
51 E6 Melitopol' Ukr.
46 G6 Melk Austria
59 H1 Melkrivier S. Africa
39 E6 Melksham U.K.
36 T3 Mellakoski Fin.
36 Q5 Mellansel Sweden
43 G2 Melle Ger.
68 B2 Mellen U.S.A.
37 N7 Mellerud Sweden
43 J4 Mellrichstadt Ger.
43 G1 Mellum *i.* Ger.
59 J4 Melmoth S. Africa
91 F2 Melo Uru.
8 B2 Melrose Austr.
40 F5 Melrose U.K.
43 H3 Melsungen Ger.
31 A5 Melta, Mt *mt* Malaysia
39 G5 Melton Mowbray U.K.
44 F2 Melun France
65 J4 Melville Can.
63 M2 Melville Bugt *b.* Greenland
6 E3 Melville, C. *c.* Austr.
31 A5 Melville, C. *c.* Phil.
6 D3 Melville Island *i.* Austr.
62 G2 Melville Island *i.* Can.
67 J3 Melville, Lake *l.* Can.
63 K3 Melville Peninsula Can.
41 C3 Melvin, Lough *l.* Rep. of Ireland/U.K.
13 T3 Melyuveyem Rus. Fed.
23 E2 Mêmar Co *salt l.* China
25 F7 Memberamo *r.* Indon.
59 H3 Memel S. Africa
43 J5 Memmelsdorf Ger.
46 E7 Memmingen Ger.
42 C5 Mémorial Américain *h.* France
33 C2 Mempawah Indon.
16 C7 Memphis Egypt
68 A5 Memphis MO U.S.A.
79 B5 Memphis TN U.S.A.
77 C5 Memphis TX U.S.A.
81 G2 Memphrémagog, Lac *l.* Can.
28 H3 Memuro-dake *mt* Japan
51 E5 Mena Ukr.
77 E5 Mena U.S.A.
54 C3 Ménaka Mali
Mènam Khong *r. see* Mekong
77 D6 Menard U.S.A.
68 C3 Menasha U.S.A.
33 D3 Mendawai *r.* Indon.
44 F4 Mende France
17 M3 Mendejīn Iran
62 B4 Mendenhall, C. *pt* U.S.A.
64 C3 Mendenhall Glacier *gl.* U.S.A.
84 C1 Méndez Mex.
56 D3 Mendī Eth.
6 E2 Mendi P.N.G.
39 E6 Mendip Hills *h.* U.K.
74 A2 Mendocino U.S.A.
72 A3 Mendocino, C. *c.* U.S.A.
95 K3 Mendocino Seascarp *sea feature* Pac. Oc.
68 E4 Mendon U.S.A.
8 G1 Mendooran Austr.
74 B3 Mendota CA U.S.A.
68 C5 Mendota IL U.S.A.
68 C4 Mendota, Lake *l.* U.S.A.
91 C2 Mendoza Arg.
91 C2 Mendoza *div.* Arg.
91 C2 Mendoza *r.* Arg.
89 C2 Mene de Mauroa Venez.
89 C2 Mene Grande Venez.
49 M5 Menemen Turkey
26 E3 Mengcheng China
16 D1 Mengen Turkey
33 C3 Menggala Indon.
27 D5 Mengshan China
26 F3 Meng Shan *mts* China
26 E3 Mengyin China
27 B6 Mengzi China
67 G3 Menihek Can.
67 G3 Menihek Lakes *l.* Can.
8 D2 Menindee Austr.
8 D2 Menindee Lake *l.* Austr.
8 B3 Meningie Austr.
17 M4 Menjān Iran
13 Q3 Menkere Rus. Fed.
44 F2 Mennecy France
68 D3 Menominee U.S.A.
68 D3 Menominee *r.* U.S.A.
68 C4 Menomonee Falls U.S.A.
68 B3 Menomonie U.S.A.
57 B5 Menongue Angola
45 J2 Menorca *i.* Spain
31 A6 Mensalong Indon.
33 A3 Mentawai, Kepulauan *is* Indon.
32 B5 Mentekab Malaysia
43 J3 Menteroda Ger.
75 H4 Mentmore U.S.A.
33 C3 Mentok Indon.
44 H5 Menton France
80 C4 Mentor U.S.A.
54 C1 Menzel Bourguiba Tunisia
48 D6 Menzel Temime Tunisia
6 C4 Menzies Austr.
92 D4 Menzies, Mt *mt* Ant.
42 E2 Meppel Neth.
42 F2 Meppen Ger.
59 K1 Mepuze Moz.
59 G4 Meqheleng S. Africa
50 G3 Mera *r.* Rus. Fed.
33 C4 Merak Indon.
36 M5 Meråker Norway
76 F4 Meramec *r.* U.S.A.
48 D1 Merano Italy
89 E3 Merari, Sa. *mt* Brazil
58 F1 Meratswe *r.* Botswana
33 E3 Meratus, Pegunungan *mts* Indon.
25 G7 Merauke Indon.
8 D3 Merbein Austr.
74 B3 Merced U.S.A.
91 B1 Mercedario, Cerro *mt* Arg.
91 E2 Mercedes *Buenos Aires* Arg.
88 E3 Mercedes *Corrientes* Arg.
91 D2 Mercedes *San Luis* Arg.
91 E2 Mercedes Uru.
80 A4 Mercer OH U.S.A.
68 B2 Mercer WI U.S.A.
64 F4 Mercoal Can.
9 E2 Mercury Islands *is* N.Z.
63 M3 Mercy, C. *hd* Can.
42 B4 Mere Belgium
39 E6 Mere U.K.
81 H3 Meredith U.S.A.
77 C5 Meredith, Lake *l.* U.S.A.
77 C5 Meredith Nat. Recreation Area, Lake *res.* U.S.A.
68 B6 Meredosia U.S.A.
51 F5 Merefa Ukr.
55 E3 Merga Oasis *oasis* Sudan
32 A2 Mergui Myanmar
32 A3 Mergui Archipelago *is* Myanmar
8 C3 Meribah Austr.
49 M4 Meriç *r.* Greece/Turkey
84 E2 Mérida Mex.
45 C3 Mérida Spain
89 C2 Mérida Venez.
89 C2 Mérida, Cordillera de *mts* Venez.
81 G4 Meriden U.S.A.
74 B2 Meridian CA U.S.A.
77 F5 Meridian MS U.S.A.
44 D4 Mérignac France
36 T4 Merijärvi Fin.
37 R6 Merikarvia Fin.
8 G4 Merimbula Austr.
8 C3 Meringur Austr.
8 C4 Merino Austr.
77 C5 Merkel U.S.A.
32 □ Merlimau, P. *i.* Sing.
55 F3 Merowe Sudan
6 B5 Merredin Austr.
40 D5 Merrick *h.* U.K.
69 K3 Merrickville Can.
68 C3 Merrill U.S.A.
68 D5 Merrillville U.S.A.
76 C3 Merriman U.S.A.
64 E4 Merritt Can.
79 D6 Merritt Island U.S.A.
8 H2 Merriwa Austr.
8 G1 Merrygoen Austr.
56 E2 Mersa Fatma Eritrea
42 E5 Mersch Lux.
43 K3 Merseburg (Saale) Ger.
39 E4 Mersey *est.* U.K.
Mersin *see* İçel
33 B2 Mersing Malaysia
37 S8 Mērsrags Latvia
22 C4 Merta India
39 D6 Merthyr Tydfil U.K.
56 D3 Merti Kenya
45 C4 Mértola Port.
92 B6 Mertz Gl. *gl.* Ant.
56 D4 Meru *volc.* Tanz.
19 F4 Merui Pak.
Merv *see* Mary
58 D6 Merweville S. Africa
16 E1 Merzifon Turkey
42 E5 Merzig Ger.
92 B2 Merz Pen. *pen.* Ant.
75 G5 Mesa U.S.A.
68 A2 Mesabi Range *h.* U.S.A.
48 G4 Mesagne Italy
49 L7 Mesara, Ormos *b.* Greece
75 H3 Mesa Verde Nat. Park U.S.A.
89 B4 Mesay *r.* Col.
43 G3 Meschede Ger.
36 P4 Meselefors Sweden
66 F3 Mesgouez L. *l.* Can.
50 J2 Meshchura Rus. Fed.
Meshed *see* Mashhad
19 E2 Meshkān Iran
51 G5 Meshkovskaya Rus. Fed.
68 E3 Mesick U.S.A.
49 K4 Mesimeri Greece
49 J5 Mesolongi Greece
17 J4 Mesopotamia *reg.* Iraq
75 E3 Mesquite NV U.S.A.
77 D5 Mesquite TX U.S.A.
75 E4 Mesquite Lake *l.* U.S.A.
57 D5 Messalo *r.* Moz.
48 F5 Messina *Sicily* Italy
59 J1 Messina S. Africa
48 F5 Messina, Stretta di *str.* Italy
69 J2 Messines Can.
49 K6 Messini Greece
49 K6 Messiniakos Kolpos *b.* Greece
63 Q2 Mesters Vig Greenland
43 K1 Mestlin Ger.
49 L5 Meston, Akra *pt* Greece
48 E2 Mestre Italy
16 F1 Mesudiye Turkey
89 C3 Meta *r.* Col./Venez.
69 G2 Metagama Can.
63 L3 Meta Incognita Pen. Can.
77 F6 Metairie U.S.A.
68 C5 Metamora U.S.A.
88 C3 Metán Arg.
96 H9 Meteor Depth *depth* Atl. Ocean
49 J6 Methoni Greece
81 H3 Methuen U.S.A.
40 E4 Methven U.K.
48 G3 Metković Croatia
64 C3 Metlakatla U.S.A.
57 D5 Metoro Moz.
33 C4 Metro Indon.
78 B4 Metropolis U.S.A.
42 C4 Mettet Belgium
43 F2 Mettingen Ger.
74 C4 Mettler U.S.A.
21 B4 Mettur India
56 D3 Metu Eth
44 H2 Metz France
42 D4 Meuse *r.* Belgium/France
43 L3 Meuselwitz Ger.
39 C7 Mevagissey U.K.
26 B3 Mêwa China
77 D6 Mexia U.S.A.
82 A2 Mexicali Mex.
75 H3 Mexican Hat U.S.A.
73 F6 Mexicanos, L. de los *l.* Mex.
75 H3 Mexican Water U.S.A.
84 C3 México Mex.
81 H2 Mexico ME U.S.A.
76 F4 Mexico MO U.S.A.
81 E3 Mexico NY U.S.A.
61 H7 Mexico *country* Central America
84 C3 México *div.* Mex.
61 J7 Mexico, Gulf of *g.* Mex./U.S.A.
18 D3 Meybod Iran
43 L1 Meyenburg Ger.
19 G3 Meymaneh Afgh.
18 C3 Meymeh Iran
18 B3 Meymeh *r.* Iran
84 D3 Mezcalapa *r.* Mex.
49 K3 Mezdra Bulg.
12 F3 Mezen' Rus. Fed.
44 G4 Mézenc, Mont *mt* France
50 J2 Mezhdurechensk Rus. Fed.
24 A1 Mezhdurechensk Rus. Fed.
12 G2 Mezhdusharskiy, O. *i.* Rus. Fed.
47 K7 Mezőtúr Hungary
84 A2 Mezquital Mex.
84 A2 Mezquital *r.* Mex.
84 B2 Mezquitic Mex.
37 U8 Mežvidi Latvia
57 D5 Mfuwe Zambia
21 A2 Mhasvad India
59 J3 Mhlume Swaziland
22 C5 Mhow India
23 H5 Mi *r.* Myanmar
84 C3 Miahuatlán Mex.
45 D3 Miajadas Spain
75 G5 Miami AZ U.S.A.
79 D7 Miami FL U.S.A.
77 E4 Miami OK U.S.A.
79 D7 Miami Beach U.S.A.
18 C4 Mīān Āb Iran
19 F5 Mianaz Pak.
18 D3 Miāndarreh Iran
18 B2 Miandowāb Iran
57 E5 Miandrivazo Madag.
18 B2 Mīāneh Iran
31 C5 Miangas *i.* Phil.
19 G5 Miani Hor *b.* Pak.
19 G3 Mianjoi Afgh.
27 B4 Mianning China
22 B2 Mianwali Pak.
26 C3 Mian Xian China
27 D4 Mianyang *Hubei* China
26 B4 Mianyang *Sichuan* China
26 B4 Mianzhu China
26 F2 Miao Dao *i.* China
26 F2 Miaodao Qundao *is* China
27 F5 Miaoli Taiwan
57 E5 Miarinarivo Madag.
12 H4 Miass Rus. Fed.
75 G5 Mica Mt *mt* U.S.A.
26 C3 Micang Shan *mts* China
47 K6 Michalovce Slovakia
65 H3 Michel Can.
43 K4 Michelau in Oberfranken Ger.
43 H5 Michelstadt Ger.
43 M2 Michendorf Ger.
68 C2 Michigamme Lake *l.* U.S.A.
68 C2 Michigamme Reservoir U.S.A.
68 D2 Michigan *div.* U.S.A.
68 D5 Michigan City U.S.A.
68 D4 Michigan, Lake *l.* U.S.A.
68 E2 Michipicoten Bay *b.* Can.
68 E2 Michipicoten I. *i.* Can.
68 E1 Michipicoten River Can.
84 B3 Michoacán *div.* Mex.
49 M3 Michurin Bulg.
50 G4 Michurinsk Rus. Fed.
83 H6 Mico *r.* Nic.
94 E5 Micronesia *is* Pac. Oc.
4 F4 Micronesia, Federated States of *country* Pac. Oc.
33 C2 Midai *i.* Indon.
96 F4 Mid-Atlantic Ridge *sea feature* Atl. Ocean
58 C6 Middelberg Pass S. Africa
42 B3 Middelburg Neth.
58 F5 Middelburg *Eastern Cape* S. Africa
59 H2 Middelburg *Mpumalanga* S. Africa
37 L9 Middelfart Denmark
42 C3 Middelharnis Neth.
58 D5 Middelpos S. Africa
59 G2 Middelwit S. Africa
72 C3 Middle Alkali Lake *l.* U.S.A.
94 N5 Middle America Trench *sea feature* Pac. Oc.
81 H4 Middleboro U.S.A.
80 E4 Middleburg U.S.A.
81 F3 Middleburgh U.S.A.
81 G2 Middlebury U.S.A.
9 C6 Middlemarch N.Z.
80 B6 Middlesboro U.S.A.
38 F3 Middlesbrough U.K.
74 A2 Middletown CA U.S.A.
81 G4 Middletown CT U.S.A.
81 F5 Middletown DE U.S.A.
81 F4 Middletown NY U.S.A.
80 A5 Middletown OH U.S.A.
68 E4 Middleville U.S.A.
39 G7 Midhurst U.K.
93 K4 Mid-Indian Basin *sea feature* Ind. Ocean
93 K6 Mid-Indian Ridge *sea feature* Ind. Ocean
69 H3 Midland Can.
69 E4 Midland MI U.S.A.
77 C5 Midland TX U.S.A.
41 C6 Midleton Rep. of Ireland
94 F4 Mid-Pacific Mountains *sea feature* Pac. Oc.
36 □ Miðvágur Faroe Is
Midway *see* Thamarīt
5 K2 Midway Islands *is* HI U.S.A.
72 F3 Midwest U.S.A.
77 D5 Midwest City U.S.A.
42 D2 Midwoud Neth.
17 H3 Midyat Turkey
40 □ Mid Yell U.K.
49 K3 Midzhur *mt* Bulg./Yugo.
37 U6 Miehikkälä Fin.
36 T3 Miekojärvi *l.* Fin.
47 K5 Mielec Pol.
57 D4 Miembwe Tanz.
36 U2 Mieraslompolo Fin.
47 M7 Miercurea-Ciuc Romania
45 D1 Mieres Spain
56 E3 Mī'ēso Eth.
43 K2 Mieste Ger.
80 E4 Mifflinburg U.S.A.
80 E4 Mifflintown U.S.A.
26 C3 Migang Shan *mt* China
59 F3 Migdol S. Africa
19 E4 Mīghān Iran
23 H3 Miging India
84 B1 Miguel Auza Mex.
16 C2 Mihalıççık Turkey
29 C7 Mihara Japan
29 F7 Mihara-yama *volc.* Japan
45 F2 Mijares *r.* Spain
42 C2 Mijdrecht Neth.
69 F3 Mikado U.S.A.
47 N4 Mikashevichy Belarus
50 F4 Mikhaylov Rus. Fed.
92 D5 Mikhaylov I. *i.* Ant.
28 C3 Mikhaylovka *Primorskiy Kray* Rus. Fed.
51 G5 Mikhaylovka *Volgograd.* Rus. Fed.
12 J4 Mikhaylovskiy Rus. Fed.
23 H4 Mikir Hills *mts* India
37 U6 Mikkeli Fin.
37 U6 Mikkelin mlk Fin.
64 G3 Mikkwa *r.* Can.
56 D4 Mikumi Tanz.
50 J2 Mikun' Rus. Fed.
29 F6 Mikuni-sammyaku *mts* Japan
29 F8 Mikura-jima *i.* Japan
76 E2 Milaca U.S.A.
21 A5 Miladhunmadulu Atoll *atoll* Maldives
48 C2 Milan Italy
79 B5 Milan U.S.A.
8 B3 Milang Austr.
57 D5 Milange Moz.
Milano *see* Milan
16 A3 Milas Turkey
48 F5 Milazzo *Sicily* Italy
76 D2 Milbank U.S.A.
39 H5 Mildenhall U.K.
8 D3 Mildura Austr.
27 B5 Mile China
72 F2 Miles City U.S.A.
41 C5 Milestone Rep. of Ireland
48 F4 Miletto, Monte *mt* Italy
41 D2 Milford Rep. of Ireland
74 B1 Milford CA U.S.A.
81 G4 Milford CT U.S.A.
81 F5 Milford DE U.S.A.
68 D5 Milford IL U.S.A.
81 H3 Milford MA U.S.A.
81 J2 Milford ME U.S.A.
81 H3 Milford NH U.S.A.
81 F3 Milford NY U.S.A.
75 F2 Milford UT U.S.A.
39 B6 Milford Haven U.K.
9 A6 Milford Sound N.Z.
9 A6 Milford Sound *in.* N.Z.
45 H4 Miliana Alg.
62 G5 Milk *r. Alta.* Can.
72 F1 Milk *r.* Can./U.S.A.
13 R4 Mil'kovo Rus. Fed.
45 F2 Millárs *r.* Spain
44 F4 Millau France
74 B1 Mill Creek *r.* U.S.A.
79 D5 Milledgeville GA U.S.A.
68 C5 Milledgeville IL U.S.A.
76 E2 Mille Lacs L. *l.* U.S.A.
66 B4 Mille Lacs, Lac des *l.* Can.
76 D2 Miller U.S.A.
68 B3 Miller Dam Flowage *resr* U.S.A.
69 G3 Miller Lake Can.
51 G5 Millerovo Rus. Fed.
75 G6 Miller Peak *summit* U.S.A.
80 C4 Millersburg OH U.S.A.
80 E4 Millersburg PA U.S.A.
80 E6 Millers Tavern U.S.A.
74 C3 Millerton Lake *l.* U.S.A.
40 C5 Milleur Point *pt* U.K.
92 C6 Mill I. *i.* Ant
8 C4 Millicent Austr.
69 F4 Millington MI U.S.A.
79 B5 Millington TN U.S.A.
81 J2 Millinocket U.S.A.
38 D3 Millom U.K.
40 D5 Millport U.K.
81 F5 Millsboro U.S.A.
64 F2 Mills Lake *l.* Can.
80 C5 Millstone U.S.A.
67 G4 Milltown Can.
41 B5 Milltown Malbay Rep. of Ireland
81 K1 Millville Can.
81 F5 Millville U.S.A.
81 J2 Milo U.S.A.
28 D3 Milogradovo Rus. Fed.
49 L6 Milos *i.* Greece
50 F4 Miloslavskoye Rus. Fed.
80 E4 Milroy U.S.A.
69 H4 Milton Can.
9 B7 Milton N.Z.
79 C6 Milton FL U.S.A.
68 A5 Milton IA U.S.A.
80 E4 Milton PA U.S.A.
81 G2 Milton VT U.S.A.
72 C2 Milton-Freewater U.S.A.
39 G5 Milton Keynes U.K.
80 C4 Milton, Lake *l.* U.S.A.
27 D4 Miluo China
68 D4 Milwaukee U.S.A.
51 G5 Milyutinskaya Rus. Fed.
44 D4 Mimizan France
56 B4 Mimongo Gabon
84 B1 Mina Mex.
74 C2 Mina U.S.A.
18 E5 Mīnāb Iran
25 E6 Minahasa, Semenanjung *pen.* Indon.
18 D5 Mina Jebel Ali U.A.E.
65 L4 Minaki Can.
29 B8 Minamata Japan
29 E7 Minami Alps National Park Japan
33 B2 Minas Indon.
91 F2 Minas Uru.
17 M7 Mīnā Sa'ūd Kuwait
67 H4 Minas Basin *b.* Can.
91 F1 Minas de Corrales Uru.
90 D2 Minas Gerais *div.* Brazil
90 D2 Minas Novas Brazil
84 D3 Minatitlán Mex.
23 H5 Minbu Myanmar
23 H5 Minbya Myanmar
88 B6 Minchinmávida *volc.* Chile
40 C2 Minch, The *str.* U.K.
48 D2 Mincio *r.* Italy
17 L2 Mincivan Azer.
31 C5 Mindanao *i.* Phil.
8 C3 Mindarie Austr.
54 □ Mindelo Cape Verde
69 H3 Minden Can.
43 G2 Minden Ger.
77 E5 Minden LA U.S.A.
74 C2 Minden NV U.S.A.
23 H6 Mindon Myanmar
8 D2 Mindona L. *l.* Austr.
31 B3 Mindoro *i.* Phil.
31 A3 Mindoro Strait *str.* Phil.
56 B4 Mindouli Congo
39 D6 Minehead U.K.
41 D6 Mine Head *hd* Rep. of Ireland
90 B2 Mineiros Brazil
77 E5 Mineola U.S.A.
74 B1 Mineral U.S.A.
74 C3 Mineral King U.S.A.
51 G6 Mineral'nyye Vody Rus. Fed.
68 B4 Mineral Point U.S.A.
77 D5 Mineral Wells U.S.A.
75 F2 Minersville U.S.A.
48 G4 Minervino Murge Italy
23 E1 Minfeng China
57 C5 Minga Congo(Zaire)
17 L1 Mingäçevir Azer.
17 L1 Mingäçevir Su Anbarı *resr* Azer.
67 H3 Mingan Can.
8 C2 Mingary Austr.
26 E3 Minggang China
45 F3 Minglanilla Spain
57 D5 Mingoyo Tanz.
27 B4 Ming-shan China
24 E2 Mingshui China
40 A4 Mingulay *i.* U.K.
27 E5 Mingxi China
26 B2 Minhe China
27 F5 Minhou China
21 A4 Minicoy *i.* India
6 B4 Minilya Austr.
67 H3 Minipi Lake *l.* Can.
65 J4 Minitonas Can.
27 F5 Min Jiang *r. Fujian* China
26 B4 Min Jiang *r. Sichuan* China
26 A2 Minle China
54 C4 Minna Nigeria
37 O5 Minne Sweden
76 E2 Minneapolis U.S.A.
65 K4 Minnedosa Can.
68 A2 Minnesota *div.* U.S.A.
71 G2 Minnesota *r.* MN U.S.A.
66 B4 Minnitaki L. *l.* Can.
45 B2 Miño *r.* Port./Spain
68 C3 Minocqua U.S.A.
68 B2 Minong U.S.A.
68 C5 Minonk U.S.A.
Minorca *i. see* Menorca
76 C1 Minot U.S.A.
26 B2 Minqin China
27 F5 Minqing China
26 B3 Min Shan *mts* China
23 H4 Minsin Myanmar
50 C4 Minsk Belarus
47 K4 Mińsk Mazowiecki Pol.
39 E5 Minsterley U.K.
22 C1 Mintaka Pass *pass* China/Jammu and Kashmir
67 G4 Minto Can.
62 G2 Minto Inlet *in.* Can.
66 F2 Minto, Lac *l.* Can.
73 F4 Minturn U.S.A.
16 C6 Minûf Egypt
24 B1 Minusinsk Rus. Fed.
23 J3 Minutang India
26 B3 Min Xian China
8 D4 Minyip Austr.
69 E3 Mio U.S.A.
66 E4 Miquelon Can.
67 J4 Miquelon *i.* N. America
89 A4 Mira *r.* Col.
19 F4 Mirabad Afgh.
81 F2 Mirabel Can.
90 D2 Mirabela Brazil
87 J5 Miracema do Norte Brazil
87 J5 Mirador, Parque Nacional de *nat. park* Brazil
89 B4 Miraflores Col.
90 D2 Miralta Brazil
91 F3 Miramar Arg.
84 E3 Miramar, L. *l.* Mex.
44 G5 Miramas France
67 G4 Miramichi *r.* Can.
49 L7 Mirampelou, Kolpos *b.* Greece
22 B2 Miram Shah Pak.
90 A3 Miranda Brazil
74 A1 Miranda U.S.A.
90 A3 Miranda *r.* Brazil
45 E1 Miranda de Ebro Spain
45 C2 Mirandela Port.
48 D2 Mirandola Italy
90 B3 Mirandópolis Brazil
17 H5 Mirā', Wādī al *watercourse* Iraq/S. Arabia
20 D6 Mirbāṭ Oman
44 E5 Mirepoix France
33 D2 Miri Malaysia
19 F4 Miri *mt* Pak.
21 B2 Mirialguda India
91 G2 Mirim, Lagoa *l.* Brazil
19 F4 Mīrjāveh Iran
50 G2 Mirnyy Rus. Fed.
13 N3 Mirnyy Rus. Fed.
92 D5 Mirnyy *Rus. Fed. Base* Ant.
65 J3 Mirond L. *l.* Can.
43 L1 Mirow Ger.
22 C2 Mirpur Pak.
22 B4 Mirpur Batoro Pak.
22 B4 Mirpur Khas Pak.
22 A4 Mirpur Sakro Pak.
64 G4 Mirror Can.
27 □ Mirs Bay *b.* H.K. China
19 E5 Mīr Shahdād Iran
49 K6 Mirtoö Pelagos *sea* Greece
30 E6 Miryang S. Korea
19 F2 Mirzachirla Turkm.
23 E4 Mirzapur India
29 C8 Misaki Japan
28 G4 Misawa Japan
67 H4 Miscou I. *i.* Can.
22 C1 Misgar Pak.
28 B2 Mishan China
18 C5 Mishāsh al Hādī *well* S. Arabia
68 D5 Mishawaka U.S.A.
68 E1 Mishibishu Lake *l.* Can.
29 B7 Mi-shima *i.* Japan
23 H3 Mishmi Hills *mts* India
6 F3 Misima I. *i.* P.N.G.
83 H6 Miskitos, Cayos *atolls* Nic.
47 K6 Miskolc Hungary
25 F7 Misoöl *i.* Indon.
68 B2 Misquah Hills *h.* U.S.A.
55 D1 Miṣrātah Libya
22 E4 Misrikh India
69 E1 Missanabie Can.
66 D3 Missinaibi *r.* Can.
69 F1 Missinaibi Lake *l.* Can.
65 J3 Missinipe Can.
76 C3 Mission SD U.S.A.
84 C1 Mission TX U.S.A.
64 E5 Mission City Can.
66 D3 Missisa L. *l.* Can.
69 F2 Missisagi *r.* Can.
69 H4 Mississauga Can.
68 E5 Mississinewa Lake *l.* U.S.A.
77 F5 Mississippi *div.* U.S.A.
69 J3 Mississippi *r.* Can.
77 F6 Mississippi *r.* U.S.A.
77 F6 Mississippi Delta *delta* U.S.A.
72 D2 Missoula U.S.A.
68 A6 Missouri *div.* U.S.A.
76 C2 Missouri *r.* U.S.A.
76 E3 Missouri Valley U.S.A.
63 L4 Mistassibi *r.* Can.
67 F4 Mistassini Can.
67 F4 Mistassini *r.* Can.
66 F3 Mistassini, L. *l.* Can.
67 H2 Mistastin Lake *l.* Can.
46 H6 Mistelbach Austria
64 C3 Misty Fjords National Monument *res.* U.S.A.
84 A2 Mita, Pta de *hd* Mex.
6 E4 Mitchell Austr.
69 G4 Mitchell Can.
76 D3 Mitchell U.S.A.
6 E3 Mitchell *r. Qld.* Austr.
8 F4 Mitchell *r. Vic.* Austr.
68 E3 Mitchell, Lake *l.* U.S.A.
79 D5 Mitchell, Mt *mt* U.S.A.
41 C5 Mitchelstown Rep. of Ireland
16 C6 Mīt Ghamr Egypt
22 B3 Mithankot Pak.
22 B4 Mithi Pak.
22 B4 Mithrani Canal *canal* Pak.
49 M5 Mithymna Greece
64 C3 Mitkof I. *i.* U.S.A.
29 G6 Mito Japan
57 D4 Mitole Tanz.
9 E4 Mitre *mt* N.Z.
7 H3 Mitre Island *i.* Solomon Is
8 H3 Mittagong Austr.
8 F4 Mitta Mitta Austr.
43 G2 Mittellandkanal *canal* Ger.
43 L5 Mitterteich Ger.
43 L4 Mittweida Ger.
89 C4 Mitú Col.
89 C4 Mituas Col.
57 C5 Mitumba, Chaîne des *mts* Congo(Zaire)
56 C4 Mitumba, Monts *mts* Congo(Zaire)
56 B3 Mitzic Gabon
29 F7 Miura Japan
17 G4 Miyah, Wādī el *watercourse* Syria
29 F7 Miyake-jima *i.* Japan
28 G5 Miyako Japan
29 B9 Miyakonojō Japan
26 B4 Miyaluo China
22 B5 Miyāni India
29 B9 Miyazaki Japan
29 D7 Miyazu Japan
27 B5 Miyi China
29 C7 Miyoshi Japan
26 E1 Miyun China
26 E1 Miyun Sk. *resr* China
19 G3 Mīzāni Afgh.
56 D3 Mīzan Teferī Eth.
55 D1 Mizdah Libya
41 B6 Mizen Head *hd* Rep. of Ireland
51 B5 Mizhhir"ya Ukr.
26 D2 Mizhi China
23 H5 Mizoram *div.* India
28 G5 Mizusawa Japan
37 O7 Mjölby Sweden
56 D4 Mkata Tanz.
56 D4 Mkomazi Tanz.
57 C5 Mkushi Zambia
46 G5 Mladá Boleslav Czech Rep.
49 J2 Mladenovac Yugo.
47 K4 Mława Pol.
48 G3 Mljet *i.* Croatia
59 G5 Mlungisi S. Africa
47 M5 Mlyniv Ukr.
59 F2 Mmabatho S. Africa
59 G1 Mmamabula Botswana
59 F2 Mmathethe Botswana
37 J6 Mo Norway
75 H2 Moab U.S.A.
6 E3 Moa I. *i.* Austr.
7 H3 Moala *i.* Fiji
18 D3 Mo'alla Iran
59 K2 Moamba Moz.
75 E3 Moapa U.S.A.
41 D4 Moate Rep. of Ireland
56 C4 Moba Congo(Zaire)
29 G7 Mobara Japan
18 C3 Mobārakeh Iran
56 C3 Mobayi-Mbongo Congo(Zaire)
76 E4 Moberly U.S.A.
79 B6 Mobile AL U.S.A.
75 F5 Mobile AZ U.S.A.
79 B6 Mobile Bay *b.* U.S.A.
76 C2 Mobridge U.S.A.
Mobutu, Lake *l. see* Albert, Lake
87 J4 Mocajuba Brazil
57 E5 Moçambique Moz.
89 D2 Mocapra *r.* Venez.
27 B6 Mộc Châu Vietnam
89 D2 Mochirma, Parque Nacional *nat. park* Venez.
57 C6 Mochudi Botswana
57 E5 Mocimboa da Praia Moz.
43 K2 Möckern Ger.
43 H5 Möckmühl Ger.
36 R4 Mockträsk Sweden
89 A4 Mocoa Col.

90 C3 Mococa Brazil
84 A1 Mocorito Mex.
84 B2 Moctezuma Mex.
57 D5 Mocuba Moz.
44 H4 Modane France
22 C5 Modasa India
58 F4 Modder r. S. Africa
48 D2 Modena Italy
75 F3 Modena U.S.A.
74 B3 Modesto U.S.A.
8 F5 Moe Austr.
39 D5 Moel Sych h. U.K.
37 M6 Moely Norway
36 Q2 Moen Norway
75 G3 Moenkopi U.S.A.
9 C6 Moeraki Pt pt N.Z.
42 E3 Moers Ger.
40 E5 Moffat U.K.
22 C3 Moga India
Mogadishu see Muqdisho
80 C4 Mogadore Reservoir resr U.S.A.
59 H1 Mogalakwena r. S. Africa
59 H2 Moganyaka S. Africa
43 L2 Mögelin Ger.
19 G2 Moghiyon Tajik.
90 C3 Mogi-Mirim Brazil
24 D1 Mogocha Rus. Fed.
48 C6 Mogod mts Tunisia
59 F2 Mogoditshane Botswana
24 B4 Mogok Myanmar
75 H5 Mogollon Baldy mt U.S.A.
75 H5 Mogollon Mts mts U.S.A.
75 G4 Mogollon Rim plat. U.S.A.
59 G2 Mogwase S. Africa
49 H2 Mohács Hungary
9 F3 Mohaka r. N.Z.
59 G5 Mohale's Hoek Lesotho
65 J5 Mohall U.S.A.
19 E3 Mohammad Iran
Moḥammadābād see Darreh Gaz
45 G5 Mohammadia Alg.
22 E3 Mohan r. India/Nepal
75 E4 Mohave, L. l. U.S.A.
75 F5 Mohawk U.S.A.
81 F3 Mohawk r. U.S.A.
75 F5 Mohawk Mts mts U.S.A.
57 E5 Moheli i. Comoros
41 D4 Mohill Rep. of Ireland
43 G3 Möhne r. Ger.
75 F4 Mohon Peak summit U.S.A.
57 D4 Mohoro Tanz.
77 C7 Mohovano Ranch Mex.
17 M5 Moh Reza Shah Pahlavi resr Iran
51 C5 Mohyliv Podil's'kyy Ukr.
37 K7 Moi Norway
59 G1 Moijabana Botswana
59 K2 Moine Moz.
47 N7 Moinești Romania
81 F2 Moira U.S.A.
36 O3 Mo i Rana Norway
23 H4 Moirang India
37 T7 Mõisaküla Estonia
91 E1 Moisés Ville Arg.
67 G3 Moisie Can.
67 G3 Moisie r. Can.
44 E4 Moissac France
74 C4 Mojave U.S.A.
74 D4 Mojave r. U.S.A.
74 D4 Mojave Desert des. U.S.A.
90 C3 Moji das Cruzes Brazil
90 C3 Moji-Guaçu r. Brazil
29 B8 Mojikō Japan
23 F4 Mokāma India
74 □1 Mokapu Pen. pen. U.S.A.
9 E3 Mokau N.Z.
9 E3 Mokau r. N.Z.
74 B2 Mokelumne r. U.S.A.
59 H4 Mokhoabong Pass Lesotho
59 H4 Mokhotlong Lesotho
48 D7 Moknine Tunisia
9 E1 Mokohinau Is is N.Z.
55 D3 Mokolo Cameroon
59 G2 Mokolo r. S. Africa
30 D6 Mokp'o S. Korea
50 G4 Moksha r. Rus. Fed.
50 H4 Mokshan Rus. Fed.
74 □1 Mokuauia I. i. U.S.A.
74 □1 Mokulua Is is U.S.A.
84 C2 Molango Mex.
45 F3 Molatón mt Spain
Moldavia country see Moldova
36 K5 Molde Norway
36 O3 Moldjord Norway
35 H4 Moldova country Europe
49 L2 Moldoveanu, Vârful mt Romania
39 D7 Mole r. U.K.
54 B4 Mole National Park Ghana
57 C6 Molepolole Botswana
37 T9 Molėtai Lith.
48 G4 Molfetta Italy
30 C2 Molihong Shan h. China
45 F2 Molina de Aragón Spain
68 B5 Moline U.S.A.
37 N7 Molkom Sweden
17 M4 Mollā Bodāgh Iran
23 H4 Mol Len mt India
43 M1 Möllenbeck Ger.
86 D7 Mollendo Peru
43 J1 Mölln Ger.
37 N8 Mölnlycke Sweden
50 F3 Molochnoye Rus. Fed.
36 X2 Molochnyy Rus. Fed.
92 D4 Molodezhnaya Rus. Fed. Base Ant.
50 E3 Molodoy Tud Rus. Fed.
74 □2 Molokai i. U.S.A.
95 K4 Molokai Fracture Zone sea feature Pac. Oc.
50 J3 Moloma r. Rus. Fed.
8 G2 Molong Austr.
58 F2 Molopo watercourse Botswana/S. Africa
55 D4 Moloundou Cameroon
65 K4 Molson L. l. Can.
Moluccas is see Maluku
25 E7 Molucca Sea g. Indon.
57 D5 Moma Moz.
8 D1 Momba Austr.
56 D4 Mombasa Kenya
23 H4 Mombi New India
90 B2 Mombuca, Serra da h. Brazil
51 C7 Momchilgrad Bulg.
68 D5 Momence U.S.A.
87 B2 Mompós Col.
37 N9 Møn i. Denmark
75 G2 Mona U.S.A.
40 A3 Monach Islands is U.K.
40 A3 Monach, Sound of chan. U.K.
34 F4 Monaco country Europe
40 D3 Monadhliath Mountains mts U.K.
41 E3 Monaghan Rep. of Ireland
77 C6 Monahans U.S.A.
83 L5 Mona, I. i. Puerto Rico
83 L5 Mona Passage chan. Dom. Rep./Puerto Rico
57 E5 Monapo Moz.
64 D4 Monarch Mt. mt Can.
73 F4 Monarch Pass U.S.A.
40 C3 Monar, Loch l. U.K.
64 F4 Monashee Mts mts Can.
48 D7 Monastir Tunisia
47 P3 Monastyrshchina Rus. Fed.
51 D5 Monastyryshche Ukr.
28 H2 Monbetsu Japan
28 H3 Monbetsu Japan
48 B2 Moncalieri Italy
45 F2 Moncayo mt Spain
36 X3 Monchegorsk Rus. Fed.
42 E3 Mönchengladbach Ger.
45 B4 Monchique Port.
79 E5 Moncks Corner U.S.A.
82 D3 Monclova Mex.
67 H4 Moncton Can.
45 C2 Mondego r. Port.
59 J3 Mondlo S. Africa
48 B2 Mondovì Italy
68 B3 Mondovi U.S.A.
48 E4 Mondragone Italy
49 K6 Monemvasia Greece
28 G1 Moneron, Ostrov i. Rus. Fed.
80 D4 Monessen U.S.A.
69 K1 Monet Can.
41 D5 Moneygall Rep. of Ireland
41 E3 Moneymore U.K.
48 E2 Monfalcone Italy
45 C1 Monforte Spain
56 C3 Monga Congo(Zaire)
27 C6 Mông Cai Vietnam
30 C4 Monggŭmp'o-ri N. Korea
32 A1 Mong Mau Myanmar
10 L5 Mongolia country Asia
22 C2 Mongora Pak.
57 C5 Mongu Zambia
81 J3 Monhegan I. i. U.S.A.
40 E5 Moniaive U.K.
74 D2 Monitor Mt mt U.S.A.
74 D2 Monitor Range mts U.S.A.
41 C4 Monivea Rep. of Ireland
69 G4 Monkton Can.
23 F3 Mon La pass China
39 E6 Monmouth U.K.
68 B5 Monmouth IL U.S.A.
81 H2 Monmouth ME U.S.A.
64 E4 Monmouth Mt. mt Can.
39 E6 Monnow r. U.K.
54 C3 Mono r. Togo
74 C3 Mono Lake l. U.S.A.
81 H4 Monomoy Pt pt U.S.A.
68 D5 Monon U.S.A.
68 B4 Monona U.S.A.
48 G4 Monopoli Italy
80 C5 Monorgahela r. U.S.A.
45 F2 Monreal del Campo Spain
48 E5 Monreale Sicily Italy
77 E5 Monroe LA U.S.A.
69 F5 Monroe MI U.S.A.
79 D5 Monroe NC U.S.A.
81 F4 Monroe NY U.S.A.
75 F2 Monroe UT U.S.A.
68 C4 Monroe WV U.S.A.
68 B6 Monroe City U.S.A.
79 C6 Monroeville U.S.A.
54 A4 Monrovia Liberia
42 B4 Mons Belgium
42 E4 Monschau Ger.
48 D2 Monselice Italy
43 F4 Montabaur Ger.
57 E5 Montagne d'Ambre, Parc National de la nat. park Madag.
58 D6 Montagu S. Africa
68 D4 Montague U.S.A.
92 C1 Montagu I. i. Atl. Ocean
48 F5 Montalto mt Italy
48 G5 Montalto Uffugo Italy
49 K3 Montana Bulg.
72 E2 Montana div. U.S.A.
44 F3 Montargis France
44 E4 Montauban France
81 G4 Montauk U.S.A.
81 H4 Montauk Pt pt U.S.A.
44 G3 Montbard France
45 G2 Montblanc Spain
44 G4 Montbrison France
44 G3 Montceau-les-Mines France
42 C5 Montcornet France
44 D5 Mont-de-Marsan France
44 F2 Montdidier France
87 H4 Monte Alegre Brazil
90 C1 Monte Alegre de Goiás Brazil
90 D1 Monte Azul Brazil
66 E4 Montebello Can.
48 F6 Montebello Ionico Italy
48 E2 Montebelluna Italy
91 D2 Monte Buey Arg.
44 H5 Monte Carlo Monaco
91 F1 Monte Caseros Arg.
59 G1 Monte Christo S. Africa
91 C2 Monte Comán Arg.
83 K5 Monte Cristi Dom. Rep.
48 D3 Montecristo, Isola di i. Italy
83 J5 Montego Bay Jamaica
44 G4 Montélimar France
88 E2 Monte Lindo r. Para.
48 F4 Montella Italy
68 C4 Montello U.S.A.
84 C1 Montemorelos Mex.
45 B3 Montemor-o-Novo Port.
49 H3 Montenegro div. Yugo.
57 D5 Montepuez Moz.
48 D3 Montepulciano Italy
44 F2 Montereau-faut-Yonne France
74 B3 Monterey CA U.S.A.
80 D5 Monterey VA U.S.A.
74 B3 Monterey Bay b. U.S.A.
89 B2 Montería Col.
86 F7 Montero Bol.
84 B1 Monterrey Mex.
48 F4 Montesano sulla Marcellana Italy
87 L6 Monte Santo Brazil
90 D2 Montes Claros Brazil
48 F3 Montesilvano Italy
48 D3 Montevarchi Italy
91 F2 Montevideo Uru.
76 E2 Montevideo U.S.A.
73 F4 Monte Vista U.S.A.
68 A5 Montezuma U.S.A.
75 G4 Montezuma Castle National Monument res. U.S.A.
75 H3 Montezuma Creek U.S.A.
74 D3 Montezuma Peak summit U.S.A.
42 D3 Montfort Neth.
39 D5 Montgomery U.K.
79 C5 Montgomery U.S.A.
46 C7 Monthey Switz.
77 F5 Monticello AR U.S.A.
79 D6 Monticello FL U.S.A.
68 B4 Monticello IA U.S.A.
68 D5 Monticello IN U.S.A.
81 K1 Monticello ME U.S.A.
68 B5 Monticello MO U.S.A.
81 F4 Monticello NY U.S.A.
75 H3 Monticello UT U.S.A.
68 C4 Monticello WV U.S.A.
91 E1 Montiel, Cuchilla de h. Arg.
44 E4 Montignac France
42 C4 Montignies-le-Tilleul Belgium
42 E5 Montigny-lès-Metz France
45 D4 Montilla Spain
67 G4 Mont Joli Can.
69 K2 Mont-Laurier Can.
67 G4 Mont Louis Can.
44 F3 Montluçon France
67 F4 Montmagny Can.
42 D5 Montmédy France
42 B6 Montmirail France
68 D5 Montmorenci U.S.A.
67 F4 Montmorency Can.
44 E3 Montmorillon France
42 B6 Montmort-Lucy France
6 F4 Monto Austr.
72 E3 Montpelier ID U.S.A.
68 E5 Montpelier IN U.S.A.
80 A4 Montpelier OH U.S.A.
81 G2 Montpelier VT U.S.A.
44 F5 Montpellier France
66 F4 Montréal Can.
69 G2 Montreal r. Can.
69 F2 Montreal r. Can.
68 E2 Montreal I. i. Can.
65 H4 Montreal Lake Can.
65 H4 Montreal Lake l. Can.
81 F2 Montréal-Mirabel Can.
68 E2 Montreal River Can.
46 C7 Montreux Switz.
40 F4 Montrose U.K.
73 F4 Montrose CO U.S.A.
69 F4 Montrose MI U.S.A.
81 F4 Montrose PA U.S.A.
58 D3 Montrose well S. Africa
61 M8 Montserrat terr. Caribbean Sea
67 G4 Monts, Pte des pt Can.
75 G3 Monument Valley reg. U.S.A.
24 B4 Monywa Myanmar
48 C2 Monza Italy
57 C5 Monze Zambia
45 G2 Monzón Spain
59 J4 Mooi r. S. Africa
58 B3 Mooifontein Namibia
59 J4 Mooirivier S. Africa
59 G1 Mookane Botswana
8 H1 Moonbi Ra. mts Austr.
8 A3 Moonta Austr.
72 F2 Moorcroft U.S.A.
80 D5 Moorefield U.S.A.
6 B4 Moore, Lake salt flat Austr.
79 E7 Moores I. i. Bahamas
81 K2 Moores Mills Can.
40 E5 Moorfoot Hills h. U.K.
76 D2 Moorhead U.S.A.
8 D2 Moornanyah Lake Austr.
8 C3 Moorook Austr.
8 E4 Mooroopna Austr.
58 C6 Moorreesburg S. Africa
66 D3 Moose r. Can.
66 D3 Moose Factory Can.
81 J2 Moosehead Lake l. U.S.A.
65 J4 Moose Jaw Can.
68 A2 Moose Lake U.S.A.
65 J4 Moose Lake l. Can.
81 H2 Mooselookmeguntic Lake l. U.S.A.
66 D3 Moose River Can.
65 J4 Moosomin Can.
66 D3 Moosonee Can.
8 D1 Mootwingee Austr.
59 H1 Mopane S. Africa
54 B3 Mopti Mali
19 G3 Moqor Afgh.
86 D7 Moquegua Peru
55 D3 Mora Cameroon
45 E3 Mora Spain
37 O6 Mora Sweden
91 B2 Mora, Cerro mt Arg./Chile
22 A3 Morad r. Pak.
22 D3 Moradabad India
57 E5 Morafenobe Madag.
21 B2 Moram India
57 E5 Moramanga Madag.
68 E3 Moran MI U.S.A.
72 E3 Moran WY U.S.A.
40 C4 Morar, Loch l. U.K.
21 C5 Moratuwa Sri Lanka
46 H6 Morava r. Austria/Slovakia
18 D2 Moraveh Tappeh Iran
81 E3 Moravia U.S.A.
40 E3 Moray Firth est. U.K.
42 F5 Morbach Ger.
48 C1 Morbegno Italy
22 B5 Morbi India
44 D4 Morcenx France
24 E1 Mordaga China
17 K3 Mor Dağı mt Turkey
65 K5 Morden Can.
8 E5 Mordialloc Austr.
50 H4 Mordoviya, Respublika div. Rus. Fed.
51 G4 Mordovo Rus. Fed.
76 C2 Moreau r. U.S.A.
38 E3 Morecambe U.K.
38 D3 Morecambe Bay b. U.K.
6 E4 Moree Austr.
6 E2 Morehead P.N.G.
80 B5 Morehead U.S.A.
79 E5 Morehead City U.S.A.
22 D4 Morel r. India
84 B3 Morelia Mex.
45 F2 Morella Spain
40 D2 More, Loch l. U.K.
84 E3 Morelos Mex.
84 C3 Morelos div. Mex.
22 D4 Morena India
45 D3 Morena, Sierra mts Spain
75 H5 Morenci AZ U.S.A.
69 E5 Morenci MI U.S.A.
49 L2 Moreni Romania
91 E2 Moreno Arg.
73 E6 Moreno Mex.
74 D5 Moreno Valley U.S.A.
64 C4 Moresby Island i. Can.
58 F1 Moreswe Pan salt pan Botswana
39 F6 Moreton-in-Marsh U.K.
42 A5 Moreuil France
16 D4 Morfou Cyprus
16 D4 Morfou Bay b. Cyprus
8 B3 Morgan Austr.
77 F6 Morgan City U.S.A.
74 B3 Morgan Hill U.S.A.
74 C3 Morgan, Mt mt U.S.A.
81 F4 Morgantown PA U.S.A.
80 D5 Morgantown WV U.S.A.
59 H3 Morgenzon S. Africa
46 C7 Morges Switz.
23 F4 Morhar r. India
28 G3 Mori Japan
75 E2 Moriah, Mt mt U.S.A.
73 F5 Moriarty U.S.A.
89 C4 Morichal Col.
89 E2 Morichal Largo r. Venez.
59 G4 Morija Lesotho
43 H3 Moringen Ger.
50 D3 Morino Rus. Fed.
28 G5 Morioka Japan
8 H2 Morisset Austr.
28 G5 Moriyoshi-zan volc. Japan
36 S3 Morjärv Sweden
19 F4 Morjen r. Pak.
50 J3 Morki Rus. Fed.
44 C2 Morlaix France
38 F4 Morley U.K.
75 G4 Mormon Lake l. U.S.A.
6 D3 Mornington I. i. Austr.
88 A7 Mornington, I. i. Chile
22 A4 Moro Pak.
6 E2 Morobe P.N.G.
68 D5 Morocco U.S.A.
52 D3 Morocco country Africa
56 D4 Morogoro Tanz.
31 B5 Moro Gulf g. Phil.
59 G4 Morojaneng S. Africa
58 E3 Morokweng S. Africa
84 B2 Moroleón Mex.
57 E6 Morombe Madag.
83 J4 Morón Cuba
24 C2 Mörön Mongolia
57 E6 Morondava Madag.
45 D4 Morón de la Frontera Spain
57 E5 Moroni Comoros
25 E6 Morotai i. Indon.
56 D3 Moroto Uganda
51 G5 Morozovsk Rus. Fed.
69 G4 Morpeth Can.
38 F2 Morpeth U.K.
90 C2 Morrinhos Brazil
65 K5 Morris Can.
68 C5 Morris IL U.S.A.
76 E2 Morris MN U.S.A.
81 F2 Morrisburg Can.
68 C5 Morrison U.S.A.
75 F5 Morristown AZ U.S.A.
81 F4 Morristown NJ U.S.A.
81 F2 Morristown NY U.S.A.
79 D4 Morristown TN U.S.A.
81 F4 Morrisville PA U.S.A.
81 G2 Morrisville VT U.S.A.
74 B4 Morro Bay U.S.A.
89 C2 Morrocoy, Parque Nacional nat. park Venez.
87 H4 Morro Grande h. Brazil
88 B3 Morro, Pta pt Chile
89 B2 Morrosquillo, Golfo de b. Col.
43 H3 Morschen Ger.
68 D5 Morse Reservoir resr U.S.A.
50 G4 Morshansk Rus. Fed.
50 E2 Morskaya Masel'ga Rus. Fed.
48 C7 Morsott Alg.
44 E2 Mortagne-au-Perche France
44 D3 Mortagne-sur-Sèvre France
39 C6 Mortehoe U.K.
91 E1 Morteros Arg.
Mortes r. see Manso
8 D5 Mortlake Austr.
Mortlock Is is see Tauu
39 G5 Morton U.K.
68 C5 Morton IL U.S.A.
72 B2 Morton WA U.S.A.
8 H3 Morton Nat. Park Austr.
8 F3 Morundah Austr.
59 G1 Morupule Botswana
8 H3 Moruya Austr.
40 C4 Morvern reg. U.K.
Morvi see Morbi
8 F5 Morwell Austr.
43 H5 Mosbach Ger.
39 F4 Mosborough U.K.
50 F4 Moscow Rus. Fed.
72 C2 Moscow U.S.A.
92 C6 Moscow Univ. Ice Shelf ice feature Ant.
92 B6 Mose, C. c. Ant.
42 F4 Mosel r. Ger.
58 E2 Moselebe watercourse Botswana
44 H2 Moselle r. France
43 K2 Möser Ger.
72 C2 Moses Lake U.S.A.
74 D1 Moses, Mt mt U.S.A.
9 C6 Mosgiel N.Z.
58 E3 Moshaweng watercourse S. Africa
56 D4 Moshi Tanz.
68 C3 Mosinee U.S.A.
36 N4 Mosjøen Norway
36 N3 Moskenesøy i. Norway
50 F4 Moskovskaya Oblast' div. Rus. Fed.
Moskva see Moscow
46 H7 Mosonmagyaróvár Hungary
89 A4 Mosquera Col.
73 F5 Mosquero U.S.A.
83 H5 Mosquitia reg. Honduras
90 E1 Mosquito r. Brazil
80 C4 Mosquito Creek Lake l. U.S.A.
83 H7 Mosquitos, Golfo de los b. Panama
65 J2 Mosquitto Lake l. Can.
37 M7 Moss Norway
40 F3 Mossat U.K.
9 B6 Mossburn N.Z.
58 E7 Mossel Bay S. Africa
58 E7 Mossel Bay b. S. Africa
56 B4 Mossendjo Congo
8 E2 Mossgiel Austr.
6 E3 Mossman Austr.
87 L5 Mossoró Brazil
8 H3 Moss Vale Austr.
46 F5 Most Czech Rep.
18 D3 Moştafaabad Iran
54 C1 Mostaganem Alg.
48 G3 Mostar Bos.-Herz.
88 F4 Mostardas Brazil
65 G3 Mostoos Hills h. Can.
51 G6 Mostovskoy Rus. Fed.
33 E2 Mostyn Malaysia
17 J3 Mosul Iraq
37 L7 Møsvatnet l. Norway
37 O7 Motala Sweden
89 C2 Motatán r. Venez.
59 K2 Motaze Moz.
59 H2 Motetema S. Africa
22 D4 Moth India
40 E5 Motherwell U.K.
23 F4 Motihari India
45 F3 Motilla del Palancar Spain
9 F2 Motiti I. i. N.Z.
30 B3 Motlan Ling h. China
58 E2 Motokwe Botswana
84 D4 Motozintla Mex.
45 E4 Motril Spain
49 K2 Motru Romania
82 G4 Motul Mex.
5 M6 Motu One i. Pac. Oc.
27 A5 Mouding China
54 A3 Moudjéria Maur.
49 L5 Moudros Greece
37 S6 Mouhijärvi Fin.
56 B4 Mouila Gabon
8 E3 Moulamein Austr.
56 B4 Moulèngui Binza Gabon
44 F3 Moulins France
32 A1 Moulmein Myanmar
79 D6 Moultrie U.S.A.
71 L5 Moultrie, Lake l. SC U.S.A.
78 B4 Mound City IL U.S.A.
76 E3 Mound City MO U.S.A.
55 D4 Moundou Chad
80 C5 Moundsville U.S.A.
22 C4 Mount Abu India
79 C5 Mountain Brook U.S.A.
68 C3 Mountain City U.S.A.
77 E4 Mountain Grove U.S.A.
77 E4 Mountain Home AR U.S.A.
72 D3 Mountain Home ID U.S.A.
59 F6 Mountain Zebra National Park S. Africa
80 C6 Mount Airy U.S.A.
9 B6 Mount Aspiring National Park N.Z.
59 H5 Mount Ayliff S. Africa
76 E3 Mount Ayr U.S.A.
8 B3 Mount Barker Austr.
8 F4 Mount Beauty Austr.
41 C4 Mount Bellew Rep. of Ireland
8 F4 Mt Bogong Nat.Park Austr.
8 F4 Mount Buffalo National Park Austr.
81 K1 Mount Carleton Provincial Park res. Can.
75 F3 Mount Carmel Junction U.S.A.
68 C4 Mount Carroll U.S.A.
9 C5 Mount Cook N.Z.
9 C5 Mount Cook National Park N.Z.
57 D5 Mount Darwin Zimbabwe
81 J2 Mount Desert Island i. U.S.A.
59 H5 Mount Fletcher S. Africa
69 G4 Mount Forest Can.
59 H5 Mount Frere S. Africa
8 C4 Mount Gambier Austr.
80 B4 Mount Gilead U.S.A.
6 E2 Mount Hagen P.N.G.
8 E2 Mount Hope N.S.W. Austr.
80 C6 Mount Hope U.S.A.
6 D4 Mount Isa Austr.
81 G4 Mount Kisco U.S.A.
8 B3 Mount Lofty Range mts Austr.
69 G2 Mount MacDonald Can.
6 B4 Mount Magnet Austr.
8 D2 Mount Manara Austr.
74 B1 Mount Meadows Reservoir U.S.A.
41 D4 Mountmellick Rep. of Ireland
59 G5 Mount Moorosi Lesotho
8 D1 Mount Murchison Austr.
68 B5 Mount Pleasant IA U.S.A.
68 E4 Mount Pleasant MI U.S.A.
78 C3 Mount Pleasant MI U.S.A.
80 D4 Mount Pleasant PA U.S.A.
79 E5 Mount Pleasant SC U.S.A.
77 E5 Mount Pleasant TX U.S.A.
75 G2 Mount Pleasant UT U.S.A.
68 C5 Mount Pulaski U.S.A.
72 B2 Mount Rainier Nat. Park U.S.A.
64 F4 Mount Robson Prov. Park res. Can.
80 C6 Mount Rogers National Recreation Area res. U.S.A.
39 B7 Mount's Bay b. U.K.
39 F5 Mountsorrel U.K.
68 B6 Mount Sterling IL U.S.A.
80 B5 Mount Sterling KY U.S.A.
80 D5 Mount Storm U.S.A.
80 E4 Mount Union U.S.A.
79 B6 Mount Vernon AL U.S.A.
68 B5 Mount Vernon IA U.S.A.
78 B4 Mount Vernon IL U.S.A.
80 A6 Mount Vernon KY U.S.A.
80 B4 Mount Vernon OH U.S.A.
72 B1 Mount Vernon WA U.S.A.
92 C3 Mt. Victor mt Ant.
6 E4 Moura Austr.
86 F4 Moura Brazil
55 E3 Mourdi, Dépression du depression Chad
41 D3 Mourne r. U.K.
41 E3 Mourne Mountains h. U.K.
42 B4 Mouscron Belgium
55 D3 Moussoro Chad
25 E6 Moutong Indon.
42 A5 Mouy France
54 C2 Mouydir, Mts de plat. Alg.
42 D5 Mouzon France
41 C4 Moy r. Rep. of Ireland
56 D3 Moyale Eth.
54 A4 Moyamba Sierra Leone
21 B4 Moyar r. India
54 B1 Moyen Atlas mts Morocco
59 G5 Moyeni Lesotho
41 E4 Moyer h. Rep. of Ireland
67 G2 Moyne, Lac le l. Can.
15 F2 Moyynty Kazak.
53 H8 Mozambique country Africa
57 E5 Mozambique Channel str. Africa
93 G5 Mozambique Ridge sea feature Ind. Ocean
51 H7 Mozdok Rus. Fed.
19 F2 Mozdūrān Iran
50 F4 Mozhaysk Rus. Fed.
19 F3 Mozhnābād Iran
23 H5 Mozo Myanmar
56 C4 Mpala Congo(Zaire)
56 D4 Mpanda Tanz.
57 D5 Mpika Zambia
59 J4 Mpolweni S. Africa
57 D4 Mporokoso Zambia
59 H2 Mpumalanga div. S. Africa
59 H5 Mqanduli S. Africa
48 G2 Mrkonjić-Grad Bos.-Herz.
54 D1 M'Saken Tunisia
50 D3 Mshinskaya Rus. Fed.
45 J5 M'Sila Alg.
50 E3 Msta r. Rus. Fed.
50 D4 Mstsislaw Belarus
59 H4 Mt-aux-Sources mt Lesotho
50 F4 Mtsensk Rus. Fed.
59 K4 Mtubatuba S. Africa
59 J4 Mtunzini S. Africa
57 E5 Mtwara Tanz.
56 B4 Muanda Congo(Zaire)
32 B2 Muang Chainat Thai.
32 A1 Muang Chiang Rai Thai.
27 B6 Muang Hiam Laos
32 B1 Muang Hôngsa Laos
32 B1 Muang Kalasin Thai.
32 C1 Muang Khammouan Laos
32 C2 Muang Không Laos
32 C2 Muang Khôngxédôn Laos
32 B1 Muang Khon Kaen Thai.
27 B6 Muang Khoua Laos
32 A3 Muang Kirirath r. Thai.
32 A1 Muang Lampang Thai.
32 A1 Muang Lamphun Thai.
32 B1 Muang Loei Thai.
32 B1 Muang Lom Sak Thai.
32 A1 Muang Long Thai.
32 A3 Muang Luang r. Thai.
32 C2 Muang Mai Thai.
32 C1 Muang Mok Laos
32 C1 Muang Nakhon Phanom Thai.
32 B2 Muang Nakhon Sawan Thai.
32 B1 Muang Nan Thai.
27 B6 Muang Ngoy Laos
32 C1 Muang Nong Laos
27 A6 Muang Ou Nua Laos
32 B1 Muang Pakxan Laos
32 C1 Muang Phalan Laos
32 A1 Muang Phan Thai.
32 A1 Muang Phayao Thai.
32 B1 Muang Phetchabun Thai.
32 B1 Muang Phiang Laos
32 B1 Muang Phichai Thai.
32 B1 Muang Phichit Thai.
32 C1 Muang Phin Laos
32 B1 Muang Phitsanulok Thai.
32 B1 Muang Phôn-Hông Laos
32 B1 Muang Phrae Thai.
32 B1 Muang Roi Et Thai.
32 C1 Muang Sakon Nakhon Thai.
32 B2 Muang Samut Prakan Thai.
32 B1 Muang Souy Laos
32 B2 Muang Uthai Thani Thai.
27 B6 Muang Va Laos
32 B1 Muang Vangviang Laos
32 B1 Muang Xaignabouri Laos
27 B6 Muang Xay Laos
27 B6 Muang Xon Laos
32 C2 Muang Yasothon Thai.
33 B2 Muar Malaysia
32 B5 Muar r. Malaysia
33 B3 Muarabungo Indon.
33 B3 Muaradua Indon.
33 A3 Muarasiberut Indon.
33 A2 Muarasipongi Indon.
33 B3 Muaratembesi Indon.
23 E4 Mubarakpur India
19 G2 Mubarek Uzbek.
17 H7 Mubarraz well S. Arabia
56 D3 Mubende Uganda
55 D3 Mubi Nigeria
89 E4 Mucajaí r. Brazil
89 E4 Mucajaí, Serra do mts Brazil
42 F4 Much Ger.
57 D5 Muchinga Escarpment esc. Zambia
27 B4 Muchuan China
40 B4 Muck i. U.K.
40 □ Muckle Roe i. U.K.
89 C3 Muco r. Col.
57 C5 Muconda Angola
89 E4 Mucucuaú r. Brazil
16 E2 Mucur Turkey
90 E2 Mucuri Brazil
90 E2 Mucuri r. Brazil
57 C5 Mucussueje Angola
32 B4 Muda r. Malaysia
21 A3 Mūdabidri India
30 E1 Mudanjiang China
30 E1 Mudan Jiang r. China
16 B1 Mudanya Turkey
17 L7 Mudayrah Kuwait
80 C5 Muddlety U.S.A.
36 R3 Muddus Nationalpark nat. park Sweden
75 G2 Muddy Creek r. U.S.A.
75 E3 Muddy Peak summit U.S.A.
19 E3 Mūd-e-Dahanāb Iran
43 F4 Mudersbach Ger.
8 G2 Mudgee Austr.
21 A2 Mudhol India
22 C3 Mudki India
74 D3 Mud Lake l. U.S.A.
32 A1 Mudon Myanmar
16 C1 Mudurnu Turkey
50 F2 Mud'yuga Rus. Fed.
57 D5 Mueda Moz.
84 D3 Muerto, Mar l. Mex.
50 H1 Muftyuga Rus. Fed.
57 C5 Mufulira Zambia
57 C5 Mufumbwe Zambia
27 E4 Mufu Shan mts China
81 K2 Mugaguadavic Lake l. Can.
17 M2 Muğan Düzü lowland Azer.
23 F2 Mugarripug China
Mughalbhin see Jati
23 E4 Mughal Sarai India
18 D3 Mūghār Iran
16 F7 Mughayrā' S. Arabia
19 H2 Mughsu r. Tajik.
16 B3 Muğla Turkey
23 H2 Mug Qu r. China
23 E3 Mugu Karnali r. Nepal
23 H2 Mugxung China
55 F2 Muhammad Qol Sudan
18 B5 Muḥayriqah S. Arabia
43 L3 Mühlanger Ger.
43 M3 Mühlberg Ger.
43 J3 Mühlhausen (Thüringen) Ger.
36 T4 Muhos Fin.
56 C4 Muhulu Congo(Zaire)
32 C3 Mui Ca Mau c. Vietnam
32 D3 Mui Dinh hd Vietnam
32 D2 Mui Nây pt Vietnam
41 E5 Muine Bheag Rep. of Ireland
40 D5 Muirkirk U.K.
40 B2 Muirneag h. U.K.
40 D3 Muir of Ord U.K.
74 A3 Muir Woods National Monument res. U.S.A.
57 D5 Muite Moz.
30 D6 Muju S. Korea
51 B5 Mukacheve Ukr.
33 D2 Mukah Malaysia
23 F3 Mukangsar China
32 C1 Mukdahan Thai.
6 B5 Mukinbudin Austr.
33 B3 Mukomuko Indon.
19 G2 Mukry Turkm.
22 C3 Muktsar India
65 K4 Mukutawa r. Can.
68 C4 Mukwonago U.S.A.
22 D5 Mul India
21 A2 Mula r. India
22 A3 Mula r. Pak.
28 A2 Mulan China
31 B3 Mulanay Phil.
57 D5 Mulanje, Mt mt Malawi
18 B5 Mulayḥ S. Arabia
77 E5 Mulberry U.S.A.
91 B3 Mulchén Chile
43 L3 Mulde r. Ger.
56 D4 Muleba Tanz.
75 H5 Mule Creek NM U.S.A.
72 F3 Mule Creek WY U.S.A.
77 C5 Muleshoe U.S.A.
45 E4 Mulhacén mt Spain
42 E3 Mülheim an der Ruhr Ger.
44 H3 Mulhouse France
27 A5 Muli China
30 F1 Muling China
30 F1 Muling China
30 G1 Muling r. China
40 C4 Mull i. U.K.
17 M3 Mulla Ali Iran
41 B5 Mullaghareirk Mts h. Rep. of Ireland
21 C4 Mullaittivu Sri Lanka
8 G1 Mullaley Austr.
8 F1 Mullengudgery Austr.
33 D2 Muller, Pegunungan mts Indon.
68 E3 Mullett Lake l. U.S.A.
6 B4 Mullewa Austr.
40 F1 Mull Head hd U.K.
81 F5 Mullica r. U.S.A.
41 D4 Mullingar Rep. of Ireland
8 G2 Mullion Cr. Austr.
40 B4 Mull, Sound of chan. U.K.
57 C5 Mulobezi Zambia
21 A2 Mulshi L. l. India
22 D5 Multai India
22 B3 Multan Pak.
37 T5 Multia Fin.
42 A6 Multien reg. France
19 F5 Mūmān Iran
Mumbai see Bombay
8 G2 Mumbil Austr.
57 C5 Mumbwa Zambia
19 H2 Mū'minobod Tajik.
51 H6 Mumra Rus. Fed.
84 E2 Muna Mex.
13 N3 Muna r. Rus. Fed.
36 C3 Munaðarnes Iceland
43 K4 Münchberg Ger.
46 E6 München Ger.
43 G4 Münchhausen Ger.
89 A4 Munchique, Co mt Col.
64 D3 Muncho Lake Can.
64 D3 Muncho Lake Provincial Park res. Can.
30 D4 Munch'ŏn N. Korea
68 E5 Muncie U.S.A.
80 E4 Muncy U.S.A.
21 B5 Mundel L. l. Sri Lanka
39 J5 Mundesley U.K.
39 H5 Mundford U.K.
6 C5 Mundrabilla Austr.
22 C4 Mundwa India
21 C2 Muneru r. India
22 D4 Mungaoli India
56 C3 Mungbere Congo(Zaire)
23 E5 Mungeli India
23 F4 Munger India
32 D5 Munggaresak, Tanjung pt Indon.
6 E4 Mungindi Austr.
Munich see München
87 K4 Munim r. Brazil
68 D2 Munising U.S.A.
90 E3 Muniz Freire Brazil
37 M7 Munkedal Sweden
36 V2 Munkelva Norway
37 N7 Munkfors Sweden
43 J4 Münnerstadt Ger.
59 H1 Munnik S. Africa
30 D5 Munsan S. Korea
46 C7 Münsingen Switz.
43 G5 Münster Hessen Ger.
43 J2 Münster Niedersachsen Ger.
42 F3 Münster Nordrhein-Westfalen Ger.
42 F3 Münsterland reg. Ger.
67 F3 Muntviel, Lac l. Can.
36 V4 Muojärvi l. Fin.
32 C1 Mương Lam Vietnam
27 B6 Mương Nhie Vietnam
36 S3 Muonio Fin.
36 S2 Muonioälven r. Fin./Sweden
30 A5 Muping China
56 E3 Muqdisho Somalia
17 M1 Müqtädır Azer.
17 J2 Muradiye Turkey
28 F5 Murakami Japan
88 B7 Murallón, Cerro mt Chile
56 C4 Muramvya Burundi
56 D4 Muranga Kenya
32 □ Mura Res. resr Sing.
50 J3 Murashi Rus. Fed.
17 H2 Murat r. Turkey
16 B2 Murat Dağı mts Turkey
16 A1 Muratlı Turkey
28 G5 Murayama Japan
18 C3 Murcheh Khvort Iran
8 E4 Murchison Austr.
6 B4 Murchison watercourse Austr.
56 D3 Murchison Falls National Park Uganda
45 F4 Murcia Spain
45 F4 Murcia div. Spain
76 C3 Murdo U.S.A.
67 G4 Murdochville Can.
57 D5 Murehwa Zimbabwe
47 M7 Mureș r. Romania
44 E5 Muret France
79 E4 Murfreesboro NC U.S.A.
79 C5 Murfreesboro TN U.S.A.
19 F2 Murgab Turkm.
19 F2 Murgab r. Turkm.
19 G3 Murghab r. Afgh.
22 B3 Murgha Kibzai Pak.
15 F3 Murghob Tajik.
19 H3 Murgh Pass Afgh.
26 A2 Muri China
23 F5 Muri India
18 E2 Mūrī Iran
90 D3 Muriaé Brazil
57 C4 Muriege Angola
43 L1 Müritz l. Ger.
43 M1 Müritz, Nationalpark nat. park Ger.
43 L1 Müritz Seenpark res. Ger.
36 X2 Murmansk Rus. Fed.
36 W2 Murmanskaya Oblast' div. Rus. Fed.
48 C4 Muro, Capo di pt Corsica France
50 G4 Murom Rus. Fed.
28 G3 Muroran Japan
45 B1 Muros Spain
29 D8 Muroto Japan
29 D8 Muroto-zaki pt Japan

68 D5 Murphey Lake, J. C. l. U.S.A.
72 C3 Murphy ID U.S.A.
79 D5 Murphy NC U.S.A.
74 B2 Murphys U.S.A.
78 B4 Murray KY U.S.A.
72 E3 Murray UT U.S.A.
8 C3 Murray r. Austr.
64 E3 Murray r. Can.
8 B3 Murray Bridge Austr.
79 D5 Murray, L. l. U.S.A.
6 E2 Murray, Lake l. P.N.G.
58 E5 Murraysburg S. Africa
95 L3 Murray Seascarp sea feature Pac. Oc.
8 C3 Murrayville Austr.
43 H6 Murrhardt Ger.
8 G3 Murringo Austr.
41 B4 Murrisk reg. Rep. of Ireland
41 B4 Murroogh Rep. of Ireland
8 G3 Murrumbateman Austr.
8 E3 Murrumbidgee r. Austr.
57 D5 Murrupula Moz.
8 H1 Murrurundi Austr.
48 G1 Murska Sobota Slovenia
8 D4 Murtoa Austr.
21 A2 Murud India
30 A2 Muruin Sum Sk. resr China
21 C4 Murunkan Sri Lanka
9 F3 Murupara N.Z.
5 O7 Mururoa i. Pac. Oc.
22 E5 Murwara India
55 D2 Murzūq Libya
46 G7 Mürzzuschlag Austria
17 H2 Muş Turkey
22 B3 Musa Khel Bazar Pak.
33 A2 Musala i. Indon.
49 K3 Musala mt Bulg.
30 E2 Musan N. Korea
18 E5 Musandam Peninsula Oman
19 G3 Musa Qala Afgh.
19 G3 Musa Qala, Rūd-i r. Afgh.
Musay'īd see Umm Sa'id
20 E5 Muscat Oman
68 B5 Muscatine U.S.A.
68 B4 Muscoda U.S.A.
81 J3 Muscongus Bay b. U.S.A.
6 D4 Musgrave Ranges mts Austr.
41 C5 Musheramore h. Rep. of Ireland
56 B4 Mushie Congo(Zaire)
21 B2 Musi r. India
33 B3 Musi r. Indon.
75 F4 Music Mt mt U.S.A.
75 G2 Musinia Peak summit U.S.A.
64 E2 Muskeg r. Can.
81 H4 Muskeget Channel chan. U.S.A.
68 D4 Muskegon U.S.A.
68 D4 Muskegon r. U.S.A.
80 C5 Muskingum r. U.S.A.
77 E5 Muskogee U.S.A.
69 H3 Muskoka Can.
69 H3 Muskoka, Lake l. Can.
64 E3 Muskwa r. Can.
16 F3 Muslimīyah Syria
55 F3 Musmar Sudan
56 D4 Musoma Tanz.
6 E2 Mussau I. i. P.N.G.
40 E5 Musselburgh U.K.
42 F2 Musselkanaal Neth.
72 E2 Musselshell r. U.S.A.
16 B1 Mustafakemalpaşa Turkey
37 S7 Mustjala Estonia
30 E3 Musu-dan pt N. Korea
8 H2 Muswellbrook Austr.
55 E2 Mut Egypt
16 D3 Mut Turkey
90 E1 Mutá, Pta do pt Brazil
57 D5 Mutare Zimbabwe
25 E7 Mutis, G. mt Indon.
8 C2 Mutooroo Austr.
57 D5 Mutorashanga Zimbabwe
28 G4 Mutsu Japan
28 G4 Mutsu-wan b. Japan
9 B7 Muttonbird Is is N.Z.
9 A7 Muttonbird Islands is N.Z.
41 B5 Mutton Island i. Rep. of Ireland
57 D5 Mutuali Moz.
90 C1 Mutunópolis Brazil
21 C4 Mutur Sri Lanka
36 U2 Mutusjärvi r. Fin.
36 T3 Muurola Fin.
26 C2 Mu Us Shamo des. China
57 B4 Muxaluando Angola
50 E2 Muyezerskiy Rus. Fed.
56 D4 Muyinga Burundi
56 C4 Muyumba Congo(Zaire)
26 D4 Muyuping China
22 C2 Muzaffarabad Pak.
22 B3 Muzaffargarh Pak.
22 D3 Muzaffarnagar India
23 F4 Muzaffarpur India
59 K1 Muzamane Moz.
19 F5 Mūzīn Iran
64 C4 Muzon, C. c. U.S.A.
22 E2 Muztag mt China
23 F1 Muztag mt China
55 E4 Mvolo Sudan
56 D4 Mvomero Tanz.
57 D5 Mvuma Zimbabwe
Mwali i. see Moheli
57 C4 Mwanza Congo(Zaire)
56 D4 Mwanza Tanz.
41 B4 Mweelrea h. Rep. of Ireland
56 C4 Mweka Congo(Zaire)
57 C5 Mwenda Zambia
56 C4 Mwene-Ditu Congo(Zaire)
57 D6 Mwenezi Zimbabwe
57 C4 Mweru, Lake l. Congo(Zaire)/Zambia
57 C4 Mwimba Congo(Zaire)
57 C5 Mwinilunga Zambia
50 C4 Myadzyel Belarus
23 H5 Myaing Myanmar
22 B4 Myājlār India
10 L7 Myanmar country Asia
29 B9 Myanoura-dake mt Japan
40 E2 Mybster U.K.
23 H5 Myebon Myanmar
25 B4 Myingyan Myanmar
32 A2 Myinmoletkat mt Myanmar
24 B4 Myitkyina Myanmar
32 A2 Myitta Myanmar
23 H5 Myittha r. Myanmar
51 E6 Mykolayiv Ukr.
49 L6 Mykonos Greece
49 L6 Mykonos i. Greece
12 G3 Myla Rus. Fed.
23 G4 Mymensingh Bangl.
37 S6 Mynämäki Fin.
39 D5 Mynydd Eppynt h. U.K.
39 C6 Mynydd Preseli h. U.K.
23 H5 Myohaung Myanmar
29 F6 Myōkō-san volc. Japan
30 E3 Myonggan N. Korea
50 C4 Myory Belarus
36 D5 Mýrdalsjökull ice cap Iceland
36 O2 Myre Norway
36 R4 Myrheden Sweden
51 E5 Myrhorod Ukr.
51 D5 Myronivka Ukr.
79 E5 Myrtle Beach U.S.A.
8 F4 Myrtleford Austr.
72 A3 Myrtle Point U.S.A.
46 G4 Myślibórz Pol.
21 B3 Mysore India
13 U3 Mys Shmidta Rus. Fed.
81 F5 Mystic Islands U.S.A.
32 C3 My Tho Vietnam
49 M5 Mytilini Greece
50 F4 Mytishchi Rus. Fed.
59 G5 Mzamomhle S. Africa
43 L5 Mže r. Czech Rep.
57 D5 Mzimba Malawi
57 D5 Mzuzu Malawi

N

43 K5 Naab r. Ger.
74 □2 Naalehu U.S.A.
37 S6 Naantali Fin.
41 E4 Naas Rep. of Ireland
58 B4 Nababeep S. Africa
21 C2 Nabarangapur India
29 E7 Nabari Japan
31 B4 Nabas Phil.
16 E5 Nabatiyet et Tahta Lebanon
43 L5 Nabburg Ger.
56 D4 Naberera Tanz.
12 G4 Naberezhnyye Chelny Rus. Fed.
55 D1 Nabeul Tunisia
22 D3 Nabha India
8 J2 Nabiac Austr.
19 E4 Nabīd Iran
25 F7 Nabire Indon.
16 E5 Nablus West Bank
59 H2 Naboomspruit S. Africa
32 A2 Nabule Myanmar
57 E5 Nacala Moz.
72 B2 Naches U.S.A.
22 B4 Nāchna India
74 B4 Nacimiento Reservoir U.S.A.
77 E6 Nacogdoches U.S.A.
82 C2 Nacozari de García Mex.
22 C5 Nadiad India
18 D4 Nadīk Iran
54 B1 Nador Morocco
18 D3 Nadūshan Iran
51 C5 Nadvirna Ukr.
12 E3 Nadvoitsy Rus. Fed.
12 J3 Nadym Rus. Fed.
37 M9 Næstved Denmark
49 J5 Nafpaktos Greece
49 K6 Nafplio Greece
17 K5 Naft r. Iraq
16 C4 Naft-e Safid Iran
17 K5 Naft Khaneh Iraq
18 B3 Naft Shahr Iran
18 B5 Nafūd al Jur'ā sand dunes S. Arabia
18 A6 Nafūd as Surrah sand dunes S. Arabia
18 B5 Nafūd Qunayfidhah sand dunes S. Arabia
18 A5 Nafy S. Arabia
31 B3 Naga Phil.
66 D4 Nagagami r. Can.
29 C8 Nagahama Japan
23 H4 Naga Hills mts India
29 G5 Nagai Japan
23 H4 Nagaland div. India
8 E4 Nagambie Austr.
29 F6 Nagano Japan
29 F6 Nagaoka Japan
23 H4 Nagaon India
21 B4 Nagappattinam India
22 D2 Nagar India
21 B2 Nāgārjuna Sāgar Reservoir India
22 B4 Nagar Parkar Pak.
23 G3 Nagarzê China
29 A8 Nagasaki Japan
29 B7 Nagato Japan
22 C4 Nagaur India
21 C2 Nagavali r. India
23 G2 Nag, Co l. China
22 C5 Nagda India
21 B4 Nagercoil India
19 G5 Nagha Kalat Pak.
22 D3 Nagina India
23 E3 Nagma Nepal
50 J3 Nagorsk Rus. Fed.
29 E7 Nagoya Japan
22 D5 Nagpur India
23 H3 Nagqu China
31 C3 Nagumbuaya Point pt Phil.
17 F1 Nagurskoye Rus. Fed.
48 G1 Nagyatád Hungary
46 H7 Nagykanizsa Hungary
24 E4 Naha Japan
22 D3 Nahan India
19 F5 Nahang r. Iran/Pak.
64 E2 Nahanni Butte Can.
64 D2 Nahanni National Park Can.
16 E5 Nahariyya Israel
18 C3 Nahāvand Iran
43 F5 Nahe r. Ger.
17 K5 Nahrawān canal Iraq
17 L6 Nahr 'Umr Iraq
91 B3 Nahuelbuta, Parque Nacional nat. park Chile
91 B4 Nahuel Huapi, L. l. Arg.
91 B4 Nahuel Huapi, Parque Nacional nat. park Arg.
79 D6 Nahunta U.S.A.
23 H2 Naij Tal China
30 A2 Naiman Qi China
67 H2 Nain Can.
18 D3 Nā'īn Iran
22 D3 Naini Tal India
22 E5 Nainpur India
40 E3 Nairn U.K.
69 G2 Nairn Centre Can.
56 D4 Nairobi Kenya
56 D4 Naivasha Kenya
30 D2 Naizishan China
18 B5 Na'jān S. Arabia
20 B4 Najd reg. S. Arabia
45 E1 Nájera Spain
22 D3 Najibabad India
30 F2 Najin N. Korea
20 B6 Najrān S. Arabia
29 A8 Nakadōri-shima i. Japan
29 B8 Nakama Japan
29 C8 Nakamura Japan
13 M3 Nakanno Rus. Fed.
29 F6 Nakano Japan
29 C6 Nakano-shima i. Japan
19 H3 Naka Pass Afgh.
29 B8 Nakatsu Japan
29 E7 Nakatsugawa Japan
56 D2 Nak'fa Eritrea
55 F1 Nakhl Egypt
24 F2 Nakhodka Rus. Fed.
32 B2 Nakhon Nayok Thai.
32 B2 Nakhon Pathom Thai.
32 B2 Nakhon Ratchasima Thai.
32 A3 Nakhon Si Thammarat Thai.
22 B5 Nakhtarana India
64 C3 Nakina B.C. Can.
66 C3 Nakina Ont. Can.
62 C4 Naknek U.S.A.
57 D4 Nakonde Zambia
37 M9 Nakskov Denmark
30 E6 Naktong r. S. Korea
56 D4 Nakuru Kenya
64 F4 Nakusp Can.
19 G5 Nal Pak.
19 G5 Nal r. Pak.
59 K2 Nalázi Moz.
23 G4 Nalbari India
51 G7 Nal'chik Rus. Fed.
21 B2 Naldurg India
21 B2 Nalgonda India
21 B3 Nallamala Hills h. India
16 C1 Nallıhan Turkey
54 D1 Nālūt Libya
30 D4 Nam r. N. Korea
59 K2 Namaacha Moz.
59 H3 Namahadi S. Africa
18 C3 Namak, Daryācheh-ye salt flat Iran
19 E4 Namakzar-e Shadad salt flat Iran
56 D4 Namanga Kenya
14 F2 Namangan Uzbek.
57 D5 Namapa Moz.
58 B3 Namaqualand reg. Namibia
58 B4 Namaqualand reg. S. Africa
6 F2 Namatanai P.N.G.
7 F4 Nambour Austr.
32 C3 Năm Căn Vietnam
23 H3 Namcha Barwa mt China
30 D4 Namch'ŏn N. Korea
24 B3 Nam Co l. China
36 N4 Namdalen v. Norway
36 M4 Namdalseid Norway
27 C6 Nam Đinh Vietnam
68 B3 Namekagon r. U.S.A.
30 E6 Namhae-do i. S. Korea
57 B6 Namib Desert des. Namibia
57 B5 Namibe Angola
53 F8 Namibia country Africa
29 G6 Namie Japan
32 B1 Nam Khan r. Laos
25 E7 Namlea Indon.
32 B1 Nam Lik r. Laos
32 A1 Nammekon Myanmar
27 B6 Nam Na r. China/Vietnam
32 B1 Nam Ngum r. Laos
8 H1 Namoi r. Austr.
27 B6 Nam Ou r. Laos
64 F3 Nampa Can.
72 C3 Nampa U.S.A.
22 E3 Nampa mt Nepal
54 B3 Nampala Mali
32 B1 Nam Pat Thai.
32 B1 Nam Phong Thai.
30 C4 Namp'o N. Korea
57 D5 Nampula Moz.
23 G2 Namru Co l. China
15 H4 Namrup India
27 B7 Nam Sam r. Laos/Vietnam
23 E3 Namsê La pass Nepal
36 N4 Namsen r. Norway
17 K3 Namshir Iran
23 H4 Namsi India
23 G3 Namsi La pass Bhutan
36 M4 Namsos Norway
13 O3 Namtsy Rus. Fed.
24 B4 Namtu Myanmar
42 C4 Namur Belgium
57 C5 Namwala Zambia
30 D6 Namwŏn S. Korea
56 B3 Nana Bakassa C.A.R.
64 E5 Nanaimo Can.
74 □1 Nanakuli U.S.A.
30 E3 Nanam N. Korea
27 F5 Nan'an China
58 B2 Nananib Plateau plat. Namibia
27 E6 Nan'ao China
29 E6 Nanao Japan
29 E6 Nanatsu-shima i. Japan
26 C4 Nanbu China
28 A1 Nancha China
27 E4 Nanchang Jiangxi China
27 E5 Nancheng China
27 C4 Nanchong China
27 C4 Nanchuan China
44 H2 Nancy France
22 E3 Nanda Devi mt India
22 E3 Nanda Kot mt India
27 C5 Nandan China
21 B2 Nānded India
22 C5 Nandgaon India
27 D6 Nandu Jiang r. China
22 C5 Nandurbar India
21 B3 Nandyal India
27 D6 Nanfeng Guangdong China
27 E5 Nanfeng Jiangxi China
55 D4 Nanga Eboko Cameroon
33 D3 Nangahpinoh Indon.
30 E2 Nangang Shan mts China/N. Korea
22 C2 Nanga Parbat mt Jammu and Kashmir
33 D3 Nangatayap Indon.
32 A3 Nangin Myanmar
30 D3 Nangnim N. Korea
30 D3 Nangnim Sanmaek mts N. Korea
26 E2 Nangong China
57 D4 Nangulangwa Tanz.
23 H3 Nang Xian China
26 A2 Nanhua China
26 F4 Nanhui China
21 B3 Nanjangud India
26 C3 Nanjiang China
27 E5 Nanjing Fujian China
26 F3 Nanjing Jiangsu China
27 E5 Nankang China
Nanking see Nanjing
29 C8 Nankoku Japan
57 B5 Nankova Angola
26 E2 Nanle China
26 F4 Nanling China
27 D5 Nan Ling mts China
27 C6 Nanliu Jiang r. China
27 C6 Nanning China
27 E6 Nan'ao Dao i. China
63 O3 Nanortalik Greenland
27 C5 Nanpan Jiang r. China
30 A3 Nanpiao China
27 F5 Nanping Fujian China
26 B3 Nanping Sichuan China
27 F5 Nanri Dao i. China
24 E4 Nansei-shotō is Japan
63 J1 Nansen Sound chan. Can.
44 D3 Nantes France
42 A5 Nanteuil-le-Haudouin France
21 C4 Nanthi Kadal lag. Sri Lanka
69 G4 Nanticoke Can.
81 F5 Nanticoke r. U.S.A.
64 G4 Nanton Can.
26 F3 Nantong Jiangsu China
26 F4 Nantong Jiangsu China
27 F6 Nant'ou Taiwan
81 H4 Nantucket U.S.A.
81 H4 Nantucket I. i. U.S.A.
81 H4 Nantucket Sound g. U.S.A.
39 E4 Nantwich U.K.
7 H2 Nanumanga i. Tuvalu
7 H2 Nanumea i. Tuvalu
90 E2 Nanuque Brazil
31 C5 Nanusa, Kepulauan is Indon.
27 B4 Nanxi China
27 C4 Nan Xian China
27 E5 Nanxiong China
26 C3 Nanyang China
30 C3 Nanzamu China
26 C4 Nanzhang China
26 C3 Nanzhao China
45 C3 Nao, Cabo de la hd Spain
67 F3 Naococane, Lac l. Can.
23 C4 Naogaon Bangl.
22 B4 Naokot Pak.
28 C1 Naoli r. China
19 F3 Naomid, Dasht-e des. Afgh./Iran
22 C2 Naoshera Jammu and Kashmir
27 D6 Naozhou Dao i. China
74 A2 Napa U.S.A.
81 K1 Napadogan Can.
69 J3 Napanee Can.
22 C4 Napasar India
63 N3 Napasoq Greenland
68 C5 Naperville U.S.A.
9 F3 Napier N.Z.
92 D4 Napier Mts mts Ant.
81 G2 Napierville Can.
48 F4 Naples Italy
79 D7 Naples FL U.S.A.
81 H3 Naples ME U.S.A.
27 B3 Napo China
86 D4 Napo r. Ecuador/Peru
80 A4 Napoleon U.S.A.
Napoli see Naples
91 D3 Naposta Arg.
91 D3 Naposta r. Arg.
68 E5 Nappanee U.S.A.
17 K3 Naqadeh Iran
16 E6 Naqb Ashtar Jordan
17 M4 Naqqash Iran
29 D7 Nara Japan
54 B3 Nara Mali
47 N3 Narach Belarus
8 C4 Naracoorte Austr.
8 F2 Naradhan Austr.
22 C4 Naraina India
22 E6 Narainpur India
84 C2 Naranjos Mex.
21 D2 Narasannapeta India
21 C2 Narasapatnam, Pt pt India
21 C2 Narasapur India
21 C2 Narasaraopet India
23 F5 Narasinghapur India
32 B4 Narathiwat Thai.
21 A2 Narayangaon India
Narbada r. see Narmada
39 C6 Narberth U.K.
44 F5 Narbonne France
45 C1 Narcea r. Spain
18 D2 Nardin Iran
48 H4 Nardò Italy
91 E1 Nare Arg.
22 B3 Narechi r. Pak.
63 M1 Nares Strait str. Can./Greenland
47 K4 Narew r. Pol.
30 D2 Narhong China
22 A3 Nari r. Pak.
57 B6 Narib Namibia
58 B5 Nariep S. Africa
51 H6 Narimanov Rus. Fed.
19 H2 Narin Afgh.
19 H3 Narin reg. Afgh.
16 G3 Narince Turkey
23 H1 Narin Gol watercourse China
29 G7 Narita Japan
22 C5 Narmada r. India
17 H1 Narman Turkey
22 D3 Narnaul India
48 E3 Narni Italy
47 O5 Narodychi Ukr.
50 F4 Naro-Fominsk Rus. Fed.
8 H4 Narooma Austr.
50 G4 Narovchat Rus. Fed.
51 D5 Narowlya Belarus
37 R5 Närpes Fin.
81 H4 Narragansett Bay b. U.S.A.
8 F3 Narrandera Austr.
8 G2 Narromine Austr.
80 C6 Narrows U.S.A.
81 F4 Narrowsburg U.S.A.
22 D5 Narsimhapur India
23 G5 Narsingdi Bangl.
22 D5 Narsinghgarh India
21 C2 Narsipatnam India
26 E1 Nart China
29 D7 Naruto Japan
37 V7 Narva Estonia
37 U7 Narva Bay b. Estonia/Rus. Fed.
31 B2 Narvacan Phil.
36 P2 Narvik Norway
37 V7 Narvskoye Vdkhr. resr Estonia/Rus. Fed.
22 D3 Narwana India
22 D4 Narwar India
12 G3 Nar'yan-Mar Rus. Fed.
15 F2 Naryn Kyrg
36 P5 Näsåker Sweden
75 H3 Naschitti U.S.A.
9 C6 Naseby N.Z.
68 A4 Nashua IA U.S.A.
81 H3 Nashua NH U.S.A.
79 C4 Nashville U.S.A.
16 F5 Nasib Syria
37 S6 Näsijärvi l. Fin.
22 C5 Nasik India
55 F4 Nasir Sudan
Nasirabad see Mymensingh
22 B3 Nasirabad Pak.
57 C5 Nasondoye Congo(Zaire)
16 C6 Nasr Egypt
18 C3 Naşrābād Iran
19 E3 Naşrābād Iran
Nasratabad see Zābol
17 L5 Nasrīān-e-Pā'īn Iran
64 D3 Nass r. Can.
79 E7 Nassau Bahamas
5 L6 Nassau i. Cook Is Pac. Oc.
55 F2 Nasser, Lake resr Egypt
37 O8 Nässjö Sweden
66 E2 Nastapoca r. Can.
66 E2 Nastapoka Islands is Can.
25 F6 Nasu-dake volc. Japan
31 B3 Nasugbu Phil.
47 P2 Nasva Rus. Fed.
57 C6 Nata Botswana
56 D4 Nata Tanz.
89 B4 Natagaima Col.
87 L5 Natal Brazil
Natal div. see Kwazulu-Natal
93 G6 Natal Basin sea feature Ind. Ocean
18 C3 Naţanz Iran
67 H3 Natashquan Can.
67 H3 Natashquan r. Can.
77 F6 Natchez U.S.A.
77 E6 Natchitoches U.S.A.
8 E4 Nathalia Austr.
22 C4 Nathdwara India
8 C4 Natimuk Austr.
74 D5 National City U.S.A.
45 H2 Nati, Pta pt Spain
54 C3 Natitingou Benin
87 J6 Natividade Brazil
28 G5 Natori Japan
56 D4 Natron, Lake salt l. Tanz.
32 A1 Nattaung mt Myanmar
33 C2 Natuna Besar i. Indon.
33 C2 Natuna, Kepulauan is Indon.
81 F2 Natural Bridge U.S.A.
75 G3 Natural Bridges National Monument res. U.S.A.
93 M6 Naturaliste Plateau sea feature Ind. Ocean
75 H2 Naturita U.S.A.
68 E2 Naubinway U.S.A.
57 B6 Nauchas Namibia
43 L2 Nauen Ger.
81 G4 Naugatuck U.S.A.
31 B3 Naujan Phil.
31 B3 Naujan, L. l. Phil.
37 S8 Naujoji Akmenė Lith.
22 C4 Naukh India
43 H3 Naumburg (Hessen) Ger.
43 K3 Naumburg (Saale) Ger.
32 A1 Naungpale Myanmar
16 E6 Na'ūr Jordan
19 G4 Nauroz Kalat Pak
4 H5 Nauru country Pac. Oc.
22 B4 Naushara Pak.
37 J6 Naustdal Norway
86 D4 Nauta Peru
58 C3 Naute Dam dam Namibia
84 C2 Nautla Mex.
19 G3 Nauzad Afgh.
23 G5 Navadwīp India
50 C4 Navahrudak Belarus
75 H4 Navajo U.S.A.
73 F4 Navajo Lake l. U.S.A.
75 G3 Navajo Mt mt U.S.A.
31 C4 Naval Phil.
45 D3 Navalmoral de la Mata Spain
45 D3 Navalvillar de Pela Spain
41 E4 Navan Rep. of Ireland
50 D4 Navapolatsk Belarus
13 T3 Navarin, Mys c. Rus. Fed.
88 C9 Navarino, I. i. Chile
45 F1 Navarra div. Spain
8 D4 Navarre Austr.
74 A2 Navarro U.S.A.
50 G4 Navashino Rus. Fed.
77 D6 Navasota U.S.A.
36 O5 Näverede Sweden
40 D2 Naver, Loch l. U.K.
91 B2 Navidad Chile
87 H3 Navio, Serra do Brazil
50 E4 Navlya Rus. Fed.
49 N2 Năvodari Romania
19 G1 Navoi Uzbek.
82 C3 Navojoa Mex.
50 G3 Navoloki Rus. Fed.
22 C5 Navsari India
22 C4 Nawa India
16 F5 Nawá Syria
23 G4 Nawabganj Bangl.
22 B4 Nawabshah Pak.
23 F4 Nawada India
19 G3 Nāwah Afgh.
22 C4 Nawalgarh India
17 K2 Naxçıvan Azer.
27 B4 Naxi China
49 L6 Naxos Greece
49 L6 Naxos i. Greece
89 A4 Naya Col.
23 F5 Nayagarh India
84 A2 Nayar Mex.
84 A2 Nayarit div. Mex.
18 D5 Nāy Band Iran
28 H2 Nayoro Japan
21 B3 Nāyudupeta India
90 E1 Nazaré Brazil
21 B4 Nazareth India
16 E5 Nazareth Israel
77 B7 Nazas Mex.
84 A1 Nazas r. Mex.
86 D6 Nazca Peru
Nazca Ridge sea feature see South-West Peru Ridge
17 K2 Nāzik Iran
17 J2 Nazik Gölü l. Turkey
19 F4 Nāzīl Iran
16 B3 Nazilli Turkey
19 G5 Nazimabad Pak.
17 G2 Nazımiye Turkey
23 H4 Nazira India
64 E4 Nazko Can.
64 E4 Nazko r. Can.
17 K3 Nāzlū r. Iran
51 H7 Nazran' Rus. Fed.
56 D3 Nazrēt Eth.
20 E5 Nazwá Oman
57 C4 Nchelenge Zambia
57 C6 Ncojane Botswana
57 B4 N'dalatando Angola
56 C3 Ndélé C.A.R.
56 B4 Ndendé Gabon
7 G3 Ndeni i. Solomon Is
55 D3 Ndjamena Chad
57 C5 Ndola Zambia
59 J4 Ndwedwe S. Africa
41 E3 Neagh, Lough l. U.K.
72 A1 Neah Bay U.S.A.
6 D4 Neale, L. salt flat Austr.
49 K5 Nea Liosia Greece
49 K6 Neapoli Greece
39 D6 Neath U.K.
39 D6 Neath r. U.K.
18 D2 Nebitdag Turkm.
50 E3 Nebolchi Rus. Fed.
75 G2 Nebo, Mount mt U.S.A.
76 C3 Nebraska div. U.S.A.
76 E3 Nebraska City U.S.A.
48 F6 Nebrodi, Monti mts Sicily Italy
77 E6 Neches r. U.S.A.
89 B3 Nechi r. Col.
56 D3 Nechisar National Park Eth.
43 G5 Neckar r. Ger.
43 H5 Neckarsulm Ger.
5 L2 Necker Island i. HI U.S.A.
91 E3 Necochea Arg.
43 M1 Neddemin Ger.
66 F2 Neddouc, Lac l. Can.
36 R2 Nedre Soppero Sweden
75 E4 Needles U.S.A.
39 F7 Needles, The stack U.K.
68 C3 Neenah U.S.A.
65 K4 Neepawa Can.
63 K2 Neergaard Lake l. Can.
42 D3 Neerijnen Neth.
42 D3 Neerpelt Belgium
17 M2 Neftçala Azer.
12 G4 Neftekamsk Rus. Fed.
51 H6 Neftekumsk Rus. Fed.
12 J3 Nefteyugansk Rus. Fed.
39 C5 Nefyn U.K.
48 C6 Nefza Tunisia
56 B4 Negage Angola
56 D3 Negēlē Eth.
90 A3 Negla r. Para.
57 D5 Negomane Moz.
21 B5 Negombo Sri Lanka
49 K4 Negotino Macedonia
86 C5 Negra, Cordillera mts Peru
86 B5 Negra, Pta pt Peru
48 B7 Négrine Alg.
86 B4 Negritos Peru
91 D4 Negro r. Arg.
90 A2 Negro r. Mato Grosso do Sul Brazil
86 F4 Negro r. S. America
91 F2 Negro r. Uru.
31 B4 Negros i. Phil.
49 N3 Negru Vodă Romania
17 M4 Nehavand Iran
19 F4 Nehbandān Iran
24 E2 Nehe China
27 B4 Neijiang China
65 H4 Neilburg Can.
30 A2 Nei Monggol Zizhiqu div. China
43 K3 Neinstedt Ger.
46 G5 Neiß r. Ger./Pol.
89 B4 Neiva Col.
26 D3 Neixiang China
65 K3 Nejanilini Lake l. Can.
18 D2 Neka Iran
56 D3 Nek'emtē Eth.
28 E2 Nekrasovka Rus. Fed.
37 O9 Neksø Denmark
50 E3 Nelidovo Rus. Fed.
76 D3 Neligh U.S.A.
13 Q3 Nel'kan Rus. Fed.
24 F1 Nel'kan Rus. Fed.
21 B3 Nellore India
64 F5 Nelson Can.
9 D4 Nelson N.Z.
38 E4 Nelson U.K.
75 E4 Nelson U.S.A.
63 J4 Nelson r. Man. Can.
65 L3 Nelson r. Can.
8 J2 Nelson Bay Austr.
8 C5 Nelson, C. c. Austr.
88 B8 Nelson, Estrecho chan. Chile
64 E3 Nelson Forks Can.
65 K3 Nelson House Can.
59 J2 Nelspruit S. Africa
54 B3 Néma Maur.
50 J3 Nema Rus. Fed.
68 A2 Nemadji r. U.S.A.
50 B4 Neman Rus. Fed.
16 F5 Nemara Syria
50 G3 Nemda r. Rus. Fed.
50 K2 Nemed Rus. Fed.
69 F2 Nemegos Can.
36 W2 Nemetskiy, Mys c. Rus. Fed.
44 F2 Nemours France
17 J2 Nemrut Dağı h. Turkey
28 J3 Nemuro Japan
28 J3 Nemuro-kaikyō chan. Japan
51 D5 Nemyriv Ukr.
41 C5 Nenagh Rep. of Ireland
39 H5 Nene r. U.K.
24 E2 Nenjiang China
42 E5 Nennig Ger.
50 F1 Nenoksa Rus. Fed.
77 E4 Neosho U.S.A.
76 E4 Neosho r. U.S.A.
10 K7 Nepal country Asia
69 K3 Nepean Can.
75 G2 Nephi U.S.A.
41 B3 Nephin h. Rep. of Ireland
41 B3 Nephin Beg Range h. Rep. of Ireland
56 C3 Nepoko r. Congo(Zaire)
81 F4 Neptune U.S.A.
44 E4 Nérac France
24 D1 Nerchinsk Rus. Fed.
50 G3 Nerekhta Rus. Fed.
48 G3 Neretva r. Bos.-Herz./Croatia
57 C5 Neriquinha Angola
37 T9 Neris r. Lith.
50 F3 Nerl' r. Rus. Fed.
90 C2 Nerópolis Brazil
24 E1 Neryungri Rus. Fed.
42 D1 Nes Neth.
37 L6 Nes Norway
37 L6 Nesbyen Norway
36 G4 Neskaupstaður Iceland
42 A5 Nesle France
36 N3 Nesna Norway
76 D4 Ness City U.S.A.
43 J4 Nesse r. Ger.
64 C3 Nesselrode, Mt mt Can./U.S.A.
40 D3 Ness, Loch l. U.K.
49 L4 Nestos r. Greece
16 E5 Netanya Israel
65 N2 Netchek, Cape c. Can.
34 F3 Netherlands country Europe
61 M8 Netherlands Antilles terr. Caribbean Sea
43 G4 Netphen Ger.
23 G4 Netrakona Bangl.
22 C5 Netrang India
63 L3 Nettilling Lake l. Can.
68 A1 Nett Lake U.S.A.
68 A1 Nett Lake l. U.S.A.
84 D3 Netzahualcóyotl, Presa resr Mex.
43 M1 Neubrandenburg Ger.
46 C7 Neuchâtel Switz.
46 C7 Neuchâtel, Lac de l. Switz.
43 J5 Neuendettelsau Ger.
42 E2 Neuenhaus Ger.
43 H1 Neuenkirchen Ger.
43 G2 Neuenkirchen (Oldenburg) Ger.
42 D5 Neufchâteau Belgium
44 G2 Neufchâteau France
44 E2 Neufchâtel-en-Bray France
43 F1 Neuharlingersiel Ger.
43 H1 Neuhaus (Oste) Ger.
43 H4 Neuhof Ger.
43 K1 Neu Kaliß Ger.
43 H4 Neukirchen Hessen Ger.
43 L4 Neukirchen Sachsen Ger.
65 K2 Neultin Lake l. Can.
43 K5 Neumarkt in der Oberpfalz Ger.
92 C2 Neumayer Ger. Base Ant.
46 D3 Neumünster Ger.
43 L5 Neunburg vorm Wald Ger.
46 H7 Neunkirchen Austria
42 F5 Neunkirchen Ger.
91 C3 Neuquén Arg.
91 C3 Neuquén div. Arg.
91 C3 Neuquén r. Arg.
43 L2 Neuruppin Ger.
79 E5 Neuse r. U.S.A.
46 H7 Neusiedler See l. Austria/Hungary
42 E3 Neuss Ger.
43 H2 Neustadt am Rübenberge Ger.
43 J5 Neustadt an der Aisch Ger.
43 L5 Neustadt an der Waldnaab Ger.
43 G5 Neustadt an der Weinstraße Ger.
43 K4 Neustadt bei Coburg Ger.
43 K1 Neustadt-Glewe Ger.
42 F4 Neustadt (Wied) Ger.
43 M1 Neustrelitz Ger.
43 L6 Neutraubling Ger.
42 F4 Neuwied Ger.
43 H1 Neu Wulmstorf Ger.
77 E4 Nevada MO U.S.A.
74 D2 Nevada div. U.S.A.
45 E4 Nevada, Sierra mts Spain
91 C2 Nevado, Cerro mt Arg.
82 D5 Nevado de Colima volc Mex.
84 B3 Nevado de Colima, Parque Nacional nat. park Mex.
84 C3 Nevado de Toluca, Parque Nacional nat. park Mex.
91 C3 Nevado, Sierra del mts Arg.
50 D3 Nevel' Rus. Fed.
44 F3 Nevers France
8 F1 Nevertire Austr.
49 H3 Nevesinje Bos.-Herz.
51 G6 Nevinnomyssk Rus. Fed.
40 C3 Nevis, Loch in. U.K.
16 E2 Nevşehir Turkey
28 C2 Nevskoye Rus. Fed.
75 E5 New r. CA U.S.A.
80 C6 New r. WV U.S.A.
78 C4 New Albany IN U.S.A.
77 F5 New Albany MS U.S.A.
81 E4 New Albany PA U.S.A.
87 G2 New Amsterdam Guyana
81 F5 Newark DE U.S.A.
81 F5 Newark MD U.S.A.
81 F4 Newark NJ U.S.A.
80 E3 Newark NY U.S.A.
80 B4 Newark OH U.S.A.
75 E2 Newark Lake l. U.S.A.
39 G4 Newark-on-Trent U.K.
81 E3 Newark Valley U.S.A.
81 H4 New Bedford U.S.A.
72 B2 Newberg U.S.A.
81 F3 New Berlin U.S.A.
79 E5 New Bern U.S.A.
68 E2 Newberry MI U.S.A.
79 D5 Newberry SC U.S.A.
74 D4 Newberry Springs U.S.A.
38 F2 Newbiggin-by-the-Sea U.K.
69 J3 Newboro Can.
81 G3 New Boston MA U.S.A.
80 B5 New Boston OH U.S.A.
77 D6 New Braunfels U.S.A.
41 E4 Newbridge Rep. of Ireland
81 G4 New Britain U.S.A.
6 E2 New Britain i. P.N.G.
81 F4 New Brunswick U.S.A.
67 G4 New Brunswick div. Can.
68 D5 New Buffalo U.S.A.
40 F3 Newburgh U.K.
81 F4 Newburgh U.S.A.
39 F6 Newbury U.K.
81 H3 Newburyport U.S.A.
38 E3 Newby Bridge U.K.
4 H7 New Caledonia terr. Pac. Oc.
67 G4 New Carlisle Can.
8 H2 Newcastle Austr.
67 G4 Newcastle N.B. Can.
69 H4 Newcastle Ont. Can.
41 E4 Newcastle Rep. of Ireland
59 H3 Newcastle S. Africa
41 F3 Newcastle N. Ireland U.K.
74 B2 Newcastle CA U.S.A.
68 E6 New Castle IN U.S.A.
80 B4 Newcastle OH U.S.A.
80 C4 New Castle PA U.S.A.
75 F3 Newcastle UT U.S.A.
80 C6 New Castle VA U.S.A.
72 F3 Newcastle WY U.S.A.
39 C5 Newcastle Emlyn U.K.
39 E4 Newcastle-under-Lyme U.K.
38 F3 Newcastle upon Tyne U.K.
41 B5 Newcastle West Rep. of Ireland
81 F6 New Church U.S.A.
75 H3 Newcomb U.S.A.
40 D5 New Cumnock U.K.
40 F3 New Deer U.K.
22 D3 New Delhi India
81 K1 New Denmark Can.
74 B3 New Don Pedro Reservoir U.S.A.
8 H1 New England Range mts Austr.
39 E6 Newent U.K.
67 J4 Newfoundland div. Can.
63 N5 Newfoundland i. Can.
96 G2 Newfoundland Basin sea feature Atl. Ocean
40 D5 New Galloway U.K.
7 F2 New Georgia i. Solomon Is
7 F2 New Georgia Islands is Solomon Is
67 H4 New Glasgow Can.
25 G7 New Guinea i. Asia
80 B4 New Hampshire OH U.S.A.
81 G3 New Hampshire div. U.S.A.
68 A4 New Hampton U.S.A.
59 J4 New Hanover S. Africa
6 F2 New Hanover i. P.N.G.
81 G4 New Haven U.S.A.
64 D3 New Hazelton Can.
74 B2 New Hogan Reservoir U.S.A.
68 C4 New Holstein U.S.A.
77 F6 New Iberia U.S.A.
59 J2 Newington S. Africa
41 D5 Newinn Rep. of Ireland
6 F2 New Ireland i. P.N.G.

81 F5 New Jersey div. U.S.A.
80 E6 New Kent U.S.A.
80 B5 New Lexington U.S.A.
68 B4 New Lisbon U.S.A.
69 H2 New Liskeard Can.
81 G4 New London CT U.S.A.
68 B5 New London IA U.S.A.
68 B6 New London MO U.S.A.
68 C3 New London WV U.S.A.
6 B4 Newman Austr.
68 D6 Newman U.S.A.
69 H3 Newmarket Can.
41 B5 Newmarket Rep. of Ireland
39 H5 Newmarket U.K.
80 D5 New Market U.S.A.
41 C5 Newmarket on-Fergus Rep. of Ireland
80 C5 New Martinsville U.S.A.
72 C2 New Meadows U.S.A.
74 B3 New Melanes L. l. U.S.A.
73 F5 New Mexico div. U.S.A.
79 C5 Newnan U.S.A.
77 F6 New Orleans U.S.A.
81 F4 New Paltz U.S.A.
80 C4 New Philadelphia U.S.A.
40 F3 New Pitsligo U.K.
9 E3 New Plymouth N.Z.
41 B4 Newport Mayo Rep. of Ireland
41 C5 Newport Tipperary Rep. of Ireland
39 E5 Newport Eng. U.K.
39 F7 Newport Eng. U.K.
39 D6 Newport Wales U.K.
77 F5 Newport AR U.S.A.
80 A5 Newport KY U.S.A.
81 J2 Newport ME U.S.A.
69 F5 Newport MI U.S.A.
81 G3 Newport NH U.S.A.
72 A2 Newport OR U.S.A.
81 H4 Newport RI U.S.A.
81 G2 Newport VT U.S.A.
72 C1 Newport WA U.S.A.
74 D5 Newport Beach U.S.A.
80 E6 Newport News U.S.A.
39 G5 Newport Pagnell U.K.
79 E7 New Providence i. Bahamas
39 B7 Newquay U.K.
67 G4 New Richmond Can.
68 A3 New Richmond U.S.A.
75 F5 New River U.S.A.
77 F6 New Roads U.S.A.
39 H7 New Romney U.K.
41 E5 New Ross Rep. of Ireland
41 E3 Newry U.K.
40 E4 New Scone U.K.
68 A5 New Sharon U.S.A.
New Siberia Islands is see Novosibirskiye Ostrova
79 D6 New Smyrna Beach U.S.A.
8 D2 New South Wales div. Austr.
27 □ New Territories reg. H.K. China
38 E4 Newton U.K.
76 E3 Newton IA U.S.A.
76 D4 Newton KS U.S.A.
81 H3 Newton MA U.S.A.
77 F5 Newton MS U.S.A.
81 F4 Newton NJ U.S.A.
39 D7 Newton Abbot U.K.
40 F3 Newtonhill U.K.
40 D5 Newton Mearns U.K.
40 D6 Newton Stewart U.K.
41 C5 Newtown Rep. of Ireland
39 E5 Newtown Eng. U.K.
39 D5 Newtown Wales U.K.
76 C1 New Town U.S.A.
41 F3 Newtownabbey U.K.
41 F3 Newtownards U.K.
41 D3 Newtownbutler U.K.
41 E4 Newtownmountkennedy Rep. of Ireland
40 F5 Newtown St Boswells U.K.
41 D3 Newtownstewart U.K.
76 E2 New Ulm U.S.A.
74 A2 Newville U.S.A.
64 E5 New Westminster Can.
81 G4 New York U.S.A.
81 E3 New York div. U.S.A.
81 G4 New York-John F. Kennedy airport U.S.A.
81 F4 New York-Newark airport U.S.A.
4 J9 New Zealand country Oceania
94 G9 New Zealand Plateau sea feature Pac. Oc.
50 G3 Neya Rus. Fed.
18 D4 Neyrīz Iran
19 E2 Neyshābūr Iran
21 B4 Neyyattinkara India
33 D2 Ngabang Indon.
56 B4 Ngabé Congo
32 A2 Nga Chong, Khao mt Myanmar/Thai.
31 C6 Ngalipaëng Indon.
57 C6 Ngami, Lake l. Botswana
23 F3 Ngamring China
23 E3 Ngangla Ringco salt l. China
22 E2 Nganglong Kangri mt China
22 E2 Nganglong Kangri mts Xizang China
23 F3 Ngangzê Co salt l. China
32 A1 Ngao Thai.
55 D4 Ngaoundéré Cameroon
9 E2 Ngaruawahia N.Z.
9 F3 Ngaruroro r. N.Z.
9 E3 Ngauruhoe, Mt volc. N.Z.
32 B1 Ngiap r. Laos
56 B4 Ngo Congo
32 C2 Ngoc Linh mt Vietnam
23 F3 Ngoin, Co salt l. China
54 D4 Ngol Bembo Nigeria
23 H2 Ngom Qu r. China
23 F2 Ngoqumaima China
24 B3 Ngoring Hu l. China
55 D3 Ngourti Niger
55 D3 Nguigmi Niger
25 F6 Ngulu i. Micronesia
54 D3 Nguru Nigeria
27 B6 Nguyên Binh Vietnam
58 E2 Ngwaketse div. Botswana
59 G3 Ngwathe S. Africa
59 J3 Ngwavuma r. Swaziland
59 J4 Ngwelezana S. Africa
57 D5 Nhamalabué Moz.
32 D2 Nha Trang Vietnam
8 C4 Nhill Austr.
59 J3 Nhlangano Swaziland
27 B6 Nho Quan Vietnam
6 D3 Nhulunbuy Austr.
65 J4 Niacam Can.
54 B3 Niafounké Mali
68 D3 Niagara U.S.A.
69 H4 Niagara Falls Can.
80 D3 Niagara Falls U.S.A.
69 H4 Niagara River r. Can./U.S.A.
54 C3 Niamey Niger
31 C5 Niampak Indon.
57 D4 Niangandu Tanz.
56 C3 Niangara Congo(Zaire)
33 A2 Nias i. Indon.
Niassa, Lago l. see Nyasa, Lake
37 R8 Nīca Latvia
61 K8 Nicaragua country Central America
83 G6 Nicaragua, Lago de l. Nic.
48 G5 Nicastro Italy
44 H5 Nice France
67 F3 Nichicun, Lac l. Can.
23 E4 Nichlaul India
79 E7 Nicholl's Town Bahamas
69 F2 Nicholson Can.
15 H6 Nicobar Islands is Andaman and Nicobar Is
16 D4 Nicosia Cyprus
83 H7 Nicoya, G. de b. Costa Rica
83 G7 Nicoya, Pen. de pen. Costa Rica
81 K1 Nictau Can.
37 R9 Nida Lith.
38 F4 Nidd r. U.K.
43 H4 Nidda Ger.
43 H4 Nidder r. Ger.
47 K4 Nidzica Pol.
46 D3 Niebüll Ger.
42 E5 Niederanven Lux.
43 H4 Niederaula Ger.
46 F7 Niedere Tauern mts Austria
43 G2 Niedersachsen div. Ger.
42 E1 Niedersächsisches Wattenmeer, Nationalpark nat. park Ger.
54 D4 Niefang Equatorial Guinea
54 B3 Niellé Côte d'Ivoire
43 H2 Nienburg (Weser) Ger.
42 E3 Niers r. Ger.
43 G5 Nierstein Ger.
87 G2 Nieuw Amsterdam Suriname
42 C2 Nieuwe-Niedorp Neth.
42 E1 Nieuwe Pekela Neth.
42 C3 Nieuwerkerk aan de IJssel Neth.
87 G2 Nieuw Nickerie Suriname
42 E1 Nieuwolda Neth.
58 C5 Nieuwoudtville S. Africa
42 A3 Nieuwpoort Belgium
42 C3 Nieuw-Vossemeer Neth.
16 E3 Niğde Turkey
52 E4 Niger country Africa
54 C4 Niger r. Africa
53 E5 Nigeria country Africa
54 C4 Niger, Mouths of the est. Nigeria
69 G1 Nighthawk Lake l. Can.
49 K4 Nigrita Greece
29 G6 Nihonmatsu Japan
29 F6 Niigata Japan
29 C8 Niihama Japan
74 □2 Niihau i. U.S.A.
29 F7 Nii-jima i. Japan
28 H3 Niikappu Japan
29 C7 Niimi Japan
29 F6 Niitsu Japan
42 D2 Nijkerk Neth.
42 D3 Nijmegen Neth.
42 E2 Nijverdal Neth.
36 W2 Nikel' Rus. Fed.
54 C4 Nikki Benin
29 F6 Nikkō Nat. Park Japan
50 H4 Nikolayevka Rus. Fed.
51 H5 Nikolayevsk Rus. Fed.
50 H4 Nikol'sk Penzen. Rus. Fed.
50 H3 Nikol'sk Vologod. Rus. Fed.
13 S4 Nikol'skoye Rus. Fed.
51 E6 Nikopol' Ukr.
17 M3 Nik Pey Iran
16 F1 Niksar Turkey
19 F5 Nīkshahr Iran
49 H3 Nikšić Yugo.
7 J2 Nikumaroro i. Kiribati
7 H2 Nikunau i. Kiribati
22 C2 Nila Pak.
23 F5 Nilagiri India
75 E5 Niland U.S.A.
22 D3 Nilang India
21 B2 Nilanga India
56 D2 Nile r. Africa
68 D5 Niles U.S.A.
21 A3 Nileswaram India
21 B4 Nilgiri Hills mts India
36 V5 Nilsiä Fin.
84 D3 Niltepec Mex.
22 C4 Nimach India
44 G5 Nîmes France
8 G4 Nimmitabel Austr.
92 B4 Nimrod Glacier gl. Ant.
55 F4 Nimule Sudan
21 A4 Nine Degree Chan. India
8 D1 Nine Mile Lake Austr.
74 D2 Ninemile Peak summit U.S.A.
27 □ Ninepin Group is H.K. China
93 K5 Ninety-East Ridge sea feature Ind. Ocean
8 F5 Ninety Mile Beach beach Austr.
9 D1 Ninety Mile Beach beach N.Z.
17 J3 Nineveh Iraq
81 F3 Nineveh U.S.A.
30 E1 Ning'an China
27 F4 Ningbo China
26 F1 Ningcheng China
27 F5 Ningde China
27 E5 Ningdu China
27 D5 Ninggang China
27 F4 Ningguo China
27 F4 Ninghai China
26 E2 Ninghe China
27 E5 Ninghua China
24 B3 Ningjing Shan mts China
26 E3 Ningling China
27 C6 Ningming China
27 B5 Ningnan China
26 C3 Ningqiang China
26 C3 Ningshan China
26 D2 Ningwu China
26 B2 Ningxia div. China
26 C3 Ning Xian China
27 D4 Ningxiang China
26 E3 Ningyang China
27 D5 Ningyuan China
27 C6 Ninh Binh Vietnam
32 D2 Ninh Hoa Vietnam
92 B6 Ninnis Gl. gl. Ant.
28 G4 Ninohe Japan
90 A3 Nioaque Brazil
76 C3 Niobrara r. U.S.A.
23 H4 Nioko India
54 A3 Niokolo Koba, Parc National du nat. park Senegal
54 B3 Niono Mali
54 B3 Nioro Mali
44 D3 Niort France
21 A2 Nipani India
65 J4 Nipawin Can.
65 J4 Nipawin Provincial Park res. Can.
66 C4 Nipigon Can.
68 C1 Nipigon Bay b. Can.
66 C4 Nipigon, Lake l. Can.
67 H3 Nipishish Lake l. Can.
69 H2 Nipissing Can.
69 G2 Nipissing, L. l. Can.
74 B4 Nipomo U.S.A.
17 K5 Nippur Iraq
75 E4 Nipton U.S.A.
90 C1 Niquelândia Brazil
18 B2 Nīr Iran
21 A2 Nira r. India
21 B2 Nirmal India
21 B2 Nirmal Range h. India
49 J3 Niš Yugo.
45 C3 Nisa Port.
18 B5 Nisah, W. watercourse S. Arabia
48 F6 Niscemi Sicily Italy
Nīshāpūr see Neyshābūr
29 B9 Nishino-'omote Japan
29 C6 Nishino-shima i. Japan
29 A8 Nishi-Sonogi-hantō pen. Japan
29 D7 Nishiwaki Japan
64 B2 Nisling r. Can.
42 C3 Nispen Neth.
37 N8 Nissan r. Sweden
47 O7 Nistrului Inferior, Câmpia lowland Moldova
64 C2 Nisutlin r. Can.
49 M6 Nisyros i. Greece
18 C5 Niṭā S. Arabia
67 F3 Nitchequon Can.
90 D3 Niterói Brazil
40 E5 Nith r. U.K.
40 E5 Nithsdale v. U.K.
22 D3 Niti Pass pass China
46 J6 Nitra Slovakia
80 C5 Nitro U.S.A.
7 J3 Niuatoputopu i. Tonga
5 L6 Niue terr. Pac. Oc.
7 H3 Niulakita i. Tuvalu
27 B5 Niulan Jiang r. China
7 H2 Niutao i. Tuvalu
30 B3 Niuzhuang China
36 T5 Nivala Fin.
42 C4 Nivelles Belgium
50 K2 Nivshera Rus. Fed.
22 C4 Niwāi India
74 C2 Nixon U.S.A.
23 E1 Niya He r. China
17 M1 Niyazoba Azer.
21 B2 Nizamabad India
21 B2 Nizam Sagar l. India
50 H3 Nizhegorodskaya Oblast' div. Rus. Fed.
13 S3 Nizhnekolymsk Rus. Fed.
24 B1 Nizhneudinsk Rus. Fed.
12 J3 Nizhnevartovsk Rus. Fed.
13 P2 Nizhneyansk Rus. Fed.
50 G4 Nizhniy Lomov Rus. Fed.
50 G3 Nizhniy Novgorod Rus. Fed.
50 K2 Nizhniy Odes Rus. Fed.
50 H3 Nizhniy Yenangsk Rus. Fed.
51 D5 Nizhyn Ukr.
47 K4 Nizina reg. Pol.
16 F3 Nizip Turkey
28 D3 Nizmennyy, Mys pt Rus. Fed.
36 R2 Njallavarri mt Norway
36 Q3 Njavve Sweden
Njazidja i. see Grande Comore
57 D4 Njinjo Tanz.
57 D4 Njombe Tanz.
37 P5 Njurundabommen Sweden
54 D4 Nkambe Cameroon
59 J4 Nkandla S. Africa
54 B4 Nkawkaw Ghana
57 C5 Nkayi Zimbabwe
57 D5 Nkhata Bay Malawi
57 D5 Nkhotakota Malawi
54 C4 Nkongsamba Cameroon
59 G5 Nkululeko S. Africa
57 B5 Nkurenkuru Namibia
59 G6 Nkwenkwezi S. Africa
23 J4 Noa Dihing r. India
23 G5 Noakhali Bangl.
23 F5 Noamundi India
41 E4 Nobber Rep. of Ireland
29 B8 Nobeoka Japan
28 G3 Noboribetsu Japan
90 A1 Nobres Brazil
84 B2 Nochistlán Mex.
69 G2 Noelville Can.
82 B2 Nogales Mex.
70 D5 Nogales AZ U.S.A.
29 B8 Nōgata Japan
44 E2 Nogent-le-Rotrou France
42 A5 Nogent-sur-Oise France
50 F4 Noginsk Rus. Fed.
29 E7 Nōgōhaku-san mt Japan
91 E2 Nogoyá Arg.
91 E2 Nogoya r. Arg.
30 E5 Nogwak-san mt S. Korea
22 C3 Nohar India
28 G4 Noheji Japan
42 F5 Nohfelden Ger.
44 C3 Noirmoutier-en-l'Île France
44 C3 Noirmoutier, Île de i. France
42 E5 Noisseville France
27 F9 Nojima-zaki c. Japan
22 C4 Nokha India
19 F4 Nok Kundi Pak.
65 J3 Nokomis Lake l. Can.
56 B3 Nola C.A.R.
50 J3 Nolinsk Rus. Fed.
81 H4 No Mans Land i. U.S.A.
62 B3 Nome AK U.S.A.
26 B1 Nomgon Mongolia
23 J1 Nomhon China
4 G4 Nomoi Islands is Micronesia
59 G5 Nomonde S. Africa
29 A8 Nomo-zaki pt Japan
50 G3 Nomzha Rus. Fed.
65 H2 Nonacho Lake l. Can.
59 J4 Nondweni S. Africa
30 C1 Nong'an China
32 C1 Nông Hèt Laos
32 B2 Nong Hong Thai.
32 B1 Nong Khai Thai.
59 J3 Nongoma S. Africa
42 E5 Nonnweiler Ger.
7 H2 Nonouti i. Kiribati
30 D5 Nonsan S. Korea
32 B2 Nonthaburi Thai.
58 F5 Nonzwakazi S. Africa
42 B3 Noordbeveland i. Neth.
42 E1 Noordbroek-Uiterburen Neth.
42 C2 Noorderhaaks i. Neth.
42 D2 Noordoost Polder reclaimed land Neth.
42 C2 Noordwijk-Binnen Neth.
64 D5 Nootka I. i. Can.
19 H2 Norak Tajik.
31 C5 Norala Phil.
69 H1 Noranda Can.
37 O6 Norberg Sweden
12 D2 Nordaustlandet i. Svalbard
42 F1 Norden Ger.
12 L2 Nordenshel'da, Arkhipelag is Rus. Fed.
42 F1 Norderland reg. Ger.
42 F1 Norderney Ger.
42 F1 Norderney i. Ger.
43 J1 Norderstedt Ger.
37 J6 Nordfjordeid Norway
36 O3 Nordfold Norway
Nordfriesische Inseln is see North Frisian Islands
43 J3 Nordhausen Ger.
43 G1 Nordholz Ger.
42 F2 Nordhorn Ger.
36 T1 Nordkapp c. Norway
36 Q2 Nordkjosbotn Norway
36 N4 Nordli Norway
46 E6 Nördlingen Ger.
36 Q5 Nordmaling Sweden
46 D3 Nord-Ostsee-Kanal canal Ger.
43 F5 Nordpfälzer Bergland reg. Ger.
63 N3 Nordre Strømfjord in. Greenland
42 F3 Nordrhein-Westfalen div. Ger.
41 D5 Nore r. Rep. of Ireland
44 F5 Nore, Pic de mt France
76 D3 Norfolk NE U.S.A.
81 F2 Norfolk NY U.S.A.
81 E6 Norfolk VA U.S.A.
7 G4 Norfolk Island terr. Pac. Oc.
94 G7 Norfolk Island Ridge sea feature Pac. Oc.
94 F7 Norfolk Island Trough sea feature Pac. Oc.
77 E4 Norfork L. l. U.S.A.
42 E1 Norg Neth.
37 K6 Norheimsund Norway
29 E6 Norikura-dake volc. Japan
12 K3 Noril'sk Rus. Fed.
17 K1 Nor Kharberd Armenia
69 H3 Norland Can.
68 C5 Normal U.S.A.
77 D5 Norman U.S.A.
6 F2 Normanby I. i. P.N.G.
Normandes, Îles terr. see Channel Islands
44 D2 Normandie reg. France
79 D5 Norman, L. l. U.S.A.
6 E3 Normanton Austr.
8 B3 Normanville Austr.
64 D1 Norman Wells Can.
91 B4 Ñorquinco Arg.
36 R5 Norra Kvarken str. Fin./Sweden
36 O4 Norra Storfjället mts Sweden
42 A4 Norrent-Fontes France
80 B6 Norris Lake l. U.S.A.
81 F4 Norristown U.S.A.
37 P7 Norrköping Sweden
37 Q7 Norrtälje Sweden
6 C5 Norseman Austr.
36 Q4 Norsjö Sweden
7 G3 Norsup Vanuatu
43 H3 Nörten-Hardenberg Ger.
91 F3 Norte, Pta pt Buenos Aires Arg.
88 D6 Norte, Pta pt Chubut Arg.
20 C6 North div. Yemen
81 G3 North Adams U.S.A.
38 F3 Northallerton U.K.
96 E4 North American Basin sea feature Atl. Ocean
6 B4 Northampton Austr.
39 G5 Northampton U.K.
81 G3 Northampton U.S.A.
80 E5 North Anna r. U.S.A.
81 J2 North Anson U.S.A.
64 G2 North Arm b. Can.
79 D5 North Augusta U.S.A.
67 H2 North Aulatsivik Island i. Can.
65 H4 North Battleford Can.
69 H2 North Bay Can.
66 E2 North Belcher Islands is Can.
72 A3 North Bend U.S.A.
40 F4 North Berwick U.K.
81 H3 North Berwick U.S.A.
68 A3 North Branch U.S.A.
92 A5 North, C. c. Ant.
67 H4 North, C. c. Can.
North Cape c. see Nordkapp
9 D1 North Cape c. N.Z.
67 H4 North Cape pt P.E.I. Can.
66 B3 North Caribou Lake l. Can.
79 D5 North Carolina div. U.S.A.
72 B1 North Cascades Nat. Park U.S.A.
69 F2 North Channel chan. Can.
41 E2 North Channel str. N. Ireland/Scot. U.K.
81 H2 North Conway U.S.A.
76 C2 North Dakota div. U.S.A.
39 H6 North Downs h. U.K.
80 D3 North East U.S.A.
96 H2 North-Eastern Atlantic Basin sea feature Atl. Ocean
79 E7 Northeast Providence Chan. chan. Bahamas
43 H3 Northeim Ger.
79 F7 North End Pt pt Bahamas
22 C1 Northern Areas div. Pak.
58 D4 Northern Cape div. S. Africa
65 K3 Northern Indian Lake l. Can.
34 E3 Northern Ireland div. U.K.
66 B4 Northern Light L. l. Can.
4 F3 Northern Mariana Islands terr. Pac. Oc.
59 H1 Northern Province div. S. Africa
6 D3 Northern Territory div. Austr.
40 F4 North Esk r. U.K.
81 G3 Northfield MA U.S.A.
76 E2 Northfield MN U.S.A.
81 G2 Northfield VT U.S.A.
39 J6 North Foreland c. U.K.
74 C3 North Fork U.S.A.
74 B2 North Fork American r. U.S.A.
74 B2 North Fork Feather r. U.S.A.
68 E3 North Fox I. i. U.S.A.
66 D3 North French r. Can.
46 C3 North Frisian Islands is Ger.
38 G3 North Grimston U.K.
81 K2 North Head Can.
9 E2 North Head hd N.Z.
65 K2 North Henik Lake l. Can.
81 G3 North Hudson U.S.A.
9 E3 North Island i. N.Z.
31 B1 North Island i. Phil.
31 B4 North Islet rf Phil.
75 G4 North Jadito Canyon U.S.A.
68 D5 North Judson U.S.A.
65 K3 North Knife r. Can.
23 E4 North Koel r. India
23 H4 North Lakhimpur India
75 E3 North Las Vegas U.S.A.
77 E5 North Little Rock U.S.A.
57 D5 North Luangwa National Park nat. park Zambia
68 E5 North Manchester U.S.A.
68 D3 North Manitou I. i. U.S.A.
64 D2 North Nahanni r. Can.
65 L5 Northome U.S.A.
74 C3 North Palisade summit U.S.A.
76 C3 North Platte U.S.A.
76 C3 North Platte r. U.S.A.
27 □ North Point H.K. China
78 D2 North Point pt U.S.A.
68 E3 Northport U.S.A.
75 F3 North Rim U.S.A.
40 F1 North Ronaldsay i. U.K.
40 F1 North Ronaldsay Firth chan. U.K.
74 B2 North San Juan U.S.A.
65 G4 North Saskatchewan r. Can.
34 F3 North Sea sea Europe
65 J3 North Seal r. Can.
38 F2 North Shields U.K.
74 D2 North Shoshone Peak summit U.S.A.
62 D3 North Slope plain U.S.A.
39 H4 North Somercotes U.K.
81 H2 North Stratford U.S.A.
38 F2 North Sunderland U.K.
9 E3 North Taranaki Bight b. N.Z.
64 F4 North Thompson r. Can.
40 A3 Northton U.K.
80 D3 North Tonawanda U.S.A.
22 D3 North Tons r. India
9 A7 North Trap rf N.Z.
81 G2 North Troy U.S.A.
66 D3 North Twin I. i. Can.
38 E2 North Tyne r. U.K.
40 A3 North Uist i. U.K.
38 E2 Northumberland National Park U.K.
67 H4 Northumberland Strait chan. Can.
64 E5 North Vancouver Can.
81 F3 Northville U.S.A.
39 J5 North Walsham U.K.
58 F3 North West div. S. Africa
6 B4 North West C. c. Austr.
22 C2 North West Frontier div. Pak.
79 E7 Northwest Providence Chan. chan. Bahamas
67 J3 North West River Can.
65 G2 Northwest Territories div. Can.
39 E4 Northwich U.K.
81 F5 North Wildwood U.S.A.
81 H2 North Woodstock U.S.A.
38 G3 North York Moors reg. U.K.
38 G3 North York Moors National Park U.K.
67 G4 Norton Can.
38 G3 Norton U.K.
76 D4 Norton KS U.S.A.
80 B6 Norton VA U.S.A.
81 H2 Norton VT U.S.A.
57 D5 Norton Zimbabwe
62 B3 Norton Sound b. AK U.S.A.
92 C2 Norvegia, K. c. Ant.
81 G4 Norwalk CT U.S.A.
80 B4 Norwalk OH U.S.A.
81 H2 Norway U.S.A.
34 F2 Norway country Europe
69 J3 Norway Bay Can.
65 K4 Norway House Can.
96 J1 Norwegian Basin sea feature Atl. Ocean
63 J2 Norwegian Bay b. Can.
34 F2 Norwegian Sea sea Atl. Ocean
69 G4 Norwich Can.
39 J5 Norwich U.K.
81 G4 Norwich CT U.S.A.
81 F3 Norwich NY U.S.A.
81 H3 Norwood MA U.S.A.
81 F2 Norwood NY U.S.A.
80 A5 Norwood OH U.S.A.
88 C2 Nos de Cachi mt Arg.
65 H1 Nose Lake l. Can.
49 M3 Nos Emine pt Bulg.
49 M3 Nos Galata pt Bulg.
28 G2 Noshappu-misaki hd Japan
28 G4 Noshiro Japan
51 D5 Nosivka Ukr.
49 N3 Nos Kaliakra pt Bulg.
50 H3 Noskovo Rus. Fed.
58 D2 Nosop r. Botswana/S. Africa
12 G3 Nosovaya Rus. Fed.
19 E4 Noṣratābād Iran
90 A1 Nossa Senhora do Livramento Brazil
37 N7 Nossebro Sweden
49 N3 Nos Shabla pt Bulg.
40 □ Noss, Isle of i. U.K.
58 C2 Nossob r. Namibia
57 E5 Nosy Be i. Madag.
57 E5 Nosy Boraha i. Madag.
57 E6 Nosy Varika Madag.
75 F2 Notch Peak summit U.S.A.
46 H4 Noteć r. Pol.
37 L7 Notodden Norway
48 F6 Noto, Golfo di g. Sicily Italy
29 E6 Noto-hantō pen. Japan
67 K4 Notre Dame Bay b. Can.
69 K3 Notre-Dame-de-la-Salette Can.
81 H2 Notre-Dame-des-Bois Can.
69 K2 Notre-Dame-du-Laus Can.
69 H2 Notre-Dame-du-Nord Can.
67 G4 Notre Dame, Monts mts Can.
69 G3 Nottawasaga Bay b. Can.
66 E3 Nottaway r. Can.
39 F5 Nottingham U.K.
80 E6 Nottoway r. U.S.A.
42 F3 Nottuln Ger.
65 H5 Notukeu Cr. r. Can.
54 A2 Nouâdhibou Maur.
54 A3 Nouakchott Maur.
54 A3 Nouâmghâr Maur.
32 C2 Nouei Vietnam
7 G4 Nouméa New Caledonia
54 B3 Nouna Burkina
58 F5 Noupoort S. Africa
36 V3 Nousu Fin.
Nouveau-Comptoir see Wemindji
Nouvelle Calédonie is see New Caledonia
90 C1 Nova América Brazil
90 B3 Nova Esperança Brazil
90 D3 Nova Friburgo Brazil
48 G2 Nova Gradiška Croatia
90 C3 Nova Granada Brazil
90 D3 Nova Iguaçu Brazil
51 E6 Nova Kakhovka Ukr.
90 D2 Nova Lima Brazil
50 D4 Novalukoml' Belarus
51 D6 Nova Odesa Ukr.
48 C2 Novara Italy
90 C1 Nova Roma Brazil
67 H5 Nova Scotia div. Can.
74 A2 Novato U.S.A.
90 E2 Nova Venécia Brazil
90 B1 Nova Xavantino Brazil
13 R2 Novaya Sibir', Ostrov i. Rus. Fed.
12 G2 Novaya Zemlya is Rus. Fed.
49 M3 Nova Zagora Bulg.
45 F3 Novelda Spain
46 J7 Nové Zámky Slovakia
50 D3 Novgorod Rus. Fed.
50 E3 Novgorodskaya Oblast' div. Rus. Fed.
51 E5 Novhorod-Sivers'kyy Ukr.
49 K3 Novi Iskŭr Bulg.
48 C2 Novi Ligure Italy
49 M3 Novi Pazar Bulg.
49 J3 Novi Pazar Yugo.
49 H2 Novi Sad Yugo.
51 G6 Novoaleksandrovsk Rus. Fed.
51 G5 Novoanninskiy Rus. Fed.
86 F5 Novo Aripuanã Brazil
51 F6 Novoazovs'k Ukr.
19 H2 Novobod Tajik.
50 H3 Novocheboksarsk Rus. Fed.
51 G6 Novocherkassk Rus. Fed.
50 G1 Novodvinsk Rus. Fed.
88 F3 Novo Hamburgo Brazil
90 C3 Novo Horizonte Brazil
46 G6 Novohradské Hory mts Czech Rep.
51 C5 Novohrad-Volyns'kyy Ukr.
14 E2 Novokazalinsk Kazak.
51 G6 Novokubansk Rus. Fed.
24 A1 Novokuznetsk Rus. Fed.
92 D3 Novolazarevskaya Rus. Fed. Base Ant.
13 M2 Novoletov'ye Rus. Fed.
48 F2 Novo Mesto Slovenia
50 F4 Novomichurinsk Rus. Fed.
51 F6 Novomikhaylovskiy Rus. Fed.
50 F4 Novomoskovsk Rus. Fed.
51 E5 Novomoskovs'k Ukr.
51 D5 Novomyrhorod Ukr.
51 G5 Novonikolayevskiy Rus. Fed.
51 E6 Novooleksiyivka Ukr.
28 D2 Novopokrovka Rus. Fed.
51 G6 Novopokrovskaya Rus. Fed.
51 J5 Novorepnoye Rus. Fed.
51 F6 Novorossiysk Rus. Fed.
13 M2 Novorybnoye Rus. Fed.
47 O2 Novorzhev Rus. Fed.
51 E6 Novoselivs'ke Ukr.
47 O1 Novosel'ye Rus. Fed.
51 F6 Novoshakhtinsk Rus. Fed.
28 C2 Novoshakhtinskiy Rus. Fed.
12 K4 Novosibirsk Rus. Fed.
13 Q2 Novosibirskiye Ostrova is Rus. Fed.
50 D3 Novosokol'niki Rus. Fed.
50 H4 Novospasskoye Rus. Fed.
51 E6 Novotroyits'ke Ukr.
51 D5 Novoukrayinka Ukr.
51 J5 Novouzensk Rus. Fed.
51 C5 Novovolyns'k Ukr.
51 F5 Novovoronezh Rus. Fed.
51 D4 Novozybkov Rus. Fed.
46 H6 Nový Jičín Czech Rep.
13 M2 Novyy Rus. Fed.
51 F5 Novyy Oskol Rus. Fed.
12 J3 Novyy Port Rus. Fed.
50 J3 Novyy Tor'yal Rus. Fed.
12 J3 Novyy Urengoy Rus. Fed.
24 F1 Novyy Urgal Rus. Fed.
14 D2 Novyy Uzen' Kazak.
18 D4 Now Iran
77 E4 Nowata U.S.A.
18 C3 Nowbarān Iran
19 E3 Now Deh Iran
17 M3 Nowdī Iran
Nowgong see Nagaon
22 D4 Nowgong Madhya Pradesh India
65 J2 Nowleye Lake l. Can.
46 G4 Nowogard Pol.
8 H3 Nowra Austr.
18 C2 Now Shahr Iran
18 C2 Nowshahr Iran
22 C2 Nowshera Pak.
47 K6 Nowy Sącz Pol.
47 K6 Nowy Targ Pol.
81 E4 Noxen U.S.A.
12 J3 Noyabr'sk r. Rus. Fed.
64 C3 Noyes I. i. U.S.A.
44 F2 Noyon France
32 C1 Noy, Xé r. Laos
32 C1 Noy, Xé r. Laos
59 F5 Nozizwe S. Africa
59 G6 Nqamakwe S. Africa
59 J4 Nqutu S. Africa
57 D5 Nsanje Malawi
56 B4 Ntandembele Congo(Zaire)
59 G3 Ntha S. Africa
56 D4 Ntungamo Uganda
55 F3 Nuba Mountains mts Sudan
17 K1 Nubarashen Armenia
55 F2 Nubian Desert des. Sudan
91 B3 Nuble r. Chile
26 D1 Nüden Mongolia
86 D7 Nudo Coropuna mt Peru
77 D6 Nueces r. U.S.A.
89 C2 Nueva Florida Venez.
91 F2 Nueva Helvecia Uru.
91 B3 Nueva Imperial Chile
89 A4 Nueva Loja Ecuador
88 B6 Nueva Lubecka Arg.
82 D3 Nueva Rosita Mex.
83 J4 Nuevitas Cuba
82 C2 Nuevo Casas Grandes Mex.
91 D4 Nuevo, Golfo g. Arg.
84 A1 Nuevo Ideal Mex.
82 E3 Nuevo Laredo Mex.
84 C1 Nuevo León div. Mex.
56 E3 Nugaal watercourse Somalia
9 B7 Nugget Pt pt N.Z.
7 F2 Nuguria Is is P.N.G.
9 F3 Nuhaka N.Z.
7 H2 Nui i. Tuvalu
32 C2 Nui Ti On mt Vietnam
24 B3 Nu Jiang r. China
7 J4 Nuku'alofa Tonga
7 H2 Nukufetau i. Tuvalu
5 N5 Nuku Hiva i. Pac. Oc.
7 H2 Nukulaelae i. Tuvalu
7 F2 Nukumanu Is is P.N.G.
7 J2 Nukunono i. Pac. Oc.
14 D2 Nukus Uzbek.
6 C4 Nullagine Austr.
6 C5 Nullarbor Plain plain Austr.
26 F1 Nulu'erhu Shan mts China
54 D4 Numan Nigeria
29 F6 Numata Japan
29 F7 Numazu Japan
37 L6 Numedal v. Norway
25 F7 Numfor i. Indon.
8 E4 Numurkah Austr.
67 H2 Nunaksaluk Island i. Can.
63 O3 Nunarsuit i. Greenland
80 E3 Nunda U.S.A.
8 H1 Nundle Austr.
39 F5 Nuneaton U.K.
66 B3 Nungesser L. l. Can.
62 B4 Nunivak I. i. AK U.S.A.
22 D2 Nunkun mt India
13 U3 Nunligran Rus. Fed.
45 C2 Nuñomoral Spain
42 D2 Nunspeet Neth.
48 C4 Nuoro Sardinia Italy
7 G3 Nupani i. Solomon Is
20 B4 Nuqrah S. Arabia
89 A3 Nuquí Col.
22 E1 Nur China
18 D2 Nur r. Iran
18 C4 Nurābād Iran
Nuremberg see Nürnberg
17 J2 Nurettin Turkey
19 G4 Nur Gamma Pak.
8 B3 Nuriootpa Austr.
19 H3 Nuristan reg. Afgh.
50 J4 Nurlaty Rus. Fed.
36 V5 Nurmes Fin.
36 S5 Nurmo Fin.
43 K5 Nürnberg Ger.
8 F1 Nurri, Mt h. Austr.
23 H1 Nur Turu China
17 H3 Nusaybin Turkey
19 G4 Nushki Pak.
67 H2 Nutak Can.
75 H5 Nutrioso U.S.A.
22 B3 Nuttal Pak.
36 U3 Nuupas Fin.
63 N2 Nuussuaq Greenland
63 N2 Nuussuaq pen. Greenland
21 C5 Nuwara Eliya Sri Lanka
58 C5 Nuwerus S. Africa
58 D6 Nuweveldberg mts S. Africa
17 K4 Nuzi Iraq
59 J1 Nwanedi National Park nat. park S. Africa
12 H3 Nyagan' Rus. Fed.
8 D3 Nyah West Austr.
23 G3 Nyainqêntanglha Feng mt China
23 G3 Nyainqêntanglha Shan mts China
23 H2 Nyainrong China
36 Q5 Nyaker Sweden
55 E3 Nyala Sudan
23 F3 Nyalam China
57 C5 Nyamandhiovu Zimbabwe
50 G2 Nyandoma Rus. Fed.
50 F2 Nyandomskiy Vozvyshennost' reg. Rus. Fed.
57 D5 Nyanga Zimbabwe
56 B4 Nyanga r. Gabon
23 H3 Nyang Qu r. Xizang China
23 G3 Nyang Qu r. Xizang China
57 D5 Nyasa, Lake l. Africa
50 C4 Nyasvizh Belarus
37 M9 Nyborg Denmark
36 V1 Nyborg Norway
37 O8 Nybro Sweden
63 N1 Nyeboe Land reg. Greenland
23 G3 Nyêmo China
56 D4 Nyeri Kenya
23 F3 Nyima China
24 B4 Nyingchi China
47 K7 Nyíregyháza Hungary
36 S5 Nykarleby Fin.
37 M9 Nykøbing Denmark
37 M9 Nykøbing Sjælland Denmark
37 P7 Nyköping Sweden
36 P5 Nyland Sweden
59 H2 Nylstroom S. Africa
8 F2 Nymagee Austr.
37 P7 Nynäshamn Sweden
8 F1 Nyngan Austr.
47 L4 Nyoman r. Belarus/Lith.
46 C7 Nyon Switz.
30 E5 Nyongwol S. Korea
23 F3 Nyonni Ri mt China
44 G4 Nyons France
12 G3 Nyrob Rus. Fed.
46 H5 Nysa Pol.
Nysa Łużycka r. see Neiß
50 J2 Nyuchpas Rus. Fed.
28 F5 Nyūdō-zaki pt Japan
56 C4 Nyunzu Congo(Zaire)
13 N3 Nyurba Rus. Fed.
50 J2 Nyuvchim Rus. Fed.
51 E6 Nyzhn'ohirs'kyy Ukr.
56 D4 Nzega Tanz.
54 B4 Nzérékoré Guinea
56 B4 N'zeto Angola
59 J1 Nzhelele Dam dam S. Africa
Nzwani i. see Anjouan

O

76 C2 Oahe, Lake l. U.S.A.
74 □1 Oahu i. U.S.A.
8 C2 Oakbank Austr.
75 F2 Oak City U.S.A.
77 E6 Oakdale U.S.A.
76 D2 Oakes U.S.A.
39 G5 Oakham U.K.
72 B1 Oak Harbor U.S.A.
80 C6 Oak Hill U.S.A.
74 C3 Oakhurst U.S.A.
68 B2 Oak I. i. U.S.A.
74 A3 Oakland CA U.S.A.
80 D5 Oakland MD U.S.A.
76 D3 Oakland NE U.S.A.
72 B3 Oakland OR U.S.A.
8 F3 Oaklands Austr.
68 D5 Oak Lawn U.S.A.
76 C4 Oakley U.S.A.
6 C4 Oakover r. Austr.
79 C4 Oak Ridge U.S.A.
72 B3 Oakridge U.S.A.
8 C2 Oakvale Austr.
69 H4 Oakville Can.
9 C6 Oamaru N.Z.
40 B5 Oa, Mull of hd U.K.
9 D5 Oaro N.Z.
31 B3 Oas Phil.
72 D3 Oasis U.S.A.
92 B5 Oates Land reg. Ant.
75 E4 Oatman U.S.A.
84 C3 Oaxaca Mex.
84 C3 Oaxaca div. Mex.

12 H3 Ob' r. Rus. Fed.
54 D4 Obala Cameroon
29 D7 Obama Japan
40 C4 Oban U.K.
28 G5 Obanazawa Japan
45 C1 O Barco Spain
66 F4 Obatogama L. l. Can.
64 F4 Obed Can.
9 B6 Obelisk mt N.Z.
43 H4 Oberaula Ger.
43 J3 Oberdorla Ger.
43 J3 Oberharz nat. park Ger.
42 E3 Oberhausen Ger.
76 C4 Oberlin KS U.S.A.
80 B4 Oberlin OH U.S.A.
43 F5 Obermoschel Ger.
8 G2 Oberon Austr.
43 L5 Oberpfälzer Wald mts Ger.
43 H4 Obersinn Ger.
43 H4 Oberthulba Ger.
43 G4 Obertshausen Ger.
43 H3 Oberwälder Land reg. Ger.
25 E7 Obi i. Indon.
87 G4 Óbidos Brazil
19 H2 Obigarm Tajik.
28 H3 Obihiro Japan
51 H6 Obil'noye Rus. Fed.
89 C2 Obispos Venez.
24 F2 Obluch'ye Rus. Fed.
50 F4 Obninsk Rus. Fed.
56 C3 Obo C.A.R.
26 A2 Obo China
56 E2 Obock Djibouti
56 C4 Obokote Congo(Zaire)
30 E3 Obŏk-tong N. Korea
56 B4 Obouya Congo
51 F5 Oboyan' Rus. Fed.
50 G2 Obozerskiy Rus. Fed.
23 E4 Obra India
23 E4 Obra Dam dam India
70 E6 Obregón, Presa resr Mex.
49 J2 Obrenovac Yugo.
16 D2 Obruk Turkey
12 J2 Obskaya Guba chan. Rus. Fed.
54 B4 Obuasi Ghana
51 D5 Obukhiv Ukr.
50 J2 Ob''yachevo Rus. Fed.
79 D6 Ocala U.S.A.
89 D4 Ocamo r. Venez.
84 B1 Ocampo Mex.
89 B2 Ocaña Col.
45 E3 Ocaña Spain
86 E7 Occidental, Cordillera mts Chile
89 A4 Occidental, Cordillera mts Col.
86 C6 Occidental, Cordillera mts Peru
64 B3 Ocean Cape pt U.S.A.
81 F5 Ocean City MD U.S.A.
81 F5 Ocean City NJ U.S.A.
64 D4 Ocean Falls Can.
96 G3 Oceanographer Fracture sea feature Atl. Ocean
74 D5 Oceanside U.S.A.
77 F6 Ocean Springs U.S.A.
51 D6 Ochakiv Ukr.
51 G7 Och'amch'ire Georgia
40 E4 Ochil Hills h. U.K.
22 C1 Ochili Pass Afgh.
43 J5 Ochsenfurt Ger.
42 F2 Ochtrup Ger.
37 P6 Ockelbo Sweden
84 D3 Ococingo Mex.
47 M7 Ocolașul Mare, Vârful mt Romania
71 K5 Oconee r. GA U.S.A.
68 C4 Oconomowoc U.S.A.
68 D3 Oconto U.S.A.
74 D5 Ocotillo Wells U.S.A.
84 B2 Ocotlán Mex.
54 B4 Oda Ghana
29 C7 Ōda Japan
36 E4 Ódáðahraun lava Iceland
30 E3 Ōdaejin N. Korea
28 G4 Ōdate Japan
29 F7 Odawara Japan
37 K6 Odda Norway
65 K3 Odei r. Can.
68 C5 Odell U.S.A.
45 B4 Odemira Port.
16 A2 Ödemiş Turkey
59 G3 Odendaalsrus S. Africa
37 M9 Odense Denmark
43 G5 Odenwald reg. Ger.
43 J3 Oder r. Ger./Pol.
46 G3 Oderbucht b. Ger.
51 D6 Odesa Ukr.
37 O7 Ödeshog Sweden
77 C6 Odessa U.S.A.
45 C4 Odiel r. Spain
54 B4 Odienné Côte d'Ivoire
50 F4 Odintsovo Rus. Fed.
32 C3 Ŏdôngk Cambodia
46 J6 Odra r. Ger./Pol.
87 K5 Oeiras Brazil
76 C3 Oelrichs U.S.A.
43 L4 Oelsnitz Ger.
68 B4 Oelwein U.S.A.
42 D1 Oenkerk Neth.
17 H1 Of Turkey
48 G4 Ofanto r. Italy
43 G4 Offenbach am Main Ger.
42 F6 Offenburg Ger.
49 M6 Ofidoussa i. Greece
28 G5 Ōfunato Japan
28 F5 Oga Japan
56 E3 Ogadēn reg. Eth.
28 E5 Oga-hantō pen. Japan
29 E7 Ōgaki Japan
76 C3 Ogallala U.S.A.
24 G4 Ogasawara-shotō is Japan
69 H2 Ogascanane, Lac l. Can.
54 C4 Ogbomoso Nigeria
76 E3 Ogden IA U.S.A.
72 E3 Ogden UT U.S.A.
64 C3 Ogden, Mt mt Can.
81 F2 Ogdensburg U.S.A.
62 E3 Ogilvie r. Can.
62 E3 Ogilvie Mts mts Can.
18 D2 Oglanly Turkm.
79 C5 Oglethorpe, Mt mt U.S.A.
48 D1 Oglio r. Italy
54 C4 Ogoja Nigeria
66 C3 Ogoki r. Can.
66 C3 Ogoki Res. resr Can.
49 K3 Ogosta r. Bulg.
37 T8 Ogre Latvia
48 F2 Ogulin Croatia
18 D2 Ogurchinskiy, Ostrov i. Turkm.
17 L1 Oğuz Azer.
9 A6 Ohai N.Z.
9 E3 Ohakune N.Z.
28 G4 Ōhata Japan
9 B6 Ohau, L. l. N.Z.
91 B2 O'Higgins div. Chile
88 B7 O'Higgins, L. l. Chile
80 B4 Ohio div. U.S.A.
78 C4 Ohio r. U.S.A.
43 G4 Ohm r. Ger.
43 J4 Ohrdruf Ger.
43 L4 Ohře r. Czech Rep.
43 K2 Ohre r. Ger.
49 J4 Ohrid Macedonia
49 J4 Ohrid, Lake l. Albania/Macedonia
59 J2 Ohrigstad S. Africa
43 H5 Öhringen Ger.
9 E3 Ohura N.Z.
87 H3 Oiapoque Brazil
40 D3 Oich, Loch l. U.K.
23 H3 Oiga China
42 A4 Oignies France
80 D4 Oil City U.S.A.
74 C4 Oildale U.S.A.
44 F2 Oise r. France
42 B5 Oise à l'Aisne, Canal de l' canal France
29 B8 Ōita Japan
49 K5 Oiti mt Greece
74 C4 Ojai U.S.A.
91 D2 Ojeda Arg.
68 B3 Ojibwa U.S.A.
82 D3 Ojinaga Mex.
84 C3 Ojitlán Mex.
29 F6 Ojiya Japan
88 C3 Ojos del Salado mt Arg.
50 G4 Oka r. Rus. Fed.
57 B6 Okahandja Namibia
9 E3 Okahukura N.Z.
57 B6 Okakarara Namibia
67 H2 Okak Islands is Can.
64 F5 Okanagan Falls Can.
64 F4 Okanagan Lake l. Can.
64 F5 Okanogan U.S.A.
72 C1 Okanogan r. Can./U.S.A.
72 B1 Okanogan Range mts U.S.A.
56 C3 Okapi, Parc National de la nat. park Congo(Zaire)
22 C3 Okara Pak.
18 D2 Okarem Turkm.
57 B5 Okaukuejo Namibia
57 C5 Okavango r. Botswana/Namibia
57 C5 Okavango Delta swamp Botswana
29 F6 Okaya Japan
29 C7 Okayama Japan
29 E7 Okazaki Japan
79 D7 Okeechobee U.S.A.
79 D7 Okeechobee, L. l. U.S.A.
79 D6 Okefenokee Swamp swamp U.S.A.
39 C7 Okehampton U.K.
54 C4 Okene Nigeria
43 J2 Oker r. Ger.
22 B5 Okha India
24 G1 Okha Rus. Fed.
23 F4 Okhaldhunga Nepal
22 B5 Okha Rann marsh India
13 Q3 Okhotka r. Rus. Fed.
13 Q4 Okhotsk Rus. Fed.
24 G2 Okhotsk, Sea of g. Rus. Fed.
51 E5 Okhtyrka Ukr.
24 E4 Okinawa i. Japan
29 B7 Okino-shima i. Japan
29 C6 Oki-shotō is Japan
77 D5 Oklahoma div. U.S.A.
77 D5 Oklahoma City U.S.A.
77 D5 Okmulgee U.S.A.
56 B4 Okondja Gabon
64 G4 Okotoks Can.
51 E4 Okovskiy Les forest Rus. Fed.
56 B4 Okoyo Congo
36 S1 Øksfjord Norway
50 F2 Oksovskiy Rus. Fed.
19 H2 Oktyabr' Tajik.
14 D2 Oktyabr'sk Kazak.
50 J4 Oktyabr'sk Rus. Fed.
50 G2 Oktyabr'skiy Archangel. Rus. Fed.
51 G6 Oktyabr'skiy Volgograd. Rus. Fed.
24 H1 Oktyabr'skiy Rus. Fed.
12 G4 Oktyabr'skiy Rus. Fed.
19 G2 Oktyabr'skiy Uzbek.
12 H3 Oktyabr'skoye Rus. Fed.
13 L2 Oktyabr'skoy Revolyutsii, Ostrov i. Rus. Fed.
50 E3 Okulovka Rus. Fed.
28 F3 Okushiri-tō i. Japan
58 E1 Okwa watercourse Botswana
36 B4 Ólafsvík Iceland
74 C3 Olancha U.S.A.
74 C3 Olancha Peak summit U.S.A.
37 P8 Öland i. Sweden
36 W3 Olanga Rus. Fed.
8 C2 Olary Austr.
8 C2 Olary r. Austr.
76 E4 Olathe U.S.A.
91 E3 Olavarría Arg.
46 H5 Oława Pol.
75 G5 Olberg U.S.A.
48 C4 Olbia Sardinia Italy
80 D3 Olcott U.S.A.
21 C2 Old Bastar India
41 D4 Oldcastle Rep. of Ireland
62 E3 Old Crow Can.
42 D1 Oldeboorn Neth.
43 G1 Oldenburg Ger.
46 E3 Oldenburg in Holstein Ger.
42 E2 Oldenzaal Neth.
36 R2 Olderdalen Norway
81 F3 Old Forge NY U.S.A.
81 F4 Old Forge PA U.S.A.
39 E4 Oldham U.K.
41 C6 Old Head of Kinsale hd Rep. of Ireland
64 G4 Oldman r. Can.
40 F3 Oldmeldrum U.K.
81 H3 Old Orchard Beach U.S.A.
67 K4 Old Perlican Can.
64 G4 Olds Can.
81 J2 Old Town U.S.A.
65 H4 Old Wives L. l. Can.
75 E4 Old Woman Mts mts U.S.A.
80 D3 Olean U.S.A.
47 L3 Olecko Pol.
13 O4 Olekma r. Rus. Fed.
13 O3 Olekminsk Rus. Fed.
51 E5 Oleksandriya Ukr.
50 H1 Olema Rus. Fed.
37 J7 Ølen Norway
36 X2 Olenegorsk Rus. Fed.
13 N3 Olenek Rus. Fed.
13 O2 Olenek r. Rus. Fed.
13 O2 Olenek B. b. Rus. Fed.
50 E3 Olenino Rus. Fed.
51 C5 Olevs'k Ukr.
28 B3 Ol'ga Rus. Fed.
45 C4 Olhão Port.
59 J4 Olifants S. Africa
58 C5 Olifants r. S. Africa
58 C2 Olifants watercourse Namibia
58 E3 Olifantshoek S. Africa
58 C6 Olifantsrivierberg mts S. Africa
91 F2 Olimar Grande r. Uru.
90 C3 Olímpia Brazil
84 C3 Olinalá Mex.
87 M5 Olinda Brazil
57 D5 Olinga Moz.
59 G2 Oliphants Drift Botswana
91 D2 Oliva Arg.
45 F3 Oliva Spain
88 C3 Oliva, Cordillera de mts Arg./Chile
91 C1 Olivares, Co del mt Chile
80 B5 Olive Hill U.S.A.
90 D3 Oliveira Brazil
45 C3 Olivenza Spain
76 E2 Olivia U.S.A.
50 G4 Ol'khi Rus. Fed.
88 C2 Ollagüe Chile
91 B1 Ollita, Cordillera de mts Arg./Chile
91 B1 Ollitas mt Arg.
86 C5 Olmos Peru
81 G3 Olmstedville U.S.A.
39 G5 Olney U.K.
78 C4 Olney U.S.A.
37 O8 Olofström Sweden
46 H6 Olomouc Czech Rep.
50 E2 Olonets Rus. Fed.
31 B3 Olongapo Phil.
44 D5 Oloron-Ste-Marie France
45 H1 Olot Spain
24 D1 Olovyannaya Rus. Fed.
22 C5 Olpad India
43 F3 Olpe Ger.
47 K4 Olsztyn Pol.
46 C7 Olten Switz.
49 M2 Oltenița Romania
17 H1 Oltu Turkey
31 B5 Olutanga i. Phil.
72 B2 Olympia U.S.A.
72 A2 Olympic Nat. Park WA U.S.A.
72 B2 Olympic Nat. Park WA U.S.A.
Olympus mt see Troödos, Mount
49 K4 Olympus mt Greece
72 B2 Olympus, Mt mt U.S.A.
13 S3 Olyutorskiy Rus. Fed.
13 T4 Olyutorskiy, Mys c. Rus. Fed.
13 S4 Olyutorskiy Zaliv b. Rus. Fed.
23 E2 Oma China
28 G4 Ōma Japan
29 E6 Ōmachi Japan
29 F7 Omae-zaki pt Japan
41 D3 Omagh U.K.
76 E3 Omaha U.S.A.
58 C1 Omaheke div. Namibia
72 C1 Omak U.S.A.
10 G8 Oman country Asia
19 E5 Oman, Gulf of g. Asia
9 B6 Omarama N.Z.
57 B6 Omaruru Namibia
57 B5 Omatako watercourse Namibia
86 D7 Omate Peru
58 E2 Omaweneno Botswana
28 G4 Ōma-zaki c. Japan
56 A4 Omboué Gabon
48 D3 Ombrone r. Italy
23 F3 Ombu China
58 E5 Omdraaisvlei S. Africa
55 F3 Omdurman Sudan
48 C2 Omegna Italy
8 F4 Omeo Austr.
56 D2 Om Häjer Eritrea
18 C4 Omīdīyeh Iran
64 D3 Omineca Mountains Can.
58 C1 Omitara Namibia
29 F7 Ōmiya Japan
64 C3 Ommaney, Cape hd U.S.A.
42 E2 Ommen Neth.
26 B1 Ömnögovĭ div. Mongolia
13 R3 Omolon r. Rus. Fed.
56 D3 Omo National Park Eth.
28 G5 Omono-gawa r. Japan
12 J4 Omsk Rus. Fed.
13 R3 Omsukchan Rus. Fed.
28 H2 Ōmu Japan
29 A8 Ōmura Japan
49 L2 Omu, Vârful mt Romania
68 B4 Onalaska U.S.A.
81 F6 Onancock U.S.A.
66 D4 Onaping Lake l. Can.
69 E3 Onaway U.S.A.
32 A2 Onbingwin Myanmar
91 D1 Oncativo Arg.
38 C3 Onchan U.K.
57 B5 Oncócua Angola
57 B5 Ondangwa Namibia
58 B1 Ondekaremba Namibia
58 D5 Onderstedorings S. Africa
57 B5 Ondjiva Angola
54 C4 Ondo Nigeria
24 D2 Öndörhaan Mongolia
30 A1 Ondor Had China
26 B1 Ondor Mod China
26 D1 Ondor Sum China
50 E2 Ondozero Rus. Fed.
58 D1 One Botswana
50 F2 Onega Rus. Fed.
50 F2 Onega r. Rus. Fed.
50 E2 Onega, Lake l. Rus. Fed.
64 E4 100 Mile House Can.
81 F3 Oneida U.S.A.
81 F3 Oneida Lake l. U.S.A.
76 D3 O'Neill U.S.A.
24 H2 Onekotan, O. i. Rus. Fed.
81 F3 Oneonta U.S.A.
9 E2 Oneroa N.Z.
47 N7 Onești Romania
50 E1 Onezhskaya Guba g. Rus. Fed.
Onezhskoye Ozero l. see Onega, Lake
23 E5 Ong r. India
56 B4 Onga Gabon
9 F3 Ongaonga N.Z.
58 E4 Ongers watercourse S. Africa
30 C5 Ongjin N. Korea
26 F1 Ongniud Qi China
21 C3 Ongole India
51 G7 Oni Georgia
57 E6 Onilahy r. Madag.
54 C4 Onitsha Nigeria
58 B1 Onjati Mountain mt Namibia
29 E7 Ōno Japan
7 J4 Ono-i-Lau i. Fiji
29 C7 Onomichi Japan
7 H2 Onotoa i. Kiribati
64 G4 Onoway Can.
58 C4 Onseepkans S. Africa
6 B4 Onslow Austr.
79 E5 Onslow Bay b. U.S.A.
30 F2 Onsong N. Korea
42 F1 Onstwedde Neth.
29 E7 Ontake-san volc. Japan
72 C2 Ontario U.S.A.
66 B3 Ontario div. Can.
69 H4 Ontario, Lake l. Can./U.S.A.
68 C2 Ontonagon U.S.A.
7 F2 Ontong Java Atoll atoll Solomon Is
6 D4 Oodnadatta Austr.
77 E4 Oologah L. resr U.S.A.
42 B3 Oostburg Neth.
Oostende see Ostend
42 D2 Oostendorp Neth.
42 C3 Oosterhout Neth.
42 B3 Oosterschelde est. Neth.
42 E2 Oosterwolde Neth.
42 A4 Oostvleteren Belgium
42 D1 Oost-Vlieland Neth.
64 D4 Ootsa Lake Can.
64 D4 Ootsa Lake l. Can.
80 E5 Opal U.S.A.
56 C4 Opala Congo(Zaire)
50 J3 Oparino Rus. Fed.
66 B3 Opasquia Can.
66 B3 Opasquia Provincial Park res. Can.
66 F3 Opataca L. l. Can.
46 H6 Opava Czech Rep.
79 C5 Opelika U.S.A.
77 E6 Opelousas U.S.A.
72 F1 Opheim U.S.A.
69 F2 Ophir Can.
33 B2 Ophir, Gunung volc. Indon.
9 C5 Opihi r. N.Z.
66 E3 Opinaca r. Can.
66 E3 Opinaca, Réservoir resr Can.
66 E3 Opinnagau r. Can.
17 K5 Opis Iraq
67 G3 Opiscotéo L. l. Can.
42 C2 Opmeer Neth.
50 D3 Opochka Rus. Fed.
46 H5 Opole Pol.
45 B2 Oporto Port.
9 F3 Opotiki N.Z.
79 C6 Opp U.S.A.
36 L5 Oppdal Norway
9 D3 Opunake N.Z.
57 B5 Opuwo Namibia
68 B5 Oquawka U.S.A.
81 H2 Oquossoc U.S.A.
75 G5 Oracle U.S.A.
75 G5 Oracle Junction U.S.A.
47 K7 Oradea Romania
36 E4 Öræfajökull gl. Iceland
49 J3 Orahovac Yugo.
22 D4 Orai India
54 B1 Oran Alg.
88 D2 Orán Arg.
32 C2 O Rang Cambodia
30 E3 Orang N. Korea
8 G2 Orange Austr.
44 G4 Orange France
81 G3 Orange MA U.S.A.
77 E6 Orange TX U.S.A.
80 D5 Orange VA U.S.A.
57 B6 Orange r. Namibia/S. Africa
79 D5 Orangeburg U.S.A.
87 H3 Orange, Cabo c. Brazil
Orange Free State div. see Free State
69 G3 Orangeville Can.
75 G2 Orangeville U.S.A.
82 G5 Orange Walk Belize
31 B3 Orani Phil.
43 M2 Oranienburg Ger.
57 B6 Oranjemund Namibia
89 C1 Oranjestad Aruba
41 C4 Oranmore Rep. of Ireland
57 C6 Orapa Botswana
31 C3 Oras Phil.
49 K2 Orăștie Romania
36 S5 Oravais Fin.
49 J2 Oravita Romania
22 E2 Orba Co l. China
48 C3 Orbetello Italy
45 C1 Orbigo r. Spain
8 G4 Orbost Austr.
92 E1 Orcadas Arg. Base Ant.
75 H2 Orchard Mesa U.S.A.
89 D2 Orchila, Isla i. Venez.
74 E4 Orcutt U.S.A.
6 C3 Ord r. Austr.
73 D4 Orderville U.S.A.
45 E1 Ordes Spain
6 C3 Ord, Mt h. Austr.
74 D4 Ord Mt mt U.S.A.
16 F1 Ordu Turkey
17 L2 Ordubad Azer.
73 G4 Ordway U.S.A.
Ordzhonikidze see Vladikavkaz
51 E6 Ordzhonikidze Ukr.
74 C1 Oreana U.S.A.
37 O7 Örebro Sweden
68 C4 Oregon IL U.S.A.
80 E4 Oregon OH U.S.A.
68 C4 Oregon WI U.S.A.
72 E3 Oregon div. U.S.A.
72 B2 Oregon City U.S.A.
50 F4 Orekhovo-Zuyevo Rus. Fed.
50 F4 Orel Rus. Fed.
24 F1 Orel', Ozero l. Rus. Fed.
75 G1 Orem U.S.A.
49 M6 Ören Turkey
16 A2 Ören Turkey
12 G4 Orenburg Rus. Fed.
91 E3 Orense Arg.
9 A7 Orepuki N.Z.
37 N9 Øresund str. Denmark
9 B7 Oreti r. N.Z.
9 E2 Orewa N.Z.
42 D4 Oreye Belgium
49 K4 Orfanou, Kolpos b. Greece
39 J5 Orford U.K.
39 J5 Orford Ness spit U.K.
75 F5 Organ Pipe Cactus National Monument res. U.S.A.
19 H3 Orgūn Afgh.
16 B2 Orhaneli Turkey
51 D7 Orhangazi Turkey
50 J3 Orichi Rus. Fed.
81 K2 Orient U.S.A.
86 E7 Oriental, Cordillera mts Bol.
89 B3 Oriental, Cordillera mts Col.
86 D6 Oriental, Cordillera mts Peru
91 E3 Oriente Arg.
45 F3 Orihuela Spain
51 E6 Orikhiv Ukr.
69 H3 Orillia Can.
37 T6 Orimattila Fin.
89 E2 Orinoco r. Col./Venez.
89 E2 Orinoco Delta delta Venez.
23 F5 Orissa div. India
37 S7 Orissaare Estonia
48 C5 Oristano Sardinia Italy
37 T6 Orivesi Fin.
36 V5 Orivesi l. Fin.
87 G4 Oriximiná Brazil
84 C3 Orizaba Mex.
36 L5 Orkanger Norway
37 N8 Örkelljunga Sweden
36 L5 Orkla r. Norway
59 G3 Orkney S. Africa
40 E1 Orkney Islands is U.K.
77 C6 Orla U.S.A.
74 A2 Orland U.S.A.
90 C3 Orlândia Brazil
79 D6 Orlando U.S.A.
44 E3 Orléans France
81 J4 Orleans MA U.S.A.
81 G2 Orleans VT U.S.A.
50 J3 Orlov Rus. Fed.
50 F4 Orlovskaya Oblast' div. Rus. Fed.
51 G6 Orlovskiy Rus. Fed.
19 G5 Ormara Pak.
19 G5 Ormara, Ras hd Pak.
31 C4 Ormoc Phil.
79 D6 Ormond Beach U.S.A.
38 E4 Ormskirk U.K.
81 G2 Ormstown Can.
44 D2 Orne r. France
36 N3 Ørnes Norway
36 Q5 Örnsköldsvik Sweden
30 D4 Oro N. Korea
89 C3 Orocué Col.
54 B3 Orodara Burkina
72 C2 Orofino U.S.A.
73 F5 Orogrande U.S.A.
67 G4 Oromocto Can.
16 E6 Oron Israel
7 J2 Orona i. Kiribati
81 J2 Orono U.S.A.
40 B4 Oronsay i. U.K.
Orontes r. see 'Āṣī, Nahr al
24 E1 Oroqen Zizhiqi China
31 B4 Oroquieta Phil.
87 L5 Orós, Açude resr Brazil
48 C4 Orosei Sardinia Italy
48 C4 Orosei, Golfo di b. Sardinia Italy
47 K7 Orosháza Hungary
75 G5 Oro Valley U.S.A.
74 B2 Oroville CA U.S.A.
72 C1 Oroville WA U.S.A.
74 B2 Oroville, Lake l. U.S.A.
8 B2 Orroroo Austr.
37 O6 Orsa Sweden
50 D4 Orsha Belarus
12 G4 Orsk Rus. Fed.
37 K5 Ørsta Norway
45 C1 Ortegal, Cabo c. Spain
44 D5 Orthez France
45 C1 Ortigueira Spain
89 D2 Ortíz Venez.
48 D1 Ortles mt Italy
38 E3 Orton U.K.
48 F3 Ortona Italy
76 D2 Ortonville U.S.A.
13 O3 Orulgan, Khrebet mts Rus. Fed.
58 B1 Orumbo Namibia
18 B2 Orūmīyeh Iran
18 B2 Orūmīyeh, Daryācheh-ye salt l. Iran
86 E7 Oruro Bol.
42 D5 Orval, Abbaye d' Belgium
48 E3 Orvieto Italy
92 B3 Orville Coast coastal area Ant.
80 C4 Orwell OH U.S.A.
81 G3 Orwell VT U.S.A.
37 M5 Os Norway
68 A4 Osage U.S.A.
76 E4 Osage r. U.S.A.
29 D7 Ōsaka Japan
83 H7 Osa, Pen. de pen. Costa Rica
37 N8 Osby Sweden
77 F5 Osceola AR U.S.A.
76 E3 Osceola IA U.S.A.
43 M3 Oschatz Ger.
43 K2 Oschersleben (Bode) Ger.
48 C4 Oschiri Sardinia Italy
69 F3 Oscoda U.S.A.
50 F4 Osetr r. Rus. Fed.
29 A8 Ōse-zaki pt Japan
69 K3 Osgoode Can.
15 F2 Osh Kyrg.
57 B5 Oshakati Namibia
28 G3 Oshamanbe Japan
69 H4 Oshawa Can.
28 G5 Oshika-hantō pen. Japan
28 F4 Ō-shima i. Japan
29 F7 Ō-shima i. Japan
76 C3 Oshkosh NE U.S.A.
68 C3 Oshkosh WI U.S.A.
18 B2 Oshnovīyeh Iran
54 C4 Oshogbo Nigeria
17 M5 Oshtorān Kūh mt Iran
17 M5 Oshtorīnān Iran
56 B4 Oshwe Congo(Zaire)
49 H2 Osijek Croatia
48 E3 Osimo Italy
22 C4 Osiyān India
59 J3 Osizweni S. Africa
48 G2 Osječenica mt Bos.-Herz.
36 O5 Ösjön l. Sweden
76 E3 Oskaloosa U.S.A.
37 P8 Oskarshamn Sweden
69 K1 Oskélanéo Can.
51 F5 Oskol r. Rus. Fed.
37 M7 Oslo Norway
31 B4 Oslob Phil.
37 M7 Oslofjorden chan. Norway
21 B2 Osmānābād India
16 E1 Osmancık Turkey
16 B1 Osmaneli Turkey
16 F3 Osmaniye Turkey
37 V7 Os'mino Rus. Fed.
43 G2 Osnabrück Ger.
49 K3 Osogovske Planine mts Bulg./Macedonia
91 B4 Osorno Chile
45 D1 Osorno Spain
91 B4 Osorno, Vol. volc. Chile
64 F5 Osoyoos Can.
37 J6 Osøyri Norway
6 E3 Osprey Reef rf Coral Sea Is Terr.
42 D3 Oss Neth.
6 E6 Ossa, Mt mt Austr.
68 B3 Osseo U.S.A.
69 F3 Ossineke U.S.A.
81 H3 Ossipee Lake l. U.S.A.
43 K3 Oßmannstedt Ger.
67 H3 Ossokmanuan Lake l. Can.
50 E3 Ostashkov Rus. Fed.
43 F2 Ostbevern Ger.
43 H1 Oste r. Ger.
42 A3 Ostend Belgium
47 P5 Oster Ukr.
43 K2 Osterburg (Altmark) Ger.
37 O8 Österbymo Sweden
37 N6 Österdalälven l. Sweden
37 M5 Østerdalen v. Norway
43 K3 Osterfeld Ger.
43 G1 Osterholz-Scharmbeck Ger.
43 J3 Osterode am Harz Ger.
36 O5 Östersund Sweden
43 J3 Osterwieck Ger.
Ostfriesische Inseln is see East Frisian Islands
42 F1 Ostfriesland reg. Ger.
37 Q6 Östhammar Sweden
46 J6 Ostrava Czech Rep.
47 J4 Ostróda Pol.
51 F5 Ostrogozhsk Rus. Fed.
43 L4 Ostrov Czech Rep.
50 D3 Ostrov Rus. Fed.
47 K5 Ostrowiec Świętokrzyski Pol.
47 K4 Ostrów Mazowiecka Pol.
46 H5 Ostrów Wielkopolski Pol.
49 L3 Osŭm r. Bulg.
29 B9 Ōsumi-Kaikyō chan. Japan
29 B9 Ōsumi-shotō is Japan
45 D4 Osuna Spain
81 F2 Oswegatchie U.S.A.
68 C5 Oswego IL U.S.A.
80 E3 Oswego NY U.S.A.
81 E3 Oswego r. U.S.A.
39 D5 Oswestry U.K.
29 F6 Ōta Japan
9 C6 Otago Peninsula pen. N.Z.
9 E4 Otaki N.Z.
36 U4 Otanmäki Fin.
89 B4 Otare, Co h. Col.
28 G3 Otaru Japan
9 B7 Otatara N.Z.
86 C3 Otavalo Ecuador
57 B5 Otavi Namibia
29 G6 Ōtawara Japan
9 C6 Otematata N.Z.
37 U7 Otepää Estonia
72 C2 Othello U.S.A.
84 A1 Otinapa Mex.
9 C5 Otira N.Z.
81 E3 Otisco Lake l. U.S.A.
67 F3 Otish, Monts mts Can.
57 B6 Otjiwarongo Namibia
38 F4 Otley U.K.
26 C2 Otog Qi China
28 H2 Otoineppu Japan
9 E3 Otorohanga N.Z.
66 C3 Otoskwin r. Can.
49 H4 Otranto Italy
49 H4 Otranto, Strait of str. Albania/Italy
13 T3 Otrozhnyy Rus. Fed.
68 E4 Otsego U.S.A.
68 E3 Otsego Lake l. MI U.S.A.
81 F3 Otsego Lake l. NY U.S.A.
81 F3 Otselic U.S.A.
29 D7 Ōtsu Japan
37 L6 Otta Norway
69 K3 Ottawa Can.
68 C5 Ottawa IL U.S.A.
76 E4 Ottawa KS U.S.A.
80 A4 Ottawa OH U.S.A.
69 H2 Ottawa r. Can.
66 D2 Ottawa Islands is Can.
38 E2 Otterburn U.K.
75 G2 Otter Creek Reservoir U.S.A.
68 D1 Otter I. i. Can.
66 D3 Otter Rapids Can.
43 H1 Ottersberg Ger.
39 C7 Ottery r. U.K.
42 C4 Ottignies Belgium
63 K1 Otto Fjord in. Can.
68 A5 Ottumwa U.S.A.
42 F5 Ottweiler Ger.
54 C4 Otukpo Nigeria
88 D3 Otumpa Arg.
86 C5 Otuzco Peru
8 D5 Otway, C. c. Austr.
77 E5 Ouachita r. U.S.A.
77 E5 Ouachita, L. l. U.S.A.
77 E5 Ouachita Mts mts U.S.A.
56 C3 Ouadda C.A.R.
55 E3 Ouaddaï reg. Chad
54 B3 Ouagadougou Burkina
54 B3 Ouahigouya Burkina
54 B3 Oualâta Maur.
56 C3 Ouanda-Djailé C.A.R.
54 B2 Ouarâne reg. Maur.
54 C1 Ouargla Alg.
54 B1 Ouarzazate Morocco
58 F6 Oubergpas pass S. Africa
42 B4 Oudenaarde Belgium
42 F1 Oude Pekela Neth.
58 E6 Oudtshoorn S. Africa
42 C3 Oud-Turnhout Belgium
45 F5 Oued Tlélat Alg.
54 B1 Oued Zem Morocco
48 B6 Oued Zénati Alg.
44 B2 Ouessant, Île d' i. France
56 B3 Ouésso Congo
54 C4 Ouidah Benin
54 B1 Oujda Morocco
36 T4 Oulainen Fin.
45 G4 Ouled Farès Alg.
36 T4 Oulu Fin.
36 U4 Oulujärvi l. Fin.
36 U4 Oulujoki r. Fin.
36 T4 Oulunsalo Fin.
44 H4 Oulx Italy
55 E3 Oum-Chalouba Chad
54 B4 Oumé Côte d'Ivoire
55 D3 Oum-Hadjer Chad
36 T3 Ounasjoki r. Fin.
39 G5 Oundle U.K.
55 E3 Ounianga Kébir Chad
42 D4 Oupeye Belgium
42 E5 Our r. Lux.
73 F4 Ouray CO U.S.A.
75 H1 Ouray UT U.S.A.
45 C1 Ourense Spain
87 K5 Ouricurí Brazil
90 C3 Ourinhos Brazil
90 C1 Ouro r. Brazil
90 D3 Ouro Preto Brazil
42 D4 Ourthe r. Belgium
42 E5 Our, Vallée de l' v. Ger./Lux.
38 G4 Ouse r. Eng. U.K.
39 H7 Ouse r. Eng. U.K.
67 G3 Outardes r. Can.
58 E6 Outeniekpas pass S. Africa
40 A2 Outer Hebrides is U.K.
68 B2 Outer I. i. U.S.A.
74 C5 Outer Santa Barbara Channel chan. U.S.A.
57 B6 Outjo Namibia
62 H4 Outlook Can.
36 V5 Outokumpu Fin.
40 Out Skerries is U.K.
7 G4 Ouvéa i. New Caledonia
27 D5 Ouyang Hai Sk. resr China
8 D3 Ouyen Austr.
39 G5 Ouzel r. U.K.
48 C4 Ovace, Pte d' mt Corsica France
17 G2 Ovacık Turkey
48 C2 Ovada Italy
7 H3 Ovalau i. Fiji
91 B1 Ovalle Chile
45 B2 Ovar Port.
91 D2 Oveja mt Arg.
8 F4 Ovens r. Austr.
42 F4 Overath Ger.
36 S3 Överkalix Sweden
75 E3 Overton U.S.A.
36 S3 Övertorneå Sweden
37 P8 Överum Sweden
42 C2 Overveen Neth.
68 E4 Ovid U.S.A.
45 D1 Oviedo Spain
36 T2 Øvre Anarjåkka Nasjonalpark nat. park Norway
36 Q2 Øvre Dividal Nasjonalpark nat. park Norway
37 M6 Øvre Rendal Norway
51 D5 Ovruch Ukr.
9 B7 Owaka N.Z.
56 B4 Owando Congo
29 E7 Owase Japan
76 E2 Owatonna U.S.A.
19 F3 Owbeh Afgh.
81 E3 Owego U.S.A.
93 H3 Owen Fracture sea feature Ind. Ocean
41 B3 Owenmore r. Rep. of Ireland
9 D4 Owen River N.Z.
74 C3 Owens r. U.S.A.
78 C4 Owensboro U.S.A.
74 D3 Owens Lake l. U.S.A.
69 G3 Owen Sound Can.
69 G3 Owen Sound in. Can.
6 E2 Owen Stanley Range mts P.N.G.
54 C4 Owerri Nigeria
64 D4 Owikeno L. l. Can.
80 B5 Owingsville U.S.A.
81 J2 Owls Head U.S.A.
54 C4 Owo Nigeria
69 E4 Owosso U.S.A.
17 L4 Owrāmān, Kūh-e mts Iran/Iraq
72 C3 Owyhee U.S.A.
72 C3 Owyhee r. U.S.A.
72 C3 Owyhee Mts mts U.S.A.
86 C6 Oxapampa Peru
36 E3 Öxarfjörður b. Iceland
65 J5 Oxbow Can.
81 J1 Oxbow U.S.A.
37 P7 Oxelösund Sweden
9 D5 Oxford N.Z.
39 F6 Oxford U.K.
69 F4 Oxford MI U.S.A.
77 F5 Oxford MS U.S.A.
81 F3 Oxford NY U.S.A.
81 F5 Oxford PA U.S.A.
65 K4 Oxford House Can.
65 K4 Oxford L. l. Can.
8 E3 Oxley Austr.
8 H1 Oxleys Pk mt Austr.
74 C4 Oxnard U.S.A.
69 H3 Oxtongue Lake Can.
36 N3 Øya Norway
29 F6 Oyama Japan
87 H3 Oyapock r. Brazil/Fr. Guiana
56 B3 Oyem Gabon
40 D3 Oykel r. U.K.
54 C4 Oyo Nigeria
44 G3 Oyonnax France
23 H5 Oyster I. i. Myanmar
43 H1 Oyten Ger.
17 J2 Özalp Turkey
31 B4 Ozamiz Phil.
79 C6 Ozark AL U.S.A.
68 E2 Ozark MI U.S.A.
77 E4 Ozark Plateau plat. U.S.A.
76 E4 Ozarks, Lake of the l. U.S.A.
18 E3 Ozbagū Iran
51 G7 Ozerget'i Georgia
24 H1 Ozernovskiy Rus. Fed.
50 E4 Ozernyy Rus. Fed.
47 L3 Ozersk Rus. Fed.
50 F4 Ozery Rus. Fed.
13 Q3 Ozhogino Rus. Fed.
48 C4 Ozieri Sardinia Italy
77 C6 Ozona U.S.A.
29 B7 Ozuki Japan

P

63 O3 Paamiut Greenland
32 A1 Pa-an Myanmar
58 C6 Paarl S. Africa
58 D4 Paballelo S. Africa
30 E3 Pabal-li N. Korea
40 A3 Pabbay i. Scot. U.K.
40 A4 Pabbay i. Scot. U.K.
47 J5 Pabianice Pol.
23 G4 Pabna Bangl.
37 T9 Pabradė Lith.
19 G5 Pab Range mts Pak.
86 F6 Pacaás Novos, Parque Nacional nat. park Brazil
89 E4 Pacaraima, Serra mts Brazil
86 C5 Pacasmayo Peru
73 E6 Pacheco Chihuahua Mex.
84 B1 Pacheco Mex.
50 H2 Pachikha Rus. Fed.
48 F6 Pachino Sicily Italy
21 B1 Pachmarhi India
22 D5 Pachore India
84 C2 Pachuca Mex.
74 B2 Pacific U.S.A.
95 L9 Pacific-Antarctic Ridge sea feature Pac. Oc.
29 F8 Pacific Ocean ocean
31 C4 Pacijan i. Phil.
33 D4 Pacitan Indon.
87 H4 Pacoval Brazil
90 D2 Pacuí r. Brazil
46 H5 Paczków Pol.
31 C5 Padada Phil.
89 D4 Padamo r. Venez.
33 B3 Padang Indon.
33 B3 Padangpanjang Indon.
33 A2 Padangsidimpuan Indon.
33 C3 Padangtikar i. Indon.
50 E2 Padany Rus. Fed.
17 M5 Padatha, Kūh-e mt Iran
89 D4 Padauiri r. Brazil
86 F8 Padcaya Bol.
64 F3 Paddle Prairie Can.
80 C5 Paden City U.S.A.
43 G3 Paderborn Ger.
49 K2 Padeșu, Vârful mt Romania
86 F7 Padilla Bol.
36 P3 Padjelanta Nationalpark nat. park Sweden
23 G5 Padma r. Bangl.
Padova see Padua
77 D7 Padre Island i. U.S.A.
48 C3 Padro, Monte mt Corsica France
39 C7 Padstow U.K.

47 N3 Padsvillye Belarus
8 C4 Padthaway Austr.
21 C2 Pādua India
48 D2 Padua Italy
78 B4 Paducah KY U.S.A.
77 C5 Paducah TX U.S.A.
22 D2 Padum Jammu and Kashmir
30 E3 Paegam N. Korea
30 C5 Paengnyŏng-do i. N. Korea
9 E2 Paeroa N.Z.
31 B3 Paete Phil.
16 D4 Pafos Cyprus
59 J1 Pafúri Moz.
48 F2 Pag Croatia
48 F2 Pag i. Croatia
31 B5 Pagadian Phil.
33 B3 Pagai Selatan i. Indon.
33 B3 Pagai Utara i. Indon.
25 G5 Pagan i. N. Mariana Is
33 E3 Pagatan Indon.
75 G3 Page U.S.A.
37 R9 Pagėgiai Lith.
88 □ Paget, Mt mt Atl. Ocean
73 F4 Pagosa Springs U.S.A.
23 G4 Pagri China
66 C3 Pagwa River Can.
74 □2 Pahala U.S.A.
22 B2 Paharpur Pak.
9 A7 Pahia Pt pt N.Z.
74 □2 Pahoa U.S.A.
79 D7 Pahokee U.S.A.
19 F3 Pahra Kariz Afgh.
75 E3 Pahranagat Range mts U.S.A.
22 D4 Pahuj r. India
74 D3 Pahute Mesa plat. U.S.A.
32 A1 Pai Thai.
37 T7 Paide Estonia
39 D7 Paignton U.K.
37 T6 Päijänne l. Fin.
23 F3 Paiku Co l. China
32 B2 Pailin Cambodia
91 B4 Paillaco Chile
74 □2 Pailolo Chan. chan. U.S.A.
37 S6 Paimio Fin.
91 B2 Paine Chile
80 C4 Painesville U.S.A.
75 G3 Painted Desert des. U.S.A.
75 F5 Painted Rock Reservoir U.S.A.
65 K3 Paint Lake Provincial Recr. Park res. Can.
80 B6 Paintsville U.S.A.
69 G3 Paisley Can.
40 D5 Paisley U.K.
86 B5 Paita Peru
31 A5 Paitan, Teluk b. Malaysia
27 D4 Paizhou China
36 S3 Pajala Sweden
87 L5 Pajeú r. Brazil
32 B4 Paka Malaysia
86 F2 Pakaraima Mountains Guyana
30 C4 Pakch'ŏn N. Korea
69 G3 Pakesley Can.
13 S3 Pakhacha Rus. Fed.
10 H7 Pakistan country Asia
Paknampho see Muang Nakhon Sawan
9 D1 Pakotai N.Z.
22 C3 Pakpattan Pak.
32 B4 Pak Phayun Thai.
37 S9 Pakruojis Lith.
47 J7 Paks Hungary
19 H3 Paktīkā reg. Afgh.
32 C2 Pakxé Laos
55 D4 Pala Chad
32 A2 Pala Myanmar
33 C4 Palabuhanratu Indon.
33 C4 Palabuhanratu, Teluk b. Indon.
48 G3 Palagruža i. Croatia
49 K7 Palaiochora Greece
44 F2 Palaiseau France
Palakkat see Palghat
21 D1 Pāla Laharha India
58 E1 Palamakoloi Botswana
45 H2 Palamós Spain
22 C4 Palana India
13 R4 Palana Rus. Fed.
31 B2 Palanan Phil.
31 B2 Palanan Point pt Phil.
19 F4 Palangān, Kūh-e mts Iran
43 D3 Palangkaraya Indon.
21 B4 Palani India
22 C4 Palanpur India
19 G5 Palantak Pak.
31 C3 Palapag Phil.
57 C6 Palapye Botswana
21 B3 Palar r. India
23 G4 Palasbari India
13 R3 Palatka Rus. Fed.
11 P9 Palau country Pac. Oc.
31 B2 Palaui i. Phil.
31 A3 Palauig Phil.
32 A2 Palauk Myanmar
94 E5 Palau Tr. sea feature Pac. Oc.
32 A2 Palaw Myanmar
31 A4 Palawan i. Phil.
31 B3 Palayan Phil.
37 T7 Paldiski Estonia
23 H5 Pale Myanmar
42 D2 Paleis Het Loo Neth.
33 B3 Palembang Indon.
88 B6 Palena Chile
45 D1 Palencia Spain
84 E3 Palenque Mex.
48 E5 Palermo Sicily Italy
77 E6 Palestine U.S.A.
23 H5 Paletwa Myanmar
21 B4 Palghat India
22 C4 Pali India
4 G4 Palikir Micronesia
31 C5 Palimbang Phil.
48 F4 Palinuro, Capo c. Italy
75 H2 Palisade U.S.A.
42 D5 Paliseul Belgium
22 B5 Palitana India
37 S7 Palivere Estonia
21 B4 Palk Bay b. Sri Lanka
50 D3 Palkino Rus. Fed.
21 C2 Pālkohda India
21 B3 Palkonda Range mts India
15 F6 Palk Strait str. India/Sri Lanka
41 C5 Pallas Green Rep. of Ireland
36 S2 Pallas-ja Ounastunturin Kansallispuisto nat. park Fin.
51 H5 Pallasovka Rus. Fed.
21 C3 Pallavaram India
21 B2 Palleru r. India
9 E4 Palliser Bay b. N.Z.
9 E4 Palliser, Cape c. N.Z.
22 C3 Pallu India
45 D4 Palma del Río Spain
45 H3 Palma de Mallorca Spain
54 A2 Palma, La i. Canary Is
89 B2 Palmar r. Venez.
89 C3 Palmarito Venez.
54 B4 Palmas, Cape c. Liberia
90 D1 Palmas de Monte Alto Brazil
79 D7 Palm Bay U.S.A.
79 D7 Palm Beach U.S.A.
74 C4 Palmdale U.S.A.
90 B4 Palmeira Brazil
87 L5 Palmeira dos Índios Brazil
87 K5 Palmeirais Brazil
62 D3 Palmer AK U.S.A.
92 B2 Palmer U.S.A. Base Ant.
92 B2 Palmer Land reg. Ant.
9 C6 Palmerston N.Z.
5 L6 Palmerston Island i. Pac. Oc.
9 E4 Palmerston North N.Z.
81 F4 Palmerton U.S.A.
79 E7 Palmetto Pt pt Bahamas
48 F5 Palmi Italy
84 C2 Palmillas Mex.
89 A4 Palmira Col.
84 A2 Palmito del Verde, Isla i. Mex.
74 D5 Palm Springs U.S.A.
Palmyra see Tadmur
68 B6 Palmyra MO U.S.A.
80 E3 Palmyra NY U.S.A.
68 C4 Palmyra WV U.S.A.
5 L4 Palmyra I. i. Pac. Oc.
23 F5 Palmyras Point pt India
74 A3 Palo Alto U.S.A.
89 A3 Palo de las Letras Col.
55 F3 Paloich Sudan
36 S2 Palojärvi Fin.
36 U2 Palomaa Fin.
84 D3 Palomares Mex.
74 D5 Palomar Mt mt U.S.A.
75 G6 Palominas U.S.A.
21 C2 Paloncha India
25 E7 Palopo Indon.
45 F4 Palos, Cabo de c. Spain
75 F5 Palo Verde AZ U.S.A.
75 E5 Palo Verde CA U.S.A.
36 U4 Paltamo Fin.
25 D7 Palu Indon.
17 G2 Palu Turkey
31 B3 Paluan Phil.
19 G2 Pal'vart Turkm.
22 D3 Palwal India
13 T3 Palyavaam r. Rus. Fed.
21 B4 Pamban Channel India
8 G4 Pambula Austr.
33 C4 Pameungpeuk Indon.
21 B3 Pamidi India
44 E5 Pamiers France
15 F3 Pamir mts Asia
79 E5 Pamlico Sound chan. U.S.A.
77 C5 Pampa U.S.A.
91 C2 Pampa de la Salinas salt pan Arg.
86 F7 Pampa Grande Bol.
91 D2 Pampas reg. Arg.
89 B3 Pamplona Col.
31 B4 Pamplona Phil.
45 F1 Pamplona Spain
43 K1 Pampow Ger.
16 C1 Pamukova Turkey
80 E6 Pamunkey r. U.S.A.
22 D2 Pamzal Jammu and Kashmir
78 B4 Pana U.S.A.
31 C5 Panabo Phil.
75 E3 Panaca U.S.A.
31 A4 Panagtaran Point pt Phil.
33 C4 Panaitan i. Indon.
21 A3 Panaji India
83 J7 Panamá Panama
61 K9 Panama country Central America
83 J7 Panama Canal canal Panama
79 C6 Panama City U.S.A.
83 J7 Panamá, Golfo de b. Panama
74 D3 Panamint Range mts U.S.A.
74 D3 Panamint Springs U.S.A.
74 D3 Panamint Valley U.S.A.
31 C4 Panaon i. Phil.
23 G4 Panar r. India
48 F5 Panarea, Isola i. Italy
33 C2 Panarik Indon.
31 C3 Panay i. Phil.
31 B4 Panay i. Phil.
31 B4 Panay Gulf b. Phil.
75 E2 Pancake Range mts U.S.A.
49 J2 Pančevo Yugo.
31 C3 Pandan Phil.
31 B4 Pandan Phil.
31 B4 Pandan B. b. Phil.
32 □ Pandan Res. resr Sing.
22 E5 Pandaria India
90 D1 Pandeiros r. Brazil
21 A2 Pandharpur India
22 D5 Pandhurna India
91 F2 Pando Uru.
39 E6 Pandy U.K.
37 T9 Panevėžys Lith.
22 C2 Pangi Range mts Pak.
33 D3 Pangkalanbuun Indon.
33 A2 Pangkalansusu Indon.
33 C3 Pangkalpinang Indon.
25 E7 Pangkalsiang, Tanjung pt Indon.
31 B4 Panglao i. Phil.
63 M3 Pangnirtung Can.
12 J3 Pangody Rus. Fed.
22 D2 Pangong Tso l. India
91 B3 Panguipulli Chile
91 B3 Panguipulli, L. l. Chile
75 F3 Panguitch U.S.A.
32 A5 Panguruan Indon.
31 B5 Pangutaran i. Phil.
31 B5 Pangutaran Group is Phil.
77 C5 Panhandle U.S.A.
56 C4 Pania-Mwanga Congo(Zaire)
22 B5 Pānikoita i. India
51 G5 Panino Rus. Fed.
22 D3 Panipat India
31 A4 Panitan Phil.
19 H2 Panj Tajik.
19 G3 Panjāb Afgh.
19 G2 Panjakent Tajik.
32 D5 Panjang i. Indon.
17 L5 Panjbarār Iran
19 G5 Panjgur Pak.
22 C5 Panjhra r. India
Panjim see Panaji
22 B2 Panjkora r. Pak.
22 B3 Panjnad r. Pak.
36 W5 Pankakoski Fin.
54 C4 Pankshin Nigeria
30 F2 Pan Ling mts China
22 D4 Panna reg. India
6 B4 Pannawonica Austr.
90 B3 Panorama Brazil
21 B4 Panruti India
30 B3 Panshan China
30 D2 Panshi China
90 A2 Pantanal de São Lourenço marsh Brazil
90 A2 Pantanal do Taquarí marsh Brazil
87 G7 Pantanal Matogrossense, Parque Nacional do nat. park Brazil
48 D6 Pantelleria Sicily Italy
48 E6 Pantelleria, Isola di i. Sicily Italy
31 C5 Pantukan Phil.
84 C2 Pánuco Mex.
84 C2 Pánuco r. Mex.
21 A2 Panvel India
27 B5 Pan Xian China
27 D6 Panyu China
56 B4 Panzi Congo(Zaire)
89 E3 Pao r. Venez.
48 G5 Paola Italy
78 C4 Paoli U.S.A.
56 B3 Paoua C.A.R.
46 H7 Pápa Hungary
9 E2 Papakura N.Z.
48 F4 Papa, Monte del mt Italy
84 C2 Papantla Mex.
21 C2 Pāparhāhandi India
9 C5 Paparoa Range mts N.Z.
40 □ Papa Stour i. U.K.
9 E2 Papatoetoe N.Z.
9 B7 Papatowai N.Z.
40 F1 Papa Westray i. U.K.
42 F1 Papenburg Ger.
70 E6 Papigochic r. Mex.
69 K2 Papineau-Labelle, Réserve faunique de res. Can.
75 E3 Papoose L. l. U.S.A.
43 J6 Pappenheim Ger.
40 B5 Paps of Jura h. U.K.
41 B5 Paps, The h. Rep. of Ireland
6 E2 Papua, Gulf of g. P.N.G.
4 F5 Papua New Guinea country Oceania
32 A1 Papun Myanmar
39 C7 Par U.K.
87 J4 Pará r. Brazil
90 D2 Pará r. Brazil
50 G4 Para r. Rus. Fed.
6 B4 Paraburdoo Austr.
31 B3 Paracale Phil.
90 C2 Paracatu Minas Gerais Brazil
90 D2 Paracatu r. Brazil
8 B1 Parachilna Austr.
49 J3 Paraćin Yugo.
90 D2 Pará de Minas Brazil
69 J1 Paradis Can.
74 B2 Paradise CA U.S.A.
68 E2 Paradise MI U.S.A.
65 H4 Paradise Hill Can.
74 D2 Paradise Peak summit U.S.A.
67 J3 Paradise River Can.
77 F4 Paragould U.S.A.
86 F6 Paragua r. Bol.
89 E3 Paragua r. Venez.
87 G7 Paraguai r. Brazil
89 C2 Paraguáipoa Venez.
89 C1 Paraguaná, Pen. de pen. Venez.
85 D5 Paraguay country S. America
88 E3 Paraguay r. Arg./Para.
87 L5 Paraíba r. Brazil
90 D3 Paraíba do Sul r. Brazil
84 D3 Paraíso Mex.
54 C4 Parakou Benin
21 D2 Parālākhemundi India
22 E6 Paralkot India
21 B4 Paramakkudi India
87 G2 Paramaribo Suriname
89 B3 Paramillo mt Col.
89 A3 Paramillo, Parque Nacional nat. park Col.
90 D1 Paramirim Brazil
89 A3 Paramo Frontino mt Col.
81 F4 Paramus U.S.A.
24 H1 Paramushir, O. i. Rus. Fed.
91 E1 Paraná Arg.
87 J6 Paranã Brazil
90 B4 Paraná div. Brazil
90 C1 Paranã r. Brazil
91 E2 Paraná r. S. America
90 C4 Paranaguá Brazil
90 B2 Paranaíba Brazil
90 B2 Paranaíba r. Brazil
91 E2 Paraná Ibicuy r. Arg.
90 B3 Paranapanema r. Brazil
90 C4 Paranapiacaba, Serra mts Brazil
90 C1 Paranã, Sa do h. Brazil
90 B3 Paranavaí Brazil
31 B5 Parang Phil.
21 B4 Parangipettai India
49 K2 Parângul Mare, Vârful mt Romania
22 C5 Parantij India
90 D2 Paraopeba r. Brazil
17 K4 Pārāpāra Iraq
9 E4 Paraparaumu N.Z.
89 D3 Paraque, Co mt Venez.
77 D7 Paras Mex.
22 D5 Paratwada India
90 B2 Paraúna Brazil
44 G3 Paray-le-Monial France
22 D4 Parbati r. India
21 B2 Parbhani India
43 K1 Parchim Ger.
68 C4 Pardeeville U.S.A.
23 G2 Parding China
90 E1 Pardo r. Bahia/Minas Gerais Brazil
90 B3 Pardo r. Mato Grosso do Sul Brazil
90 D1 Pardo r. Minas Gerais Brazil
90 C3 Pardo r. São Paulo Brazil
46 G5 Pardubice Czech Rep.
22 D2 Pare Chu r. China
23 G4 Pare Chu r. India
86 F6 Parecis, Serra dos h. Brazil
84 B1 Paredón Mex.
18 B2 Pareh Iran
9 D1 Parengarenga Harbour in. N.Z.
66 E4 Parent, Lac l. Can.
9 C6 Pareora N.Z.
33 E3 Parepare Indon.
91 D2 Parera Arg.
50 G3 Parfen'yevo Rus. Fed.
47 P2 Parfino Rus. Fed.
49 J5 Parga Greece
37 S6 Pargas Fin.
89 D2 Pariaguán Venez.
89 E2 Paria, Gulf of g. Trinidad/Venez.
89 E2 Paria, Península de pen. Venez.
75 F3 Paria Plateau plat. U.S.A.
37 V6 Parikkala Fin.
Parima r. see Uatatás
89 D4 Parima, Serra mts Brazil
89 D4 Parima-Tapirapecó, Parque Nacional nat. park Venez.
86 B4 Pariñas, Pta pt Peru
8 C3 Paringa Austr.
87 G4 Parintins Brazil
69 G4 Paris Can.
44 F2 Paris France
80 A5 Paris KY U.S.A.
79 B4 Paris TN U.S.A.
77 E5 Paris TX U.S.A.
68 E2 Parisienne, Île i. Can.
18 D4 Pārīz Iran
41 D3 Park U.K.
19 E5 Parkā Bandar Iran
21 B2 Parkal India
37 S5 Parkano Fin.
67 J3 Parke Lake l. Can.
75 E4 Parker U.S.A.
75 E4 Parker Dam dam U.S.A.
65 K2 Parker Lake l. Can.
27 □ Parker, Mt h. H.K. China
68 A4 Parkersburg IA U.S.A.
80 C5 Parkersburg WV U.S.A.
8 G2 Parkes Austr.
68 B3 Park Falls U.S.A.
68 D5 Park Forest U.S.A.
69 F2 Parkinson Can.
76 E2 Park Rapids U.S.A.
64 E5 Parksville Can.
81 F4 Parksville U.S.A.
21 D2 Parla Kimedi India
21 B2 Parli Vaijnath India
48 D2 Parma Italy
72 C3 Parma ID U.S.A.
80 C4 Parma OH U.S.A.
89 D3 Parmana Venez.
87 K4 Parnaíba Brazil
87 K4 Parnaíba r. Brazil
49 K5 Parnassos mt Greece
9 D5 Parnassus N.Z.
68 A5 Parnell U.S.A.
49 K6 Parnon mts Greece
37 T7 Pärnu Estonia
37 T7 Pärnu-Jaagupi Estonia
19 F3 Paropamisus mts Afgh.
49 L6 Paros Greece
49 L6 Paros i. Greece
75 F3 Parowan U.S.A.
91 B3 Parral Chile
81 F6 Parramore I. i. U.S.A.
84 B1 Parras Mex.
91 F3 Parravicini Arg.
39 E6 Parrett r. U.K.
67 H4 Parrsboro Can.
62 F2 Parry, Cape pt Can.
62 G2 Parry Islands is Can.
63 L2 Parry, Kap c. Greenland
69 G3 Parry Sound Can.
77 E4 Parsons KS U.S.A.
80 D5 Parsons WV U.S.A.
43 H4 Partenstein Ger.
44 D3 Parthenay France
28 C3 Partizansk Rus. Fed.
39 H4 Partney U.K.
41 B4 Partry Rep. of Ireland
41 B4 Partry Mts h. Rep. of Ireland
87 H4 Paru r. Brazil
89 D3 Parucito r. Venez.
21 C2 Parvatipuram India
22 C4 Parvatsar India
22 D4 Parwan r. India
23 E3 Paryang China
59 G3 Parys S. Africa
74 C4 Pasadena CA U.S.A.
77 E6 Pasadena TX U.S.A.
86 B4 Pasado, C. pt Ecuador
18 D4 Pasargadae Iran
33 B3 Pasarseblat Indon.
32 A1 Pasawng Myanmar
77 F6 Pascagoula U.S.A.
69 J1 Pascalis Can.
47 N7 Paşcani Romania
72 C2 Pasco U.S.A.
90 E2 Pascoal, Monte h. Brazil
31 B3 Pascual Phil.
Pas de Calais str. see Dover, Strait of
46 G4 Pasewalk Ger.
65 H3 Pasfield Lake l. Can.
50 E2 Pasha Rus. Fed.
31 B3 Pasig Phil.
17 H2 Pasinler Turkey
32 □ Pasir Gudang Malaysia
32 □ Pasir Panjang Sing.
33 B1 Pasir Putih Malaysia
74 A2 Paskenta U.S.A.
19 F5 Paskūh Iran
19 E5 Pasni Pak.
84 E3 Paso Caballos Guatemala
89 B4 Paso de las Cruces mt Col.
91 F2 Paso de los Toros Uru.
88 B7 Paso Río Mayo Arg.
74 B4 Paso Robles U.S.A.
65 J4 Pasquia Hills h. Can.
18 D4 Pasrūdak Iran
81 J2 Passadumkeag U.S.A.
68 C1 Passage I. i. U.S.A.
46 F6 Passau Ger.
31 B4 Passi Phil.
88 F3 Passo Fundo Brazil
90 C3 Passos Brazil
50 C4 Pastavy Belarus
86 C4 Pastaza r. Peru
65 J4 Pas, The Can.
89 A4 Pasto Col.
75 H3 Pastora Peak summit U.S.A.
31 B2 Pasuquin Phil.
33 D4 Pasuruan Indon.
37 T8 Pasvalys Lith.
31 B5 Pata i. Phil.
75 G6 Patagonia U.S.A.
85 C8 Patagonia reg. Arg.
23 G4 Patakata India
19 F4 Patambar Iran
22 C5 Patan Gujarat India
22 D5 Patan Madhya Pradesh India
Patan see Somnath
23 F4 Patan Nepal
8 D3 Patchewollock Austr.
9 E3 Patea N.Z.
9 E3 Patea r. N.Z.
38 F3 Pateley Bridge U.K.
23 G5 Patenga Point pt Bangl.
58 F6 Patensie S. Africa
48 F6 Paternò Sicily Italy
8 H2 Paterson Austr.
81 F4 Paterson U.S.A.
22 C2 Pathankot India
72 F3 Pathfinder Res. resr U.S.A.
32 A3 Pathiu Thai.
21 B2 Pathri India
32 B2 Pathum Thani Thai.
33 D4 Pati Indon.
89 A4 Patía r. Col.
22 D3 Patiala India
49 M6 Patmos i. Greece
23 F4 Patna India
23 E5 Patnagarh India
31 B3 Patnanongan i. Phil.
17 J2 Patnos Turkey
22 E3 Paton India
49 H4 Patos Albania
87 L5 Patos Brazil
90 C2 Patos de Minas Brazil
88 F4 Patos, Lagoa dos l. Brazil
91 C1 Patquía Arg.
49 J5 Patra Greece
36 B4 Patreksfjörður Iceland
90 C2 Patrocínio Brazil
36 V2 Patsoyoki r. Europe
32 B4 Pattani Thai.
32 B4 Pattani r. Thai.
32 B2 Pattaya Thai.
81 J2 Patten U.S.A.
43 H2 Pattensen Ger.
74 B3 Patterson U.S.A.
80 D5 Patterson r. U.S.A.
64 C2 Patterson, Mt mt Can.
74 C3 Patterson Mt mt U.S.A.
68 E3 Patterson, Pt pt U.S.A.
36 T4 Pattijoki Fin.
36 R2 Pättikkä Fin.
21 B3 Pattikonda India
64 D3 Pattullo, Mt mt Can.
23 G5 Patuakhali Bangl.
65 H3 Patuanak Can.
80 E5 Patuxent r. U.S.A.
92 B3 Patuxent Ra. mts Ant.
84 B3 Pátzcuaro Mex.
44 D5 Pau France
44 D4 Pauillac France
23 H5 Pauktaw Myanmar
75 F4 Paulden U.S.A.
80 A4 Paulding U.S.A.
67 H2 Paul Island i. Can.
87 K5 Paulistana Brazil
87 L5 Paulo Afonso Brazil
59 J3 Paulpietersburg S. Africa
59 G4 Paul Roux S. Africa
81 F2 Paul Smiths U.S.A.
77 D5 Pauls Valley U.S.A.
89 C3 Pauto r. Col.
90 E2 Pavão Brazil
18 B3 Pāveh Iran
48 C2 Pavia Italy
37 R8 Pāvilosta Latvia
50 H3 Pavino Rus. Fed.
49 L3 Pavlikeni Bulg.
15 F1 Pavlodar Kazak.
51 E5 Pavlohrad Ukr.
50 H4 Pavlovo Rus. Fed.
50 G4 Pavlovo Rus. Fed.
51 G5 Pavlovsk Rus. Fed.
51 F6 Pavlovskaya Rus. Fed.
89 B4 Pavon Col.
22 E3 Pawayan India
68 E4 Paw Paw U.S.A.
81 H4 Pawtucket U.S.A.
32 A2 Pawut Myanmar
68 C5 Paxton U.S.A.
33 B3 Payakumbuh Indon.
32 □ Paya Lebar Sing.
89 B4 Paya, Parque Nacional la nat. park Col.
72 C2 Payette U.S.A.
12 H3 Pay-Khoy, Khrebet h. Rus. Fed.
66 F2 Payne, Lac l. Can.
74 B1 Paynes Creek U.S.A.
91 E2 Paysandú Uru.
75 G4 Payson AZ U.S.A.
75 G1 Payson UT U.S.A.
91 C3 Payún, Cerro volc. Arg.
16 D1 Pazar Turkey
17 H1 Pazar Turkey
16 F3 Pazarcık Turkey
49 L3 Pazardzhik Bulg.
89 C3 Paz de Ariporo Col.
89 B3 Paz de Rio Col.
48 E2 Pazin Croatia
64 G3 Peace r. Can.
62 G4 Peace r. U.S.A.
64 F3 Peace River Can.
75 F4 Peach Springs U.S.A.
39 F4 Peak District National Park U.K.
67 G4 Peaked Mt. h. U.S.A.
31 A4 Peaked Point pt Phil.
8 G2 Peak Hill Austr.
75 H2 Peale, Mt mt U.S.A.
75 H6 Pearce U.S.A.
68 C1 Pearl Can.
77 F6 Pearl r. U.S.A.
74 □1 Pearl City U.S.A.
74 □1 Pearl Harbor in. U.S.A.
77 D6 Pearsall U.S.A.
79 D6 Pearson U.S.A.
63 H2 Peary Channel Can.
62 C2 Peawanuck Can.
57 D5 Pebane Moz.
49 J3 Peć Yugo.
90 D2 Peçanha Brazil
36 W2 Pechenga Rus. Fed.
12 G3 Pechora Rus. Fed.
50 C3 Pechory Rus. Fed.
69 F4 Peck U.S.A.
77 C6 Pecos U.S.A.
77 C6 Pecos r. U.S.A.
49 H1 Pécs Hungary
59 G6 Peddie S. Africa
36 S5 Pedersöre Fin.
23 E3 Pêdo La pass China
90 E1 Pedra Azul Brazil
89 C2 Pedraza La Vieja Venez.
89 C2 Pedregal Venez.
90 C3 Pedregulho Brazil
87 K4 Pedreiras Brazil
84 B1 Pedriceña Mex.
87 J5 Pedro Afonso Brazil
89 C4 Pedro Chico Col.
88 C2 Pedro de Valdivia Chile
90 A2 Pedro Gomes Brazil
89 D4 Pedro II, Ilha i. Brazil
88 E2 Pedro Juan Caballero Para.
87 K4 Pedro II Brazil
91 G1 Pedro Osório Brazil
21 C4 Pedro, Pt pt Sri Lanka
40 E5 Peebles U.K.
79 E5 Pee Dee r. U.S.A.
81 G4 Peekskill U.S.A.
38 C3 Peel U.K.
8 H1 Peel r. Austr.
62 E3 Peel r. N.W.T. Can.
42 D3 Peer Belgium
64 F4 Peers Can.
9 D5 Pegasus Bay b. N.Z.
43 K5 Pegnitz Ger.
43 K5 Pegnitz r. Ger.
25 B5 Pegu Myanmar
50 J2 Pegysh Rus. Fed.
91 E2 Pehuajó Arg.
27 F6 Peikang Taiwan
43 J2 Peine Ger.
Peipsi Järve l. see Peipus, Lake
37 U7 Peipus, Lake l. Estonia/Rus. Fed.
49 K6 Peiraias Greece
43 K3 Peißen Ger.
26 E3 Peitun China
87 J6 Peixe Brazil
90 B1 Peixe r. Goiás Brazil
90 B3 Peixe r. São Paulo Brazil
26 E3 Pei Xian Jiangsu China
26 F3 Pei Xian Jiangsu China
90 A2 Peixo de Couro r. Brazil
59 G4 Peka Lesotho
33 C4 Pekalongan Indon.
32 B5 Pekan Malaysia
33 B2 Pekanbaru Indon.
68 C5 Pekin U.S.A.
32 B5 Pelabuhan Kelang Malaysia
69 F5 Pelee I. i. Can.
69 F5 Pelee Pt pt Can.
25 E7 Peleng i. Indon.
50 J2 Peles Rus. Fed.
68 A1 Pelican Lake l. MN U.S.A.
68 C3 Pelican Lake l. WV U.S.A.
65 J3 Pelican Narrows Can.
36 U3 Pelkosenniemi Fin.
58 C4 Pella S. Africa
65 H1 Pellat Lake l. Can.
6 E2 Pelleluhu Is is P.N.G.
68 C4 Pell Lake U.S.A.
36 S3 Pello Fin.
64 B2 Pelly r. Can.
63 K3 Pelly Bay Can.
64 B2 Pelly Crossing Can.
65 J1 Pelly Lake l. Can.
64 C2 Pelly Mountains mts Can.
91 G1 Pelotas Brazil
88 F3 Pelotas, R. das r. Brazil
16 D6 Pelusium Egypt
44 H4 Pelvoux, Massif du mts France
81 J2 Pemadumcook Lake l. U.S.A.
33 C4 Pemalang Indon.
33 C2 Pemangkat Indon.
33 A2 Pematangsiantar Indon.
57 E5 Pemba Moz.
57 C5 Pemba Zambia
56 D4 Pemba I. i. Tanz.
76 D1 Pembina U.S.A.
64 F4 Pembina r. Can.
69 J3 Pembroke Can.
39 C6 Pembroke U.K.
81 K2 Pembroke U.S.A.
39 B5 Pembrokeshire Coast National Park U.K.
21 A2 Pen India
23 H5 Pen r. Myanmar
45 D1 Peña Cerredo mt Spain
45 E2 Peñalara mt Spain
84 C2 Peñamiller Mex.
84 C2 Peña Nevada, Cerro mt Mex.
90 B3 Penápolis Brazil
45 D1 Peña Prieta mt Spain
45 D2 Peñaranda de Bracamonte Spain
8 D3 Penarie Austr.
45 F2 Peñarroya mt Spain
45 D3 Peñarroya-Pueblonuevo Spain
39 D6 Penarth U.K.
45 D1 Peñas, Cabo de c. Spain
82 B2 Peñasco, Pto Mex.
88 A7 Penas, Golfo de b. Chile
89 E2 Peñas, Pta pt Venez.
45 D1 Peña Ubiña mt Spain
22 D5 Pench r. India
92 D5 Penck, C. c. Ant.
54 C3 Pendjari, Parc National de la nat. park Benin
38 E4 Pendle Hill h. U.K.
72 C2 Pendleton U.S.A.
64 D4 Pendleton Bay Can.
72 C1 Pend Oreille r. U.S.A.
72 C2 Pend Oreille L. l. U.S.A.
23 E5 Pendra India
69 H3 Penetanguishene Can.
26 C4 Peng'an China
21 B2 Penganga r. India
22 D6 Penganga r. India
27 □ Peng Chau i. H.K. China
27 G5 P'eng-chia Hsü i. Taiwan
56 C4 Penge Congo(Zaire)
59 J2 Penge S. Africa
27 F6 P'eng-hu Lieh-tao is Taiwan
27 F6 Peng-hu Tao i. Taiwan
32 □ Peng Kang h. Sing.
26 F2 Penglai China
27 B4 Pengshan China
27 C4 Pengshui China
27 B4 Pengxi China
27 E4 Pengze China
59 G5 Penhoek Pass S. Africa
45 B3 Peniche Port.
40 E5 Penicuik U.K.
43 L4 Penig Ger.
50 E2 Peninga Rus. Fed.
33 B2 Peninsular Malaysia pen. Malaysia
17 K4 Penjwin Iraq
48 E3 Penne Italy
92 A5 Pennell Coast coastal area Ant.
21 B3 Penner r. India
8 A3 Penneshaw Austr.
38 E3 Pennines h. U.K.
59 J5 Pennington S. Africa
81 F5 Pennsville U.S.A.
80 D4 Pennsylvania div. U.S.A.
80 E3 Penn Yan U.S.A.
63 M3 Penny Icecap ice cap Can.
65 H2 Pennylan Lake l. Can.
92 B4 Penny Pt pt Ant.
81 J2 Penobscot r. U.S.A.
81 J2 Penobscot Bay b. U.S.A.
8 C4 Penola Austr.
84 A1 Peñón Blanco Mex.
6 D5 Penong Austr.
38 E3 Penrith U.K.
79 C6 Pensacola U.S.A.
92 B3 Pensacola Mts mts Ant.
17 M2 Pensär Azer.
8 D4 Penshurst Austr.
7 G3 Pentecost I. i. Vanuatu
64 F5 Penticton Can.
39 B7 Pentire Point pt U.K.
40 E2 Pentland Firth chan. U.K.
40 E5 Pentland Hills h. U.K.
68 D4 Pentwater U.S.A.
21 B3 Penukonda India
39 D5 Penygadair h. U.K.
38 E3 Pen-y-Ghent h. U.K.
50 H4 Penza Rus. Fed.
39 B7 Penzance U.K.
50 H4 Penzenskaya Oblast' div. Rus. Fed.
13 S3 Penzhino Rus. Fed.
13 S3 Penzhinskaya Guba b. Rus. Fed.
75 F5 Peoria AZ U.S.A.
68 C5 Peoria IL U.S.A.
32 B4 Perai Malaysia
32 A4 Perak i. Malaysia
32 B4 Perak r. Malaysia
45 F2 Perales del Alfambra Spain
21 B4 Perambalur India
Perämeri g. see Bottenviken
67 H4 Percé Can.
81 H2 Percy U.S.A.
6 F4 Percy Is is Austr.
69 J3 Percy Reach l. Can.
45 G1 Perdido, Monte mt Spain
12 H3 Peregrebnoye Rus. Fed.
89 B3 Pereira Col.
90 B3 Pereira Barreto Brazil
50 D3 Perekhoda r. Rus. Fed.
51 G5 Perelazovskiy Rus. Fed.
68 D4 Pere Marquette r. U.S.A.
92 C6 Peremennyy, C. c. Ant.
47 M6 Peremyshlyany Ukr.
50 F3 Pereslavl'-Zalesskiy Rus. Fed.
50 H4 Perevoz Rus. Fed.
51 D5 Pereyaslav-Khmel'nyts'kyy Ukr.
91 E2 Pergamino Arg.
32 B4 Perhentian Besar i. Malaysia
36 T5 Perho Fin.
67 F3 Péribonca, Lac l. Can.
88 C2 Perico Arg.
84 A1 Pericos Mex.
44 E4 Périgueux France
89 B2 Perijá, Parque Nacional nat. park Venez.
89 B2 Perija, Sierra de mts Venez.
88 B7 Perito Moreno Arg.
68 D3 Perkins U.S.A.
83 H6 Perlas, Pta de pt Nic.
43 K1 Perleberg Ger.
12 G4 Perm' Rus. Fed.
50 H3 Permas Rus. Fed.
49 K3 Pernik Bulg.
44 F2 Péronne France
84 C3 Perote Mex.
44 F5 Perpignan France
39 B7 Perranporth U.K.
75 D5 Perris U.S.A.
44 C2 Perros-Guirec France
79 D6 Perry FL U.S.A.
79 D5 Perry GA U.S.A.
76 E3 Perry IA U.S.A.
77 D4 Perry OK U.S.A.
80 B4 Perrysburg U.S.A.
77 C4 Perryton U.S.A.
77 F4 Perryville U.S.A.
39 E5 Pershore U.K.
17 G2 Pertek Turkey
6 B5 Perth Austr.
69 J3 Perth Can.
40 E4 Perth U.K.
81 F4 Perth Amboy U.S.A.
81 K1 Perth-Andover Can.
50 F1 Pertominsk Rus. Fed.
44 G5 Pertuis France
37 U6 Pertunmaa Fin.
48 C4 Pertusato, Capo pt Corsica France
68 C5 Peru U.S.A.
85 C3 Peru country S. America
95 N7 Peru Basin sea feature Pac. Oc.
95 P7 Peru-Chile Trench sea feature Pac. Oc.
48 E3 Perugia Italy
90 C4 Peruíbe Brazil
42 B4 Péruwelz Belgium
50 G4 Pervomaysk Rus. Fed.
51 D5 Pervomays'k Ukr.
50 K2 Pervomayskaya Rus. Fed.
51 E6 Pervomays'ke Ukr.
50 G4 Pervomayskiy Rus. Fed.
51 F5 Pervomays'kyy Ukr.
48 E3 Pesaro Italy
74 A3 Pescadero U.S.A.
75 H4 Pescado U.S.A.
48 F3 Pescara Italy
48 F3 Pescara r. Italy
51 G6 Peschanokopskoye Rus. Fed.
32 □ Pesek, P. i. Sing.
22 B2 Peshawar Pak.
49 J4 Peshkopi Albania
49 L3 Peshtera Bulg.
68 D3 Peshtigo U.S.A.
68 C3 Peshtigo r. U.S.A.
19 F2 Peski Turkm.
48 F1 Pesnica Slovenia
44 D4 Pessac France
43 L2 Pessin Ger.
50 E3 Pestovo Rus. Fed.
50 G4 Pet r. Rus. Fed.
84 B3 Petacalco, Bahía de b. Mex.
16 E5 Petah Tiqwa Israel
49 L5 Petalioi i. Greece
74 A2 Petaluma U.S.A.
42 D5 Pétange Lux.
33 E3 Petangis Indon.
89 D2 Petare Venez.
84 B3 Petatlán Mex.
84 B3 Petatlán, Morro de hd Mex.
57 D5 Petauke Zambia
69 J3 Petawawa Can.
68 C3 Petenwell Lake l. U.S.A.
92 A3 Peter I Øy i. Ant.
8 B2 Peterborough S.A. Austr.
8 D5 Peterborough Vic. Austr.
69 H3 Peterborough Can.
39 G5 Peterborough U.K.
40 F3 Peterculter U.K.
40 G3 Peterhead U.K.
65 L2 Peter Lake l. Can.
38 F3 Peterlee U.K.
6 C4 Petermann Ranges mts Austr.
91 B2 Peteroa, Vol. volc. Chile
65 H3 Peter Pond L. l. Can.
43 H4 Petersberg Ger.
64 C3 Petersburg AK U.S.A.
68 C6 Petersburg IL U.S.A.
80 E6 Petersburg VA U.S.A.
80 D5 Petersburg WV U.S.A.
39 G6 Petersfield U.K.
43 G2 Petershagen Ger.
67 F2 Peters, Lac l. Can.
48 G5 Petilia Policastro Italy
66 E2 Petite Rivière de la Baleine r. Can.
67 G3 Petit Lac Manicouagan l. Can.
81 K2 Petit Manan Pt pt U.S.A.
67 J3 Petit Mécatina r. Can.
64 E3 Petitot r. Can.
84 C3 Petlalcingo Mex.
82 G4 Peto Mex.
68 E3 Petoskey U.S.A.
16 E6 Petra Jordan
24 F2 Petra Velikogo, Zaliv b. Rus. Fed.
69 J4 Petre, Pt pt Can.
49 K4 Petrich Bulg.
75 H4 Petrified Forest Nat. Park U.S.A.
48 G2 Petrinja Croatia

49 K3 Petrokhanski Prokhod pass Bulg.
69 F4 Petrolia Can.
87 K5 Petrolina Brazil
51 G5 Petropavlovka Rus. Fed.
12 H4 Petropavlovsk Kazak.
24 H1 Petropavlovsk-Kamchatskiy Rus. Fed.
49 K2 Petroşani Romania
51 H4 Petrovsk Rus. Fed.
24 C1 Petrovsk-Zabaykal'skiy Rus. Fed.
51 H5 Petrov Val Rus. Fed.
50 E2 Petrozavodsk Rus. Fed.
59 F4 Petrusburg S. Africa
59 H3 Petrus Steyn S. Africa
58 F5 Petrusville S. Africa
42 C2 Petten Neth.
41 D3 Pettigo U.K.
12 H4 Petukhovo Rus. Fed.
32 A4 Peureula Indon.
13 T3 Pevek Rus. Fed.
46 H6 Pezinok Slovakia
43 F5 Pfälzer Wald forest Ger.
43 G6 Pforzheim Ger.
46 D7 Pfullendorf Ger.
43 G5 Pfungstadt Ger.
22 C3 Phagwara India
59 G4 Phahameng Free State S. Africa
59 H2 Phahameng Northern Province S. Africa
59 J1 Phalaborwa S. Africa
22 C4 Phalodi India
22 B4 Phalsund India
21 A2 Phaltan India
32 A3 Phangnga Thai.
32 D3 Phan Rang Vietnam
32 D3 Phan Ri Vietnam
32 D3 Phan Thiêt Vietnam
77 D7 Pharr U.S.A.
27 C6 Phat Diêm Vietnam
32 B4 Phatthalung Thai.
23 H4 Phek India
65 J3 Phelps Lake l. Can.
32 B1 Phen Thai.
79 C5 Phenix City U.S.A.
32 A2 Phet Buri Thai.
32 C2 Phiafai Laos
77 F5 Philadelphia MS U.S.A.
81 F2 Philadelphia NY U.S.A.
81 F5 Philadelphia PA U.S.A.
76 C2 Philip U.S.A.
42 C4 Philippeville Belgium
80 C5 Philippi U.S.A.
42 B3 Philippine Neth.
11 O8 Philippines country Asia
31 C2 Philippine Sea sea Phil.
94 D5 Philippine Trench sea feature Pac. Oc.
59 F5 Philippolis S. Africa
43 G5 Philippsburg Ger.
80 D4 Philipsburg U.S.A.
42 C3 Philipsdam barrage Neth.
62 D3 Philip Smith Mts U.S.A.
58 F5 Philipstown S. Africa
8 E5 Phillip I. i. Austr.
81 H2 Phillips ME U.S.A.
68 B3 Phillips WI U.S.A.
76 D4 Phillipsburg KS U.S.A.
81 F4 Phillipsburg NJ U.S.A.
63 J1 Phillips Inlet in. Can.
80 D4 Phillipston U.S.A.
81 G3 Philmont U.S.A.
65 G3 Philomena Can.
80 C6 Philpott Reservoir resr U.S.A.
32 B2 Phimae Thai.
32 C2 Phimun Mangsahan Thai.
59 G3 Phiritona S. Africa
Phnom Penh see Phnum Penh
32 C2 Phnum Aôral mt Cambodia
32 C3 Phnum Penh Cambodia
75 F5 Phoenix U.S.A.
7 J2 Phoenix Islands is Pac. Oc.
59 G3 Phomolong S. Africa
25 C4 Phôngsali Laos
27 B6 Phong Thô Vietnam
32 B1 Phon Phisai Thai.
32 B1 Phou Bia mt Laos
32 C1 Phou Cô Pi mt Laos/Vietnam
27 B6 Phou Sam Sao mts Laos/Vietnam
32 A1 Phrao Thai.
32 B2 Phra Phutthabat Thai.
27 B6 Phuc Yên Vietnam
32 D2 Phu Hôi Vietnam
32 A4 Phuket Thai.
22 C4 Phulera India
23 G5 Phultala Bangl.
27 B6 Phu Ly Vietnam
32 B2 Phumĭ Bânhchok Kon Cambodia
32 C3 Phumĭ Chhuk Cambodia
32 C2 Phumĭ Kâmpóng Trâlach Cambodia
32 B3 Phumĭ Kaôh Kŏng Cambodia
32 B2 Phumĭ Kiliĕk Cambodia
32 C2 Phumĭ Mlu Prey Cambodia
32 B2 Phumĭ Moŭng Cambodia
32 B2 Phumĭ Prâmaôy Cambodia
32 B2 Phumĭ Sâmraông Cambodia
32 C2 Phumĭ Toêng Cambodia
32 D2 Phu My Vietnam
32 D2 Phu Nhon Vietnam
32 C3 Phuoc Long Vietnam
32 C3 Phu Quôc Vietnam
59 H4 Phuthaditjhaba S. Africa
27 B6 Phu Tho Vietnam
32 B1 Phu Wiang Thai.
87 J5 Piaca Brazil
48 C2 Piacenza Italy
26 D2 Pianguan China
48 D3 Pianosa, Isola i. Italy
47 N7 Piatra Neamţ Romania
87 K5 Piauí r. Brazil
48 E1 Piave r. Italy
55 F4 Pibor r. Sudan
55 F4 Pibor Post Sudan
68 D1 Pic r. Can.
75 F4 Pica U.S.A.
75 G5 Picacho AZ U.S.A.
75 E5 Picacho CA U.S.A.
44 F2 Picardie reg. France
79 B6 Picayune U.S.A.
88 D2 Pichanal Arg.
91 C2 Pichi Ciego Arg.
91 B2 Pichilemu Chile
70 D7 Pichilingue Mex.
91 D3 Pichi Mahuida Arg.
22 D4 Pichor India
84 D3 Pichucalco Mex.
68 D1 Pic, I. i. Can.
38 G3 Pickering U.K.
38 G3 Pickering, Vale of v. U.K.
68 E2 Pickford U.S.A.
66 B3 Pickle Lake Can.
34 C5 Pico i. Port.
89 C2 Pico Bolívar mt Venez.
89 D4 Pico da Neblina mt Brazil
89 D4 Pico da Neblina, Parque Nacional do nat. park Brazil
84 C3 Pico de Orizaba, Parque Nacional nat. park Mex.
84 B3 Pico de Tancítaro, Parque Nacional nat. park Mex.
83 K5 Pico Duarte mt Dom. Rep.
89 E4 Pico Redondo summit Brazil
89 E4 Pico Rondon summit Brazil
87 K5 Picos Brazil
88 C7 Pico Truncado Arg.
68 D1 Pic River Can.
8 H3 Picton Austr.
69 J4 Picton Can.
67 H4 Pictou Can.
68 D2 Pictured Rocks National Lakeshore res. U.S.A.
91 C3 Picún Leufú r. Arg.
19 F5 Pidarak Pak.
21 C5 Pidurutalagala mt Sri Lanka
89 B3 Piedecuesta Col.
91 C1 Pie de Palo, Sa mts Arg.
79 C5 Piedmont U.S.A.
80 C4 Piedmont Lake l. U.S.A.
82 D3 Piedras Negras Coahuila Mex.
84 C3 Piedras Negras Veracruz Mex.
91 F2 Piedras, Punta pt Arg.
86 D6 Piedras, Río de las r. Peru
68 C1 Pie Island i. Can.
36 U5 Pieksämäki Fin.
36 U5 Pielavesi Fin.
36 V5 Pielinen l. Fin.
59 H2 Pienaarsrivier S. Africa
68 E5 Pierceton U.S.A.
74 A2 Piercy U.S.A.
49 K4 Pieria mts Greece
40 F1 Pierowall U.K.
76 C2 Pierre U.S.A.
44 G4 Pierrelatte France
59 J4 Pietermaritzburg S. Africa
59 H1 Pietersburg S. Africa
48 G5 Pietra Spada, Passo di pass Italy
59 J3 Piet Retief S. Africa
47 M7 Pietrosa mt Romania
69 F4 Pigeon U.S.A.
69 F5 Pigeon Bay b. Can.
80 D6 Pigg r. U.S.A.
77 F4 Piggott U.S.A.
59 J2 Pigg's Peak Swaziland
91 D3 Pigüé Arg.
84 C2 Piguicas mt Mex.
22 E4 Pihani India
26 E3 Pi He r. China
37 V6 Pihlajavesi l. Fin.
37 R6 Pihlava Fin.
36 T5 Pihtipudas Fin.
36 T4 Piippola Fin.
36 V4 Piispajärvi Fin.
84 D4 Pijijiapan Mex.
50 E3 Pikalevo Rus. Fed.
80 D3 Pike U.S.A.
69 G3 Pike Bay Can.
4 G4 Pikelot i. Micronesia
58 C6 Piketberg S. Africa
80 B6 Pikeville U.S.A.
30 B4 Pikou China
91 E3 Pila Arg.
46 H4 Piła Pol.
59 G2 Pilanesberg National Park S. Africa
91 E2 Pilar Arg.
88 E3 Pilar Para.
31 B5 Pilas i. Phil.
91 B4 Pilcaniyeu Arg.
88 E2 Pilcomayo r. Bol./Para.
31 B3 Pili Phil.
22 D3 Pilibhit India
27 □ Pillar Pt pt H.K. China
91 E2 Pillo, Isla del i. Arg.
90 C2 Pilões, Serra dos mts Brazil
74 D2 Pilot Peak summit U.S.A.
8 G4 Pilot, The mt Austr.
77 F6 Pilottown U.S.A.
37 R8 Piltene Latvia
86 F6 Pimenta Bueno Brazil
22 C5 Pimpalner India
22 D2 Pin r. India
75 F6 Pinacate, Cerro del summit Mex.
22 D4 Pinahat India
75 G5 Pinaleno Mts mts U.S.A.
31 B3 Pinamalayan Phil.
91 F3 Pinamar Arg.
33 B1 Pinang i. Malaysia
16 F2 Pınarbaşı Turkey
83 H4 Pinar del Río Cuba
51 C7 Pinarhisar Turkey
47 K5 Pińczów Pol.
22 D3 Pindar r. India
87 J4 Pindaré r. Brazil
22 C2 Pindi Gheb Pak.
49 J5 Pindos mts Greece
Pindu Pass see Pêdo La
Pindus Mts mts see Pindos
75 G4 Pine AZ U.S.A.
68 E4 Pine r. MI U.S.A.
68 E3 Pine r. MI U.S.A.
68 C3 Pine r. WI U.S.A.
77 E5 Pine Bluff U.S.A.
72 F3 Pine Bluffs U.S.A.
67 K4 Pine, C. c. Can.
68 A3 Pine City U.S.A.
6 D3 Pine Creek Austr.
80 E4 Pine Creek r. U.S.A.
74 B2 Pinecrest U.S.A.
74 C3 Pinedale CA U.S.A.
72 E3 Pinedale WY U.S.A.
65 K4 Pine Falls Can.
74 C3 Pine Flat Lake l. U.S.A.
50 G1 Pinega Rus. Fed.
50 G1 Pinega r. Rus. Fed.
81 E4 Pine Grove U.S.A.
79 D6 Pine Hills U.S.A.
65 H3 Pinehouse Can.
68 A3 Pine Island U.S.A.
92 A3 Pine Island Bay b. Ant.
81 F3 Pine Lake U.S.A.
77 E6 Pineland U.S.A.
74 B4 Pine Mt mt U.S.A.
75 F4 Pine Peak summit U.S.A.
64 G2 Pine Point Can.
76 C3 Pine Ridge U.S.A.
74 C3 Pineridge U.S.A.
48 B2 Pinerolo Italy
77 E5 Pines, Lake O' the l. U.S.A.
59 J4 Pinetown S. Africa
80 B6 Pineville KY U.S.A.
77 E6 Pineville LA U.S.A.
80 C6 Pineville WV U.S.A.
26 B2 Ping'an China
27 B6 Pingbian China
26 F3 Ping Dao i. China
26 D2 Pingding China
26 D3 Pingdingshan China
26 F2 Pingdu China
30 C2 Pinggang China
27 C6 Pingguo China
27 E5 Pinghe China
27 D4 Pingjiang China
27 D5 Pingle China
26 C3 Pingli China
26 C3 Pingliang China
26 D2 Pinglu China
26 C2 Pingluo China
27 F5 Pingnan Fujian China
27 D6 Pingnan Guangxi China
26 F1 Pingquan China
26 E2 Pingshan China
27 D5 Pingshi China
27 F5 Pingtan China
27 C5 Pingtang China
27 F6 P'ing-tung Taiwan
26 B3 Pingwu China
27 C6 Pingxiang Guangxi China
27 D5 Pingxiang Jiangxi China
27 F5 Pingyang China
26 D2 Pingyao China
26 E3 Pingyi China
26 E2 Pingyin China
26 E3 Pingyu China
27 E5 Pingyuan China
27 B6 Pingyuanjie China
27 □ Ping Yuen Ho r. H.K. China
27 C5 Pingzhai China
87 J4 Pinheiro Brazil
91 G1 Pinheiro Machado Brazil
39 D7 Pinhoe U.K.
33 A2 Pini i. Indon.
64 E3 Pink Mountain Can.
9 D4 Pinnacle mt N.Z.
8 C3 Pinnaroo Austr.
43 H1 Pinneberg Ger.
74 C4 Pinos, Mt mt U.S.A.
84 C3 Pinotepa Nacional Mex.
7 G4 Pins, Î. des i. New Caledonia
51 C4 Pinsk Belarus
69 G4 Pins, Pointe aux pt Can.
86 □ Pinta, Isla i. Galapagos Is Ecuador
75 F5 Pinta, Sierra summit U.S.A.
75 F3 Pintura U.S.A.
75 E3 Pioche U.S.A.
57 C4 Piodi Congo(Zaire)
12 K1 Pioner, O. i. Rus. Fed.
47 K3 Pionerskiy Rus. Fed.
47 K5 Pionki Pol.
9 E3 Piopio N.Z.
86 F4 Piorini, Lago l. Brazil
47 J5 Piotrków Trybunalski Pol.
19 F5 Pīp Iran
30 E2 Pipa Dingzi mt China
22 C4 Pipar India
22 D5 Piparia India
49 L5 Piperi i. Greece
74 D3 Piper Peak summit U.S.A.
75 F3 Pipe Spring Nat. Mon. nat. park U.S.A.
76 D3 Pipestone U.S.A.
66 B3 Pipestone r. Can.
9 E3 Pipiriki N.Z.
22 C3 Pipli India
67 F4 Pipmuacan, Réservoir resr Can.
23 E4 Pipra Dam dam India
80 A4 Piqua U.S.A.
90 A2 Piquiri r. Mato Grosso do Sul Brazil
90 B4 Piquiri r. Paraná Brazil
90 C2 Piracanjuba Brazil
90 C3 Piracicaba Brazil
90 D2 Piracicaba r. Minas Gerais Brazil
90 C3 Piracicaba r. São Paulo Brazil
90 C3 Piraçununga Brazil
87 K4 Piracuruca Brazil
Piraeus see Peiraias
90 C4 Piraí do Sul Brazil
90 C3 Pirajuí Brazil
22 C5 Piram I. i. India
90 B2 Piranhas Brazil
90 B2 Piranhas r. Goiás Brazil
87 L5 Piranhas r. Paraíba/Rio Grande do Norte Brazil
89 C4 Piraparaná r. Col.
90 B3 Pirapó r. Brazil
90 D2 Pirapora Brazil
91 G1 Piratini Brazil
91 G1 Piratini r. Brazil
22 D4 Pirawa India
91 C4 Pire Mahuida, Sa mts Arg.
90 C2 Pires do Rio Brazil
23 G4 Pirganj Bangl.
87 K4 Piripiri Brazil
89 C2 Piritu Venez.
90 A2 Pirizal Brazil
42 F5 Pirmasens Ger.
49 K3 Pirot Yugo.
22 C2 Pir Panjal Pass India
22 C2 Pir Panjal Range mts India/Pak.
89 A3 Pirre, Co mt Panama
17 M2 Pirsaat Azer.
17 M1 Pirsaatçay r. Azer.
25 E7 Piru Indon.
48 D3 Pisa Italy
88 B1 Pisagua Chile
9 B6 Pisa, Mt mt N.Z.
81 F4 Piscataway U.S.A.
86 C6 Pisco Peru
86 C6 Pisco, B. de b. Peru
81 F3 Piseco Lake l. U.S.A.
46 G6 Písek Czech Rep.
19 F5 Pishin Iran
22 A3 Pishin Pak.
19 G4 Pishin Lora r. Pak.
88 C3 Pissis, Cerro mt Arg.
48 G4 Pisticci Italy
48 D3 Pistoia Italy
45 D1 Pisuerga r. Spain
72 B3 Pit r. U.S.A.
54 A3 Pita Guinea
67 G3 Pitaga Can.
84 E3 Pital Mex.
89 A4 Pitalito Col.
90 B4 Pitanga Brazil
90 D2 Pitangui Brazil
8 D3 Pitarpunga L. l. Austr.
5 P7 Pitcairn Islands i. Pitcairn Is Pac. Oc.
5 P7 Pitcairn Islands terr. Pac. Oc.
36 R4 Piteå Sweden
36 R4 Piteälven r. Sweden
51 H5 Piterka Rus. Fed.
49 L2 Piteşti Romania
21 C2 Pithapuram India
73 D6 Pitiquito Mex.
50 D2 Pitkyaranta Rus. Fed.
40 E4 Pitlochry U.K.
91 B3 Pitrufquén Chile
59 F2 Pitsane Siding Botswana
40 F4 Pitscottie U.K.
64 D4 Pitt I. i. Can.
7 J6 Pitt Island i. Pac. Oc.
77 E4 Pittsburg U.S.A.
80 D4 Pittsburgh U.S.A.
68 B6 Pittsfield IL U.S.A.
81 G3 Pittsfield MA U.S.A.
81 J2 Pittsfield ME U.S.A.
81 H3 Pittsfield NH U.S.A.
81 G3 Pittsfield VT U.S.A.
65 K2 Pitz Lake l. Can.
90 D3 Piumhí Brazil
86 B5 Piura Peru
74 C4 Piute Peak summit U.S.A.
23 E3 Piuthan Nepal
47 O6 Pivdennyy Buh r. Ukr.
48 F2 Pivka Slovenia
22 D1 Pixa China
84 E3 Pixoyal Mex.
46 E7 Piz Buin mt Austria/Switz.
50 H3 Pizhma Rus. Fed.
50 H3 Pizhma r. Rus. Fed.
67 K4 Placentia Can.
67 K4 Placentia B. b. Can.
31 B4 Placer Phil.
31 C4 Placer Phil.
74 B2 Placerville U.S.A.
83 J4 Placetas Cuba
81 H4 Plainfield CT U.S.A.
68 C5 Plainfield IL U.S.A.
68 C3 Plainfield WI U.S.A.
68 A3 Plainview MN U.S.A.
76 D3 Plainview NE U.S.A.
77 C5 Plainview TX U.S.A.
81 J1 Plaisted U.S.A.
13 T3 Plamennyy Rus. Fed.
64 G4 Plamondon Can.
33 E4 Plampang Indon.
43 L5 Planá Czech Rep.
74 B3 Planada U.S.A.
90 C1 Planaltina Brazil
91 B2 Planchón, P. de pass Arg.
89 B2 Planeta Rica Col.
94 F6 Planet Deep depth Pac. Oc.
76 D3 Plankinton U.S.A.
68 C5 Plano IL U.S.A.
77 D5 Plano TX U.S.A.
79 D7 Plantation U.S.A.
77 F6 Plaquemine U.S.A.
45 C2 Plasencia Spain
81 K1 Plaster Rock Can.
28 E2 Plastun Rus. Fed.
86 B4 Plata, I. la i. Ecuador
48 E6 Platani r. Sicily Italy
91 F2 Plata, Río de la chan. Arg./Uru.
59 H4 Platberg mt S. Africa
13 V4 Platinum U.S.A.
89 B2 Plato Col.
76 C3 Platte r. U.S.A.
68 B4 Platteville U.S.A.
43 L6 Plattling Ger.
81 G2 Plattsburgh U.S.A.
76 E3 Plattsmouth U.S.A.
43 L1 Plau Ger.
43 L4 Plauen Ger.
43 L1 Plauer See l. Ger.
50 F4 Plavsk Rus. Fed.
73 E6 Playa Noriega, L. l. Mex.
86 B4 Playas Ecuador
32 D2 Plây Cu Vietnam
65 K4 Playgreen L. l. Can.
84 A1 Playón Mex.
91 C3 Plaza Huincul Arg.
81 J4 Pleasant Bay b. U.S.A.
75 G1 Pleasant Grove U.S.A.
75 F5 Pleasant, Lake l. U.S.A.
75 H5 Pleasanton NM U.S.A.
77 D6 Pleasanton TX U.S.A.
9 C6 Pleasant Point N.Z.
75 H2 Pleasant View U.S.A.
81 F5 Pleasantville U.S.A.
78 C4 Pleasure Ridge Park U.S.A.
44 F4 Pleaux France
32 C2 Plei Doch Vietnam
43 J5 Pleinfeld Ger.
9 F2 Plenty, Bay of b. N.Z.
72 F1 Plentywood U.S.A.
50 G2 Plesetsk Rus. Fed.
67 F3 Plétipi L. l. Can.
43 F3 Plettenberg Ger.
58 E7 Plettenberg Bay S. Africa
49 L3 Pleven Bulg.
49 H3 Pljevlja Yugo.
47 J4 Płock Pol.
48 G3 Pločno mt Bos.-Herz.
50 D2 Plodovoye Rus. Fed.
44 C3 Ploemeur France
49 M2 Ploieşti Romania
65 H3 Plonge, Lac la l. Can.
47 P2 Ploskosh' Rus. Fed.
50 G3 Ploskoye Rus. Fed.
46 G4 Płoty Pol.
44 B2 Ploudalmézeau France
44 B2 Plouzané France
49 L3 Plovdiv Bulg.
68 C3 Plover U.S.A.
68 C3 Plover r. U.S.A.
27 □ Plover Cove Res. resr H.K. China
84 C2 Pluma Hidalgo Mex.
81 G4 Plum I. i. U.S.A.
72 C2 Plummer U.S.A.
37 R9 Plungė Lith.
47 N2 Plyeshchanitsy Belarus
32 A1 Ply Huey Wati, Khao mt Myanmar/Thai.
83 M5 Plymouth Montserrat
39 C7 Plymouth U.K.
74 B2 Plymouth CA U.S.A.
68 D5 Plymouth IN U.S.A.
81 H4 Plymouth MA U.S.A.
81 H3 Plymouth NH U.S.A.
78 E5 Plymouth PA U.S.A.
68 D4 Plymouth WI U.S.A.
81 H4 Plymouth Bay b. U.S.A.
39 D5 Plynlimon h. U.K.
46 F6 Plzeň Czech Rep.
54 B3 Pô Burkina
93 L8 Pobeda Ice Island ice feature Ant.
12 K5 Pobedy, Pik mt China/Kyrg.
77 F4 Pocahontas U.S.A.
80 C6 Pocatalico r. U.S.A.
72 D3 Pocatello U.S.A.
51 C5 Pochayiv Ukr.
50 E4 Pochep Rus. Fed.
50 H4 Pochinki Rus. Fed.
50 E4 Pochinok Rus. Fed.
41 B6 Pocket, The h. Rep. of Ireland
46 F6 Pocking Ger.
38 G4 Pocklington U.K.
90 E1 Poções Brazil
81 F6 Pocomoke City U.S.A.
81 F6 Pocomoke Sound b. U.S.A.
90 A2 Poconé Brazil
81 F4 Pocono Mountains h. U.S.A.
81 F4 Pocono Summit U.S.A.
90 C3 Poços de Caldas Brazil
50 D3 Poddor'ye Rus. Fed.
51 F5 Podgorenskiy Rus. Fed.
49 H3 Podgorica Yugo.
12 K4 Podgornoye Rus. Fed.
21 B3 Podile India
13 L3 Podkamennaya r. Rus. Fed.
86 C4 Podocarpus, Parque Nacional nat. park Ecuador
50 F4 Podol'sk Rus. Fed.
50 E2 Podporozh'ye Rus. Fed.
48 G1 Podravina reg. Hungary
49 J3 Podujevo Yugo.
50 H2 Podvoloch'ye Rus. Fed.
50 J2 Podz' Rus. Fed.
58 C4 Pofadder S. Africa
69 G2 Pogamasing Can.
51 E4 Pogar Rus. Fed.
48 D3 Poggibonsi Italy
49 J4 Pogradec Albania
90 A2 Poguba r. Brazil
30 E5 P'ohang S. Korea
4 G4 Pohnpei i. Micronesia
51 D5 Pohrebyshche Ukr.
22 D4 Pohri India
49 K3 Poiana Mare Romania
56 C4 Poie Congo(Zaire)
92 C6 Poinsett, C. c. Ant.
74 A2 Point Arena U.S.A.
69 K2 Point-Comfort Can.
83 M5 Pointe-à-Pitre Guadeloupe
69 G3 Pointe au Baril Sta. Can.
56 B4 Pointe-Noire Congo
62 B3 Point Hope U.S.A.
64 G1 Point Lake l. Can.
69 F5 Point Pelee National Park Can.
81 F4 Point Pleasant NJ U.S.A.
80 B5 Point Pleasant WV U.S.A.
69 K3 Poisson Blanc, Lac du l. Can.
44 E3 Poitiers France
27 □ Poi Toi I. i. H.K. China
44 D3 Poitou reg. France
90 E1 Pojuca Brazil
22 B4 Pokaran India
23 E3 Pokhara Nepal
56 C3 Poko Congo(Zaire)
22 A4 Pokran Pak.
28 C2 Pokrovka Rus. Fed.
28 B3 Pokrovka Rus. Fed.
13 O3 Pokrovsk Rus. Fed.
51 F6 Pokrovskoye Rus. Fed.
50 H2 Pokshen'ga r. Rus. Fed.
31 B3 Pola Phil.
75 G4 Polacca U.S.A.
75 G4 Polacca Wash r. U.S.A.
45 D1 Pola de Lena Spain
45 D1 Pola de Siero Spain
81 F3 Poland U.S.A.
34 G3 Poland country Europe
66 D3 Polar Bear Provincial Park res. Can.
16 D2 Polatlı Turkey
50 D4 Polatsk Belarus
47 N3 Polatskaya Nizina lowland Belarus
21 C2 Polavaram India
36 R3 Polcirkeln Sweden
50 G2 Poldarsa Rus. Fed.
18 B2 Pol Dasht Iran
19 F2 Pol-e-Khatum Iran
19 H3 Pol-e-Khomrī Afgh.
50 B4 Polessk Rus. Fed.
33 E3 Polewali Indon.
55 D4 Poli Cameroon
46 G4 Police Pol.
48 G4 Policoro Italy
44 G3 Poligny France
31 B3 Polillo i. Phil.
31 B3 Polillo Islands is Phil.
31 B3 Polillo Strait chan. Phil.
16 D4 Polis Cyprus
51 D5 Polis'ke Ukr.
46 H5 Polkowice Pol.
21 B4 Pollachi India
43 H3 Polle Ger.
45 H3 Pollença Spain
48 G5 Pollino, Monte mt Italy
36 U1 Polmak Norway
36 V4 Polo Fin.
68 C5 Polo U.S.A.
51 F6 Polohy Ukr.
50 J3 Polom Rus. Fed.
31 C5 Polomoloc Phil.
21 C5 Polonnaruwa Sri Lanka
51 C5 Polonne Ukr.
39 C7 Polperro U.K.
72 D2 Polson U.S.A.
50 G1 Polta r. Rus. Fed.
51 E5 Poltava Ukr.
28 B2 Poltavka Rus. Fed.
37 T7 Põltsamaa Estonia
37 U7 Põlva Estonia
36 V5 Polvijärvi Fin.
36 X2 Polyarnyy Rus. Fed.
13 T3 Polyarnyy Rus. Fed.
36 X3 Polyarnyye Zori Rus. Fed.
49 K4 Polygyros Greece
49 K4 Polykastro Greece
94 H6 Polynesia is Pac. Oc.
37 S6 Pomarkku Fin.
90 D3 Pomba r. Brazil
45 B3 Pombal Port.
90 B3 Pombo r. Brazil
59 J4 Pomeroy S. Africa
41 D3 Pomeroy U.K.
80 B5 Pomeroy U.S.A.
48 E4 Pomezia Italy
58 E2 Pomfret S. Africa
6 E2 Pomio P.N.G.
74 D4 Pomona U.S.A.
49 M3 Pomorie Bulg.
46 G3 Pomorska, Zatoka b. Pol.
50 E1 Pomorskiy Bereg coastal area Rus. Fed.
Pomo Tso l. see Puma Yumco
79 D7 Pompano Beach U.S.A.
90 D2 Pompéu Brazil
50 H3 Ponazyrevo Rus. Fed.
77 D4 Ponca City U.S.A.
83 L5 Ponce Puerto Rico
73 F4 Poncha Springs U.S.A.
66 E3 Poncheville, Lac l. Can.
21 B4 Pondicherry India
63 L2 Pond Inlet Can.
67 J3 Ponds, Island of i. Can.
45 C1 Ponferrada Spain
9 F4 Pongaroa N.Z.
55 E4 Pongo watercourse Sudan
59 J3 Pongola r. S. Africa
59 J3 Pongolapoort Dam resr S. Africa
47 P3 Ponizov'ye Rus. Fed.
21 B3 Ponnaivar r. India
21 A4 Ponnani India
23 H5 Ponnyadaung Range mts Myanmar
64 G4 Ponoka Can.
54 □ Ponta do Sol Cape Verde
90 B4 Ponta Grossa Brazil
90 C2 Pontalina Brazil
44 H2 Pont-à-Mousson France
90 A3 Ponta Porã Brazil
44 H3 Pontarlier France
77 F6 Pontchartrain, L. l. U.S.A.
42 C4 Pont-de-Loup Belgium
45 B3 Ponte de Sôr Port.
38 F4 Pontefract U.K.
38 F2 Ponteland U.K.
87 G7 Pontes-e-Lacerda Brazil
45 B1 Pontevedra Spain
68 C5 Pontiac IL U.S.A.
69 F4 Pontiac MI U.S.A.
33 C3 Pontianak Indon.
44 C2 Pontivy France
44 B3 Pont-l'Abbé France
44 F2 Pontoise France
65 K4 Ponton Can.
77 F5 Pontotoc U.S.A.
48 C2 Pontremoli Italy
42 A5 Pont-Ste-Maxence France
69 H3 Pontypool Can.
39 D6 Pontypool U.K.
39 D6 Pontypridd U.K.
48 E4 Ponza, Isola di i. Italy
48 E4 Ponziane, Isole is Italy
39 F7 Poole U.K.
Poona see Pune
8 D2 Pooncarie Austr.
8 E1 Poopelloe, L. l. Austr.
86 E7 Poopó, Lago de l. Bol.
9 E1 Poor Knights Is is N.Z.
54 B3 Pô, Parc National de nat. park Burkina
89 A4 Popayán Col.
42 A4 Poperinge Belgium
13 M2 Popigay r. Rus. Fed.
8 C2 Popiltah Austr.
8 C2 Popilta L. l. Austr.
72 F1 Poplar U.S.A.
65 K4 Poplar r. Can.
77 F4 Poplar Bluff U.S.A.
80 C6 Poplar Camp U.S.A.
77 F6 Poplarville U.S.A.
84 C3 Popocatépetl volc. Mex.
56 B4 Popokabaka Congo(Zaire)
49 M3 Popovo Bulg.
43 J3 Poppenberg h. Ger.
47 K6 Poprad Slovakia
19 G5 Porali r. Pak.
9 F4 Porangahau N.Z.
90 C1 Porangatu Brazil
22 B5 Porbandar India
89 B3 Porce r. Col.
64 C4 Porcher I. i. Can.
62 E3 Porcupine r. Can./U.S.A.
67 J3 Porcupine, Cape c. Can.
65 J4 Porcupine Hills h. Can.
68 C2 Porcupine Mts mts U.S.A.
65 J4 Porcupine Plain Can.
65 J4 Porcupine Prov. Forest res. Can.
89 C3 Pore Col.
48 E2 Poreč Croatia
50 H4 Poretskoye Rus. Fed.
37 R6 Pori Fin.
9 E4 Porirua N.Z.
50 D3 Porkhov Rus. Fed.
89 E2 Porlamar Venez.
44 C3 Pornic France
31 C4 Poro i. Phil.
24 G2 Poronaysk Rus. Fed.
49 K6 Poros Greece
50 E2 Porosozero Rus. Fed.
92 C6 Porpoise Bay b. Ant.
36 T1 Porsangen chan. Norway
37 L7 Porsgrunn Norway
16 C2 Porsuk r. Turkey
8 B3 Port Adelaide Austr.
41 E3 Portadown U.K.
41 F3 Portaferry U.K.
81 J1 Portage ME U.S.A.
68 E4 Portage MI U.S.A.
68 C4 Portage WI U.S.A.
65 K5 Portage la Prairie Can.
76 C1 Portal U.S.A.
64 E5 Port Alberni Can.
8 F5 Port Albert Austr.
45 C3 Portalegre Port.
77 C5 Portales U.S.A.
64 C3 Port Alexander U.S.A.
59 G6 Port Alfred S. Africa
64 D4 Port Alice Can.
80 D4 Port Allegany U.S.A.
77 F6 Port Allen U.S.A.
72 B1 Port Angeles U.S.A.
41 D4 Portarlington Rep. of Ireland
6 E6 Port Arthur Austr.
77 E6 Port Arthur U.S.A.
40 B5 Port Askaig U.K.
8 A2 Port Augusta Austr.
83 K5 Port-au-Prince Haiti
69 F3 Port Austin U.S.A.
67 J3 Port aux Choix Can.
41 F3 Portavogie U.K.
58 D7 Port Beaufort S. Africa
15 H5 Port Blair Andaman and Nicobar Is
69 H3 Port Bolster Can.
45 H1 Portbou Spain
69 G4 Port Burwell Can.
8 D5 Port Campbell Austr.
69 H3 Port Carling Can.
9 C6 Port Chalmers N.Z.
79 D7 Port Charlotte U.S.A.
81 G4 Port Chester U.S.A.
64 C4 Port Clements Can.
80 B4 Port Clinton U.S.A.
81 J3 Port Clyde U.S.A.
69 H4 Port Colborne Can.
64 E5 Port Coquitlam Can.
69 H4 Port Credit Can.
83 K5 Port-de-Paix Haiti
32 B5 Port Dickson Malaysia
80 C3 Port Dover Can.
68 D3 Porte des Morts chan. U.S.A.
64 C4 Port Edward Can.
59 J5 Port Edward S. Africa
68 C3 Port Edwards U.S.A.
90 D1 Porteirinha Brazil
87 H4 Portel Brazil
69 G3 Port Elgin Can.
59 F6 Port Elizabeth S. Africa
40 B5 Port Ellen U.K.
8 B3 Port Elliot Austr.
38 C3 Port Erin U.K.
65 H2 Porter Lake l. Can.
64 C3 Porter Landing Can.
58 C6 Porterville S. Africa
74 C3 Porterville U.S.A.
8 D5 Port Fairy Austr.
9 E2 Port Fitzroy N.Z.
Port Fuad see Bûr Fu'ad
56 A4 Port-Gentil Gabon
8 B2 Port Germein Austr.
77 F6 Port Gibson U.S.A.
40 D5 Port Glasgow U.K.
54 C4 Port Harcourt Nigeria
64 D4 Port Hardy Can.
Port Harrison see Inukjuak
67 H4 Port Hawkesbury Can.
39 D6 Porthcawl U.K.
6 B4 Port Hedland Austr.
81 G2 Port Henry U.S.A.
39 B7 Porthleven U.K.
39 C5 Porthmadog U.K.
69 H4 Port Hope Can.
67 J3 Port Hope Simpson Can.
69 F4 Port Huron U.S.A.
17 M2 Port-İliç Azer.
45 B4 Portimão Port.
27 □ Port Island i. H.K. China
8 H2 Port Jackson in. Austr.
81 G4 Port Jefferson U.S.A.
81 F4 Port Jervis U.S.A.
86 G2 Port Kaituma Guyana
8 H3 Port Kembla Austr.
8 G2 Portland N.S.W. Austr.
8 C5 Portland Vic. Austr.
68 E5 Portland IN U.S.A.
81 H3 Portland ME U.S.A.
72 B2 Portland OR U.S.A.
64 C3 Portland Canal in. Can.
9 F3 Portland I. i. N.Z.
39 E7 Portland, Isle of pen. U.K.
41 D4 Portlaoise Rep. of Ireland
77 D6 Port Lavaca U.S.A.
41 D5 Portlaw Rep. of Ireland
40 F3 Portlethen U.K.
6 D5 Port Lincoln Austr.
54 A4 Port Loko Sierra Leone
8 C5 Port MacDonnell Austr.
64 D4 Port McNeill Can.
7 F5 Port Macquarie Austr.
67 H2 Port Manvers in. Can.
67 H4 Port-Menier Can.
62 B4 Port Moller b. U.S.A.
72 B1 Port Moody Can.
6 E2 Port Moresby P.N.G.
40 B2 Portnaguran U.K.
40 B5 Portnahaven U.K.
79 F7 Port Nelson Bahamas
40 B2 Port Nis U.K.
58 B4 Port Nolloth S. Africa
Port-Nouveau-Québec see Kangiqsualujjuaq
Porto see Oporto
86 E5 Porto Acre Brazil
90 B3 Porto Alegre Mato Grosso do Sul Brazil
88 F4 Porto Alegre Rio Grande do Sul Brazil
87 G6 Porto Artur Brazil
87 G6 Porto dos Gaúchos Óbidos Brazil
87 G7 Porto Esperidião Brazil
48 D3 Portoferraio Italy
87 J5 Porto Franco Brazil
89 E2 Port of Spain Trinidad and Tobago
48 E2 Portogruaro Italy
54 □ Porto Inglês Cape Verde
90 A2 Porto Jofre Brazil
74 B2 Portola U.S.A.
48 D2 Portomaggiore Italy
87 G8 Porto Murtinho Brazil
87 J6 Porto Nacional Brazil
54 C4 Porto-Novo Benin
Porto Novo see Parangipettai
90 B3 Porto Primavera, Represa resr Brazil
72 A3 Port Orford U.S.A.
87 H4 Porto Santana Brazil
90 E2 Porto Seguro Brazil
48 E2 Porto Tolle Italy
48 C4 Porto Torres Sardinia Italy
48 C4 Porto-Vecchio Corsica France
86 F5 Porto Velho Brazil
86 B4 Portoviejo Ecuador
40 C6 Portpatrick U.K.
69 H3 Port Perry Can.
8 E5 Port Phillip Bay b. Austr.
8 B2 Port Pirie Austr.
39 B7 Portreath U.K.
40 B3 Portree U.K.
64 E5 Port Renfrew Can.
69 G4 Port Rowan Can.
80 E5 Port Royal U.S.A.
41 E2 Portrush U.K.
55 F1 Port Said Egypt
79 C6 Port St Joe U.S.A.
59 H5 Port St Johns S. Africa
38 C3 Port St Mary U.K.
41 D2 Portsalon Rep. of Ireland
69 F4 Port Sanilac U.S.A.
69 H3 Port Severn Can.
27 □ Port Shelter b. H.K. China
59 J5 Port Shepstone S. Africa
64 C4 Port Simpson Can.
39 F7 Portsmouth U.K.
81 H3 Portsmouth NH U.S.A.
80 B5 Portsmouth OH U.S.A.
81 E6 Portsmouth VA U.S.A.
40 F3 Portsoy U.K.
41 E2 Portstewart U.K.
55 F3 Port Sudan Sudan
79 B6 Port Sulphur U.S.A.
39 D6 Port Talbot U.K.
36 U2 Porttipahdan tekojärvi l. Fin.
34 E5 Portugal country Europe
89 C2 Portuguesa r. Venez.
41 C4 Portumna Rep. of Ireland
44 F5 Port-Vendres France
7 G3 Port Vila Vanuatu
36 X2 Port Vladimir Rus. Fed.
9 E2 Port Waikato N.Z.
8 B3 Port Wakefield Austr.
68 D4 Port Washington U.S.A.
40 D6 Port William U.K.
68 B2 Port Wing U.S.A.
91 D2 Porvenir Arg.
37 T6 Porvoo Fin.
45 D1 Posada de Llanera Spain
88 E3 Posadas Arg.
49 H2 Posavina reg. Bos.-Herz./Croatia
69 F3 Posen U.S.A.
17 L5 Posht-é-Kūh mts Iran
18 C2 Posht Kūh h. Iran
36 V3 Posio Fin.
25 E7 Poso Indon.
17 J1 Posof Turkey
30 D6 Posŏng S. Korea
90 C1 Posse Brazil
92 A5 Possession Is is Ant.
43 K4 Pößneck Ger.
77 C5 Post U.S.A.
66 E2 Poste-de-la-Baleine Can.

58 E4 Postmasburg S. Africa
67 J3 Postville Can.
68 B4 Postville U.S.A.
48 G3 Posušje Bos.-Herz.
28 B3 Pos'yet Rus. Fed.
59 G3 Potchefstroom S. Africa
77 E5 Poteau U.S.A.
87 L5 Potengi r. Brazil
48 F4 Potenza Italy
9 A7 Poteriteri, L. l. N.Z.
58 F5 Potfontein S. Africa
59 H2 Potgietersrus S. Africa
77 D6 Poth U.S.A.
66 F2 Potherie, Lac La l. Can.
51 G7 P'ot'i Georgia
87 K5 Poti r. Brazil
21 C2 Potikal India
54 D3 Potiskum Nigeria
72 D2 Pot Mt. mt U.S.A.
80 E5 Potomac r. U.S.A.
80 D5 Potomac South Branch r. U.S.A.
86 E7 Potosí Bol.
76 F4 Potosi U.S.A.
75 E4 Potosi Mt mt U.S.A.
31 B4 Pototan Phil.
43 M2 Potsdam Ger.
81 F2 Potsdam U.S.A.
39 E6 Potterne U.K.
39 G6 Potters Bar U.K.
81 F4 Pottstown U.S.A.
81 E4 Pottsville U.S.A.
21 C5 Pottuvil Sri Lanka
64 E3 Pouce Coupe Can.
67 K4 Pouch Cove Can.
81 G4 Poughkeepsie U.S.A.
81 G3 Poultney U.S.A.
38 E4 Poulton-le-Fylde U.K.
32 B1 Pou San mt Laos
90 D3 Pouso Alegre Brazil
32 B2 Poŭthĭsăt Cambodia
47 J6 Považská Bystrica Slovakia
50 E2 Povenets Rus. Fed.
9 F3 Poverty Bay b. N.Z.
49 H2 Povlen mt Yugo.
45 B2 Póvoa de Varzim Port.
51 G5 Povorino Rus. Fed.
28 C3 Povorotnyy, Mys hd Rus. Fed.
74 D5 Poway U.S.A.
72 F2 Powder r. U.S.A.
72 F3 Powder River U.S.A.
72 E2 Powell U.S.A.
80 B6 Powell r. U.S.A.
75 G3 Powell, Lake resr U.S.A.
74 C2 Powell Mt mt U.S.A.
79 E7 Powell Pt pt Bahamas
64 E5 Powell River Can.
68 D3 Powers U.S.A.
80 E6 Powhatan U.S.A.
90 A1 Poxoréu Brazil
27 E4 Poyang Hu l. China
32 □ Poyan Res. resr Sing.
68 C3 Poygan, Lake l. U.S.A.
16 E3 Pozantı Turkey
49 J2 Požarevac Yugo.
84 C2 Poza Rica Mex.
48 G2 Požega Croatia
49 J3 Požega Yugo.
28 D1 Pozharskoye Rus. Fed.
46 H4 Poznań Pol.
45 D3 Pozoblanco Spain
48 F4 Pozzuoli Italy
33 B3 Prabumulih Indon.
46 G6 Prachatice Czech Rep.
23 F6 Prachi r. India
32 B2 Prachin Buri Thai.
32 A3 Prachuap Khiri Khan Thai.
44 F5 Prades France
90 E2 Prado Brazil
46 G5 Prague Czech Rep.
Praha see Prague
54 □ Praia Cape Verde
59 K2 Praia do Bilene Moz.
90 A1 Praia Rica Brazil
68 E5 Prairie Creek Reservoir U.S.A.
77 C5 Prairie Dog Town Fork r. U.S.A.
68 B4 Prairie du Chien U.S.A.
32 B2 Prakhon Chai Thai.
32 B2 Pran r. Thai.
21 B2 Pranhita r. India
33 A2 Prapat Indon.
53 K6 Praslin i. Seychelles
49 M7 Prasonisi, Akra pt Greece
90 C2 Prata Brazil
90 C2 Prata r. Brazil
48 D3 Prato Italy
77 D4 Pratt U.S.A.
77 G5 Prattville U.S.A.
21 A2 Pravara r. India
47 K3 Pravdinsk Rus. Fed.
33 E4 Praya Indon.
32 C2 Preăh Vihear Cambodia
47 O3 Prechistoye Rus. Fed.
65 J4 Preeceville Can.
50 B4 Pregolya r. Rus. Fed.
37 U8 Preiļi Latvia
69 H1 Preissac, Lac l. Can.
32 C3 Prêk Tnaôt l. Cambodia
8 G1 Premer Austr.
44 F3 Prémery France
43 L2 Premnitz Ger.
68 B3 Prentice U.S.A.
46 F4 Prenzlau Ger.
28 C3 Preobrazheniye Rus. Fed.
46 H6 Přerov Czech Rep.
81 F2 Prescott Can.
75 F4 Prescott U.S.A.
75 F4 Prescott Valley U.S.A.
49 J3 Preševo Yugo.
76 C3 Presho U.S.A.
88 D3 Presidencia Roque Sáenz Peña Arg.
87 K5 Presidente Dutra Brazil
90 B3 Presidente Epitácio Brazil
86 F6 Presidente Hermes Brazil
90 B3 Presidente Prudente Brazil
90 B3 Presidente Venceslau Brazil
77 B6 Presidio U.S.A.
49 M3 Preslav Bulg.
47 K6 Prešov Slovakia
49 J4 Prespa, Lake l. Europe
81 K1 Presque Isle U.S.A.
68 D2 Presque Isle Pt pt U.S.A.
39 D5 Presteigne U.K.
38 E4 Preston U.K.
72 E3 Preston ID U.S.A.
68 A4 Preston MN U.S.A.
77 E4 Preston MO U.S.A.
75 E2 Preston NV U.S.A.
40 F5 Prestonpans U.K.
80 B6 Prestonsburg U.S.A.
40 D5 Prestwick U.K.
90 E1 Preto r. Bahia Brazil
90 C2 Preto r. Minas Gerais Brazil
59 H2 Pretoria S. Africa
80 E5 Prettyboy Lake l. U.S.A.
43 L3 Pretzsch Ger.
49 J5 Preveza Greece
32 C3 Prey Vêng Cambodia
13 V4 Pribilof Islands is U.S.A.
49 H3 Priboj Yugo.
67 G4 Price Can.
75 G2 Price U.S.A.
64 D4 Price I. i. Can.
79 B6 Prichard U.S.A.
37 R8 Priekule Latvia
37 T8 Priekuļi Latvia
37 S9 Prienai Lith.
58 E4 Prieska S. Africa
72 C1 Priest L. l. U.S.A.
72 C1 Priest River U.S.A.
47 J6 Prievidza Slovakia
43 L1 Prignitz reg. Ger.
48 G2 Prijedor Bos.-Herz.
49 H3 Prijepolje Yugo.
12 F5 Prikaspiyskaya Nizmennost' lowland Kazak./Rus. Fed.
49 J4 Prilep Macedonia
84 C2 Primavera Mex.
43 L5 Přimda Czech Rep.
91 D1 Primero r. Arg.
37 V6 Primorsk Rus. Fed.
28 C2 Primorskiy Kray div. Rus. Fed.
51 F6 Primorsko-Akhtarsk Rus. Fed.
65 H4 Primrose Lake l. Can.
65 H4 Prince Albert Can.
58 E6 Prince Albert S. Africa
92 B5 Prince Albert Mts mts Ant.
65 H4 Prince Albert National Park Can.
62 G2 Prince Albert Peninsula Can.
58 D6 Prince Albert Road S. Africa
62 G2 Prince Albert Sound chan. Can.
62 F2 Prince Alfred, C. c. Can.
63 L3 Prince Charles I. Can.
92 D4 Prince Charles Mts mts Ant.
67 H4 Prince Edward Island div. Can.
93 G7 Prince Edward Islands is Ind. Ocean
69 J4 Prince Edward Pt pt Can.
80 E5 Prince Frederick U.S.A.
64 E4 Prince George Can.
62 B3 Prince of Wales, Cape c. U.S.A.
63 J2 Prince of Wales I. N.W.T. Can.
6 E3 Prince of Wales I. i. Austr.
64 C3 Prince of Wales Island i. U.S.A.
62 G2 Prince of Wales Strait chan. Can.
62 F2 Prince Patrick I. i. Can.
63 J2 Prince Regent Inlet chan. Can.
64 C4 Prince Rupert Can.
65 K2 Princess Mary Lake l. Can.
81 F5 Princess Anne U.S.A.
92 D3 Princess Astrid Coast coastal area Ant.
6 E3 Princess Charlotte Bay b. Austr.
92 D5 Princess Elizabeth Land reg. Ant.
92 D3 Princess Ragnhild Coast coastal area Ant.
64 D4 Princess Royal I. i. Can.
64 E5 Princeton Can.
74 A2 Princeton CA U.S.A.
68 C5 Princeton IL U.S.A.
78 C4 Princeton IN U.S.A.
78 C4 Princeton KY U.S.A.
81 K2 Princeton ME U.S.A.
76 E3 Princeton MO U.S.A.
81 F4 Princeton NJ U.S.A.
68 C4 Princeton WV U.S.A.
80 C6 Princeton WV U.S.A.
81 K2 Prince William Can.
62 D3 Prince William Sound b. U.S.A.
54 C4 Príncipe i. Sao Tome and Principe
72 B2 Prineville U.S.A.
12 C2 Prins Karls Forland i. Svalbard
83 H6 Prinzapolca Nic.
50 D2 Priozersk Rus. Fed.
Pripet r. see Pryp"yat
36 W2 Prirechnyy Rus. Fed.
49 J3 Priština Yugo.
43 K1 Pritzier Ger.
43 L1 Pritzwalk Ger.
44 G4 Privas France
48 F2 Privlaka Croatia
50 G3 Privolzhsk Rus. Fed.
50 H4 Privolzhskaya Vozvyshennost' reg. Rus. Fed.
51 G6 Priyutnoye Rus. Fed.
49 J3 Prizren Yugo.
33 D4 Probolinggo Indon.
43 K4 Probstzella Ger.
39 C7 Probus U.K.
68 A2 Proctor MN U.S.A.
81 G3 Proctor VT U.S.A.
87 G3 Professor van Blommestein Meer resr Suriname
82 G5 Progreso Honduras
77 C7 Progreso Coahuila Mex.
84 C2 Progreso Hidalgo Mex.
84 E2 Progreso Yucatán Mex.
51 H7 Prokhladnyy Rus. Fed.
12 K4 Prokop'yevsk Rus. Fed.
49 J3 Prokuplje Yugo.
50 D3 Proletariy Rus. Fed.
51 G6 Proletarsk Rus. Fed.
90 A2 Promissão Brazil
62 F4 Prophet r. Can.
64 E3 Prophet River Can.
68 C5 Prophetstown U.S.A.
6 E4 Proserpine Austr.
81 F3 Prospect U.S.A.
31 C4 Prosperidad Phil.
58 D7 Protem S. Africa
68 A4 Protivin U.S.A.
49 M3 Provadiya Bulg.
Prøven see Kangersuatsiaq
44 H5 Provence reg. France
81 H4 Providence U.S.A.
69 F3 Providence Bay Can.
9 A7 Providence, Cape c. N.Z.
77 F5 Providence, Lake U.S.A.
86 B1 Providencia, Isla de i. Col.
62 A3 Provideniya Rus. Fed.
81 H3 Provincetown U.S.A.
75 G1 Provo U.S.A.
65 G4 Provost Can.
90 B4 Prudentópolis Brazil
62 D2 Prudhoe Bay U.S.A.
42 E4 Prüm Ger.
42 E4 Prüm r. Ger.
48 C3 Prunelli-di-Fiumorbo Corsica France
47 K4 Pruszków Pol.
51 D6 Prut r. Moldova/Romania
92 D5 Prydz Bay b. Ant.
51 E5 Pryluky Ukr.
51 F6 Prymors'k Ukr.
71 G4 Pryor OK U.S.A.
47 M5 Pryp"yat r. Ukr.
47 N4 Prypyats' r. Belarus
47 L6 Przemyśl Pol.
49 L5 Psara i. Greece
51 G6 Psebay Rus. Fed.
51 F6 Pshish r. Rus. Fed.
50 D3 Pskov Rus. Fed.
37 U7 Pskov, Lake l. Estonia/Rus. Fed.
50 D3 Pskovskaya Oblast' div. Rus. Fed.
49 J4 Ptolemaïda Greece
48 F1 Ptuj Slovenia
26 C3 Pu r. China
91 D3 Puán Arg.
27 B5 Pu'an China
30 D6 Puan S. Korea
27 C6 Pubei China
86 D5 Pucallpa Peru
27 F5 Pucheng Fujian China
26 C3 Pucheng Shaanxi China
50 G3 Puchezh Rus. Fed.
30 D5 Puch'ŏn S. Korea
31 B4 Pucio Pt pt Phil.
46 J3 Puck Pol.
68 C4 Puckaway Lake l. U.S.A.
91 B3 Pucón Chile
Pudai watercourse see Dor
18 D3 Pūdanū Iran
36 U4 Pudasjärvi Fin.
58 F3 Pudimoe S. Africa
50 F2 Pudozh Rus. Fed.
38 F4 Pudsey U.K.
Puduchcheri see Pondicherry
21 B4 Pudukkottai India
84 C3 Puebla Mex.
84 C3 Puebla div. Mex.
45 C1 Puebla de Sanabria Spain
73 F4 Pueblo U.S.A.
89 C2 Pueblo Nuevo Venez.
84 D3 Pueblo Viejo Mex.
91 D3 Puelches Arg.
91 C3 Puelén Arg.
91 B2 Puente Alto Chile
84 C3 Puente de Ixtla Mex.
45 D4 Puente-Genil Spain
89 C2 Puente Torres Venez.
86 F6 Puerto Alegre Bol.
84 C4 Puerto Angel Mex.
84 D4 Puerto Arista Mex.
83 H7 Puerto Armuelles Panama
89 A4 Puerto Asís Col.
89 D3 Puerto Ayacucho Venez.
82 G5 Puerto Barrios Guatemala
89 B3 Puerto Berrío Col.
89 C2 Puerto Cabello Venez.
83 H6 Puerto Cabezas Nic.
89 D3 Puerto Carreño Col.
88 E2 Puerto Casado Para.
88 B6 Puerto Cisnes Chile
88 C8 Puerto Coig Arg.
83 H7 Puerto Cortés Costa Rica
89 C2 Puerto Cumarebo Venez.
84 C4 Puerto Escondido Mex.
89 C1 Puerto Estrella Col.
86 F6 Puerto Frey Bol.
88 E2 Puerto Guarani Para.
86 E6 Puerto Heath Bol.
89 D4 Puerto Inírida Col.
87 G7 Puerto Isabel Bol.
89 D2 Puerto La Cruz Venez.
86 D4 Puerto Leguízamo Col.
45 D3 Puertollano Spain
91 D4 Puerto Lobos Arg.
89 B3 Puerto Lopéz Col.
84 D4 Puerto Madero Mex.
91 D4 Puerto Madryn Arg.
86 E6 Puerto Maldonado Peru
86 B4 Puerto Máncora Peru
90 A4 Puerto Mendes Para.
89 D3 Puerto Miranda Venez.
91 B4 Puerto Montt Chile
88 B8 Puerto Natáles Chile
89 C3 Puerto Nuevo Col.
89 A2 Puerto Obaldia Panama
89 E2 Puerto Ordaz Venez.
89 D3 Puerto Páez Venez.
88 E2 Puerto Pinasco Para.
91 D4 Puerto Pirámides Arg.
83 K5 Puerto Plata Dom. Rep.
86 D5 Puerto Portillo Peru
31 A4 Puerto Princesa Phil.
89 A2 Puerto Rey Col.
61 M8 Puerto Rico terr. Caribbean Sea
92 E4 Puerto Rico Trench sea feature Atl. Ocean
88 E2 Puerto Sastre Para.
89 A4 Puerto Tejado Col.
84 A2 Puerto Vallarta Mex.
91 B4 Puerto Varas Chile
51 J4 Pugachev Rus. Fed.
22 C3 Pugal India
27 B5 Puge China
18 D5 Pūhāl-e Khamīr, Kūh-e mts Iran
45 H3 Puig Major mt Spain
45 H1 Puigmal mt France/Spain
27 □ Pui O Wan b. H.K. China
27 F4 Pujiang China
30 D3 Pujŏn Reservoir resr N. Korea
30 E3 Pujonryong Sanmaek mts N. Korea
9 C6 Pukaki, Lake l. N.Z.
68 E1 Pukaskwa r. Can.
68 E1 Pukaskwa National Park Can.
65 J3 Pukatawagan Can.
30 C3 Pukchin N. Korea
30 E3 Pukch'ŏng N. Korea
9 E2 Pukekohe N.Z.
9 D5 Puketeraki Ra. mts N.Z.
9 F4 Puketoi Range h. N.Z.
9 C6 Pukeuri Junction N.Z.
47 P3 Pukhnovo Rus. Fed.
50 G2 Puksoozero Rus. Fed.
30 D3 Puksubaek-san mt N. Korea
48 E2 Pula Croatia
86 E8 Pulacayo Bol.
30 A4 Pulandian Wan b. China
31 C5 Pulangi r. Phil.
81 E3 Pulaski NY U.S.A.
79 C5 Pulaski TN U.S.A.
80 C6 Pulaski VA U.S.A.
68 C3 Pulaski WV U.S.A.
47 K5 Puławy Pol.
42 E3 Pulheim Ger.
21 C3 Pulicat L. b. India
21 B3 Pulivendla India
21 B4 Puliyangudi India
36 T4 Pulkkila Fin.
72 C2 Pullman U.S.A.
36 X2 Pulozero Rus. Fed.
22 E1 Pulu China
17 G2 Pülümür Turkey
31 C5 Pulutan Indon.
23 G3 Puma Yumco l. China
86 B4 Puná, Isla i. Ecuador
23 G4 Punakha Bhutan
22 C2 Punch Jammu and Kashmir
64 E4 Punchaw Can.
23 G3 Püncogling China
59 J1 Punda Maria S. Africa
22 D3 Pundri India
21 A2 Pune India
32 □ Punggol Sing.
30 E3 P'ungsan N. Korea
57 D5 Púngoè r. Moz.
56 C4 Punia Congo(Zaire)
91 B1 Punitaqui Chile
22 C3 Punjab div. India
22 B3 Punjab div. Pak.
22 D2 Punmah Gl. gl. China/Jammu and Kashmir
23 F4 Punpun r. India
91 D3 Punta Alta Arg.
88 B8 Punta Arenas Chile
48 C4 Punta Balestrieri mt Italy
83 L5 Punta, Cerro de mt Puerto Rico
91 D4 Punta Delgada Arg.
82 G5 Punta Gorda Belize
79 D7 Punta Gorda U.S.A.
91 D4 Punta Norte Arg.
83 H6 Puntarenas Costa Rica
89 C2 Punto Fijo Venez.
80 D4 Punxsutawney U.S.A.
36 U4 Puokio Fin.
36 U4 Puolanka Fin.
27 D4 Puqi China
18 E5 Pūr Iran
12 J3 Pur r. Rus. Fed.
89 A4 Puracé, Parque Nacional nat. park Col.
89 A4 Purace, Volcán de volc. Col.
77 D5 Purcell U.S.A.
64 F4 Purcell Mts mts Can.
91 B3 Purén Chile
73 G4 Purgatoire r. U.S.A.
23 F6 Puri India
42 C2 Purmerend Neth.
21 B2 Purna India
22 D5 Purna r. Maharashtra India
22 D6 Purna r. Maharashtra India
21 B1 Purna r. India
23 G4 Purnabhaba r. India
23 F4 Pūrnia India
91 B4 Purranque Chile
84 B2 Puruandiro Mex.
23 F5 Puruliya India
86 F4 Purus r. Brazil
37 V6 Puruvesi l. Fin.
33 C4 Purwakarta Indon.
33 D4 Purwodadi Indon.
33 C4 Purwokerto Indon.
30 E2 Puryŏng N. Korea
22 D6 Pus r. India
22 D6 Pusad India
30 E6 Pusan S. Korea
81 J2 Pushaw Lake l. U.S.A.
50 H2 Pushemskiy Rus. Fed.
22 C4 Pushkar India
50 D3 Pushkin Rus. Fed.
51 H5 Pushkino Rus. Fed.
50 D3 Pushkinskiye Gory Rus. Fed.
19 F4 Pusht-i-Rud reg. Afgh.
47 O2 Pustoshka Rus. Fed.
47 L4 Puszcza Augustowska forest Pol.
46 G4 Puszcza Natecka forest Pol.
24 B4 Putao Myanmar
27 F5 Putian China
33 D3 Puting, Tanjung pt Indon.
84 C3 Putla Mex.
19 G4 Putla Khan Afgh.
43 L1 Putlitz Ger.
49 M2 Putna r. Romania
81 H4 Putnam U.S.A.
81 G3 Putney U.S.A.
23 H3 Putrang La pass China
58 D4 Putsonderwater S. Africa
21 B4 Puttalam Sri Lanka
21 B4 Puttalam Lagoon lag. Sri Lanka
42 E5 Puttelange-aux-Lacs France
42 D2 Putten Neth.
42 C3 Puttershoek Neth.
46 E3 Puttgarden Ger.
86 D4 Putumayo r. Col.
16 G2 Pütürge Turkey
33 D2 Putusibau Indon.
50 G4 Putyatino Rus. Fed.
51 E5 Putyvl' Ukr.
37 V6 Puumala Fin.
74 □2 Puuwai U.S.A.
66 E1 Puvurnituq Can.
72 B2 Puyallup U.S.A.
26 E3 Puyang China
91 B4 Puyehue Chile
91 B4 Puyehue, Parque Nacional nat. park Chile
44 F5 Puylaurens France
9 A7 Puysegur Pt pt N.Z.
57 C4 Pweto Congo(Zaire)
39 C5 Pwllheli U.K.
50 E2 Pyal'ma Rus. Fed.
50 H4 P'yana r. Rus. Fed.
22 B1 Pyandzh r. Afgh./Tajik.
36 W3 Pyaozero, Ozero l. Rus. Fed.
36 W4 Pyaozerskiy Rus. Fed.
12 K2 Pyasina r. Rus. Fed.
51 G6 Pyatigorsk Rus. Fed.
51 E5 P"yatykhatky Ukr.
25 B5 Pyè Myanmar
9 B7 Pye, Mt h. N.Z.
51 D4 Pyetrykaw Belarus
36 T4 Pyhäjoki Fin.
36 T4 Pyhäjoki r. Fin.
36 U4 Pyhäntä Fin.
36 T5 Pyhäsalmi Fin.
36 V5 Pyhäselkä l. Fin.
23 H5 Pyingaing Myanmar
39 D6 Pyle U.K.
12 K3 Pyl'karamo Rus. Fed.
49 J6 Pylos Greece
80 C4 Pymatuning Reservoir U.S.A.
30 C5 Pyŏksŏng N. Korea
30 C3 Pyŏktong N. Korea
30 D4 P'yŏnggang N. Korea
30 C4 P'yŏnghae S. Korea
30 C4 P'yŏngsong N. Korea
30 D5 P'yŏngt'aek S. Korea
30 C4 P'yŏngyang N. Korea
8 E4 Pyramid Hill Austr.
74 C1 Pyramid Lake l. U.S.A.
68 E3 Pyramid Pt pt U.S.A.
74 C2 Pyramid Range mts U.S.A.
34 E4 Pyrenees mts France/Spain
49 J6 Pyrgos Greece
51 E5 Pyryatyn Ukr.
46 G4 Pyrzyce Pol.
50 H3 Pyshchug Rus. Fed.
47 N2 Pytalovo Rus. Fed.
49 K5 Pyxaria mt Greece

Q

63 M2 Qaanaaq Greenland
18 D6 Qābil Oman
17 J6 Qabr Bandar Iraq
59 H5 Qacha's Nek Lesotho
17 K4 Qādir Karam Iraq
17 J4 Qadissiya Dam dam Iraq
26 C1 Qagan Ders China
26 C2 Qagan Nur China
26 D1 Qagan Nur China
30 C1 Qagan Nur l. Jilin China
26 E1 Qagan Nur l. Nei Monggol China
26 E1 Qagan Nur resr China
26 D1 Qagan Teg China
26 E1 Qagan Us China
23 H3 Qagbasêrag China
23 E2 Qagcaka China
63 O3 Qagssimiut Greenland
26 D1 Qahar Youyi Qianqi China
26 D1 Qahar Youyi Zhongqi China
24 B3 Qaidam Pendi basin China
19 G3 Qaisar Afgh.
19 G3 Qaisar, Koh-i- mt Afgh.
17 K3 Qalā Diza Iraq
19 H2 Qal'aikhum Tajik.
19 G3 Qala Shinia Takht Afgh.
19 G3 Qalāt Afgh.
18 D4 Qalat Iran
17 H4 Qal'at as Sālihīyah Syria
16 E6 Qal'at el Hasal Jordan
17 L6 Qal'at Sālih Iraq
17 L6 Qal'at Sukkar Iraq
19 F3 Qala Vali Afgh.
18 B2 Qal'eh D. mt Iran
19 F3 Qal 'eh-ye Now Afgh.
19 G4 Qal 'eh-ye Bost Afgh.
17 M5 Qal'eh-ye-Now Iran
17 K7 Qalīb Bāqūr well Iraq
16 C6 Qalyūb Egypt
59 G5 Qamata S. Africa
22 B4 Qambar Pak.
22 B3 Qamruddin Karez Pak.
18 C3 Qamṣar Iran
18 B2 Qandaranbashi mt Iran
26 E1 Qangdin Sum China
17 M2 Qaraçala Azer.
17 J4 Qarachōq, J. mts Iraq
17 K4 Qara D. r. Iraq
17 H7 Qārah S. Arabia
19 H3 Qarah Bāgh Afgh.
18 A5 Qa'rah, J. al h. S. Arabia
17 L3 Qaranqu r. Iran
56 E3 Qardho Somalia
17 L3 Qareh Āqāj Iran
17 L2 Qareh D. mts Iran
17 L3 Qareh Dāsh, Kūh-e mt Iran
18 B2 Qareh Sū r. Iran
17 L3 Qareh Urgān, Kūh-e mt Iran
23 H1 Qarhan China
19 G2 Qarqīn Afgh.
17 K6 Qaryat al Gharab Iraq
18 B5 Qaryat al Ulyā S. Arabia
18 E3 Qasamī Iran
19 F3 Qasa Murg mts Afgh.
18 C4 Qash Qai reg. Iran
63 N3 Qasigiannguit Greenland
17 J5 Qasr al Khubbāz Iraq
17 M7 Qaṣr aṣ Ṣabīyah Kuwait
16 F6 Qasr el Azraq Jordan
19 F5 Qaṣr-e-Qand Iran
18 B3 Qasr-e-Shirin Iran
17 L6 Qaṣr Shaqrah Iraq
16 F5 Qaṭanā Syria
10 G7 Qatar country Asia
16 F6 Qatrāna Jordan
16 C7 Qaṭrāni, Gebel esc. Egypt
55 E2 Qattâra Depression depression Egypt
17 L1 Qax Azer.
19 E3 Qāyen Iran
23 H3 Qayü China
17 J4 Qayyarah Iraq
17 L2 Qazangödağ mt Azer.
17 K1 Qazax Azer.
22 B4 Qazi Ahmad Pak.
17 M1 Qazımämmäd Azer.
18 C2 Qazvīn Iran
26 A1 Qeh China
55 F2 Qena Egypt
63 N3 Qeqertarsuatsiaat Greenland
63 N3 Qeqertarsuatsiaq i. Greenland
63 N3 Qeqertarsuup Tunua b. Greenland
18 B3 Qeshlag r. Iran
17 L4 Qeshlaq Iran
18 E5 Qeshm Iran
18 C2 Qeydār Iran
18 D5 Qeys i. Iran
18 C2 Qezel Owzan r. Iran
16 E6 Qeẓi'ot Israel
26 C3 Qian r. China
26 F2 Qian'an China
30 C1 Qian'an China
27 C5 Qiancheng China
26 F3 Qiang r. China
30 C1 Qian Gorlos China
27 D4 Qianjiang Hubei China
27 C4 Qianjiang Sichuan China
30 E1 Qianjin China
26 A4 Qianning China
30 B1 Qianqihao China
30 B3 Qian Shan mts China
27 C5 Qianxi China
26 C3 Qian Xian China
27 D5 Qianyang Hunan China
26 C3 Qianyang Shaanxi China
27 F4 Qianyang Zhejiang China
26 D2 Qiaocun China
27 B5 Qiaojia China
17 K2 Qīās Iran
18 B5 Qibā' S. Arabia
59 G4 Qibing S. Africa
27 D5 Qidong Hunan China
26 F4 Qidong Jiangsu China
23 H2 Qidukou China
15 G3 Qiemo China
26 E2 Qihe China
27 C4 Qijiang China
12 L5 Qijiaojing China
19 G4 Qila Abdullah Pak.
19 F5 Qila Ladgasht Pak.
26 E1 Qilaotu Shan mts China
19 F4 Qila Safed Pak.
22 B3 Qila Saifullah Pak.
24 B3 Qilian Shan mts China
63 P3 Qillak i. Greenland
23 G1 Qimantag mts China
27 E4 Qimen China
26 D3 Qin r. China
26 B3 Qin'an China
30 C2 Qing r. China
30 B3 Qingchengzi China
26 F2 Qingdao China
26 A2 Qinghai div. China
26 A2 Qinghai Hu salt l. China
24 B3 Qinghai Nanshan mts China
28 A1 Qinghe China
30 C3 Qinghecheng China
26 D2 Qingjian China
26 F3 Qingjiang Jiangsu China
27 E4 Qingjiang Jiangxi China
27 D4 Qing Jiang r. China
27 E5 Qingliu China
27 B5 Qinglong Guizhou China
26 F1 Qinglong Hebei China
26 F2 Qinglong r. China
27 C6 Qingping China
26 F4 Qingpu China
26 C3 Qingshui China
26 D2 Qingshuihe China
27 F4 Qingtian China
26 E2 Qing Xian China
26 D2 Qingxu China
27 E4 Qingyang Anhui China
26 C2 Qingyang Gansu China
27 D6 Qingyuan Guangdong China
27 F5 Qingyuan Zhejiang China
30 C2 Qingyuan China
27 C5 Qingzhen China
26 F2 Qinhuangdao China
26 C3 Qin Ling mts China
26 C2 Qintongxia China
26 D2 Qin Xian China
26 D3 Qinyang China
26 D2 Qinyuan China
27 C6 Qinzhou China
27 C6 Qinzhou Wan b. China
27 D7 Qionghai China
27 B4 Qionglai China
26 B4 Qionglai Shan mts China
27 D7 Qiongshan China
27 C6 Qiongzhou Haixia str. China
24 E2 Qiqihar China
17 M5 Qīr Iran
18 D4 Qīr Iran
22 E1 Qira China
16 E6 Qiryat Gat Israel
16 F6 Qitab ash Shāmah crater S. Arabia
28 B2 Qitaihe China
27 B5 Qiubei China
26 F2 Qixia China
26 E3 Qi Xian Henan China
26 D2 Qi Xian Shanxi China
28 C1 Qixing r. China
27 D5 Qiyang China
26 C2 Qiying China
27 D7 Qizhou Liedao i. China
17 M2 Qızılağac Körfäzi b. Azer.
Qogir Feng mt see K2
26 C1 Qog Qi China
18 B2 Qojūr Iran
18 C3 Qom Iran
13 H3 Qomdo China
18 C3 Qomishēh Iran
Qomolangma Feng mt see Everest, Mt
17 M1 Qonaqkänd Azer.
18 C3 Qonāq, Kūh-e h. Iran
23 G3 Qonggyai China
26 C1 Qongi China
16 F4 Qornet es Saouda mt Lebanon
18 B3 Qorveh Iran
18 E5 Qoṭbābād Iran
17 K2 Qoṭūr Iran
81 G3 Quabbin Reservoir U.S.A.
74 D4 Quail Mts mts U.S.A.
43 F2 Quakenbrück Ger.
81 F4 Quakertown U.S.A.
65 K2 Quamarirjung Lake l. Can.
8 D3 Quambatook Austr.
8 F1 Quambone Austr.
77 D5 Quanah U.S.A.
26 D3 Quanbao Shan mt China
32 D2 Quang Ngai Vietnam
32 C1 Quang Tri Vietnam
27 C6 Quang Yen Vietnam
27 E5 Quannan China
27 F5 Quanzhou Fujian China
27 D5 Quanzhou Guangxi China
65 J4 Qu'Appelle Can.
65 J4 Qu'Appelle r. Can.
91 F1 Quaraí Brazil
91 F1 Quaraí r. Brazil
27 □ Quarry Bay H.K. China
48 C5 Quartu Sant'Elena Sardinia Italy
74 D3 Quartzite Mt mt U.S.A.
75 E5 Quartzsite U.S.A.
64 D4 Quatsino Sound in. Can.
17 M1 Quba Azer.
19 E2 Quchan Iran
8 G3 Queanbeyan Austr.
67 F4 Québec Can.
63 L4 Quebec div. Can.
90 C2 Quebra Anzol r. Brazil
89 C2 Quebrada del Toro, Parque Nacional de la nat. park Venez.
91 B4 Quedal, C. hd Chile
43 K3 Quedlinburg Ger.
64 E4 Queen Bess, Mt mt Can.
64 C4 Queen Charlotte Can.
64 C4 Queen Charlotte Islands is Can.
64 D4 Queen Charlotte Sound chan. Can.
64 D4 Queen Charlotte Str. chan. Can.
63 H1 Queen Elizabeth Islands Can.
56 D3 Queen Elizabeth National Park nat. park Uganda
92 C5 Queen Mary Land reg. Ant.
62 H3 Queen Maud Gulf b. Can.
Queen Maud Land reg. see Dronning Maud Land
92 B4 Queen Maud Mts mts Ant.
6 E4 Queensland div. Austr.
6 E6 Queenstown Austr.
9 B6 Queenstown N.Z.
59 G5 Queenstown S. Africa
32 □ Queenstown Sing.
81 E5 Queenstown U.S.A.
72 A2 Queets U.S.A.
91 F2 Queguay Grande r. Uru.
91 D3 Quehué Arg.
87 H4 Queimada ou Serraria, Ilha i. Brazil
57 D5 Quelimane Moz.
88 B6 Quellón Chile
Quelpart Island i. see Cheju-do
75 H4 Quemado U.S.A.
91 B4 Quemchi Chile
91 D3 Quemú-Quemú Arg.
91 E3 Quequén Grande r. Arg.
90 B3 Querência do Norte Brazil
84 B2 Querétaro Mex.
84 C2 Querétaro div. Mex.
43 K3 Querfurt Ger.
26 E3 Queshan China
64 E4 Quesnel Can.
64 E4 Quesnel r. Can.
64 E4 Quesnel L. l. Can.
68 B1 Quetico Provincial Park res. Can.
22 A3 Quetta Pak.
91 B3 Queuco Chile
91 B3 Queule Chile
82 F6 Quezaltenango Guatemala
31 A4 Quezon Phil.
31 B3 Quezon City Phil.
26 E3 Qufu China
57 B5 Quibala Angola
57 B4 Quibaxe Angola
89 A3 Quibdó Col.
44 C3 Quiberon France
57 B4 Quiçama, Parque Nacional do nat. park Angola
32 C1 Qui Châu Vietnam
75 F5 Quijotoa U.S.A.
91 D1 Quilino Arg.
44 F5 Quillan France
65 J4 Quill Lakes l. Can.
91 B2 Quillota Chile
91 E2 Quilmes Arg.
21 B4 Quilon India
6 E4 Quilpie Austr.
91 B2 Quilpué Chile
56 B4 Quimbele Angola
88 D3 Quimilí Arg.
44 B3 Quimper France
44 C3 Quimperlé France
86 D6 Quince Mil Peru
74 B2 Quincy CA U.S.A.
79 C6 Quincy FL U.S.A.
68 B6 Quincy IL U.S.A.
81 H3 Quincy MA U.S.A.
91 D2 Quines Arg.
32 D2 Qui Nhon Vietnam
75 E3 Quinn Canyon Range mts U.S.A.
45 E3 Quintanar de la Orden Spain
91 B2 Quintero Chile
45 F2 Quinto Spain
91 D2 Quinto r. Arg.
57 E5 Quionga Moz.
57 B5 Quipungo Angola
91 B3 Quirihue Chile
57 B5 Quirima Angola
8 H1 Quirindi Austr.
91 E2 Quiroga Arg.
57 D6 Quissico Moz.
57 B5 Quitapa Angola
90 B2 Quitéria r. Brazil
79 D6 Quitman GA U.S.A.
79 B5 Quitman MS U.S.A.
86 C4 Quito Ecuador
73 D6 Quitovac Mex.
75 F4 Quivero U.S.A.
87 L4 Quixadá Brazil
27 D5 Qujiang China
27 C4 Qu Jiang r. China
27 D6 Qujie China
27 B5 Qujing China
17 L7 Qulbān Layyah well Iraq
19 H2 Qullai Garmo mt Tajik.
23 H2 Qumar He r. China
23 H2 Qumarlêb China
23 H2 Qumarrabdün China
23 H2 Qumaryan China
59 H5 Qumbu S. Africa
59 G6 Qumrha S. Africa
18 B6 Qunayy well S. Arabia
65 L2 Quoich r. Can.
40 C3 Quoich, Loch l. U.K.
41 F3 Quoile r. U.K.
58 C7 Quoin Pt pt S. Africa
23 E2 Quong Muztag mt China
58 F1 Quoxo r. Botswana
17 L3 Qurābeh Iran
19 E6 Qurayat Oman
19 H2 Qŭrghonteppa Tajik.
Qurlurtuuq see Coppermine
67 G2 Qurlutu r. Can.
17 K2 Qūrū Gol pass Iran
17 M1 Qusar Azer.
55 F2 Quseir Egypt
18 B2 Qūshchī Iran
17 L2 Qūsheh D. mts Iran
18 C3 Qūtīābād Iran
26 B2 Quwu Shan mts China
26 C4 Qu Xian China
23 G3 Qüxü China
32 C1 Quynh Luu Vietnam
27 B6 Quynh Nhai Vietnam
69 J3 Quyon Can.
26 E2 Quzhou Hebei China
27 F4 Quzhou Zhejiang China
51 H7 Qvareli Georgia
Qyteti Stalin see Kuçovë

R

46 H7 Raab r. Austria
36 T4 Raahe Fin.
36 V5 Rääkkylä Fin.
42 E2 Raalte Neth.
36 T3 Raanujärvi Fin.
33 D4 Raas i. Indon.
40 B3 Raasay i. U.K.
40 B3 Raasay, Sound of chan. U.K.
56 F2 Raas Caseyr c. Somalia
33 E4 Raba Indon.
22 E2 Rabang China
48 F7 Rabat Malta
54 B1 Rabat Morocco
19 E3 Rabāt-e Kamah Iran
6 F2 Rabaul P.N.G.
64 D3 Rabbit r. Can.
20 A5 Rābigh S. Arabia
23 G5 Rabnabad Islands is Bangl.
51 D6 Râbniţa Moldova
18 E4 Rābor Iran
80 B5 Raccoon Creek r. U.S.A.
67 K4 Race, C. c. Can.
81 H3 Race Pt pt U.S.A.
16 E5 Rachaïya Lebanon
77 D7 Rachal U.S.A.
75 E3 Rachel U.S.A.
32 C3 Rach Gia Vietnam
46 J5 Racibórz Pol.
68 D4 Racine U.S.A.
69 F1 Racine Lake l. Can.
68 E2 Raco U.S.A.

47 M7 Rădăuţi Romania
78 C4 Radcliff U.S.A.
80 C6 Radford U.S.A.
22 B5 Radhanpur India
66 E3 Radisson Can.
64 F4 Radium Hot Springs Can.
49 L3 Radnevo Bulg.
47 K5 Radom Pol.
49 K3 Radomir Bulg.
55 E4 Radom National Park Sudan
47 J5 Radomsko Pol.
51 D5 Radomyshl' Ukr.
49 K4 Radoviš Macedonia
39 E6 Radstock U.K.
50 C4 Radun' Belarus
37 S9 Radviliškis Lith.
47 M5 Radyvyliv Ukr.
22 E4 Rae Bareli India
64 F2 Rae-Edzo Can.
64 F2 Rae Lakes Can.
9 E3 Raetihi N.Z.
91 E1 Rafaela Arg.
16 E6 Rafah Gaza
56 C3 Rafaï C.A.R.
20 B4 Rafḩā S. Arabia
18 E4 Rafsanjān Iran
31 C5 Ragang, Mt volc. Phil.
31 B3 Ragay Gulf b. Phil.
43 L1 Rägelin Ger.
81 J3 Ragged I. i. U.S.A.
18 B4 Raghwah S. Arabia
43 L2 Ragösen Ger.
43 L3 Raguhn Ger.
48 F6 Ragusa Sicily Italy
26 A3 Ra'gyagoinba China
6 C2 Raha Indon.
50 D4 Rahachow Belarus
Rahaeng see Tak
43 G2 Rahden Ger.
17 J5 Rahhālīyah Iraq
21 A2 Rahimatpur India
22 B3 Rahimyar Khan Pak.
18 C3 Rāhjerd Iran
91 B3 Rahue mt Chile
21 A2 Rahuri India
19 F3 Rahzanak Afgh.
21 B2 Raichur India
23 G4 Raiganj India
23 E5 Raigarh India
75 E2 Railroad Valley v. U.S.A.
67 G3 Raimbault, Lac l. Can.
8 D3 Rainbow Austr.
75 G3 Rainbow Bridge Nat. Mon. res. U.S.A.
64 F3 Rainbow Lake Can.
80 C6 Rainelle U.S.A.
72 B2 Rainier, Mt volc. U.S.A.
22 B3 Raini N. r. Pak.
66 B4 Rainy r. U.S.A.
63 J5 Rainy Lake l. Can.
65 L5 Rainy River Can.
23 E5 Raipur Madhya Pradesh India
22 C4 Raipur Rajasthan India
37 S6 Raisio Fin.
42 B4 Raismes France
21 C2 Rajahmundry India
36 V2 Raja-Jooseppi Fin.
21 B3 Rajampet India
33 D2 Rajang r. Malaysia
21 B4 Rajapalaiyam India
21 A2 Rajapur India
22 C4 Rajasthan div. India
22 C3 Rajasthan Canal canal India
23 F4 Rajauli India
23 G5 Rajbari Bangl.
22 C3 Rajgarh Rajasthan India
22 D4 Rajgarh Rajasthan India
16 F6 Rajil, W. watercourse Jordan
23 E5 Rajim India
22 B5 Rajkot India
23 F4 Rajmahal India
23 F4 Rajmahal Hills h. India
22 E5 Raj Nandgaon India
22 D3 Rajpura India
23 G4 Rajshahi Bangl.
21 B2 Rajura India
23 F3 Raka China
5 L5 Rakahanga i. Pac. Oc.
9 C5 Rakaia r. N.Z.
22 C1 Rakaposhi mt Pak.
23 F3 Raka Zangbo r. China
51 C5 Rakhiv Ukr.
22 B3 Rakhni Pak.
19 G5 Rakhshan r. Pak.
51 E5 Rakitnoye Belgorod. Obl. Rus. Fed.
28 D2 Rakitnoye Primorskiy Kray Rus. Fed.
37 U7 Rakke Estonia
37 M7 Rakkestad Norway
22 B3 Rakni r. Pak.
37 U7 Rakvere Estonia
79 E5 Raleigh U.S.A.
4 H4 Ralik Chain is Marshall Is
68 D2 Ralph U.S.A.
64 E2 Ram r. Can.
67 H2 Ramah Can.
75 H4 Ramah U.S.A.
90 D1 Ramalho, Serra do h. Brazil
16 E6 Ramallah West Bank
21 B3 Ramanagaram India
21 B4 Ramanathapuram India
94 E3 Ramapo Deep depth Pac. Oc.
21 A3 Ramas, C. c. India
59 F2 Ramatlabama S. Africa
6 E2 Rambutyo I. i. P.N.G.
21 A3 Ramdurg India
39 C7 Rame Head hd U.K.
57 E5 Ramena Madag.
50 F3 Rameshki Rus. Fed.
21 B4 Rameswaram India
22 D4 Ramganga r. India
23 G5 Ramgarh Bangl.
23 F5 Ramgarh Bihar India
22 B4 Ramgarh Rajasthan India
18 C4 Rāmhormoz Iran
16 E7 Ram, Jebel mt Jordan
16 E6 Ramla Israel
Ramlat Rabyānah des. see Rebiana Sand Sea
Ramnad see Ramanathapuram
22 D3 Ramnagar India
49 M2 Râmnicu Sărat Romania
49 L2 Râmnicu Vâlcea Romania
74 D5 Ramona U.S.A.
69 G1 Ramore Can.
57 C6 Ramotswa Botswana
22 D3 Rampur India
22 C4 Rampura India
Rampur Boalia see Rajshahi
23 F4 Rampur Hat India
23 H6 Ramree I. i. Myanmar
36 P5 Ramsele Sweden
69 F2 Ramsey Can.
38 C3 Ramsey Isle of Man
39 G5 Ramsey Eng. U.K.
39 B6 Ramsey Island i. U.K.
69 F2 Ramsey Lake l. Can.
39 J6 Ramsgate U.K.
22 D5 Ramtek India
37 T9 Ramygala Lith.
89 C4 Rana, Co h. Col.
23 G5 Ranaghat India
22 C5 Ranapur India
33 E1 Ranau Malaysia
91 B2 Rancagua Chile
23 F5 Ranchi India
91 B4 Ranco, L. de l. Chile
8 F3 Rand Austr.
41 E3 Randalstown U.K.
48 F6 Randazzo Sicily Italy
37 M8 Randers Denmark
81 H3 Randolph MA U.S.A.
81 G3 Randolph VT U.S.A.
37 N5 Randsjö Sweden
36 S4 Råneå Sweden
9 C6 Ranfurly N.Z.
32 B4 Rangae Thai.
23 H5 Rangamati Bangl.
9 D1 Rangaunu Bay b. N.Z.
81 H2 Rangeley U.S.A.
81 H2 Rangeley Lake l. U.S.A.
75 H1 Rangely U.S.A.
69 F2 Ranger Lake Can.
9 D5 Rangiora N.Z.
5 N6 Rangiroa i. Pac. Oc.
9 F3 Rangitaiki r. N.Z.
9 C5 Rangitata r. N.Z.
9 E4 Rangitikei r. N.Z.
Rangoon see Yangon
23 G4 Rangpur Bangl.
21 A3 Ranibennur India
23 F5 Raniganj India
23 E5 Ranijula Peak mt India
22 B4 Ranipur Pak.
77 C6 Rankin U.S.A.
65 L2 Rankin Inlet Can.
65 L2 Rankin Inlet in. Can.
8 F2 Rankin's Springs Austr.
37 U7 Ranna Estonia
40 D4 Rannoch, L. l. U.K.
40 D4 Rannoch Moor moorland U.K.
22 B4 Rann of Kachchh marsh India
32 A3 Ranong Thai.
32 B4 Ranot Thai.
50 G4 Ranova r. Rus. Fed.
17 M5 Rānsa Iran
37 N6 Ransby Sweden
25 F7 Ransiki Indon.
37 V5 Rantasalmi Fin.
33 A2 Rantauprapat Indon.
68 C5 Rantoul U.S.A.
47 R2 Rantsevo Rus. Fed.
36 T4 Rantsila Fin.
36 U4 Ranua Fin.
17 K3 Rānya Iraq
28 C1 Raohe China
27 E6 Raoping China
5 K7 Raoul i. N.Z.
5 N7 Rapa i. Pac. Oc.
48 C2 Rapallo Italy
22 B5 Rapar India
19 E5 Rapch watercourse Iran
91 B2 Rapel r. Chile
63 M3 Raper, C. pt Can.
41 D3 Raphoe Rep. of Ireland
80 E5 Rapidan r. U.S.A.
8 B3 Rapid Bay Austr.
76 C2 Rapid City U.S.A.
69 H2 Rapide-Deux Can.
69 H2 Rapide-Sept Can.
68 D3 Rapid River U.S.A.
37 T7 Rapla Estonia
80 E5 Rappahannock r. U.S.A.
23 E4 Rapti r. India
22 B5 Rapur India
31 C3 Rapurapu i. Phil.
81 F2 Raquette r. U.S.A.
81 F3 Raquette Lake U.S.A.
81 F3 Raquette Lake l. U.S.A.
81 F4 Raritan Bay b. U.S.A.
5 M7 Rarotonga i. Pac. Oc.
31 A4 Rasa i. Phil.
20 E5 Ra's al Ḩadd pt Oman
18 D5 Ra's al Khaymah U.A.E.
91 D4 Rasa, Pta pt Arg.
56 D2 Ras Dashen mt Eth.
37 S9 Raseiniai Lith.
16 C6 Rashîd Egypt
19 G4 Rashid Qala Afgh.
18 D3 Rashm Iran
18 C2 Rasht Iran
21 B4 Rasipuram India
19 F5 Rāsk Iran
22 C1 Raskam mts China
19 G4 Raskoh mts Pak.
55 F2 Ras Muhammad c. Egypt
63 J3 Rasmussen Basin b. Can.
88 C6 Raso, C. pt Arg.
50 D4 Rasony Belarus
23 E4 Rasra India
48 D6 Rass Jebel Tunisia
50 G4 Rasskazovo Rus. Fed.
20 D4 Ras Tannūrah S. Arabia
43 G1 Rastede Ger.
43 K1 Rastow Ger.
18 D5 Rasūl watercourse Iran
4 J3 Ratak Chain is Marshall Is
37 O5 Rätan Sweden
59 H3 Ratanda S. Africa
22 C3 Ratangarh India
23 E5 Ratanpur India
37 O5 Rätansbyn Sweden
32 A2 Rat Buri Thai.
22 D4 Rath India
41 E4 Rathangan Rep. of Ireland
41 D5 Rathdowney Rep. of Ireland
41 E5 Rathdrum Rep. of Ireland
23 H5 Rathedaung Myanmar
43 L2 Rathenow Ger.
41 E3 Rathfriland U.K.
41 C5 Rathkeale Rep. of Ireland
41 E2 Rathlin Island i. U.K.
41 C5 Rathluirc Rep. of Ireland
42 E3 Ratingen Ger.
22 C3 Ratiya India
22 C5 Ratlam India
21 A2 Ratnagiri India
21 C5 Ratnapura Sri Lanka
51 C5 Ratne Ukr.
22 B4 Rato Dero Pak.
73 F4 Raton U.S.A.
40 G3 Rattray Head hd U.K.
37 O6 Rättvik Sweden
43 J1 Ratzeburg Ger.
64 C3 Ratz, Mt mt Can.
32 B5 Raub Malaysia
91 E3 Rauch Arg.
17 L7 Raudhatain Kuwait
43 K4 Rauenstein Ger.
36 F3 Raufarhöfn Iceland
9 G2 Raukumara mt N.Z.
9 F3 Raukumara Range mts N.Z.
37 R6 Rauma Fin.
23 F5 Raurkela India
28 J2 Rausu Japan
36 V5 Rautavaara Fin.
37 V6 Rautjärvi Fin.
72 D2 Ravalli U.S.A.
17 L4 Ravānsar Iran
18 E4 Rāvar Iran
42 C3 Ravels Belgium
81 G3 Ravena U.S.A.
38 D3 Ravenglass U.K.
48 E2 Ravenna Italy
46 D7 Ravensburg Ger.
80 C5 Ravenswood U.S.A.
22 C3 Ravi r. Pak.
19 F2 Ravnina Turkm.
19 F2 Ravnina Turkm.
17 H4 Rāwah Iraq
5 K5 Rawaki i. Kiribati
22 C2 Rawalpindi Pak.
17 K3 Rawāndiz Iraq
22 C3 Rawatsar India
46 H5 Rawicz Pol.
80 D5 Rawley Springs U.S.A.
72 F3 Rawlins U.S.A.
88 C6 Rawson Arg.
23 F4 Raxaul India
21 B3 Rayachoti India
21 B3 Rayadurg India
21 C2 Rayagarha India
16 F5 Rayak Lebanon
67 J4 Ray, C. hd Can.
24 E2 Raychikhinsk Rus. Fed.
39 H6 Rayleigh U.K.
64 G5 Raymond Can.
81 H3 Raymond NH U.S.A.
72 B2 Raymond WA U.S.A.
8 H2 Raymond Terrace Austr.
77 D7 Raymondville U.S.A.
32 B2 Rayong Thai.
80 D4 Raystown Lake l. U.S.A.
18 C3 Razan Iran
17 M5 Rāzān Iran
Razdan see Hrazdan
28 B3 Razdol'noye Rus. Fed.
18 C3 Razeh Iran
49 M3 Razgrad Bulg.
49 N2 Razim, Lacul lag. Romania
49 K4 Razlog Bulg.
44 B2 Raz, Pte du pt France
39 G6 Reading U.K.
81 F4 Reading U.S.A.
68 B4 Readstown U.S.A.
59 G2 Reagile S. Africa
91 D2 Realicó Arg.
44 F5 Réalmont France
32 B3 Reäng Kesei Cambodia
84 B1 Reata Mex.
42 B6 Rebais France
55 E2 Rebiana Sand Sea des. Libya
50 D2 Reboly Rus. Fed.
28 G2 Rebun-tō i. Japan
6 C5 Recherche, Archipelago of the is Austr.
22 C3 Rechna Doab lowland Pak.
51 D4 Rechytsa Belarus
87 M5 Recife Brazil
59 F7 Recife, Cape c. S. Africa
42 F3 Recklinghausen Ger.
88 E3 Reconquista Arg.
88 C3 Recreo Arg.
65 K5 Red r. Can./U.S.A.
77 E6 Red r. U.S.A.
32 B4 Redang i. Malaysia
81 F4 Red Bank NJ U.S.A.
79 C5 Red Bank TN U.S.A.
67 J3 Red Bay Can.
74 A1 Red Bluff U.S.A.
75 F4 Red Butte summit U.S.A.
38 F3 Redcar U.K.
65 G4 Redcliff Can.
8 D3 Red Cliffs Austr.
76 D3 Red Cloud U.S.A.
64 G4 Red Deer Alta. Can.
65 G4 Red Deer r. Alta. Can.
65 J4 Red Deer r. Sask. Can.
65 J4 Red Deer L. l. Can.
81 F5 Redden U.S.A.
59 G4 Reddersburg S. Africa
72 B3 Redding U.S.A.
39 F5 Redditch U.K.
81 F3 Redfield NY U.S.A.
76 D2 Redfield SD U.S.A.
8 B2 Redhill Austr.
75 H4 Red Hill U.S.A.
77 D4 Red Hills h. U.S.A.
67 J4 Red Indian L. l. Can.
68 E5 Redkey U.S.A.
75 E4 Red L. U.S.A.
65 L4 Red L. l. Can.
65 L4 Red Lake Can.
76 E1 Red Lakes l. U.S.A.
72 E2 Red Lodge U.S.A.
72 B2 Redmond U.S.A.
76 E3 Red Oak U.S.A.
45 C3 Redondo Port.
68 C1 Red Rock Can.
81 E4 Red Rock U.S.A.
52 H3 Red Sea sea Africa/Asia
64 E4 Redstone Can.
64 D2 Redstone r. Can.
65 L4 Red Sucker L. l. Can.
64 G4 Redwater Can.
67 H3 Red Wine r. Can.
68 A3 Red Wing U.S.A.
74 A3 Redwood City U.S.A.
76 E2 Redwood Falls U.S.A.
72 B3 Redwood Nat. Park U.S.A.
74 A2 Redwood Valley U.S.A.
68 E4 Reed City U.S.A.
74 C3 Reedley U.S.A.
68 C4 Reedsburg U.S.A.
72 A3 Reedsport U.S.A.
81 E6 Reedville U.S.A.
92 B4 Reedy Gl. gl. Ant.
9 C5 Reefton N.Z.
41 D4 Ree, Lough l. Rep. of Ireland
42 E3 Rees Ger.
16 G2 Refahiye Turkey
77 D6 Refugio U.S.A.
46 F6 Regen Ger.
43 L5 Regen r. Ger.
43 L5 Regensburg Ger.
43 L5 Regenstauf Ger.
54 C2 Reggane Alg.
48 F5 Reggio di Calabria Italy
48 D2 Reggio nell'Emilia Italy
47 M7 Reghin Romania
65 J4 Regina Can.
19 G4 Registan reg. Afgh.
36 W4 Regozero Rus. Fed.
43 L4 Rehau Ger.
43 H2 Rehburg Ger.
22 D5 Rehli India
43 K1 Rehna Ger.
57 B6 Rehoboth Namibia
75 H4 Rehoboth U.S.A.
81 F5 Rehoboth Bay b. U.S.A.
81 F5 Rehoboth Beach U.S.A.
16 E6 Rehovot Israel
43 L3 Reibitz Ger.
43 L4 Reichenbach Ger.
43 F6 Reichshoffen France
79 E4 Reidsville U.S.A.
39 G6 Reigate U.K.
44 D3 Ré, Île de i. France
75 G5 Reiley Peak summit U.S.A.
44 G2 Reims France
88 B8 Reina Adelaida, Archipiélago de la is Chile
68 A4 Reinbeck U.S.A.
43 J1 Reinbek Ger.
65 J3 Reindeer r. Can.
65 K4 Reindeer I. i. Can.
65 J3 Reindeer Lake l. Can.
36 N3 Reine Norway
43 J1 Reinfeld (Holstein) Ger.
9 D1 Reinga, Cape c. N.Z.
45 D1 Reinosa Spain
42 E5 Reinsfeld Ger.
36 B4 Reiphólsfjöll mt Iceland
36 R2 Reisaelva r. Norway
36 S2 Reisa Nasjonalpark nat. park Norway
36 T5 Reisjärvi Fin.
59 H3 Reitz S. Africa
58 F3 Reivilo S. Africa
89 D3 Rejunya Venez.
42 F3 Reken Ger.
65 H2 Reliance Can.
54 C1 Relizane Alg.
43 H1 Rellingen Ger.
42 F4 Remagen Ger.
8 B2 Remarkable, Mt Austr.
19 E5 Remeshk Iran
58 B1 Remhoogte Pass Namibia
46 C6 Remiremont France
22 D2 Remo Gl. gl. India
51 G6 Remontnoye Rus. Fed.
42 F3 Remscheid Ger.
68 E4 Remus U.S.A.
37 M6 Rena Norway
21 B2 Renapur India
78 B4 Rend L. l. U.S.A.
7 F2 Rendova i. Solomon Is
46 D3 Rendsburg Ger.
69 J3 Renfrew Can.
40 D5 Renfrew U.K.
91 B2 Rengo Chile
26 C3 Ren He r. China
26 E4 Renheji China
27 D5 Renhua China
27 C5 Renhuai China
51 D6 Reni Ukr.
Renland reg. see Tuttut Nunaat
8 C3 Renmark Austr.
7 G3 Rennell i. Solomon Is
43 G4 Rennerod Ger.
44 D2 Rennes France
92 B5 Rennick Gl. gl. Ant.
65 H2 Rennie Lake l. Can.
74 C2 Reno U.S.A.
48 D2 Reno r. Italy
80 E4 Renovo U.S.A.
26 E2 Renqiu China
27 B4 Renshou China
68 D5 Rensselaer IN U.S.A.
81 G3 Rensselaer NY U.S.A.
42 D2 Renswoude Neth.
72 B2 Renton U.S.A.
23 E4 Renukut India
9 D4 Renwick N.Z.
54 B3 Réo Burkina
25 E7 Reo Indon.
19 F2 Repetek Turkm.
72 C1 Republic U.S.A.
76 D3 Republican r. U.S.A.
63 K3 Repulse Bay Can.
86 D5 Requena Peru
45 F3 Requena Spain
16 F1 Reşadiye Turkey
17 J2 Reşadiye Turkey
90 B4 Reserva Brazil
18 C2 Reshteh-ye Alborz mts Iran
18 E2 Reshteh-ye Esfarayen mts Iran
88 E3 Resistencia Arg.
49 J2 Reşiţa Romania
63 J2 Resolute Can.
63 M3 Resolution Island i. N.W.T. Can.
9 A6 Resolution Island i. N.Z.
84 E4 Retalhuleu Guatemala
32 □ Retan Laut, P. i. Sing.
39 G4 Retford U.K.
44 G2 Rethel France
43 H2 Rethem (Aller) Ger.
49 L7 Rethymno Greece
28 C2 Rettikhovka Rus. Fed.
43 L2 Reuden Ger.
53 K8 Réunion terr. Ind. Ocean
45 G2 Reus Spain
43 L1 Reuterstadt Stavenhagen Ger.
46 D6 Reutlingen Ger.
74 D3 Reveille Peak summit U.S.A.
44 F5 Revel France
64 F4 Revelstoke Can.
64 C3 Revillagigedo I. i. U.S.A.
82 B5 Revillagigedo, Islas is Mex.
42 C5 Revin France
16 E6 Revivim Israel
22 E4 Rewa India
22 D3 Rewari India
72 E3 Rexburg U.S.A.
67 H4 Rexton Can.
74 C4 Reyes Peak summit U.S.A.
74 A2 Reyes, Point pt U.S.A.
16 F3 Reyhanlı Turkey
36 C4 Reykir Iceland
96 G2 Reykjanes Ridge sea feature Atl. Ocean
36 B5 Reykjanestá pt Iceland
36 C4 Reykjavík Iceland
84 C1 Reynosa Mex.
37 U8 Rēzekne Latvia
17 M3 Rezvanshahr Iran
16 F5 Rharaz, W. watercourse Syria
39 D5 Rhayader U.K.
43 G3 Rheda-Wiedenbrück Ger.
42 E3 Rhede Ger.
Rhein r. Ger./Switz. see Rhine
42 F2 Rheine Ger.
42 E4 Rheinisches Schiefergebirge h. Ger.
42 F5 Rheinland-Pfalz div. Ger.
43 L1 Rheinsberg Ger.
43 G6 Rheinstetten Ger.
Rhin r. France see Rhine
46 C5 Rhine r. Europe
81 G4 Rhinebeck U.S.A.
68 C3 Rhinelander U.S.A.
43 L2 Rhinkanal canal Ger.
43 L2 Rhinluch marsh Ger.
43 L2 Rhinow Ger.
48 C2 Rho Italy
81 H4 Rhode Island div. U.S.A.
49 N6 Rhodes Greece
49 N6 Rhodes i. Greece
72 D2 Rhodes Pk summit U.S.A.
39 D6 Rhondda U.K.
44 G4 Rhône r. France/Switz.
39 D4 Rhyl U.K.
90 E2 Riachão Brazil
90 D1 Riacho de Santana Brazil
91 D4 Riachos, Is de los i. Arg.
90 C1 Rialma Brazil
90 C1 Rianópolis Brazil
22 C2 Riasi Jammu and Kashmir
33 B2 Riau, Kepulauan is Indon.
45 C1 Ribadeo Spain
45 D1 Ribadesella Spain
90 B3 Ribas do Rio Pardo Brazil
57 D5 Ribáuè Moz.
38 E4 Ribble r. U.K.
37 L9 Ribe Denmark
42 A5 Ribécourt-Dreslincourt France
90 C4 Ribeira r. Brazil
90 C3 Ribeirão Preto Brazil
42 B5 Ribemont France
44 E4 Ribérac France
86 E6 Riberalta Bol.
46 F3 Ribnitz-Damgarten Ger.
46 G6 Říčany Czech Rep.
75 E4 Rice U.S.A.
68 B3 Rice Lake U.S.A.
69 F2 Rice Lake l. Can.
68 A4 Riceville IA U.S.A.
80 D4 Riceville PA U.S.A.
59 K4 Richards Bay S. Africa
77 D5 Richardson U.S.A.
65 G3 Richardson r. Can.
81 H2 Richardson Lakes l. U.S.A.
62 E3 Richardson Mts N.W.T. Can.
9 B6 Richardson Mts mts N.Z.
75 F2 Richfield U.S.A.
81 F3 Richfield Springs U.S.A.
81 E3 Richford NY U.S.A.
81 G2 Richford VT U.S.A.
70 C2 Richland WA U.S.A.
68 B5 Richland U.S.A.
68 B4 Richland Center U.S.A.
80 C6 Richlands U.S.A.
8 H2 Richmond N.S.W. Austr.
6 E4 Richmond Austr.
69 K3 Richmond Can.
9 D4 Richmond N.Z.
59 J4 Richmond Kwazulu-Natal S. Africa
58 E5 Richmond Northern Cape S. Africa
38 F3 Richmond U.K.
68 E6 Richmond IN U.S.A.
80 A6 Richmond KY U.S.A.
81 J2 Richmond ME U.S.A.
69 F4 Richmond MI U.S.A.
80 E6 Richmond VA U.S.A.
81 G2 Richmond VT U.S.A.
69 H3 Richmond Hill Can.
9 D4 Richmond, Mt mt N.Z.
58 B4 Richtersveld National Park S. Africa
80 B4 Richwood OH U.S.A.
80 C5 Richwood WV U.S.A.
69 K3 Rideau r. Can.
69 J3 Rideau Lakes l. Can.
74 D4 Ridgecrest U.S.A.
80 D4 Ridgway U.S.A.
65 J4 Riding Mountain Nat. Park Can.
46 D6 Riedlingen Ger.
42 D4 Riemst Belgium
43 M3 Riesa Ger.
88 B8 Riesco, Isla i. Chile
58 D5 Riet r. S. Africa
37 R9 Rietavas Lith.
58 E6 Rietbron S. Africa
58 D3 Rietfontein S. Africa
48 E3 Rieti Italy
73 F4 Rifle U.S.A.
36 E3 Rifstangi pt Iceland
23 H3 Riga India
37 T8 Rīga Latvia
37 S8 Riga, Gulf of g. Estonia/Latvia
19 E4 Rīgān Iran
Rigas Jūras Līcis g. see Riga, Gulf of
81 F2 Rigaud Can.
72 C2 Riggins U.S.A.
67 J3 Rigolet Can.
40 E5 Rigside U.K.
18 E3 Rīgū Iran
23 E4 Rihand r. India
23 E4 Rihand Dam dam India
Riia Laht g. see Riga, Gulf of
37 T6 Riihimäki Fin.
92 D4 Riiser-Larsenhalvøya pen. Ant.
92 C3 Riiser-Larsenisen ice feature Ant.
92 D3 Riiser-Larsen Sea sea Ant.
73 D5 Riito Mex.
48 F2 Rijeka Croatia
Rijn r. Neth. see Rhine
28 G5 Rikuzen-takata Japan
49 K3 Rila mts Bulg.
72 C3 Riley U.S.A.
44 G4 Rillieux-la-Pape France
47 K6 Rimavská Sobota Slovakia
64 G4 Rimbey Can.
48 E2 Rimini Italy
67 G4 Rimouski Can.
43 H5 Rimpar Ger.
40 D2 Rimsdale, Loch l. U.K.
23 G3 Rinbung China
84 B2 Rincón de Romos Mex.
22 E4 Rind r. India
36 L5 Rindal Norway
22 C4 Ringas India
23 G2 Ring Co salt l. China
42 E2 Ringe Ger.
37 M6 Ringebu Norway
37 L8 Ringkøbing Denmark
41 E2 Ringsend U.K.
37 M9 Ringsted Denmark
36 Q2 Ringvassøy i. Norway
39 F7 Ringwood U.K.
91 B3 Riñihue Chile
91 B3 Riñihue, L. l. Chile
33 E4 Rinjani, G. volc. Indon.
43 H2 Rinteln Ger.
68 C4 Rio U.S.A.
90 A2 Rio Alegre Brazil
86 C4 Riobamba Ecuador
75 H2 Rio Blanco U.S.A.
86 E6 Rio Branco Brazil
90 C4 Rio Branco do Sul Brazil
89 E4 Rio Branco, Parque Nacional do nat. park Brazil
90 A3 Rio Brilhante Brazil
91 B4 Río Bueno Chile
89 E2 Río Caribe Venez.
91 D1 Río Ceballos Arg.
90 C3 Rio Claro Brazil
89 E2 Rio Claro Trinidad and Tobago
91 D3 Río Colorado Arg.
91 D2 Río Cuarto Arg.
90 D3 Rio de Janeiro Brazil
90 D3 Rio de Janeiro div. Brazil
88 G3 Rio do Sul Brazil
88 C8 Río Gallegos Arg.
88 C8 Río Grande Arg.
91 G2 Rio Grande Brazil
84 B2 Río Grande Mex.
86 F7 Río Grande r. Bol.
82 C2 Rio Grande r. Mex./U.S.A.
77 D7 Rio Grande City U.S.A.
96 G7 Rio Grande Rise sea feature Atl. Ocean
89 B2 Ríohacha Col.
86 C5 Rioja Peru
87 L5 Rio Largo Brazil
44 F4 Riom France
86 E7 Río Mulatos Bol.
90 C4 Rio Negro Brazil
91 C4 Río Negro div. Arg.
91 F2 Río Negro, Embalse del resr Uru.
51 G7 Rioni r. Georgia
91 G1 Rio Pardo Brazil
90 D1 Rio Pardo de Minas Brazil
91 D1 Río Primero Arg.
73 F5 Rio Rancho U.S.A.
75 G6 Rio Rico U.S.A.
91 D1 Río Segundo Arg.
89 A3 Ríosucio Col.
91 D2 Río Tercero Arg.
86 C4 Río Tigre Ecuador
31 A4 Rio Tuba Phil.
90 B2 Rio Verde Brazil
84 C2 Río Verde Mex.
90 A2 Rio Verde de Mato Grosso Brazil
74 B2 Rio Vista U.S.A.
90 A2 Riozinho r. Brazil
47 P5 Ripky Ukr.
38 F3 Ripley Eng. U.K.
39 F4 Ripley Eng. U.K.
80 B5 Ripley OH U.S.A.
79 B5 Ripley TN U.S.A.
80 C5 Ripley WV U.S.A.
45 H1 Ripoll Spain
38 F3 Ripon U.K.
74 B3 Ripon CA U.S.A.
68 C4 Ripon WI U.S.A.
39 D6 Risca U.K.
18 C4 Rīshahr Iran
28 G2 Rishiri-tō i. Japan
16 E6 Rishon Le Ẕiyyon Israel
19 F5 Rish Pish Iran
37 L7 Risør Norway
36 L5 Rissa Norway
37 U6 Ristiina Fin.
36 V4 Ristijärvi Fin.
36 W2 Ristikent Rus. Fed.
58 F4 Ritchie S. Africa
36 P3 Ritsem Sweden
43 G1 Ritterhude Ger.
73 C4 Ritter, Mt mt U.S.A.
45 E2 Rituerto r. Spain
72 C2 Ritzville U.S.A.
91 C2 Rivadavia Mendoza Arg.
91 D2 Rivadavia Pampas Arg.
88 D2 Rivadavia Salta Arg.
91 B1 Rivadavia Chile
48 D2 Riva del Garda Italy
83 G6 Rivas Nic.
19 E3 Rīvash Iran
91 D3 Rivera Arg.
91 F1 Rivera Uru.
54 B4 River Cess Liberia
81 G4 Riverhead U.S.A.
8 E3 Riverina reg. Austr.
58 D7 Riversdale S. Africa
59 H5 Riverside S. Africa
74 D5 Riverside U.S.A.
8 B3 Riverton Austr.
65 K4 Riverton Can.
9 B7 Riverton N.Z.
72 E3 Riverton U.S.A.
67 H4 Riverview Can.
44 F5 Rivesaltes France
79 D7 Riviera Beach U.S.A.
81 J1 Rivière Bleue Can.
67 G4 Rivière-du-Loup Can.
51 C5 Rivne Ukr.
9 D4 Riwaka N.Z.
20 C5 Riyadh S. Arabia
26 A2 Riyue Shankou pass China
18 D3 Riza well Iran
17 H1 Rize Turkey
26 F3 Rizhao China
16 E4 Rizokarpason Cyprus
18 E4 Rīzū'īyeh Iran
37 L7 Rjukan Norway
37 K7 Rjuvbrokkene mt Norway
54 A3 Rkîz Maur.
22 D3 Rnyar r. India
37 M6 Roa Norway
39 G5 Roade U.K.
36 M4 Roan Norway
75 H2 Roan Cliffs cliff U.S.A.
44 G3 Roanne France
79 C5 Roanoke AL U.S.A.
68 C5 Roanoke IL U.S.A.
80 D6 Roanoke VA U.S.A.
78 E4 Roanoke r. VA U.S.A.
79 E4 Roanoke Rapids U.S.A.
75 H2 Roan Plateau plat. U.S.A.
41 B6 Roaringwater Bay b. Rep. of Ireland
36 R5 Röbäck Sweden
18 E4 Robāţ Iran
19 F4 Robat r. Afgh.
18 E3 Robāţ-e Khān Iran
19 F4 Robat Thana Pak.
6 E6 Robbins I. i. Austr.
8 B4 Robe Austr.
41 B4 Robe r. Rep. of Ireland
43 L1 Röbel Ger.
8 C1 Robe, Mt h. Austr.
77 C6 Robert Lee U.S.A.
72 D3 Roberts U.S.A.
74 D2 Roberts Creek Mt mt U.S.A.
36 R4 Robertsfors Sweden
23 E4 Robertsganj India
77 E5 Robert S. Kerr Res. resr U.S.A.
58 C6 Robertson S. Africa
92 B2 Robertson I. i. Ant.
54 A4 Robertsport Liberia
8 B2 Robertstown Austr.
67 F4 Roberval Can.
63 M1 Robeson Channel chan. Can./Greenland
38 G3 Robin Hood's Bay U.K.
27 □ Robin's Nest h. H.K. China
78 C4 Robinson U.S.A.
95 O8 Robinson Crusoe i. Pac. Oc.
6 B4 Robinson Ranges h. Austr.
8 D3 Robinvale Austr.
75 G5 Robles Junction U.S.A.
75 G5 Robles Pass U.S.A.
65 J4 Roblin Can.
64 F4 Robson, Mt mt Can.
77 D7 Robstown U.S.A.
84 D3 Roca Partida, Pta hd Mex.
48 E6 Rocca Busambra mt Sicily Italy
91 F2 Rocha Uru.
38 E4 Rochdale U.K.
90 A2 Rochedo Brazil
42 D4 Rochefort Belgium
44 D4 Rochefort France
66 F2 Rochefort, Lac l. Can.
50 G2 Rochegda Rus. Fed.
68 C5 Rochelle U.S.A.
8 E4 Rochester Austr.
39 H6 Rochester U.K.
68 D5 Rochester IN U.S.A.
68 A3 Rochester MN U.S.A.
81 H3 Rochester NH U.S.A.
80 E3 Rochester NY U.S.A.
39 H6 Rochford U.K.
43 L3 Rochlitz Ger.
44 C2 Roc'h Trévezel h. France
64 D2 Rock r. Can.
68 B5 Rock r. U.S.A.
96 H2 Rockall Bank sea feature Atl. Ocean
92 B4 Rockefeller Plateau plat. Ant.
68 C4 Rockford U.S.A.
65 H5 Rockglen Can.
6 F4 Rockhampton Austr.
68 C1 Rock Harbor U.S.A.
79 D5 Rock Hill U.S.A.
6 B5 Rockingham Austr.
79 E5 Rockingham U.S.A.
81 G2 Rock Island Can.
68 B5 Rock Island U.S.A.
76 D1 Rocklake U.S.A.
81 F2 Rockland Can.
81 H3 Rockland MA U.S.A.
81 J2 Rockland ME U.S.A.
68 C2 Rockland MI U.S.A.
8 D4 Rocklands Reservoir Austr.
75 H3 Rock Point U.S.A.
81 H3 Rockport U.S.A.
76 D3 Rock Rapids U.S.A.
72 F2 Rock Springs MT U.S.A.
72 E3 Rock Springs WY U.S.A.
77 C6 Rocksprings U.S.A.
8 F3 Rock, The Austr.
80 D3 Rockton Can.
68 D6 Rockville IN U.S.A.
80 E5 Rockville MD U.S.A.
81 J2 Rockwood U.S.A.
73 G4 Rocky Ford U.S.A.
80 B5 Rocky Fork Lake l. U.S.A.
69 F2 Rocky Island Lake l. Can.
79 E5 Rocky Mount NC U.S.A.
80 D6 Rocky Mount VA U.S.A.
64 G4 Rocky Mountain House Can.
72 F3 Rocky Mountain Nat. Park U.S.A.
60 E4 Rocky Mountains Can./U.S.A.
64 F4 Rocky Mountains Forest Reserve res. Can.
42 B5 Rocourt-St-Martin France
42 C5 Rocroi France
37 L6 Rodberg Norway
37 M9 Rødbyhavn Denmark
67 J3 Roddickton Can.
40 B3 Rodel U.K.
42 E1 Roden Neth.
43 K4 Rödental Ger.
91 C1 Rodeo Arg.
84 A1 Rodeo Mex.
75 H6 Rodeo U.S.A.
44 F4 Rodez France
43 L5 Roding Ger.
19 G5 Rodkhan Pak.
50 G3 Rodniki Rus. Fed.
49 L4 Rodopi Planina mts Bulg./Greece
Rodos see Rhodes
Rodos i. see Rhodes
93 J5 Rodrigues i. Ind. Ocean
93 J5 Rodrigues Fracture sea feature Ind. Ocean
6 B4 Roebourne Austr.
6 C3 Roebuck Bay b. Austr.
59 H2 Roedtan S. Africa
42 D3 Roermond Neth.
42 B4 Roeselare Belgium
63 K3 Roes Welcome Sound chan. Can.
86 E6 Rogaguado, Lago l. Bol.
43 K2 Rogätz Ger.
77 E4 Rogers U.S.A.
69 F3 Rogers City U.S.A.
74 D4 Rogers Lake l. U.S.A.
72 D3 Rogerson U.S.A.
80 B6 Rogersville U.S.A.
66 E3 Roggan r. Can.
58 D6 Roggeveld plat. S. Africa
58 D6 Roggeveldberge esc. S. Africa
36 O3 Rognan Norway
72 A3 Rogue r. U.S.A.
74 A2 Rohnert Park U.S.A.
46 F6 Rohrbach in Oberösterreich Austria
42 F5 Rohrbach-lès-Bitche France
22 B4 Rohri Pak.
22 D3 Rohtak India
5 N6 Roi Georges, Îles du is Pac. Oc.
42 B5 Roisel France
37 S8 Roja Latvia
91 E2 Rojas Arg.
22 B3 Rojhan Pak.
84 C2 Rojo, C. c. Mex.
33 B2 Rokan r. Indon.
37 T9 Rokiškis Lith.
36 R4 Roknäs Sweden
51 C5 Rokytne Ukr.
23 G2 Rola Co salt l. China
90 B3 Rolândia Brazil
76 F4 Rolla U.S.A.
37 L6 Rollag Norway
9 D5 Rolleston N.Z.
69 H2 Rollet Can.
79 F7 Rolleville Bahamas
69 J2 Rolphton Can.
6 E4 Roma Austr.
Roma see Rome
59 G4 Roma Lesotho
37 Q8 Roma Sweden
25 E7 Roma i. Indon.
79 E5 Romain, Cape c. U.S.A.
67 H3 Romaine r. Can.
47 N7 Roman Romania

96 H6 Romanche Gap sea feature Atl. Ocean
16 D6 Românî Egypt
35 H4 Romania country Europe
51 G5 Romanovka Rus. Fed.
24 D1 Romanovka Rus. Fed.
44 G4 Romans-sur-Isère France
62 B3 Romanzof, Cape c. U.S.A.
44 H2 Rombas France
31 B3 Romblon Phil.
31 B3 Romblon i. Phil.
48 E4 Rome Italy
79 C5 Rome GA U.S.A.
81 J2 Rome ME U.S.A.
81 F3 Rome NY U.S.A.
69 F4 Romeo U.S.A.
39 H6 Romford U.K.
44 F2 Romilly-sur-Seine France
19 G2 Romitan Uzbek.
80 D5 Romney U.S.A.
39 H6 Romney Marsh reg. U.K.
51 E5 Romny Ukr.
37 L9 Rømø i. Denmark
44 E3 Romorantin-Lanthenay France
32 B5 Rompin r. Malaysia
39 F7 Romsey U.K.
21 A3 Ron India
32 C1 Ron Vietnam
40 C3 Rona i. Scot. U.K.
40 C1 Rona i. Scot. U.K.
40 □ Ronas Hill h. U.K.
7 F2 Roncador Reef rf Solomon Is
87 H6 Roncador, Serra do h. Brazil
45 D4 Ronda Spain
37 L6 Rondane Nasjonalpark nat. park Norway
89 C3 Rondón Col.
86 F6 Rondônia Brazil
90 A2 Rondonópolis Brazil
15 F3 Rondu Jammu and Kashmir
27 C5 Rong'an China
27 B4 Rongchang China
30 B5 Rongcheng China
30 B5 Rongcheng Wan b. China
23 G3 Rong Chu r. China
65 H3 Ronge, Lac la l. Can.
94 G5 Rongelap i. Pac. Oc.
27 C5 Rongjiang China
27 C6 Rong Jiang r. China
23 H5 Rongklang Range mts Myanmar
9 E4 Rongotea N.Z.
27 C5 Rongshui China
27 D6 Rong Xian Guangxi China
27 B4 Rong Xian Sichuan China
37 O9 Rønne Denmark
37 O8 Ronneby Sweden
92 B3 Ronne Entrance str. Ant.
92 B3 Ronne Ice Shelf ice feature Ant.
43 H2 Ronnenberg Ger.
42 B4 Ronse Belgium
42 E1 Roodeschool Neth.
42 D1 Roordahuizum Neth.
22 D3 Roorkee India
42 C3 Roosendaal Neth.
75 G5 Roosevelt AZ U.S.A.
75 G1 Roosevelt UT U.S.A.
75 G5 Roosevelt Dam dam U.S.A.
92 A4 Roosevelt I. i. Ant.
64 D3 Roosevelt, Mt mt Can.
64 E2 Root r. Can.
68 B4 Root r. U.S.A.
50 K2 Ropcha Rus. Fed.
44 D4 Roquefort France
89 E4 Roraima div. Brazil
86 F2 Roraima, Mt mt Guyana
36 M5 Røros Norway
36 M4 Rørvik Norway
47 P6 Ros' r. Ukr.
86 □ Rosa, C. pt Galapagos Is Ecuador
74 C4 Rosamond U.S.A.
74 C4 Rosamond Lake l. U.S.A.
91 E2 Rosario Arg.
82 A2 Rosario Baja California Mex.
77 C7 Rosario Coahuila Mex.
84 A2 Rosario Mex.
31 B2 Rosario Phil.
31 B3 Rosario Phil.
89 B2 Rosario Venez.
91 E2 Rosario del Tala Arg.
91 F1 Rosário do Sul Brazil
90 A1 Rosário Oeste Brazil
48 F5 Rosarno Italy
81 F4 Roscoe U.S.A.
44 C2 Roscoff France
41 C4 Roscommon Rep. of Ireland
68 E3 Roscommon U.S.A.
41 D5 Roscrea Rep. of Ireland
83 M5 Roseau Dominica
65 K5 Roseau U.S.A.
67 J4 Rose Blanche Can.
72 B3 Roseburg U.S.A.
69 E3 Rose City U.S.A.
38 G3 Rosedale Abbey U.K.
55 F3 Roseires Reservoir Sudan
74 C2 Rose, Mt mt U.S.A.
77 E6 Rosenberg U.S.A.
37 K7 Rosendal Norway
59 G4 Rosendal S. Africa
46 F7 Rosenheim Ger.
64 C4 Rose Pt pt Can.
79 F7 Roses Bahamas
48 F3 Roseto degli Abruzzi Italy
65 H4 Rosetown Can.
Rosetta see Rashîd
65 J4 Rose Valley Can.
74 B2 Roseville CA U.S.A.
68 B5 Roseville IL U.S.A.
50 D2 Roshchino Leningrad. Rus. Fed.
28 D2 Roshchino Primorskiy Kray Rus. Fed.
19 E3 Roshkhvār Iran
58 B3 Rosh Pinah Namibia
19 H2 Roshtqal'a Tajik.
48 D3 Rosignano Marittimo Italy
49 L2 Roşiori de Vede Romania
37 N9 Roskilde Denmark
50 E4 Roslavl' Rus. Fed.
36 X2 Roslyakovo Rus. Fed.
9 C5 Ross N.Z.
64 C2 Ross r. Can.
48 G5 Rossano Italy
41 C3 Rossan Point pt Rep. of Ireland
77 F5 Ross Barnett Res. l. U.S.A.
67 G3 Ross Bay Junction Can.
41 B6 Ross Carbery Rep. of Ireland
92 A5 Ross Dependency reg. Ant.
7 F3 Rossel Island i. P.N.G.
92 B4 Ross Ice Shelf ice feature Ant.
67 H5 Rossignol, L. l. Can.
92 B5 Ross Island i. Ant.
41 E5 Rosslare Rep. of Ireland
39 A5 Rosslare Harbour Rep. of Ireland
43 L3 Roßlau Ger.
69 J3 Rossmore Can.
9 E4 Ross, Mt mt N.Z.
54 A3 Rosso Maur.
48 C3 Rosso, Capo pt Corsica France
39 E6 Ross-on-Wye U.K.
51 F5 Rossosh' Rus. Fed.
68 D1 Rossport Can.
64 C2 Ross River Can.
92 A5 Ross Sea sea Ant.
43 J5 Roßtal Ger.
36 O4 Røssvatnet l. Norway
68 D5 Rossville U.S.A.
43 M3 Roßwein Ger.
64 D3 Rosswood Can.
17 K3 Rōst Iraq
19 H2 Rostāq Afgh.
18 D5 Rostāq Iran
65 H4 Rosthern Can.
46 F3 Rostock Ger.
50 F3 Rostov Rus. Fed.
51 F6 Rostov-na-Donu Rus. Fed.
51 G6 Rostovskaya Oblast' div. Rus. Fed.
36 R4 Rosvik Sweden
79 C5 Roswell GA U.S.A.
73 F5 Roswell NM U.S.A.
25 G5 Rota i. N. Mariana Is
43 J5 Rot am See Ger.
25 E8 Rote i. Indon.
43 H1 Rotenburg (Wümme) Ger.
43 K4 Roter Main r. Ger.
43 K5 Roth Ger.
43 G4 Rothaargebirge reg. Ger.
38 F2 Rothbury U.K.
38 F2 Rothbury Forest forest U.K.
43 J5 Rothenburg ob der Tauber Ger.
39 G7 Rother r. U.K.
92 B2 Rothera U.K. Base Ant.
9 D5 Rotherham N.Z.
39 F4 Rotherham U.K.
40 E5 Rothes U.K.
40 C5 Rothesay U.K.
68 C3 Rothschild U.S.A.
92 B2 Rothschild I. i. Ant.
39 G5 Rothwell U.K.
Roti i. see Rote
8 E2 Roto Austr.
9 C5 Rotomanu N.Z.
48 C3 Rotondo, Monte mt Corsica France
9 D4 Rotoroa, L. l. N.Z.
9 F3 Rotorua N.Z.
9 F3 Rotorua, L. l. N.Z.
46 F6 Rott r. Ger.
43 K5 Röttenbach Ger.
43 J5 Rottendorf Ger.
46 G7 Rottenmann Austria
42 C3 Rotterdam Neth.
43 J3 Rottleberode Ger.
42 E1 Rottumeroog i. Neth.
42 E1 Rottumerplaat i. Neth.
46 D6 Rottweil Ger.
7 H3 Rotuma i. Fiji
36 O5 Rötviken Sweden
43 L5 Rötz Ger.
44 F1 Roubaix France
44 E2 Rouen France
9 B6 Rough Ridge ridge N.Z.
Roulers see Roeselare
67 F3 Roundeyed, Lac l. Can.
38 F3 Round Hill h. U.K.
74 D2 Round Mountain U.S.A.
75 H3 Round Rock U.S.A.
72 E2 Roundup U.S.A.
40 E1 Rousay i. U.K.
81 G2 Rouses Point U.S.A.
44 F5 Roussillon reg. France
Routh Bank sand bank see Seahorse Bank
59 G5 Rouxville S. Africa
69 H1 Rouyn Can.
36 T3 Rovaniemi Fin.
51 F5 Roven'ki Rus. Fed.
48 D2 Rovereto Italy
32 C2 Rôviĕng Tbong Cambodia
48 D2 Rovigo Italy
48 E2 Rovinj Croatia
51 H5 Rovnoye Rus. Fed.
18 C3 Row'ān Iran
31 B4 Roxas Phil.
31 B4 Roxas Phil.
31 A4 Roxas Phil.
31 B3 Roxas Phil.
31 B2 Roxas Phil.
79 E4 Roxboro U.S.A.
9 B6 Roxburgh N.Z.
73 F4 Roy U.S.A.
41 E4 Royal Canal canal Rep. of Ireland
68 C1 Royale, Isle i. U.S.A.
59 H4 Royal Natal National Park S. Africa
69 F4 Royal Oak U.S.A.
44 D4 Royan France
42 A5 Roye France
66 E2 Roy, Lac le l. Can.
39 G5 Royston U.K.
51 D6 Rozdil'na Ukr.
51 E6 Rozdol'ne Ukr.
51 F6 Rozivka Ukr.
18 C3 Rozveh Iran
51 G4 Rtishchevo Rus. Fed.
48 E2 Rt Kamenjak pt Croatia
39 D5 Ruabon U.K.
57 B5 Ruacana Namibia
56 D4 Ruaha National Park Tanz.
9 E3 Ruapehu, Mt volc. N.Z.
9 B7 Ruapuke I. i. N.Z.
9 F3 Ruarine Range mts N.Z.
9 G2 Ruatoria N.Z.
50 D4 Ruba Belarus
20 C6 Rub' al Khālī des. S. Arabia
28 H3 Rubeshibe Japan
40 C2 Rubha Coigeach pt U.K.
40 B3 Rubha Hunish pt U.K.
40 C3 Rubha Reidh pt U.K.
74 B2 Rubicon r. U.S.A.
51 F5 Rubizhne Ukr.
12 K4 Rubtsovsk Rus. Fed.
62 C3 Ruby U.S.A.
75 E1 Ruby Lake l. U.S.A.
75 E1 Ruby Mountains U.S.A.
27 D5 Rucheng China
80 D5 Ruckersville U.S.A.
18 E5 Rudan Iran
23 E4 Rudauli India
19 F4 Rudbar Afgh.
17 M3 Rūdbār Iran
18 E2 Rūd-e Kāl-Shūr r. Iran
19 E4 Rūd-i-Shur watercourse Iran
37 M9 Rudkøbing Denmark
24 F2 Rudnaya Pristan' Rus. Fed.
50 K3 Rudnichnyy Rus. Fed.
50 D4 Rudnya Rus. Fed.
14 E1 Rudnyy Kazak.
28 D2 Rudnyy Rus. Fed.
12 G1 Rudolfa, O. i. Rus. Fed.
43 K4 Rudolstadt Ger.
26 F3 Rudong China
18 C2 Rūdsar Iran
68 E2 Rudyard U.S.A.
57 D4 Rufiji r. Tanz.
91 D2 Rufino Arg.
54 A3 Rufisque Senegal
57 C5 Rufunsa Zambia
26 F3 Rugao China
39 F5 Rugby U.K.
76 C1 Rugby U.S.A.
39 F5 Rugeley U.K.
46 F3 Rügen i. Ger.
80 B4 Ruggles U.S.A.
43 J5 Rügland Ger.
18 B5 Ruḩayyat al Ḩamr'ā' waterhole S. Arabia
56 C4 Ruhengeri Rwanda
37 S8 Ruhnu i. Estonia
42 E4 Ruhr r. Ger.
27 F5 Rui'an China
73 F5 Ruidoso U.S.A.
27 E5 Ruijin China
65 N2 Ruin Point pt Can.
57 D4 Ruipa Tanz.
84 A2 Ruiz Mex.
89 B3 Ruiz, Nevado del volc. Col.
37 T8 Rūjiena Latvia
18 C5 Rukbah well S. Arabia
23 E3 Rukumkot Nepal
56 D4 Rukwa, Lake l. Tanz.
18 E5 Rūl Ḑadnah U.A.E.
19 E3 Rūm Iran
40 B4 Rum i. Scot. U.K.
49 H2 Ruma Yugo.
18 B5 Rumāh S. Arabia
55 E4 Rumbek Sudan
79 F7 Rum Cay i. Bahamas
81 H2 Rumford U.S.A.
44 G4 Rumilly France
6 D3 Rum Jungle Austr.
28 G3 Rumoi Japan
26 E3 Runan China
9 C5 Runanga N.Z.
9 F2 Runaway, Cape c. N.Z.
39 E4 Runcorn U.K.
57 B5 Rundu Namibia
36 Q5 Rundvik Sweden
26 E3 Runheji China
26 A3 Ru'nying China
37 V6 Ruokolahti Fin.
24 A3 Ruoqiang China
23 H4 Rupa India
91 B4 Rupanco, L. l. Chile
8 D4 Rupanyup Austr.
33 B2 Rupat i. Indon.
72 D3 Rupert U.S.A.
66 E3 Rupert r. Can.
66 E3 Rupert Bay b. Can.
92 A4 Ruppert Coast coastal area Ant.
57 D5 Rusape Zimbabwe
49 L3 Ruse Bulg.
30 A5 Rushan China
39 G5 Rushden U.K.
68 B4 Rushford U.S.A.
68 C4 Rush Lake l. U.S.A.
23 H3 Rushon India
19 H2 Rushon Tajik.
68 B5 Rushville IL U.S.A.
76 C3 Rushville NE U.S.A.
8 E4 Rushworth Austr.
77 E6 Rusk U.S.A.
79 D7 Ruskin U.S.A.
65 J4 Russell Man. Can.
81 F2 Russell Ont. Can.
9 E1 Russell N.Z.
76 D4 Russell U.S.A.
64 F2 Russell Lake l. Can.
63 J2 Russell I. i. Can.
7 F2 Russell Is is Solomon Is
79 C4 Russellville AL U.S.A.
77 E5 Russellville AR U.S.A.
78 C4 Russellville KY U.S.A.
43 G4 Rüsselsheim Ger.
10 E3 Russian Federation country Asia/Europe
28 C3 Russkiy, Ostrov i. Rus. Fed.
17 K1 Rust'avi Georgia
59 G2 Rustenburg S. Africa
77 E5 Ruston U.S.A.
25 E7 Ruteng Indon.
75 E2 Ruth U.S.A.
43 G3 Rüthen Ger.
69 H2 Rutherglen Can.
39 D4 Ruthin U.K.
50 H3 Rutka r. Rus. Fed.
81 G3 Rutland U.S.A.
39 G5 Rutland Water resr U.K.
65 G2 Rutledge Lake l. Can.
22 D2 Rutog China
69 G2 Rutter Can.
36 T4 Ruukki Fin.
18 E5 Rū'us al Jibāl pen. Oman
57 D5 Ruvuma r. Moz./Tanz.
16 F5 Ruwayshid, Wādī watercourse Jordan
18 D5 Ruweis U.A.E.
27 D5 Ruyuan China
14 E1 Ruzayevka Kazak.
50 H4 Ruzayevka Rus. Fed.
47 J6 Ružomberok Slovakia
53 G6 Rwanda country Africa
18 D2 Ryābād Iran
50 H2 Ryadovo Rus. Fed.
40 C5 Ryan, Loch b. U.K.
50 F4 Ryazan' Rus. Fed.
50 G4 Ryazanskaya Oblast' div. Rus. Fed.
50 G4 Ryazhsk Rus. Fed.
12 E2 Rybachiy, Poluostrov pen. Rus. Fed.
50 F3 Rybinsk Rus. Fed.
50 F3 Rybinskoye Vdkhr. resr Rus. Fed.
50 J4 Rybnaya Sloboda Rus. Fed.
47 J5 Rybnik Pol.
50 F4 Rybnoye Rus. Fed.
64 F3 Rycroft Can.
37 O8 Ryd Sweden
92 B3 Rydberg Pen. pen. Ant.
39 F7 Ryde U.K.
39 H7 Rye U.K.
38 G3 Rye r. U.K.
51 E5 Ryl'sk Rus. Fed.
8 G2 Rylstone Austr.
30 D5 Ryoju S. Korea
29 F5 Ryōtsu Japan
47 L5 Rzeszów Pol.
51 G4 Rzhaksa Rus. Fed.
50 E3 Rzhev Rus. Fed.

S

18 E3 Sa'ābād Iran
18 D4 Sa'ādatābād Iran
18 D4 Sa'ādatābād Iran
43 K6 Saal an der Donau Ger.
43 K3 Saale r. Ger.
43 K4 Saalfeld Ger.
42 E5 Saar r. Ger.
42 E5 Saarbrücken Ger.
37 S7 Saaremaa i. Estonia
36 T3 Saarenkylä Fin.
42 E5 Saargau reg. Ger.
36 T5 Saarijärvi Fin.
36 U3 Saari-Kämä Fin.
36 R2 Saarikoski Fin.
42 E5 Saarland div. Ger.
42 E5 Saarlouis Ger.
17 M2 Saatlı Azer.
91 D3 Saavedra Arg.
16 F5 Şab' Ābār Syria
49 H2 Šabac Yugo.
45 H2 Sabadell Spain
29 E7 Sabae Japan
33 E1 Sabah div. Malaysia
32 B5 Sabak Malaysia
33 E4 Sabalana, Kep. is Indon.
22 D4 Sabalgarh India
83 H4 Sabana, Arch. de is Cuba
89 B2 Sabanalarga Col.
16 D1 Şabanözü Turkey
90 D2 Sabará Brazil
21 C2 Sābari r. India
22 C5 Sabarmati r. India
48 E4 Sabaudia Italy
19 E3 Sabeh Iran
58 E5 Sabelo S. Africa
55 D2 Sabhā Libya
18 B6 Şabḩā' S. Arabia
22 D3 Sabi r. India
59 K2 Sabie Moz.
59 J2 Sabie S. Africa
59 K2 Sabie r. Moz./S. Africa
82 D3 Sabinas Mex.
82 D3 Sabinas Hidalgo Mex.
77 E6 Sabine L. l. U.S.A.
17 M1 Sabirabad Azer.
31 B3 Sablayan Phil.
79 D7 Sable, Cape c. U.S.A.
7 F3 Sable, Île de i. New Caledonia
63 N5 Sable Island i. N.S. Can.
69 F2 Sables, River aux r. Can.
92 C6 Sabrina Coast coastal area Ant.
31 B1 Sabtang i. Phil.
45 C2 Sabugal Port.
68 B4 Sabula U.S.A.
20 B6 Şabyā S. Arabia
Sabzawar see Shīndand
19 E2 Sabzevār Iran
49 N2 Sacalinul Mare, Insula i. Romania
49 L2 Săcele Romania
57 B5 Sachanga Angola
66 B3 Sachigo r. Can.
66 B3 Sachigo L. l. Can.
22 C5 Sachin India
30 E6 Sach'on S. Korea
22 D2 Sach Pass India
43 L3 Sachsen div. Ger.
43 K3 Sachsen-Anhalt div. Ger.
43 H6 Sachsenheim Ger.
62 F2 Sachs Harbour Can.
81 E3 Sackets Harbor U.S.A.
43 G4 Sackpfeife h. Ger.
67 H4 Sackville Can.
81 H3 Saco ME U.S.A.
72 F1 Saco MT U.S.A.
31 B5 Sacol i. Phil.
74 B2 Sacramento U.S.A.
74 B2 Sacramento r. U.S.A.
73 F5 Sacramento Mts mts U.S.A.
72 B3 Sacramento Valley v. U.S.A.
59 G6 Sada S. Africa
45 F1 Sádaba Spain
18 C4 Sa'dabad Iran
16 F4 Şadad Syria
32 B4 Sadao Thai.
59 J2 Saddleback pass S. Africa
32 C3 Sa Đec Vietnam
23 H3 Sadêng China
19 E5 Sadīj watercourse Iran
22 B3 Sadiqabad Pak.
22 C1 Sad Istragh mt Afgh./Pak.
17 L5 Sa'dīyah, Hawr as l. Iraq
18 D5 Sa'diyyat i. U.A.E.
18 E2 Sad-Kharv Iran
45 B3 Sado r. Port.
29 F6 Sadoga-shima i. Japan
24 F3 Sado-Shima i. Japan
45 H3 Sa Dragonera i. Spain
37 M8 Sæby Denmark
Safad see Zefat
17 L6 Safayal Maqūf well Iraq
19 H2 Safed Khirs mts Afgh.
19 G3 Safed Koh mts Afgh.
37 N7 Säffle Sweden
75 H5 Safford U.S.A.
39 H5 Saffron Walden U.K.
16 E6 Safi Jordan
54 B1 Safi Morocco
18 C2 Safīd r. Iran
18 D3 Safīd Ab Iran
19 F4 Safidabeh Iran
17 M5 Safīd Dasht Iran
16 F4 Şāfītā Syria
36 X2 Safonovo Murmansk. Rus. Fed.
50 E4 Safonovo Smolensk. Rus. Fed.
12 F3 Safonovo Rus. Fed.
18 A5 Safrā' al Asyāḩ esc. S. Arabia
16 D1 Safranbolu Turkey
17 L6 Safwān Iraq
23 F3 Saga China
29 B8 Saga Japan
29 F7 Sagamihara Japan
29 F7 Sagami-nada g. Japan
29 F7 Sagami-wan b. Japan
89 B3 Sagamoso r. Col.
32 A2 Saganthit Kyun i. Myanmar
21 B2 Sagar Karnataka India
21 A3 Sagar Karnataka India
22 D5 Sagar Madhya Pradesh India
51 H7 Sagarejo Georgia
23 G5 Sagar I. i. India
13 O2 Sagastyr Rus. Fed.
18 D3 Saghand Iran
19 F3 Saghar Afgh.
21 B3 Sagileru r. India
69 F4 Saginaw U.S.A.
69 F4 Saginaw Bay b. U.S.A.
67 H2 Saglek Bay b. Can.
48 C3 Sagone, Golfe de b. Corsica France
45 B4 Sagres Port.
23 H5 Sagu Myanmar
73 F4 Saguache U.S.A.
83 H4 Sagua la Grande Cuba
75 G5 Saguaro National Monument res. U.S.A.
67 F4 Saguenay r. Can.
45 F3 Sagunto-Sagunt Spain
22 C5 Sagwara India
89 B2 Sahagún Col.
45 D1 Sahagún Spain
17 L3 Sahand, Kūh-e mt Iran
52 D3 Sahara des. Africa
Saharan Atlas mts see Atlas Saharien
22 D3 Saharanpur India
23 F4 Saharsa India
22 D3 Sahaswan India
18 C6 Sahba', W. as watercourse S. Arabia
22 C3 Sahiwal Pak.
19 E3 Sahlābād Iran
17 L4 Şaḩneh Iran
17 K6 Şaḩrā al Ḩijārah reg. Iraq
75 G6 Sahuarita U.S.A.
84 B2 Sahuayo Mex.
32 D2 Sa Huynh Vietnam
Sahyadri mts see Western Ghats
22 C5 Sahyadriparvat Range h. India
22 E4 Sai r. India
32 B4 Sai Buri Thai.
32 B4 Sai Buri r. Thai.
Saïda see Sidon
18 D4 Sa'īdābād Iran
32 B2 Sai Dao Tai, Khao mt Thai.
19 F5 Sa'īdī Iran
23 G4 Saidpur Bangl.
22 C2 Saidu Pak.
29 C6 Saigō Japan
Saigon see Hô Chi Minh
23 H5 Saiha India
26 A1 Saihan Toroi China
29 C8 Saijō Japan
29 B8 Saiki Japan
27 □ Sai Kung H.K. China
37 V6 Saimaa l. Fin.
16 F2 Saimbeyli Turkey
18 D4 Sā'īn Iran
84 B2 Sain Alto Mex.
19 F4 Saindak Pak.
18 B2 Sa'īndezh Iran
40 F5 St Abb's Head hd U.K.
39 B7 St Agnes U.K.
39 A8 St Agnes i. U.K.
67 J4 St Alban's Can.
39 G6 St Albans U.K.
81 G2 St Albans VT U.S.A.
80 C5 St Albans WV U.S.A.
39 E7 St Alban's Head hd U.K.
64 G4 St Albert Can.
42 B4 St-Amand-les-Eaux France
44 F3 St-Amand-Montrond France
44 G3 St-Amour France
81 K2 St Andrews Can.
40 F4 St Andrews U.K.
83 J5 St Ann's Bay Jamaica
41 F6 St Ann's Head hd U.K.
67 J3 St Anthony Can.
72 E3 St Anthony U.S.A.
8 D4 St Arnaud Austr.
9 D5 St Arnaud Range mts N.Z.
67 J3 St-Augustin Can.
42 F4 St Augustin Ger.
79 D6 St Augustine U.S.A.
39 C7 St Austell U.K.
44 E3 St-Avertin France
42 E5 St-Avold France
83 M5 St Barthélémy i. Guadeloupe
38 D3 St Bees U.K.
38 D3 St Bees Head hd U.K.
39 B6 St Bride's Bay b. U.K.
44 C2 St-Brieuc France
75 G5 St Carlos Lake l. U.S.A.
69 H4 St Catharines Can.
79 D6 St Catherines I. i. U.S.A.
39 F7 St Catherine's Point pt U.K.
44 E4 St-Céré France
81 G2 St-Césaire Can.
44 G4 St-Chamond France
72 E3 St Charles ID U.S.A.
80 E5 St Charles MD U.S.A.
68 A4 St Charles MN U.S.A.
76 F4 St Charles MO U.S.A.
69 F4 St Clair U.S.A.
69 F4 St Clair Shores U.S.A.
44 G3 St-Claude France
39 C6 St Clears U.K.
76 E2 St Cloud U.S.A.
83 M5 St Croix i. Virgin Is
67 G4 St Croix r. Can.
68 A2 St Croix r. U.S.A.
68 A3 St Croix Falls U.S.A.
75 G6 St David U.S.A.
41 F6 St David's U.K.
39 B6 St David's Head hd U.K.
42 A6 St-Denis France
44 H2 St-Dié France
44 G2 St-Dizier France
65 K5 Ste Anne Can.
67 F4 Ste-Anne-de-Beaupré Can.
81 J1 Sainte-Anne-de-Madawaska Can.
69 K2 Sainte-Anne-du-Lac Can.
67 G3 Ste Anne, L. l. Can.
81 H1 Ste-Camille-de-Lellis Can.
44 G4 St-Égrève France
81 H1 Sainte-Justine Can.
81 J1 St-Éleuthère Can.
64 B2 St Elias Mountains Can.
67 G3 Ste Marguerite r. Can.
44 H5 Ste-Maxime France
44 D4 Saintes France
81 G2 Ste-Thérèse Can.
44 G4 St-Étienne France
81 F2 St Eugene Can.
81 G2 St-Eustache Can.
83 M5 St Eustatius i. Neth. Ant.
67 F4 St-Félicien Can.
41 F3 Saintfield U.K.
48 C3 St-Florent Corsica France
44 F3 St-Florent-sur-Cher France
56 C3 St. Floris, Parc National nat. park C.A.R.
76 C4 St Francis KS U.S.A.
81 J1 St Francis ME U.S.A.
81 J1 St-Francis r. Can./U.S.A.
77 F4 St Francis r. U.S.A.
67 K4 St Francis, C. c. Can.
81 J1 St Froid Lake l. U.S.A.
46 D7 St Gallen Switz.
44 E5 St-Gaudens France
81 H2 St-Gédéon Can.
6 E4 St George Austr.
81 K2 St George Can.
79 D5 St George SC U.S.A.
75 F3 St George UT U.S.A.
7 F2 St George, C. pt P.N.G.
79 C6 St George I. i. U.S.A.
72 A3 St George, Pt pt U.S.A.
67 F4 St Georges Can.
83 M6 St George's Grenada
67 J4 St George's B. b. Can.
6 F2 St George's Channel P.N.G.
39 A6 St George's Channel Rep. of Ireland/U.K.
39 C6 St Govan's Head hd U.K.
68 E3 St Helen U.S.A.
74 A2 St Helena U.S.A.
53 D7 St Helena terr. Atl. Ocean
58 C6 St Helena Bay S. Africa
58 C6 St Helena Bay b. S. Africa
96 J7 St Helena Fracture sea feature Atl. Ocean
39 E4 St Helens U.K.
72 B2 St Helens U.S.A.
72 B2 St Helens, Mt volc. U.S.A.
44 C2 St Helier Channel Is U.K.
42 D4 St-Hubert Belgium
66 F4 St-Hyacinthe Can.
68 E3 St Ignace U.S.A.
68 C1 St Ignace I. i. Can.
39 C6 St Ishmael U.K.
39 B7 St Ives Eng. U.K.
39 G5 St Ives Eng. U.K.
81 J1 St-Jacques Can.
68 E3 St James U.S.A.
64 C4 St James, Cape pt Can.
44 D4 St-Jean-d'Angély France
44 C3 St-Jean-de-Monts France
67 F4 St-Jean, Lac l. Can.
66 F4 St-Jean-sur-Richelieu Can.
66 F4 St-Jérôme Can.
72 C2 St Joe r. U.S.A.
67 G4 St John Can.
75 F1 St John U.S.A.
83 M5 St John i. Virgin Is
81 K2 St John r. Can./U.S.A.
83 M5 St John's Antigua
67 K4 St John's Can.
75 H4 St Johns AZ U.S.A.
68 E4 St Johns MI U.S.A.
79 D6 St Johns r. U.S.A.
81 H2 St Johnsbury U.S.A.
38 E3 St John's Chapel U.K.
67 F4 St Joseph Can.
68 D4 St Joseph MI U.S.A.
76 E4 St Joseph MO U.S.A.
68 E5 St Joseph r. U.S.A.
69 F2 St Joseph I. i. Can.
77 D7 St Joseph I. i. U.S.A.
66 B3 St Joseph, Lac l. Can.
66 F4 St-Jovité Can.
44 E4 St-Junien France
39 B7 St Just U.K.
42 A5 St-Just-en-Chaussée France
39 B7 St Keverne U.K.
61 M8 St Kitts-Nevis country Caribbean Sea
42 B3 St-Laureins Belgium
87 H2 St Laurent Fr. Guiana
St-Laurent, Golfe du g. see St Lawrence, Gulf of
67 K4 St Lawrence Nfld Can.
67 G4 St Lawrence in. Que. Can.
67 H4 St Lawrence, Gulf of g. Can./U.S.A.
62 B3 St Lawrence I. i. AK U.S.A.
69 K3 St Lawrence Islands National Park Can.
81 F2 St Lawrence Seaway chan. Can./U.S.A.
67 G4 St-Léonard Can.
67 J3 St Lewis Can.
67 J3 Saint Lewis r. Can.
44 D2 St-Lô France
54 A3 St Louis Senegal
68 E4 St Louis MI U.S.A.
76 F4 St Louis MO U.S.A.
68 A2 St Louis r. U.S.A.
61 M8 St Lucia country Caribbean Sea
59 K4 St Lucia Estuary S. Africa
59 K3 St Lucia, Lake l. S. Africa
83 M5 St Maarten i. Neth. Ant.
40 □ St Magnus Bay b. U.K.
44 D3 St-Maixent-l'École France
44 C2 St-Malo France
44 C2 St-Malo, Golfe de g. France
59 G6 St Marks S. Africa
83 M5 Saint Martin i. Guadeloupe
58 B6 St Martin, Cape hd S. Africa
68 D3 St Martin I. i. U.S.A.
65 K4 St Martin, L. l. Can.
39 A8 St Martin's i. U.K.
23 H5 St Martin's I. i. Bangl.
8 B1 St Mary Pk mt Austr.
69 G4 St Mary's Can.
40 F2 St Mary's U.K.
80 A4 St Marys OH U.S.A.
80 D4 St Marys PA U.S.A.
80 C5 Saint Marys U.S.A.
39 A8 St Mary's i. U.K.
80 A4 St Marys r. U.S.A.
67 K4 St Mary's, C. hd Can.
62 A3 St Matthew I. i. AK U.S.A.
6 E2 St Matthias Group is P.N.G.
66 F4 St Maurice r. Can.
39 B7 St Mawes U.K.
44 D4 St-Médard-en-Jalles France
67 J3 St Michaels Bay b. Can.
46 D7 St Moritz Switz.
44 C3 St-Nazaire France
39 G5 St Neots U.K.
44 H2 St-Nicolas-de-Port France
42 C3 St-Niklaas Belgium
44 F1 St-Omer France
81 J1 St-Pamphile Can.
67 G4 St Pascal Can.
65 G4 St Paul Can.
68 A3 St Paul MN U.S.A.
76 D3 St Paul NE U.S.A.
80 B6 St Paul VA U.S.A.
93 K6 St Paul, Île i. Ind. Ocean
44 C2 St Peter Port Channel Is U.K.
50 D3 St Petersburg Rus. Fed.
79 D7 St Petersburg U.S.A.
67 J4 St-Pierre St Pierre and Miquelon N. America
44 G5 St-Pierre mt France
63 N5 St Pierre and Miquelon terr. N. America
44 D4 St-Pierre-d'Oléron France
66 F4 St-Pierre, Lac l. Can.
44 F3 St-Pierre-le-Moûtier France
42 A4 St-Pol-sur-Ternoise France
46 G6 St Pölten Austria
44 F3 St-Pourçain-sur-Sioule France
81 H1 Saint-Prosper Can.
44 F2 St-Quentin France
44 H5 St-Raphaël France
81 F2 St Regis r. U.S.A.
81 F2 St Regis Falls U.S.A.
81 G2 St-Rémi Can.
81 H2 St-Sébastien Can.
67 G4 St Siméon Can.
79 D6 St Simons I. i. U.S.A.
81 K2 St Stephen Can.
79 E5 St Stephen U.S.A.
81 H2 St-Théophile Can.
65 L4 St Theresa Point Can.
69 G4 St Thomas Can.
44 H5 St-Tropez France
42 D4 St-Truiden Belgium
65 K5 St Vincent U.S.A.
61 M8 St Vincent and the Grenadines country Caribbean Sea
St Vincent, Cape c. see São Vicente, Cabo de
8 A3 St. Vincent, Gulf Austr.
42 E4 St-Vith Belgium
65 H4 St Walburg Can.
42 F5 St Wendel Ger.
69 G4 St Williams Can.
44 E4 St-Yrieix-la-Perche France
22 E3 Saipal mt Nepal
25 G5 Saipan i. N. Mariana Is
23 H5 Saitlai Myanmar
36 T3 Saittanulkki h. Fin.
27 □ Sai Wan H.K. China
86 E7 Sajama, Nevado mt Bol.
18 B5 Sājir S. Arabia
58 D5 Sak watercourse S. Africa
29 D7 Sakai Japan
29 C7 Sakaide Japan
29 C7 Sakaiminato Japan
20 B3 Sakākah S. Arabia
19 G5 Saka Kalat Pak.
76 C2 Sakakawea, Lake l. U.S.A.
66 E3 Sakami Can.
66 F3 Sakami r. Can.
66 E3 Sakami, Lac l. Can.
49 M4 Sakar mts Bulg.
16 C1 Sakarya Turkey
16 C1 Sakarya r. Turkey
28 F5 Sakata Japan
30 C3 Sakchu N. Korea
32 B2 Sa Keo r. Thai.
54 C4 Sakété Benin
24 G2 Sakhalin i. Rus. Fed.
24 G1 Sakhalinskiy Zaliv b. Rus. Fed.
22 C3 Sakhi India
59 H3 Sakhile S. Africa
18 C2 Sakht-Sar Iran
17 L1 Şäki Azer.
37 S9 Šakiai Lith.
22 A3 Sakir mt Pak.
24 E4 Sakishima-guntō is Japan
22 B4 Sakrand Pak.
32 □ Sakra, P. i. Sing.
58 D5 Sakrivier S. Africa
29 B9 Sakura-jima volc. Japan
51 E6 Saky Ukr.
37 S6 Säkylä Fin.
54 □ Sal i. Cape Verde
51 G6 Sal r. Rus. Fed.
37 S8 Sala Latvia
37 P7 Sala Sweden
66 F4 Salaberry-de-Valleyfield Can.
37 T8 Salacgrīva Latvia
48 F4 Sala Consilina Italy
75 E5 Salada, Laguna salt l. Mex.
91 E2 Saladillo Buenos Aires Arg.
91 D2 Saladillo r. Córdoba Arg.
91 E2 Salado r. Buenos Aires Arg.
91 C2 Salado r. Mendoza/San Luis Arg.
91 D4 Salado r. Rio Negro Arg.
91 E1 Salado r. Santa Fé Arg.
82 E3 Salado r. Mex.
88 B3 Salado, Quebrada de r. Chile
54 B4 Salaga Ghana
58 F1 Salajwe Botswana
55 D3 Salal Chad
20 D6 Şalālah Oman
84 E4 Salamá Guatemala
91 B1 Salamanca Chile
84 B2 Salamanca Mex.
45 D2 Salamanca Spain
80 D3 Salamanca U.S.A.
59 K3 Salamanga Moz.
18 B3 Salamatabad Iran
89 B3 Salamina Col.
16 F4 Salamīyah Syria
68 E5 Salamonie r. U.S.A.
68 E5 Salamonie Lake l. U.S.A.
23 F5 Salandi r. India
37 R8 Salantai Lith.
88 C2 Salar de Arizaro salt flat Arg.
88 C2 Salar de Atacama salt flat Chile
45 C1 Salas Spain
37 T8 Salaspils Latvia
25 F7 Salawati i. Indon.
22 B5 Salaya India
25 E7 Salayar i. Indon.
5 R7 Sala y Gómez, Isla i. Chile
91 D3 Salazar Arg.
37 T9 Šalčininkai Lith.
39 D7 Salcombe U.K.
45 D1 Saldaña Spain
89 B4 Saldaña r. Col.
58 B6 Saldanha S. Africa
58 B6 Saldanha Bay b. S. Africa
91 E3 Saldungaray Arg.
37 S8 Saldus Latvia
8 F5 Sale Austr.
17 L5 Şālehābād Iran
18 C3 Şāleḩābād Iran
12 H3 Salekhard Rus. Fed.
21 B4 Salem India
81 H3 Salem MA U.S.A.
77 F4 Salem MO U.S.A.
78 F4 Salem NJ U.S.A.
81 G3 Salem NY U.S.A.
80 C4 Salem OH U.S.A.
72 B2 Salem OR U.S.A.
78 D4 Salem VA U.S.A.
40 C4 Salen U.K.
40 C4 Salen U.K.
48 F4 Salerno Italy
48 F4 Salerno, Golfo di g. Italy
39 E4 Salford U.K.
87 L5 Salgado r. Brazil
47 J6 Salgótarján Hungary
87 L5 Salgueiro Brazil
19 F4 Salian Afgh.
31 C6 Salibabu i. Indon.
70 E4 Salida CO U.S.A.
44 D5 Salies-de-Béarn France
16 B2 Salihli Turkey
50 C4 Salihorsk Belarus
57 D5 Salima Malawi

57 D5 Salimo Moz.
76 D4 Salina KS U.S.A.
75 G2 Salina UT U.S.A.
84 D3 Salina Cruz Mex.
91 D4 Salina Gualicho salt flat Arg.
48 F5 Salina, Isola i. Italy
91 C2 Salina Llancanelo salt flat Arg.
90 D2 Salinas Brazil
86 B4 Salinas Ecuador
84 B2 Salinas Mex.
74 B3 Salinas CA U.S.A.
74 B3 Salinas r. CA U.S.A.
88 C4 Salinas Grandes salt flat Arg.
73 F5 Salinas Peak summit U.S.A.
77 E5 Saline r. AR U.S.A.
76 C4 Saline r. KS U.S.A.
45 H3 Salines, Cap de ses pt Spain
74 D3 Saline Valley v. U.S.A.
87 J4 Salinópolis Brazil
86 C6 Salinosó Lachay, Pta pt Peru
39 F6 Salisbury U.K.
81 F5 Salisbury MD U.S.A.
79 D5 Salisbury NC U.S.A.
39 E6 Salisbury Plain plain U.K.
87 K6 Salitre r. Brazil
16 F5 Şalkhad Syria
23 F5 Salki r. India
36 V3 Salla Fin.
91 D3 Salliqueló Arg.
77 E5 Sallisaw U.S.A.
63 L3 Salluit Can.
23 E3 Sallyana Nepal
18 B2 Salmās Iran
50 D2 Salmi Rus. Fed.
64 F5 Salmo Can.
72 D2 Salmon U.S.A.
72 D2 Salmon r. U.S.A.
64 F4 Salmon Arm Can.
81 F3 Salmon Reservoir resr U.S.A.
72 D2 Salmon River Mountains U.S.A.
42 E5 Salmtal Ger.
37 S6 Salo Fin.
23 E4 Salon India
44 G5 Salon-de-Provence France
56 C4 Salonga Nord, Parc National de la nat. park Congo(Zaire)
56 C4 Salonga Sud, Parc National de la nat. park Congo(Zaire)
47 K7 Salonta Romania
91 D1 Salsacate Arg.
51 G6 Sal'sk Rus. Fed.
48 C2 Salsomaggiore Terme Italy
16 E5 Salt Jordan
75 G5 Salt r. AZ U.S.A.
68 B6 Salt r. MO U.S.A.
58 E5 Salt watercourse S. Africa
88 C2 Salta Arg.
39 C7 Saltash U.K.
40 D5 Saltcoats U.K.
80 B5 Salt Creek r. U.S.A.
41 E5 Saltee Islands is Rep. of Ireland
36 O3 Saltfjellet Svartisen Nasjonalpark nat. park Norway
77 B6 Salt Flat U.S.A.
80 C4 Salt Fork Lake l. U.S.A.
84 B1 Saltillo Mex.
72 E3 Salt Lake City U.S.A.
91 E2 Salto Arg.
90 C3 Salto Brazil
91 F1 Salto Uru.
90 E2 Salto da Divisa Brazil
88 E4 Salto Grande, Embalse de resr Uru.
75 E5 Salton Sea salt l. U.S.A.
22 C2 Salt Ra. h. Pak.
65 G2 Salt River Can.
80 B5 Salt Rock U.S.A.
79 D5 Saluda SC U.S.A.
80 E6 Saluda VA U.S.A.
22 C4 Salumbar India
21 C2 Salur India
48 B2 Saluzzo Italy
91 D1 Salvador Arg.
90 E1 Salvador Brazil
77 F6 Salvador, L. l. U.S.A.
84 B2 Salvatierra Mex.
75 G2 Salvation Creek r. U.S.A.
18 C5 Salwah Qatar
25 B5 Salween r. Myanmar
17 M2 Salyan Azer.
80 B6 Salyersville U.S.A.
58 B2 Salzbrunn Namibia
46 F7 Salzburg Austria
43 J2 Salzgitter Ger.
43 J1 Salzhausen Ger.
43 G3 Salzkotten Ger.
43 K3 Salzmünde Ger.
43 K2 Salzwedel Ger.
22 B4 Sam India
18 B4 Samāh well S. Arabia
18 B3 Samaida Iran
31 C5 Samal i. Phil.
31 B5 Samales Group is Phil.
21 C2 Samalkot India
16 E3 Samandağı Turkey
28 H3 Samani Japan
16 C6 Samannûd Egypt
31 C4 Samar i. Phil.
12 G4 Samara Rus. Fed.
89 D3 Samariapo Venez.
33 E3 Samarinda Indon.
28 D2 Samarka Rus. Fed.
19 G2 Samarkand Uzbek.
19 H2 Samarkand, Pik mt Tajik.
17 J4 Sāmarrā' Iraq
31 C4 Samar Sea g. Phil.
50 J4 Samarskaya Oblast' div. Rus. Fed.
17 M1 Şamaxı Azer.
56 C4 Samba Congo(Zaire)
33 E2 Sambaliung mts Indon.
23 F5 Sambalpur India
33 D3 Sambar, Tanjung pt Indon.
33 C2 Sambas Indon.
57 F5 Sambava Madag.
23 G4 Sambha India
22 D3 Sambhal India
22 C4 Sambhar L. l. India
51 B5 Sambir Ukr.
87 K5 Sambito r. Brazil
91 F2 Samborombón, Bahía b. Arg.
42 B4 Sambre r. Belgium/France
89 A3 Sambú r. Panama
30 E5 Samch'ŏk S. Korea
30 E6 Samch'ŏnp'o S. Korea
17 K3 Samdi Dag mt Turkey
56 D4 Same Tanz.
Samirum see Yazd-e Khvāst
30 E3 Samjiyŏn N. Korea
17 L1 Şämkir Azer.
18 D3 Samnan va Damghan reg. Iran
48 F2 Samobor Croatia
50 G2 Samoded Rus. Fed.
49 K3 Samokov Bulg.
46 H6 Šamorín Slovakia
49 M6 Samos i. Greece
33 A2 Samosir i. Indon.
49 L4 Samothraki Greece
49 L4 Samothraki i. Greece
31 B3 Sampaloc Point pt Phil.
33 D3 Sampit Indon.
33 D3 Sampit, Teluk b. Indon.
57 C4 Sampwe Congo(Zaire)
30 E6 Samrangjin S. Korea
77 E6 Sam Rayburn Res. resr U.S.A.
23 E3 Samsang China
32 C1 Sâm Sơn Vietnam
16 F1 Samsun Turkey
51 G7 Samtredia Georgia
51 J7 Samur r. Azer./Rus. Fed.
32 B2 Samut Sakhon Thai.
32 B2 Samut Songkhram Thai.
23 G3 Samyai China
54 B3 San Mali
20 B6 Şan'ā Yemen
92 C3 Sanae S. Africa Base Ant.
55 D4 Sanaga r. Cameroon
89 A4 San Agustín Col.
31 C5 San Agustin, Cape c. Phil.
18 B6 Sanām S. Arabia
85 C5 San Ambrosio i. Chile
18 B3 Sanandaj Iran
74 B2 San Andreas U.S.A.
31 C3 San Andres Phil.
86 B1 San Andrés, Isla de i. Col.
73 F5 San Andres Mts mts U.S.A.
84 D3 San Andrés Tuxtla Mex.
77 C6 San Angelo U.S.A.
91 B2 San Antonio Chile
31 B3 San Antonio Phil.
77 D6 San Antonio U.S.A.
45 G3 San Antonio Abad Spain
83 H4 San Antonio, C. pt Cuba
91 F3 San Antonio, Cabo pt Arg.
88 C2 San Antonio de los Cobres Arg.
89 D2 San Antonio de Tamanaco Venez.
74 D4 San Antonio, Mt mt U.S.A.
91 D4 San Antonio Oeste Arg.
74 B4 San Antonio Reservoir U.S.A.
74 B3 San Ardo U.S.A.
91 E3 San Augustín Arg.
91 C1 San Augustín de Valle Fértil Arg.
22 D5 Sanawad India
84 B2 San Bartolo Mex.
48 E3 San Benedetto del Tronto Italy
82 B5 San Benedicto, I. i. Mex.
77 D7 San Benito U.S.A.
74 B3 San Benito r. U.S.A.
74 B3 San Benito Mt mt U.S.A.
74 D4 San Bernardino U.S.A.
73 C5 San Bernardino Mts mts U.S.A.
91 B2 San Bernardo Chile
84 A1 San Bernardo Mex.
29 C7 Sanbe-san volc. Japan
84 A2 San Blas Mex.
79 C6 San Blas, C. c. U.S.A.
86 E6 San Borja Bol.
81 H3 Sanbornville U.S.A.
70 F6 San Buenaventura Mex.
91 C2 San Carlos Arg.
91 B3 San Carlos Chile
77 C6 San Carlos Coahuila Mex.
84 C1 San Carlos Tamaulipas Mex.
31 B3 San Carlos Luzon Phil.
31 B4 San Carlos Negros Phil.
91 F2 San Carlos Uru.
75 G5 San Carlos U.S.A.
89 D4 San Carlos Amazonas Venez.
89 C2 San Carlos Cojedes Venez.
91 E1 San Carlos Centro Arg.
91 B4 San Carlos de Bariloche Arg.
91 E3 San Carlos de Bolívar Arg.
89 C2 San Carlos del Zulia Venez.
73 D6 San Carlos, Mesa de h. Mex.
26 C2 Sancha Gansu China
26 D2 Sancha Shanxi China
30 D1 Sanchahe China
27 C5 Sancha He r. China
27 B6 San Chien Pau mt Laos
22 B4 Sanchor India
26 D2 Sanchuan r. China
50 H3 Sanchursk Rus. Fed.
84 C2 San Ciro de Acosta Mex.
91 B2 San Clemente Chile
74 D5 San Clemente U.S.A.
74 C5 San Clemente I. i. U.S.A.
44 F3 Sancoins France
91 E1 San Cristóbal Arg.
89 B3 San Cristóbal Venez.
7 G3 San Cristobal i. Solomon Is
84 D3 San Cristóbal de las Casas Mex.
86 □ San Cristóbal, Isla i. Galapagos Is Ecuador
75 F5 San Cristobal Wash r. U.S.A.
83 J4 Sancti Spíritus Cuba
59 H1 Sand r. S. Africa
28 D3 Sandagou Rus. Fed.
40 C5 Sanda Island i. U.K.
33 E1 Sandakan Malaysia
37 K6 Sandane Norway
49 K4 Sandanski Bulg.
43 L2 Sandau Ger.
40 F1 Sanday i. U.K.
40 F1 Sanday Sound chan. U.K.
39 E4 Sandbach U.K.
37 M7 Sandefjord Norway
92 D4 Sandercock Nunataks nunatak Ant.
75 H4 Sanders U.S.A.
43 K3 Sandersleben Ger.
77 C6 Sanderson U.S.A.
40 D6 Sandhead U.K.
68 B2 Sand I. i. U.S.A.
86 E6 Sandia Peru
74 D5 San Diego U.S.A.
88 C8 San Diego, C. c. Arg.
16 C2 Sandıklı Turkey
22 E4 Sandila India
84 E3 San Dimas Campeche Mex.
84 A1 San Dimas Durango Mex.
68 E2 Sand Lake Can.
37 J7 Sandnes Norway
36 N3 Sandnessjøen Norway
57 C4 Sandoa Congo(Zaire)
47 K5 Sandomierz Pol.
89 A4 Sandoná Col.
48 E2 San Donà di Piave Italy
25 B5 Sandoway Myanmar
39 F7 Sandown U.K.
58 C7 Sandown Bay b. S. Africa
36 □ Sandoy i. Faroe Is
72 C1 Sandpoint U.S.A.
40 A4 Sandray i. U.K.
47 N7 Şandrul Mare, Vârful mt Romania
37 O6 Sandsjö Sweden
64 C4 Sandspit Can.
77 D4 Sand Springs U.S.A.
74 C2 Sand Springs Salt Flat salt flat U.S.A.
68 A2 Sandstone U.S.A.
75 F5 Sand Tank Mts mts U.S.A.
27 C5 Sandu Guizhou China
27 D5 Sandu Hunan China
69 F4 Sandusky MI U.S.A.
80 B4 Sandusky OH U.S.A.
80 B4 Sandusky Bay b. U.S.A.
58 C5 Sandveld mts S. Africa
58 B3 Sandverhaar Namibia
37 M7 Sandvika Norway
36 N5 Sandvika Sweden
37 P6 Sandviken Sweden
67 J3 Sandwich Bay b. Can.
40 □ Sandwick U.K.
23 G5 Sandwip Ch. chan. Bangl.
81 H2 Sandy r. U.S.A.
65 J3 Sandy Bay Can.
7 F4 Sandy Cape c. Austr.
80 B5 Sandy Hook U.S.A.
81 F4 Sandy Hook pt U.S.A.
19 F2 Sandykachi Turkm.
66 B3 Sandy L. l. Can.
66 B3 Sandy Lake Can.
81 E3 Sandy Pond U.S.A.
90 A4 San Estanislao Para.
31 B2 San Fabian Phil.
91 B2 San Felipe Chile
82 B2 San Felipe Baja California Norte Mex.
84 B2 San Felipe Guanajuato Mex.
89 C2 San Felipe Venez.
85 B5 San Félix i. Chile
91 E2 San Fernando Arg.
91 B2 San Fernando Chile
84 C1 San Fernando Mex.
31 B2 San Fernando Luzon Phil.
31 B3 San Fernando Luzon Phil.
45 C4 San Fernando Spain
89 E2 San Fernando Trinidad and Tobago
74 C4 San Fernando U.S.A.
89 D3 San Fernando de Apure Venez.
89 D3 San Fernando de Atabapo Venez.
74 D5 San Filipe Creek r. U.S.A.
79 D6 Sanford FL U.S.A.
81 H3 Sanford ME U.S.A.
79 E5 Sanford NC U.S.A.
68 E4 Sanford Lake l. U.S.A.
91 D1 San Francisco Arg.
74 A3 San Francisco CA U.S.A.
75 H5 San Francisco r. NM U.S.A.
74 A3 San Francisco Bay in. U.S.A.
84 B2 San Francisco del Rincón Mex.
83 K5 San Francisco de Macoris Dom. Rep.
88 C7 San Francisco de Paula, C. pt Arg.
45 G3 San Francisco Javier Spain
88 C3 San Francisco, Paso de pass Arg.
89 A4 San Gabriel Ecuador
74 C4 San Gabriel Mts mts U.S.A.
86 C4 Sangai, Parque Nacional nat. park Ecuador
22 C6 Sangamner India
68 C6 Sangamon r. U.S.A.
19 G3 Sangan Afgh.
19 F4 Sangān Iran
19 G3 Sangan, Koh-i- mt Afgh.
13 O3 Sangar Rus. Fed.
22 B3 Sangar r. Pak.
21 B2 Sangāreddi India
48 C5 San Gavino Monreale Sardinia Italy
19 E3 Sang Bast Iran
31 B5 Sangboy Islands is Phil.
33 E4 Sangeang i. Indon.
26 B1 Sangejing China
74 C3 Sanger U.S.A.
43 K3 Sangerhausen Ger.
26 E1 Sanggan r. China
26 B3 Sanggarmai China
33 D2 Sanggau Indon.
30 B5 Sanggou Wan b. China
56 B3 Sangha r. Congo
22 B4 Sanghar Pak.
89 B3 San Gil Col.
48 G5 San Giovanni in Fiore Italy
48 F4 San Giovanni Rotondo Italy
31 C6 Sangir i. Indon.
25 E6 Sangir, Kepulauan is Indon.
33 E2 Sangkulirang Indon.
21 A2 Sangli India
19 H2 Sanglich Afgh.
54 D4 Sangmélima Cameroon
22 D3 Sangnam India
23 H3 Sangngagqoling China
30 E3 Sang-ni N. Korea
57 D6 Sango Zimbabwe
21 A2 Sāngole India
74 D4 San Gorgonio Mt mt U.S.A.
46 D7 San Gottardo, Passo del pass Switz.
73 F4 Sangre de Cristo Range mts U.S.A.
89 E2 Sangre Grande Trinidad and Tobago
22 C3 Sangrur India
23 F3 Sangsang China
64 G4 Sangudo Can.
87 G6 Sangue r. Brazil
59 K1 Sangutane r. Moz.
19 H2 Sangvor Tajik.
27 D4 Sangzhi China
82 B3 San Hipólito, Pta pt Mex.
16 C7 Sanhûr Egypt
86 E6 San Ignacio Beni Bol.
86 F7 San Ignacio Santa Cruz Bol.
66 E2 Sanikiluaq Can.
31 B2 San Ildefonso, Cape c. Phil.
31 B2 San Ildefonso Peninsula Phil.
31 C4 San Isidro Phil.
31 B3 San Jacinto Phil.
74 D5 San Jacinto U.S.A.
74 D5 San Jacinto Peak summit U.S.A.
23 F5 Sanjai, R r. India
91 E1 San Javier Arg.
91 B2 San Javier de Loncomilla Chile
22 B3 Sanjawi Pak.
57 D4 Sanje Tanz.
89 A3 San Jerónimo, Serranía de mts Col.
27 C5 Sanjiang China
30 B2 Sanjiangkou China
30 B2 Sanjiazi China
29 F6 Sanjō Japan
74 B3 San Joaquin CA U.S.A.
74 B3 San Joaquin r. CA U.S.A.
74 B3 San Joaquin Valley v. U.S.A.
91 E1 San Jorge Arg.
89 B2 San Jorge r. Col.
88 C7 San Jorge, Golfo de g. Arg.
83 H7 San José Costa Rica
31 B3 San Jose Phil.
74 B3 San Jose U.S.A.
82 B4 San José i. Mex.
89 E2 San José de Amacuro Venez.
31 B4 San Jose de Buenavista Phil.
86 F7 San José de Chiquitos Bol.
91 E1 San José de Feliciano Arg.
84 A1 San José de Gracia Mex.
89 D2 San José de Guanipa Venez.
91 C1 San Jose de Jáchal Arg.
91 D1 San José de la Dormida Arg.
91 B3 San José de la Mariquina Chile
82 C4 San José del Cabo Mex.
89 B4 San José del Guaviare Col.
91 F2 San José de Mayo Uru.
89 C3 San José de Ocuné Col.
84 B1 San José de Raíces Mex.
91 D4 San José, Golfo g. Arg.
91 C2 San José, Vol. volc. Chile
30 E5 Sanju S. Korea
91 C1 San Juan Arg.
77 C7 San Juan Mex.
31 C4 San Juan Phil.
83 L5 San Juan Puerto Rico
89 D3 San Juan Venez.
91 C1 San Juan div. Arg.
89 A3 San Juan r. Col.
83 H6 San Juan r. Costa Rica/Nic.
74 B4 San Juan r. CA U.S.A.
75 H3 San Juan r. UT U.S.A.
88 E3 San Juan Bautista Para.
45 G3 San Juan Bautista Spain
84 C3 San Juan Bautista Tuxtepec Mex.
91 B4 San Juan dela Costa Chile
89 C2 San Juan de los Cayos Venez.
89 C2 San Juan de los Morros Venez.
84 A1 San Juan del Río Durango Mex.
84 C2 San Juan del Río Querétaro Mex.
75 F4 San Juan Mts mts U.S.A.
22 C1 Sanju He watercourse China
88 C7 San Julián Arg.
91 E1 San Justo Arg.
21 A2 Sankeshwar India
23 F5 Sankh r. India
Sankt-Peterburg see St Petersburg
16 G3 Şanlıurfa Turkey
91 E2 San Lorenzo Arg.
86 F8 San Lorenzo Bol.
86 C3 San Lorenzo Ecuador
73 F6 San Lorenzo Mex.
45 E1 San Lorenzo mt Spain
88 E7 San Lorenzo, Cerro mt Arg./Chile
86 C6 San Lorenzo, I. i. Peru
45 C4 Sanlúcar de Barrameda Spain
82 C4 San Lucas Mex.
91 C2 San Luis Arg.
75 E5 San Luis AZ U.S.A.
75 G5 San Luis AZ U.S.A.
91 C2 San Luis div. Arg.
84 B2 San Luis de la Paz Mex.
86 F6 San Luis, Lago de l. Bol.
74 B4 San Luis Obispo U.S.A.
74 B4 San Luis Obispo Bay b. U.S.A.
84 B2 San Luis Potosí Mex.
84 B2 San Luis Potosí div. Mex.
74 B3 San Luis Reservoir U.S.A.
82 B2 San Luis Río Colorado Mex.
91 C2 San Luis, Sa de mts Arg.
48 E6 San Marco, Capo c. Sicily Italy
84 E4 San Marcos Guatemala
84 C3 San Marcos Mex.
77 D6 San Marcos U.S.A.
48 E3 San Marino San Marino
34 E4 San Marino country Europe
88 C3 San Martín Catamarca Arg.
91 C2 San Martín Mendoza Arg.
89 B4 San Martín Col.
86 F6 San Martín r. Bol.
91 B4 San Martín de los Andes Arg.
88 B7 San Martín, L. l. Arg./Chile
74 A3 San Mateo U.S.A.
91 D4 San Matías, Golfo g. Arg.
89 D2 San Mauricio Venez.
27 F4 Sanmen China
27 F4 Sanmen Wan b. China
26 D3 Sanmenxia China
84 E3 San Miguel El Salvador
75 G6 San Miguel AZ U.S.A.
74 B4 San Miguel CA U.S.A.
86 F6 San Miguel r. Bol.
89 B4 San Miguel r. Col.
75 H2 San Miguel r. U.S.A.
31 B3 San Miguel Bay b. Phil.
84 B2 San Miguel de Allende Mex.
91 E2 San Miguel del Monte Arg.
88 C3 San Miguel de Tucumán Arg.
74 B4 San Miguel I. i. U.S.A.
31 A5 San Miguel Islands is Phil.
84 C3 San Miguel Sola de Vega Mex.
27 E5 Sanming China
31 B3 San Narciso Phil.
48 F4 Sannicandro Garganico Italy
91 E2 San Nicolás de los Arroyos Arg.
74 C5 San Nicolas I. i. U.S.A.
59 F3 Sannieshof S. Africa
54 B4 Sanniquellie Liberia
47 L6 Sanok Pol.
84 C2 San Pablo Mex.
31 B3 San Pablo Phil.
91 E2 San Pedro Buenos Aires Arg.
88 D2 San Pedro Jujuy Arg.
86 F7 San Pedro Bol.
54 B4 San-Pédro Côte d'Ivoire
88 E2 San Pedro Para.
31 B3 San Pedro Phil.
75 G5 San Pedro r. U.S.A.
74 C5 San Pedro Channel U.S.A.
89 C3 San Pedro de Arimena Col.
89 E3 San Pedro de las Bocas Venez.
84 B1 San Pedro de las Colonias Mex.
45 C3 San Pedro, Sierra de mts Spain
82 G5 San Pedro Sula Honduras
48 C5 San Pietro, Isola di i. Sardinia Italy
40 E5 Sanquhar U.K.
86 C3 Sanquianga, Parque Nacional nat. park Col.
82 A2 San Quintín Mex.
91 C2 San Rafael Arg.
74 A3 San Rafael U.S.A.
89 C2 San Rafael Venez.
75 G2 San Rafael r. U.S.A.
75 G2 San Rafael Knob summit U.S.A.
74 C4 San Rafael Mts mts U.S.A.
86 F6 San Ramón Bol.
48 B3 San Remo Italy
89 C1 San Román, C. pt Venez.
45 B1 San Roque Spain
77 D6 San Saba U.S.A.
91 E1 San Salvador Arg.
82 G6 San Salvador El Salvador
83 K4 San Salvador i. Bahamas
88 C2 San Salvador de Jujuy Arg.
86 □ San Salvador, Isla i. Galapagos Is Ecuador
22 D5 Sansar India
45 F1 San Sebastián Spain
45 E2 San Sebastián de los Reyes Spain
48 E3 Sansepolcro Italy
48 F4 San Severo Italy
27 F5 Sansha China
27 D6 Sanshui China
48 G2 Sanski Most Bos.-Herz.
27 C5 Sansui China
32 C2 San, T. r. Cambodia
86 E7 Santa Ana Bol.
82 G6 Santa Ana El Salvador
74 D5 Santa Ana U.S.A.
7 G3 Santa Ana i. Solomon Is
77 D6 Santa Anna U.S.A.
89 B3 Sta Bárbara Col.
82 C3 Santa Bárbara Mex.
74 C4 Santa Barbara U.S.A.
74 B4 Santa Barbara Channel U.S.A.
74 C5 Santa Barbara I. i. U.S.A.
88 C3 Sta Catalina Chile
45 B1 Santa Catalina de Armada Spain
74 D5 Santa Catalina, Gulf of b. U.S.A.
74 C5 Santa Catalina I. i. U.S.A.
84 B1 Sta Catarina Mex.
86 E4 Santa Clara Col.
83 J4 Santa Clara Cuba
74 B3 Santa Clara CA U.S.A.
75 F3 Santa Clara UT U.S.A.
91 F2 Santa Clara de Olimar Uru.
74 C4 Santa Clarita U.S.A.
48 F6 Sta Croce, Capo c. Sicily Italy
86 F7 Santa Cruz Bol.
91 B2 Sta Cruz Chile
31 B3 Santa Cruz Luzon Phil.
31 B2 Santa Cruz Luzon Phil.
31 A3 Sta Cruz Phil.
74 A3 Santa Cruz U.S.A.
88 C8 Santa Cruz r. Arg.
73 E5 Santa Cruz r. U.S.A.
84 E4 Sta Cruz Barillas Guatemala
90 E2 Santa Cruz Cabrália Brazil
45 F3 Santa Cruz de Moya Spain
54 A2 Santa Cruz de Tenerife Canary Is
88 F3 Santa Cruz do Sul Brazil
74 C4 Santa Cruz I. i. U.S.A.
86 □ Santa Cruz, Isla i. Galapagos Is Ecuador
7 G3 Santa Cruz Islands is Solomon Is
88 C8 Santa Cruz, Pto Arg.
91 E1 Sta Elena Arg.
86 B4 Sta Elena, B. de b. Ecuador
82 G6 Sta Elena, C. hd Costa Rica
48 G5 Sta Eufemia, Golfo di g. Italy
91 E1 Santa Fé Arg.
73 F5 Santa Fe U.S.A.
91 E1 Santa Fé div. Arg.
90 B2 Santa Helena de Goiás Brazil
26 B4 Santai China
88 B8 Santa Inés, Isla i. Chile
91 C3 Santa Isabel Arg.
7 F2 Santa Isabel i. Solomon Is
84 E4 Sta Lucia Guatemala
91 F2 Sta Lucia r. Uru.
73 B4 Santa Lucia Range mts U.S.A.
90 A2 Santa Luisa, Serra de h. Brazil
54 □ Santa Luzia i. Cape Verde
82 B4 Sta Margarita i. Mex.
88 C3 Sta María Arg.
87 G4 Santa Maria Amazonas Brazil
88 F3 Santa Maria Rio Grande do Sul Brazil
54 □ Santa Maria Cape Verde
84 A1 Sta María Mex.
86 D4 Santa María Peru
74 B4 Santa Maria U.S.A.
34 C5 Santa Maria i. Azores Port.
91 F1 Santa Maria r. Brazil
73 F6 Sta María r. Mex.
82 C2 Sta Maria r. Mex.
45 C4 Santa Maria, Cabo de c. Port.
59 K3 Santa Maria, Cabo de pt Moz.
87 J5 Santa Maria das Barreiras Brazil
90 D1 Santa Maria da Vitória Brazil
89 D2 Sta María de Ipire Venez.
84 B2 Sta María del Río Mex.
49 H5 Sta Maria di Leuca, Capo c. Italy
91 B3 Santa María, I. i. Chile
7 G3 Santa Maria I. i. Vanuatu
86 □ Santa María, Isla i. Galapagos Is Ecuador
70 E5 Sta María, L. de l. Mex.
79 F7 Sta Marie, Cape c. Bahamas
89 B2 Santa Marta Col.
89 B2 Santa Marta, Sierra Nevada de mts Col.
74 C4 Santa Monica U.S.A.
74 C5 Santa Monica Bay b. U.S.A.
87 K6 Santana Brazil
90 B2 Santana r. Brazil
91 G1 Santana da Boa Vista Brazil
91 F1 Santana do Livramento Brazil
89 A4 Santander Col.
45 E1 Santander Spain
75 G5 Santan Mt mt U.S.A.
48 C5 Sant'Antioco Sardinia Italy
48 C5 Sant'Antioco, Isola di i. Sardinia Italy
74 C4 Santa Paula U.S.A.
87 K4 Santa Quitéria Brazil
87 H4 Santarém Brazil
45 B3 Santarém Port.
89 C2 Sta Rita Venez.
90 B2 Sta Rita do Araguaia Brazil
74 B3 Santa Rita Park U.S.A.
91 D3 Santa Rosa La Pampa Arg.
91 C4 Santa Rosa Rio Negro Arg.
86 D5 Santa Rosa Acre Brazil
88 F3 Sta Rosa Brazil
74 A2 Santa Rosa CA U.S.A.
73 F5 Santa Rosa NM U.S.A.
82 G6 Santa Rosa de Copán Honduras
91 D1 Sta Rosa del Río Primero Arg.
74 B5 Santa Rosa I. i. U.S.A.
82 B3 Sta Rosalía Mex.
72 C3 Sta Rosa Ra. mts U.S.A.
75 G5 Santa Rosa Wash r. U.S.A.
91 G2 Sta Vitória do Palmar Brazil
74 D5 Santee U.S.A.
79 E5 Santee r. U.S.A.
84 B3 San Telmo, Pta pt Mex.
88 F3 Santiago Brazil
91 B2 Santiago Chile
83 K5 Santiago Dom. Rep.
84 A1 Santiago Mex.
83 H7 Santiago Panama
31 B2 Santiago Phil.
91 B2 Santiago div. Chile
84 D3 Santiago Astata Mex.
45 B1 Santiago de Compostela Spain
83 J4 Santiago de Cuba Cuba
84 A2 Santiago Ixcuintla Mex.
84 A2 Santiago, Río Grande de r. Mex.
91 F2 Santiago Vazquez Uru.
84 A1 Santiaguillo, L. de l. Mex.
65 N2 Santianna Point pt Can.
45 G2 Sant Jordi, Golf de g. Spain
90 E1 Santo Amaro Brazil
90 E3 Santo Amaro de Campos Brazil
90 C4 Sto Amaro, I. de i. Brazil
90 C3 Santo André Brazil
88 F3 Santo Angelo Brazil
54 □ Santo Antão i. Cape Verde
90 D2 Sto Antônio r. Brazil
90 E1 Sto Antônio, Cabo c. Brazil
90 B3 Santo Antônio da Platina Brazil
90 E1 Sto Antônio de Jesus Brazil
90 A1 Sto Antônio de Leverger Brazil
86 E4 Santo Antônio do Içá Brazil
90 D3 Santo Antônio do Monte Brazil
87 G7 Santo Corazón Bol.
83 L5 Santo Domingo Dom. Rep.
84 B2 Sto Domingo Mex.
89 C2 Sto Domingo r. Venez.
70 E4 Santo Domingo Pueblo NM U.S.A.
45 E1 Santoña Spain
30 D2 Santong r. China
90 D1 Sto Onofre r. Brazil
49 L6 Santorini i. Greece
90 C3 Santos Brazil
90 D3 Santos Dumont Brazil
86 D6 Santo Tomás Peru
88 E3 Santo Tomé Arg.
75 F3 Sanup Plateau plat. U.S.A.
88 B7 San Valentín, Cerro mt Chile
82 G6 San Vicente El Salvador
31 B2 San Vicente Phil.
86 C6 San Vicente de Cañete Peru
89 B4 San Vicente del Caguán Col.
48 D3 San Vincenzo Italy
48 E5 San Vito, Capo c. Sicily Italy
27 C7 Sanya China
26 C3 Sanyuan China
30 C2 Sanyuanpu China
56 B4 Sanza Pombo Angola
90 C3 São Bernardo do Campo Brazil
88 E3 São Borja Brazil
90 C3 São Carlos Brazil
90 C1 São Domingos Brazil
90 B2 São Domingos r. Brazil
87 H6 São Félix Mato Grosso Brazil
87 H5 São Félix Pará Brazil
90 E3 São Fidélis Brazil
54 □ São Filipe Cape Verde
90 D1 São Francisco Brazil
87 L5 São Francisco r. Brazil
88 G3 São Francisco do Sul Brazil
91 F1 São Gabriel Brazil
90 D3 São Gonçalo Brazil
90 D2 São Gotardo Brazil
90 C1 São João da Aliança Brazil
90 E3 São João da Barra Brazil
90 C3 São João da Boa Vista Brazil
45 B2 São João da Madeira Port.
90 D1 São João do Paraíso Brazil
90 D3 São João Nepomuceno Brazil
90 C3 São Joaquim da Barra Brazil
34 C5 São Jorge i. Port.
89 D5 São José Brazil
90 E3 São José do Calçado Brazil
91 G2 São José do Norte Brazil
90 C3 São José do Rio Preto Brazil
90 D3 São José dos Campos Brazil
90 C4 São José dos Pinhais Brazil
90 D3 São Lourenço Brazil
90 A2 São Lourenço r. Brazil
91 G1 São Lourenço do Sul Brazil
87 K4 São Luís Brazil
90 C3 São Manuel Brazil
90 C2 São Marcos r. Brazil
87 K4 São Marcos, Baía de b. Brazil
90 E2 São Mateus Brazil
90 E2 São Mateus r. Brazil
34 C5 São Miguel i. Azores Port.
90 C2 São Miguel r. Brazil
44 G3 Saône r. France
54 □ São Nicolau i. Cape Verde
90 C3 São Paulo Brazil
90 C3 São Paulo div. Brazil
96 H5 São Pedro e São Paulo is Atl. Ocean
87 K5 São Raimundo Nonato Brazil
90 D2 São Romão Brazil
87 L5 São Roque, Cabo de pt Brazil
90 D3 São Sebastião Brazil
90 C3 São Sebastião do Paraíso Brazil
90 D3 São Sebastião, Ilha de i. Brazil
91 G1 São Sepé Brazil
90 B2 São Simão Brazil
90 B2 São Simão, Barragem de resr Brazil
25 E6 Sao-Siu Indon.
54 □ São Tiago i. Cape Verde
54 C4 São Tomé i. Sao Tome and Principe
53 E5 São Tomé and Príncipe country Africa
90 E3 São Tomé, Cabo de c. Brazil
90 C3 São Vicente Brazil
54 □ São Vicente i. Cape Verde
45 B4 São Vicente, Cabo de c. Port.
16 C1 Sapanca Turkey
6 C2 Saparua Indon.
16 C2 Şaphane Dağı mt Turkey
54 B4 Sapo National Park nat. park Liberia
28 G3 Sapporo Japan
48 F4 Sapri Italy
33 D4 Sapudi i. Indon.
77 D4 Sapulpa U.S.A.
19 E3 Sāqī Iran
18 B2 Saqqez Iran
18 B2 Sarāb Iran
17 L5 Sarābe Meymeh Iran
32 B2 Sara Buri Thai.
Saragossa see Zaragoza
86 C4 Saraguro Ecuador
49 H3 Sarajevo Bos.-Herz.
19 F2 Sarakhs Iran
14 D1 Saraktash Rus. Fed.
23 H4 Saramati mt India
81 G2 Saranac r. U.S.A.
81 F2 Saranac Lake U.S.A.
66 E5 Saranac Lakes l. U.S.A.
49 J5 Sarandë Albania
91 F2 Sarandí del Yí Uru.
91 F2 Sarandí Grande Uru.
31 C5 Sarangani i. Phil.
31 C5 Sarangani Bay b. Phil.
31 C5 Sarangani Islands is Phil.
31 C5 Sarangani Str. chan. Phil.
33 D3 Saran, Gunung mt Indon.
50 H4 Saransk Rus. Fed.
12 G4 Sarapul Rus. Fed.
89 C3 Sarare r. Venez.
79 D7 Sarasota U.S.A.
22 B5 Saraswati r. India
51 D6 Sarata Ukr.
72 F3 Saratoga U.S.A.
81 G3 Saratoga Springs U.S.A.
33 D2 Saratok Malaysia
51 H5 Saratov Rus. Fed.
51 H5 Saratovskaya Oblast' div. Rus. Fed.
50 J4 Saratovskoye Vdkhr. resr Rus. Fed.
19 F5 Saravan Iran
32 C2 Saravan Laos
32 A2 Sarawa r. Myanmar
33 D2 Sarawak div. Malaysia
16 A1 Saray Turkey
16 B3 Sarayköy Turkey
16 D2 Sarayönü Turkey
19 F5 Sarbāz Iran
19 F5 Sarbāz r. Iran
19 E3 Sarbīsheh Iran
48 D2 Sarca r. Italy
17 M3 Sarcham Iran
22 E3 Sarda r. India/Nepal
23 E3 Sarda r. Nepal
22 C3 Sardarshahr India
18 B2 Sar Dasht Iran
17 M5 Sardasht Iran
Sardegna i. see Sardinia
89 B2 Sardinata Col.
48 C4 Sardinia i. Sardinia Italy
17 L3 Sardrūd Iran
18 C5 Sareb, Rās-as pt U.A.E.
36 P3 Sareks Nationalpark nat. park Sweden
36 P3 Sarektjåkkå mt Sweden
19 G2 Sar-e Pol Afgh.
18 B3 Sar-e-Pol-e-Zahāb Iran
18 D4 Sare Yazd Iran
96 E4 Sargasso Sea sea Atl. Ocean
22 C2 Sargodha Pak.
55 D4 Sarh Chad
18 D2 Sārī Iran
49 M7 Saria i. Greece
16 B2 Sarıgöl Turkey
17 J1 Sarıkamış Turkey
16 D3 Sarıkavak Turkey
22 D4 Sarila India
32 □ Sarimbun Res. resr Sing.
6 E4 Sarina Austr.
16 E2 Sarıoğlan Turkey
19 G3 Sar-i-Pul Afgh.
55 D2 Sarīr Tibesti des. Libya
17 J2 Sarısu Turkey
30 C4 Sariwŏn N. Korea
16 C2 Sarıyar Barajı resr Turkey
16 B1 Sarıyer Turkey
16 F2 Sarız Turkey
22 E4 Sarju r. India
15 F2 Sarkand Kazak.
22 B4 Sarkāri Tala India
16 C2 Şarkikaraağaç Turkey
16 F2 Şarkışla Turkey
51 C7 Şarköy Turkey
19 G4 Sarlath Range mts Afgh./Pak.
44 E4 Sarlat-la-Canéda France
25 F7 Sarmi Indon.
37 N6 Särna Sweden
17 L5 Sarneh Iran
48 C1 Sarnen Switz.
69 F4 Sarnia Can.
51 C5 Sarny Ukr.
33 B3 Sarolangun Indon.
28 H2 Saroma-ko l. Japan
49 K6 Saronikos Kolpos g. Greece
51 C7 Saros Körfezi b. Turkey
22 C4 Sarotra India
50 G4 Sarova Rus. Fed.
19 H3 Sarowbī Afgh.
51 H6 Sarpa, Ozero l. Kalmykiya Rus. Fed.
51 H5 Sarpa, Ozero l. Volgograd. Rus. Fed.
37 M7 Sarpsborg Norway
44 H2 Sarrebourg France
42 F5 Sarreguemines France
45 C1 Sarria Spain
45 F2 Sarrión Spain
42 C6 Sarry France
48 C4 Sartène Corsica France
18 C3 Sarud r. Iran
19 G5 Saruna Pak.
17 M4 Saruq Iran
17 K2 Şärur Azer.
19 F4 Saru Tara Afgh.
17 L4 Sarvabad Iran
46 H7 Sárvár Hungary
18 D4 Sarvestān Iran
20 E1 Sarykamyshkoye Ozero salt l. Turkm.

15 F2 Saryozek Kazak.
15 F2 Saryshagan Kazak.
15 F3 Sary-Tash Kyrg.
19 F2 Sary Yazikskoye Vdkhr. *resr* Turkm.
75 G6 Sasabe U.S.A.
23 F4 Sasaram India
29 A8 Sasebo Japan
65 H4 Saskatchewan *div.* Can.
65 J4 Saskatchewan *r.* Can.
65 H4 Saskatoon Can.
13 N2 Saskylakh Rus. Fed.
59 G3 Sasolburg S. Africa
50 G4 Sasovo Rus. Fed.
81 F5 Sassafras U.S.A.
54 B4 Sassandra Côte d'Ivoire
48 C4 Sassari *Sardinia* Italy
43 G3 Sassenberg Ger.
46 F3 Sassnitz Ger.
51 H6 Sasykoli Rus. Fed.
54 A3 Satadougou Mali
29 B9 Sata-misaki *c.* Japan
22 C5 Satana India
21 A2 Satara India
59 J2 Satara S. Africa
51 G4 Satinka Rus. Fed.
23 G5 Satkhira Bangl.
21 B2 Satmala Range *h.* India
22 E4 Satna India
22 C5 Satpura Range *mts* India
29 B9 Satsuma-hantō *pen.* Japan
43 J5 Satteldorf Ger.
22 D2 Satti Jammu and Kashmir
47 L7 Satu Mare Romania
32 B4 Satun Thai.
91 E1 Sauce Arg.
84 B1 Sauceda Mex.
75 F5 Sauceda Mts *mts* U.S.A.
37 K7 Sauda Norway
36 D4 Sauðárkrókur Iceland
10 F7 Saudi Arabia *country* Asia
43 F3 Sauerland *reg.* Ger.
68 D4 Saugatuck U.S.A.
81 G3 Saugerties U.S.A.
76 E2 Sauk Center U.S.A.
68 C4 Sauk City U.S.A.
44 G3 Saulieu France
69 E2 Sault Ste Marie Can.
68 E2 Sault Ste Marie U.S.A.
25 F7 Saumlakki Indon.
44 D3 Saumur France
92 A4 Saunders Coast *coastal area* Ant.
92 C1 Saunders I. *i.* Atl. Ocean
23 F4 Saura *r.* India
57 C4 Saurimo Angola
49 J2 Sava *r.* Europe
7 J3 Savaii *i.* Western Samoa
51 G5 Savala *r.* Rus. Fed.
54 C4 Savalou Benin
Savanat *see* Eşţahbānāt
68 B4 Savanna U.S.A.
79 D6 Savannah *GA* U.S.A.
79 B5 Savannah *TN* U.S.A.
79 D5 Savannah *r.* U.S.A.
79 E7 Savannah Sound Bahamas
32 C1 Savannakhét Laos
83 J5 Savanna la Mar Jamaica
66 B3 Savant Lake Can.
21 A3 Savanur India
36 R5 Sävar Sweden
49 M5 Savaştepe Turkey
54 C4 Savè Benin
57 D6 Save *r.* Moz.
18 C3 Sāveh Iran
36 V5 Saviaho Fin.
12 F3 Savinskiy Rus. Fed.
44 H4 Savoie *reg.* France
48 C2 Savona Italy
37 V6 Savonlinna Fin.
36 V5 Savonranta Fin.
17 J1 Şavşat Turkey
37 O8 Sävsjö Sweden
36 V3 Savukoski Fin.
17 H3 Savur Turkey
22 D4 Sawai Madhopur India
32 A1 Sawankhalok Thai.
73 F4 Sawatch Mts *mts* U.S.A.
40 A6 Sawel Mt *h.* U.K.
68 B2 Sawtooth Mountains *h.* U.S.A.
25 E7 Sawu Sea *g.* Indon.
39 G4 Saxilby U.K.
39 J5 Saxmundham U.K.
36 O4 Saxnäs Sweden
24 B1 Sayano-Shushenskoye Vdkhr. *resr* Rus. Fed.
19 F2 Sayat Turkm.
84 E3 Sayaxché Guatemala
20 D6 Sayḩūt Yemen
51 H5 Saykhin Kazak.
56 E2 Säylac Somalia
24 D2 Saynshand Mongolia
45 F1 Sayoa *mt* Spain
28 E2 Sayon Rus. Fed.
77 D5 Sayre *OK* U.S.A.
80 E4 Sayre *PA* U.S.A.
84 B3 Sayula *Jalisco* Mex.
84 D3 Sayula *Veracruz* Mex.
22 C2 Sazin Pak.
50 E3 Sazonovo Rus. Fed.
54 B2 Sbaa Alg.
54 C1 Sbeitla Tunisia
38 D3 Scafell Pike *mt* U.K.
40 B4 Scalasaig U.K.
48 F5 Scalea Italy
40 □ Scalloway U.K.
41 C5 Scalp *h.* Rep. of Ireland
40 C3 Scalpay *i. Scot.* U.K.
40 B3 Scalpay *i. Scot.* U.K.
40 A5 Scalp Mountain *h.* Rep. of Ireland
40 E2 Scapa Flow *in.* U.K.
40 C4 Scarba *i.* U.K.
69 H4 Scarborough Can.
89 E2 Scarborough Trinidad and Tobago
38 G3 Scarborough U.K.
31 A3 Scarborough Shoal *sand bank* Phil.
40 A2 Scarp *i.* U.K.
Scarpanto *i. see* Karpathos
43 J1 Schaale *r.* Ger.
43 J1 Schaalsee *l.* Ger.
42 C4 Schaerbeek Belgium
46 D7 Schaffhausen Switz.
43 K3 Schafstädt Ger.
42 C2 Schagen Neth.
42 C2 Schagerbrug Neth.
58 B3 Schakalskuppe Namibia
19 F4 Schao *watercourse* Afgh./Iran
46 F6 Schärding Austria
42 B3 Scharendijke Neth.
43 J5 Schebheim Ger.
43 H1 Scheeßel Ger.
67 G3 Schefferville Can.
42 C3 Schelde *r.* Belgium
75 E2 Schell Creek Range *mts* U.S.A.
43 J2 Schellerten Ger.
81 G3 Schenectady U.S.A.
43 H1 Schenefeld Ger.
42 C2 Schermerhorn Neth.
40 D4 Schiehallion *mt* U.K.
43 L6 Schierling Ger.
42 E1 Schiermonnikoog Neth.
42 E1 Schiermonnikoog *i.* Neth.
42 E1 Schiermonnikoog Nationaal Park *nat. park* Neth.
43 G1 Schiffdorf Ger.
43 K1 Schilde *r.* Ger.
42 D4 Schinnen Neth.
48 D2 Schio Italy
43 L3 Schkeuditz Ger.
42 E4 Schleiden Ger.
43 K4 Schleiz Ger.
46 D3 Schleswig Ger.
43 H1 Schleswig-Holstein *div.* Ger.
43 J4 Schleusingen Ger.
43 H4 Schlitz Ger.
43 G3 Schloß Holte-Stukenbrock Ger.
43 H4 Schlüchtern Ger.
43 J5 Schlüsselfeld Ger.
43 G3 Schmallenberg Ger.
43 L4 Schneeberg Ger.
43 K3 Schneidlingen Ger.
43 H1 Schneverdingen Ger.
81 G3 Schodack Center U.S.A.
68 C3 Schofield U.S.A.
74 □1 Schofield Barracks U.S.A.
43 L1 Schönebeck Ger.
43 K2 Schönebeck (Elbe) Ger.
43 J2 Schöningen Ger.
43 H5 Schöntal Ger.
81 J2 Schoodic Lake *l.* U.S.A.
68 E4 Schoolcraft U.S.A.
42 C3 Schoonhoven Neth.
43 J5 Schopfloch Ger.
43 J2 Schöppenstedt Ger.
43 F1 Schortens Ger.
6 E2 Schouten Islands *is* P.N.G.
68 D1 Schreiber Can.
81 G3 Schroon Lake *l.* U.S.A.
75 F5 Schuchuli U.S.A.
41 B6 Schull Rep. of Ireland
65 K2 Schultz Lake *l.* Can.
74 C2 Schurz U.S.A.
42 F2 Schüttorf Ger.
81 G3 Schuylerville U.S.A.
43 K5 Schwabach Ger.
43 H5 Schwäbisch Hall Ger.
46 E6 Schwabmünchen Ger.
43 G2 Schwaförden Ger.
43 H4 Schwalmstadt-Ziegenhain Ger.
43 L5 Schwandorf Ger.
33 D3 Schwaner, Pegunungan *mts* Indon.
43 G1 Schwanewede Ger.
43 H2 Schwarmstedt Ger.
43 M3 Schwarze Elster *r.* Ger.
43 J1 Schwarzenbek Ger.
43 L4 Schwarzenberg Ger.
42 E4 Schwarzer Mann *h.* Ger.
58 B2 Schwarzrand *mts* Namibia
46 E7 Schwaz Austria
46 G4 Schwedt Ger.
43 G5 Schwegenheim Ger.
42 E5 Schweich Ger.
43 J4 Schweinfurt Ger.
43 M3 Schweinitz Ger.
43 L1 Schweinrich Ger.
59 F3 Schweizer-Reneke S. Africa
42 F3 Schwelm Ger.
46 D6 Schwenningen Ger.
43 K1 Schwerin Ger.
43 K1 Schweriner See *l.* Ger.
43 G5 Schwetzingen Ger.
46 D7 Schwyz Switz.
48 E6 Sciacca *Sicily* Italy
39 A8 Scilly, Isles of *is* U.K.
80 B5 Scioto *r.* U.S.A.
75 F2 Scipio U.S.A.
72 F1 Scobey U.S.A.
39 J5 Scole U.K.
46 H2 Scone Austr.
63 Q2 Scoresby Land *reg.* Greenland
63 Q2 Scoresby Sund *chan.* Greenland
96 F9 Scotia Ridge *sea feature* Atl. Ocean
85 E8 Scotia Sea *sea* Atl. Ocean
69 G4 Scotland Can.
34 E3 Scotland *div.* U.K.
92 B5 Scott Base *N.Z. Base* Ant.
59 J5 Scottburgh S. Africa
64 D4 Scott, C. *c.* Can.
76 C4 Scott City U.S.A.
92 B5 Scott Coast *coastal area* Ant.
80 D4 Scottdale U.S.A.
92 B4 Scott Gl. *gl.* Ant.
63 L2 Scott Inlet *in.* Can.
92 A5 Scott Island *i.* Ant.
65 H3 Scott Lake *l.* Can.
92 D4 Scott Mts *mts* Ant.
76 C3 Scottsbluff U.S.A.
79 C5 Scottsboro U.S.A.
78 C4 Scottsburg U.S.A.
73 E5 Scottsdale U.S.A.
74 A3 Scotts Valley U.S.A.
68 D4 Scottville U.S.A.
74 D3 Scotty's Junction U.S.A.
40 C2 Scourie U.K.
40 □ Scousburgh U.K.
40 E2 Scrabster U.K.
81 F4 Scranton U.S.A.
40 B4 Scridain, Loch *in.* U.K.
38 G4 Scunthorpe U.K.
39 H7 Seaford U.K.
81 F5 Seaford U.S.A.
69 G4 Seaforth Can.
31 A4 Seahorse Bank *sand bank* Phil.
65 K3 Seal *r.* Can.
8 D3 Sea Lake Austr.
58 E7 Seal, Cape *pt* S. Africa
81 J3 Seal I. *i.* U.S.A.
67 H3 Seal Lake *l.* Can.
58 F7 Seal Point *pt* S. Africa
75 E3 Seaman Range *mts* U.S.A.
38 G3 Seamer U.K.
75 E4 Searchlight U.S.A.
77 F5 Searcy U.S.A.
74 D4 Searles Lake *l.* U.S.A.
68 E4 Sears U.S.A.
81 J2 Searsport U.S.A.
74 B3 Seaside *CA* U.S.A.
72 B2 Seaside *OR* U.S.A.
40 D3 Seaton *Eng.* U.K.
38 D3 Seaton U.K.
72 B2 Seattle U.S.A.
81 F5 Seaville U.S.A.
81 H3 Sebago Lake *l.* U.S.A.
82 B3 Sebastián Vizcaíno, Bahía *b.* Mex.
81 J2 Sebasticook *r.* U.S.A.
33 E2 Sebatik *i.* Indon.
16 C1 Seben Turkey
49 K2 Sebeş Romania
33 C4 Sebesi *i.* Indon.
69 F4 Sebewaing U.S.A.
50 D3 Sebezh Rus. Fed.
16 E3 Şebil Turkey
16 G1 Şebinkarahisar Turkey
81 J2 Seboeis Lake *l.* U.S.A.
81 J2 Seboomook U.S.A.
81 J2 Seboomook Lake *l.* U.S.A.
79 D7 Sebring U.S.A.
51 G5 Sebrovo Rus. Fed.
86 B5 Sechura Peru
86 B5 Sechura, Bahía de *b.* Peru
43 H5 Seckach Ger.
81 H2 Second Lake *l.* U.S.A.
9 A6 Secretary Island *i.* N.Z.
59 H3 Secunda S. Africa
21 B2 Secunderabad India
76 E4 Sedalia U.S.A.
21 B2 Sedam India
8 B3 Sedan Austr.
44 G2 Sedan France
9 E4 Seddon N.Z.
9 C4 Seddonville N.Z.
19 E3 Sedeh Iran
81 J2 Sedgwick U.S.A.
54 A3 Sédhiou Senegal
46 G6 Sedlčany Czech Rep.
16 E6 Sedom Israel
75 G4 Sedona U.S.A.
48 B6 Sédrata Alg.
37 S9 Šeduva Lith.
43 J1 Seedorf Ger.
41 D5 Seefin *h.* Rep. of Ireland
43 K2 Seehausen Ger.
43 K2 Seehausen (Altmark) Ger.
57 B6 Seeheim Namibia
43 G5 Seeheim-Jugenheim Ger.
58 E6 Seekoegat S. Africa
75 E5 Seeley U.S.A.
92 B3 Seelig, Mt *mt* Ant.
43 H2 Seelze Ger.
44 E2 Sées France
43 J3 Seesen Ger.
43 J1 Seevetal Ger.
54 A4 Sefadu Sierra Leone
59 G1 Sefare Botswana
49 M5 Seferihisar Turkey
59 G1 Sefophe Botswana
37 M6 Segalstad Norway
32 B5 Segamat Malaysia
43 L2 Segeletz Ger.
50 E2 Segezha Rus. Fed.
45 F3 Segorbe Spain
54 B3 Ségou Mali
89 B3 Segovia Col.
45 D2 Segovia Spain
Segovia *r. see* Coco
50 E2 Segozerskoye, Oz. *resr* Rus. Fed.
45 G1 Segre *r.* Spain
55 D2 Séguédine Niger
54 B4 Séguéla Côte d'Ivoire
77 D6 Seguin U.S.A.
91 D1 Segundo *r.* Arg.
45 F3 Segura *r.* Spain
57 C6 Sehithwa Botswana
59 H4 Sehlabathebe National Park Lesotho
22 D5 Sehore India
36 S1 Seiland *i.* Norway
77 D4 Seiling U.S.A.
36 S5 Seinäjoki Fin.
66 B4 Seine *r.* Can.
44 E2 Seine *r.* France
44 D2 Seine, Baie de *b.* France
44 F2 Seine, Val de *v.* France
47 L3 Sejny Pol.
33 B3 Sekayu Indon.
58 F2 Sekhutlane *watercourse* Botswana
58 E2 Sekoma Botswana
54 B4 Sekondi Ghana
19 F4 Sekūheh Iran
32 D5 Sekura Indon.
72 B2 Selah U.S.A.
25 F7 Selaru *i.* Indon.
33 D3 Selatan, Tanjung *pt* Indon.
32 □ Selat Johor *chan.* Malaysia/Sing.
32 □ Selat Jurong *chan.* Sing.
32 □ Selat Pandan *chan.* Sing.
62 B3 Selawik U.S.A.
43 L4 Selb Ger.
36 L5 Selbekken Norway
36 M5 Selbu Norway
38 F4 Selby U.K.
76 C2 Selby U.S.A.
57 C6 Selebi-Phikwe Botswana
24 F1 Selemdzhinsky Khr. *mts* Rus. Fed.
16 B2 Selendi Turkey
44 H2 Sélestat France
32 □ Seletar Sing.
32 □ Seletar, P. *i.* Sing.
32 □ Seletar Res. *resr* Sing.
15 F1 Seletyteniz, Ozero *l.* Kazak.
Seleucia Pieria *see* Samandağı
76 C2 Selfridge U.S.A.
50 J2 Selib Rus. Fed.
54 A3 Sélibabi Maur.
43 G4 Seligenstadt Ger.
50 E3 Seliger, Oz. *l.* Rus. Fed.
75 F4 Seligman U.S.A.
55 E2 Selīma Oasis *oasis* Sudan
69 J5 Selinsgrove U.S.A.
47 Q2 Selishche Rus. Fed.
51 H6 Selitrennoye Rus. Fed.
47 Q2 Selizharovo Rus. Fed.
37 L7 Seljord Norway
43 K3 Selke *r.* Ger.
65 K4 Selkirk Can.
40 F5 Selkirk U.K.
64 F4 Selkirk Mountains *mts* Can.
38 D3 Sellafield U.K.
75 G6 Sells U.S.A.
42 F3 Selm Ger.
79 C5 Selma *AL* U.S.A.
74 C3 Selma *CA* U.S.A.
79 B5 Selmer U.S.A.
19 F4 Selseleh-ye Pīr Shūrān *mts* Iran
39 G7 Selsey Bill *hd* U.K.
32 C4 Seluan *i.* Indon.
86 D5 Selvas *reg.* Brazil
65 J3 Selwyn Lake *l.* Can.
64 C2 Selwyn Mountains *mts* Can.
62 E3 Selwyn Mts Can.
6 D4 Selwyn Range *h.* Austr.
33 D4 Semarang Indon.
33 C2 Sematan Malaysia
33 E3 Semayang, Danau *l.* Indon.
31 A6 Sembakung *r.* Indon.
32 □ Sembawang Sing.
56 B3 Sembé Congo
17 K3 Şemdinli Turkey
33 D4 Semenanjung Blambangan *pen.* Indon.
51 E4 Semenivka Ukr.
50 H3 Semenov Rus. Fed.
51 G6 Semikarakorsk Rus. Fed.
51 F5 Semiluki Rus. Fed.
72 F3 Seminoe Res. *resr* U.S.A.
77 C5 Seminole U.S.A.
79 C6 Seminole, L. *l.* U.S.A.
15 G1 Semipalatinsk Kazak.
31 B3 Semirara *i.* Phil.
31 B4 Semirara Islands *is* Phil.
18 C4 Semīrom Iran
18 D3 Semnān Iran
42 D5 Semois *r.* Belgium
42 D5 Semois, Vallée de la *v.* Belgium/France
33 E2 Semporna Malaysia
33 D4 Sempu *i.* Indon.
31 A5 Senaja Malaysia
51 G7 Senaki Georgia
86 E5 Sena Madureira Brazil
21 C5 Senanayake Samudra *l.* Sri Lanka
57 C5 Senanga Zambia
29 B9 Sendai Japan
28 G5 Sendai Japan
23 H3 Sêndo China
32 B5 Senebui, Tanjung *pt* Indon.
75 G5 Seneca *AZ* U.S.A.
68 C5 Seneca *IL* U.S.A.
72 C2 Seneca *OR* U.S.A.
80 E3 Seneca Falls U.S.A.
80 E3 Seneca Lake *l.* U.S.A.
80 D5 Seneca Rocks U.S.A.
80 C5 Senecaville Lake *l.* U.S.A.
52 C4 Senegal *country* Africa
54 A3 Sénégal *r.* Maur./Senegal
59 G4 Senekal S. Africa
68 E2 Seney U.S.A.
46 G5 Senftenberg Ger.
22 D4 Sengar *r.* India
56 D4 Sengerema Tanz.
50 J4 Sengiley Rus. Fed.
87 K6 Senhor do Bonfim Brazil
48 E3 Senigallia Italy
48 F2 Senj Croatia
36 P2 Senja *i.* Norway
17 J1 Şenkaya Turkey
22 D2 Senku Jammu and Kashmir
58 E2 Senlac S. Africa
30 F2 Senlin Shan *mt* China
44 F2 Senlis France
32 C2 Senmonorom Cambodia
39 B7 Sennen U.K.
69 J1 Senneterre Can.
59 H5 Senqu *r.* Lesotho
44 F2 Sens France
42 B4 Sensée *r.* France
82 G6 Sensuntepeque El Salvador
49 J2 Senta Yugo.
22 D3 Senthal India
75 F5 Sentinel U.S.A.
64 E3 Sentinel Pk *summit* Can.
92 B3 Sentinel Ra. *mts* Ant.
32 □ Sentosa *i.* Sing.
17 H3 Şenyurt Turkey
22 D5 Seoni India
23 E5 Seorinarayan India
30 D5 Seoul S. Korea
9 D4 Separation Pt *pt* N.Z.
17 L4 Separ Shāhābād Iran
90 D3 Sepetiba, Baía de *b.* Brazil
18 C4 Sepīdān Iran
6 E2 Sepik *r.* P.N.G.
30 D4 Sep'o N. Korea
67 G3 Sept-Îles Can.
74 C3 Sequoia National Park U.S.A.
17 L3 Serā Iran
51 G5 Serafimovich Rus. Fed.
19 F2 Serakhs Turkm.
25 E7 Seram *i.* Indon.
25 F7 Seram Sea *g.* Indon.
33 C4 Serang Indon.
32 □ Serangoon Harbour *chan.* Sing.
32 D5 Serasan *i.* Indon.
33 C2 Serasan, Selat *chan.* Indon.
32 D5 Seraya *i.* Indon.
32 □ Seraya, P. *i.* Sing.
49 J3 Serbia *div.* Yugo.
Serbija *div. see* Serbia
Serdar *see* Kaypak
56 E2 Serdo Eth.
51 H4 Serdoba *r.* Rus. Fed.
51 H4 Serdobsk Rus. Fed.
50 D3 Seredka Rus. Fed.
16 D2 Şereflikoçhisar Turkey
33 B2 Seremban Malaysia
56 D4 Serengeti National Park Tanz.
57 D5 Serenje Zambia
50 H4 Sergach Rus. Fed.
28 C3 Sergeyevka Rus. Fed.
50 F3 Sergiyev Posad Rus. Fed.
33 D2 Seria Brunei
33 D2 Serian Malaysia
49 L6 Serifos *i.* Greece
67 G2 Sérigny, Lac *l.* Can.
16 C3 Serik Turkey
25 E7 Sermata, Kepulauan *is* Indon.
50 J3 Sernur Rus. Fed.
19 E2 Sernyy Zavod Turkm.
51 H6 Seroglazka Rus. Fed.
12 H4 Serov Rus. Fed.
57 C6 Serowe Botswana
45 C4 Serpa Port.
89 E2 Serpent's Mouth *chan.* Trinidad/Venez.
50 F4 Serpukhov Rus. Fed.
90 C3 Serra da Canastra, Parque Nacional da *nat. park* Brazil
89 D4 Serranía de la Neblina, Parque Nacional *nat. park* Venez.
90 B2 Serranópolis Brazil
42 B5 Serre *r.* France
49 K4 Serres Greece
91 D1 Serrezuela Arg.
87 L6 Serrinha Brazil
90 D2 Sêrro Brazil
91 B4 Serrucho *mt* Arg.
48 C6 Sers Tunisia
90 C3 Sertãozinho Brazil
50 D2 Sertolovo Rus. Fed.
32 A4 Seruai Indon.
33 D3 Seruyan *r.* Indon.
24 B3 Sêrxu China
33 E2 Sesayap Indon.
31 A6 Sesayap *r.* Indon.
66 B3 Seseganaga L. *l.* Can.
69 G1 Sesekinika Can.
57 B5 Sesfontein Namibia
59 H1 Seshego S. Africa
57 C5 Sesheke Zambia
48 E4 Sessa Aurunca Italy
48 C2 Sestri Levante Italy
50 D2 Sestroretsk Rus. Fed.
28 F3 Setana Japan
44 F5 Sète France
90 D2 Sete Lagoas Brazil
36 Q2 Setermoen Norway
37 K7 Setesdal *v.* Norway
23 F4 Seti *r. Gandakhi* Nepal
22 E3 Seti *r. Seti* Nepal
54 C1 Sétif Alg.
29 E7 Seto Japan
32 C2 Set, P. *mt* Laos
54 B1 Settat Morocco
38 E3 Settle U.K.
45 B3 Setúbal Port.
45 B3 Setúbal, Baía de *b.* Port.
68 E3 Seul Choix Pt *pt* U.S.A.
66 B3 Seul, Lac *l.* Can.
17 K1 Sevan Armenia
Sevana Lich *l. see* Sevan, Lake
17 K1 Sevan, Lake *l.* Armenia
51 E6 Sevastopol' Ukr.
67 H2 Seven Islands Bay *b.* Can.
39 H6 Sevenoaks U.K.
Seven Pagodas *see* Māmallapuram
44 F4 Sévérac-le-Château France
58 E3 Severn S. Africa
66 B3 Severn *r.* Can.
39 E6 Severn *r.* U.K.
50 G2 Severnaya Dvina *r.* Rus. Fed.
51 H7 Severnaya Osetiya, Respublika *div.* Rus. Fed.
13 M1 Severnaya Zemlya *is* Rus. Fed.
66 B3 Severn L. *l.* Can.
12 H3 Severnyy Rus. Fed.
24 D1 Severo Baykal'skoye Nagorye *mts* Rus. Fed.
50 F1 Severodvinsk Rus. Fed.
13 R4 Severo-Kuril'sk Rus. Fed.
36 X2 Severomorsk Rus. Fed.
12 L3 Severo-Yeniseyskiy Rus. Fed.
51 F6 Severskaya Rus. Fed.
73 D4 Sevier *r.* U.S.A.
75 G2 Sevier Bridge Reservoir U.S.A.
75 F2 Sevier Desert. U.S.A.
75 F2 Sevier Lake *salt l.* U.S.A.
89 B3 Sevilla Col.
Sevilla *see* Seville
45 D4 Seville Spain
49 L3 Sevlievo Bulg.
22 C3 Sewāni India
62 D3 Seward *AK* U.S.A.
76 D3 Seward U.S.A.
62 B3 Seward Peninsula *AK* U.S.A.
64 F3 Sexsmith Can.
70 E6 Sextín *r.* Mex.
19 F3 Seyah Band Koh *mts* Afgh.
17 K2 Seyah Cheshmeh Iran
12 J2 Seyakha Rus. Fed.
84 E3 Seybaplaya Mex.
53 K6 Seychelles *country* Ind. Ocean
19 F2 Seydi Turkm.
16 C3 Seydişehir Turkey
36 F4 Seyðisfjörður Iceland
18 B2 Seydvān Iran
Seyhan *see* Adana
16 E3 Seyhan *r.* Turkey
51 E5 Seym *r.* Rus. Fed.
13 R3 Seymchan Rus. Fed.
8 E4 Seymour Austr.
59 G6 Seymour S. Africa
78 C4 Seymour *IN* U.S.A.
77 D5 Seymour *TX* U.S.A.
19 H3 Seyyedābād Afgh.
44 F2 Sézanne France
49 L7 Sfakia Greece
49 L2 Sfântu Gheorghe Romania
54 D1 Sfax Tunisia
49 K4 Sfikia, Limni *resr* Greece
42 D2 's-Graveland Neth.
's-Gravenhage *see* The Hague
40 C4 Sgurr Dhomhnuill *h.* U.K.
40 C3 Sgurr Mor *mt* U.K.
26 E2 Sha *r.* China
26 C3 Shaanxi *div.* China
18 B2 Shabestar Iran
67 G3 Shabogamo Lake *l.* Can.
56 C4 Shabunda Congo(Zaire)
15 F3 Shache China
92 B4 Shackleton Coast *coastal area* Ant.
92 B4 Shackleton Gl. *gl.* Ant.
92 D6 Shackleton Ice Shelf *ice feature* Ant.
92 C3 Shackleton Ra. *mts* Ant.
22 A4 Shadadkot Pak.
18 C4 Shādegān Iran
22 A3 Shadikhak Pass Pak.
18 D4 Shādkām *watercourse* Iran
68 D5 Shafer, Lake *l.* U.S.A.
92 B5 Shafer Pk *summit* Ant.
74 C4 Shafter U.S.A.
39 E6 Shaftesbury U.K.
62 C3 Shageluk U.S.A.
9 C6 Shag Pt *pt* N.Z.
92 B2 Shag Rocks *is* Atl. Ocean
18 C2 Shah *r.* Iran
21 B2 Shahabad *Karnataka* India
22 E4 Shahabad *Uttar Pradesh* India
22 C5 Shahada India
33 B2 Shah Alam Malaysia
21 A3 Shahapur India
22 A4 Shahbandar Pak.
19 G5 Shahbaz Kalat Pak.
23 G5 Shahbazpur *chan.* Bangl.
19 E4 Shahdāb Iran
22 E5 Shahdol India
19 G3 Shah Fuladi *mt* Afgh.
22 B4 Shahgarh India
17 K3 Shāhīdān Iraq
17 K3 Shahi Pen. *pen.* Iran
19 G4 Shah Ismail Afgh.
22 D4 Shahjahanpur India
18 E2 Shāh Jehān, Kūh-e *mts* Iran
19 E4 Shāh Kūh *mt* Iran
18 D3 Shahmīrzād Iran
21 B2 Shahpur India
22 B3 Shahpur Pak.
22 E5 Shahpura *Madhya Pradesh* India
22 D4 Shahpura *Rajasthan* India
19 G3 Shahrak Afgh.
19 F3 Shahrakht Iran
18 D4 Shahr-e Bābāk Iran
18 C3 Shahr-e Kord Iran
Shahrezā *see* Qomisheh
18 C3 Shahr Rey Iran
19 H2 Shahrtuz Tajik.
18 D3 Shahrud Bustam *reg.* Iran
19 G4 Shaikh Husain *mt* Pak.
18 C5 Shaj'ah, J. *h.* S. Arabia
30 C3 Shajianzi China
17 L3 Shakar Bolāghī Iran
59 J4 Shakaville S. Africa
19 H2 Shakh Tajik.
19 H2 Shakhdara *r.* Tajik.
19 E3 Shākhen Iran
50 E3 Shakhovskaya Rus. Fed.
19 G2 Shakhrisabz Uzbek.
51 G6 Shakhty Rus. Fed.
50 H3 Shakhun'ya Rus. Fed.
76 E2 Shakopee U.S.A.
28 G3 Shakotan-hantō *pen.* Japan
28 G3 Shakotan-misaki *c.* Japan
50 G2 Shalakusha Rus. Fed.
24 B3 Shaluli Shan *mts* China
23 J3 Shaluni *mt* India
65 L3 Shamattawa Can.
27 □ Sham Chun *h. H.K.* China
18 E5 Shamīl Iran
18 D6 Shamis U.A.E.
80 E4 Shamokin U.S.A.
77 C5 Shamrock U.S.A.
57 D5 Shamva Zimbabwe
41 B6 Shanacrane Rep. of Ireland
19 F4 Shand Afgh.
19 F4 Shāndak Iran
26 A2 Shandan China
17 M3 Shānderman Iran
26 E1 Shandian *r.* China
19 E2 Shandiz Iran
74 B4 Shandon U.S.A.
30 A5 Shandong *div.* China
26 F2 Shandong Bandao *pen.* China
17 K5 Shandrūkh Iraq
22 C1 Shandur Pass *pass* Pak.
57 C5 Shangani *r.* Zimbabwe
26 E3 Shangcai China
27 C5 Shangchao China
26 E4 Shangcheng China
23 G3 Shang Chu *r.* China
27 D6 Shangchuan Dao *i.* China
26 D1 Shangdu China
27 E4 Shanggao China
26 F4 Shanghai China
26 F4 Shanghai *div.* China
27 E5 Shanghang China
26 E2 Shanghe China
30 C3 Shanghekou China
26 D3 Shangjin China
27 C6 Shanglin China
26 D3 Shangman China
26 E3 Shangqiu *Henan* China
26 E3 Shangqiu *Henan* China
27 E4 Shangrao *Jiangxi* China
27 E4 Shangrao *Jiangxi* China
26 E3 Shangshui China
27 C6 Shangsi China
27 E4 Shangtang China
26 D1 Shangyi China
27 E5 Shangyou China
27 F4 Shangyu China
30 D1 Shangzhi China
26 C3 Shangzhou China
30 D1 Shanhetun China
41 C5 Shannon *est.* Rep. of Ireland
41 C4 Shannon *r.* Rep. of Ireland
60 R2 Shannon Island *i.* Greenland
41 B5 Shannon, Mouth of the *est.* Rep. of Ireland
30 D2 Shansonggang China
23 G5 Shāntipur India
27 E6 Shantou China
27 E6 Shanwei China
26 D2 Shanxi *div.* China
26 E3 Shan Xian China
26 C3 Shanyang China
26 D2 Shanyin China
27 D5 Shaodong China
27 D5 Shaoguan China
27 E5 Shaowu China
27 F4 Shaoxing China
27 D5 Shaoyang *Hunan* China
27 D5 Shaoyang *Hunan* China
38 E3 Shap U.K.
27 D6 Shapa China
40 F1 Shapinsay *i.* U.K.
20 C4 Shaqrā' S. Arabia
17 J6 Sharaf *well* Iraq
22 B3 Sharan Jogizai Pak.
19 G2 Shargun Uzbek.
51 D5 Sharhorod Ukr.
28 J3 Shari-dake *volc.* Japan
20 E4 Sharjah U.A.E.
47 N3 Sharkawshchyna Belarus
6 B4 Shark Bay *b.* Austr.
18 D2 Sharlouk Turkm.
81 G4 Sharon *CT* U.S.A.
80 C4 Sharon *PA* U.S.A.
27 □ Sharp Peak *h. H.K.* China
16 E5 Sharqi, Jebel esh *mts* Lebanon/Syria
50 H3 Shar'ya Rus. Fed.
57 C6 Shashe *r.* Botswana/Zimbabwe
56 D3 Shashemenē Eth.
27 D4 Shashi China
72 B3 Shasta L. *l.* U.S.A.
72 B3 Shasta, Mt *volc.* U.S.A.
27 □ Sha Tin *H.K.* China
50 H4 Shatki Rus. Fed.
17 M7 Shatt al Arab *r.* Iran/Iraq
17 K6 Shatt al Hillah *r.* Iraq
18 C4 Shaţţ, Ra's osh *pt* Iran
50 F4 Shatura Rus. Fed.
16 E6 Shaubak Jordan
65 H5 Shaunavon Can.
80 D5 Shavers Fork *r.* U.S.A.
81 F4 Shawangunk Mts *h.* U.S.A.
68 C3 Shawano U.S.A.
68 C3 Shawano Lake *l.* U.S.A.
66 F4 Shawinigan Can.
16 F4 Shawmarīyah, Jebel ash *mts* Syria
77 D5 Shawnee U.S.A.
27 F5 Sha Xi *r.* China
27 E5 Sha Xian China
27 D4 Shayang China
6 C4 Shay Gap Austr.
17 L5 Shaykh Jūwī Iraq
17 L5 Shaykh Sa'd Iraq
18 D4 Shaytūr Iran
19 J2 Shazud Tajik.
50 F4 Shchekino Rus. Fed.
13 S3 Shcherbakovo Rus. Fed.
51 F5 Shchigry Rus. Fed.
51 D5 Shchors Ukr.
50 C4 Shchuchyn Belarus
51 F5 Shebekino Rus. Fed.
19 G2 Sheberghān Afgh.
68 D4 Sheboygan U.S.A.
54 D4 Shebshi Mountains Nigeria
67 H4 Shediac Can.
64 D3 Shedin Pk *summit* Can.
41 D4 Sheelin, Lough *l.* Rep. of Ireland
41 D2 Sheep Haven *b.* Rep. of Ireland
59 J3 Sheepmoor S. Africa
75 E3 Sheep Peak *summit* U.S.A.
39 H6 Sheerness U.K.
67 H5 Sheet Harbour Can.
9 D5 Sheffield N.Z.
39 F4 Sheffield U.K.
79 C5 Sheffield *AL* U.S.A.
68 C5 Sheffield *IL* U.S.A.
80 D4 Sheffield *PA* U.S.A.
77 C6 Sheffield *TX* U.S.A.
69 G3 Sheguiandah Can.
26 B4 Shehong China
16 E5 Sheikh, Jebel esh *mt* Lebanon/Syria
22 C3 Shekhupura Pak.
27 □ Shek Kwu Chau *i. H.K.* China
27 □ Shek Pik Reservoir *H.K.* China
50 F3 Sheksna Rus. Fed.
27 □ Shek Uk Shan *h. H.K.* China
19 F4 Shelag *watercourse* Afgh./Iran
13 T2 Shelagskiy, Mys *pt* Rus. Fed.
68 A6 Shelbina U.S.A.
67 G5 Shelburne *N.S.* Can.
69 G3 Shelburne *Ont.* Can.
81 G3 Shelburne Falls U.S.A.
68 D4 Shelby *MI* U.S.A.
72 E1 Shelby *MT* U.S.A.
79 D5 Shelby *NC* U.S.A.
80 B4 Shelby *OH* U.S.A.
78 C4 Shelbyville *IN* U.S.A.
68 A6 Shelbyville *MO* U.S.A.
79 C5 Shelbyville *TN* U.S.A.
75 H5 Sheldon *AZ* U.S.A.
68 D5 Sheldon *IL* U.S.A.
81 G2 Sheldon Springs U.S.A.
67 H3 Sheldrake Can.
13 R3 Shelikhova, Zaliv *g.* Rus. Fed.
62 C4 Shelikof Strait U.S.A.
65 H4 Shellbrook Can.
72 D3 Shelley U.S.A.
8 H3 Shellharbour Austr.
74 A1 Shell Mt *mt* U.S.A.
64 F4 Shelter Bay Can.
74 A1 Shelter Cove U.S.A.
27 □ Shelter I. *i. H.K.* China
81 G4 Shelter I. *i.* U.S.A.
9 B7 Shelter Pt *pt* N.Z.
76 E3 Shenandoah *IA* U.S.A.
81 E4 Shenandoah *PA* U.S.A.
80 D5 Shenandoah *VA* U.S.A.
80 D5 Shenandoah *r.* U.S.A.
80 D5 Shenandoah Mountains U.S.A.
80 D5 Shenandoah National Park U.S.A.
80 C4 Shenango River Lake *l.* U.S.A.
54 C4 Shendam Nigeria
28 C1 Shending Shan *h.* China
26 G4 Shengsi China
27 F4 Sheng Xian China
50 G2 Shenkursk Rus. Fed.
26 D2 Shenmu China
26 D4 Shennongjia China
26 E3 Shenqiu China
28 A1 Shenshu China
30 B3 Shenwo Sk. *resr* China
30 B3 Shenyang China
27 E6 Shenzhen China
51 C5 Shepetivka Ukr.
7 G3 Shepherd Is *is* Vanuatu
8 E4 Shepparton Austr.
39 H6 Sheppey, Isle of *i.* U.K.
19 G2 Sherabad Uzbek.
39 E7 Sherborne U.K.
67 H4 Sherbrooke *N.S.* Can.
67 F4 Sherbrooke *Que.* Can.
81 F3 Sherburne U.S.A.
41 E4 Shercock Rep. of Ireland
19 H3 Sher Dahan Pass Afgh.
55 F3 Shereiq Sudan
22 C4 Shergarh India
77 E5 Sheridan *AR* U.S.A.
72 F2 Sheridan *WY* U.S.A.
39 J5 Sheringham U.K.
77 D5 Sherman U.S.A.
81 J2 Sherman Mills U.S.A.
75 E1 Sherman Mtn *mt* U.S.A.
23 G4 Sherpur Bangl.
65 J3 Sherridon Can.
42 D3 's-Hertogenbosch Neth.
39 F4 Sherwood Forest *reg.* U.K.
64 C3 Sheslay Can.
12 A3 Shetland *i.* U.K.
14 D2 Shetpe Kazak.
27 □ Sheung Shui *H.K.* China
27 □ Sheung Sze Mun *chan. H.K.* China
21 B4 Shevaroy Hills *mts* India
27 F4 She Xian China
26 F3 Sheyang China
76 D2 Sheyenne U.S.A.
76 D2 Sheyenne *r.* U.S.A.
18 D5 Sheykh Sho'eyb *i.* Iran
40 B3 Shiant Islands *is* U.K.
24 H2 Shiashkotan, O. *i.* Rus. Fed.
69 E4 Shiawassee *r.* U.S.A.
20 C6 Shibām Yemen
19 H3 Shibar Pass *pass* Afgh.
29 F6 Shibata Japan
28 J3 Shibetsu Japan
28 H2 Shibetsu Japan
16 C6 Shibīn el Kōm Egypt
29 F6 Shibukawa Japan
27 E5 Shicheng China
30 B4 Shicheng Dao *i.* China
81 E4 Shickshinny U.S.A.
16 G6 Shidād al Mismā' *h.* S. Arabia
30 B5 Shidao China
30 B5 Shidao Wan *b.* China
40 C4 Shiel, Loch *l.* U.K.
26 B4 Shifang China
50 J4 Shigony Rus. Fed.
26 D1 Shiguaigou China
15 G2 Shihezi China
26 E2 Shijiazhuang China
19 F4 Shikar *r.* Pak.
21 A3 Shikarpur India
22 B4 Shikarpur Pak.
22 D4 Shikohabad India
29 C8 Shikoku *i.* Japan
29 C8 Shikoku-sanchi *mts* Japan
28 G3 Shikotsu-Tōya National Park Japan
38 F3 Shildon U.K.
50 H1 Shilega Rus. Fed.
23 G4 Shiliguri India
27 D4 Shilipu China
22 D2 Shilla *mt* India
41 E5 Shillelagh Rep. of Ireland

69 G1 **Shillington** Can.
23 G4 **Shillong** India
51 J5 **Shil'naya Balka** Kazak.
81 F5 **Shiloh** U.S.A.
26 D2 **Shilou** China
50 G4 **Shilovo** Rus. Fed.
29 B8 **Shimabara** Japan
29 F7 **Shimada** Japan
24 E1 **Shimanovsk** Rus. Fed.
27 D4 **Shimen** China
27 B4 **Shimian** China
29 F7 **Shimizu** Japan
22 D3 **Shimla** India
29 F7 **Shimoda** Japan
21 A3 **Shimoga** India
56 D4 **Shimoni** Kenya
29 B8 **Shimonoseki** Japan
22 C1 **Shimshal** Jammu and Kashmir
50 D3 **Shimsk** Rus. Fed.
27 C6 **Shinan** China
19 F3 **Shīndand** Afgh.
22 B3 **Shinghar** Pak.
22 C1 **Shinghshal Pass** Pak.
68 D2 **Shingleton** U.S.A.
27 □ **Shing Mun Res.** *resr* H.K. China
29 E8 **Shingū** Japan
59 J1 **Shingwedzi** S. Africa
59 J1 **Shingwedzi** *r.* S. Africa
39 E4 **Shining Tor** *h.* U.K.
69 G2 **Shining Tree** Can.
28 G5 **Shinjō** Japan
19 G4 **Shīnkāy** Afgh.
40 D2 **Shin, Loch** *l.* U.K.
29 E6 **Shinminato** Japan
81 J1 **Shin Pond** U.S.A.
56 D4 **Shinyanga** Tanz.
28 G5 **Shiogama** Japan
29 D8 **Shiono-misaki** *c.* Japan
29 G6 **Shioya-zaki** *pt* Japan
79 E7 **Ship Chan Cay** *i.* Bahamas
27 B6 **Shiping** China
22 D3 **Shipki Pass** China/India
38 F4 **Shipley** U.K.
67 H4 **Shippegan** Can.
80 E4 **Shippensburg** U.S.A.
75 H3 **Shiprock** U.S.A.
75 H3 **Shiprock Peak** *summit* U.S.A.
27 F4 **Shipu** China
27 C5 **Shiqian** China
26 C3 **Shiquan** China
22 E2 **Shiquan He** *r.* China
26 C3 **Shiquan Sk.** *resr* China
17 M2 **Shīrābād** Iran
29 G6 **Shirakawa** Japan
24 F3 **Shirane-san** *mt* Japan
29 F6 **Shirane-san** *volc.* Japan
92 D4 **Shirasebreen** *ice feature* Ant.
92 A4 **Shirase Coast** *coastal area* Ant.
18 D4 **Shīrāz** Iran
16 C6 **Shirbīn** Egypt
28 J2 **Shiretoko-misaki** *c.* Japan
19 G4 **Shirinab** *r.* Pak.
28 G4 **Shiriya-zaki** *c.* Japan
81 G4 **Shirley** U.S.A.
81 J2 **Shirley Mills** U.S.A.
29 E7 **Shirotori** Japan
22 C5 **Shirpur** India
19 E2 **Shīrvān** Iran
17 L5 **Shīrvān** Iran
27 D4 **Shishou** China
27 E4 **Shitai** China
27 F4 **Shitang** China
17 J5 **Shithāthah** Iraq
22 B4 **Shiv** India
70 C4 **Shively** U.S.A.
22 D4 **Shivpuri** India
75 F3 **Shivwits Plateau** *plat.* U.S.A.
19 H2 **Shiwal** *l.* Afgh.
27 C6 **Shiwan Dashan** *mts* China
27 E5 **Shixing** China
26 D3 **Shiyan** China
27 C4 **Shizhu** China
27 B5 **Shizong** China
28 G5 **Shizugawa** Japan
26 C2 **Shizuishan** China
29 F7 **Shizuoka** Japan
50 D4 **Shklow** Belarus
49 H3 **Shkodër** Albania
12 K1 **Shmidta, Ostrov** *i.* Rus. Fed.
29 C7 **Shōbara** Japan
28 G3 **Shokanbetsu-dake** *mt* Japan
50 J2 **Shomvukva** Rus. Fed.
22 D2 **Shor** India
81 B4 **Shoranur** India
19 G5 **Shorap** Pak.
19 G4 **Shorawak** *reg.* Afgh.
17 K3 **Shor Gol** Iran
22 C3 **Shorkot** Pak.
28 G2 **Shosanbetsu** Japan
74 D4 **Shoshone** *CA* U.S.A.
72 D3 **Shoshone** *ID* U.S.A.
72 E2 **Shoshone** *r.* U.S.A.
72 E2 **Shoshone L.** *l.* U.S.A.
73 C4 **Shoshone Mts** *mts* U.S.A.
59 G1 **Shoshong** Botswana
72 E3 **Shoshoni** U.S.A.
51 E5 **Shostka** Ukr.
26 F2 **Shouguang** China
27 F5 **Shouning** China
26 E3 **Shou Xian** China
26 D2 **Shouyang** China
26 C3 **Shouyang Shan** *mt* China
23 E3 **Shovo Tso** *salt l.* China
75 G4 **Show Low** U.S.A.
51 G6 **Shpakovskoye** Rus. Fed.
51 D5 **Shpola** Ukr.
77 E5 **Shreveport** U.S.A.
39 E5 **Shrewsbury** U.K.
21 A2 **Shrigonda** India
23 G5 **Shrirampur** India
26 F3 **Shu** *r.* China
17 L6 **Shu'aiba** Iraq
27 E5 **Shuangbai** China
30 D1 **Shuangcheng** China
26 C4 **Shuanghechang** China
30 B2 **Shuangliao** China
27 D5 **Shuangpai** China
30 A3 **Shuangtaizihe Kou** *b.* China
30 C2 **Shuangyang** China
28 B1 **Shuangyashan** China
14 D2 **Shubarkuduk** Kazak.
26 E4 **Shucheng** China
27 F5 **Shuiji** China
26 A2 **Shuiquanzi** China
22 B3 **Shujaabad** Pak.
18 C4 **Shūl** *watercourse* Iran
30 D1 **Shulan** China
26 E2 **Shulu** China
28 H2 **Shumarinai-ko** *l.* Japan
57 C5 **Shumba** Zimbabwe
49 M3 **Shumen** Bulg.
50 H4 **Shumerlya** Rus. Fed.
47 O3 **Shumilina** Belarus
75 G4 **Shumway** U.S.A.
50 E4 **Shumyachi** Rus. Fed.
27 E5 **Shunchang** China
27 D6 **Shunde** China
62 C3 **Shungnak** U.S.A.
26 E1 **Shunyi** China
27 C6 **Shuolong** China
26 D2 **Shuo Xian** China
20 C7 **Shuqrah** Yemen
19 F3 **Shūr** *r.* Iran
18 D4 **Shūr** *r.* Iran
18 D4 **Shūr** *r.* Iran
19 E3 **Shūr** *watercourse* Iran
18 D4 **Shūr** *watercourse* Iran
18 D5 **Shūr** *watercourse* Iran
18 E3 **Shūrāb** Iran
18 D3 **Shūrāb** Iran
18 C3 **Shūr Āb** Iran
18 E4 **Shūr Āb** *watercourse* Iran
19 G2 **Shurchi** Uzbek.
18 D3 **Shureghestan** Iran
19 E4 **Shūr Gaz** Iran
18 D4 **Shūrjestān** Iran
57 D5 **Shurugwi** Zimbabwe
17 K6 **Shuruppak** Iraq
19 F4 **Shusf** Iran
18 C3 **Shūsh** Iran
18 C3 **Shushtar** Iran
64 F4 **Shuswap L.** *l.* Can.
19 G3 **Shutar Khun Pass** Afgh.
50 G3 **Shuya** Rus. Fed.
26 F3 **Shuyang** China
18 D4 **Shūzū** Iran
32 A1 **Shwegun** Myanmar
14 E2 **Shymkent** Kazak.
22 D2 **Shyok** Jammu and Kashmir
22 D2 **Shyok** *r.* India
51 F5 **Shypuvate** Ukr.
51 E6 **Shyroke** Ukr.
25 F7 **Sia** Indon.
22 D2 **Siachen Gl.** *gl.* India
19 F5 **Siahan Range** *mts* Pak.
19 G3 **Siah Koh** *mts* Afgh.
18 D3 **Siāh Kūh** *mts* Iran
19 G4 **Siah Sang Pas** Afgh.
22 C2 **Sialkot** Pak.
32 C5 **Siantan** *i.* Indon.
89 D4 **Siapa** *r.* Venez.
19 F4 **Sīāreh** Iran
31 C4 **Siargao** *i.* Phil.
31 B5 **Siasi** Phil.
31 B5 **Siasi** *i.* Phil.
31 B4 **Siaton** Phil.
37 S9 **Šiauliai** Lith.
19 F5 **Sib** Iran
18 C3 **Sībak** Iran
59 J1 **Sibasa** S. Africa
31 B4 **Sibay** *i.* Phil.
59 K3 **Sibayi, Lake** *l.* S. Africa
92 B5 **Sibbald, C.** *c.* Ant.
48 F3 **Šibenik** Croatia
33 A3 **Siberut** *i.* Indon.
22 A3 **Sibi** Pak.
56 D3 **Sibiloi National Park** Kenya
28 C2 **Sibirtsevo** Rus. Fed.
56 B4 **Sibiti** Congo
49 L2 **Sibiu** Romania
33 A2 **Sibolga** Indon.
32 A5 **Siborongborong** Indon.
23 H4 **Sibsagar** India
33 D2 **Sibu** Malaysia
31 B5 **Sibuco** Phil.
31 B5 **Sibuguey** *r.* Phil.
31 B5 **Sibuguey Bay** *b.* Phil.
56 B3 **Sibut** C.A.R.
31 A5 **Sibutu** *i.* Phil.
31 A5 **Sibutu Passage** *chan.* Phil.
31 B3 **Sibuyan** *i.* Phil.
31 B3 **Sibuyan Sea** *sea* Phil.
31 B2 **Sicapoo** *mt* Phil.
27 B4 **Sichuan** *div.* China
27 B4 **Sichuan Pendi** *basin* China
44 G5 **Sicié, Cap** *c.* France
Sicilia *i. see* **Sicily**
48 E6 **Sicilian Channel** Italy/Tunisia
48 E6 **Sicily** *i.* Italy
86 D6 **Sicuani** Peru
28 D2 **Sidatun** Rus. Fed.
22 C5 **Siddhapur** India
21 B2 **Siddipet** India
49 M7 **Sideros, Akra** *pt* Greece
58 E6 **Sidesaviwa** S. Africa
45 H5 **Sidi Aïssa** Alg.
45 G4 **Sidi Ali** Alg.
54 B1 **Sidi Bel Abbès** Alg.
48 C7 **Sidi Bouzid** Tunisia
48 D7 **Sidi El Hani, Sebkhet de** *salt pan* Tunisia
54 A2 **Sidi Ifni** Morocco
54 B1 **Sidi Kacem** Morocco
32 A5 **Sidikalang** Indon.
40 E4 **Sidlaw Hills** *h.* U.K.
92 A4 **Sidley, Mt** *mt* Ant.
39 D7 **Sidmouth** U.K.
64 E5 **Sidney** Can.
72 F2 **Sidney** *MT* U.S.A.
76 C3 **Sidney** *NE* U.S.A.
81 F3 **Sidney** *NY* U.S.A.
80 A4 **Sidney** *OH* U.S.A.
79 D5 **Sidney Lanier, L.** *l.* U.S.A.
23 H5 **Sidoktaya** Myanmar
16 E5 **Sidon** Lebanon
50 G3 **Sidorovo** Rus. Fed.
90 A3 **Sidrolândia** Brazil
59 J3 **Sidvokodvo** Swaziland
44 F5 **Sié, Col de** *pass* France
47 L4 **Siedlce** Pol.
43 G4 **Siegen** Ger.
32 B2 **Siĕmréab** Cambodia
48 D3 **Siena** Italy
47 J5 **Sieradz** Pol.
77 B6 **Sierra Blanca** U.S.A.
91 C4 **Sierra Colorada** Arg.
75 F5 **Sierra Estrella** *mts* U.S.A.
91 D4 **Sierra Grande** Arg.
52 C5 **Sierra Leone** *country* Africa
96 H5 **Sierra Leone Basin** *sea feature* Atl. Ocean
96 H5 **Sierra Leone Rise** *sea feature* Atl. Ocean
74 C4 **Sierra Madre Mts** *mts* U.S.A.
74 B1 **Sierra Nevada** *mts* U.S.A.
89 B2 **Sierra Nevada de Santa Marta, Parque Nacional** *nat. park* Col.
89 C2 **Sierra Nevada, Parque Nacional** *nat. park* Venez.
91 D4 **Sierra, Punta** *pt* Arg.
74 B2 **Sierraville** U.S.A.
75 G6 **Sierra Vista** U.S.A.
46 C7 **Sierre** Switz.
36 T5 **Sievi** Fin.
27 C6 **Sifang Ling** *mts* China
49 L6 **Sifnos** *i.* Greece
45 F5 **Sig** Alg.
47 L7 **Sighetu Marmaţiei** Romania
47 M7 **Sighişoara** Romania
32 □ **Siglap** Sing.
33 A1 **Sigli** Indon.
36 D3 **Siglufjörður** Iceland
31 B4 **Sigma** Phil.
46 D6 **Sigmaringen** Ger.
42 E4 **Signal de Botrange** *h.* Belgium
75 E5 **Signal Peak** *summit* U.S.A.
92 B1 **Signy** *U.K. Base* Ant.
42 C5 **Signy-l'Abbaye** France
68 A5 **Sigourney** U.S.A.
49 L5 **Sigri, Akra** *pt* Greece
45 E2 **Sigüenza** Spain
54 B3 **Siguiri** Guinea
37 T8 **Sigulda** Latvia
32 B3 **Sihanoukville** Cambodia
26 F3 **Sihong** China
22 E5 **Sihora** India
27 D6 **Sihui** China
36 T4 **Siikajoki** Fin.
36 U5 **Siilinjärvi** Fin.
17 H3 **Siirt** Turkey
33 B3 **Sijunjung** Indon.
22 B5 **Sika** India
64 E3 **Sikanni Chief** Can.
64 E3 **Sikanni Chief** *r.* Can.
22 C4 **Sikar** India
19 H3 **Sikaram** *mt* Afgh.
54 B3 **Sikasso** Mali
77 F4 **Sikeston** U.S.A.
24 F2 **Sikhote-Alin'** *mts* Rus. Fed.
49 L6 **Sikinos** *i.* Greece
23 G4 **Sikkim** *div.* India
36 P4 **Siksjö** Sweden
33 E1 **Sikuati** Malaysia
45 C1 **Sil** *r.* Spain
31 C4 **Silago** Phil.
37 S9 **Šilalė** Lith.
82 D4 **Silao** Mex.
31 B4 **Silay** Phil.
43 H1 **Silberberg** *h.* Ger.
23 H4 **Silchar** India
16 B1 **Şile** Turkey
21 C2 **Sileru** *r.* India
22 E3 **Silgarhi** Nepal
48 C6 **Siliana** Tunisia
16 D3 **Silifke** Turkey
23 G3 **Siling Co** *salt l.* China
Silistat *see* **Bozkır**
49 M2 **Silistra** Bulg.
16 B1 **Silivri** Turkey
37 O6 **Siljan** *l.* Sweden
37 L8 **Silkeborg** Denmark
37 U7 **Sillamäe** Estonia
22 C5 **Sillod** India
59 J3 **Silobela** S. Africa
23 G3 **Silong** China
77 E6 **Silsbee** U.S.A.
36 U3 **Siltaharju** Fin.
19 F5 **Sīlūp** *r.* Iran
37 R9 **Šilutė** Lith.
17 H2 **Silvan** Turkey
22 C5 **Silvassa** India
68 B2 **Silver Bay** U.S.A.
73 E5 **Silver City** U.S.A.
68 C1 **Silver Islet** Can.
72 B3 **Silver Lake** U.S.A.
74 D4 **Silver Lake** *l. CA* U.S.A.
68 D2 **Silver Lake** *l. MI* U.S.A.
41 C5 **Silvermine Mts** *h.* Rep. of Ireland
74 D3 **Silver Peak Range** *mts* U.S.A.
80 E5 **Silver Spring** U.S.A.
74 C2 **Silver Springs** U.S.A.
8 C1 **Silverton** Austr.
39 D7 **Silverton** U.K.
69 F3 **Silver Water** Can.
84 E3 **Silvituc** Mex.
33 D2 **Simanggang** Malaysia
31 B3 **Simara** *i.* Phil.
69 H2 **Simard, Lac** *l.* Can.
17 L5 **Sīmareh** *r.* Iran
23 F4 **Simaria** India
16 B2 **Simav** Turkey
16 B2 **Simav Dağları** *mts* Turkey
56 C3 **Simba** Congo(Zaire)
Simbirsk *see* **Ul'yanovsk**
Simbor *i. see* **Pānikoita**
69 G4 **Simcoe** Can.
69 H3 **Simcoe, Lake** *l.* Can.
23 F5 **Simdega** India
56 D2 **Simēn Mountains** *mts* Eth.
33 A2 **Simeuluë** *i.* Indon.
51 E6 **Simferopol'** Ukr.
23 E3 **Simikot** Nepal
89 B3 **Simití** Col.
74 C4 **Simi Valley** U.S.A.
73 F4 **Simla** U.S.A.
47 L7 **Şimleu Silvaniei** Romania
42 E4 **Simmerath** Ger.
42 F5 **Simmern (Hunsrück)** Ger.
74 C4 **Simmler** U.S.A.
75 F4 **Simmons** U.S.A.
79 F7 **Simms** Bahamas
36 U3 **Simojärvi** *l.* Fin.
64 F4 **Simonette** *r.* Can.
65 J4 **Simonhouse** Can.
46 D7 **Simplon Pass** Switz.
6 D4 **Simpson Desert** Austr.
68 D1 **Simpson I.** *i.* Can.
74 D2 **Simpson Park Mts** *mts* U.S.A.
37 O9 **Simrishamn** Sweden
31 A5 **Simunul** *i.* Phil.
24 H2 **Simushir, O.** *i.* Rus. Fed.
21 A2 **Sina** *r.* India
33 A2 **Sinabang** Indon.
33 A2 **Sinabung** *volc.* Indon.
55 F2 **Sinai** *reg.* Egypt
42 C5 **Sinai, Mont** *h.* France
84 A1 **Sinaloa** *div.* Mex.
48 D3 **Sinalunga** Italy
27 C5 **Sinan** China
30 C4 **Sinanju** N. Korea
23 H5 **Sinbyugyun** Myanmar
16 F2 **Sincan** Turkey
89 B2 **Sincé** Col.
89 B2 **Sincelejo** Col.
79 D5 **Sinclair, L.** *l.* U.S.A.
64 E4 **Sinclair Mills** Can.
58 B2 **Sinclair Mine** Namibia
40 E2 **Sinclair's Bay** *b.* U.K.
22 D4 **Sind** *r.* India
31 B4 **Sindañgan** Phil.
33 C4 **Sindangbarang** Indon.
22 B4 **Sindari** India
46 D6 **Sindelfingen** Ger.
21 B2 **Sindgi** India
22 B4 **Sindh** *div.* Pak.
21 B3 **Sindhnur** India
16 B2 **Sındırgı** Turkey
22 D6 **Sindkhed** India
22 C5 **Sindkheda** India
30 C4 **Sin-do** *i.* China
50 J2 **Sindor** Rus. Fed.
23 F5 **Sindri** India
22 B3 **Sind Sagar Doab** *lowland* Pak.
50 J3 **Sinegor'ye** Rus. Fed.
49 M4 **Sinekçi** Turkey
45 B4 **Sines** Port.
45 B4 **Sines, Cabo de** *pt* Port.
36 T3 **Sinettä** Fin.
54 B4 **Sinfra** Côte d'Ivoire
55 F3 **Singa** Sudan
22 E3 **Singahi** India
30 D3 **Sin'galp'a** China
22 D2 **Singa Pass** *pass* India
32 B5 **Singapore** Sing.
11 M9 **Singapore** *country* Asia
32 B5 **Singapore, Strait of** *chan.* Indon./Sing.
33 E4 **Singaraja** Indon.
32 B2 **Sing Buri** Thai.
69 G3 **Singhampton** Can.
56 D4 **Singida** Tanz.
6 C2 **Singkang** Indon.
33 C2 **Singkawang** Indon.
32 A5 **Singkil** Indon.
8 H2 **Singleton** Austr.
Singora *see* **Songkhla**
30 D4 **Sin'gye** N. Korea
30 D3 **Sinhŭng** N. Korea
48 C4 **Siniscola** *Sardinia* Italy
48 G3 **Sinj** Croatia
6 C2 **Sinjai** Indon.
17 H3 **Sinjār** Iraq
17 H3 **Sinjār, Jabal** *mt* Iraq
17 K3 **Sinji** Iran
55 F3 **Sinkat** Sudan
Sinkiang Uighur Aut. Region *div. see* **Xinjiang Uygur Zizhiqu**
30 C4 **Sinmi I.** *i.* N. Korea
43 G4 **Sinn** Ger.
87 H2 **Sinnamary** Fr. Guiana
Sinneh *see* **Sanandaj**
49 N2 **Sinoie, Lacul** *lag.* Romania
51 E7 **Sinop** Turkey
30 D3 **Sinpa** N. Korea
30 E3 **Sinp'o** N. Korea
30 E3 **Sinp'ung-dong** N. Korea
30 D4 **Sinp'yŏng** N. Korea
30 D4 **Sinsang** N. Korea
43 G5 **Sinsheim** Ger.
33 D2 **Sintang** Indon.
77 D6 **Sinton** U.S.A.
89 A2 **Sinú** *r.* Col.
30 C3 **Sinŭiju** N. Korea
42 F4 **Sinzig** Ger.
31 B5 **Siocon** Phil.
46 J7 **Siófok** Hungary
46 C7 **Sion** Switz.
41 D3 **Sion Mills** U.K.
76 D3 **Sioux Center** U.S.A.
76 D3 **Sioux City** U.S.A.
76 D3 **Sioux Falls** U.S.A.
66 B3 **Sioux Lookout** Can.
31 B4 **Sipalay** Phil.
30 C2 **Siping** China
65 K3 **Sipiwesk** Can.
65 K3 **Sipiwesk L.** *l.* Can.
92 B4 **Siple Coast** *coastal area* Ant.
92 A4 **Siple, Mt** *mt* Ant.
22 C5 **Sipra** *r.* India
79 C5 **Sipsey** *r.* U.S.A.
33 A3 **Sipura** *i.* Indon.
83 H6 **Siquia** *r.* Nic.
31 B4 **Siquijor** Phil.
31 B4 **Siquijor** *i.* Phil.
22 B5 **Sir** *r.* Pak.
21 B3 **Sira** India
37 K7 **Sira** *r.* Norway
18 D5 **Şīr Abū Nu'āyr** *i.* U.A.E.
Siracusa *see* **Syracuse**
64 E4 **Sir Alexander, Mt** *mt* Can.
17 G1 **Şiran** Turkey
19 G5 **Siranda Lake** *l.* Pak.
18 D5 **Şīr Banī Yās** *i.* U.A.E.
17 M3 **Sīrdān** Iran
6 D3 **Sir Edward Pellew Group** *is* Austr.
68 A3 **Siren** U.S.A.
19 F5 **Sīrgān** Iran
32 B1 **Siri Kit Dam** *dam* Thai.
18 D4 **Sīrīz** Iran
64 D2 **Sir James McBrien, Mt** *mt* Can.
Sirjan *see* **Sa'īdābād**
18 D4 **Sīrjan** *salt flat* Iran
18 E5 **Sirk** Iran
22 E4 **Sirmour** India
17 J3 **Şırnak** Turkey
21 C2 **Sironcha** India
22 D4 **Sironj** India
21 B2 **Sirpur** India
74 C4 **Sirretta Peak** *summit* U.S.A.
18 D5 **Sīrrī, Jazīreh-ye** *i.* Iran
22 C3 **Sirsa** *Haryana* India
22 E4 **Sirsa** *Uttar Pradesh* India
64 F4 **Sir Sanford, Mt** *mt* Can.
21 A3 **Sirsi** *Karnataka* India
22 D3 **Sirsi** India
21 B2 **Sirsilla** India
55 D1 **Sirte** Libya
55 D1 **Sirte, Gulf of** *g.* Libya
21 A2 **Sirur** India
17 J2 **Şirvan** Turkey
37 T9 **Širvintos** Lith.
17 K4 **Sīrwān** *r.* Iraq
64 F4 **Sir Wilfred Laurier, Mt** *mt* Can.
48 G2 **Sisak** Croatia
32 C2 **Sisaket** Thai.
18 C4 **Sīsakht** Iran
84 E2 **Sisal** Mex.
58 E3 **Sishen** S. Africa
17 L2 **Sisian** Armenia
68 C2 **Siskiwit Bay** *b.* U.S.A.
32 B2 **Sisŏphŏn** Cambodia
74 B4 **Sisquoc** *r.* U.S.A.
76 D2 **Sisseton** U.S.A.
81 K1 **Sisson Branch Reservoir** Can.
19 F4 **Sīstan** *reg.* Iran
19 F4 **Sīstan, Daryācheh-ye** *marsh* Afgh.
22 C5 **Sitamau** India
31 A5 **Sitangkai** Phil.
22 E4 **Sitapur** India
49 M7 **Siteia** Greece
59 J3 **Siteki** Swaziland
49 K4 **Sithonia** *pen.* Greece
90 C1 **Sítio da Abadia** Brazil
90 D1 **Sítio do Mato** Brazil
64 B3 **Sitka** U.S.A.
22 B3 **Sitpur** Pak.
42 D4 **Sittard** Neth.
23 H4 **Sittaung** Myanmar
43 H1 **Sittensen** Ger.
39 H6 **Sittingbourne** U.K.
23 H5 **Sittwe** Myanmar
27 □ **Siu A Chau** *i.* H.K. China
23 F5 **Siuri** India
21 B4 **Sivaganga** India
21 B4 **Sivakasi** India
18 D4 **Sīvand** Iran
16 F2 **Sivas** Turkey
16 B2 **Sivaslı** Turkey
17 G3 **Siverek** Turkey
17 G2 **Sivrice** Turkey
16 C2 **Sivrihisar** Turkey
59 H3 **Sivukile** S. Africa
55 E2 **Siwa** Egypt
22 D3 **Siwalik Range** *mts* India/Nepal
23 F4 **Siwan** India
22 C4 **Siwana** India
44 G5 **Six-Fours-les-Plages** France
26 E3 **Si Xian** China
68 E4 **Six Lakes** U.S.A.
41 D3 **Sixmilecross** U.K.
59 H2 **Siyabuswa** S. Africa
26 F3 **Siyang** China
17 M1 **Siyäzän** Azer.
26 C1 **Siyitang** China
18 D3 **Sīyunī** Iran
26 D1 **Siziwang Qi** China
Sjælland *i. see* **Zealand**
49 J3 **Sjenica** Yugo.
37 N9 **Sjöbo** Sweden
36 P2 **Sjøvegan** Norway
89 E2 **S. Juan** *r.* Venez.
51 E6 **Skadovs'k** Ukr.
36 E4 **Skaftafell National Park** Iceland
36 E5 **Skaftárós** *est.* Iceland
36 D3 **Skagafjörður** *in.* Iceland
37 M8 **Skagen** Denmark
37 L8 **Skagerrak** *str.* Denmark/Norway
72 B1 **Skagit** *r.* Can./U.S.A.
64 B3 **Skagway** U.S.A.
36 T1 **Skaidi** Norway
36 P2 **Skaland** Norway
36 O4 **Skalmodal** Sweden
37 L8 **Skanderborg** Denmark
81 E3 **Skaneateles Lake** *l.* U.S.A.
68 C2 **Skanee** U.S.A.
49 L5 **Skantzoura** *i.* Greece
37 N7 **Skara** Sweden
37 R7 **Skärgårdshavet Nationalpark** *nat. park* Fin.
37 M6 **Skarnes** Norway
47 K5 **Skarżysko-Kamienna** Pol.
36 R3 **Skaulo** Sweden
47 J6 **Skawina** Pol.
64 D3 **Skeena** *r.* Can.
64 D3 **Skeena Mountains** *mts* Can.
39 H4 **Skegness** U.K.
36 R4 **Skellefteå** Sweden
36 Q4 **Skellefteälven** *r.* Sweden
36 R4 **Skelleftehamn** Sweden
41 A6 **Skellig Rocks** *is* Rep. of Ireland
38 E4 **Skelmersdale** U.K.
41 E4 **Skerries** Rep. of Ireland
37 M7 **Ski** Norway
49 K5 **Skiathos** *i.* Greece
41 B6 **Skibbereen** Rep. of Ireland
36 R2 **Skibotn** Norway
38 D3 **Skiddaw** *mt* U.K.
37 L7 **Skien** Norway
47 K5 **Skierniewice** Pol.
54 C1 **Skikda** Alg.
38 G4 **Skipsea** U.K.
8 D4 **Skipton** Austr.
38 E4 **Skipton** U.K.
37 L8 **Skive** Denmark
36 E4 **Skjálfandafljót** *r.* Iceland
37 L9 **Skjern** Denmark
37 K6 **Skjolden** Norway
36 K5 **Skodje** Norway
36 T2 **Skoganvarre** Norway
41 F6 **Skokholm Island** *i.* U.K.
68 D4 **Skokie** U.S.A.
39 B6 **Skomer Island** *i.* U.K.
49 K5 **Skopelos** *i.* Greece
50 F4 **Skopin** Rus. Fed.
49 J4 **Skopje** Macedonia
51 F5 **Skorodnoye** Rus. Fed.
37 N7 **Skövde** Sweden
81 J2 **Skowhegan** U.S.A.
37 S8 **Skrunda** Latvia
64 B2 **Skukum, Mt** *mt* Can.
59 J2 **Skukuza** S. Africa
74 D3 **Skull Peak** *summit* U.S.A.
68 B5 **Skunk** *r.* U.S.A.
37 R8 **Skuodas** Lith.
37 N9 **Skurup** Sweden
37 P6 **Skutskär** Sweden
51 D5 **Skvyra** Ukr.
40 B3 **Skye** *i.* U.K.
49 L5 **Skyros** Greece
49 L5 **Skyros** *i.* Greece
92 B3 **Skytrain Ice Rise** *ice feature* Ant.
37 M9 **Slagelse** Denmark
36 Q4 **Slagnäs** Sweden
33 C4 **Slamet, Gunung** *volc.* Indon.
41 E4 **Slane** Rep. of Ireland
41 E5 **Slaney** *r.* Rep. of Ireland
50 D3 **Slantsy** Rus. Fed.
51 G5 **Slashchevskaya** Rus. Fed.
68 D1 **Slate Is** *is* Can.
48 G2 **Slatina** Croatia
49 L2 **Slatina** Romania
65 G2 **Slave** *r.* Can.
54 C4 **Slave Coast** *coastal area* Africa
64 G3 **Slave Lake** Can.
15 F1 **Slavgorod** Rus. Fed.
47 O2 **Slavkovichi** Rus. Fed.
49 H2 **Slavonija** *reg.* Croatia
49 H2 **Slavonski Brod** Croatia
51 C5 **Slavuta** Ukr.
51 D5 **Slavutych** Ukr.
28 B3 **Slavyanka** Rus. Fed.
51 F6 **Slavyansk-na-Kubani** Rus. Fed.
50 D4 **Slawharad** Belarus
46 H3 **Sławno** Pol.
39 G4 **Sleaford** U.K.
41 A5 **Slea Head** *hd* Rep. of Ireland
40 C3 **Sleat** *pen.* U.K.
40 C3 **Sleat, Sound of** *chan.* U.K.
66 E2 **Sleeper Islands** *is* Can.
68 D3 **Sleeping Bear Dunes National Seashore** *res.* U.S.A.
68 D3 **Sleeping Bear Pt** *pt* U.S.A.
51 H7 **Sleptsovskaya** Rus. Fed.
92 C3 **Slessor Glacier** *gl.* Ant.
77 F6 **Slidell** U.S.A.
41 A5 **Slievanea** *h.* Rep. of Ireland
41 D3 **Slieve Anierin** *h.* Rep. of Ireland
41 D5 **Slieveardagh Hills** *h.* Rep. of Ireland
41 C4 **Slieve Aughty Mts** *h.* Rep. of Ireland
41 D3 **Slieve Beagh** *h.* Rep. of Ireland/U.K.
41 C5 **Slieve Bernagh** *h.* Rep. of Ireland
41 D4 **Slieve Bloom Mts** *h.* Rep. of Ireland
41 B5 **Slievecallan** *h.* Rep. of Ireland
41 B3 **Slieve Car** *h.* Rep. of Ireland
41 F3 **Slieve Donard** *h.* U.K.
41 B4 **Slieve Elva** *h.* Rep. of Ireland
41 C3 **Slieve Gamph** *h.* Rep. of Ireland
41 C3 **Slieve League** *h.* Rep. of Ireland
41 B5 **Slieve Mish Mts** *h.* Rep. of Ireland
41 B5 **Slieve Miskish Mts** *h.* Rep. of Ireland
41 A3 **Slieve More** *h.* Rep. of Ireland
41 D4 **Slieve na Calliagh** *h.* Rep. of Ireland
41 D5 **Slievenamon** *h.* Rep. of Ireland
41 D2 **Slieve Snaght** *mt* Rep. of Ireland
40 B3 **Sligachan** U.K.
41 C3 **Sligo** Rep. of Ireland
41 C3 **Sligo Bay** *b.* Rep. of Ireland
37 Q8 **Slite** Sweden
49 M3 **Sliven** Bulg.
50 H2 **Sloboda** Rus. Fed.
50 J2 **Slobodchikovo** Rus. Fed.
49 M2 **Slobozia** Romania
64 F5 **Slocan** Can.
42 E1 **Slochteren** Neth.
50 C4 **Slonim** Belarus
42 C2 **Slootdorp** Neth.
42 D2 **Sloten** Neth.
42 D2 **Slotermeer** *l.* Neth.
7 F2 **Slot, The** *chan.* Solomon Is
39 G6 **Slough** U.K.
35 G4 **Slovakia** *country* Europe
34 G4 **Slovenia** *country* Europe
48 F1 **Slovenj Gradec** Slovenia
51 F5 **Slov"yans'k** Ukr.
46 H3 **Słupsk** Pol.
36 P4 **Slussfors** Sweden
50 C4 **Slutsk** Belarus
41 A4 **Slyne Head** *hd* Rep. of Ireland
13 M4 **Slyudyanka** Rus. Fed.
81 J3 **Small Pt** *pt* U.S.A.
67 H3 **Smallwood Reservoir** Can.
50 D4 **Smalyavichy** Belarus
47 N3 **Smarhon'** Belarus
58 E5 **Smartt Syndicate Dam** *resr* S. Africa
65 J4 **Smeaton** Can.
49 J2 **Smederevo** Yugo.
49 J2 **Smederevska Palanka** Yugo.
80 D4 **Smethport** U.S.A.
51 D5 **Smila** Ukr.
42 E2 **Smilde** Neth.
37 T8 **Smiltene** Latvia
64 G3 **Smith** Can.
74 C2 **Smith** U.S.A.
80 C6 **Smith** *r.* U.S.A.
62 C2 **Smith Bay** *b.* U.S.A.
64 D4 **Smithers** Can.
59 G5 **Smithfield** S. Africa
79 E5 **Smithfield** *NC* U.S.A.
72 E3 **Smithfield** *UT* U.S.A.
92 A3 **Smith Glacier** *gl.* Ant.
92 B2 **Smith I.** *i. S. Shetland Is* Ant.
81 E5 **Smith I.** *i. MD* U.S.A.
81 F6 **Smith I.** *i. VA* U.S.A.
80 D6 **Smith Mountain Lake** *l.* U.S.A.
64 D3 **Smith River** Can.
69 J3 **Smiths Falls** Can.
63 L2 **Smith Sound** *str.* Can./Greenland
74 C1 **Smoke Creek Desert** U.S.A.
64 F4 **Smoky** *r.* Can.
76 C4 **Smoky** *r.* U.S.A.
66 D3 **Smoky Falls** Can.
76 D4 **Smoky Hills** *h.* U.S.A.
64 G4 **Smoky Lake** Can.
36 K5 **Smøla** *i.* Norway
50 E4 **Smolensk** Rus. Fed.
50 E4 **Smolenskaya Oblast'** *div.* Rus. Fed.
49 L4 **Smolyan** Bulg.
28 C3 **Smolyaninovo** Rus. Fed.
66 D4 **Smooth Rock Falls** Can.
66 C3 **Smoothrock L.** *l.* Can.
65 H4 **Smoothstone Lake** *l.* Can.
36 T1 **Smørfjord** Norway
92 B3 **Smyley I.** *i.* Ant.
81 F5 **Smyrna** *DE* U.S.A.
79 C5 **Smyrna** *GA* U.S.A.
80 C4 **Smyrna** *OH* U.S.A.
81 J1 **Smyrna Mills** U.S.A.
38 C3 **Snaefell** *h.* U.K.
36 F4 **Snæfell** *mt* Iceland
64 A2 **Snag** Can.
72 D3 **Snake** *r.* U.S.A.
75 E2 **Snake Range** *mts* U.S.A.
72 D3 **Snake River Plain** *plain* U.S.A.
79 E7 **Snap Pt** *pt* Bahamas
64 G2 **Snare Lake** Can.
7 G6 **Snares Is** *is* N.Z.
36 N4 **Snasa** Norway
42 D1 **Sneek** Neth.
41 B6 **Sneem** Rep. of Ireland
58 F6 **Sneeuberg** *mts* S. Africa
67 H3 **Snegamook Lake** *l.* Can.
39 H5 **Snettisham** U.K.
12 K3 **Snezhnogorsk** Rus. Fed.
48 F2 **Snežnik** *mt* Slovenia
47 K4 **Śniardwy, Jezioro** *l.* Pol.
51 E6 **Snihurivka** Ukr.
40 B3 **Snizort, Loch** *b.* U.K.
72 B2 **Snohomish** U.S.A.
72 B2 **Snoqualmie Pass** U.S.A.
36 N3 **Snøtinden** *mt* Norway
65 J2 **Snowbird Lake** *l.* Can.
39 C4 **Snowdon** *mt* U.K.
39 D5 **Snowdonia National Park** U.K.
75 G4 **Snowflake** U.S.A.
81 F5 **Snow Hill** *MD* U.S.A.
79 E5 **Snow Hill** *NC* U.S.A.
65 J4 **Snow Lake** Can.
8 B2 **Snowtown** Austr.
72 D3 **Snowville** U.S.A.
8 G4 **Snowy** *r.* Austr.
8 G4 **Snowy Mts** *mts* Austr.
67 J3 **Snug Harbour** *Nfld* Can.
69 G3 **Snug Harbour** *Ont.* Can.
32 C2 **Snuŏl** Cambodia
77 D5 **Snyder** *OK* U.S.A.
77 C5 **Snyder** *TX* U.S.A.
57 E5 **Soalala** Madag.
57 E5 **Soanierana-Ivongo** Madag.
30 D6 **Soan kundo** *i.* S. Korea
89 B3 **Soata** Col.
40 B3 **Soay** *i.* U.K.
30 D6 **Sobaek Sanmaek** *mts* S. Korea
55 F4 **Sobat** *r.* Sudan
43 F5 **Sobernheim** Ger.
25 G7 **Sobger** *r.* Indon.
29 B8 **Sobo-san** *mt* Japan
87 K6 **Sobradinho, Barragem de** *resr* Brazil
87 K4 **Sobral** Brazil
So-chaoson-man *g. see* **Korea Bay**
51 F7 **Sochi** Rus. Fed.
30 D5 **Sŏch'on** S. Korea
5 M6 **Society Islands** *is* Pac. Oc.
90 C3 **Socorro** Brazil
89 B3 **Socorro** Col.
73 F5 **Socorro** U.S.A.
82 B5 **Socorro, I.** *i.* Mex.
20 D7 **Socotra** *i.* Yemen
32 C3 **Soc Trăng** Vietnam
45 E3 **Socuéllamos** Spain
74 D4 **Soda Lake** *l.* U.S.A.
36 U3 **Sodankylä** Fin.
22 D2 **Soda Plains** *plain* China/Jammu and Kashmir
72 E3 **Soda Springs** U.S.A.
37 P6 **Söderhamn** Sweden
37 P7 **Söderköping** Sweden
37 P7 **Södertälje** Sweden
55 E3 **Sodiri** Sudan
56 D3 **Sodo** Eth.
37 Q6 **Södra Kvarken** *str.* Fin./Sweden
59 H1 **Soekmekaar** S. Africa
42 D3 **Soerendonk** Neth.
43 G3 **Soest** Ger.
42 D2 **Soest** Neth.
8 G2 **Sofala** Austr.
49 K3 **Sofia** Bulg.
Sofiya *see* **Sofia**
36 W4 **Sofporog** Rus. Fed.
29 G10 **Sōfu-gan** *i.* Japan
89 B3 **Sogamoso** Col.
17 G1 **Soğanlı Dağları** *mts* Turkey
42 F2 **Sögel** Ger.
37 K7 **Søgne** Norway
37 J6 **Sognefjorden** *in.* Norway
31 C4 **Sogod** Phil.
26 A1 **Sogo Nur** *l.* China
50 H2 **Sogra** Rus. Fed.
26 A3 **Sogruma** China
16 C1 **Söğüt** Turkey
30 D7 **Sŏgwip'o** S. Korea
23 H3 **Sog Xian** China
55 F2 **Sohâg** Egypt
22 D5 **Sohagpur** India
39 H5 **Soham** U.K.
22 B2 **Sohan** *r.* Pak.
7 F2 **Sohano** P.N.G.
23 E5 **Sohela** India
22 D3 **Sohna** India
30 E3 **Sŏho-ri** N. Korea
30 C6 **Sŏhŭksan** *i.* S. Korea
42 C4 **Soignes, Forêt de** *forest* Belgium
42 C4 **Soignies** Belgium
36 T5 **Soini** Fin.
44 F2 **Soissons** France
22 C4 **Sojat** India
31 B4 **Sojoton Point** *pt* Phil.
51 C5 **Sokal'** Ukr.
30 E4 **Sokch'o** S. Korea
49 M6 **Söke** Turkey
51 G7 **Sokhumi** Georgia
54 C4 **Sokodé** Togo
27 □ **Soko Islands** *is* H.K. China
50 G3 **Sokol** Rus. Fed.
47 L4 **Sokółka** Pol.
54 B3 **Sokolo** Mali
43 L4 **Sokolov** Czech Rep.
28 C3 **Sokolovka** Rus. Fed.
47 L4 **Sokołów Podlaski** Pol.
54 C3 **Sokoto** Nigeria
54 C3 **Sokoto** *r.* Nigeria
51 C5 **Sokyryany** Ukr.
22 D3 **Solan** India
9 A7 **Solander I.** *i.* N.Z.
21 A2 **Solāpur** India
89 B2 **Soledad** Col.
74 B3 **Soledad** U.S.A.
89 E2 **Soledad** Venez.
84 C3 **Soledad de Doblado** Mex.
51 G6 **Solenoye** Rus. Fed.
39 F7 **Solent, The** *str.* U.K.
36 N3 **Solfjellsjøen** Norway
17 H2 **Solhan** Turkey
50 G3 **Soligalich** Rus. Fed.
39 F5 **Solihull** U.K.
12 G4 **Solikamsk** Rus. Fed.
12 G4 **Sol'-Iletsk** Rus. Fed.
42 F3 **Solingen** Ger.
58 A1 **Solitaire** Namibia
17 M1 **Şollar** Azer.
36 P5 **Sollefteå** Sweden
43 L3 **Söllichau** Ger.
43 H3 **Solling** *h.* Ger.
43 J3 **Sollstedt** Ger.
43 G4 **Solms** Ger.
50 F3 **Solnechnogorsk** Rus. Fed.
33 B3 **Solok** Indon.
84 E4 **Sololá** Guatemala
4 H5 **Solomon Islands** *country* Pac. Oc.
6 F2 **Solomon Sea** *sea* P.N.G./Solomon Is
68 B2 **Solon Springs** U.S.A.
25 E7 **Solor, Kepulauan** *is* Indon.
46 C7 **Solothurn** Switz.
50 E1 **Solovetskiye Ostrova** *is* Rus. Fed.
50 H3 **Solovetskoye** Rus. Fed.
48 G3 **Šolta** *i.* Croatia
18 C4 **Soltānābād** Iran
19 E3 **Soltānābād** Iran
19 E2 **Soltānābād** Iran
43 H2 **Soltau** Ger.
50 D3 **Sol'tsy** Rus. Fed.
81 E3 **Solvay** U.S.A.
37 O8 **Sölvesborg** Sweden
40 E6 **Solway Firth** *est.* U.K.
57 C5 **Solwezi** Zambia
29 G6 **Sōma** Japan
16 A2 **Soma** Turkey
42 B4 **Somain** France
53 J5 **Somalia** *country* Africa
93 H3 **Somali Basin** *sea feature* Ind. Ocean
57 C4 **Sombo** Angola
49 H2 **Sombor** Yugo.
84 B2 **Sombrerete** Mex.
22 C4 **Somdari** India
81 J2 **Somerest Junction** U.S.A.
37 S6 **Somero** Fin.
78 C4 **Somerset** *KY* U.S.A.
68 E4 **Somerset** *MI* U.S.A.
80 D5 **Somerset** *PA* U.S.A.
59 F6 **Somerset East** S. Africa
63 J2 **Somerset Island** *i.* Can.

81 G3 Somerset Reservoir U.S.A.
58 C7 Somerset West S. Africa
81 H3 Somersworth U.S.A.
77 D6 Somerville Res. *resr* U.S.A.
37 O7 Sommen *l.* Sweden
43 K3 Sömmerda Ger.
67 G3 Sommet, Lac du *l.* Can.
22 B5 Somnath India
68 C5 Somonauk U.S.A.
91 C4 Somuncurá, Mesa Volcánica de *plat.* Arg.
23 F4 Son *r.* India
23 F5 Sonamukhi India
23 G5 Sonamura India
23 E5 Sonapur India
22 D4 Sonar *r.* India
23 H4 Sonari India
30 C4 Sŏnch'ŏn N. Korea
50 E2 Sondaly Rus. Fed.
37 L9 Sønderborg Denmark
43 J3 Sondershausen Ger.
63 N3 Søndre Strømfjord *in.* Greenland
48 C1 Sondrio Italy
21 B2 Sonepet India
22 B5 Songad India
26 E4 Songbu China
32 D2 Sông Cau Vietnam
32 C1 Song Con *r.* Vietnam
27 B6 Sông Đa *r.* Vietnam
32 D2 Sông Đa Răng *r.* Vietnam
57 D5 Songea Tanz.
30 D3 Songgan N. Korea
32 C3 Song Hâu Giang *r.* Vietnam
30 D2 Songhua Hu *resr* China
30 C1 Songhua Jiang China
28 B1 Songhua Jiang *r.* China
26 F4 Songjiang China
30 D2 Songjianghe China
27 C4 Songkan China
32 B4 Songkhla Thai.
27 C6 Sông Ky Cung *r.* Vietnam
24 E2 Songling China
26 F1 Song Ling *mts* China
27 B6 Sông Ma *r.* Laos/Vietnam
30 D5 Sŏngnam S. Korea
32 C1 Sông Ngan Sau *r.* Vietnam
30 C4 Songnim N. Korea
56 B4 Songo Angola
57 D5 Songo Moz.
26 B3 Songpan China
32 C3 Song Saigon *r.* Vietnam
23 G4 Songsak India
30 D7 Sŏngsan S. Korea
26 D3 Song Shan *mt* China
30 D3 Songshuzhen China
27 C4 Songtao China
27 F5 Songxi China
26 D3 Song Xian China
27 D4 Songzi China
32 D2 Sơn Ha Vietnam
26 D1 Sonid Youqi China
26 D1 Sonid Zuoqi China
22 D3 Sonipat India
36 U5 Sonkajärvi Fin.
27 B6 Sơn La Vietnam
19 G5 Sonmiani Pak.
19 G5 Sonmiani Bay *b.* Pak.
43 K4 Sonneberg Ger.
90 D2 Sono *r. Minas Gerais* Brazil
87 J6 Sono *r. Tocantins* Brazil
75 G6 Sonoita U.S.A.
75 F6 Sonoita *r.* Mex.
74 B3 Sonora *CA* U.S.A.
77 C6 Sonora *TX* U.S.A.
70 D6 Sonora *div.* Mex.
82 B3 Sonora *r.* Mex.
75 F6 Sonoyta Mex.
18 B3 Sonqor Iran
89 B3 Sonsón Col.
82 G6 Sonsonate El Salvador
27 B6 Sơn Tây Vietnam
59 H5 Sonwabile S. Africa
91 F1 Sopas *r.* Uru.
13 S4 Sopka Shiveluch *mt* Rus. Fed.
55 E4 Sopo *watercourse* Sudan
49 L3 Sopot Bulg.
47 J3 Sopot Pol.
46 H7 Sopron Hungary
48 E4 Sora Italy
23 F6 Sorada India
37 P5 Soråker Sweden
30 E4 Sŏraksan *mt* S. Korea
66 F4 Sorel Can.
6 E6 Sorell Austr.
16 E2 Sorgun Turkey
45 E2 Soria Spain
12 C2 Sørkappøya *i.* Svalbard
18 D3 Sorkheh Iran
18 D3 Sorkh, Kūh-e *mts* Iran
36 N4 Sørli Norway
23 F5 Soro India
51 D5 Soroca Moldova
90 C3 Sorocaba Brazil
12 G4 Sorochinsk Rus. Fed.
25 G6 Sorol *i.* Micronesia
25 F7 Sorong Indon.
56 D3 Soroti Uganda
36 S1 Sørøya *i.* Norway
45 B3 Sorraia *r.* Port.
36 Q2 Sorreisa Norway
8 E5 Sorrento Austr.
57 B6 Sorris Sorris Namibia
92 D3 Sør-Rondane *mts* Ant.
36 P4 Sorsele Sweden
31 C3 Sorsogon Phil.
50 D2 Sortavala Rus. Fed.
36 O2 Sortland Norway
50 J2 Sortopolovskaya Rus. Fed.
50 J3 Sorvizhi Rus. Fed.
30 D5 Sŏsan S. Korea
59 H2 Soshanguve S. Africa
51 F4 Sosna *r.* Rus. Fed.
91 C2 Sosneado *mt* Arg.
50 K2 Sosnogorsk Rus. Fed.
50 H2 Sosnovka *Archangel.* Rus. Fed.
50 G4 Sosnovka *Tambov.* Rus. Fed.
12 F3 Sosnovka Rus. Fed.
36 X4 Sosnovyy Rus. Fed.
37 V7 Sosnovyy Bor Rus. Fed.
47 J5 Sosnowiec Pol.
51 F6 Sosyka *r.* Rus. Fed.
89 A4 Sotara, Volcán *volc.* Col.
36 V4 Sotkamo Fin.
91 D1 Soto Arg.
84 C2 Soto la Marina Mex.
56 B3 Souanké Congo
54 B4 Soubré Côte d'Ivoire
81 F4 Souderton U.S.A.
49 M4 Soufli Greece
44 E4 Souillac France
42 D5 Souilly France
54 C1 Souk Ahras Alg.
Sŏul *see* Seoul
44 D5 Soulom France
Soûr *see* Tyre
45 H4 Sour el Ghozlane Alg.
65 J5 Souris *Man.* Can.
67 H4 Souris *P.E.I.* Can.
65 J5 Souris *r.* Can./U.S.A.
87 L5 Sousa Brazil
54 D1 Sousse Tunisia
44 D5 Soustons France
20 C7 South *div.* Yemen
53 G9 South Africa, Republic of *country* Africa
69 G3 Southampton Can.
39 F7 Southampton U.K.
81 G4 Southampton U.S.A.
63 K3 Southampton I. Can.
65 M2 Southampton Island *i.* Can.
80 E6 South Anna *r.* U.S.A.
39 F4 South Anston U.K.
67 H2 South Aulatsivik Island *i.* Can.
6 D5 South Australia *div.* Austr.
93 N6 South Australian Basin *sea feature* Ind. Ocean
77 F5 Southaven U.S.A.
73 F5 South Baldy *mt* U.S.A.
38 F3 South Bank U.K.
80 B4 South Bass I. *i.* U.S.A.
65 N2 South Bay *b.* Can.
69 F3 South Baymouth Can.
68 D5 South Bend *IN* U.S.A.
72 B2 South Bend *WA* U.S.A.
79 E7 South Bight *chan.* Bahamas
80 D6 South Boston U.S.A.
9 D5 Southbridge N.Z.
81 G3 Southbridge U.S.A.
South Cape *c. see* Ka Lae
79 D5 South Carolina *div.* U.S.A.
81 J2 South China U.S.A.
33 C1 South China Sea *sea* Pac. Oc.
76 C2 South Dakota *div.* U.S.A.
81 G3 South Deerfield U.S.A.
39 G7 South Downs *h.* U.K.
59 F2 South East *div.* Botswana
8 F5 South East Cape *Vic.* Austr.
6 E6 South East Cape *c.* Austr.
95 N10 South-East Pacific Basin *sea feature* Pac. Oc.
65 J3 Southend Can.
40 C5 Southend U.K.
39 H6 Southend-on-Sea U.K.
68 A5 South English U.S.A.
9 C5 Southern Alps *mts* N.Z.
6 B5 Southern Cross Austr.
65 K3 Southern Indian Lake *l.* Can.
55 E4 Southern National Park Sudan
3 □ Southern Ocean *ocean*
79 E5 Southern Pines U.S.A.
92 C1 Southern Thule I. *i.* Atl. Ocean
40 D5 Southern Uplands *reg.* U.K.
40 F4 South Esk *r.* U.K.
68 B6 South Fabius *r.* U.S.A.
94 G7 South Fiji Basin *sea feature* Pac. Oc.
73 F4 South Fork U.S.A.
74 A2 South Fork Eel *r.* U.S.A.
74 C4 South Fork Kern *r.* U.S.A.
80 D5 South Fork South Branch *r.* U.S.A.
68 E3 South Fox I. *i.* U.S.A.
92 C5 South Geomagnetic Pole Ant.
85 G8 South Georgia *i.* Atl. Ocean
40 A3 South Harris *i.* U.K.
23 G5 South Hatia I. *i.* Bangl.
68 D4 South Haven U.S.A.
65 K2 South Henik Lake *l.* Can.
81 G2 South Hero U.S.A.
80 D6 South Hill U.S.A.
94 E4 South Honshu Ridge *sea feature* Pac. Oc.
65 K3 South Indian Lake Can.
81 G4 Southington U.S.A.
9 C6 South Island *i.* N.Z.
31 A4 South Islet *rf* Phil.
23 F5 South Koel *r.* India
74 B2 South Lake Tahoe U.S.A.
57 D5 South Luangwa National Park Zambia
92 B6 South Magnetic Pole Ant.
68 D3 South Manitou I. *i.* U.S.A.
79 D7 South Miami U.S.A.
39 H6 Southminster U.K.
65 J4 South Moose L. *l.* Can.
80 E5 South Mts *h.* U.S.A.
64 D2 South Nahanni *r.* Can.
40 □ South Nesting Bay *b.* U.K.
85 F9 South Orkney Islands *is* Ant.
81 H2 South Paris U.S.A.
72 G3 South Platte *r.* U.S.A.
92 B4 South Pole Ant.
69 G1 South Porcupine Can.
38 D4 Southport U.K.
81 H3 South Portland U.S.A.
69 H3 South River Can.
40 F2 South Ronaldsay *i.* U.K.
81 G3 South Royalton U.S.A.
59 J5 South Sand Bluff *pt* S. Africa
85 H8 South Sandwich Islands *terr.* Atl. Ocean
96 H9 South Sandwich Trench *sea feature* Atl. Ocean
65 H4 South Saskatchewan *r.* Can.
65 K3 South Seal *r.* Can.
85 E9 South Shetland Islands *is* Ant.
38 F2 South Shields U.K.
38 G4 South Skirlaugh U.K.
68 A5 South Skunk *r.* U.S.A.
9 E3 South Taranaki Bight *b.* N.Z.
75 G2 South Tent *summit* U.S.A.
23 E4 South Tons *r.* India
66 E3 South Twin I. *i.* Can.
38 E3 South Tyne *r.* U.K.
40 A3 South Uist *i.* U.K.
9 A7 South West Cape *c.* N.Z.
93 H6 South-West Indian Ridge *sea feature* Ind. Ocean
95 J8 South-West Pacific Basin *sea feature* Pa. Oc.
95 O7 South-West Peru Ridge *sea feature* Pac. Oc.
68 E5 South Whitley U.S.A.
81 H3 South Windham U.S.A.
39 J5 Southwold U.K.
59 H1 Soutpansberg *mts* S. Africa
48 G5 Soverato Italy
50 B4 Sovetsk *Kaliningrad.* Rus. Fed.
50 J3 Sovetsk *Kirovsk.* Rus. Fed.
24 G2 Sovetskaya Gavan' Rus. Fed.
50 D2 Sovetskiy *Leningrad.* Rus. Fed.
50 J3 Sovetskiy *Mariy El.* Rus. Fed.
12 H3 Sovetskiy Rus. Fed.
59 G3 Soweto S. Africa
18 E4 Sowghān Iran
84 D3 Soyaló Mex.
28 G2 Sōya-misaki *c.* Japan
30 D4 Soyang-ho *l.* S. Korea
47 P4 Sozh *r.* Belarus
49 M3 Sozopol Bulg.
42 D4 Spa Belgium
92 B3 Spaatz I. *i.* Ant.
34 E4 Spain *country* Europe
39 G5 Spalding U.K.
39 D6 Span Head *h.* U.K.
69 F2 Spanish Can.
69 G2 Spanish *r.* Can.
75 G1 Spanish Fork U.S.A.
83 J5 Spanish Town Jamaica
74 C2 Sparks U.S.A.
80 C6 Sparta *NC* U.S.A.
68 B4 Sparta *WV* U.S.A.
79 D5 Spartanburg U.S.A.
49 K6 Sparti Greece
48 G6 Spartivento, Capo *c.* Italy
64 G5 Sparwood Can.
50 E4 Spas-Demensk Rus. Fed.
50 E2 Spasskaya Guba Rus. Fed.
24 F2 Spassk-Dal'niy Rus. Fed.
49 K7 Spatha, Akra *pt* Greece
64 D3 Spatsizi Plateau Wilderness Provincial Park *res.* Can.
76 C2 Spearfish U.S.A.
77 C4 Spearman U.S.A.
81 F3 Speculator U.S.A.
76 E3 Spencer *IA* U.S.A.
72 D2 Spencer *ID* U.S.A.
80 C5 Spencer *WV* U.S.A.
64 B3 Spencer, Cape *c.* U.S.A.
6 D5 Spencer Gulf *est.* Austr.
64 E4 Spences Bridge Can.
38 F3 Spennymoor U.K.
41 D3 Sperrin Mountains *h.* U.K.
80 D5 Sperryville U.S.A.
43 H5 Spessart *reg.* Ger.
49 K6 Spetses *i.* Greece
40 E3 Spey *r.* U.K.
43 G5 Speyer Ger.
19 G4 Spezand Pak.
43 F1 Spiekeroog *i.* Ger.
46 C7 Spiez Switz.
42 E1 Spijk Neth.
42 C3 Spijkenisse Neth.
48 E1 Spilimbergo Italy
39 H4 Spilsby U.K.
19 G4 Spīn Būldak Afgh.
22 B3 Spintangi Pak.
64 F3 Spirit River Can.
68 C3 Spirit River Flowage *resr* U.S.A.
65 H4 Spiritwood Can.
19 G3 Spirsang Pass *pass* Afgh.
47 K6 Spišská Nová Ves Slovakia
17 K1 Spitak Armenia
22 D3 Spiti *r.* India
12 C2 Spitsbergen *i.* Svalbard
46 F7 Spittal an der Drau Austria
48 G3 Split Croatia
65 K3 Split Lake Can.
65 K3 Split Lake *l.* Can.
72 C2 Spokane U.S.A.
48 E3 Spoleto Italy
32 C2 Spong Cambodia
68 B3 Spooner U.S.A.
43 K1 Spornitz Ger.
72 F2 Spotted Horse U.S.A.
67 J3 Spotted Island Can.
69 F2 Spragge Can.
64 E4 Spranger, Mt *mt* Can.
72 C2 Spray U.S.A.
46 G5 Spree *r.* Ger.
42 D4 Sprimont Belgium
69 F3 Spring Bay Can.
58 B4 Springbok S. Africa
67 J4 Springdale Can.
77 E4 Springdale U.S.A.
43 H2 Springe Ger.
73 F4 Springer U.S.A.
75 H4 Springerville U.S.A.
77 C4 Springfield *CO* U.S.A.
68 C6 Springfield *IL* U.S.A.
81 G3 Springfield *MA* U.S.A.
81 J2 Springfield *ME* U.S.A.
76 E2 Springfield *MN* U.S.A.
77 E4 Springfield *MO* U.S.A.
80 B5 Springfield *OH* U.S.A.
77 C4 Springfield *OR* U.S.A.
81 G3 Springfield *VT* U.S.A.
80 D5 Springfield *WV* U.S.A.
68 C6 Springfield, Lake *l.* U.S.A.
59 F5 Springfontein S. Africa
68 B4 Spring Green U.S.A.
68 B4 Spring Grove U.S.A.
67 H4 Springhill Can.
79 D6 Spring Hill U.S.A.
68 D4 Spring Lake U.S.A.
75 E3 Spring Mountains *mts* U.S.A.
9 D5 Springs Junction N.Z.
68 A4 Spring Valley U.S.A.
80 D3 Springville *NY* U.S.A.
75 G1 Springville *UT* U.S.A.
39 J5 Sprowston U.K.
64 G4 Spruce Grove Can.
80 D5 Spruce Knob-Seneca Rocks National Recreation Area *res.* U.S.A.
72 D3 Spruce Mt. *mt* U.S.A.
38 H4 Spurn Head *c.* U.K.
64 E5 Spuzzum Can.
64 E5 Squamish Can.
81 H3 Squam Lake *l.* U.S.A.
81 J1 Squapan Lake *l.* U.S.A.
81 J1 Square Lake *l.* U.S.A.
48 G5 Squillace, Golfo di *g.* Italy
82 A2 S. Quintín, C. *pt* Mex.
32 B3 Srê Âmběl Cambodia
13 R4 Sredinnyy Khrebet *mts* Rus. Fed.
49 K3 Sredna Gora *mts* Bulg.
13 R3 Srednekolymsk Rus. Fed.
12 E4 Sredne-Russkaya Vozvyshennost' *reg.* Rus. Fed.
13 M3 Sredne-Sibirskoye Ploskogor'ye *plat.* Rus. Fed.
36 W4 Sredneye Kuyto, Oz. *l.* Rus. Fed.
49 L3 Srednogorie Bulg.
32 C2 Srêpok, T. *r.* Cambodia
24 D1 Sretensk Rus. Fed.
21 C3 Sriharikota I. *i.* India
21 D2 Srikakulam India
21 B3 Sri Kālahasti India
22 D3 Sri Kanta *mt* India
10 K9 Sri Lanka *country* Asia
22 D3 Srinagar India
22 C2 Srinagar Jammu and Kashmir
21 B4 Srirangam India
32 B1 Sri Thep Thai.
21 B4 Srivaikuntam India
21 A2 Srivardhan India
21 B4 Srivilliputtur India
21 C2 Srungavarapukota India
43 H1 Stade Ger.
42 B4 Staden Belgium
42 E2 Stadskanaal Neth.
43 H4 Stadtallendorf Ger.
43 H2 Stadthagen Ger.
43 K4 Stadtilm Ger.
42 E3 Stadtlohn Ger.
43 H3 Stadtoldendorf Ger.
43 K4 Stadtroda Ger.
40 B4 Staffa *i.* U.K.
43 K4 Staffelberg *h.* Ger.
43 J4 Staffelstein Ger.
39 E5 Stafford U.K.
80 E5 Stafford U.S.A.
37 T8 Staicele Latvia
39 G6 Staines U.K.
51 F5 Stakhanov Ukr.
39 E7 Stalbridge U.K.
39 J5 Stalham U.K.
Stalingrad *see* Volgograd
64 E3 Stalin, Mt *mt* Can.
47 L5 Stalowa Wola Pol.
49 L3 Stamboliyski Bulg.
39 G5 Stamford U.K.
81 G4 Stamford *CT* U.S.A.
81 F3 Stamford *NY* U.S.A.
Stampalia *i. see* Astypalaia
57 B6 Stampriet Namibia
36 N2 Stamsund Norway
76 E3 Stanberry U.S.A.
42 C3 Standdaarbuiten Neth.
59 H3 Standerton S. Africa
69 F4 Standish U.S.A.
78 C4 Stanford U.S.A.
59 J4 Stanger S. Africa
79 E7 Staniard Ck Bahamas
49 K3 Stanke Dimitrov Bulg.
43 M5 Staňkov Czech Rep.
81 K1 Stanley Can.
27 □ Stanley *H.K.* China
88 E8 Stanley Falkland Is
38 F3 Stanley U.K.
72 D2 Stanley *ID* U.S.A.
76 C1 Stanley *ND* U.S.A.
68 B3 Stanley *WV* U.S.A.
56 C3 Stanley, Mount *mt* Congo(Zaire)/Uganda
21 B4 Stanley Reservoir India
38 F2 Stannington U.K.
13 R3 Stanovaya Rus. Fed.
24 D1 Stanovoye Nagor'ye *mts* Rus. Fed.
24 E1 Stanovoy Khrebet *mts* Rus. Fed.
39 H5 Stanton U.K.
80 B6 Stanton *KY* U.S.A.
68 E4 Stanton *MI* U.S.A.
76 C3 Stapleton U.S.A.
47 K5 Starachowice Pol.
Stara Planina *see* Balkan Mts
50 H4 Staraya Kulatka Rus. Fed.
51 H5 Staraya Poltavka Rus. Fed.
50 D3 Staraya Russa Rus. Fed.
47 P2 Staraya Toropa Rus. Fed.
50 J4 Staraya Tumba Rus. Fed.
49 L3 Stara Zagora Bulg.
5 M5 Starbuck I. *i.* Kiribati
46 G4 Stargard Szczeciński Pol.
50 E3 Staritsa Rus. Fed.
79 D6 Starke U.S.A.
77 F5 Starkville U.S.A.
46 E7 Starnberger See *l.* Ger.
51 F5 Starobil's'k Ukr.
47 O4 Starodub Rus. Fed.
47 J4 Starogard Gdański Pol.
51 C5 Starokostyantyniv Ukr.
51 F6 Starominskaya Rus. Fed.
51 F6 Staroshcherbinovskaya Rus. Fed.
74 C1 Star Peak *mt* U.S.A.
39 D7 Start Point *pt* U.K.
47 O4 Staryya Darohi Belarus
51 F5 Staryy Oskol Rus. Fed.
43 K3 Staßfurt Ger.
80 E4 State College U.S.A.
79 D5 Statesboro U.S.A.
79 D5 Statesville U.S.A.
43 M3 Stauchitz Ger.
43 G4 Staufenberg Ger.
80 D5 Staunton U.S.A.
37 J7 Stavanger Norway
39 F4 Staveley U.K.
51 G6 Stavropol' Rus. Fed.
51 G6 Stavropol'skaya Vozvyshennost' *reg.* Rus. Fed.
51 G6 Stavropol'skiy Kray *div.* Rus. Fed.
8 D4 Stawell Austr.
59 H4 Steadville S. Africa
74 C2 Steamboat U.S.A.
72 F3 Steamboat Springs U.S.A.
92 B2 Steele I. *i.* Ant.
80 E4 Steelton U.S.A.
42 E2 Steenderen Neth.
59 J2 Steenkampsberge *mts* S. Africa
64 F3 Steen River Can.
72 C3 Steens Mt. *mt* U.S.A.
63 N2 Steenstrup Gletscher *gl.* Greenland
42 A4 Steenvoorde France
42 E2 Steenwijk Neth.
92 D4 Stefansson Bay *b.* Ant.
62 H2 Stefansson I. *i.* Can.
43 J5 Steigerwald *forest* Ger.
43 K5 Stein Ger.
43 K4 Steinach Ger.
65 K5 Steinbach Can.
43 G2 Steinfeld (Oldenburg) Ger.
42 F2 Steinfurt Ger.
57 B6 Steinhausen Namibia
43 H3 Steinheim Ger.
43 H2 Steinhuder Meer *l.* Ger.
36 M4 Steinkjer Norway
58 B4 Steinkopf S. Africa
75 H5 Steins U.S.A.
36 M4 Steinsdalen Norway
58 F3 Stella S. Africa
58 C6 Stellenbosch S. Africa
48 C3 Stello, Monte *mt Corsica* France
42 D5 Stenay France
43 K2 Stendal Ger.
27 □ Stenhouse, Mt *h. H.K.* China
40 E4 Stenhousemuir U.K.
37 M7 Stenungsund Sweden
Stepanakert *see* Xankändi
51 H7 Step'anavan Armenia
65 K5 Stephen U.S.A.
8 C2 Stephens *r.* Austr.
9 D4 Stephens, Cape *c.* N.Z.
8 C1 Stephens Creek Austr.
68 D3 Stephenson U.S.A.
64 C3 Stephens Passage *chan.* U.S.A.
67 J4 Stephenville Can.
77 D5 Stephenville U.S.A.
51 H5 Stepnoye Rus. Fed.
59 H4 Sterkfontein Dam *resr* S. Africa
59 G5 Sterkstroom S. Africa
58 F5 Sterling S. Africa
72 G3 Sterling *CO* U.S.A.
68 C5 Sterling *IL* U.S.A.
76 C2 Sterling *ND* U.S.A.
75 G2 Sterling *UT* U.S.A.
77 C6 Sterling City U.S.A.
69 F4 Sterling Hgts U.S.A.
14 D1 Sterlitamak Rus. Fed.
43 K1 Sternberg Ger.
64 G4 Stettler Can.
68 D2 Steuben U.S.A.
80 C4 Steubenville U.S.A.
39 G6 Stevenage U.K.
65 K4 Stevenson L. *l.* Can.
68 C3 Stevens Point U.S.A.
62 D3 Stevens Village U.S.A.
64 D3 Stewart Can.
64 B2 Stewart *r.* Can.
64 B2 Stewart Crossing Can.
9 A7 Stewart Island *i.* N.Z.
7 G2 Stewart Islands *is* Solomon Is
63 K3 Stewart Lake *l.* Can.
40 D5 Stewarton U.K.
68 A4 Stewartville U.S.A.
59 F5 Steynsburg S. Africa
46 G6 Steyr Austria
58 F6 Steytlerville S. Africa
42 D1 Stiens Neth.
64 C3 Stikine *r.* Can./U.S.A.
64 C3 Stikine Ranges *mts* Can.
58 D7 Stilbaai S. Africa
68 A3 Stillwater *MN* U.S.A.
74 C2 Stillwater *NV* U.S.A.
77 D4 Stillwater *OK* U.S.A.
73 C4 Stillwater Ra. *mts* U.S.A.
39 G5 Stilton U.K.
49 K4 Štip Macedonia
8 B3 Stirling Austr.
40 E4 Stirling U.K.
74 B2 Stirling City U.S.A.
8 A2 Stirling North Austr.
36 M5 Stjørdalshalsen Norway
46 H6 Stockerau Austria
43 K4 Stockheim Ger.
37 Q7 Stockholm Sweden
81 J1 Stockholm U.S.A.
39 E4 Stockport U.K.
74 B3 Stockton *CA* U.S.A.
76 D4 Stockton *KS* U.S.A.
75 F1 Stockton *UT* U.S.A.
68 B2 Stockton I. *i.* U.S.A.
77 E4 Stockton L. *l.* U.S.A.
38 F3 Stockton-on-Tees U.K.
81 J2 Stockton Springs U.S.A.
37 P5 Stöde Sweden
32 B2 Stœng Sângke *r.* Cambodia
32 C2 Stœng Sên *r.* Cambodia
32 C2 Stœng Trêng Cambodia
40 C2 Stoer, Point of *pt* U.K.
39 E4 Stoke-on-Trent U.K.
38 F3 Stokesley U.K.
36 C5 Stokkseyri Iceland
36 N3 Stokkvågen Norway
36 O2 Stokmarknes Norway
49 G3 Stolac Bos.-Herz.
42 E4 Stolberg (Rheinland) Ger.
51 C5 Stolin Belarus
43 L4 Stollberg Ger.
43 H2 Stolzenau Ger.
39 E5 Stone U.K.
69 J2 Stonecliffe Can.
81 F5 Stone Harbor U.S.A.
40 F4 Stonehaven U.K.
64 E3 Stone Mountain Prov. Park *res.* Can.
75 H3 Stoner U.S.A.
81 F4 Stone Ridge U.S.A.
65 K4 Stonewall Can.
80 C5 Stonewall Jackson Lake *l.* U.S.A.
69 F4 Stoney Point Can.
81 J2 Stonington U.S.A.
74 A2 Stonyford U.S.A.
81 E3 Stony Pt *pt* U.S.A.
65 H3 Stony Rapids Can.
36 Q3 Stora Inlevatten *l.* Sweden
36 P3 Stora Sjöfallets Nationalpark *nat. park* Sweden
36 Q4 Storavan *l.* Sweden
37 M9 Store Bælt *chan.* Denmark
36 M5 Støren Norway
36 O3 Storforshei Norway
36 O3 Storjord Norway
62 H2 Storkerson Peninsula Can.
59 G5 Stormberg S. Africa
59 G5 Stormberg *mts* S. Africa
76 E3 Storm Lake U.S.A.
37 K6 Stornosa *mt* Norway
40 B2 Stornoway U.K.
50 K2 Storozhevsk Rus. Fed.
51 C5 Storozhynets' Ukr.
81 G4 Storrs U.S.A.
40 B3 Storr, The *h.* U.K.
36 P4 Storseleby Sweden
36 O5 Storsjön *l.* Sweden
37 L5 Storskrymten *mt* Norway
36 R2 Storslett Norway
42 D1 Stortemelk *chan.* Neth.
36 P4 Storuman Sweden
36 P4 Storuman *l.* Sweden
37 P6 Storvik Sweden
37 M8 Storvorde Denmark
37 P7 Storvreta Sweden
39 G5 Stotfold U.K.
68 C4 Stoughton U.S.A.
39 E7 Stour *r. Eng.* U.K.
39 F5 Stour *r. Eng.* U.K.
39 J6 Stour *r. Eng.* U.K.
39 H6 Stour *r. Eng.* U.K.
39 E5 Stourbridge U.K.
39 E5 Stourport-on-Severn U.K.
65 L4 Stout L. *l.* Can.
50 C4 Stowbtsy Belarus
81 F4 Stowe U.S.A.
39 H5 Stowmarket U.K.
71 H3 St Peter *MN* U.S.A.
41 D3 Strabane U.K.
41 D4 Stradbally Rep. of Ireland
39 J5 Stradbroke U.K.
48 C2 Stradella Italy
75 G3 Straight Cliffs *cliff* U.S.A.
46 F6 Strakonice Czech Rep.
46 F3 Stralsund Ger.
58 C7 Strand S. Africa
36 K5 Stranda Norway
79 E7 Strangers Cay *i.* Bahamas
41 F3 Strangford U.K.
41 F3 Strangford Lough *l.* U.K.
40 C6 Stranraer U.K.
44 H2 Strasbourg France
80 D5 Strasburg U.S.A.
8 F4 Stratford Austr.
69 G4 Stratford Can.
9 E3 Stratford N.Z.
77 C4 Stratford *TX* U.S.A.
68 B3 Stratford *WV* U.S.A.
39 F5 Stratford-upon-Avon U.K.
8 B3 Strathalbyn Austr.
40 D5 Strathaven U.K.
40 G3 Strathbeg, Loch of *l.* U.K.
40 D3 Strathcarron *v.* U.K.
64 D5 Strathcona Prov. Park *res.* Can.
40 D3 Strathconon *v.* U.K.
40 D3 Strath Dearn *v.* U.K.
40 D2 Strath Fleet *v.* U.K.
64 G4 Strathmore Can.
64 E4 Strathnaver Can.
40 D2 Strathnaver *v.* U.K.
40 E2 Strath of Kildonan *v.* U.K.
69 G4 Strathroy Can.
40 E3 Strathspey *v.* U.K.
40 E2 Strathy U.K.
40 D2 Strathy Point *pt* U.K.
39 C7 Stratton U.K.
81 H2 Stratton U.S.A.
43 L6 Straubing Ger.
36 B3 Straumnes *pt* Iceland
68 B4 Strawberry Point U.S.A.
75 G1 Strawberry Reservoir U.S.A.
6 D5 Streaky Bay Austr.
6 D5 Streaky Bay *b.* Austr.
68 C5 Streator U.S.A.
39 E6 Street U.K.
49 K2 Strehaia Romania
43 M3 Strehla Ger.
13 R3 Strelka Rus. Fed.
37 T8 Strenči Latvia
43 L5 Stříbro Czech Rep.
40 F3 Strichen U.K.
49 K4 Strimonas *r.* Greece
91 D4 Stroeder Arg.
41 C4 Strokestown Rep. of Ireland
40 E2 Stroma, Island of *i.* U.K.
48 F5 Stromboli, Isola *i.* Italy
40 E2 Stromness U.K.
76 D3 Stromsburg U.S.A.
37 M7 Strömstad Sweden
36 O5 Strömsund Sweden
80 C4 Strongsville U.S.A.
40 F1 Stronsay *i.* U.K.
8 H2 Stroud Austr.
39 E6 Stroud U.K.
8 H2 Stroud Road Austr.
81 F4 Stroudsburg U.S.A.
37 L8 Struer Denmark
49 J4 Struga Macedonia
50 D3 Strugi-Krasnyye Rus. Fed.
58 D7 Struis Bay S. Africa
43 J5 Strullendorf Ger.
49 K4 Struma *r.* Bulg.
39 B5 Strumble Head *hd* U.K.
49 K4 Strumica Macedonia
49 L3 Stryama *r.* Bulg.
58 E4 Strydenburg S. Africa
37 K6 Stryn Norway
51 B5 Stryy Ukr.
79 D7 Stuart *FL* U.S.A.
80 C6 Stuart *VA* U.S.A.
64 E4 Stuart Lake *l.* Can.
80 D5 Stuarts Draft U.S.A.
8 G2 Stuart Town Austr.
9 C6 Studholme Junction N.Z.
36 Q5 Studsviken Sweden
77 C6 Study Butte U.S.A.
65 L4 Stull L. *l.* Can.
32 C2 Stung Chinit *r.* Cambodia
50 F4 Stupino Rus. Fed.
92 A6 Sturge I. *i.* Ant.
68 D2 Sturgeon *r.* U.S.A.
68 D3 Sturgeon Bay *WV* U.S.A.
65 K4 Sturgeon Bay *b.* Can.
68 E3 Sturgeon Bay *b.* U.S.A.
68 D3 Sturgeon Bay Canal *chan.* U.S.A.
69 H2 Sturgeon Falls Can.
66 B3 Sturgeon L. *l.* Can.
78 C4 Sturgis *KY* U.S.A.
68 E5 Sturgis *MI* U.S.A.
76 C2 Sturgis *SD* U.S.A.
6 C3 Sturt Creek *r.* Austr.
6 E4 Sturt Desert *des.* Austr.
59 G6 Stutterheim S. Africa
46 D6 Stuttgart Ger.
77 F5 Stuttgart U.S.A.
36 B4 Stykkishólmur Iceland
47 M5 Styr *r.* Ukr.
90 D2 Suaçuí Grande *r.* Brazil
55 F3 Suakin Sudan
27 F5 Su'ao Taiwan
73 E6 Suaqui Gde Mex.
89 B3 Suárez *r.* Col.
47 M3 Subačius Lith.
23 H4 Subansiri *r.* India
23 F5 Subarnarekha *r.* India
17 G6 Şubayḩah S. Arabia
33 C2 Subi Besar *i.* Indon.
49 H1 Subotica Yugo.
47 N7 Suceava Romania
28 C3 Suchan *r.* Rus. Fed.
41 C4 Suck *r.* Rep. of Ireland
43 K1 Suckow Ger.
86 E7 Sucre Bol.
89 B2 Sucre Col.
89 C3 Sucuaro Col.
90 B2 Sucuriú *r.* Brazil
51 E6 Sudak Ukr.
52 G4 Sudan *country* Africa
50 G3 Suday Rus. Fed.
17 K6 Sudayr *watercourse* Iraq
69 G2 Sudbury Can.
39 H5 Sudbury U.K.
55 E4 Sudd *swamp* Sudan
43 K1 Sude *r.* Ger.
46 H5 Sudety *mts* Czech Rep./Pol.
81 F5 Sudlersville U.S.A.
50 G4 Sudogda Rus. Fed.
16 D7 Sudr Egypt
36 □ Suðuroy *i.* Faroe Is
55 E4 Sue *watercourse* Sudan
45 F3 Sueca Spain
55 F2 Suez Egypt
55 F1 Suez Canal *canal* Egypt
55 F2 Suez, Gulf of *g.* Egypt
80 E6 Suffolk U.S.A.
18 B2 Sūfiān Iran
68 C4 Sugar *r.* U.S.A.
81 H2 Sugarloaf Mt. *mt* U.S.A.
31 C4 Sugbuhan Point *pt* Phil.
33 E1 Sugut *r.* Malaysia
31 A5 Sugut, Tg *pt* Malaysia
26 B2 Suhait China
20 E5 Şuḩār Oman
24 C1 Sühbaatar Mongolia
43 J4 Suhl Ger.
43 J2 Suhlendorf Ger.
16 C2 Şuhut Turkey
22 B3 Sui Pak.
28 B1 Suibin China
27 F4 Suichang China
27 E5 Suichuan China
26 D2 Suide China
30 F1 Suifenhe China
22 B4 Suigam India
24 E2 Suihua China
27 B4 Suijiang China
27 D5 Suining *Hunan* China
26 E3 Suining *Jiangsu* China
27 B4 Suining *Sichuan* China
26 E3 Suiping China
42 C5 Suippes France
41 D5 Suir *r.* Rep. of Ireland
26 E3 Suixi China
26 E3 Sui Xian China
27 C5 Suiyang China
26 F1 Suizhong China
26 D4 Suizhou China
26 C1 Suj China
22 C4 Sujangarh India
22 D3 Sujanpur India
22 B4 Sujawal Pak.
33 C4 Sukabumi Indon.
33 C3 Sukadana Indon.
29 G6 Sukagawa Japan
31 A5 Sukau Malaysia
30 C4 Sukch'ŏn N. Korea
28 C1 Sukhanovka Rus. Fed.
50 E4 Sukhinichi Rus. Fed.
50 H2 Sukhona *r.* Rus. Fed.
32 A1 Sukhothai Thai.
50 E2 Sukkozero Rus. Fed.
22 B4 Sukkur Pak.
21 C2 Sukma India
22 C4 Sukri *r.* India
50 F3 Sukromny Rus. Fed.
29 C8 Sukumo Japan
37 J6 Sula *i.* Norway
22 B3 Sulaiman Ranges *mts* Pak.
51 H7 Sulak *r.* Rus. Fed.
25 E7 Sula, Kepulauan *is* Indon.
18 C4 Sūlār Iran
40 B1 Sula Sgeir *i.* U.K.
33 E3 Sulawesi *i.* Indon.
17 K4 Sulaymān Beg Iraq
18 C2 Suledeh Iran
40 D1 Sule Skerry *i.* U.K.
40 D1 Sule Stack *i.* U.K.
16 F3 Süleymanlı Turkey
54 A4 Sulima Sierra Leone
43 G2 Sulingen Ger.
36 P3 Sulitjelma Norway
37 V6 Sulkava Fin.
86 B4 Sullana Peru
76 F4 Sullivan U.S.A.
65 G4 Sullivan L. *l.* Can.
81 J1 Sully Can.
48 E3 Sulmona Italy
77 E6 Sulphur U.S.A.
77 E5 Sulphur Springs U.S.A.
69 F2 Sultan Can.
Sultanabad *see* Arāk
16 C2 Sultan Dağları *mts* Turkey
16 D2 Sultanhanı Turkey
19 F4 Sultan, Koh-i- *mts* Pak.
23 E4 Sultanpur India
31 B5 Sulu Archipelago *is* Phil.
19 H2 Sülüktü Kyrg.
16 F2 Sulusaray Turkey
31 A4 Sulu Sea *sea* Phil.
43 K5 Sulzbach-Rosenberg Ger.
92 A4 Sulzberger Bay *b.* Ant.
19 E6 Sumāil Oman
88 D3 Sumampa Arg.
89 B4 Sumapaz, Parque Nacional *nat. park* Col.
17 K5 Sūmar Iran
33 B3 Sumatera *i.* Indon.
Sumatra *i. see* Sumatera
46 F6 Šumava *mts* Czech Rep.
25 E7 Sumba *i.* Indon.
18 D2 Sumbar *r.* Turkm.
25 D7 Sumba, Selat *chan.* Indon.
33 E4 Sumbawa *i.* Indon.
33 E4 Sumbawabesar Indon.
57 D4 Sumbawanga Tanz.
57 B5 Sumbe Angola
40 □ Sumburgh U.K.
40 □ Sumburgh Head *hd* U.K.
22 D2 Sumdo China/Jammu and Kashmir
17 M3 Sume'eh Sarā Iran
33 D4 Sumenep Indon.
Sumgait *see* Sumqayıt
29 F9 Sumisu-jima *i.* Japan
17 J3 Summēl Iraq
66 C3 Summer Beaver Can.
67 K4 Summerford Can.
68 D3 Summer I. *i.* U.S.A.
40 C2 Summer Isles *is* U.K.
67 H4 Summerside Can.
80 C5 Summersville U.S.A.
80 C5 Summersville Lake *l.* U.S.A.
64 E4 Summit Lake Can.
68 E5 Summit Lake *l.* U.S.A.
74 D2 Summit Mt *mt* U.S.A.
22 D2 Sumnal China/India
9 D5 Sumner N.Z.
68 A4 Sumner U.S.A.
9 D5 Sumner, L. *l.* N.Z.
64 C3 Sumner Strait *chan.* U.S.A.
29 F6 Sumon-dake *mt* Japan
29 D7 Sumoto Japan
46 H6 Šumperk Czech Rep.
17 M1 Sumqayıt Azer.
17 M1 Sumqayıt *r.* Azer.
22 B4 Sumrahu Pak.
79 D5 Sumter U.S.A.
51 E5 Sumy Ukr.
72 D2 Sun *r.* U.S.A.
50 J3 Suna Rus. Fed.
28 G3 Sunagawa Japan
23 G4 Sunamganj Bangl.
30 C4 Sunan N. Korea
40 C4 Sunart, Loch *in.* U.K.
18 D6 Şunaynah Oman
17 K4 Sunbula Kuh *mts* Iran
72 E1 Sunburst U.S.A.
8 E4 Sunbury Austr.
80 B4 Sunbury *OH* U.S.A.
80 E4 Sunbury *PA* U.S.A.
91 E1 Sunchales Arg.
30 C4 Sunch'ŏn N. Korea
30 D6 Sunch'ŏn S. Korea
59 G2 Sun City S. Africa
81 H3 Suncook U.S.A.
72 F2 Sundance U.S.A.
23 F5 Sundargarh India
22 D3 Sundarnagar India
33 C4 Sunda, Selat *chan.* Indon.
93 M4 Sunda Trench *sea feature* Ind. Ocean
38 F3 Sunderland U.K.
43 G3 Sundern (Sauerland) Ger.
16 C2 Sündiken Dağları *mts* Turkey
69 H3 Sundridge Can.
37 P5 Sundsvall Sweden

19 F2 Sundukli, Peski des. Turkm.
59 J4 Sundumbili S. Africa
22 D4 Sunel India
32 B5 Sungaikabung Indon.
33 C3 Sungailiat Indon.
33 B2 Sungai Pahang r. Malaysia
33 B3 Sungaipenuh Indon.
33 B1 Sungei Petani Malaysia
32 □ Sungei Seletar Res. resr Sing.
16 E1 Sungurlu Turkey
23 F4 Sun Kosi r. Nepal
37 K6 Sunndal Norway
36 L5 Sunndalsøra Norway
37 N7 Sunne Sweden
72 C2 Sunnyside U.S.A.
74 A3 Sunnyvale U.S.A.
68 C4 Sun Prairie U.S.A.
74 □1 Sunset Beach U.S.A.
75 G4 Sunset Crater National Monument res. U.S.A.
13 N3 Suntar Rus. Fed.
19 F5 Suntsar Pak.
72 D3 Sun Valley U.S.A.
30 C5 Sunwi Do i. N. Korea
54 B4 Sunyani Ghana
36 U3 Suolijärvet l. Fin.
68 C1 Suomi Can.
36 V4 Suomussalmi Fin.
29 B8 Suō-nada b. Japan
36 U5 Suonenjoki Fin.
32 C3 Suŏng Cambodia
27 B7 Suong r. Laos
50 E2 Suoyarvi Rus. Fed.
21 A3 Supa India
75 F3 Supai U.S.A.
89 E3 Supamo r. Venez.
23 F4 Supaul India
75 G5 Superior AZ U.S.A.
76 D3 Superior NE U.S.A.
68 A2 Superior WI U.S.A.
84 D3 Superior, L. l. Mex.
68 C2 Superior, Lake l. Can./U.S.A.
32 B2 Suphan Buri Thai.
17 J2 Süphan Dağı mt Turkey
50 E4 Suponevo Rus. Fed.
92 B3 Support Force Glacier gl. Ant.
30 C3 Supung N. Korea
17 L6 Sūq ash Shuyūkh Iraq
26 F3 Suqian China
Suquṭrā i. see Socotra
20 E5 Şūr Oman
50 H4 Sura Rus. Fed.
50 H4 Sura r. Rus. Fed.
17 M1 Şuraabad Azer.
19 G4 Surab Pak.
33 D4 Surabaya Indon.
19 E5 Sūrak Iran
33 D4 Surakarta Indon.
22 C5 Surat India
22 C3 Suratgarh India
32 A3 Surat Thani Thai.
50 E4 Surazh Rus. Fed.
17 K4 Sūrdāsh Iraq
49 K3 Surdulica Yugo.
42 E5 Sûre r. Lux.
22 B5 Surendranagar India
74 B4 Surf U.S.A.
12 J3 Surgut Rus. Fed.
21 B2 Suriapet India
31 C4 Surigao Phil.
31 C4 Surigao Str. chan. Phil.
32 B2 Surin Thai.
85 E2 Suriname country S. America
19 H3 Surkhab r. Afgh.
19 G2 Surkhandar'ya r. Uzbek.
23 E3 Surkhet Nepal
19 H2 Surkhob r. Tajik.
18 D4 Surmāq Iran
17 H1 Sürmene Turkey
51 G5 Surovikino Rus. Fed.
74 B3 Sur, Pt pt U.S.A.
91 F3 Sur, Pta pt Arg.
80 E6 Surry U.S.A.
50 H4 Sursk Rus. Fed.
Surt see Sirte
Surt, Khalīj g. see Sirte, Gulf of
36 C5 Surtsey i. Iceland
16 G3 Sürüç Turkey
29 F7 Suruga-wan b. Japan
33 B3 Surulangun Indon.
31 C5 Surup Phil.
42 F2 Surwold Ger.
17 L2 Şuşa Azer.
29 B7 Susa Japan
29 C8 Susaki Japan
18 C4 Süsangerd Iran
50 G3 Susanino Rus. Fed.
74 B1 Susanville U.S.A.
17 G1 Suşehri Turkey
32 A4 Suso Thai.
27 E4 Susong China
81 E4 Susquehanna r. U.S.A.
67 G4 Sussex Can.
81 F4 Sussex U.S.A.
33 A5 Susul Malaysia
13 Q3 Susuman Rus. Fed.
16 B2 Susurluk Turkey
22 D2 Sutak Jammu and Kashmir
74 C2 Sutcliffe U.S.A.
58 D6 Sutherland S. Africa
76 C3 Sutherland U.S.A.
22 C3 Sutlej r. Pak.
74 B2 Sutter Creek U.S.A.
39 G5 Sutterton U.K.
81 G2 Sutton Can.
39 H5 Sutton U.K.
80 C5 Sutton U.S.A.
66 D3 Sutton r. Can.
39 F5 Sutton Coldfield U.K.
39 F4 Sutton in Ashfield U.K.
66 D3 Sutton L. l. Can.
80 C5 Sutton Lake l. U.S.A.
28 G3 Suttsu Japan
28 D1 Sutungu Rus. Fed.
7 H3 Suva Fiji
50 F4 Suvorov Rus. Fed.
5 L6 Suvorov Island i. Pac. Oc.
29 F6 Suwa Japan
47 L3 Suwałki Pol.
32 B2 Suwannaphum Thai.
79 D6 Suwannee r. U.S.A.
17 K6 Suwayqīyah, Hawr as l. Iraq
17 H6 Suwayr well S. Arabia
30 D5 Suwŏn S. Korea
29 F6 Suzaka Japan
50 G3 Suzdal' Rus. Fed.
26 E3 Suzhou Anhui China
26 F4 Suzhou Jiangsu China
30 C3 Suzi r. China
29 E6 Suzu Japan
29 E7 Suzuka Japan
29 E6 Suzu-misaki pt Japan
36 U1 Sværholthalvøya pen. Norway
34 G1 Svalbard terr. Arctic Ocean
63 N2 Svartenhuk Halvø pen. Greenland
51 F5 Svatove Ukr.
32 C3 Svay Riĕng Cambodia
37 O5 Sveg Sweden
37 U8 Sveki Latvia
37 J6 Svelgen Norway
36 L5 Svellingen Norway
37 T9 Švenčionėliai Lith.
37 U9 Švenčionys Lith.
37 M9 Svendborg Denmark
36 Q2 Svensby Norway
36 O5 Svenstavik Sweden
Sverdlovsk see Yekaterinburg
51 F5 Sverdlovs'k Ukr.
63 J1 Sverdrup Channel Can.
49 J4 Sveti Nikole Macedonia
24 F2 Svetlaya Rus. Fed.
12 K3 Svetlogorsk Rus. Fed.
50 B4 Svetlogorsk Rus. Fed.
51 G6 Svetlograd Rus. Fed.
50 B4 Svetlyy Rus. Fed.
51 H5 Svetlyy Yar Rus. Fed.
50 D2 Svetogorsk Rus. Fed.
36 E4 Sviahnúkar volc. Iceland
49 M4 Svilengrad Bulg.
49 K2 Svinecea Mare, Vârful mt Romania
50 C4 Svir Belarus
50 E2 Svir' r. Rus. Fed.
49 L3 Svishtov Bulg.
46 H6 Svitava r. Czech Rep.
46 H6 Svitavy Czech Rep.
51 E5 Svitlovods'k Ukr.
50 J4 Sviyaga r. Rus. Fed.
24 E1 Svobodnyy Rus. Fed.
36 O2 Svolvær Norway
49 K3 Svrljiške Planine mts Yugo.
51 D4 Svyetlahorsk Belarus
39 F5 Swadlincote U.K.
39 H5 Swaffham U.K.
6 F4 Swain Reefs rf Austr.
79 D5 Swainsboro U.S.A.
5 K6 Swains I. i. Pac. Oc.
57 B6 Swakopmund Namibia
38 F3 Swale r. U.K.
7 G3 Swallow Is is Solomon Is
65 J4 Swan r. Can.
39 F7 Swanage U.K.
8 D3 Swan Hill Austr.
64 F4 Swan Hills Can.
83 H5 Swan Islands is Honduras
65 J4 Swan L. l. Can.
39 H6 Swanley U.K.
8 B3 Swan Reach Austr.
65 J4 Swan River Can.
8 H2 Swansea N.S.W. Austr.
39 D6 Swansea U.K.
39 D6 Swansea Bay b. U.K.
81 J2 Swans I. i. U.S.A.
81 G2 Swanton U.S.A.
59 G2 Swartruggens S. Africa
75 F2 Swasey Peak summit U.S.A.
69 G1 Swastika Can.
22 B2 Swat r. Pak.
Swatow see Shantou
53 H8 Swaziland country Africa
34 G2 Sweden country Europe
72 B2 Sweet Home U.S.A.
79 C5 Sweetwater TN U.S.A.
77 C5 Sweetwater TX U.S.A.
72 E3 Sweetwater r. U.S.A.
58 D7 Swellendam S. Africa
46 H5 Świdnica Pol.
46 G4 Świdwin Pol.
46 G4 Świebodzin Pol.
47 J4 Świecie Pol.
81 H2 Swift r. U.S.A.
65 H4 Swift Current Can.
65 H5 Swiftcurrent Cr. r. Can.
64 C2 Swift River Can.
41 D2 Swilly, Lough in. Rep. of Ireland
39 F6 Swindon U.K.
41 C4 Swinford Rep. of Ireland
46 G4 Świnoujście Pol.
40 F5 Swinton U.K.
34 F4 Switzerland country Europe
41 E4 Swords Rep. of Ireland
28 D1 Syain Rus. Fed.
50 E2 Syamozero, Oz. l. Rus. Fed.
50 G2 Syamzha Rus. Fed.
47 O3 Syanno Belarus
50 E2 Syas'troy Rus. Fed.
50 H3 Syava Rus. Fed.
68 C5 Sycamore U.S.A.
8 H2 Sydney Austr.
67 H4 Sydney Can.
65 L4 Sydney L. l. Can.
67 H4 Sydney Mines Can.
51 F5 Syeverodonets'k Ukr.
43 G2 Syke Ger.
50 J2 Syktyvkar Rus. Fed.
79 C5 Sylacauga U.S.A.
36 N5 Sylarna mt Norway/Sweden
23 G4 Sylhet Bangl.
50 G2 Syloga Rus. Fed.
46 D3 Sylt i. Ger.
79 D5 Sylvania GA U.S.A.
80 B4 Sylvania OH U.S.A.
64 G4 Sylvan Lake Can.
79 D6 Sylvester U.S.A.
64 E3 Sylvia, Mt mt Can.
49 M6 Symi i. Greece
84 B1 Symon Mex.
51 E5 Synel'nykove Ukr.
92 D4 Syowa Japan Base Ant.
48 F6 Syracuse Sicily Italy
76 C4 Syracuse KS U.S.A.
81 E3 Syracuse NY U.S.A.
14 E2 Syrdar'ya r. Kazak.
10 E6 Syria country Asia
20 A3 Syrian Desert des. Asia
49 M6 Syrna i. Greece
49 L6 Syros i. Greece
37 T6 Sysmä Fin.
50 J2 Sysola r. Rus. Fed.
50 J4 Syzran' Rus. Fed.
46 G4 Szczecin Pol.
46 H4 Szczecinek Pol.
47 K4 Szczytno Pol.
47 K7 Szeged Hungary
47 J7 Székesfehérvár Hungary
47 J7 Szekszárd Hungary
47 K7 Szentes Hungary
46 H7 Szentgotthárd Hungary
48 G1 Szigetvár Hungary
47 K7 Szolnok Hungary
46 H7 Szombathely Hungary

T

31 B3 Taal, L. l. Phil.
31 B3 Tabaco Phil.
59 H5 Tabankulu S. Africa
16 G4 Ţabaqah Syria
6 F2 Tabar Is is P.N.G.
16 E4 Tabarja Lebanon
48 C6 Tabarka Tunisia
18 E3 Ţabas Iran
84 D3 Tabasco div. Mex.
18 D3 Tabāsin Iran
18 C4 Tābask, Kūh-e mt Iran
86 E4 Tabatinga Col.
31 B2 Tabayoo, Mt mt Phil.
8 E3 Tabbita Austr.
54 B2 Tabelbala Alg.
65 G5 Taber Can.
23 F3 Tabia Tsaka salt l. China
7 H2 Tabiteuea i. Kiribati
37 U7 Tabivere Estonia
31 B3 Tablas i. Phil.
31 B3 Tablas Strait chan. Phil.
9 F3 Table Cape c. N.Z.
58 C6 Table Mountain mt S. Africa
77 E4 Table Rock Res. resr U.S.A.
90 A2 Tabocó r. Brazil
46 G6 Tábor Czech Rep.
56 D4 Tabora Tanz.
54 B4 Tabou Côte d'Ivoire
18 B2 Tabrīz Iran
5 M4 Tabuaeran i. Kiribati
20 A4 Tabūk S. Arabia
7 G3 Tabwémasana mt Vanuatu
37 O7 Täby Sweden
84 B3 Tacámbaro Mex.
89 A2 Tacarcuna, Cerro mt Panama
15 G2 Tacheng China
46 F6 Tachov Czech Rep.
31 C4 Tacloban Phil.
86 D7 Tacna Peru
72 B2 Tacoma U.S.A.
91 F1 Tacuarembó Uru.
91 G2 Tacuarí r. Uru.
89 E4 Tacutu r. Brazil
38 F4 Tadcaster U.K.
54 C2 Tademaït, Plateau du plat. Alg.
7 G4 Tadine New Caledonia
56 E2 Tadjoura Djibouti
16 G4 Tadmur Syria
65 K3 Tadoule Lake l. Can.
67 G4 Tadoussac Can.
30 D4 T'aebaek Sanmaek mts N. Korea/S. Korea
30 D5 Taech'ŏn S. Korea
30 C5 Taech'ŏngdo i. N. Korea
30 C4 Taedasa-do N. Korea
30 D4 Taedong r. N. Korea
30 C5 Taedong man b. N. Korea
30 E6 Taegu S. Korea
30 C6 Taehŭksan-kundo i. S. Korea
30 D5 Taejŏn S. Korea
30 D7 Taejŏng S. Korea
30 E5 T'aepaek S. Korea
39 C6 Taf r. U.K.
7 J3 Tafahi i. Tonga
45 F1 Tafalla Spain
18 D4 Tafihān Iran
16 E6 Tafila Jordan
54 B4 Tafiré Côte d'Ivoire
88 C3 Tafí Viejo Arg.
18 C3 Tafresh Iran
18 D4 Taft Iran
74 C4 Taft U.S.A.
19 F4 Taftān, Kūh-e mt Iran
51 F6 Taganrog Rus. Fed.
51 F6 Taganrog, Gulf of b. Rus. Fed./Ukr.
31 C3 Tagapula i. Phil.
31 B3 Tagaytay City Phil.
31 B4 Tagbilaran Phil.
23 E2 Tagchagpu Ri mt China
41 E5 Taghmon Rep. of Ireland
64 C2 Tagish Can.
48 E1 Tagliamento r. Italy
45 J4 Tagma, Col de pass Alg.
31 C4 Tagoloan r. Phil.
31 B4 Tagolo Point pt Phil.
7 F3 Tagula I. i. P.N.G.
31 C5 Tagum Phil.
45 B3 Tagus r. Port./Spain
64 F4 Tahaetkun Mt. mt Can.
32 B4 Tahan, Gunung mt Malaysia
54 C2 Tahat, Mt mt Alg.
24 E1 Tahe China
9 D1 Taheke N.Z.
5 N6 Tahiti i. Pac. Oc.
19 F4 Tahlab r. Iran/Pak.
19 F4 Tahlab, Dasht-i plain Pak.
77 E5 Tahlequah U.S.A.
74 B2 Tahoe City U.S.A.
62 H3 Tahoe Lake l. Can.
74 B2 Tahoe, Lake l. U.S.A.
77 C5 Tahoka U.S.A.
54 C3 Tahoua Niger
64 D4 Tahtsa Pk summit Can.
31 C6 Tahuna Indon.
27 □ Tai a Chau i. H.K. China
30 B3 Tai'an Liaoning China
26 E2 Tai'an Shandong China
26 C3 Taibai Shan mt China
26 E1 Taibus Qi China
27 F5 T'ai-chung Taiwan
9 C6 Taieri r. N.Z.
26 D2 Taigu China
26 D2 Taihang Shan mts China
9 E3 Taihape N.Z.
26 E3 Taihe Anhui China
27 E5 Taihe Jiangxi China
27 E4 Taihu China
24 E3 Tai Hu l. China
27 C5 Taijiang China
26 E3 Taikang China
27 □ Tai Lam Chung Res. resr H.K. China
8 B3 Tailem Bend Austr.
27 □ Tai Long Bay b. H.K. China
27 F5 T'ai-lu-ko Taiwan
19 F3 Taimani reg. Afgh.
27 □ Tai Mo Shan h. H.K. China
27 F6 T'ainan Taiwan
27 F6 T'ai-nan Taiwan
49 K6 Tainaro, Akra pt Greece
27 E5 Taining China
27 □ Tai O H.K. China
90 D1 Taiobeiras Brazil
54 B4 Taï, Parc National de nat. park Côte d'Ivoire
27 F5 T'ai-pei Taiwan
27 F4 Taiping Anhui China
27 D6 Taiping Guangxi China
33 B2 Taiping Malaysia
26 A2 Taipingbao China
30 B1 Taipingchuan China
27 □ Tai Po H.K. China
28 H3 Taisetsu-zan National Park Japan
29 C7 Taisha Japan
27 D6 Taishan China
27 F5 Taishun China
42 C5 Taissy France
9 D5 Taitanu N.Z.
88 E7 Taitao, Península de pen. Chile
27 F6 T'ai-tung Taiwan
36 V4 Taivalkoski Fin.
36 T2 Taivaskero h. Fin.
11 O7 Taiwan country Asia
27 F6 Taiwan Shan mts Taiwan
27 F5 Taiwan Strait str. China/Taiwan
26 F3 Tai Xian China
26 F3 Taixing China
26 D2 Taiyuan China
26 D2 Taiyue Shan mts China
26 F3 Taizhou China
27 F4 Taizhou Wan b. China
30 C3 Taizi r. China
20 B7 Ta'izz Yemen
22 B4 Tajal Pak
82 F5 Tajamulco, Volcano de volc. Guatemala
48 C7 Tajerouine Tunisia
10 H6 Tajikistan country Asia
Tajo r. see Tagus
32 A1 Tak Thai.
18 B2 Takāb Iran
29 C7 Takahashi Japan
9 D4 Takaka N.Z.
22 D5 Takal India
29 D7 Takamatsu Japan
22 D4 Takanpur India
29 E6 Takaoka Japan
9 F4 Takapau N.Z.
9 E2 Takapuna N.Z.
29 F6 Takasaki Japan
58 F2 Takatokwane Botswana
58 D1 Takatshwaane Botswana
29 C8 Takatsuki-yama mt Japan
29 E6 Takayama Japan
32 B4 Tak Bai Thai.
29 E7 Takefu Japan
29 B8 Takeo Japan
29 B9 Take-shima i. Japan
Take-shima i. see Tok-tō
18 C2 Takestān Iran
29 B8 Taketa Japan
32 C3 Takêv Cambodia
17 K7 Takhādīd well Iraq
20 E1 Takhiatash Uzbek.
32 C3 Ta Khmau Cambodia
19 F3 Takhta-Bazar Turkm.
17 M5 Takht Apān, Kūh-e mt Iran
19 G4 Takhta Pul Post Afgh.
22 B3 Takht-i-Sulaiman mt Pak.
18 C2 Takht-i-Suleiman mt Iran
65 G1 Takijuq Lake l. Can.
28 G3 Takikawa Japan
28 H2 Takinoue Japan
9 A6 Takitimu Mts mts N.Z.
64 D3 Takla Lake l. Can.
64 D3 Takla Landing Can.
Taklimakan Desert des. see Taklimakan Shamo
15 G3 Taklimakan Shamo des. China
19 H2 Takob Tajik.
23 H3 Takpa Shiri mt China
64 C3 Taku r. Can.
54 C4 Takum Nigeria
91 F2 Tala Uru.
50 D4 Talachyn Belarus
21 B4 Talaimannar Sri Lanka
22 C5 Talaja India
23 H4 Talap India
86 B4 Talara Peru
19 F5 Talar-i-Band mts Pak.
25 E6 Talaud, Kepulauan is Indon.
45 D3 Talavera de la Reina Spain
13 R3 Talaya Rus. Fed.
31 C5 Talayan Phil.
63 L2 Talbot Inlet b. Can.
8 G2 Talbragar r. Austr.
91 B2 Talca Chile
91 B3 Talcahuano Chile
23 F5 Talcher India
15 F2 Taldykorgan Kazak.
17 M5 Taleh Zang Iran
18 C2 Tālesh Iran
39 D6 Talgarth U.K.
25 E7 Taliabu i. Indon.
31 C4 Talibon Phil.
21 B2 Talikota India
19 G2 Talimardzhan Uzbek.
17 J1 T'alin Armenia
21 A3 Taliparamba India
31 B4 Talisay Phil.
31 C4 Talisayan Phil.
17 M2 Tališ Dağları mts Azer./Iran
50 H3 Talitsa Rus. Fed.
33 E4 Taliwang Indon.
79 C5 Talladega U.S.A.
17 J3 Tall 'Afar Iraq
79 C6 Tallahassee U.S.A.
8 F4 Tallangatta Austr.
79 C5 Tallassee U.S.A.
16 F6 Tall as Suwaysh h. Jordan
17 H3 Tall Baydar Syria
17 H4 Tall Fadghāmī Syria
37 T7 Tallinn Estonia
16 F4 Tall Kalakh Syria
17 J3 Tall Kayf Iraq
41 C5 Tallow Rep. of Ireland
77 F5 Tallulah U.S.A.
17 J3 Tall 'Uwaynāt Iraq
44 D3 Talmont-St-Hilaire France
51 D5 Tal'ne Ukr.
55 F3 Talodi Sudan
67 G2 Talon, Lac l. Can.
19 H2 Tāloqān Afgh.
51 G5 Talovaya Rus. Fed.
63 J3 Taloyoak Can.
22 C2 Tal Pass pass Pak.
37 S8 Talsi Latvia
88 B3 Taltal Chile
65 G2 Taltson r. Can.
18 B3 Talvar r. Iran
36 S1 Talvik Norway
51 G5 Taly Rus. Fed.
8 D2 Talyawalka r. Austr.
68 A4 Tama U.S.A.
89 B2 Tamalameque Col.
54 B4 Tamale Ghana
7 H2 Tamana i. Kiribati
89 A3 Tamana mt Col.
29 C7 Tamano Japan
54 C2 Tamanrasset Alg.
23 H4 Tamanthi Myanmar
89 B3 Tama, Parque Nacional el nat. park Venez.
81 F4 Tamaqua U.S.A.
39 C7 Tamar r. U.K.
59 G1 Tamasane Botswana
84 C1 Tamaulipas div. Mex.
84 A1 Tamazula Mex.
84 C3 Tamazulápam Mex.
84 C2 Tamazunchale Mex.
56 D3 Tambach Kenya
54 A3 Tambacounda Senegal
23 F4 Tamba Kosi r. Nepal
31 A5 Tambisan Malaysia
8 F4 Tambo r. Austr.
33 E4 Tambora, Gunung volc. Indon.
8 F4 Tamboritha mt Austr.
50 G4 Tambov Rus. Fed.
50 G4 Tambovskaya Oblast' div. Rus. Fed.
45 B1 Tambre r. Spain
31 A5 Tambunan, Bukit h. Malaysia
55 E4 Tambura Sudan
31 A5 Tambuyukon, Gunung mt Malaysia
54 A3 Tâmchekket Maur.
89 C3 Tame Col.
45 C2 Tâmega r. Port.
23 H4 Tamenglong India
48 B7 Tamerza Tunisia
84 C2 Tamiahua Mex.
84 C2 Tamiahua, Lag. de lag. Mex.
32 A4 Tamiang, Ujung pt Indon.
21 B4 Tamil Nadu div. India
50 F1 Tamitsa Rus. Fed.
16 C7 Tāmīya Egypt
32 D2 Tam Ky Vietnam
79 D7 Tampa U.S.A.
79 D7 Tampa Bay b. U.S.A.
19 E5 Tamp-e Gīrān Iran
37 S6 Tampere Fin.
84 C2 Tampico Mex.
32 □ Tampines Sing.
24 D2 Tamsagbulag Mongolia
26 B1 Tamsag Muchang China
46 F7 Tamsweg Austria
23 H4 Tamu Myanmar
84 C2 Tamuín Mex.
23 F4 Tamur r. Nepal
8 H1 Tamworth Austr.
39 F5 Tamworth U.K.
56 D4 Tana r. Kenya
29 D8 Tanabe Japan
36 V1 Tana Bru Norway
36 V1 Tanafjorden chan. Norway
T'ana Hāyk' l. see Tana, Lake
33 E3 Tanahgrogot Indon.
25 E7 Tanahjampea i. Indon.
33 A3 Tanahmasa i. Indon.
31 A6 Tanahmerah Indon.
32 B4 Tanah Merah Malaysia
33 C4 Tanah, Tanjung pt Indon.
56 D2 Tana, Lake l. Eth.
6 D3 Tanami Desert Austr.
32 C3 Tân An Vietnam
62 C3 Tanana U.S.A.
48 C2 Tanaro r. Italy
31 C4 Tanauan Phil.
26 F3 Tancheng China
30 E3 Tanch'ŏn N. Korea
84 B3 Tancitaro, Cerro de mt Mex.
54 B4 Tanda Côte d'Ivoire
23 E4 Tanda India
31 C4 Tandag Phil.
49 M2 Țăndărei Romania
31 A5 Tandek Malaysia
22 D2 Tandi India
91 E3 Tandil Arg.
91 E3 Tandil, Sa del h. Arg.
22 B4 Tando Adam Pak.
22 B4 Tando Bago Pak.
8 D2 Tandou L. l. Austr.
41 E3 Tandragee U.K.
21 B2 Tandur India
9 F3 Taneatua N.Z.
29 B9 Tanega-shima i. Japan
32 A1 Tanen Taunggyi mts Thai.
80 E5 Taneytown U.S.A.
54 B2 Tanezrouft reg. Alg./Mali
56 D4 Tanga Tanz.
9 E2 Tangaehe N.Z.
23 G4 Tangail Bangl.
7 F2 Tanga Is is P.N.G.
21 C5 Tangalla Sri Lanka
56 C4 Tanganyika, Lake l. Africa
18 D2 Tangar Iran
21 B4 Tangasseri India
27 B5 Tangdan China
92 D4 Tange Prom. hd Ant.
Tanger see Tangier
33 C4 Tangerang Indon.
43 K2 Tangerhütte Ger.
43 K2 Tangermünde Ger.
26 B3 Tanggor China
23 G2 Tanggula Shan mts China
23 G2 Tanggula Shankou pass China
26 D3 Tanghe China
22 B2 Tangi Pak.
54 B1 Tangier Morocco
81 E6 Tangier I. i. U.S.A.
30 D5 Tangjin S. Korea
23 G4 Tangla India
32 □ Tanglin Sing.
23 H3 Tangmai China
23 F3 Tangra Yumco salt l. China
26 F2 Tangshan China
31 B4 Tangub Phil.
54 C3 Tanguieta Benin
28 A1 Tangwang r. China
27 C4 Tangyan He r. China
26 E3 Tangyin China
28 A1 Tangyuan China
36 U3 Tanhua Fin.
32 C3 Tani Cambodia
23 H3 Taniantaweng Shan mts China
25 F7 Tanimbar, Kepulauan is Indon.
31 B4 Tanjay Phil.
Tanjore see Thanjavur
32 A5 Tanjungbalai Indon.
33 C4 Tanjungkarang Telukbetung Indon.
33 C3 Tanjungpandan Indon.
33 B2 Tanjungpinang Indon.
32 A5 Tanjungpura Indon.
33 E2 Tanjungredeb Indon.
33 E2 Tanjungselor Indon.
22 B2 Tank Pak.
22 D2 Tankse Jammu and Kashmir
23 F4 Tankuhi India
7 G3 Tanna i. Vanuatu
40 F4 Tannadice U.K.
37 N5 Tannäs Sweden
24 B1 Tannu Ola, Khrebet mts Rus. Fed.
31 B4 Tañon Strait chan. Phil.
22 B4 Tanot India
54 C3 Tanout Niger
23 E4 Tansen Nepal
27 F5 Tan-shui Taiwan
55 F1 Tanta Egypt
54 A2 Tan-Tan Morocco
8 C4 Tantanoola Austr.
84 C2 Tantoyuca Mex.
21 C2 Tanuku India
37 M7 Tanumshede Sweden
8 B3 Tanunda Austr.
30 E5 Tanyang S. Korea
53 H6 Tanzania country Africa
30 B1 Tao'an China
30 B1 Tao'er r. China
26 B3 Tao He r. China
27 D4 Taojiang China
26 C2 Taole China
94 G5 Taongi i. Pac. Oc.
32 □ Tao Payoh Sing.
48 F6 Taormina Sicily Italy
73 F4 Taos U.S.A.
54 B2 Taoudenni Mali
54 B1 Taourirt Morocco
27 E5 Taoxi China
27 D4 Taoyuan China
27 F5 T'ao-yuan Taiwan
37 T7 Tapa Estonia
31 B5 Tapaan Passage chan. Phil.
84 D4 Tapachula Mex.
87 G4 Tapajós r. Brazil
33 A2 Tapaktuan Indon.
91 E3 Tapalqué Arg.
84 D3 Tapanatepec Mex.
32 A5 Tapanuli, Teluk b. Indon.
86 F5 Tapauá Brazil
86 E5 Tapauá r. Brazil
54 B4 Tapeta Liberia
22 C5 Tāpi r. India
31 B5 Tapiantana i. Phil.
68 C2 Tapiola U.S.A.
32 B4 Tapis mt Malaysia
23 F4 Taplejung Nepal
27 □ Tap Mun Chau i. H.K. China
80 E6 Tappahannock U.S.A.
80 C4 Tappan Lake l. U.S.A.
18 C3 Tappeh, Kūh-e h. Iran
9 D4 Tapuaenuku mt N.Z.
31 B5 Tapul Phil.
31 B5 Tapul Group is Phil.
89 D5 Tapurucuara Brazil
17 L4 Tāq-e Bostan mt Iraq
17 K4 Ţaqţaq Iraq
90 B1 Taquaral, Serra do h. Brazil
90 B2 Taquari Brazil
87 G7 Taquari r. Brazil
90 A2 Taquari, Serra do h. Brazil
90 C3 Taquaritinga Brazil
90 B3 Taquaruçu r. Brazil
41 D5 Tar r. Rep. of Ireland
54 D4 Taraba r. Nigeria
86 E7 Tarabuco Bol.
Ţarābulus see Tripoli
89 C4 Taracua Brazil
41 E4 Tara, Hill of h. Rep. of Ireland
22 B4 Tar Ahmad Rind Pak.
22 E4 Tarahuwan India
23 G4 Tarai reg. India
33 E2 Tarakan Indon.
31 A6 Tarakan i. Indon.
16 C1 Taraklı Turkey
8 G3 Taralga Austr.
8 G2 Tarana Austr.
22 D5 Tarana India
22 C3 Tārānagar India
Taranaki, Mt volc. see Egmont, Mt
45 E2 Tarancón Spain
47 J3 Taran, Mys pt Rus. Fed.
40 A3 Taransay i. U.K.
48 G4 Taranto Italy
48 G4 Taranto, Golfo di g. Italy
86 C5 Tarapoto Peru
9 E4 Tararua Range mts N.Z.
47 P6 Tarashcha Ukr.
86 D5 Tarauacá Brazil
86 E5 Tarauacá r. Brazil
4 J4 Tarawa Kiribati
9 F3 Tarawera N.Z.
9 F3 Tarawera, Mt mt N.Z.
45 F2 Tarazona Spain
45 F3 Tarazona de la Mancha Spain
15 G2 Tarbagatay, Khrebet mts Kazak.
40 E3 Tarbat Ness pt U.K.
22 C2 Tarbela Dam dam Pak.
41 B5 Tarbert Rep. of Ireland
40 B3 Tarbert Scot. U.K.
40 C5 Tarbert Scot. U.K.
44 E5 Tarbes France
79 E5 Tarboro U.S.A.
8 F3 Tarcutta Austr.
24 F2 Tardoki-Yani, Gora mt Rus. Fed.
7 F5 Taree Austr.
12 L2 Tareya Rus. Fed.
72 E2 Targhee Pass pass U.S.A.
49 L2 Târgoviște Romania
49 K2 Târgu Jiu Romania
47 M7 Târgu Mureș Romania
47 N7 Târgu Neamț Romania
47 N7 Târgu Secuiesc Romania
18 B3 Tarhān Iran
26 C2 Tarian Gol China
18 D5 Tarif U.A.E.
45 D4 Tarifa Spain
45 D4 Tarifa o Marroqui, Pta de pt Spain
86 F8 Tarija Bol.
25 F7 Tariku r. Indon.
20 C6 Tarim Yemen
Tarim Basin basin see Tarim Pendi
15 G3 Tarim Pendi basin China
19 G3 Tarīn Kowt Afgh.
25 F7 Taritatu r. Indon.
17 K4 Tarjīl Iraq
59 F6 Tarka r. S. Africa
59 G6 Tarkastad S. Africa
76 E3 Tarkio U.S.A.
12 J3 Tarko-Sale Rus. Fed.
54 B4 Tarkwa Ghana
31 B3 Tarlac Phil.
43 H1 Tarmstedt Ger.
44 F4 Tarn r. France
36 O4 Tärnaby Sweden
19 G3 Tarnak r. Afgh.
47 M7 Târnăveni Romania
47 K5 Tarnobrzeg Pol.
50 G2 Tarnogskiy Gorodok Rus. Fed.
47 K5 Tarnów Pol.
23 E3 Tarok Tso salt l. China
18 D4 Ţārom Iran
54 B1 Taroudannt Morocco
8 C4 Tarpeena Austr.
79 E7 Tarpum Bay Bahamas
18 C3 Tarq Iran
48 D3 Tarquinia Italy
45 G2 Tarragona Spain
36 Q3 Tårrajaur Sweden
8 F2 Tarran Hills h. Austr.
9 B6 Tarras N.Z.
45 G2 Tàrrega Spain
16 E3 Tarsus Turkey
88 D2 Tartagal Arg.
17 L1 Tärtär Azer.
17 L1 Tärtär r. Azer.
44 D5 Tartas France
37 U7 Tartu Estonia
16 E4 Ţarţūs Syria
90 E2 Tarumirim Brazil
51 H6 Tarumovka Rus. Fed.
32 A5 Tarutung Indon.
48 E1 Tarvisio Italy
18 E4 Tarz Iran
66 E4 Taschereau Can.
21 A2 Tasgaon India
30 A3 Tashan China
23 G4 Tashigang Bhutan
Tashio Chho see Thimphu
17 K1 Tashir Armenia
18 D4 Tashk Iran
18 D4 Tashk, Daryācheh-ye l. Iran
14 E2 Tashkent Uzbek.
19 F2 Tashkepri Turkm.
66 F2 Tasiat, Lac l. Can.
63 P3 Tasiilaq Greenland
33 C4 Tasikmalaya Indon.
67 G2 Tasiujaq Can.
15 G2 Taskesken Kazak.
16 E1 Taşköprü Turkey
17 J2 Taşlıçay Turkey
94 F8 Tasman Basin sea feature Pac. Oc.
9 D4 Tasman Bay b. N.Z.
6 E6 Tasmania div. Austr.
9 D4 Tasman Mountains mts N.Z.
94 E9 Tasman Plateau sea feature Pac. Oc.
7 F5 Tasman Sea sea Pac. Oc.
16 F1 Taşova Turkey
74 B3 Tassajara Hot Springs U.S.A.
67 F2 Tassialujjuaq, Lac l. Can.
54 C2 Tassili du Hoggar plat. Alg.
54 C2 Tassili n'Ajjer plat. Alg.
17 K2 Tasūj Iran
13 N3 Tas-Yuryakh Rus. Fed.
47 J7 Tatabánya Hungary
51 D6 Tatarbunary Ukr.
12 J4 Tatarsk Rus. Fed.
24 G1 Tatarskiy Proliv str. Rus. Fed.
50 J4 Tatarstan, Respublika div. Rus. Fed.
18 B2 Tatavi r. Iran
29 F7 Tateyama Japan
29 E6 Tate-yama volc. Japan
64 F2 Tathlina Lake l. Can.
20 B5 Tathlīth, W. watercourse S. Arabia
8 G4 Tathra Austr.
65 K2 Tatinnai Lake l. Can.
51 H5 Tatishchevo Rus. Fed.
72 A1 Tatla Lake Can.
64 D3 Tatlatui Prov. Park res. Can.
25 E7 Tat Mailau, G. mt Indon.
8 F4 Tatong Austr.
47 J6 Tatry reg. Pol.
64 B3 Tatshenshini r. Can.
51 G5 Tatsinskiy Rus. Fed.
29 D7 Tatsuno Japan
22 A4 Tatta Pak.
90 C3 Tatuí Brazil
64 E4 Tatuk Mtn mt Can.
77 C5 Tatum U.S.A.
8 E4 Tatura Austr.
17 J2 Tatvan Turkey
37 J7 Tau Norway
87 K5 Taua Brazil
90 D3 Taubaté Brazil
43 H5 Tauber r. Ger.
43 H5 Tauberbischofsheim Ger.
43 L3 Taucha Ger.
43 H4 Taufstein h. Ger.
58 F3 Taung S. Africa
25 B4 Taung-gyi Myanmar
32 A2 Taungnyo Range mts Myanmar
39 D6 Taunton U.K.
81 H4 Taunton U.S.A.
43 F4 Taunus h. Ger.
9 F3 Taupo N.Z.
9 E3 Taupo, Lake l. N.Z.
37 S9 Tauragė Lith.
9 F2 Tauranga N.Z.
48 G5 Taurianova Italy
9 D1 Tauroa Pt pt N.Z.
7 F2 Tauu is P.N.G.
16 B3 Tavas Turkey
39 J5 Taverham U.K.
45 C4 Tavira Port.
39 C7 Tavistock U.K.
32 A2 Tavoy Myanmar
32 A2 Tavoy Pt pt Myanmar
28 B3 Tavrichanka Rus. Fed.
16 B2 Tavşanlı Turkey
39 C6 Taw r. U.K.
69 F3 Tawas Bay b. U.S.A.
69 F3 Tawas City U.S.A.
33 E2 Tawau Malaysia
39 D6 Tawe r. U.K.
22 C2 Tawi r. India
31 A5 Tawitawi i. Phil.
27 F6 T'a-wu Taiwan
84 C3 Taxco Mex.
15 F3 Taxkorgan China
64 C2 Tay r. Can.
40 E4 Tay r. U.K.
31 B3 Tayabas Bay b. Phil.
36 X2 Taybola Rus. Fed.
40 E4 Tay, Firth of est. U.K.
40 C5 Tayinloan U.K.
40 D4 Tay, Loch l. U.K.
64 E3 Taylor Can.
75 G4 Taylor AZ U.S.A.
69 F4 Taylor MI U.S.A.
68 B6 Taylor MO U.S.A.
76 D3 Taylor NE U.S.A.
77 D6 Taylor TX U.S.A.
81 E5 Taylors Island U.S.A.
78 B4 Taylorville U.S.A.
20 A4 Taymā' S. Arabia
13 L3 Taymura r. Rus. Fed.
13 M2 Taymyr, Ozero l. Rus. Fed.
13 L2 Taymyr, Poluostrov pen. Rus. Fed.
32 C3 Tây Ninh Vietnam
31 A4 Taytay Phil.
31 B3 Taytay Phil.
31 A4 Taytay Bay b. Phil.
19 F3 Tayyebād Iran
13 K2 Taz r. Rus. Fed.
54 B1 Taza Morocco
17 K4 Tāza Khurmātū Iraq
17 L2 Tazeh Kand Azer.
80 B6 Tazewell TN U.S.A.
80 C6 Tazewell VA U.S.A.
65 H2 Tazin r. Can.
65 H3 Tazin Lake l. Can.
55 E2 Tāzirbū Libya
45 J4 Tazmalt Alg.
12 J3 Tazovskaya Guba chan. Rus. Fed.

17 J1 Tba Khozap'ini l. Georgia
51 H7 T'bilisi Georgia
51 G6 Tbilisskaya Rus. Fed.
56 B4 Tchibanga Gabon
55 D2 Tchigaï, Plateau du plat. Niger
55 D4 Tcholliré Cameroon
47 J3 Tczew Pol.
84 A2 Teacapán Mex.
9 A6 Te Anau N.Z.
9 A6 Te Anau, L. l. N.Z.
84 D3 Teapa Mex.
9 G2 Te Araroa N.Z.
9 E2 Te Aroha N.Z.
9 E3 Te Awamutu N.Z.
38 E3 Tebay U.K.
65 K2 Tebesjuak Lake l. Can.
54 C1 Tébessa Alg.
48 B7 Tébessa, Monts de mts Alg.
88 E3 Tebicuary r. Para.
33 A2 Tebingtinggi Indon.
33 B3 Tebingtinggi Indon.
48 C6 Tébourba Tunisia
48 C6 Téboursouk Tunisia
51 H7 Tebulos Mt'a mt Georgia/Rus. Fed.
54 B4 Techiman Ghana
88 B6 Tecka Arg.
42 F2 Tecklenburger Land reg. Ger.
84 C2 Tecolutla Mex.
84 B3 Tecomán Mex.
74 D4 Tecopa U.S.A.
84 B3 Técpan Mex.
47 N7 Tecuci Romania
69 F5 Tecumseh U.S.A.
19 F2 Tedzhen Turkm.
19 F2 Tedzhen r. Turkm.
19 F2 Tedzhenstroy Turkm.
75 H3 Teec Nos Pos U.S.A.
15 H1 Teeli Rus. Fed.
38 F3 Tees r. U.K.
38 E3 Teesdale reg. U.K.
31 A4 Teeth, The mt Phil.
86 E4 Tefé r. Brazil
16 B3 Tefenni Turkey
33 C4 Tegal Indon.
43 M2 Tegel airport Ger.
39 D5 Tegid, Llyn l. U.K.
82 G6 Tegucigalpa Honduras
54 C3 Teguidda-n-Tessoumt Niger
74 C4 Tehachapi U.S.A.
73 C5 Tehachapi Mts mts U.S.A.
74 C4 Tehachapi Pass U.S.A.
65 K2 Tehek Lake l. Can.
Teheran see Tehrān
54 B4 Téhini Côte d'Ivoire
18 C3 Tehrān Iran
22 D3 Tehri Uttar Pradesh India
Tehri see Tikamgarh
84 C3 Tehuacán Mex.
84 D4 Tehuantepec, Golfo de g. Mex.
84 D3 Tehuantepec, Istmo de isth. Mex.
95 N5 Tehuantepec Ridge sea feature Pac. Oc.
84 C3 Tehuitzingo Mex.
39 C5 Teifi r. U.K.
39 D7 Teign r. U.K.
39 D7 Teignmouth U.K.
Tejo r. see Tagus
74 C4 Tejon Pass U.S.A.
9 D1 Te Kao N.Z.
9 C5 Tekapo, L. l. N.Z.
23 F4 Tekari India
82 G4 Tekax Mex.
56 D2 Tekezē Wenz r. Eritrea/Eth.
22 E1 Tekiliktag mt China
16 A1 Tekirdağ Turkey
21 D2 Tekkali India
17 H2 Tekman Turkey
23 H5 Teknaf Bangl.
68 E4 Tekonsha U.S.A.
9 E3 Te Kuiti N.Z.
23 E5 Tel r. India
51 H7 T'elavi Georgia
16 E5 Tel Aviv-Yafo Israel
46 G6 Telč Czech Rep.
82 G4 Telchac Puerto Mex.
64 C3 Telegraph Creek Can.
44 G3 Télégraphe, Le h. France
90 B4 Telêmaco Borba Brazil
91 D3 Telén Arg.
33 E2 Telen r. Indon.
49 L2 Teleorman r. Romania
74 D3 Telescope Peak summit U.S.A.
87 G5 Teles Pires r. Brazil
39 E5 Telford U.K.
43 F3 Telgte Ger.
54 A3 Télimélé Guinea
17 J3 Tel Kotchek Syria
64 D4 Telkwa Can.
62 B3 Teller AK U.S.A.
21 A4 Tellicherry India
42 D4 Tellin Belgium
17 L6 Telloh Iraq
32 □ Telok Blangah Sing.
84 C3 Teloloapán Mex.
91 C4 Telsen Arg.
37 S9 Telšiai Lith.
43 M2 Teltow Ger.
32 B2 Teluk Anson Malaysia
33 A2 Telukdalam Indon.
69 H2 Temagami Can.
69 H2 Temagami Lake l. Can.
33 D4 Temanggung Indon.
59 H2 Temba S. Africa
33 C2 Tembelan, Kepulauan is Indon.
13 L3 Tembenchi r. Rus. Fed.
33 B3 Tembilahan Indon.
59 H3 Tembisa S. Africa
56 B4 Tembo Aluma Angola
39 E5 Teme r. U.K.
74 D5 Temecula U.S.A.
16 D2 Temelli Turkey
33 B2 Temerloh Malaysia
17 M5 Temīleh Iran
15 F1 Temirtau Kazak.
69 H2 Temiscaming Can.
69 H2 Témiscamingue, Lac l. Can.
67 G4 Témiscouata, L. l. Can.
36 T4 Temmes Fin.
50 G4 Temnikov Rus. Fed.
8 F3 Temora Austr.
75 G5 Tempe U.S.A.
43 M2 Tempelhof airport Ger.
48 C4 Tempio Pausania Sardinia Italy
68 E3 Temple MI U.S.A.
77 D6 Temple TX U.S.A.
39 C5 Temple Bar U.K.
41 D5 Templemore Rep. of Ireland
31 A4 Templer Bank sand bank Phil.
38 E3 Temple Sowerby U.K.
43 M1 Templin Ger.

84 C2 Tempoal Mex.
51 F6 Temryuk Rus. Fed.
91 B3 Temuco Chile
9 C6 Temuka N.Z.
86 C4 Tena Ecuador
74 D1 Tenabo, Mt mt U.S.A.
21 C2 Tenali India
84 C3 Tenancingo Mex.
32 A2 Tenasserim Myanmar
32 A2 Tenasserim r. Myanmar
39 E5 Tenbury Wells U.K.
39 C6 Tenby U.K.
69 F2 Tenby Bay Can.
56 E2 Tendaho Eth.
44 H4 Tende France
15 H6 Ten Degree Chan. Andaman and Nicobar Is
28 G5 Tendō Japan
17 J2 Tendürük Dağı mt Turkey
54 B3 Ténenkou Mali
54 D3 Ténéré reg. Niger
54 D2 Ténéré du Tafassâsset des. Niger
54 A2 Tenerife i. Canary Is
45 G4 Ténès Alg.
33 E4 Tengah, Kepulauan is Indon.
32 □ Tengeh Res. resr Sing.
26 B2 Tengger Shamo des. China
32 B4 Tenggul i. Malaysia
14 E1 Tengiz, Oz. l. Kazak.
27 C7 Tengqiao China
54 B3 Tengréla Côte d'Ivoire
27 D6 Teng Xian Guangxi China
26 E3 Teng Xian Shandong China
92 B2 Teniente Jubany Arg. Base Ant.
92 B2 Teniente Rodolfo Marsh Chile Base Ant.
57 C5 Tenke Congo(Zaire)
13 Q2 Tenkeli Rus. Fed.
54 B3 Tenkodogo Burkina
6 D3 Tennant Creek Austr.
80 B6 Tennessee div. U.S.A.
79 C5 Tennessee r. U.S.A.
73 F4 Tennessee Pass U.S.A.
36 P2 Tennevoll Norway
91 B2 Teno r. Chile
36 U2 Tenojoki r. Fin./Norway
84 E3 Tenosique Mex.
72 F2 Ten Sleep U.S.A.
6 C2 Tenteno Indon.
39 H6 Tenterden U.K.
79 D7 Ten Thousand Islands is U.S.A.
45 C3 Tentudia mt Spain
90 B3 Teodoro Sampaio Brazil
90 E2 Teófilo Otôni Brazil
84 D3 Teopisca Mex.
84 C3 Teotihuacán Mex.
73 E6 Tepachi Mex.
9 D1 Te Paki N.Z.
84 B3 Tepalcatepec Mex.
84 B2 Tepatitlán Mex.
17 H3 Tepe Turkey
17 J3 Tepe Gawra Iraq
84 A1 Tepehuanes Mex.
84 C3 Tepeji Mex.
49 J4 Tepelenë Albania
84 C3 Tepelmemec Mex.
43 L5 Tepelská Vrchovina reg. Czech Rep.
89 E4 Tepequem, Serra mts Brazil
84 A2 Tepic Mex.
9 C5 Te Pirita N.Z.
46 F5 Teplice Czech Rep.
50 K2 Teplogorka Rus. Fed.
50 F4 Teploye Rus. Fed.
9 F2 Te Puke N.Z.
84 D3 Tequisistlán Mex.
84 C2 Tequisquiapán Mex.
45 H1 Ter r. Spain
5 L4 Teraina i. Kiribati
22 D2 Teram Kangri mt China/Jammu and Kashmir
48 E3 Teramo Italy
8 D5 Terang Austr.
42 F2 Ter Apel Neth.
22 B3 Teratani r. Pak.
51 F4 Terbuny Rus. Fed.
17 H2 Tercan Turkey
34 C5 Terceira i. Port.
47 M6 Terebovlya Ukr.
51 H7 Terek Rus. Fed.
51 H7 Terek r. Rus. Fed.
50 J4 Teren'ga Rus. Fed.
90 A3 Terenos Brazil
89 C2 Terepaima, Parque Nacional nat. park Venez.
50 H4 Tereshka r. Rus. Fed.
87 K5 Teresina Brazil
90 D3 Teresópolis Brazil
42 B5 Tergnier France
16 F1 Terme Turkey
19 G2 Termez Uzbek.
48 E6 Termini Imerese Sicily Italy
84 E3 Términos, Lag. de lag. Mex.
48 F4 Termoli Italy
39 E5 Tern r. U.K.
25 E6 Ternate Indon.
42 B3 Terneuzen Neth.
28 E2 Terney Rus. Fed.
48 E3 Terni Italy
51 C5 Ternopil' Ukr.
8 B2 Terowie Austr.
24 G2 Terpeniya, Mys c. Rus. Fed.
24 G2 Terpeniya, Zaliv g. Rus. Fed.
64 D4 Terrace Can.
68 D1 Terrace Bay Can.
58 E2 Terra Firma S. Africa
36 N4 Terråk Norway
48 C5 Terralba Sardinia Italy
67 K4 Terra Nova Nat. Pk Can.
92 B6 Terre Adélie reg. Ant.
77 F6 Terre Bonne Bay b. U.S.A.
78 C4 Terre Haute U.S.A.
67 K4 Terrenceville Can.
72 F2 Terry U.S.A.
51 G5 Tersa r. Rus. Fed.
42 D1 Terschelling i. Neth.
48 C5 Tertenia Sardinia Italy
45 F2 Teruel Spain
32 A4 Terutao i. Thai.
36 T3 Tervola Fin.
48 G2 Tešanj Bos.-Herz.
56 D2 Teseney Eritrea
50 G4 Tesha r. Rus. Fed.
62 C2 Teshekpuk Lake l. U.S.A.
28 J3 Teshikaga Japan
28 G2 Teshio Japan
28 H3 Teshio-dake mt Japan
28 G2 Teshio-gawa r. Japan
64 C2 Teslin Can.
64 C2 Teslin r. Can.
64 C2 Teslin Lake l. Can.
90 B1 Tesouras r. Brazil
90 B2 Tesouro Brazil
54 C3 Tessaoua Niger
39 F6 Test r. U.K.

48 C6 Testour Tunisia
88 B2 Tetas, Pta pt Chile
57 D5 Tete Moz.
9 F3 Te Teko N.Z.
47 P5 Teteriv r. Ukr.
43 L1 Teterow Ger.
47 O6 Tetiyiv Ukr.
38 G4 Tetney U.K.
72 E2 Teton r. U.S.A.
72 E3 Teton Ra. mts U.S.A.
54 B1 Tetouan Morocco
49 J3 Tetovo Macedonia
22 B5 Tetpur India
50 J4 Tetyushi Rus. Fed.
88 D2 Teuco r. Arg.
58 B1 Teufelsbach Namibia
43 G1 Teufels Moor reg. Ger.
28 G2 Teuri-tō i. Japan
43 G2 Teutoburger Wald h. Ger.
37 R5 Teuva Fin.
Teverya see Tiberias
40 F5 Teviot r. U.K.
40 F5 Teviotdale v. U.K.
9 A7 Te Waewae Bay b. N.Z.
59 G1 Tewane Botswana
7 F4 Tewantin Austr.
9 E4 Te Wharau N.Z.
39 E6 Tewkesbury U.K.
26 B3 Têwo China
64 E5 Texada I. i. Can.
77 E5 Texarkana U.S.A.
77 D6 Texas div. U.S.A.
77 E6 Texas City U.S.A.
84 C3 Texcoco Mex.
42 C1 Texel i. Neth.
77 C4 Texhoma U.S.A.
77 D5 Texoma, Lake l. U.S.A.
59 G4 Teyateyaneng Lesotho
50 G3 Teykovo Rus. Fed.
19 G3 Teyvareh Afgh.
50 G3 Teza r. Rus. Fed.
84 C3 Teziutlán Mex.
23 H4 Tezpur India
23 J4 Tezu India
65 K2 Tha-anne r. Can.
59 H4 Thabana-Ntlenyana mt Lesotho
59 G4 Thaba Nchu S. Africa
59 G4 Thaba Putsoa mt Lesotho
59 H4 Thaba-Tseka Lesotho
59 G2 Thabazimbi S. Africa
32 B1 Tha Bo Laos
59 G3 Thabong S. Africa
18 B5 Thādiq S. Arabia
32 A2 Thagyettaw Myanmar
27 C6 Thai Binh Vietnam
22 B3 Thai Desert des. Pak.
11 M8 Thailand country Asia
32 B3 Thailand, Gulf of g. Asia
27 B6 Thai Nguyên Vietnam
18 C5 Thaj S. Arabia
22 E5 Thakurtola India
43 J4 Thal Ger.
22 B2 Thal Pak.
48 C7 Thala Tunisia
32 A3 Thalang Thai.
Thalassery see Tellicherry
43 K3 Thale (Harz) Ger.
32 B4 Thale Luang lag. Thai.
32 B1 Tha Li Thai.
19 G4 Thalo Pak.
59 F2 Thamaga Botswana
20 D6 Thamarīt Oman
20 C7 Thamar, J. mt Yemen
39 G5 Thame r. U.K.
9 E2 Thames N.Z.
39 H6 Thames est. Eng. U.K.
39 G6 Thames r. Eng. U.K.
69 G4 Thamesville Can.
32 A2 Thanbyuzayat Myanmar
22 C5 Thandla India
22 B5 Thangadh India
32 D2 Thăng Binh Vietnam
32 C1 Thanh Hoa Vietnam
21 B4 Thanjavur India
32 B1 Tha Pla Thai.
32 A3 Thap Put Thai.
32 A3 Thap Sakae Thai.
22 B4 Tharad India
22 B4 Thar Desert des. India/Pak.
49 L4 Thasos i. Greece
75 H5 Thatcher U.S.A.
27 C6 Thât Khê Vietnam
25 B5 Thaton Myanmar
23 H4 Thaungdut Myanmar
32 A1 Thaungyin r. Myanmar/Thai.
25 B5 Thayetmyo Myanmar
75 F5 Theba U.S.A.
76 C3 Thedford U.S.A.
42 C2 The Hague Neth.
32 A3 Theinkun Myanmar
65 H2 Thekulthili Lake l. Can.
65 J2 Thelon r. Can.
65 J2 Thelon Game Sanctuary res. Can.
43 J4 Themar Ger.
58 F6 Thembalesizwe S. Africa
59 H3 Thembalihle S. Africa
45 H4 Thenia Alg.
45 H5 Theniet El Had Alg.
86 F5 Theodore Roosevelt r. Brazil
75 G5 Theodore Roosevelt Lake l. U.S.A.
76 C2 Theodore Roosevelt Nat. Park U.S.A.
42 A5 Thérain r. France
81 F2 Theresa U.S.A.
49 K4 Thermaïkos Kolpos g. Greece
74 B2 Thermalito U.S.A.
72 E3 Thermopolis U.S.A.
42 A4 Thérouanne France
62 F2 Thesiger Bay b. Can.
69 F2 Thessalon Can.
49 K4 Thessaloniki Greece
39 H5 Thet r. U.K.
39 H5 Thetford U.K.
67 F4 Thetford Mines Can.
32 C1 Theun r. Laos
59 G4 Theunissen S. Africa
77 F6 Thibodaux U.S.A.
65 K3 Thicket Portage Can.
76 D1 Thief River Falls U.S.A.
92 B4 Thiel Mts mts Ant.
44 F4 Thiers France
54 A3 Thiès Senegal
56 D4 Thika Kenya
21 A5 Thiladhunmathee Atoll atoll Maldives
23 G4 Thimphu Bhutan
44 H2 Thionville France
Thira i. see Santorini
49 L6 Thirasia i. Greece
38 F3 Thirsk U.K.
Thiruvananthapuram see Trivandrum
37 L8 Thisted Denmark
49 K5 Thiva Greece
65 K2 Thlewiaza r. Can.

65 H2 Thoa r. Can.
59 J1 Thohoyandou S. Africa
42 C3 Tholen Neth.
42 F5 Tholey Ger.
80 D5 Thomas U.S.A.
79 C5 Thomaston GA U.S.A.
81 J2 Thomaston ME U.S.A.
81 K2 Thomaston Corner Can.
41 D5 Thomastown Rep. of Ireland
79 D6 Thomasville U.S.A.
42 E4 Thommen Belgium
65 K3 Thompson Man. Can.
68 D3 Thompson MI U.S.A.
81 F4 Thompson PA U.S.A.
64 E4 Thompson r. Can.
76 E3 Thompson r. U.S.A.
72 D2 Thompson Falls U.S.A.
79 D5 Thomson U.S.A.
32 C1 Thôn Cư Lai Vietnam
46 C7 Thonon-les-Bains France
32 D3 Thôn Sơn Hai Vietnam
73 E5 Thoreau U.S.A.
42 D3 Thorn Neth.
38 F3 Thornaby-on-Tees U.K.
68 E4 Thornapple r. U.S.A.
39 E6 Thornbury U.K.
69 H2 Thorne Can.
38 G4 Thorne U.K.
74 C2 Thorne U.S.A.
64 C3 Thorne Bay U.S.A.
68 D5 Thorntown U.S.A.
68 B3 Thorp U.S.A.
92 D3 Thorshavnheiane mts Ant.
59 G4 Thota-ea-Moli Lesotho
44 D3 Thouars France
81 E2 Thousand Islands is Can.
75 G2 Thousand Lake Mt mt U.S.A.
74 C4 Thousand Oaks U.S.A.
49 L4 Thrakiko Pelagos sea Greece
72 E2 Three Forks U.S.A.
64 G4 Three Hills Can.
9 D1 Three Kings Is is N.Z.
68 C3 Three Lakes U.S.A.
68 D5 Three Oaks U.S.A.
32 A2 Three Pagodas Pass Myanmar/Thai.
54 B4 Three Points, Cape c. Ghana
68 E5 Three Rivers MI U.S.A.
77 D6 Three Rivers TX U.S.A.
72 B2 Three Sisters mt U.S.A.
Thrissur see Trichur
77 D5 Throckmorton U.S.A.
65 G2 Thubun Lakes l. Can.
32 C3 Thu Dâu Môt Vietnam
42 C4 Thuin Belgium
Thule see Qaanaaq
57 C6 Thuli Zimbabwe
46 C7 Thun Switz.
68 C1 Thunder Bay Can.
68 C1 Thunder Bay b. Can.
69 F3 Thunder Bay b. U.S.A.
43 H5 Thüngen Ger.
32 A3 Thung Song Thai.
32 A4 Thung Wa Thai.
43 J4 Thüringen div. Ger.
43 K3 Thüringer Becken reg. Ger.
43 J4 Thüringer Wald mts Ger.
41 D5 Thurles Rep. of Ireland
80 E5 Thurmont U.S.A.
46 F7 Thurn, Paß pass Austria
81 F2 Thurso Can.
40 E2 Thurso U.K.
40 E2 Thurso r. Scot. U.K.
92 A3 Thurston I. i. Ant.
43 H2 Thüster Berg h. Ger.
38 E3 Thwaite U.K.
92 A3 Thwaites Gl. gl. Ant.
37 L8 Thyborøn Denmark
26 A1 Tiancang China
26 F3 Tianchang China
27 C6 Tiandeng China
27 C6 Tiandong China
27 C5 Tian'e China
87 K4 Tianguá Brazil
26 E2 Tianjin China
26 E2 Tianjin div. China
24 B3 Tianjun China
27 C5 Tianlin China
27 D4 Tianmen China
27 F4 Tianmu Shan mts China
30 E2 Tianqiaoling China
27 B4 Tianquan China
30 C3 Tianshifu China
26 B3 Tianshui China
22 D2 Tianshuihai China/Jammu and Kashmir
27 F4 Tiantai China
26 E1 Tiantaiyong China
27 C6 Tianyang China
26 B2 Tianzhu Gansu China
27 C5 Tianzhu Guizhou China
54 C1 Tiaret Alg.
54 B4 Tiassalé Côte d'Ivoire
90 B4 Tibagi r. Brazil
17 J5 Tibal, Wādī watercourse Iraq
55 D4 Tibati Cameroon
48 E3 Tiber r. Italy
16 E5 Tiberias Israel
Tiberias, Lake l. see Galilee, Sea of
72 E1 Tiber Res. resr U.S.A.
55 D2 Tibesti mts Chad
Tibet Aut. Region div. see Xizang Zizhiqu
Tibet, Plateau of plat. see Xizang Gaoyuan
6 E4 Tibooburra Austr.
23 E3 Tibrikot Nepal
23 E3 Tibrikot Nepal
37 O7 Tibro Sweden
82 B3 Tiburón i. Mex.
31 B3 Ticao i. Phil.
39 H6 Ticehurst U.K.
69 J3 Tichborne Can.
54 B3 Tîchît Maur.
54 A2 Tichla Western Sahara
46 D7 Ticino r. Switz.
81 G3 Ticonderoga U.S.A.
82 G4 Ticul Mex.
37 N7 Tidaholm Sweden
23 H5 Tiddim Myanmar
54 C2 Tidikelt, Plaine du plain Alg.
54 A3 Tidjikja Maur.
42 D3 Tiel Neth.
28 A1 Tieli China
30 B2 Tieling China
22 D2 Tielongtan China/Jammu and Kashmir
42 B4 Tielt Belgium
54 B4 Tiémé Côte d'Ivoire
42 C4 Tienen Belgium
10 K5 Tien Shan mts China/Kyrg.
Tientsin see Tianjin
37 P6 Tierp Sweden
73 F4 Tierra Amarilla U.S.A.
84 C3 Tierra Blanca Mex.
84 C3 Tierra Colorada Mex.

88 C8 Tierra del Fuego, Isla Grande de i. Arg./Chile
45 D2 Tiétar r. Spain
45 D2 Tiétar, Valle de v. Spain
90 C3 Tietê Brazil
90 B3 Tietê r. Brazil
80 B4 Tiffin U.S.A.
Tiflis see T'bilisi
79 D6 Tifton U.S.A.
49 L3 Tigheciului, Dealurile h. Moldova
51 D6 Tighina Moldova
23 F5 Tigiria India
55 D4 Tignère Cameroon
67 H4 Tignish Can.
86 C4 Tigre r. Ecuador/Peru
89 E2 Tigre r. Venez.
17 L5 Tigris r. Iraq/Turkey
20 B6 Tihāmah reg. S. Arabia
16 D7 Tîh, Gebel el plat. Egypt
82 A2 Tijuana Mex.
90 C2 Tijuco r. Brazil
22 D4 Tikamgarh India
51 G6 Tikhoretsk Rus. Fed.
50 E3 Tikhvin Rus. Fed.
50 E3 Tikhvinskaya Gryada ridge Rus. Fed.
9 F3 Tikokino N.Z.
7 G3 Tikopia i. Solomon Is
17 J4 Tikrīt Iraq
36 W3 Tikshozero, Oz. l. Rus. Fed.
13 O2 Tiksi Rus. Fed.
23 E3 Tila r. Nepal
23 F4 Tilaiya Reservoir India
18 D2 Tilavar Iran
42 D3 Tilburg Neth.
39 H6 Tilbury U.K.
88 C2 Tilcara Arg.
23 H5 Tilin Myanmar
54 C3 Tillabéri Niger
72 B2 Tillamook U.S.A.
40 E4 Tillicoultry U.K.
69 G4 Tillsonburg Can.
40 F3 Tillyfourie U.K.
49 M6 Tilos i. Greece
8 E1 Tilpa Austr.
51 F5 Tim Rus. Fed.
50 K1 Timanskiy Kryazh ridge Rus. Fed.
17 J2 Timar Turkey
9 C6 Timaru N.Z.
51 F6 Timashevsk Rus. Fed.
54 B3 Timbedgha Maur.
8 D3 Timber Creek Austr.
74 D3 Timber Mt mt U.S.A.
80 D5 Timberville U.S.A.
8 D5 Timboon Austr.
54 B3 Timétrine reg. Mali
54 C2 Timimoun Alg.
49 J2 Timişoara Romania
69 G1 Timmins Can.
50 F3 Timokhino Rus. Fed.
87 K5 Timon Brazil
25 E7 Timor i. Indon.
6 C3 Timor Sea sea Austr./Indon.
50 H3 Timoshino Rus. Fed.
91 D2 Timote Arg.
37 P5 Timrå Sweden
79 C5 Tims Ford L. l. U.S.A.
22 D5 Timurni Muafi India
89 C2 Tinaco Venez.
21 B3 Tindivanam India
54 B2 Tindouf Alg.
32 C5 Tinggi i. Malaysia
27 E5 Ting Jiang r. China
23 F3 Tingri China
37 O8 Tingsryd Sweden
91 B2 Tinguiririca, Vol. volc. Chile
36 L5 Tingvoll Norway
40 E1 Tingwall U.K.
90 E1 Tinharé, Ilha de i. Brazil
32 C1 Tinh Gia Vietnam
25 G5 Tinian i. N. Mariana Is
88 C3 Tinogasta Arg.
49 L6 Tinos i. Greece
42 B5 Tinqueux France
54 C2 Tinrhert, Plateau du plat. Alg.
23 H4 Tinsukia India
39 C7 Tintagel U.K.
8 C3 Tintinara Austr.
40 E5 Tinto h. U.K.
80 E4 Tioga r. U.S.A.
33 B2 Tioman i. Malaysia
69 F1 Tionaga Can.
80 D4 Tionesta Lake l. U.S.A.
81 E3 Tioughnioga r. U.S.A.
45 H4 Tipasa Alg.
68 D5 Tippecanoe r. U.S.A.
68 E5 Tippecanoe Lake l. U.S.A.
41 C5 Tipperary Rep. of Ireland
23 F4 Tiptala Bhanjyang pass Nepal
68 B5 Tipton IA U.S.A.
68 D5 Tipton IN U.S.A.
75 E4 Tipton, Mt mt U.S.A.
68 E1 Tip Top Hill h. Can.
39 H6 Tiptree U.K.
89 C4 Tiquié r. Brazil
87 J4 Tiracambu, Serra do h. Brazil
49 H4 Tirana Albania
Tiranë see Tirana
48 D1 Tirano Italy
51 D6 Tiraspol Moldova
58 B3 Tiraz Mts mts Namibia
16 A2 Tire Turkey
40 B4 Tiree i. U.K.
22 B1 Tirich Mir mt Pak.
21 B2 Tirna r. India
21 A3 Tirthahalli India
23 F5 Tirtol India
21 B4 Tiruchchendur India
21 B4 Tiruchchirāppalli India
21 B4 Tiruchengodu India
21 B4 Tirunelveli India
21 B3 Tirupati India
21 B3 Tiruppattur India
21 B4 Tiruppur India
21 B4 Tirutturaippundi India
21 B3 Tiruvannamalai India
21 B4 Tisaiyanvilai India
65 J4 Tisdale Can.
21 C5 Tissamaharama Sri Lanka
45 G5 Tissemsilt Alg.
23 G4 Tista r. India
92 B4 Titan Dome ice feature Ant.
13 O2 Tit-Ary Rus. Fed.
86 E7 Titicaca, Lago l. Bol./Peru
23 E5 Titlagarh India
48 G2 Titov Drvar Bos.-Herz.
69 E4 Tittabawassee r. U.S.A.
49 L2 Titu Romania
79 D6 Titusville FL U.S.A.
80 D4 Titusville PA U.S.A.
69 G3 Tiverton Can.
39 D7 Tiverton U.K.
48 E4 Tivoli Italy

84 C3 Tixtla Mex.
84 B2 Tizapán el Alto Mex.
45 H4 Tizi El Arba h. Alg.
82 G4 Tizimín Mex.
45 J4 Tizi Ouzou Alg.
89 D2 Tiznados r. Venez.
54 B2 Tiznit Morocco
84 B1 Tizoc Mex.
59 J2 Tjaneni Swaziland
36 Q4 Tjappsåive Sweden
42 D2 Tjeukemeer l. Neth.
37 K7 Tjorhom Norway
84 C3 Tlacolula Mex.
84 D3 Tlacotalpán Mex.
84 B1 Tlahualilo Mex.
84 C3 Tlalnepantla Mex.
84 C3 Tlapa Mex.
84 B2 Tlaquepaque Mex.
84 C3 Tlaxcala Mex.
84 C3 Tlaxcala div. Mex.
84 C3 Tlaxiaco Mex.
54 B1 Tlemcen Alg.
58 E4 Tlhakalatlou S. Africa
59 H4 Tlholong S. Africa
59 F2 Tlokweng Botswana
64 D3 Toad River Can.
57 E5 Toamasina Madag.
91 D3 Toay Arg.
29 E7 Toba Japan
32 A5 Toba, Danau l. Indon.
86 F1 Tobago i. Trinidad and Tobago
22 A3 Toba & Kakar Ranges mts Pak.
25 E6 Tobelo Indon.
69 G3 Tobermory Can.
40 B4 Tobermory U.K.
65 J4 Tobin L. l. Can.
74 D1 Tobin, Mt mt U.S.A.
81 K1 Tobique r. Can.
28 F5 Tobi-shima i. Japan
33 C3 Toboali Indon.
12 H4 Tobol r. Kazak./Rus. Fed.
32 D2 Tô Bong Vietnam
87 J5 Tocantinópolis Brazil
87 J4 Tocantins r. Brazil
90 C1 Tocantinzinha r. Brazil
79 D5 Toccoa U.S.A.
22 B2 Tochi r. Pak.
37 M7 Töcksfors Sweden
88 B2 Tocopilla Chile
8 E3 Tocumwal Austr.
89 C2 Tocuyo r. Venez.
48 E3 Todi Italy
46 D7 Todi mt Switz.
28 H5 Todoga-saki pt Japan
28 G4 Todohokke Japan
86 E7 Todos Santos Bol.
74 D6 Todos Santos, Bahía de b. Mex.
64 G4 Tofield Can.
64 D5 Tofino Can.
40 □ Toft U.K.
68 B2 Tofte U.S.A.
7 J3 Tofua i. Tonga
25 E7 Togian, Kepulauan is Indon.
68 A2 Togo U.S.A.
53 E5 Togo country Africa
26 D1 Togtoh China
75 H4 Tohatchi U.S.A.
36 T5 Toholampi Fin.
26 B1 Tohom China
37 S6 Toijala Fin.
29 B9 Toi-misaki pt Japan
37 U5 Toivakka Fin.
74 D2 Toiyabe Range mts U.S.A.
19 H2 Tojikobod Tajik.
62 D3 Tok U.S.A.
29 F6 Tōkamachi Japan
9 B7 Tokanui N.Z.
55 F3 Tokar Sudan
24 E4 Tokara-rettō is Japan
16 F1 Tokat Turkey
30 D5 Tŏkchoktŏ i. S. Korea
30 D4 Tŏkch'ŏn N. Korea
5 K5 Tokelau terr. Pac. Oc.
15 F2 Tokmak Kyrg.
51 E6 Tokmak Ukr.
9 G3 Tokomaru Bay N.Z.
9 E3 Tokoroa N.Z.
59 H3 Tokoza S. Africa
12 K5 Toksun China
29 B6 Tok-tō i. Japan
29 D7 Tokushima Japan
29 B7 Tokuyama Japan
29 F7 Tōkyō Japan
29 F7 Tōkyō-wan b. Japan
19 G3 Tokzār Afgh.
9 G3 Tolaga Bay N.Z.
57 E6 Tôlañaro Madag.
84 C2 Toleant Mex.
90 B4 Toledo Brazil
45 D3 Toledo Spain
68 A5 Toledo IA U.S.A.
80 B4 Toledo OH U.S.A.
77 E6 Toledo Bend Reservoir U.S.A.
45 D3 Toledo, Montes de mts Spain
91 B3 Tolhuaca, Parque Nacional nat. park Chile
57 E6 Toliara Madag.
89 B3 Tolima, Nev. del volc. Col.
25 E6 Tolitoli Indon.
12 K3 Tol'ka Rus. Fed.
43 M1 Tollensesee l. Ger.
50 D3 Tolmachevo Rus. Fed.
48 E1 Tolmezzo Italy
27 □ Tolo Channel chan. H.K. China
27 □ Tolo Harbour b. H.K. China
45 E1 Tolosa Spain
30 D6 Tolsan-do i. S. Korea
69 F3 Tolsmaville Can.
40 B2 Tolsta Head hd U.K.
89 B2 Tolú Col.
84 C3 Toluca Mex.
70 B4 Tolumne r. CA U.S.A.
36 W3 Tolvand, Oz. l. Rus. Fed.
50 J4 Tol'yatti Rus. Fed.
68 B4 Tomah U.S.A.
68 C3 Tomahawk U.S.A.
28 G3 Tomakomai Japan
28 G2 Tomamae Japan
7 H3 Tomanivi mt Fiji
89 E5 Tomar Brazil
45 B3 Tomar Port.
16 E2 Tomarza Turkey
91 F1 Tomás Gomensoro Uru.
47 L5 Tomaszów Lubelski Pol.
47 K5 Tomaszów Mazowiecki Pol.
40 E3 Tomatin U.K.
84 A3 Tomatlán Mex.
79 B6 Tombigbee r. U.S.A.
56 B4 Tomboco Angola
90 D3 Tombos Brazil
54 B3 Tombouctou Mali
75 G6 Tombstone U.S.A.
57 B5 Tombua Angola

59 H1 Tom Burke S. Africa
91 B3 Tomé Chile
59 L1 Tome Moz.
37 N9 Tomelilla Sweden
45 E3 Tomelloso Spain
69 H2 Tomiko Can.
8 G2 Tomingley Austr.
54 B3 Tominian Mali
25 E7 Tomini, Teluk g. Indon.
40 E3 Tomintoul U.K.
75 G3 Tomislavgrad Bos.-Herz.
36 O3 Tømmerneset Norway
13 O4 Tommot Rus. Fed.
89 D4 Tomo Col.
89 C3 Tomo r. Col.
26 D1 Tomortei China
13 P3 Tompo Rus. Fed.
6 B4 Tom Price Austr.
24 A1 Tomsk Rus. Fed.
37 O8 Tomtabacken h. Sweden
13 Q3 Tomtor Rus. Fed.
28 H3 Tomuraushi-yama mt Japan
51 G6 Tomuzlovka r. Rus. Fed.
84 D3 Tonalá Mex.
75 G3 Tonalea U.S.A.
86 E4 Tonantins Brazil
72 C1 Tonasket U.S.A.
39 H6 Tonbridge U.K.
25 E6 Tondano Indon.
37 L9 Tønder Denmark
39 E6 Tone r. U.K.
5 K7 Tonga country Pac. Oc.
59 J4 Tongaat S. Africa
8 E4 Tongala Austr.
27 F5 Tong'an China
5 M5 Tongareva i. Pac. Oc.
9 E3 Tongariro National Park nat. park N.Z.
7 J4 Tongatapu Group is Tonga
94 H7 Tonga Tr. sea feature Pac. Oc.
26 D3 Tongbai China
26 D3 Tongbai Shan mts China
26 E4 Tongcheng Anhui China
27 D4 Tongcheng Hubei China
30 D4 T'ongch'ŏn N. Korea
26 C3 Tongchuan China
27 C5 Tongdao China
26 A3 Tongde China
30 D5 Tongduch'ŏn S. Korea
42 D4 Tongeren Belgium
27 E4 Tonggu China
27 D7 Tonggu Jiao pt China
30 E5 Tonghae S. Korea
27 B5 Tonghai China
28 A2 Tonghe China
30 C3 Tonghua Jilin China
30 C3 Tonghua Jilin China
26 C4 Tongjiang China
30 B2 Tongjiangkou China
30 D4 Tongjosŏn Man b. N. Korea
27 C6 Tongking, Gulf of g. China/Vietnam
27 C4 Tongliang China
30 B2 Tongliao China
26 E4 Tongling China
27 F4 Tonglu China
30 E6 Tongnae S. Korea
27 B4 Tongnan China
31 B5 Tongquil i. Phil.
27 C5 Tongren Guizhou China
26 A3 Tongren Qinghai China
23 G4 Tongsa r. Bhutan
27 E4 Tongshan China
23 H2 Tongtian He r. China
40 D2 Tongue U.K.
72 F2 Tongue r. U.S.A.
79 E7 Tongue of the Ocean chan. Bahamas
26 B3 Tongwei China
26 E2 Tong Xian China
26 B2 Tongxin China
26 E4 Tongyanghe China
30 B1 Tongyu China
30 B3 Tongyuanpu China
27 C4 Tongzi China
68 C5 Tonica U.S.A.
22 C4 Tonk India
18 C2 Tonkābon Iran
27 B6 Tonkin reg. Vietnam
50 H3 Tonkino Rus. Fed.
32 C3 Tônle Basăk r. Cambodia
32 C2 Tônle Repou r. Laos
32 B2 Tônlé Sab l. Cambodia
28 G5 Tōno Japan
74 D2 Tonopah U.S.A.
89 E2 Tonoro r. Venez.
37 M7 Tønsberg Norway
37 K7 Tonstad Norway
75 G5 Tonto National Monument res. U.S.A.
23 H5 Tonzang Myanmar
72 D3 Tooele U.S.A.
8 D3 Tooleybuc Austr.
8 G3 Tooma r. Austr.
8 F5 Toora Austr.
8 G1 Tooraweenah Austr.
58 F6 Toorberg mt S. Africa
6 F4 Toowoomba Austr.
75 G6 Topawa U.S.A.
74 C2 Topaz U.S.A.
76 E4 Topeka U.S.A.
84 A1 Topia Mex.
64 D4 Topley Landing Can.
43 L2 Töplitz Ger.
91 B2 Topocalma, Pta pt Chile
75 E4 Topock U.S.A.
46 J6 Topoľčany Slovakia
82 C3 Topolobampo Mex.
49 M3 Topolovgrad Bulg.
36 W4 Topozero, Oz. l. Rus. Fed.
72 B2 Toppenish U.S.A.
81 K2 Topsfield U.S.A.
75 F3 Toquerville U.S.A.
56 D3 Tor Eth.
49 M5 Torbalı Turkey
19 E3 Torbat-e-Heydarīyeh Iran
19 F3 Torbat-e-Jām Iran
50 G4 Torbeyevo Rus. Fed.
68 E3 Torch Lake l. U.S.A.
45 D2 Tordesillas Spain
36 S4 Töre Sweden
45 H1 Torelló Spain
42 D2 Torenberg h. Neth.
43 L3 Torgau Ger.
51 H5 Torgun r. Rus. Fed.
42 B3 Torhout Belgium
Torino see Turin
29 G9 Tori-shima i. Japan
55 F4 Torit Sudan
90 B2 Torixoreu Brazil
17 L3 Torkamān Iran
50 G3 Tor'kovskoye Vdkhr. resr Rus. Fed.
45 D2 Tormes r. Spain
36 S3 Torneälven r. Fin./Sweden
36 Q2 Torneträsk Sweden
36 Q2 Torneträsk l. Sweden

67 H2 Torngat Mountains Can.
36 T4 Tornio Fin.
91 D3 Tornquist Arg.
45 D2 Toro Spain
24 F1 Torom r. Rus. Fed.
8 H2 Toronto Austr.
69 H4 Toronto Can.
50 D3 Toropets Rus. Fed.
84 B1 Toro, Pico del mt Mex.
74 D5 Toro Pk summit U.S.A.
56 D3 Tororo Uganda
16 D3 Toros Dağları mts Turkey
40 F3 Torphins U.K.
39 D7 Torquay U.K.
74 C5 Torrance U.S.A.
45 B3 Torrão Port.
45 C2 Torre mt Port.
45 G2 Torreblanca Spain
48 F4 Torre del Greco Italy
45 D1 Torrelavega Spain
45 D4 Torremolinos Spain
8 A1 Torrens, Lake Austr.
45 F3 Torrent Spain
84 B1 Torreón Mex.
7 G3 Torres Islands is Vanuatu
45 B3 Torres Novas Port.
6 E2 Torres Strait str. Austr.
45 B3 Torres Vedras Port.
45 G3 Torreta, Sa h. Spain
45 F4 Torrevieja Spain
75 G2 Torrey U.S.A.
39 C7 Torridge r. U.K.
40 C3 Torridon, Loch in. U.K.
45 D3 Torrijos Spain
81 G4 Torrington CT U.S.A.
72 F3 Torrington WY U.S.A.
45 H1 Torroella de Montgrí Spain
37 N6 Torsby Sweden
36 □ Tórshavn Faroe Is
91 C1 Tórtolas, Cerro Las mt Chile
48 C5 Tortolì Sardinia Italy
48 C2 Tortona Italy
45 G2 Tortosa Spain
17 H1 Tortum Turkey
18 D3 Torūd Iran
17 G1 Torul Turkey
47 J4 Toruń Pol.
41 C2 Tory Island i. Rep. of Ireland
41 C2 Tory Sound chan. Rep. of Ireland
50 E3 Torzhok Rus. Fed.
29 C8 Tosa Japan
29 C8 Tosashimizu Japan
36 N4 Tosbotn Norway
58 E2 Tosca S. Africa
48 C3 Toscano, Arcipelago is Italy
28 G4 Tōshima-yama mt Japan
50 D3 Tosno Rus. Fed.
88 D3 Tostado Arg.
43 H1 Tostedt Ger.
29 B8 Tosu Japan
16 E1 Tosya Turkey
50 G3 Tot'ma Rus. Fed.
84 C3 Totolapan Mex.
92 C6 Totten Glacier gl. Ant.
39 F7 Totton U.K.
29 D7 Tottori Japan
54 B4 Touba Côte d'Ivoire
54 A3 Touba Senegal
54 B1 Toubkal, Jbel mt Morocco
26 B2 Toudaohu China
54 B3 Tougan Burkina
54 C1 Touggourt Alg.
54 A3 Tougue Guinea
44 G2 Toul France
44 G5 Toulon France
44 E5 Toulouse France
54 B4 Toumodi Côte d'Ivoire
25 B5 Toungoo Myanmar
27 D5 Toupai China
32 B1 Tourakom Laos
42 B4 Tourcoing France
42 B4 Tournai Belgium
44 G4 Tournon-sur-Rhône France
44 G3 Tournus France
87 L5 Touros Brazil
44 E3 Tours France
58 D6 Touwsrivier S. Africa
43 L4 Toužim Czech Rep.
89 C2 Tovar Venez.
39 F5 Tove r. U.K.
17 K1 Tovuz Azer.
28 G4 Towada Japan
28 G5 Towada-Hachimantai National Park Japan
28 G4 Towada-ko l. Japan
9 E1 Towai N.Z.
81 E4 Towanda U.S.A.
75 H3 Towaoc U.S.A.
39 G5 Towcester U.K.
41 C6 Tower Rep. of Ireland
68 A2 Tower U.S.A.
65 J5 Towner U.S.A.
74 D3 Townes Pass U.S.A.
72 E2 Townsend U.S.A.
8 G4 Townsend, Mt mt Austr.
6 E3 Townsville Austr.
25 E7 Towori, Teluk b. Indon.
80 E5 Towson U.S.A.
28 G3 Tōya-ko l. Japan
29 E6 Toyama Japan
29 E6 Toyama-wan b. Japan
29 F7 Toyohashi Japan
29 E7 Toyokawa Japan
29 D7 Toyonaka Japan
29 D7 Toyooka Japan
29 E7 Toyota Japan
54 C1 Tozeur Tunisia
51 G7 Tqibuli Georgia
51 G7 Tqvarch'eli Georgia
42 F5 Traben Ger.
16 E5 Trâblous Lebanon
49 K4 Trabotivište Macedonia
17 G1 Trabzon Turkey
81 K2 Tracy Can.
74 B3 Tracy CA U.S.A.
76 E2 Tracy MN U.S.A.
68 A4 Traer U.S.A.
45 C4 Trafalgar, Cabo pt Spain
91 B3 Traiguén Chile
64 F5 Trail Can.
37 T9 Trakai Lith.
50 J2 Trakt Rus. Fed.
41 B5 Tralee Rep. of Ireland
41 B5 Tralee Bay b. Rep. of Ireland
89 E3 Tramán Tepui mt Venez.
41 D5 Tramore Rep. of Ireland
37 O7 Tranås Sweden
88 C3 Trancas Arg.
37 N8 Tranemo Sweden
40 F5 Tranent U.K.
32 A4 Trang Thai.
25 F7 Trangan i. Indon.
8 F2 Trangie Austr.
91 F1 Tranqueras Uru.
92 B5 Transantarctic Mountains Ant.
65 G4 Trans Canada Highway Can.
65 K5 Transcona Can.
48 E5 Trapani Sicily Italy
8 F5 Traralgon Austr.
48 E3 Trasimeno, Lago l. Italy
45 E3 Trasvase, Canal de canal Spain
32 B2 Trat Thai.
46 F7 Traunsee l. Austria
46 F7 Traunstein Ger.
8 D2 Travellers L. l. Austr.
92 C1 Traversay Is is Atl. Ocean
68 E3 Traverse City U.S.A.
9 D5 Travers, Mt mt N.Z.
32 C3 Tra Vinh Vietnam
77 D6 Travis, L. l. U.S.A.
48 G2 Travnik Bos.-Herz.
48 F1 Trbovlje Slovenia
7 F2 Treasury Is is Solomon Is
43 M2 Trebbin Ger.
46 G6 Třebíč Czech Rep.
49 H3 Trebinje Bos.-Herz.
47 K6 Trebišov Slovakia
48 F2 Trebnje Slovenia
43 G5 Trebur Ger.
43 J3 Treffurt Ger.
68 B3 Trego U.S.A.
40 D4 Treig, Loch l. U.K.
91 F2 Treinta-y-Tres Uru.
88 C6 Trelew Arg.
37 N9 Trelleborg Sweden
42 C4 Trélon France
39 C5 Tremadoc Bay b. U.K.
66 F4 Tremblant, Mt h. Can.
48 F3 Tremiti, Isole is Italy
72 D3 Tremonton U.S.A.
45 G1 Tremp Spain
68 B3 Trempealeau r. U.S.A.
39 B7 Trenance U.K.
46 J6 Trenčín Slovakia
43 H3 Trendelburg Ger.
91 D2 Trenque Lauquen Arg.
38 G4 Trent r. U.K.
48 D1 Trento Italy
69 J3 Trenton Can.
76 E3 Trenton MO U.S.A.
81 F4 Trenton NJ U.S.A.
67 K4 Trepassey Can.
91 F2 Tres Árboles Uru.
91 E3 Tres Arroyos Arg.
39 A8 Tresco i. U.K.
90 D3 Três Corações Brazil
89 B4 Tres Esquinas Col.
40 B4 Treshnish Isles is U.K.
90 B3 Três Lagoas Brazil
88 B7 Tres Lagos Arg.
91 D3 Tres Lomas Arg.
90 D2 Três Marias, Represa resr Brazil
84 D4 Tres Picos Mex.
91 B4 Tres Picos mt Arg.
91 E3 Tres Picos, Cerro mt Arg.
73 F4 Tres Piedras U.S.A.
90 D3 Três Pontas Brazil
88 C7 Tres Puntas, C. pt Arg.
90 D3 Três Rios Brazil
84 C3 Tres Valles Mex.
84 D3 Tres Zapotes Mex.
37 M6 Tretten Norway
43 J6 Treuchtlingen Ger.
43 L2 Treuenbrietzen Ger.
37 L7 Treungen Norway
48 C2 Treviglio Italy
48 E2 Treviso Italy
39 B7 Trevose Head hd U.K.
49 M6 Tria Nisia i. Greece
49 N6 Trianta Greece
22 B2 Tribal Areas div. Pak.
49 H5 Tricase Italy
21 B4 Trichur India
42 A5 Tricot France
8 E2 Trida Austr.
42 E5 Trier Ger.
48 E2 Trieste Italy
48 E1 Triglav mt Slovenia
49 J5 Trikala Greece
16 D4 Trikomon Cyprus
25 F7 Trikora, Pk mt Indon.
41 E4 Trim Rep. of Ireland
21 C4 Trincomalee Sri Lanka
90 C2 Trindade Brazil
96 G7 Trindade, Ilha da i. Atl. Ocean
86 F6 Trinidad Bol.
89 C3 Trinidad Col.
83 J4 Trinidad Cuba
91 F2 Trinidad Uru.
73 F4 Trinidad U.S.A.
86 F1 Trinidad i. Trinidad and Tobago
61 M8 Trinidad and Tobago country Caribbean Sea
67 K4 Trinity Bay b. Can.
62 C4 Trinity Islands is U.S.A.
74 C1 Trinity Range mts U.S.A.
79 C5 Trion U.S.A.
43 K1 Tripkau Ger.
49 K6 Tripoli Greece
Tripoli see Trâblous
55 D1 Tripoli Libya
21 B4 Tripunittura India
23 G5 Tripura div. India
53 C9 Tristan da Cunha i. Atl. Ocean
22 D3 Trisul mt India
23 F4 Trisul Dam dam Nepal
43 J1 Trittau Ger.
42 E5 Trittenheim Ger.
21 B4 Trivandrum India
48 F4 Trivento Italy
46 H6 Trnava Slovakia
6 F2 Trobriand Islands is P.N.G.
36 N4 Trofors Norway
48 G3 Trogir Croatia
48 F4 Troia Italy
42 F4 Troisdorf Ger.
42 D4 Trois-Ponts Belgium
67 F4 Trois-Rivieres Can.
51 H6 Troitskoye Rus. Fed.
37 N7 Trollhättan Sweden
87 G3 Trombetas r. Brazil
53 K7 Tromelin, Île i. Ind. Ocean
91 B3 Tromen, Volcán volc. Arg.
59 F5 Trompsburg S. Africa
36 Q2 Tromsø Norway
74 D4 Trona U.S.A.
91 B4 Tronador, Monte mt Arg.
36 M5 Trondheim Norway
36 M5 Trondheimsfjorden chan. Norway
16 D4 Troodos Cyprus
16 D4 Troödos, Mount mt Cyprus
40 D5 Troon U.K.
90 D1 Tropeiros, Serra dos h. Brazil
75 F3 Tropic U.S.A.
40 D4 Trossachs, The reg. U.K.
41 E2 Trostan h. U.K.
40 F3 Troup Head hd U.K.
64 E2 Trout r. Can.
69 H3 Trout Creek Can.
75 F2 Trout Creek U.S.A.
66 B3 Trout L. l. Can.
64 G3 Trout Lake Alta. Can.
64 E2 Trout Lake N.W.T. Can.
68 E2 Trout Lake U.S.A.
64 E2 Trout Lake l. Can.
68 C2 Trout Lake l. U.S.A.
72 E2 Trout Peak summit U.S.A.
80 E4 Trout Run U.S.A.
39 E6 Trowbridge U.K.
79 C6 Troy AL U.S.A.
72 D2 Troy MT U.S.A.
81 G3 Troy NH U.S.A.
81 G3 Troy NY U.S.A.
80 A4 Troy OH U.S.A.
80 E4 Troy PA U.S.A.
49 L3 Troyan Bulg.
44 G2 Troyes France
74 D4 Troy Lake l. U.S.A.
75 E2 Troy Peak summit U.S.A.
49 J3 Trstenik Yugo.
51 E4 Trubchevsk Rus. Fed.
45 C1 Truchas Spain
50 E3 Trud Rus. Fed.
28 C3 Trudovoye Rus. Fed.
83 G5 Trujillo Honduras
86 C5 Trujillo Peru
45 D3 Trujillo Spain
89 C2 Trujillo Venez.
42 F5 Trulben Ger.
81 G4 Trumbull U.S.A.
75 F3 Trumbull, Mt mt U.S.A.
33 A2 Trumon Indon.
8 F2 Trundle Austr.
32 C2 Trung Hiệp Vietnam
27 C6 Trung Khanh China
67 H4 Truro Can.
39 B7 Truro U.K.
41 C3 Truskmore h. Rep. of Ireland
64 E3 Trutch Can.
73 F5 Truth or Consequences U.S.A.
46 G5 Trutnov Czech Rep.
49 L7 Trypiti, Akra pt Greece
37 N6 Trysil Norway
46 G3 Trzebiatów Pol.
24 A2 Tsagaannuur Mongolia
51 H6 Tsagan Aman Rus. Fed.
51 H6 Tsagan-Nur Rus. Fed.
51 G7 Ts'ageri Georgia
17 K1 Tsalka Georgia
57 E5 Tsaratanana, Massif du mts Madag.
58 B2 Tsaris Mts mts Namibia
51 H5 Tsatsa Rus. Fed.
58 A3 Tsaukaib Namibia
56 D4 Tsavo National Park Kenya
51 G6 Tseina Rus. Fed.
57 B6 Tses Namibia
57 C6 Tsetseng Botswana
24 C2 Tsetserleg Mongolia
57 C6 Tshabong Botswana
57 C6 Tshane Botswana
51 F6 Tshchikskoye Vdkhr. resr Rus. Fed.
56 B4 Tshela Congo(Zaire)
56 C4 Tshibala Congo(Zaire)
56 C4 Tshikapa Congo(Zaire)
56 C4 Tshikapa r. Congo(Zaire)
59 G3 Tshing S. Africa
59 J1 Tshipise S. Africa
57 C4 Tshitanzu Congo(Zaire)
56 C4 Tshofa Congo(Zaire)
59 J2 Tshokwane S. Africa
56 C4 Tshuapa r. Congo(Zaire)
51 G6 Tsimlyansk Rus. Fed.
51 G6 Tsimlyanskoye Vdkhr. resr Rus. Fed.
58 E3 Tsineng S. Africa
Tsingtao see Qingdao
27 □ Tsing Yi i. H.K. China
57 E6 Tsiombe Madag.
57 E5 Tsiroanomandidy Madag.
58 E6 Tsitsikamma Forest and Coastal National Park S. Africa
64 D4 Tsitsutl Pk summit Can.
50 H4 Tsivil'sk Rus. Fed.
51 G7 Ts'khinvali Georgia
50 G4 Tsna r. Rus. Fed.
22 D2 Tsokr Chumo l. India
59 H5 Tsolo S. Africa
59 G6 Tsomo S. Africa
22 D2 Tso Morari L. l. India
51 G7 Tsqaltubo Georgia
29 E7 Tsu Japan
29 G6 Tsuchiura Japan
27 □ Tsuen Wan H.K. China
28 G4 Tsugarū-Kaikyō str. Japan
57 B5 Tsumeb Namibia
57 B6 Tsumis Park Namibia
57 C5 Tsumkwe Namibia
23 G4 Tsunthang India
29 E7 Tsuruga Japan
29 D8 Tsurugi-san mt Japan
28 F5 Tsuruoka Japan
29 A7 Tsushima i. Japan
Tsushima-kaikyō str. see Korea Strait
29 D7 Tsuyama Japan
58 D1 Tswaane Botswana
59 F4 Tswaraganang S. Africa
59 F3 Tswelelang S. Africa
47 M4 Tsyelyakhany Belarus
36 X2 Tsyp-Navolok Rus. Fed.
51 E6 Tsyurupyns'k Ukr.
25 F7 Tual Indon.
41 C4 Tuam Rep. of Ireland
9 D4 Tuamarina N.Z.
5 N6 Tuamotu Archipelago arch. Pac. Oc.
27 B6 Tuân Giao Vietnam
32 A5 Tuangku i. Indon.
51 F6 Tuapse Rus. Fed.
32 □ Tuas Sing.
9 A7 Tuatapere N.Z.
75 G3 Tuba City U.S.A.
33 D4 Tuban Indon.
88 G3 Tubarão Brazil
31 A4 Tubbataha Reefs rf Phil.
41 C3 Tubbercurry Rep. of Ireland
46 D6 Tübingen Ger.
54 A4 Tubmanburg Liberia
31 B4 Tubod Phil.
55 E1 Tubruq Libya
5 M7 Tubuai Islands is Pac. Oc.
87 L6 Tucano Brazil
91 B3 Tucapel, Pta pt Chile
87 G7 Tucavaca Bol.
43 L1 Tüchen Ger.
43 L2 Tuchheim Ger.
64 D2 Tuchitua Can.
81 F5 Tuckerton U.S.A.
75 G5 Tucson U.S.A.
75 G5 Tucson Mts mts U.S.A.
89 B2 Tucuco r. Venez.
73 G5 Tucumcari U.S.A.
89 E2 Tucupita Venez.
87 J4 Tucuruí Brazil
87 J4 Tucuruí, Represa resr Brazil
17 M5 Tū Dār Iran
45 F1 Tudela Spain
45 C2 Tuela r. Port.
27 □ Tuen Mun H.K. China
23 H4 Tuensang India
18 C5 Ţufayḩ S. Arabia
59 J4 Tugela r. S. Africa
31 C4 Tugnug Point pt Phil.
31 B2 Tuguegarao Phil.
13 F4 Tugur Rus. Fed.
26 F2 Tuhai r. China
32 A5 Tuhemberua Indon.
45 B1 Tui Spain
89 A2 Tuira r. Panama
25 E7 Tukangbesi, Kepulauan is Indon.
66 E2 Tukarak Island i. Can.
9 F3 Tukituki r. N.Z.
62 E3 Tuktoyaktuk Can.
37 S8 Tukums Latvia
84 C2 Tula Mex.
50 F4 Tula Rus. Fed.
23 H1 Tulagt Ar Gol r. China
84 C2 Tulancingo Mex.
74 C3 Tulare U.S.A.
74 C4 Tulare Lake Bed l. U.S.A.
73 F5 Tularosa U.S.A.
21 C2 Tulasi mt India
58 C6 Tulbagh S. Africa
86 C3 Tulcán Ecuador
49 N2 Tulcea Romania
51 D5 Tul'chyn Ukr.
74 C3 Tule r. U.S.A.
18 D3 Tuleh Iran
23 G4 Tule-la Pass pass Bhutan
65 J2 Tulemalu Lake l. Can.
77 C5 Tulia U.S.A.
16 E5 Tulkarm West Bank
41 C5 Tulla Rep. of Ireland
79 C5 Tullahoma U.S.A.
8 F2 Tullamore Austr.
41 D4 Tullamore Rep. of Ireland
44 E4 Tulle France
36 O5 Tulleråsen Sweden
8 F2 Tullibigeal Austr.
77 E6 Tullos U.S.A.
41 E5 Tullow Rep. of Ireland
6 E3 Tully Austr.
40 D3 Tully U.K.
81 E3 Tully U.S.A.
50 D2 Tulos Rus. Fed.
77 D4 Tulsa U.S.A.
50 F4 Tul'skaya Oblast' div. Rus. Fed.
89 A3 Tuluá Col.
62 B3 Tuluksak AK U.S.A.
91 C1 Tulum, Valle de v. Arg.
24 C1 Tulun Rus. Fed.
33 D4 Tulungagung Indon.
23 H4 Tulung La pass China
31 A4 Tuluran i. Phil.
89 A4 Tumaco Col.
59 G3 Tumahole S. Africa
51 J6 Tumak Rus. Fed.
37 P7 Tumba Sweden
56 B4 Tumba, Lac l. Congo(Zaire)
33 D3 Tumbangsamba Indon.
31 C5 Tumbao Phil.
86 B4 Tumbes Peru
64 E3 Tumbler Ridge Can.
26 D1 Tumd Youqi China
26 D1 Tumd Zuoqi China
30 E2 Tumen China
30 E2 Tumen Jiang r. China/N. Korea
26 B2 Tumenzi China
86 F2 Tumereng Guyana
31 A5 Tumindao i. Phil.
21 B3 Tumkur India
23 G3 Tum La pass China
40 E4 Tummel, Loch l. U.K.
24 G2 Tumnin r. Rus. Fed.
19 F5 Tump Pak.
32 B4 Tumpat Malaysia
54 B3 Tumu Ghana
87 G3 Tumucumaque, Serra h. Brazil
8 G3 Tumut Austr.
18 D5 Tunb al Kubrā i. Iran
39 H6 Tunbridge Wells, Royal U.K.
17 G2 Tunceli Turkey
27 D7 Tunchang China
22 D4 Tundla India
57 D5 Tunduru Tanz.
49 M3 Tundzha r. Bulg.
21 B3 Tungabhadra r. India
21 A3 Tungabhadra Reservoir India
23 H3 Tunga Pass pass China/India
31 B5 Tungawan Phil.
27 □ Tung Chung Wan b. H.K. China
36 D4 Tungnaá r. Iceland
64 D2 Tungsten Can.
50 E1 Tunguda Rus. Fed.
24 C1 Tunguska, Nizhnyaya r. Rus. Fed.
27 □ Tung Wan b. H.K. China
22 C5 Tuni India
54 D1 Tunis Tunisia
48 D6 Tunis, Golfe de g. Tunisia
52 E2 Tunisia country Africa
8 G3 Tuniut r. Austr.
89 B3 Tunja Col.
26 D2 Tunliu China
36 N4 Tunnsjøen l. Norway
39 J5 Tunstall U.K.
36 V3 Tuntsa Fin.
36 W3 Tuntsayoki r. Fin./Rus. Fed.
67 H2 Tunungayualok Island i. Can.
91 C2 Tunuyán Arg.
91 C2 Tunuyán r. Arg.
26 E3 Tuo He r. China
26 F2 Tuoji Dao i. China
32 C3 Tuŏl Khpos Cambodia
74 B3 Tuolumne U.S.A.
74 C3 Tuolumne Meadows U.S.A.
27 B5 Tuoniang Jiang r. China
23 H2 Tuotuo He r. China
23 H2 Tuotuoyan China
90 B3 Tupã Brazil
90 C2 Tupaciguara Brazil
17 L3 Tūp Āghāj Iran
88 F3 Tupanciretã Brazil
89 C3 Tuparro r. Col.
77 F5 Tupelo U.S.A.
86 E8 Tupiza Bol.
81 F2 Tupper Lake U.S.A.
81 F2 Tupper Lake l. U.S.A.
91 C2 Tupungato Arg.
91 C2 Tupungato, Cerro mt Arg./Chile
17 K7 Tuqayyid well Iraq
30 A1 Tuquan China
89 A4 Túquerres Col.
27 C7 Tuqu Wan b. China
23 G4 Tura India
13 M3 Tura Rus. Fed.
20 B5 Turabah S. Arabia
89 D3 Turagua, Serranía mt Venez.
9 E4 Turakina N.Z.
18 E3 Turan Iran
24 F1 Turana, Khrebet mts Rus. Fed.
9 E3 Turangi N.Z.
18 E2 Turan Lowland lowland Asia
16 G6 Turayf S. Arabia
18 C5 Turayf well S. Arabia
37 T7 Turba Estonia
89 B2 Turbaco Col.
19 F5 Turbat Pak.
89 A2 Turbo Col.
47 L7 Turda Romania
18 C3 Tūreh Iran
Turfan see Turpan
14 E2 Turgay Kazak.
49 M3 Tŭrgovishte Bulg.
16 C2 Turgut Turkey
16 A2 Turgutlu Turkey
16 F1 Turhal Turkey
37 T7 Türi Estonia
45 F3 Turia r. Spain
89 D2 Turiamo Venez.
48 B2 Turin Italy
28 B2 Turiy Rog Rus. Fed.
51 C5 Turiys'k Ukr.
56 D3 Turkana, Lake salt l. Eth./Kenya
49 M4 Türkeli Adası i. Turkey
14 E2 Turkestan Kazak.
19 G2 Turkestan Range mts Asia
10 E6 Turkey country Asia
68 B4 Turkey r. U.S.A.
51 G5 Turki Rus. Fed.
12 G6 Turkmenbashi Turkm.
16 C2 Türkmen Dağı mt Turkey
10 G6 Turkmenistan country Asia
19 F2 Turkmen-Kala Turkm.
18 D2 Turkmenskiy Zaliv b. Turkm.
16 F3 Türkoğlu Turkey
61 L7 Turks and Caicos Islands terr. Caribbean Sea
83 K4 Turks Islands is Turks and Caicos Is
37 S6 Turku Fin.
56 D3 Turkwel watercourse Kenya
74 B3 Turlock U.S.A.
74 B3 Turlock L. l. U.S.A.
9 F4 Turnagain, Cape c. N.Z.
40 D5 Turnberry U.K.
75 G5 Turnbull, Mt mt U.S.A.
82 G5 Turneffe Is is Belize
69 F3 Turner U.S.A.
42 C3 Turnhout Belgium
65 H3 Turnor Lake l. Can.
49 L3 Turnu Măgurele Romania
8 G2 Turon r. Austr.
50 G3 Turovets Rus. Fed.
24 A2 Turpan China
24 A2 Turpan Pendi China
83 J4 Turquino mt Cuba
40 F3 Turriff U.K.
17 K5 Tursāq Iraq
20 F1 Turtkul' Uzbek.
68 B2 Turtle Flambeau Flowage resr U.S.A.
65 H4 Turtleford Can.
68 A3 Turtle Lake U.S.A.
15 F2 Turugart Pass China/Kyrg.
90 B2 Turvo r. Goiás Brazil
90 C3 Turvo r. São Paulo Brazil
75 F4 Tusayan U.S.A.
79 C5 Tuscaloosa U.S.A.
80 C4 Tuscarawas r. U.S.A.
80 E4 Tuscarora Mts h. U.S.A.
68 C6 Tuscola IL U.S.A.
77 D5 Tuscola TX U.S.A.
18 E3 Tusharīk Iran
79 C5 Tuskegee U.S.A.
80 D4 Tussey Mts h. U.S.A.
19 E4 Tūtak Iran
17 J2 Tutak Turkey
50 F3 Tutayev Rus. Fed.
21 B4 Tuticorin India
76 D4 Tuttle Creek Res. resr U.S.A.
46 D7 Tuttlingen Ger.
63 Q2 Tuttut Nunaat reg. Greenland
7 J3 Tutuila i. Pac. Oc.
57 C6 Tutume Botswana
84 C3 Tututepec Mex.
30 D3 Tuun, Mt mt N. Korea
36 W5 Tuupovaara Fin.
36 V5 Tuusniemi Fin.
4 J5 Tuvalu country Pac. Oc.
18 B5 Tuwayq, Jabal h. S. Arabia
84 B3 Tuxpan Jalisco Mex.
84 C2 Tuxpan Veracruz Mex.
84 D3 Tuxtla Gutiérrez Mex.
89 D2 Tuy r. Venez.
32 C2 Tuy Duc Vietnam
27 B6 Tuyên Quang Vietnam
32 D2 Tuy Hoa Vietnam
18 C3 Tūysarkān Iran
16 D2 Tuz Gölü salt l. Turkey
75 F4 Tuzigoot National Monument res. U.S.A.
17 K4 Tuz Khurmātū Iraq
49 H2 Tuzla Bos.-Herz.
17 H2 Tuzla r. Turkey
Tuz, Lake salt l. see Tuz Gölü
51 F6 Tuzlov r. Rus. Fed.
37 L7 Tvedestrand Norway
50 E3 Tver' Rus. Fed.
50 E3 Tverskaya Oblast' div. Rus. Fed.
69 J3 Tweed Can.
40 F5 Tweed r. Eng./Scot. U.K.
64 D4 Tweedsmuir Prov. Park res. Can.
58 C6 Tweefontein S. Africa
58 C2 Twee Rivier Namibia
42 E2 Twente reg. Neth.
74 D4 Twentynine Palms U.S.A.
67 K4 Twillingate Can.
72 D2 Twin Bridges U.S.A.
77 C6 Twin Buttes Res. resr U.S.A.
67 H3 Twin Falls Can.
72 D3 Twin Falls U.S.A.
64 F3 Twin Lakes Can.
81 H2 Twin Mountain U.S.A.
80 C6 Twin Oaks U.S.A.
74 B2 Twin Peak summit U.S.A.
43 G2 Twistringen Ger.
8 G4 Twofold B. b. Austr.
75 G4 Two Guns U.S.A.
68 B2 Two Harbors U.S.A.
65 G4 Two Hills Can.
72 D1 Two Medicine r. U.S.A.
68 D3 Two Rivers U.S.A.
23 H5 Tyao r. India/Myanmar
36 M5 Tydal Norway
80 D5 Tygart Lake l. U.S.A.
80 D5 Tygart Valley v. U.S.A.
24 E1 Tygda Rus. Fed.
77 E5 Tyler U.S.A.
77 F6 Tylertown U.S.A.
24 E1 Tynda Rus. Fed.
64 A2 Tyndall Gl. gl. U.S.A.
40 F4 Tyne r. U.K.
38 F2 Tynemouth U.K.
37 M5 Tynset Norway
16 E5 Tyre Lebanon
65 H2 Tyrell Lake l. Can.
36 T4 Tyrnävä Fin.
49 K5 Tyrnavos Greece
80 D4 Tyrone U.S.A.
8 D3 Tyrrell r. Austr.
8 D3 Tyrrell, L. l. Austr.
48 D4 Tyrrhenian Sea sea France/Italy
13 Q3 Tyubelyakh Rus. Fed.
12 J4 Tyukalinsk Rus. Fed.
94 D4 Tyukyu Trench sea feature Pac. Oc.
12 H4 Tyumen' Rus. Fed.
13 N3 Tyung r. Rus. Fed.
39 C6 Tywi r. U.K.
39 C5 Tywyn U.K.
59 J1 Tzaneen S. Africa

U

57 C5 Uamanda Angola
89 E4 Uatatás r. Brazil
87 L5 Uauá Brazil
89 D5 Uaupés Brazil
89 C4 Uaupés r. Brazil
18 B4 U'aywij well S. Arabia
17 J7 U'aywij, W. watercourse S. Arabia
90 D3 Ubá Brazil
90 D2 Ubaí Brazil
90 E1 Ubaitaba Brazil
56 B3 Ubangi r. C.A.R./Congo(Zaire)
89 B3 Ubate Col.
17 J5 Ubayyid, Wādī al watercourse Iraq/S. Arabia
29 B8 Ube Japan
45 E3 Úbeda Spain
90 C2 Uberaba Brazil
87 G7 Uberaba, Lagoa l. Bol./Brazil
90 C2 Uberlândia Brazil
32 □ Ubin, Pulau i. Sing.
32 B1 Ubolratna Res. resr Thai.
59 K3 Ubombo S. Africa
32 C2 Ubon Ratchathani Thai.
43 G5 Ubstadt-Weiher Ger.
56 C4 Ubundu Congo(Zaire)
17 L1 Ucar Azer.
86 D5 Ucayali r. Peru
22 B3 Uch Pak.
19 F2 Uch-Adzhi Turkm.
18 C2 Ūchān Iran
15 G2 Ucharal Kazak.
28 G3 Uchiura-wan b. Japan
43 G2 Uchte Ger.
43 K2 Uchte r. Ger.
24 F1 Uchur r. Rus. Fed.
39 H7 Uckfield U.K.
64 D5 Ucluelet Can.
75 H3 Ucolo U.S.A.
72 F2 Ucross U.S.A.
13 P4 Uda r. Rus. Fed.
51 H6 Udachnoye Rus. Fed.
13 N3 Udachnyy Rus. Fed.
21 B4 Udagamandalam India
22 C4 Udaipur Rajasthan India
23 G5 Udaipur Tripura India
23 E5 Udanti r. India/Myanmar
21 B3 Udayagiri India
37 M7 Uddevalla Sweden
40 D5 Uddingston U.K.
36 P4 Uddjaure l. Sweden
42 D3 Uden Neth.
21 B2 Udgir India
50 H2 Udimskiy Rus. Fed.
48 E1 Udine Italy
67 J2 Udjuktok Bay b. Can.
50 E3 Udomlya Rus. Fed.
32 B1 Udon Thani Thai.
24 F1 Udskaya Guba b. Rus. Fed.
21 B4 Udumalaippetai India
21 A3 Udupi India
24 F1 Udyl', Ozero l. Rus. Fed.
46 G4 Ueckermünde Ger.
29 F6 Ueda Japan
6 C2 Uekuli Indon.
56 C3 Uele r. Congo(Zaire)
62 B3 Uelen Rus. Fed.
43 J2 Uelzen Ger.
56 C3 Uere r. Congo(Zaire)
43 H1 Uetersen Ger.
43 H5 Uettingen Ger.
43 J2 Uetze Ger.
12 G4 Ufa Rus. Fed.
43 J5 Uffenheim Ger.
57 B6 Ugab watercourse Namibia
56 D4 Ugalla r. Tanz.
53 H5 Uganda country Africa
59 H5 Ugie S. Africa
24 G2 Uglegorsk Rus. Fed.
28 C3 Uglekamensk Rus. Fed.
50 F3 Uglich Rus. Fed.
48 F2 Ugljan i. Croatia
50 E3 Uglovka Rus. Fed.
28 C3 Uglovoye Rus. Fed.
13 Q3 Ugol'naya Zyryanka Rus. Fed.
13 T3 Ugol'nyye Kopi Rus. Fed.
50 E4 Ugra Rus. Fed.
46 H6 Uherské Hradiště Czech Rep.
80 C4 Uhrichsville U.S.A.
40 B3 Uig U.K.
56 B4 Uíge Angola
30 D5 Ŭijŏngbu S. Korea
30 C3 Ŭiju N. Korea
36 W5 Uimaharju Fin.
75 F3 Uinkaret Plateau plat. U.S.A.
72 E3 Uinta Mts mts UT U.S.A.
57 B6 Uis Mine Namibia
41 D4 Uisneach h. Rep. of Ireland
30 E5 Ŭisŏng S. Korea
59 F6 Uitenhage S. Africa
42 C2 Uithoorn Neth.
42 E1 Uithuizen Neth.
67 H2 Uivak, Cape hd Can.
29 D7 Uji Japan
29 A9 Uji-guntō is Japan
22 C5 Ujjain India
33 E4 Ujung Pandang Indon.
17 J5 Ukhaydir Iraq
23 H4 Ukhrul India
50 K2 Ukhta Rus. Fed.
50 K2 Ukhta r. Rus. Fed.
74 A2 Ukiah CA U.S.A.
72 C2 Ukiah OR U.S.A.
63 N2 Ukkusissat Greenland
37 T9 Ukmergė Lith.
35 H4 Ukraine country Europe
50 J2 Uktym Rus. Fed.
29 A8 Uku-jima i. Japan
58 D1 Ukwi Botswana
58 D1 Ukwi Pan salt pan Botswana
24 C2 Ulaanbaatar Mongolia
24 B2 Ulaangom Mongolia
8 G2 Ulan Austr.
Ulan Bator see Ulaanbaatar
26 C1 Ulan Buh Shamo des. China
51 H6 Ulan Erge Rus. Fed.
51 H6 Ulan-Khol Rus. Fed.
26 C1 Ulansuhai Nur l. China
26 A1 Ulan Tohoi China
24 C1 Ulan-Ude Rus. Fed.
23 G2 Ulan Ul Hu l. China
16 F2 Ulaş Turkey
7 G2 Ulawa I. i. Solomon Is
19 E4 Ulāy, Kūh-e h. Iran
30 E5 Ulchin S. Korea
37 L7 Ulefoss Norway
37 U7 Ülenurme Estonia
21 A2 Ulhasnagar India
24 B2 Uliastay Mongolia
42 C3 Ulicoten Neth.
36 X2 Ulita r. Rus. Fed.
25 F6 Ulithi i. Micronesia
8 H3 Ulladulla Austr.
40 C3 Ullapool U.K.
36 S5 Ullava Fin.
38 E3 Ullswater l. U.K.
30 F5 Ullŭng-do i. S. Korea
46 D6 Ulm Ger.
42 E4 Ulmen Ger.
37 N8 Ulricehamn Sweden
42 E1 Ulrum Neth.
30 E6 Ulsan S. Korea
36 L5 Ulsberg Norway
41 D3 Ulster Canal canal Rep. of Ireland/U.K.
8 D3 Ultima Austr.
16 B1 Ulubat Gölü l. Turkey
16 C2 Uluborlu Turkey
16 B1 Uludağ mt Turkey
32 B5 Ulu Kali, Gunung mt Malaysia
16 E3 Ulukışla Turkey
59 J4 Ulundi S. Africa
24 A2 Ulungur Hu l. China
32 □ Ulu Pandan Sing.
Uluru h. see Ayers Rock
16 D1 Ulus Turkey
40 B4 Ulva i. U.K.
42 C3 Ulvenhout Neth.
38 D3 Ulverston U.K.
37 O6 Ulvsjön Sweden
19 H1 Ul'yanovo Uzbek.
50 J4 Ul'yanovsk Rus. Fed.
50 H4 Ul'yanovskaya Oblast' div. Rus. Fed.
77 C4 Ulysses U.S.A.
84 E2 Umán Mex.
51 D5 Uman' Ukr.
19 G4 Umarao Pak.
22 E5 Umaria India
22 D6 Umarkhed India
23 E6 Umarkot India
22 B4 Umarkot Pak.
72 C2 Umatilla U.S.A.
12 E3 Umba Rus. Fed.
81 H2 Umbagog Lake l. U.S.A.
6 E2 Umboi i. P.N.G.
36 R5 Umeå Sweden
36 Q4 Umeälven r. Sweden
59 J4 Umfolozi r. S. Africa
17 L7 Umgharah Kuwait
59 J4 Umhlanga S. Africa
62 H3 Umingmaktok Can.
66 E2 Umiujaq Can.
59 J5 Umkomaas S. Africa
59 J4 Umlazi S. Africa
17 K6 Umma Iraq
18 D5 Umm al Qaywayn U.A.E.
18 C5 Umm Bāb Qatar
55 E3 Umm Keddada Sudan
17 L6 Umm Qasr Iraq
55 F3 Umm Ruwaba Sudan
55 E1 Umm Sa'ad Libya
18 C5 Umm Sa'id Qatar
72 A3 Umpqua r. U.S.A.
57 B5 Umpulo Angola
22 D5 Umred India
22 C5 Umreth India
59 H5 Umtata S. Africa
59 J5 Umtentweni S. Africa
54 C4 Umuahia Nigeria
90 B3 Umuarama Brazil
59 H5 Umzimkulu S. Africa
59 J5 Umzinto S. Africa
90 E1 Una Brazil
48 G2 Una r. Bos.-Herz./Croatia
16 F6 'Unāb, W. al watercourse Jordan
90 C2 Unaí Brazil
19 H3 Unai Pass pass Afgh.
62 B3 Unalakleet U.S.A.
40 C2 Unapool U.K.
89 D2 Unare r. Venez.
16 E6 'Unayzah Jordan
20 B4 'Unayzah S. Arabia
17 G5 'Unayzah, Jabal h. Iraq
73 E4 Uncompahgre Plateau plat. U.S.A.
59 H4 Underberg S. Africa
8 C3 Underbool Austr.
76 C2 Underwood U.S.A.
50 E4 Unecha Rus. Fed.
8 F2 Ungarie Austr.
67 G2 Ungava Bay b. Can.
66 F1 Ungava, Péninsule d' pen. Can.
30 F2 Unggi N. Korea
51 C6 Ungheni Moldova
19 E2 Unguz, Solonchakovyye Vpadiny salt flat Turkm.
50 J3 Uni Rus. Fed.
90 B4 União da Vitória Brazil
89 B4 Unilla r. Col.
86 F4 Unini r. Brazil
90 A4 Unión Para.
81 J2 Union ME U.S.A.
79 D5 Union SC U.S.A.
80 C6 Union WV U.S.A.
68 E5 Union City OH U.S.A.
80 D4 Union City PA U.S.A.
79 B4 Union City TN U.S.A.
58 E6 Uniondale S. Africa
75 F4 Union, Mt mt U.S.A.
79 C5 Union Springs U.S.A.
80 D5 Uniontown U.S.A.
69 F4 Unionville U.S.A.
72 E3 Unita Mts. mts U.S.A.
10 G7 United Arab Emirates country Asia
34 E3 United Kingdom country Europe

61 H6 United States of America country N. America
65 H4 Unity Can.
81 J2 Unity ME U.S.A.
72 C2 Unity OR U.S.A.
22 C5 Unjha India
43 F3 Unna Ger.
22 E4 Unnão India
30 C4 Ŭnp'a N. Korea
30 C3 Unsan N. Korea
30 D4 Ŭnsan N. Korea
40 □ Unst i. U.K.
43 K3 Unstrut r. Ger.
23 G2 Unuli Horog China
23 F5 Upar Ghat reg. India
82 E2 Upata Venez.
57 C4 Upemba, Lac l. Congo(Zaire)
57 C4 Upemba, Parc National de l' nat. park Congo(Zaire)
31 C5 Upi Phil.
89 B3 Upía r. Col.
58 D4 Upington S. Africa
22 B5 Upleta India
36 W3 Upoloksha Rus. Fed.
7 J3 Upolu i. Western Samoa
80 B4 Upper Arlington U.S.A.
64 F4 Upper Arrow L. l. Can.
9 E4 Upper Hutt N.Z.
68 B4 Upper Iowa r. U.S.A.
81 K1 Upper Kent Can.
72 B3 Upper Klamath L. l. U.S.A.
72 B3 Upper L. l. U.S.A.
74 A2 Upper Lake U.S.A.
64 D2 Upper Liard Can.
41 D3 Upper Lough Erne l. U.K.
80 E5 Upper Marlboro U.S.A.
32 □ Upper Peirce Res. resr Sing.
67 J4 Upper Salmon Reservoir Can.
80 B4 Upper Sandusky U.S.A.
81 F2 Upper Saranac Lake l. U.S.A.
9 D4 Upper Takaka N.Z.
37 P7 Uppsala Sweden
66 B4 Upsala Can.
81 H2 Upton U.S.A.
17 L7 Uqlat al 'Udhaybah well Iraq
17 L6 Ur Iraq
89 A2 Urabá, Golfo de b. Col.
26 C1 Urad Qianqi China
26 C1 Urad Zhongqi Lianheqi China
18 E4 Ūrāf Iran
28 H3 Urakawa Japan
8 F2 Ural h. Austr.
8 H1 Uralla Austr.
35 M2 Ural Mountains mts Rus. Fed.
14 D1 Ural'sk Kazak.
Ural'skiy Khrebet mts see Ural Mountains
56 D4 Urambo Tanz.
8 F3 Urana Austr.
8 F3 Urana, L. l. Austr.
90 D1 Urandi Brazil
65 H3 Uranium City Can.
8 F3 Uranquity Austr.
89 E4 Uraricoera Brazil
89 E4 Uraricoera r. Brazil
89 E4 Uraricuera r. Brazil
89 E3 Uraucaima, Sa mt Brazil
75 H2 Uravan U.S.A.
18 B5 'Urayq ad Duḩūl sand dunes S. Arabia
51 F5 Urazovo Rus. Fed.
68 C5 Urbana IL U.S.A.
80 B4 Urbana OH U.S.A.
48 E3 Urbino Italy
86 D6 Urcos Peru
51 H5 Urda Kazak.
50 J2 Urdoma Rus. Fed.
38 F3 Ure r. U.K.
50 H3 Uren' Rus. Fed.
12 J3 Urengoy Rus. Fed.
7 G3 Uréparapara i. Vanuatu
9 F3 Urewera National Park N.Z.
50 H4 Urga r. Rus. Fed.
14 E2 Urgench Uzbek.
16 E2 Ürgüp Turkey
19 G2 Urgut Uzbek.
36 V2 Urho Kekkosen Kansallispuisto nat. park Fin.
89 B2 Uribia Col.
37 S6 Urjala Fin.
42 D2 Urk Neth.
51 H7 Urkarakh Rus. Fed.
45 M5 Urla Turkey
41 D5 Urlingford Rep. of Ireland
19 H2 Urmetan Tajik.
Urmia see Orūmīyeh
Urmia, Lake salt l. see Orūmīyeh, Daryācheh-ye
27 □ Urmston Road chan. H.K. China
49 J3 Uroševac Yugo.
19 H2 Ŭroteppa Tajik.
23 F3 Urru Co salt l. China
26 A1 Urt Mongolia
90 C1 Uruaçu Brazil
84 B3 Uruapan Mex.
86 D6 Urubamba r. Peru
87 G4 Urucara Brazil
87 K5 Uruçuí Brazil
90 D2 Urucuia r. Brazil
87 K5 Uruçuí Preto r. Brazil
87 G4 Urucurituba Brazil
88 E3 Uruguaiana Brazil
85 E6 Uruguay country S. America
88 E4 Uruguay r. Arg./Uru.
Uruk see Erech
Urumchi see Ürümqi
24 A2 Ürümqi China
51 G6 Urup r. Rus. Fed.
24 H2 Urup, O. i. Rus. Fed.
51 H7 Urus-Martan Rus. Fed.
51 G5 Uryupinsk Rus. Fed.
50 J3 Urzhum Rus. Fed.
49 M2 Urziceni Romania
29 B8 Usa Japan
50 J4 Usa r. Rus. Fed.
16 B2 Uşak Turkey
57 B6 Usakos Namibia
92 B5 Usarp Mts mts Ant.
88 E8 Usborne, Mt h. Falkland Is
12 J1 Ushakova, O. i. Rus. Fed.
18 B5 'Ushayrah S. Arabia
29 B8 Ushibuka Japan
15 F2 Ushtobe Kazak.
88 C8 Ushuaia Arg.
43 G4 Usingen Ger.
12 G3 Usinsk Rus. Fed.
39 E6 Usk U.K.
39 E6 Usk r. U.K.
23 E4 Uska India
50 C4 Uskhodni Belarus
43 H3 Uslar Ger.
51 F4 Usman' Rus. Fed.
37 S8 Usmas Ezers l. Latvia
50 J2 Usogorsk Rus. Fed.
24 C1 Usol'ye-Sibirskoye Rus. Fed.
44 F4 Ussel France
28 D1 Ussuri r. China/Rus. Fed.
24 F2 Ussuriysk Rus. Fed.
50 H3 Usta r. Rus. Fed.
13 M4 Ust'-Barguzin Rus. Fed.
51 G5 Ust'-Buzulukskaya Rus. Fed.
51 G6 Ust'-Donetskiy Rus. Fed.
48 E5 Ustica, Isola di i. Sicily Italy
24 C4 Ust'Ilimsk Rus. Fed.
24 C1 Ust'-Ilimskiy Vdkhr. resr Rus. Fed.
12 G3 Ust'-Ilych Rus. Fed.
46 G5 Ústí nad Labem Czech Rep.
Ustinov see Izhevsk
46 H3 Ustka Pol.
13 S4 Ust'-Kamchatsk Rus. Fed.
15 G2 Ust'-Kamenogorsk Kazak.
24 C1 Ust'-Kut Rus. Fed.
13 P2 Ust'-Kuyga Rus. Fed.
51 F6 Ust'-Labinsk Rus. Fed.
37 V7 Ust'-Luga Rus. Fed.
13 P3 Ust'-Maya Rus. Fed.
12 G3 Ust'-Nem Rus. Fed.
13 Q3 Ust'-Nera Rus. Fed.
50 J2 Ust'-Ocheya Rus. Fed.
13 N2 Ust'-Olenek Rus. Fed.
13 Q3 Ust'omchug Rus. Fed.
24 C1 Ust'-Ordynskiy Rus. Fed.
13 S3 Ust'-Penzhino Rus. Fed.
12 K3 Ust'-Port Rus. Fed.
50 G2 Ust'-Shonosha Rus. Fed.
12 G3 Ust'-Tsil'ma Rus. Fed.
50 H2 Ust'-Ura Rus. Fed.
50 G2 Ust'-Vayen'ga Rus. Fed.
50 H2 Ust'-Vyyskaya Rus. Fed.
50 G2 Ust'ya r. Rus. Fed.
50 F3 Ust'ye Rus. Fed.
50 F3 Ust'ye r. Rus. Fed.
12 G5 Ustyurt Plateau plat. Kazak./Uzbek.
50 F3 Ustyuzhna Rus. Fed.
29 B8 Usuki Japan
84 E3 Usumacinta r. Guatemala/Mex.
50 D4 Usvyaty Rus. Fed.
75 G2 Utah div. U.S.A.
75 G1 Utah Lake l. U.S.A.
36 U4 Utajärvi Fin.
18 C5 Utayyiq S. Arabia
37 T9 Utena Lith.
19 G5 Uthal Pak.
32 A2 U Thong Thai.
32 C2 Uthumphon Phisai Thai.
81 F3 Utica U.S.A.
45 F3 Utiel Spain
64 F3 Utikuma Lake l. Can.
59 F3 Utlwanang S. Africa
23 E4 Utraula India
42 D2 Utrecht Neth.
59 J3 Utrecht S. Africa
45 D4 Utrera Spain
36 U2 Utsjoki Fin.
29 F6 Utsunomiya Japan
51 H6 Utta Rus. Fed.
32 B1 Uttaradit Thai.
22 D4 Uttar Pradesh div. India
39 F5 Uttoxeter U.K.
7 G3 Utupua i. Solomon Is
63 M2 Uummannaq Greenland
63 N2 Uummannaq Fjord in. Greenland
63 O4 Uummannarsuaq c. Greenland
36 T5 Uurainen Fin.
37 R6 Uusikaupunki Fin.
89 C4 Uva r. Col.
77 D6 Uvalde U.S.A.
51 G5 Uvarovo Rus. Fed.
56 D4 Uvinza Tanz.
59 J5 Uvongo S. Africa
24 B1 Uvs Nuur l. Mongolia
29 C8 Uwajima Japan
55 E2 Uweinat, Jebel mt Sudan
39 G6 Uxbridge U.K.
26 C2 Uxin Ju China
26 C2 Uxin Qi China
84 E2 Uxmal Mex.
24 B1 Uyar Rus. Fed.
26 C1 Üydzin Mongolia
13 Q3 Uyega Rus. Fed.
54 C4 Uyo Nigeria
86 E8 Uyuni, Salar de salt flat Bol.
50 H4 Uza r. Rus. Fed.
17 K4 'Uẓaym, Nahr al r. Iraq
10 H5 Uzbekistan country Asia
44 G4 Uzès France
51 B5 Uzhhorod Ukr.
49 H3 Užice Yugo.
50 F4 Uzlovaya Rus. Fed.
50 G3 Uzola r. Rus. Fed.
16 C3 Üzümlü Turkey
19 H2 Uzun Uzbek.
17 L3 Üzün Darreh r. Iran
51 C7 Uzunköprü Turkey
51 D5 Uzyn Ukr.

V

37 T5 Vaajakoski Fin.
58 H3 Vaal r. S. Africa
36 U4 Vaala Fin.
58 F4 Vaalbos National Park nat. park S. Africa
59 H3 Vaal Dam dam S. Africa
59 H2 Vaalwater S. Africa
36 R5 Vaasa Fin.
19 G1 Vabkent Uzbek.
47 J7 Vác Hungary
88 F3 Vacaria Brazil
90 A3 Vacaria r. Mato Grosso do Sul Brazil
90 D2 Vacaria r. Minas Gerais Brazil
90 A3 Vacaria, Serra h. Brazil
74 B2 Vacaville U.S.A.
50 G4 Vad r. Rus. Fed.
22 C6 Vada India
37 K7 Vadla Norway
22 C5 Vadodara India
36 V1 Vadsø Norway
46 D7 Vaduz Liechtenstein
36 N3 Værøy i. Norway
50 G2 Vaga r. Rus. Fed.
37 L6 Vågåmo Norway
48 F2 Vaganski Vrh mt Croatia
36 □ Vágar i. Faroe Is
36 Q4 Vägsele Sweden
36 □ Vágur Faroe Is
36 S5 Vähäkyrö Fin.
37 T7 Vaida Estonia
21 B4 Vaigai r. India
75 G5 Vail U.S.A.
42 B5 Vailly-sur-Aisne France
7 H2 Vaitupu i. Tuvalu
19 J2 Vakhan Tajik.
19 H2 Vakhsh Tajik.
21 C5 Valachchenai Sri Lanka
69 K2 Val-Barrette Can.
37 P6 Valbo Sweden
91 C4 Valcheta Arg.
48 D2 Valdagno Italy
50 E3 Valday Rus. Fed.
50 E3 Valdayskaya Vozvyshennost' reg. Rus. Fed.
45 D3 Valdecañas, Embalse de resr Spain
37 S8 Valdemārpils Latvia
37 P7 Valdemarsvik Sweden
44 G2 Val-de-Meuse France
45 E3 Valdepeñas Spain
44 E2 Val-de-Reuil France
69 K3 Val-des-Bois Can.
91 D4 Valdés, Península pen. Arg.
62 D3 Valdez U.S.A.
91 B3 Valdivia Chile
69 J1 Val-d'Or Can.
79 D6 Valdosta U.S.A.
37 L6 Valdres v. Norway
17 J1 Vale Georgia
72 C2 Vale U.S.A.
64 F4 Valemount Can.
90 E1 Valença Brazil
44 G4 Valence France
45 F3 Valencia Spain
89 D2 Valencia Venez.
45 F3 Valencia div. Spain
45 C3 Valencia de Alcántara Spain
45 D1 Valencia de Don Juan Spain
45 G3 Valencia, Golfo de g. Spain
41 A6 Valencia Island i. Rep. of Ireland
44 F1 Valenciennes France
28 D3 Valentin Rus. Fed.
75 F4 Valentine AZ U.S.A.
76 C3 Valentine NE U.S.A.
77 B6 Valentine TX U.S.A.
31 B3 Valenzuela Phil.
37 M6 Våler Norway
89 C2 Valera Venez.
49 H2 Valjevo Yugo.
37 U8 Valka Latvia
37 T6 Valkeakoski Fin.
42 D3 Valkenswaard Neth.
51 E5 Valky Ukr.
92 C4 Valkyrjedomen ice feature Ant.
82 G4 Valladolid Mex.
45 D2 Valladolid Spain
45 F3 Vall de Uxó Spain
37 K7 Valle Norway
89 D2 Valle de la Pascua Venez.
84 B2 Valle de Santiago Mex.
89 B2 Valledupar Col.
91 C1 Valle Fértil, Sa de mts Arg.
86 F7 Valle Grande Bol.
84 C1 Valle Hermoso Mex.
74 A2 Vallejo U.S.A.
84 C3 Valle Nacional Mex.
48 F7 Valletta Malta
39 C4 Valley U.K.
76 D2 Valley City U.S.A.
72 B3 Valley Falls U.S.A.
80 C5 Valley Head U.S.A.
64 F3 Valleyview Can.
45 G2 Valls Spain
65 H5 Val Marie Can.
37 T8 Valmiera Latvia
45 E1 Valnera mt Spain
50 C4 Valozhyn Belarus
66 E4 Val-Paradis Can.
90 B3 Valparaíso Brazil
91 B2 Valparaíso Chile
84 B2 Valparaíso Mex.
68 D5 Valparaiso U.S.A.
91 B2 Valparaíso div. Chile
44 G4 Valréas France
22 C5 Valsād India
58 F3 Valspan S. Africa
25 F7 Vals, Tanjung c. Indon.
50 H1 Val'tevo Rus. Fed.
36 V5 Valtimo Fin.
51 G6 Valuyevka Rus. Fed.
51 F5 Valuyki Rus. Fed.
45 C4 Valverde del Camino Spain
32 C3 Vam Co Tay r. Vietnam
37 S6 Vammala Fin.
21 C2 Vamsadhara r. India
17 J2 Van Turkey
17 K1 Vanadzor Armenia
77 E5 Van Buren AR U.S.A.
81 K1 Van Buren ME U.S.A.
32 D2 Vân Canh Vietnam
81 K2 Vanceboro U.S.A.
80 B5 Vanceburg U.S.A.
64 E5 Vancouver Can.
72 B2 Vancouver U.S.A.
64 D5 Vancouver Island i. Can.
64 A2 Vancouver, Mt mt Can./U.S.A.
78 B4 Vandalia IL U.S.A.
80 A5 Vandalia OH U.S.A.
59 G3 Vanderbijlpark S. Africa
68 E3 Vanderbilt U.S.A.
80 D4 Vandergrift U.S.A.
64 E4 Vanderhoof Can.
58 F5 Vanderkloof Dam resr S. Africa
6 D3 Vanderlin I. i. Austr.
75 H4 Vanderwagen U.S.A.
6 D3 Van Diemen Gulf b. Austr.
37 T7 Vändra Estonia
37 N7 Vänern l. Sweden
37 N7 Vänersborg Sweden
80 E3 Van Etten U.S.A.
57 E6 Vangaindrano Madag.
17 J2 Van Gölü salt l. Turkey
77 B6 Van Horn U.S.A.
69 K3 Vanier Can.
7 G3 Vanikoro Is is Solomon Is
6 E2 Vanimo P.N.G.
24 G2 Vanino Rus. Fed.
21 B3 Vanivilasa Sagara resr India
21 B3 Vaniyambadi India
19 H2 Vanj Tajik.
19 H2 Vanj, Qatorkŭhi mts Tajik.
13 V3 Vankarem Rus. Fed.
81 F2 Vankleek Hill Can.
Van, Lake salt l. see Van Gölü
36 R1 Vanna i. Norway
36 Q5 Vännäs Sweden
44 C3 Vannes France
25 F7 Van Rees, Pegunungan mts Indon.
58 C5 Vanrhynsdorp S. Africa
37 O6 Vansbro Sweden
37 T6 Vantaa Fin.
7 G3 Vanua Lava i. Vanuatu
7 H3 Vanua Levu i. Fiji
4 H6 Vanuatu country Pac. Oc.
80 A4 Van Wert U.S.A.
58 D5 Vanwyksvlei S. Africa
58 D5 Vanwyksvlei l. S. Africa
27 B6 Văn Yên Vietnam
58 E3 Van Zylsrus S. Africa
21 A3 Varada r. India
37 U8 Varakļāni Latvia
18 C3 Varāmīn Iran
23 E4 Varanasi India
36 V1 Varangerfjorden chan. Norway
36 V1 Varangerhalvøya pen. Norway
48 G1 Varaždin Croatia
37 N8 Varberg Sweden
21 B2 Vardannapet India
49 K4 Vardar r. Macedonia
37 L9 Varde Denmark
18 B1 Vardenis Armenia
36 W1 Vardø Norway
43 G1 Varel Ger.
91 C2 Varela Arg.
37 T9 Varėna Lith.
48 C2 Varese Italy
28 C2 Varfolomeyevka Rus. Fed.
37 N7 Vårgårda Sweden
90 D3 Varginha Brazil
42 D3 Varik Neth.
36 U5 Varkaus Fin.
49 M3 Varna Bulg.
37 O8 Värnamo Sweden
37 N6 Värnäs Sweden
50 H3 Varnavino Rus. Fed.
16 D4 Varosia Cyprus
36 U5 Varpaisjärvi Fin.
46 J7 Várpalota Hungary
19 H2 Varsaj Afgh.
17 H2 Varto Turkey
23 E4 Varuna r. India
80 D3 Varysburg U.S.A.
18 D3 Varzaneh Iran
90 D2 Várzea da Palma Brazil
50 H2 Vashka r. Rus. Fed.
Vasht see Khāsh
50 H2 Vasilevo Rus. Fed.
37 U7 Vasknarva Estonia
47 N7 Vaslui Romania
69 F4 Vassar U.S.A.
37 P7 Västerås Sweden
37 N6 Västerdalälven r. Sweden
36 P3 Västerfjäll Sweden
37 Q7 Vasterhaninge Sweden
37 P8 Västervik Sweden
48 F3 Vasto Italy
51 D5 Vasyl'kiv Ukr.
44 E3 Vatan France
40 A4 Vatersay i. U.K.
21 A2 Vathar India
49 M6 Vathy Greece
34 G4 Vatican City country Europe
36 E4 Vatnajökull ice cap Iceland
47 M7 Vatra Dornei Romania
37 O7 Vättern l. Sweden
73 F5 Vaughn U.S.A.
42 B4 Vaulx Belgium
89 C4 Vaupés r. Col.
45 F4 Vauvert France
7 J3 Vava'u Group is Tonga
54 B4 Vavoua Côte d'Ivoire
21 C4 Vavuniya Sri Lanka
50 C4 Vawkavysk Belarus
37 O8 Växjö Sweden
21 B3 Vāyalpād India
50 H1 Vazhgort Rus. Fed.
57 E5 Vazobe mt Madag.
32 B2 Veal Vêng Cambodia
43 G2 Vechta Ger.
42 E2 Vechte r. Ger.
43 H3 Veckerhagen (Reinhardshagen) Ger.
21 B4 Vedaranniyam India
37 N8 Veddige Sweden
49 L3 Vedea r. Romania
51 H7 Vedeno Rus. Fed.
17 K2 Vedi Armenia
91 E2 Vedia Arg.
50 E2 Vedlozero Rus. Fed.
68 D5 Veedersburg U.S.A.
42 E1 Veendam Neth.
42 D2 Veenendaal Neth.
77 C5 Vega U.S.A.
36 M4 Vega i. Norway
65 G4 Vegreville Can.
37 U6 Vehkalahti Fin.
22 B3 Vehoa r. Pak.
22 B4 Veirwaro Pak.
43 H5 Veitshöchheim Ger.
45 D4 Vejer de la Frontera Spain
37 L9 Vejle Denmark
89 B1 Vela, Cabo de la pt Col.
21 B4 Velanai I. i. Sri Lanka
42 F3 Velbert Ger.
49 K3 Velbŭzhdki Prokhod pass Macedonia
58 C6 Velddrif S. Africa
48 F2 Velebit mts Croatia
42 E3 Velen Ger.
48 F1 Velenje Slovenia
49 J4 Veles Macedonia
89 B3 Vélez Col.
45 D4 Vélez-Málaga Spain
45 E4 Vélez-Rubio Spain
90 D2 Velhas r. Brazil
51 H6 Velichayevskoye Rus. Fed.
48 G2 Velika Gorica Croatia
49 J2 Velika Plana Yugo.
50 J3 Velikaya Rus. Fed.
50 D3 Velikaya r. Rus. Fed.
13 T3 Velikaya r. Rus. Fed.
50 E2 Velikaya Guba Rus. Fed.
28 E2 Velikaya Kema Rus. Fed.
50 D3 Velikiye Luki Rus. Fed.
50 H2 Velikiy Ustyug Rus. Fed.
21 B3 Velikonda Ra. h. India
47 Q2 Velikooktyabr'skiy Rus. Fed.
49 L3 Veliko Tŭrnovo Bulg.
50 F3 Velikoye Rus. Fed.
50 F3 Velikoye, Oz. l. Rus. Fed.
50 G4 Velikoye, Oz. l. Rus. Fed.
48 F2 Veli Lošinj Croatia
54 A3 Vélingara Senegal
47 P3 Velizh Rus. Fed.
46 H7 Veľký Meder Slovakia
7 F2 Vella Lavella i. Solomon Is
21 B4 Vellar r. India
43 H5 Vellberg Ger.
43 H3 Vellmar Ger.
21 B3 Vellore India
43 J2 Velpke Ger.
50 G2 Vel'sk Rus. Fed.
43 M2 Velten Ger.
42 D2 Veluwe reg. Neth.
42 E2 Veluwezoom, Nationaal Park nat. park Neth.
65 J5 Velva U.S.A.
96 G5 Vema Fracture sea feature Atl. Ocean
93 J4 Vema Trough sea feature Ind. Ocean
21 B4 Vembanād L. l. India
40 D4 Venachar, Loch l. U.K.
91 E2 Venado Tuerto Arg.
48 F4 Venafro Italy
89 E3 Venamo r. Guyana/Venez.
89 E3 Venamo, Co mt Venez.
90 C3 Venceslau Bráz Brazil
44 E3 Vendôme France
50 F4 Venev Rus. Fed.
Venezia see Venice
48 E2 Venezia, Golfo di g. Europe
85 D2 Venezuela country S. America
89 C2 Venezuela, Golfo de g. Venez.
96 E4 Venezuelan Basin sea feature Atl. Ocean
21 A3 Vengurla India
48 E2 Venice Italy
79 D7 Venice U.S.A.
44 G4 Vénissieux France
21 B3 Venkatagiri India
21 C2 Venkatapuram India
42 E3 Venlo Neth.
37 K7 Vennesla Norway
42 D3 Venray Neth.
37 S8 Venta Lith.
37 R8 Venta r. Latvia/Lith.
91 D3 Ventana, Serra de la h. Arg.
59 G4 Ventersburg S. Africa
59 G3 Ventersdorp S. Africa
59 F5 Venterstad S. Africa
39 F7 Ventnor U.K.
44 G4 Ventoux, Mont mt France
37 R8 Ventspils Latvia
89 D3 Ventuari r. Venez.
74 C4 Ventucopa U.S.A.
74 C4 Ventura U.S.A.
8 E5 Venus B. b. Austr.
88 D3 Vera Arg.
45 F4 Vera Spain
84 C3 Veracruz Mex.
84 C2 Veracruz div. Mex.
22 B5 Veraval India
48 C2 Verbania Italy
48 C2 Vercelli Italy
36 M5 Verdalsøra Norway
91 D4 Verde r. Arg.
90 C2 Verde r. Goiás Brazil
90 C2 Verde r. Goiás/Minas Gerais Brazil
90 B2 Verde r. Mato Grosso do Sul Brazil
70 E6 Verde r. Mex.
88 E2 Verde r. Para.
75 G4 Verde r. U.S.A.
90 D1 Verde Grande r. Brazil
31 B3 Verde Island Pass. chan. Phil.
43 H2 Verden (Aller) Ger.
91 D3 Verde, Pen. pen. Arg.
77 E4 Verdigris r. U.S.A.
44 H5 Verdon r. France
44 G2 Verdun France
59 G3 Vereeniging S. Africa
69 J2 Vérendrye, Réserve faunique La res. Can.
91 G2 Vergara Uru.
81 G2 Vergennes U.S.A.
45 C2 Verín Spain
51 F6 Verkhnebakanskiy Rus. Fed.
47 Q3 Verkhnedneprovskiy Rus. Fed.
12 K3 Verkhneimbatskoye Rus. Fed.
36 W2 Verkhnetulomskiy Rus. Fed.
13 O3 Verkhnevilyuysk Rus. Fed.
50 D1 Verkhneye Kuyto, Oz. l. Rus. Fed.
51 H5 Verkhniy Baskunchak Rus. Fed.
51 J5 Verkhniy Kushum Rus. Fed.
36 W3 Verkhnyaya Pirenga, Oz. l. Rus. Fed.
50 H2 Verkhnyaya Toyma Rus. Fed.
50 G2 Verkhovazh'ye Rus. Fed.
50 F4 Verkhov'ye Rus. Fed.
51 C5 Verkhovyna Ukr.
13 P3 Verkhoyansk Rus. Fed.
13 O3 Verkhoyanskiy Khrebet mts Rus. Fed.
42 B5 Vermand France
90 B1 Vermelho r. Brazil
65 G4 Vermilion Can.
68 C5 Vermilion r. U.S.A.
75 F3 Vermilion Cliffs cliff U.S.A.
68 A2 Vermilion Lake l. U.S.A.
68 A2 Vermilion Range h. U.S.A.
76 D3 Vermillion U.S.A.
65 L5 Vermillion Bay Can.
81 G3 Vermont div. U.S.A.
92 B2 Vernadsky Ukr. Base Ant.
72 E3 Vernal U.S.A.
69 G2 Verner Can.
58 D5 Verneuk Pan salt pan S. Africa
64 F4 Vernon Can.
75 H4 Vernon AZ U.S.A.
81 G4 Vernon CT U.S.A.
77 D5 Vernon TX U.S.A.
75 F1 Vernon UT U.S.A.
79 D7 Vero Beach U.S.A.
49 K4 Veroia Greece
48 D2 Verona Italy
91 F2 Verónica Arg.
44 F2 Versailles France
43 G2 Versmold Ger.
44 D3 Vertou France
59 J4 Verulam S. Africa
42 D4 Verviers Belgium
44 F2 Vervins France
42 C5 Verzy France
48 C3 Vescovato Corsica France
12 G4 Veselaya, G. mt Rus. Fed.
51 E6 Vesele Ukr.
51 G6 Veselovskoye Vdkhr. resr Rus. Fed.
51 G5 Veshenskaya Rus. Fed.
42 B5 Vesle r. France
44 H3 Vesoul France
28 D3 Vesselyy Yar Rus. Fed.
42 D3 Vessem Neth.
36 O2 Vesterålen is Norway
36 N2 Vesterålsfjorden chan. Norway
92 C3 Vestfjella mts Ant.
37 L7 Vestfjorddalen v. Norway
36 N3 Vestfjorden chan. Norway
36 □ Vestmanna Faroe Is
36 C5 Vestmannaeyjar Iceland
36 C5 Vestmannaeyjar is Iceland
36 K5 Vestnes Norway
36 F4 Vesturhorn hd Iceland
Vesuvio volc. see Vesuvius
48 F4 Vesuvius volc. Italy
50 F3 Ves'yegonsk Rus. Fed.
46 H7 Veszprém Hungary
36 S5 Veteli Fin.
37 O8 Vetlanda Sweden
50 H3 Vetluga Rus. Fed.
50 H3 Vetluga r. Rus. Fed.
48 E3 Vettore, Monte mt Italy
42 A3 Veurne Belgium
46 C7 Vevey Switz.
75 F3 Veyo U.S.A.
18 C4 Veys Iran
44 E4 Vézère r. France
16 E1 Vezirköprü Turkey
37 P5 Vi Sweden
86 C6 Viajas, I. de las i. Peru
87 K4 Viana Brazil
45 B2 Viana do Castelo Port.
42 D3 Vianen Neth.
Viangchan see Vientiane
90 C2 Vianópolis Brazil
48 D3 Viareggio Italy
37 L8 Viborg Denmark
48 G5 Vibo Valentia Italy
45 H2 Vic Spain
92 B2 Vicecomodoro Marambio Arg. Base Ant.
74 C5 Vicente, Pt pt U.S.A.
48 D2 Vicenza Italy
89 C3 Vichada r. Col.
86 D3 Vichada r. Col.
50 G3 Vichuga Rus. Fed.
91 B2 Vichuquén Chile
44 F3 Vichy France
75 F5 Vicksburg AZ U.S.A.
77 F5 Vicksburg MS U.S.A.
90 D3 Viçosa Brazil
68 A5 Victor U.S.A.
8 B3 Victor Harbour Austr.
91 E2 Victoria Arg.
64 E5 Victoria Can.
91 B3 Victoria Chile
Victoria see Labuan
48 F6 Victoria Malta
77 D6 Victoria U.S.A.
8 E4 Victoria div. Austr.
6 D3 Victoria r. Austr.
63 L2 Victoria and Albert Mts mts Can.
83 J4 Victoria de las Tunas Cuba
57 C5 Victoria Falls waterfall Zambia/Zimbabwe
63 O1 Victoria Fjord in. Greenland
27 □ Victoria Harbour chan. H.K. China
79 F7 Victoria Hill Bahamas
62 G2 Victoria Island i. Can.
56 D4 Victoria, Lake l. Africa
8 C2 Victoria, Lake l. N.S.W. Austr.
8 F5 Victoria, Lake l. Vic. Austr.
67 J4 Victoria Lake l. Can.
92 B5 Victoria Land reg. Ant.
23 H5 Victoria, Mt mt Myanmar
6 E2 Victoria, Mt mt P.N.G.
56 D3 Victoria Nile r. Sudan/Uganda
9 D5 Victoria Range mts N.Z.
6 D3 Victoria River Downs Austr.
67 F4 Victoriaville Can.
58 E5 Victoria West S. Africa
91 D3 Victorica Arg.
92 D3 Victor, Mt mt Ant.
74 D4 Victorville U.S.A.
91 D2 Vicuña Mackenna Arg.
75 E4 Vidal Junction U.S.A.
49 L2 Videle Romania
49 K3 Vidin Bulg.
22 D5 Vidisha India
40 □ Vidlin U.K.
50 E2 Vidlitsa Rus. Fed.
47 N3 Vidzy Belarus
50 J2 Vidz'yuyar Rus. Fed.
43 L5 Viechtach Ger.
91 D4 Viedma Arg.
88 B7 Viedma, L. l. Arg.
43 K1 Vielank Ger.
42 D4 Vielsalm Belgium
43 J3 Vienenburg Ger.
46 H6 Vienna Austria
78 B4 Vienna IL U.S.A.
81 F5 Vienna MD U.S.A.
80 C5 Vienna WV U.S.A.
44 G4 Vienne France
44 E3 Vienne r. France
32 B1 Vientiane Laos
91 B3 Viento, Cordillera del mts Arg.
83 L5 Vieques i. Puerto Rico
36 U5 Vieremä Fin.
42 E3 Viersen Ger.
46 D7 Vierwaldstätter See l. Switz.
44 F3 Vierzon France
84 B1 Viesca Mex.
37 T8 Viesīte Latvia
48 G4 Vieste Italy
36 Q3 Vietas Sweden
11 M8 Vietnam country Asia
27 B6 Viêt Tri Vietnam
31 B2 Vigan Phil.
48 C2 Vigevano Italy
42 A4 Vignacourt France
44 D5 Vignemale mt France
48 D2 Vignola Italy
45 B1 Vigo Spain
36 T4 Vihanti Fin.
22 C3 Vihari Pak.
37 T6 Vihti Fin.
36 T5 Viitasaari Fin.
22 C3 Vijainagar India
21 A2 Vijayadurg India
21 C2 Vijayawada India
36 D5 Vík Iceland
36 U3 Vikajärvi Fin.
65 G4 Viking Can.
36 M4 Vikna i. Norway
37 K6 Vikøyri Norway
54 □ Vila da Ribeira Brava Cape Verde
54 □ Vila de Sal Rei Cape Verde
54 □ Vila do Tarrafal Cape Verde
45 B3 Vila Franca de Xira Port.
45 B1 Vilagarcía de Arousa Spain
59 K2 Vila Gomes da Costa Moz.
45 C1 Vilalba Spain
45 B2 Vila Nova de Gaia Port.
45 G2 Vilanova i la Geltrú Spain
54 □ Vila Nova Sintra Cape Verde
45 C2 Vila Real Port.
45 C2 Vilar Formoso Port.
21 B4 Vilavankod India
90 E3 Vila Velha Brazil
86 D6 Vilcabamba, Cordillera mts Peru
36 P4 Vilhelmina Sweden
86 F6 Vilhena Brazil
37 T7 Viljandi Estonia
59 G3 Viljoenskroon S. Africa
37 S9 Vilkaviškis Lith.
37 S9 Vilkija Lith.
13 L2 Vil'kitskogo, Proliv str. Rus. Fed.
84 C3 Villa Alta Mex.
86 E6 Villa Bella Bol.
45 C1 Villablino Spain
91 E2 Villa Cañás Arg.
45 E3 Villacañas Spain
46 F7 Villach Austria
48 C5 Villacidro Sardinia Italy
91 E2 Villa Constitución Arg.
70 D6 Villa Constitución Mex.
84 B3 Villa de Alvarez Mex.
84 B2 Villa de Cos Mex.
91 D1 Villa del Rosario Arg.
91 D1 Villa del Totoral Arg.
91 D1 Villa Dolores Arg.
84 D3 Villa Flores Mex.
77 F5 Village, Lake U.S.A.
91 F3 Villa Gesell Arg.
84 C1 Villagrán Mex.
91 E1 Villaguay Arg.
84 D3 Villahermosa Mex.
91 D2 Villa Huidobro Arg.
91 D3 Villa Iris Arg.
45 F3 Villajoyosa Spain
84 B1 Villaldama Mex.
91 D3 Villalonga Arg.
91 D2 Villa María Arg.
91 E1 Villa María Grande Arg.
86 F8 Villa Montes Bol.
57 E5 Villandro, Tanjona pt Madag.
59 H1 Villa Nora S. Africa
89 B2 Villanueva Col.
84 B2 Villanueva Mex.
45 D3 Villanueva de la Serena Spain
45 E3 Villanueva de los Infantes Spain
88 E3 Villa Ocampo Arg.
77 B7 Villa O. Pereyra Mex.
48 C5 Villaputzu Sardinia Italy
91 C3 Villa Regina Arg.
91 B3 Villarrica Chile
88 E3 Villarrica Para.
91 B3 Villarrica, L. l. Chile
91 B3 Villarrica, Parque Nacional nat. park Chile
91 B3 Villarrica, Volcán volc. Chile
45 E3 Villarrobledo Spain
48 F5 Villa San Giovanni Italy
91 E2 Villa San José Arg.
91 C1 Villa Santa Rita de Catuna Arg.
88 C3 Villa Unión Arg.
84 A2 Villa Unión Durango Mex.
84 A2 Villa Unión Sinaloa Mex.
91 D2 Villa Valeria Arg.
89 B3 Villavicencio Col.
86 E8 Villazon Bol.
44 F4 Villefranche-de-Rouergue France
44 G4 Villefranche-sur-Saône France
69 H2 Ville-Marie Can.
45 F3 Villena Spain
44 E4 Villeneuve-sur-Lot France
44 F2 Villeneuve-sur-Yonne France
77 E6 Ville Platte U.S.A.
42 B5 Villers-Cotterêts France
42 D5 Villerupt France
44 G4 Villeurbanne France
59 H3 Villiers S. Africa
46 D6 Villingen Ger.
65 G4 Vilna Can.
37 T9 Vilnius Lith.
51 E6 Vil'nyans'k Ukr.
37 T5 Vilppula Fin.
43 K5 Vils r. Ger.
21 B4 Viluppuram India
42 C4 Vilvoorde Belgium
50 C4 Vilyeyka Belarus
13 O3 Vilyuy r. Rus. Fed.
13 M3 Vilyuyskoye Vdkhr. resr Rus. Fed.
37 O8 Vimmerby Sweden
42 A4 Vimy France
74 A2 Vina U.S.A.
91 B2 Viña del Mar Chile
81 J2 Vinalhaven U.S.A.
45 G2 Vinaròs Spain
78 C4 Vincennes U.S.A.
92 C6 Vincennes Bay b. Ant.
36 Q4 Vindelälven r. Sweden
36 Q4 Vindeln Sweden
22 C5 Vindhya Range h. India
81 F5 Vineland U.S.A.
81 H4 Vineyard Haven U.S.A.
32 C1 Vinh Vietnam
32 C1 Vinh Linh Vietnam
32 C3 Vinh Long Vietnam
32 C3 Vinh Rach Gia b. Vietnam
27 B6 Vinh Yên Vietnam
77 E4 Vinita U.S.A.
49 H2 Vinkovci Croatia
51 D5 Vinnytsya Ukr.
92 B3 Vinson Massif mt Ant.
37 L6 Vinstra Norway
68 A4 Vinton U.S.A.
21 B2 Vinukonda India
48 D1 Vipiteno Italy
43 L1 Vipperow Ger.
31 C3 Virac Phil.
22 C5 Viramgam India
17 G3 Viranşehir Turkey
22 B4 Virawah Pak.
65 J5 Virden Can.
44 D2 Vire France
57 B5 Virei Angola
90 D2 Virgem da Lapa Brazil
69 H1 Virginatown Can.
41 D4 Virginia Rep. of Ireland
59 G4 Virginia S. Africa
68 A2 Virginia U.S.A.
80 D6 Virginia div. U.S.A.
81 E6 Virginia Beach U.S.A.
74 C2 Virginia City U.S.A.
61 M8 Virgin Islands (U.K.) terr. Caribbean Sea
61 M8 Virgin Islands (U.S.A.) terr. Caribbean Sea
75 F3 Virgin Mts mts U.S.A.
37 T6 Virkkala Fin.
32 C2 Virôchey Cambodia
68 B4 Viroqua U.S.A.
48 G2 Virovitica Croatia
37 S5 Virrat Fin.
42 D5 Virton Belgium
37 S7 Virtsu Estonia
21 B4 Virudunagar India
56 C3 Virunga, Parc National des nat. park Congo(Zaire)
48 G3 Vis i. Croatia
37 U9 Visaginas Lith.
74 C3 Visalia U.S.A.
22 B5 Visavadar India
31 B4 Visayan Sea sea Phil.
43 G2 Visbek Ger.
37 Q8 Visby Sweden
62 G2 Viscount Melville Sound str. Can.
42 D4 Visé Belgium
49 H3 Višegrad Bos.-Herz.

12 J2 Vise, O. i. Rus. Fed.
87 J4 Viseu Brazil
45 C2 Viseu Port.
21 C2 Vishakhapatnam India
37 U8 Viški Latvia
22 C5 Visnagar India
49 H3 Visoko Bos.-Herz.
48 B2 Viso, Monte mt Italy
46 C7 Visp Switz.
43 H2 Visselhövede Ger.
74 D5 Vista U.S.A.
90 A2 Vista Alegre Brazil
49 L4 Vistonida, Limni lag. Greece
89 C3 Vita r. Col.
22 B3 Vitakri Pak.
48 E3 Viterbo Italy
48 G2 Vitez Bos.-Herz.
86 E8 Vitichi Bol.
45 C2 Vitigudino Spain
7 H3 Viti Levu i. Fiji
24 D1 Vitim r. Rus. Fed.
24 D1 Vitimskoye Ploskogor'ye plat. Rus. Fed.
90 E3 Vitória Brazil
Vitoria see Vitoria-Gasteiz
90 E1 Vitória da Conquista Brazil
45 E1 Vitoria-Gasteiz Spain
44 D2 Vitré France
42 A4 Vitry-en-Artois France
44 G2 Vitry-le-François France
50 D4 Vitsyebsk Belarus
36 R3 Vittangi Sweden
48 F6 Vittoria Sicily Italy
48 E2 Vittorio Veneto Italy
94 F3 Vityaz Depth depth Pac. Oc.
45 C1 Viveiro Spain
59 H1 Vivo S. Africa
Vizagapatam see Vishakhapatnam
82 B3 Vizcaíno, Sierra mts Mex.
51 C7 Vize Turkey
21 C2 Vizianagaram India
50 J2 Vizinga Rus. Fed.
42 C3 Vlaardingen Neth.
47 L7 Vlădeasa, Vârful mt Romania
51 H7 Vladikavkaz Rus. Fed.
28 D3 Vladimir Primorskiy Kray Rus. Fed.
50 G3 Vladimir Vladimir. Obl. Rus. Fed.
28 C3 Vladimiro-Aleksandrovskoye Rus. Fed.
24 F2 Vladivostok Rus. Fed.
50 G4 Vlaimirskaya Oblast' div. Rus. Fed.
59 H2 Vlakte S. Africa
49 K3 Vlasotince Yugo.
58 D7 Vleesbaai b. S. Africa
42 C1 Vlieland i. Neth.
42 B3 Vlissingen Neth.
49 H4 Vlorë Albania
43 G2 Vlotho Ger.
46 G6 Vltava r. Czech Rep.
46 F6 Vöcklabruck Austria
50 F2 Vodlozero, Ozero l. Rus. Fed.
40 □ Voe U.K.
42 D4 Voerendaal Neth.
43 H4 Vogelsberg h. Ger.
48 C2 Voghera Italy
43 L4 Vogtland reg. Ger.
43 L5 Vohenstrauß Ger.
Vohimena, Cape c. see Vohimena, Tanjona
57 E6 Vohimena, Tanjona c. Madag.
43 G3 Vöhl Ger.
37 T7 Võhma Estonia
56 D4 Voi Kenya
54 B4 Voinjama Liberia
44 G4 Voiron France
37 L9 Vojens Denmark
49 H2 Vojvodina div. Yugo.
50 H3 Vokhma Rus. Fed.
50 D1 Voknavolok Rus. Fed.
72 F2 Volborg U.S.A.
91 B1 Volcán, Co del mt Chile
Volcano Bay b. see Uchiura-wan
Volcano Is is see Kazan-rettō
37 K5 Volda Norway
42 D2 Volendam Neth.
51 H6 Volga r. Rus. Fed.
68 B4 Volga r. U.S.A.
51 G6 Volgodonsk Rus. Fed.
12 F5 Volgograd Rus. Fed.
51 H5 Volgogradskaya Oblast' div. Rus. Fed.
46 G7 Völkermarkt Austria
50 E3 Volkhov Rus. Fed.
50 D3 Volkhov r. Rus. Fed.
42 E5 Völklingen Ger.
59 H3 Volksrust S. Africa
28 B3 Vol'no-Nadezhdinskoye Rus. Fed.
51 F6 Volnovakha Ukr.
13 L2 Volochanka Rus. Fed.
51 C5 Volochys'k Ukr.
51 F6 Volodars'ke Ukr.
51 J6 Volodarskiy Rus. Fed.
14 E1 Volodarskoye Kazak.
47 O5 Volodars'k-Volyns'kyy Ukr.
47 N5 Volodymyrets' Ukr.
51 C5 Volodymyr-Volyns'kyy Ukr.
50 F3 Vologda Rus. Fed.
50 G3 Vologodskaya Oblast' div. Rus. Fed.
51 F5 Volokonovka Rus. Fed.
49 K5 Volos Greece
50 D3 Volosovo Rus. Fed.
47 P2 Volot Rus. Fed.
51 F4 Volovo Rus. Fed.
51 H4 Vol'sk Rus. Fed.
54 B4 Volta, Lake resr Ghana
90 D3 Volta Redonda Brazil
48 F4 Volturno r. Italy
49 K4 Volvi, L. l. Greece
50 J4 Volzhsk Rus. Fed.
51 H5 Volzhskiy Rus. Fed.
57 E6 Vondrozo Madag.
50 G1 Vonga Rus. Fed.
36 F4 Vopnafjörður Iceland
36 F4 Vopnafjörður b. Iceland
50 B2 Vörå Fin.
47 M3 Voranava Belarus
50 J3 Vorchanka Rus. Fed.
50 E2 Vorenzha Rus. Fed.
12 H3 Vorkuta Rus. Fed.
37 S7 Vormsi i. Estonia
51 G5 Vorona r. Rus. Fed.
51 F5 Voronezh Rus. Fed.
51 F5 Voronezh r. Rus. Fed.
51 G5 Voronezhskaya Oblast' div. Rus. Fed.
50 G3 Voron'ye Rus. Fed.
Voroshilovgrad see Luhans'k
47 O3 Vorot'kovo Rus. Fed.
51 E5 Vorskla r. Rus. Fed.
37 T7 Võrtsjärv l. Estonia
37 U8 Võru Estonia
19 H2 Vorukh Tajik.
58 E5 Vosburg S. Africa
19 H2 Vose Tajik.
44 H2 Vosges mts France
37 K6 Voss Norway
Vostochno-Sibirskoye More sea see East Siberian Sea
24 B1 Vostochnyy Sayan mts Rus. Fed.
28 D1 Vostok Rus. Fed.
92 C5 Vostok Rus. Fed. Base Ant.
5 M6 Vostok I. i. Kiribati
28 D2 Vostretsovo Rus. Fed.
12 G4 Votkinsk Rus. Fed.
90 C3 Votuporanga Brazil
42 C5 Vouziers France
44 E2 Voves France
50 J3 Voya r. Rus. Fed.
78 A1 Voyageurs Nat. Park nat. park U.S.A.
36 W4 Voynitsa Rus. Fed.
50 G2 Vozhega Rus. Fed.
50 F2 Vozhe, Ozero l. Rus. Fed.
51 D6 Voznesens'k Ukr.
28 C3 Vrangel' Rus. Fed.
13 V4 Vrangelya, O. i. U.S.A.
49 J3 Vranje Yugo.
49 M3 Vratnik pass Bulg.
49 K3 Vratsa Bulg.
49 H2 Vrbas Yugo.
48 G2 Vrbas r. Bos.-Herz.
59 H3 Vrede S. Africa
59 G3 Vredefort S. Africa
58 B6 Vredenburg S. Africa
58 C5 Vredendal S. Africa
42 C5 Vresse Belgium
21 B4 Vriddhachalam India
42 E1 Vries Neth.
37 O8 Vrigstad Sweden
49 J2 Vršac Yugo.
58 F3 Vryburg S. Africa
59 J3 Vryheid S. Africa
50 D2 Vsevolozhsk Rus. Fed.
49 J3 Vučitrn Yugo.
49 H2 Vukovar Croatia
12 G3 Vuktyl' Rus. Fed.
59 H3 Vukuzakhe S. Africa
48 F5 Vulcano, Isola i. Italy
75 F5 Vulture Mts mts U.S.A.
32 C3 Vung Tau Vietnam
37 U6 Vuohijärvi Fin.
36 U4 Vuolijoki Fin.
36 R3 Vuollerim Sweden
36 U3 Vuostimo Fin.
50 H4 Vurnary Rus. Fed.
57 D4 Vwawa Tanz.
22 C5 Vyara India
50 J3 Vyatka Rus. Fed.
50 J3 Vyatka r. Rus. Fed.
50 E4 Vyaz'ma Rus. Fed.
50 G3 Vyazniki Rus. Fed.
51 H5 Vyazovka Rus. Fed.
50 D2 Vyborg Rus. Fed.
50 J2 Vychegda r. Rus. Fed.
50 H2 Vychegodskiy Rus. Fed.
50 C4 Vyerkhnyadzvinsk Belarus
50 D4 Vyetryna Belarus
50 E2 Vygozero, Ozero l. Rus. Fed.
50 G4 Vyksa Rus. Fed.
51 D6 Vylkove Ukr.
47 L6 Vynohradiv Ukr.
50 E3 Vypolzovo Rus. Fed.
50 D3 Vyritsa Rus. Fed.
39 D5 Vyrnwy, Lake l. U.K.
51 F6 Vyselki Rus. Fed.
50 G4 Vysha Rus. Fed.
51 D5 Vyshhorod Ukr.
50 E3 Vyshnevolotskaya Gryada ridge Rus. Fed.
50 E3 Vyshniy-Volochek Rus. Fed.
46 H6 Vyškov Czech Rep.
51 D5 Vystupovychi Ukr.
50 F2 Vytegra Rus. Fed.

W

54 B3 Wa Ghana
42 D3 Waal r. Neth
42 D3 Waalwijk Neth.
66 B3 Wabakimi L. l. Can.
64 G3 Wabasca Can.
64 G3 Wabasca r. Can.
68 E5 Wabash U.S.A.
68 E5 Wabash r. U.S.A.
68 A3 Wabasha U.S.A.
69 E1 Wabatongushi Lake l. Can.
56 E3 Wabē Gestro r. Eth.
56 E3 Wabē Shebelē Wenz r. Eth.
65 K4 Wabowden Can.
66 C2 Wabuk Pt pt Can.
67 G3 Wabush Can.
67 G3 Wabush L. l. Can.
74 C2 Wabuska U.S.A.
79 D6 Waccasassa Bay b. U.S.A.
43 H4 Wächtersbach Ger.
77 D6 Waco U.S.A.
19 G5 Wad Pak.
8 G4 Wadbilliga Nat. Park Austr.
50 D2 Waddān Libya
42 C1 Waddeneilanden is Neth.
42 C2 Waddenzee chan. Neth.
64 D4 Waddington, Mt mt Can.
42 C2 Waddinxveen Neth.
39 C7 Wadebridge U.K.
65 J4 Wadena Can.
76 E2 Wadena U.S.A.
42 E5 Wadern Ger.
21 A2 Wadgaon India
42 E5 Wadgassen Ger.
55 E3 Wadi el Milk watercourse Sudan
55 F2 Wadi Halfa Sudan
55 E3 Wadi Howar watercourse Sudan
55 F3 Wad Medani Sudan
74 C2 Wadsworth U.S.A.
30 B4 Wafangdian China
17 L7 Wafra Kuwait
43 G2 Wagenfeld Ger.
43 J2 Wagenhoff Ger.
63 K3 Wager Bay b. Can.
8 F3 Wagga Wagga Austr.
22 C2 Wah Pak.
74 □1 Wahiawa U.S.A.
43 H3 Wahlhausen Ger.
76 D3 Wahoo U.S.A.
76 D2 Wahpeton U.S.A.
75 F2 Wah Wah Mts mts U.S.A.
21 A2 Wai India
74 □1 Waialee U.S.A.
74 □1 Waialua U.S.A.
74 □1 Waialua Bay b. U.S.A.
74 □1 Waianae U.S.A.
74 □1 Waianae Ra. mts U.S.A.
9 D5 Waiau r. N.Z.
46 G7 Waidhofen an der Ybbs Austria
25 F7 Waigeo i. Indon.
9 E2 Waiharoa N.Z.
9 E2 Waiheke Island i. N.Z.
9 E2 Waihi N.Z.
9 E2 Waihou r. N.Z.
25 D7 Waikabubak Indon.
9 B6 Waikaia r. N.Z.
74 □1 Waikane U.S.A.
9 D5 Waikari N.Z.
9 E2 Waikato r. N.Z.
9 F2 Waikawa Pt pt N.Z.
8 B3 Waikerie Austr.
74 □1 Waikiki Beach beach U.S.A.
9 C6 Waikouaiti N.Z.
74 □2 Wailuku U.S.A.
9 D5 Waimakariri r. N.Z.
74 □1 Waimanalo U.S.A.
9 C4 Waimangaroa N.Z.
9 F3 Waimarama N.Z.
9 C6 Waimate N.Z.
74 □1 Waimea HI U.S.A.
74 □2 Waimea HI U.S.A.
22 D5 Wainganga r. India
25 E7 Waingapu Indon.
39 C7 Wainhouse Corner U.K.
65 G4 Wainwright Can.
62 C2 Wainwright AK U.S.A.
9 E3 Waiouru N.Z.
9 E3 Waipa r. N.Z.
9 B7 Waipahi N.Z.
74 □1 Waipahu U.S.A.
9 F3 Waipaoa r. N.Z.
9 B7 Waipapa Pt pt N.Z.
9 D5 Waipara N.Z.
9 F3 Waipawa N.Z.
9 F3 Waipukurau N.Z.
9 F3 Wairakei N.Z.
9 E4 Wairarapa, L. l. N.Z.
9 D4 Wairau r. N.Z.
9 F3 Wairoa N.Z.
9 F3 Wairoa r. Hawke's Bay N.Z.
9 E1 Wairoa r. Northland N.Z.
9 F3 Waitahanui N.Z.
9 B6 Waitahuna N.Z.
9 E2 Waitakaruru N.Z.
9 C6 Waitaki r. N.Z.
9 E3 Waitara N.Z.
9 E2 Waitoa N.Z.
9 E2 Waiuku N.Z.
9 B7 Waiwera South N.Z.
27 F5 Waiyang China
29 E6 Wajima Japan
56 E3 Wajir Kenya
29 D7 Wakasa-wan b. Japan
9 B6 Wakatipu, Lake l. N.Z.
65 H4 Wakaw Can.
29 D7 Wakayama Japan
76 D4 Wa Keeney U.S.A.
69 K3 Wakefield Can.
9 D4 Wakefield N.Z.
38 F4 Wakefield U.K.
68 C2 Wakefield MI U.S.A.
81 H4 Wakefield RI U.S.A.
80 E6 Wakefield VA U.S.A.
Wakeham see Kangiqsujuaq
4 H3 Wake Island i. Pac. Oc.
28 G4 Wakinosawa Japan
28 G2 Wakkanai Japan
59 J3 Wakkerstroom S. Africa
8 E3 Wakool Austr.
8 D3 Wakool r. Austr.
67 G2 Wakuach, Lac l. Can.
46 H5 Wałbrzych Pol.
8 H1 Walcha Austr.
46 E7 Walchensee l. Ger.
42 C4 Walcourt Belgium
46 H4 Wałcz Pol.
81 F4 Walden Montgomery U.S.A.
46 F6 Waldkraiburg Ger.
39 C7 Waldon r. U.K.
80 E5 Waldorf U.S.A.
92 C6 Waldron, C. c. Ant.
34 E3 Wales div. U.K.
6 E5 Walgett Austr.
92 A3 Walgreen Coast coastal area Ant.
56 C4 Walikale Congo(Zaire)
68 B4 Walker IA U.S.A.
76 E2 Walker MN U.S.A.
74 C2 Walker r. U.S.A.
58 C7 Walker Bay b. S. Africa
79 E7 Walker Cay i. Bahamas
74 C2 Walker Lake l. U.S.A.
92 A3 Walker Mts mts Ant.
74 C4 Walker Pass pass U.S.A.
69 G3 Walkerton Can.
76 C2 Wall U.S.A.
72 C2 Wallace U.S.A.
69 F4 Wallaceburg Can.
8 A2 Wallaroo Austr.
39 D4 Wallasey U.K.
8 F3 Walla Walla Austr.
72 C2 Walla Walla U.S.A.
43 H5 Walldürn Ger.
58 B5 Wallekraal S. Africa
8 G3 Wallendbeen Austr.
81 F4 Wallenpaupack, Lake l. U.S.A.
39 F6 Wallingford U.K.
81 G4 Wallingford U.S.A.
5 K6 Wallis and Futuna terr. Pac. Oc.
7 J3 Wallis, Îles is Pac. Oc.
81 F6 Wallops I. i. U.S.A.
72 C2 Wallowa Mts mts U.S.A.
40 □ Walls U.K.
65 H2 Walmsley Lake l. Can.
38 D3 Walney, Isle of i. U.K.
68 C5 Walnut U.S.A.
75 G4 Walnut Canyon National Monument res. U.S.A.
77 F4 Walnut Ridge U.S.A.
23 J3 Walong India
39 F5 Walsall U.K.
73 F4 Walsenburg U.S.A.
43 H2 Walsrode Ger.
21 C2 Waltair India
79 D5 Walterboro U.S.A.
79 C6 Walter F. George Res. resr U.S.A.
69 J3 Waltham Can.
78 C4 Walton KY U.S.A.
81 F3 Walton NY U.S.A.
57 B6 Walvis Bay Namibia
96 K7 Walvis Ridge sea feature Atl. Ocean
56 C3 Wamba Congo(Zaire)
22 B2 Wana Pak.
9 B6 Wanaka N.Z.
9 B6 Wanaka, L. l. N.Z.
27 E5 Wan'an China
69 G2 Wanapitei Lake l. Can.
81 F4 Wanaque Reservoir U.S.A.
8 C3 Wanbi Austr.
9 C6 Wanbrow, Cape c. N.Z.
28 C2 Wanda Shan mts China
60 R1 Wandel Sea sea Greenland
43 J4 Wandersleben Ger.
43 M2 Wandlitz Ger.
30 D6 Wando S. Korea
9 E3 Wanganui N.Z.
9 E3 Wanganui r. N.Z.
8 F4 Wangaratta Austr.
26 C3 Wangcang China
27 D4 Wangcheng China
43 F1 Wangerooge Ger.
43 F1 Wangerooge i. Ger.
30 A3 Wanghai Shan h. China
27 E4 Wangjiang China
27 C5 Wangmo China
30 E2 Wangqing China
22 B5 Wankaner India
56 E3 Wanlaweyn Somalia
43 G1 Wanna Ger.
27 E4 Wannian China
27 D7 Wanning China
26 E1 Wanquan China
42 D3 Wanroij Neth.
27 D6 Wanshan Qundao is China
9 F4 Wanstead N.Z.
39 F6 Wantage U.K.
69 G2 Wanup Can.
27 C4 Wan Xian China
27 C4 Wanxian China
26 C3 Wanyuan China
27 E4 Wanzai China
42 D4 Wanze Belgium
80 A4 Wapakoneta U.S.A.
68 B5 Wapello U.S.A.
66 C3 Wapikopa L. l. Can.
64 F4 Wapiti r. Can.
77 F4 Wappapello, L. resr U.S.A.
68 A5 Wapsipinicon r. U.S.A.
26 B3 Waqên China
18 C6 Waqr well S. Arabia
22 A4 Warah Pak.
21 B2 Warangal India
8 E4 Waranga Reservoir Austr.
22 E5 Waraseoni India
8 F5 Waratah B. b. Austr.
43 H3 Warburg Ger.
6 C4 Warburton Austr.
6 D4 Warburton watercourse Austr.
65 G2 Warburton Bay l. Can.
59 H3 Warden S. Africa
43 G1 Wardenburg Ger.
22 D5 Wardha India
22 D6 Wardha r. India
9 A6 Ward, Mt mt Southland N.Z.
9 B5 Ward, Mt mt West Coast N.Z.
64 D3 Ware Can.
81 G3 Ware U.S.A.
39 E7 Wareham U.K.
81 H4 Wareham U.S.A.
42 D4 Waremme Belgium
43 L1 Waren Ger.
43 F3 Warendorf Ger.
8 H1 Warialda Austr.
43 K1 Warin Ger.
32 C2 Warin Chamrap Thai.
9 E2 Warkworth N.Z.
38 F2 Warkworth U.K.
42 A4 Warloy-Baillon France
65 H4 Warman Can.
53 C4 Warmbad Namibia
59 H2 Warmbad S. Africa
39 E6 Warminster U.K.
81 F4 Warminster U.S.A.
42 C2 Warmond Neth.
74 D2 Warm Springs NV U.S.A.
80 D5 Warm Springs VA U.S.A.
58 D6 Warmwaterberg mts S. Africa
81 H3 Warner U.S.A.
72 B3 Warner Mts mts U.S.A.
79 D5 Warner Robins U.S.A.
86 F7 Warnes Bol.
22 D5 Warora India
8 D4 Warracknabeal Austr.
8 H3 Warragamba Reservoir Austr.
8 E5 Warragul Austr.
6 E4 Warrego r. Austr.
8 F1 Warren Austr.
69 G2 Warren Can.
77 E5 Warren AR U.S.A.
69 F4 Warren MI U.S.A.
76 D1 Warren MN U.S.A.
80 C4 Warren OH U.S.A.
80 D4 Warren PA U.S.A.
80 C4 Warrendale U.S.A.
41 E3 Warrenpoint U.K.
76 E4 Warrensburg MO U.S.A.
81 G3 Warrensburg NY U.S.A.
58 F4 Warrenton S. Africa
80 E5 Warrenton U.S.A.
54 C4 Warri Nigeria
9 C6 Warrington N.Z.
39 E4 Warrington U.K.
79 C6 Warrington U.S.A.
8 D5 Warrnambool Austr.
76 E1 Warroad U.S.A.
8 G1 Warrumbungle Ra. mts Austr.
47 K4 Warsaw Pol.
68 E5 Warsaw IN U.S.A.
76 E4 Warsaw MO U.S.A.
80 D3 Warsaw NY U.S.A.
80 E6 Warsaw VA U.S.A.
43 G3 Warstein Ger.
Warszawa see Warsaw
46 G4 Warta r. Pol.
6 F4 Warwick Austr.
39 F5 Warwick U.K.
81 F4 Warwick NY U.S.A.
81 H4 Warwick RI U.S.A.
73 E4 Wasatch Range mts U.S.A.
59 J4 Wasbank S. Africa
74 C4 Wasco U.S.A.
76 E2 Waseca U.S.A.
19 F5 Washap Pak.
68 C5 Washburn IL U.S.A.
81 J1 Washburn ME U.S.A.
76 C2 Washburn ND U.S.A.
68 B2 Washburn WV U.S.A.
22 D5 Wāshīm India
80 E5 Washington DC U.S.A.
79 D5 Washington GA U.S.A.
68 C5 Washington IL U.S.A.
78 C4 Washington IN U.S.A.
76 F4 Washington MO U.S.A.
79 E5 Washington NC U.S.A.
81 F4 Washington NJ U.S.A.
80 C4 Washington PA U.S.A.
75 F3 Washington UT U.S.A.
72 B2 Washington div. U.S.A.
92 B5 Washington, C. c. Ant.
80 B5 Washington Court House U.S.A.
68 D3 Washington Island i. U.S.A.
63 M1 Washington Land reg. Greenland
81 H2 Washington, Mt mt U.S.A.
77 D5 Washita r. U.S.A.
39 H5 Wash, The b. U.K.
19 G5 Washuk Pak.
18 B5 Wasi' S. Arabia
17 L5 Wasit Iraq
66 E3 Waskaganish Can.
65 K3 Waskaiowaka Lake l. Can.
42 C2 Wassenaar Neth.
58 C3 Wasser Namibia
43 H4 Wasserkuppe h. Ger.
43 J5 Wassertrüdingen Ger.
74 C2 Wassuk Range mts U.S.A.
66 E4 Waswanipi, Lac l. Can.
25 E7 Watampone Indon.
81 G4 Waterbury CT U.S.A.
81 G2 Waterbury VT U.S.A.
65 H3 Waterbury Lake l. Can.
41 D5 Waterford Rep. of Ireland
80 D4 Waterford U.S.A.
41 E5 Waterford Harbour harbour Rep. of Ireland
41 C5 Watergrasshill Rep. of Ireland
42 C4 Waterloo Belgium
69 G4 Waterloo Can.
68 A4 Waterloo IA U.S.A.
81 H3 Waterloo ME U.S.A.
80 E3 Waterloo NY U.S.A.
68 C4 Waterloo WV U.S.A.
39 F7 Waterlooville U.K.
59 H1 Waterpoort S. Africa
68 C2 Watersmeet U.S.A.
64 G5 Waterton Lakes Nat. Park Can.
81 E3 Watertown NY U.S.A.
76 D2 Watertown SD U.S.A.
68 C4 Watertown WV U.S.A.
59 J2 Waterval-Boven S. Africa
8 B2 Watervale Austr.
81 J2 Waterville U.S.A.
65 G3 Waterways Can.
69 G4 Watford Can.
39 G6 Watford U.K.
76 C2 Watford City U.S.A.
65 J3 Wathaman r. Can.
43 J2 Wathlingen Ger.
80 E3 Watkins Glen U.S.A.
Watling i. see San Salvador
77 D5 Watonga U.S.A.
65 H4 Watrous Can.
56 C3 Watsa Congo(Zaire)
68 D5 Watseka U.S.A.
56 C4 Watsi Kengo Congo(Zaire)
65 J4 Watson Can.
64 D2 Watson Lake Can.
74 B3 Watsonville U.S.A.
40 E2 Watten U.K.
40 E2 Watten, Loch l. U.K.
65 J2 Watterson Lake l. Can.
64 F3 Watt, Mt h. Can.
39 H5 Watton U.K.
68 C2 Watton U.S.A.
6 D2 Watubela, Kepulauan is Indon.
6 E2 Wau P.N.G.
55 E4 Wau Sudan
68 D3 Waucedah U.S.A.
79 D7 Wauchula U.S.A.
68 D4 Waukegan U.S.A.
68 C4 Waukesha U.S.A.
68 B4 Waukon U.S.A.
68 C3 Waupaca U.S.A.
68 C4 Waupun U.S.A.
77 D5 Waurika U.S.A.
68 C3 Wausau U.S.A.
80 A4 Wauseon U.S.A.
68 C3 Wautoma U.S.A.
68 C4 Wauwatosa U.S.A.
39 J5 Waveney r. U.K.
68 A4 Waverly IA U.S.A.
80 B5 Waverly OH U.S.A.
79 C4 Waverly TN U.S.A.
80 E6 Waverly VA U.S.A.
42 C4 Wavre Belgium
68 E1 Wawa Can.
54 C4 Wawa Nigeria
68 E5 Wawasee, Lake l. U.S.A.
74 C3 Wawona U.S.A.
77 D5 Waxahachie U.S.A.
79 D6 Waycross U.S.A.
80 B6 Wayland KY U.S.A.
68 E5 Wayland MO U.S.A.
76 D3 Wayne U.S.A.
79 D5 Waynesboro GA U.S.A.
77 F6 Waynesboro MS U.S.A.
80 E5 Waynesboro PA U.S.A.
80 D5 Waynesboro VA U.S.A.
80 C5 Waynesburg U.S.A.
77 E4 Waynesville U.S.A.
77 D4 Waynoka U.S.A.
55 D3 Waza, Parc National de nat. park Cameroon
22 C2 Wazirabad Pak.
54 C3 W du Niger, Parcs Nationaux du nat. park Niger
66 B3 Weagamow L. l. Can.
39 H6 Weald, The reg. U.K.
38 E3 Wear r. U.K.
6 E3 Weary B. b. Austr.
77 D5 Weatherford U.S.A.
72 B3 Weaverville U.S.A.
69 G2 Webbwood Can.
66 C3 Webequie Can.
64 D3 Weber, Mt mt Can.
56 E3 Webi Shabeelle r. Somalia
81 H3 Webster MA U.S.A.
76 D2 Webster SD U.S.A.
68 A3 Webster WV U.S.A.
76 E3 Webster City U.S.A.
80 C5 Webster Springs U.S.A.
88 D8 Weddell I. i. Falkland Is
92 B2 Weddell Sea sea Ant.
8 D4 Wedderburn Austr.
43 H1 Wedel (Holstein) Ger.
72 B3 Weed U.S.A.
80 D4 Weedville U.S.A.
59 J4 Weenen S. Africa
42 F1 Weener Ger.
42 E2 Weerribben, Nationaal Park De nat. park Neth.
42 D3 Weert Neth.
8 F2 Weethalle Austr.
42 E3 Wegberg Ger.
47 K3 Węgorzewo Pol.
26 B2 Wei r. Henan China
26 D3 Wei r. Shaanxi China
26 E1 Weichang China
43 L4 Weida Ger.
43 K5 Weidenberg Ger.
43 L5 Weiden in der Oberpfalz Ger.
26 F2 Weifang China
30 B5 Weihai China
30 D2 Weihu Ling mts China
43 G4 Weilburg Ger.
43 K4 Weimar Ger.
26 C3 Weinan China
43 G5 Weinheim Ger.
27 B5 Weining China
43 H5 Weinsberg Ger.
6 E3 Weipa Austr.
65 L3 Weir River Can.
80 C4 Weirton U.S.A.
72 C2 Weiser U.S.A.
26 E3 Weishan China
26 E3 Weishan Hu l. China
26 E3 Weishi China
43 J5 Weißenburg in Bayern Ger.
43 K3 Weißenfels Ger.
79 C5 Weiss L. l. U.S.A.
58 C2 Weissrand Mts mts Namibia
43 G5 Weiterstadt Ger.
27 B5 Weixin China
26 B3 Weiyuan Gansu China
27 B4 Weiyuan Sichuan China
46 G7 Weiz Austria
27 C6 Weizhou Dao i. China
30 B3 Weizi China
46 J3 Wejherowo Pol.
65 K4 Wekusko Can.
65 K4 Wekusko Lake l. Can.
80 C6 Welch U.S.A.
81 H2 Weld U.S.A.
56 D2 Weldiya Eth.
74 C4 Weldon U.S.A.
56 D3 Welk'īt'ē Eth.
59 G3 Welkom S. Africa
69 H4 Welland Can.
39 G5 Welland r. U.K.
69 H4 Welland Canal canal Can.
21 C5 Wellawaya Sri Lanka
69 G4 Wellesley Can.
6 D3 Wellesley Is is Austr.
64 B2 Wellesley Lake l. Can.
81 H4 Wellfleet U.S.A.
42 D4 Wellin Belgium
39 G5 Wellingborough U.K.
8 G2 Wellington N.S.W. Austr.
8 B3 Wellington S.A. Austr.
9 E4 Wellington N.Z.
58 C6 Wellington S. Africa
39 D7 Wellington Eng. U.K.
39 E5 Wellington Eng. U.K.
72 F3 Wellington CO U.S.A.
77 D4 Wellington KS U.S.A.
74 C2 Wellington NV U.S.A.
80 B4 Wellington OH U.S.A.
77 C5 Wellington TX U.S.A.
75 G2 Wellington UT U.S.A.
88 A7 Wellington, I. i. Chile
8 F5 Wellington, L. l. Austr.
68 B5 Wellman U.S.A.
64 E4 Wells Can.
39 E6 Wells U.K.
72 D3 Wells NV U.S.A.
81 F3 Wells NY U.S.A.
80 E4 Wellsboro U.S.A.
9 E2 Wellsford N.Z.
64 E4 Wells Gray Prov. Park res. Can.
6 C4 Wells, L. salt flat Austr.
39 H5 Wells-next-the-Sea U.K.
80 B5 Wellston U.S.A.
80 E3 Wellsville U.S.A.
75 E5 Wellton U.S.A.
46 G6 Wels Austria
81 K2 Welshpool Can.
39 D5 Welshpool U.K.
43 M3 Welsickendorf Ger.
39 G6 Welwyn Garden City U.K.
43 H6 Welzheim Ger.
39 E5 Wem U.K.
59 H4 Wembesi S. Africa
64 F3 Wembley Can.
66 E3 Wemindji Can.
79 E7 Wemyss Bight Bahamas
26 F3 Wen r. China
72 B2 Wenatchee U.S.A.
27 D7 Wenchang China
27 F5 Wencheng China
54 B4 Wenchi Ghana
26 B4 Wenchuan China
43 K5 Wendelstein Ger.
43 F4 Wenden Ger.
75 F5 Wenden U.S.A.
30 B5 Wendeng China
56 D3 Wendo Eth.
72 D3 Wendover U.S.A.
69 F2 Wenebegon Lake l. Can.
27 C5 Weng'an China
27 E5 Wengyuan China
26 B4 Wenjiang China
27 F4 Wenling China
86 □ Wenman, Isla i. Galapagos Is Ecuador
68 C5 Wenona U.S.A.
27 B6 Wenshan China
39 H5 Wensum r. U.K.
43 J1 Wentorf bei Hamburg Ger.
8 C3 Wentworth Austr.
81 H3 Wentworth U.S.A.
26 B3 Wen Xian China
27 F5 Wenzhou China
43 L2 Wenzlow Ger.
59 G4 Wepener S. Africa
33 A1 We, Pulau i. Indon.
43 K2 Werben (Elbe) Ger.
58 E2 Werda Botswana
43 L4 Werdau Ger.
43 L2 Werder Ger.
43 F3 Werdohl Ger.
43 F3 Werl Ger.
43 L5 Wernberg-Köblitz Ger.
42 F3 Werne Ger.
64 C2 Wernecke Mountains Can.
43 J3 Wernigerode Ger.
43 H3 Werra r. Ger.
8 E4 Werribee Austr.
8 C3 Werrimull Austr.
8 H1 Werris Creek Austr.
43 H5 Wertheim Ger.
42 B4 Wervik Belgium
42 E3 Wesel Ger.
42 E3 Wesel-Datteln-Kanal canal Ger.
43 L1 Wesenberg Ger.
43 J2 Wesendorf Ger.
43 G1 Weser chan. Ger.
43 H2 Weser r. Ger.
43 G2 Wesergebirge h. Ger.
76 C4 Weskan U.S.A.
69 J3 Weslemkoon Lake l. Can.
81 K2 Wesley U.S.A.
67 K4 Wesleyville Can.
6 D3 Wessel, C. c. Austr.
6 D3 Wessel Is is Austr.
59 H3 Wesselton S. Africa
76 D2 Wessington Springs U.S.A.
68 C4 West Allis U.S.A.
92 A4 West Antarctica reg. Ant.
93 L5 West Australian Basin sea feature Ind. Ocean
93 L6 West Australian Ridge sea feature Ind. Ocean
22 B5 West Banas r. India
16 E5 West Bank terr. Asia
67 J3 West Bay Can.
77 F6 West Bay b. U.S.A.
68 C4 West Bend U.S.A.
23 F5 West Bengal div. India
69 E3 West Branch U.S.A.
80 D4 West Branch Susquehanna r. U.S.A.
39 F5 West Bromwich U.K.
81 H3 Westbrook U.S.A.
40 □ West Burra i. U.K.
39 E6 Westbury U.K.
8 F3 Westby Austr.
68 B4 Westby U.S.A.
94 E5 West Caroline Basin sea feature Pac. Oc.
81 F5 West Chester U.S.A.
81 G2 West Danville U.S.A.
69 F3 West Duck Island i. Can.
79 E7 West End Bahamas
74 D4 Westend U.S.A.
79 E7 West End Pt pt Bahamas
43 F4 Westerburg Ger.
42 F1 Westerholt Ger.
46 D3 Westerland Ger.
42 C3 Westerlo Belgium
81 H4 Westerly U.S.A.
65 H1 Western r. Can.
6 C4 Western Australia div. Austr.
58 D6 Western Cape div. S. Africa
55 E2 Western Desert des. Egypt
21 A2 Western Ghats mts India
8 E5 Western Port b. Austr.
52 C3 Western Sahara terr. Africa
5 K6 Western Samoa country Pac. Oc.
42 B3 Westerschelde est. Neth.
43 F1 Westerstede Ger.
43 F4 Westerwald reg. Ger.
88 D8 West Falkland i. Falkland Is
76 D2 West Fargo U.S.A.
68 D5 Westfield IN U.S.A.
81 G3 Westfield MA U.S.A.
81 K1 Westfield ME U.S.A.
80 D3 Westfield NY U.S.A.
42 E1 Westgat chan. Neth.
81 K2 West Grand Lake l. U.S.A.
43 J6 Westhausen Ger.
40 F3 Westhill U.K.
76 C1 Westhope U.S.A.
92 D5 West Ice Shelf ice feature Ant.
42 B3 Westkapelle Neth.
27 □ West Lamma Chan. H.K. China
80 B5 West Lancaster U.S.A.
9 B5 Westland National Park N.Z.
39 J5 Westleton U.K.
74 B3 Westley U.S.A.
80 B6 West Liberty KY U.S.A.
80 B4 West Liberty OH U.S.A.
40 E5 West Linton U.K.
40 B2 West Loch Roag b. U.K.
64 G4 Westlock Can.
69 G4 West Lorne Can.
42 C3 Westmalle Belgium
77 F5 West Memphis U.S.A.
80 E5 Westminster MD U.S.A.
79 D5 Westminster SC U.S.A.
80 C5 Weston U.S.A.
39 E6 Weston-super-Mare U.K.
81 F5 Westover U.S.A.
79 D7 West Palm Beach U.S.A.
77 F4 West Plains U.S.A.
77 F5 West Point MS U.S.A.
81 F4 West Point NY U.S.A.
69 J3 Westport Can.
9 C4 Westport N.Z.
41 B4 Westport Rep. of Ireland
74 A2 Westport U.S.A.
65 J4 Westray Can.
40 E1 Westray i. U.K.
69 G2 Westree Can.
42 F5 Westrich reg. Ger.
64 E4 West Road r. Can.
81 H2 West Stewartstown U.S.A.
42 D1 West-Terschelling Neth.
81 H4 West Tisbury U.S.A.
81 G2 West Topsham U.S.A.
81 G3 West Townshend U.S.A.
68 B4 West Union IA U.S.A.
80 B5 West Union OH U.S.A.
80 C5 West Union WV U.S.A.
68 D5 Westville U.S.A.
80 C5 West Virginia div. U.S.A.
74 C2 West Walker r. U.S.A.
74 B1 Westwood U.S.A.
8 F2 West Wyalong Austr.
72 E2 West Yellowstone U.S.A.
42 C2 Westzaan Neth.
25 E7 Wetar i. Indon.
64 G4 Wetaskiwin Can.
68 D2 Wetmore U.S.A.
43 G4 Wetter r. Ger.
43 K3 Wettin Ger.
43 G4 Wetzlar Ger.
6 E2 Wewak P.N.G.
41 E5 Wexford Rep. of Ireland
65 H4 Weyakwin Can.
68 C3 Weyauwega U.S.A.
39 G6 Weybridge U.K.
65 J5 Weyburn Can.
43 G2 Weyhe Ger.
39 E7 Weymouth U.K.
81 H3 Weymouth U.S.A.
42 E2 Wezep Neth.
9 F2 Whakatane N.Z.
9 F3 Whakatane r. N.Z.
32 A3 Whale B. b. Myanmar
64 B3 Whale B. b. U.S.A.
79 E7 Whale Cay i. Bahamas
65 L2 Whale Cove Can.
40 □ Whalsay i. U.K.
9 E2 Whangamata N.Z.
9 E3 Whangamomona N.Z.
9 E1 Whangarei N.Z.
66 E2 Whapmagoostui Can.
38 F4 Wharfe r. U.K.
69 F2 Wharncliffe Can.
65 J2 Wharton Lake l. Can.
68 A5 What Cheer U.S.A.
72 F3 Wheatland U.S.A.
68 C5 Wheaton U.S.A.
73 F4 Wheeler Peak summit NM U.S.A.
75 E2 Wheeler Peak summit NV U.S.A.
80 C4 Wheeling U.S.A.
91 E2 Wheelwright Arg.
38 E3 Whernside h. U.K.

72 B3 Whiskeytown-Shasta-Trinity Nat. Recreation Area res. U.S.A.
40 E5 Whitburn U.K.
69 H4 Whitby Can.
38 G3 Whitby U.K.
39 E5 Whitchurch U.K.
64 A2 White r. AK/Y.T. Can./U.S.A.
77 E4 White r. AR U.S.A.
75 G5 White r. AZ U.S.A.
72 E3 White r. CO U.S.A.
78 C4 White r. IN U.S.A.
68 D4 White r. MI U.S.A.
75 E2 White r. NV U.S.A.
76 C3 White r. SD U.S.A.
68 B2 White r. WV U.S.A.
67 J3 White Bay b. Can.
76 C2 White Butte mt U.S.A.
68 E4 White Cloud U.S.A.
64 F4 Whitecourt Can.
68 A2 Whiteface Lake l. U.S.A.
81 H2 Whitefield U.S.A.
69 G2 Whitefish Can.
72 D1 Whitefish MT U.S.A.
68 D3 Whitefish r. MI U.S.A.
65 H2 Whitefish Lake l. Can.
68 E2 Whitefish Pt pt U.S.A.
41 D5 Whitehall Rep. of Ireland
40 F1 Whitehall U.K.
81 G3 Whitehall NY U.S.A.
68 B3 Whitehall WV U.S.A.
38 D3 Whitehaven U.K.
41 F3 Whitehead U.K.
39 G6 Whitehill U.K.
64 B2 Whitehorse Can.
75 E1 White Horse Pass U.S.A.
39 F6 White Horse, Vale of v. U.K.
92 D4 White I. i. Ant.
9 F2 White I. i. N.Z.
77 E6 White L. l. LA U.S.A.
68 D4 White L. l. MI U.S.A.
6 C4 White, L. salt flat Austr.
81 H2 White Mountains mts U.S.A.
74 C3 White Mt Peak summit U.S.A.
55 F3 White Nile r. Sudan/Uganda
58 C1 White Nossob watercourse Namibia
75 E2 White Pine Range mts U.S.A.
81 G4 White Plains U.S.A.
66 C4 White River Can.
75 H5 Whiteriver U.S.A.
81 G3 White River Junction U.S.A.
75 E2 White River Valley v. U.S.A.
75 E2 White Rock Peak summit U.S.A.
73 F5 White Sands Nat. Mon. res. U.S.A.
80 B6 Whitesburg U.S.A.
12 E3 White Sea g. Rus. Fed.
65 K4 Whiteshell Prov. Park res. Can.
72 E2 White Sulphur Springs MT U.S.A.
80 C6 White Sulphur Springs WV U.S.A.
79 E5 Whiteville U.S.A.
54 B4 White Volta r. Ghana
68 C4 Whitewater U.S.A.
66 C3 Whitewater L. l. Can.
65 J4 Whitewood Can.
8 F4 Whitfield Austr.
39 J6 Whitfield U.K.
40 D6 Whithorn U.K.
9 E2 Whitianga N.Z.
81 K2 Whiting U.S.A.
39 C6 Whitland U.K.
38 F2 Whitley Bay U.K.
79 D5 Whitmire U.S.A.
69 H3 Whitney Can.
74 C3 Whitney, Mt mt U.S.A.
81 K2 Whitneyville U.S.A.
39 J6 Whitstable U.K.
6 E4 Whitsunday I. i. Austr.
8 E4 Whittlesea Austr.
39 G5 Whittlesey U.K.
8 F3 Whitton Austr.
65 H2 Wholdaia Lake l. Can.
75 F5 Why U.S.A.
8 A2 Whyalla Austr.
32 A1 Wiang Phran Thai.
32 B1 Wiang Sa Thai.
69 G3 Wiarton Can.
42 B3 Wichelen Belgium
77 D4 Wichita U.S.A.
77 D5 Wichita Falls U.S.A.
77 D5 Wichita Mts mts U.S.A.
40 E2 Wick U.K.
75 F5 Wickenburg U.S.A.
39 H6 Wickford U.K.
41 E5 Wicklow Rep. of Ireland
41 F5 Wicklow Head hd Rep. of Ireland
41 E5 Wicklow Mountains Rep. of Ireland
41 E4 Wicklow Mountains National Park Rep. of Ireland
39 E4 Widnes U.K.
30 D6 Wi-do i. S. Korea
43 G2 Wiehengebirge h. Ger.
42 F4 Wiehl Ger.
47 J5 Wieluń Pol.
Wien see Vienna
46 H7 Wiener Neustadt Austria
42 E2 Wierden Neth.
43 J2 Wieren Ger.
42 C2 Wieringermeer Polder reclaimed land Neth.
42 D2 Wieringerwerf Neth.
43 G4 Wiesbaden Ger.
43 L5 Wiesenfelden Ger.
43 J5 Wiesentheid Ger.
43 G5 Wiesloch Ger.
43 F1 Wiesmoor Ger.
43 H2 Wietze Ger.
43 H2 Wietzendorf Ger.
46 J3 Wieżyca h. Pol.
38 E4 Wigan U.K.
77 F6 Wiggins U.S.A.
39 F7 Wight, Isle of i. U.K.
65 H2 Wignes Lake l. Can.
39 F5 Wigston U.K.
38 D3 Wigton U.K.
40 D6 Wigtown U.K.
40 D6 Wigtown Bay b. U.K.
42 D3 Wijchen Neth.
42 E2 Wijhe Neth.
42 C3 Wijnegem Belgium
75 F4 Wikieup U.S.A.
69 G3 Wikwemikong Can.
72 C2 Wilbur U.S.A.
8 D1 Wilcannia Austr.
43 L2 Wildberg Ger.
65 J4 Wildcat Hill Wilderness Area res. Can.
74 D2 Wildcat Peak summit U.S.A.
59 H5 Wild Coast coastal area S. Africa
43 G2 Wildeshausen Ger.
68 C1 Wild Goose Can.
64 F4 Wildhay r. Can.
68 A2 Wild Rite Lake l. U.S.A.
46 E7 Wildspitze mt Austria
79 D6 Wildwood FL U.S.A.
81 F5 Wildwood NJ U.S.A.
59 H3 Wilge r. Free State S. Africa
59 H2 Wilge r. Gauteng/Mpumalanga S. Africa
92 C5 Wilhelm II Land reg. Ant.
80 C4 Wilhelm, Lake l. U.S.A.
6 E2 Wilhelm, Mt mt P.N.G.
43 G1 Wilhelmshaven Ger.
81 F4 Wilkes-Barre U.S.A.
92 B6 Wilkes Coast coastal area Ant.
92 B6 Wilkes Land reg. Ant.
65 H4 Wilkie Can.
92 B2 Wilkins Coast coastal area Ant.
92 B2 Wilkins Ice Shelf ice feature Ant.
72 B2 Willamette r. U.S.A.
39 D7 Willand U.K.
8 E2 Willandra Billabong r. Austr.
72 B1 Willapa B. b. U.S.A.
80 B4 Willard U.S.A.
81 F5 Willards U.S.A.
75 H5 Willcox U.S.A.
43 H3 Willebadessen Ger.
42 C3 Willebroek Belgium
83 L6 Willemstad Neth. Ant.
65 H3 William r. Can.
8 D4 William, Mt mt Austr.
75 F4 Williams AZ U.S.A.
74 A2 Williams CA U.S.A.
68 A5 Williamsburg IA U.S.A.
80 A6 Williamsburg KY U.S.A.
68 E3 Williamsburg MI U.S.A.
80 E6 Williamsburg VA U.S.A.
79 E7 Williams I. i. Bahamas
64 E4 Williams Lake Can.
67 H1 William Smith, Cap c. Can.
80 E3 Williamson NY U.S.A.
80 B6 Williamson WV U.S.A.
68 D5 Williamsport IN U.S.A.
80 E4 Williamsport PA U.S.A.
79 E5 Williamston U.S.A.
81 G3 Williamstown MA U.S.A.
81 F3 Williamstown NY U.S.A.
80 C5 Williamstown WV U.S.A.
81 G4 Willimantic U.S.A.
58 D5 Williston S. Africa
79 D6 Williston FL U.S.A.
76 C1 Williston ND U.S.A.
64 E3 Williston Lake l. Can.
39 D6 Williton U.K.
74 A2 Willits U.S.A.
76 E2 Willmar U.S.A.
64 F4 Willmore Wilderness Prov. Park res. Can.
64 D3 Will, Mt mt Can.
8 A1 Willochra r. Austr.
64 E4 Willow r. Can.
65 H5 Willow Bunch Can.
80 E4 Willow Hill U.S.A.
64 F2 Willow Lake l. Can.
58 E6 Willowmore S. Africa
68 C3 Willow Reservoir U.S.A.
74 A2 Willows U.S.A.
77 F4 Willow Springs U.S.A.
8 H1 Willow Tree Austr.
59 H6 Willowvale S. Africa
81 G2 Willsboro U.S.A.
6 C4 Wills, L. salt flat Austr.
8 B3 Willunga Austr.
8 B2 Wilmington Austr.
81 F5 Wilmington DE U.S.A.
79 E5 Wilmington NC U.S.A.
80 B5 Wilmington OH U.S.A.
81 G3 Wilmington VT U.S.A.
39 E4 Wilmslow U.K.
43 G4 Wilnsdorf Ger.
8 B1 Wilpena r. Austr.
43 H1 Wilseder Berg h. Ger.
76 D4 Wilson KS U.S.A.
79 E5 Wilson NC U.S.A.
92 B5 Wilson Hills h. Ant.
73 F4 Wilson, Mt mt CO U.S.A.
75 E2 Wilson, Mt mt NV U.S.A.
76 D4 Wilson Res. resr U.S.A.
81 H2 Wilsons Mills U.S.A.
8 F5 Wilson's Promontory pen. Austr.
8 F5 Wilson's Promontory Nat. Park Austr.
42 E2 Wilsum Ger.
68 B5 Wilton IA U.S.A.
81 H2 Wilton ME U.S.A.
42 D5 Wiltz Lux.
6 C4 Wiluna Austr.
39 J7 Wimereux France
8 D4 Wimmera r. Austr.
68 D5 Winamac U.S.A.
59 G4 Winburg S. Africa
39 E6 Wincanton U.K.
81 G3 Winchendon U.S.A.
66 E4 Winchester Can.
39 F6 Winchester U.K.
68 B6 Winchester IL U.S.A.
68 E5 Winchester IN U.S.A.
80 A6 Winchester KY U.S.A.
81 G3 Winchester NH U.S.A.
79 C5 Winchester TN U.S.A.
80 D5 Winchester VA U.S.A.
62 E3 Wind r. N.W.T. Can.
72 E3 Wind r. U.S.A.
76 C3 Wind Cave Nat. Park U.S.A.
38 E3 Windermere U.K.
38 E3 Windermere l. U.K.
57 B6 Windhoek Namibia
76 E3 Windom U.S.A.
6 E4 Windorah Austr.
75 H4 Window Rock U.S.A.
68 D4 Wind Pt pt U.S.A.
72 E3 Wind River Range mts U.S.A.
39 F6 Windrush r. U.K.
43 J5 Windsbach Ger.
8 H2 Windsor Austr.
67 J4 Windsor Nfld Can.
67 H5 Windsor N.S. Can.
69 F4 Windsor Ont. Can.
67 F4 Windsor Que. Can.
39 G6 Windsor U.K.
81 G4 Windsor CT U.S.A.
79 E5 Windsor NC U.S.A.
81 F3 Windsor NY U.S.A.
80 E6 Windsor VA U.S.A.
81 G3 Windsor VT U.S.A.
81 G4 Windsor Locks U.S.A.
83 M5 Windward Islands is Caribbean Sea
83 K5 Windward Passage chan. Cuba/Haiti
79 C5 Winfield AL U.S.A.
68 B5 Winfield IA U.S.A.
77 D4 Winfield KS U.S.A.
38 F3 Wingate U.K.
8 H1 Wingen Austr.
42 B3 Wingene Belgium
42 F6 Wingen-sur-Moder France
69 G4 Wingham Can.
66 C2 Winisk Can.
66 C2 Winisk r. Can.
66 C3 Winisk L. l. Can.
66 C3 Winisk River Provincial Park res. Can.
32 A2 Winkana Myanmar
65 K5 Winkler Can.
81 J2 Winn U.S.A.
54 B4 Winneba Ghana
68 C3 Winnebago, Lake l. U.S.A.
68 C3 Winneconne U.S.A.
72 C3 Winnemucca U.S.A.
74 C1 Winnemucca Lake l. U.S.A.
76 D3 Winner U.S.A.
77 E6 Winnfield U.S.A.
76 E2 Winnibigoshish L. l. U.S.A.
65 K5 Winnipeg Can.
65 K4 Winnipeg r. Can.
65 K4 Winnipeg, Lake l. Can.
65 J4 Winnipegosis Can.
65 J4 Winnipegosis, Lake l. Can.
81 H3 Winnipesaukee, L. l. U.S.A.
77 F5 Winnsboro U.S.A.
75 G4 Winona AZ U.S.A.
68 C2 Winona MI U.S.A.
68 B3 Winona MN U.S.A.
77 F5 Winona MS U.S.A.
81 G2 Winooski U.S.A.
81 G2 Winooski r. U.S.A.
42 F1 Winschoten Neth.
43 H2 Winsen (Aller) Ger.
43 J1 Winsen (Luhe) Ger.
39 E4 Winsford U.K.
75 G4 Winslow U.S.A.
81 G4 Winsted U.S.A.
79 D4 Winston-Salem U.S.A.
43 G3 Winterberg Ger.
79 D6 Winter Haven U.S.A.
81 J2 Winterport U.S.A.
74 B2 Winters U.S.A.
42 E3 Winterswijk Neth.
46 D7 Winterthur Switz.
59 H4 Winterton S. Africa
81 J1 Winterville U.S.A.
81 J2 Winthrop U.S.A.
6 E4 Winton Austr.
9 B7 Winton N.Z.
39 G5 Winwick U.K.
8 B2 Wirrabara Austr.
39 D4 Wirral pen. U.K.
8 C4 Wirrega Austr.
39 H5 Wisbech U.K.
81 J2 Wiscasset U.S.A.
43 H1 Wischhafen Ger.
68 C3 Wisconsin div. U.S.A.
68 B4 Wisconsin r. U.S.A.
68 C4 Wisconsin Dells U.S.A.
68 C4 Wisconsin, Lake l. U.S.A.
68 C3 Wisconsin Rapids U.S.A.
80 B6 Wise U.S.A.
40 E5 Wishaw U.K.
47 J4 Wisła r. Pol.
46 E4 Wismar Ger.
39 J7 Wissant France
68 B3 Wissota L. l. U.S.A.
64 D4 Wistaria Can.
59 H2 Witbank S. Africa
58 C2 Witbooisvlei Namibia
39 H6 Witham U.K.
39 G4 Witham r. U.K.
81 G2 Witherbee U.S.A.
38 H4 Withernsea U.K.
42 D1 Witmarsum Neth.
39 F6 Witney U.K.
59 J2 Witrivier S. Africa
42 C5 Witry-lès-Reims France
59 G5 Witteberg mts S. Africa
68 C3 Wittenberg U.S.A.
43 K2 Wittenberge Ger.
43 K1 Wittenburg Ger.
44 H3 Wittenheim France
43 J2 Wittingen Ger.
42 E5 Wittlich Ger.
43 F1 Wittmund Ger.
43 L1 Wittstock Ger.
6 E2 Witu Is is P.N.G.
57 B6 Witvlei Namibia
43 H3 Witzenhausen Ger.
30 D3 Wiwon N. Korea
46 J3 Władysławowo Pol.
47 J4 Włocławek Pol.
81 H2 Woburn Can.
8 F4 Wodonga Austr.
43 F6 Woerth France
42 D5 Woëvre, Plaine de la plain France
43 G4 Wohra r. Ger.
42 E5 Woippy France
25 F7 Wokam i. Indon.
28 B1 Woken r. China
23 H4 Wokha India
39 G6 Woking U.K.
39 G6 Wokingham U.K.
68 D5 Wolcott IN U.S.A.
80 E3 Wolcott NY U.S.A.
43 M1 Woldegk Ger.
42 F1 Woldendorp Neth.
64 C2 Wolf r. Can.
68 C3 Wolf r. U.S.A.
72 D2 Wolf Creek U.S.A.
73 F4 Wolf Creek Pass pass U.S.A.
81 H3 Wolfeboro U.S.A.
69 J3 Wolfe I. i. Can.
43 L3 Wolfen Ger.
43 J2 Wolfenbüttel Ger.
43 H3 Wolfhagen Ger.
64 C2 Wolf Lake l. Can.
72 F1 Wolf Point U.S.A.
46 G7 Wolfsberg Austria
43 J2 Wolfsburg Ger.
42 F5 Wolfstein Ger.
67 H4 Wolfville Can.
86 Wolf, Volcán volc. Galapagos Is Ecuador
46 F3 Wolgast Ger.
46 G4 Wolin Pol.
88 C9 Wollaston, Islas is Chile
65 J3 Wollaston Lake Can.
65 J3 Wollaston Lake l. Can.
62 G3 Wollaston Peninsula Can.
8 H3 Wollongong Austr.
59 F3 Wolmaransstad S. Africa
43 K2 Wolmirstedt Ger.
8 C4 Wolseley Austr.
58 C6 Wolseley S. Africa
38 F3 Wolsingham U.K.
42 E2 Wolvega Neth.
39 E5 Wolverhampton U.K.
68 E3 Wolverine U.S.A.
42 C3 Wommelgem Belgium
42 F5 Womrather Höhe h. Ger.
8 E1 Wongalarroo Lake l. Austr.
8 G2 Wongarbon Austr.
23 G4 Wong Chu r. Bhutan
27 Wong Chuk Hang H.K. China
30 D5 Wŏnju S. Korea
8 F4 Wonnangatta Moroka Nat. Park Austr.
30 D4 Wŏnsan N. Korea
8 E5 Wonthaggi Austr.
6 D3 Woodah, Isle i. Austr.
39 J5 Woodbridge U.K.
80 E5 Woodbridge U.S.A.
64 G3 Wood Buffalo National Park Can.
72 B2 Woodburn U.S.A.
68 E4 Woodbury MI U.S.A.
81 F5 Woodbury NJ U.S.A.
80 A6 Wood Creek Lake l. U.S.A.
74 C2 Woodfords U.S.A.
74 C3 Woodlake U.S.A.
74 B2 Woodland U.S.A.
73 F4 Woodland Park U.S.A.
32 Woodlands Sing.
7 F2 Woodlark I. i. P.N.G.
6 D4 Woodroffe, Mt mt Austr.
72 E3 Woodruff U.S.A.
80 C5 Woodsfield U.S.A.
8 F5 Woodside Austr.
6 D3 Woods, L. salt flat Austr.
65 L5 Woods, Lake of the l. Can./U.S.A.
8 F4 Woods Pt Austr.
67 G4 Woodstock N.B. Can.
69 G4 Woodstock Ont. Can.
68 C4 Woodstock IL U.S.A.
80 D5 Woodstock VA U.S.A.
81 F5 Woodstown U.S.A.
81 G2 Woodsville U.S.A.
9 E4 Woodville N.Z.
80 E3 Woodville NY U.S.A.
77 E6 Woodville TX U.S.A.
77 D4 Woodward U.S.A.
38 E2 Wooler U.K.
6 D5 Woomera Austr.
81 H4 Woonsocket U.S.A.
80 C4 Wooster U.S.A.
43 J3 Worbis Ger.
58 C6 Worcester S. Africa
39 E5 Worcester U.K.
81 H3 Worcester U.S.A.
46 F7 Wörgl Austria
38 D3 Workington U.K.
39 F4 Worksop U.K.
42 D2 Workum Neth.
72 F2 Worland U.S.A.
43 L3 Wörlitz Ger.
42 C2 Wormerveer Neth.
43 G5 Worms Ger.
39 C6 Worms Head hd U.K.
58 B1 Wortel Namibia
43 G5 Wörth am Rhein Ger.
39 G7 Worthing U.K.
76 E3 Worthington U.S.A.
95 G5 Wotje i. Pac. Oc.
25 E7 Wotu Indon.
42 C3 Woudrichem Neth.
76 C3 Wounded Knee U.S.A.
42 F5 Woustviller France
25 E7 Wowoni i. Indon.
64 C3 Wrangell U.S.A.
64 C3 Wrangell I. i. U.S.A.
62 C4 Wrangell Mountains U.S.A.
40 C2 Wrath, Cape c. U.K.
76 C3 Wray U.S.A.
39 F5 Wreake r. U.K.
58 B4 Wreck Point pt S. Africa
43 J2 Wrestedt Ger.
39 E4 Wrexham U.K.
31 C4 Wright Phil.
72 F3 Wright U.S.A.
77 E5 Wright Patman L. l. U.S.A.
75 G6 Wrightson, Mt mt U.S.A.
64 E2 Wrigley Can.
46 H5 Wrocław Pol.
46 H4 Września Pol.
26 E2 Wu'an China
26 D2 Wubu China
30 D1 Wuchang Heilongjiang China
27 E4 Wuchang Hubei China
27 D6 Wuchuan Guangdong China
27 C4 Wuchuan Guizhou China
26 D1 Wuchuan Nei Monggol China
26 C2 Wuda China
26 D3 Wudang Shan mt China
26 C3 Wudang Shan mts China
30 A4 Wudao China
23 H2 Wudaoliang China
26 E2 Wudi China
27 B5 Wuding China
26 D2 Wuding r. China
26 B3 Wudu China
27 D4 Wufeng China
27 D5 Wugang China
26 C3 Wugong China
26 C2 Wuhai China
27 E4 Wuhan China
26 E3 Wuhe China
26 F4 Wuhu China
27 E6 Wuhua China
22 D2 Wūjang China
27 C6 Wujia China
27 C4 Wu Jiang r. China
54 C4 Wukari Nigeria
23 H3 Wulang China
22 C2 Wular L. l. India
30 B5 Wuleidao Wan l. China
26 F3 Wulian China
27 B4 Wulian Feng mts China
24 C4 Wuliang Shan mts China
25 F7 Wuliaru i. Indon.
27 C4 Wuling Shan mts China
27 C4 Wulong China
27 B5 Wumeng Shan mts China
27 C6 Wuming China
43 H1 Wümme r. Ger.
26 A4 Wungda China
27 E4 Wuning China
43 G3 Wünnenberg Ger.
43 L4 Wunsiedel Ger.
43 H2 Wunstorf Ger.
24 B4 Wuntho Myanmar
75 G4 Wupatki National Monument res. U.S.A.
27 E5 Wuping China
42 F3 Wuppertal Ger.
58 C6 Wuppertal S. Africa
26 C2 Wuqi China
26 E2 Wuqiao China
26 E2 Wuqing China
43 H5 Würzburg Ger.
43 L3 Wurzen Ger.
26 B3 Wushan Gansu China
26 C4 Wushan Sichuan China
26 D4 Wu Shan mts China
27 C4 Wusheng China
27 C6 Wushi China
43 H3 Wüstegarten h. Ger.
Wusuli Jiang r. see Ussuri
26 D2 Wutai China
26 D2 Wutai Shan mt China
6 E2 Wuvulu I. i. P.N.G.
26 E4 Wuwei Anhui China
26 B2 Wuwei Gansu China
26 F4 Wuxi Jiangsu China
26 C4 Wuxi Sichuan China
Wuxing see Huzhou
27 C6 Wuxu China
27 C6 Wuxuan China
26 D3 Wuyang China
27 F4 Wuyi China
24 E2 Wuyiling China
27 E5 Wuyi Shan mts China
27 E4 Wuyuan Jiangxi China
26 C1 Wuyuan Nei Monggol China
26 D2 Wuzhai China
26 D4 Wuzhen China
26 C2 Wuzhong China
27 D6 Wuzhou China
68 B5 Wyaconda r. U.S.A.
8 F2 Wyalong Austr.
69 F4 Wyandotte U.S.A.
68 C5 Wyanet U.S.A.
8 G2 Wyangala Reservoir Austr.
8 D4 Wycheproof Austr.
39 E6 Wye r. U.K.
39 F6 Wylye r. U.K.
39 J5 Wymondham U.K.
6 C3 Wyndham Austr.
77 F5 Wynne U.S.A.
62 G2 Wynniatt Bay b. Can.
65 J4 Wynyard Can.
68 C5 Wyoming IL U.S.A.
68 E4 Wyoming MI U.S.A.
72 E3 Wyoming div. U.S.A.
72 E3 Wyoming Peak summit U.S.A.
8 H2 Wyong Austr.
8 D3 Wyperfeld Nat. Park Austr.
38 E4 Wyre r. U.K.
81 E4 Wysox U.S.A.
47 K4 Wyszków Pol.
39 F5 Wythall U.K.
80 C6 Wytheville U.S.A.
81 J2 Wytopitlock U.S.A.

X

56 F2 Xaafuun Somalia
17 M1 Xaçmaz Azer.
58 E1 Xade Botswana
23 H3 Xagquka China
22 D1 Xaidulla China
23 G3 Xainza China
57 D6 Xai Xai Moz.
Xalapa see Jalapa Enríquez
25 C4 Xam Hua Laos
32 B1 Xan r. Laos
57 C6 Xanagas Botswana
26 B1 Xangd China
26 D1 Xangdin Hural China
57 B5 Xangongo Angola
17 L2 Xankändi Azer.
49 L4 Xanthi Greece
32 C2 Xan, Xé r. Vietnam
86 E6 Xapuri Brazil
17 M2 Xaraba Şähär Sayı i. Azer.
17 M2 Xärä Zirä Adası is Azer.
23 F3 Xarba La pass China
26 B1 Xar Burd China
26 F1 Xar Moron r. Nei Monggol China
26 D1 Xar Moron r. Nei Monggol China
45 F3 Xàtiva Spain
57 C6 Xau, Lake l. Botswana
87 J6 Xavantes, Serra dos h. Brazil
32 C3 Xa Vo Đat Vietnam
80 B5 Xenia U.S.A.
30 A3 Xi r. China
30 F1 Xiachengzi China
27 D6 Xiachuan Dao i. China
26 B3 Xiahe China
27 E5 Xiajiang China
26 E2 Xiajin China
27 F5 Xiamen China
26 C3 Xi'an China
26 E3 Xiancheng China
26 C2 Xianchengbu China
27 C4 Xianfeng China
26 D3 Xiangcheng China
26 D3 Xiangfan China
26 D1 Xianghuang Qi China
32 B1 Xiangkhoang Laos
22 D3 Xiangquan He r. China
27 F4 Xiangshan China
27 D5 Xiangtan China
27 D5 Xiangxiang China
27 D4 Xiangyin China
27 F4 Xianju China
27 E4 Xianning China
27 E5 Xianxia Ling mts China
26 E2 Xian Xian China
26 C3 Xianyang China
27 F5 Xianyou China
27 C6 Xiaodong China
27 D4 Xiaogan China
24 E1 Xiao Hinggan Ling mts China
26 B4 Xiaojin China
23 H2 Xiaonanchuan China
27 F4 Xiaoshan China
27 E5 Xiaotao China
26 E2 Xiaowutai Shan mt China
26 E3 Xiao Xian China
27 B4 Xiaoxiang Ling mts China
26 D2 Xiaoyi China
27 F5 Xiapu China
30 A2 Xiawa China
26 D3 Xiayukou China
27 B5 Xichang China
26 B4 Xichong China
27 B6 Xichou China
26 D3 Xichuan China
27 B4 Xide China
89 D4 Xié r. Brazil
27 C6 Xieyang Dao i. China
26 E3 Xifei He r. China
27 C5 Xifeng Guizhou China
30 C2 Xifeng Liaoning China
26 C3 Xifengzhen China
15 G4 Xigazê China
26 C3 Xihan Shui r. China
26 B3 Xihe China
26 A1 Xi He watercourse China
26 B3 Xiji China
27 D6 Xi Jiang r. China
23 G2 Xijir China
23 G2 Xijir Ulan Hu salt l. China
26 B2 Xijishui China
26 D1 Xil China
30 B2 Xiliao r. China
27 B5 Xilin China
26 E1 Xilinhot China
26 D1 Xilin Qagan Obo Mongolia
26 A1 Ximiao China
27 F4 Xin'anjiang China
27 F4 Xin'anjiang Sk. resr China
59 K2 Xinavane Moz.
30 C3 Xinbin China
26 E3 Xincai China
27 F4 Xinchang China
26 A2 Xincheng Gansu China
27 C5 Xincheng Guangxi China
26 C2 Xincheng Ningxia China
26 C2 Xinchengbu China
27 D6 Xindu Guangxi China
26 B4 Xindu Sichuan China
27 E5 Xinfeng Guangdong China
27 E5 Xinfeng Jiangxi China
27 E6 Xinfengjiang Sk. resr China
27 E5 Xingan China
27 D5 Xing'an China
30 A4 Xingangzhen China
26 F1 Xingcheng China
27 E5 Xingguo China
15 H3 Xinghai China
26 D1 Xinghe China
26 F3 Xinghua China
27 F5 Xinghua Wan b. China
28 C2 Xingkai China
27 E5 Xingning China
27 D4 Xingou China
26 C3 Xingping China
27 B5 Xingren China
26 A3 Xingsagoinba China
26 D4 Xingshan China
26 E2 Xingtai China
87 H4 Xingu r. Brazil
87 H6 Xingu, Parque Indígena do nat. park Brazil
27 B4 Xingwen China
26 D2 Xing Xian China
26 D3 Xingyang China
27 B5 Xingyi China
27 E4 Xingzi China
27 D5 Xinhua China
26 B2 Xinhuacun China
27 C5 Xinhuang China
27 D6 Xinhui China
26 A2 Xining China
27 E4 Xinjian China
26 D3 Xinjiang China
24 A2 Xinjiang Uygur Zizhiqu div. China
26 C2 Xinjie China
27 B4 Xinjin Sichuan China
30 B4 Xinjin China
30 B1 Xinkai r. China
30 B3 Xinmin China
27 D5 Xinning China
27 A5 Xinping China
27 E5 Xinquan China
27 D5 Xinshao China
26 E3 Xintai China
27 D5 Xintian China
26 E4 Xin Xian Henan China
26 D2 Xin Xian Shanxi China
26 D3 Xinxiang China
27 D6 Xinxing China
26 E3 Xinyang Henan China
26 E3 Xinyang Henan China
26 D3 Xinye China
26 F3 Xinyi r. China
27 D6 Xinyi Guangdong China
26 F3 Xinyi Jiangsu China
27 C7 Xinying China
27 E5 Xinyu China
26 D2 Xinzhou China
45 C1 Xinzo de Limia Spain
30 B3 Xiongyuecheng China
26 D3 Xiping Henan China
26 E3 Xiping Henan China
26 A3 Xiqing Shan mts China
87 K6 Xique Xique Brazil
27 C4 Xishui Guizhou China
27 E4 Xishui Hubei China
24 D2 Xi Ujimqin Qi China
27 F4 Xiuning China
27 C4 Xiushan China
27 E4 Xiushui China
27 E4 Xiu Shui r. China
27 C5 Xiuwen China
26 D3 Xiuwu China
30 B3 Xiuyan China
27 D6 Xiuying China
23 F3 Xixabangma Feng mt China
26 D3 Xixia China
26 E3 Xi Xian Henan China
26 D2 Xi Xian Shanxi China
26 C3 Xi Xiang China
27 F5 Xiyang Dao i. China
27 B5 Xiyang Jiang r. China
15 G3 Xizang Gaoyuan plat. China
24 B3 Xizang Zizhiqu div. China
30 A4 Xizhong Dao i. China
23 H3 Xoka China
32 C3 Xom An Lôc Vietnam
32 C3 Xom Duc Hanh Vietnam
26 F4 Xuancheng China
27 C4 Xuan'en China
26 C4 Xuanhan China
26 B2 Xuanhepu China
26 E1 Xuanhua China
32 C3 Xuân Lôc Vietnam
27 B5 Xuanwei China
26 D3 Xuchang China
17 M1 Xudat Azer.
56 E3 Xuddur Somalia
27 C5 Xuefeng Shan mts China
23 H2 Xugui China
23 E2 Xungba China
23 F3 Xungru China
26 C3 Xun He r. China
27 D6 Xun Jiang r. China
27 E5 Xunwu China
26 E3 Xun Xian China
26 C3 Xunyang China
26 C3 Xunyi China
27 D5 Xupu China
23 F3 Xuru Co salt l. China
26 E2 Xushui China
27 D6 Xuwen China
26 F3 Xuyi China
27 B4 Xuyong China
26 E3 Xuzhou China

Y

27 B4 Ya'an China
8 D3 Yaapeet Austr.
54 C4 Yabassi Cameroon
56 D3 Yabēlo Eth.
24 C1 Yablonovyy Khrebet mts Rus. Fed.
26 B2 Yabrai Shan mts China
26 B2 Yabrai Yanchang China
16 F5 Yabrūd Syria
30 E1 Yabuli China
89 C2 Yacambu, Parque Nacional nat. park Venez.
27 C7 Yacheng China
27 C5 Yachi He r. China
86 E6 Yacuma r. Bol.
21 B2 Yadgir India
71 K4 Yadkin r. NC U.S.A.
50 H4 Yadrin Rus. Fed.
28 G2 Yagishiri-tō i. Japan
18 D2 Yagman Turkm.
55 D3 Yagoua Cameroon
23 E3 Yagra China
23 H2 Yagradagzê Shan mt China
91 F1 Yaguari r. Uru.
Yaguarón r. see Jaguarão
32 B4 Yaha Thai.
16 D2 Yahşihan Turkey
16 E2 Yahyalı Turkey
19 H4 Yahya Wana Afgh.
29 F6 Yaita Japan
29 F7 Yaizu Japan
27 A4 Yajiang China
16 F3 Yakacık Turkey
19 G4 Yakhehal Afgh.
72 B2 Yakima U.S.A.
72 B2 Yakima r. U.S.A.
18 D3 Yakinish Iran
19 G2 Yakkabag Uzbek.
19 F4 Yakmach Pak.
54 B3 Yako Burkina
64 B3 Yakobi I. i. U.S.A.
28 C2 Yakovlevka Rus. Fed.
28 G3 Yakumo Japan
29 B9 Yaku-shima i. Japan
64 B3 Yakutat U.S.A.
64 B3 Yakutat Bay b. U.S.A.
13 O3 Yakutsk Rus. Fed.
51 E6 Yakymivka Ukr.
32 B4 Yala Thai.
69 F4 Yale U.S.A.
8 F5 Yallourn Austr.
27 A5 Yalong Jiang r. China
16 B1 Yalova Turkey
51 F6 Yalta Donets'k Ukr.
51 E6 Yalta Krym Ukr.
30 C3 Yalu Jiang r. China/N. Korea
30 C4 Yalujiang Kou river mouth N. Korea
16 C2 Yalvaç Turkey
28 G5 Yamada Japan
28 G5 Yamagata Japan
29 B9 Yamagawa Japan
29 B7 Yamaguchi Japan
12 H2 Yamal, Poluostrov pen. Rus. Fed.
65 G2 Yamba Lake l. Can.
89 C4 Yambi, Mesa de h. Col.
55 E4 Yambio Sudan
49 M3 Yambol Bulg.
12 J3 Yamburg Rus. Fed.
26 A2 Yamenzhuang China
29 G6 Yamizo-san mt Japan
37 V7 Yamm Rus. Fed.
54 B4 Yamoussoukro Côte d'Ivoire
72 E3 Yampa r. U.S.A.
51 D5 Yampil' Ukr.
22 E4 Yamuna r. India
22 D3 Yamunanagar India
23 G3 Yamzho Yumco l. China
26 D2 Yan r. China
13 P3 Yana r. Rus. Fed.
8 C4 Yanac Austr.
21 C2 Yanam India
26 C2 Yan'an China
86 D6 Yanaoca Peru
27 A5 Yanbian China
20 A5 Yanbu' al Baḥr S. Arabia
26 F3 Yancheng China
6 B5 Yanchep Austr.
26 C2 Yanchi China
26 D2 Yanchuan China
8 F3 Yanco Austr.
8 C1 Yanco Glen Austr.
8 E1 Yanda r. Austr.
54 B3 Yanfolila Mali
26 E1 Yang r. China
23 H3 Ya'ngamdo China
23 G3 Yangbajain China
26 D3 Yangcheng China
27 D6 Yangchun China
30 D4 Yangdok N. Korea
26 D1 Yanggao China
26 E2 Yanggu China
19 G2 Yangi-Nishan Uzbek.
19 G1 Yangirabad Uzbek.
27 D6 Yangjiang China
25 B5 Yangon Myanmar
26 D4 Yangping China
26 D2 Yangquan China
27 D5 Yangshan China
27 D5 Yangshuo China
27 E4 Yangtze r. China
26 F4 Yangtze, Mouth of the est. China
56 E2 Yangudi Nassa National Park Eth.
26 C3 Yang Xian China
30 E5 Yangyang S. Korea
26 E1 Yangyuan China
26 F3 Yangzhou China
27 C4 Yanhe China
23 E2 Yanhuqu China
30 E2 Yanji China
27 B4 Yanjin China
54 C4 Yankara National Park Nigeria
76 D3 Yankton U.S.A.
13 P2 Yano-Indigirskaya Nizmennost' lowland Rus. Fed.
21 C4 Yan Oya r. Sri Lanka
26 E1 Yanqing China
26 E2 Yanshan Hebei China
27 E4 Yanshan Jiangxi China
27 B6 Yanshan Yunnan China
26 E1 Yan Shan mts China
23 H2 Yanshiping China
30 E1 Yanshou China
13 P2 Yanskiy Zaliv g. Rus. Fed.
30 A5 Yantai China
47 J3 Yantarnyy Rus. Fed.
30 D2 Yantongshan China
27 A5 Yanyuan China
26 E3 Yanzhou China
54 D4 Yaoundé Cameroon
26 C3 Yao Xian China
25 F6 Yap i. Micronesia
89 D4 Yapacana, Co mt Venez.
25 F7 Yapen i. Indon.
25 F7 Yapen, Selat chan. Indon.
94 E5 Yap Tr. sea feature Pac. Oc.
82 C3 Yaqui r. Mex.
89 C2 Yaracuy r. Venez.
6 E4 Yaraka Austr.
50 H3 Yaransk Rus. Fed.
16 C3 Yardımcı Burnu pt Turkey
17 M2 Yardımlı Azer.

39 J5 Yare r. U.K.
50 K2 Yarega Rus. Fed.
7 G2 Yaren Nauru
50 J2 Yarensk Rus. Fed.
89 B4 Yari r. Col.
29 E6 Yariga-take mt Japan
89 C2 Yaritagua Venez.
69 J3 Yarker Can.
22 C1 Yarkhun r. Pak.
67 G5 Yarmouth Can.
39 F7 Yarmouth U.K.
81 H4 Yarmouth Port U.S.A.
75 F4 Yarnell U.S.A.
50 F3 Yaroslavl' Rus. Fed.
50 F3 Yaroslavskaya Oblast' div. Rus. Fed.
28 C2 Yaroslavskiy Rus. Fed.
8 F5 Yarram Austr.
8 E4 Yarra Yarra r. Austr.
23 H3 Yartö Tra La pass China
50 E4 Yartsevo Rus. Fed.
12 K3 Yartsevo Rus. Fed.
89 B3 Yarumal Col.
23 F5 Yasai r. India
7 H3 Yasawa Group is Fiji
51 F6 Yasenskaya Rus. Fed.
51 G6 Yashalta Rus. Fed.
51 H6 Yashkul' Rus. Fed.
28 E2 Yasnaya Polyana Rus. Fed.
8 G3 Yass Austr.
8 G3 Yass r. Austr.
18 C4 Yāsūj Iran
16 B3 Yatağan Turkey
7 G4 Yaté New Caledonia
77 E4 Yates Center U.S.A.
65 K2 Yathkyed Lake l. Can.
29 F7 Yatsuga-take volc. Japan
29 B8 Yatsushiro Japan
39 E6 Yatton U.K.
27 □ Yau Tong H.K. China
86 D5 Yavari r. Brazil/Peru
22 D5 Yavatmāl India
17 H2 Yavi Turkey
89 D3 Yaví, Co mt Venez.
51 B5 Yavoriv Ukr.
29 C8 Yawatahama Japan
23 E1 Yawatongguz He r. China
23 H5 Yaw Ch. r. Myanmar
84 E3 Yaxchilan Guatemala
18 D4 Yazd Iran
19 F3 Yazdān Iran
18 D4 Yazd-e Khvāst Iran
16 G2 Yazıhan Turkey
77 F5 Yazoo r. U.S.A.
77 F5 Yazoo City U.S.A.
37 L9 Yding Skovhøj h. Denmark
49 K6 Ydra i. Greece
32 A2 Ye Myanmar
8 E4 Yea Austr.
39 D7 Yealmpton U.K.
15 F3 Yecheng China
79 D7 Yeehaw Junction U.S.A.
50 F4 Yefremov Rus. Fed.
17 K2 Yeghegnadzor Armenia
51 G6 Yegorlyk r. Rus. Fed.
51 G6 Yegorlykskaya Rus. Fed.
28 E2 Yegorova, Mys pt Rus. Fed.
50 F4 Yegor'yevsk Rus. Fed.
55 F4 Yei Sudan
26 E4 Yejiaji China
12 H4 Yekaterinburg Rus. Fed.
51 G5 Yelan' Rus. Fed.
51 G5 Yelan' r. Rus. Fed.
19 F2 Yelbarsli Turkm.
51 F4 Yelets Rus. Fed.
54 A3 Yélimané Mali
40 □ Yell i. U.K.
21 C2 Yellandu India
21 A3 Yellapur India
68 B3 Yellow r. U.S.A.
80 D4 Yellow Creek U.S.A.
62 G3 Yellowknife Can.
8 F2 Yellow Mt h. Austr.
Yellow River r. see Huang He
30 B6 Yellow Sea sea Pac. Oc.
72 F2 Yellowstone r. U.S.A.
72 E2 Yellowstone L. l. U.S.A.
72 E2 Yellowstone Nat. Park U.S.A.
72 E2 Yellowtail Res. resr U.S.A.
40 □ Yell Sound chan. U.K.
19 F2 Yeloten Turkm.
51 D5 Yel'sk Belarus
63 K1 Yelverton Bay b. Can.
10 F8 Yemen country Asia
50 G2 Yemetsk Rus. Fed.
50 G2 Yemtsa Rus. Fed.
50 J2 Yemva Rus. Fed.
36 W3 Yena Rus. Fed.
51 F5 Yenakiyeve Ukr.
23 H5 Yenangyat Myanmar
23 H5 Yenangyaung Myanmar
23 H6 Yenanma Myanmar
27 B6 Yên Bai Vietnam
8 F3 Yenda Austr.
54 B4 Yendi Ghana
56 B4 Yénéganou Congo
17 L3 Yengejeh Iran
16 D1 Yeniçağa Turkey
16 E3 Yenice Turkey
49 M5 Yenice Turkey
16 D2 Yeniceoba Turkey
16 B1 Yenişehir Turkey
12 L4 Yenisey r. Rus. Fed.
12 L4 Yeniseysk Rus. Fed.
12 L4 Yeniseyskiy Kryazh ridge Rus. Fed.
12 J2 Yeniseyskiy Zaliv in. Rus. Fed.
27 B6 Yên Minh Vietnam
51 H6 Yenotayevka Rus. Fed.
22 C5 Yeola India
Yeotmal see Yavatmāl
8 G2 Yeoval Austr.
39 E7 Yeovil U.K.
Yeo Yeo r. see Bland
6 F4 Yeppoon Austr.
19 E2 Yerbent Turkm.
13 M3 Yerbogachen Rus. Fed.
17 K1 Yerevan Armenia
51 H6 Yergeni h. Rus. Fed.
74 C2 Yerington U.S.A.
16 E2 Yerköy Turkey
21 A2 Yerla r. India
15 F1 Yermentau Kazak.
84 A1 Yermo Mex.
74 D4 Yermo U.S.A.
51 J5 Yershov Rus. Fed.
50 G2 Yertsevo Rus. Fed.
Yerushalayim see Jerusalem
51 H5 Yeruslan r. Rus. Fed.
30 D5 Yesan S. Korea
14 E1 Yesil' Kazak.
16 E2 Yeşilhisar Turkey
16 F1 Yeşilırmak r. Turkey
16 B3 Yeşilova Turkey
51 G6 Yessentuki Rus. Fed.
13 M3 Yessey Rus. Fed.
39 C7 Yes Tor h. U.K.
24 B4 Yeu Myanmar
44 C3 Yeu, Île d' i. France
17 L1 Yevlax Azer.
51 E6 Yevpatoriya Ukr.
26 D3 Ye Xian Henan China
26 F2 Ye Xian Shandong China
51 F6 Yeya r. Rus. Fed.
23 E1 Yeyik China
51 F6 Yeysk Rus. Fed.
50 H1 Yezhuga r. Rus. Fed.
50 D4 Yezyaryshcha Belarus
26 D3 Yi r. Henan China
26 F3 Yi r. Shandong China
91 F2 Yí r. Uru.
27 B4 Yibin China
23 F2 Yibug Caka salt l. China
27 D4 Yichang Hubei China
27 D4 Yicheng Hubei China
26 D4 Yicheng Hubei China
26 D3 Yicheng Shanxi China
26 D3 Yichuan China
24 E2 Yichun Heilongjiang China
27 E5 Yichun Jiangxi China
27 D4 Yidu Hubei China
26 F2 Yidu Shandong China
27 E4 Yifeng China
27 E5 Yihuang China
26 C3 Yijun China
28 A1 Yilan China
49 M4 Yıldız Dağları mts Turkey
16 F2 Yıldızeli Turkey
27 B5 Yiliang Yunnan China
27 B5 Yiliang Yunnan China
26 C4 Yilong China
27 B6 Yilong Hu l. China
27 B5 Yimen China
30 E1 Yimianpo China
26 F3 Yinan China
26 C2 Yinchuan China
30 C2 Yingchengzi China
27 D5 Yingde China
27 C7 Yinggehai China
26 E3 Ying He r. China
30 B3 Yingkou Liaoning China
30 B3 Yingkou Liaoning China
26 B2 Yingpanshui China
27 E4 Yingshan Hubei China
26 C4 Yingshan Sichuan China
26 E3 Yingshang China
27 E4 Yingtan China
26 D2 Ying Xian China
15 G2 Yining China
27 C5 Yinjiang China
30 C1 Yinma r. China
23 H5 Yinmabin Myanmar
26 C1 Yin Shan mts China
23 H3 Yi'ong Zangbo r. China
27 A5 Yipinglang China
56 D3 Yirga Alem Eth.
23 G2 Yirna Tso l. China
27 C5 Yishan China
26 F2 Yi Shan mt China
26 F3 Yishui China
32 □ Yishun Sing.
30 C2 Yitong China
30 C1 Yitong r. China
24 B2 Yiwu China
30 A3 Yiwulü Shan mts China
27 E4 Yi Xian Anhui China
30 A3 Yi Xian China
26 F4 Yixing China
27 D4 Yiyang Hunan China
27 E4 Yiyang Jiangxi China
27 D5 Yizhang China
37 S6 Yläne Fin.
36 S5 Ylihärmä Fin.
36 T4 Yli-Ii Fin.
36 T4 Yli-Kärppä Fin.
36 U4 Ylikiiminki Fin.
36 V3 Yli-kitka l. Fin
36 S5 Ylistaro Fin.
36 S3 Ylitornio Fin.
36 T4 Ylivieska Fin.
37 S6 Ylöjärvi Fin.
77 D6 Yoakum U.S.A.
28 G3 Yobetsu-dake volc. Japan
33 D4 Yogyakarta Indon.
64 F4 Yoho Nat. Park Can.
55 D4 Yokadouma Cameroon
29 E7 Yokkaichi Japan
55 D4 Yoko Cameroon
29 F7 Yokohama Japan
29 F7 Yokosuka Japan
28 G5 Yokote Japan
28 G4 Yokotsu-dake mt Japan
55 D4 Yola Nigeria
84 C3 Yoloxóchitl Mex.
54 B4 Yomou Guinea
30 D5 Yŏnan N. Korea
29 G6 Yonezawa Japan
8 B2 Yongala Austr.
30 D6 Yongam S. Korea
27 E5 Yong'an China
30 E3 Yŏng-an N. Korea
26 A2 Yongchang China
26 E3 Yongcheng China
30 E6 Yŏngch'ŏn S. Korea
27 F5 Yongchun China
26 B2 Yongdeng China
27 E5 Yongding China
26 E2 Yongding r. China
30 E5 Yŏngdŏk S. Korea
27 C5 Yongfu China
30 D6 Yŏnggwang S. Korea
23 H3 Yonggyap pass India
30 D4 Yŏnghŭng N. Korea
30 D4 Yŏnghŭng-man b. N. Korea
30 D2 Yongji China
27 F4 Yongjia China
26 B3 Yongjing China
30 E5 Yŏngju S. Korea
27 F4 Yongkang China
30 C3 Yongling China
26 E2 Yongnian China
27 C6 Yongning China
27 A5 Yongren China
30 D6 Yŏngsan r. S. Korea
30 D6 Yŏngsanp'o S. Korea
27 C4 Yongshun China
27 F5 Yongtai China
27 D5 Yongxin China
27 E5 Yongxing China
27 E4 Yongxiu China
27 D5 Yongzhou China
30 D3 Yŏnhwa, Mt mt N. Korea
81 G4 Yonkers U.S.A.
44 F2 Yonne r. France
89 B3 Yopal Col.
6 B5 York Austr.
38 F4 York U.K.
76 D3 York NE U.S.A.
80 E5 York PA U.S.A.
79 D5 York SC U.S.A.
6 E3 York, C. c. Austr.
8 A3 Yorke Peninsula Austr.
8 A3 Yorketown Austr.
63 M2 York, Kap c. Greenland
38 E3 Yorkshire Dales National Park U.K.
38 G4 Yorkshire Wolds reg. U.K.
65 J4 Yorkton Can.
80 E6 Yorktown U.S.A.
38 F3 York, Vale of v. U.K.
54 B3 Yorosso Mali
74 C3 Yosemite National Park U.S.A.
74 C3 Yosemite Village U.S.A.
29 C8 Yoshino-gawa r. Japan
29 D7 Yoshino-Kumano National Park Japan
50 H3 Yoshkar-Ola Rus. Fed.
30 D6 Yŏsu S. Korea
16 E7 Yotvata Israel
41 D6 Youghal Rep. of Ireland
80 D5 Youghiogheny River Lake l. U.S.A.
27 C6 You Jiang r. China
8 G3 Young Austr.
91 F2 Young Uru.
8 B3 Younghusband Pen. pen. Austr.
92 A6 Young I. i. Ant.
80 C4 Youngstown U.S.A.
27 D4 You Shui r. China
54 B3 Youvarou Mali
27 F5 Youxi China
27 D5 You Xian China
27 C4 Youyang China
28 B1 Youyi China
26 D2 Youyu China
19 H2 Yovon Tajik.
16 E2 Yozgat Turkey
90 A3 Ypané r. Para.
90 A3 Ypé-Jhú Para.
72 B3 Yreka U.S.A.
Yr Wyddfa mt see Snowdon
42 A4 Yser r. France
42 D3 Ysselsteyn Neth.
37 N9 Ystad Sweden
39 D5 Ystwyth r. U.K.
15 F2 Ysyk-Köl Kyrg.
15 F2 Ysyk-Köl l. Kyrg.
40 F3 Ythan r. U.K.
13 P3 Ytyk-Kyuyel Rus. Fed.
27 F6 Yüalin Taiwan
26 D4 Yuan'an China
27 C5 Yuanbao Shan mt China
27 D4 Yuanjiang Hunan China
27 A6 Yuanjiang Yunnan China
27 D4 Yuan Jiang r. Hunan China
27 B6 Yuan Jiang r. Yunnan China
27 F5 Yüanli Taiwan
27 D4 Yuanling China
27 A5 Yuanmou China
26 D2 Yuanping China
26 D3 Yuanqu China
27 B6 Yuanyang China
74 B2 Yuba r. U.S.A.
74 B2 Yuba City U.S.A.
28 G3 Yūbari Japan
84 E2 Yucatán div. Mex.
82 F5 Yucatán pen. Mex.
82 G4 Yucatan Channel str. Cuba/Mex.
75 E4 Yucca U.S.A.
74 D3 Yucca L. l. U.S.A.
74 D4 Yucca Valley U.S.A.
26 E2 Yucheng China
26 D2 Yuci China
13 P4 Yudoma r. Rus. Fed.
27 E5 Yudu China
27 C4 Yuechi China
6 D4 Yuendumu Austr.
27 □ Yuen Long H.K. China
27 F4 Yueqing China
27 E4 Yuexi Anhui China
27 B4 Yuexi Sichuan China
27 D4 Yueyang China
27 E4 Yugan China
35 H4 Yugoslavia country Europe
13 R3 Yugo-Tala Rus. Fed.
50 K2 Yugydtydor Rus. Fed.
27 F4 Yuhuan China
26 E2 Yuhuang Ding mt China
27 E4 Yujiang China
27 D6 Yu Jiang r. China
13 R3 Yukagirskoye Ploskogor'ye plat. Rus. Fed.
16 E2 Yukarısarıkaya Turkey
56 B4 Yuki Congo(Zaire)
62 C3 Yukon r. Can./U.S.A.
64 B2 Yukon Territory div. Can.
17 K3 Yüksekova Turkey
79 D6 Yulee U.S.A.
27 F6 Yüli Taiwan
27 D6 Yulin Guangxi China
27 C7 Yulin Hainan China
26 C2 Yulin Shaanxi China
75 E5 Yuma U.S.A.
75 E5 Yuma Desert des. U.S.A.
89 A4 Yumbo Col.
24 B3 Yumen China
16 E3 Yumurtalık Turkey
16 C2 Yunak Turkey
27 D6 Yunan China
26 E3 Yuncheng Shandong China
26 D3 Yuncheng Shanxi China
27 D6 Yunfu China
27 B5 Yun Gui Gaoyuan plat. China
27 F4 Yunhe China
27 D6 Yunkai Dashan mts China
26 D4 Yunmeng China
27 A5 Yunnan div. China
26 D4 Yun Shui r. China
8 B2 Yunta Austr.
27 D6 Yunwu Shan mts China
26 D3 Yunxi China
26 D3 Yun Xian China
27 E6 Yunxiao China
26 D3 Yunyang Henan China
26 C4 Yunyang Sichuan China
27 C5 Yuping China
26 E1 Yuqiao Sk. resr China
27 C5 Yuqing China
24 A1 Yurga Rus. Fed.
86 C5 Yurimaguas Peru
89 E3 Yuruán r. Venez.
89 E3 Yuruari r. Venez.
89 C2 Yurubí, Parque Nacional nat. park Venez.
22 E1 Yurungkax He r. China
50 J3 Yur'ya Rus. Fed.
50 G3 Yur'yevets Rus. Fed.
50 F3 Yur'yev-Pol'skiy Rus. Fed.
27 F4 Yushan China
27 F6 Yü Shan mt Taiwan
26 D2 Yushe China
50 E1 Yushkozero Rus. Fed.
30 D1 Yushu China
24 B3 Yushu China
50 J3 Yushut r. Rus. Fed.
51 H6 Yusta Rus. Fed.
17 H1 Yusufeli Turkey
26 E3 Yutai China
23 E1 Yutian China
26 C2 Yuwang China
27 B5 Yuxi China
26 E2 Yu Xian Hebei China
26 D3 Yu Xian Henan China
26 D2 Yu Xian Shanxi China
27 F4 Yuyao China
28 G5 Yuzawa Japan
50 G3 Yuzha Rus. Fed.
24 D1 Yuzhno Muyskiy Khrebet mts Rus. Fed.
24 G2 Yuzhno-Sakhalinsk Rus. Fed.
51 H6 Yuzhno-Sukhokumsk Rus. Fed.
51 D6 Yuzhnoukrayinsk Ukr.
28 H1 Yuzhnoye Rus. Fed.
51 G6 Yuzhnyy Rus. Fed.
26 B3 Yuzhong China
18 B3 Yūzīdar Iran
46 C7 Yverdon Switz.
44 E2 Yvetot France
32 A1 Ywathit Myanmar

Z

19 H2 Zaamin Uzbek.
42 C2 Zaandam Neth.
24 D2 Zabaykal'sk Rus. Fed.
18 B2 Zab-e Kuchek r. Iran
20 B7 Zabīd Yemen
19 F4 Zābol Iran
19 F5 Zābolī Iran
82 G5 Zacapa Guatemala
84 B3 Zacapu Mex.
84 B2 Zacatecas Mex.
84 B2 Zacatecas div. Mex.
84 C3 Zacatlán Mex.
49 J6 Zacharo Greece
48 F2 Zadar Croatia
32 A3 Zadetkale Kyun i. Myanmar
32 A3 Zadetkyi Kyun i. Myanmar
23 H2 Zadoi China
51 F4 Zadonsk Rus. Fed.
17 L4 Zafarābād Iran
49 M6 Zafora i. Greece
45 C3 Zafra Spain
55 F1 Zagazig Egypt
18 E3 Zaghdeh well Iran
17 M5 Zāgheh Iran
48 D6 Zaghouan Tunisia
48 F2 Zagreb Croatia
18 B3 Zagros, Kūhhā-ye mts Iran
Zagros Mountains mts see Zagros, Kūhhā-ye
23 G3 Za'gya Zangbo r. China
19 F4 Zāhedān Iran
19 H3 Zahidabad Afgh.
16 E5 Zahlé Lebanon
Zaïre country see Congo
Zaïre r. see Congo
49 K3 Zaječar Yugo.
19 F2 Zakhmet Turkm.
17 J3 Zākhō Iraq
55 D3 Zakouma, Parc National de nat. park Chad
49 J6 Zakynthos Greece
Zakynthos i. see Zante
46 H7 Zalaegerszeg Hungary
46 H7 Zalai-domsag h. Hungary
45 D3 Zalamea de la Serena Spain
47 L7 Zalău Romania
50 F3 Zales'ye Rus. Fed.
55 E3 Zalingei Sudan
47 M6 Zalishchyky Ukr.
50 D3 Zaluch'ye Rus. Fed.
16 E2 Zamanti r. Turkey
31 B3 Zambales Mts mts Phil.
57 D5 Zambeze r. Moz.
57 C5 Zambezi Zambia
57 C5 Zambezi r. Africa
53 G7 Zambia country Africa
31 B5 Zamboanga Phil.
31 B5 Zamboanga Peninsula Phil.
86 C4 Zamora Ecuador
45 D2 Zamora Spain
84 B3 Zamora de Hidalgo Mex.
47 L5 Zamość Pol.
23 A3 Zamtang China
89 C2 Zamuro, Pta pt Venez.
89 E3 Zamuro, Sierra del mts Venez.
22 D3 Zanda China
59 J2 Zandamela Moz.
42 C3 Zandvliet Belgium
80 C5 Zanesville U.S.A.
22 D2 Zangla Jammu and Kashmir
18 C2 Zanjān Iran
17 L3 Zanjān r. Iran
49 J6 Zante i. Greece
56 D4 Zanzibar Tanz.
56 D4 Zanzibar I. i. Tanz.
27 D4 Zaoshi China
54 C2 Zaouatallaz Alg.
26 D3 Zaoyang China
24 B1 Zaozernyy Rus. Fed.
26 E3 Zaozhuang China
17 J3 Zap r. Turkey
50 E3 Zapadnaya Dvina Rus. Fed
Zapadnaya Dvina r. see Dvina, Western
49 K4 Zapadni Rodopi mts Bulg.
12 K3 Zapadno-Sibirskaya Ravnina plain Rus. Fed.
36 Y2 Zapadnyy Kil'din Rus. Fed.
15 G1 Zapadnyy Sayan reg. Rus. Fed.
91 B3 Zapala Arg.
77 D7 Zapata U.S.A.
89 B3 Zapatoca Col.
36 W2 Zapolyarnyy Rus. Fed.
51 E6 Zaporizhzhya Ukr.
28 D2 Zapovednik mt Rus. Fed.
22 E2 Zapug China
17 L1 Zaqatala Azer.
23 H2 Zaqên China
23 H2 Za Qu r. China
16 F2 Zara Turkey
19 G2 Zarafshon, Qatorkŭhi mts Tajik.
89 B3 Zaragoza Col.
73 F6 Zaragoza Chihuahua Mex.
45 F2 Zaragoza Spain
18 E4 Zarand Iran
19 F4 Zaranj Afgh.
16 E6 Zararikh Reserve res. Egypt
37 U9 Zarasai Lith.
91 E2 Zárate Arg.
89 D2 Zaraza Venez.
19 H1 Zarbdar Uzbek.
17 L1 Zärdab Azer.
36 W3 Zarechensk Rus. Fed.
17 M4 Zāreh Iran
64 C3 Zarembo I. i. U.S.A.
22 A3 Zargun mt Pak.
54 C3 Zaria Nigeria
51 C5 Zarichne Ukr.
18 B2 Zarīneh r. Iran
19 F3 Zarmardan Afgh.
17 L5 Zarneh Iran
49 L2 Zărneşti Romania
16 F5 Zarqā' Jordan
18 D4 Zarqān Iran
18 D3 Zarrīn Iran
28 B3 Zarubino Rus. Fed.
46 G5 Żary Pol.
89 A3 Zarzal Col.
55 D1 Zarzis Tunisia
36 W3 Zasheyek Rus. Fed.
22 D2 Zaskar r. India
22 D2 Zaskar Mts mts India
50 C4 Zaslawye Belarus
59 G5 Zastron S. Africa
43 L2 Zauche reg. Ger.
18 B3 Zavareh Iran
49 H2 Zavidoviči Bos.-Herz.
24 E1 Zavitinsk Rus. Fed.
26 A2 Zawa China
47 J5 Zawiercie Pol.
15 G2 Zaysan, Ozero l. Kazak.
24 B4 Zayü China
46 G6 Žďár nad Sázavou Czech Rep.
51 C5 Zdolbuniv Ukr.
37 M9 Zealand i. Denmark
17 K3 Zēbār Iraq
26 E3 Zecheng China
42 B3 Zedelgem Belgium
42 B3 Zeebrugge Belgium
59 G2 Zeerust S. Africa
42 B3 Zeeuwsch-Vlaanderen reg. Neth.
16 E5 Zefat Israel
43 M2 Zehdenick Ger.
43 J4 Zeil am Main Ger.
42 D2 Zeist Neth.
43 L3 Zeitz Ger.
26 A3 Zêkog China
36 X3 Zelenoborskiy Rus. Fed.
50 J4 Zelenodol'sk Rus. Fed.
37 V6 Zelenogorsk Rus. Fed.
50 F3 Zelenograd Rus. Fed.
50 B4 Zelenogradsk Rus. Fed.
51 G6 Zelenokumsk Rus. Fed.
50 H3 Zelentsovo Rus. Fed.
46 F7 Zell am See Austria
43 H5 Zellingen Ger.
42 B3 Zelzate Belgium
26 A3 Zêmdasam China
50 G4 Zemetchino Rus. Fed.
56 C3 Zémio C.A.R.
12 F1 Zemlya Aleksandry i. Rus. Fed.
Zemlya Frantsa-Iosifa is see Franz Josef Land
12 F2 Zemlya Georga i. Rus. Fed.
12 H1 Zemlya Vil'cheka i. Rus. Fed.
45 G5 Zemmora Alg.
84 C3 Zempoala Pyramids Mex.
84 D3 Zempoaltepetl mt Mex.
27 D6 Zengcheng China
30 E2 Zengfeng Shan mt China
74 A1 Zenia U.S.A.
49 G2 Zenica Bos.-Herz.
39 B7 Zennor U.K.
74 C2 Zephyr Cove U.S.A.
43 L3 Zerbst Ger.
42 E5 Zerf Ger.
43 J1 Zernien Ger.
43 L2 Zernitz Ger.
51 G6 Zernograd Rus. Fed.
51 G7 Zestap'oni Georgia
23 G3 Zêtang China
43 F1 Zetel Ger.
43 K4 Zeulenroda Ger.
43 H1 Zeven Ger.
42 E3 Zevenaar Neth.
24 E1 Zeya Rus. Fed.
24 E1 Zeya r. Rus. Fed.
19 F5 Zeyarat-e Shamil Iran
18 D4 Zeydābād Iran
19 E2 Zeydar Iran
18 E4 Zeynalābād Iran
24 E1 Zeyskoye Vdkhr. resr Rus. Fed.
45 C3 Zêzere r. Port.
47 J5 Zgierz Pol.
50 C4 Zhabinka Belarus
14 E1 Zhaltyr Kazak.
14 F2 Zhambyl Kazak.
26 E2 Zhang r. China
26 E1 Zhangbei China
30 E1 Zhangguangcai Ling mts China
30 B2 Zhanggutai China
26 E1 Zhangjiakou China
26 B3 Zhangla China
27 E5 Zhangping China
27 E5 Zhangpu China
30 B2 Zhangqiangzhen China
26 E2 Zhangwei Xinhe r. China
30 B2 Zhangwu China
26 B3 Zhang Xian China
26 A2 Zhangye China
27 E5 Zhangzhou China
26 D2 Zhangzi China
30 B4 Zhangzi Dao i. China
26 F2 Zhanhua China
27 D6 Zhanjiang China
27 B5 Zhanyi China
27 E6 Zhao'an China
27 B4 Zhaojue China
27 D5 Zhaoping China
27 D6 Zhaoqing China
30 B2 Zhaosutai r. China
27 B5 Zhaotong China
26 E2 Zhao Xian China
30 C1 Zhaoyuan China
27 D6 Zhapo China
23 F3 Zhari Namco salt l. China
15 G2 Zharkent Kazak.
50 E4 Zharkovskiy Rus. Fed.
15 G2 Zharma Kazak.
51 D5 Zhashkiv Ukr.
26 C3 Zhashui China
23 F2 Zhaxi Co salt l. China
22 D2 Zhaxigang China
27 F4 Zhejiang div. China
12 H2 Zhelaniya, M. c. Rus. Fed.
51 E4 Zheleznogorsk Rus. Fed.
26 C3 Zhen'an China
26 C3 Zhenba China
27 C4 Zheng'an China
26 E2 Zhengding China
27 F5 Zhenghe China
26 E1 Zhenglan Qi China
26 C3 Zhengning China
26 E1 Zhengxiangbai Qi China
26 E3 Zhengyang China
26 D3 Zhengzhou China
27 F4 Zhenhai China
26 F3 Zhenjiang China
26 B3 Zhenjiangguan China
27 B5 Zhenning China
26 D3 Zhenping China
27 B5 Zhenxiong China
26 C3 Zhenyuan Gansu China
27 C5 Zhenyuan Guizhou China
51 G5 Zherdevka Rus. Fed.
27 F5 Zherong China
50 J2 Zheshart Rus. Fed.
27 D4 Zhexi Sk. resr China
14 E2 Zhezkazgan Kazak.
27 D4 Zhicheng China
26 C2 Zhidan China
23 H2 Zhidoi China
13 O3 Zhigansk Rus. Fed.
27 D6 Zhigong China
23 G3 Zhigung China
27 D4 Zhijiang Hubei China
27 C5 Zhijiang Hunan China
27 E6 Zhijin China
Zhi Qu r. see Tongtian He
51 H5 Zhirnovsk Rus. Fed.
51 H5 Zhitkur Rus. Fed.
17 L4 Zhīvār Iran
50 D4 Zhlobin Belarus
51 D5 Zhmerynka Ukr.
22 B3 Zhob Pak.
22 B3 Zhob r. Pak.
13 R2 Zhokhova, O. i. Rus. Fed.
23 F3 Zhongba China
24 B4 Zhongdian China
26 B4 Zhongjiang China
26 B2 Zhongning China
27 D6 Zhongshan Guangdong China
27 D5 Zhongshan Guangxi China
92 D5 Zhongshan China Base Ant.
26 D3 Zhongtiao Shan mts China
26 B2 Zhongwei China
27 C4 Zhong Xian China
27 E5 Zhongxin China
27 B5 Zhongyicun China
27 D7 Zhongyuan China
26 C4 Zhou He r. China
26 B2 Zhoujiajing China
26 E3 Zhoukou China
27 F5 Zhouning China
26 D1 Zhouzi China
51 E5 Zhovti Vody Ukr.
30 B4 Zhuanghe China
26 B3 Zhuanglang China
26 F3 Zhucheng China
26 B3 Zhugqu China
27 D6 Zhuhai China
27 F4 Zhuji China
50 E4 Zhukovka Rus. Fed.
26 E2 Zhulong r. China
26 E3 Zhumadian China
26 E1 Zhuolu China
26 E2 Zhuo Xian China
26 D2 Zhuozang r. China
26 D3 Zhushan China
26 C3 Zhuxi China
27 D5 Zhuzhou Hunan China
27 D5 Zhuzhou Hunan China
51 C5 Zhydachiv Ukr.
51 C4 Zhytkavichy Belarus
51 D5 Zhytomyr Ukr.
26 F2 Zi r. China
47 J6 Žiar nad Hronom Slovakia
17 J3 Zībār Iraq
26 F2 Zibo China
26 C2 Zichang China
6 D4 Ziel, Mt mt Austr.
46 G5 Zielona Góra Pol.
43 H3 Zierenberg Ger.
43 L2 Ziesar Ger.
16 C6 Zifta Egypt
17 M1 Zığ Azer.
23 H5 Zigaing Myanmar
27 B4 Zigong China
27 D4 Zigui China
54 A3 Ziguinchor Senegal
37 U8 Žīguri Latvia
84 B3 Zihuatanejo Mex.
27 B5 Zijin China
42 E2 Zijpenberg h. Neth.
16 E5 Zikhron Ya'aqov Israel
16 E1 Zile Turkey
47 J6 Žilina Slovakia
24 C1 Zima Rus. Fed.
84 C2 Zimapán Mex.
84 C3 Zimatlán Mex.
57 C5 Zimba Zambia
53 G7 Zimbabwe country Africa
18 B3 Zimkan r. Iran
54 A4 Zimmi Sierra Leone
49 L3 Zimnicea Romania
51 G6 Zimovniki Rus. Fed.
16 E4 Zimrin Syria
19 F3 Zindajan Afgh.
54 C3 Zinder Niger
54 B3 Ziniaré Burkina
26 B2 Zinihu China
75 F3 Zion Nat. Park U.S.A.
66 B3 Zionz L. l. Can.
89 B3 Zipaquirá Col.
23 H2 Ziqudukou China
43 J5 Zirndorf Ger.
23 H4 Ziro India
27 D4 Zi Shui r. China
46 H6 Zistersdorf Austria
84 B3 Zitácuaro Mex.
46 G5 Zittau Ger.
17 K3 Zīveh Iran
27 E5 Zixi China
27 D5 Zixing China
26 E2 Ziya r. China
26 C3 Ziyang Shaanxi China
27 B4 Ziyang Sichuan China
27 D5 Ziyuan China
27 C5 Ziyun China
27 B4 Zizhong China
46 H6 Zlín Czech Rep.
51 D4 Zlynka Rus. Fed.
51 F5 Zmiyiv Ukr.
50 E4 Znamenka Rus. Fed.
51 E5 Znam"yanka Ukr.
46 H6 Znojmo Czech Rep.
58 D6 Zoar S. Africa
17 L4 Zobeyrī Iran
42 C2 Zoetermeer Neth.
17 K4 Zohāb Iran
26 B3 Zoigê China
22 C2 Zoji La pass India
59 G6 Zola S. Africa
42 D3 Zolder Belgium
51 E5 Zolochiv Kharkiv Ukr.
51 C5 Zolochiv L'viv Ukr.
51 E5 Zolotonosha Ukr.
51 F4 Zolotukhino Rus. Fed.
57 D5 Zomba Malawi
Zongga see Gyirong
56 B3 Zongo Congo(Zaire)
16 C1 Zonguldak Turkey
23 G3 Zongxoi China
27 E4 Zongyang China
48 C4 Zonza Corsica France
43 L3 Zörbig Ger.
54 B3 Zorgo Burkina
54 B4 Zorzor Liberia
42 B4 Zottegem Belgium
55 D2 Zouar Chad
54 A2 Zouérat Maur.
26 E2 Zouping China
27 D4 Zoushi China
26 E3 Zou Xian China
26 D2 Zouyun China
49 J2 Zrenjanin Yugo.
43 M4 Zschopau Ger.
43 L3 Zschornewitz Ger.
89 D2 Zuata r. Venez.
91 D3 Zubillaga Arg.
50 G4 Zubova Polyana Rus. Fed.
54 B4 Zuénoula Côte d'Ivoire
46 D7 Zug Switz.
51 G7 Zugdidi Georgia
46 D7 Zuger See l. Switz.
46 E7 Zugspitze mt Austria/Ger
Zuider Zee l. see IJsselmeer
42 E1 Zuidhorn Neth.
42 C2 Zuid-Kennemerland Nationaal Park nat. park Neth.
45 D3 Zújar r. Spain
89 B2 Zulia r. Col.
42 E4 Zülpich Ger.
57 D5 Zumbo Moz.
68 A3 Zumbro r. U.S.A.
68 A3 Zumbrota U.S.A.
84 C3 Zumpango Mex.
54 C4 Zungeru Nigeria
26 F1 Zunhua China
75 H4 Zuni U.S.A.
75 H4 Zuni Mts mts U.S.A.
27 C5 Zunyi Guizhou China
27 C5 Zunyi Guizhou China
27 C6 Zuo Jiang r. China/Vietnam
26 D2 Zuoquan China
17 K2 Zūrābād Iran
17 L5 Zurbāṭīyah Iraq
46 D7 Zürich Switz.
19 H3 Zurmat reg. Afgh.
42 E2 Zutphen Neth.
59 F6 Zuurberg National Park S. Africa
55 D1 Zuwārah Libya
50 J3 Zuyevka Rus. Fed.
37 T8 Zvejniekciems Latvia
50 J4 Zvenigovo Rus. Fed.
51 D5 Zvenyhorodka Ukr.
57 D6 Zvishavane Zimbabwe
47 J6 Zvolen Slovakia
49 H2 Zvornik Bos.-Herz.
54 B4 Zwedru Liberia
42 E2 Zweeloo Neth.
42 F5 Zweibrücken Ger.
59 G6 Zwelitsha S. Africa
43 M3 Zwethau Ger.
46 G6 Zwettl Austria
43 L4 Zwickau Ger.
43 L3 Zwochau Ger.
42 E2 Zwolle Neth.
43 L4 Zwönitz Ger.
13 R3 Zyryanka Rus. Fed.

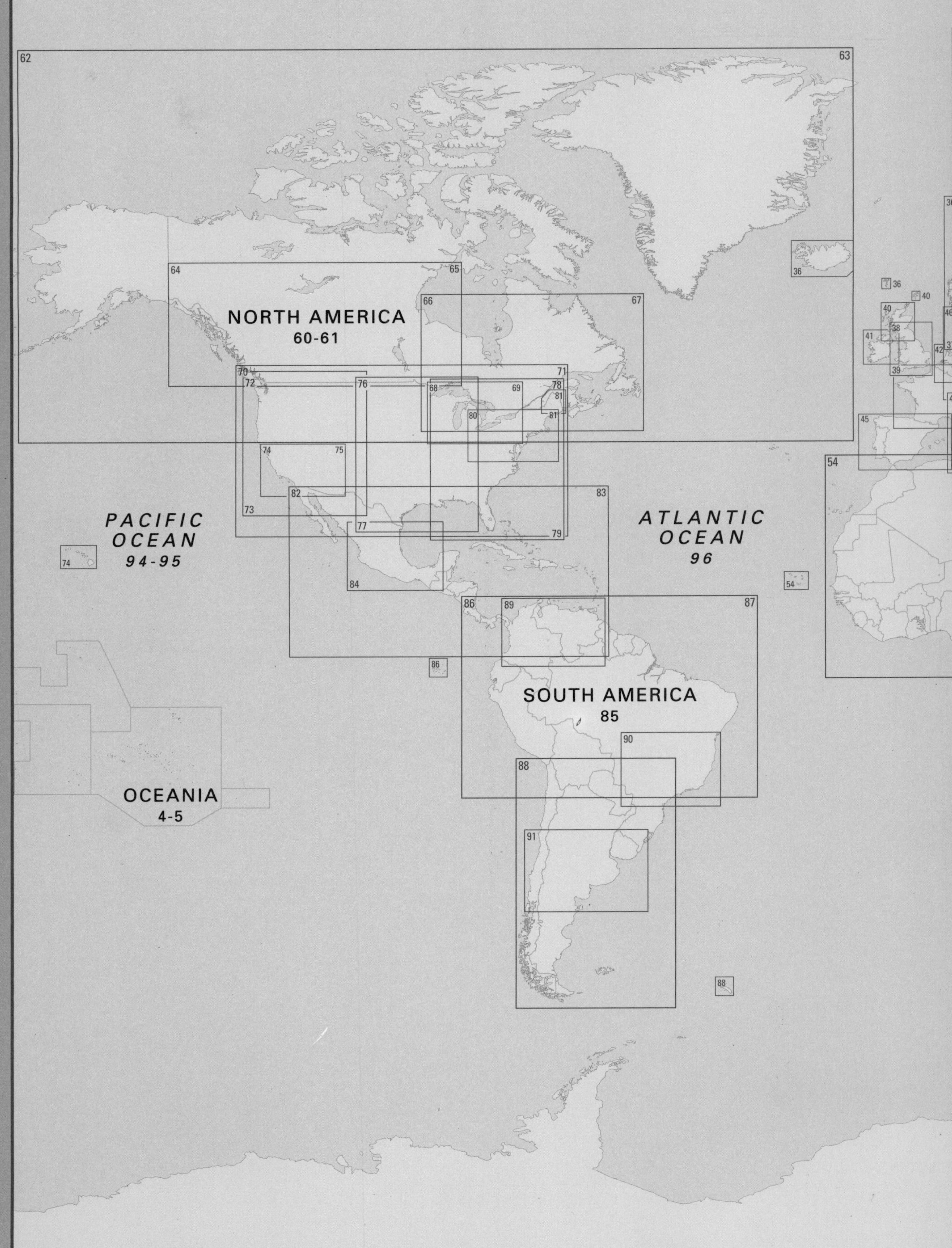

62
63
64
65
66
67
NORTH AMERICA
60-61
70
71
72
76
68
69
78
81
80
81
74
75
73
82
83
77
79
PACIFIC
OCEAN
94-95
74
ATLANTIC
OCEAN
96
84
54
86
89
87
86
SOUTH AMERICA
85
90
88
91
88
OCEANIA
4-5
36
36
40
40
38
41
39
42
37
46
48
45
54